Consumer and Trading Law
Cases and Materials

C. J. Miller BA, LLM
of Lincoln's Inn, Barrister,
Professor of Law, University
of Warwick

Brian W. Harvey MA, LLM
Solicitor, Professor of Law,
University of Birmingham

Butterworths
London
1985

England   Butterworth & Co (Publishers) Ltd, 88 Kingsway, LONDON WC2B 6AB

Australia   Butterworths Pty Ltd, SYDNEY, MELBOURNE, BRISBANE, ADELAIDE, PERTH, CANBERRA and HOBART

Canada   Butterworth & Co (Canada) Ltd, TORONTO and VANCOUVER

New Zealand   Butterworths of New Zealand Ltd, WELLINGTON and AUCKLAND

Singapore   Butterworth & Co (Asia) Pte Ltd, SINGAPORE

South Africa   Butterworth Publishers (Pty) Ltd, DURBAN and PRETORIA

USA   Butterworth Legal Publishers,
               ST PAUL, Minnesota, SEATTLE, Washington, BOSTON, Massachusetts, AUSTIN, Texas and D & S Publishers, CLEARWATER, Florida

Miller, C.J.
    Consumer and trading law: cases and materials.
    1. Consumer protection—Law and legislation
    —Great Britain
    I. Title   II. Harvey, Brian W.
    344.103'71   KD2204

ISBN Softcover 0 406 01261 X
     Hardcover 0 406 01260 1

Front cover photograph reproduced by kind permission of The Bridgeman Art Library and Guildhall Art Gallery London.

Typeset by Phoenix Photosetting, Chatham, Kent
Printed and bound in Great Britain by
Billing & Sons Ltd, Worcester.

Law

Preface

Our main aim in writing this book is to provide the student of consumer law with a wide range of materials on this increasingly important subject. The materials include extracts both from cases and statutes and Government, Law Commission, Office of Fair Trading and National Consumer Council publications, along with extracts illustrating the approach of other jurisdictions, notably within the Commonwealth, North America and the Continent of Europe. Much of the material is not otherwise readily accessible to students or indeed to trading standards officers or advice agencies who we believe will benefit from it also. The subject has been defined broadly as including private law remedies (both their content and enforcement), codes of practice and fair trading and public law controls.

In preparing the text we have received a great deal of help from many sources—not least, of course, from the individuals whose writings have contributed to it. We are grateful to them and especially so for the admirable research and related assistance provided by our erstwhile students Marilyn Thompson, Peggy Clapham and Diane Mellett. Marilyn Thompson and Peggy Clapham assisted also in the odious task of proof-reading. As always the kindness and efficiency of our publishers, Butterworths, have matched our by now perhaps unfairly high expectations, and we are grateful to them.

We delivered the manuscript to the publishers on 28 September 1984 but have been able to incorporate some later developments and references, most notably the decision of the House of Lords in *Wings v Ellis*. Some other developments came too late for inclusion, for example the relevant provisions of the Insolvency Bill.

January, 1985

C. J. Miller, Warwick
Brian Harvey, Birmingham

Contents

Chapter 7
The enforcement of private law remedies:
I   Some problems of individual redress   290

Chapter 8
The enforcement of private law remedies:
II   Collective redress   352

Chapter 9
The consumer and codes of practice   386

Chapter 13
False price claims and bargain offers   525

Chapter 14
General statutory defences in consumer protection legislation   552

Acknowledgments

Grateful acknowledgment is made to all authors and publishers of extract material. In particular the following permissions are noted:

American Journal of Comparative Law: extracts are printed by kind permission of the publishers.

American Law Institute: extracts from Restatement of Torts (2d) s 402(A) copyright (1965) by the American Law Institute, reprinted with permission of the American Law Institute.

Australian Law Reform Commission: extracts from Discussion Paper No 11 reprinted by kind permission.

British Code of Advertising Practice Committee: extracts from the British Code of Advertising Practice reprinted by kind permission.

British Insurance Association: extracts from Statements of Insurance Practice reprinted by kind permission.

Civil Justice Quarterly: extracts reprinted by kind permission of Sweet & Maxwell Ltd.

Consumer Protection Law and Theory (by Duggan and Darvall): extracts reprinted by kind permission of The Law Book Co Ltd, Australia.

Dominion Law Reports: extracts reprinted by kind permission of Canada Law Book Inc.

Estates Gazette: extracts reprinted by kind permission of the publishers.

HMSO: extracts from publications reprinted by kind permission of the Controller of Her Majesty's Stationery Office.

Insurance Ombudsman Bureau: extracts from the Annual Report 1983 reprinted by kind permission.

Journal of Business Law: extracts reprinted by kind permission of Sweet & Maxwell Ltd.

Law and the Weaker Party, Vols I-III: extracts reprinted by kind permission of the editors, Alan C. Neal and S. D. Anderman, and Professional Books Ltd.

The Law Reports, The Weekly Law Reports: extracts reprinted by kind permission of the Incorporated Council of Law Reporting for England and Wales.

Lloyd's List Law Reports: extracts reprinted by kind permission of Lloyd's of London Press Ltd.

Modern Law Review: extracts reprinted by kind permission of the publishers.

National Consumer Council: extracts from publications reprinted by kind permission.

National Newspapers' Mail Order Protection Scheme: extract reprinted from the Mail Order Protection Scheme by kind permission.

Office of Fair Trading: extracts from Annual Reports and other publications reprinted by kind permission.

Oyez Longman: extracts from *The Solicitors' Journal* reprinted by kind permission.

Road Traffic Reports: extracts reprinted by kind permission of Kenneth Mason Publications Ltd, The Old Harbourmaster's, 8 North Street, Emsworth, Hampshire PO10 7DD.

Scots Law Times: extracts reprinted by kind permission of W. Green & Son Ltd.

Society of Public Teachers of Law: extract from *Legal Studies* reprinted by kind permission of the Society and of Dr Richard Tur.

Times: extracts from Law Reports of 13 January 1932 and 29 June 1978 reprinted by kind permission of Times Newspapers Ltd.

Toronto Ministry of Government Services: extract from reports of the Ontario Law Reform Commission reprinted by kind permission.

Trading Law: extracts reprinted by kind permission of Barry Rose Law Periodicals Ltd.

Unfair Contracts (by Sina Deutsch): extracts reprinted by kind permission (Lexington, Mass: Lexington Books, D. C. Heath and Company, Copyright 1977, D. C. Heath and Company).

Tony Weir, Fellow, Trinity College, Cambridge: translation of the West German Law Against Unfair Competition printed by kind permission.

West Publishing Company: extracts from the *Pacific Reporter, Atlantic Reporter, Federal Supplement* and *North Eastern Reporter* reprinted by kind permission. Copyright © by West Publishing Co.

Table of statutes

References in this Table to *Statutes* are to Halsbury's Statutes of England (Third Edition) showing the volume and page at which the annotated text of the Act will be found. Page references printed in bold type indicate where the Act is set out in part or in full.

List of cases

Page numbers marked with an asterisk i.e. * indicate where a case is set out

CHAPTER 1

The framework of remedies: representations, warranties and guarantees

Introduction

The first part of this book is concerned with the content, scope and effectiveness of the private law remedies available to consumers where damage or loss is caused by some fault in the provision of goods or services. The following information indicates the range of recorded complaints about such matters:

Annual Report of the Director General of Fair Trading (1983) pp 69–70

CONSUMER COMPLAINTS AND CONVICTIONS UNDER CONSUMER LEGISLATION REPORTED IN THE YEAR ENDING 30 SEPTEMBER 1983

Table 1 gives a summary of detailed complaint statistics provided by local enforcement authorities and advice agencies (who also supplied an analysis of the trading practices involved). Ratios of complaints to consumer expenditure are included only for comparison between different goods and services sectors. Inflation has the effect of reducing these ratios and comparisons with previous years would be misleading.
. . .

Table 1—An analysis of the consumer complaints recorded by local enforcement authorities and advice agencies

Goods	No of complaints 1982–83	Complaints per £m spent 1982–83
Food and drink	34,628[1]	0.87
Footwear	22,475	10.74
Clothing and textiles	49,791	4.65
Furniture and floor coverings	63,060	14.28
Household appliances	82,471	23.57
Toilet requisites, soaps, detergents, etc	1,938	1.16
Toys, games, sports goods, etc	10,242	10.72
Solid and liquid fuels	5,714	0.72
Motor vehicles and accessories	65,815	6.62
Other consumer goods	87,534	—
Non-consumer goods	4,390	—
Land, including houses	1,694	—

Services		
Home repairs and improvements	18,185	2.99
Repairs and servicing to domestic electrical appliances (excluding radio and TV)	4,607	20.10
Repairs and servicing to motor vehicles	10,701	7.17
Other repairs and servicing	12,237	32.55
Cleaning	7,967	29.51
Public utilities and transport	15,553	0.68

1

Table 1—*cont.*

Services—*cont.*	No of complaints 1982–83	Complaints per £m spent 1982–83
Consumer credit	9,300	—
Entertainment and accommodation	11,473[1]	—
Holidays	9,129	2.02
Professional services	15,178	2.48
General services, etc	20,616	—

[1] Includes complaints recorded by Environmental Health Officers as follows:

Food and drink	13,268
Entertainment and accommodation	7,189

For further information see, for example, the following National Consumer Council papers and reports, 'Consumer Concerns Survey' (1981), 'Faulty Goods' (1981), 'Buying Problems' (1984). Of course such recorded complaints will be only a small proportion of the total number of problems experienced by consumers: see further below, at pp 290–295.

Whether a consumer will have a legal remedy in respect of any given complaint involving goods or services will be affected by a variety of factors. One is the relationship, if any, between the parties and in particular whether it is contractual. Another is whether the defendant is a trader or a private individual, a consumer's rights being more extensive in the former case. Again the position may depend on the nature of the damage or loss suffered, and in particular on whether physical injury or property damage is involved. Other things being equal a remedy will be available more readily in such cases than in cases where, for example, the complaint is that the goods are shoddy or that a service has not had the promised effect.

Statements of opinion, fact and contractual promise

If B makes a statement to A about the condition or quality of goods or about services to be provided, or if such a statement is contained in a written contract, it may fall into any one of three broad categories. Some such statements are mere puffs of the 'whiter than white' variety and of no legal effect. They are controlled, if at all, through such voluntary measures as the Code of Advertising Practice (see below pp 398–403). Similarly the statement may be no more than an honest expression of opinion or an estimate and as such it will again not normally ground liability in damages if it proves to be ill-informed. (Cf, however, the position under the Trade Descriptions Act 1968, s 3(3) especially and *Holloway v Cross* [1981] 1 All ER 1012 (QBD), below p 489.) The second broad category encompasses statements of fact or 'mere representations' which may induce a person (A) to enter a contract in reliance on the statement being true but which do not form part of the contract. Nowadays there will be a remedy in damages in such cases if the statement is false provided at least that the person making the statement (B) did not have reasonable grounds for believing it to be true (see generally the Misrepresentation Act 1967, s 2). Also it may be open to A to rescind or set aside the contract. Thirdly the statment may constitute a contractual term or promise in the sense that B has 'warranted', for example, that his goods have certain attributes or has 'guaranteed' that his services will conform to a particular description or produce a particular result. A will then have a remedy for damages for breach of contract if the goods or services are not as warranted or if the promise is not fulfilled. He may also, depending on the nature of the term broken (whether a condition or a warranty) or perhaps on the consequences of the breach (innominate term) be entitled to treat the contract as having been repudiated. Such express terms are commonplace in a wide range of everyday consumer transactions including the sale of goods (especially when they are second-hand), home improvements, car servicing and the provision of holidays.

The above matters are dealt with fully in the standard texts of the law of contract and sale of goods: see, for example, Cheshire and Fifoot, *The Law of Contract* (10th edn, 1981) at pp 110–115, 128–138 and 235 et seq; Smith and Thomas, *A Casebook on Contract* (7th edn, 1982) Chs 9 and 11; Atiyah, *The Sale of Goods* (6th edn, 1980) Ch 6 and *Benjamin's Sale of Goods* (2nd edn, 1981) Ch 10.

The following cases illustrate the distinction between statements of opinion, fact and promise.

Dick Bentley Productions Ltd v Harold Smith (Motors) Ltd [1965] 2 All ER 65, [1965] 1 WLR 623, Court of Appeal

The facts are set out in the judgment of Lord Denning MR:

Lord Denning MR: The second plaintiff, Mr Charles Walter Bentley, sometimes known as Dick Bentley, brings an action against Harold Smith (Motors) Ltd for damages for breach of warranty on the sale of a car. Mr Bentley had been dealing with Mr Smith (to whom I shall refer in the stead of the defendant company) for a couple of years and told Mr Smith he was on the look-out for a well vetted Bentley car. In January, 1960, Mr Smith found one and bought it for £1,500 from a firm in Leicester. He wrote to Mr Bentley and said: 'I have just purchased a Park Ward power operated hood convertible. It is one of the nicest cars we have had in for quite a long time.' Mr Smith had told Mr Bentley earlier that he was in a position to find out the history of cars. It appears that with a car of this quality the makers do keep a complete biography of it.

Mr Bentley went to see the car. Mr Smith told him that a German baron had had this car. He said that it had been fitted at one time with a replacement engine and gearbox, and had done twenty thousand miles only since it had been so fitted. The speedometer on the car showed only twenty thousand miles. Mr Smith said the price was £1,850, and he would guarantee the car for twelve months, including parts and labour. That was on the morning of Jan 23, 1960. In the afternoon Mr Bentley took his wife over to see the car. Mr Bentley repeated to his wife in Mr Smith's presence what Mr Smith had told him in the morning. In particular that Mr Smith said it had done only twenty thousand miles since it had been refitted with a replacement engine and gearbox. Mr Bentley took it for a short run. He bought the car for £1,850, gave his cheque and the sale was concluded. The car was a considerable disappointment to him. He took it back to Mr Smith from time to time. [His Lordship referred briefly to some work done on the car and continued:] Eventually he brought this action for breach of warranty. The county court judge found that there was a warranty, that it was broken, and that the damages were more than £400, but as the claim was limited to £400, he gave judgment for the plaintiffs for that amount.

The first point is whether this representation, namely that the car had done twenty thousand miles only since it had been fitted with a replacement engine and gearbox, was an innocent misrepresentation (which does not give rise to damages), or whether it was a warranty. It was said by Holt, C J,[1] and repeated in *Heilbut, Symons & Co v Buckleton*[2].

'An affirmation at the time of the sale is a warranty, provided it appear on evidence to be so intended.'

But that word 'intended' has given rise to difficulties. I endeavoured to explain in *Oscar Chess Ltd v Williams*[3] that the question whether a warranty was intended depends on the conduct of the parties, on their words and behaviour, rather than on their thoughts. If an intelligent bystander would reasonably infer that a warranty was intended, that will suffice. What conduct, then? What words and behaviour, lead to the inference of a warranty?

Looking at the cases once more, as we have done so often, it seems to me that if a representation is made in the course of dealings for a contract for the very purpose of inducing the other party to act on it, and it actually induces him to act on it by entering into the contract, that is prima facie ground for inferring that the representation was intended as a warranty. It is not necessary to speak of it as being collateral. Suffice it that the representation was intended to be acted on and was in fact acted on. But the maker of the representation can rebut this inference if he can show that it really was an innocent misrepresentation, in that he was in fact innocent of fault in making it, and that it would not be reasonable in the circumstances for him to be bound by it. In the *Oscar Chess* case[4] the inference was rebutted. There a man had bought a second-hand car and received with it a log-book, which stated the year of the car, 1948. He afterwards resold the car. When he resold it he simply repeated what was in the log-book and passed it on to the buyer. He honestly believed on reasonable grounds that it was true. He was completely innocent of any fault. There was no warranty by him but only an innocent misrepresentation. Whereas in the present case it is very different. The inference is not rebutted. Here we have a dealer Mr Smith, who was in a position to know, or at least to find out, the history of the car. He could get it by writing to the makers. He did not do so. Indeed it was done later. When the history of this car was examined, his statement turned out to be quite wrong. He ought to have known better. There was no reasonable foundation for it.

[His Lordship summarised the history of the car, and continued:] The county court judge found that the representations were not dishonest. Mr Smith was not guilty of fraud. But he made the statement as to twenty thousand miles without any foundation. And the judge was well justified in finding that there was a warranty. He said:

'I have no hesitation that as a matter of law the statement was a warranty. Mr Smith stated a fact that should be within his own knowledge. He had jumped to a conclusion and stated it as a fact. A fact that a buyer would act on.'

That is ample foundation for the inference of a warranty. So much for this point.

I hold that the appeal fails and should be dismissed.

Danckwerts LJ: I agree with the judgment of Lord Denning MR.

Salmon LJ: I agree. I have no doubt at all that the learned county court judge reached a correct conclusion when he decided that Mr Smith gave a warranty to the second plaintiff, Mr Bentley, and that that warranty was broken. Was what Mr Smith said intended and understood as a legally binding promise? If so, it was a warranty and as such may be part of the contract of sale or collateral to it. In effect, Mr Smith said: 'If you will enter into a contract to buy this motor car from me for £1,850, I undertake that you will be getting a motor car which has done no more than twenty thousand miles since it was fitted with a new engine and a new gearbox.' I have no doubt at all that what was said by Mr Smith was so understood and was intended to be so understood by Mr Bentley.

I accordingly agree that the appeal should be dismissed.

Appeal dismissed.

1. In *Crosse v Gardner* (1688) Carth 90 and *Medina v Stoughton* (1700) 1 Salk 210.
2. [1911–13] All ER Rep 83 at 92; [1913] AC 30 at 49. The words quoted were ascribed by Lord Moulton to Holt CJ. They appear in the judgment of Buller J, in *Pasley v Freeman* ((1789) 3 Term Rep 51 at 57, 100 ER 450 at 453) where he said '. . . it was rightly held by Holt CJ, [in *Crosse v Gardner* (1688) Carth 90, 90 ER 656 and *Medina v Stoughton* (1700) 1 Salk 210, 91 ER 188], and has been uniformly adopted ever since, that an affirmation at the time of sale is a warranty, provided it appear on evidence to have been so intended'.
3. [1957] 1 All ER 325 at pp 328, 329.
4. [1957] 1 All ER 325.

NOTES

It is generally agreed that Lord Denning's emphasis on the question of fault is somewhat misplaced. If B warrants to A that an article has certain characteristics it is not in point that he was honestly and reasonably mistaken in believing this to be so. Indeed this is the essence of a guarantee properly so-called. (Cf the position under the Misrepresentation Act 1967, s 2). Nonetheless presumably an intelligent bystander will infer a warranty much more readily where a person is in a position to know the truth and often such a person will be at fault in failing to discover it. As between a dealer and a consumer obviously it is generally the former who will fill this role. In the *Oscar Chess* case to which Lord Denning referred the seller was a private individual.

For a more recent unreported case involving the breach of an express warranty that a Rolls Royce car was 'in excellent condition' see *Peter Symmons & Co v Cook* (1981) 131 NLJ 758 (R Rougier, QC: QBD); see also below p 76 and p 259 for further references.

Esso Petroleum Co Ltd v Mardon [1976] 2 All ER 5, [1976] QB 801, Court of Appeal

The Plaintiffs 'Esso' had acquired a site on a busy main street for development as a petrol filling station. Their original calculations showed an estimated annual throughput of some 200,000 gallons from the third year of operation. However the conditions on which planning permission was subsequently granted were such that this estimate should have been revised to a much lower figure. This was not done. During negotiations with the defendant for the tenancy of the site Esso's experienced local manager told him of this estimate and in April 1963 an agreement for three years was concluded. An annual throughput of some 60,000–70,000 gallons was all that could be expected realistically and the agreement was a financial disaster for the tenant. In July 1964 he tendered notice to quit but he was granted rather a new tenancy to run from September 1964 and at a reduced rent. Matters did not improve and Esso claimed possession of the station and moneys due. The defendant, Mardon, counter-claimed for damages in respect of the manager's representation. The trial judge, Lawson J, rejected his claim for breach of warranty but held that Esso were liable in tort for breach of their own duty of care when advising him of the estimated throughput. However he limited damages to the loss suffered up to September 1964. The defendant, Mardon, appealed.

Lord Denning MR, having stated the facts, continued:

Such being the facts, I turn to consider the law. It is founded on the representation that the estimated throughput of the service station was 200,000 gallons. No claim can be brought under the Misrepresentation Act 1967 because that Act did not come into force until 22nd April 1967, whereas this representation was made in April 1963. So the claim is put in two ways: first, that the representation was a collateral warranty; second, that is was a negligent misrepresentation. I will take them in order.

Collateral warranty
Ever since *Heilbut, Symons & Co v Buckleton*[1] we have had to contend with the law as laid down by the House of Lords that an innocent misrepresentation gives no right to damages. In order to escape from that rule, the pleader used to allege—I often did it myself—that the misrepresentation was fraudulent, or alternatively a collateral warranty. At the trial we nearly always succeeded on collateral warranty. We had to reckon, of course, with the dictum of

Lord Moulton[2] that 'such collateral contracts must from their very nature be rare'. But more often than not the court elevated the innocent misrepresentation into a collateral warranty; and thereby did justice—in advance of the Misrepresentation Act 1967. I remember scores of cases of that kind, especially on the sale of a business. A representation as to the profits that had been made in the past was invariably held to be a warranty. Besides that experience, there have been many cases since I have sat in this court where we have readily held a representation—which induces a person to enter into a contract—to be a warranty sounding in damages. I summarised them in *Dick Bentley Productions Ltd v Harold Smith (Motors) Ltd*[3] . . .

Counsel for Esso retaliated, however, by citing *Bisset v Wilkinson*[4] where the Privy Council said that a statement by a New Zealand farmer that an area of land 'would carry 2,000 sheep' was only an expression of opinion. He submitted that the forecast here of 200,000 gallons was an expression of opinion and not a statement of fact; and that it could not be interpreted as a warranty or promise.

Now, I would quite agree with counsel for Esso that it was not a warranty—in this sense—that it did not *guarantee* that the throughput *would be* 200,000 gallons. But, nevertheless, it was a forecast made by a party, Esso, who had special knowledge and skill. It was the yardstick (the 'e a c') by which they measured the worth of a filling station. They knew the facts. They knew the traffic in the town. They knew the throughput of comparable stations. They had much experience and expertise at their disposal. They were in a much better position than Mr Mardon to make a forecast. It seems to me that if such a person makes a forecast—intending that the other should act on it and he does act on it—it can well be interpreted as a warranty that the forecast is sound and reliable in this sense that they made it with reasonable care and skill. It is just as if Esso said to Mr Mardon: 'Our forecast of throughput is 200,000 gallons. You can rely on it as being a sound forecast of what the service station should do. The rent is calculated on that footing.' If the forecast turned out to be an unsound forecast, such as no person of skill or experience should have made, there is a breach of warranty. Just as there is a breach of warranty when a forecast is made 'expected to load' by a certain date if the maker has no reasonable grounds for it: see *Samuel Sanday & Co v Keighley, Maxted & Co*[5]; or bunkers 'expected 600/700 tons': see *The Pantanassa*[6] by Diplock J. It is very different from the New Zealand case[7] where the land had never been used as a sheep farm and both parties were equally able to form an opinion as to its carrying capacity.

In the present case it seems to me that there was a warranty that the forecast was sound, that is that Esso had made it with reasonable care and skill. That warranty was broken. Most negligently Esso made a 'fatal error' in the forecast they stated to Mr Mardon, and on which he took the tenancy. For this they are liable in damages. The judge, however, declined to find a warranty[8]. So I must go further.

Negligent misrepresentation

Assuming that there was no warranty, the question arises whether Esso are liable for negligent mis-statement under the doctrine of *Hedley Byrne & Co Ltd v Heller & Partners Ltd*[9]. It has been suggested that *Hedley Byrne*[9] cannot be used so as to impose liability for negligent pre-contractual statements; and that, in a pre-contract situation, the remedy (at any rate before the 1967 Act) was only in warranty or nothing . . .

. . . [I] cannot accept counsel for Esso's proposition. It seems to me that *Hedley Byrne*[9], properly understood, covers this particular proposition: if a man, who has or professes to have special knowledge or skill, makes a representation by virtue thereof to another—be it advice, information or opinion—with the intention of inducing him to enter into a contract with him, he is under a duty to use reasonable care to see that the representation is correct, and that the advice, information or opinion is reliable. If he negligently gives unsound advice or misleading information or expresses an erroneous opinion, and thereby induces the other side into a contract with him, he is liable in damages. This proposition is in line with what I said in *Candler v Crane Christmas & Co*[10], which was approved by the majority of the Privy Council in *Mutual Life and Citizens' Assurance Ltd v Evatt*[11]. And the judges of the Commonwealth have shown themselves quite ready to apply *Hedley Byrne*[9] between contracting parties: see, in Canada, *Sealand of the Pacific Ltd v Ocean Cement Ltd*[12] and, in New Zealand, *Capital Motors Ltd v Beecham*[13].

Applying this principle, it is plain that Esso professed to have—and did in fact have—special knowledge or skill in estimating the throughput of a filling station. They made the representation—they forecast a throughput of 200,000 gallons—intending to induce Mr Mardon to enter into a tenancy on the faith of it. They made it negligently. It was a 'fatal error'. And thereby induced Mr Mardon to enter into a contract of tenancy that was disastrous to him. For this misrepresentation they are liable in damages.

Damages

Now for the measure of damages. Mr Mardon is not to be compensated here for 'loss of a bargain'. He was given no bargain that the throughput *would* amount to 200,000 gallons a year. He is only to be compensated for having been induced to enter into a contract which turned out to be disastrous for him. Whether it be called breach of warranty or negligent misrepresentation, its effect was *not* to warrant the throughput, but only to induce him to enter into the contract. So the damages in either case are to be measured by the loss he suffered. Just as in the case of *Doyle v Olby (Ironmongers) Ltd*[14], he can say: 'I would not have entered into this contract at all but for your representation. Owing to it, I have lost all the capital I put into it. I also incurred a large overdraft. I have spent four years of my life in wasted endeavour without reward; and it will take me some time to re-establish myself.'

For all such loss he is entitled to recover damages. It is to be measured in a similar way as the loss due to a personal injury. You should look into the future so as to forecast what would have been likely to happen if he had never entered into this contract; and contrast it with his position as it is now as a result of entering into it. The future is necessarily problematical and can only be a rough-and-ready estimate. But it must be done in assessing the loss.

Now for the new agreement of 1st September 1964. The judge limited the loss to the period from April 1963 to September 1964, when the new agreement was made. He said that from 1st September 1964 Mr Mardon was carrying on the business 'on an entirely fresh basis, of which the negligent mis-statement formed no part'.

I am afraid I take a different view. It seems to me that from 1st September 1964, Mr Mardon acted most reasonably. He was doing what he could to retrieve the position, not only in his own interest, but also in the interest of Esso. It was Esso who were anxious for him to stay on. They had no other suitable tenant to replace him. They needed him to keep the station as a going concern and sell their petrol. It is true that by this time the truth was known, that the throughput was very far short of 200,000 gallons, but nevertheless, the effect of the original mis-statement was still there. It laid a heavy hand on all that followed. The new agreement was an attempt to mitigate the effect. It was not a fresh cause which eliminated the past. It seems to me that the losses after 1st September 1964 can be attributed to the original mis-statement, just as those before . . .

Ormrod and Shaw LJJ agreed that the appeal should be allowed.

Appeal allowed; cross-appeal dismissed.
Subsequently the court approved the terms of a settlement between the parties as to the damages to be paid to Mr Mardon which were indorsed on counsels' briefs but not made public.

1. [1913] AC 30, [1911–13] All ER Rep 83.
2. [1913] AC [30] at 47, [1911–13] All ER Rep [83] at 90.
3. [1965] 2 All ER 65 at 67, [1965] 1 WLR 623 at 627 [above p 3].
4. [1927] AC 177, [1926] All ER Rep 343.
5. (1922) 27 Com Cas 296.
6. [1958] 2 Lloyd's Rep 449 at 455–7.
7. See particularly [1927] AC at 183, 184, [1926] All ER Rep at 346, 347.
8. [1975] 1 All ER at 215, 216, [1975] QB at 825, 826.
9. [1963] 2 All ER 575, [1964] AC 465.
10. [1951] 1 All ER 426 at 433, 434, [1951] 2 KB 164 at 179, 180.
11. [1971] 1 All ER 150, [1971] AC 793.
12. (1973) 33 DLR (3d) 625.
13. [1975] 1 NZLR 576.
14. [1969] 2 All ER 119, [1969] 2 QB 158.

As the above cases and *Lambert v Lewis* [1980] 1 All ER 978, CA, below p 35, indicate there is a wide range of options available in the classification of statements made in a contractual context. The English approach, requiring that contractual warranties be dependent on promissory intent (see *Heilbut, Symons & Co v Buckleton* [1913] AC 30, HL), has not found favour in other common law jurisdictions. For example in the United States Uniform Commercial Code Art 2–313 the test is whether the relevant affirmation of fact or promise is 'part of the basis of the bargain'. An alternative approach is to place emphasis on the question of 'reliance'. This is the position under the American Uniform Sales Act 1906, s 12, which provides in part that:

> Any affirmation of fact or any promise by the seller relating to the goods is an express warranty if the natural tendency of such affirmation or promise is to induce the buyer to purchase the goods, and if the buyer purchases the goods relying thereon.

A proviso to s 12 adds that 'No affirmation of the value of the goods, nor any statement purporting to be a statement of the seller's opinion only shall be construed as a warranty'.

Reliance, rather than the 'basis of the bargain' or contractual intention, is the approach preferred also by the Ontario Law Reform Commission in its 'Report on Sale of Goods' (1979) (see Ch 6, pp 135–145). The accompanying draft Bill contains the following provision.

Report on Sale of Goods 1979 (Ontario Law Reform Commission)

5.10   Express warranties by seller, etc
(1) A representation or promise in any form relating to goods that are the subject of a contract of sale made by the seller, manufacturer or distributor of the goods is an express warranty and binding upon the person making it,
   (a) if the natural tendency of such representation or promise is to induce the buyer, or buyers generally if the representation or promise is made to the public, to rely thereon; and
   (b) if, in the case of a representation or promise not made to the public, the buyer acts in reliance upon the representation or promise.

Irrelevant factors
(2) Subsection 1 applies to a representation or promise made before or at the time the contract was made and whether or not,
   (a) it was made fraudulently or negligently;
   (b) there is privity of contract between the person making the representation or promise and the buyer;
   (c) it was made with a contractual intention; or
   (d) any consideration was given in respect of it.

Express warranties by buyer
(3) This section applies *mutatis mutandis* to a representation or promise made by the buyer.

(For further reference to manufacturers' express warranties see below p 31 et seq.)

In English law the importance of distinguishing between contractual terms and 'mere representations' has been considerably reduced by two developments referred to in *Esso Petroleum Co Ltd v Mardon* [1976] 2 All ER 5, [1976] 2 WLR 583, above p 5. The first is the decision in *Hedley Byrne & Co Ltd v Heller & Partners Ltd* [1964] AC 465, [1963] 2 All ER 575, HL, and the second is the Misrepresentation Act 1967. Both now provide a remedy in damages for negligent misrepresentations. The *Hedley Byrne* decision is discussed in detail in the standard texts on the law of tort: see for example Street *The Law of Torts* (7th edn, 1983) p 201 et seq especially; *Winfield and Jolowicz on Tort* (12th edn, 1984) p 273 et seq. For discussion of the Misrepresentation Act 1967 see Cheshire and Fifoot, op cit, at p 250 et seq; Smith and Thomas, op cit, at p 271 et seq and Atiyah and Treitel (1967) 30 MLR 369.

By s 2(1) of the 1967 Act it is the person making the statement who has the onus of proving a reasonable ground for believing it to be true. In this the Act has an advantage over the *Hedley Byrne* principle where it is the plaintiff representee who must establish negligence. The Act may have an advantage also where the representation is made innocently and without fault since by s 2(2) damages may be awarded in lieu of the traditional remedy of rescission.

It is in relation to the approach to quantifying damages that it is most likely that the distinction between representations and warranties will remain important. In very general terms damages for breach of contract are awarded to place the plaintiff in the position he would have enjoyed if the contract had been performed and the promise fulfilled whereas in tort damages are awarded to compensate for losses incurred through reliance on the representation. There are differences also in the rules governing remoteness of damage where the 'reasonable foreseeability' test in tort is perhaps somewhat less restrictive than the equivalent 'reasonable contemplation of the parties' test in contract. For more detailed discussion of damages in contract and tort respectively see Cheshire and Fifoot, op cit, at p 537 et seq; Smith and Thomas, op cit, Chapter 16; Street, op cit, p 133 et seq and Winfield and Jolowicz, op cit, p 120 et seq.

It is clear that it is the tort-based approach which applies where the claim is based on the *Hedley Byrne* principle. Similarly the better view is that the same approach is applicable to actions based on the Misrepresentation Act 1967, s 2: see *Andre & Cie SA v Ets Michel Blanc & Fils* [1977] 2 Lloyds Rep 166 at 181 (Ackner J); *F & H Entertainments Ltd v Leisure Enterprises Ltd* (1976) 120 Sol Jo 331 (Walton J); *Benjamin's Sale of Goods,* para 885, but contrast *Jarvis v Swan's Tours Ltd* [1973] QB 233, [1973] 1 All ER 71, CA; *Watts v Spence* [1976] Ch 165, [1975] 2 All ER 528.

Finally it is important to note that the *Hedley Byrne* principle applies even though there is no contract between the parties. Indeed this is its principal sphere of application. Conversely it has been held that the 1967 Act applies only where there is a contractual relationship between the parties and not, for example, when the defendant is merely acting as an agent for a third party: see *Resolute Maritime Inc v Nippon Kaiji Kyokai, The Skopas* [1983] 2 All ER 1, [1983] 1 WLR 857). The point may be of some importance when consumers deal with travel agents, estate agents and other agents.

Problems

In the light of the above materials consider the following cases.
1. Boswell owns an art gallery in which he displays an unsigned painting. Jonson, a private collector, shows an interest in the work and asks Boswell who painted it. Boswell replies, 'It is almost certainly an early Picasso'. Jonson then agrees to buy the painting for £5,000. In fact, and unbeknown to Boswell, it is by another artist and worth only £500. As an early Picasso it would have been worth £10,000. Twelve months later Jonson discovers the true facts.

Advise Jonson. Would your advice be different if Boswell had been a private collector selling off part of his collection?
2. Gnome wishes to acquire a boat for general cruising and for use in water skiing. He approaches Quick, a specialist dealer in second-hand boats who has the Mary Rose for sale in his yard. Quick is not told of Gnome's precise requirements for the boat but on being asked her speed

he replies, 'I estimate she will do a good fifteen miles per hour'. This would have been sufficient for Gnome's purposes. Having bought the Mary Rose Gnome discovers that she is capable of only ten miles per hour, a speed which is too low for water skiing.

Advise Gnome. (See *J J Savage & Sons Pty Ltd v Blakney* (1970) 119 CLR 435 (Aust. HC).

3.   Ada is approached by Bert, a seller of double-glazing systems. Bert asks her what her annual heating bill is and Ada replies, '£600'. Bert says, 'We estimate that in an average year you would save a good £150 with our system'. Ada has the system installed at a cost of £1,000. In the following year (when the weather is 'normal') Ada's savings are only £50. She expects to continue to live in the house for another thirty or so years.

Advise Ada. How, if at all, would it affect the position if Bert had added, 'At the very least we can guarantee savings of £100'?

4.   Chisel, a private collector of objets d'art, approaches Hammer, an auctioneer, and asks him to sell a vase on his behalf. Chisel describes it as 'early Ming' and this description is printed in Hammer's catalogue. Chisel knows that the description is entirely erroneous but Hammer believes it to be correct. The vase is bought by Sickle, a private collector. Six months later Sickle discovers the truth.

Advise Sickle as to any remedy which he may have against (i) Chisel and (ii) Hammer, assuming there are no relevant conditions of sale.

The classification of contractual terms

Traditionally English law has classified contractual terms as either conditions or warranties, the classification being important to the consequences of breach. Prima facie breach of a condition will give the 'innocent' party the right to treat the contract as having been repudiated and also free him from an obligation to perform his own contractual undertakings, whereas breach of a warranty will give rise only to an entitlement to damages. In many consumer transactions there are important implied terms as to quality etc which by statute are designated 'conditions' (see, for example, the Supply of Goods (Implied Terms) Act 1973, ss 9 and 10, below p 62, the Sale of Goods Act 1979, ss 13 and 14, below p 61 and the Supply of Goods and Services Act 1982, ss 3, 4, 8 and 9, below p 64 and p 65). In other contracts the parties themselves may choose to describe a stipulation as a condition, as where an insurance contract provides that the answers to certain questions shall form the 'basis of the contract' (see below p 138 et seq). Alternatively an attempt may be made to stipulate the contrary, as where a contract to instal fitted cupboards or double-glazing provides that 'time shall not be of the essence of the contract'. The use by the parties of the word 'condition' will not necessarily be taken as a conclusive indication that they intended that any breach, no matter how trivial, would give rise to an entitlement to treat the contract as having been repudiated: see *Schuler AG v Wickman Machine Tool Sales Ltd* [1974] AC 235, [1973] 2 All ER 39, HL.

Many consumer contracts will contain express terms of varying degrees of importance, for example contracts for the provision of services such as home removals, dry-cleaning, car servicing (where the terms may be incorporated by reference to the manufacturer's handbook) and holidays.

In holiday contracts it is obvious that some terms will be more important than others. For example it may be assumed that the absence of a swimming pool or of air conditioning in a hot and humid climate is far more important than (say) the temporary suspension of afternoon tea. The one might justify the holidaymaker in cancelling the holiday whereas probably the other would not. Again much may depend on the individual consumer. The absence of a promised 'disco' may ruin a holiday for a group of teenagers and be a positive boon to others. This suggests that there are benefits in a flexible approach to such matters.

The Law Commission Working Paper No 85 on the 'Sale and Supply of Goods' (1983) contains a helpful discussion of the notion of an innominate or intermediate term.

Sale and supply of goods (1983) (Law Commission Working Paper No 85) pp 26–34

I. SALE OF GOODS

2.24 The first question which we consider is the extent to which the buyer's remedies for breach of one of the statutory implied terms depend on whether the term is classified as a condition or warranty. The position is different in English and Scots law but in both jurisdictions the existing law on this point is, in our view, open to criticism.

The buyer's remedies: conditions and warranties

(i) *English law*
2.25 *The statutory distinction between conditions and warranties.*　The word 'condition' is not specifically defined in the Sale of Goods Act, though section 11(3) of the 1979 Act defines it by inference when it states that:

> Whether a stipulation in a contract of sale is a condition, the breach of which may give rise to a right to treat the contract as repudiated, or a warranty, the breach of which may give rise to a claim for damages but not a right to reject the goods and treat the contract as repudiated, depends in each case on the construction of the contract . . .

In addition to being defined by inference in this provision, 'warranty' is also defined expressly in section 61(1) of the 1979 Act as:

> an agreement with reference to goods which are the subject of a contract of sale, but collateral to the main purpose of such contract, the breach of which gives rise to a claim for damages, but not to a right to reject the goods and treat the contract as repudiated.

The statutory implied terms as to title, description, quality, fitness for purpose and correspondence with sample are all classified as conditions in the Act. The statutory implied terms as to freedom from encumbrances and quiet possession are classified as warranties.

2.26 *Effect of the statutory distinction.*　It will be seen that whether a statutory implied term is a condition or a warranty has a profound effect on the buyer's remedies for breach. If the term is a condition, the buyer (provided that he has not waived the condition,[1] or elected to treat its breach as a mere breach of warranty[2] or accepted the goods within the meaning of the Act[3]) can reject the goods,[4] treat the contract as repudiated and recover the price if it has already been paid.[5] If the term is a warranty the buyer is confined to a claim for damages.[6]

2.27 *Developments in the common law.*　It was at one time thought[7] that in English law the distinction between conditions and warranties was the main criterion for determining the effects of breach of contract in general. However, this supposition was rejected in *Hongkong Fir Shipping Co Ltd v Kawasaki Kisen Kaisha Ltd*[8] where the stipulation as to seaworthiness in a charterparty was held to be neither a condition nor a warranty but an intermediate or innominate term. It was held that because such a term could be broken in many different ways, ranging from the most trivial to the most serious, the innocent party's right to treat the contract as at an end depended on the nature and effect of the breach in question. The right of the innocent party to treat the contract as at an end depended on whether he had been deprived 'of substantially the whole benefit which it was intended he should obtain from the contract.'[9] This test which is the same as that for frustration makes it extremely difficult for the innocent party to reject. It was extended into the law of sale in *Cehave v Bremer*[10] where an express term that the goods were to be shipped in good condition was breached but it was held that the circumstances were not sufficiently serious to justify rejection. The court relied on section 61(2) of the Sale of Goods Act 1893 in holding that the common law rules preserved by that subsection prevented an exclusive distinction between condition and warranty and allowed the court, where appropriate, to regard a particular express term as innominate.

2.28 This important development has been approved by the House of Lords in more recent cases[11] and it is clear that the statutory classification of terms in the Sale of Goods Act as conditions or warranties is not to be treated as an indication that the law knows no terms other than conditions and warranties.[12] Whether a term is a condition or a warranty or an innominate term depends on the intention of the parties, as ascertained from the construction of the contract. Even if the parties do not expressly classify a term as a condition it may nevertheless be construed as a condition if it is clear what the parties intended. This is more likely if certainty is very important in the context, if the term is one the breach of which is likely to be clearly established one way or the other, or if compliance with the term is necessary to enable the other party to perform another term. In *Bunge Corpn v Tradax*, for example, a stipulation as to time in an f.o.b. contract was held to be a condition: the stipulation regulated a series of acts to be done one after another by parties to a string of contracts.[13] The House of Lords in that case specifically drew attention to the distinction between such a term and a term with a flexible content such as the seaworthiness clause in the *Hongkong Fir*[14] case. The seaworthiness clause can be 'broken by the presence of trivial defects easily and rapidly remediable as well as by defects which must inevitably result in a total loss of the vessel'.[15] Where the same term can be broken both by slight and unimportant departures from the contract and by important and serious defects, it is unlikely, in the absence of some express indication to the contrary, to be the intention of the parties that the innocent party can terminate for every breach (ie the term is a condition) or for no breach (ie the term is a warranty).

2.29 *Assessment of the statutory distinction.* It is, in our view, necessary to assess the statutory classification of implied terms in contracts for the sale or supply of goods in the light of these common law developments. The first point to be made is that it is an essential feature of the implied term as to quality in a sale of goods contract that a breach may vary from the trivial to one which renders the goods wholly useless. Some matters can be easily and rapidly repaired; some defective or unsuitable goods can, and in most cases in practice normally will, be replaced at once. For example, in *Jackson v Rotax Motor and Cycle Co*[16] a large proportion of motor horns delivered under a contract of sale were dented and badly polished but could easily have been made merchantable at a trifling cost. Other departures from the contract, however, cannot be promptly and simply repaired, and either replacement is impracticable or to substitute goods will amount to a new contract. There are many cases in which seriously defective goods have been delivered which could not be replaced or rapidly repaired. Replacement within the terms of the contract may, moreover, be impossible.

2.30 In our view, if the Sale of Goods Act did not classify the implied terms as to quality and fitness as conditions of the contract, a court today would not so classify them in the absence of a clear indication that this was what the parties to the particular contract intended. The present classification of these terms is inconsistent with the developed common law.

2.31 Another, and perhaps more serious, criticism of the classification of most of the implied terms in the Sale of Goods Act as conditions is that it leads to inflexibility and to a danger that the obligation of the seller to supply goods of the appropriate quality will be watered down. If a defect is a minor one the court may be reluctant to allow rejection and so, under the present law, may be tempted to hold that there is no breach at all of the implied term as to quality. This is illustrated by two recent cases to which we have already referred. In *Millars of Falkirk Ltd v Turpie*[17] it was held that it was not a breach of contract to deliver a car in a condition which was admittedly defective and required repair; while in *Cehave v Bremer* Lord Denning MR said[18] that the implied condition was only broken if the defect was so serious that a commercial man would have thought that the buyer should be able to reject the goods. These cases illustrate the difficulties to which the rigid classification gives rise, and lower courts are bound by the precedents thus created. There has, moreover, been express criticism[19] of the inflexibility of the present law as to compliance with description. In several earlier cases[20] the court, in deciding whether the buyer should be entitled to terminate the contract, concentrated entirely on whether there had been a breach of the implied term as to description and not at all on the effect that such a breach had had on the contract as a whole. In one of these cases[21] it was expressly found that the goods were commercially within the specification. Some of these decisions were recently said in the House of Lords to be 'excessively technical'.[22]

2.32 There has also been criticism[23] of the concept of the implied warranty for the breach of which the buyer is only entitled to damages. This criticism has been highlighted by a recent development in the common law relating to remedies for breach of express terms. Although the present state of the law is unclear on the point,[24] recent judicial dicta[25] and some academic opinion[26] have suggested that there may well be circumstances in the law of sale where a deliberate breach of a minor express term or an accumulation of breaches of such a minor term would entitle the injured party to treat the contract as at an end. In other words, the argument runs, there should not be a category of express terms or warranties for the breach of which rejection is never available.

(ii)   *Scots Law*
. . .

(iii)   *Conclusion for both jurisdictions*
2.37 The conclusion we reach is that in both English and Scots law the classification of the statutory implied terms as conditions or warranties is inappropriate and liable to produce unreasonable results.

1. Section 11(2).
2. Ibid.
3. Section 11(4). See paras 2.48 to 2.60, below.
4. We discuss later whether the seller has the right to require the buyer to accept repair or replacement of rejected goods. See para 2.38, below.
5. The right to recover the price would appear to be a right in restitution and to be preserved by s 54 of the 1979 Act; see *Chitty on Contracts* 25th edn, (1983) Vol 1, para 4376; *Benjamin's Sale of Goods* 2nd edn, (1981) para 929 and Treitel *The Law of Contract* 5th edn, (1979) at p 774.
6. See also s 53.
7. *Benjamin's Sale of Goods* 2nd edn, (1981), para 757.
8. [1962] 2 QB 26.
9. Ibid, per Diplock LJ at 70.
10. [1976] QB 44.
11. *Reardon Smith Line Ltd v Hansen-Tangen* [1976] 1 WLR 989 at 998, per Lord Wilberforce; *Bunge Corpn v Tradax SA* [1981] 1 WLR 711.
12. *Bunge Corpn v Tradax SA* (above) per Lord Scarman at 718.
13. Whether a clause laying down the time by which an act must be done is or is not a condition still depends, however, on the true construction of the particular clause in question: *Bremer Handelsgesellschaft mbH v Vanden Avenne-Izegem PVBA* [1978] 2 Lloyd's Rep 109. Where earlier authorities (eg *Bowes v Shand* (1877) 2 App Cas 455, HL and *Behn v Burness* (1863) 3 B & S 751) have held a clause to be a condition, it is likely that later parties using a similar clause will also be assumed to intend their term to be a condition.
14. [1962] 2 QB 26; see also *The Ymnos* [1982] 2 Lloyd's Rep 574 at 583 per Goff J.
15. Ibid at 71 per Diplock LJ; see also *Toepfer v Lenersan-Poortman NV* [1978] 2 Lloyd's Rep 555.
16. [1910] 2 KB 937, CA.
17. 1976 SLT (Notes) 66.
18. [1976] QB 44 at 62.
19. *Reardon Smith Line Ltd v Hansen-Tangen* [1976] 1 WLR 989 per Lord Wilberforce at 998.
20. See eg *Arcos Ltd v Ronaasen* [1933] AC 470, HL and *Re Moore & Co Ltd & Landauer & Co* [1921] 2 KB 519, CA.
21. *Arcos Ltd v Ronaasen,* (above).
22. *Reardon Smith Line Ltd v Hansen-Tangen* [1976] 1 WLR 989 per Lord Wilberforce at 998. The seller may in some circumstances have the right to replace the goods: for the difficulties and uncertainties that surround this right see para 2.38, below.
23. *Benjamin's Sale of Goods* 2nd edn, (1981), para 758.
24. Ibid.
25. *Cehave v Bremer* [1976] QB 44 per Lord Denning MR at 60, per Ormrod LJ at 82 to 84.
26. Treitel *The Law of Contract* 5th edn, (1979) at pp 608 to 610.

The Ontario Law Reform Commission also has recommended the abandonment of the distinction between conditions and warranties in contracts for the sale of goods. In its 'Report on Consumer Warranties and Guarantees in the Sale of Goods' (1972) it commented at p 31:

The distinction between warranties and conditions has been frequently criticized and we endorse the criticism . . . American sales law has never adopted the distinction and apparently has not suffered from its absence.[1] It has been rightly pointed out that the distinction focuses on an *a priori* classification of the obligation rather than on the severity of the breach of the obligation . . .

The Commission sees no merit in maintaining the distinction. It is therefore recommended that the distinction between warranties and conditions be aboished with respect to consumer sales and replaced by the single concept of 'warranty'.

1. See Williston, *Rescission for Breach of Warranty* (1903), 16 Harv L Rev 465.

The Commission's 'Report on Sale of Goods' (1979) reviewed the above recommendation and concluded that it was appropriate for contracts for the sale of goods generally and not only for consumer sales. It recommended at p 151:

. . .

5. The revised Act should eliminate the distinction between warranty and condition and, where appropriate, substitute the single term 'warranty'.
6. In order to determine the remedies available to an aggrieved buyer or seller and when he may cancel the contract because of breach by the other, the revised Act should adopt a unitary concept of substantial breach in place of the existing classification of warranties and conditions.

Problems

The above conclusions and recommendations are concerned with contracts for the supply of goods where there are sound arguments for adopting the 'wait and see' approach of the *Hongkong Fir Shipping* case. However such an approach may be difficult to apply in practice in other consumer contracts.

Consider the following cases.

1.   A contract for the provision of a package tour holiday with the Oz travel company states that 'Baby sitting facilities are always available at our Belleview Hotel'. On arrival at the airport prior to departure clients are informed that these facilities have been withdrawn. Benjamin and Chitty both wish to cancel their holiday. Benjamin has eight young children. Chitty has no children but he fears that the lack of such facilities will mean that dinners will be far less peaceful than he had expected.

Advise Benjamin and Chitty.

2.   Wotan has booked a two-week package holiday for himself and his family with the Valhalla Travel Company. The contract provides for accommodation at the Hotel Freia which is a four-star hotel. Two weeks before the departure date Valhalla writes to Wotan saying, 'We have been informed that the Hotel Freia may not be ready for the first two days of your stay. Local labour problems are delaying completion. During this period you will be accommodated in the Hotel Fricka which is a pleasant one-star hotel. We are confident that your transfer to the Freia should not be delayed by more than two days. An appropriate price adjustment is being made'. Wotan does not like one-star hotels and is in any event sceptical about the delay being for two days only. He wishes to cancel the holiday and make alternative arrangements.

Advise Wotan.

Adopting a manufacturer's representations

Later in this chapter we consider the extent to which manufacturers of goods may be held liable for failure to meet their own express assurances and more general advertising or promotional claims (see below at pp 31–52). Here we raise a related and similarly basic issue on which there seems to be a curious dearth of English authority or discussion in point.

Cochran v McDonald. 161 Pacific Reporter, 2d series 305 (1945) Supreme Court of Washington

The facts are stated in the judgment of Grady J.

Grady Justice: This action was originally brought by O. K. Cochran against Winterine Manufacturing Company, a corporation, to recover damages for breach of warranty. In an amended complaint H. D. McDonald, doing business as McDonald & Company, was joined as a defendant. The plaintiff was unable to secure legal service of process upon Winterine Manufacturing Company, and the case proceeded to trial against McDonald & Company as the sole defendant. At the close of the evidence submitted by the plaintiff its sufficiency was challenged by the defendant, which challenge was sustained by the court and a judgment was entered dismissing the action. The motion of the plaintiff for a new trial was denied and this appeal followed.

The factual situation as disclosed by the record is as follows: Winterine Manufacturing Company manufactured a product known as Antarctic Antifreeze to be used in motor vehicles to prevent freezing in cold weather. The company assigned to respondent the western part of Washington for the distribution of its product and he purchased from it a large quantity of the antifreeze. The antifreeze was put up in sealed gallon jugs and to each jug the manufacturer affixed a label upon which was printed the following:

'Antarctic Antifreeze. The Manufacturer's Guarantee on Antarctic Antifreeze is Insured by an Old Line Casualty Company. Manufactured by Winterine Manufacturing Company, Denver, Colorado.

'Guarantee. The Manufacturer of this Antifreeze Guarantees: 1. If used according to directions, in a normal cooling system, Antarctic Antifreeze will protect the cooling system from freezing for a full winter season. 2. It will not cause rust or deteriorate the hose, radiator or engine of your car. 3. It will not cause damage to the finish of your car. 4. It will not evaporate. 5. It will not leak out of a cooling system tight enough to hold water.

'Directions for Use. Do not mix with any other antifreeze. Drain cooling system, make certain it is clean and leakproof. Put in proper amount of Antarctic to afford the required freezing protection. (See your dealer's 'Protective Chart.') Add water. Fill to within about 2 inches of top of radiator.'

The respondent sold a quantity of the antifreeze to Huletz Auto Electric Co and it resold to a Texaco service station. The appellant purchased a gallon jug of the antifreeze from the service station. Before making the purchase appellant read what was on the label. He testified that this induced him to buy the antifreeze and that he relied upon the representations printed thereon. Appellant put the antifreeze in the radiator of his automobile. Damage was done to the radiator and motor of appellant's automobile. An analysis of the antifreeze showed that it contained highly corrosive elements and was unfit for the purpose designed. The inherently dangerous character of the article was not known to respondent and there was nothing about it as handled by him indicating anything out of the ordinary. It was only upon use of the antifreeze that its character became known.

The appellant presents three grounds of liability of respondent to him:

(1) Upon the express warranty printed upon the label affixed to the article by the manufacturer.

(2) Upon an implied warranty of fitness for the purpose intended when the article resold is noxious and dangerous to property.

(3) Upon an implied warranty of fitness for the purpose intended under the Uniform Sales Act.

We shall discuss the foregoing in the order set forth.

(1) The question presented is whether a wholesaler, who purchases goods from the manufacturer of them who has affixed a written warranty of quality or fitness for the purpose intended by reselling the goods to a vendee is liable upon the warranty to an ultimate purchaser who relies upon the warranty in making his purchase, puts the goods to use and suffers damage to his property by reason of a breach of the warranty.

In our discussion of this branch of the case we shall refer only to express warranties as the subject of implied warranty is treated later in this opinion.

[1] We have not found in our research many cases dealing with the precise question we are now considering, but the courts passing upon the question, and the text writers, seem to agree that the applicable principle of law is that a dealer is not liable upon an express warranty of a manufacturer which is put out with or attached to the goods manufactured unless he, in some way, adopts the warranty and makes it his own when selling the goods to others, and that by merely selling the goods he does not adopt the warranty of the manufacturer as his own. *Pemberton v Dean* 88 Minn 60, 92 NW 478, 60 LRA 311, 97 Am St Rep 503; *Cool v Fighter* 239 Mich 42, 214 NE 162; *Wallace et al v McCampbell* 178 Tenn 224, 156 SW2d 442, 55 CJ Sales, 684, § 687.

In 55 CJ, supra, the author states:

'A purchaser of personal property with warranty, who in reselling it to another adopts, by his conduct at the resale, the warranty of his seller, thereby assumes a warranty of the same character as that which was expressly accorded to him. The fact of resale does not of itself constitute an adoption of prior warranties so as to render the seller liable for failure of the goods to comply with such warranties; and this is true even though the words of warranty are physically affixed to the goods.'

The *Pemberton* case, supra, although not citing any supporting authority, is a leading case on the subject and is the basis for the text pronouncing the foregoing rule in 24 RCL Sales, 158, § 430, and 46 Am Jur Sales, 495, § 313 . . . We think, under the foregoing authorities, that the correct rule of law is that a vendor of goods is not liable upon the express warranty of the manufacturer unless in making a sale he adopts the warranty as his own, or such warranty is specifically assigned to his vendee.

[2] The respondent in this case did not sell the antifreeze to appellant, and having had no transaction with him did not either adopt the warranty as to him or assign the warranty to him. It must follow, therefore, that the respondent is not liable to appellant upon the express warranty of the manufacturer . . .

[The court then considered and dismissed the alternate theories on which it was sought to ground liability and concluded:]

The judgment is affirmed.

Beals C J and **Simpson** and **Jeffers JJ**, concur.

Steinert J, concurs in the result.

NOTES

1.   In the *Cochran* case the respondent was a wholesale rather than a retail dealer but there is no reason to suppose that the court would have adopted a different approach to the express warranty issue if the plaintiff had sued the Texaco garage which sold the antifreeze to him. The *Pemberton* case cited in the judgment involved a retailer (emery wheel warranted as able to operate at 1,800 revolutions per minute).

2.   The Ontario Law Reform Commission (OLRC) commented on the decision as follows in its 'Report on Consumer Warranties and Guarantees in the Sale of Goods' (1972) at p 35:

Taken to its logical conclusion, it would absolve the typical retailer of responsibility for the accuracy of the labelling of most of the goods displayed on his shelves, since it is evident that he does not affix them himself. The common assumption of commercial lawyers, and indeed the assumption implicit in many Anglo-Canadian decisions, has been that a retailer does adopt as his own at least the descriptive parts of such labels by the mere act of displaying the goods. If this assumption is correct, the distinction would appear to lie between such descriptive materials and express undertakings by the manufacturer guaranteeing satisfaction and promising some form of redress if the goods are found defective.

The distinction is a difficult one to apply and may give rise to anomalous results. There is some evidence in the *Uniform Commercial Code*[1] that the draftsmen may have intended to hold the seller responsible for all the contents of the labels on his goods. In our opinion, this is a sound approach. The Commission therefore recommends that, in the proposed Act, the rule in section 14 be changed in order to provide that, in a consumer sale, promises or affirmations of fact made on the label or container or otherwise accompanying te goods shall be deemed to be part of the description of the goods, or otherwise an express warranty by the seller, whether the labels or containers originated from the seller or not. It is appreciated that this will impose a heavy onus on the seller, but it appears to us in quality to be no different from the strict liability that is imposed on him under the existing law for breach of the implied warranties and conditions.

1. UCC 2–314

(For the implied condition of correspondence with description see generally below at pp 67–71)
3. The following provision of a Canadian statute provides a possible model for dealing with the point.

Saskatchewan Consumer Products Warranties Act 1977

10. Express warranties in labels or packages, in advertising, deemed part of description
(1) A retail seller shall be deemed to be a party to express warranties contained on labels or packages accompanying or attached to a consumer product sold by him to a consumer unless he has made it clear to the consumer prior to the sale that he does not adopt the express warranties.
(2) Subject to subsection (3), no retail seller shall be deemed to be a party to any express warranties contained in any advertisement originating from or carried out by a manufacturer unless he expressly or impliedly adopts such warranties.
(3) Notwithstanding that a retail seller does not adopt the express warranties mentioned in subsections (1) and (2), any descriptive statements that appear on the label or container or otherwise accompany the consumer product shall, for the purposes of paragraph 3 of section 11, be deemed to be part of the description of the product.

Section 2 of this Act contains the following definitions of the terms 'consumer' and 'consumer product':

. . . (d) 'consumer' means a person who buys a consumer product from a retail seller and
   includes a non-profit organization, whether incorporated or not, that has objects of a benevolent, charitable, educational, cultural or recreational nature and that acquires a consumer product from a retail seller, but no person who:
   (i) acquires a consumer product for the purpose of resale shall be a consumer with respect to that product;
   (ii) intends to use a consumer product in a business, or who intends to use the product predominantly for business purposes but also for personal, family or household purposes, shall be a consumer with respect to that product, except that, where goods are consumer products within the meaning of subclause (ii) of clause (e), the individual or the corporation shall be a consumer for the purposes of this Act;
  (e) 'consumer product':
   (i) means any goods ordinarily used for personal, family or household purposes and, without restricting the generality of the foregoing, includes any goods ordinarily used for personal, family or household purposes that are designed to be attached to or installed in any real or personal property, whether or not they are so attached or installed; and

(ii) includes any goods bought for agricultural or fishing purposes by an individual or by a family farming corporation but does not include any implement the sale of which is governed by the provisions of The Agricultural Implements Act 1968; . . .

(See also s 17 (1) of this Act which is printed below, p 51).

4.   Another way of approaching the question is via the implied condition of merchantable quality (see generally below p 73 et seq). The Uniform Commercial Code contains the following provision:

2-314.(2) Goods to be merchantable must be at least such as . . .
(f) conform to the promises or affirmations of fact made on the container or label if any.

In a later report on Sale of Goods (1979) the OLRC commends this provision (at p 205) as striking 'a reasonable balance between providing no guidance as to what types of representations the merchant-seller is deemed to adopt as his own, and holding him responsible for everything the manufacturer may say . . .'

5.   It seems clear that some representations will not be impliedly adopted if only because buyers will not assume that retailers are in any way associated with them. For example a manufacturer may invite consumers to return goods to him directly 'if not fully satisfied' (the goods being entirely merchantable and fit for their purpose). At the other extreme it cannot be doubted that a retailer will be liable (under s 13 of the Sale of Goods Act 1979, below p 61) if a manufacturer makes incorrect statements (for example on labels or elsewhere) forming part of the goods' description. In between these two extremes there is room for doubt.

Problems

Consider the civil liability of a retail seller B to a consumer buyer A when B sells to A goods manufactured by D in the following cases:

(i) A buys a garment with a label sewn in reading 'Guaranteed Shrinkproof'. The garment is not shrinkproof.

(ii) A buys a fertiliser on the packet of which is a statement, 'Guaranteed to Double your Yield'. A's yield is not doubled. Would it affect the position if D had made the statement in its general television advertising rather than on the packet and B was (a) aware, (b) unaware of it?

(iii) A buys a cosmetic marked, 'Absolutely safe for all skins'. The cosmetic is neither unmerchantable (see below p 73 et seq) nor otherwise defective (see below p 150 et seq) but A suffers an unpleasant allergic reaction.

(The position of D may be considered in the light of the materials printed below at pp 31–52.)

Privity of contract

In English law the privity of contract doctrine assumes considerable importance in relation to everyday consumer transactions. Briefly it produces the following consequences for the scope of liability for breach of the implied conditions as to quality etc in a contract for the sale of consumer goods.

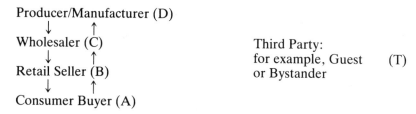

Producer/Manufacturer (D)

Wholesaler (C)

Third Party:
for example, Guest   (T)
Retail Seller (B)   or Bystander

Consumer Buyer (A)

(The arrows indicate respectively goods which are sold 'down' the chain (↓), and a buyer (A) suing (B) who sues (C) and so on (↑)).

In terms of the above diagram the consumer buyer, A, may sue only the retail seller, B, who will then sue the wholesaler, C, and so on up to the manufacturers, D. The corresponding implied conditions will run down the chain from D–C–B–A. If B is insolvent or cannot be traced A cannot leapfrog over him and seek to sue C or D directly, basing his claim on the implied conditions. Nor for that matter may B sue D directly if he cannot trace C: see *Lambert v Lewis* [1980] 1 All ER 978, CA, (revsd in part [1982] AC 225, HL), below p 35. Of course this is without prejudice to any claims which the parties may formulate on some other basis, typically in tort. This limitation is now widely referred to as the 'vertical' privity barrier. The other barrier of 'horizontal' privity effectively prevents third parties, T, from availing themselves of the benefits of the implied conditions of a contract. Such third parties are not parties to the contract and in a formal sense it is easy enough to understand that they may not benefit from its terms. However as the following case illustrates the results may be indefensible in practice. The case is helpful also as illustrating the inter-relation of contract (sale) and tort in this area.

Daniels and Daniels v R White & Sons Ltd and Tarbard [1938] 4 All ER 258, King's Bench Divisional Court

The facts appear in the judgment.

Lewis J: The first plaintiff, Mr Daniels, is a street trader. He hawks and trades in secondhand clothing and secondhand furniture. Mr Daniels claims damages for negligence against R. White & Sons, Ltd, who are manufacturers and bottlers of, amongst other things, lemonade. The second plaintiff, his wife, also claims damages for negligence against R. White & Sons, Ltd. The negligence alleged is that the defendants, in breach of the duty which they owed to the plaintiffs, supplied a bottle of lemonade which in fact contained carbolic acid. The bottle of lemonade was in fact obtained by the male plaintiff from a Mrs Tarbard, the licensee of a public-house known as the Falcon Arms, Falcon Terrace, Battersea, in the county of London. Both plaintiffs allege as against the first defendants, who are, as I say, manufacturers and bottlers, that they did not exercise reasonable care as manufacturers to prevent injury being done to the consumers or purchasers of their wares. The male plaintiff also sues Mrs Tarbard, from whom the bottle of lemonade was actually obtained, alleging, first of all, that, under the Sale of Goods Act, in the circumstances there was an implied warranty that the lemonade was reasonably fit for the purpose of drinking, that it contained no deleterious and noxious matter, and/or that it was of merchantable quality, relying, as I read that plea, upon the Sale of Goods Act 1893, s 14 (1), (2).

On July 23, the male plaintiff, who was a customer of the Falcon Arms, went into the Falcon Arms at about 7 pm with a jug, in order to purchase a jug of beer, and, as he said, a bottle of R. White's lemonade, which is the lemonade made and bottled by the first defendants . . .

Having obtained his jug of beer and his bottle of lemonade, he then proceeded quite a short distance to his own home. It was a very hot day. On arriving home, the first thing he did was to take out the stopper of the lemonade bottle, having first of all torn away the paper label which was stuck over the top of the bottle, which paper label I find was intact when it was sold to him. Having opened the bottle, he then poured a little lemonade into the jug of beer . . . Both husband and wife drank almost simultaneously, and they both immediately realised that there was something burning in the liquid which they had taken, and they at once thought they had been poisoned. I need not go into the details, but in fact it was estimated, on an analysis of what remained in the bottle, that that bottle of lemonade contained 38 grains of carbolic acid, and that would amount to half-a-teaspoonful . . .

That was the case for the plaintiffs, and at the end of the plaintiffs' case a submission that there was no case to answer was made to me by counsel for the first defendants. The position was this. After a certain discussion for the purpose of the submission, it was said that they had to assume and accept that here was a bottle which, when purchased, quite properly had its stopper in, and also had the label pasted over the top, but which, on the evidence called by the plaintiffs at that stage, contained carbolic acid, and that, as a result of drinking the contents of the bottle, the two plaintiffs had suffered damage. That, said counsel for the first defendants—and he said it quite accurately—is the only evidence in the case. He prayed in aid a statement which is to be found at the end of the opinion of Lord Macmillan in *M'Alister (or Donoghue) v Stevenson*[1], in which, said counsel, Lord Macmillan was saying that those facts are not sufficient to establish a *prima facie* case. Lord Macmillan said, at p 622:

> The burden of proof must always be upon the injured party to establish that the defect which caused the injury was present in the article when it left the hands of the party whom he sues, that the defect was occasioned by the carelessness of that party, and that the circumstances are such as to cast upon the defender a duty to take care not to injure the pursuer. There is no presumption of negligence in such a case as the present, nor is there any justification for applying the maxim, *res ipsa loquitur*. Negligence must be both averred and proved. The appellant accepts this burden of proof, and in my opinion she is entitled to have an opportunity of discharging it if she can . . .

His Lordship considered the evidence against the manufacturer and continued:

Even if the true view be that there was here a case for the defendants to answer, I am quite satisfied that they have answered it, and that the plaintiffs, as a result, have entirely failed to prove to my satisfaction that the defendant company were guilty of a breach of their duty towards the plaintiffs—namely, a duty to take reasonable care to see that there should be no defect which might injure the plaintiffs. For that reason, I think that the plaintiffs' claim against the first defendants fails . . .

With regard to the other defendant, I confess that there is one consideration which ought really perhaps to be taken into account, and that is this. She was, of course, entirely innocent and blameless in the matter. She had received the bottle three days before from the first defendants, and she sold it over the counter to the husband, and the husband, of course, is the only one who has any rights in contract and breach of warranty against her. There is no issue of fact between the husband and Mrs Tarbard. They entirely agree as to what happened— namely, that Mr Daniels came into the public-house, the licensed premises, and said, 'I want a bottle of R. White's lemonade,' and R. White's lemonade was what she gave him. The question which arises is, on those facts, the bottle in fact containing carbolic acid, and, the lemonade, therefore, not being of merchantable quality, whether or not the second defendant is liable.

. . . If it is a case of goods sold by description by a seller who deals in goods of that description, there is an implied condition that the goods shall be of merchantable quality. Unfortunately for Mrs Tarbard, through no fault of hers, the goods were not of merchantable quality. It was suggested by Mr Block that there was an opportunity of examination so as to bring the matter within the priviso to s 14(2) of the Act, and he cited an authority to me, but I do not think that that authority takes him the length which he would wish it to do. I therefore find that this was a sale by description, and therefore hold—with some regret, because it is rather hard on Mrs Tarbard, who is a perfectly innocent person in the matter—that she is liable for the injury sustained by Mr Daniels through drinking this bottle of lemonade. However, that, as I understand it, is the law and therefore I think that there must be judgment for Mr Daniels, who is the only person who can recover against Mrs Tarbard.

Judgment for the male plaintiff against the second defendant for £21 15s, and judgment for the first defendants against both plaintiffs. Costs on the High Court scale.

1. [1932] AC 562.

Some of the points which emerge from this case are discussed in later chapters, for example the fact that Mrs Tarbard was liable although she was 'perfectly innocent' (see below pp 89–90) and the standard of care demanded of manufacturers (see below p 150 et seq). As to the latter it may be said that negligence would be inferred much more readily nowadays, thus enabling Mrs Daniels to recover against R. White and Sons.

One limited way of escaping from the constraints of horizontal privity is suggested by the following case.

Lockett v A & M Charles Ltd [1938] 4 All ER 170, King's Bench Divisional Court

The plaintiffs, who were husband and wife, stopped for lunch at a hotel at Bray owned by the defendant company. The meal included whitebait, and the female plaintiff, having swallowed a mouthful, refused to eat the remainder. Subsequently she was taken ill. The plaintiffs claimed that the food was unfit for human consumption and that there was a breach of an implied term of the contract under which the meal was supplied. Tucker J: having stated that he was satisfied that the plaintiff's food poisoning had been caused by the whitebait, continued:

With regard to the female plaintiff's position in respect of breach of warranty, every proprietor of a restaurant is under a duty to take reasonable care to see that the food which he supplies to his guests is fit for human consumption. If he does not take such reasonable steps, and if he is negligent, a person who buys the food which he supplies can recover damages from him based on his negligence. As, however, there is no allegation of such negligence in this case, it must be assumed that the proprietor of the hotel and his servants could not be at fault in any way, and either plaintiff can recover only if he or she establishes that there was a contract between him or her and the proprietor of the hotel.

Counsel for the defendants submitted that, where a man and a woman, be they husband and wife or not, go into a restaurant and the man orders the dinner, *prima facie* the only inference is that the man alone makes himself liable in contract to the proprietor of the hotel. He agreed that every case must depend on its own circumstances, and that there might very easily be circumstances in which that inference could not be drawn, and that there might be a case where it was quite apparent that the woman was going to pay, and that in fact, to use counsel's expression, she was in charge of the proceedings. Counsel also agreed that, where somebody orders a private room at a hotel, entertains a large party, and makes arrangements beforehand, there is no question but that he is the only person who is contracting with the hotel, and that his guests who attend have no contractual relationship with the proprietor of the hotel. Counsel, however, argues that, in the ordinary case where a man and a woman go into a hotel, it is naturally assumed that the man is going to pay for the meal, and that he is the one making the contract, unless there is evidence to the contrary.

In this particular case, there is very little evidence to show precisely what happened in the hotel in that respect . . . It is what may be described as completely neutral evidence, and simply a case where a man and a woman sat down at a table and ordered their food, and I think that I am entitled to assume that the man asked the woman what she would have, and that she accordingly ordered her meal. There was no specific evidence as to who actually paid for the lunch, but everybody is agreed in fact that the husband did.

Counsel for the plaintiffs is, in my opinion, right when he submits that, when persons go into a restaurant and order food, they are making a contract of sale in exactly the same way as they are making a contract of sale when they go into a shop and order any other goods. I think that the inference is that the person who orders the food in a hotel or restaurant *prima facie* makes himself or herself liable to pay for it, and when two people—whether or not they happen to be husband and wife—go into a hotel and each orders and is supplied with food, then, as between those persons and the proprietor of the hotel, each of them is making himself liable for the food which he orders, whatever may be the arrangement between the two persons who are eating at the hotel. On the facts in this case, it is, in my opinion, right to hold that there was a contract implied by the conduct of the parties between the plaintiff, Mrs Lockett, and the defendants when she ordered and was supplied with the whitebait at the Hotel de Paris.

. . . [Where] there is no evidence to indicate to the proprietor of the hotel what the relationship between the parties is, and where there is no evidence that one or the other is in charge of the proceedings, and yet one or the other takes on himself the position of a host entertaining his guests, the proper inference of law is that the person who orders and consumes the food is liable to pay for it as between himself and the proprietor of the restaurant. If that is so, it follows beyond all doubt that there is an implied warranty that the food supplied is reasonably fit for human consumption. I hold that the whitebait delivered in this case were not reasonably fit for human consumption, and that there was a breach of warranty. Accordingly I give judgment for the male plaintiff for the agreed sum of £99 8s, and for Mrs Lockett for £100.

NOTE

The case was decided well before the rise of the feminist movement and some may find it surprising that Tucker J made the assumption on which the plaintiff's success depended. For others cases see *Daly v General Steam Navigation Co Ltd, The Dragon* [1980] 3 All ER 696, [1981] 1 WLR, 120 (boat tickets) and *Benjamin's Sale of Goods* (2nd edn, 1981), para 1079. Of course in a different context a similar assumption may lead to less welcome results. By s 3 of the Theft Act 1978 a person commits an offence if he or she 'makes off' without paying, knowing that payment on the spot for a service is 'required or expected' from him or her.

Question

Would the result have been different if the evidence was that the husband had ordered for both himself and his wife? Suppose that they had been accompanied by a child and that he had been poisoned. Would the child have recovered in contract?

Perhaps predictably it was Lord Denning, MR, who sought in the following case to make a somewhat more substantial inroad into the privity limitation.

Jackson v Horizon Holidays Ltd [1975] 3 All ER 92, [1975] 1 WLR 1468, Court of Appeal

The plaintiff, a successful young businessman, had contracted with the defendants for a family holiday in Ceylon for himself, his wife and two young children. The total cost was £1,200. The holiday was a disaster. The defendants admitted liability and disputed only the amount of damages payable. The trial court judge had awarded £1,100, having taken into account the mental distress and inconvenience suffered (see also below p 127), but had not itemised the award.

Lord Denning MR, having stated the facts of the case, continued:

Counsel for Horizon Holidays suggests that the judge gave £100 for diminution in value and £1,000 for the mental distress. But counsel for Mr Jackson suggested that the judge gave £600 for the diminution in value and £500 for the mental distress. If I were inclined myself to speculate, I think the suggestion of counsel for Mr Jackson may well be right. The judge took the cost of the holidays at £1,200. The family only had about half the value of it. Divide it by two and you get £600. Then add £500 for the mental distress.

On this question a point of law arises. The judge said that he could only consider the mental distress to Mr Jackson himself, and that he could not consider the distress to his wife and children. He said:

'. . . the damages are the Plaintiff's; that I can consider the effect upon his mind of his wife's discomfort, vexation and the like, although I cannot award a sum which represents her vexation.'

Counsel for Mr Jackson disputes that proposition. He submits that damages can be given not only for the leader of the party, in this case, Mr Jackson's own distress, discomfort and vexation, but also for that of the rest of the party.

We have had an interesting discussion as to the legal position when one person makes a contract for the benefit of a party. In this case it was a husband making a contract for the benefit of himself, his wife and children. Other cases readily come to mind. A host makes a contract with a restaurant for a dinner for himself and his friends. The vicar makes a contract for a coach trip for the choir. In all these cases there is only one person who makes the contract. It is the husband, the host or the vicar, as the case may be. Sometimes he pays the whole price himself. Occasionally he may get a contribution from the others. But in any case it is he who makes the contract. It would be a fiction to say that the contract was made by all the family, or all the guests, or all the choir, and that he was only an agent for them. Take this very case. It would be absurd to say that the twins of three years old were parties to the contract or that the father was making the contract on their behalf as if they were principals. It would equally be a mistake to say that in any of these instances there was a trust. The transaction bears no resemblance to a trust. There was no trust fund and no trust property. No, the real truth is that in each instance, the father, the host or the vicar, was making a contract himself for the benefit of the whole party. In short, a contract by one for the benefit of third persons.

What is the position when such a contract is broken? At present the law says that the only one who can sue is the one who made the contract. None of the rest of the party can sue, even though the contract was made for their benefit. But when that one does sue, what damages can he recover? Is he limited to his own loss? Or can he recover for the others? Suppose the holiday firm puts the family into a hotel which is only half built and the visitors have to sleep on the floor? Or suppose the restaurant is fully booked and the guests have to go away, hungry and angry, having spent so much on fares to get there? Or suppose the coach leaves the choir stranded half-way and they have to hire cars to get home? None of them individually can sue. Only the father, the host or the vicar can sue. He can, of course, recover his own damages. But can he not recover for the others? I think he can. The case comes within the principle stated by Lush LJ in *Lloyd's v Harper*[1]:

'. . . I consider it to be an established rule of law that where a contract is made with *A*. for the benefit of *B*., *A*. can sue on the contract for the benefit of *B*, and recover all that *B*. could have recovered if the contract had been made with *B* himself.'

It has been suggested that Lush LJ was thinking of a contract in which A was trustee for B. But I do not think so. He was a common lawyer speaking of the common law. His words were quoted with considerable approval by Lord Pearce in *Beswick v Beswick*[2]. I have myself often quoted them. I think they should be accepted as correct, at any rate so long as the law forbids the third persons themselves to sue for damages. It is the only way in which a just result can be achieved. Take the instance I have put. The guests ought to recover from the restaurant their wasted fares. The choir ought to recover the cost of hiring the taxis home. There is no one to recover for them except the one who made the contract for their benefit. He should be able to recover the expense to which they have been put, and pay it over to them. Once recovered, it will be money had and received to their use. (They might even, if desired, be joined as plaintiffs.) If he can recover for the expense, he should also be able to recover for the discomfort, vexation and upset which the whole party have suffered by reason of the breach of contract, recompensing them accordingly out of what he recovers.

Applying the principles to this case, I think that the figure of £1,100 was about right. It would, I think, have been excessive if it had been awarded only for the damage suffered by Mr Jackson himself. But when extended to his wife and children, I do not think it is excessive. People look forward to a holiday. They expect the promises to be fulfilled. When it fails, they are greatly disappointed and upset. It is difficult to assess in terms of money; but it is the task of the judges to do the best they can. I see no reason to interfere with the total award of £1,100.

I would therefore dismiss this appeal.

Orr LJ. I agree.

James LJ. In this case Mr Jackson, as found by the judge on the evidence, was in need of a holiday at the end of 1970. He was able to afford a holiday for himself and his family. According to the form which he completed, which was the form of Horizon Holidays Ltd, he booked what was a family holiday. The wording of that form might in certain circumstances give rise to a contract in which the person signing the form is acting as his own principal and as agent for others. In the circumstances of this case, as indicated by Lord Denning MR, it would be wholly unrealistic to regard this contract as other than one made by Mr Jackson for a family holiday. The judge found that he did not get a family holiday. The costs were some £1,200. When he came back he felt no benefit. His evidence was to the effect that, without any exaggeration, he felt terrible. He said: 'The only thing, I was pleased to be back, very pleased, but I had nothing at all from that holiday.' For my part, on the issue of damages in this matter, I am quite content to say that £1,100 awarded was the right and proper figure in those circumstances. I would dismiss the appeal.

Appeal dismissed. Leave to appeal to the House of Lords refused.

1. (1880) 16 Ch D 290 at 321, CA.
2. [1967] 2 All ER 1197 at 1212, [1968] AC 58 at 88.

Although the result of *Jackson's* case is sensible and probably correct, Lord Denning's reasoning has since been disapproved in the House of Lords in *Woodar Investment Development Ltd v Wimpey Construction UK Ltd* [1980] 1 All ER 571, [1980] 1 WLR 277, HL. In a case in which A had contracted with B to pay a sum of money to T Lord Wilberforce said (at pp 576–577):

1. The majority of the Court of Appeal followed, in the case of Goff LJ with expressed reluctance, its previous decision in *Jackson v Horizon Holidays Ltd*[1]. I am not prepared to dissent from the actual decision in that case. It may be supported either as a broad decision on the measure of damages (per James LJ) or possibly as an example of a type of contract, examples of which are persons contracting for family holidays, ordering meals in restaurants for a party, hiring a taxi for a group, calling for special treatment. As I suggested in *New Zealand Shipping Co Ltd v A M Satterthwaite & Co Ltd*[2], there are many situations of daily life which do not fit neatly into conceptual analysis, but which require some flexibility in the law of contract. *Jackson's* case[1] may well be one.

I cannot agree with the basis on which Lord Denning MR put his decision in that case. The extract on which he relied from the judgment of Lush LJ in *Lloyd's v Harper*[3] was part of a passage in which Lush LJ was stating as an 'established rule of law' that an agent (sc an insurance broker) may sue on a contract made by him on behalf of the principal (sc the assured) if the contract gives him such a right, and is no authority for the proposition required in *Jackson's* case[1], still less for the proposition, required here, that, if Woodar made a contract for a sum of money to be paid to Transworld, Woodar can, without showing that it has itself suffered loss or that Woodar was agent or trustee for Transworld, sue for damages for non-payment of that sum. That would certainly not be an established rule of law, nor was it quoted as such authority by Lord Pearce in *Beswick v Beswick*[4].

1. [1975] 3 All ER 92, [1975] 1 WLR 1468.
2. [1974] 1 All ER 1015 at 1020, [1975] AC 154 at 167.
3. (1880) 16 Ch D 290 at 321.
4. [1967] 2 All ER 1197, [1968] AC 58.

A similar view was expressed by Lord Russell (ibid at p 585). Whether the disapproval will make any difference in practice to the quantum of damages awarded in family holiday cases is unclear. A sympathetic judge might choose to place more emphasis on the distress of the contracting party in witnessing the family suffering.

Both the above cases mention agency as a qualification to the privity rule and there is no doubt that this doctrine may have a part to play. Where A contracts with B as an agent for a third party, T, T will have a contract with B and benefit from its terms. However, as Lord Denning noted in *Jackson's* case, above p 23, agency doctrines usually cannot be applied realistically in everyday consumer transactions. Also they can work in reverse since where A contracts only as an agent for T he will acquire no personal rights under the contract.

Problem

Claude asks his son Al, aged five, to go to the local corner shop owned by Bert to buy a tin of corned beef. Al does so, saying to Bert, 'Dad says will you put it on his account please'. Al eats the corned beef for his supper and suffers food poisoning.

Advise Al. See *Heil v Hedges* [1951] 1 TLR 512.

A further implication of privity is that usually a third party is not entitled to benefit from any protection purportedly conferred on him in a contract between A and B. So in the well-known case of *Adler v Dickson* [1955] 1 QB 158, [1954] 3 All ER 397, CA, the master and boatswain of the P and O ship *Himalaya* were not protected by a general exclusion clause in a contract between an injured passenger and the P and O company. The same conclusion was reached on very different facts involving a contract for the carriage of goods by sea in the leading case of *Scruttons Ltd v Midland Silicones Ltd* [1962] AC 446, [1962] 1 All ER 1, HL (stevedores denied protection under bill of lading). However in this latter case Lord Reid noted a number of ways (including agency) in which such third parties as stevedores might be accorded contractual protection. Not unnaturally those responsible for drafting commercial contracts have since sought—and with some success—so to re-word their contracts as to produce the desired result: see *New Zealand Shipping Co Ltd v A M Satterthwaite & Co Ltd* [1975] AC 154, [1974] 1 All ER 1015, PC; *Port Jackson Stevedoring Pty Ltd v Salmond and Spraggon (Australia) Pty Ltd, The New York Star* [1980] 3 All ER 257, [1981] 1 WLR 138, PC. For comment on these cases see Reynolds (1980) 96 LQR 506, Coote [1981] CLJ 13 and Clarke [1981] CLJ 17.

The recent cases have a distinctly commercial flavour and the precise route to protection (whether agency or the offer of a unilateral contract to the third party) is not always clear. However the important point is that the higher courts now seem willing to extend protection to third parties on appropriate facts. This may have implications for consumer contracts. The following is an extract from the standard form contract of a major cross-channel operator. (Exemption clauses, generally, are discussed in Ch 6, below.)

Passenger/Accompanied Vehicle Tickets Terms and Conditions for Carriage of Passengers and Accompanied Vehicles and Property

. . . 7. (A) The purpose of this Clause is to confer on the servants and agents of the Carrier, and on independent contractors engaged from time to time by the Carrier or its servants or agents ('Protected Persons'), the benefit of protection from liability for claims which may be made by the Passenger.

   (B) By accepting this Ticket the Passenger shall be deemed to offer to the Carrier as agent for each of the Protected Persons (and the Carrier so accepts such offer) to confer on them the following protections:-

   (1) Where acceptance of the offer constitutes a contract of which English law is the

proper law, the benefit of every limitation of or exemption from liability, and of every defence or immunity from claims, provided for the benefit of the Carrier under this Ticket; or

(2) In any other case, complete and total exemption from all liability and immunity from all claims howsoever arising and whether or not involving any negligence or fault on the part of the Protected Person.

(C) The consideration for such offer and for any contract made pursuant thereto shall be the provision or prospective provision by any of the Protected Persons of any services for the benefit, whether direct or indirect, of the Passenger or in connection with the performance by the Carrier of its obligations under this Ticket.

(D) Acceptance by the Carrier of such offer shall be deemed to be ratified severally by the Protected Persons (whether or not any of them then has actual knowledge of the terms of the offer) upon their providing any such service as aforesaid whether or not the Passenger has notice thereof.

Question

Ignoring the provisions of the Athens Convention (see below p 284) is this clause effective in achieving its objective? Is it realistic to regard individual employees who, for example, may deal with customers' cars as principals of the Carrier? Is it in any event desirable that they should enjoy such protection as the law permits to the contracting Carrier?

In spite of the opportunities afforded by agency and similar doctrines English law is still committed to the essentials of the privity of contract requirement in both its horizontal and vertical form. However this is not true of some other jurisdictions and no doubt readers will draw their own conclusions as to which, if any, of the following approaches might usefully be adopted in English law. A complete picture can be obtained only after considering a manufacturer's liability in tort, especially for economic loss: see below Ch 4, p 165 et seq. In reading the various provisions particular attention should be paid to whether they breach horizontal or vertical privity or both.

The following is a provision of the American Uniform Commercial Code (individual States being free to adopt any—or indeed none—of the three alternatives).

Uniform Commercial Code

§ 2–318 THIRD PARTY BENEFICIARIES OF WARRANTIES EXPRESS OR IMPLIED

Alternative A

A seller's warranty whether express or implied extends to any natural person who is in the family or household of his buyer or who is a guest in his home if it is reasonable to expect that such person may use, consume or be affected by the goods and who is injured in person by breach of the warranty. A seller may not exclude or limit the operation of this section.

Alternative B

A seller's warranty whether express or implied extends to any natural person who may reasonably be expected to use, consume or be affected by the goods and who is injured in person by breach of the warranty. A seller may not exclude or limit the operation of this section.

Alternative C

A seller's warranty whether express or implied extends to any person who may reasonably be expected to use, consume or be affected by the goods and who is injured by breach of the warranty. A seller may not exclude or limit the operation of this section with respect to injury to the person of an individual to whom the warranty extends . . .

Question

Jo, a pensioner, buys two tins of salmon from his local supermarket. The salmon is served to Jo and to two guests as part of their afternoon tea. Owing to a defect in the canning process which took place in Canada the salmon is contaminated and the parties become seriously ill. The foreign manufacturer is highly reputable and the supermarket is innocent of all fault.

Advise Jo and his guests on the basis of (i) English law, (ii) UCC Art 2–318.

The following American case is of general interest as a landmark decision even if the theory of liability which it espouses has since been overtaken by a widespread acceptance of an alternative theory of strict liability in tort (see below Ch 4 pp 176–192).

Henningsen v Bloomfield Motors, Inc. 161 A.2d 69 (1960), Supreme Court of New Jersey

The plaintiffs had acquired a new Plymouth sedan car manufactured by the Chrysler Corporation and sold through an authorised dealer. The car had been purchased by a husband as a gift for his wife and the wife was injured when faulty steering caused it to go out of control as she was driving it. There was no evidence of negligence to go to the jury and the case proceeded solely on the issues of the implied warranty of merchantability. The manufacturer's attempted disclaimer contained in a limited warranty or guarantee (described as 'a sad commentary upon the automobile manufacturers' marketing practices') was held to be void as being inimical to the public good. The husband's claim against the dealer (Bloomfield Motors) was straightforward but the remaining claims were more difficult to establish. The court dealt first with the husband's claim against Chrysler.

Francis J . . . Chrysler points out that an implied warranty of merchantability is an incident of a contract of sale. It concedes, of course, the making of the original sale to Bloomfield Motors, Inc., but maintains that this transaction marked the terminal point of its contractual connection with the car. Then Chrysler urges that since it was not a party to the sale by the dealer to Henningsen, there is no privity of contract between it and the plaintiffs, and the absence of this privity eliminates any such implied warranty.

There is no doubt that under early common-law concepts of contractual liability only those persons who were parties to the bargain could sue for a breach of it. In more recent times a noticeable disposition has appeared in a number of jurisdictions to break through the narrow barrier of privity when dealing with sales of goods in order to give realistic recognition to a universally accepted fact. The fact is that the dealer and the ordinary buyer do not, and are not expected to, buy goods, whether they be foodstuffs, or automobiles, exclusively for their own consumption or use . . .

Although only a minority of jurisdictions have thus far departed from the requirement of privity, the movement in that direction is most certainly gathering momentum. Liability to the ultimate consumer in the absence of direct contractual connection has been predicated upon a variety of theories. Some courts hold that the warranty runs with the article like a covenant running with land; others recognize a third-party beneficiary thesis; still others rest their decision on the ground that public policy requires recognition of a warranty made directly to the consumer . . .

Under modern conditions the ordinary layman, on responding to the importuning of colorful advertising, has neither the opportunity nor the capacity to inspect or to determine the fitness of an automobile for use; he must rely on the manufacturer who has control of its construction, and to some degree on the dealer who, to the limited extent called for by the manufacturer's instructions, inspects and services it before delivery. In such a marketing milieu his remedies and those of persons who properly claim through him should not depend 'upon the intricacies of the law of sales'. The obligation of the manufacturer should not be based alone on privity of contract. It should rest, as was once said, upon 'the demands of social justice.' *Mazetti v Armour & Co*, 75 Wash 622, 135 P 633, 635, 48 LRANS, 213 (Sup Ct 1913) . . .

Accordingly, we hold that under modern marketing conditions, when a manufacturer puts a new automobile in the stream of trade and promotes its purchase by the public, an implied warranty that it is reasonably suitable for use as such accompanies it into the hands of the ultimate purchaser. Absence of agency between the manufacturer and the dealer who makes the ultimate sale is immaterial . . .

THE DEFENCE OF LACK OF PRIVITY AGAINST MRS HENNINGSEN

Both defendants contend that since there was no privity of contract between them and Mrs Henningsen, she cannot recover for breach of any warranty made by either of them. On the facts, as they were developed, we agree that she was not a party to the purchase agreement. *Faber v Creswick* 31 NJ 234, 156 A2d 252 (1959). Her right to maintain the action, therefore, depends upon whether she occupies such legal status thereunder as to permit her to take advantage of a breach of defendants' implied warranties.

[26] For the most part the cases that have been considered dealt with the right of the buyer or consumer to maintain an action against the manufacturer where the contract of sale was with a dealer and the buyer had no contractual relationship with the manufacturer. In the present matter, the basic contractual relationship is between Claus Henningsen, Chrysler, and Bloomfield Motors, Inc. The precise issue presented is whether Mrs Henningsen, who is not a party to their respective warranties, may claim under them. In our judgment, the principles of those cases and the supporting texts are just as proximately applicable to her situation. We are convinced that the cause of justice in this area of the law can be served only by recognizing that she is such a person who, in the reasonable contemplation of the parties to the warranty, might be expected to become a user of the automobile . . .

[28] It is important to express the right of Mrs Henningsen to maintain her action in terms of a general principle. To what extent may lack of privity be disregarded in suits on such warranties? . . . It is our opinion that an implied warranty of merchantability chargeable to either an automobile manufacturer or a dealer extends to the purchaser of the car, members of his family, and to other persons occupying or using it with his consent. It would be wholly opposed to reality to say that use by such persons is not within the anticipation of parties to such a warranty of reasonable suitability of an automobile for ordinary highway operation. Those persons must be considered within the distributive chain . . .

It is not necessary in this case to establish the outside limits of the warranty protection. For present purposes, with respect to automobiles, it suffices to promulgate the principle set forth above . . .

Under all of the circumstances outlined above, the judgments in favor of the plaintiffs and against the defendants are affirmed.

NOTES

1. The general approach of the New Jersey Supreme Court may be compared with the traditional approach of Lewis J, in *Daniels and Daniels v R White & Sons Ltd and Tarbard* [1938] 4 All ER 258, above p 19.

2. For an interesting case decided under the civil law system of Quebec see *General Motors Products of Canada Ltd v Kravitz* (1979) 93 DLR (3d) 481 (Can, SC). The respondent, Kravitz, had purchased a new 1968 General Motors (GM) Oldsmobile car from an authorised dealer, Plamondon. The car had serious latent defects which rendered it unfit for use and on the basis of which the respondent brought an action both against Plamondon and GM. It was held that Kravitz was entitled to succeed against GM by suing on the legal warranty against defects in the contract between GM and Plamondon. Moreover an exemption clause did not defeat the claim.

The reasoning in this case may seem strange to common lawyers but it has implications which should not be overlooked. The inability of Plamondon to rely on an exemption clause as against Kravitz is parallelled by our own provisions in the Unfair Contract Terms Act 1977, s 6 (see below p 240). However the same section enables such clauses to operate within the distributive chain (for example as between manufacturer and dealer) provided that they satisfy a requirement of reasonableness. If the equivalent of the French 'action directe' were to be adopted in English law presumably it would be necessary to ensure that such protection was not effectively by-passed, so depriving a manufacturer of the protection he would otherwise enjoy. The point is discussed further when considering a manufacturer's liability in tort for economic loss (see below Ch 4, p 165 et seq). Meanwhile it is of interest to note that the Onario Law Reform Commission had this factor in mind in its 'Report on Sale of Goods' (1979): see Chapter 10 especially. In addition to recommendations concerning implied terms as to quality etc the draft Bill contains the following provisions:

Report on Sale of Goods (1979) (Ontario Law Reform Commission)

5.18*   Interpretation
(1) In this section,
    (a) 'goods' includes goods that have been converted into, incorporated in, or attached to, other goods or that have been incorporated in or attached to land;
    (b) 'immediate buyer' means a buyer who buys goods from a prior seller;
    (c) 'injury' means injury to the person, damage to property, or any economic loss;
    (d) 'prior seller' means a seller who sells goods that are subsequently resold;
    (e) 'subsequent buyer' means a buyer who buys goods that have previously been sold by a prior seller to an immediate buyer.

Prior seller's warranty
(2) Without prejudice to a subsequent buyer's rights under section 5.10, a prior seller's warranty, express or implied, and any remedies for breach thereof, enure in favour of any subsequent buyer of the goods who suffers injury because of a breach of the warranty.

Subsequent buyer's rights
(3) A subsequent buyer's rights under subsection 2 are subject to any defence that would have been available to such prior seller in an action against him for breach of the same warranty by his immediate buyer.

Subsequent buyer's damages
(4) The measure of damages recoverable by a subsequent buyer for breach of warranty by a prior seller shall be no greater than the damages that the immediate buyer could have recovered from such prior seller if a successful claim had been brought against the immediate buyer by the subsequent buyer for breach of the same warranty and the immediate buyer had made a claim over against the prior seller.

Application of section
(5) This section applies notwithstanding any agreement to the contrary.

*The Commission makes no recommendation concerning the enactment of this section. It has been inserted in the Draft Bill to draw attention to the issue and to stimulate discussion.

(For clause 5.10 of the draft Bill see above p 8).

A statute of another Canadian province contains the following provisions.

Saskatchewan Consumer Products Warranties Act 1977

4.   Subsequent owners
(1) Subject to subsection (2), persons who derive their property or interest in a product from or through the consumer, whether by purchase, gift, operation of law or otherwise, shall, regardless of their place in the sequence of dealings with respect to the product, be deemed to be given by the retail seller or manufacturer the same statutory warranties that the consumer was deemed to have been given under sections 11 and 13 and shall be deemed to receive from the warrantor the same additional written warranties that the consumer received under section 17 and shall, for the purposes of any provision of this Act unless otherwise provided in this Act, have rights and remedies against the retail seller, manufacturer or warrantor equal to but not greater than the rights and remedies the consumer has under this Act and shall be subject to any defences or rights of set-off that could be raised against the consumer under this Act.
(2) No retail seller who acquires a product from or through a consumer for the purposes of resale or for use predominantly in a business shall have any rights under subsection (1) with respect to that product . . .

13.   Manufacturers deemed to give statutory warranties; 'retail seller'
. . . (2) Subject to subsection (3), the manufacturer of consumer products shall be deemed to give to consumers of his products the same statutory warranties with respect to his products as the retail seller is deemed to have given under paragraphs 2 to 8 of section 11.
(3) A manufacturer of consumer products shall be liable only for his own breach of the statutory warranties or of any express or additional written warranties that he has given to consumers and, without limiting the generality of the foregoing, the application of subsection (2) shall be subject to the following: . . .
    (b)   no manufacturer shall b bound by any description applied by the retail seller to the consumer products without the authority or consent of the manufacturer;
    (c)   for the purpose of paragraph 4 of section 11, the consumer shall be deemed to have notice of a defect if disclosure of such a defect was made directly or indirectly to the retail seller and was intended by the manufacturer to reach the consumer and in the normal course of events could reasonably be expected by the manufacturer to reach the consumer;
    (d)   no provision of paragraph 5 of section 11 shall apply where, without the consent of the manufacturer, any consumer product is sold by a retail seller to a consumer as being fit for a purpose that is not the ordinary purpose of such a product.

14.   No privity of contract required and consideration deemed to be received; awareness or reliance irrelevant
(1) In any action brought under this Act against a manufacturer, retail seller or warrantor for breach of a statutory, express or additional written warranty, lack of privity of contract between the person bringing the action and the retail seller, manufacturer or warrantor shall not be a defence and the retail seller, manufacturer or warrantor shall be conclusively presumed to have received consideration.
(2) In any action brought to enforce the terms of an additional written warranty, the fact that at the time of the sale of the consumer product the consumer was or was not aware of the existence of the additional written warranty or the consumer did or did not rely upon the additional written warranty shall be irrelevant.

(For sections 11 and 17 of the Saskatchewan Act see below at p 89 and p 51 respectively. For the definition of 'consumer' and 'consumer products' see above p 17).

Similarly, and as further evidence of what now seems to be a widespread trend against insistence on privity of contract requirements, Australia has adopted the following provision.

Australian Trade Practices Act 1974 (as amended by the Trade Practices Amendment Act 1978)

74D. Action in respect of goods of unmerchantable quality
(1) Where—
    (a) a corporation, in trade or commerce, supplies goods manufactured by the corporation to another person who acquires the goods for re-supply;
    (b) a person (whether or not the person who acquired the goods from the corporation) supplies the goods (otherwise than by way of sale by auction) to a consumer;
    (c) the goods are not of merchantable quality; and
    (d) the consumer or any person who derives title to the goods through or under the consumer suffers loss or damage by reason that the goods are not of merchantable quality,
the corporation is liable to compensate the consumer or person who so derives title to the goods for the loss or damage and the consumer or person who so derives title to the goods may recover the amount of the compensation by action against the corporation in a court of competent jurisdiction.
(2) Sub-section (1) does not apply—
    (a) if the goods are not of merchantable quality by reason of—
        (i) an act or default of any person (not being the corporation or a servant or agent of the corporation); or
        (ii) a cause independent of human control,
    occurring after the goods have left the control of the corporation;
    (b) as regards defects specifically drawn to the consumer's attention before the making of the contract for the supply of the goods to the consumer; or
    (c) if the consumer examines the goods before that contract is made, as regards defects that the examination ought to reveal . . .

Manufacturers' express warranties and guarantees

INTRODUCTION

An earlier section raised the question of the extent to which retailers may be said impliedly to adopt the unsubstantiated claims and misdescriptions of manufacturers whose goods they are selling: see above, pp 15–18. This section is concerned with the liability of manufacturers themselves. It falls into two parts. First their civil liability (other than under a straightforward contract of sale) for express warranties and general advertising or promotional claims. Second the position with respect to manufacturers' guarantees and the undertakings contained in them. The wider question of manufacturers' liability for defective products generally is discussed in Chapter 4.

EXPRESS WARRANTIES AND PROMOTIONAL CLAIMS

When manufacturers or producers give a personal assurance to a consumer who later acquires the goods through a third party or takes some equivalent step there should be no difficulty in holding them liable under a collateral contract. There are several well-known English cases in point, including *Wells (Merstham) Ltd v Buckland Sand and Silica Co Ltd* [1965] 2 QB 170, [1964] 1 All ER 41 and *Shanklin Pier Ltd v Detel Products Ltd* [1951] 2 KB 854, [1951] 2 All ER 471. For the facts of the latter case see below p 38. In addition such cases as *Brown v Sheen and Richmond Car Sales Ltd* ([1950] 1 All ER 1102), *Andrews v Hopkinson* ([1957] 1 QB 229,

[1956] 3 All ER 422) and *Yeoman Credit Ltd v Odgers* ([1962] 1 All ER 789, [1962] 1 WLR 215) were all concerned with the common situation in which assurances are given by a motor dealer with the consumer entering a credit transaction with a finance company thereafter. (For the liability of the finance company on such facts see now s 56 of the Consumer Credit Act 1974, p 223, below).

It is possible to use a similar approach to hold manufacturers civilly liable to consumers where the claims or assurances are not given directly and personally but are contained rather in leaflets and general advertising material. So in *Carlill v Carbolic Smoke Ball Co* [1893] 1 QB 256, CA, the plaintiff was held to be contractually entitled to the £100 reward which the defendants had advertised in the *Pall Mall Gazette* as being payable to anyone who contracted influenza after using the carbolic smoke ball in the prescribed manner. The following case is noted in Borrie and Diamond *The Consumer, Society and the Law* (4th edn, 1981) at pp 108–109.

Wood v Letrik Ltd (1932) Times, 12 January, King's Bench Divisional Court

AN ELECTRIC COMB: £500 AWARDED ON A GUARANTEE

Before Mr Justice Rowlatt
His Lordship gave judgment for the plaintiff for the amount claimed in this action, in which Mr Francis Arthur Wood, of Bronwen, Newlands-avenue, Radlett, Herts, sought to recover from Letrik, Limited, of 70, Milton-street, EC, vendors of the 'Letrik' electric comb, £500, which he said the defendants guaranteed in an advertisement that they would pay if the comb failed to cure grey hair after 10 days' use.

The case for the plaintiff was that, having read in a periodical an advertisement of the defendants which began: 'New hair in 72 hours. Letrik Electric Comb. Great news for hair sufferers. What is *your* trouble?

Is it grey hair? In 10 days not a grey hair left. £500 guarantee.'
He bought one of the combs and used it as directed, the only result being that, instead of restoring the original colour of his hair, which was prematurely turning grey, it scratched his head and made him feel uncomfortable.

The defendants denied that they guaranteed to pay £500 in such circumstances. That sum, they said, was intended to cover only the return of the price of the combs.

Mr T Eastham KC and Mr Rober Fortune appeared for the plaintiff; Mr F S Laskey for the defendants.

Mr Eastham, addressing his Lordship, said that the plaintiff bought and used the comb on the terms of the offer which he accepted by performing the conditions. The words were a pledge or undertaking to pay £500 in the event of a grey hair being left on the plaintiff's head at the end of 10 days' use of the comb. If an intelligent meaning could be given to the words it could not be said that the phrase meant nothing and was illusory. The point that performance was impossible was a bad one because the advertisement itself stated that the comb actually did what was promised. No coupon qualifying the defendants' guarantee was inserted: they did not alter the advertisement or withdraw the offer, and until they did so it was effective.

JUDGMENT

His Lordship, in giving judgment, said that the plaintiff sought to recover £500 under a contract to be found in an advertisement which, according to the construction for which he contended, offered him that sum if he used the comb and it did not cure his grey hair. He said that he had used the comb, that it did not cure his grey hair, and that he wanted the £500.

Claims of that nature had been before the Courts for many years since *Carlill v Carbolic Smoke Ball Company* (9 *The Times* LR 124; [1893] 1 QB 256) and it was quite clear that there was no reason in law why one person should not say to another: 'You use this comb, or this article of mine, and I guarantee to you that it will have certain effects; and I contract with you that if it does not have those effects I will pay you a certain sum.' That was a perfectly good contract. If the conditions were complied with by the user of the article it was simply a question of the meaning of the advertisement and proof of compliance with its terms.

In the advertisement before him it was not specifically stated to whom it was addressed—whether to the purchaser or the user. The present plaintiff was both purchaser and user, but it seemed to him (his Lordship) that the advertisement was clearly addressed, and must be addressed, to the user; and the act of using would certainly be sufficient compliance with the advertisement and a sufficient consideration for the promise.

What did the advertisement mean? In the first place, was it intended as a contract at all or as a mere puff—meaningless but attractive words? The word 'guarantee' was about as emphatic a word in the contract as one could well imagine. He had construed the advertisement according to the plain meaning which ordinary sensible people would attach to it. When people read the word 'guarantee' they understood that the person using it was offering to bind himself to be responsible for the happening, continuance, or existence of a certain state of facts.

As regarded the £500, he was asked to say that that was a mere flourish. He had inquired of Mr Atkinson [director of the defendant company] whether it was, and he replied, 'Yes.' He (his Lordship) did not think that the £500 guarantee could be treated as a mere flourish. It might be a question of what it meant, but it must be treated as a serious statement.

There was another question. It was suggested that the defendants were not really bound by that advertisement at all; that it was not there by their authority. It appeared that the advertisement was inserted through the instrumentality of an advertising agency. The agency might have been contractors, but on behalf of the defendants they put in that advertisement and had sent in their bill including it. It had never been repudiated, nor had any complaint been made about it. He could not take a view other than that the defendants were bound by it.

THE QUESTION OF THE COUPON

In another case the defendants had inserted a coupon which very much limited the meaning of the words '£500 guarantee'. It explained that they only guaranteed £500 as fortifying the repayment of 3s 6d spent on the comb. That was perfectly futile and merely misleading, but the defendants had not put the coupon into the advertisement in the present case, and they were bound by the advertisement as it appeared.

With regard to the impossibility of performance, it was said that to enable the plaintiff to recover he would have to show that the promise was that the hair, already grey, and he (his Lordship) supposed dead, would be rejuvenated, and the actual cells turned to their original colour by the use of the comb; and that, as that was an obvious impossibility, the contract was void, and there was no reality in the consideration.

If a man contracted to do a thing which was obviously impossible it was merely nonsense. If a man contracted to go to the moon he was talking nonsense, and the law recognized no contract of that kind. If a man 100 years ago had contracted that his voice would be audible many miles away it would have been held to be impossible, but he did not see why anybody should think that it was impossible for living grey hair to resume its original hue.

The defendants put in their advertisement the picture of a man whose hair was said to have been thin and going grey, that he looked about 45 and was only 35, and that on the tenth day the greyness had gone entirely, 'the comb having done the trick.' The defendants had also stated in the advertisement that 'not one has failed to do everything we claim for it.'

Then it was said that after all there was no real proof that the advertisement had ever been complied with or the money really earned. One did not regard an action of that kind with favour, but it was not his business to regard it with favour or disfavour. It was rather a windfall for the plaintiff, but he (his Lordship) did not see why Mr Wood should not say: 'Here is a man who says that my hair will be turned to the colour of my boyhood and if it is not I shall get £500. I will try it. I shall be pleased to have my hair dark again.' There was no reason why a man should not take that attitude in all seriousness.

It was contended that the plaintiff did not properly try the comb. The advertisement stated: 'You simply use it in place of your ordinary comb and in the same way.' In the box supplied there was a little blue paper which said: 'To get the full benefit you should use it for five minutes.' The plaintiff said that he combed his hair for several minutes in the morning when he got up and in the evening and that he also took the comb to his office and had a comb now and again when he felt inclined to spare a few moments in going on with the cure. (Laughter.) That was the most natural thing in the world to do.

Then it was said that on the true construction the advertisement could only mean that the comb made the hair grow again through the roots, and that it did not appear that the plaintiff's hair was not growing again from the roots. He (his Lordship) was not impressed by that. If that comb had ever made anybody's hair grow again from the roots he would have listened to evidence on that point with great pleasure, because it would have been very material. Possibly there were numerous persons who could have come and said that the comb had made their hair grow brown again from the roots, though the plaintiff had said that it had not done that for him. The defendants might have called the man at Forest-hill, whose picture appeared in the advertisement and whose hair was said to have been very thin and going grey. If they had called him and he said that the comb had done what was stated he (his Lordship) might have doubted whether the plaintiff had gripped at the roots with his comb.

So soon as the claim was made it was open to the defendants to say to the plaintiff: 'Make an appointment so that somebody may inspect your hair and report on its condition.' That was often done in cases in those Courts, but no such step was taken. He could not doubt that the comb failed in its operation. It was a comb which had a battery in it and if all went well there was probably a circuit set up between the teeth of the comb so that electricity passed to the scalp.

He thought the plaintiff was entitled to recover, that he had complied with the advertisement which amounted to a contract, and that there was no answer to the action.

Judgment for the plaintiff was accordingly entered for the £500 claimed.

A stay of execution for 14 days was granted on the terms that the money was paid into Court.

Questions

To what extent should it affect the issue if the suggested contract is to do something which is apparently impossible (like going to the moon in 1932)? Was the plaintiff gullible or credulous? Should this matter? (See further below p 40). What would you estimate to be the equivalent value today of £500 in 1932?

Both *Carlill v Carbolic Smoke Ball Co* (see below p 37) and the above case involved undertakings that a specific sum would be paid in certain eventualities. Unlike the *Wells* case the undertakings were made to the world at large and not to the plaintiff personally, although in all cases their terms were specific and unambiguous. It is likely that the same will be true of many situations in which manufacturers invite consumers to contact them directly, perhaps through 'flash offers' on the goods themselves.

Consider the following cases.

1. Art buys a bar of Brand X chocolate from his local shop. The wrapper has an undertaking which reads, 'Brand X aims to give complete satisfaction with all its products. Return this to us for a complete refund if not fully satisfied. This does not affect your statutory rights.' Art agrees that the chocolate is quite wholesome but he does not like its taste. He returns it to Brand X which declines to make a refund.

Advise Art.

2. The Coffee company markets its 200 grammes jars of coffee with the following statement on the label, 'This coupon is worth 20p. Collect 5 coupons, send them to us and we will give you £1'. Bert does so but does not receive £1.

Advise Bert.

3. Washwhite markets its washing powder with a coupon stating, 'Save 15p towards your next purchase. *To the Consumer*: This coupon entitles you to a saving of 15p on the retail price of any size of E10 or E20 New System Washwhite Automatic . . . Redemption of this coupon against any other item would constitute fraud. *To the Trader*: Washwhite will refund the face value of this coupon provided that you have accepted this in part payment for any size of E10 or E20 New System Washwhite Automatic and no other item . . .'.

Sam goes to his local Downtown Supermarket, takes a selection of goods (including an E10 packet of Washwhite) off the shelves and they are duly rung up at the checkout point. He then presents his coupon and Downtown declines to refund 15p.

Is Downtown bound by the terms of its contract with Sam to refund the 15p? If it refuses is Washwhite obliged to do so? If the coupon is redeemed against another item does this 'constitute fraud'?

A more difficult issue is whether liability should be extended beyond cases of the type outlined above to include claims for unliquidated damages based on a manufacturer's general advertising. In principle there is no reason why this step should not be taken but in practice the opportunities afforded by such seminal cases as *Carlill v Carbolic Smoke Ball Co* (below p 37) and more recently by the developing law of negligence have not been exploited fully in English law. Our apparent reluctance to venture into this area may be contrasted with developments in both the United States of America and the Commonwealth (see below pp 41–46). However it is relevant also to note that where it is claimed that goods have characteristics (for example, being 'waterproof' or 'shrinkproof') which they do not possess there will be potential criminal liability under the Trade Descriptions Act 1968 (see below Ch 12) and the possibility of a compensation order in favour of consumers who are affected thereby: see below pp 326–330.

The following case provided an opportunity for the Court of Appeal to discuss the possible lines of argument which are available. Because the facts were complex and unusual they are stated fully.

Lambert v Lewis [1980] 1 All ER 978, Court of Appeal

The plaintiffs, a mother and daughter, were travelling in a Reliant car driven by the father in which the son was also a passenger. As their car approached an oncoming Land-Rover, driven by a farmer's employee, a trailer being towed by the Land-Rover became unhitched and slewed across the road into the path of the plaintiff's car. In the ensuing accident the father and son were killed and the mother and daughter injured. They sued (i) the employee-driver, (ii) the owner of the Land-Rover, (iii) the garage which had supplied and fitted the coupling (Lexmead (Basingstoke) Ltd), and (iv) the coupling's manufacturer (B-Dixon-Bate Ltd). The trial court Judge, Stocker J, awarded the plaintiffs £45,000 agreed damages and apportioned liability on the basis of 75% to the manufacturers, who had been negligent in designing the coupling, and 25% to the farmer-owner, who had been negligent in continuing to use it. The plaintiffs claim against the supplier was dismissed: see [1978] 1 Lloyd's Rep 610. Thereafter the case was concerned solely with who (as between the farmer-owner, the supplier, and the manufacturer) was to be ultimately responsible for the payment of this 25%.

In the third party proceedings the owner claimed an indemnity against the supplier (Lexmead), basing his claim on the implied warranties of fitness for purpose and merchantability of s 14 of the Sale of Goods Act (see below p 61). In fourth party proceedings Lexmead, being unable to trace the identity of its own supplier (and so having no claim under a contract of sale) sought to sue the manufacturer (Dixon-Bate) directly. Stocker J dismissed the claim in the third party proceedings on the ground that the owner's negligence in continuing to use the coupling over a prolonged period when it was in an obviously damaged state was too remote a consequence of Lexmead's breach of contract. On this view the loss would lie with the owner and the fourth party proceedings would have no practical importance, there being no loss to pass on. However he added that he would have dismissed Lexmead's claim against Dixon-Bate.

On appeal to the Court of Appeal the Court allowed the owner's appeal in the third party proceedings, holding that Lexmead was responsible for all damage which flowed naturally and directly from its breach of contract, and this damage included the accident because it should have foreseen that some such negligence might occur. The fourth party proceedings then assumed practical importance and the Court dealt as follows with the issues raised.

Stephenson LJ read the following judgment of the court: From the judgment we have already given in the third party proceedings allowing the owner's appeal and holding the suppliers liable to indemnify the owner arises the necessity to decide the fourth party proceedings brought by the suppliers against the manufacturers. The necessity for taking those proceedings arose simply from the fact that the suppliers were unable to identify the stockist or distributor who sold to them the particular Dixon-Bate towing hitch (or trailer coupling) which they sold to the owner. If they could have identified that party they could, in the absence of special contractual terms, have obtained an indemnity from that party for his breach of contractual condition or warranty, or perhaps for negligent misrepresentation under the Misrepresentation Act 1967, and that party could in turn have been indemnified by the seller of the hitch to him, probably the manufacturers themselves, but without that identification the suppliers must have recourse direct to the manufacturers, with whom they had no contract of sale, but who may be considered in part responsible because they do not identify each coupling by a serial number.

Counsel for the suppliers have addressed to us an ingenious argument that they are none the worse off for that lack of identification. The argument was put before us, as it was put before Stocker J, in three different ways. Having dismissed the third party proceedings it was not necessary for him to consider the argument or pronounce on it; but he did so for the sake of completeness should it be held on appeal, as it has been, that he was wrong to dismiss the third party proceedings, and after considering the argument he rejected it and stated that he would have dismissed the fourth party proceedings.

We agree with him that they should be dismissed and in deference to the interesting arguments of counsel for the suppliers, and also because the judge did not expressly deal with the third way in which they put their case, we shall state our reasons more fully perhaps than we need . . .

(His Lordship then referred to the suppliers' (Lexmead's) claim and continued:)

The suppliers relied on the manufacturers' representations, reputation and warranties and carried out no test or examination and fitted the towing hitch to the owner's Land-Rover in such reliance. The suppliers therefore claim under the heads above specified: (1) damages for negligent misrepresentation, and/or (2) damages for the breach of the warranty alleged to have been given to them as distributors. They also alleged (in para 6) a breach of the duty alleged in para 2(4) and claimed damages for that.

The judge dealt first, and so will we, with the argument that the suppliers could succeed on a breach of warranty. The allegation of implied collateral warranty, he said—

'. . . is based on a submission that the following facts are established: 1. The [manufacturers] were well known in the trade as manufacturers of a variety of towing hitches. 2. [They] had justly acquired not only a good trade reputation but also a reputation for quality and safety. 3. [They] sought to improve their reputation by obtaining approval of certain of their products from Messrs Rovers, the Ministry of Defence, and so on. 4. To the trade and to the public [they] expressly claimed in relation to the safe towing trailer coupling that it requires 'no maintenance', is 'foolproof' and 'once the pin is pushed home it is locked—absolutely'. They also claimed that the pin 'locked positively and automatically' and 'no metallic springs to break or rust'. 5. [They] were thus making these claims seriously and intending that any purchaser should rely on them. It is said that Mr Dixon-Bate said in his evidence 'Such claims were intended to be serious and to be acted on by users'. 6. The [manufacturers] did not consider or publicly claim that any instruction or warning in relation to a hitch was necessary, nor did they give any indication with regard to restrictions of user in relation to the suitability for that purpose of their coupling. 7. [They] expressly or by implication claimed no instruction or warning was necessary.'

The evidence of the suppliers' witnesses, Mr Baldwin, their parts manager, Mr Curtis, their salesman, and Mr Wallace, their storeman, was mainly related to documents put out by the manufacturers in 1960, 1963 and 1966, which were not concerned with the dual-purpose towing hitch, or put out in 1973 after the purchase of this hitch by the suppliers. But it was rightly assumed that there was a document put out by the manufacturers after the manufacture of the dual-purpose hitch in 1968 and before this purchase by the suppliers and in the same terms as the 1973 literature. The judge rightly acted on that assumption and found that Mr Wallace read the claims then made and relying on the manufacturers' reputation rather than on them believed them to be true.

Counsel for the suppliers relied before the judge, and also before us, on the evidence of Mr Dixon-Bate himself that the manufacturers intended these claims to be taken seriously, and on the decisions of this court in *Carlill v Carbolic Smoke Ball Co*[1] and of McNair J in *Shanklin Pier Ltd v Detel Products Ltd*[2].

We accept counsel for the suppliers' submission that not much is needed to conclude that when a warranty of suitability for a particular purpose is expressed or implied in a contract of sale that warranty has been relied on by the purchaser: see *Henry Kendall & Sons Ltd (a firm) v William Lillico & Sons Ltd*[3] per Lord Reid and Lord Pearce; *Ashington Piggeries Ltd v Christopher Hill Ltd*[4] per Lord Wilberforce. But the difficulty is to show that what the manufacturers stated in the literature advertising and accompanying their products as to their safety and suitability was intended to be a contractual warranty or binding promise. It is one thing to express or imply it in a contract of sale, another to treat it as expressed or implied as a contract, or a term of a contract, collateral to a contract of sale. There may be cases where the purchase from an intermediate seller may be regarded as fortuitous and the original supplier or seller can properly be held liable for breaches of warranty given by the intermediate seller as well as for those given by him: see *Wells (Merstham) Ltd v Buckland Sand and Silica Co Ltd*[5]. But that is not, in our judgment, this case.

In the *Carbolic Smoke Ball* case[1] this court had no difficulty in holding that the suppliers of the ball made a binding promise to pay £100 to any users of the ball on the stated conditions if it failed to prevent them from getting influenza. Their statement that they had deposited £1,000 with a bank showed that their statements were not a mere 'puff' but a sincere promise, and we cannot agree with counsel for the suppliers that the promise to pay £100 merely showed that they were serious and quantified the damages which they would have been liable to pay to an unsuccessful user of their ball as the loss naturally and directly resulting from their breach of contract. It appears from the report of the argument before Hawkins J[6] that the plaintiff there put her case as a claim for liquidated damages for breach of a contract of warranty of prevention of disease; but it could have been put as a claim for a debt. That case is no authority for holding that the manufacturers were saying to the suppliers: 'If you acquire our product we promise it is safe and merchantable and if it is not we will pay you such damages as the law requires.'

A statement relating to the marketed product may be more than a puff and less than a warranty: it may be so important that it may induce a contract, may now amount to a negligent misrepresentation, and may nearly amount to a warranty: see *Howard Marine and Dredging Co Ltd v Ogden & Sons (Excavations) Ltd*[7], where Lord Denning MR and Bridge LJ (Shaw LJ dubitante) held that oral statements made in pre-contract negotiations as to deadweight capacity were not warranties (though, as Roskill LJ pointed out in the course of the argument, any terms as to deadweight capacity in the charterparty, which was the resulting contract, are not given in the reports of the case). But whether the statement is oral or written, made contemporaneously with the contract or earlier, the question is whether it is intended to be binding. When it is written, as here, we doubt if parol evidence of the intention of the person who made it is admissible, though here admitted without objection, but the intention must, we think, be inferred from the construction of the writings against the background of all the circumstances. The construction of these documents in the circumstances of this case leads us to the same conclusion as the judge, that the claims in them 'were not intended to be, nor were they acted on as being express warranties and (though this further finding, if it adds anything, is not strictly necessary) the [suppliers] did not purchase the coupling in reliance on such warranties'.

Nor do we think that the development of the law in the *Shanklin Pier Co* case[2] (and, it may be, in the unreported case of *Independent Broadcasting Authority v EMI Electronics Ltd*[8]) helps the suppliers to a different result. The effect and ratio of the former decision are correctly stated by the judge in his judgment in these terms:

> 'In that case the defendant paint company made certain express representations as to the quality of its paint and its suitability for use on the plaintiffs' pier which was then to be repaired by contractors. On the strength of that representation the plaintiffs caused the specification for their works to be carried out by contractors to be amended by substituting the defendants' paint for that previously specified. The contractors bought and used the paint, which was unsatisfactory and unsuitable for use on the pier. It was held that the plaintiff company could recover damages on the warranty from the defendant paint company despite the fact that there was no contract other than a collateral one between the plaintiff pier company and the defendant paint company. In my judgment the basis of this decision was that consideration for the representation was the procurement by the plaintiffs of a contract of sale by their contractors with the defendants.'

There the express representation was clearly an express warranty, for which the consideration was the procurement of a particular contract, as the judge pointed out; but here was no warranty and we find it unnecessary to consider whether that decision could be extended to the contract of purchase made by the suppliers, or the contract of resale made by them, and to hold that in consideration of either of those contracts, both in fact unknown to the manufacturers, they are promising or warranting, either expressly or by implication, that their claims for their hitch are true, and they are prepared to stand by their warranties and pay the suppliers and any other distributors in their position damages for breach of them, as long (counsel for the suppliers was constrained to add) as the user of the hitch is reasonable.

The judge went on to hold that this finding that the manufacturers' claims were not warranted precluded the suppliers from recovering damages from the manufacturers in tort for negligent misrepresentation. The basis of his finding against counsel's second submission was that the House of Lords in *Hedley Byrne & Co Ltd v Heller & Partners Ltd*[9], had 'limited the ambit of those entitled to sue in respect of negligent misstatement to the person to whom [we add the words 'the answer to'] 'the enquiry was directed and for the purposes for which the enquiry was made'. And he appears to have held that even if the ambit could have been extended to the suppliers they would be defeated by the fact that they did not rely on the manufacturer's misstatements.

Counsel for the suppliers does not dispute that a special relationship is necessary between the maker of the misstatement and the person who suffers damage by acting on it before the former can be liable for the damage to the latter on the *Hedley Byrne*[9] principle. He concedes also that it is easier to prove that relationship and the consequent duty of care if the information or advice contained in the statement is asked for. But he submits that if the statement is made seriously, not casually, and is intended to be acted on and is in fact acted on and it is negligent, it is actionable at the suit of him who acts on it notwithstanding the maker has forestalled an enquiry for the information or advice it contains by volunteering the one or the other.

This may sometimes be so. A doctor who goes to the help of an unconscious patient will be liable to him if he injures him by negligent treatment. But we cannot regard the manufacturer and supplier of an article as putting himself into a special relationship with every distributor who obtains his product and reads what he says or prints about it and so owing him a duty to take reasonable care to give him true information or good advice. Bearing in mind what, for instance, Lord Reid and what Lord Pearce said in the *Hedley Byrne* case[10], we consider that cases of liability for statements volunteered negligently must be rare and that statements made in such circumstances as these are not actionable at the suit of those who have not asked for them. To make such statements with the serious intention that others will or may rely on them (and here parol evidence of intent may be admissible) is not, in our opinion, enough to establish a special relationship with those others or a duty to them.

So we are again in agreement with the judge's rejection of leading counsel for the suppliers' argument . . .

(His Lordship then considered and rejected the third way in which the suppliers had put their case, namely that the manufacturers were in breach of a duty of care owed by them under general principles of *Donoghue v Stevenson* ([1932] AC 562, HL, see below p 150 et seq) and concluded:)

Putting aside any sympathy we may feel for the suppliers, or their insurers, we would therefore reject all three grounds on which their appeal is put and dismiss it.

Appeal by driver against plaintiffs allowed by consent. Appeal by owner in third party proceedings allowed. Appeal by owner against manufacturers in main action be dismissed. Appeal of suppliers in fourth party proceedings be dismissed. Suppliers application for leave to appeal to House of Lords refused.

1. [1893] 1 QB 256, [1891–4] All ER Rep 127.
2. [1951] 2 All ER 471, [1951] 2 KB 854.
3. [1968] 2 All ER 444 at 457, 483, [1969] 2 AC 31 at 84, 115.
4. [1971] 1 All ER 847 at 876–877, [1972] AC 441 at 495.
5. [1964] 1 All ER 41, [1965] 2 QB 170.
6. [1892] 2 QB 484 at 486.
7. [1978] 2 All ER 1134, [1978] QB 574.
8. [1978] Court of Appeal Transcript 670; [(1981) 14 BLR 1].
9. [1963] 2 All ER 575, [1964] AC 465.
10. [1963] 2 All ER 575 at 580, 616–617, [1964] AC 465 at 482, 539.

NOTES

1.   On further appeal to the House of Lords (see [1981] 1 All ER 1185) it was held that Stocker J has been correct in concluding that the suppliers (Lexmead) were not liable to indemnify the owner-farmer. His negligence in using the coupling was not a consequence which flowed directly and naturally in the ordinary course of events from their breach of contract. Neither had they warranted that it was safe to use a damaged coupling on a public road and the loss to the owner which resulted from his doing so was not recoverable as damages for breach of contract. Accordingly the third party proceedings failed and the fourth party proceedings again lost their practical significance. Nevertheless the reasoning of the Court of Appeal remains important. For a general comment on the case see Hervey, 'Winner Takes All' (1981) 44 MLR 575.

2.   In *Lambert v Lewis* the claims made by the manufacturers of the dangerously-designed coupling were unequivocal enough. It was said to require 'no maintenance', to be 'foolproof' and to lock 'absolutely', 'positively and automatically'. Yet it was a dealer who was seeking to found liability on the unsubstantiated claims and the judgment of the Court of Appeal neither confirms nor denies that the result would have been the same if an injured consumer had been suing.

3.   Of the two routes to recovery considered in the above passages the collateral contract or warranty has the advantage that liability may be independent of any requirement of proof of negligence. Knowledge of the warranty is essential although probably it is not strictly speaking necessary for the plaintiff to show that he relied on it. The *Hedley Byrne v Heller* approach depends on establishing negligence. Both approaches in principle accommodate claims for purely economic losses as well as for personal injury.

4.   It is likely that any development of English law in this area will reflect a compromise between two competing considerations. One is that manufacturers should not feel aggrieved if unsubstantiated advertising claims form a basis for civil liability. Indeed one may have some sympathy with the view of Professor Trebilcock when he writes (in 'Private Law Remedies for Misleading Advertising' (1972) 22 Univ Toronto Law Jo 1,4):

> It should never lie in the mouth of an advertiser to argue that a claim was a mere puff and ought not to have been paid attention to. He ought irrebuttably to be presumed to have made the claim for a purpose and if somebody, as intended, acts on the claim, no matter how irrationally, the seller should be obliged to live with it.'

The competing consideration is a concern not to introduce an open-ended liability – more especially where such liability may both be strict and encompass economic losses. However, in the case of economic loss generally there has been a marked increase in the potential scope of liability in recent years: see *Ross v Caunters (a firm)* [1980] Ch 297, [1979] 3 All ER 580; *Yianni v Edwin Evans & Sons* [1982] QB 438, [1981] 3 All ER 592: *Junior Books Ltd v Veitchi Co Ltd* [1983] AC 520, [1982] 3 All ER 201, HL; *JEB Fastners Ltd v Marks Bloom & Co (a firm)* [1983] 1 All ER 583, CA and below pp 165–176.

5.   If a somewhat more wide-ranging liability were to be imposed in respect of manufacturers' advertising claims a key issue would be the degree of intelligence or scepticism to be attributed to the typical consumer to whom the words are addressed. The issue has been discussed in Canada and, in particular, in the USA. *R v Imperial Tobacco Products Ltd* (1970) 16 DLR (3d) 470 (cited by Trebilcock, op cit at p 5) involved a prosecution charging misleading advertising contrary to the then Combines Investigation Act 1952, s 33D (1). The defendants had promoted a new brand of cigarettes with a campaign stating '\$5 in Every Pack of New Casino'. In fact the packs contained no more than an entry to a game which gave a 1 in 400 chance of winning \$5. Dealing with a suggestion that the average person or reasonable man 'would not have been so incredulous as to believe that Imperial Tobacco was going to give \$5 in cash in exchange for the purchase price of the package', Sinclair J said (at p 472):

> In my view, that is not the test to be applied. Section 33D makes no reference to standards such as those. It seems to me the protection afforded by the section is for 'the public—that vast multitude which includes the ignorant, the unthinking and the credulous', to use an expression that appears in Federal Trade Commission Prosecution cases in the United States, and of which *Charles of the Ritz Distributors Corp v Federal Trade Com'n* (1944) 143 F 2d 676, is an example.

The conviction was upheld on appeal to the Appellate Division: see (1972) 22 DLR (3d) 51. For another interesting Canadian case see *Ranger v Herbert A Watts (Quebec) Ltd* (1970) 10 DLR (3d) 395; affd (1971) 20 DLR (3d) 650 (Ont CA) ('cash certificates' to be found in cigarette packets).

For references to other FTC cases under 15 USC ¶ 45 (Unfair Methods of Competition) see the annotations to the section in the United States Code Annotated (USCA), notes 54–61 especially. The annotations contain a wealth of references to advertising techniques which are familiar on both sides of the Atlantic. For a case noting that there are limits to the 'ignorant, unthinking and credulous' test see *Standard Oil Co of California v FTC* 577 F 2d 653 (1978) (CA, 9th Circ) where Kennedy J said (at 657), 'We do not think that any television viewer would have a level of credulity so primitive that he could expect to breath fresh air if he stuck his head into a bag inflated by exhaust, no matter how clean it looked.' (A television advertisement for a petrol additive had shown a balloon attached to the exhaust of a car being inflated with transparent vapour.)

6. For further discussion of advertising controls in the United Kingdom see Lawson, *Advertising Law* (Macdonald & Evans, 1978) Ch 1 especially; Mitchell (ed) *Marketing and the Consumer Movement* (McGraw-Hill, 1978) and in general below at pp 397–413.

Both in the USA and the Commonwealth there has been much less reluctance to extend the scope of civil liability to cover unsubstantiated advertising claims. For general discussion see Miller and Lovell *Product Liability* (1977), pp 58 et seq; Legh-Jones, 'Product Liability: Consumer Protection in America' (1969) CLJ 54, pp 57–61; Ontario Law Reform Commission, 'Report on Consumer Warranties and Guarantees in the Sale of Goods (1972), Ch 5 especially, 'Report on Sale of Goods' (1979), Ch 10 especially; 2 Frumer and Friedman *Product Liability*, ¶ 16.04[4]. The following is a leading American case.

Randy Knitwear Inc v American Cyanamid Co 11 NY 2d 5, 181 NE 2d 399 (1962), Court of Appeals of New York

The facts appear in the judgment of Judge Fuld. (Footnotes omitted.)

Fuld J: 'The assault upon the citadel of privity', Chief Judge Cardozo wrote in 1931, 'is proceeding in these days apace.' (Ultramares Corp v Touche 255 NY 170, 180, 174 NE 441, 445, 74 ALR 1139.) In these days, too, for the present appeal, here by leave of the Appellate Division on a certified question, calls upon us to decide whether, under the facts disclosed, privity of contract is essential to maintenance of an action against a manufacturer for breach of express warranty.

American Cyanamid Company is the manufacturer of chemical resins, marketed under the registered trade-mark 'Cyana', which are used by textile manufacturers and finishers to process fabrics in order to prevent them from shrinking. Apex Knitted Fabrics and Fairtex Mills are manufacturers of fabrics who were licensed or otherwise authorised by Cyanamid to treat their goods with 'Cyana' and to sell such goods under the 'Cyana' label and, with the guaranty that they were 'Cyana' finished. Randy Knitwear, a manufacturer of children's knitted sportswear and play clothes, purchased large quantities of these 'Cyana' treated fabrics from Apex and Fairtex. After most of such fabrics had been made up into garments and sold by Randy to customers, it was claimed that ordinary washing caused them to shrink and to lose their shape. This action for breach of express warranty followed, each of the 3 parties being made the subject of a separate count. After serving its answer, Cyanamid, urging lack of privity of contract, moved for summary judgment dismissing the cause of action asserted against it, and it is solely with this cause of action that we are concerned.

Insofar as relevant, the complaint alleges that Cyanamid 'represented' and 'warranted' that the 'Cyana' finished fabrics sold by Fairtex and Apex to the plaintiff would not shrink or lose their shape when washed and that the plaintiff purchased the fabrics and agreed to pay the additional charge for the cost involved in rendering them shrink-proof 'in reliance upon' Cyanamid's representations. However, the complaint continues, the fabrics were not as represented since, when manufactured into garments and subjected to ordinary washing, they shrank and failed to hold their shape. The damages suffered are alleged to be over $208,000.

According to the complaint and the affidavits submitted in opposition to Cyanamid's motion, the representations relied upon by the plaintiff took the form of written statements expressed not only in numerous advertisements appearing in trade journals and in direct mail pieces to clothing manufacturers, but also in labels or garment tags furnished by Cyanamid. These labels bore the legend,

'A
CYANA
FINISH
This Fabric Treated for
SHRINKAGE
CONTROL
Will Not Shrink or
Stretch Out of Fit
CYANAMID',

and were issued to fabric manufacturers using the 'Cyana Finish' only after Cyanamid had tested samples of the fabrics and approved them. Cyanamid delivered a large number of these labels to Fairtex and Apex and they, with Cyanamid's knowledge and approval, passed them on to garment manufacturers, including the plaintiff, so that they might attach them to the clothing which they manufactured from the fabrics purchased.

As noted, Cyanamid moved for summary judgment dismissing the complaint against it on the ground that there was no privity of contract to support the plaintiff's action. The court at Special Term denied the motion and the Appellate Division unanimously affirmed the resulting order . . .

It was in this precise type of case, where express representations were made by a manufacturer to induce reliance by remote purchasers, that 'the citadel of privity' was successfully breached in the State of Washington in 1932. (See *Baxter v Ford Motor Co*, 168 Wash 456, 12 P2d 409, 15 P2d 1118, 88 ALR 521; same case after new trial, 179 Wash 123, 35 P2d 1090.) It was the holding in the *Baxter* case that the manufacturer was liable for breach of express warranty to one who purchased an automobile from a retailer since such purchaser had a right to rely on representations made by the manufacturer in its sales literature, even though there was no privity of contract between them. And in the 30 years which have passed since that decision, not only have the courts throughout the country shown a marked, and almost uniform, tendency to discard the privity limitation and hold the manufacturer strictly accountable for the truthfulness of representations made to the public and relied upon by the plaintiff in making his purchase, but the vast majority of the authoritative commentators have applauded the trend and approved the result.

The rationale underlying the decisions rejecting the privity requirement is easily understood in the light of present-day commercial practices. It may once have been true that the warranty which really induced the sale was normally an actual term of the contract of sale. Today, however, the significant warranty, the one which effectively induces the purchase, is frequently that given by the manufacturer through mass advertising and labeling to ultimate business users or to consumers with whom he has no direct contractual relationship.

The world of merchandising is, in brief, no longer a world of direct contract; it is, rather, a world of advertising and, when representations expressed and disseminated in the mass communications media and on labels (attached to the goods themselves) prove false and the user or consumer is damaged by reason of his reliance on those representations, it is difficult to justify the manufacturer's denial of liability on the sole ground of the absence of technical privity. Manufacturers make extensive use of newspapers, periodicals and other media to call attention, in glowing terms, to the qualities and virtues of their products, and this advertising is directed at the ultimate consumer or at some manufacturer or supplier who is not in privity with them. Equally sanguine representations on packages and labels frequently accompany the article throughout its journey to the ultimate consumer and, as intended, are relied upon by remote purchasers. Under these circumstances, it is highly unrealistic to limit a purchaser's protection to warranties made directly to him by his immediate seller. The protection he really needs is against the manufacturer whose published representations caused him to make the purchase.

The policy of protecting the public from injury, physical or pecuniary, resulting from misrepresentations outweighs allegiance to an old and out-moded technical rule of law which, if observed, might be productive of great injustice. The manufacturer places his product upon the market and, by advertising and labeling it, represents its quality to the public in such a way as to induce reliance upon his representations. He unquestionably intends and expects that the product will be purchased and used in reliance upon his express assurance of its quality and, in fact, it is so purchased and used. Having invited and solicited the use, the manufacturer should not be permitted to avoid responsibility, when the expected use leads to injury and loss, by claiming that he made no contract directly with the user.

It is true that in many cases the manufacturer will ultimately be held accountable for the falsity of his representations, but only after an unduly wasteful process of litigation. Thus, if the consumer or ultimate business user sues and recovers, for breach of warranty, from his immediate seller and if the latter in turn, sues and recovers against his supplier in recoupment of his damages and costs, eventually, after several separate actions by those in the chain of distribution, the manufacturer may finally be obliged 'to shoulder the responsibility which should have been his in the first instance.' (*Hamon v Digliani* 148 Conn 710, 717, 174 A.2d 294, 297; see *Kasler & Cohen v Slavouski* [1928] 1 KB 78, where there was a series of 5 recoveries, the manufacturer ultimately paying the consumer's damages, plus a much larger sum covering the costs of the entire litigation.) As is manifest, and as Dean Prosser observes this circuity of action is 'an expensive, time-consuming and wasteful process, and it may be interrupted by insolvency, lack of jurisdiction, disclaimers, or the statute of limitations'. (Prosser, 'The Assault upon the Citadel [Strict Liability to the Consumer]', 69 Yale LJ 1099, 1124.)

Indeed, and it points up the injustice of the rule, insistence upon the privity requirement may well leave the aggrieved party, whether he be ultimate business user or consumer, without a remedy in a number of situations. For instance, he would be remediless either where his immediate seller's representations as to quality were less extravagant or enthusiastic than those of the manufacturer or where—as is asserted by Fairtex in this very case . . . there has been an effective disclaimer of any and all warranties by the plaintiff's immediate seller. Turning to the case before us, even if the representations respecting 'Cyana' treated fabric were false, the plaintiff would be foreclosed of all remedy against Fairtex, if it were to succeed on its defense of disclaimer, and against Cyanamid because of a lack of privity . . . Although we believe that it has already been made clear, it is to be particularly remarked that in the present case the plaintiff's reliance is not on newspaper advertisements alone. It places heavy emphasis on the fact that the defendant not only made representations (as to the nonshrinkable character of 'Cyana Finish' fabrics) in newspapers and periodicals, but also repeated them on its own labels and tags which accompanied the fabrics purchased by the plaintiff from Fairtex and Apex. There is little in reason or logic to support Cyanamid's submission that it should not be held liable to the plaintiff even though the representations prove false in fact and it is ultimately found that the plaintiff relied to its harm upon such representations in making its purchases.

We perceive no warrant for holding—as the appellant urges—that strict liability should not here be imposed because the defect involved, fabric shrinkage, is not likely to cause personal harm or injury. Although there is language in some of the opinions which appears to support Cyanamid's contention [References omitted.], most of the courts which have dispensed with the requirement of privity in this sort of case have not limited their decisions in this manner [References omitted.] And this makes sense. Since the basis of liability turns not upon the character of the product but upon the representation, there is no justification for a distinction on the basis of the type of injury suffered or the type of article or goods involved . . .

In concluding that the old court-made rule should be modified to dispense with the requirement of privity, we are doing nothing more or less than carrying out an historic and necessary function of the court to bring the law into harmony 'with modern-day needs and with concepts of justice and fair dealing.' [References omitted.]

The order appealed from should be affirmed, with costs, and the question certified answered in the negative.

Froessel J (concurring): We concur in result only. We agree with Judge Fuld that defendant, American Cyanamid Company, may be held liable for its express representations (as to the non-shrinkable character of 'Cyana Finish' fabrics) in newspapers and periodicals where they have been repeated on its own labels and tags delivered by Cyanamid to fabric manufacturers such as Fairtex and Apex, to be passed on to garment manufacturers such as plaintiff, so that they might attach them to the clothing cut from the fabrics purchased, all allegedly with Cyanamid's knowledge and authorization.

We do not agree that the so-called 'old court-made rule' should be modified to dispense with the requirement of privity without limitation. We decide cases as they arise, and would affirm in this case under the facts here disclosed.

Desmond C J, and **Burke** and **Foster JJ,** concur with **Fuld J.**

Froessel J, concurs in result only in a separate opinion in which **Dye** and **Van Voorhis JJ,** concur.

Order affirmed, etc.

In the *Baxter* case decided in the Washington Supreme Court in 1932 and referred to by Judge Fuld the Ford Motor Company had made the following claims in its catalogues and printed matter:

> Triplex Shatter-Proof Glass Windshield. All of the new Ford cars have a Triplex shatter-proof glass windshield—so made that it will not fly or shatter under the hardest impact. This is an important safety factor because it eliminates the dangers of flying glass—the cause of most of the injuries in automobile accidents. In these days of crowded, heavy traffic, the use of this Triplex glass is an absolute necessity. Its extra margin of safety is something that every motorist should look for in the purchase of a car—especially where there are women and children'.

The plaintiff who had purchased a Ford sedan car from a dealer was partially blinded when a pebble from a passing car struck and broke his windscreen. Denying that the absence of a contract of sale between Ford and the plaintiff was a sufficient reason to preclude recovery Herman J, said in a much-cited passage (see 88 ALR 521, 525–526):

> Since the rule of caveat emptor was first formulated, vast changes have taken place in the economic structures of the English speaking peoples. Methods of doing business have undergone a great transition. Radio, bill-boards, and the products of the printing press have become the means of creating a large part of the demand that causes goods to depart from factories to the ultimate consumer. It would be unjust to recognize a rule that would permit manufacturers of goods to create a demand for their products by representing that they possess qualities which they, in fact, do not possess, and then, because there is no privity of contract existing between the consumer and the manufacturer, deny the consumer the right to recover if damages result from the absence of those qualities, when such absence is not readily noticeable.

Frequently it will be possible in such cases to view the product and the statement as one and so conclude that the product itself was 'defective'. For example, a statement may be attached to or otherwise accompany a product, as by being included on a label, package or instruction leaflet; and a product may be defective specifically because it is accompanied by unwarranted representations of safety or inadequate warnings or directions for safe use (see below p 154 et seq). If physical injury or property damage is suffered and negligence can be proved liability may then be imposed under the principles of *Donoghue v Stevenson* ([1932] AC 562, HL). However there will be cases in which this is at best an unnatural use of language and where separate provision should be made for false statements themselves. The Ontario Law Reform Commission illustrated the point in its 'Report on Products Liability' (1979), pp 28–29, with the following example:

> Damage may be caused, not by a defect in the product itself, but by something said about the product. For example, a wire cable perfectly capable of lifting a one-half ton weight may become very dangerous if it is inaccurately described as capable of supporting two tons. If the cable is accompanied by the misleading description, it would be possible to classify the cable and its descriptive material, taken as a whole, as a 'defective' product. The misleading statement and the product may, however, come from separate sources. For example, the product may come from a retailer and the descriptive material may come from a manufacturer. In this kind of situation, it is difficult to describe the product as 'defective'. The real complaint is that the statement is misleading.

The Commission made provision for this distinction in clause 4 of its Draft Bill to impose Strict Liability on Business Suppliers of Defective Products. Clause 4 provides as follows:

Strict liability for false statements about products
(1) Where in the course of his business a person supplies a product of a kind that it is his business to supply and makes a false statement concerning the product, reliance upon which causes personal injury or damage to property, that person is liable in damages,
  (a) for the injury or damage so caused; and
  (b) for any economic loss directly consequent upon such injury or damage,
whether or not the reliance is that of the person suffering the injury or damage.

Exception for business losses
(2) A supplier is not liable under clause a or b of subsection 1 for damage to property used in the course of carrying on a business.

For this purpose a 'false statement' includes 'any misstatement of fact, whether made by words, pictures, conduct or otherwise': see 1(1)(b) of the Draft Bill. It has already been noted that the Commission recommended the making of very substantial inroads into the privity doctrine in Chapter 10 of its 'Report on Sale of Goods' (1979): see above p 29 and draft clause 5.10, above p 8. For an interesting Canadian case arising out of the alleged breach of an express warranty see *Naken v General Motors of Canada Ltd* (1979) 92 DLR (3d) 100 (Ont CA), below p 359.

Again, and as further evidence of a widespread trend, reference may be made to a somewhat differently worded provision contained in the Australian Trade Practices Amendment Act 1978, inserting a new Division 2A into Part V of the Trade Practices Act 1974.

Australian Trade Practices Act 1974

74G. Actions in respect of non-compliance with express warranty
(1) Where—
    (a) a corporation, in trade or commerce, supplies goods manufactured by the corporation to another person who acquires the goods for re-supply;
    (b) a person (whether or not the person who acquired the goods from the corporation) supplies the goods (otherwise than by way of sale by auction) to a consumer;
    (c) the corporation fails to comply with an express warranty given or made by the corporation in relation to the goods; and
    (d) the consumer suffers loss or damage by reason of the failure,
the corporation is liable to compensate the consumer for the loss or damage and the consumer may recover the amount of the compensation by action against the corporation in a court of competent jurisdiction.
(2) For the purposes of any action instituted by a consumer against a corporation under this section, where—
    (a) an undertaking, assertion or statement in relation to the quality, performance or characteristics of goods was given or made in connexion with the supply of the goods or in connexion with the promotion by any means of the supply or use of the goods; and
    (b) the undertaking, assertion or statement would, if it had been given or made by the corporation or a person acting on its behalf, have constituted an express warranty in relation to the goods,
it shall be presumed that the undertaking, assertion or statement was given or made by the corporation or a person acting on its behalf unless the corporation proves that it did not give or make, and did not cause or permit the giving or making of, the undertaking, assertion or statement.

By section 74A(1):

In this Division—
'express warranty', in relation to goods, means an undertaking, assertion or statement in relation to the quality, performance or characteristics of the goods given or made in connexion with the supply of the goods, or in connexion with the promotion by any means of the supply or use of the goods, the natural tendency of which is to induce persons to acquire the goods;
'manufactured' includes grown, extracted, produced, processed and assembled.

Consider the following cases on the basis of the position (i) in English civil law; (ii) in the *Randy Knitwear* case and (iii) under the various provisions cited including draft clause 5.10 of the Ontario Sales Report, above p 8.

1. The Carbolic Smoke Ball Company advertises as follows: 'Use our Smoke Ball according to instructions and you will be free from Influenza this winter. Results guaranteed'. Alfredo buys a Smoke Ball from his local chemist shop, uses it according to instructions and contracts influenza. He is off work for two weeks with an agreed loss of income of £500.

Advise Alfredo.

2. Frogman publishes an advertisement in the Sunday press which portrays a swimmer emerging from a pool with a watch on his wrist. The advertisement reads, 'You need never be without a Frogman's watch'. Pamina purchases a Frogman's watch and on diving into a pool finds that it is not waterproof. The retailer who sold the watch to her is insolvent.

Advise Pamina. Suppose further that Pamina had given the watch to a friend, Tamino, as a present and that Tamino, having read the advertisement, dives into a pool with the same result.

3. Giles, a farmer, attends a local Town and Country Fair where he visits a trade stand and explains to a representative of the XY Tractor Company that he is looking for a new harvester. The representative hands him a brochure containing details of XY's Greenfield Harvester and a list of approved dealers. The brochure claims: 'You'll harvest over 65 tons per hour with ease'. Giles buys a Greenfield Harvester from his local dealer and finds that it is quite incapable of harvesting at the rate claimed. However it is well able to harvest at the average rate for a harvester of this size and power. The dealer is now insolvent.

Advise Giles. (See *Murray v Sperry Rand Corpn* (1979) 96 DLR (3d) 113 (Ont) and cf *International Harvester Co of Australia Pty Ltd v Carrigan's Hazeldene Pastoral Co* (1958) 100 CLR 644 (Aust HC).

Would it affect your advice if it had been the local dealer who had given XY's brochure to Giles? Suppose further that the dealer is solvent and that Giles wishes to rescind the contract or reject the harvester. Against whom should he proceed? To whom should he seek to return it? (Consider also in this context the position of the manufacturer of the various products in the cases (i)–(iii) above p 18).

MANUFACTURERS' GUARANTEES

Manufacturers' guarantees may take a variety of forms. Some may be little more than expressions of general company policy, for example an assurance of 'aiming to give complete satisfaction'. Others may provide consumers with benefits going well beyond the demands imposed by the general law, as when a manufacturer of cassettes promises, 'Every recording as good as the first or we will give you a new tape'. Yet others may be positively detrimental or misleading, as by seeking to substitute strictly limited rights for those which would otherwise be conferred by statute or the common law. So far English law has been primarily concerned with this last category of so-called guarantees, rather than with seeking, for example, to prescribe minimum contents for such guarantees. For example, it will be seen later that s 5 of the Unfair Contract Terms Act 1977 invalidates 'guarantees' of consumer goods which seek to exclude or restrict liability under a contract to supply the goods in question: see below at p 240 and p 258, and for a comment on the Scottish equivalent of this section see Cusine, 'Manufacturers' Guarantees and the Unfair Contract

Terms Act' [1980] Juridical Review 185. Another approach has been to create a criminal offence under Part II of the Fair Trading Act 1973 (below p 415 et seq) in the following circumstances.

The Consumer Transactions (Restrictions on Statements) Order 1976 (SI 1976 1813, as amended by SI 1978 127)

Article 5
(1) This Article applies to goods which are supplied in the course of a business by one person ('the supplier') to another where, at the time of the supply, the goods were intended by the supplier to be, or might reasonably be expected by him to be, the subject of a subsequent consumer transaction.
(2) A supplier shall not—
    (a) supply goods to which this Article applies if the goods bear, or are in a container bearing, a statement which sets out or describes or limits obligations (whether legally enforceable or not) accepted or to be accepted by him in relation to the goods; or
    (b) furnish a document in relation to the goods which contains such a statement, unless there is in close proximity to any such statement another statement which is clear and conspicuous and to the effect that the first mentioned statement does not or will not affect the statutory rights of a consumer.
(3) A person does not contravene paragraph (2) above—
    (i) in a case to which sub-paragraph (a) of that paragraph applies, unless the goods have become the subject of a consumer transaction;
    (ii) in a case to which sub-paragraph (b) applies, unless the document has been furnished to a consumer in relation to goods which were the subject of a consumer transaction, or to a person likely to become a consumer pursuant to such a transaction; or
    (iii) by virtue of any statement if before the date on which this Article comes into operation the document containing, or the goods or container bearing, the statement has ceased to be in his possession.

NOTE

For Article 3 of this Order see below p 281 et seq.

Question

What is the underlying mischief which the above provision seeks to control?

So far as the content of guarantees is concerned the Office of Fair Trading has issued the following guidelines.

A Guide for Manufacturers prepared by the Office of Fair Trading, (Office of Fair Trading) (1979)

1. THE BASIC UNDERTAKING

The OFT believes that a manufacturer's guarantee should:
    (a) undertake for a stated period to repair or replace specified (or all) defective parts within a specified and reasonable time of being asked to do so;
    (b) undertake to do this free of any charge, including charges for labour, call out and return carriage;
    (c) undertake to extend the specified period by any significant period (eg 3 weeks or more) during which the consumer is without the product because a defect is being repaired under the guarantee.

2.   CLARITY

The OFT suggests that manufacturers should word a guarantee plainly and simply, so that the following essential points are clear to the consumer:
  (a) the name and address of the guarantor;
  (b) the products or parts covered by, or excluded from, the guarantee;
  (c) the duration (or durations, if they differ for particular parts) of the guarantee;
  (d) the procedure which the consumer should follow in order to present a claim under the guarantee;
  (e) the remedies which the guarantor undetakes to provide in response to a valid claim under the guarantee;
  (f) whether in order to benefit under the guarantee the consumer must complete and return a guarantee registration card.

3.   UNDESIRABLE RESTRICTIONS

While recognising that a manufacturer's guarantee is a voluntarily provided supplement to the consumer's rights in contract, the OFT regards a number of restrictive terms as producing difficult—and often entirely unexpected—problems for consumers. We suggest therefore that the following restrictive terms should be avoided:
  (a) terms which do not allow the consumer a reasonable time in which to return a guarantee registration card, where this is made a condition for claiming under the guarantee;
  (b) terms which impose unreasonable territorial limitations on the guarantee, in particular the exclusion of certain parts of the United Kingdom;
  (c) terms which restrict the assignment of the benefits of the guarantee to a person other than the original purchaser;
  (d) terms under which guarantors reserve to themselves the absolute right to decide whether goods returned to them are defective or not;
  (e) terms requiring that goods must be returned in the original packaging;
  (f) terms which make the guarantee conditional upon the full list price having been paid, or the goods having been purchased from an appointed dealer;
  (g) terms which require the consumer to certify that the goods have been satisfactorily installed.

4.   ADVERTISEMENTS

In advertisements the term 'guarantee' should be used in accordance with Section II 4.9 of the British Code of Advertising Practice . . .

5.   RETAIL DISPLAY

In the case of expensive goods (eg goods priced at over £20) a manufacturer's guarantee is of particular importance to the consumer who is well advised to take its terms into account when comparing brands and reaching a decision about what to buy. We suggest therefore that for these goods consumers should be given the opportunity to read the guarantee prior to purchase and that manufacturers and retailers should act to make this possible.

6.   MANUFACTURER/REPAIRER RELATIONS

Guarantors should ensure that:
  (a) both they and their repair agencies deal with claims quickly, effectively and, for the consumer, conveniently;
  (b) both they and their repair agencies maintain adequate stocks of spare parts;
  (c) where claims are dealt with by independent repair agencies, these are adequately compensated for all reasonable expenses.

7.   OTHER IMPORTANT POINTS

The following points may be found to be helpful:
  (a) guarantors should not claim that particular guarantees have in any way been endorsed by the Office of Fair Trading: such a statement may contravene the Trade Descriptions Act;
  (b) before any agreement is reached or a trade association makes any recommendation to its members about the terms of a guarantee or the use of a model form they should

    seek advice from this Office as to whether the agreement is registrable in accordance with the Restrictive Trade Practices Act 1976;

(c) when issuing a guarantee, or similar document, the guarantor is required by the Consumer Transactions (Restrictions on Statements) Order 1976 (as amended) to include a statement that the terms of a guarantee do not affect the consumer's statutory rights;

(d) the Unfair Contract Terms Act 1977 (Section 5) states that 'In the case of goods of a type ordinarily supplied for private use or consumption, where loss or damage—

    (a) arises from the goods proving defective while in consumer use; and

    (b) results from the negligence of a person concerned in the manufacture or distribution of the goods,

liability for the loss or damage cannot be excluded or restricted by reference to any contract term or notice contained in or operating by reference to a guarantee of the goods.'

NOTES

1. For the British Code of Advertising Practice see below p 398.

2. For other helpful surveys of guarantees see Trebilcock, 'Manufacturers' Guarantees' (1972) 18 McGill Law Journal 1; Ontario Law Reform Commission 'Report on Consumer Warranties and Guarantees in the Sale of Goods' (1972), Chs 6 and 7 especially. Some of the economic implications of guarantees are discussed in perceptive articles by Priest, 'A Theory of the Consumer Product Warranty' (1981) 90 Yale Law Journal 1297 and Whitford, 'Comment on A Theory of the Consumer Product Warranty' (1982) 91 Yale Law Journal 1371.

3. The Consumer Association magazine *Which?* contains regular evaluations of guarantees, warranties, extended warranties and mechanical breakdown insurance schemes: see, for example, 'Guarantees', April 1976 p 78, 'Guarantees', January 1980, p 30 (new and second-hand cars), 'Extended Guarantees and Maintenance Contracts,' May 1984, p 214 (electrical appliances).

4. The problems associated with long-term guarantees offered by firms which may have a short life-expectancy are currently being studied by the Office of Fair Trading: see 'Annual Report of the Director General of Fair Trading 1983,' p 15. A discussion paper has been issued: see 'Consumer Guarantees—a discussion paper' (Office of Fair Trading, 1984).

    Some of the points mentioned in the Office of Fair Trading guidelines printed above are the subject of statutory control in other jurisdictions. Perhaps the best known example is the United States Magnusson-Moss Warranty Act 1975. The Act is administered by the Federal Trade Commission and some of its principal features have been summarised as follows:

'Warranties Guaranteed' by Vickers (1979) JBL 406

WARRANTY INFORMATION DEMANDED

Under the Act the issue of warranties by a manufacturer is not mandatory but when they are given, the regulations of the FTC now set out the duties of the warrantors[1] and sellers, and the rights of the consumers, where the cost of the product is more than $15 (approximately £7). As from January 9, 1977, the warrantor is required to clearly and conspicuously disclose in a single document and in readily understood language the following items of information[2]:

(1) The identity of the party to whom the warranty is extended, and whether it is limited to the original consumer purchaser, or subject to other limitations.
(2) A clear description and identification of the products, parts, etc., covered, or as the case may be, excluded.
(3) What the warrantor will do if the product is defective, and what services or items the warrantor will or will not pay for, or provide.
(4) The exact period of time covered by the warranty.
(5) A detailed explanation of what the consumer should do to get repair or replacement of the product. This should include the name and address of the warrantor, and/or the title and address of the department responsible for warranty performance, and/or a telephone number that the customer can use, free of charge, to get warranty information.
(6) Information about any informal dispute settlement procedure provided by the warrantor . . .
(7) A statement whether or not the return of any card, eg warranty registration card, is a condition precedent to warranty coverage and performance.[3] (Under a 'full' warranty—see post—a requirement that the return of a card is a condition of performance is an unreasonable duty and therefore not permitted.)[4]

WARRANTY COMPARISONS

Prior to the Act, a warranty was usually only given to the purchaser after the contract of sale had taken place, and its contents were, in most instances, examined at home when the goods were unpacked.

The rules now require the seller to give consumers the opportunity to read and compare warranties before sale takes place.[5] This may be done by displaying a text of the warranty close to the product, and/or maintaining a binder(s) which contains all the warranties in each department of the store. The binders must be conspicuously placed, indexed and kept up to date.[6] Where the warranty is printed on the package itself the latter must be clearly visible.[7] It is the duty of the warrantor to provide the seller with all the materials to make the above possible.[8]

Where a seller offers for sale by mail order catalogue a warranted product he must disclose on the same or facing page of the advertised product either the contents of the warranty, or where a free copy can be obtained.[9] In the case of door-to-door sales,[10] the representative must tell the purchaser that he has copies of the warranties which may be inspected before sale.[11]

Under the Act, all warranties costing the consumer more than $10 (excluding tax) must be labelled 'full' or 'limited.'[12] The 'full' warranties[13] are required to meet the Federal minimum standard,[14] viz a product with a defect or malfunction must be repaired within a reasonable time without charge, and if it cannot be repaired the purchaser is entitled to a replacement or full refund. If unreasonable delays cause extra expense, compensation must be provided. No charge is payable for returning the product to the factory for repair. Consequential damage arising from breach of written or implied warranty may be excluded if this appears conspicuously on the face of the warranty (provided State laws permit this). All warranties falling short of these standards must be designated 'limited.' The duration may be added if desired and the rules set out the means by which 'duration' should be calculated.[15] . . .

1. Supplier or other person who gives or offers to give a written warranty—16 CFR [Code of Federal Regulations] 701.1 (g).
2. 16 CFR 701.3 (a).
3. 16 CFR 701.4.
4. 16 CFR 700.7.
5. 16 CFR 702.3 (a) (1).
6. 16 CFR 702.3 (a) (1) (i) and (ii).
7. 16 CFR 702.3 (a) (1) (iii).
8. 16 CFR 702.3 (b) (1).
9. 16 CFR 702.3 (c) (2).
10. Where the offer to purchase is made at a place other than the seller's place of business.
11. 16 CFR 702.3 (d).
12. s 103.
13. Designated 'full (statement of duration) warranties'.
14. s 104.
15. 16 CFR 700.6.

Another interesting North American example contains the following provisions:

Saskatchewan Consumer Products Warranties Act 1977 (as amended by the Saskatchewan Consumer Products Warranties Amendment Act 1981, ss 8 and 9)

ADDITIONAL WRITTEN WARRANTIES

17. Additional written warranties, guidelines
(1) Nothing in this Act shall prevent a warrantor from giving additional written warranties in addition to the statutory warranties set out in section 11.
(2) Any additional written warranty shall contain:
  (a) the name and address of the warrantor;
  (b) the parts of the consumer product covered warranty;
  (c) the duration of the warranty;
  (d) the conditions that the person claiming under the warranty must fulfill before the warrantor will perform his obligation under the warranty;
  (e) the costs, if any, that must be borne by the person claiming under the warranty;
  (f) a statement to the effect that the provisions of the additional written warranty are in addition to and not a modification of or subtraction from the statutory warranties and other rights and remedies contained in this or any other Act;
  (g) the procedure a person claiming under the warranty has to follow for the presentation of a claim under the warranty;
  (h) the location of the repair facility that the consumer product is to be sent to for repair or that a request is to be sent to for the repair of the product in the home of the person claiming under the warranty.
(2.1) No additional written warranty is void by reason only that it does not contain the information mentioned in subsection (2).
(3) No additional written warranty shall:
  (a) purport to make the warrantor or his agent the sole judge in deciding whether or not there is a valid claim under the warranty;
  (b) purport to exclude or limit any express or statutory warranty or any of the rights or remedies contained in this Act;
  (c) purport to make a claim under the warranty dependent upon the consumer product's being returned to the warrantor, when it would be unreasonable to so return the product;
  (d) purport to limit the benefit of the warranty to the consumer or purport to exclude persons mentioned in subsection 4(1) from receiving the benefit of the warranty; or
  (e) be deceptively worded.

17.1 Retail seller deemed warrantor
Where an additional written warranty accompanies or is attached to a consumer product sold by a retail seller, the retail seller is deemed to be a warrantor with respect to the additional written warranty regardless of whether or not the additional written warranty is given by another warrantor, unless the retail seller has, in writing prior to the sale, made it clear to the consumer that he does not adopt the additional written warranty as his own.

18. When unreasonable to require return of product
For the purposes of clause (c) of subsection (3) of section 17, it shall be unreasonable to require a person claiming under the warranty to return to a warrantor any consumer product that, because of its size, weight or method of attachment or installation, cannot be removed or transported without significant cost to such person.

. . .

24. Remedy for breach of additional written warranty to repair or replace
Where a consumer makes a valid claim under an additional written warranty for repair or replacement of a consumer product and the warrantor does not, within a reasonable period of time after the claim is made, perform the repair or replacement in accordance with the terms of the additional written warranty, the consumer shall be entitled to have the defect remedied elsewhere and to recover reasonable repair costs from the warrantor as well as damages for losses that the consumer suffered and that were reasonably foreseeable as liable to result from the failure of the warrantor to honour the warranty.

. . .

ADMINISTRATION OF THE ACT

35.   Offences and penalties
(1) Every manufacturer, retail seller or warrantor who without lawful excuse, the proof of which lies upon him, provides an additional written warranty that does not comply with section 17 or who contravenes subsection (2) of section 7 or any provision of the regulations is guilty of an offence and liable on summary conviction to a fine of not more than $1,000 or to imprisonment for a period not exceeding six months or to both such a fine and imprisonment and, in default of payment, to imprisonment for a term not exceeding six months.

. . .

NOTES

For the definition of a 'consumer' and a 'consumer product' see above p 17. An extract from the statutory warranties of s 11 of the Act is printed below p 89.

Questions

1. Would you favour the adoption of similar provisions to those contained in the above Saskatchewan legislation?
2. What benefits do manufacturers derive from issuing guarantees which confer rights over and above those required by law?

Problem

Art purchases an electric toaster from Ben's shop. On returning home and opening the package he finds that the toaster has an unconditional six months guarantee issued by the manufacturer, Claude. Two months later the toaster stops working. Ben is in liquidation and Claude declines to honour the guarantee, claiming that it is not legally binding. Advise Art as to any legal arguments which he may have to be prepared to meet. Would it affect your advice if he had posted off a slip to register his purchase?

CHAPTER 2

Contracts for the supply of goods

Introduction

The statistics published annually by the Office of Fair Trading (see above p 1) indicate the range of consumer complaints related to goods and services generally. The following extract is concerned with the specific problem of faulty goods.

Faulty Goods (National Consumer Council Occasional Paper) (June 1981)

INTRODUCTION

1.1 This paper looks at consumers' experiences and problems connected with faulty goods, and particularly with goods not lasting as well as expected.

. . .

The information comes from the National Consumer Council's survey, *Consumer Concerns,* which looked at consumer experiences across a wide range of activities and services: housing, local services, shopping, transport, fuels and water, personal finance, tax and work, health, education, welfare and communications.

The survey
1.2 The survey, based on nearly 2,000 interviews with people throughout the United Kingdom aged 18 or over, was carried out for the NCC by Research Services Limited (RSL), who used a two-stage probability sample. The interviews were conducted over two periods: 512 interviews beween mid-November 1979 and mid-February 1980 (which we call the 'pilot'), and 1,456 interviews between mid-September 1980 and mid-November 1980 (which we call the 'mainstage'). All the interviews were completed within one year.

. . .

General findings
1.4 In comparison with many sections of the survey, faulty goods—and getting faulty goods repaired—raised a considerable number of problems. This is particularly marked when we look not at overall numbers of problems but at the proportion of 'users' or 'those at risk' experiencing problems. Some one in ten consumer durables bought by our respondents in the year previous to the interview were claimed to be faulty. And with a quarter of these faulty goods, respondents told us they had problems getting the fault put right. Cars and car servicing, dealt with separately in this paper, also caused a number of problems.
1.5 Durability of goods was one of the problems most frequently-mentioned by respondents. Over 15 per cent of the sample told us about goods they had bought which had not lasted as well as expected—particularly furniture, electrical appliances, and shoes. We deal with the issues raised concerning durability at some length.
1.6 Analysis of the quantitative and qualitative data is not yet complete, so this paper contains only preliminary findings. We rely heavily on the qualitative data because this gives a very useful indication of the kind of problems people experience buying goods, and of what happens when goods are considered faulty.

BUYING AND REPAIRING CONSUMER DURABLES

2.1 We asked whether people had bought any of the following goods in the year previous to the interview: gas cooker, electric cooker, gas fire, electric fire, washing machine, refrigerator, deep freeze, vacuum cleaner, central heating, separate water heater, television (bought or rented), and hi-fi or stereo.
2.2 Of those people who had bought any of these goods, we asked first if the product had any faults in it when new; and second if they had any difficulties getting the fault put right. Overall, roughly one in ten products bought by respondents had faults when newly acquired—cookers, central heating systems, separate water heaters and hi-fi's being particularly prone. A high proportion of people (over one in four) reported difficulties getting the fault put right—and half of these considered the problem to be serious . . .

The National Consumer Council obtained further information in an interesting report from which the following extract is taken:

Buying problems: consumers, unsatisfactory goods and the Law, pp 1–3 (National Consumer Council) (1984)

INTRODUCTION AND SUMMARY

What happens to consumers when they complain about goods which have gone wrong or which are unsatisfactory in other ways? What would they like to happen? What legal changes are needed to get a fairer deal for the consumer?

This report tries to answer some of these questions. It is based upon a detailed survey of the experiences and attitudes of 369 consumers who (during a two-week period) consulted a representative sample of citizens' advice bureaux and consumer aid centres with problems about unsatisfactory goods. We also draw upon 646 case-related questionnaires which were completed by the consumer advisers. This survey was undertaken by the National Consumer Council in connection with the review by the English and Scottish Law Commissions of aspects of the law relating to the sale and supply of goods. The Law Commission had indicated to us that it would like to have firm evidence from consumers on which to base its final recommendations . . .

SUMMARY OF MAJOR FINDINGS FROM THE SURVEY

(1) The most common causes of complaint were with personal items and household goods: shoes, clothing, furniture and—to a lesser extent—cars were a particular source of problems.
(2) Approximately one-eighth of the unsatisfactory goods cost more than £500, the current 'small claims limit' in county courts. More than two-thirds of the goods had been bought by cash or cheque rather than on credit.
(3) Half the goods had been bought within the previous three months, and for more than one quarter of informants the fault had been serious immediately the item was used.
(4) Approximately half the items were described as being not fit for their intended purpose, and approximately a quarter were described as scratched, dented or faulty in some way.
(5) One-third of all informants told us that the unsatisfactory item had been under a manufacturer's guarantee when the fault had first developed: one-fifth claimed that the item had been under a seller's guarantee.
(6) All except six per cent of clients had taken some action in an attempt to solve the problem before their visit to the Citizens' Advice Bureau or Consumer Advice Centre. Almost ninety per cent of clients had previously contacted the seller. Just over one-third of the sellers had accepted responsibility and done or attempted some replacement or repair: clients were not satisfied with what had been done, hence their visit to the bureau/centre. The majority of informants described themselves as being extremely dissatisfied with the way the seller had dealt with their problem.
(7) Just over half the total sample said that their preferred solution to the problem would be a refund of the full price that had been paid. A slightly smaller number said that they wanted the faulty product replaced by a new one.
(8) Advisers were asked about the advice they had given to clients and about the action that should be taken in future. The advisers put great emphasis on personal contact between the buyer and the seller.

(9) In some sixty per cent of cases overall, the advisers felt that the client had some entitlement to a remedy. This assessment should, however, be treated with caution. There was considerable uncertainty about whether or not clients would obtain remedy and/or their entitlement.

(10) A follow-up survey carried out some six months after the main study suggested that, though in more than ten per cent of cases no progress had been made, one-fifth of informants had had their product replaced and approximately the same number had received a full refund.

. . .

The following additional information from p 83 of the report is also of interest:

THE FINDINGS

A. What is going wrong?: The product and its purchase

i *Which goods are unsatisfactory?*
Data from both the clients and from the advice workers suggested that the most common causes of complaint were personal items and household goods. A full list of the products about which data was obtained is included in *Appendix B* to this report: the key summary data is set out below in Table 1. Approximately one third of all unsatisfactory goods were personal items: clothing and shoes were a particular source of complaint though leisure goods (items as various as cameras, records and fishing equipment are included) were also important. Approximately a quarter of all complaints related to household goods of one sort or another: in particular, furniture was a source of problems. Amongst the electrical goods, fridges, fridge/freezers and washing machines were the items mentioned most frequently. There is little difference between the CAB and the CAC information, though household goods in general were a less frequent source of complaint for those consulting CACs.

Table 1: Type of goods

	CAB		CAC	
Base: All clients	(176)		(193)	
1a. Totals	No	%	No	%
Personal items	58	33	64	33
Household goods	52	30	46	24
Electrical goods	27	15	26	13
Audio-visual	22	13	25	13
Vehicles	15	9	31	16
1b. Major individual items				
Shoes	17	10	22	11
Clothing	21	12	20	10
Furniture	18	10	27	14
Cars	9	5	16	8

	CAB		CAC	
Base: All advice workers	(306)		(340)	
1c. Totals	No	%	No	%
Personal items	105	34	129	38
Household goods	87	28	68	20
Electrical goods	35	11	43	13
Audio-visual	36	12	50	15
Vehicles	39	13	47	14
1d. Major individual items				
Shoes	28	9	42	12
Clothing	38	12	44	13
Furniture	42	14	41	12
Cars	23	8	25	7

For more detailed discussion of problems within particular sectors see 'Home Improvements: A Report by the Director General of Fair Trading'

(June 1983), 'Consumer Difficulties in the Used-Car sector: A report and recommendations made by the Director General of Fair Trading' (November 1980), 'Car Servicing and Repairs: A Discussion Paper' (OFT, September 1983).

Where consumers have such complaints relating to faulty goods the remedies for breach of express contractual terms or following a mis-representation (see above p 2 et seq) have long been supplemented by an important range of implied terms as to quality and related matters. These terms which are styled 'conditions' (see above p 10 and below p 61 et seq) generally apply only where goods are supplied 'in the course of a business'. Moreover they cannot be excluded as against one who 'deals as consumer': see the Unfair Contract Terms Act 1977, ss 6(2) and 7(2), below p 240. This chapter is concerned with their content and scope.

Sales and related transactions

Until recently it was important to distinguish between the various types of legal transaction under which the property in or the possession of goods might pass from a supplier to a consumer. If the contract was of sale terms were implied by the Sale of Goods Act 1979 (see ss 13–14 especially, below p 61). Statutory terms were implied also in hire-purchase transactions (see the Supply of Goods (Implied Terms) Act 1973, ss 9–10, below p 62) and on the redemption of trading stamps for goods (see the Trading Stamps Act 1964, s 4). These provisions remain in force. However there are many everyday consumer transactions which do not fall into the above legal categories. For example consumers may hire such goods as television sets and do-it-yourself equipment or acquire goods by way of barter or a contract for work and materials. This last and perhaps arcane expression covers such important and expensive transactions as the installation of central heating, double glazing, cavity insulation and the repair of cars, all of which involve the supply of both goods and services in one contract. For many years there were no statutory implied terms in such transactions although frequently a court was willing to imply terms as to quality etc under the guise of giving effect to the parties' intentions.

THE DISTINCTION BETWEEN SALE AND ANALOGOUS TRANSACTIONS

The distinction between a contract of sale which envisages a transfer of property in goods 'for a money consideration, called the price' (see s 2(1) of the 1979 Act) and a contract of hire where possession only is transferred creates few problems. However the distinction between contracts of sale and contracts of barter and for work and materials is far less clear-cut. In a Working Paper which led eventually to statutory reform the Law Commission referred to a number of commonplace consumer transactions which might have been classified as barter rather than sale. Having discussed the position in the case of a trade-in or part-exchange the Commission continued:

Implied terms in Contracts for the Supply of Goods (Law Commission Working Paper No 71) (1977)

Barter

. . .

20. Another kind of transaction that may be outside the provisions of the Sale of Goods Act involves the supply of goods in return for stamps, coupons, wrappers or labels. Sometimes goods are offered in return for such things without requiring the payment of money; more often the acceptance of the offer requires the payment of a sum in cash as well. The supply of goods on the redemption of trading stamps was recognised as being outside the ambit of the Sale of Goods Act 1893, so special provision was made for it.[1] However there remain other transactions for which no provision has yet been made, transactions involving the supply of goods in return for things other than stamps, with or without the payment of money in addition. For example, in *Chappell & Co Ltd v Nestlé Co Ltd*[2] the defendants advertised a gramophone record for supply to members of the public for a sum of money together with three of their chocolate wrappers. The essential nature of the transaction was not put in issue in the case but one of the Law Lords was disposed to think that it was not, strictly speaking, a sale.[3] Such transactions are a regular feature of ordinary retail trade. The promotion of particular products often involves the distribution of coupons, vouchers and the like; the customer may trade these in as part of the consideration for the supply of the goods in order to get a reduction in the price that would otherwise be payable. There is, as yet, no clear authority on the status of such a transaction; either it is a sale and subject to the provisions of the Sale of Goods Act 1893 or it is barter and subject only to the rules established at common law.

. . .

35. Another difficulty could arise on facts such as occurred in *Chappell & Co Ltd v Nestlé Co Ltd* to which we referred earlier.[4] What if the record supplied by the chocolate manufacturers had been unfit to play or of unmerchantable quality? It might be argued that since the suppliers were not 'dealers' in records and it was not in the course of their business to supply records, no terms relevant to the quality of the record should be implied. Such an argument might be sustainable on an analogy with the original wording of section 14 of the Sale of Goods Act 1893.[5] This section has been amended since and, in the case of a sale, terms as to quality are now implied wherever the goods are supplied in the course of a business, whether or not the seller deals in the goods in question or sells them as a regular feature of his business.[6] The position on sale has thus been put on a slightly different footing by the Supply of Goods (Implied Terms) Act 1973, but of course that Act does not apply to contracts of barter. The common law position remains unclear.
36. There seems to be a need for greater clarity in relation to contracts for work and materials as well . . .

1. Trading Stamps Act 1964, s 4, now amended by Supply of Goods (Implied Terms) Act 1973, s 16.
2. [1960] AC 87.
3. Ibid, at p 109, per Lord Reid.
4. [1960] AC 87; see para 20, above.
5. See, however, the Canadian case of *Buckley v Lever Bros Ltd* [1953] 4 DLR 16 in which it was assumed on similar facts that the Sale of Goods Act *did* apply and the argument just put was rejected.
6. Sale of Goods Act 1893, ss 14(2) and 14(3) . . . These sections were put in their present form by Supply of Goods (Implied Terms) Act 1973, s 3.

NOTE

For further discussion of the distinction between sale and related transactions see *Benjamin's Sale of Goods* (2nd edn, 1981) p 23 et seq; Atiyah *Sale of Goods* (6th edn, 1980) Ch 2; the Law Commission Report, 'Implied Terms in Contracts for the Supply of Goods' (Law Com No 95 1979) para 27 et seq and materials there cited.

Fortunately the question whether such transactions are to be classified as sale or barter is no longer of practical importance since the coming into force on 4 January 1983 of the Supply of Goods and Services Act 1982. This Act (see ss 3–4 and 8–9, below pp 64–65) applies to any such contract, and to contracts for work and materials and of hire, equivalent obligations as to correspondence with description, quality and fitness for purpose as are implied in a contract of sale: see Palmer (1983) 46 MLR 619. However it is still important to determine whether goods have been supplied contractually rather than gratuitously and it may be important also to determine when or where any such contract was formed.

CONTRACTS AND THEIR FORMATION

The general principles of the law of contract which assist in determining whether goods have been supplied pursuant to a contract are discussed in the standard texts on the law of contract: see, for example, Cheshire and Fifoot *Law of Contract* (10th edn, 1981) at p 26 et seq especially; Smith and Thomas *A Casebook on Contract* (7th edn, 1982) Ch 1. Their importance in the present context is that they may affect such issues as a consumer's entitlement both to complain if goods are faulty and to recover damages if they are dangerous and cause injury. As was seen in *Daniels and Daniels v R White & Sons Ltd and Tarbard* [1938] 4 All ER 258 (above p 19) a retail seller is strictly liable where unmerchantable goods cause physical injury, but such liability arises only where a contract can be established. Otherwise liability depends on proof of negligence. Of course the rules governing the formation of a contract will determine also when a consumer is contractually bound to buy or otherwise acquire goods. The following extract from a Law Commission report indicates an area where the distinction between contracts and gifts may not be entirely clear.

Implied terms in contracts for the supply of goods (Law Commission) (Law Com No 95) (1979)

The contract of supply
30. In our working paper we explained that we would not be concerned with non-contractual transactions such as gift where there was no *contract* to supply the goods in question.[1] However, the borderlines separating (a) gift from sale and (b) gift and sale from contracts analogous to sale are not always clear, a point which is well illustrated by *Esso Petroleum Co Ltd v Commissioners of Customs and Excise*.[2] Esso had devised a petrol sales promotion scheme which involved the distribution of coins to petrol stations. Each coin was stamped with the likeness of one of the English footballers selected for the 1970 World Cup Competition, and the object of the scheme was that the petrol station proprietor should offer to give away a coin for every four gallons of Esso petrol which motorists bought. The coins were of little intrinsic value but it was hoped that motorists would wish to build up a full set of 30. The coins were advertised as 'Going free, at your Esso Action Station now'. The question to be decided was whether the coins were being 'sold' and were accordingly chargeable to purchase tax. Pennycuick V-C held that the coins were being sold; the Court of Appeal, reversing his decision, held that the coins were not being sold but were being distributed as gifts and that no tax was due. In the House of Lords, opinions were divided. Lord Fraser's opinion was that there was a sale; Viscount Dilhorne and Lord Russell thought that the Court of Appeal were right in holding that the coins were being distributed as gifts. Lord Simon and Lord Wilberforce both concluded that the supply of the coins to the motorists was contractual but without there being a sale; the consideration for the transfer of the coin or coins was not a money payment but the undertaking by the motorist to enter into a collateral contract to

purchase the appropriate quantity of Esso petrol; accordingly it was not a gift, but it was not a sale either.

31. The result of the *Esso* case was that the House of Lords decided, Lord Fraser dissenting, that the coins had not been 'sold' and that they were therefore exempt from purchase tax. For our purposes the significance of the case is on a more general point. It shows that the distinctions between gifts and sales and contracts analogous to sale are not always easy to draw and that the consequences of the distinction can be important.

32. Under the existing law a person who receives a gift has no right of redress against the donor merely because the gift is of unmerchantable quality or does not correspond with the donor's description of it. The person receiving the gift may have a remedy in tort if the gift causes injury or damage which is attributable to negligence on the donor's part. But that is another matter: he has no remedy in contract against the donor for the simple reason that there is no contract between them. To the extent that the offer of worthless goods, without charge, as part of a sales promotion, is against the public interest it is primarily the concern of the Office of Fair Trading. We therefore do not intend to examine the law of gift in this report.

1. Working Paper No 71, para 11.
2. [1976] 1 WLR 1.

In the case of sales in supermarkets it is well known that the basic rule is that a contract is not concluded by a consumer buyer taking goods off a shelf and putting them into a trolley or basket. Usually it is concluded only at the check-out point: see generally *Pharmaceutical Society of Great Britain v Boots Cash Chemists Southern Ltd* [1953] 1 QB 401, [1953] 1 All ER 482, CA; and *Fisher v Bell* [1961] 1 QB 394, [1960] 3 All ER 731. The position has been discussed in some detail in relation to the law of theft where the following case as reported in *The Times* is of interest and importance. However it should be noted that in a prosecution for theft the emphasis is on when property in and possession of the goods (as opposed to mere custody) passes to the consumer and this may occur after the parties have agreed to buy and sell the goods in question.

Davies v Leighton (1978) Times, 29 June, (1978) 68 Cr App Rep 4, [1978] Crim LR 575 (Queen's Bench Divisional Court)

The prosecutor was appealing on a case stated by Clwyd Justices who had dismissed an information against the defendant, Myra Leighton, alleging theft of one bag of apples and one of tomatoes, contrary to sections 1 and 7 of the Theft Act 1968.

Mr Justice Ackner said that the defendant was alleged to have stolen the apples and tomatoes, valued at 13p and 20p respectively, at a store in Wrexham, in May, 1976. The store had a self-service area for the purchase of foodstuffs. Within that area there was a counter for the sale of fruit and vegetables manned by an assistant, who weighed the quantity required by a customer, and bagged and priced it. The bag was handed to the customer, who was expected to pay the cashier at the exit.

On the day in question the defendant was observed by a store detective to acquire the bags of apples and tomatoes from the assistant and to carry them in her hand to an off-licence section of the store. There she bought some wine, which she paid for and placed in her own shopping trolley. She also placed the apples and tomatoes in the trolley and, after joining a queue at the exit, left the store without paying for the apples and tomatoes.

She was stopped outside by the detective, and when she returned to the store she claimed that she had paid for the goods although she could not produce a receipt.

At the conclusion of the prosecution case before the justices, a submission was made on behalf of the defendant that ownership of the goods in question passed to the defendant when she received them from the assistant and, therefore, unless there was prima facie evidence that she had not intended to pay for them before they were handed to her, the justices could not convict because the Theft Act required that there should be a dishonest appropriation of property belonging to another. The contention was that when she took the goods through the check-out, the property had already passed to her.

Although the justices were referred to *Edwards v Ddin* ([1976] 1 WLR 942), the report was not produced to them. If it had been, they would have realised that it was inapplicable.

The law was well settled in relation to purchases in a supermarket. In *Lacis v Cashmarts* ([1969] 2 QB 400, [at] 407) Lord Parker, Lord Chief Justice, said: 'The fundamental question . . . is: what is the intention of the parties . . . In my judgment when one is dealing with a case such as this, particularly a shop of the supermarket variety . . . the intention of the parties quite clearly as it seems to me is that the property shall not pass until the price is paid. That as it seems to me is in accordance with the reality and in accordance with commercial practice.'

Edwards v Ddin was particularly relied on by the defendant. A motorist drove to a garage forecourt and had his petrol tank filled: he then drove away without paying. The petrol intermingled with petrol already in the tank and it was held that the garage owner did not reserve the right to dispose of the petrol once it was in the tank and therefore theproperty in it had passed to the motorist in accordance with section 18, rule 5 of the Sale of Goods, 1893.

Mr Pitman argued that a similar situation arose in the present case because there was a finding that the goods were not only bagged but weighed, so that the case was taken out of the general principles applicable to supermarket sales.

In *Martin v Puttick* ([1968] 2 QB 82) Mr Justice Winn said that 'the limit of the authority of the meat counter assistant is clearly merely to hand over and wrap up the meat and not to deal in any way with any transfer of property from the owner of the shop to the customer'. That statement seemed applicable to the present case, where the customer asked the assistant for the quantity required.

There was no reference to the assistant being in a managerial or other special category, when a different situation might arise. The justices had come to the wrong conclusion, namely, that the property had passed when the defendant received the goods. In fact and in law, the property never passed because she never paid for the goods.

Mr Justice Talbot and the Lord Chief Justice agreed.

The appeal was allowed, and the case was ordered to be sent back for the hearing to continue.

NOTES

1.   The leading case on theft in supermarkets is now *R v Morris, Anderton v Burnside* [1984] AC 320, [1983] 3 All ER 288.

2.   For a reference to some of the problems of determining when a contract is completed in more modern methods of selling through the medium of television see the Office of Fair Trading paper, 'Micro-electronics and Retailing' (September 1982), para 3.56 et seq.

Question

For what reasons may consumers sometimes have difficulty in establishing that defective goods were purchased from a particular shop or other source?

Problems

1.   The Pennymede Courier publishes the following advertisement which has been inserted by Pinetree Kitchens, 'Free Double Oven Worth £400 when you buy a Pinetree Luxury Fitted Kitchen'. Andrea has such a kitchen installed by Pinetree and finds that the oven is defective and does not work.

Advise Andrea.

2. Supersave operates a supermarket in Littletown. It has a section which deals in cheese and paté and a separate counter which sells wines and spirits. One Saturday evening when the shop is about to close Amantha asks the assistant for a pound of duck paté and half of a fine Stilton cheese. The paté is cut out of a bowl and the Stilton cut in two. Both are then placed in polythene bags and the price is marked on the bags to be paid at the check-out point. Bill goes to the wines and spirits counter and pays for two bottles of sparkling wine. Amantha decides that she does not wish to buy the paté and cheese but the shop assistant refuses to take them back. As Bill is waiting in the check-out queue to pay for other goods one of his bottles explodes, causing him facial injury.

Advise Amantha and Bill.

3. Multistores is a company with a head office in London and some one hundred retail shops in the United Kingdom. Meg buys a cassette recorder from Multistores when on holiday in Plymouth and on returning home to Newcastle she discovers that it is defective. The Newcastle branch agrees that it is defective but declines to deal with the matter.

Advise Meg.

STATUTORY IMPLIED TERMS AS TO QUALITY AND RELATED MATTERS

As has been noted above (p 56) statutory terms as to the quality of goods and materials supplied are now implied in most important consumer transactions including contracts of sale, hire-purchase, work and materials and hire. Although the terms are virtually identical it is convenient to set out the statutory text of the various provisions before examining their main requirements and implications.

Sale of Goods Act 1979

13. Sale by description
(1) Where there is a contract for the sale of goods by description, there is an implied condition that the goods will correspond with the description.
(2) If the sale is by sample as well as by description it is not sufficient that the bulk of the goods corresponds with the sample if the goods do not also correspond with the description.
(3) A sale of goods is not prevented from being a sale by description by reason only that, being exposed for sale or hire, they are selected by the buyer.

. . .

14. Implied terms about quality or fitness
(1) Except as provided by this section and section 15 below and subject to any other enactment, there is no implied condition or warranty about the quality or fitness for any particular purpose of goods supplied under a contract of sale.
(2) Where the seller sells goods in the course of a business, there is an implied condition that the goods supplied under the contract are of merchantable quality, except that there is no such condition—
    (a) as regards defects specifically drawn to the buyer's attention before the contract is made; or
    (b) if the buyer examines the goods before the contract is made, as regards defects which that examination ought to reveal.
(3) Where the seller sells goods in the course of a business and the buyer, expressly or by implication, makes known—
    (a) to the seller, or

(b) where the purchase price or part of it is payable by instalments and the goods were previously sold by a credit-broker to the seller, to that credit-broker,

any particular purpose for which the goods are being bought, there is an implied condition that the goods supplied under the contract are reasonably fit for that purpose, whether or not that is a purpose for which such goods are commonly supplied, except where the circumstances show that the buyer does not rely, or that it is unreasonable for him to rely, on the skill or judgment of the seller or credit-broker.

(4) An implied condition or warranty about quality or fitness for a particular purpose may be annexed to a contract of sale by usage.

(5) The preceding provisions of this section apply to a sale by a person who in the course of a business is acting as agent for another as they apply to a sale by a principal in the course of a business, except where that other is not selling in the course of a business and either the buyer knows that fact or reasonable steps are taken to bring it to the notice of the buyer before the contract is made.

(6) Goods of any kind are of merchantable quality within the meaning of subsection (2) above if they are as fit for the purpose or purposes for which goods of that kind are commonly bought as it is reasonable to expect having regard to any description applied to them, the price (if relevant) and all the other relevant circumstances.

(7) Paragraph 5 of Schedule 1 below applies in relation to a contract made on or after 18 May 1973 and before the appointed day, and paragraph 6 in relation to one made before 18 May 1973.

(8) In subsection (7) above and paragraph 5 of Schedule 1 below references to the appointed day are to the day appointed for the purposes of those provisions by an order of the Secretary of State made by statutory instrument.

NOTE

The 'appointed day' is 19 May 1985: see the Sale of Goods Act 1979 (Appointed Day) Order 1983, SI 1983/1572. The provisions of Sch 1, para 5 which apply until this date (see s 14(7) above) differ only in terminology from the text printed above. The new terminology reflects the changes brought about by the Consumer Credit Act 1974.

Supply of Goods (Implied Terms) Act 1973

9. Bailing or hiring by description

(1) Where under a hire-purchase agreement goods are bailed or (in Scotland) hired by description, there is an implied condition that the goods will correspond with the description, and if under the agreement the goods are bailed or hired by reference to a sample as well as a description, it is not sufficient that the bulk of the goods corresponds with the sample if the goods do not also correspond with the description.

(2) Goods shall not be prevented from being bailed or hired by description by reason only that, being exposed for sale, bailment or hire, they are selected by the person to whom they are bailed or hired.

10. Implied undertakings as to quality or fitness

(1) Except as provided by this section and section 11 below and subject to the provisions of any other enactment, including any enactment of the Parliament of Northern Ireland or the Northern Ireland Assembly, there is no implied condition or warranty as to the quality or fitness for any particular purpose of goods bailed or (in Scotland) hired under a hire-purchase agreement.

(2) Where the creditor bails or hires goods under a hire-purchase agreement in the course of a business, there is an implied condition that the goods are of merchantable quality, except that there is no such condition—

(a) as regards defects specifically drawn to the attention of the person to whom the goods are bailed or hired before the agreement is made; or

(b) if that person examines the goods before the agreement is made, as regards defects which that examination ought to reveal.

(3) Where the creditor bails or hires goods under a hire-purchase agreement in the course of

a business and the person to whom the goods are bailed or hired, expressly or by implication, makes known—

(a) to the creditor in the course of negotiations conducted by the creditor in relation to the making of the hire-purchase agreement, or

(b) to a credit-broker in the course of negotiations conducted by that broker in relation to goods sold by him to the creditor before forming the subject matter of the hire-purchase agreement,

any particular purpose for which the goods are being bailed or hired, there is an implied condition that the goods supplied under the agreement are reasonably fit for that purpose, whether or not that is a purpose for which such goods are commonly supplied, except where the circumstances show that the person to whom the goods are bailed or hired does not rely, or that it is unreasonable for him to rely, on the skill or judgment of the creditor or credit-broker.

(4) An implied condition or warranty as to quality or fitness for a particular purpose may be annexed to a hire-purchase agreement by usage.

(5) The preceding provisions of this section apply to a hire-purchase agreement made by a person who in the course of a business is acting as agent for the creditor as they apply to an agreement made by the creditor in the course of a business, except where the creditor is not bailing or hiring in the course of a business and either the person to whom the goods are bailed or hired knows that fact or reasonable steps are taken to bring it to the notice of that person before the agreement is made.

(6) In subsection (3) above and this subsection—

(a) 'credit-broker' means a person acting in the course of a business of credit brokerage;

(b) 'credit brokerage' means the effecting of introductions of individuals desiring to obtain credit—

(i) to persons carrying on any business so far as it relates to the provision of credit, or

(ii) to other persons engaged in credit brokerage.

NOTE

These sections are printed as substituted by the Consumer Credit Act 1974, s 192(3)(a) and Sch 4, para 35. By virtue of the Consumer Credit Act 1974 (Commencement No 8) Order 1983, SI 1983/1551 the substitutions take effect from 19 May 1985.

Supply of Goods and Services Act 1982, Part I (Supply of Goods)

CONTRACTS FOR THE TRANSFER OF PROPERTY IN GOODS

1. The contracts concerned

(1) In this Act a 'contract for the transfer of goods' means a contract under which one person transfers or agrees to transfer to another the property in goods, other than an excepted contract.

(2) For the purposes of this section an excepted contract means any of the following:—

(a) a contract of sale of goods;

(b) a hire-purchase agreement;

(c) a contract under which the property in goods is (or is to be) transferred in exchange for trading stamps on their redemption;

(d) a transfer or agreement to transfer which is made by deed and for which there is no consideration other than the presumed consideration imported by the deed;

(e) a contract intended to operate by way of mortgage, pledge, charge or other security.

(3) For the purposes of this Act a contract is a contract for the transfer of goods whether or not services are also provided or to be provided under the contract, and (subject to subsection (2) above) whatever is the nature of the consideration for the transfer or agreement to transfer.

. . .

3.   Implied terms where transfer is by description
(1) This section applies where, under a contract for the transfer of goods, the transferor transfers or agrees to transfer the property in the goods by description.
(2) In such a case there is an implied condition that the goods will correspond with the description.
(3) If the transferor transfers or agrees to transfer the property in the goods by sample as well as by description it is not sufficient that the bulk of the goods corresponds with the sample if the goods do not also correspond with the description.
(4) A contract is not prevented from falling within subsection (1) above by reason only that, being exposed for supply, the goods are selected by the transferee.

4.   Implied terms about quality or fitness
(1) Except as provided by this section and section 5 below and subject to the provisions of any other enactment, there is no implied condition or warranty about the quality or fitness for any particular purpose of goods supplied under a contract for the transfer of goods.
(2) Where, under such a contract, the transferor transfers the property in goods in the course of a business, there is (subject to subsection (3) below) an implied condition that the goods supplied under the contract are of merchantable quality.
(3) There is no such condition as is mentioned in subsection (2) above—
   (a) as regards defects specifically drawn to the transferee's attention before the contract is made; or
   (b) if the transferee examines the goods before the contract is made, as regards defects which that examination ought to reveal.
(4) Subsection (5) below applies where, under a contract for the transfer of goods, the transferor transfers the property in goods in the course of a business and the transferee, expressly or by implication, makes known—
   (a) to the transferor, or
   (b) where the consideration or part of the consideration for the transfer is a sum payable by instalments and the goods were previously sold by a credit-broker to the transferor, to that credit-broker,
any particular purpose for which the goods are being acquired.
(5) In that case there is (subject to subsection (6) below) an implied condition that the goods supplied under the contract are reasonably fit for that purpose, whether or not that is a purpose for which such goods are commonly supplied.
(6) Subsection (5) above does not apply where the circumstances show that the transferee does not rely, or that it is unreasonable for him to rely, on the skill or judgment of the transferor or credit-broker.
(7) An implied condition or warranty about quality or fitness for a particular purpose may be annexed by usage to a contract for the transfer of goods.
(8) The preceding provisions of this section apply to a transfer by a person who in the course of a business is acting as agent for another as they apply to a transfer by a principal in the course of a business, except where that other is not transferring in the course of a business and either the transferee knows that fact or reasonable steps are taken to bring it to the transferee's notice before the contract concerned is made.
(9) Goods of any kind are of merchantable quality within the meaning of subsection (2) above if they are as fit for the purpose or purposes for which goods of that kind are commonly supplied as it is reasonable to expect having regard to any description applied to them, the price (if relevant) and all the other relevant circumstances.

. . .

CONTRACTS FOR THE HIRE OF GOODS

6.   The contracts concerned
(1) In this Act a 'contract for the hire of goods' means a contract under which one person bails or agrees to bail goods to another by way of hire, other than an excepted contract.
(2) For the purposes of this section an excepted contract means any of the following:—
   (a) a hire-purchase agreement;
   (b) a contract under which goods are (or are to be) bailed in exchange for trading stamps on their redemption.
(3) For the purposes of this Act a contract is a contract for the hire of goods whether or not services are also provided or to be provided under the contract, and (subject to subsection (2) above) whatever is the nature of the consideration of the bailment or agreement to bail by way of hire.

. . .

8. Implied terms where hire is by description

(1) This section applies where, under a contract for the hire of goods, the bailor bails or agrees to bail the goods by description.

(2) In such a case there is an implied condition that the goods will correspond with the description.

(3) If under the contract the bailor bails or agrees to bail the goods by reference to a sample as well as a description it is not sufficient that the bulk of the goods corresponds with the sample if the goods do not also correspond with the description.

(4) A contract is not prevented from falling within subsection (1) above by reason only that, being exposed for supply, the goods are selected by the bailee.

9. Implied terms about quality or fitness

(1) Except as provided by this section and section 10 below and subject to the provisions of any other enactment, there is no implied condition or warranty about the quality or fitness for any particular purpose of goods bailed under a contract for the hire of goods.

(2) Where, under such a contract, the bailor bails goods in the course of a business, there is (subject to subsection (3) below) an implied condition that the goods supplied under the contract are of merchantable quality.

(3) There is no such condition as is mentioned in subsection (2) above—

    (a) as regards defects specifically drawn to the bailee's attention before the contract is made; or

    (b) if the bailee examines the goods before the contract is made, as regards defects which that examination ought to reveal.

(4) Subsection (5) below applies where, under a contract for the hire of goods, the bailor bails goods in the course of a business and the bailee, expressly or by implication, makes known—

    (a) to the bailor in the course of negotiations conducted by him in relation to the making of the contract, or

    (b) to a credit-broker in the course of negotiations conducted by that broker in relation to goods sold by him to the bailor before forming the subject matter of the contract,

any particular purpose for which the goods are being bailed.

(5) In that case there is (subject to subsection (6) below) an implied condition that the goods supplied under the contract are reasonably fit for that purpose, whether or not that is a purpose for which such goods are commonly supplied.

(6) Subsection (5) above does not apply where the circumstances show that the bailee does not rely, or that it is unreasonable for him to rely, on the skill or judgment of the bailor or credit-broker.

(7) An implied condition or warranty about quality or fitness for a particular purpose may be annexed by usage to a contract for the hire of goods.

(8) The preceding provisions of this section apply to a bailment by a person who in the course of a business is acting as agent for another as they apply to a bailment by a principal in the course of a business, except where that other is not bailing in the course of a business and either the bailee knows that fact or reasonable steps are taken to bring it to the bailee's notice before the contract concerned is made.

(9) Goods of any kind are of merchantable quality within the meaning of subsection (2) above if they are as fit for the purpose or purposes for which goods of that kind are commonly supplied as it is reasonable to expect having regard to any description applied to them, the consideration for the bailment (if relevant) and all the other relevant circumstances.

THE SCOPE OF PART I OF THE SUPPLY OF GOODS AND SERVICES ACT 1982

Although Part I of the above Act imposes obligations as to the quality of the goods supplied in the most important types of consumer contracts which are neither contracts for the sale of goods nor hire-purchase agreements the precise scope of its coverage is not wholly clear. Part II which imposes an obligation of reasonable care in the provision of services (see s 13) is noted below p 114. Professor Palmer has discussed some areas of doubt and omissions within Part I as follows:

'The Supply of Goods and Services Act 1982' (1983) 46 MLR 619, 621–22

The Act may also apply to goods which are, according to usual practice, supplied as an adjunct to services and abandoned when those services are completed: for example, the provision for tea chests by a removal company.[1] But its application to other title-transferring transactions may not have been so clearly envisaged and may occasion surprise to trading organisations. Some, it is true, may be an acceptable subject-matter for sections 1 to 5: for example, the award of prizes in competitions; the supply of products to agents or canvassers in return for (or for use in) services which they perform for the supplier; the provision of 'free' meals to employees as part of their contract of employment; the use by a hotel guest or perhaps by a tenant of consumable goods supplied on the premises, for which no independent consideration is required; the supply of a replacement chattel by a trader to a customer who is dissatisfied with the goods already supplied to him (where the buyer's consideration is presumably, at least in part, his forbearance from taking legal action under the original, compromised contract); and the collateral contract between the dealer and the debtor under a hire-purchase agreement, where the debtor's consideration is his entry into the hire-purchase agreement with a distinct party, the finance house.[2] The prospect of exposing other transactions to sections 1 to 5 is more alarming: for example, the transfer by an employer-corporation of its property in a company car to an employee as part of a dismissal or redundancy settlement . . .

This apparent elasticity is the more curious in view of the fact that certain aspects of the supply of goods do not appear to enjoy the benefit of sections 2 to 5 because the contract involves no passing of property. An example is the use of materials which are consumed in the course of their application by the supplier, such as dyes, lotions, solvents and shampoos. It seems that the consumer cannot be a transferee within section 1 (1) because there can be no property in goods which are dissipated[3]. Although terms similar to those in section 4 of the 1982 Act seem impliable in such a case at common law,[4] the lack of statutory treatment is regrettable, especially since there is no statutory formulation of the implied terms governing quality of services beyond the anaemic obligation of reasonable care and skill in section 13. The silence of the statute on these points shows the peril of segregating provisions upon the quality of goods and services[5] and consigns contracts like that in *Ingham v Emes*[6] to the very state of uncertainty and inferiority which, in comparable areas, the Act is concerned to relieve . . .

1. *Sed quaere*: must there be a contractual *right* to the transfer in the transferee? Possibly the question may be answered by holding that the abandonment of property is not a transfer *to him*.
2. Tentatively recognised by McNair J in *Andrews v Hopkinson* [1957] 1 QB 229 as capable of generating similar implied terms to those in the Sale of Goods Act. The application of the 1982 Act to such a contract, whereby property is transferred to the transferee via a third (and independently-contracting) party, seems probable but somewhat problematic.
3. Cf *Borden (UK) Ltd v Scottish Timber Products Ltd* [1979] 3 All ER 961.
4. *Ingham v Emes* [1955] 2 QB 366.
5. Cf Law Com No 95 (1979), paras 61–63.
6. [1955] 2 QB 366; see also *Parker v Oloxo Ltd* [1937] 3 All ER 524, (1980) 43 MLR 193, 197.

Questions

1. Art and Ben have each received a National Health prescription from their doctor. Blacks, the chemists, dispenses the prescribed drug from a batch which is contaminated and both Art and Ben become seriously ill. Art has a certificate which exempts him from payment and Ben has paid the standard prescription charge.

Is either transaction subject to (i) the Sale of Goods Act 1979 or (ii) the Supply of Goods and Services Act 1982? See generally *Appelby v Sleep* [1968] 2 All ER 265 at 269 per Lord Parker, CJ, *Pfizer v Ministry of Health* [1965] AC 512 [1965] 1 All ER 450, HL. (For the definition of a contract for the sale of goods see above, p 56.)

2. Is a dentist subject to the implied terms of Part I of the 1982 Act as to the quality of the materials 'supplied' to a private fee-paying patient when he (i) fills a cavity, (ii) injects a pain-killing substance into his gums and (iii) uses gas as an anaesthetic before extracting a tooth?

3. Claude and Dick own adjoining terrace houses both of which have been attacked by dry rot. They call in the services of Pestakill, a specialist contractor, who carries out the standard form of treatment by painting replacement timber with a fungicide which is also pumped under pressure into holes drilled into the walls. Owing to an error by the manufacturer and unknown to all concerned the fungicide is fifty times its normal concentration. Standard precautions which have been taken are insufficient to ensure safety. Claude is burned when he touches a window and some fluid comes into contact with his hand. Two days later when the fungicide has dried out Dick returns home and becomes ill when breathing in the resultant fumes.

Advise Claude and Dick as to whether they benefit from the implied terms of Part I of the 1982 Act.

CORRESPONDENCE WITH DESCRIPTION

The implied condition of correspondence with description may be important in a substantial number of consumer transactions. This is especially true of cases where a consumer has not seen the goods and is ordering them in response to an advertisement or by reference to a catalogue. Mail order transactions provide a notable example. The leading cases on the scope and implications of s 13 of the Sale of Goods Act 1979 have a strongly commercial flavour: see in particular *Ashington Piggeries Ltd v Christopher Hill Ltd* [1972] AC 441, [1971] 1 All ER 847, HL; *Arcos Ltd v E A Ronaasen & Son* [1933] AC 470, HL and *Re Moore & Co Ltd and Landauer & Co* [1921] 2 KB 519, CA. They establish that the section is concerned only with matters which touch on the identity or essential characteristics of the goods and not with matters which affect quality alone: see the *Ashington Piggeries* case where toxic herring-meal was still within the contract description although it was lethal to mink. However if the matter does affect the goods' description it seems that precise compliance is required if breach of s 13 is to be avoided. At least this is true of such matters as measurements and quantity: see *Arcos Ltd v E A Ronaasen & Son* above, where in a well-known passage Lord Atkin said (ibid at p 479):

> If the written contract specifies conditions of weight, measurement and the like, those conditions must be complied with. A ton does not mean about a ton, or a yard about a yard. Still less when you descend to minute measurements does ½ inch mean about ½ inch. If the seller wants a margin he must and in my experience does stipulate for it.

Moreover, the implied term as to correspondence with description being designated an implied condition, its breach will prima facie entitle the other party to reject the goods. As Professor Diamond has said, with due allowance for de minimis deviations, 'If the term broken is a condition, the buyer can reject however little harm has been done. There is no such thing as a "slight breach of condition"': see Diamond, 'Commerce, Customers and Contracts' (1978) 11 Melbourne University Law Review 563, 567. See also Coote, 'Correspondence with Description in the Law of Sale of Goods' (1976) 50 ALJ 17; Stoljar, 'Conditions, Warranties and Descriptions of Quality in Sale of Goods II' (1953) 16 MLR 174.

A further feature of this implied condition is that, unlike the implied conditions as to quality and fitness for purpose below, it applies to private transactions no less than to occasions where goods are supplied 'in the course of a business'. The importance of this point and the borderline between matters of description and quality are illustrated in the following cases.

Beale v Taylor [1967] 3 All ER 253, [1967] 1 WLR 1193, Court of Appeal

The facts are set out in the judgment.

Sellers LJ: . . . The defendant seller, Mr Taylor, had a car which he believed to be a Herald convertible, 1961, 1200 twin-carburetter car. He apparently had driven it for some time and done a considerable mileage with it and wished to dispose of it. I think that it had been in an accident, and certainly it was not in very good condition. The seller inserted an advertisement in about April, 1966, in a well-known paper for the sale of secondhand cars. That was in these terms: 'Herald convertible, white, 1961, twin carbs., £190. Telephone Welwyn Garden', and it gives a telephone number, 'after 6.0 p.m.'. The plaintiff buyer, who was born in 1946 and has been driving cars for some little time, or his mother, or both, saw that advertisement, got in touch with the seller, and went along to his home to see the car.. They saw it and had a run in it. The buyer did not drive because there was no insurance for him. I do not know whether his mother went in the car too. After that run and some discussion the buyer made an offer, or his mother made an offer, to buy the car for £160, which the seller accepted. There was a little delay while the balance of the purchase price was paid, and then the buyer drove it away. From the outset apparently the buyer found that the steering was pulling to the left-hand side, so much so that he said that, in his journey from Welwyn Garden City to St Albans, his arms ached; and he eventually after a short time put it in a garage to be checked over. Then it was found by the garage people that, instead of being a car of that description—that being a 1961 1200 Triumph Herald convertible—it was in fact a car which was made up of two cars. The back portion apparently was of that description but the front portion, which had been welded on about half-way, somewhere under the driver's seat, and which contained the engine, was an older, earlier model, the 948 cc model, and these two parts had been made into this one structure. Having regard to the nature of the welding of the two chassis together, as described by the expert who was called, it is not surprising that the car was not running properly. It had also apparently had an accident, as I have said, and it was condemned as being unsafe to take on the road.

The question then arose what was to happen with regard to the purchase price which the buyer had paid to the seller. Instead of the matter being settled amicably, which might have been the wisest thing to do in order to save the money which has been involved in costs, the matter went to court. The buyer relied on the fact that there had been a description of this vehicle as a Triumph Herald 1200 motor car with the registration number 400 RDH and that the vehicle which was delivered did not correspond with that description. The seller, who conducted his own defence and apparently put in his written defence as well, denied that it was a sale by description and said that, on the contrary, it was

> 'the sale of a particular car as seen, tried and approved, the [buyer] having an abundant opportunity to inspect and test the car.'

He denied that the buyer had in the circumstances suffered any loss or damage. Of course a person may purchase a commodity relying entirely on his own judgment in the matter, and there may be no representation at all. Perhaps one hundred years ago more credence might have been given to the seller's defence than is given now, but, since the Sale of Goods Act 1893, the rule caveat emptor has been very much modified. Section 13 of the Sale of Goods Act, 1893, provides that

> 'Where there is a contract for the sale of goods by decription, there is an implied condition that the goods shall correspond with that description; . . .'

and certainly there is good authority for saying that, if the buyer has not seen the goods, then in the ordinary way the contract would be one where the buyer relied on the description alone. Sale of goods by description may, however, apply where the buyer has seen the goods if the deviation of the goods from the description is not apparent; but even then (and I am quoting now from a well-known text book, *Chalmers' Sale of Goods* (15th edn), when the parties are really agreed on the thing sold a misdescription of it in the contract may be immaterial.

The question in this case is whether this was a sale by description or whether, as the seller contends, this was a sale of a particular thing seen by the buyer and bought by him purely on his own assessment of the value of the thing to him. We were referred to a passage in the speech of Lord Wright in *Grant v Australian Knitting Mills Ltd*[1], which I think is apt as far as this case is concerned. Lord Wright said:

'It may also be pointed out that there is a sale by description even though the buyer is buying something displayed before him on the counter; a thing is sold by description, though it is specific, so long as it is sold not merely as the specific thing but as a thing corresponding to a description, eg, woollen under-garments, a hot water bottle, a secondhand reaping machine, to select a few obvious illustrations'

—and, I might add, a secondhand motor car. I think that, on the facts of this case, the buyer, when he came along to see this car, was coming along to see a car as advertised, that is, a car described as a 'Herald convertible, white, 1961'. When he came along he saw what ostensibly was a Herald convertible, white, 1961, because the evidence shows that the '1200' which was exhibited on the rear of this motor car is the first model of the '1200' which came out in 1961; it was on that basis that he was making the offer and in the belief that the seller was advancing his car as that which his advertisement indicated. Apart from that, the selling of a car of that make, I would on the face of it rather agree with the submission of the seller that he was making no warranties at all and making no contractual terms; but fundamentally he was selling a car of that description. The facts as revealed very shortly afterwards show that that description was false. It was unfortunately not false to the knowledge of the owner who was selling nor of the buyer, because no one could see from looking at the car in the ordinary sort of examination which would be made that it was anything other than that which it purported to be. It was only afterwards that, on examination, it was found to be in two parts. I think that that is a sufficient ground on which to decide this case in favour of the buyer . . .

Danckwerts LJ: I agree.

Baker J: I agree.

Appeal allowed. No order as to costs of the appeal.

1. [1935] All ER Rep 209 at 215, [1936] AC 85 at 100.

Smith v Lazarus (1981) (unreported) 23 June, Court of Appeal (Lexis transcript)

Lawton LJ: This is an appeal by a Mr Lazarus, who was the defendant at the trial, against a judgment given against him by His Honour Judge Taylor in the Southend County Court on 29 July 1980 whereby the learned judge gave judgment for the plaintiff, Mr George Smith, in the sum of £351, including interest of £49, together with the costs of the claim.

Mr Lazarus is a gentleman who did not see fit to go into the witness box in the county court. It may be he was very wise to keep out of the witness box. Apparently one of the things he does is to advertise motor cars for sale. He has certainly done so on two occasions. Unfortunately we have not before us the form of the advertisement which led to the series of untoward events with which we are concerned. It suffices to say, however, that early in December 1978 he advertised a motor car for sale in the *Evening Echo*, which circulates in the Southend area. The probabilities are that, in the course of describing the motor car in the advertisement, he put something like this in it: 'Full MOT'. The plaintiff saw the advertisement, went round to Mr Lazarus's house to have a look at the car. It was dark when he arrived. He only examined it cursorily. He then decided to buy it. Mr Lazarus then drove him to his house and the car was left outside.

The next morning Mr Smith had a better look at what he had bought and was appalled, as well he might have been, at what Mr Lazarus had sold him. It seemed to Mr Smith—and he was right in the assumptions which he made—that the motor car was not roadworthy. This being December there was some delay before the Automobile Association could make an inspection. They did make an inspection on 2 January 1979 and they came to the conclusion, as the learned judge found, that the vehicle was unfit for use on the road because its structure was so badly corroded that it would be unsafe to drive it; and anyway, the engine had frozen up during the time it was standing outside Mr Smith's house, and the consequence of so freezing was to cause a good deal of damage to the mechanics of the motor car.

If Mr Lazarus had been an upright man one would have expected him, when these defects were brought to his attention, to take the car back and return the price; but that, apparently, is not Mr Lazarus's way of dealing. He took his stand on caveat emptor: Mr Smith had bought a pig in a poke and had to put up with the pig, having got it. Was Mr Lazarus entitled in law to refuse to return the price?

Mr Smith and his advisers suspected that Mr Lazarus was in trade as a motor dealer, selling his motor cars, as is well-known some dishonest motor dealers do, by pretending to be a private individual and inserting advertisements in local newspapers. The reason they suspected that that is what he was up to was that it came to their notice that there had been an earlier advertisement in the *Evening Echo* in respect of another motor car. On the basis of their suspicions they put their claim in this way: firstly, that there had been a breach by Mr Lazarus of implied warranties of fitness under the provisions of section 14 of the Sale of Goods Act 1979 as amended. Secondly—and this was by a late amendment—that as there had been a reference, in the course of the negotiations for the sale, to a recent MOT certificate having been obtained in respect of the car, as one had been obtained about a fortnight before the sale it followed, so it was submitted, that Mr Lazarus was impliedly warranting that the motor car was structurally safe for use on the road. And thirdly the suggestion was made that what had been sold by Mr Lazarus to Mr Smith was not a motor car at all but a piece of useless machinery; and it was said to be a piece of useless machinery because the AA report suggested that the defects were so grave that it would be a waste of money to try and put them right.

As I have already said, Mr Lazarus prudently kept out of the witness box, and the result was that all the learned judge had was evidence of advertising two vehicles for sale over a short period in the *Evening Echo*. He came to the conclusion that that was not enough to prove that Mr Lazarus was selling in the course of business. That finding cannot, in my judgment, be challenged.

He also found that any reference during the course of negotiations to the MOT certificate did not amount to a warranty of fitness. The court has looked at that possibility and has come to the conclusion that the learned judge was right in that respect, because all the MOT certificate does is to say that on a particular date the car was examined and was found by an engineer to comply with the statutory regulations relating to the condition of motor cars; and it is worth noting that the MOT certificate itself bears on its face this warning in biggish type: 'Warning. A test certificate should not be accepted as evidence of the satisfactory mechanical condition of a used vehicle offered for sale'. The learned county court judge, however, clearly sympathised with Mr Smith, as I do, and seems to have been anxious to have found some way of compensating him for what, clearly, was a shady trading practice by Mr Lazarus. The conclusion he came to, according to the note of his judgment which was taken by Mr Matthews, was this—and I read from the note—

> 'Mr Smith paid Lazarus £310 for a car. He did not get a car. A car is something you can use and drive. The vehicle was unroadworthy. He paid for a car. What he got was almost valueless piece of machinery. Having regard to contents of report the consideration fails'.

Mr Matthews, on behalf of Mr Lazarus, has challenged the judgment on that point. He has pointed out that this is a classic case of caveat emptor: Mr Smith bought what he was shown by Mr Lazarus. Because of the circumstances, and perhaps because of Mr Smith's lack of knowledge about motor cars, he did not make a thorough examination of the motor car, and in the ordinary way, unless warranties can be implied, or express warranties are given, a purchaser has to take what he is shown, with all its faults. It is up to him to discover what the faults are.

There was no evidence here that there was any misrepresentation which would bring into operation the Misrepresentation Act. There was not enough evidence to show that Mr Lazarus was selling the car in the course of business. It follows that the ordinary common law principles of caveat emptor did apply. And if Mr Smith did get a motor car which was a useless motor car, unfortunately he has to bear the resulting loss. The problem is: Did he get a motor car?

The learned judge may have had in mind, when giving his judgment, the case of *Karsales (Harrow) Ltd v Wallis* [1956] 2 All ER 866, [1956] 1 WLR 936. In the course of his judgment in that case Lord Justice Denning (as he then was) said this:

> 'When the defendant inspected the car prior to signing the application form, the car was in excellent condition and would go, whereas the car which was subsequently

delivered to him was no doubt the same car but it was in a deplorable state and would not go. That breach went to the root of the contract and disentitles the lender from relying on the exempting clause'.

No question of an exempting clause arises in this case, and in any event the case of *Karsales (Harrow) Ltd v Wallis* is distinguishable on its facts, because in the passage in the judgment to which I have referred Lord Justice Denning was saying that what the purchaser was shown was not what he got; whereas in this case what Mr Smith was shown was what he got. It follows, therefore, that it is impossible to say that there was any change in the identity of the subject matter of the sale.

For my part, with very great regret, I find I am unable to accept the learned judge's finding that what was delivered to Mr Smith was not a motor car: it was a motor car, but one of very poor quality indeed. Mr Smith's mistake as to the quality of what he was buying is not a reason why he should not pay for what he was buying.

I would allow the appeal.

Shaw LJ: I agree.

Fortunately for Mr Lazarus we have to decide this appeal on the legalities and not the moralities of this mater. In all but the strict sense of the law Mr Lazarus cheated Mr Smith out of £310. In find it a matter of great regret that this court can do nothing to enable Mr Smith to recover his money.

I would allow this appeal

Sir Stanley Rees: I agree with both judgments.

Appeal allowed, with costs; defendant to have no costs in the court below; order of County Court judge set aside.

NOTES

1. For the offence which is committed when it can be proved that a person is disguising the fact that a sale is 'in the course of a business' see the Business Advertisements (Disclosure) Order 1977, SI 1977/1918 and below p 418 et seq.

2. For discussion of the extent to which retailers impliedly adopt descriptions and promotional claims of the manufacturers whose goods they are selling see above p 15 et seq.

Questions

1. In the following advertisement, which words form part of the contract description: '1982 Mini Metro Y Registration 27,000 miles. One careful lady owner'?

2. In the example in Lord Wright's speech in *Grant v Australian Knitting Mills* [1936] AC 85 at 100, cited above p 69 would there have been a 'sale by description' if the hot water bottle had not been marked or otherwise labelled as such? Suppose that it had been so labelled and that it had burst the first time it was used, being quite incapable of holding hot water: would there then have been a breach of s 13?

MERCHANTABLE QUALITY AND FITNESS FOR PURPOSE

The implied terms of, for example, s 14 or the Sale of Goods Act 1979, above p 61, constitute the cornerstone of consumers' rights in relation to the quality and fitness for purpose of goods and materials supplied. Subject to a provision for sales through agents (see s 14(5) of the 1979 Act) the terms are implied only where goods are supplied 'in the course of a business'.

In the course of a business

The delimitation according to whether an act is done 'in the course of a business' appears in a variety of contexts. The expression is considered further when discussing a similar limitation in the Trade Descriptions Act 1968, s 1, below pp 470–75, and the Business Advertisements (Disclosure) Order 1977, below p 418. (See in particular the contrasting cases of *Davies v Sumner* [1984] 1 WLR 405; affd [1984] 3 All ER 831, HL, below p 470, and *Blakemore v Bellamy* [1983] RTR 303, below p 421). Its origins in the present context may be seen in the following extract.

Exemption clauses in contracts—Law Commission's First Report: Amendments to the Sale of Goods Act 1893 (1969) (Law Com No 24)

Subsection (1) of section 14

. . .

Recommendations for amending the subsection
31.   The Molony Committee recommended two amendments to subsection (1). The first of these concerned the requirement that, in order to give rise to the implied condition of fitness, the goods must be 'of a description which it is in the course of the seller's business to supply'. The Molony Committee took the view that if a retailer sells an article in the course of business, he should be answerable for both its merchantability and its fitness for purpose, whether or not he has traded in the same line previously. 'The test should be whether he sells by way of trade to the particular purchaser and not whether he makes a habit of trading in similar goods, which is a circumstance not necessarily known to the purchaser.'[1] We associate ourselves with these arguments and recommend that the condition of fitness for purpose should be implied into all sales other than those in which the seller sells in a private capacity. In other words, the condition should be implied whenever the seller is acting in the course of a business[2] even though he may not be a dealer in goods of the relevant description.[3]

. . .

1. Final Report, paragraph 443; the arguments there advanced with reference to merchantable quality were adopted in paragraph 447 with reference to fitness for purpose.
2. The Molony Committee, in the text quoted from paragraph 443 of their Final Report, suggested that the test should be whether the seller sells 'by way of trade'. We prefer the formula 'in the course of a business' which, unlike the phrase 'by way of trade', does not lend itself to a restrictive interpretation tending in the direction of making the seller's particular trade the applicable test. Such a restrictive interpretation would defeat our main purpose which is to ensure that the conditions implied by section 14 are imposed on every trade seller, no matter whether he is or is not habitually dealing in goods of the type sold.
3. Thus, for example, where a coal merchant whose business it is to supply coal sells one of his delivery vehicles the condition of fitness should be implied; for the sale is part of the seller's business activities, even though he is not a dealer in vehicles.

NOTES

1.   Section 14(1) of the Sale of Goods Act 1893 has since been re-numbered s 14(3).
2.   The word 'business' is defined by the Sale of Goods Act 1979, s 61(1) to

include 'a profession and the activities of any government department (including a Northern Ireland department) or local or public authority'. See also the Supply of Goods and Services Act 1982, s 18(1).

The following Scottish case is of some assistance in indicating the scope of the expression 'in the course of a business' as used in the present context.

Buchanan-Jardine v Hamilink 1981 SLT (Notes) 60

A contract for the sale of a farm and estate provided that the purchasers would take over the livestock at a valuation. Thereafter two cows reacted positively to tests for tuberculosis. The purchasers retained part of the purchase price and counter-claimed for damages in respect of their losses. Lord Dunpark, having stated the facts of the case, is reported as adding:

The legal basis of the purchasers' claim was stated thus: 'Prior to the sale the seller had carried on business as a farmer on said land and estate and had acquired the stock in the course of that business. The sale of the stock to the purchasers was made in the course of the seller's said business. It was accordingly a term of the contract of sale that the stock should be of merchantable quality. The two cows which were discovered to be tuberculosis reactors were such reactors when the contract of sale was concluded on 21 December 1977 and therefore at that date they were not of merchantable quality.'

The case came in procedure roll before Lord Dunpark sitting in the Outer House. In indicating that a proof would be appropriate provided that the purchasers gave more specification of their losses the Lord Ordinary dealt with several preliminary arguments on behalf of the seller. In considering and rejecting a submission that s 14(2) of the Sale of Goods Act did not apply to the sale of the livestock his Lordship said:

'Counsel's second ground of irrelevancy was that s 14(2) did not apply to the sale of this livestock in respect that this was not a sale "in the course of a business", notwithstanding the defenders' averment that it was. His short point was that this was a private sale of a whole enterprise and that such a sale, which terminated the business, was not a sale "in the course of a business". He did not suggest that farming was not a business or that the pursuer had not been carrying on such a business when he sold his farm, with stock and implements, to the defenders . . . In my opinion anyone who sells any part of his business equipment must sell that part "in the course of his business". It can make no difference whether he sells only one item or the whole of the goods used by him for the purpose of a business. Moreover, it is significant, although not relevant to this case, that since 1973 the warranty of merchantable quality has applied to all goods sold "in the course of a business", whether or not the seller "deals" in the goods sold. I have no doubt that this sale of livestock was made by the pursuer "in the course of a business".'

Questions

If the farmer had sold off his combine harvester rather than his cattle would such a sale have attracted the implied terms of s 14 of the Act?
  Would it be desirable in principle that it should have done so?

Merchantable quality

The present statutory definitions of 'merchantable quality' have been set out above: see, for example, the Sale of Goods Act 1979, s 14(6), above p 62 and the Supply of Goods and Services Act 1982, s 9(9), above p 65. They originate in the Law Commissions' report of 1969, the following extracts from which indicate the variety of approaches which had been adopted at common law.

Exemption clauses in contracts First Report: Amendments to the Sale of Goods Act 1893 (Law Commission) (Law Com No 24) (1969)

41. The Sale of Goods Act contains no definition of merchantable quality, and this expression has been interpreted in different ways by the courts. In the case of *Cammell Laird & Co Ltd v Manganese Bronze & Brass Co Ltd* Lord Wright said:

> 'What subsection (2) now means by "merchantable quality" is that the goods in the form in which they were tendered were of no use for any purpose for which such goods would normally be used and hence were not saleable under that description.'[1]

In the earlier case, however, of *Bristol Tramways etc Carriage Co Ltd v Fiat Motors Ltd* Farwell LJ said:

> 'The phrase in s 14 subsection (2) [ie, merchantable quality] is, in my opinion, used as meaning that the article is of such quality and in such condition that a reasonable man acting reasonably would after a full examination accept it under the circumstances of the case in performance of his offer to buy that article whether he buys for his own use or to sell again.'[2]

In the recent *Hardwick Game Farm* case[3] the House of Lords had occasion to consider the meaning of the phrase though their Lordships' observaations were obiter. Lords Guest, Pearce and Wilberforce expressed a preference for Farwell LJ's definition as amplified by Dixon J in *Australian Knitting Mills v Grant*[4] namely, the goods

> 'should be in such an actual state that a buyer fully acquainted with the facts and therefore, knowing what hidden defects exist and not being limited to their apparent condition would buy them without abatement of the price obtainable for such goods if in reasonable sound order and condition and without special terms . . .'

though each of their Lordships placed a slightly different interpretation on this definition. On the other hand, Lord Morris of Borth-y-Gest preferred Lord Wright's approach, while Lord Reid was critical of all three definitions but suggested that with certain qualifications both Lord Wright's and Dixon J's were helpful.

1. [1934] AC 402 at 430.
2. [1910] 2 KB 831 at 841.
3. [*Henry Kendall & Sons v Lillico & Sons Ltd* [1969] 2 AC 31, [1968] 2 All ER 444].
4. (1933) 50 CLR 387 at 418.

The Law Commission Working Paper which preceded the above report had favoured an amplified version of Dixon J's definition but this was criticised as being unduly complicated. The test which was recommended and adopted was based on the deceptively simple notion of fitness for purpose. Thereafter doubts were expressed as to whether the new statutory definition adequately covered both cosmetic defects which did not affect the functioning of the goods and cases where defects were individually minor and yet cumulatively serious. In 1978 the Consumers' Association became involved in such a case based on the sale of a new Reliant Scimitar car which had many defects of varying degrees of importance. Counsel had advised that the buyer was not entitled to reject the car as being unmerchantable and this led to the Association organising a seminar in which academics and practitioners presented papers. An edited version of the proceedings was published under the title *Merchantable Quality: What Does it Mean?* (CA, 1979, editor Professor J Macleod). After the seminar Mr Donald Stewart, MP, was persuaded to introduce a private member's bill to reform the law. The Bill was withdrawn on the matter being referred by the Lord Chancellor to the Law Commission which was asked to consider:

(a) whether the undertakings as to quality and fitness of goods implied under the law relating to the sale of goods, hire-purchase and other contracts for the supply of goods require amendment;

(b) the circumstances in which a person to whom goods are supplied under a contract of sale, hire-purchase or other contract for the supply of goods is entitled, where there has been a breach by the supplier of a term implied by statute, to:
    (i)   reject the goods and treat the contract as repudiated;
    (ii) claim against the supplier a diminution or extinction of the price;
    (iii) claim damages against the supplier;
(c) the circumstances in which, by reason of the Sale of Goods Act 1893,[1] a buyer loses the right to reject the goods; and to make recommendations.'

1. The various enactments relating to the sale of goods are now consolidated in the Sale of Goods Act 1979.

This reference has led to the publication of a Working Paper (No 85, 1983) on which comments have been invited. Extracts are printed below. First, however, the following cases and notes provide a further indication of some of the issues raised by the present definition.

Jackson v Rotax Motor and Cycle Co [1910] 2 KB 937, Court of Appeal

The plaintiff was a manufacturer of motor horns and the defendants were dealers in motor accessories. The defendants placed an order with the plaintiff for about six hundred horns. On delivery some 360 of the horns were claimed to be defective and not immediately saleable as being either dented, badly polished, badly finished or otherwise faulty. The defendants rejected the entire consignment and the plaintiff claimed the contract price (£450) less some £16 which had been paid on account. The official referee found that the consignment was not unmerchantable so as to justify rejection and that the plaintiffs were entitled to the sum claimed less an allowance of £35 in respect of the defects. The Divisional Court dismissed the defendants' appeal and the defendants now appealed to the Court of Appeal. There was a cross notice of appeal by the plaintiff as to costs.

Cozens-Hardy MR, having outlined part of the background to the case, continued.

The official referee has found not merely that the horns were damaged in transit, but that owing to defective packing many of the horns as delivered were not in a merchantable state in the sense that they could without more have been disposed of reasonably and properly by the buyers as dealers in horns to any customer who wanted then and there a horn for a motor car, but that in order to make them merchantable they required to be polished and otherwise dealt with at a cost which he said would have been trifling.

I will read a passage from his judgment. [The Master of the Rolls read the passage set out in the statement of facts, and proceeded.] What does that amount to? The plaintiff is suing for the contract price of the goods and the official referee has held the defendants bound to take the goods, part of which were, as the official referee finds, unmerchantable, with an allowance of 35*l*. The case then went to the Divisional Court, and the Divisional Court put what so far as I am aware is an entirely new meaning on the word 'merchantable,' namely, that goods are 'merchantable' if they only want some trifling thing done to make them immediately saleable—that they are to be considered as merchantable, although not immediately saleable, and although a further expenditure of money is required by the purchaser to make them saleable. I am not aware of any authority for that view. It seems to me to be inconsistent with the language of the Sale of Goods Act to which our attention has been called . . .

Here the fact that the buyers have accepted the first consignment seems to me to have no bearing at all upon their right to reject, if they have a right to reject, the goods which were delivered in pursuance of later requirements. Now had they a right to reject? It seems to me plain on the face of the finding of the official referee, which I see no reason to doubt, that they had a right to reject. The goods were not in accordance with the contract. They were not merchantable. It is true that a large proportion of the goods were merchantable, but that does not justify an action by the vendor for the price of the goods unless he can prove that he was ready and willing to deliver and had delivered or had tendered all the goods in a merchantable condition and of the quality required, subject, of course, to the qualification, if it be necessary to mention it, that the law does not regard as an exception to that to which the rule of de minimis can apply; but, subject only to that qualification, it is for the vendor in a case like this to prove that he has delivered or has tendered delivery of goods which were in accordance with the contract.

For these reasons it seems to me that the decisions of the official referee and the Divisional Court were wrong and that this appeal ought to be allowed and judgment entered for the defendants.

Farwell LJ. I am of the same opinion. The point is an interesting one, and I am grateful to counsel on both sides for the assistance they have given me in arriving at a conclusion. The first question is one of fact. The official referee has found that both the tubes and the horns were in fact unmerchantable, but that the goods as an entire consignment were not unmerchantable. That requires a little consideration. Of the tubes in question more than half were defective, and of the horns also a very considerable number were defective, so that a very large number of the aggregate were in fact unmerchantable. It may well be that in the case of a single horn out of hundreds or a tube or two out of hundreds the rule de minimis would apply, and it would be open to the jury, or to the official referee, to find that, notwithstanding the fact that one or two items were unmerchantable, the consignment as a whole, treating the contract as for a consignment, was merchantable; but the official referee has not taken that view, and, as I understand his finding, I think it is untenable. 'True it is,' he says, 'that I find that each individual horn of, say, half the consignment is unmerchantable, so that the purchasers could not be compelled to take it, but I do not find that the amount of injury or bad workmanship or the like is sufficient to make it very unmerchantable, and therefore, if one half only of the horns comprising the consignment are unmerchantable, I think the buyers must take the whole.' In my opinion that is not what is meant by 'merchantable' as applied to a consignment. If the individual horns are to any appreciable extent unmerchantable, it is not open to the official referee or any one else to say 'Although you would not be bound to take one horn because it does not answer the description of being merchantable, still you must take the whole because more than half are merchantable.' I do not think that is the meaning of de minimis, and on no other ground do I see how it is possible to hold that a consignment can be merchantable when the individual articles making it up, or a large number of them, are not merchantable. I find therefore on the facts before me that the articles are unmerchantable . . .

For these reasons I am unable to take the same view as has been taken in the Divisional Court, where Darling J has invented a novel meaning of the word 'merchantable.'

Kennedy LJ. I agree . . . I also have a difficulty in appreciating the language used in the Divisional Court, where a distinction is drawn between goods which are of unmerchantable quality within the Act of Parliament and goods which by reason of being damaged cannot be honestly sold at the time as merchantable goods, but which can be made saleable if some labour is spent upon them. I do not think we can treat 'merchantable quality' as meaning something which can be made merchantable—it is something which is merchantable at the time when the tender is made by the seller . . .

Appeal allowed.
Cross-appeal dismissed.

Peter Symmons & Co v Cook (1981) 31 March (unreported) Queen's Bench Divisional Court (Lexis transcript)

The plaintiffs were a firm of surveyors with two partners, a Mr Symmons and a Mr Buckley. The defendant was a motor dealer who had once been the sales manager at Jack Barclays (the well-known Rolls Royce agents) but who was now trading on his own account. In May 1978 the defendant had sold to the plaintiffs a 1964 Silver Cloud Mark III Rolls Royce car with a mileage of some 62,000 miles. The plaintiffs alleged that the defendant had represented that, apart from a minor scrape, the car was in 'absolutely tip top condition', but there was a conflict of evidence on this point. A further issue (discussed below p 259) was whether the transaction was one in which the plaintiffs had dealt as consumers within the meaning of s 12 of the Unfair Contract Terms Act 1977.

Mr R Rougier QC, having discussed the background to the case, continued:

So the deal was done and after the car found its way to Mr Buckley's possession it was not long before he became concerned about the consumption of the oil and he ultimately put the car into Owen's Garage for a full check and a report. That document is No 5 in the agreed bundle. When he received that report and discussed it with the staff of H.R. Owen, Mr Buckley received an unpleasant shock. The amount of repairs or even redecoration which Owen's considered desirable involved a very large sum indeed and there were certain defects in the car by the time it arrived at Owen's which made it potentially dangerous to drive . . . Now having seen and heard the three protagonists I have reached the conclusion that by one form of words or another the Defendant did indeed represent that this car was in very good condition for its age and that he made deliberate use of his connection with Jack Barclay to add authority to this statement. Those two features were specifically recollected by Mr Buckley in his evidence and I should put it on record that I consider Mr Buckley to be both a truthful and accurate witness . . .

It is admitted that the car was sold by Mr Cook in the course of his business. From that and from my other findings it follows that I also hold that it was an implied term that the car should be of merchantable quality. I also hold that the Plaintiffs were impressed by the earlier employment history of the Defendant and relied upon his skill and judgment. Consequently there was also an implied term that the car would be reasonably fit for the purpose of being driven on the road as a prestigious car. For the purposes of this action the counsel are agreed that the two last implied terms in reality amounted to the same thing.

I next turn to consider whether there was a breach of any of these terms. I have the benefit of an estimate and evidence from a Mr Calvert, the service manager of H.R. Owen, also very well known and reputable Rolls Royce dealers. Now I am bound to say that I regard the written estimate with the very greatest reserve. Mr Cook tells me, and I entirely accept, that the service departments of the best known Rolls Royce dealers operate (and this is not said in criticism) to a standard of near perfection. Put a not so new Rolls Royce into their hands and their view of what needs to be done when translated into terms of money will often exceed the value of the car itself. I also have in mind that the car had done something in the region of 2,000 miles before Owen's were asked to report. At the same time it seems to me that this is a point where the evidence of Mr Cook himself cuts both ways, for, as he was the first to say, a car of this nature does not develop all these faults within a mere 2,000 miles. Even making due allowance for those reflections it seems to me that this car had an astonishing amount of things wrong with it. One other similar case was I believe called a congeries of defects. Spectacular among these was that the engine was in such a condition that it was in fact cheaper to have a replacement than repair it; and there were other defects, notably in the brakes and steering which rendered the car positively dangerous to drive, or potentially dangerous at any rate. Indeed, Owen's warned the Plaintiffs that they should drive it as little as possible until the more serious of these defects had been rectified.

In summary I think that some of the matters listed in the estimate and report may represent the counsel of perfection; others may have manifested themselves subsequent to the sale; but I am however satisfied that the majority, both in terms of numbers and seriousness, were present at the time of the sale and their presence rendered the car anything but a car which was in excellent condition for its 14 years. As one witness said, 14 years is not particularly old for a Rolls Royce.

I therefore hold that there was a breach of the express warranty that car was in excellent condition. In view of this it is, strictly speaking, unnecessary for me to go on to consider whether the implied terms of s 14 were breached. However, having considered the authorites cited to me, notably *Bartlett v Sidney Marcus Ltd* [1965] 2 All ER 753, [1965] 1 WLR 1013, *Lee v York Coach and Marine Co Ltd* [1977] RTR 35, *Crowther v Shannon Motor Co* [1975] 1 All ER 139, [1975] 1 WLR 30, and *MacDonald v Empire Garage,* reported in The Times of October 8th, 1975, I think that whether one considers the matter in terms of roadworthiness, or in terms of the expense of rectification, or, which I believe to be correct, as a mixture of both those and all other relevant factors, this car was not of merchantable quality within the meaning of s 62 of the Sale of Goods Act, 1893; nor for that matter was it reasonably fit for its purpose.

Lastly I have to decide what is the proper measure of damages. The formula which I accept is that put forward by Mr Bartlett on behalf of the Plaintiffs, namely, the difference in value between the car as it actually was and as it was warranted to be. Herein I accept the evidence broadly speaking of Mr Candy. His view was that the value of the car as it was to a purchaser was between £7,000 and £7,500, whereas the value of a car of this type if it had been in excellent condition but lacked a service history was between £11,500 and £12,000. This produces a bracket of between £4,000 and £5,000, but bearing in mind that it is for the Plaintiffs to prove not only the nature but the extent of their loss, I think that Miss Bowman is perfectly right to suggest that I would not be justified in taking other than the lower end of these two figures. Consequently, in my view, there must be judgment for the Plaintiffs in the sum of £4,000.

Judgment for the Plaintiff of £4,000 with interest of 12½% as from date of service of the writ, and costs.

Millars of Falkirk Ltd v Turpie 1976 SLT 66 (Notes)

On 14 July 1973 a solicitor, as purchaser, took delivery from dealers in motor cars of a new Ford Granada motor car. On the same date he delivered to the motor car dealers in part-exchange a Zodiac motor car and it was arranged that he would pay the balance by cheque within a few days. He failed to do so and the dealers raised an action in the sheriff court for payment of that balance. The defender averred in defence that he had validly rejected the new car on the ground that it was not of 'merchantable quality' as defined by s 62(1A) of the Sale of Goods Act 1893 as amended by the Supply of Goods (Implied Terms) Act 1973 and that the pursuers were in breach of the implied conditions defined by s 14(2) and (3) introduced into the principal Act by the later statute. He also counter-claimed for return of his Zodiac or its agreed value of £542.42 and for damages. Proof was allowed. It was established that when the defender took delivery of his new car he drove it straight home and into his garage. On the morning of Monday, 16 July it was found that some oil had leaked on to the garage floor from what was later shown to be the power-assisted steering box. On receiving the defender's report of this, and a minor complaint about a loose bonnet catch, the pursuers collected the car that day and after making certain adjustments of or in connection with the power-assisted steering box in their repair shop, returned it to the defender on 17 July 1973 in the stated belief that the source of the leakage had been eliminated. On the morning of the following day, however, the defender again found that oil had leaked on to his garage floor. He thereupon intimated rejection of the new car to the pursuers who declined to accept it and asked to be allowed to collect the car again in order to remedy the defect properly. The defender refused to allow them to remove the car for this purpose and the car has remained in the defender's garage ever since. The leakage came from the power steering unit. The trouble was (and this was the evidence of the expert witness led for the defender) a comparatively minor matter which could readily have been cured by the pursuers with very great ease, and at very little cost. All that might have been required was the tightening of a nut at the union between the valve assembly and the return pipe, and at worst the problem would be eliminated by replacing the power steering unit at a cost which would not exceed £25. In addition the leak, and its association with the power-assisted steering unit were obvious, and although, if the car were to be driven for long enough with a leak from this unit, the hydraulic oil reservoir would become dry, causing the pump providing the pressure required for power steering to fail fairly suddenly. If that were to happen the unexpected change from power-assisted to ordinary unassisted steering might cause danger but, as the defender's expert agreed, there was no question of such leakage continuing 'for a long time with a possibly dangerous result without being noticed'. Many new cars have, on delivery to a purchaser, some defects, and it was not exceptional that a car should come from a manufacturer in the condition of the defender's new car on delivery.

Upon these facts the sheriff held that the new car was of merchantable quality as defined by s 62(1A) of the principal Act as amended, that the pursuers were not in breach of either of the implied conditions relied on by the defender and that accordingly he was not entitled to reject the car. For these reasons he granted decree in favour of the pursuers for the sum sued for and refused the counter claim.

On appeal to the sheriff principal the defender appeared on his own behalf. The sheriff principal, by interlocutor dated 19 December 1974, refused the appeal and adhered to the interlocutor of the sheriff in so far as it disposed of the pursuers' action. Quoad the counter claim, however, he recalled the interlocutor, finding that in respect of a minor breach of contract by the pursuers the defender was entitled to nominal damages of £5. In so disposing of the appeal the sheriff principal made no additional findings in fact nor did he vary any of those made by the sheriff. It appeared from his note, that the sheriff principal purported to differ from the sheriff in that he was of opinion that breach of the implied conditions set out in s 14(2) and (3) had been made out. He nevertheless held that the defect in the car was a minor one which could be easily and cheaply rectified and the pursuers were offering to rectify it. In these circumstances he concluded that the pursuers had not failed to perform any material part of the contract within the meaning of s 11(2) of the principal Act with the result that the defender was not entitled to reject the car.

The defender appealed. He argued that if there was a breach of the implied conditions prescribed by s 14(2) and (3) of the principal Act as amended, however trivial, it followed that the sellers had failed to perform a material part of the contract which entitled the buyer to reject. Alternatively he contended that the alleged breaches were so serious that his right to reject under s 11(2) was clear. Counsel for the pursuers challenged the defender's submissions and argued that the sheriff, having directed himself correctly as to the meaning of 'merchantable quality' and 'reasonable fitness' in s 14(2) and (3) of the Act, was entitled to reach the conclusion which he did and that it was not open to the sheriff principal on the same facts to substitute his own conclusion for that of the judge who heard the proof (*Thomas v Thomas* 1947 SC (HL) 45, 1948 SLT 2). The court *refused* the appeal and *recalled* the interlocutor of the sheriff principal in so far as it awarded damages to the defender. In his opinion the Lord President (Emslie) said: 'There is no doubt that the question of whether an article sold is of "merchantable quality" or is "reasonably fit" for a relevant purpose in terms of s 14(3) is a question of fact, once the court has correctly understood the meaning of these expressions. Support for this view is, I think, to be found in the opinion of Roskill LJ in *Cehave NV v Bremer mbH* [1975] 3 WLR 447 at 468. In this case, bearing in mind that the defender has throughout relied upon showing that the new car was not of "merchantable quality" and has at no time argued that if he failed so to show he could be in any stronger or different position under s 14(3), the sheriff approached his judgment by appreciating perfectly correctly the meaning of the expression "merchantable quality" in s 14(2) . . . With Lord Denning MR in *Cehave* I am of opinion that this definition is the best that has yet been devised, and that in any particular case in which the question of merchantable quality arises it is to be answered as a commercial man would be likely to answer it having regard to the various matters mentioned in the statutory definition. As I read his note, the sheriff has approached the question in precisely this way and in light of all the relevant circumstances upon which his judgment proceeded, and which I have already set out, he reached the conclusion that the car sold to the defender was of merchantable quality and reasonably fit for the purpose which a new motor car is designed to serve. In my opinion he was entitled to reach that conclusion on the facts of this case and I would not quarrel with that conclusion. I have in mind particularly that the relevant circumstances included these: (i) the defect was a minor one which could readily and very easily be cured at very small cost; (ii) the pursuers were willing and anxious to cure the defect: (iii) the defect was obvious and the risk of the car being driven long enough to create some danger if the steering unexpectedly ceased to be assisted was slight; (iv) many new cars have, on delivery to a purchaser, some defects, and it was not exceptional for a new car to be delivered in the condition in which the defender's car was delivered. I have only to add that it appears to have been common ground in the evidence that the car was sold with a manufacturer's repair warranty although it was not produced or examined at the proof. If I am right in holding that the conclusion reached by the sheriff was one which was open to him in all the proved relevant circumstances, was the sheriff principal sitting as an appellate judge entitled to substitute his own conclusion? In my opinion he was not . . . He should not, in my opinion, have disturbed the conclusion of the sheriff unless he was satisfied that it was one he was not entitled to reach in all the relevant proved circumstances of this case derived from the evidence which he had heard. There are no grounds upon which he or we could be so satisfied given the particular circumstances of this case, and on this whole matter I hold that the pursuers' submission is well founded, and that the case stands in the position that the defender has failed to establish the breach of either of the implied conditions which formed the starting point of his claim of rejection and for damages . . . In the result we do not reach the interesting and difficult question of whether mere breach of the implied conditions prescribed by s 14(2) and (3), however minor or readily remediable the defect which led to the finding of breach, constitutes a failure to perform a material part of the contract within the meaning of s 11(2) . . . In England the problem does not arise for the law is not the same and because, in particular, in terms of s 11(1), the breach of any "condition" affords, subject only to the de minimis rule the right to reject. Whether the same result should follow, standing the language of s 11(2) which applies only to Scotland, is another matter, and it could only follow if it were to be held that failure to fulfil one of the statutory implied conditions amounts, irrespective of the degree of failure, to failure to perform a material part of the contract which would entitle the buyer to reject.'

Lord Johnston and Lord Avonside agreed with the Lord President . . .

NOTES

1. For general discussion of merchantable quality and fitness for purpose see, in addition to the sources noted above, *Benjamin's Sale of Goods* (2nd edn, 1981) para 790 et seq; Atiyah *Sale of Goods* (6th edn, 1980) p 98 et seq; Goode *Commercial Law* (1982) p 256 et seq; Miller and Lovell *Product Liability* p 82 et seq and the Ontario Law Reform Commission 'Report on Sale of Goods' (1979) p 206 et seq.

2. The *Cehave* case (*The Hansa Nord*) [1976] QB 44, [1975] 3 All ER 739, CA, to which the Lord President referred in *Millars of Falkirk Ltd v Turpie*, above, is an extreme example of goods being held to be merchantable although badly damaged. The citrus pulp pellets could still be used as a base for cattle feed in spite of their being damaged through overheating. Indeed the buyers had repurchased them at a price which was well below the contract price (£32,000 as against some £100,000) and used them in accordance with their original intentions. The facts of the case are so peculiar that it is unlikely that they can be regarded as being of general application.

3. For examples of cases holding goods to be unmerchantable although the defects were relatively minor see *International Business Machines Co v Shcherban* [1925] 1 DLR 864 (Sask CA) (computing scale with broken glass dial costing 30 cents to replace); *Winsley Bros v Woodfield Importing Co* [1929] NZLR 480 (planing machine with a defect which could be remedied at a cost of approximately one per cent of the purchase price).

4. In two important cases decided before there was a statutory definition of 'merchantable quality' the House of Lords held that goods were merchantable when fit for one of the purposes for which they might be used although unfit (and indeed in one case lethal) when used for another purpose: see *Henry Kendall & Sons v William Lillico & Sons Ltd* [1969] 2 AC 31, [1968] 2 All ER 444 (groundnut extractions unfit for poultry but safe for use as cattle food) and *BS Brown & Son Ltd v Craiks Ltd* [1970] 1 All ER 823, [1970] 1 WLR 752, HL (cloth unfit for use as dress material but suitable for industrial purposes). In the former case the buyers were able to invoke what is now s 14(3) of the Act since their 'particular purpose' (compounding into feed for animals and poultry *generally*) had been made known to the sellers. It is arguable that the present statutory definition of merchantable quality (with its reference to 'purpose or purposes') might affect the issue in either or both of the above cases by requiring that the goods be fit for all normal purposes, at least unless there is an indication to the contrary.

5. The Law Commission's Working Paper No 85 (1983, below p 85) favours consideration of replacing the phrase 'merchantable quality' with 'proper quality' or 'acceptable quality in all respects'.

Questions

1. Should a new dishwasher be regarded as unmerchantable when delivered if it (i) has an unsightly scratch across the front panel but washes dishes to perfection; (ii) does not work at all but the problem can be rectified by a small amount of rewiring; (iii) is electrically dangerous but again the fault can be rectified easily; (iv) lacks baskets to hold the cutlery there being a three week delay in obtaining them from the manufacturers?

2. Professor Goode has noted that,

> It is clear that merchantability is not a fixed or immutable conception but changes as commercial attitudes change. An article readily saleable despite its faults in one age may be quite unacceptable in another because of rising standards in the market and a greater sophistication on the part of buyers.

—see *Commercial Law* p 269. Is the reverse also true? If prolonged 'teething troubles' become the norm, even in the case of established products, does the standard of merchantable quality fall correspondingly?

Fitness for purpose

The implied condition of reasonable fitness for purpose of, for example, s 14(3) of the Sale of Goods Act 1979 overlaps considerably with the implied condition of merchantable quality of s 14(2). This is especially true where a definition of merchantable quality is itself based on the notion of fitness for purpose: see, for example, s 14(6) of the 1979 Act, above p 62. However there are cases in which the position of the buyer will vary according to which sub-section is being considered. For example in *Baldry v Marshall* [1925] 1 KB 260, CA the specified particular purpose was a comfortable car suitable for touring and this was not satisfied by the supply of an eight-cylinder Bugatti. Similarly the House of Lords showed itself willing to define the relevant purpose very broadly in both *Henry Kendall & Sons v William Lillico & Sons Ltd* [1969] 2 AC 31, [1968] 2 All ER 444 (compounding groundnut extraction into feed for animals and poultry generally) and the *Ashington Piggeries* case [1972] AC 441, [1971] 1 All ER 847 (compounding herring-meal into animal feeding-stuffs), so facilitating recovery under what is now s 14(3) of the Act. The cases which follow were both argued in terms of the same provision (then s 14(1) of the Act) but they introduce also additional points of general interest.

Griffiths v Peter Conway Ltd [1939] 1 All ER 685, Court of Appeal

The facts are set out in the judgment

Sir Wilfred Greene, MR: This is an appeal by the plaintiff in the action, Mrs Griffiths, against the judgment of the judge who dismissed her action. The defendants are retail tailors, and in June, 1937, the plaintiff bought from them a Harris tweed coat, which was specially made for her. Shortly after she began to wear the coat, she developed dermatitis, and suffered from a very severe and prolonged attack of that disease. She brought the present action to recover damages against the defendants on the ground of breach of warranty, and the only breach of warranty relied upon before us is that dealt with by the Sale of Goods Act 1893, s 14(1) . . .

The judge found, and his finding of fact is not challenged in this court, as follows:

> '. . . the real cause of the trouble was not in the cloth alone, because there was nothing in the cloth that would have affected a normal person's skin. The trouble was that, because Mrs Griffiths' skin was not normal, it had what Dr O'Donovan has called an idiosyncratic effect, so that what the plaintiff got was idiosyncratic contact dermatitis, a thing which no purveyor of cloth or wearing apparel could really guard against to any further extent than purveyors of this cloth have guarded against there being anything harmful in its texture.'

That finding is, of course, that no normal skin would have been affected by this cloth. There was nothing in it which would affect a normal skin, but the plaintiff unfortunately had an idiosyncrasy, and that was the real reason why she contracted this disease.

On the basis of that finding, which is not challenged, Mr Morris says: 'Take the language of the section, and the present case falls within it.' He says that the buyer, Mrs Griffiths, expressly made known to the defendants the particular purpose for which the coat was required—that is to say, for the purpose of being worn by her, Mrs Griffiths, when it was made. Once that state of affairs is shown to exist, Mr Morris says that the language of the section relentlessly and without any escape imposes upon the seller the oligation which the section imports.

It seems to me that there is one quite sufficient answer to that argument. Before the condition as to reasonable fitness is implied, it is necessary that the buyer should make known, expressly or by implication, first of all the particular purpose for which the goods are required. The particular purpose for which the goods were required was the purpose of being worn by a woman suffering from an abnormality. It seems to me that, if a person suffering from such an abnormality requires an article of clothing for his or her use, and desires to obtain the benefit of the implied condition, he or she does not make known to the seller the particular purpose merely by saying: 'The article of clothing is for my own wear.' The essential matter for the seller to know in such cases with regard to the purposes for which the article is required consists in the particular abnormality or idiosyncrasy from which the buyer suffers. It is only when he has that knowledge that he is in a position to exercise his skill or judgment, because how can he decide and exercise skill or judgment in relation to the suitability of the goods that he is selling for the use of the particular individual who is buying from him unless he knows the essential characteristics of that individual? The fact that those essential characteristics are not known, as in the present case they were not known, to the buyer does not seem to me to affect the question. When I speak of 'essential characteristics,' I am not, of course, referring to any variations which take place and exist within the class of normal people. No two normal people are precisely alike, and, in the matter of sensitiveness of skin, among people who would be described as normal their sensitiveness must vary in degree.

This does not mean that there is a line which it is the function of the court, or of a medical witness, to draw with precision, so as to define all cases where normality ceases and abnormality begins. The impossibility of drawing such a line by reference to some scientific formula or something of that kind does not mean that, for the present purpose, the difference between normality and abnormality is a thing that must be disregarded, or cannot be ascertained. It is a question that no judge and no jury would have any real difficulty in deciding on the evidence in any particular case. In this particular case, the judge has found the existence of abnormality, and, that being so, it seems to me impossible to say that the seller here had the particular purpose pointed out to him so as to show that the buyer relied on his skill or judgment. After all, the object of that is to enable the seller to make up his mind whether or not he will accept the burden of the implied condition, and the effect of the argument addressed to us would be to impose that implied condition upon the seller without his having the opportunity of knowing the vital matter which would affect his mind.

. . .

MacKinnon, LJ: I agree. If Mr Morris had not so abundantly proved to the contrary, I should have thought that this appeal was unarguable.

Goddard, LJ: I agree with both judgments.

Appeal dismissed, with costs.

NOTE

For a general discussion of the questions raised by allergies and peculiar susceptibilities see Miller and Lovell *Product Liability,* pp 324–326 and sources there cited.

Questions

1. Should the position have been altered by the fact that the buyer did not know of her abnormality and so could not communicate it? Does this decision in any way qualify the strict nature of the liability (see below p 89) usually associated with s 14 of the Act? See also below pp 199–201 for discussion of a similar issue in the context of the law of tort.

2. In what circumstances is it realistic in an age of national brand-name advertising to conclude that there has been reliance on the skill and judgment of the seller?

See *Junior Books Ltd v Veitchi Co Ltd* [1982] 3 All ER 201 at 214 per Lord Roskill, below p 171 and the questions which follow the extracts from that case.

3. Greenfingers has a large overgrown garden. He sees a newspaper advertisement in a Sunday magazine which shows a Greenbelt Mower cutting through long wet grass in an overgrown orchard. Since this corresponds closely with his requirements he buys such a mower from his local garden centre. In fact the mower is incapable of cutting grass in the manner indicated.

Consider the garden centre's liability under s 14(3) of the 1979 Act. Would it affect the position if the garden centre had displayed a large placard featuring the same advertisement?

(See also above, pp 15–18).

Durability, spare parts and servicing facilities

There is no doubt that a major source of consumer dissatisfaction and complaint is that goods are insufficiently durable and are liable to break down or wear out in an unreasonably short period of time. The extent of the problem was noted in the National Consumer Council survey 'Faulty Goods', June 1981, to which reference was made above, p 53. According to this survey (para 3.2), 'over 15 per cent of the sample told us about goods that had not lasted as well as expected'. These included 'white goods'—for example washing machines and tumble dryers—shoes, cookers, cars, carpets, and 'brown goods'—for example television sets and stereo systems. Certain remarks of Lord Denning MR in the following case have sometimes been regarded as casting doubt on the extent to which a requirement of reasonable durability is embodied in the present law.

Crowther v Shannon Motor Co (a firm) [1975] 1 All ER 139, [1975] 1 WLR 30, Court of Appeal

The facts are set out in the judgment of Lord Denning MR

Lord Denning MR. The plaintiff, Mr Crowther, is a young man interested in art. In 1972 he bought a secondhand motor car from the defendants who were reputable dealers in Southampton. It was a 1964 Jaguar. He bought it on 17th July 1972 for the sum of £390. The dealers commended it. They said that 'it would be difficult to find a 1964 Jaguar of this quality inside and out'. They added that for a Jaguar 'it is hardly run in'. Mr Crowther looked carefully at it. He took it for a trial run. The next day it was tested by the Ministry of Transport officials. The report of the test was satisfactory. So Mr Crowther bought the Jaguar. He did not take the words of puff seriously. But he relied on the sellers' skill and judgment. There was clearly an implied condition under s 14(1) of the Sale of Goods Act 1893 that the car was reasonably fit for the purpose for which he required it and which he made known to the sellers.

That was 17th July 1972. The mileage as stated on the mileometer at that time was 82,165 miles. Mr Crowther took the car. He drove it on some long journeys. He went up to the north of England and back. He went round Hampshire. He went over 2,000 miles in it. He found that it used a great deal of oil. But he managed to drive it for three weeks. Then on 8th August 1972, when he was driving up the M3 motorway, it came to a full stop. The engine seized up. The car was towed into a garage. The engine was found to be in an extremely bad condition. So much so that it had to be scrapped and replaced by a reconditioned engine. The car was out of use for a couple of months or so.

Mr Crowther brought an action in the county court for damages from the dealers. He called as a witness a previous owner of the car, a Mr Hall. He gave evidence that he had bought it from these selfsame dealers about eight months before. He had paid them about £400 for it. He had used it for those eight months and then sold it back in July 1972 to these very dealers. When he resold it to them he knew the engine was in a very bad state, but he did not disclose it to them. He left them to find out for themselves. He was himself an engineer. He gave a trenchant description of the engine:

> 'At the time of resale I thought the engine was clapped out. I do not think this engine was fit to be used on a road, not really, it needed a rebore.'

The judge accepted the evidence of Mr Hall. He held that there was a breach of s 14(1) of the 1893 Act. He awarded Mr Crowther damages in the sum of £460.37 with costs. Now there is an appeal to this court by the dealers. They say there was no justification for the finding that this car was not reasonably fit for the purpose. The mileage when they sold it was 82,165 miles. The mileage when it 'clapped out' was 84,519 miles. So that in the three weeks it had gone 2,354 miles.

Counsel for the dealers, who put the case very cogently before us, submitted that a car which had covered 2,354 miles must have been reasonably fit for the purpose of driving along the road. He drew attention to a case some years ago in this court, *Bartlett v Sidney Marcus Ltd*[1]. We emphasised then that a buyer, when he buys a secondhand car, should realise that defects may appear sooner or later. In that particular case a defect did appear in the clutch. It was more expensive to repair than had been anticipated. It was held by this court that the fact that the defect was more expensive than had been anticipated did not mean that there had been any breach of the implied condition. But that case seems to me to be entirely distinguishable from the present case. In that case it was a minor repair costing £45 after 300 miles. Here we have a very different case. On the dealers' own evidence, a buyer could reasonably expect to get 100,000 miles life out of a Jaguar engine. Here the Jaguar had only done 80,000 miles. Yet it was in such a bad condition that it was 'clapped out' and after some 2,300 miles it failed altogether. That is very different from a minor repair. The dealers themselves said that if they had known that the engine would blow up after 2,000 miles, they would not have sold it. The reason obviously was because it would not have been reasonably fit for the purpose.

Some criticism was made of a phrase used by the judge. He said: 'What does "fit for the purpose" mean?' He answered: 'To go as a car for a reasonable time.' I am not quite sure that that is entirely accurate. The relevant time is the time of sale. But there is no doubt what the judge meant. If the car does not go for a reasonable time but the engine breaks up within a short time, that is evidence which goes to show it was not reasonably fit for the purpose at the time it was sold. On the evidence in this case, the engine was liable to go at any time. It was 'nearing the point of failure', said the expert, Mr Wise. The time interval was merely 'staving off the inevitable'. That shows that at the time of the sale it was not reasonably fit for the purpose of being driven on the road. I think the judge on the evidence was quite entitled to find there was a breach of s 14(1) of the 1893 Act and I would therefore dismiss the appeal.

Orr and Browne LLJ agreed with Lord Denning. *Appeal dismissed.*

1. [1965] 2 All ER 753, [1965] 1 WLR 1013.

NOTES

1.   If the failure of the engine was only evidence going to show that the car was not reasonably fit for its purpose when sold presumably it would have been open to the seller to seek to establish the contrary. In the case of new goods which break down after a relatively short period considerable weight might be attached to evidence establishing the excellence of a manufacturer's quality control system.

2.   For a statement which appears to recognise an obligation of reasonable durability see *Lee v York Coach and Marine* [1977] RTR 35, CA per Stevenson LJ, below p 94.

An alternative way of expressing the extent of the seller's obligations is to be seen in the following passage from Lord Diplock's opinion in *Lambert v Lewis* [1981] 1 All ER 1185 at 1191, HL, the facts of which are set out above p 35. His Lordship said:

> The implied warranty of fitness for a particular purpose relates to the goods at the time of delivery under the contract of sale in the state in which they were delivered. I do not doubt that it is a continuing warranty that the goods will continue to be fit for that purpose for a reasonable time after delivery, so long as they remain in the same apparent state as that in which they were delivered, apart from normal wear and tear. What is a reasonable time will depend on the nature of the goods, but I would accept that in the case of the coupling the warranty was still continuing up to the date, some three to six months before the accident, when it first became known to the farmer that the handle of the locking mechanism was missing. Up to that time the farmer would have had a right to rely on the dealers' warranty as excusing him from making his own examination of the coupling to see if it were safe; but, if the accident had happened before then, the farmer would not have been held to have been guilty of any negligence to the plaintiff.

Although the context in which this statement was made may cast some doubt on whether Lord Diplock was recognising an implied term of durability as such (see Goode *Commercial Law*, p 289) it nonetheless provides support for those who argue in favour of such a term. Yet it would be preferable for the obligation to be made explicit. The Law Commission discusses the point as follows:

Sale and Supply of Goods Law Commission Working Paper No 85 (1983)

Durability

2.14 Although it seems clear that the term as to quality falls to be satisfied at the time of delivery and not at some later date, it also seems clear in law that goods will not be of merchantable quality unless they are of reasonable durability.[1] What is reasonable durability will, of course, depend on the nature of the goods and the other circumstances of the case. The courts will, where relevant, examine later events in order to determine whether goods measured up to the appropriate standard at the time of delivery.

2.15 There is, however, no express reference in the Act to the concept of durability or to the time when the term as to quality must be satisfied. It may not therefore be sufficiently clear outside the courts that the goods must be of reasonable durability and, in the absence of any such statutory provision, there is some uncertainty at least in the context of consumer complaints. It appears that complaints and queries are frequently raised with consumer protection agencies and associations concerning such goods as carpets, shoes and sofas which wear out, beyond any hope of repair or refurbishing, in an unreasonably short time.[2] Cases arising from such complaints are rarely in practice heard by the higher courts and it is said that judicial attitudes expressed in some of the lower courts on the question of durability make it harder for consumers to achieve a satisfactory settlement. It is true that there are codes of practice governing the general standard, including the durability, of certain consumer articles but, as we have already pointed out, the observance of a code by a manufacturer is generally voluntary and cannot be enforced by a consumer.[3] In its report on *Implied Terms in Contracts for the Supply of Goods*[4] the Law Commission recommended the introduction of an express provision on durability into the Sale of Goods Act. Both Commissions now take the view that the absence of an express reference to durability constitutes a justifiable criticism of the present law and that the provision of such a reference should make it easier in many cases for a consumer to establish a breach of contract.[5]

1. See *Lambert v Lewis* [1982] AC 225, especially per Lord Diplock at 276; *Crowther v Shannon* [1975] 1 WLR 30.
2. See *Faulty Goods* (1981), published by the National Consumer Council.
3. See para 1.12, above. Under some codes there is provision for arbitration and conciliation procedures.
4. Law Com No 95, (1979) at para 113.
5. See R. M. Goode *Commercial Law* (1982) at pp 288 to 290. A term of reasonable durability has been accepted in, eg, some Canadian Provinces: see the Nova Scotia Consumer Protection Act RSNS 1967 c 53 as amended by SNS 1975 c 19, s 20 c(3)(j); the Saskatchewan Consumer Products Warranties Act 1977, s 11(7) [see below p 89].

A further important issue is whether there should be any legal obligation to ensure that spare parts and servicing facilities remain available over a reasonable or even a specified period. The issue is closely related to such matters as the existence and legal status of manufacturers' express warranties and guarantees (see above pp 31–52) and the extent of their liability for economic loss (see below pp 165–176). In principle it seems clear that there would be benefits to consumers in recognising such an obligation since the unavailability of even a cheap spare part may render an expensive consumer durable quite unusable. Moreover the modern tendency to replace and discard is not apt to encourage the craftsman whose repairing skills might make good the deficiency. However there are serious practical problems involved and the Law Commission does not favour the imposition of additional legal obligations of this kind. The Commission's reasoning appears in the following extract.

Implied terms in contracts for the supply of goods (Law Commission) (Law Com No 95) (1979)

Spare parts and servicing facilities
115. In our working paper[1] we raised questions about the obligations on the suppliers of goods in relation to spare parts and servicing. When goods break down or are damaged they may become useless unless they can be repaired and unless spare parts are available, but there appears to be no legal obligation on the seller or supplier, let alone on the manufacturer, to maintain stocks or to provide servicing facilities. We invited comments on the problems which arose in practice and on the need for law reform. This part of the working paper stirred up considerable interest, particularly amongst manufacturers, retailers and consumer organisations, and we received many informative and useful comments and proposals.

Additional obligations on the retailer

. . .

117. If an obligation to stock spares and to provide servicing of goods is to be imposed on the retailer alone then the obligation can be formulated as an additional implied term in the contract of sale or supply. Conceptually the notion presents no difficulty (we come to the practical problems later).

. . .

119. As we said earlier, there would be no conceptual difficulty in including an additional term in contracts of sale or supply to the effect that the retailer should maintain a stock of spares and servicing facilities.[2] However, hardly any support for this idea was received on consultation. If applied to all kinds of contract involving all kinds of goods it could, in many cases, impose hardship on the retailer. It is unrealistic to suppose that the small shop-keeper could or should maintain a stock of spares for every product which he sells. For example, if he orders goods for a customer which he does not usually stock it would be unjust to require him to lay in a stock of spare parts as well. Even if one considers large department stores, there is a limit to the amount of space which is available for the stocking of spares and to the number of staff who can be retained for servicing the goods supplied. If such extra stocks and facilities were made obligatory by law the cost would have to be passed on to the consumer, and we are informed that the extra cost would be considerable. In some Provinces in Canada,[3]

manufacturers, distributors and dealers in agricultural machinery are required to maintain stocks of spares and servicing facilities for ten years, and we were told on consultation that their machinery is, as a result, considerably more expensive. English farmers tend to prefer to buy more cheaply and either to do their own servicing and maintenance or to have the work done by experts engaged either under a maintenance contract or from time to time as the need arises.

120. It may be said that the retailer need not be placed under a duty to keep stocks of spares on the premises but that the risk of their being unavailable should be placed on him rather than on the customer. Even so, the acceptance of the extra risk would mean an increase in price which would not be welcomed. Many commentators went further and said that it would be oppressive to hold the retailer liable for the parts becoming unavailable, for example on the manufacturer going out to business. But anything less would be ineffective. If the retailer were only liable to provide spares as long as they were available the position would be no different, in practice, from that which obtains under the existing law.

. . .

122. The conclusion at which we have arrived, and which received wide support on consultation, is that it would be wrong to make it an additional term in contracts of sale (or supply) that the seller (or supplier) should maintain stocks of spares or servicing facilities. We recommend accordingly.

Additional obligations on the manufacturer

123. Having reached this conclusion we might end this report at this stage. However, we did raise the question of manufacturers' liabilities in our working paper, and although it takes us beyond 'implied terms' into another branch of the law we feel that, in fairness to those who sent us comments, we should say something further.

124. The question of manufacturers' liabilities in the matter of spares and servicing facilities has to be considered in the context of manufacturers' liabilities generally. In jurisdictions where manufacturers are under a legal duty to keep spares and servicing facilities available[4] they are also liable to answer for defects in the products themselves as, for example, where the products do not correspond with the description applied to them by the manufacturer, where the goods do not perform in the way claimed by the manufacturer, and where the manufacturer has broken an express 'warranty', by which is meant not only warranties set out in the "manufacturers' guarantee" but also undertakings, assertions and statements made by or on behalf of the manufacturer in advertisements and promotional material relating to the goods in question. This is in keeping with the pattern of the Ontario Report which recommended that manufacturers should be under a duty to maintain stocks of spares for their products and also repair facilities,[5] not as a single recommendation but as part of the whole new body of obligations which it recommended should be borne by manufacturers.

125. In 1977 we concluded a study, jointly with the Scottish Law Commission, on the remedies which are or should be available in respect of defective products. In our report we recommended, amongst other things, that manufacturers should be strictly liable for defects in their products but that the liability should be confined to personal injury and death; we recommended that the régime of strict liability should not cover damage to property or pure economic loss.[6] We also recommended that the test whether a product was defective should be whether it was unsafe, not whether it was unmerchantable in a more general sense. Our conclusion, in which we were supported by a majority of commentators, was that liability for 'safe but shoddy' products should be regulated by the law of contract as at present and not included in the régime of strict liability in tort.[7]

. . .

127. When preparing our consultative document on Liability for Defective Products,[8] we did not examine the law relating to misrepresentation, and what may loosely be called "manufacturers' warranties". These are among the matters to be considered as part of our work on the general law of contract.[9] Representations about the availability of spare parts and servicing facilities are some of the many kinds of representation to be examined in that context.[10]

Voluntary codes of practice

128. We intend in due course to produce a consultative document on the topic of misrepresentation which will consider the need for reform and for additional remedies to be provided in respect of representations made by manufacturers (and others) in respect of their goods. However we are not the only body with an interest in this branch of the law. The

Office of Fair Trading has, as part of its responsibility, the control of consumer trade practices which are prejudicial to the economic interests of consumers in the United Kingdom,[11] and the Director General has a duty to keep commercial activities affecting consumers under review.[12] We have learnt from the Office of Fair Trading that manufacturing industries are working with them to produce voluntary codes of practice which provide for, amongst other things, their advertisements regarding their products, the terms set out in guarantees, and the obligations undertaken in regard to spare parts and servicing. A number of industries in which spare parts and servicing present a real problem (including the motor trade and electrical industries) have already agreed codes with the Office of Fair Trading, though the codes vary as to the obligations laid down with regard to spare parts. Those in the electrical industry require that spares will be kept for a specified period after production of the goods in question has ceased; whilst motor manufacturers go no further than accepting a responsibility for ensuring a reasonable availability of spare parts throughout the distribution chain. The formulation of codes of practice has the support of the Confederation of British Industry and of the Consumers' Association, amongst others, and, provided the codes are clear in their terms, specific in their obligations as to spare parts and are in fact honoured, we think that many of the problems concerning spare parts (and servicing) are best solved by this means.[13]

1. Working Paper No 71, paras 76–78.
2. Para 117, above; and see s 11(8) of the Saskatchewan Consumer Products Warranties Act 1977.
3. Alberta (Farm Implement Act, Revised Statutes of Alberta 1970, c 136), Manitoba (Farm Machinery and Equipment Act 1971, c 83), Prince Edward Island (Farm Implement Act, Revised Statutes of Prince Edward Island 1974, c F-3) and Saskatchewan (Agricultural Implements Act 1968).
4. We have studied in particular the Manufacturers Warranties Act 1974 which is in force in South Australia, the Law Reform (Manufacturers Warranties) Ordinance 1977 (Australian Capital Territory No 12 of 1977) and the Consumer Products Warranties Act 1977 in Saskatchewan.
5. Report by the Ontario Law Reform Commission on Consumer Warranties and Guarantees in the Sale of Goods (1972), pp 44–46, 76–77.
6. Report on Liability for Defective Products (1977), Law Com No 82, Scot Law Com No 45, Cmnd 6831 paras 117–121.
7. *Ibid*, paras 45–47.
8. Law Commission Working Paper No 64, Scottish Law Commission Memorandum No 20.
9. Thirteenth Annual Report (1977–78), Law Com No 92 para 2.9.
10. Also of interest is a draft EEC Directive on Misleading and Unfair Advertising which has been prepared in the Commission of the European Communities in Brussels. There has been opposition to the draft Directive in this country (see eg *Hansard* (HL), 4 July 1978, vol 394, cols 848–911; *Hansard* (HC), 16 November 1978, vol 958, cols 705–758; *Hansard* (HL), 28 November 1978, vol 396, cols 1189–1241; and the report of the House of Lords Select Committee on the European Communities, (1977–78) HL 38), and we understand that it has now been under consideration by the Council of Ministers for some time.
11. Fair Trading Act 1973, s 13 and s 17.
12. *Ibid*, s 2.
13. On the operation of voluntary codes of practice in the motor trade, see Motoring Which? January 1977 pp 14–17.

NOTES

1.   The Law Commission reached the same conclusion when it returned to the question in its Working Paper No 85 on the Sale and Supply of Goods (1983), para 2.17. The opposite conclusion favouring a warranty of spare parts and repair facilities was reached by the Ontario Law Reform Commission in its 'Report on Sale of Goods' (1979), pp 216–217.

2.   For an example of a code of practice which provides for the availability of spare parts see the AMDEA code, 'Principles for Domestic Electrical Appliance Servicing', below p 388. See also the Council of Europe Resolution (78) 38 on Adequate After-Sales Service.

Section 11 of the Saskatchewan Consumer Products Warranties Act 1977, to which reference was made in para 124, note 4 above, provides in part (and as amended by the Consumer Products Warranties Act 1980, s 5) as follows:

11. Statutory warranties
Where a consumer product is sold by a retail seller, the following warranties shall be deemed to be given by the retail seller to the consumer:

. . .

7. *Durability* that the product and all its components shall be durable for a reasonable period of time, having regard to all the relevant circumstances of the sale, including the description and nature of the product, the purchase price, the express warranties of the retail seller or manufacturer, the necessary maintenance the product normally requires and the manner in which it has been used;
8. *Spare parts and repair facilities* where the product normally requires repairs, that spare parts and [repair facilities will be reasonably] available for a reasonable period of time after the date of sale of the product.

Section 13(2) of the 1977 Act provides in part that 'the manufacturer of consumer products shall be deemed to give to consumers of his products the same statutory warranties with respect to his products as the retail seller is deemed to have given under paragraphs 2 to 8 of section 11'. Accordingly obligations as to durability, spare parts and repair facilities are imposed on manufacturers directly. See also above p 30. For the definition of a 'consumer product' see above p 17.

Strict contractual liability

Contractual liability in respect of goods which are unmerchantable or unfit for their purpose is not dependent on proof that the seller had failed to exercise reasonable care: see *Daniels and Daniels v R White & Sons Ltd and Tarbard* [1938] 4 All ER 258, above p 19. The point has been confirmed in modern decisions of the House of Lords. Thus in *Henry Kendall & Sons v William Lillico & Sons* Lord Reid said that s 14(1) (now 14(3)) covers 'defects which are latent in the sense that even the utmost skill and judgment on the part of the seller would not have detected them' ([1969] 2 AC 31, 84). Similarly, liability was imposed in the *Ashington Piggeries* case even though, in the words of Lord Diplock, 'in the then state of knowledge, scientific and commercial, no deliberate exercise of human skill or judgment could have prevented the meal from having its toxic effect upon mink. It was sheer bad luck' ([1972] AC 441, 498).

An equivalent strict liability is imposed in hire-purchase transactions (see the Supply of Goods (Impled Terms) Act 1973, ss 9 and 10, above p 62) and the Supply of Goods and Services Act 1982 has removed doubts as to the strictness of the obligation where the property in goods is transferred under a contract which falls within the scope of that Act, notably contracts for work and materials and contracts of hire.

In the context of consumer transactions the supplier may accordingly be liable when, for example, goods are supplied in a container or pre-packed and even though the defect is discoverable only by a minute chemical analysis: see, for example, *Jackson v Watson & Sons* [1909] 2 KB 193, CA (tinned salmon); *Frost v Aylesbury Dairy Co* [1905] 1 KB 608, CA (milk containing typhoid germs); *Grant v Australian Knitting Mills Ltd* [1936]

AC 85 at 100, PC (excess of free sulphites in underpants); *Wren v Holt*
[1903] 1 KB 610 (arsenic in beer). The point is frequently overlooked by
those who argue against the imposition of strict liability on manufacturers
or producers of defective products: see below Ch 4 at p 196 et seq.

Problem

For many years Smith has run a corner shop in Bridgtown where he sells a
range of commodities including cigarettes and fruit. Jones, one of his most
faithful and long-standing customers, always makes a point of buying his
cigarettes from Smith's. Jones, who smokes some thirty cigarettes a day,
has now contracted lung cancer and it is accepted that this has been caused
by his smoking. Thomas buys six oranges from Smith's shop and on eating
them becomes seriously ill. Chemical analysis establishes that they were
part of a consignment which had been injected with a poison in furtherance
of a political campaign.

Advise Jones and Thomas.

REMEDIES FOR BREACH OF THE IMPLIED TERMS

In illustrating the remedies available for breach of the implied terms as to
quality and related matters noted above an initial distinction must be taken
between contracts for the sale of goods and other contracts of supply. The
former are covered by statutory provisions whereas the latter are subject
only to the common law and general contractual principles. The area is one
in which there is considerable uncertainty even as to matters which are of
everyday concern.

Contracts for the sale of goods

The following are the principal provisions which govern the remedies
available to the buyer on breach of the implied conditions of sections 13
and 14 of the Sale of Goods Act 1979: see above pp 61–62.

Sale of Goods Act 1979

11.   When condition to be treated as warranty
(1) Subsections (2) to (4) and (7) below do not apply to Scotland and subsection (5) below
applies only to Scotland.
(2) Where a contract of sale is subject to a condition to be fulfilled by the seller, the buyer
may waive the condition, or may elect to treat the breach of the condition as a breach of
warranty and not as a ground for treating the contract as repudiated.
(3) Whether a stipulation in a contract of sale is a condition, the breach of which may give
rise to a right to treat the contract as repudiated, or a warranty, the breach of which may give
rise to a claim for damages but not to a right to reject the goods and treat the contract as
repudiated, depends in each case on the construction of the contract; and a stipulation may
be a condition, though called a warranty in the contract.
(4) Where a contract of sale is not severable and the buyer has accepted the goods or part of
them, the breach of a condition to be fulfilled by the seller can only be treated as a breach of
warranty, and not as a ground for rejecting the goods and treating the contract as repudiated,
unless there is an express or implied term of the contract to that effect.

(5) In Scotland, failure by the seller to perform any material part of a contract of sale is a breach of contract, which entitles the buyer either within a reasonable time after delivery to reject the goods and treat the contract as repudiated, or to retain the goods and treat the failure to perform such material part as a breach which may give rise to a claim for compensation or damages.

. . .

34. Buyer's right of examining the goods
(1) Where goods are delivered to the buyer, and he has not previously examined them, he is not deemed to have accepted them until he has had a reasonable opportunity of examining them for the purpose of ascertaining whether they are in conformity with the contract.
(2) Unless otherwise agreed, when the seller tenders delivery of goods to the buyer, he is bound on request to afford the buyer a reasonable opportunity of examining the goods for the purpose of ascertaining whether they are in conformity with the contract.

35. Acceptance
(1) The buyer is deemed to have accepted the goods when he intimates to the seller that he has accepted them, or (except where section 34 above otherwise provides) when the goods have been delivered to him and he does any act in relation to them which is inconsistent with the ownership of the seller, or when after the lapse of a reasonable time he retains the goods without intimating to the seller that he has rejected them.

. . .

36. Buyer not bound to return rejected goods
Unless otherwise agreed, where goods are delivered to the buyer, and he refuses to accept them, having the right to do so, he is not bound to return them to the seller, but it is sufficient if he intimates to the seller that he refuses to accept them.

. . .

53. Remedy for breach of warranty
(1) Where there is a breach of warranty by the seller, or where the buyer elects (or is compelled) to treat any breach of a condition on the part of the seller as a breach of warranty, the buyer is not by reason only of such breach of warranty entitled to reject the goods; but he may—
    (a) set up against the seller the breach of warranty in diminution or extinction of the price, or
    (b) maintain an action against the seller for damages for the breach of warranty.
(2) The measure of damages for breach of warranty is the estimated loss directly and naturally resulting, in the ordinary course of events, from the breach of warranty.
(3) In the case of breach of warranty of quality such loss is prima facie the difference between the value of the goods at the time of delivery to the buyer and the value they would have had if they had fulfilled the warranty.
(4) The fact that the buyer has set up the breach of warranty in diminution or extinction of the price does not prevent him from maintaining an action for the same breach of warranty if he has suffered further damage.

. . .

Rejection

The terminology of s 11(3) and (4) of the 1979 Act suggests that a breach of condition, for example as to correspondence with description or merchantable quality, will give rise to a right to reject the goods and treat the contract as repudiated. In addition the buyer may claim damages for breach of contract, and these may include compensation for personal injury and property damage. A breach of warranty will give rise to a right to damages only. However, the precise implications of the entitlement to reject are less clear. For general discussion see *Benjamin's Sale of Goods* (2nd edn) para 887 et seq; Goode *Commercial Law* Chs 10 and 11; Atiyah *Sale of Goods* (6th edn, 1980) Ch 26.

Consider the following cases:

1.   On 1 June Butter and Worth both agree to buy new 'Washcleen 1000' dishwashers from their local department store. The store does not have any machines in stock but it assures both Butter and Worth that it will obtain one from the manufacturer for delivery within ten days. Butter pays cash in advance and Worth agrees to pay cash on delivery. On 6 June the store delivers to Butter a 'Washcleen 800' dishwasher. Butter telephones to point out that this is the wrong model and the store apologises, stating that it will deliver the correct model from stock the following day. Butter who has discovered that he can buy the machine much more cheaply elsewhere demands the return of his money and declines the suggested arrangement. On 7 June the store delivers to Worth a 'Washcleen 1000'. The machine is defective and floods the kitchen floor without causing any damage. Worth telephones to complain, the store apologises and promises to send a service-man around immediately. The service-man explains that the defect can be remedied by changing a faulty part and that he has the necessary part in his van. Worth insists that the machine be removed, adding that he would rather buy another machine elsewhere.

Advise the store.

2.   Ada goes to her local delicatessen shop where she buys a Snorter pork pie. When she cuts it at home she finds that it is mouldy and unwholesome. She returns to the shop to complain and demands her money back but the shop offers rather a replacement pie which Ada declines to accept.

Advise Ada.

3.   In January 1981 Chalmers bought an expensive Britekleen washing machine from his local department store, paying £300 in cash. In January 1984 the programmer failed so that the machine was no longer usable. When Chalmers returned to the store to complain he was told that replacement programmers had once been available at a cost of £65 but were no longer produced as Britekleen had gone out of business. All stocks had been sold and reconditioned programmers could not be found. Neither could they be repaired. The store agreed that an average life for such a washing machine was ten years. Chalmers then bought a new machine of equivalent quality for £400.

Advise Chalmers: see generally *Bacon v Cooper (Metals) Ltd* [1982] 1 All ER 397. How, if at all, would it affect your advice if the failure of the programmer had been caused by the store supplying an entirely different replacement part which was itself faulty?

NOTE

Article 2-508 of the United States Uniform Commercial Code contains the following provision:

Cure by seller of improper tender or delivery; replacement
(1) Where any tender or delivery by the seller is rejected because non-conforming and the time for performance has not yet expired, the seller may seasonably notify the buyer of his intention to cure and may then within the contract time make a conforming delivery.
(2) Where the buyer rejects a non-conforming tender which the seller had reasonable grounds to believe would be acceptable with or without money allowance the seller may if he seasonably notifies the buyer have a further reasonable time to substitute a conforming tender.

Question

Would it be desirable to introduce such a provision into English law? (See further below p 107 et seq where the matter is discussed in an extract from a Law Commission Working Paper.)

The loss of the right to reject

Assuming that the circumstances are such that a consumer buyer has the right to reject goods two further issues may then arise. One is whether the goods have been effectively rejected. The other is whether the right to reject has been lost through acceptance of the goods within s 11(4) and ss 34 and 35 of the 1979 Act. The first issue arose in the following case.

Lee v York Coach and Marine [1977] RTR 35, Court of Appeal

On 7 March 1974 the defendant garage sold to the plaintiff a 1967 Morris 1100 car at a purchase price of £355. The car had a number of defects affecting its safety and the plaintiff gave the defendants several opportunities to rectify them. She then took it to another garage, Dutton-Forshaw, which declined to issue a test certificate. The plaintiff's claim for the return of the purchase price was dismissed by Judge Merrilees who held that the defendants were not in breach of s 14 of the Sale of Goods Act. The plaintiff then appealed to the Court of Appeal.

Cairns LJ, having outlined the facts of the case continued:

The plaintiff took the car to the defendants again, but they were still unwilling to do any further work on it, and so she took it home and stood it in her drive and there it has stood ever since. Nobody has had any use of it since April 1974.

On the 26 April 1974 the plaintiff's solicitors, whom in the meanwhile she had consulted, wrote a letter to the defendants complaining of numerous defects in the car, and saying: 'We must ask you please to remedy all these defects without delay or to refund £355 to Mrs Lee'. Clearly up to this stage there had been no actual rejection of the car by the plaintiff, and the highest that it can be put in relation to this letter from her solicitors would be that there was a conditional rejection, in the sense that she would reject if the defendants were not willing to do the necessary repairs. The defendants replied to that letter on 29 April saying that they had done certain work on the car after delivery, and continuing:

> 'This work was carried out some three weeks ago without you taking this vehicle back for MOT to Forshaws, as we did agree to bleed brakes and fit extra brake pipes if required by Forshaws, also repair horn and speedo. This we will do in order that MOT standard is attained for Forshaws'.

It appears from that that the defendants were offering to do some work, but not everything that had been asked for by the plaintiff's solicitors in their letter.

The next step that was taken on behalf of the plaintiff was to have the vehicle examined by a Mr Stone, who is a Department of the Environment vehicle examiner. He made his examination on 8 May and he listed six defects:

> '(1) Severe corrosion of brake pipings at off side front near to hose union, and at near side front hose union. (2) Corrosion of rear brake pipings. (3) Play in near side steering swivels bottom. (4) Horn button broken and horn not working. (5) Off side drive shaft inner flange loose. (6) Rear subframe weakened by extensive corrosion.'

On the strength of that report the plaintiff's solicitors wrote to the defendants again on 10 May further complaining of the defects, and saying in the course of the letter:

> 'Mrs Lee would have been justified in rescinding the contract on that basis'—that is on the basis that the car was unroadworthy—'In our opinion she may still be entitled to do so'.

Again I observe that that was not absolute rejection on the part of the solicitors as agents for the plaintiff. Indeed, if the earlier letter could have been considered to be a conditional rejection, they were in this letter in effect saying merely as a matter of opinion that she would have been entitled to rescind in the past, and she might still be entitled to do so, without saying that she did so.

In reply to that letter the defendants wrote on the 16 May offering to do certain further work to the car, but saying that they would require a signed satisfaction note from Mrs Lee that the work had been carried out to her satisfaction before the vehicle left their premises. She was unwilling, having regard to the previous history, to sign any satisfaction note without further opportunity of having the car tested, and accordingly she did not take the car back to them for any further attempt to put it in order, and, indeed, did nothing more about it until the 19 September, when she started the county court proceedings.

In her particulars of claim allegations were made that the car was not of merchantable quality and was not fit for the purpose of being driven safely on the road, in breach of the conditions in the Sale of Goods Act 1893, as amended by the Supply of Goods (Implied Terms) Act 1973. It was then stated: 'In the premises the plaintiff is entitled to and does reject the said car' and she claimed repayment of purchase price of £355 and, in the alternative, damages. The defendants' defence we have not seen, but we understand that it was a comprehensive denial of the allegations in the particulars of claim.

. . .

The first and main question for this court is whether the judge's conclusion that the car was of merchantable quality and fit for its purpose is sustainable. In my opinion, it is not. Having regard to all the circumstances of this case, I think it is clear that the car was not fit for the purpose for which it was intended, namely, for driving on the road. I also think that it was not of merchantable quality . . . I feel no doubt, having regard to the relevant circumstances of this case, that part of what constituted merchantable quality was that the car should be in a state in which it could be safely driven. That really overlaps, as so often happens, the other statutory implied condition.

. . .

I reach the clear conclusion that there was a breach of both implied statutory conditions here, and that in those circumstances the plaintiff would have been entitled to reject. But I do not think she ever did reject. I have indicated what in my view is the effect of the two letters written on her behalf by her solicitors, which are the high water mark of any case for rejection before the action was started. She purported to reject in her particulars of claim. That will not do; it is too late. I, therefore, consider that she is entitled not to the return of the purchase money, but to damages, and as no issue has been raised as to the correctness of the amount of damages, I would allow the appeal and award her £100 damages.

Stephenson LJ. I agree. This second hand car was not, in my opinion of the evidence which the judge accepted, of merchantable quality within section 14(2) and section 62(1A) of the Act of 1893, or reasonably fit for the particular purpose for which it was bought by Mrs Lee within section 14(3). To be fit for that purpose—and I think to be merchantable—it had to be, broadly speaking, roadworthy. More precisely, I would regard that purpose as the purpose of being driven lawfully and safely on the road immediately on delivery and for a reasonable time thereafter. A car which is likely to break up if the driver breaks hard in an emergency is unmerchantable and unfit for that purpose. If the car could have been made merchantable and fit for that purpose at small expense, that would not, in my opinion, necessarily make it merchantable or fit for the purpose at the relevant time, which was the time of delivery, and would not have made it so in the circumstances of this case. I therefore agree that the judge was wrong in finding no breach of either implied statutory condition. But I also agree that Mrs Lee did not, for the reasons given by Cairns LJ, reject the car or treat the contract of sale as repudiated, at least until she brought this action in September 1974. She must, therefore, be taken to have accepted the car and compelled by section 11(1)(c) of the Act of 1893 [see now s 11(4)] to treat the sellers' breaches of condition as breaches of warranty. She is not entitled to reject the car, but she is entitled to damages by section 53 of the Act of 1893. She must keep what is left of the car and be content with the now agreed damages of £100 which the judge would have awarded her.

I agree to that extent the appeal should be allowed.

Bridge LJ. I agree . . .

Appeal allowed. Plaintiff awarded £100 damages. Order below for defendant's costs set aside and an order substituted for plaintiff's costs below on the scale appropriate to £100 damages. No order for costs in the Court of Appeal.

If the requirement of an unequivocal rejection is satisfied it will be effective only if the goods have not been accepted. The rules as to what constitutes acceptance are printed above: see ss 34 and 35 of the 1979 Act. The following case is concerned with the loss of the right to rescind for misrepresentation rather than with the loss of the right to reject for breach of condition. However it seems clear that the two situations have much in common. In reading the case it should be noted that s 1 of the Misrepresentation Act 1967 has since reversed the rule denying rescission of a contract which had been completed or performed. The scope of this rule was the question of principle which had been left open in *Leaf v International Galleries* [1950] 2 KB 86, [1950] 1 All ER 693 and to which Pearce LJ, refers in his judgment.

Long v Lloyd [1958] 2 All ER 402, [1958] 1 WLR 753, Court of Appeal

Jenkins LJ: The judgment which is about to be read by Pearce LJ, is the judgment of the court in this case.

Pearce LJ: The plaintiff appeals from a judgment of Glyn-Jones J, dismissing the plaintiff's claim to rescission of an executed contract of sale on the ground of innocent misrepresentation. The learned judge in a clear and careful judgment made findings of fact that may be summarised as follows.

Both parties carry on business as haulage contractors, the plaintiff at Sevenoaks, the defendant at Hampton Court. On Friday, Oct 19, 1956, the plaintiff read a newspaper advertisement inserted by the defendant, offering for sale at £850 a 1947 Dennis twelve/fourteen ton lorry described as in 'exceptional condition'. On the telephone that evening the defendant said to the plaintiff that it was 'in first-class condition'. The next day, Saturday, the plaintiff saw it at the defendant's premises. The defendant said that it was capable of forty miles per hour. The plaintiff said that he would be willing to pay £750 for it, if he was satisfied on a trial run, and it was agreed that on the plaintiff paying £5 the defendant would hold the vehicle for him until Monday. That night it was arranged on the telephone that the plaintiff might pay one half of the purchase price in cash and the remainder a few days later. The defendant repeated that it was a good vehicle. On Monday, Oct 22, the plaintiff took trade plates to the defendant's premises in order to take the lorry (which was unlicensed) for a trial run on the road. The defendant made various representations as to the lorry, one of which was that it would do eleven miles to the gallon. The defendant and the plaintiff drove it in turn. The speedometer was not working, there was a wire which had to be pulled in order to decelerate since the spring was missing from the accelerator pedal, and the plaintiff had difficulty with the fifth (or top) gear. The defendant having assured the plaintiff that there was nothing wrong with the vehicle about which he had not told him, the plaintiff there and then bought the lorry for £750 paying a cheque of £370 which together with the £5 already paid made up half the purchase price and left a balance of £375 to be paid later. Before leaving, the plaintiff said: 'If I find anything wrong your phone won't stop ringing'. The defendant answered: 'It's quite all right'.

On Tuesday, Oct 23, a receipt was posted to the plaintiff by the defendant:

> 'Received from Mr S. E. Long the sum of £375 by cheque being half payment of Dennis vehicle DDW 864 as tried and approved by the above. Balance remaining £375.'

On Wednesday, Oct 24, the plaintiff drove the lorry to Rochester to pick up a small load. On the journey the dynamo ceased to function and the plaintiff was advised that night to fit a reconstructed dynamo. He noticed also that an oil seal was allowing oil to escape, that there was a crack in one of the wheels, and that he had used eight gallons of fuel for about forty miles. That night he told the defendant of these defects. The defendant said that the dynamo was 'all right' when the lorry left him and offered to pay half the cost of the reconstructed dynamo. This the plaintiff accepted. The defendant denied any knowledge of the broken oil seal.

The next day, Thursday, Oct 25, the dynamo was fitted and the lorry was driven by the plaintiff's brother on a journey to Middlesbrough. On the night of Friday, Oct 26, the plaintiff heard from his brother that the lorry had broken down on its journey. In consequence, the plaintiff wrote to the defendant complaining of leakage or consumption of oil from the sump, of a fuel consumption of only nine miles per gallon instead of eleven, and of the fact that instead of the lorry being a forty mph vehicle it was an effort to keep it at twenty-five mph with the four ton load. He ended:

'The above in addition to the oil cup retainer, the rear offside spring retaining bolt, and also one cracked wheel (one to my knowledge) the dodgy accelerator, has convinced me that you have wilfully and deliberately misrepresented the state of the vehicle and under these circumstances I ask for the return of my money, and the vehicle will be returned to you by about Tuesday (I hope it lasts that long).'

He has not persisted in that charge of fraud. On Nov 14 the lorry was examined by an expert who gave evidence of many serious defects which he found, sufficient, in his opinion, to make it unroadworthy.

The learned judge found that the defendant honestly made the misrepresentations complained of, that the vehicle had probably deteriorated while out of use, and that it had the defects alleged. He said this:

'The fact remains that the plaintiff was induced to buy this vehicle by material representations made to him by the defendant which, though honestly made, were untrue, and I must therefore deal with [counsel for the plaintiff's] argument that in the circumstances of this case his client is entitled to rescind the contract.'

Counsel for the plaintiff's argument is founded on the view expressed on this somewhat vexed question by Denning, LJ, in the comparatively recent cases of *Solle v Butcher* ([1949] 2 All ER 1107 at 1119) and *Leaf v International Galleries* ([1950] 1 All ER 693 at 694).

. . .

The question was thus left open in *Leaf v International Galleries* but the court was unanimous in holding that on the assumption that the innocent misrepresentation did give rise to a right to claim rescission after the contract had been completed such right had in the circumstances of the case been lost by the time that the buyer purported to exercise it. Counsel for the plaintiff's able argument has not sufficed to resolve our doubts on the question of principle, but we think that it is unnecessary here, as it was in *Leaf's* case, to decide whether the innocent misrepresentation relied on by the plaintiff gave rise to a right to rescission after completion of the contract, because we are satisfied that his right to do so, if it ever existed, had been lost by the time that he purported to reject the lorry.

We should next refer to the facts of *Leaf's* case and the observations made by the members of the court on those facts. The contract was a contract for the sale of a picture which the sellers innocently misrepresented to have been painted by Constable. The buyer took delivery of the picture and kept it for a matter of five years. He was then informed on attempting to sell the picture that it was not a Constable. Thereupon he brought his action for rescission on the ground that the sellers had misrepresented, albeit innocently, the identity of the artist. He could have claimed damages for breach of warranty but refrained from doing so. On these facts Denning, LJ, after referring to s 11(1)(c) and s 35 of the Sale of Goods Act, 1893, said this ([1950] 1 All ER at p 695):

'In this case this buyer took the picture into his house, and five years passed before he intimated any rejection. That, I need hardly say, is much more than a reasonable time. It is far too late for him at the end of five years to reject this picture for breach of any condition. His remedy after that length of time is for damages only, a claim which he has not brought before the court . . . although rescission may in some cases be a proper remedy, nevertheless it is to be remembered that an innocent misrepresentation is much less potent than a breach of condition. A condition is a term of the contract of a most material character, and, if a claim to reject for breach of condition is barred, it seems to me a fortiori that a claim to rescission on the ground of innocent misrepresentation is also barred. So, assuming that a contract for the sale of goods may be rescinded in a proper case for innocent misrepresentation, nevertheless, once the buyer has accepted, or is deemed to have accepted, the goods, the claim is barred. In this case the buyer must clearly be deemed to have accepted the picture. He had ample opportunity to examine it in the first few days after he bought it. Then was the time to see if the condition or representation was fulfilled, yet he has kept it all this time and five years have elapsed without any notice of rejection. In my judgment, he cannot now claim to rescind . . .'

Jenkins LJ, founded himself on the five years' delay as being far in excess of the reasonable time within which the right to claim rescission, if it ever existed, should have been exercised; and while expressing no dissent from, did not advert to, Denning LJ's view to the effect that the buyer's acceptance of the picture in itself barred any right there might otherwise have been to claim rescission. Sir Raymond Evershed MR, said (ibid, at p 696):

'I also agree that this appeal should be dismissed, for the reasons which have already been given. On the facts of this case it seems to me that the buyer ought not now to be allowed to rescind this contract . . . [ibid, at p 697] If a man elects to buy a work of art or any other chattel on the faith of some representation, innocently made, and delivery of the article is accepted, then it seems to me that there is much to be said for the view that on acceptance there is an end of that particular transaction, and that, if it were otherwise, business dealings in these things would become hazardous, difficult, and uncertain.'

As to the facts of the present case, counsel for the plaintiff contrasts the period of only a few days between the delivery of the lorry to the plaintiff and his purported rescission of the contract with the period of five years in *Leaf's* case. He says the plaintiff was entitled to a reasonable time within which to ascertain the true condition of the lorry and to exercise (if so advised) the right of rescission which for the present purpose he must be assumed to have had. It is of course obvious that so far as time is concerned this case bears no resemblance to *Leaf's* case. Nevertheless, a strict application to the facts of the present case of Denning LJ's view to the effect that the right (if any) to rescind after completion on the ground of innocent misrepresentation is barred by acceptance of the goods must necessarily prove fatal to the plaintiff's case. Apart from special circumstances, the place of delivery is the proper place for examination and for acceptance. It was open to the plaintiff to have the lorry examined by an expert before driving it away but he chose not to do so. It is true, however, that the truth of certain of the representations, for example, that the lorry would do eleven miles to the gallon could not be ascertained except by user and therefore the plaintiff should have a reasonable time to test it. Until he had had such an opportunity it might well be said that he had not accepted the lorry, always assuming, of course, that he did nothing inconsistent with the ownership of the seller. An examination of the facts, however, shows that on any view he must have accepted the lorry before he purported to reject it.

Thus, to recapitulate the facts, after the trial run the plaintiff drove the lorry home from Hampton Court to Sevenoaks, a not inconsiderable distance. After that experience he took it into use in his business by driving it on the following day to Rochester and back to Sevenoaks with a load. By the time he returned from Rochester he knew that the dynamo was not charging, that there was an oil seal leaking, that he had used eight gallons of fuel for a journey of forty miles and that a wheel was cracked. He must also, as we think, have known by this time that the vehicle was not capable of forty miles per hour. As to oil consumption, we should have thought that, if it was so excessive that the sump was practically dry after three hundred miles, the plaintiff could have reasonably been expected to discover that the rate of consumption was unduly high by the time he had made the journey from Hampton Court to Sevenoaks and thence to Rochester and back. On his return from Rochester the plaintiff telephoned to the defendant and complained about the dynamo, the excessive fuel consumption, the leaking oil seal and the cracked wheel. The defendant then offered to pay half the cost of the reconstructed dynamo which the plaintiff had been advised to fit, and the plaintiff accepted the defendant's offer. We find this difficult to reconcile with the continuance of any right of rescission which the plaintiff might have had down to that time.

The matter does not rest there. On the following day the plaintiff, knowing all that he did about the condition and performance of the lorry, despatched it, driven by his brother, on a business trip to Middlesbrough. That step, at all events, appears to us to have amounted, in all the circumstances of the case, to a final acceptance of the lorry by the plaintiff for better or for worse, and to have conclusively extinguished any right of rescission remaining to the plaintiff after completion of the sale. Accordingly, even if the plaintiff should be held, notwithstanding *Seddon v North Eastern Salt Co Ltd* ((1905) 1 Ch 326) to have had a right to rescission which survived the completion of the contract, we think that on the facts of this case he lost any such right before his purported exercise of it. For these reasons we would dismiss this appeal.

Appeal dismissed. Leave to appeal to the House of Lords granted.

NOTE

For a case in which the buyer of a new and defective Chrysler car was successful in claiming damages but too late to reject see *Jackson v Chrysler Acceptances Ltd* [1978] RTR 474, CA.

Questions

1. Was Denning LJ correct in saying in *Leaf's* case (see above p 96) that 'if a claim to reject for breach of condition is barred it seems to me a fortiori that a claim to rescission on the ground of innocent misrepresentation is also barred'?

Might not a buyer 'accept' goods without knowing their true condition and yet not be barred from rescission for misrepresentation on ascertaining the truth soon thereafter? For a reference to the principles of affirmation see below p 99 et seq. Note, however, that the Misrepresentation Act 1967, s 2(2) gives a court the power to declare a contract subsisting and to award damages in lieu of rescission.

2. Does *Long v Lloyd* assist in determining whether a buyer prejudices his position by agreeing to allow the seller an opportunity to carry out a repair? Referring to this point Professor Goode has written:

> Not uncommonly, the seller will offer either to repair the goods himself or to send them back to the manufacturer for repair. If the buyer accepts this offer, does he thereby adopt the sale so as to bar rejection if the repairs are not satisfactorily carried out? Plainly the answer is no. His acceptance is conditional only. What he is in effect saying is that if the goods are satisfactorily repaired he will take them, and if not he expects his money back . . .

—see *Commercial Law* p 310. If this is correct would the position be the same if the buyer attempted to settle the matter by paying part of the cost of repair?

3. To the extent that the implied condition of merchantable quality includes a requirement of reasonable durability (see above p 83 et seq) will this be vindicated only by a remedy in damages?

Problems

1. Wedgwood buys an expensive twelve-cover set of china from his local antique shop. It is delivered by the store's van and he signs a delivery note which reads 'I confirm that these goods have been received in good condition'. On opening the box containing the china two days later Wedgwood discovers that several items have been badly chipped during package or transit. He wishes to reject the china.

Advise Wedgwood.

2. Margaux orders two cases of 1982 claret as part of an opening offer from a specialist vintner, Palmer. He expects to drink the wine in 1990. He wishes to know how the provisions as to acceptance may affect him should the wine prove to be unmerchantable.

Advise Margaux.

3. On 1 January 1984 Beatle buys a new stereo set from his local dealer, Fastbuck, paying £200 cash. When he opens the package at home he finds that the set has a guarantee provided by the manufacturer, Ginushi, which reads as follows: 'We guarantee this stereo set for three months from the date of purchase. Any necessary replacement part will be provided free of charge within this period'. The set works quite satisfactorily for two weeks and then stops working on 15 January. On the same day Beatle takes it back to Fast-buck, who returns it to Ginushi. The set is ready for collection on 1 February and is collected by Beatle from Fastbuck on that day. It works satisfactorily until 15 March and then breaks down again. Beatle takes it back to Fastbuck saying, 'Look, I am getting fed up with this. Make sure it is fixed properly this time or I shall be wanting my money back'. The set is returned to Ginushi for repair and is collected by Beatle from Fastbuck on 30 March. It works well until 15 April and then breaks down again.

Advise Beatle as to what remedies, if any, he may have against (i) Fastbuck and (ii) Ginushi. For the position of Ginushi see also above pp 31–52.

Other contracts for the supply of goods

The position where goods are supplied other than under a contract of sale has been summarised conveniently in the following extract from a Law Commission Working Paper.

Sale and Supply of Goods (1983) Law Commission Working Paper No 85

English law: affirmation
2.61 In this section we are concerned not only with contracts of hire, hire-purchase, barter and for work and materials but also with consumer conditional sale agreements, which are equated with hire-purchase agreements for the purpose of 'acceptance'[1] and are subject to the same common law principle of affirmation.
2.62 Unlike a buyer, the customer in any of the other contracts for the supply of goods does not lose his right to bring the contract to an end by virtue of provisions similar to those contained in the Sale of Goods Act, but by virtue of the common law doctrine of affirmation. If he is held to have affirmed the contract he can thereafter only sue for damages. The following principles have emerged in the general law of contract and appear to be of general application:
　(i)　on discovering the breach, an innocent party must elect between his available remedies;[2]
　(ii)　it seems that as a general[3] rule an innocent party cannot be held to have affirmed the contract, unless he had knowledge of the breach;
　(iii)　affirmation may be express if the innocent party expressly refuses to accept the other party's repudiation of the contract;[4]
　(iv)　affirmation may be implied if the innocent party does some act such as pressing for the performance of the contract from which it may be inferred that he recognises the continued existence of the contract;[5]
　(v)　mere inactivity by the innocent party after discovering the breach will not of itself constitute affirmation, unless (a) the other party would be prejudiced by the delay in treating the contract as repudiated or (b) the delay is of such length as to constitute evidence of a decision to affirm the contract;[6]
　(vi)　affirmation must be total in the sense that the innocent party cannot affirm part of the contract and disaffirm the rest.[7]
2.63 In applying the doctrine of affirmation to hire-purchase agreements the tendency of the courts has been wherever possible to protect the right of the hirer to reject defective goods. However, authority in this area of the law is scanty.[8] There are no reported cases in which the doctrine of affirmation has been applied to contracts of barter or for work and materials, but there is no reason to suppose that it would not be applicable. The doctrine appears to have been applied in a contract of hire.[9]

1. Supply of Goods (Implied Terms) Act 1973, s 14.
2. *Kammins Ballrooms Co Ltd v Zenith Investments (Torquay) Ltd* [1971] AC 850 per Lord Diplock at p 853.
3. See however *Panchaud Freres SA v Etablissements General Grain Co* [1970] 1 Lloyd's Rep 53, where the Court of Appeal, stressing the need for finality in commercial transactions, created a limited exception of uncertain ambit to the general rule. It held that a buyer who rejected shipping documents on an inadmissible ground could not subsequently justify this on grounds which he could have detected, but did not detect at the time and which he only discovered three years later.
4. *White and Carter (Councils) Ltd v McGregor* [1962] AC 413.
5. *Suisse Atlantique Société d'Armement Maritime SA v Rotterdamsche Kolen Centrale NV* [1967] 1 AC 361.
6. *Allen v Robles* [1969] 1 WLR 1193.
7. *Suisse Atlantique* case (above).
8. See *Yeoman Credit Ltd v Apps* [1962] 2 QB 508; *Farnworth Finance Ltd v Attryde* [1970] 1 WLR 1053.
9. *Guarantee Trust of Jersey Ltd v Gardner* (1973) 117 Sol Jo 564.

The following case is perhaps the single most important example discussing the notion of affirmation in relation to a consumer hire-purchase transaction.

Farnworth Finance Facilities Ltd v Attryde [1970] 2 All ER 774, [1970] 1 WLR 1053, Court of Appeal

Lord Denning MR. The first defendant is a civil servant employed by the Ministry of Aviation at Aberporth in Cardiganshire. In 1964, when he was aged 23, he wanted a new motor cycle. He read an advertisement issued by the Enfield Cycle Co Ltd and decided to get a Royal Enfield Interceptor. He went to dealers, the second defendants, King's Motors (Oxford) Ltd of Wolverhampton. They got a machine from the makers and supplied it to him on hire-purchase terms. The finance company was Farnworth Finance Facilities Ltd of Cardiff, the plaintiffs. The second defendants had the forms in their office at Wolverhampton. The first defendant signed them and took delivery of the machine. The cash price was £427 5s 10d. The finance charges were £89 16s. Add £1 option to purchase. Thus making a total hire-purchase price of £518 1s 10d. The first defendant paid £155 5s 10d down, with instalments payable over the next three years of £10 1s a month.

The first defendant took delivery of the machine on 11 July 1964. But he had a lot of trouble with it. He took it back to the second defendants. They tried to correct the faults, but did not succeed. So he took it back to the makers, the Enfield Cycle Co Ltd at Redditch. They had it for nine days—from 21 to 31 July 1964. They remedied some defects, but they did not succeed in remedying all the faults. On 13 August, the first defendant took it back again to the Enfield Cycle Co Ltd. They had it this time for some weeks. He did not get it back until 15 October 1964. They had remedied some defects, but not all. He used it for five weeks, from 15 October to 23 November. But he found that there were still serious faults. The last straw was on Saturday, 21 November 1964. As he was turning out from a drive, the rear chain broke. The broken chain knocked a hole in the crank case and caused considerable damage. It would be a very expensive repair. He decided that he would not go on with it any further. He wrote on Monday, 23 November 1964:

> 'I am not making any further effort to get Enfields or things to put things right. I have tried hard enough and got nowhere. Obviously I will not continue to pay hire charges for a machine I cannot use and which has been a troublesome burden ever since I've had it. Please come and repossess the bike you will find it at the address given at the start of this letter.'

That was his address in Cardiganshire. So being utterly disappointed, he rejected the machine.

It was a big loss to him: for he had paid £155 10s down. He had paid four instalments of £10 1s. So he had paid £195 14s. The plaintiffs, or someone on their behalf, came and took possession of the machine. They sold it for £142 5s. They then sued the first defendant for a further £149 1s. He no longer had the motor cycle, and he was now being sued for a further £149 1s. He resisted the claim on the ground that the plaintiffs had been guilty of a fundamental breach of their obligations under the contract. He put in a counterclaim for his own loss. The plaintiffs said that, if they were in breach, they could claim indemnity from the second defendants. So they joined them as defendants.

The action was tried by his Honour Judge Temple-Morris QC at Cardiff. He accepted the first defendant's evidence in its entirety . . .

His Lordship then discussed the position of the second defendants and referred to the doctrine of fundamental breach (see below p 235) and continued:

As between the plaintiffs and the first defendant, there was no express term about the condition of the machine. But there were implied terms. It has been established by a series of cases in this court that, in a hire-purchase agreement of a motor vehicle there are a number of implied terms which are of fundamental importance. These cases are: *Yeoman Credit Ltd v Apps*[1], *Astley Industrial Trust Ltd v Grimley*[2] and *Charterhouse Credit Co Ltd v Tolly*[3]. These cases show that it is an implied condition that the machine should correspond with the description and that it should be reasonably fit for the purpose for which it was hired; which means, of course, that it should be roadworthy. In addition, the machine in this case was expressly described as 'new', which adds emphasis to the implied terms. A new motor cycle should at any rate be a workman-like motor cycle which is safe to be used on the roads.

There were clearly breaches of those implied terms . . .

The next question is whether the first defendant affirmed the contract. Counsel for the second defendants points out that the first defendant had ridden this bicycle for 4,000 miles. Even after he got it back from the makers on 15 October he had used it for five or six weeks till 23 November and had ridden 3,000 miles on it. Counsel said that by using it all that time the first defendant had affirmed the contract and it was too late for him to repudiate it. But as the argument proceeded, I think that counsel for the first defendant gave the right answer. He pointed out that affirmation is a matter of election. A man only affirms a contract when he knows of the defects and by his conduct elects to go on with the contract despite them. In this case the first defendant complained from the beginning of the defects and sent the machine back for them to be remedied. He did not elect to accept it unless they were remedied. But the defects were never satisfactorily remedied. When the rear chain broke, it was the last straw. It showed that the machine could not be relied on. This knowledge was not brought home to him until this last final incident. The first defendant was entitled to say then: 'I am not going on with this machine any longer. I have tried it long enough.' After all, it was a contract of hiring. The machine was not his until the three years had been completed—and the price paid. Owing to the defects, the first defendant was entitled to throw up the hiring; to say he would have no more to do with it; and to claim damages. The judge found that the first defendant did not affirm the contract and I agree with him.

. . .

There is one other point, and that is on damages. Counsel for the second defendants said that the first defendant ought to give credit for the use which he had of the motor cycle for some 4,000 miles. He relied on *Charterhouse Credit Co Ltd v Tolly*[3] when such a credit was allowed. But it seems to me that the value of any use had by the first defendant is offset by the great amount of trouble he had. So no credit need be given for the use. I see no reason for interfering with the award of the judge on damages.

So the plaintiffs are liable to the first defendant. But they are entitled to claim over against the second defendants on the express promise that the machine was in a roadworthy condition. They can recover against them the full amount of £149 1s, and for the £195 9s 10d that they have to pay the first defendant. The judge so ordered. I find that there is no fault to be found with the judgment of the judge in this case, and I would dismiss the appeal.

Fenton Atkinson and Megaw LLJ agreed with Lord Denning's judgment.

Appeal dismissed.

1. [1961] 2 All ER 281, [1962] 2 QB 508.
2. [1963] 2 All ER 33, [1963] 1 WLR 584.
3. [1963] 2 All ER 432, [1963] 2 QB 683.

NOTES

1. The entitlement of a consumer to recover in quasi-contract all the money he has paid out by way of a deposit or instalments will depend on his establishing a total failure of consideration. In the above case the use 'enjoyed' by the hirer was offset by the trouble which he had suffered. In *Charterhouse Credit Co Ltd v Tolly* [1963] 2 QB 683, [1963] 2 All ER 432, CA, where it was conceded that some element of benefit had been received, Donovan LJ explained the method of calculating damages as follows (at p 439):

This point again seems to be free from direct authority, but an application of basic principle does, I think, yield the true and just solution. The general rule in cases of breach of contract is that a plaintiff is entitled to be placed, so far as money can do it, in the same position as he would have been in had the contract been performed (per Parke B. in *Robinson v Harman*[1]). This involves considering what would have been the hirer's position had there been no continuing breach of the contract by the finance company. He would then have had a suitable car delivered to him on hire-purchase terms. He would have been liable for the initial payment plus three monthly instalments. These payments would have been much higher than payments for mere hire alone, on account of the eventual option to purchase for the purely nominal sum of £1. The hirer has, in fact, paid the initial payment of £90, and under this judgment must pay the three instalments amounting to £47 4s. For this outlay, however, he has received nothing, owing to the finance company's breach of contract, except the two rides to Greenwich. What is required to put him, so far as money can, in the same position as if the contract had been performed? To my mind, it is a sum equal to the cost of hiring a similar car on similar terms as to the eventual option to purchase for £1. There is no reason why one should not adopt as the figure of that cost what the hirer actually has to pay to the finance company for the like hiring in the present case, to wit, £90 and £47 4s. less a small sum for the two journeys he made in the car, which I would put at £5. The net figure thus becomes £132 4s.

I reject counsel for the finance company's argument that all to which the hirer is entitled is the cost of hiring another similar car. That would not of itself be restitutio in integrum, for the contract here was not one of simple hire but of hire-purchase.

1. (1848) 1 Exch 850 at 855.

See also Diamond *Commercial and Consumer Credit: An Introduction* (1982), Ch 28.

2. In contracts of hire-purchase, hire, barter and conditional sales usually it will be possible for the defective goods to be made available for collection by the supplier. Sometimes this will be true of contracts of work and materials. For exampe if a contract to supply and fit a carpet is so classified it may not be unduly difficult for the supplier to take up any that he has laid. However there will be many situations in which at best this would create serious practical problems. The following case provides an interesting example of the position of the contractor and his customer in such a situation.

Bolton v Mahadeva [1972] 2 All ER 1322, [1972] 1 WLR 1009, Court of Appeal

The plaintiff agreed with the defendant to install central heating in the defendant's house. The contract price for the central heating installation was a lump sum of £560. On completion of the work the defendant complained that the work was defective and refused to pay. At the trial the county court judge found that because of a defective flue fumes affected the condition of the air in the living rooms. Moreover the house was on average ten per cent less warm than it should have been with such a system, but the deficiency varied from room to room and in some rooms it was much greater. In each case the expenditure necessary to cure these defects was £40. The judge held that because of those and other deficiencies the defendant was entitled to set off £174.50 against the contract price. He gave judgment for the plaintiff for the balance accordingly. The defendant appealed.

Cairns LJ, having outlined the facts of the case, continued:

The main question in the case is whether the defects in workmanship found by the judge to be such as to cost £174 to repair—ie between one-third and one-quarter of the contract price—were of such a character and amount that the plaintiff could not be said to have substantially performed his contract. That is, in my view, clearly the legal principle which has to be applied to cases of this kind.

The rule which was laid down many years ago in *Cutter v Powell*[1] in relation to lump sum contracts was that, unless the contracting party had performed the whole of his contract, he was not entitled to recover anything. That strong rule must now be read in the light of certain more recent cases to which I shall briefly refer. The first of those cases is *H Dakin & Co Ltd v Lee*[2] a decision of the Court of Appeal, in which it was held that, where the amount of work which had not been carried out under a lump sum contract was very minor in relation to the contract as a whole, the contractor was entitled to be paid the lump sum, subject to such deduction as might be proper in respect of the uncompleted work. It is necessary to observe that the headnote of *H Dakin & Co Ltd v Lee*[2] was based, not on the judgments in the Court of Appeal, but on the judgments that had been delivered in the Divisional Court; and , as was pointed out in *Vigers v Cook*[3] that headnote does not properly represent the grounds of the decision of the Court of Appeal in that case. The basis on which the Court of Appeal did decide *H Dakin & Co Ltd v Lee*[2] is to be found in a passage of the judgment of Lord Cozens-Hardy MR[4]. I do not think it is necessary to read it in full, but I read this short passage[5]:

> 'But to say that a builder cannot recover from a building owner merely because some item of the work has been done negligently or inefficiently or improperly is a proposition which I should not listen to unless compelled by a decision of the House of Lords. Take a contract for a lump sum to decorate a house; the contract provides that there shall be three coats of oil paint, but in one of the rooms only two coats of paint are put on. Can anybody say that under these circumstances the building owner could go and occupy the house and take the benefit of all the decorations which had been done in the other rooms without paying a penny for all the work done by the builder, just because only two coats of paint had been put on in one room where they ought to have been three?'

. . .

Perhaps the most helpful case is the most recent one of *Hoenig v Isaacs*[6]. That was a case where the plaintiff was an interior decorator and designer of furniture who had entered into a contract to decorate and furnish the defendant's flat for a sum of £750; and, as appears from the statement of facts, the Official Referee who tried the case at first instance found that the door of a wardrobe required replacing, that a bookshelf which was too short would have to be remade, which would require alterations being made to a bookcase, and that the cost of remedying the defects was £55 18s 2d. That is on a £750 contract. The ground on which the Court of Appeal in that case held that the plaintiff was entitled to succeed, notwithstanding that there was not complete performance of the contract, was that there was substantial performance of the contract and that the defects in the work which there existed were not sufficient to amount to a substantial degree of non-performance.

In considering whether there was substantial performance I am of opinion that it is relevant to take into account both the nature of the defects and the proportion between the cost of rectifying them and the contract price. It would be wrong to say that the contractor is only entitled to payment if the defects are so trifling as to be covered by the de minimis rule.

. . .

Now, certainly it appears to me that the nature and amount of the defects in this case were far different from those which the court had to consider in *H Dakin & Co Ltd v Lee*[2] and

Hoenig v Isaacs[6]. For my part, I find it impossible to say that the judge was right in reaching the conclusion that in those circumstances the contract had been substantially performed. The contract was a contract to install a central heating system. If a central heating system when installed is such that it does not heat the house adequately and is such, further, that fumes are given out, so as to make living rooms uncomfortable, and if the putting right of those defects is not something which can be done by some slight amendment of the system, then I think that the contract is not substantially performed.

The actual amounts of expenditure which the judge assessed as being necessary to cure those particular defects were £40 in each case. Taking those matters into account and the other matters making up the total of £174, I have reached the conclusion that the judge was wrong in saying that this contract had been substantially completed; and, on my view of the law, it follows that the plaintiff was not entitled to recover under that contract.

. . .

So far as the defendant's claim in respect of fees for the report which he obtained from his expert is concerned, it seems to me clear that that report was obtained in view of a dispute which had arisen and with a view to being used in evidence if proceedings did become necessary, and in the hope that it would assist in the settlement of the dispute without proceedings being started. In those circumstances, I think that the judge was right in reaching the conclusion that that report was something the fees for which, if recoverable at all, would be recoverable only under an order for costs.

So far as concerns the damages in respect of the inconvenience to which the defendant was put, the judge, as I have said, assessed that inconvenience at £15. I must say that, on the evidence, it seems to me to be a low figure; but obviously it is a figure which is incapable of any exact assessment. and I am not prepared to say that the judge was wrong in assessing that sum.

. . .

It appears to me that the result should be this, that the appeal should be allowed and the judgment in favour of the plaintiff should be set aside. It is not, I think, contested that there is in respect of the extras a sum of £61 which was due to the plaintiff at the commencement of the action; that, of course, is far less than the £400 which had been paid into court. If Sachs and Buckley LJJ agree with the judgment which I have delivered, it will be for consideration then as to the exact form of the order that this court should make.

Buckley LJ I agree and do not wish to add anything.

Sachs LJ I agree that this appeal should be allowed, for the reasons given by Cairns LJ.

. . .

When, however, one looks at the aggregate of the number of defects that he held to have been established, at the importance of some of those defects, and at the way in which some of them prevented the installation being one that did what was intended, I find myself, like Cairns LJ, quite unable to agree that there was a substantial performance by the plaintiff of this lump sum contract. It is not merely that so very much of the work was shoddy, but it is the general ineffectiveness of it for its primary purpose that leads me to that conclusion.

So far as the law is concerned, I would merely add that it seems to me to be compactly and accurately stated in Cheshire and Fifoot[7] in the following terms:

'. . . the present rule is that "so long as there is substantial performance the contractor is entitled to the stipulated price, subject only to a cross-action or counter-claim for the omissions or defects in execution[8]"';

and, to 'cross-action or counter-claim', I would of course add 'set-off'. The converse, however, is equally correct—if there is not a substantial performance, the contractor cannot recover. It is on the application of that converse rule that the plaintiff's case here fails. This rule does not work hardly on a contractor if only he is prepared to remedy the defects before seeking to resort to litigation to recover the lump sum. It is entirely the fault of the plaintiff contractor in this instant case that he has placed himself in a difficulty by his refusal on 4 December 1969 to remedy the defects of which complaint was being made.

. . .

Appeal allowed; judgment set aside, there being substituted therefore judgment for the plaintiff for £46; plaintiff to repay the balance of £354 within 14 days.

1. (1795) 6 Term Rep 320, [1775–1802] All ER Rep 159.
2. [1916] 1 KB 566.
3. [1919] 2 KB 475 at 483.
4. [1916] 1 KB at 578 at 579.
5. [1916] 1 KB at 579.
6. [1952] 2 All ER 176.
7. The Law of Contract (7th Edn, 1969), p 492.
8. 2 Smith's Leading Cases (13th Edn), p 19.

For discussion of the doctrine of substantial performance see Cheshire and Fifoot *Law of Contract* (10th edn, 1981), p 479 et seq; Smith and Thomas *A Casebook on Contract* (7th edn, 1982), p 345 et seq. See also the Law Commission Working Paper No 65, 'Pecuniary Restitution on Breach of Contract' (1975).

Questions

1. Would the result of this case have been the same if the contractor had wished to remedy the defects but the defendant had denied him the opportunity, fearing that his apparent incompetence might only make things worse? Is there a risk that a consumer will be taken to have affirmed the contract if he allows a contractor an opportunity to rectify gross defects?

2. Suppose that in the above case the householder had paid the full cost of the installation in advance. Would he have recovered his prepayment in full or only some lesser sum? Is the overall position satisfactory?

Problem

Fangio owns an old Daimler car which has serious defects both in the engine and in the brakes. He takes it to Jeff's Garage for repair. The estimated cost of repair is £2,500 of which half is attributable to the engine and half to the brakes. Similarly half the overall cost is for labour charges and the other for parts. Jeff assures Fangio that 'the car will be in tip-top condition when I have finished with it'. Four weeks later Fangio collects the car and Jeff agrees to send on his account. After driving the car for some two days and 500 miles Fangio discovers that although the repair to the engine has been carried out satisfactorily the brakes are still dangerous since defective spare parts have been used. Jeff is pressing for payment.

Advise Fangio. What advice would you give if, on collecting the car, Fangio had settled the account by cheque which had not yet been presented for payment?

Reform of the law

As has been noted the English and Scottish Law Commissions have been asked to consider the undertakings as to quality and fitness in contracts for the supply of goods. Their terms of reference are set out above pp 74–75. It has been noted also that in their Working Paper No 85, 1983 the two Commissions concluded that 'the classification of the statutory implied terms as conditions or warranties is inappropriate and liable to produce unreasonable results' (see above p 13). A more flexible approach was preferred. Part IV of the Working Paper discussed the position with respect to contracts of sale. The following extracts point to some of the difficulties and to possible solutions.

Sale and Supply of Goods (1983) (Law Commission Working Paper No 85)

LAW REFORM PROPOSALS: CONTRACTS OF SALE

A. Content of the implied term as to quality

Requirements of the implied term
4.5 We have no doubt that the implied term as to quality should be expressed in such a way that it unambiguously covers all those minor defects which should constitute a breach of contract. The difficulty arises from the need to state in words what is the appropriate standard of quality which should be possessed by goods of every kind and description (excluding obvious defects and defects specifically drawn to the buyer's attention). 'Goods' includes an almost unimaginable range of items. It includes, for example, brand new and very old motor-cars, vegetables sold in the High Street, ships, aircraft, animals, children's toys, commodities such as iron ore, corn and wheat, consumer 'white goods' such as refrigerators and washing machines, building materials, works of art whether modern or antique and specialised artefacts involving complicated modern technology, such as computers.
4.6 Most of the criticisms of the present law . . . have concerned new consumer durables rather than goods supplied under commercial contracts or second-hand goods. We do not, however, think that it is practical to provide different standards of quality for different types of transaction, different types of goods or even different classes of buyer and seller. Goods do not fall into neat categories and the result of such categorisation would be a regime of great complexity in which arguments as to which category applied would become of major and recurring importance. We think that in principle the term should be the same for all types of goods and all types of transaction, both consumer and non-consumer, and should have the necessary flexibility built into its wording . . .

The Commissions then discuss the difficulty of finding a qualitative adjective which would be sufficiently flexible to indicate the appropriate standard by reference to which goods are to be judged. For example the adjectives 'good' or 'sound' would be inappropriate when applied to 'rejects' or 'seconds'. There are difficulties also with an alternative approach whereby the standard would be expressed as a quality which was 'fully acceptable to a reasonable buyer' who had full knowledge of the goods' condition, quality and characteristics. This standard of 'acceptability in all respects' (see para 4.10 of the Working Paper) might be considered artificial and difficult to apply. Having discussed the objections to this approach and the benefits and problems associated with using a neutral standard (such as 'proper' or 'appropriate') the Commissions list the various matters which might be relevant to the quality of the goods. This part of the discussion concludes:

What a new term might look like
4.24 In order to draw together the various elements in the above discussion and to make it easier for readers to assess the type of provision we have in mind, we set out below what it might look like. This is set out for purposes of consultation only and does not represent our concluded views. We have put the words 'proper quality' and 'acceptable quality in all respects' in brackets to indicate that we would particularly welcome views on which of these phrases is the more appropriate or whether another word or phrase would be preferable. It will be noted that the clause does not refer to 'state or condition' as aspects of quality. That is because section 61(1) of the 1979 Act already provides that 'quality', in relation to goods, includes their state or condition. The clause might look like this.
(1) Where the seller sells goods in the course of a business, there is an implied term that the goods supplied under the contract are of [proper quality] [acceptable quality in all respects] except that there is no such term—

   (a) as regards defects specifically drawn to the buyer's attention before the contract is made; or

   (b) if the buyer examines the goods before the contract is made, as regards defects which that examination ought to reveal.[1]

(2) For the purposes of paragraph (1) above 'quality' in relation to goods includes, where appropriate, the following matters:

   (a) fitness for the purpose or purposes for which goods of that kind are commonly bought;

   (b) appearance, finish, suitability for immediate use and freedom from minor defects;

   (c) safety;

   (d) durability;

and in determining whether goods supplied under a contract are of [proper quality] [acceptable quality in all respects] regard shall be had to any description applied to them, the price (if relevant) and all the other relevant circumstances.

1. These two exclusions already appear in s 14(2).

NOTES

1. In relation to the view expressed in para 4.6 above compare the definition of a 'consumer product' in, for example, the Saskatchewan Consumer Products Warranties Act 1977, s 2(e), above p 17. The same Act uses the expression 'acceptable quality' in formulating the warranty given by the retail seller to the consumer (see s 11(4)).

2. The above draft clause may be compared with the following provision from another major common law jurisdiction.

Uniform Commercial Code

§2–314. IMPLIED WARRANTY: MERCHANTABILITY; USAGE OF TRADE

(1) Unless excluded or modified (Section 2–316), a warranty that the goods shall be merchantable is implied in a contract for their sale if the seller is a merchant with respect to goods of that kind. Under this section the serving for value of food or drink to be consumed either on the premises or elsewhere is a sale.

(2) Goods to be merchantable must be at least such as

   (a) pass without objection in the trade under the contract description; and

   (b) in the case of fungible goods, are of fair average quality within the description; and

   (c) are fit for the ordinary purposes for which such goods are used; and

   (d) run, within the variations permitted by the agreement, of even kind, quality and quantity within each unit and among all units involved; and

   (e) are adequately contained, packaged, and labelled as the agreement may require; and

   (f) conform to the promises or affirmations of fact made on the container or label if any.

(3) Unles excluded or modified (Section 2–316) other implied warranties may arise from course of dealing or usage of trade.

3. For a reference to Art 2–314(2)(f) see above p 18.

4. The version recommended by the Ontario Law Reform Commission in its 'Report on Sale of Goods' (1979), pp 219–220 includes a provision whereby 'in the case of new goods, unless the circumstances indicate otherwise, that spare parts and repair facilities, if relevant, will be available for a reasonable period of time.' For further reference to such provisions see above p 83 et seq.

   In a later part of its Working Paper No 85 the Law Commissions discuss the question of remedies for breach of the implied terms, suggesting three possible schemes all of which recognise and encourage 'the reasonable use of cure [that is, repair or replacement] as a commonly practised solution to consumer disputes' (see para 4.37). The second scheme which is provisionally preferred is described as follows:

4.43 The second scheme of remedies which we put forward—and the scheme which we provisionally favour—is as follows: where the seller is in breach of one of the implied terms contained in sections 13 to 15 of the Sale of Goods Act the buyer should be entitled:

(a) to reject the goods outright and claim his money back (without any deduction being made for his use or possession of them) except where the seller can show that the nature and consequences of the breach are slight and in the circumstances it is reasonable that the buyer should be required to accept cure (ie repair or replacement of the goods);

(b) where cure (whether the buyer is required to accept it or, though not so bound, has requested it) is not effected satisfactorily and promptly, having regard to the nature of the breach, to reject the goods (and claim his money back as in (a) above);

(c) in all cases to claim damages.

4.44 The essential difference between this scheme and the first is that, under this scheme, the buyer can reject the goods, however slight the breach, if cure is not practicable or is not effected. Where one of the terms is broken, there would be no question of the buyer being restricted to a claim in damages.

4.45 Once again the reference to the slightness of the breach affirms the central role which is to be played by the buyer's right of rejection. Superimposed upon this right is a limited right to cure in favour of the seller. There will be cases where the buyer justifiably does not wish to submit to such a process because of the time it might take and the uncertainty it might create. Even where cure or replacement could be effected easily and quickly, there will be cases where a buyer has lost confidence in the seller or in the product and wishes to buy elsewhere or not buy at all. On the other hand, there may be cases (eg of complex products of a sort which often require adjustment soon after supply) where a refusal to accept cure is quite unreasonable. To give the seller a limited right to cure, placing the burden on him to show that rejection is unreasonable, seems to us to represent an acceptable balance between these interests. In considering reasonableness a court can taken into account such factors as the ease of cure, the likelihood of its proving effective, the time it would take, whether the contract itself involves a time factor, inconvenience caused to the buyer, and the uncertainty caused by loss of confidence in the supplier and in the goods. We do not, however, suggest that this scheme should be complicated by the formal articulation of such factors.

4.46 Cure must obviously be effected quickly; a buyer who receives defective goods is entitled to have satisfactory ones as near as possible to the original time of delivery, whether or not he can prove loss as a result of delayed cure. For present purposes we think that the concept is adequately expressed by the word 'promptly'. If the seller cannot cure the defect promptly or at all, the buyer's right of rejection becomes exercisable. This means that even if the defect is minor but it cannot be repaired the buyer will be entitled to reject the goods. In some cases this might seem to be a wholly unreasonable result at which to arrive. For example, the cigarette lighter in an expensive new car might be defective and yet many months' delay might be inevitable before the necessary spare part could be obtained from the manufacturer. Nevertheless we prefer such a result to the first regime of remedies under which the buyer may in some cases only have a right in damages. A decision of policy has to be taken on this issue and in our view it is necessary for the protection of consumer buyers that the ultimate sanction of rejection should always (subject to the acceptance rules) be available to them. If this were not so, we think that the consumer buyer's bargaining position would be seriously weakened vis-a-vis the seller. The risk that there will be some unreasonable buyers who insist on rejection where it seems harsh on the seller to allow it would have to be accepted, since the policy of the law here should, we think, be in favour of the buyer rather than the seller.

4.47 In other cases, where the seller has no right to impose cure on the buyer, the buyer can simply reject. We have considered whether in such cases the right should shift to the buyer, so that he is entitled to *demand* cure. We think however that this is not appropriate: such a right could be exercised unreasonably, and there will in any case be situations where cure is impossible or impracticable. However, it is obvious that any buyer can, and many buyers will, *request* cure; and we think that the formulation should take this into account and even encourage it. This generates two requirements. First, it must be provided that requests for cure and submission to attempts to cure, do not bar rejection: to this we return below.[1] Second, the sanction of rejection when cure fails must apply to cases where the buyer requests cure as well as to cases where he initially can be required to accept it. This is reflected in the formulation above.

1. See paras. 4.74 to 4.75, below.

Question

Do you consider that the above scheme represents an acceptable compromise between the respective interests of consumers and retailers?

NOTE

For a reference to Article 2–508 of the United States Uniform Commercial Code see above p 92. For further discussion of rejection, acceptance and cure see the Ontario Law Reform Commission 'Report on Sale of Goods' (1979) at p 444 et seq.

In discussing the loss of the right to reject, the Law Commissions provisionally conclude that 'as under the present law, rejection should be permitted only during a relatively short period after delivery' (para 4.72). The following additional comments and provisional recommendations are of particular interest in relation to consumer sales:

The statutory bar to rejection
4.73 The present provisions of the Sale of Goods Act dealing with the loss of the right to reject do not distinguish between consumers and commercial buyers. There are, however, two points in particular which should be borne in mind in relation to consumers. The first is that a consumer may be less vigilant than a commercial buyer in checking and scrutinising goods delivered to him, and indeed it may not be reasonable to expect the same standard of vigilance in both cases. Secondly the unravelling of commercial contracts is likely to be more complex than in the case of consumer contracts. This may suggest that the policy behind the acceptance rules should be applied less strictly to consumers than to commercial buyers . . .

(i) *Effect of request to cure or replace and of attempts to cure*
4.74 In our suggested regime of remedies for consumers we put forward a scheme whereby the seller had a limited right to cure defects in the goods.[1] But if such a scheme is to work successfully it must not be possible to argue that a request for cure or an agreement that cure should be attempted amounts to acceptance—whether as a species of implied intimation of acceptance, or as contributing to the running of the whole or part of a reasonable time (both of which bar rejection under the present section 35(1)). We think that this would be clear from any formulation of our suggested regime for rejection; but we also think that the point may well need attention again in connection with acceptance, in the interest of general clarity.

. . .

1. See para 4.43 to 4.48, above.

(iii) *Intimation of acceptance*

. . .

4.82 . . . We have already referred to the problems caused by so-called 'acceptance notes' which the buyer unwittingly signs, and which may contain a statement to the effect that he has examined the goods and has accepted them. It seems to us that a consumer, at any rate, should not be barred from rejection by the signature of such a document. A possible solution would be to prevent express acceptance from ever barring the right to reject in consumer transactions. Another solution would be to outlaw such acceptance notes unless, at least, the buyer has had an opportunity to inspect the goods. However, we do not consider that it would be sufficient simply to provide that 'acceptance notes' were ineffective. To do this would leave the problem of an oral statement to the same effect as a note. In our view the policy should be that a consumer cannot lose his right to reject . . . unless he has had a reasonable opportunity to examine the goods and that any purported exclusion or limitation of this right would be ineffective. We would not however suggest extending this protection to non-consumer buyers, who do not appear to us to need it. We invite comments.

(iv)   The lapse of a reasonable time
4.83   A further bar on the right to reject is created by the lapse of a reasonable time. It is generally thought that a reasonable time, in this context, means a fairly short period, but there is in fact little authority on the point . . . There is however one factor which is doubtless taken into account by the courts and which could perhaps be mentioned specifically in the legislation: the fact that on rejection the buyer is entitled to recover the whole price.
4.84   There are, however, two further matters which arise in relation to the 'reasonable' time. First, as we proposed in paragraph 4.74 above, time which is taken in negotiating or in effecting repair or replacement by the seller should be excluded from the calculation of a reasonable time. Secondly, we also think that a relevant factor should be whether any earlier defects had been notified to the seller but the buyer did not reject on account of them. This would put beyond doubt that the court may have regard to the history of the defects which appeared in the article and may take account of that history in considering what is a reasonable time. Such a provision should enable the court in the case of the so-called 'Friday car' to reach the conclusion that even though a considerable time had elapsed from delivery a reasonable time had still not elapsed having regard to the time taken in repairing and to the number of defects which had been notified to the seller during the period after delivery.

(v)   An act inconsistent with the ownership of the seller
4.85   Finally . . . we provisionally recommend that, even if retained in non-consumer transactions, the 'inconsistent act' rule should not apply to consumer sales; and that the only bars on the consumer's right of rejection, so long as the goods remain in substantially the same condition as when delivered, should be express acceptance after an opportunity to examine, and the lapse of a reasonable time . . .

The following extract is of interest as an example of a modern statutory provision which covers substantially the same ground as the Law Commission Working Paper with a similar emphasis on the importance of cure.

Saskatchewan Consumer Products Warranties Act 1977

20.   Remedies for breach of statutory or express warranties
(1)   Where there is a breach by a manufacturer or retail seller of a statutory warranty set out in section 11 or of an express warranty mentioned in section 8:
    (a)   and where the breach is remediable and not of a substantial character:
        (i)   the party in breach shall, within a reasonable period of time, make good the breach free of charge to the consumer but, where the breach has not been remedied within such reasonable period of time, the consumer shall be entitled to have the breach remedied elsewhere and to recover from the party in breach all reasonable costs incurred in having the breach remedied;
        (ii)   the consumer shall be entitled to recover damages for losses that he has suffered and that were reasonably foreseeable as liable to result from the breach regardless of whether the breach is remedied;
    (b)   and where the breach is of a substantial character or is not remediable, the consumer may, at his option, exercise the remedies under clause (a) or, subject to the provisions of subsections (2) and (3), he may reject the consumer product and, if he exercises his right to reject, he shall be entitled to recover the purchase price from the party in breach and to recover damages for any other losses that he has suffered and that were reasonably foreseeable as liable to result from the breach.
(2)   The consumer shall exercise his right to reject the consumer product under clause (b) of subsection (1) within a reasonable period of time as mentioned in subsection (3), except where the consumer delays the exercise of his right to reject because he has relied upon assurances made by the party in breach or his agent that the breach will be remedied when in fact the breach is not so remedied.
(3)   For the purposes of subsection (2), regardless of whether the right to reject is being exercised by the consumer or a person mentioned in subsection (1) of section 4, a reasonable period of time shall run from the time of delivery of the product to the consumer and shall consist of a period of time sufficient to permit such testing, trial or examination of the consumer product as may be normally required by consumers of that product and as may be appropriate considering the nature of the product, for the purpose of determining the conformity of the product to the obligations imposed under this Act on the party in breach.

. . .

22. Where party in breach must repair product

(1) Where the provisions of subsection (1) of section 20 apply so that the party in breach is required to repair the consumer product, the consumer shall return the product to the place of business of, or to any repair facility or service outlet operated by:

    (a) the retail seller, where he is the party in breach;

    (b) the manufacturer, where he is the party in breach; or

    (c) either of them, where both are in breach.

(2) No consumer shall be obliged to return the consumer product pursuant to subsection (1) to the party in breach if, by reason of the nature of the breach or the size, weight or method of attachment or installation of the product, it cannot be removed or transported without significant cost to the consumer: and in that event the party in breach shall collect and arrange for the transportation and return of the product at his own expense or shall cause the repair to be made at the site where the product is located.

(3) For the purposes of subclause (i) of clause (a) or subsection (1) of section 20, the reasonable period of time shall run from the time when the party in breach receives the consumer product but, where subsection (2) of this section applies, the reasonable period of time shall run from the time when the consumer advises the party in breach of the defect in the consumer product.

Turning to other contracts for the supply of goods the Law Commissions favour the adoption of the same implied terms as those applicable to contracts of sale. However the question of complete equivalence in remedies and the loss of the right to terminate the contract is more problematic as the following extracts from the Law Commission Working Paper No 85 indicate:

LAW REFORM PROPOSALS: OTHER CONTRACTS FOR THE SUPPLY OF GOODS

    . . .

B. Remedies for breach of the implied terms

    . . .

Consumer transactions

5.5 . . . We . . . propose that, subject to the two important qualifications which we discuss below, the scheme of remedies set out in paragraph 4.43 for breach of the implied terms should apply also to the other consumer contracts for the supply of goods.

5.6 The first qualification concerns the right of rejection. As far as contracts of sale are concerned, we have proposed that whenever the buyer is entitled to reject for breach of an implied term he should be entitled to claim his money back without any deduction being made for his use or possession of the goods.[1] This proposal would seem to accord with the present position in the law of sale, where the buyer will be unlikely to have had any significant use or possession of the goods before he loses his right to reject them.

5.7 In the other contracts for the supply of goods the innocent party may be entitled to terminate the contract and return the goods a considerable period after they have been delivered to him. Under English law he loses his right only if, with knowledge of the breach, he affirms the contract . . .

5.8 The question thus arises whether the innocent party in such contracts should, as in contracts of sale, automatically be entitled to recover all the money he has paid under the contract. As we noted in paragraphs 2.39 to 2.47, above there is uncertainty in English and Scots law as to whether in these circumstances the innocent party is so entitled; or whether a deduction should be made for his use or possession of the goods; or whether he is only entitled to damages. It would not therefore be satisfactory to leave this matter to the operation of the common law.

5.9 In our view it would be unreasonable to permit an innocent party under a contract for the supply of goods both to return them, even after a substantial period of time, and automatically to recover all the money he has paid under the contract. We provisionally recommend that, in view of the length of time during which the innocent party will in the majority of cases be entitled to return the goods, he should be entitled either to an action for damages or to recover the money he has paid under the contract subject to a deduction for his use and possession of the goods—whichever yields the greater sum. We invite comments as to whether this choice of remedies would be appropriate in this context.

5.10 The second qualification to the scheme of remedies proposed for breach of the implied terms in contracts of sale concerns the obligation to pay hire or hire-purchase instalments which fall due during any period when the goods are either being repaired or replaced. It may be argued that the suspension of the obligation would constitute both a negotiating weapon for the consumer and an incentive for the owner to effect the cure promptly and satisfactorily. It seems that the case for such a provision is stronger in the case of hire than hire-purchase since in the former the instalments are being paid only for the use of the goods and yet pending their repair or replacement the hirer has no use of them.[2] Although we have formed no firm views on this point, we provisionally propose that a hirer under a contract of hire should be under no legal obligation to continue to make payments whilst the goods are being repaired or replaced in accordance with our provisions as to cure set out above.[3]

5.11   The position is less straightforward in hire-purchase transactions. In such cases it is possible that any provision permitting the suspension of the payment of instalments might be used by hire-purchasers seeking an excuse to delay the obligation to make payment. In this situation goods might be returned not in order that they might be repaired but in order to suspend the obligation to pay instalments. Another problem would arise if any such suspension of payment were to necessitate a complex re-scheduling of the debt. Such calculations, if necessary, would increase the costs of administration which would probably be passed on to consumers. One way of avoiding this problem might be to provide that any instalments which were suspended (and unpaid) would become due on the date of the first instalment after cure had been satisfactorily carried out. Because of the potential problems, we make no provisional recommendation with regard to the suspension of instalments during the period of cure in hire-purchase contracts. We welcome comments on this question.

. . .

C.   The loss of the right to terminate the contract

5.15   In the light of our provisional recommendation that statutory rules, rather than the common law rules, should govern the loss of the right to reject in contracts of sale, the question now arises whether similar statutory rules should be applied to other contracts for the supply of goods. These other contracts include conditional sale contracts where the buyer deals as a consumer.[4] The question is, in short, whether the law should be altered so as to bring the other contracts in line with sale of goods contracts.

5.16   In many respects there is a special legal regime which applies to many[5] contracts of hire-purchase and conditional sale contracts. When he enters into such a contract the customer is generally contracting with a finance company whose activities were, in the past, considered to have many similarities with those of a money-lender. Special statutory provisions were enacted to protect the customer in these circumstances. For example, he is given a special right to terminate the contract upon payment of the appropriate proportion of the instalments.[6] He is permitted to cancel the contract in the early period without penalty.[7] There are special rules relating to the contract forms to be used[8] and to statements as to the cash price of the goods.[9] As a matter of the development of the law, the principles of 'acceptance' which applied to sale of goods contracts did not apply to other contracts for the supply of goods and this is now an accepted part of the special regime relating to hire-purchase and to consumer conditional sale contracts.[4] In our view, a very strong case would have to be made out for removing from the customer part of his existing legal rights. It is our provisional conclusion, on which we invite comments, that the law should remain as it is in relation to the other contracts for the supply of goods.

. . .

5.18   Under a contract of hire there is, essentially, a continuing relationship between the parties and the very nature of the contract itself seems, in our view, to lead to the conclusion that a continuing right to return the goods and bring the contract to an end is appropriate. When the hirer returns the goods to the owner, the latter will often be able to make further use of them by hiring them out again once they have been repaired. It is, perhaps, more difficult to justify a similar right in the case of a contract for work and materials. No difficulties in this area of the law appear to us to have arisen and, on balance, we think that the present position should be maintained.

. . .

1. See paras 4.39 and 4.66 to 4.72, above.
2. Under a hire-purchase contract the instalments are in effect partly going towards the acquisition of the title.
3. See paras. 4.43 to 4.48, above.
4. Supply of Goods (Implied Terms) Act 1973, s 14.
5. This regime applies to those contracts of hire-purchase and conditional sale agreements

which are within the scope of the Hire-Purchase Act 1965 and the Hire-Purchase (Scotland) Act 1965. In order to come within these Acts the total purchase price must not exceed £7,500: SI 1983/611.

6. Section 27, Hire-Purchase Act 1965 and s 27, Hire-Purchase (Scotland) Act 1965.

7. Section 11 to 15, Hire-Purchase Act 1965 and ss 11 to 15, Hire-Purchase (Scotland) Act 1965.

8. Section 7, Hire-Purchase Act 1965 and s 7, Hire-Purchase (Scotland) Act 1965.

9. Section 6, Hire-Purchase Act 1965 and s 6, Hire-Purchase (Scotland) Act 1965.

NOTE

The above provisional conclusions are qualified by a suggestion that in contracts of barter and 'trading-in' the statutory rules as to the loss of the right to reject should apply.

CHAPTER 3

Contracts for the supply of services

Introduction

Examples of consumer complaints involving the provision of services are noted in the extract from the Annual Report of the Director General of Fair Trading 1983 printed above p 1. Such contracts for the supply of services fall into two broad categories: (i) those including provision of goods or materials and (ii) those not including such provision. Frequently any given sector (for example home repairs and improvements or repairs and servicing to motor vehicles) will include both types of complaint. For instance a plumber may contract for the supply of work and materials, as when he installs a central heating system, or he may provide a service simpliciter, as when he unblocks a drain. Other contracts will fall predominantly or exclusively into what may be termed the 'pure services' category, notably those for the provision of holidays or entertainment, cleaning or film processing or a service of a professional nature.

In the last chapter reference was made to Part I of the Supply of Goods and Services Act 1982 and its statutory implied terms as to the quality of materials supplied: see above p 63. Part II of the 1982 Act also is important as introducing other implied terms into contracts for the supply of services. It originates in a National Consumer Council paper, 'Services Please' (1981) and is intended to be only an interim measure in as much as the Law Commission has been asked to consider, in the light of Part II of the 1982 Act:

> (a) what reforms, if any, should be made to the terms to be implied by law in a contract for the supply of a service; (b) whether, as against a consumer, the exclusion or restriction of the supplier's liability for breach of any of such implied terms should be prohibited; (c) the consequences of breach by a supplier of any such terms.

The relevant terms of Part II of the 1982 Act provide as follows:

Supply of Goods and Services Act 1982

PART II (SUPPLY OF SERVICES)

12. The contracts concerned
(1) In this Act a 'contract for the supply of a service' means, subject to subsection (2) below, a contract under which a person ('the supplier') agrees to carry out a service.
(2) For the purposes of this Act, a contract of service or apprenticeship is not a contract for the supply of a service.
(3) Subject to subsection (2) above, a contract is a contract for the supply of a service for the purposes of this Act whether or not goods are also—
    (a) transferred or to be transferred, or
    (b) bailed or to be bailed by way of hire,

under the contract, and whatever is the nature of the consideration for which the service is to be carried out.

(4) The Secretary of State may by order provide that one or more of sections 13 to 15 below shall not apply to services of a description specified in the order, and such an order may make different provision for different circumstances.

(5) The power to make an order under subsection (4) above shall be exercisable by statutory instrument subject to annulment in pursuance of a resolution of either House of Parliament.

13. Implied term about care and skill

In a contract for the supply of a service where the supplier is acting in the course of a business, there is an implied term that the supplier will carry out the service with reasonable care and skill.

14. Implied term about time for performance

(1) Where, under a contract for the supply of a service by a supplier acting in the course of a business, the time for the service to be carried out is not fixed by the contract, left to be fixed in a manner agreed by the contract or determined by the course of dealing between the parties, there is an implied term that the supplier will carry out the service within a reasonable time.

(2) What is a reasonable time is a question of fact.

15. Implied term about consideration

(1) Where, under a contract for the supply of a service, the consideration for the service is not determined by the contract, left to be determined in a manner agreed by the contract or determined by the course of dealing between the parties, there is an implied term that the party contracting with the supplier will pay a reasonable charge.

(2) What is a reasonable charge is a question of fact.

16. Exclusion of implied terms, etc

(1) Where a right, duty or liability would arise under a contract for the supply of a service by virtue of this Part of this Act, it may (subject to subsection (2) below and the 1977 Act) be negatived or varied by express agreement, or by the course of dealing between the parties, or by such usage as binds both parties to the contract.

(2) An express term does not negative a term implied by this Part of this Act unless inconsistent with it.

(3) Nothing in this Part of this Act prejudices—

    (a) any rule of law which imposes on the supplier a duty stricter than that imposed by section 13 or 14 above; or

    (b) subject to paragraph (a) above, any rule of law whereby any term not inconsistent with this Part of this Act is to be implied in a contract for the supply of a service.

(4) This Part of this Act has effect subject to any other enactment which defines or restricts the rights, duties or liabilities arising in connection with a service of any description.

The remainder of this chapter is divided into two parts. The first covers some points of general interest or application especially in relation to the 1982 Act. The second covers some particular sectors such as holidays and insurance which are of concern to consumers. Inevitably this second section is highly selective and many important sectors are not covered. For example professional services are touched on only briefly and we have not sought to cover such areas as the services provided by the nationalised industries. Further discussion may be found in both general and specialist works: see for example Harvey *The Law of Consumer Protection and Fair Trading* (2nd edn, 1982), p 162 et seq; Dugdale and Stanton *Professional Negligence* (1982); Palmer *Bailment* (1979): *Banking Services and the Consumer* (National Consumer Council, 1983); 'Home Improvements: A Report by the Director General of Fair Trading' (1983); 'Consumer Difficulties in the Used-Car Sector' (Office of Fair Trading, 1980); 'Car Servicing and Repairs: A Discussion Paper' (Office of Fair Trading, 1983); 'The Nationalised Industries' (National Consumer Council, 1981).

Some general considerations

As s 12(3) of the 1982 Act makes clear a contract for the provision of a service is within the scope of the Act whether or not it is accompanied by the transfer of property in or possession of goods. The reverse is true also, so that by s 1(3) of the Act, above p 63, 'a contract is a contract for the transfer of goods whether or not services are also provided'. So the service or 'work' element in a contract for work and materials is subject to the terms of sections 13–15, above. The same provisions may apply to contracts of hire which may have a servicing element also, notably in the case of television rentals and similar long-term arrangements. By s 12(4) and (5) of the Act the Secretary of State is empowered to exempt services from the obligations which would otherwise be imposed. As in the case of Part I of the Act the various obligations apply only where the service is supplied by way of contract and 'in the course of a business': see above pp 58 and 72. For comment and discussion see Murdoch, 'Contracts for the Supply of Services under the 1982 Act' (1983) Lloyd's Maritime and Commercial Law 652; Palmer (1983) 46 MLR 619, 627 et seq. See also the National Consumer Council report 'Service Please' (1981) on which Part II of the Act was based; Woodroffe *Goods and Services – The New Law* (1982); Lawson *The Supply of Goods and Services Act 1982* (1982).

FAULTY WORK

The following case serves to illustrate some of the distinctions which may result from treating obligations relating to work and materials as falling into separate categories.

Stewart v Reavell's Garage [1952] 1 All ER 1191, [1952] 2 QB 545, Queen's Bench Divisional Court

The plaintiff was a motorist with no technical knowledge who owned a 1929 Bentley speed model with powerful brakes. He took the car to the defendants, an experienced firm of car repairers, to have the brake-drums and brake-shoes re-lined. The re-lining of brake-drums was work of a specialist nature which the defendants did not undertake. The plaintiff preferred to have brake-drums made from an unwelded circle of metal and he suggested a particular firm. However the price they quoted was too high. A quotation was obtained from another firm, Re-Lined Brake-Drums, whom the defendants recommended and who duly did the work as sub-contractors of the defendants. Unknown to the plaintiff their method involved welding. The re-lined brake-drums were fitted and tested by the defendants. Soon after the plaintiff had taken delivery of the car he applied the brakes. There was a loud noise and vibration and the car swung to the right and hit a tree. The accident was caused by the lining on a front brake-drum coming away from the drum. It seems that such strip metal lining was unsatisfactory for brake-drums and moreover that the sub-contractors had not fitted it properly. There was no negligence on the defendants' part, whether in their choice of sub-contractors or in their fitting or testing of the drums.

Sellers J, having referred to the facts of the case, continued:

The somewhat difficult question of the liability of the defendants depends on the terms, expressed or implied, of the contract, and must be determined on their true effect. This was not a contract for the sale of goods to which s 14 of the Sale of Goods Act, 1893, could be applied. It was a contract for work done and materials supplied. Into that type of contract there may also be implied an absolute warranty of fitness for the intended purpose, if the circumstances show that the particular purpose is made known to the repairer and that the work of repair is of the type which the repairer holds himself out to perform either by himself or others as his sub-contractors, and, no less important, if the circumstances show that the purpose was made known so as to show that the customer relied on the repairer's skill and judgment in the matter.

I would adapt to this kind of contract some words of Lord Wright which state the standard of proof in a case of the sale of goods in *Cammell Laird & Co Ltd v Manganese Bronze & Brass Co Ltd* ([1934] AC 423). The standard of proof is equally applicable to the present case. Such a reliance must be affirmatively shown. The customer must bring home to the mind of the repairer that he is relying on him in such a way that the repairer can be taken to have contracted on that footing. The reliance is to be the basis of a contractual obligation. There is a passage in the judgment of Du Parcq J, in *G H Myers & Co v Brent Cross Service Co*, which provides a concise statement of the law applicable ([1934] 1 KB 55):

> '. . . I think that the true view is that a person contracting to do work and supply materials warrants that the materials which he uses will be of good quality and reasonably fit for the purpose for which he is using them, unless the circumstances of the contract are such as to exclude any such warranty. There may be circumstances which would clearly exclude it. A man goes to a repairer and says: "Repair my car; get the parts from the makers of the car and fit them". In such a case it is made plain that the person ordering the repairs is not relying upon any warranty except that the parts used will be parts ordered and obtained from the makers. On the other hand, if he says "Do this work, fit any necessary parts", then he is in no way limiting the person doing the repair work, and the person doing the repair work is, in my view, liable if there is any defect in the materials supplied, even if it was one which reasonable care could not have discovered.'

The present case does not fall precisely under either of the classes the learned judge enumerated. If the plaintiff's first suggestion had been accepted and those sub-contractors had done the work, I think it would have beeen very much the same as saying: 'Get the parts from the makers of the car' and the facts would have negatived any reliance by the plaintiff on the defendants' skill and judgment in respect of the lining to the brake-drums. The particular purpose of the work which the plaintiff contracted to have done was obvious. It was the very object of the arrangement, namely, to be provided with an efficient braking system for his Bentley car, which was a car specially designed for speed, and, therefore, required a braking system adequate for such speeds as were in contemplation. The size and type of the drums themselves indicated a powerful braking system. The question arises whether this purpose, made known, as it was, to the defendants, was made known to them so as to show that the plaintiff relied on their skill and judgment. I find that the effect of what was said and done when the parties entered into the contract was that the plaintiff did rely on the defendants as experienced repairers to repair the brakes in a suitable and efficient manner, and it was left to them to obtain suitable sub-contractors to do the lining of the drums and to arrange for a suitable type of drum lining to be fitted. The plaintiff's original request for a cast-iron sleeve—that is a sleeve without a weld—was not carried out. The defendants and not the plaintiff substituted for that a strip-metal sleeve with a weld and, although some mention of the Re-Lined Brake-Drums, Ltd's quotation was made known to the plaintiff, more particularly as to price, he was not informed that this sleeve involved a weld. Once the defendants departed from the plaintiff's suggestion of a cast-iron sleeve, the type of lining was a matter within their province as repairers. It was their duty, in the circumstances, to provide good workmanship, materials of good quality, and a braking system reasonably fit for its purpose, and they failed to do so by reason of the faulty off-side front brake-drum lining. In fact, though unwittingly, the defendants handed over to the plaintiff a highly dangerous vehicle. The faulty lining caused the accident and the damage to the plaintiff's car, and the plaintiff is, therefore, entitled to recover damages in this action.

Learned counsel for the defendants sought to apply to this case the reasoning of Tucker LJ, in *Edwards v Newland* ([1950] 1 All ER 1080), and to allege that this was a complex contract where the defendants would be liable for such work as they did themselves if it were faulty, but with regard to work which it was known, indeed intended, would be sub-contracted, they were only under a duty to take reasonable care to employ suitable sub-contractors and were not to be liable for their default and were entitled to assume without further detailed examination that their work would be satisfactory. *Edwards v Newland* was a case of the storage of furniture for reward, and the furniture was stored elsewhere than in the defendant's premises without the knowledge of the plaintiff, the bailor and owner of the furniture. As the defendant had never fulfilled his obligation to be a bailee for storage, he was held to have been in breach of his contract ab initio. I do not find it possible to apply similar considerations to the facts of this case which are so essentially different. I would add that I have considered also the other authorities referred to on behalf of the defendants, but I do not regard them as sufficiently relevant to call for further examination.

Judgment for plaintiff for £283 2s 4d damages, less an amount set off in respect of work done. Counterclaim dismissed.

NOTES

1. For the potential liability of the sub-contractor to the plaintiff where goods are dangerous or simply defective see below Ch 4 and in particular *Junior Books Ltd v Veitchi Co Ltd* [1983] AC 520, [1982] 3 All ER 201, HL, below p 168 et seq.
2. It seems that in *Stewart v Reavell's Garage* the source of the problem with the brakes was two-fold: (i) the choice of an unsatisfactory material as a lining and (ii) the fact that the fitting was done incorrectly.

Questions

1. In such cases precisely what are the respective spheres of application of ss 4 (above p 64) and 13 of the 1982 Act?
2. Will 'goods supplied under the contract' be 'reasonably fit for that purpose' within s 4(5) of the Act or of merchantable quality within s 4(9) if they are sound and in no way defective but fitted incorrectly?
3. Suppose that Bodgit Plumbers have contracted with Greenpeace to service and maintain her central heating system and that the contract provides for an annual visit, with Greenpeace paying the cost of any replacement parts which may be needed. What is the source and nature of Bodgit's obligations under the 1982 Act when it causes damage to Greenpeace's property by (i) fitting a faulty replacement part correctly; (ii) fitting a non-faulty replacement part incorrectly; (iii) making an incorrect adjustment to an existing part?

DELAYS

Delays in carrying out servicing, repairs and building work (including double-glazing) are discussed in 'Simple Justice', pp 13–17 especially, from which it appears that problems are widespread and a major source of dissatisfaction. The National Consumer Council refers to two aspects of the problem at p 13 of the above paper:

> Work started late or performed slowly can cause as many problems as work done badly. Complaints about the time element in a service fall into two categories. There are those cases where a date for the commencement or completion of the work has been agreed between both parties and subsequently ignored by the contractor. And there are others—more common in our experience—where no time limit is agreed but the consumer thinks the contractor has taken unreasonably long to perform the service.

Section 14 of the 1982 Act, above p 115, restates the common law applicable to the latter situation. The following case provides an example of a delay which the Court of Appeal agreed was unreasonable in the circumstances. It also raises a further point of general interest and application.

Charnock v Liverpool Corpn [1968] 3 All ER 473, [1968] 1 WLR 1498, Court of Appeal

The plaintiff owned a car which was involved in a collision caused by negligence on the part of the driver of the other vehicle. He took it to the defendant repairers where he met his insurers' assessor and an estimate was agreed. A reasonable time for carrying out the repairs was at most five weeks. The repairers took eight weeks to complete the work, having given priority to warranty repairs on cars made by the Rootes Group. The plaintiff, who had not been warned of the delay, claimed as damages the cost of hiring a replacement car over this additional three-week period. The Presiding Judge of the Court of Passage at Liverpool awarded the plaintiff £53 damages and the defendant repairers now appealed to the Court of Appeal.

Harman LJ, having referred to the facts of the case, continued:

The argument before us has been that there is a contract thus formed between the insurance company and the repairers to repair the car for the money stated and no other contract at all. It is said that the plaintiff who took the car in did not make any contract: he was merely a bystander and in the hands of the insurance company and that as far as he was concerned he had nothing to say, neither to make nor meddle in the matter. . . .

'Oh', say the repairers, 'there was no contract between us and the plaintiff: our only contract was to do the work for the insurance company for a sum of money and to do it as far as they were concerned reasonably well and within a reasonable time: but the plaintiff cannot take advantage of that because he is a stranger to that contract and he has made no contract himself at all.'

I must confess that when I first heard that proposition put it seemed to me that in spite of the strenuous advocacy of counsel for the repairers it was 'all my eye', if I may use a vulgar phrase, and that it would not do at all, and that when a man takes his car into a garage and asks them to repair it, as is done every day, and the garage agrees to do so, there a contract is made to do the repairs with reasonable skill and in a reasonable time. The fact that the insurance company will indemnify the owner is well known in all insurance cases to both parties. The practice has grown up that the insurance company shall agree the sum for which they will stand surety and a contract is very often made by the repairer with the insurance company. Let it be so in this case. That does not in my view at all rule out the existence of a contract between the person who owns the car and the repairers. The owner takes the car in to the repairers and he asks them to repair it, at whatever cost the insurance company will be willing to go to, and everybody knows that the insurance company will within that limit pay. Whether there is any obligation on the owner himself to pay if the insurance company does not is another matter; but I cannot see why there is as regards the owner not a contract on which the repairers are liable first if they do not do the work with reasonable skill and secondly if they do not do it within a reasonable time; and it is on that contract that the present case turns.

The court I think was inclined to take the view that the judge—who held that there were two contracts, one between the insurers and the repairers and one between the plaintiff and the repairers—was clearly right; but counsel for the repairers has held over us two cases in the Court of Appeal, not cited to the judge, which he says make it impossible that we should decide in that way. Those two cases were both cases arising out of the collapse of the same insurance company. The insurance company collapsed, did not pay 6d in the pound, and the repairers who had done the work in each case then sued the owners of the cars. The Court of Appeal in each case held that there was no liability on the owners. The only point at which they looked was whether there was a liability to pay for the repairs in question and they held that on the facts that were before them there was not in either case such a liability; but they did not, I think, hold that there was no contract at all—only that there was no contract in respect of the sum due for repairs. Though there is a sort of family resemblance between those two cases and this, I think they are quite clearly distinguishable. It seems to me that it is quite reasonable to leave standing the view that there was a contract between the repairers and the insurance company and that the only person liable to pay on that was the insurance company, they having chosen to make the contract as principals, and that the only thing that the Court of Appeal decided was that they did not make it as agents so as to bring in the owners as disclosed principals liable on the agency contract.

. . . I would therefore for my part affirm the judge's decision and dismiss this appeal.

Salmon LJ: I agree. . . . I have no doubt at all, on the facts of the present case, that the judge's finding that there were in fact two contracts is unassailable. In my view there was a clear contract to be inferred from the facts between the repairers and the plaintiff car owner that in consideration of the plaintiff leaving his car with the repairers for repair the repairers would carry out the repairs with reasonable expedition and care, and that they would be paid by the insurance company. No doubt on the documents here the repairers took the precaution of entering into another contract with the insurers that the insurers would pay; and if they had not paid the insurers could have been sued; but this does not relieve the repairers from their obligations to the car owner. So much for the first point.

The second point is even shorter. The judge found that the repairers broke their contract with the plaintiff in that they failed to repair the car within a reasonable time. There was ample evidence before him that a reasonable time for carrying out these repairs should not have exceeded five weeks. Since the repairers in fact took eight weeks, they were in breach of their contract. Counsel for the repairers has argued vigorously that the finding that the work was not done within a reasonable time is not supportable; but I confess that I am quite unable to detect any real substance in the argument. The reason why the repairers were unable to do the work within a reasonable time, namely five weeks, was that when they took on the work their labour force was very much under strength. Moreover the holiday period was approaching; and, further, and perhaps most importantly, they had an arrangement (which no doubt was commercially of great value to them) with the Rootes Group that any warranty work should be given precedence. Warranty work, as the phrase was used in this case, related to cases in which cars which had been sold developed some fault in breach of the warranty given to the car owner: the car was then brought in and repaired so that it should comply with the warranty. As this arrangement with the Rootes Group was of great commercial value to these garage owners, they gave precedence to any warranty work and let any work such as the work for the present plaintiff wait. I cannot see for myself how the fact that they chose to take on the work knowing of the three factors to which I have referred can possibly entitle them to say 'Well, we could have done it within five weeks' (which is generally recognised in the trade as a reasonable time in which to perform the work) 'but for these three factors which prevented us from doing so'. . . . I agree that the appeal should be dismissed.

[**Winn, LJ** agreed.] *Appeal dismissed.*

NOTE

The cases to which Harman LJ referred were *Godfrey Davis Ltd v Culling and Hecht* [1962] 2 Lloyd's Rep 349 and *Cooter & Green Ltd v Tyrrell* [1962] 2 Lloyd's Rep 377, CA.

Questions

1. If an insurance company has contracted with a repairer to pay the full cost of repair, what consideration does the car owner furnish to support the repairer's contractual obligations to do the work in a reasonable time etc? Presumably the question does not arise if, as is usually the case, the car owner's insurance policy is subject to an excess which he pays to the repairer directly.

2. If a consumer has contracted with a specialist firm for the supply and installation of, for example, bedroom cupboards of a standard size, what would be a reasonable time for the completion of the work:
(i) ten days, (ii) three weeks, (iii) two months or (iv) some longer period?

Is this a matter which is governed by the delay which is typical in the trade or by the expectations of a reasonable consumer? At what point should one feel confident in advising a consumer to cancel such a contract and engage another supplier? What are the risks of purporting to cancel before 'a reasonable time' has passed?

PROBLEMS OF COST

Some of the problems associated with the cost of services are discussed in the following extract:

Services and the law: a consumer view (National Consumer Council, 1981) (p 17 et seq)

When shoppers make a purchase they nearly always know the price in advance. If they are unhappy about the price being asked they do not buy the goods. The same is true of some types of service. Dry cleaners, shoe repairers, furniture removers and hairdressers usually indicate their prices for the job they are asked to do, enabling consumers to shop around until they find a price which suits them.

However, with some jobs the contractor may be reluctant to give a firm quotation because he has little idea until he starts work of what the job will entail. This is true of car and electrical repairs, for example. A consumer who has been given no idea of what the price will be is clearly in a very vulnerable position. And those who need work carried out in an emergency are especially at risk, as the Price Commission pointed out in its 1977 report on call-out charges. With reference to 24-hour emergency plumbers it stated: 'In the worst cases, particularly in an emergency where for example leaking water is harming furnishings and decorations, the total bill may be as high as an irresponsible plumber thinks he can get away with.' The Commission found examples of householders who had been charged £26 for a replacement tap washer and £120 for fitting twenty feet of copper pipe in four hours—and these, it should be remembered, were 1974–76 prices.

. . .

Even if the consumer suspects that the charge is exorbitant, it takes courage to refuse to pay for work already done. Once the job is completed he is likely to pay the bill either because he wants his goods back (as in the case of cars and small electrical repairs) or because he fears retaliatory action by the contractor, in the form of a county court summons or worse.

. . .

The OFT [the Office of Fair Trading] encourages members of trade associations to offer customers an estimate of the likely cost of work wherever possible so that they can shop around before choosing a contractor. But when an estimate is only a rough guide, the contractor who discovers that the job is more complicated than he originally thought can charge more. Some have been known to take advantage of this fact.

Mr W was given a verbal estimate of £200 by an emergency plumbing service to unblock a drain. When the work was completed five hours later the firm demanded £426.75. Mr W paid but alleged that the price was unreasonable, took the firm to court and won back £200. (*Which?* Personal Service)

. . .

Mr C, an ex-policeman, authorised a repair to his car which, he was told, would cost in the region of £300. On collecting the vehicle he was handed a bill for £678. He refused to pay and was sued by the garage. The court ordered him to pay £375 for the work. (*Which?* Personal Service)

. . .

So far we have considered cases where a charge for the work was not fixed in advance. But what of consumers who do agree a price with a contractor, only to discover later that this was extortionate? This might apply where it is impractical for consumers to collect comparison quotations in advance. Most domestic appliance repairers, for example, levy a call-out charge simply for giving an estimate. A consumer who has already paid £12 or more for a diagnosis is likely to accept the engineer's quotation, however high.

. . .

Garages handling breakdown and serious crash repairs are also in a strong position because they know customers may be unable to compare prices. The July 1980 issue of the AA magazine *Drive* contained evidence of extortionate prices charged by some garages for crash repairs. The magazine took a crashed Ford Fiesta to twenty garages and asked for estimates for repair. These ranged from £276 plus parts to £2,225 (the true cost was estimated by the Motor Insurance Research Centre at around £800). Even among members of the Vehicle Builders and Repairers Association—which has negotiated a code of practice with the OFT—there was up to 100 per cent difference in labour charges. 'The vehicle accident repair trade is full of inconsistencies, incompetence and irregularities,' the report concluded.

NOTES

1. Where a service is supplied under circumstances which fall within section 15 of the 1982 Act, above p 115, the consumer is obliged to pay only a 'reasonable charge'.

2. It is generally agreed that a 'quotation' indicates a fixed price which cannot be exceeded even when unexpected difficulties are encountered whereas the use of the word 'estimate' allows for a margin.

Questions

1. What are the factors which may fairly be taken into account in deciding the extent, if any, to which an account may exceed an estimate?

2. Is it possible to say that there is a maximum percentage increase (if only in theory) which should never be exceeded or does it depend also on the sums of money involved? Other things being equal which is likely to be the more acceptable in a consumer contract (i) a bill for £4.00 compared with an estimate of £2.50 or (ii) a bill for £1,500 compared with an estimate of £1,000? Is a consumer entitled to insist on paying a sum which is *less* than the estimate if the work proves to be easier or quicker than expected?

3. Protection against extortionate credit bargains is now provided by the Consumer Credit Act 1974, ss 137–140, below p 219. Is there any reason of principle or insuperable practical difficulty to prevent a similar measure of protection being extended to persons who pay extortionate cash prices? Is it not likely that some of the most vulnerable members of society, notably the elderly, will save money and pay cash rather than buy on credit? See generally below p 265 et seq for discussion of protection against unjust contract terms.

4. Consider the following case.

Vulnerable lives in a cottage which is in need of some modernisation. She returns home one evening to find that an unlagged pipe has burst, causing water to pour down from the attic. She contacts Shark, a plumber, who comes over immediately, turns off the water at the mains and fixes the burst joint. There has been no discussion of the price for the work which takes about half an hour including travelling time. He has now presented a bill for £125.

The burst pipe necessitates extensive redecoration of the main rooms of the cottage and Vulnerable accepts a quotation of £1,200 from Renoir, a decorator. Renoir has now explained that he has miscalculated the cost of the materials involved. He has presented a bill for £1,700.

Vulnerable's septic tank is in need of renewal. She obtains an estimate of £3,200 from Drainaway for fitting a new tank and associated piping. Of this £1,700 is the cost of the tank itself. When he begins the work Drainaway discovers that Vulnerable's garden is built on rock. Instead of the work taking him two days as he had calculated it takes him four. Moreover he has to hire specialist excavating machinery at an additional cost of £200. He wishes to know what price he may legitimately charge.

Advise Vulnerable and Drainway.

STRICTER CONTRACTUAL OBLIGATIONS

As s 16(3)(a) of the 1982 Act makes clear the implied obligations of s 13 of the Act operate without prejudice to any stricter obligations which have been undertaken. The following commercial case provides a good example of a situation in which such an obligation was held to have arisen.

Greaves & Co (Contractors) Ltd v Baynham Meikle & Partners [1975] 3 All ER 99, [1975] 1 WLR 1095, Court of Appeal
Lord Denning MR. This case arises out of a new kind of building contract called a 'package deal'. The building owners were Alexander Duckham & Co Ltd. They wanted a new factory, warehouse and offices to be constructed at Aldridge in Staffordshire. The warehouse was needed as a store in which barrels of oil could be kept until they were needed and despatched, and in which they could be moved safely from one point to another. The 'package deal' meant that the building owners did not employ their own architects or engineers. They employed one firm of contractors, the plaintiffs, to do everything for them. It was the task of the contractors not only to provide the labour and materials in the usual way but also to employ the architects and engineers as sub-contractors. The contractors were to do everything as a 'package deal' for the owners.

Now, as between the owners and the contractors, it is plain that the owners made known to the contractors the purpose for which the building was required, so as to show that they relied on the contractors' skill and judgment. It was therefore the duty of the contractors to see that the finished work was reasonably fit for the purpose for which they knew it was required. It was not merely an obligation to use reasonable care. The contractors were obliged to ensure that the finished work was reasonably fit for the purpose. That appears from the recent cases in which a man employs a contractor to build a house: *Miller v Cannon Hill Estates Ltd*[1]; *Hancock v B W Brazier (Anerley) Ltd*[2]. It is a term implied by law that the builder will do his work in a good and workmanlike manner; that he will supply good and proper materials; and it will be reasonably fit for human habitation. Similarly in this case the contractors undertook an obligation towards the owners that the warehouse should be reasonably fit for the purpose for which, they knew it was required, that is as a store in which to keep and move barrels of oil. In order to get the warehouse built, the contractors found they needed expert skilled assistance, particularly in regard to the structural steel work. The warehouse was to be built according to a new system which was just coming into use. It was a composite construction system in structural steel and concrete. First there would be a steel frame erected to carry the walls and floors. Next they would get planks made of pre-cast concrete and bring them on to the site. They would place these planks in position along the floors, etc. Then, in order to bind those planks firmly together, they would pour ready-mixed concrete in and above the planks, thus forming a solid floor. This method of construction had recently been introduced into use in England. It is governed by the British Standard Code of Practice 1965, CP 117.

The contractors employed a firm of experts, the defendants, Messrs Baynham Meikle and Partners, structural engineers, to design the structure of the building and, in particular, the first floor of it. There were discussions with them about it. It was made known to them—and this is important—that the floors had to take the weight of stacker trucks—sometimes called fork-lift trucks. These were to run to and fro over the floors carrying the drums of oil. The structural engineers, Baynham Meikle, were given the task of designing the floors for that purpose.

Mr Baynham made his designs; the warehouse was built and put into use. It was used for the transport of these oil drums with the stacker trucks. But, after a little time, there was a lot of trouble. The floors began to crack. The men took strong objection to working there. They thought it was dangerous. The cracks seemed to be getting worse. So much so that the experts were called in. Attempts were made to cure the trouble, but without success. The position now is that the warehouse is of very limited use. It is anticipated that remedial works will have to take place at great expense. The damages are said to come to £100,000.

What was the cause of this cracking of the floors? The structural engineers said that it was due to the shrinkage of the concrete for which they were not responsible. There was nothing wrong, they said, with the design which they produced. But the judge did not accept that view. He found[3] that the majority of the cracks were caused by vibration and not by shrinkage. He held[4] that the floors were not designed with sufficient strength to withstand the vibration which was produced by the stacker trucks.

On those findings the first question is: what was the duty of the structural engineers towards the contractors? The judge found[4] that there was an implied term that the design should be fit for the use of loaded stacker trucks; and that it was broken. Alternatively, that the structural engineers owed a duty of care in their design, which was a higher duty than the law in general imposes on a professional man; and that there was a breach of that duty.

To resolve this question, it is necessary to distinguish between a term which is implied by law and a term which is implied in fact. A term implied by law is said to rest on the *presumed* intention of both parties; whereas, a term implied in fact rests on their *actual* intention.

It has often been stated that the law will only imply a term when it is reasonable and necessary to do so in order to give business efficacy to the transaction; and, indeed, so obvious that both parties must have intended it. But those statements must be taken with considerable qualification. In the great majority of cases it is no use looking for the intention of both parties. If you asked the parties what they intended, they would say that they never gave it a thought; or, if they did, the one would say that he intended something different from the other. So the courts imply—or, as I would say, impose—a term such as is just and reasonable in the circumstances. Take some of the most familiar of implied terms in the authorities cited to us. Such as the implied condition of fitness on a sale of goods at first implied by the common law and afterwards embodied in the Sale of Goods Act 1893. Or the implied warranty of fitness on a contract for work and materials: *Young & Marten Ltd v McManus Childs Ltd*[5]. Or the implied warranty that a house should be reasonably fit for human habitation: see *Hancock v B W Brazier*[2]. And dozens of other implied terms. If you should read the discussions in the cases, you will find that the judges are not looking for the intention of both parties; nor are they considering what the parties would answer to an officious bystander. They are only seeking to do what is 'in all the circumstances reasonable'. That is how Lord Reid put it in *Young & Marten Ltd v McManus Childs Ltd*[6]; and Lord Upjohn[7] said quite clearly that the implied warranty is 'imposed by law'.

Apply this to the employment of a professional man. The law does not usually imply a warranty that he will achieve the desired result, but only a term that he will use reasonable care and skill. The surgeon does not warrant that he will cure the patient. Nor does the solicitor warrant that he will win the case. But, when a dentist agrees to make a set of false teeth for a patient, there is an implied warranty that they will fit his gums: see *Samuels v Davis*[8].

What then is the position when an architect or an engineer is employed to design a house or a bridge? Is he under an implied warranty that, if the work is carried out to his design, it will be reasonably fit for the purpose? Or is he only under a duty to use reasonable care and skill? This question may require to be answered some day as a matter of law. But in the present case I do not think we need answer it. For the evidence shows that both parties were of one mind on the matter. Their common intention was that the engineer should design a warehouse which would be fit for the purpose for which it was required. That common intention gives rise to a term implied *in fact*. . . .

In the light of that evidence it seems to me that there was implied in fact a term that, if the work was completed in accordance with the design, it would be reasonably fit for the use of loaded stacker trucks. The engineers failed to make such a design and are, therefore, liable.

If there was, however, no such absolute warranty of fitness, but only an obligation to use reasonable care and skill, the question arises: what is the degree of care required? The judge said[4]:

> 'In the special circumstances of this case, by his knowledge of the requirement and the warning about vibration, it can be said that there was a higher duty imposed on him than the law in general imposes on a medical or other professional man.'

I do not think that was quite accurate. It seems to me that in the ordinary employment of a professional man, whether it is a medical man, a lawyer, or an accountant, an architect or an engineer, his duty is to use reasonable care and skill in the course of his employment. The extent of this duty was described by McNair J in *Bolam v Friern Hospital Management Committee*[9], approved by the Privy Council in *Chin Keow v Government of Malaysia*[10]:

'. . . where you get a situation which involves the use of some special skill or competence, then the test whether there has been negligence or not is not the test of the man on the top of a Clapham omnibus, because he has not got this special skill. The test is the standard of the ordinary skilled man exercising and professing to have that special skill . . . It is well-established law that it is sufficient if he exercises the ordinary skill of an ordinary competent man exercising that particular art.'

In applying that test, it must be remembered that the measures to be taken by a professional man depend on the circumstances of the case. Although the judge talked about a 'higher duty'[4], I feel sure that what he meant was that in the circumstances of this case special steps were necessary in order to fulfil the duty of care: see *Readhead v Midland Rly Co*[11]. In this case a new mode of construction was to be employed. The Council of British Standards Institution had issued a circular which contained this note:

'The designer should satisfy himself that no undesirable vibrations can be caused by the imposed loading. Serious vibrations may result when dynamic forces are applied at a frequency near to one of the natural frequencies of the members.'

Mr Baynham was aware of that note but he read it as a warning against resonances, i e rhythmic impulses, and not as a warning against vibrations in general. So he did not take measures to deal with the random impulses of stacker trucks. There was evidence, too, that other competent designers might have done the same as Mr Baynham. On that ground the judge seems to have thought that Mr Baynham had not failed in the ordinary duty of care. But that does not excuse him. Other designers might have fallen short too. It is for the judge to set the standard of what a competent designer would do. And the judge, in the next breath, used words which seem to me to be a finding that Mr Baynham did fail. It is a key passage[3];

'I do, however, find that he knew, or ought to have known, that the purpose of the floor was safely to carry heavily laden trucks and that he was warned about the dangers of vibration and did not take these matters sufficiently into account. The design was inadequate for the purpose.'

It seems to me that that means that Mr Baynham did not take the matters sufficiently into account which he ought to have done. That amounts to a finding of breach of the duty to use reasonable care and skill. On each of the grounds, therefore, I think the contractors are entitled to succeed. They are entitled to a declaration of liability and indemnity. I would, accordingly, dismiss the appeal.

[**Browne** and **Geoffrey Lane** LJJ agreed.] *Appeal dismissed.*

1. [1931] 2 KB 113, [1931] All ER Rep 93.
2. [1966] 2 All ER 901, [1966] 1 WLR 1317.
3. [1974] 3 All ER 666 at 672, [1974] 1 WLR 1261 at 1268.
4. [1974] 3 All ER at 672, [1974] 1 WLR at 1269.
5. [1968] 2 All ER 1169, [1969] 1 AC 454.
6. [1968] 2 All ER at 1171, 1172, [1969] 1 AC at 465, 466.
7. [1968] 2 All ER at 1175, [1969] 1 AC at 471.
8. [1943] 2 All ER 3, [1943] 1 KB 526.
9. [1957] 2 All ER 118 at 121, [1957] 1 WLR 582 at 586.
10. [1967] 1 WLR 813.
11. (1869) LR 4 QB 379 at 393, [1861–73] All ER Rep 30 at 39.

NOTES

1. For a further case involving an obligation stricter than the exercising of reasonable care see *G K Serigraphics (a firm) v Dispro Ltd* (1980) CA (available on Lexis) cited by Palmer (1983) 46 MLR 619. In this case

Arnolds required some educational material which the respondents contracted to supply. By a separate contract with the respondents the appellants undertook to carry out the process of lamination whereby a laminated surface would be made to adhere to printed boards. The lamination was not carried out successfully and the work had to be done again by a different contractor. In resultant proceedings Cumming-Bruce LJ held that an 'absolute obligation' had been undertaken. Griffiths LJ with whom O'Connor LJ agreed, reached the following conclusion.

I agree with the judge that the appellants are liable to pay damages to the respondents, but I arrive at my conclusion by a different route to that taken by the judge. The judge held the appellants liable upon the ground that the contract was subject to an implied term that the film would adhere securely to the boards and to a further implied term that the bulk of the lamination would be free from any defect rendering it unmerchantable.

In my judgment, this case can be solved without recourse to any implied term in the contract. The appellants failed to perform that which they had contracted to do: the very essence of lamination is the bonding of the transparent protective film and this they failed to achieve. Accordingly, for this failure to perform their contract they are liable in damages unless they can point to a term in the contract that exonerates them from that liability. As their breach goes to the root of the contractual obligation, a term excluding their liability would have to be very clearly expressed indeed.

Mr Englehart, in an attractively presented argument, has sought to escape from this view of the contract by submitting that the appellants' obligation was not to laminate the boards but to use all reasonable skill and care in the lamination process and to use materials of merchantable quality and reasonably fit for the purpose. If this is right it would place customers at a grave disadvantage, for the burden would be upon the customer in a case such as this to point to the fault that caused the failure of the lamination. Lamination is a skilled and a technical process. The customer does not know what materials are used, the customer does not know the processes involved, and it would be wholly unreasonable, in the absence of any express term in the contract, to saddle the customer with a burden that would be so difficult to discharge. The law certainly ought not to imply a term into this contract limiting the obligation of the laminator in the way suggested by Mr Englehart.

2. The Australian Trade Practices Act 1974 contains the following provision which is of general application:

74. (1) In every contract for the supply by a corporation in the course of a business of services to a consumer there is an implied warranty that the services will be rendered with due care and skill and that any materials supplied in connexion with those services will be reasonably fit for the purpose for which they are supplied.
(2) Where a corporation supplies services to a consumer in the course of a business and the consumer, expressly or by implication, makes known to the corporation any particular purpose for which the services are required or the result that he desires the services to achieve, there is an implied warranty that the services supplied under the contract for the supply of the services and any materials supplied in connexion with those services will be reasonably fit for that purpose or are of such a nature and quality that they might reasonably be expected to achieve that result, except where the circumstances show that the consumer does not rely, or that it is unreasonable for him to rely, on the corporation's skill or judgment.
(3) In this section, 'services' means services by way of—

    (a) the construction, maintenance, repair, treatment, processing, cleaning or alteration of goods or of fixtures on land;
    (b) the alteration of the physical state of land; or
    (c) the transportation of goods otherwise than for the purposes of a business, trade, profession or occupation carried on or engaged in by the person for whom the goods are transported.

3. For the potential criminal liability which may be incurred in respect of false statements concerning services (although not a simple failure to keep

a contractual promise) see the Trade Descriptions Act 1968, s 14, below
p 500 et seq.

Some particular examples

HOLIDAYS

Contracts for the provision of holidays are a good example of an area in
which consumers may suffer extreme inconvenience and disappointment
through failure to provide an agreed service. Here some protection is
afforded through the Association of British Travel Agents' (ABTA) codes
of practice. See generally as to codes Chapter 9 below. The following case
establishes a point of general significance.

Jarvis v Swans Tours Ltd [1973] 1 All ER 71, [1973] QB 233, Court of Appeal

Lord Denning MR. The plaintiff, Mr Jarvis, is a solicitor employed by a local authority at
Barking. In 1969 he was minded to go for Christmas to Switzerland. He was looking forward
to a ski-ing holiday. It is his one fortnight's holiday in the year. He prefers it in the winter
rather than in the summer.

Mr Jarvis read a brochure issued by Swans Tours Ltd. He was much attracted by the
description of Morlialp, Giswil, Central Switzerland. I will not read the whole of it, but just
pick out some of the principal attractions:

> 'HOUSE PARTY CENTRE with special resident host . . . MÖRLIALP is a most wonderful
> little resort on a sunny plateau . . . Up there you will find yourself in the midst of
> beautiful alpine scenery, which in winter becomes a wonderland of sun, snow and ice,
> with a wide variety of fine ski-runs, a skating-rink and an exhilarating toboggan run
> . . . Why did we choose the Hotel Krone . . . mainly and most of all, because of the
> 'GEMUTLICHKEIT' and friendly welcome you will receive from Herr and Frau Weibel
> . . . The Hotel Krone has its own Alphütte Bar which will be open several evenings a
> week . . . No doubt you will be in for a great time, when you book this houseparty
> holiday . . . Mr. Weibel, the charming owner, speaks English.'

On the same page, in a special yellow box, it was said:

> 'SWANS HOUSEPARTY IN MORLIALP. *All these Houseparty arrangements are included in
> the price of your holiday.* Welcome party on arrival. Afternoon tea and cake for 7 days.
> Swiss Dinner by candlelight. Fondue-party. Yodler evening. Chali farewell party in the
> 'Alphutte Bar'. Service of representative.'

Alongside on the same page there was a special note about ski-packs: 'Hire of Skis, Sticks and
Boots . . . 12 days £11.10.'

In August 1969, on the faith of that brochure, Mr Jarvis booked a 15 day holiday, with
ski-pack. The total charge was £63.45, including Christmas supplement. He was to fly from
Gatwick to Zurich on 20 December 1969 and return on 3 January 1970.

The plaintiff went on the holiday, but he was very disappointed. He was a man of about 35
and he expected to be one of a houseparty of some 30 or so people. Instead, he found there
were only 13 during the first week. In the second week there was no houseparty at all. He was
the only person there. Mr Weibel could not speak English. So there was Mr Jarvis, in the
second week, in this hotel with no houseparty at all, and no one could speak English, except
himself. He was very disappointed, too, with the ski-ing. It was some distance away at Giswil.
There were no ordinary length skis. There were only mini-skis, about 3 ft long. So he did not
get his ski-ing as he wanted to. In the second week he did get some longer skis for a couple of
days, but then, because of the boots, his feet got rubbed and he could not continue even with
the long skis. So his ski-ing holiday, from his point of view, was pretty well ruined.

There were many other matters, too. They appear trivial when they are set down in writing,
but I have no doubt they loomed large in Mr Jarvis's mind, when coupled with the other

disappointments. He did not have the nice Swiss cakes which he was hoping for. The only cakes for tea were potato crisps and little dry nutcakes. The yodler evening consisted of one man from the locality who came in his working clothes for a little while, and sang four or five songs very quickly. The 'Alphütte Bar' was an unoccupied annexe which was only open one evening. There was a representative, Mrs Storr, there during the first week, but she was not there during the second week. The matter was summed up by the learned judge:

'. . . during the first week he got a holiday in Switzerland which was to some extent inferior . . . and, as to the second week he got a holiday which was very largely inferior [to what he was led to expect].'

What is the legal position? I think that the statements in the brochure were representations or warranties. The breaches of them give Mr Jarvis a right to damages. It is not necessary to decide whether they were representations or warranties; because, since the Misrepresentation Act 1967, there is a remedy in damages for misrepresentation as well as for breach of warranty.

The one question in the case is: what is the amount of damages? The judge seems to have taken the difference in value between what he paid for and what he got. He said that he intended to give 'the difference between the two values and no other damages' under any other head. He thought that Mr Jarvis had got half of what he paid for. So the judge gave him half the amount which he had paid, namely, £31.72. Mr Jarvis appeals to this court. He says that the damages ought to have been much more.

There is one point I must mention first. Counsel together made a very good note of the judge's judgment. They agreed it. It is very clear and intelligible. It shows plainly enough the ground of the judge's decision; but, by an oversight, it was not submitted to the judge, as it should have been: see *Bruen v Bruce*[1]. In some circumstances we should send it back to the judge for his comments. But I do not think we need do so here. The judge received the notice of appeal and made notes for our consideration. I do not think he would have wished to add to them. We will, therefore, decide the case on the material before us.

What is the right way of assessing damages? It has often been said that on a breach of contract damages cannot be given for mental distress. Thus in *Hamlin v Great Northern Rly Co*[2] Pollock CB said that damages cannot be given 'for the disappointment of mind occasioned by the breach of contract'. And in *Hobbs v London South Western Rly Co*[3] Mellor J said that—

'. . . for the mere inconvenience, such as annoyance and loss of temper, or vexation, or for being disappointed in a particular thing which you have set your mind upon, without real physical inconvenience resulting, you cannot recover damages.'

The courts in those days only allowed the plaintiff to recover damages if he suffered physical inconvenience, such as, having to walk five miles home, as in *Hobb's case*[4]; or to live in an overcrowded house: see *Bailey v Bullock*[5].

I think that those limitations are out of date. In a proper case damages for mental distress can be recovered in contract, just as damages for shock can be recovered in tort. One such case is a contract for a holiday, or any other contract to provide entertainment and enjoyment. If the contracting party breaks his contract, damages can be given for the disappointment, the distress, the upset and frustration caused by the breach. I know that it is difficult to assess in terms of money, but it is no more difficult than the assessment which the courts have to make every day in personal injury cases for loss of amenities. Take the present case. Mr Jarvis has only a fortnight's holiday in the year. He books it far ahead, and looks forward to it all that time. He ought to be compensated for the loss of it.

A good illustration was given by Edmund Davies LJ in the course of the argument. He put the case of a man who has taken a ticket for Glyndebourne. It is the only night on which he can get there. He hires a car to take him. The car does not turn up. His damages are not limited to the mere cost of the ticket. He is entitled to general damages for the disappointment he has suffered and the loss of the entertainment which he should have had. Here, Mr Jarvis's fortnight's winter holiday has been a grave disappointment. It is true that he was conveyed to Switzerland and back and had meals and bed in the hotel. But that is not what he went for. He went to enjoy himself with all the facilities which the defendants said he would have. He is entitled to damages for the lack of those facilities, and for his loss of enjoyment.

A similar case occurred in 1951. It was *Stedman v Swan's Tours*[6]. A holiday-maker was awarded damages because he did not get the bedroom and the accommodation which he was promised. The county court judge awarded him £13 15s. This court increased it to £50.

I think the judge was in error in taking the sum paid for the holiday, £63.45, and halving it. The right measure of damages is to compensate him for the loss of entertainment and enjoyment which he was promised, and which he did not get. Looking at the matter quite broadly, I think the damages in this case should be the sum of £125. I would allow the appeal accordingly.

Edmund Davies LJ. . . . When a man has paid for and properly expects an invigorating and amusing holiday and, through no fault of his, returns home dejected because his expectations have been largely unfulfilled, in my judgment it would be quite wrong to say that his disappointment must find no reflection in the damages to be awarded. And it is right to add that, in the course of his helpful submissions, counsel for the defendants did not go so far as to submit anything of the kind. Judge Alun Pugh took that view in *Feldman v Allways Travel Services*[7]. That, too, was a holiday case. The highly experienced senior county court judge there held that the correct measure of damages was the difference between the price paid and the value of the holiday in fact furnished, 'taking into account the plaintiff's feelings of annoyance and frustration'.

The learned trial judge clearly failed to approach his task in this way, which in my judgment is the proper way to be adopted in the present case. He said:

> 'There is no evidence of inconvenience or discomfort, other than that arising out of the breach of contract and covered by my award. [There was] no evidence of physical discomfort, eg bedroom not up to standard.'

His failure is manifested, not only by these words, but also by the extremely small damages he awarded, calculated, be it noted, as one half of the cost of the holiday. Instead of 'a great time', the plaintiff's reasonable and proper hopes were largely and lamentably unfulfilled. To arrive at a proper compensation for the defendants' failure is no easy matter. But in my judgment we should not be compensating the plaintiff excessively were we to award him the £125 damages proposed by Lord Denning MR. I therefore concur in allowing this appeal.

[**Stephenson LJ** agreed.] *Appeal allowed; damages of £125 awarded.*

1. [1959] 2 All ER 375, [1959] 1 WLR 684.
2. (1856) 1 H & N 408 at 411.
3. (1875) LR 10 QB 111 at 122, [1874–80] All ER Rep 458 at 463.
4. (1875) LR 10 QB 111, [1874–80] All ER Rep 458.
5. [1950] 2 All ER 1167.
6. (1951) 95 Sol Jo 727.
7. [1957] CLY 934.

NOTES

1. For further cases involving the award of damages to disappointed holidaymakers see, for example, *Jackson v Horizon Holidays Ltd* [1975] 3 All ER 92, [1975] 1 WLR 1468, CA, above p 22 and *Adcock v Blue Sky Holidays Ltd* (CA, 13 May 1980, unreported but available on Lexis). See also *Which?* June 1980 p 372, May 1983 p 249 and August 1983 p 384. In the *Adcock* case where the Court of Appeal increased the damages awarded to £500, a figure which was broadly equivalent to the cost of the holiday, Cumming-Bruce LJ is reported as having described the position as follows:

Contracts for holidays vary on their facts very greatly. The facilities offered by the tour company vary enormously from case to case. It would be a grave mistake to look at the facts in, for example, the *Jackson* case or the *Jarvis* case and compare those facts with the facts in another case as a means of establishing the measure of damages. In the present case, which was a contract for the provision of facilities for a ski-ing holiday in the first week of January . . . the representation that the accommodation would be warm and friendly and that the bedrooms would have the amenities of central heating, hot baths or showers and hot water, were of the greatest importance—or great importance if only because, in temperatures many degrees below freezing when it is dark at about half past 4, the holidaymaker is likely, on return from the snow, to need the facilities of warmth and hot water in order to obtain the capacity for any sort of enjoyment. On the facts found by the Judge, those facilities were so markedly absent that the holiday provided was such that the enjoyment of all the members of the party was very substantially reduced; and they are entitled to compensation not only for their physical sufferings, but also for the distress that they experienced instead of obtaining enjoyment for their expenditure.

2. For examples of holiday cases involving a potential liability under the Trade Descriptions Act 1968, s 14, see *R v Sunair Holidays Ltd* [1973] 2 All ER 1233, [1973] 1 WLR 1105, CA below p 502, and *Wings Ltd v Ellis* [1984] 3 All ER 577, [1984] 3 WLR 965, below p 516.

3. In an article 'Tour Operators—For Services Rendered', (1983) Law Society's Gazette 2047, Messrs Nelson-Jones and Stewart note that the standard obligation which A owes to B in respect of the activities of an independent contractor, C, is one of reasonable care in C's selection. They add, at p 2048, 'An examination of holiday brochures will, in fact, show that most tour operators do seek to establish that they provide a service of arranging for other people to provide services (hotels, airlines, etc) and that the tour operator does not himself own or provide the airlines hotels etc which form part of the holiday package.' See also Grant, 'The Tour Operator as Agent' (1975) Trading Law 34.

Question

Do tour operators who provide such a service owe a duty which is more stringent than this standard obligation? (For an unreported decision cited by the authors of the above article which seems to support the view that tour operators do not, see *Wall v Silver Wing Surface Arrangements Ltd* (Hodgson, J 1981).)

Problems

1. Artemus enters the Spa Town travel agency in Leamington. He books a fully-inclusive winter package holiday with Walhalla Tours for a fifteen-day holiday in the Hotel Espana in Westpool. He pays Spa Town in advance. Walhalla has dealt with the Hotel Espana over many years and has always found it to be entirely reliable. During the fifteen days when Artemus is at the hotel the central heating breaks down, the food is well below standard and there are many other disappointments.

Advise Artemus as to the potential liability, if any, of (i) Spa Town, (ii) Walhalla and (iii) the Hotel Espana. (As to the position of agents under the Misrepresentation Act 1967 see *Resolute Maritime Inc v Nippon Kaiji Kyokai, The Skopas* [1983] 2 All ER 1, [1983] 1 WLR 857.)

2. On 1 June Bertram enters the Castle travel agency to enquire about a coach service operated by Motorway Travel. He buys a ticket for Motorway's service from Warwick to Heathrow Airport for 10 June explaining to the girl on the desk that this is the last date on which his transatlantic airline ticket is valid. Because it has been maintained badly Motorway's coach breaks down and Bertram misses his flight. Advise Bertram.

If Motorway Travel had become insolvent and ceased trading on 5 June what advice would you give the Castle travel agency from whom Bertram is reclaiming the £15 which he has paid for his ticket?

BAILMENT

Contracts of bailment cover a wide range of transactions in which a consumer's goods are handed over into the possession of a business. For example a car may be sent to a garage for repair, a coat to the cleaners, a film for processing or household goods may be transported or stored. Frequently in such cases the issue will be the effectiveness of an exemption or limitation clause. This matter is discussed in the extracts in Chapter 6 below. See, for example, *Woodman v Photo Trade Processing Ltd* (His Honour Judge Clarke, May 1981), below p 245; *Waldron-Kelly v British Railways Board* (His Honour Judge Brown, March 1981), below p 250; *McCutcheon v David MacBrayne Ltd* [1964] 1 All ER 430, [1964] 1 WLR 125, HL. The following case involved a limitation clause and the doctrine of fundamental breach of contract, but it is important also as illustrating a further point of some practical importance.

Levison v Patent Steam Carpet Cleaning Co Ltd [1977] 3 All ER 498, [1978] QB 69, Court of Appeal

The plaintiffs, Mr and Mrs Levison, owned a Chinese carpet which was worth £900. They arranged to have it cleaned by the defendant company. When it was collected by the defendants' van driver Mr Levison signed a form of which clause 2(a) stated that the maximum value of the carpet, based on its area, was deemed to be £40. By clause 5 it was further provided that, 'All merchandise is expressly accepted at the owner's risk'. The defendants recommended that owners should insure their goods. The carpet was never returned—presumably because it had been stolen—and the plaintiffs (or effectively their insurers) sued to recover its full value. Judgment was given for this amount, that is £900, and the defendants appealed to the Court of Appeal. On the issue of the burden of proof the following points were made:

Lord Denning MR. . . . . I am clearly of opinion that, in a contract of bailment, when a bailee seeks to escape liability on the ground that he was not negligent or that he was excused by an exception or limitation clause, then he must show what happened to the goods. He must prove all the circumstances known to him in which the loss or damage occurred. If it appears that the goods were lost or damaged without any negligence on his part, then, of course, he is not liable. If it appears that they were lost or damaged by a slight breach, not going to the root of the contract, he may be protected by the exemption or limitation clause. But, if he leaves the cause of loss or damage undiscovered and unexplained, then I think he is liable: because it is then quite likely that the goods were stolen by one of his servants; or delivered by a servant to the wrong address; or damaged by reckless or wilful misconduct; all of which the offending servant will conceal and not make known to his employer. Such conduct would be a fundamental breach against which the exemption or limitation clause will not protect him.

The cleaning company in this case did not show what had happened to the carpet. They did not prove how it was lost. They gave all sorts of excuses for non-delivery and eventually said it had been stolen. Then I would ask: by whom was it stolen? Was it by one of their own servants? or with his connivance? Alternatively, was it delivered by one of their servants to the wrong address? In the absence of any explanation, I would infer that it was one of these causes. In none of them would the cleaning company be protected by the exemption or limitation clause.

Conclusion. I think the judge was quite right in holding that the burden of proof was on the cleaning company to exclude fundamental breach. As they did not exclude it, they cannot rely on the exemption or limitation clauses. I would, therefore, dismiss this appeal.

Sir David Cairns . . . In *J Spurling Ltd v Bradshaw*[1] Denning LJ said:

> 'A bailor, by pleading and presenting his case properly, can always put the burden of proof on the bailee. In the case of non-delivery, for instance, all he need plead is the contract and a failure to deliver on demand. That puts on the bailee the burden of proving either loss without his fault (which would be a complete answer at common law) or, if the loss was due to his fault, that it was a fault from which he is excluded by the exempting clause: see *Cunard SS Co v Buerger*[2] and *Woolmer v Delmer Price Ltd*[3]. I do not think the Court of Appeal in *Alderslade v Hendon Laundry Ltd*[4] had the burden of proof in mind at all.'

I respectfully agree with that passage. Parker LJ[5] expressly refrained from considering whether *Woolmer v Delmer Price Ltd*[3] was wrongly decided. It is in my judgment open to this court either to approve or to overrule McNair J's decision[6] and for my part I would approve it because, however difficult it may sometimes be for a bailee to prove a negative, he is at least in a better position than the bailor to know what happened to the goods while in his possession.

The considerations applicable to bills of lading and to policies of marine insurance (see *The Glendarroch*[7]; *Munro, Brice & Co v War Risks Association Ltd*[8]) are not in my judgment applicable to cases such as the present.

Accordingly I would hold that the onus was on the defendants, that they did not discharge it and that the appeal should be dismissed.

[**Orr LJ** agreed.] *Appeal dismissed.*

1. [1956] 2 All ER 121 at 125, [1956] 1 WLR 461 at 466.
2. [1927] AC 1, [1926] All ER Rep 103.
3. [1955] 1 All ER 377, [1955] 1 QB 291.
4. [1945] 1 All ER 244, [1945] KB 189.
5. [1956] 2 All ER 121 at 128, [1956] 1 WLR 461 at 470.
6. [1955] 1 All ER 377, [1955] 1 QB 291.
7. [1894] P 226, [1891–4] All ER Rep 484.
8. [1918] 2 KB 78, [1916–17] All ER Rep 981.

NOTE

The above case is important as indicating the incidence of the onus of proof where goods have been lost. However it may be necessary to establish initially that there is an obligation to exercise reasonable care in relation to the safeguarding of a customer's property. The point is discussed in detail in Palmer *Bailment* (1979) (see Ch V especially). It arose in the following case.

Ashby v Tolhurst [1937] 2 All ER 837, [1937] 2 KB 242, Court of Appeal

The plaintiff drove his motor car on to a piece of ground belonging to the defendants, paid 1s, and was handed a ticket marked 'Sea Way Car Park. Car Park Ticket'. The ticket contained an exemption clause stating that:

> The proprietors do not take any responsibility for the safe custody of any cars or articles there, nor for any damage to the cars or articles however caused, nor for any injuries to any persons, all cars being left in all respects entirely at their owners' risk. Owners are requested to show ticket when required

When the plaintiff returned to the car park he found that the car was no longer there whereupon the attendant explained that it had been removed by the plaintiff's 'friend' who wanted it to ride to Thorpe Bay. The plaintiff who did not have any such friend in the area brought an action which succeeded at first instance. The defendants now appealed to the Court of Appeal.

Sir Wilfrid Greene MR, having stated the facts of the case, continued:

It seems to me that reading the document as a whole, including its own description of itself, namely, 'car park ticket,' it really means no more than this: the holder of this ticket is entitled to park his car in the Sea Way Car Park, but reading it quite shortly, this does not mean that the proprietors are going to be responsible for it. If that be the true construction of the document, and I think it is, the argument that the presence of these exempting conditions points to the view that they are inserted in order to remove a contractual liability which would otherwise be there disappears and, in my opinion, the argument, when applied to a document of this kind, is not one of any real weight. If that be the true view, the relationship was a relationship of licensor and licensee alone, and that relationship in itself would carry no obligations of the licensor towards the licensee in relation to the chattel left there, no obligation to provide anybody to look after it, no liability for any negligent act of any person in the employment of the licensor who happened to be there.

There is one other way, I think, of usefully testing the position, and that is to consider in whom possession of this car was at the relevant time. In doing that, of course, one has to be careful to see that one is not unconsciously begging the whole question; but it would be a surprising result, I think, if the effect of the relationship between these parties was that when the car was left on this piece of ground possession of the car in the legal sense became vested in the owners of the park. It would involve the consequence that the owners of the park could maintain an action of trespass, they could maintain an action of conversion if their special property in the car was interfered with. As I say, that argument must not be used in such a way as to beg the question, but it would be rather a surprising result if, when a man left his car on land like this and paid 1s for the privilege of doing so, the possession passed in a way in which it certainly would not pass if he left it in a public park in a square in London and paid the attendant 6d for the ticket, or whatever he has to pay. In such a case possession, it seems to me, clearly would not pass; I quite fail to see why possession should pass in a case such as this. That, as I say, is merely a way of looking at the matter and is not, of course, a conclusive argument.

. . .

Romer LJ: I agree. . . . [In] order that there shall be a bailment there must be a delivery by the bailor, that is to say, he must part with his possession of the chattel in question. In the present case there is no evidence whatever of any delivery in fact of the motor car to the attendant on behalf of the defendants. All I can see is that the plaintiff left his car on the car park, paying the sum of 1s for the privilege of doing so. It is true that, if the car had been left there for any particular purpose that required that the defendant should have possession of the car, a delivery would rightly be inferred, and, if the car had been left at the car park for the purposes of being sold or by way of pledge or for the purposes of being driven away to some other place or indeed for the purposes of safe custody, delivery of the car, although not actually made, would readily be inferred. It is perfectly plain in this case that the car was not delivered to the defendants for safe custody. You cannot infer a contract by A to perform a certain act out of circumstances in which A has made it perfectly plain that he declines to be under any contractual liability to perform that act. The defendants made it as clear as writing can make it in the ticket which was delivered to the plaintiff that they would not take any responsibility for the safe custody of any car. One cannot infer, therefore, in those circumstances that the car was left in the car park for the purpose of being in the custody of the defendants. It is perfectly plain that the car was not left there for any other purpose. That being so, it is impossible, it seems to me, to find that the car was delivered to the defendants or that there was any contract of bailment.

. . .

[**Scott LJ** agreed.] *Appeal allowed.*

Consider the following cases—

1. Groucho takes his car to the Downtown garage for repair. When he returns to collect it two days later the garage owner explains that it has been extensively damaged by a burglar who has broken into the premises to steal car radios. He adds that his burglar alarm system which is usually reliable failed to operate on the night in question.

Advise Groucho.

2. Eva dines at the Goodfood restaurant, leaving her valuable fur jacket on a peg close to her table. The jacket is stolen by a sneak-thief whose general appearance should have alerted the waiters to the fact that he was not an ordinary diner. The restaurant has not taken any precautions to safeguard its customers' property.

Advise Eva. Would the position be different if the jacket had been stolen from the ladies' cloakroom where Eva had left it with an attendant?

CONTRACTS OF INSURANCE

Contracts of insurance provide a further example of an area which is of considerable importance to consumers and in which, it may be argued, reform is long overdue. In this section reference is made to some of the more central issues of this complex and specialist subject. For further discussion see Birds *Modern Insurance Law* (1982) and 'Aspects of Consumer Insurance Law', LAG Bulletin, March 1980, p 65; the Law Commission Report on Non-Disclosure and Breach of Warranty (Law Com No 104, Cmnd 8064, 1980) and the Annual Reports of the Insurance Ombudsman Bureau. For critical discussion of the draft EEC Directive on the Coordination of Laws, Regulations and Administrative Provisions Relating to Insurance Contracts, see the 64th Report of the House of Lords Select Committee on the European Communities (HL 348, 1979–80).

Duty of disclosure

The general rule of English law is that a person must refrain from making positive misrepresentations and yet is not obliged to volunteer information as such. However as may be seen from the following case the position is markedly different where contracts of insurance are concerned.

Woolcott v Sun Alliance and London Insurance Ltd [1978] 1 All ER 1253, [1978] 1 WLR 493, Queen's Bench Divisional Court

In 1961 the defendant insurers issued a block insurance policy against fire and other risks. The policy was in favour of the Bristol and West Building Society, as mortgagees, and the several mortgagors recorded in its annex from time to time. In 1972 the plaintiff applied to the society for an advance of £12,000 to enable him to purchase certain property. In the standard application form he was asked to state the amount for which he wished the Society to insure the property, but there was no question which related to his moral character. Neither was he asked to complete a separate proposal form for insurance. He did not disclose the fact that he had several convictions including one for robbery, for which he had been sentenced to twelve years' imprisonment. Some two years after the purchase of the property it was destroyed by fire. The defendants indemnified the society to the extent of its security but, having learnt of the plaintiff's convictions, repudiated his claim for the excess. In subsequent proceedings it was held that the policy of insurance was not a joint insurance but rather an insurance by two persons, that is the mortgagee and the mortgagor, for their respective interests.

Caulfield J, having stated the facts of the case and reached the above conclusion on the first issue, continued:

On the second issue in this action I refer to s 17 and 18 of the Marine Insurance Act 1906. By s 17: 'A contract of marine insurance is a contract based upon the utmost good faith and if the utmost good faith be not observed by either party the contract may be avoided by the other party', and s 18:

'(1) Subject to the provisions of this section, the assured must disclose to the insurer, before the contract is concluded, every material circumstance which is known to the assured, and the assured is deemed to know every circumstance which in the ordinary course of business ought to be known by him. If the assured fails to make such disclosure, the insurer may avoid the contract.
'(2) Every circumstance is material which would influence the judgment of a prudent insurer in fixing the premium or determining whether he will take the risk.'

I refer now to the judgment of MacKenna J in *Lambert v Co-operative Insurance Society*[1]. This judgment I have found most comprehensive and most helpful, and I have followed the principles which are fully explained in the judgment of MacKenna J (who was giving the first judgment of the Court of Appeal)[2]:

'Everyone agrees that the assured is under a duty of disclosure and that the duty is the same when he is applying for a renewal as it is when he is applying for the original policy. The extent of that duty is the matter in controversy. There are, at least in theory, four possible rules or tests which I shall state: (1) The duty is to disclose such facts only as the particular assured believes to be material; (2) It is to disclose such facts as a reasonable man would believe to be material; (3) It is to disclose such facts as the particular insurer would regard as material; (4) It is to disclose such facts as a reasonable or prudent insurer might have treated as material.'

Ultimately, in a most comprehensive judgment, the learned judge then went on to conclude that the proper test was the fourth test, and the principles which he has explained in that case I have followed in reaching my judgment on this particular issue.

The duty, in my judgment, rested on the plaintiff, when he completed his application form for a loan, to disclose his criminal record for, by that application, he was accepting that the society would effect insurance of his property on his behalf as well as their own behalf. I do not think the absence of a proposal form for insurance modifies in any degree the duty of disclosure on the plaintiff. The plaintiff knew the society would be effecting a policy of insurance on their own behalf and on his behalf, and accordingly, in my judgment, there was a duty on the plaintiff to disclose such facts as a reasonable or prudent insurer might have treated as material.

On the third issue I have accepted the evidence of the underwriters who have given evidence. I accept that the criminal record of an assured can affect the moral hazard which insurers have to assess; indeed this is almost self-evident. I therefore hold that on the particular facts of this case the non-disclosure of a serious criminal offence like robbery by the plaintiff was a material non-disclosure.

For these reasons the defendants, in my judgment, are entitled to avoid the policy insofar as that policy affects the plaintiff's separate interest. There will be judgment accordingly.

Judgment for the defendants.

1. [1975] 2 Lloyd's Rep 485.
2. [1975] 2 Lloyd's Rep 485 at 487.

NOTE

In the *Lambert* case to which Caufield J referred it was held that the defendants were entitled to avoid liability under an 'all risks' policy covering jewellery when the insured did not disclose her husband's convictions for theft. Characteristically Mackenna J added, 'The defendant company would act decently if, having established the point of principle, they were to pay her.': [1975] 2 Lloyd's Rep 485 at 491. For a critical comment on this case see Merkin (1976) 39 MLR 478.

Although there is general agreement that a broadly-based duty of disclosure is inappropriate for consumer contracts there is no overall consensus as to how precisely the law should be reformed. The differing views expressed by the Law Commission and the National Consumer Council (NCC) may be seen in the following extracts from the NCC response to the Law Commission's report. Having argued in favour of a separate régime for consumer insurance contracts the NCC continues:

Insurance law—non-disclosure and breach of warranty (National Consumer Council) (1981)

THE DUTY OF DISCLOSURE

. . .

4.6.1   The Law Commission has stuck to the approach of its working-paper that changes should be limited to reform, but not abolition, of the duty of disclosure. The precise reforms now proposed, however, are not as favourable to policyholders as those of the working-paper. The reforms cover:—
   (i)   The extent of the duty where there is no proposal form
   (ii) The extent of the duty where there is a proposal form
   (iii) Renewals.

Where there is no proposal form
4.6.2   Most consumer insurance is taken out on the basis of a completed proposal form, but there are exceptions such as:—
   ★ temporary cover (eg motor insurance) pending completion of proposal form;
   ★ some holiday insurance (tick in brochure);
   ★ slot machine insurance (eg at airports).
The Law Commission rejected the abolition of the duty of disclosure and, where there is no proposal form, they recommended instead that the duty of disclosure should be reduced so that it should extend to a fact which is:—
   (i)   material to the risk
   (ii) known to the applicant or within his assumed knowledge
      and
   (iii) one which a reasonable man in the position of the applicant would disclose to his insurers.
4.6.3   The test of 'materiality' would remain largely the same as the present law, which is that a fact is material if it would influence a prudent insurer. The restriction of the duty to facts within the insured person's knowledge is a clear improvement on the present law which enables insurers to seek disclosures of facts not known to the insured. The Commission spells out that a person should be assumed to know a material fact if it would have been ascertainable by reasonable enquiry and if a reasonable man applying for the insurance in question would have ascertained it. In other words, the insured person cannot say that he did not know facts which were obviously relevant and which he could easily find out, but he is not expected to engage in an elaborate investigation into all possible facts.
4.6.4   The third element in the above formulation introduces the objectivity which the present law lacks. A reasonable man would not disclose facts which apparently had no bearing on the risks to be insured. The wording proposed ignores personal idiosyncracies, but effectively puts the reasonable man into the shoes of the person actually taking out insurance. Thus, more would be expected of a large business than an individual.
4.6.5   The Law Commission claims that the above formulation would remove one of the major mischiefs in the present law and would be in accordance with common sense and fair to both parties. It is undeniable that the proposals outlined are a considerable improvement on the present law. The problem remains, however, that there is no proposal form to be completed by the consumer and he is given no specific opportunity to consider the duty of disclosure, let alone actually to disclose material facts. It is suggested that it is simply not realistic ever to expect consumers either to know that they have to make 'voluntary' disclosures or to have any sensible idea as to what sort of information has to be disclosed . . .
4.6.6   Formulations of this nature involve the exercise of several judicial judgments which can only lead to uncertainty and litigation. The whole point of insurance is to provide cover against the unexpected. NCC therefore regards the proposals of the Law Commission and of

the draft EEC directive as both unworkable and unfair in principle. One example may illustrate the unsatisfactory nature of the Law Commission's proposal. A householder who arranges cover over the telephone, and who is not asked for such information, may well fail to mention subsidence which affected a house two streets away. Is that fact material to the risk? If he didn't know about the subsidence, was it ascertainble by reasonable enquiry? Would a reasonable man have ascertained it? Would a reasonable man in his position have disclosed the fact? The decision of the court, as to whether there had been a material non-disclosure in such circumstances, cannot be predicted with any certainty at all. The same example exposes the difficulties with the EEC proposal with even greater force.

4.6.7   If the insurers want information they should ask for it, rather than expect the law to require consumers to do the impossible. *NCC considers that where there is no proposal form the duty of disclosure on consumers should (apart from deliberate concealment) be abolished.* It is accepted that the insurer should have the right to repudiate the policy later on full investigation, but that he should be on risk with regard to claims occurring in any interim period of investigation.

Where there is a proposal form

4.6.8   Nearly all consumer insurance is initiated by the completion of a proposal form. The Law Commission do not foresee any difficulty in separately identifying these and propose that applications for insurance made in connection with applications for mortgages should be treated as proposal forms. The major criticism of the present law is that the insured may well be unaware that he is under a residual duty to disclose material facts *after* answering a series of questions in the proposal form. This is, the Law Commission say, 'a trap for the insured . . . which requires reform for the protection of the insured'.

4.6.9.   The *provisional* recommendations made by the Law Commission in 1979 were welcomed by NCC. Subject to deliberate concealment, the suggestion then made was that there should be *no* duty beyond accurate answers to specific questions and that no general questions (eg 'Is there anything else . . .') should be permitted. The effect would be to abolish the residual duty.

4.6.10   The final recommendation is different. The insurance industry has persuaded the Commission that, despite the superficial attractions of the provisional solution, proposal forms can only elicit information of a standard nature and that the provisional solution would result in lengthy, detailed and complex proposal forms. It is said that proposers might be aware of facts which any reasonable person would realise should be disclosed, but about which insurers could not reasonably be expected to ask questions. The examples quoted relate to business insurance (eg a business many who knows that his quality control system is inadequate). Accordingly, the Law Commission have now recommended:—

(i)   A duty to volunteer information in addition to answering all questions should be retained.

(ii)   The duty should be reduced to the same level as for cases where there is no proposal form (see above).

(iii)   All proposal forms should have clear and explicit warnings about the existence and the extent of the duty to volunteer information and of the consequences of failure.

(iv)   A copy of the completed proposal form should be supplied to the insured persons.

4.6.11   The new recommendations are clearly less satisfactory for consumers and perhaps illustrate most vividly the need for separate treatment of consumer insurance. Whilst there may be unlimited factors affecting business insurance, consumer insurance is reasonably standardised. There must be a limit to the types of factors relevant to, say, household or motor insurance. In its 1979 working paper the Law Commission itself pointed out that 'in practice insurers do not often rely merely on the insured's duty to volunteer information' and 'if the insurer wishes to have information to enable him to assess the risk he must ask the insured for it'.

4.6.12   Relevant questions usually appear on proposal forms already. If they do not, and the insurer considers the type of information to be relevant, then specific questions should be devised and included. Longer forms are not necessarily more difficult to complete. Indeed, the work of the Plain English Campaign suggests that they are easier. The achievements of some insurance companies reveal that proposal forms can be designed to elicit all relevant information in a way which is clear and acceptable to consumers. Despite warnings (and despite the limitation to information which a reasonable person would disclose) private consumers should not be expected to cast their minds in unspecified directions. The Scottish Consumer Council's analysis of proposal forms indicates strongly that comparable warnings which are already included on proposal forms are frequently neither clear nor prominent. However plain the warnings may be, they are unlikely to mean very much to most consumers.

If the type of information sought can be described, there should be a question. *If it cannot be described, consumers should not be expected to think of it for themselves.*
4.6.13   *NCC is therefore firmly of the view that for consumer insurance where proposal forms are used*:—
  (i)   Insurance should be confined to specific questions in all cases.
  (ii) Any residual duty of disclosure should be abolished.
  (iii) General questions should be outlawed (or only permitted with the approval of the Director-General of Fair Trading).
  (iv) Insurers should supply a copy of completed proposal forms.
  (v)   *Prescribed* warnings should be prominently displayed with regard to whatever duties are finally imposed upon people taking out insurance.

Renewals
4.8.1   The vast majority of insurance contracts are made by way of renewal which creates a new contract. The present law imposes a fresh duty to disclose all facts which are material at the date of renewal. The extent of the duty is the same as on the original application. This usually means, assuming original compliance, that the duty extends to material changes in circumstances. In practice, if people do not know of the duty when they take out the original insurance, they are even less likely to be aware of its existence on renewal. Moreover, even if the duty is known about, the insured person is usually unable to refer to the documents which record information which he previously supplied.
4.8.2   The Law Commission solutions are conditioned by their previous proposals. They recommended:—
  (i)   The duty of disclosure on renewal should be retained and the same standard of duty should apply as for the original application (ignoring, of course, information previously disclosed).
  (ii) Specific questions should be answered to the best of the person's knowledge and belief.
  (iii) Renewal notices should contain warnings about the duty of disclosure.
  (iv) Insurers should supply copies of renewal notices containing relevant information.
4.8.3   The last three points are completely acceptable, but the primary recommendation is defective for the same reasons as outlined in connection with the original policy. *NCC believes that for consumer insurances*:—
  (i)   Where there was previously a proposal form, the renewal notice should specifically ask about material changes in the disclosed information.
  (ii) Otherwise, if there was no proposal form, there should be no duty of disclosure on renewal. If specific types of information are wanted, appropriate questions should be asked on renewal.

Misstatements, warranties and 'basis of the contract' clauses

In principle it may be thought that consumers seeking assurance or insurance will be less deserving of sympathy if they give an incorrect answer when filling in a proposal form rather than merely omit to volunteer information the relevance of which they may not appreciate. However there may be unfairness also in making an entitlement to claim under a policy wholly dependent on answering all questions correctly. The following case provides an example of the importance of giving complete and truthful answers.

Kumar v Life Insurance Corpn of India [1974] 1 Lloyd's Rep 147, Queen's Bench Divisional Court

Mr Justice Kerr: This action arises out of a claim by Mr Kumar as administrator of the estate of his wife. It is a claim for £1500, the sum insured under a life policy issued by the defendants. Mrs Kumar unfortunately died on June 10, 1968 and this is how this claim arises. The defendants contend that the policy is void under its terms or that it has been avoided because of incorrect answers given in the personal statement which accompanied the proposal form. Alternatively, they claim the same result because of a non-disclosure of material facts. The facts said not to have been disclosed are the same as those which in their submission falsified the answers which were given in the personal statement. In the alternative to his main claim the plaintiff claims the return of the premium which has been paid under the policy.

Mr Kumar is of Indian nationality and his wife was also Indian. He came to this country in 1960 and she came in 1965. He is a dentist by profession. She worked as dentist's receptionist. They were both well educated, and Mrs Kumar was described by one witness as an intelligent, agreeable and educated woman.

On Feb 4, 1966, at the Central Middlesex Hospital, Mrs Kumar then being 23, gave birth to a child by a Caesarean operation; to be precise, by a lower segment Caesarean incision. It is necessary shortly to describe this well-known procedure. It takes place under the administration of a general anaesthetic and consists of surgically opening the abdominal wall, entering the peritoneal cavity, and then making a surgical division of the lower section of the uterus and delivering the baby through these openings, which are then stitched. In this case it was a so-called elective Caesarean in that it was planned in advance due to an inadequate pelvis and a breech presentation.

Having successfully had her baby in this way, Mrs Kumar was advised not to become pregnant for two years. The reason was that there is a small degree of risk that the scar in the uterus may rupture if a pregnancy occurs within a year or two. Having come out of hospital and got over her pregnancy, Mrs Kumar first tried to use a contraceptive cap but did not like this. In June, 1966, she then consulted Dr Gregory at her local Family Planning Centre. She asked whether she could be put on the 'pill', ie to be prescribed oral contraceptives to avoid another pregnancy because of the advice she had been given in relation to her Caesarean.

Dr Gregory was called for the plaintiff and I fully accept her evidence. It is of some significance how Mrs Kumar informed Dr Gregory of her past medical history. Having been asked if she had had an operation, she said 'No', and Dr Gregory wrote down this answer. She was then asked about the history of her pregnancy and mentioned the Caesarean. Dr Gregory said in evidence that she did not make the correction, and commented that she is often amused by the fact that ladies from the East do not consider a Caesarean to be an operation. Since this is a crucial issue it is right to expand it shortly at this stage.

Dr Gregory, and indeed all the doctors who were called on both sides, had no hesitation in considering that a Caesarean was an operation. One doctor described it as a major operation. I have no doubt whatever it is properly to be described as an operation, both as a matter of ordinary English and as a matter of medical terminology. It is unnecessary and undesirable to define or to circumscribe the limits of the word 'operation' for present purposes. Many examples were given in argument, such as the extraction of a tooth under anaesthetic, dealing with an ingrown toe nail, piercing somebody's ears under a local anaesthetic, or an operative delivery of a baby with forceps.

Mr Nevin, for the plaintiff, relied on the Oxford English Dictionary definition as follows: 'A thing done with hand or instrument to some part of the body to remedy a deformity, injury, disease, pain, etc'. But even on that basis a Caesarean at any rate on facts such as in this case, is clearly an operation, because there was risk, or perhaps an impossibility, of delivering this baby by natural means so that the operative procedure of a Caesarean was adopted for that purpose. I therefore decide without any doubt that a Caesarean is an operation.

In October, 1966, Mrs Kumar then took out a policy out of which this action arises. There is considerable conflict of evidence about the circumstances in which this happened, and I must deal with these in a moment. Before doing so it is convenient to go to the end of this unhappy story. She remained on the 'pill' until about January, 1968. She then wanted to have another baby and became pregnant. She unfortunately died on June 10, 1968, following an operation for a ruptured ectopic gestation. This was due to the fact that the foetus became implanted in the fallopian tubes instead of in the uterus. It is common ground that Mrs Kumar's death, although in the course of pregnancy, had no causal connection whatever with her Caesarean operation. But it is also common ground that this is not directly relevant and that it does not affect the issues which I have to decide.

. . .

I then come finally to the forms which had to be completed by any would-be insured. The forms are in three parts which are bound together as seven numbered pages. Pages 1 and 2 consist of a proposal and declaration; pp 2 to 5 consist of a personal statement, the contents of which are 'to be obtained from the life to be assured by the Medical Examiner and a Declaration by the proposer'. Then finally on pp 6 and 7 there is the confidential report of the medical examiner which is to be signed by him together with his qualifications, and he is instructed 'to satisfy himself completely about the identity of the life to be insured'. It is necessary for me to read certain parts of the two declarations. At the end of the proposal form the proposer declares as follows:

'I, the person whose life is hereinbefore proposed to be assured do hereby declare that the foregoing statements and answers are true in every particular and agree and declare that those statements and this declaration along with the further statements made or to be made before the Medical Examiner and the declaration relative thereto shall be the basis of the contract of insurance between me and the Life Insurance Corporation of India and that if any untrue averment be contained therein, the said contract shall be absolutely null and void and all monies which shall have been paid in respect thereof shall stand forfeited to the Corporation.'

Then at the end of the personal statement the proposer declares:

'I do hereby declare that the foregoing answers have been given by me after fully understanding the questions and the same are true in every particular and that I have not withheld any information and I do hereby agree that this declaration together with the proposal for assurance shall be the basis of the contract made between me and the Life Insurance Corporation of India.'

Then he had to sign this, and it also had to be signed by the medical examiner.

The effect of these declarations was incorporated in the insurance policy which was subsequently issued to Mrs Kumar so that no question about the contractual effectiveness of these declarations arises.

His Lordship then considered the conflict of evidence as to whether Mr or Mrs Kumar had discussed the Caesarean delivery in the presence of Mr Koley, the defendants' agent who had completed the form. He continued:

I must read what are now the crucial questions and answers in the personal statement of Mrs Kumar.

'[Question 4(d):] Have you consulted a medical practitioner within the last five years, if so give details. [Answer:] No.'

The defendants contend that this answer was incorrect or untrue because she had consulted Dr Gregory in the way in which I have described.

'[Question 8(a):] Did you ever have any operation, accident or injury, if so give details. [Answer:] No,'

and the defendants contend that that is incorrect because of her Caesarean.

'[Question 9(b):] Have you ever been in any hospital, asylum or sanatorium for a check-up, observation, treatment or an operation, if so give details. [Answer:] No (only delivery).'

The defendants say that that is inaccurate because the words 'only delivery' suggest normal delivery and not delivery by means of a Caesarean.

. . .

I then turn to the main issue whether the Caesarean was ever mentioned to Mr Koley. In the light of my assessment of him as a witness and of the matters with which I have already dealt I reject as a contrived afterthought Mr Kumar's evidence that this was specially mentioned by him or in his hearing to Mr Koley at the dinner party where he says he first met him. If any one of the two persons, Mr Kumar or Mr Koley, knew whether or not the Caesarean was material to the issue of a policy, it would have been Mr Koley from his employment with the company, his experience as their agent and from the references to Caesareans in the literature which I have already mentioned. I also reject Mr Kumar's evidence that Mrs Kumar mentioned the Ceasarean when the questions in the personal statement were read out to her on Oct 3, and the answers were written down by Mr Koley. I think that Mrs Kumar gave her answers to Mr Koley in October in exactly the same way as she had given them to Dr Gregory in June. She did not regard a Caesarean as an operation but merely as part and parcel of having a baby. Just as she said to Dr Gregory in answer to the question whether she had ever had an operation that the answer was 'No', so I think she did the same in relation to Mr Koley. I do not think that it ever crossed her or Mr Kumar's mind at that time or at any other time that the Caesarean should have been disclosed. I accept Mr Koley's evidence that, having written down the answers first at their place and then in relation to the personal statement at his place, Mr and Mrs Kumar read through these answers perhaps fairly quickly, but were content with them and then signed these forms.

It follows from what I have said that the answer to question 8(a), whether Mrs Kumar had ever had an operation, was incorrect and that Mr Koley did not know that it was incorrect. The answer to question 4(d) is more diffiicult. The question was whether or not Mrs Kumar had ever consulted a medical practitioner within the last five years. It is obvious that every visit to a doctor is not a consultation for the purposes of that question. I think that it must be shown that the visit was for a purpose material to a life assurance policy and not merely of such negligible potential materiality that it should be ignored.

For instance, to get a prescription for sleeping pills without any pre-existing illness or a 'flu. injection or vaccination would in my view be negligible matters. For a woman to go on the 'pill', merely as a convenient means of achieving birth control without any pre-existing health factor being involved, is also in my view irrelevant for the purposes of such a question. This was also the view of the medical witnesses who were called. But here there was a pre-existing health factor which involved some risk, though only a small degree of risk, if Mrs Kumar should become pregnant again. She had been advised not to have a baby for two years, and she went to see Dr Gregory to ask whether in these circumstances and in the light of this advice she could and should go on the 'pill'. I think on balance that this was a consultation within question 4(d), but I am thankful not to have to decide this case on that issue alone, as I should have been unhappy to do so. I would, however, have been forced to decide this case against Mr Kumar even on the basis of that question, as I see it. However, the clearly incorrect answer to question 8(a) in relation to the operation relieves me from the necessity of deciding this case solely on that point. For the sake of completeness I should add that I regard the answer to question 9(b), 'No (only delivery)' as not being accurate. The question, in effect for present purposes, is whether Mrs Kumar had ever been in any hospital for, among other things, an operation. The answer, 'No (only delivery)' was in my view sufficiently accurate not to be a false answer. I reject the suggestion that 'only delivery' excludes the possibility of a Caesarean since the question contains a reference to an operation.

It follows that it is irrelevant that Mr Koley, the agent, wrote out the proposal form and the personal statement in his own handwriting, since he did so correctly and in accordance with the answers given. It also follows that the various cases cited to me about the effect of an agent's knowledge do not apply. In these circumstances it is also irrelevant to consider whether, apart from the incorrect answers given, the non-disclosure of the Caesarean was the non-disclosure of a material fact. That question arises in life assurance generally in relation to questions of a general nature about the assured's health and his answers thereto. In the present case we are dealing with specific questions specifically answered, and in my judgment incorrectly answered, and no question of any non-disclosure of a material fact arises outside the ambit of the question and answers.

That only leaves one issue. As I mentioned, Mr Kumar alternatively claims the return of the premium paid, which amounts to a little over £100 in relation to Mrs Kumar's policy. He says that he is entitled to recover this because the defendants have claimed to avoid the policy ab initio and have succeeded in doing so. The defendants resist this by virtue of the words which would make the premium forfeited in the event of incorrect answers being given. It is right to say that they had already offered to return the premium ex gratia in full settlement, but that this was refused. They have also undertaken through their Counsel to repay this premium in any event ex gratia, whatever the result of this case, but they want to have the point decided.

I had some doubts, without looking at the books, whether in the absence of any fraud (and there was clearly no fraud in this case), such a term might not be unenforceable as being a penalty. But these doubts have been set at rest by a long and clear line of authority to which I have been referred. I need only mention the names of three cases: *Duckett v Williams* (1834) 2 Cromp & M 348; *Thomson v Weems* in the House of Lords per Lord Blackburn, (1884) 9 App Cas 671, and *Sparenborg v Edinburgh Life Assurance Company*, [1912] 1 KB 195. These cases clearly show that it is settled law that if the provision is clear and explicit and provides for the forfeiture of a premium in the event of a proposal form or similar document being incorrectly answered, such a provision can be enforced by the insurance company even in the absence of fraud. It follows that the claim for return of premium fails and that this action must be dismissed.

Judgment for the defendants.

Questions

1. Would you have described a Caesarian delivery as an 'operation'?
2. Would the plaintiff have been entitled to recover the premiums if the

'basis of the contract' clause had not contained a provision for forfeiture of the premiums?

NOTE

The leading case most directly in point is the decision of the House of Lords in *Dawsons Ltd v Bonnin* [1922] 2 AC 413. A firm of contractors in Glasgow had insured a motor vehicle against damage by fire and third party risks. A term of the contract provided that

> 'material misstatement or concealment of any circumstance by the insured material to assessing the premium herein, or in connection with any claim, shall render the policy void.'

In reply to a question in the proposal form, 'State full address at which the vehicle will usually be garaged,' the answer given was 'Above Address,' meaning the firm's ordinary place of business in Glasgow. This was not true, as the lorry was usually garaged at a farm on the outskirts of Glasgow. The inaccurate answer in the proposal was given by inadvertence. The lorry having been destroyed by fire at the garage, the insured claimed payment under the policy. The House of Lords held that, although the misstatement was not material, the recital in the policy that the proposal should be the basis of the contract made the truth of the statements a condition of the insurer's liability. Hence the claim failed. Viscount Haldane added (at p 424):

> It is clear that the answer was textually inaccurate. I think that the words employed in the body of the policy can only be properly construed as having made its accuracy a condition. The result may be technical and harsh, but if the parties have so stipulated we have no alternative, sitting as a Court of justice, but to give effect to the words agreed on. Hard cases must not be allowed to make bad law.

The views of the National Consumer Council and the recommendations of the Law Commission may be seen in the following additional extracts from the paper referred to above:

Insurance law—non-disclosure and breach of warranty (National Consumer Council) (1981)

5.   WARRANTIES

5.1   A warranty is an assurance or promise made by the insured person as part of the contract of insurance. It may be a stipulation about the existence or continuation of a state of affairs or about the performance or non performance of an act by the insured. The following are examples:—
   * that a car is, and will remain, roadworthy
   * that a house has, and will continue to have, two fire extinguishers
   * that the insured person will notify the insurer of any increase in the risk or of any possible claim.
5.2   Warranties can be (and are) created in a number of ways and can be classified as relating to past, present or future fact or behaviour. Strict compliance is required and any breach, however trivial, entitles the insurer to repudiate the policy. This is the case regardless of the materiality of the term, the insured person's state of mind or any connection between breach and loss. This means, to take the above examples, that a claim could be *rejected*:—
   * for theft of the car which had faulty steering
   * for flood damage caused to the house with only one fire extinguisher
   * for a holiday cancelled due to a broken leg where the insured person did not notify additional business commitments which might have (but did not) cause the holiday to be cancelled.
5.3   The Law Commission identified three major defects in the present law:—
   1. It is quite wrong that the insurer should be entitled to repudiate a policy for breach of a warranty which *is not material to the risk*.

2. It is unjust that rejection should be available for *any breach* of a warranty which is material, no matter how irrelevant the breach may be to the loss.
3. Material warranties should be ascertainable from a written document which is available to the consumer.

5.4 The Law Commission concluded that there is a formidable case for reform and that, again, it is not sufficient to rely upon the self regulating statements of practice. The reforms proposed by the Law Commission are largely consistent with NCC's evidence. It is therefore proposed only to set out the main elements, which are as follows:—
  (i) A contractual term should only be treated as a warranty if it is material to the risk.
  (ii) There should be a presumption that a contractual provision is a warranty, but this should be rebuttable if the insured person can show that it relates to a matter which is not material to the risk.
  (iii) To be effective, a warranty must be contained in a written document furnished to the insured person.
  (iv) Breach of warranty should not entitle the insurer to reject claims where the insured person can show:—
     (a) the loss is of a different *type* from the particular type of loss which the broken warranty was intended to safeguard against; or
     (b) even if the loss is of the same type, the breach could not have increased the risk that the loss would occur in the way in which it did in fact occur.
  (v) Insurers should still be able to repudiate a policy for the future on account of breach of warranty, but there should be no retrospective effect.

5.5 There are, however, two features which NCC opposes, both concerned with the burden of proof. The first concerns the decision whether a contractual provision is a warranty. The Law Commission's working paper originally proposed that the insurer should have the burden of proving that the broken warranty was material. It was pointed out that since the materiality or otherwise of a particular warranty depends on its influence on the judgment of a prudent insurer it would be inappropriate and unduly harsh on the insured person if the onus of disproving materiality were placed on him. Without giving specific reasons, the Law Commission now consider that the onus of proof should be reversed so that the 'inappropriate and unduly harsh' result is in fact achieved. *NCC opposes this*.

5.6 The second point of concern to NCC relates to the consequences of breach of warranty. The Law Commission envisaged that the burden should be on the insured person to show that the loss was of a different type or that the breach could not have increased the risk of the actual loss (see (iv) above). NCC feels this would place an undue burden upon individuals. NCC believes that this formulation should be reversed so that the insurer wishing to reject a claim would have to prove that the loss was of the same type *and* that the breach could have increased the risk of the actual loss.

5.7 Although (in its evidence) NCC wanted the Law Commission to devise a different word for 'warranty' (which is a technical word to which the law attaches a variety of meanings according to context), the package of reforms relating to warranties amounts to a substantial improvement in the position of the insured person. Subject to the detail points mentioned above, *NCC therefore welcomes these proposals*. NCC rejects the view of the Department of Trade that these reforms are not necessary in relation to warranties of past or present facts.

6. 'BASIS OF THE CONTRACT' CLAUSES

6.1 Insurers often pre-empt the issue as to whether a particular fact is 'material' by including in the proposal form a declaration whereby the insured person warrants the accuracy of all answers to questions, usually declaring that all answers are to form the basis of the contract. The legal effect is to make all answers into warranties so as to entitle repudiation for any breach of warranty regardless of materiality to the risk. This double security for insurance companies compounds the law's unfairness and has been widely criticised.

6.2 The Law Commission agreed with the criticism and concluded that any basis of the contract clause should be ineffective to the extent that it converts statements about past or present facts into warranties. The result would be, for example, that a statement that a house is constructed of brick and slate would not constitute a warranty. The situation is different with regard to future (promissory) warranties because they are necessary, from the insurers' point of view, to minimise the risk and the insured person will be protected by the measures which are proposed for warranties generally.

6.3 *NCC agrees with the Law Commission's proposals for dealing with 'basis of the contract' clauses.* The Department of Trade's contrary conclusions are not thought to be convincing.

NOTE

At the time of writing the above suggestions for reform have not been implemented although the Department of Trade has issued proposals based on the Law Commission recommendations. Pending the implementation of such recommendations English law remains as potentially draconian as before. However the full rigours of the law are mitigated by two developments. First insurance companies (as represented by the British Insurance Association and Lloyd's) have adopted statements of good insurance practice—apparently as a quid pro quo for insurance contracts being outside the scope of the Unfair Contract Terms Act 1977. For discussion of the first statement see Birds, (1977) 40 MLR 677. The statements as revised and reissued in December 1981 are as follows:

Statement of (non-life) insurance practice (British Insurance Association)

The following Statement of normal insurance practice applies to non-life insurances of policyholders resident in the UK and insured in their private capacity only.

1. Proposal forms
  (a) The declaration at the foot of the proposal form should be restricted to completion according to the proposer's knowledge and belief.
  (b) If not included in the declaration, prominently displayed on the proposal form should be a statement:—
    (i) drawing the attention of the proposer to the consequences of the failure to disclose all material facts, explained as those facts an insurer would regard as likely to influence the acceptance and assessment of the proposal;
    (ii) warning that if the proposer is in any doubt about facts considered material, he should disclose them.
  (c) Those matters which insurers have found generally to be material will be the subject of clear questions in proposal forms.
  (d) So far as is practicable, insurers will avoid asking questions which would require expert knowledge beyond that which the proposer could reasonably be expected to possess or obtain or which would require a value judgement on the part of the proposer.
  (e) Unless the prospectus or the proposal form contains full details of the standard cover offered, and whether or not it contains an outline of that cover, the proposal form shall include a statement that a copy of the policy form is available on request.
  (f) Unless the completed form or a copy of it has been sent to a policyholder, a copy will be made available when an insurer raises an issue under the proposal form.

2. Claims
  (a) Under the conditions regarding notification of a claim, the policyholder shall not be asked to do more than report a claim and subsequent developments as soon as reasonably possible except in the case of legal processes and claims which a third party requires the policyholder to notify within a fixed time where immediate advice may be required.
  (b) Except where fraud, deception or negligence is involved, an insurer will not unreasonably repudiate liability to indemnify a policyholder:—
    (i) on the grounds of non-disclosure or misrepresentation of a material fact where knowledge of the fact would not materially have influenced the insurer's judgement in the acceptance or assessment of the insurance;
    (ii) on the grounds of a breach of warranty or condition where the circumstances of the loss are unconnected with the breach.
    The previous paragraph 2(b) does not apply to Marine and Aviation policies.
  (c) Liability under the policy having been established and the amount payable by the insurer agreed, payment will be made without avoidable delay.

3. Renewals
Renewal notices should contain a warning about the duty of disclosure including the necessity

to advise changes affecting the policy which have occurred since the policy inception or last renewal date, whichever was the later.

4. Commencement
Any changes to insurance documents will be made as and when they need to be reprinted, but the Statement will apply in the meantime.

5. Policy documents
Insurers will continue to develop clearer and more explicit proposal forms and policy documents whilst bearing in mind the legal nature of insurance contracts.

6. EEC
This Statement will need reconsideration when the EEC Contract Law Directive is taken into English/Scots Law.

Application
It should be borne in mind that there will sometimes be exceptional circumstances which will require exceptional treatment.

Statement of long-term insurance practice

This statement relates to long-term insurance effected by individuals resident in the UK in a private capacity. Although the statement is not mandatory, it has been recognised by members of The Life Offices' Association and Associated Scottish Life Offices as an indication of insurance practice, it being understood that there will sometimes be exceptional circumstances where the statement would be inappropriate.

Industrial life assurance policyholders are already protected by The Industrial Assurance Acts 1923 to 1968 and regulations issued thereunder, to an extent not provided for ordinary branch policyholders. The statement has, therefore, been modified in its application to industrial assurance business in discussion with the Industrial Assurance Commissioner.

Life assurance is either very largely or else entirely a mutual enterprise and the aim of the industry in recent years has been to reduce to a minimum the formalities (and therefore the expense to the policyholder) involved in issuing a new life policy subject only to the need to protect the general body of policyholders from the effects of non-disclosure by a small minority of proposers.

1. Claims
    (a) An insurer will not unreasonably reject a claim. (However, fraud or deception will, and negligence or non-disclosure or misrepresentation of a material fact may, result in adjustment or constitute grounds for rejection.) In particular, an insurer will not reject a claim on grounds of non-disclosure or misrepresentation of a matter that was outside the knowledge of the proposer.

    (b) Under any conditions regarding a time limit for notification of a claim, the claimant will not be asked to do more than report a claim and subsequent developments as soon as reasonably possible.

    (c) Payment of claims will be made without avoidable delay once the insured event has been proved and the entitlement of the claimant to receive payment has been established.

2. Proposal forms
    (a) If the proposal form calls for the disclosure of material facts a statement should be included in the declaration, or prominently displayed elsewhere on the form or in the document of which it forms part:—

        (i) drawing attention to the consequences of failure to disclose all material facts and explaining that these are facts that an insurer would regard as likely to influence the assessment and acceptance of a proposal;

        (ii) warning that if the signatory is in any doubt about whether certain facts are material, these facts should be disclosed.

    (b) Those matters which insurers have commonly found to be material should be the subject of clear questions in proposal forms.

    (c) Insurers should avoid asking questions which would require knowledge beyond that which the signatory could reasonably be expected to possess.

    (d) The proposal form or a supporting document should include a statement that a copy of the policy form or of the policy conditions is available on request.

    (e) A copy of the proposal should be made available to the policyholder when an insurer raises an issue under that proposal, information not relevant to that issue being deleted where necessary to preserve confidentiality.

3.   Policies and accompanying documents

    (a) Insurers will continue to develop clearer and more explicit proposal forms and policy documents whilst bearing in mind the legal nature of insurance contracts.

    (b) Life assurance policies or accompanying documents should indicate:—

        (i) the circumstances in which interest would accrue after the assurance has matured; and

        (ii) whether or not there are rights to surrender values in the contract and, if so, what those rights are.

(*Note:* The appropriate sales literature should endeavour to impress on proposers that a whole life or endowment assurance is intended to be a long-term contract and that surrender values, especially in the early years, are frequently less than the total premiums paid.)

4.   Commencement

Any changes to insurance documents will be made as and when they need to be reprinted but the statement will apply in the meantime.

The second development to which further reference is made below, at pp 324–326, is the establishment in March 1981 of an Insurance Ombudsman Bureau. The Ombudsman's powers and duties which again refer to the principles of 'good insurance practice' are in part as follows:

> To make awards up to £100,000—or up to £10,00 per annum in personal health insurance cases—binding on members.
> When making an award, to have regard to the terms of the contract, to act in conformity with any applicable rule of law or relevant judicial authority, general principles of good insurance practice, his Terms of Reference and the standards of insurance practice and codes of practice, but not to be bound by precedent.

NOTES

1. Not all the major insurance companies are parties to the above scheme. Some subscribe rather to the Personal Insurance Arbitration Service. For details see the note, 'Guidance on the Handling of Consumer Complaints about Insurance' (prepared jointly by the Department of Trade and Industry and the Office of Fair Trading, July 1983).

2. In relation to household insurance the Office of Fair Trading has recently issued 'Household Insurance: A Discussion Paper' (July 1984).

SURVEYORS, VALUERS AND OTHER PROFESSIONALS

In recent years there have been notable developments in the range of liability for professional negligence some of which may benefit consumers in the wide sense of the word. One such development is illustrated by the following case. For a text on the subject see Dugdale and Stanton *Professional Negligence* (1982).

Yianni v Edwin Evans & Sons (a firm) [1981] 3 All ER 592, [1982] QB 438, Queen's Bench Divisional Court

In October 1974 the then owners of an end-of-terrace house, 1 Seymour Road in North London, discovered serious defects in its foundations. Without remedying the defects they sold it to P in about April 1975. P carried out extensive, but essentially cosmetic repairs and redecoration, and then offered to resell the house to the plaintiffs for £15,000. The plaintiffs approached the Halifax Building Society for a loan of £12,000 and paid the society a survey fee of £33 for the valuation which the society was required by s 25 of the Building Societies Act 1962 to arrange to have carried out. The society instructed the defendants, a well-established firm of valuers and surveyors, to inspect and value the house. They named the plaintiffs as the purchasers, the purchase price and the loan required. The defendants inspected the house and reported to the society that it was adequate security for a loan of £12,000. The offer of an advance was duly made and the plaintiffs received a copy of the society's booklet which stated that it did not accept responsibility for the condition of the property offered as security. Borrowers were advised that the valuer's report was confidential to the society and that if they required a survey for their own information they should instruct an independent surveyor. The society also sent to the plaintiffs a notice under s 30 of the 1962 Act stating that the making of an advance would not imply that it was warranting that the purchase price was reasonable. The plaintiffs, in common with 90 per cent of applicants for mortgages to purchase lower-priced houses, accepted the society's offer without having the house surveyed independently. In January 1976 they completed the purchase and soon thereafter discovered cracks in the foundations which, it was estimated, would cost some £18,000 to repair. In subsequent proceedings the defendants admitted negligence in inspecting the house and reporting that it was adequate security for a loan of £12,000 but denied that they owed the plaintiffs a duty of care.

Park J, having stated the facts of the case and referred to the judgment of Denning LJ in *Candler v Crane, Christmas & Co* [1951] 2 KB 164, [1951] 1 All ER 426 at 433–436, CA and the decisions of the House of Lords in such cases as *Hedley Byrne & Co Ltd v Heller & Partners Ltd* [1964] AC 465, [1963] 2 All ER 575, HL and *Anns v Merton London Borough Council* [1978] AC 728, [1977] 2 All ER 492, HL continued:

Accordingly, guided by the passages in the judgment of Denning LJ in *Candler's* case and by the speeches in the House of Lords cases, I conclude that, in this case, the duty of care would arise if, on the evidence, I am satisfied that the defendants knew that their valuation of 1 Seymour Road, in so far as it stated that the property provided adequate security for an advance of £12,000, would be passed on to the plaintiffs who, notwithstanding the building society's literature and the service of the notice under s 30 of the 1962 Act, in the defendants' reasonable contemplation would place reliance on its correctness in making their decision to buy the house and mortgage it to the building society. What therefore does the evidence establish?

These defendants are surveyors and valuers. It is their profession and occupation to survey and make valuations of houses and other property. They make reports about the condition of property they have surveyed. Their duty is not merely to use care in their reports, they also have a duty to use care in their work which results in their reports. On the instructions of the building society, the defendants sent a representative to 1 Seymour Road to make a survey and valuation of that property. He knew that the object of the survey was to enable the defendants, his employers, to submit a report to the building society for the use of the directors in discharging their duty under s 25 of the Act. The report, therefore, had to be directed to the value of the property and to any matter likely to affect its value. The defendants knew, therefore, that the director or other officer in the building society who considered their report would use it for the purpose of assessing the adequacy of 1 Seymour Road as security for an advance. There is no evidence that the building society had access to any other reports or information for this purpose or that the defendants believed or assumed that the building society would have any information beyond that contained in their report. Accordingly, the defendants knew that the director or other officer of the building society who dealt with the plaintiffs' application would rely on the correctness of this report in making on behalf of the Society the offer of a loan on the security of 1 Seymour Road. The defendants therefore knew that the plaintiffs would receive from the building society an offer to lend £12,000, which sum, as the defendants also knew, the plaintiffs desired to borrow. It was argued that, as the information contained in the defendants' report was confidential to the directors, the defendants could not have foreseen that the contents of their report would be passed on to the plaintiffs. But the contents of the report never were passed on. This case is not about the contents of the entire report, it is about that part of the report which said that 1 Seymour Road was suitable as security for a loan of £12,000. The defendants knew that that part would have to be passed on to the plaintiffs, since the reason for the plaintiffs' application was to obtain a loan of £12,000. Accordingly, the building society's offer of £12,000, when passed on to the plaintiffs, confirmed to them that 1 Seymour Road was sufficiently valuable to cause the building society to advance on its security 80% of the purchase price. Since that was also the building society's view the plaintiffs' belief was not unreasonable.

It was argued that there was no reasonable likelihood that the plaintiffs would rely on the fact that the defendants had made a valuation report to the building society or, alternatively, that the defendants could not reasonably have foreseen or contemplated first, that the plaintiffs would rely on the valuation in the report or, second, that they would act unreasonably in failing to obtain an independent surveyor's report for their own guidance. These submissions were founded on the fact that the defendants would know that the plaintiffs would have been provided with the building society's literature and that the building society, for its own protection, would have served with their offer the statutory notice pursuant to s 30 of the 1962 Act. Now these defendants, plainly, are in a substantial way of business in London as surveyors and valuers. The documents show that they have an address at Down Street, Mayfair, and another in Lavender Hill, London SW11. They must have on their staff some members of the Royal Institute of Chartered Surveyors. The terms of the building society's request to them to value 1 Seymour Road indicated that they had regularly carried out valuations for the Halifax, and no doubt for other building societies. Mr Hunter's evidence is that for some six years over 90% of applicants for a building society mortgage have relied on the building society's valuation, as represented by the building society's offer of an advance, as a statement that the house in question is worth at least that sum. These applicants, and in particular applicants seeking to buy houses at the lower end of the property market, do not read building society literature, or, if they do, they ignore the advice to have an independent survey and also the terms of the statutory notice. Mr Hunter's evidence was unchallenged. No witness was called to suggest that he had in any way misrepresented the beliefs, conduct and practice of the typical applicant. I think that Mr Hunter was telling me what was common knowledge in the professional world of building societies and of surveyors and valuers employed or instructed by them. I am satisfied that the defendants were fully aware of all these matters.

The defendants' representative who surveyed and valued 1 Seymour Road noted the type of dwelling house it was, its age, its price and the locality in which it was situated. It was plainly a house at the lower end of the property market. The applicant for a loan would therefore almost certainly be a person of modest means who, for one reason or another, would not be expected to obtain an independent valuation, and who would be certain to rely, as the plaintiffs in fact did, on the defendants' valuation as communicated to him in the building society's offer. I am sure that the defendants knew that their valuation would be passed on to the plaintiffs and that the defendants knew that the plaintiffs would rely on it when they decided to accept the building society's offer.

For these reasons I have come to the conclusion that the defendants owed a duty of care to the plaintiffs because, to use the words of Lord Wilberforce in *Anns v London Borough of Merton*, there was a sufficient relationship of proximity such that in the reasonable contemplation of the defendants carelessness on their part might be likely to cause damage to the plaintiffs.

I turn now to consider whether there are any considerations which ought to negative or to reduce or limit the scope of the duty or the class of person to whom it is owed. Counsel for the defendants submitted that for a number of reasons of policy the plaintiffs should have no remedy against the defendants. First he said a decision in favour of the plaintiffs would encourage applicants for a mortgage to have no independent survey of the house they wished to buy. I can see nothing objectionable in a practice which would result in a house being surveyed once by one surveyor. In my view, the Abbey National, since September 1980, have adopted a sensible procedure for dealing with the survey problem, if it is a problem. Mr Hunter said that as a matter of courtesy the Abbey National now disclose their valuation report to applicants. He also said: 'We felt that we had information which had been obtained by qualified and experienced people and it was of benefit to give that information to the applicant.' In addition, the Abbey National are about to introduce a report on condition and valuation so that, as Mr Hunter put it, the applicant has the choice of either the standard building society mortgage valuation report or the report on condition and valuation which covers the popular conception of structural survey, market valuation and mortgage valuation.

Counsel also submitted that if the defendants were held liable to the plaintiffs no professional man would be able to limit his liability to a third party, even if he could do so to his own client. He would be at the mercy of a client who might pass on his report to a third party and, as defects in the property he had surveyed might not manifest themselves for many years, he would be likely to remain under a liability for those defects he ought to have detected for a very long period, and at the end of the period, for an unlimited amount by way of damages. In my view, the only person to whom the surveyor is liable is the party named in the building society's 'Instructions to Valuer' addressed to him. That party, as well as the building society, has to be regarded as his client. That does not seem to me to be unreasonable, since, to his knowledge, his fee for the valuation is paid by that party to the building society which hands it over to him. On this submission, it can also be said that the surveyor's report is concerned with the valuation of a dwelling house, the condition of which is important only in so far as it affects its value at that time. It is common knowledge that in the ordinary way, the market value of a dwelling house is not static. Consequently, a valuation made at one time for the purpose of assessing its suitability as security for a loan would be of limited use. . . .

. . . Finally counsel said that the plaintiffs should be held guilty of contributory negligence because they failed to have an independent survey, made no inquiries with the object of discovering what had been done to the house before they decided to buy it, failed to read the literature provided by the building society and generally took no steps to discover the true condition of the house. It is true that the plaintiffs failed in all these respects, but that failure was due to the fact that they relied on the defendants to make a competent valuation of the house. I have been given no reason why they were unwise to do so. I have earlier read the paragraph under the heading 'Valuation' in the building society's handbook which Mr Yianni did not read. No doubt if the paragraph had been in stronger terms, and had included a warning that it would be dangerous to rely on the valuer's report, then I think that the plaintiffs might well have been held to be negligent. But, in my judgment, on the evidence the allegation of contributory negligence fails.

In my judgment for these reasons the defendants are liable to pay damages to the plaintiffs for the grievous loss they have suffered by the defendants' negligence.

Judgment for the plaintiffs.

Questions

1. Suppose that a similar incompetence were displayed when carrying out a building society survey in the top end of the price range where independent surveys are more common. Should a house-owner who had not had such a survey recover then? Is it open to a court to reduce the damages payable to such a house-owner on the ground of contributory negligence?

2. If failure to discover the need for re-building and under-pinning the plaintiffs' house had caused damage to the adjoining terrace house should the plaintiffs' neighbour have been entitled to recover against the defendant surveyors?

3. Should one's attitude to the result of such cases differ according to whether the hapless occupier has an operative first-party property insurance covering the results of subsidence?

CHAPTER 4

Product liability

Introduction

Strict contractual liability for breach of the implied terms as to quality in contracts for the sale of goods has long been a feature of English law. So in *Daniels and Daniels v R White & Sons Ltd and Tarbard* [1938] All ER 258, above p 19, the retail vendor of a bottle of lemonade contaminated by carbolic acid during its bottling process was liable although she was 'perfectly innocent'; see also above pp 89–90. However such strict liability extends only to contracting parties (like Mr Daniels in the above case), the privity of contract limitation preventing third parties (like Mrs Daniels) from benefiting from the implied terms: see above p 18 et seq. For many years this strict contractual liability was paralleled by a supposed rule of non-liability in tort: see *Winterbottom v Wright* (1842) 10 M & W 109. It was only in 1932 in the leading case of *Donoghue v Stevenson* [1932] AC 562, HL that it was established authoritatively in the House of Lords that a manufacturer is prima facie liable on proof of negligence when a defect in his goods causes personal injury or property damage to a consumer. The background of the case was of shock and severe gastro-enteritis allegedly suffered as a result of drinking a bottle of ginger beer contaminated by the remnants of a decomposed snail and Lord Atkin said at p 599:

> My Lords, if your Lordships accept the view that this pleading discloses a relevant cause of action you will be affirming the proposition that by Scots and English law alike a manufacturer of products, which he sells in such a form as to show that he intends them to reach the ultimate consumer in the form in which they left him with no reasonable possibility of intermediate examination, and with the knowledge that the absence of reasonable care in the preparation or putting up of the products will result in an injury to the consumer's life or property, owes a duty to the consumer to take that reasonable care.
>
> It is a proposition which I venture to say no one in Scotland or England who was not a lawyer would for one moment doubt. It will be an advantage to make it clear that the law in this matter, as in most others, is in accordance with sound common sense.

In fact two fellow-members of the House of Lords *did* doubt the 'proposition' and the duty of care was established on the basis of a bare three to two majority. In recent years discussion has centred on a move from the present system which requires proof of negligence to a system of strict liability. The point is discussed below. However the following cases are of interest as indicating the scope of liability under the present system. In reading them it is helpful to consider (i) the various respects in which it was alleged that the product was defective and (ii) the standard of care required. For more detailed discussion see Miller and Lovell *Product Liability* (1977); Miller *Product Liability and Safety Encyclopaedia* and the Law Commission report on 'Liability for Defective Products' (Law Com No 82, Cmnd 6831, 1977).

Liability in negligence

Hill v James Crowe (Cases) Ltd [1978] 1 All ER 812, Queen's Bench Divisional Court

The facts are set out in the judgment:

Mackenna J read the following judgment: On 25 January 1973 the plaintiff, Mr Hill, was working as a lorry driver employed by A A Kent Ltd. His work took him that day to a warehouse owned by Newbold Shipping Services at Silvertown in the East End of London, where he had to load on to his lorry a number of packed wooden cases and also cartons containing television sets. A fork-lift truck, operated by one of Newbold's men, lifted the cases on to the floor of the lorry, where Mr Hill moved them into a suitable position. The cases covered the floor of the lorry, which was then ready to receive the cartons which would also be brought to him by the truck. He was standing on one of the cases waiting for the first load of cartons when he fell to the ground, injuring his ankle and, more seriously, his right hand.

He brings this action against James Crowe (Cases) Ltd, whom I shall call 'Crowe', claiming that his accident was caused by their negligence. Crowe are in business as packers of goods for shipment overseas, and in the course of this business they manufacture wooden cases. They had made at least one of the cases which had been loaded on to Mr Hill's lorry to carry a quantity of household goods from London to Lagos in West Africa for delivery to a Miss Ronke Allison. Mr Hill alleges that just before he fell he had been standing on the end of this case when some of the boards stove in, causing him to lose his balance and fall. He says that the case was badly nailed. The fact of his accident, he argues, by itself proves bad manufacture, and if it does not he says that he has proved by the testimony of a credible witness that not enough nails were used to fasten the boards. Crowe, he says, owed a duty to those who were likely to come in contact with the case in transit to make it strong enough to withstand the foreseeable hazards of its journey; and one of these was the likelihood of persons standing on it in the course of loading who might be injured if the boards caved in. They had neglected this duty, and their negligence was the cause of this accident for which they are liable in damages.

On liabilty there are four issues (1) Did Mr Hill fall because the boards of the packing case he was standing on caved in? If so, (2) was the packing case badly made? If so, (3) ought the maker to have foreseen that if it were badly made persons in Mr Hill's position might suffer injury in some such way as Mr Hill was injured and to have taken care to make it properly, so that their failure to do so was in law negligence? If so, (4) had the case on which Mr Hill was standing been made by Crowe? I have no hesitation in answering all these questions in Mr Hill's favour.

. . .

In spite of Mr Crowe's evidence, I find that the accident happened while the plaintiff was standing on the packing case which Crowe had made; that it was caused by the end caving in; and that it caved in because it had been very badly nailed. If the case can be brought within the rule in *Donoghue v Stevenson*[1] liability is established.

. . .

Counsel for Crowe relied on *Daniels and Daniels v R White & Sons Ltd and Tarbard*[2]. The plaintiff in that case had bought at a public house a sealed bottle of lemonade made by the defendant manufacturers and sold by them to the public house. The bottle contained, in addition to the lemonade, a quantity of carbolic acid which it was contended had caused injury to the plaintiff, who sued the manufacturers. His action failed. The manufacturers satisfied Lewis J, the trial judge, that they had a good system of work in their factory and provided adequate supervision. He said[3]:

> 'I am quite satisfied, however, on the evidence before me, that the work of this factory is carried on under proper supervision, and, therefore, that there has been no failure of the duty owed by the defendant company to the plaintiffs.'

With respect, I do not think that this was a sufficient reason for dismissing the claim. The manufacturer's liability in negligence did not depend on proof that he had either a bad system of work or that his supervision was inadequate. He might also be vicariously liable for the negligence of his workmen in the course of their employment. If the plaintiff's injuries were a reasonably foreseeable consequence of such negligence, the manufacturer's liability would be established under *Donoghue v Stevenson*[1]. *Daniels and Daniels v R White & Sons Ltd and Tarbard*[2] has been criticised, I think justly, in *Charlesworth on Negligence*[4] and I do not propose to follow it.

I hold Crowe liable in negligence. I find that there was no contributory negligence on Mr Hill's part, and I turn to the question of damages.

[His Lordship then considered the extent of the plaintiff's injuries and the medical evidence relating thereto and assessed total damages in the sum of £8,298.81]

Judgment for the plaintiff.

1. [1932] AC 562, [1932] All ER Rep 1.
2. [1938] 4 All ER 258.
3. [1938] 4 All ER 258 at 263.
4. 5th Edn (1971), p 398.

Questions

Obviously wooden packing cases, unlike ladders, are not built for people to stand on. Would the decision have been different if the case had been nailed together correctly but was still insufficiently strong to carry the lorry driver's weight?

Suppose it had been marked 'Danger. Do not stand on this case'. Would the plaintiff have recovered then?

It is clear from this decision that negligence may be found in the fault of an individual employee as well as in the manufacturer's quality control system. The Privy Council had made the same point in *Grant v Australian Knitting Mill Ltd* [1936] AC 85 where the plaintiff had contracted dermatitis as a result, it was alleged, of wearing the defendants' undergarments. Distinguishing between the position of the retail seller and the manufacturers Lord Wright said at pp 100–101:

The retailers, accordingly, in their Lordships' judgment are liable in contract: so far as they are concerned, no question of negligence is relevant to the liability in contract. But when the position of the manufacturers is considered, different questions arise: there is no privity of contract between the appellant and the manufacturers: between them the liability, if any, must be in tort, and the gist of the cause of action is negligence. The facts set out in the foregoing show, in their Lordships' judgment, negligence in manufacture. According to the evidence, the method of manufacture was correct: the danger of excess sulphites being left was recognised and was guarded against: the process was intended to be fool proof. If excess sulphites were left in the garment, that could only be because some one was at fault. The appellant is not required to lay his finger on the exact person in all the chain who was responsible, or to specify what he did wrong. Negligence is found as a matter of inference from the existence of the defects taken in connection with all the known circumstances: even if the manufacturers could by apt evidence have rebutted that inference they have not done so.

Question

If circumstances are such that the defects must have been present from the time the product left the manufacturer's control are there any advantages in establishing the excellence of a quality control system?

Evans v Triplex Safety Glass Co Ltd [1936] 1 All ER 283, King's Bench Divisional Court

The facts are set out in the judgment:

Porter J: This is an action brought by Mr Evans and his wife against the Triplex Safety Glass Co Ltd. In June, 1934, the plaintiff bought a Vauxhall Saloon car and at the time Vauxhall cars were fitted with 'Triplex Toughened Safety Glass.' Mr Evans bought the car in 1934 with a windscreen fitted with this particular type of glass and drove it until 7 July 1935. On that day he was driving with his wife and boy down to Devonshire and after passing through Salisbury and then leaving Shaftesbury at a moderate pace of 30 mph there was a report and the windscreen cracked in the form shown in the photograph produced, disintegrated, and great care had to be exercised in pulling up. It disintegrated into small pieces and the centre portion fell out causing small cuts to the boy; a portion fell on to Mr Evans, and a considerable portion fell over his wife and she suffered in consequence a severe shock.

Now the plaintiff could have made a claim against either the seller of the car or against the manufacturers of the windscreen. The plaintiff suggested that a claim should be made against the defendants, and I can see many good reasons why a claim should be made against them. There was a contractual relationship between the plaintiff and the sellers of the Vauxhall car and the plaintiff could have sued them for breach of contract but the effect of bringing the claim in negligence is that all the contract goes and the action is brought in tort. The result is that the plaintiff must show negligence on the part of the defendants as there is no breach of warranty as in contract. The plaintiff has therefore framed his case on *M'Alister (or Donoghue) v Stevenson*. In that case the court by a majority of three judges to two held that the defendants had been guilty of negligence and I am bound by that decision which makes it clear that an action may be brought in tort against a manufacturer for negligence by an ultimate consumer. One has, however, to consider the limitations which give rise to user. The plaintiff must prove negligence and there must not be an opportunity for examination by an intermediate party or an ultimate purchaser. The article must reach the purchaser in the form in which it left the manufacturer. Now in this case I do not propose to make new law or to lay down exact limits and so far as this case is concerned the negligence has been put in this way. The plaintiff says that the proper inference for me to draw is that a flaw in this kind of glass is more susceptible to cause damage than a flaw in other glass, and the fact that it may disintegrate is in itself dangerous and especially as it does so without any warning, and therefore the plaintiff should be able to recover. That is the way in which the plaintiff puts his case.

The evidence given in support of the act of negligence is as follows. The plaintiff, who does not know anything about the technical aspect of the case, said he was driving along the road when the windscreen exploded without any apparent cause. I am not sure that the actual cause of the damage was a light blow on the windscreen which was not noticed by the plaintiff, but a light blow according to defendants ought not to break the windscreen, and I am inclined to agree with this. Now the evidence given by another witness for the plaintiff was that 'toughened glass' was not suitable for use in motor cars at all because he said that even if the glass was properly made and manufactured changes of temperature would cause it to disintegrate. He also said that there were other causes which might make the glass disintegrate, namely improperly manufactured glass or a stone jumping up and striking the windscreen or a scratch on the surface. According to the evidence given by the defendants it would need a good deal more than a scratch to cause the glass to disintegrate. They say that it will stand up to ordinary heat and a light blow will not cause disintegration. They point out that the glass is carefully manufactured and properly examined. It is heated up to 600 degrees and they say that this glass would stand up to an ordinary blow from a non-cutting instrument better than ordinary glass and that the usual cause of disintegration was a breakage of the outside surface. In those circumstances am I to infer that properly made glass would never disintegrate without fault?

In this case I do not think that I ought to infer negligence on the part of the defendants . . . No doubt this glass does suffer from disadvantages. If the outside surface is broken by cutting or if it is strained when it is being screwed into its frame we have disintegration. In this case I cannot draw the inference that the cause of the disintegration was the faulty manufacture. It is true that the human element may fail and then the manufacturers would be liable for negligence of their employee, but then that was not proved in this case. The disintegration may have been caused by any accident. There was every opportunity for failure on the part of the human element in fastening the windscreen, and I think that the disintegration was due rather to the fitting of the windscreen than to faulty manufacture having regard to its use on the road and the damage done to a windscreen in the course of user.

It is true that, as Mr Macaskie points out, in these cases he has not got to eliminate every possible element, but he has got to eliminate every probable element. He has not displaced sufficiently the balance of probabilities in this case. I think that this glass is reasonably safe and possibly more safe than other glasses. One cannot help seeing that in all these cases one has to look with considerable care. One has to consider the question of time. The plaintiff had had the windscreen for about a year. Then there is the possibility of examination. The suppliers of the car had every opportunity to examine the windscreen. I do not propose to lay down any rule of law; it is a question of degree and these elements must be taken into consideration. This article was put into a frame and screwed; one must consider that. As I have said there is the element of time, the opportunity of examination and the opportunity of damage from other causes. One must consider all these factors.

In *Donoghue v Stevenson* there was a snail in the ginger beer bottle and there was no opportunity of seeing it as you could not see through the glass. In *Grant v Australian Knitting Mills Ltd* the article passed on to the purchaser and it is quite clear that a reasonable examination of the garment would not have revealed the presence of the sulphite. That case is different from this. In that case there was found in some of the garments an excess of sulphites and that clearly was the cause of the injury. Here are a number of causes which might have caused disintegration. I do not find any negligence proved against the defendants and I give the defendants judgment with costs.

Questions

1. Is it likely that the plaintiff would have recovered if he had sued (i) the manufacturer of the Vauxhall saloon car; (ii) the manufacturers of the car and the windscreen jointly?

2. Should the manufacturer of a complex product be held responsible for any negligence on the part of a component producer? See *Taylor v Rover Co Ltd* [1966] 2 All ER 181, [1966] 1 WLR 1491, Miller and Lovell, op cit, pp 199–207.

Problem

Jumbo, a manufacturer of executive jet aeroplanes, buys in altimeters from Telstar, a specialist producer. A faulty altimeter is fitted to one of Jumbo's planes causing it to crash with consequent loss of life. The fault is attributable to negligence on the part of Telstar. It is accepted that Jumbo has exercised reasonable care in testing and fitting the altimeter.

Consider the liability of (i) Telstar, (ii) Jumbo.

Vacwell Engineering Co Ltd v B.D.H. Chemicals Ltd (formerly British Drug Houses Ltd) [1969] 3 All ER 1681, [1971] 1 QB 88, Queen's Bench Divisional Court

The defendants manufactured a chemical, boron tribromide, which they marketed for industrial use in glass ampoules bearing a warning label 'harmful vapour'. Following discussion with the defendants, the plaintiffs used the chemical in their business of manufacturing transistor materials. In order to prepare the chemical the labels were washed off the ampoules in sinks containing water and a detergent. In April 1966 a visiting Russian physicist was engaged in this task when there was a violent explosion resulting in his death and in extensive damage to the plaintiffs' premises. In all probability one of the ampoules had been dropped into the sink where it had shattered, releasing the chemical into the water. The ensuing reaction had broken the glass of the other ampoules, causing a major explosion. At the time the explosive properties of boron tribromide on contact with water were unknown to the defendants; neither were they referred to in a standard work on the industrial hazards of chemicals, nor in three other modern works which the defendants had apparently consulted. Nonetheless the dangers had been detailed in scientific literature dating from 1878. The present proceedings were based on both contract and tort.

Rees J, having held that the defendants, B.D.H., were liable in contract for breach of an implied condition of fitness for purpose (above p 81) continued:

The duty which Vacwell allege rested on B.D.H. was to take reasonable care to ascertain major industrial hazards of chemicals marketed by them and to give warning of such hazards to their customers. It was not argued before me that there was an absolute duty on B.D.H. to give warning of industrial hazards of dangerous chemicals, whether they could have discovered them by the exercise of reasonable care or not. I find that the duty to take reasonable care as stated above is the duty which rested on B.D.H. in the circumstances of this case. I have already reviewed the evidence in relation to this aspect of the matter and I need not repeat it. I am satisfied that B.D.H. failed to comply with their duty in two respects: first, they failed to provide and maintain a system for carrying out an adequate research into scientific literature to ascertain known hazards; secondly, by Mr Hill and Dr Muir they failed to carry out an adequate research into the scientific literature available to them in order to discover the industrial hazards of a new, or little-known, chemical. If that duty had been complied with, I have no doubt that the explosion hazard noted by Gautier and others would have come to light and a suitable warning been given, which would have prevented Vacwell dealing with the ampoules of boron tribromide as they did. The greater part of the observations which I have made earlier in this judgment in relation to causation and remoteness of damage apply in the present context also. But in tort, foreseeability of damage is the paramount test.

. . .

Here, it was a forseeable consequence of the supply of boron tribromide without a warning—and a fortiori with an irrelevant warning about harmful vapour—that, in the ordinary course of industrial user, it could come into contact with water and cause a violent reaction and possibly an explosion. It would also be foreseeable that some damage to property would, or might, result. In my judgment, the explosion and the type of damage being foreseeable, it matters not in the law that the magnitude of the former and the extent of the latter were not.

Finally, I turn to the question of the contributory negligence of Vacwell. The conduct of Vacwell must be looked at in the context that they knew of the risks arising from the harmful fumes caused on contact between boron tribromide and air or water. They also knew that there was some reaction between boron tribromide and water. Consequently, they dealt with the chemical on the footing that some minor harm might arise from inhaling the vapour or from the splashing of the chemical; they did not know, and it is not now alleged that they ought to have known, of the uniquely dangerous explosion hazard. Further, one must also take into account that the positive warning given to them by B.D.H. itself supported a reasonable inference that there was no other major hazard likely to arise in the ordinary course of industrial process. It is alleged against Vacwell that, even if it were justifiable to immerse one or a few ampoules of boron tribromide in water, it was obviously dangerous to immerse between 40 and 100 ampoules in each of two adjacent sinks. It is further alleged that there was carelessness on the part of the Russian scientist in using detergent which made the ampoules slippery and in allowing one or more of the ampoules to fall from his hand into the sink. I have considered these allegations with great care.

Having regard to all the circumstances and to the evidence which I accept, I do not find it negligent on the part of Vacwell to have decided to place 200 ampoules in water in two adjacent sinks. The evidence does not justify a finding that they ought to have known that there was a risk by so doing that the breaking of one or two ampoules would cause anything but the minimal harm for which they had adequate protection available in the form of gas-masks; nor that the breaking of one or two ampoules could cause the remainder to disintegrate. I have hesitated whether a finding of negligence should be made against the Russian scientist on the footing that, if he dropped an ampoule, it necessarily means that he was careless. There is no evidence as to precisely what happened, and in all the circumstances I am not prepared to hold that he was negligent. Even if such a finding had been justified by the evidence, in the context of this case the blame to be apportioned in respect of this negligence is so minimal as perhaps to fall into that category of which the law would refuse to take account.

Judgment for Vacwell.

NOTE

Subsequently the Court of Appeal approved the terms of a settlement on the basis that Rees J had been correct in adopting this approach to the question of remoteness of damage in tort. However a reduction of 20% in the damages to be assessed by an Official Referee was agreed to take account of the possibility of contributory negligence: see [1971] 1 QB 88, pp 111–112.

On the general question of failure to give adequate warnings and directions for use see Miller and Lovell, op cit, Ch 12; Macleod, 'Instructions as to the Use of Consumer Goods' (1981) 97 LQR 550.

Question

What are the principal factors of which account should be taken in deciding whether warnings or directions for use are (i) necessary, (ii) sufficient?

Problem

Kleenit markets a household product containing caustic soda. The product carries a prominent label reading, 'Danger. Keep Away from Children'. The container which is not childproof is opened and the substance ingested by Percy, aged three, who has taken it from beneath the kitchen sink. He becomes seriously ill.

Advise Percy's next friend.

Albery & Budden v BP Oil Ltd & Shell UK Ltd (1980) 2 May (Lexis transcript), (1980) 124 Sol Jo 376, Court of Appeal

The infant plaintiffs lived near the Westway in North Kensington. They claimed damages and an injunction restraining the defendant companies from using organo-lead additives in their petrol at the maximum level then permitted by regulations made by the Secretary of State under the Control of Pollution Act 1974. Judge Leonard, sitting at the Mayor's and City of London Court, had struck out the particulars of claim insofar as they alleged a cause of action in public nuisance but allowed the claims in negligence to proceed. The defendants now appealed against the judge's refusal to strike out the claims in negligence and the plaintiffs cross-appealed on the issue of nuisance. The form of the proceedings was accordingly such that the action would be dismissed only if there was no real chance of success. Megaw LJ, having outlined the facts of the case, read the following judgment of the court.

The defendants rightly and necessarily concede that, for the purpose of the decision of these applications, it is to be assumed that the plaintiffs in each action would be able, on the hearing of the actions, to establish that each of these two infant plaintiffs had, by July 1978, sustained physical injury as a result of excess lead content in the blood; that that excess of lead content had been caused, in part, by particles of lead emitted from motor vehicles as a result of the combustion of petrol to which lead had been deliberately added; that a proportion of that petrol was petrol which had been manufactured and sold by the first defendant, BP Oil Ltd, and that a further proportion of it had been manufactured and sold by the second defendant, Shell UK Ltd. It is thus to be assumed for the purpose of these applications, that each of the infant plaintiffs had, when the actions began, suffered some physical injury which had been caused, in part, by the fact that the defendants' petrol included lead.

But in order to establish his cause of action a plaintiff has to show, not merely causation, but also negligence on the part of the defendant . . .

For the plaintiffs, it is rightly submitted that it is not for them at this stage, in respect of an application of this nature, to produce the evidence which they will hope to have available and to use when the actions come on for trial, if they were allowed to proceed. But they have indicated in outline the nature of the evidence which they would be minded to produce. They refer to various reports and articles by experts, medical and scientific, showing over many years increasing awareness and concern as to the dangers of the ingestion by human beings of particles of lead from the atmosphere, and from things, including food such as vegetables, which may have been contaminated by the fall of lead particles from the atmosphere: particularly in relation to persons living in areas close to highways where there is much motor traffic; and particularly in relation to young children. The plaintiffs also refer to what has happened in countries other than the United Kingdom: in particular, the Soviet Union, West Germany, Japan and the United States of America, in which it appears that legislation has provided for the reduction of the lead content in petrol to be used in motor vehicles to a much lower limit than is the so-called 'maximum permitted amount' in the United Kingdom. Such reductions, it would seem, in at least some of those countries, have not only proceeded much further, but also started earlier and were required to be achieved on a substantially quicker time-scale, than has been required by corresponding legislative provisions in the United Kingdom. It is submitted for the plaintiffs, making all the assumptions in favour of the plaintiffs which must be made in applications of this nature, and having regard to the facilities available to the two defendants to receive and collate information as to all such matters, and with the duty which they had to give it careful consideration in order to avoid creating hazards to the public or to classes of the public, the court could not properly reach the conclusion that the case of negligence against the defendants must fail.

For the defendants on this issue there are put forward certain matters which are not in dispute. In 1972, there was a British Standard, BS4040, with which the oil industry in the United Kingdom voluntarily complied. It prescribed a maximum permitted content of lead in petrol of 0.84 grammes per litre. In that year it was announced by the then Secretary of State for the Environment that while the Chief Medical Officer of Health had advised that present levels of lead emissions did not offer a danger to health, it was desirable that they should not be exceeded, and, if possible, reduced. There had thereafter been agreement between the Secretary of State for the Environment and the Secretary of State for Trade and Industry that there should be what was described as a 'phased reduction' in the lead content of petrol. By the end of 1972, the previous 0.84 grammes per litre was to be reduced to 0.64 grammes per litre; by the end of 1973 to 0.55, and by the end of 1975 to 0.45. The oil and motor industries had been consulted and had given an assurance of co-operation. The programme was to be backed by legislation. In fact, the planned reduction to 0.55 was postponed by the Government, because of the oil crisis of that time, from January 1974 to November 1974. The further reduction to 0.45 planned for January 1976 was deferred by the Government pending further review of medical and economic issues and was overtaken by the first statutory reduction under legislation to which we now turn. It is not in dispute that both the defendants adhered in full to these planned reductions.

In 1974, the Control of Pollution Act 1974 was enacted. Section 75 made provision for regulations about motor fuel . . .

Section 77 provided that failure to comply with a provision or regulation under, inter alia, section 75 should be an offence, and provisions were made as to the penalties for such offences.

On 9 November 1976 there were laid before Parliament the Motor Fuel (Lead Content of Petrol) Regulations, 1976. They came into force on 30 November 1976 . . . There is no dispute but that the defendants have at all times complied with the regulations. They have not exceeded the permitted amount.

A submission was made on behalf of the defendants that the combined effect of section 75(1) of the 1974 Act, and the regulations, provided the defendants with an unanswerable statutory defence to the claim. Parliament authorised the Secretary of State to impose requirements. The Secretary of State has imposed requirements. These requirements are that the lead content of petrol shall not exceed a certain amount, which is a 'permitted' amount. The defendants have not exceeded the permitted amount. Hence what they have done was expressly permitted by subordinate legislation authorised by statute.

We do not think it is desirable to say more about that submission than this: it is at least arguable that the suggested interpretation of the statute is not correct. Hence it would not be right to dismiss these actions at this stage on that ground. But there remains to be considered the suggested relevance of these same matters, not as a statutory defence, but as necessarily defeating claims in these actions that the defendants were negligent.

. . .

A consideration which is of crucial importance on this aspect of the case is this: regulations such as were contemplated by section 75 of the 1974 Act could not be other than general in their application. It would not be possible to prescribe that petrol which is likely to be used in a motor vehicle which is likely to travel in a congested urban area near traffic-ridden roads should have a content of lead different from, and lower than, petrol which is likely to be used in a vehicle which will probably emit its fumes, for the most part, while travelling in rural areas. Any limitation, or a total prohibition, of lead content would have to be of general application. The fact that the dangers to health, whatever they are, are likely to be greater in areas such as those in which these two infant plaintiffs live is a matter which would most certainly be proper to take into account. But separate and different requirements for different areas or for the protection of different ages or groups of persons would not be possible.

There is no suggestion that the 1976 regulations could be attacked as being, or resulting from, an abuse of the Secretary of State's powers under the Act, or as being otherwise ultra vires. Hence it is to be assumed that he duly carried out the required consultations and that he took into account all the factors which he ought to have taken into account, and that he did not take into account any factor which he should not have considered, in arriving at his decision embodied in the provisions in the regulations.

That conclusion of the Secretary of State, accepted by Parliament, may have been right or it may have been wrong. It may be—and the plaintiffs would no doubt so contend—that it was a conclusion which was not in the public interest: the public interest, they believe, required a much more drastic limitation, if not an immediate and a total exclusion, of lead in petrol, whatever the practical consequences might have been. It is not for the court to express a view whether the Secretary of State was right or wrong.

. . .

It is true that the regulations provide for criminal penalties. But the criterion which the Secretary of State must surely be assumed to have applied is the criterion of the public interest, taking the country as a whole, and giving weight to all the relevant considerations. We find it difficult to believe that there is, in a matter of this nature, any reason to suppose that a different standard should be, or would be, applied in fixing a permitted limit by reference to criminal or civil liability. The limit must be a limit of general application, consistent, in the view of the Secretary of State and of Parliament, with the public interest.

The question which the defendants ought to have asked themselves, at whatever may have been the relevant date or dates for the purposes of the negligence here alleged, is the identical question which the Secretary of State had to decide. Precisely the same considerations applied as being relevant. Any decision as to lead content had to relate to the manufacture and sale throughout the country. It could not be a decision to have different levels for petrol which might be used in cars travelling in one area rather than another. The standard to be applied was the standard of the public interest. Manufacturers or suppliers of petrol could not be negligent in a matter such as this, where there cannot be varied limits for varied circumstances, if the limit to which they adhered was a limit which they were entitled reasonably to believe to be consistent with the public interest. There is no suggestion, and any such suggestion has been disclaimed, that there was available to either of the defendants at any relevant time any relevant information which they failed properly to disclose or which would not have been available to the Secretary of State and his advisers in carrying out the task imposed on him by Parliament and in reaching his decision.

In these circumstances, we are unable to see how a court could hold that a reasonable person, with the knowledge which the defendants had or should have had, objectively weighing all relevant considerations, had failed in his duty, owed to the plaintiffs, in following and complying with the requirements prescribed by the Secretary of State and approved, impliedly, by Parliament, after the investigations which had been made of the very matters which were relevant for the defendant's decisions.

This is not to say that the courts are bound to hold, where a limit has been prescribed in the interests of safety by statute or statutory regulations, that one who keeps within these limits cannot be guilty of negligence at common law.

. . .

But if . . . the defendants are liable here and are subject to injunctions restricting them to some limit which would be below the limits laid down under the 1974 Act and regulations, the same would apply in all the subsequent actions which would, no doubt, perfectly properly follow against all other manufacturers and suppliers of petrol in this country. The courts would thus necessarily be, in effect, laying down a permissible limit which would be of universal application: that is, not related to, or confined to, particular areas or particular circumstances. The permissible limit thus ordained by the courts, to be enforced as being orders of the courts, would be different from, and inconsistent with, the permissible limit prescribed by the authority of Parliament. That would result in a constitutional anomaly which in our view would be wholly unacceptable. The authority of Parliament must prevail. Where Parliament has decided a matter of general policy, the courts cannot properly be asked to make decisions, by way of litigation under the adversary procedure, the effect of which would, or might, be that the courts would lay down, and require to be enforced with the authority of the courts, a different and inconsistent policy.

We stress again that this does not mean that where Parliament prescribes a limit the courts may not hold a defendant liable in negligence even though he does not go above the limit. But that does not arise where what the court is asked to do, as here, is to lay down a limit which must necessarily be inconsistent with a limit of general application prescribed under the authority of Parliament, by reference to the self-same criterion – here, the general public interest in the extent and time-scale of limitations of the lead content in petrol—as Parliament has applied.

We therefore allow the appeals and dismiss the cross-appeals. We would order that the particulars of claim be struck out and the two actions be dismissed.

Appeals allowed; cross-appeals dismissed; costs below to be paid by next friends, such order not to be enforced without leave of court; costs of appeal adjourned, with liberty to Law Society to be represented; leave to appeal to House of Lords refused; legal aid taxation, both plaintiffs.

NOTE

For further discussion of the relevance of such standards see Miller and Lovell, op cit, p 264 et seq.

Question

Do you agree with the views of Megaw LJ, as to the relationship between the courts, government and Parliament on such matters?

Walton and Walton v British Leyland UK Ltd (1978) (unreported), Judgment of 12 July, Queen's Bench Divisional Court

The Honourable Mr Justice Willis: The facts and tragic results of the accident which gave rise to this claim are not in dispute and can be shortly stated. Mr and Mrs Victor Walton, the Plaintiffs, were on holiday in this country from Australia. During the evening of 22 April 1976 they were travelling northwards on the M1 motorway as passengers in an Austin Allegro motor car, owned and driven by the first Plaintiff's brother, Mr Albert Walton. At a point near Newport Pagnell when the car was travelling at 50–60 mph the *rear nearside wheel* came off, the driver lost control and the vehicle collided with the central crash barrier. Both plaintiffs are elderly, in their sixties. Miraculously the first plaintiff, who is a handicapped person, escaped with minor injuries; his wife was thrown from the car; she suffered catastrophic injuries which it is not necessary to detail, and has been left a quadriplegic.

Although both the first and second defendants saw fit in their pleadings to allege negligence on the part of the driver, Albert Walton, those allegations were properly withdrawn by Counsel on the first day of the trial: during the course of the case by the first defendant an agreement inter partes was announced that both plaintiffs are entitled to recover their damages in full—the sums to be assessed later—subject to a reservation immaterial to these proceedings, for the negligence of one or more or all the defendants. From that point my sole task has been to decide whether one of the three defendants is solely to blame or, if more than one, to apportion the degrees of negligence. The Allegro, as a new range to replace the Austin 1300, had been introduced in May 1973. The car in question was manufactured by Leylands and left their works in February 1974. Its intermediate history is unrecorded by the evidence, save that it must be assumed to have remained in the possession and under the control of a franchise holder or authorised Leyland dealer until it was sold as a new car by Duttons to Mr Walton, its first owner, on 1 November 1974.

It is now necessary to go back somewhat in the history of the Allegro. A significant alteration in its design compared with eg the Maxi and 1300 range was the introduction of tapered roller bearings in the rear hub assembly which had to be adjusted in a different way from earlier models fitted with roller bearings. The Marina was designed in a similar way. This was a bearing designed by the well-known firm of Timken, and it is fitted to a great many makes of car world wide; it is a tried method and no criticism is sought to be made of Leylands for using it in the Marina and Allegro. Its proper adjustment involves what is technically described as 'end float', to produce a certain amount of play in the wheel which is apparent upon its rotation and rocking after it has been properly adjusted.

According to the documents I have seen, the first rumblings that all was not well with the rear hub assembly of the Allegro had been heard by Leylands by at least October 1973, and probably earlier. On the 17th of that month Leylands circulated a 'Product Bulletin' to the Service Managers of (inter alios) all their accredited dealers, with a request to bring the information therein to all workshop personnel. This drew attention to the change in the method of adjusting the new rear hub bearing and emphasised the importance of correct 'end float' and the risk of bearings seizing up if enough 'end float' was not provided.

The information contained in this Bulletin, as in certain later ones was, according to a note on the document, to be treated as confidential by the recipients. It seems to have been a very ineffective method of averting the gathering storm.

It does not appear that any similar Bulletins on this topic were issued until 9 August 1974, when a diagrammatic illustration of the importance of the difference between torque tightening (for ball bearings) and end float (for roller bearings) was issued, with a similar distribution. This was followed by a Bulletin of 25 September 1974 to all dealers (and some others whom it is immaterial to try to identify) in which the recipients were told that all cars produced since a certain chassis number (in fact about 16 September 1974) incorporated a larger retaining washer in the rear hub assembly 'to improve bearing security', and urging the importance of fitting such washers 'when servicing the rear hub bearings or brakes of earlier vehicles'. I shall have to return to this document together with a letter from Leylands, dated 24 October, which followed it addressed to 'All distributors and Retail Dealers (Cars) UK for the attention of their Managing Directors and Service Managers'. In the background Leylands realised they had a very serious problem on their hands with, and in the context of the problem, only with the Allegro. Speaking with the experience of an engineer with Leylands and its various predecessors since 1940, Mr de Lassalle, the only Company witness, could recall nothing similar in scope and seriousness. By the 12 December 1973 some diagnosis of the problem had been made, and on that day a 'major' modification to the Allegro was authorised, namely a new special washer 'to provide an additional bearing retention safety feature'.

The alarming story of what was happening to Allegros in this country and abroad can be gleaned in part from Leyland's 'Product Problem Progress Card'. The 'problem' was identified as 'Rear wheel bearing failure—Wheel Adrift'; it runs from an entry on 17 December 1973, with many entries month by month through 1974 as the evidence accumulated until its conclusion in early March 1975.

I only propose to select entries to illustrate the scale of the problem as it was presented to Leylands.

In the month to 22 August not less than 10 cases of bearing failures, some with wheels adrift, had been reported from the continent.

By 5 September a total of 50 cases of failure had been reported to Leylands.

By 26 October no less than '100 cases of wheel adrift to date' are recorded as having been reported, ie 50 more in seven weeks.

In January 1975, three further failures were reported 'thought to be due to corrosion'. A further case from this cause is entered on 7 February.

Leylands were naturally anxious to identify, if they could, the cause of so many bearing failures, many involving wheels coming off, or 'adrift', if there is any sensible difference. It could discover none. Lives were plainly at risk, but so were sales, and a solution or at least a palliative had to be found urgently. It is clear from the documents and the evidence of Mr de Lassalle that early on in Leyland's investigation the expert consensus was to put the blame for the bearing failure on mechanics, careless or unfamiliar with the new technique of 'end float' adjustment, and so producing overtightening. This in turn would lead to overheating, then to bearing collapse, and in the worst cases to wheels coming off. The design was satisfactory, there was little evidence of corrosion being the cause, proper adjustment and greasing of the bearing was accepted as having been correctly done at the factory, and so the conclusion was reached that the fault lay with mechanics when working on the brakes or other parts of the rear hub assembly, and particularly at 12,000 miles service when the brakes had to be attended to. This conclusion appears to leave quite unexplained why similar problems did not appear to affect Marinas which had made their debut a little earlier, and were fitted with similar roller bearings. Mr Barber, the Deputy Chairman, at least, was writing urgently on 10 September 1974 about a serious Allegro accident in Italy a letter addressed to senior officials saying (inter alia) 'I am still not satisfied with the solution to the loss of rear wheels on the Allegro. The larger washer will certainly stop the wheels coming off in some cases but there has been at least one example of the hub itself fracturing and the larger washer obviously cannot help when that happens. To my untutored eye it looks as if the bearing is not up to the job. Will you please have this investigated.'

The reference to the larger washer is explained by the tests which had been carried out during the summer. These assumed the cause of failure basically to be due to negligent mechanics, and involved the simulation of such negligence by deliberately overtightening and testing to failure. The tests were not designed, therefore, to diagnose the cause of bearing failure but to try to find a palliative to avert the worse results should bearing failure occur. The proposal finally adopted to remedy the assumed basic cause was a limited education programme directed to mechanics working in distributors' garages.

Meantime the tests had satisfied most of Leyland's experts (but not Mr de Lassalle) that the worst potential and possibly fatal consequences of roller bearing failure could be mitigated by incorporating a larger diameter washer. With the above exception, all the experts before me agreed that the larger washer, while not preventing hub bearing failure, would prevent the wheel coming off and give a driver sufficient warning to enable him with luck to control or regain control of his car and so avoid the sort of disaster which befell the Plaintiffs. This was the Test conclusion expressed on 2 October 1974. 'The (larger) washer is effective in preventing the wheel from coming adrift when bearing failure occurs.' The decision to incorporate the larger washer had been effective on Allegros since 16 September: the Princess model was modified to provide this ab initio, and the Allegro dealers had been alerted.

It is, however, necessary to advert to the letter of 16 September 1974 from Mr Griffin, the Chief Engineer, advising Mr Perry and Mr King how to reply to Mr Barber's memorandum referred to above:

> '*Rear Hubs and Bearings*
> The design was introduced to satisfy performance demands at lower cost, and it is true to state that provided design requirements are adhered to no problem would be experienced. Unfortunately the design is not idiot proof and will therefore continuously involve risk. The risk becomes greater as vehicles become older and evermore carelessly maintained. *Had we incorporated the large washer from the commencement the risk would have been tolerable* . . . Engineering have considered the possibility of recall action but do not favour it owing to the fact that it would *damage the product*, and historically the response is too low to guarantee fixing the problem and thereby remove our liability.'

'Damage the product' is agreed to be a euphemism for 'be bad for sales'.

The extent to which the public at large was given any inkling of the true state of affairs was a television programme on 14 October 1974 having reference to a single case of a wheel 'becoming detached', and a Press release next day which read

> 'We have had a small number of rear wheel bearing failures reported and the evidence shows that failure can be brought about by corrosion arising from water ingress and/or maladjustment during vehicle servicing. Action has already been taken to correct any irregularities in new vehicle production and any cases arising in service are being dealt with as necessary.'

This form of commercial camouflage of the true state of affairs was no doubt thought to be justified in the circumstances.

Meantime on 17 October 1974 'Engineering and Service' were recommending that a recall campaign at a cost of £300,000 was not justified, that an intensive education campaign to 'franchise outlets' should be mounted and that authority should be given for fitting the larger washer when attention was being given to the rear hub or rear brake servicing. 'This should protect the customer against subsequent malpractice.'

I have thought it right to set out as briefly as I can, from such documents as I have seen, which are plainly incomplete, what information was available to Leylands about the appalling record of 'wheels adrift' on the Allegro, the problem as they saw it and the steps they took to try to remedy or palliate it, and considerations which seem to have influenced the course they took. I have done so because all these events occurred prior to 1 November 1974 when Mr Walton bought his car. I now return to that car. It had not been fitted with the recommended washers before sale.

Mr Walton is a meticulous owner: he was, up to the purchase of the Allegro in question a loyal customer of Leyland products. That he is no longer need occasion no surprise. He had owned a succession of Austin and other Leyland models. Apart from the dealer services, his cars have been serviced over the past 30 years, to his complete satisfaction, by the Third Defendants—Blue House—and still are. The drivers' handbook was in the car at all material times. The Allegro he bought was a thoroughly bad car: it was in and out of Duttons throughout 1975 for various defects to be remedied and parts replaced under warranty: by way of example only, the clutch had to be replaced on no less than four occasions. Mr Walton was so dissatisfied with it that he tried in effect to get the year's warranty extended beyond 1975; Leylands authorised an examination by Duttons who reported only minor defects on 24 November 1975. The first trouble connected with the ultimate disaster occurred in January 1975 when Mr Walton noticed a noise in the *rear offside wheel* and took the car to Duttons. I am asked to infer and Duttons admit that on that occasion they fitted the larger washer when they replaced the bearing on the rear offside wheel only. The case against them proceeds on that basis. The mileage was 1,614.

The 6,000 miles service was carried out by Blue House on 6 June 1975 at a mileage of 5,014, and the 12,000 mile service on 9 March 1976 at a mileage of 11,906. At that service the brakes were attended to, the bearings adjusted on each side, and the wheels replaced. When the accident occurred without any warning on 22 April 1976 the mileage was 13,335, so that a distance of some 1,400 miles had been covered since the service, this includes five runs of about 150 miles each. I pass over for the moment the condition of the rear assembly when it was examined after the accident, in order to complete the sorry history of this car. It was repaired at a Bedford Garage of a Leyland agent on a special Allegro jig and was collected by Mr Walton in July 1976 and driven back to Washington, a distance of about 200 miles. The next day he heard a grinding noise in the *rear offside wheel*. He was taking no chances and sent for a low loader from Blue House. On examination the outer bearing was found to have collapsed but the larger washer was there and the wheel had not come off.

The car was examined by an experienced police vehicle examiner about an hour after the accident. The outer bearing had collapsed and the inner cone had been welded by excessive heat onto the stub axle. His view was that the basic cause of the bearing collapse was overtightening of the retaining nut exacerbated by lack of grease, although the destruction was such that there was nothing to point one way or another to overtightening or lack of grease by looking at the parts themselves. He agreed with other experts that there are other, though less likely, explanations of bearing collapse. He found nothing to indicate that the rear offside wheel, which was undamaged, had been overtightened.

The case against Duttons now is that they should have fitted the larger diameter washer to both hubs when the car was brought to them in January 1975 to attend to Mr Walton's complaint about the noise in the rear offside wheel . . .

His Lordship considered the evidence on this point and concluded that 'Duttons were blameless in this matter'. He then considered the suggestion that Blue House Garage had overtightened the retaining nut, so causing the bearing to collapse, and continued:

It is no more than speculation in favour of one theory where other possibilities cannot be excluded, and I decline to hold that it was overtightening which caused the bearing to collapse.

What then of Leyland's responsibility in the matter? In my judgment it is total. It is not being wise after the event to state that had the larger washer been fitted to Mr Walton's car the accident would, in all probability, not have happened. Over a period of about a year, until October 1974, Leylands were faced with mounting and horrifying evidence of Allegro wheels coming adrift. Any of the cases reported to them could have had fatal results for the occupants of the cars concerned and other road users. They assumed, rightly or wrongly, that apart from isolated cases of corrosion, human error on the part of mechanics was the cause of the bearing failures. The Deputy Chairman was gravely disturbed; the view of the Chief Engineer by 16 September 1974 was that the design, not being 'idiot proof', would continuously involve risk, a risk which he thought would have been tolerable had the larger washer been fitted from the start.

From that date, therefore, if not before, the Engineering Section considered the risk to those who were driving Allegros which had not been fitted with the larger washers on both rear hub assemblies of their wheels coming adrift to be 'intolerable'. What, in such circumstances, is the standard of care towards users of their products to be expected of a manufacturer in the position of Leylands? They were entirely satisfied that the large washer provided a safety factor which could confidently be expected, following stringent tests, to prevent a wheel coming adrift if the bearing failed. All cars manufactured after 16 September 1974 were fitted with the approved safety device. Some steps, in my view totally inadequate, were taken to give instructions on the lines of what Dutton Forshaw were recommended to do but only to dealers. Outside this limited safety net were left, in ignorance of the risk to which Leylands knew they were subject, a very large number of Allegro owners, including Mr Walton and his passengers. In my view, the duty of care owed by Leylands to the public was to make a clean breast of the problem and recall all cars which they could in order that the safety washers could be fitted. I accept, of course, that manufactures have to steer a course between alarming the public unnecessarily and so damaging the reputation of their products, and observing their duty of care towards those whom they are in a position to protect from dangers of which they and they alone are aware. The duty seems to me to be the higher when they can palliate the worst effects of a failure which, if Leyland's view is right, they could never decisively guard against. They knew the full facts; they saw to it that no-one else did. They seriously considered recall and made an estimate of the cost at a figure which seems to me to have been in no way out of proportion to the risks involved. It was decided not to follow this course for commercial reasons. I think this involved a failure to observe their duty to care for the safety of the many who were bound to remain at risk, irrespective of the recommendations made to Leyland dealers and to them alone.

If I am wrong in equating the duty to take reasonable care in the circumstances of this case with the obligation to have recalled cars for fitting of safety washers, and so have put it too high, it was in my view at least their duty to ensure that all cars still in stock and unsold by the time the washer palliative was proven were fitted with this safety feature before sale. It is sufficient for Mr Walton's purposes that the duty is put no higher than that. This would have saved Mr Walton and his passengers and, in my judgment, Leylands were negligent in having failed to do so.

NOTE

For a further reference to the question of product recall see below Ch 11 pp 458–460. See also the Code of Practice on Action Concerning Vehicle Safety Defects reproduced in Miller *Product Liability and Safety Encyclopaedia*, Div VII, para [100].

Question

If manufacturers are to be subject to the potentially onerous requirement of recalling dangerously defective products would it be in point to enquire whether they had been negligent in failing to discover the dangers when marketing the products?

The position of retailers

Although most of the reported cases involve the liability of manufacturers or producers of allegedly defective products it is clear that on appropriate facts retailers and others may incur liability in tort as well as in contract. The following is a leading case in point.

Fisher v Harrods Ltd [1966] Lloyd's Rep 500, Queen's Bench Divisional Court

The defendants, the renowned London store, had sold a jewellery cleaning fluid, Couronne, which contained isopropyl alcohol and ammonium oleate and which was purchased by a third party for the use of the plaintiff. The fluid was supplied in a plastic bottle with a plastic bung and a screw top. As the plaintiff was squeezing the bottle the bung shot out and some fluid splashed into and damaged her eye. Couronne had been manufactured by a company which had few assets and which was uninsured. The action was brought in negligence.

McNair J, having referred to the facts of the case and the plaintiff's evidence, continued:

In addition to the evidence of the plaintiff herself as to the ejection of the fluid from the container in the quantity she described, I had the evidence of a number of ladies who had had similar but not identical experiences. Lady Carrington purchased a bottle of Couronne from the defendants in the first half of September, 1963, but had no occasion to use it until November, 1963, when she was minded to clean her jewellery. It had no sticky label on it, but, after unscrewing the red cap, she assumed that there must be a hole in the plug though it was invisible to the eye. She held it over a small bowl, and as nothing came out she shook it twice slowly over the bowl, then gave it a gentle pressure and, as soon as she did this, the bung flew out and all the liquid came out over a polished table; the French polish on the table was quite burnt away. The bung was found quite a distance away and the bottle was destroyed.

. . .

I now turn to the question of the defendants' liability. First as to the facts in relation to the putting of Couronne on the market. The defendants first came into contact with Couronne when, in May, 1962, Mr Nash, the experienced buyer for the jewellery department, was approached by Mr Meyer (whom he had never met before) with a proposal that the defendants might market for him his Couronne Jewellery Cleaner . . . According to Mr Nash it was not the practice of the defendants, even when an unknown salesman approached a buyer with a new product from an unknown manufacturer, to make any inquiries as to the status of the manufacturer . . . Though Mr Meyer told him that he had just started to manufacture, he made no inquiries as to his previous experience, or whether he had any qualifications, or had had the proposed compound tested by a chemist. The defendants have an analytical department but it did not occur to Mr Nash to send it to them (though now he thinks it would have been wise to have done so); but if told by the analytical department that it contained 50 per cent alcohol this would not have conveyed to him that it was more dangerous than any other cleaner.

. . .

Though the question of duty to make inquiries must depend on the facts of each particular case, since in the end the question must always be whether the party charged has exercised reasonable care in all the circumstances, I was referred to a number of authorities in which questions very similar to those in the present case have arisen. Perhaps the nearest is the decision of Mr Justice Stable in *Watson v Buckley, Osborne, Garrett & Co Ltd and Wyrovoys Products Ltd* [1940] 1 All ER 174, in which the learned Judge found the distributors of hair dye were liable for failure to make proper inquiries and tests when purchasing a hair dye from a stranger. At p 181, the learned Judge says this:

'. . . Ogee Ltd [—the distributors—] were not dealing with an old-established manufacturer who had been supplying them for years. They were, in essence, dealing with a gentleman who had emerged quite unexpectedly from Spain . . . They never saw where it was manufactured. They took no steps to ascertain under what sort of supervision the manufacture was carried on. When deliveries were made, no test of any sort, kind or description was made . . .'

The learned Judge is emphasizing, as I think rightly, the standard of care to be exercised by a distributor when dealing with an unknown supplier.

. . .

Without attempting to lay down any rule of law of general application I have reached the conclusion, on the facts of this case, that the defendants did not measure up to the standard of care which should have been exercised in their acceptance of Mr Meyer's request that they should market Couronne. If they had made any inquiries they would have found out that Mr Meyer was a man of no qualifications for, or experience in, the manufacture of a cleaning product and no qualifications for making a proper choice of its constituent.

. . .

Mr Moir, an experienced industrial chemist called on behalf of the plaintiff, expressed the view that he would not expect a substance of this kind to be put on the market without some warning, this view being based on his experience of substances which are accompanied by a warning when put on the market . . .

In my judgment this Couronne should not have been put on the market even with a pierced plug without instructions as to the manner in which the liquid was to be got out of the container and without a warning as to the danger if it came into contact with the eyes; *a fortiori* it should not have been put on the market with a blind plug without a similar or more stringent warning—such as was used later—namely, 'Keep away from the eyes.'

It may be said, however, that the defendants, though initially at fault for putting it on the market in July, 1962, were not at fault in September, 1963, when the particular bottle which caused the plaintiff's injuries was sold, in view of the lack of complaints to them of any untoward occurrences in the intervening months. There is some force in this point, though it has to be borne in mind that several of the ladies who gave evidence as to their mishaps with the Couronne did not report to the defendants.

. . .

In my judgment the defendants' initial fault in putting this commodity on the market without making proper inquiries, and without seeing that an adequate warning of danger was affixed to the bottles, was and remained the effective cause of the plaintiff's injuries.

. . .

There will accordingly be judgment for the plaintiff for £1995 18s and that judgment carries costs.

NOTE

See also *Devilez v Boots Pure Drug Co Ltd* (1962) 106 Sol Jo 552 and in general Miller and Lovell *Product Liability,* Ch 15.

Economic loss

Although the two cases which follow have a strong commercial flavour both raise difficult issues of practical importance for everyday consumer transactions.

Rivtow Marine Ltd v Washington Iron Works (1973) 40 DLR (3d) 530, Supreme Court of Canada

The plaintiff was the charterer of a log barge, the Rivtow Carrier, which was equipped with two pintle-type cranes designed and manufactured by the first defendants, Washington. In September 1966, some eighteen months after the commencement of the charter and at a time when the coastal logging business was at its height, the charterers learned that a crane which was virtually identical to their own and which had also been designed and manufactured by Washington had collapsed, killing its operator. As a precautionary measure, they ordered the Rivtow Carrier to return to Vancouver for inspection. This revealed that both cranes had serious structural defects in the legs of the pintle masts, necessitating extensive dismantling, modification, repair and reassembly lasting some thirty days. The plaintiff claimed compensation for the cost of repair and for loss of profits during the period in which the barge was inoperative. Washington admitted that the cracking in the legs of the crane was caused by defects in design attributable to the carelessness of their engineers; that by February 1966 they were aware that other cranes of this type had developed similar structural defects in operation; and that thirty days was a reasonable period in which to carry out the necessary modifications. They denied, however, that they had any liability to compensate in respect of the loss suffered. This view was accepted by the British Columbia Court of Appeal. The charterers then appealed to the Supreme Court of Canada. The court was unanimous in allowing the appeal and in awarding damages, but divided about the basis on which damages were to be assessed. The majority view was expressed in the following extract.

Ritchie J. . . . . As I have indicated, the judgment of the Court of Appeal in this case appears to me to proceed on the assumption that Walkem and Washington owed a duty of care to the appellant as being a person '. . . so closely and directly affected' by the faulty design of the cranes that they ought reasonably to have had it in contemplation as being so affected in directing their mind to the known defects which are here called in question.

Proceeding on this assumption, I take it that the Court of Appeal would have treated the respondents as being liable for damages attributable to personal injury or damage to property resulting from defects in the cranes, but Mr Justice Tysoe, in concluding his reasons for judgment at p 579 said:

> In my opinion the law of British Columbia as it exists today is that neither a manufacturer of a potentially dangerous or defective article nor other person who is within the proximity of relationship contemplated in *Donoghue v Stevenson* is liable in tort, as distinct from contract, to an ultimate consumer or user for damage arising in the article itself, or for economic loss resulting from the defect in the article, but only for personal injury and damage to other property caused by the article or its use. It is my view that to give effect to the claims of Rivtow it would be necessary to extend the rule of liability laid down in *Donoghue's* case beyond what it now is. I do not feel this Court would be justified in extending it so that it covers the character of damage suffered by Rivtow. I think that, if that is to be done, it must be left to a higher Court to do it.

Mr Justice Tysoe's conclusion was based in large measure on a series of American cases, and particularly *Trans World Airlines Inc v Curtiss-Wright Corpn et al* (1955) 148 NYS 2d 284, where it is pointed out that the liability for the cost of repairing damage to the defective article itself and for the economic loss flowing directly from the negligence, is akin to liability under the terms of an express or implied warranty of fitness and as it is contractual in origin cannot be enforced against the manufacturer by a stranger to the contract. It was, I think, on this basis that the learned trial Judge disallowed the appellant's claim for repairs and for such economic loss as it would, in any event, have sustained even if the proper warning had been given. I agree with this conclusion for the same reasons; but while this finding excludes recovery for damage to the article and economic loss directly flowing from Washington's negligence and faulty design, it does not exclude the additional damage occasioned by breach of the duty to warn of the danger.

In the present case, both Washington as manufacturer and Walkem as its representative, knew that the appellant relied on them for advice concerning the operation of the pintle cranes, and in my opinion a clear duty lay upon them both to warn the appellant of the necessity for repairs as soon as they had become aware of the defects and the potential danger attendant thereon.

. . .

That liability for this damage does not flow from negligence in design and manufacture is illustrated by the fact that Walkem, which was not a party to such negligence, is equally liable with Washington for failing to warn the appellant. The difference between the two types of liability and consequent damage is that one may arise without the manufacturer having any knowledge of the defect, whereas the other stems from his awareness of the danger to which the defect gives rise.

. . .

[In quantifying damages the court agreed with the approach of the trial court judge whose figures of $90,000 (earnings in the high season) *less* $30,000 (average monthly earnings), leaving $60,000, were accepted].

Laskin J (dissenting in part) . . . I agree with the award of damages so far as it goes, but I would enlarge it to include as well the cost of repairs.

I would do this because I do not agree that the liability of the respondents should be rested on the one basis of a failure to warn of the probability of injury by reason of the defective design of the crane. The failure to warn is, of course, the only basis upon which, on the facts herein, liability could be imposed upon Walkem. However, Washington, as the designer and manufacturer of the crane, was under an anterior duty to prevent injury which foreseeably would result from its negligence in the design and manufacture of this piece of equipment. If physical harm had resulted, whether personal injury or damage to property (other than to the crane itself), Washington's liability to the person affected, under its anterior duty as a designer and manufacturer of a negligently-produced crane, would not be open to question. Should it then be any less liable for the direct economic loss to the appellant resulting from the faulty crane merely because the likelihood of physical harm, either by way of personal injury to a third person or property damage to the appellant, was averted by the withdrawal of the crane from service so that it could be repaired?

. . .

[A] manufacturer's liability for negligence . . . rests upon a conviction that manufacturers should bear the risk of injury to consumers or users of their products when such products are carelessly manufactured because the manufacturers create the risk in the carrying on of their enterprises, and they will be more likely to safeguard the members of the public to whom their products are marketed if they must stand behind them as safe products to consume or to use. They are better able to insure against such risks, and the cost of insurance, as a business expense, can be spread with less pain among the buying public than would be the case if an injured consumer or user was saddled with the entire loss that befalls him.

This rationale embraces, in my opinion, threatened physical harm from a negligently-designed and manufactured product resulting in economic loss. I need not decide whether it extends to claims for economic loss where there is no threat of physical harm or to claims for damage, without more, to the defective product.

It is foreseeable injury to person or to property which supports recovery for economic loss suffered by a consumer or user who is fortunate enough to avert such injury. If recovery for economic loss is allowed when such injury is suffered, I see no reason to deny it when the threatened injury is forestalled. Washington can be no better off in the latter case than in the former. On the admitted facts, a crane on another person's barge, of similar design to that installed on the appellant's barge, had collapsed, killing its operator. It was when this fact came to its notice that the appellant took its crane out of service. Its crane had the same cracks in it that were found in the collapsed crane, and they were due to the same faulty design in both cases. Here then was a piece of equipment whose use was fraught with danger to person and property because of negligence in its design and manufacture; one death had already resulted from the use of a similar piece of equipment that had been marketed by Washington. I see nothing untoward in holding Washington liable in such circumstances for economic loss resulting from the down time necessary to effect repairs to the crane. The case is not one where a manufactured product proves to be merely defective (in short, where it has not met promised expectations), but rather one where by reason of the defect there is a foreseeable risk of physical harm from its use and where the alert avoidance of such harm gives rise to economic loss. Prevention of threatened harm resulting directly in economic loss should not be treated differently from post-injury cure.

. . .

I would, accordingly, allow the appeal, set aside the judgment of the British Columbia Court of Appeal and restore the judgment of Ruttan J, but would vary it to add the cost of repair of the crane to the amount of economic loss for which he found Washington liable. I agree with the disposition as to costs made by my brother Ritchie.

Appeal allowed; trial judgment restored.

NOTE

For an English case which may have recognised a duty to warn of subsequently discovered dangers see *Wright v Dunlop Rubber Co Ltd* (1972) 13 KIR 255, CA (carcinogenic properties of anti oxidant). See generally Miller and Lovell *Product Liability* pp 247–251.

Junior Books Ltd v Veitchi Co Ltd [1982] 3 All ER 201, [1983] 1 AC 520, House of Lords

The respondents (or pursuers) had engaged a building company, Ogilvie, to build a factory for them, nominating the appellants (or defenders) as specialist sub-contractors to lay a concrete floor. The appellants duly entered into a contract with Ogilvie but there was no contractual relationship between the appellants and the respondents. Two years after the floor had been laid it developed cracks and the respondents alleged that its defective condition was the result of the sub-contractors' negligence. The sub-contractors countered by asserting that in the absence of any contractual relationship between the parties or any plea that the defective floor was a danger to the health or safety of any person or constituted a risk of damage to any other property of the owners, the owners' pleading did not disclose a good cause of action. The Lord Ordinary and, on appeal, the Court of Session rejected the sub-contractors' contention and held that the owners were entitled to proceed with their action. The sub-contractors appealed.

Lord Roskill. My Lords, this appeal against an interlocutor of the Second Division of the Court of Session (the Lord Justice-Clerk (Lord Wheatley), Lord Kissen and Lord Robertson) dated 1 September 1980 refusing a reclaiming motion against an interlocutor of the Lord Ordinary (Grieve) dated 22 November 1979 raises a question of fundamental importance in the law of delict. Since it was accepted in the courts below and in argument before your Lordships' House that there was no relevant difference between the Scots law of delict and the English law of neligence, it follows that this appeal equally raises a question of fundamental importance in the development of the latter law . . . The Lord Ordinary started his opinion by stating that there was no Scottish authority directly in point and, while in argument before your Lordships' House much Scottish, English and indeed Commonwealth authority was cited, it remains the fact that no decision in any court that was cited to your Lordships conclusively shows the correct route to be taken, though many may be said greatly to illuminate that route.

. . .

My Lords, I have already said that there is no decided case which clearly points the way. But it is, I think, of assistance to see how far the various decisions have gone. I shall restrict my citation to the more important decisions both in this country and overseas. In *Dutton* [*Dutton v Bognor Regis United Building Co Ltd*], which, as already stated, your Lordships' House expressly approved in *Anns,* the Court of Appeal held that the plaintiff, who bought the house in question long after it had been built and its foundations inadequately inspected by the defendants' staff, was entitled to recover from the defendants, inter alia, the estimated cost of repairing the house as well as other items of loss including diminution in value. There was in that case physical damage to the house. It was argued that the defendants were not liable for the cost of repairs or diminution in value. This argument was expressly rejected by Lord Denning MR and by Sachs LJ (see [1972] 1 All ER 462 at 474 480–481, [1972] 1 QB 373 at 396, 403–404). Stamp LJ was however more sympathetic to this argument. He said ([1972] 1 All ER 462 at 489–490, [1972] 1 QB 373 at 414–415):

'It is pointed out that in the past a distinction has been drawn between constructing a dangerous article and constructing one which is defective or of inferior quality. I may be liable to one who purchases in the market a bottle of ginger beer which I have carelessly manufactured and which is dangerous and causes injury to person or property; but it is not the law that I am liable to him for the loss he suffers because what is found inside the bottle and for which he has paid money is not ginger beer but water. I do not warrant, except to an immediate purchaser and then by contract and not in tort, that the thing I manufacture is reasonably fit for its purpose. The submission is I think a formidable one and in my view raises the most difficult point for decision in this case. Nor can I see any valid distinction between the case of a builder who carelessly builds a house which, although not a source of danger to person or property, nevertheless owing to a concealed defect in its foundations starts to settle and crack and becomes valueless, and the case of a manufacturer who carelessly manufactures an article which, though not a source of danger to a subsequent owner or to his other property, nevertheless owing to a hidden defect quickly disintegrates. To hold that either the builder or the manufacturer was liable, except in contract, would be to open up a new field of liability, the extent of which could not I think be logically controlled, and since it is not in my judgment necessary to do so for the purposes of this case, I do not, more particularly because of the absence of the builder, express an opinion whether the builder has a higher or lower duty than the manufacturer. But the distinction between the case of a manufacturer of a dangerous thing which causes damage and that of a thing which turns out to be defective and valueless lies I think not in the nature of the injury but in the character of the duty. I have a duty not carelessly to put out a dangerous thing which may cause damage to one who may purchase it, but the duty does not extend to putting out carelessly a defective or useless or valueless thing. So again one goes back to consider what was the character of the duty, if any, owed to the plaintiff, and one finds on authority that the injury which is one of the essential elements of the tort of negligence is not confined to physical damage to personal property but may embrace economic damage which the plaintifff suffers through buying a worthless thing, as is shown by the *Hedley Byrne* case.'

Thus it was on the character of the duty that Stamp LJ founded and was able to agree with the other members of the Court of Appeal in that case.

My Lords, a similar question arose some years later in *Batty v Metropolitan Property Realizations Ltd* [1978] 2 All ER 445, [1978] QB 554. By the date of this decision the Court of Appeal had the benefit of the decision in your Lordships' House in *Anns*. Megaw LJ (see [1978] 2 All ER 445 at 456, [1978] QB 554 at 570) regarded the doubts raised by Stamp LJ as resolved by Lord Wilberforce's speech in *Anns*. Once again the argument based on absence of physical damage was advanced, as it had been in *Dutton*. Once again it was rejected, but on the basis that there was in this case as in *Dutton* the requisite degree of physical damage. Bridge LJ ([1978] 2 All ER 445 at 459, [1978] QB 554 at 573) however seems to me to use somewhat wider language and indeed he refers to two sentences at the end of Lord Wilberforce's speech in *Anns* [1977] 2 All ER 492 at 505, [1978] AC 728 at 759 where Lord Wilberforce said: 'Subject always to adequate proof of causation, these damages may include damages for personal injury and damage to property. In my opinion they may also include damage to the dwelling-house itself . . .'

My Lords, I am inclined to think that that last sentence was directed to the facts in *Anns* where there was, as in the other cases to which I have referred, the element of physical damage present due to trouble with the foundations, rather than directed to the full breadth of the proposition for which the respondents in the present appeal contended. None the less the three decisions, *Dutton, Anns* and *Batty*, seem to me to demonstrate how far the law has developed in the relevant respect in recent years.

My Lords, I turn next to the three main Commonwealth decisions. They are *Rivtow Marine Ltd v Washington Iron Works* [1974] SCR 1189, a decision of the Supreme Court of Canada, *Caltex Oil (Australia) Pty Ltd v Dredge Willemstad* (1976) 136 CLR 529, a decision of the High Court of Australia, and *Bowen v Paramount Builders (Hamilton) Ltd* [1977] 1 NZLR 394, a decision of the Court of Appeal of New Zealand. All three of these cases were decided before *Anns* reached your Lordships' House.

My Lords, in the first of this trilogy the Supreme Court by a majority held that the manufacturer of a dangerously defective article is not liable in tort to an ultimate consumer or user of that article for the cost of repairing damage arising in the article itself or for such economic loss as would have been sustained in any event as a result of the need to effect repairs. But there was, if I may respectfully say so, a powerful dissenting judgment by Laskin J with which Hall J concurred. The judge posed as the first question (see [1974] SCR 1189 at 1217) whether the defendants' liability for negligence should embrace economic loss where there has been no physical harm in fact. He gave an affirmative answer. After pointing out (at 1221) that the judicial limitation on liability was founded on what I have called 'the floodgates' argument rather than on principle, he adopted the view that economic loss resulting from threatened physical loss from a negligently designed or manufactured product was recoverable. It was this judgment which Lord Wilberforce described in his speech in *Anns* [1977] 2 All ER 492 at 505, [1978] AC 728 at 759—760 as of strong persuasive force. In the *Caltex* case the High Court of Australia elaborately reviewed all the relevant English authorities and indeed others as well. My Lords, I hope I shall not be thought lacking in respect for those elaborate judgments or failing to acknowledge the help which I have derived from them if I do not cite from them, for to some extent certain of the difficulties there discussed have been subsequently resolved by the decision of this House in *Anns*. In *Bowen*, to which Lord Wilberforce also referred in *Anns* as having afforded him much assistance, the Court of Appeal in New Zealand followed the Court of Appeal decision in *Dutton*. Cooke J took the view that it was enough for the purpose of the case in question to say that the damage was basically physical. But, as the report shows, he would have been prepared in agreement with the judgments of Lord Denning MR and of Sachs LJ in *Dutton* to go further (see [1977] 1 NZLR 394 at 423).

My Lords, to my mind in the instant case there is no physical damage to the flooring in the sense in which that phrase was used in *Dutton*, *Batty* and *Bowen* and some of the others cases. As my noble and learned friend Lord Russell said during the argument, the question which your Lordships' House now has to decide is whether the relevant Scots and English law today extends the duty of care beyond a duty to prevent harm being done by faulty work to a duty to avoid such faults being present in the work itself. It was powerfully urged on behalf of the appellants that were your Lordships so to extend the law a pursuer in the position of the pursuer in *Donoghue v Stevenson* could in addition to recovering for any personal injury suffered have also recovered for the diminished value of the offending bottle of ginger beer. Any remedy of that kind it was argued must lie in contract and not in delict or tort. My Lords, I seem to detect in that able argument reflections of the previous judicial approach to comparable problems before *Donoghue v Stevenson* was decided. That approach usually resulted in the conclusion that in principle the proper remedy lay in contract and not outside it. But that approach and its concomitant philosophy ended in 1932 and for my part I should be reluctant to countenance its re-emergence some fifty years later in the instant case. I think today the proper control lies not in asking whether the proper remedy should lie in contract or instead in delict or tort, not in somewhat capricious judicial determination whether a particular case falls on one side of the line or the other, not in somewhat artificial distinctions between physical and economic or financial loss when the two sometimes go together and sometimes do not (it is sometimes overlooked that virtually all damage including physical damage is in one sense financial or economic for it is compensated by an award of damages) but in the first instance in establishing the relevant principles and then in deciding whether the particular case falls within or without those principles. To state this is to do no more than to restate what Lord Reid said in the *Dorset Yacht* case and Lord Wilberforce in *Anns*. Lord Wilberforce . . . enunciated the two tests which have to be satisfied. The first is 'sufficient relationship of proximity', the second any considerations negativing, reducing or limiting the scope of the duty or the class of person to whom it is owed or the damages to which a breach of the duty may give rise. My Lords, it is I think in the application of those two principles that the ability to control the extent of liability in delict or in negligence lies. The history of the development of the law in the last fifty years shows that fears aroused by the 'floodgates' argument have been unfounded. Cooke J in *Bowen* [1977] 1 NZLR 394 at 472 described the 'floodgates' argument as specious and the argument against allowing a cause of action such as was allowed in *Dutton*, *Anns* and *Bowen* as 'in terrorem or doctrinaire'.

Turning back to the present appeal I therefore ask first whether there was the requisite degree of proximity so as to give rise to the relevant duty of care relied on by the respondents. I regard the following facts as of crucial importance in requiring an affirmative answer to that question: (1) the appellants were nominated sub-contractors; (2) the appellants were specialists in flooring; (3) the appellants knew what products were required by the appellants and their main contractors and specialised in the production of those products; (4) the appellants alone were responsible for the composition and construction of the flooring; (5) the respondents relied on the appellants' skill and experience; (6) the appellants as nominated sub-contractors must have known that the respondents relied on their skill and experience; (7) the relationship between the parties was as close as it could be short of actual privity of contract; (8) the appellants must be taken to have known that if they did the work negligently (as it must be assumed that they did) the resulting defects would at some time require remedying by the respondents expending money on the remedial measures as a consequence of which the respondents would suffer financial or economic loss.

My Lords, reverting to Lord Devlin's speech in *Hedley Byrne*, it seems to me that all the conditions existed which give rise to the relevant duty of care owed by the appellants to the respondents.

I then turn to Lord Wilberforce's second proposition. On the facts I have just stated, I see nothing whatever to restrict the duty of care arising from the proximity of which I have spoken. During the argument it was asked what the position would be in a case where there was a relevant exclusion clause in the main contract. My Lords, that question does not arise for decision in the instant appeal, but in principle I would venture the view that such a clause according to the manner in which it was worded might in some circumstances limit the duty of care just as in the *Hedley Byrne* case the plaintiffs were ultimately defeated by the defendants' disclaimer of responsibility. But in the present case the only suggested reason for limiting the damage (ex hypothesi economic or financial only) recoverable for the breach of the duty of care just enunciated is that hitherto the law has not allowed such recovery and therefore ought not in the future to do so. My Lords, with all respect to those who find this a sufficient answer I do not. I think this is the next logical step forward in the development of this branch of the law. I see no reason why what was called during the argument 'damage to the pocket' simpliciter should be disallowed when 'damage to the pocket' coupled with physical damage has hitherto always been allowed. I do not think that this development, if development it be, will lead to untoward consequences. The concept of proximity must always involve, at least in most cases, some degree of reliance; I have already mentioned the words 'skill' and 'judgment' in the speech of Lord Morris in *Hedley Byrne*. These words seem to me to be an echo, be it conscious or unconscious, of the language of s 14(1) of the Sale of Goods Act 1893. My Lords, though the analogy is not exact, I do not find it unhelpful for I think the concept of proximity of which I have spoken and the reasoning of Lord Devlin in the *Hedley Byrne* case involve factual considerations not unlike those involved in a claim under s 14(1); and as between an ultimate purchaser and a manufacturer would not easily be found to exist in the ordinary everyday transaction of purchasing chattels when it is obvious that in truth the real reliance was on the immediate vendor and not on the manufacturer.

My Lords, I have not thought it necessary to review all the cases cited in argument. If my conclusion be correct, certain of them can no longer be regarded as good law and others may have to be considered afresh hereafter, for example whether the decision of the majority of the Court of Appeal in *Spartan Steel and Alloys Ltd v Martin & Co (Contractors) Ltd* [1972] 3 All ER 557, [1973] QB 27 is correct or whether the reasoning of Edmund-Davies LJ in his dissenting judgment is to be preferred, and whether the decision of the First Division of the Inner House of the Court of Session in *Dynamco Ltd v Holland & Hannen & Cubitts (Scotland) Ltd* 1971 SC 257, a decision given after the *Dorset Yacht* case but before *Anns*, but seemingly without reference to the *Dorset Yacht* case, is correct.

My Lords, for all these reasons I would dismiss this appeal and allow this action to proceed to proof before answer.

My Lords, I would add two further observations. First, since preparing this speech I have had the advantage of reading in draft the speech of Lord Fraser, with which I agree. Second, my attention has been drawn to the decision of the Court of Appeal in New Zealand in *Mount Albert Borough Council v Johnson* [1979] 2 NZLR 234. The judgment of Cooke and Somers JJ in which the decision in *Bowen v Paramount Builders (Hamilton) Ltd* [1977] 1 NZLR 394 is stated to reflect the present law in New Zealand (see [1979] 2 NZLR 234 at 238–239) is consonant with the views I have expressed in this speech.

Lord Fraser of Tullybelton. My Lords, I have had the advantage of reading in draft the speech of my noble and learned friend Lord Roskill, and I am in full agreement with his conclusion and with the reasons on which he bases it . . .

. . . As I agree with my noble and learned friend Lord Roskill that the appeal fails, I only add to his speech in order to deal in my own words with two important matters that arise.

The first is the concern, which has been repeatedly expressed by judges in the United Kingdom and elsewhere, that the effect of relaxing strict limitations on the area of liability of delict (tort) would be, in the words of Cardozo CJ in *Ultramares Corpn v Touche* (1931) 255 NY 170 at 179, to introduce 'liability in an indeterminate amount for an indeterminate time to an indeterminate class'. This is the floodgates argument, if I may use the expression as a convenient description, and not in any dismissive or question-begging sense. The argument appears to me unattractive, especially if it leads, as I think it would in this case, to drawing an arbitrary and illogical line just because a line has to be drawn somewhere. But it has to be considered, because it has had a significant influence in leading judges to reject claims for economic loss which were not consequent on physical danger to persons or other property of the pursuer/plaintiff . . . The proximity between the parties is extremely close, falling only just short of a direct contractual relationship. The injury to the respondents was a direct and foreseeable result of negligence by the appellants. The respondents, or their architects, nominated the appellants as specialist sub-contractors and they must therefore have relied on their skill and knowledge. It would surely be wrong to exclude from probation a claim which is so strongly based, merely because of anxiety about the possible effect of the decision on other cases where the proximity may be less strong. If and when such other cases arise they will have to be decided by applying sound principles to their particular facts. The present case seems to me to fall well within limits already recognised in principle for this type of claim, and I would decide this appeal strictly on its own facts. I rely particularly on the very close proximity between the parties which in my view distinguishes this case from the case of producers of goods to be offered for sale to the public.

The second matter which might be thought to justify rejecting the respondents' claim as irrelevant is the difficulty of ascertaining the standard of duty owed by the appellants to the respondents. A manufacturer's duty to take care not to make a product that is dangerous sets a standard which is, in principle, easy to ascertain. The duty is owed to all who are his 'neighbours'. It is imposed on him by the general law and is in addition to his contractual duties to other parties to the contract. It cannot be discharged or escaped by pleading that it conflicts with his contractual duty. But a duty not to produce a *defective* article sets a standard which is less easily ascertained, because it has to be judged largely by reference to the contract. As Windeyer J said in *Voli v Inglewood Shire Council* (1963) 110 CLR 74 at 85, if an architect undertakes 'to design a stage to bear only some specified weight, he would not be liable for the consequences of someone thereafter negligently permitting a greater weight to be put upon it'. Similarly a building constructed in fulfilment of a contract for a price of £100,000 might justly be regarded as defective, although the same building constructed in fulfilment of a contract for a price of £50,000 might not. Where a building is erected under a contract with a purchaser, then, provided the building, or part of it, is not dangerous to persons or to other property and subject to the law against misrepresentation, I see no reason why the builder should not be free to make with the purchaser whatever contractual arrangements about the quality of the product the purchaser wishes. However jerry-built the product, the purchaser would not be entitled to damages from the builder if it came up to the contractual standard. I do not think a subsequent owner could be in any better position, but in most cases he would not know the details of the contractual arrangements and, without such knowledge, he might well be unable to judge whether the product was defective or not. But in this case the respondents, although not a party to the contract with the appellants, had full knowledge of the appellants' contractual duties, and this difficulty does not arise. What the position might have been if the action had been brought by a subsequent owner is a matter which does not have to be decided now.

For the reasons given by my noble and learned friend Lord Roskill, and for the additional reasons which I have stated, I would dismiss this appeal.

Lord Russell of Killowen. My Lords, I have had the advantage of reading in draft the speeches prepared by my noble and learned friends Lord Fraser and Lord Roskill. I agree with them and with their conclusion that this appeal fails. In my respectful opinion the view of my noble and learned friend Lord Brandon unnecessarily confines the relevant principles of delict to exclude cases of such immediate proximity as the present.

Lord Keith of Kinkel agreed that the appeal should be dismissed on the narrow ground that the authorities allowed recovery of expenditure in averting economic loss, and this included the loss of profits attributable to the burden of maintaining a defective floor. He continued:

Having thus reached a conclusion in favour of the respondents on the somewhat narrow ground which I have indicated, I do not consider this to be an appropriate case for seeking to advance the frontiers of the law of negligence on the lines favoured by certain of your Lordships. There are a number of reasons why such an extension would, in my view, be wrong in principle. In the first place, I am unable to regard the deterioration of the flooring which is alleged in this case as being damage to the respondents' property such as to give rise to a liability falling directly within the principle of *Donoghue v Stevenson*. The flooring had an inherent defect in it from the start. The appellants did not, in any sense consistent with the ordinary use of language or contemplated by the majority in *Donoghue v Stevenson* damage the respondents' property. They supplied them with a defective floor. Such an act can, in accordance with the views I have expressed above, give rise to liability in negligence in certain circumstances. But it does not do so merely because the flooring is defective or valueless or useless and requires to be replaced. So to hold would raise very difficult and delicate issues of principle having a wide potential application. I think it would necessarily follow that any manufacturer of products would become liable to the ultimate purchaser if the product, owing to negligence in manufacture, was, without being harmful in any way, useless or worthless or defective in quality so that the purchaser wasted the money he spent on it. One instance mentioned in argument and adverted to by Stamp LJ in *Dutton v Bognor Regis*

United Building Co Ltd [1972] 1 All ER 462 at 489, [1972] 1 QB 373 at 414 was a product purchased as ginger beer which turned out to be only water, and many others may be figured. To introduce a general liability covering such situations would be disruptive of commercial practice, under which manufacturers of products commonly provide the ultimate purchaser with limited guarantees, usually undertaking only to replace parts exhibiting defective workmanship and excluding any consequential loss. There being no contractual relationship between manufacturer and ultimate consumer, no room would exist, if the suggested principle were accepted, for limiting the manufacturer's liability. The policy considerations which would be involved in introducing such a state of affairs appear to me to be such as a court of law cannot properly assess, and the question whether or not it would be in the interests of commerce and the public generally is, in my view, much better left for the legislature. The purchaser of a defective product normally can proceed for breach of contract against the seller who can bring his own supplier into the proceedings by third party procedure, so it cannot be said that the present state of the law is unsatisfactory from the point of view of available remedies. I refer to *Young & Martin Ltd v McManus Childs Ltd* [1968] 2 All ER 1169, [1969] 1 AC 454. In the second place, I can foresee that very considerable difficulties might arise in assessing the standards of quality by which the allegedly defective product is to be judged. This aspect is more fully developed in the speech to be delivered by my noble and learned friend Lord Brandon, with whose views on the matter I respectfully agree.

My Lords, for the reasons which I have given I would concur in the dismissal of the appeal.

Lord Brandon of Oakbrook dissented:

. . .

My Lords, a good deal of the argument presented to your Lordships during the hearing of the appeal was directed to the question whether a person can recover, in an action founded on delict alone, purely pecuniary loss which is independent of any physical damage to persons or their property. If that were the question to be decided in the present case, I should have no hesitation in holding that, in principle and depending on the facts of a particular case, purely pecuniary loss may be recoverable in an action founded on delict alone. Two examples can be given of such cases. First, there is the type of case where a person suffers purely pecuniary loss as a result of relying on another person's negligent misstatements: see *Hedley Byrne & Co Ltd v Heller & Partners Ltd* [1963] 2 All ER 575, [1964] AC 465. Second, there may be a type of case where a person, who has a cause of action based on *Donoghue v Stevenson* reasonably incurs pecuniary loss in order to prevent or mitigate imminent danger of damage to the persons or property exposed to that danger: see the dissenting judgment of Laskin J in the Canadian Supreme Court case of *Rivtow Marine Ltd v Washington Iron Works* [1974] SCR 1189, referred to with approval in the speech of Lord Wilberforce in *Anns v Merton London Borough* [1977] 2 All ER 492 at 505, [1978] AC 728 at 760.

I do not, however, consider that the question of law for decision in this case is whether a person can, in an action founded in delict alone, recover for purely pecuniary loss.

. . .

His Lordship then referred to the two questions or tests formulated by Lord Wilberforce in the *Anns* case (see above p 170), held that the first test had been satisfied, and continued:

That first question having been answered in the affirmative, however, it is necessary . . . to ask oneself a second question, namely whether there are any considerations which ought, inter alia, to limit the scope of the duty which exists.

To that second question I would answer that there are two important considerations which ought to limit the scope of the duty of care which it is common ground was owed by the defenders to the pursuers on the assumed facts of the present case.

The first consideration is that, in *Donoghue v Stevenson* itself and in all the numerous cases in which the principle of that decision has been applied to different but analogous factual situations, it has always been either stated expressly, or taken for granted, that an essential ingredient in the cause of action relied on was the existence of danger, or the threat of danger, of physical damage to persons or their property, excluding for this purpose the very piece of property from the defective condition of which such danger, or threat of danger, arises. To dispense with that essential ingredient in a cause of action of the kind concerned in the present case would, in my view, involve a radical departure from long-established authority.

The second consideration is that there is no sound policy reason for substituting the wider scope of the duty of care put forward for the pursuers for the more restricted scope of such duty put forward by the defenders. The effect of accepting the pursuers' contention with regard to the scope of the duty of care involved would be, in substance, to create, as between two persons who are not in any contractual relationship with each other, obligations of one of those two persons to the other which are only really appropriate as between persons who do have such a relationship between them.

In the case of a manufacturer or distributor of goods, the position would be that he warranted to the ultimate user or consumer of such goods that they were as well designed, as merchantable and as fit for their contemplated purpose as the exercise of reasonable care could make them.

In the case of sub-contractors such as those concerned in the present case, the position would be that they warranted to the building owner that the flooring, when laid, would be as well designed, as free from defects of any kind and as fit for its contemplated purpose as the exercise of reasonable care could make it.

In my view, the imposition of warranties of this kind on one person in favour of another, when there is no contractual relationship between them, is contrary to any sound policy requirement.

It is, I think, just worth while to consider the difficulties which would arise if the wider scope of the duty of care put forward by the pursuers were accepted. In any case where complaint was made by an ultimate consumer that a product made by some persons with whom he himself had no contract was defective, by what standard or standards of quality would the question of defectiveness fall to be decided? In the case of goods bought from a retailer, it could hardly be the standard prescribed by the contract between the retailer and the wholesaler, or between the wholesaler and the distributor, or between the distributor and the manufacturer, for the terms of such contracts would not even be known to the ultimate buyer. In the case of sub-contractors such as the defenders in the present case, it could hardly be the standard prescribed by the contract between the sub-contractors and the main contractors, for, although the building owner would probably be aware of those terms, he could not, since he was not a party to such contract, rely on any standard or standards prescribed in it. It follows that the question by what standard or standards alleged defects in a product complained of by its ultimate user or consumer are to be judged remains entirely at large and cannot be given any just or satisfactory answer.

If, contrary to the views expressed above, the relevant contract or contracts can be regarded in order to establish the standard or standards of quality by which the question of defectiveness falls to be judged, and if such contract or contracts happen to include provisions excluding or limiting liability for defective products or defective work, or for negligence generally, it seems that the party sued in delict should in justice be entitled to rely on such provisions. This illustrates with especial force the inherent difficulty of seeking to impose what are really contractual obligations by unprecedented and, as I think, wholly undesirable extensions of the existing law of delict.

By contrast, if the scope of the duty of care contended for by the defenders is accepted, the standard of defectiveness presents no problem at all. The sole question is whether the product is so defective that, when used or consumed in the way in which it was intended to be, it gives rise to a danger of physical damage to persons or their property, other than the product concerned itself.

My Lords, for the reasons which I have given, I would decide the question of relevancy in favour of the defenders and allow the appeal accordingly.

Appeal dismissed.

NOTE

For general discussion of some of the issues raised by the above cases see Miller and Lovell, op cit, p 326 et seq; Peter Cane, 'Physical Loss, Economic Loss and Products Liability', (1979) 95 LQR 117. For comment on the *Junior Books* case itself see Palmer and Murdoch, (1983) 46 MLR 213; Jaffey, (1983) CLJ 37. See also above p 83 et seq for discussion of a possible liability based on the unavailability of spare parts.

Questions

1. Do you agree with Lord Roskill when he says (above p 171) that 'as between an ultimate purchaser and a manufacturer [proximity] would not easily be found to exist in the ordinary everyday transaction of purchasing chattels when it is obvious that in truth the real reliance was on the immediate vendor and not on the manufacturer'? If this is true of some cases in which a purchaser has a particular purpose in mind which he communicates to the retailer (see now s 14(3) of the Sale of Goods Act 1979, above p 61) is it true also of cases in which the complaint is simply that the product is unmerchantable?

2. If there were a relevant and reasonable exclusion clause in a contract between A and B would it be legitimate to reason as against a third party C as Lord Roskill was prepared to do (above p 171) that, 'such a clause according to the manner in which it was worded might in some circumstances limit the duty of care just as in the *Hedley Byrne* case the plaintiffs were ultimately defeated by the defendants' disclaimer of responsibility?

Would this depend on whether C knew of the existence of the clause? (For exclusion clauses generally see below Ch 6). Compare also the position in *General Motor Products of Canada Ltd v Kravitz* (1979) 93 DLR (3d) 481 (Supreme Court of Canada, above p 28) and draft clause 5.18(2) and (3) appended to the Ontario Law Reform Commission's Report on Sale of Goods (1979), above p 29.

3. If a consumer were to be allowed to recover from a manufacturer the costs of making a dangerously defective product safe should the entitlement usually be dependent on the manufacturer being given an opportunity to repair or replace the product under the provision of his guarantee?

See also above p 107 et seq for discussion of the not dissimilar issue of rejection of goods and allowing a retail seller the opportunity of carrying out a prompt repair.

4. If a consumer were to be allowed to sue the manufacturer of allegedly shoddy goods would the *Junior Books* case give a clear answer to the question of the qualitative standard by reference to which the goods were to be judged? To what extent would this be a practical problem in everyday consumer transactions? Do you agree with Lord Brandon when he says (above p 174) that 'the imposition of warranties of this kind on one person in favour of another, when there is no contractual relationship between them, is contrary to any sound policy requirement'? Cf, for example, the Australian Trade Practices Act 1974, s 74(D), above p 31.

5. Does the *Junior Books* case give any satisfactory explanation as to why *Dutton's* case was thought to involve physical damage to the dwelling-house itself whereas there was no such 'damage' to the factory? How would you classify the disintegration within the legs of the crane in the *Rivtow Marine* case? If the engine mountings of a car rust away prematurely does this constitute physical damage (i) before the mountings collapse or (ii) once they have done so?

Consider the following cases:
1. Recently Gerryhatrick has purchased a new television set from a retailer who is now insolvent. A defective valve implodes, causing the set

to shatter but no personal injury or damage to any other item of property follows. The set was manufactured by Blowout and the valve had been supplied by Component Ltd, a specialist producer. Gerryhatrick cannot afford to buy a new set.

Advise Gerryhatrick as to the liability, if any, of (i) Blowout and (ii) Component Ltd. Would Component Ltd's liability be different according to whether the valve had been (a) part of the original set or (b) a replacement part?

2. Danegeld is a manufacturer of coffee pots all of which have been sold to consumers through an independent mail order company which is now insolvent. Altogether some 10,000 such pots have been sold. It is now apparent that all the pots are dangerously defective owing to a defect in the glue which has been used to stick on the handles. The glue was supplied by an independent company which is also insolvent. Amanda has been scalded when her coffee pot broke. Ben, knowing of her injuries, feels that it is not safe to use his pot any further. Claude owns a coffee pot but is unaware of the danger. Both Amanda and Ben wish to claim compensation from Danegeld.

Advise Amanda and Ben. Consider also whether Danegeld is legally obliged to take any steps to safeguard the owners of the pots. Would it affect the position if the pots had been sold through numerous retailers rather than the one mail order company?

3. By the terms of a commercial contract beween Bardolph and Pistol, Bardolph agrees to sell to Pistol a large quantity of carpet which is described as being 'for heavy domestic use'. The agreement contains an exemption clause which, it is accepted, is enforceable as between the parties when the carpet proves not to be of merchantable quality under the contract. Some of the carpet is resold by Pistol to a private purchaser, Hal, at a price which is somewhat lower than that which would usually be paid for a carpet which was suitable for heavy domestic use, but somewhat higher than that which would be paid for a bedroom carpet. The carpet is suitable for use in a bedroom but Hal requires it for use in his hall. However he has not discussed the matter with Pistol and the carpet is not labelled or otherwise described as being of any particular quality. After buying the carpet Hal learns of the terms of the contract between Bardolph and Pistol.

Advise Hal as to any remedies which he may have against (i) Pistol and (ii) Bardolph. As to the position of Pistol see also above p 73 et seq.

4. Recently Computer Programmers have supplied a range of expensive computers and calculating machines which, because of gross errors in manufacture, will not, as they admit, fulfil their normal functions. Indeed some have been wired up incorrectly and will not work at all. The sole dealer is in liquidation.

Advise Fidelio who has purchased one such machine from the dealer and Leonora who has received one as a Christmas gift.

Some North American developments

The insistence within the United Kingdom on proof of negligence has long since ceased to be a feature of the law of some other jurisdictions, especially the United States of America. The theories of liability based on breach of express and implied warranties have been noted already: see respectively *Randy Knitwear Inc v American Cyanamid Co* 181 NE 2d 399, above p 41, and *Henningsen v Bloomfield Motors Inc* (1960) 161 A 2d 69, above p 27. This section contains material illustrating some of the principal developments through a theory which was freed from the intricacies of the law of sales and based squarely on the law of tort. The following case is seen generally as the most important in establishing the theory of strict liability in tort.

STRICT LIABILITY IN TORT

Greenman v Yuba Power Products Inc 377 P 2d 897 (1962) Supreme Court of California

Traynor Justice. Plaintiff brought this action for damages against the retailer and the manufacturer of a Shopsmith, a combination power tool that could be used as a saw, drill, and wood lathe. He saw a Shopsmith demonstrated by the retailer and studied a brochure prepared by the manufacturer. He decided he wanted a Shopsmith for his home workshop, and his wife bought and gave him one for Christmas in 1955. In 1957 he bought the necessary attachments to use the Shopsmith as a lathe for turning a large piece of wood he wished to make into a chalice. After he had worked on the piece of wood several times without difficulty, it suddenly flew out of the machine and struck him on the forehead, inflicting serious injuries. About ten and a half months later, he gave the retailer and the manufacturer written notice of claimed breaches of warranties and filed a complaint against them alleging such breaches and negligence.

After a trial before a jury, the court ruled that there was no evidence that the retailer was negligent or had breached any express warranty and that the manufacturer was not liable for the breach of any implied warranty. Accordingly, it submitted to the jury only the cause of action alleging breach of implied warranties against the retailer and the causes of action alleging negligence and breach of express warranties against the manufacturer. The jury returned a verdict for the retailer against plaintiff and for plaintiff against the manufacturer in the amount of $65,000. The trial court denied the manufacturer's motion for a new trial and entered judgment on the verdict. The manufacturer and plaintiff appeal. Plaintiff seeks a reversal of the part of the judgment in favor of the retailer, however, only in the event that the part of the judgment against the manufacturer is reversed.

Plaintiff introduced substantial evidence that his injuries were caused by defective design and construction of the Shopsmith . . . The jury could therefore reasonably have concluded that the manufacturer negligently constructed the Shopsmith. The jury could also reasonably have concluded that statements in the manufacturer's brochure were untrue, that they constituted express warranties,[1] and that plaintiff's injuries were caused by their breach.

[1] The manufacturer contends, however, that plaintiff did not give it notice of breach of warranty within a reasonable time and that therefore his cause of action for breach of warranty is barred by section 1769 of the Civil Code. Since it cannot be determined whether the verdict against it was based on the negligence or warranty cause of action or both, the manufacture concludes that the error in presenting the warranty cause of action to the jury was prejudicial.

. . .

The notice requirement of section 1769, however, is not an appropriate one for the court to adopt in actions by injured consumers against manufacturers with whom they have not dealt. (*La Hue v Coca-Cola Bottling* 50 Wash 2d 645, 314 P 2d 421 at 422; *Chapman v Brown* DC 198 F Supp 78, 85; affd *Brown v Chapman* 9 Cir, 304 F 2d 149.) 'As between the immediate parties to the sale [the notice requirement] is a sound commercial rule, designed to protect the seller against unduly delayed claims for damages. As applied to personal injuries, and notice to a remote seller, it becomes a booby-trap for the unwary. The injured consumer is seldom "steeped in the business practice which justified the rule," [James, Product Liability, 34 Texas L Rev 44, 192 197] and at least until he has had legal advice it will not occur to him to give notice to one with whom he has had no dealings.' (Prosser, Strict Liability to the Consumer, 69 Yale LJ 1099, 1130, footnotes omitted.) . . . We conclude, therefore, that even if plaintiff did not give timely notice of breach of warranty to the manufacturer, his cause of action based on the representations contained in the brochure was not barred.

[2] Moreover, to impose strict liability on the manufacturer under the circumstances of this case, it was not necessary for plaintiff to establish an express warranty as defined in section 1732 of the Civil Code.[2] A manufacturer is strictly liable in tort when an article he places on the market, knowing that it is to be used without inspection for defects, proves to have a defect that causes injury to a human being. Recognized first in the case of unwholesome food products, such liability has now been extended to a variety of other products that create as great or greater hazards if defective. [Citations omitted.] . . .

[3] Although in these cases strict liability has usually been based on the theory of an express or implied warranty running from the manufacturer to the plaintiff, the abandonment of the requirement of a contract between them, the recognition that the liability is not assumed by agreement but imposed by law [Citation omitted] and·the refusal to permit the manufacturer to define the scope of its own responsibility for defective products [citations omitted] make clear that the liability is not one governed by the law of contract warranties but by the law of strict liability in tort. Accordingly, rules defining and governing warranties that were developed to meet the needs of commercial transactions cannot properly be invoked to govern the manufacturer's liability to those injured by their defective products unless those rules also serve the purposes for which such liability is imposed.

[4] We need not recanvass the reasons for imposing strict liability on the manufacturer. They have been fully articulated in the cases cited above. (See also 2 Harper and James, Torts, §§ 28.15–28.16, pp 1569–1574; Prosser, Strict Liability to the Consumer, 69 Yale LJ 1099; *Escola v Coca-Cola Bottling Co* 24 Cal 2d 453 at 461, 150 P 2d 436, concurring opinion.) The purpose of such liability is to insure that the costs of injuries resulting from defective products are borne by the manufacturers that put such products on the market rather than by the injured persons who are powerless to protect themselves. Sales warranties serve this purpose fitfully at best. (See Prosser, Strict Liability to the Consumer, 69 Yale LJ 1099, 1124–1134.) In the present case, for example, plaintiff was able to plead and prove an express warranty only because he read and relied on the representations of the Shopsmith's ruggedness contained in the manufacturer's brochure. Implicit in the machine's presence on the market, however, was a representation that it would safely do the jobs for which it was built. Under these circumstances, it should not be controlling whether plaintiff selected the machine because of the statements in the brochure, or because of the machine's own appearance of excellence that belied the defect lurking beneath the surface, or because he merely assumed that it would safely do the jobs it was built to do. It should not be controlling whether the details of the sales from manufacturer to retailer and from retailer to plaintiff's wife were such that one or more of the implied warranties of the sales act arose. (Civ Code, § 1735.) 'The remedies of injured consumers ought not to be made to depend upon the intricacies of the law of sales.' (*Ketterer v Armour & Co* DC 200 F 322 at 323; *Klein v Duchess Sandwich Co* 14 Cal 2d 272, 282, 93 P 2d 799.) To establish the manufacturer's liability it was sufficient that plaintiff proved that he was injured while using the Shopsmith in a way it was intended to be used as a result of a defect in design and manufacture of which plaintiff was not aware that made the Shopsmith unsafe for its intended use.

[5] The manufacturer contends that the trial court erred in refusing to give three instruction requested by it. It appears from the record, however, that the substance of two of the requested instructions was adequately covered by the instructions given and that the third instructions was not supported by the evidence.

The judgment is affirmed.

Gibson C J, and **Schauer, McComb, Peters, Tobriner** and **Peek JJ**, concur.

1. In this respect the trial court limited the jury to a consideration of two statements in the manufacturer's brochure.
(1) 'WHEN SHOPSMITH IS IN HORIZONTAL POSITION—Rugged construction of frame provides rigid support from end to end. Heavy centerless-ground steel tubing insures perfect alignment of components.' (2) 'SHOPSMITH maintains its accuracy because every component has positive locks that hold adjustments through rough or precision work.' [For manufacturers' express warranties see above p 31 et seq.]
2. 'Any affirmation of fact or any promise by the seller relating to the goods is an express warranty if the natural tendency of such affirmation or promise is to induce the buyer to purchase the goods, and if the buyer purchases the goods relying thereon. No affirmation of the value of the goods, nor any statement purporting to be a statement of the seller's opinion only shall be construed as a warranty.' [For reference to the differing definitions of an express warranty see above pp 7–8.]

One of the more remarkable features of this case was the relative brevity of the judgment through which a proposition of such far-reaching importance was propounded. Thereafter general acceptance of the theory was assisted (if not assured) by its being adopted by the influential American Law Institute whose provision and some of whose comments are printed below:

Restatement (second) of Torts (1965)

§ 402A. Special Liability of Seller of Product for Physical Harm to User or Consumer
(1) One who sells any product in a defective condition unreasonably dangerous to the user or consumer or to his property is subject to liability for physical harm thereby caused to the ultimate user or consumer, or to his property, if
   (a) the seller is engaged in the business of selling such a product, and
   (b) it is expected to and does reach the user or consumer without substantial change in the condition in which it is sold.
(2) The rule stated in subsection (1) applies although
   (a) the seller has exercised all possible care in the preparation and sale of his product, and
   (b) the user or consumer has not bought the product from or entered into any contractual relation with the seller.

Caveat:
The Institute expresses no opinion as to whether the rules stated in this section may not apply
   (1) to harm to persons other than users or consumers;
   (2) to the seller of a product expected to be processed or otherwise substantially changed before it reaches the user or consumer; or
   (3) to the seller of a component part of a product to be assembled.

Comment:
   a.   This section states a special rule applicable to sellers of products. The rule is one of strict liability, making the seller subject to liability to the user or consumer even though he has exercised all possible care in the preparation and sale of the product.

. . .

   f.   Business of selling. The rule stated in this Section applies to any person engaged in the business of selling products for use or consumption. It therefore applies to any manufacturer of such a product, to any wholesale or retail dealer or distributor, and to the operator of a restaurant. It is not necessary that the seller be engaged solely in the business of selling such products. Thus the rule applies to the owner of a motion picture theatre who sells popcorn or ice cream, either for consumption on the premises or in packages to be taken home.
   The rule does not, however, apply to the occasional seller of food or other such products who is not engaged in that activity as a part of his business . . .
   g.   Defective condition. The rule stated in this Section applies only where the product is, at the time it leaves the seller's hands, in a condition not contemplated by the ultimate consumer, which will be unreasonably dangerous to him. The seller is not liable when he delivers the product in a safe condition, and subsequent mishandling or other causes make it harmful by the time it is consumed. The burden of proof that the product was in a defective condition at the time that it left the hands of the particular seller is upon the injured plaintiff; and unless evidence can be produced which will support the conclusion that it was then defective, the burden is not sustained.
   Safe condition at the time of delivery by the seller will, however, include proper packaging, necessary sterilisation, and other precautions required to permit the product to remain safe for a normal length of time when handled in a normal manner.
   h.   A product is not in a defective condition when it is safe for normal handling and consumption. If the injury result from abnormal handling, as where a bottled beverage is knocked against a radiator to remove the cap, or from abnormal preparation for use, as where too much salt is added to food, or from abnormal consumption, as where a child eats too much candy and is made ill, the seller is not liable. Where, however, he has reason to anticipate that danger may result from a particular use, as where a drug is sold which is safe only in limited doses, he may be required to give adequate warning of the danger (see Comment *j*), and a product sold without such warning is in a defective condition.

The defective condition may arise not only from harmful ingredients, not characteristic of the product itself either as to presence or quantity, but also from foreign objects contained in the product, from decay or deterioration before sale, or from the way in which the product is prepared or packed . . .

i.   Unreasonably dangerous. The rule stated in this Section applies only where the defective condition of the product makes it unreasonably dangerous to the user or consumer. Many products cannot possibly be made entirely safe for all consumption, and any food or drug necessarily involves some risk of harm, if only from over-consumption. Ordinary sugar is a deadly poison to diabetics, and castor oil found use under Mussolini as an instrument of torture. That is not what is meant by "unreasonably dangerous" in this section. The article sold must be dangerous to an extent beyond that which would be contemplated by the ordinary consumer who purchases it, with the ordinary knowledge common to the community as to its characteristics. Good whiskey is not unreasonably dangerous merely because it will make some people drunk, and is especially dangerous to alcoholics; but bad whisky, containing a dangerous amount of fusel oil, is unreasonably dangerous . . .

j.   Directions or warning. In order to prevent the product from being unreasonably dangerous, the seller may be required to give directions or warning, on the container, as to its use. The seller may reasonably assume that those with common allergies, as for example to eggs or strawberries, will be aware of them, and he is not required to warn against them. Where, however, the product contains an ingredient to which a substantial number of the population are allergic, and the ingredient is one whose danger is not generally known, or if known is one which the consumer would reasonably not expect to find in the product, the seller is required to give warning against it, if he has knowledge, or by the application of reasonable, developed human skill and foresight should have knowledge, of the presence of the ingredient and the danger. Likewise in the case of poisonous drugs, or those unduly dangerous for other reasons, warning as to use may be required . . .

k.   Unavoidably unsafe products. There are some products which, in the present state of human knowledge, are quite incapable of being made safe for their intended and ordinary use. These are especially common in the field of drugs. An outstanding example is the vaccine for the Pasteur treatment of rabies, which not uncommonly leads to very serious and damaging consequences when it is injected. Since the disease itself invariably leads to a dreadful death, both the marketing and the use of the vaccine are fully justified, notwithstanding the unavoidable high degree of risk which they involve. Such a product, properly prepared, and accompanied by proper directions and warning, is not defective, nor is it *unreasonably* dangerous. The same is true of many other drugs, vaccines, and the like, many of which for this very reason cannot legally be sold except to physicians, or under the prescription of a physician. It is also true in particular of many new or experimental drugs as to which, because of lack of time and opportunity for sufficient medical experience, there can be no assurance of safety, or perhaps even of purity of ingredients, but such experience as there is justifies the marketing and use of the drug notwithstanding a medically recognizable risk. The seller of such products, again with the qualification that they are properly prepared and marketed, and proper warning is given, where the situation calls for it, is not to be held to strict liability for unfortunate consequences attending their use, merely because he has undertaken to supply the public with an apparently useful and desirable product, attended with a known but apparently reasonable risk.

l.   User or consumer. In order for the rule stated in this Section to apply, it is not necessary that the ultimate user or consumer have acquired the product directly from the seller, although the rule applies equally if he does so. He may have acquired it through one or more intermediate dealers. It is not even necessary that the consumer have purchased the product at all. He may be a member of the family of the final purchaser, or his employee, or a guest at his table, or a mere donee from the purchaser. The liability stated is one in tort, and does not require any contractual relation, or privity of contract, between the plaintiff and the defendant . . .

NOTES

1. As comment *f.* makes clear strict liability is regarded as being applicable to all who are engaged in the business of 'selling' products. It does not apply only to manufacturers or producers. The same view has been adopted by the courts: see, for example, *Vandermark v Ford Motor Co* 391 P 2d 168 (1964) (Supreme Court of California) (seller of car) and in general

Frumer and Friedman *Products Liability,* Vol 2, §16A[4][b]. Some decisions have gone further to include business suppliers generally, for example those who hire out a defective product: see *Citrone v Hertz Truck Leasing and Rental Service* 212 A 2d 769 (New Jersey, 1965) (motor vehicle). Others have extended the doctrine to those who use a product when providing a service (for example, hairdressing) without necessarily 'supplying' it as such: see, for example, *Newmark v Gimbels Inc* 258 A 2d 697 (New Jersey, 1969) (permanent wave solution in beauty parlour). The Ontario Law Reform Commission has recommended in its 'Report on Products Liability' (1979) that strict liability be applied to business suppliers. Contrast the views of the Law Commission and the proposed EEC directive, below pp 196–197.

2. Another question which has attracted substantial comment and differences of opinion is whether American courts should follow the *Restatement* formula and require that the product be shown to be both 'in a defective condition' and 'unreasonably dangerous'. One view is that the 'unreasonably dangerous' requirement is apt to introduce an element of negligence or fault into a strict liability system. *Cronin v JBE Olson Corpn* 104 Cal Rptr 433 (1972) is an early and leading decision of the Californian Supreme Court. The plaintiff was driving a bread delivery van which collided with another vehicle when the force of the collision broke an aluminium safety hasp, releasing bread trays which, in turn, propelled him through the windscreen. There was evidence that the safety hasp was porous and defective with a low tolerance to force but the defendants contended that they had been prejudiced by the lack of a finding that it was unreasonably dangerous. Dismissing the objection the court said (at 443):

> We believe the *Greenman* formulation is consonant with the rationale and development of products liability law in California because it provides a clear and simple test for determining whether the injured plaintiff is entitled to recovery. We are not persuaded to the contrary by the formulation of s 402A which inserts the factor of an 'unreasonably dangerous' condition into the equation.

Predictably the courts of some other States have disagreed and stressed the importance of establishing that the product is 'unreasonably dangerous'. A collection of cases is to be found in Frumer and Friedman, op cit, § 16 A[4][g]. Two leading articles which continue to be influential are Keeton, 'Products Liability: liability without fault and the requirement of a defect', 41 Texas LR 855 (1963); Traynor, 'The Ways and Meanings of Defective Products and Strict Liability', 32 Tenn LR 363 (1965).

For further discussion of the notion of a 'defect' and its relation to the so-called 'state of the art' see below, pp 199–202.

3. The *Restatement* formula applies both to physical injury and property damage but not where the loss is purely economic. As in English law (see above p 165 et seq) there has been considerable difficulty in deciding where the line is to be drawn. Indeed Professor Phillips, a leading American authority, has written in a conference paper for the 1984 UKNCCL Colloquium on 'Product Liability' that 'the decisions are in disarray'. He adds: 'The alleged majority position is that the plaintiff suffering only economic loss (for example decrease in market value of the product, or lost profits) must sue either in express warranty, with or without privity of contract, or in implied warranty and then only if there is privity between the plaintiff and defendant. There is no agreement as to what constitutes physical harm, or whether the concept includes harm to the product itself.'

For two of the more important contrasting cases see *Santor v A and M Karagheusian Inc* 207 A 2d 305 (New Jersey Supreme Court, 1965) and *Seely v White Motor Co* 45 Cal Rptr 17 (California Supreme Court, 1965), discussed in Miller and Lovell, op cit, pp 338–342. For further cases and discussion see Frumer and Friedman, op cit, § 16 A[4][k].

The following case is a good example of the innovatory approach which some American courts have been prepared to adopt when dealing with complex product liability claims.

Judith Sindell v Abbott Laboratories, Maureen Rogers v Rexall Drug Company 607 P 2d 924 (1980) Supreme Court of California

(Footnotes omitted unless otherwise indicated)

Mosk Justice. This case involves a complex problem both timely and significant: may a plaintiff, injured as the result of a drug administered to her mother during pregnancy, who knows the type of drug involved but cannot identify the manufacturer of the precise product, hold liable for her injuries a maker of a drug produced from an identical formula?

Plaintiff Judith Sindell brought an action against eleven drug companies . . . on behalf of herself and other women similarly situated. The complaint alleges as follows:

Between 1941 and 1971, defendants were engaged in the business of manufacturing, promoting, and marketing diethylstilbesterol (DES), a drug which is a synthetic compound of the female hormone estrogen. The drug was administered to plaintiff's mother and the mothers of the class she represents,[1] for the purpose of preventing miscarriage. In 1947, the Food and Drug Administration authorised the marketing of DES as a miscarriage preventative, but only on an experimental basis, with a requirement that the drug contain a warning label to that effect.

DES may cause cancerous vaginal and cervical growths in the daughters exposed to it before birth, because their mothers took the drug during pregnancy. The form of cancer from which these daughters suffer is known as adenocarcinoma, and it manifests itself after a minimum latent period of 10 or 12 years. It is a fast-spreading and deadly disease, and radical surgery is required to prevent it from spreading. DES also causes adenosis, precancerous vaginal and cervical growths which may spread to other areas of the body. The treatment for adenosis is cauterization, surgery, or cryosurgery. Women who suffer from this condition must be monitored by biopsy or colposcopic examination twice a year, a painful and expensive procedure. Thousands of women whose mothers received DES during pregnancy are unaware of the effect of the drug.

In 1971, the Food and Drug Administration ordered defendants to cease marketing and promoting DES for the purpose of preventing miscarriages, and to warn physicians and the public that the drug should not be used by pregnant women because of the danger to their unborn children.

. . .

As a result of the DES ingested by her mother, plaintiff developed a malignant bladder tumor which was removed by surgery. She suffers from adenosis and must constantly be monitored by biopsy or colposcopy to insure early warning of further malignancy.

The first cause of action alleges that defendants were jointly and individually negligent in that they manufactured, marketed and promoted DES as a safe and efficacious drug to prevent miscarriage, without adequate testing or warning, and without monitoring or reporting its effects.

A separate cause of action alleges that defendants are jointly liable regardless of which particular brand of DES was ingested by plaintiff's mother because defendants collaborated in marketing, promoting and testing the drug, relied upon each other's tests, and adhered to an industry-wide safety standard. DES was produced from a common and mutually agreed upon formula as a fungible drug interchangeable with other brands of the same product; defendants knew or should have known that it was customary for doctors to prescribe the drug by its generic rather than its brand name and that pharmacists filled prescriptions from whatever brand of the drug happened to be in stock.

Other causes of action are based upon theories of strict liability, violation of express and implied warranties, false and fraudulent representations, misbranding of drugs in violation of federal law, conspiracy and 'lack of consent.'

Each cause of action alleges that defendants are jointly liable because they acted in concert, on the basis of express and implied agreements, and in reliance upon and ratification and exploitation of each other's testing and marketing methods.

Plaintiff seeks compensatory damages of $1 million and punitive damages of $10 million for herself. For the members of her class, she prays for equitable relief in the form of an order that defandants warn physicians and others of the danger of DES and the necessity of performing certain tests to determine the presence of disease caused by the drug, and that they establish free clinics in California to perform such tests.

Defendants demurred to the complaint. While the complaint did not expressly allege that plaintiff could not identify the manufacturer of the precise drug ingested by her mother, she stated in her points and authorities in opposition to the demurrers filed by some of the defendants that she was unable to make the identification, and the trial court sustained the demurrers of these defendants without leave to amend on the ground that plaintiff did not and stated she could not identify which defendant had manufactured the drug responsible for her injuries. Thereupon, the court dismissed the action. This appeal involves only five of ten defendants named in the complaint. . . .

This case is but one of a number filed throughout the country seeking to hold drug manufacturers liable for injuries allegedly resulting from DES prescribed to the plaintiffs' mothers since 1947.[2] According to a note in the Fordham Law Review, estimates of the number of women who took the drug during pregnancy range from 1½ million to 3 million. Hundreds, perhaps thousands, of the daughters of these women suffer from adenocarcinoma, and the incidence of vaginal adenosis among them is 30 to 90 percent. (Comment, *DES and a Proposed Theory of Enterprise Liability* (1978) 46 Fordham L Rev 963, 964–967 [hereafter Fordham Comment].) Most of the cases are still pending. With two exceptions,[3] those that have been decided resulted in judgments in favour of the drug company defendants because of the failure of the plaintiffs to identify the manufacturer of the DES prescribed to their mothers.[4] The same result was reached in a recent California case. (*McCreery v Eli Lilly & Co* (1978) 87 Cal App 3d 77 [at] 82–84, 150 Cal Rptr 730.) The present action is another attempt to overcome this obstacle to recovery.

[1] We begin with the proposition that, as a general rule, the imposition of liability depends upon a showing by the plaintiff that his or her injuries were caused by the act of the defendant or by an instrumentality under the defendant's control . . .

There are, however, exceptions to this rule. Plaintiff's complaint suggests several bases upon which defendants may be held liable for her injuries even though she cannot demonstrate the name of the manufacturer which produced the DES actually taken by her mother. The first of these theories, classically illustrated by *Summers v Tice* (1948) 33 Cal 2d 80, 199 P 2d 1, places the burden of proof of causation upon tortious defendants in certain circumstances. The second basis of liability emerging from the complaint is that defendants acted in concert to cause injury to plaintiff. There is a third and novel approach to the problem, sometimes called the theory of 'enterprise liability,' but which we prefer to designate by the more accurate term of 'industry-wide' liability, which might obviate the necessity for identifying the manufacturer of the injury-causing drug. We shall conclude that these doctrines, as previously interpreted, may not be applied to hold defendants liable under the allegations of this complaint. However, we shall propose and adopt a fourth basis for permitting the action to be tried, grounded upon an extension of the *Summers* doctrine.

. . .

Should we require that plaintiff identify the manufacturer which supplied the DES used by her mother or that all DES manufacturers be joined in the action, she would effectively be precluded from any recovery. As defendants candidly admit, there is little likelihood that all the manufacturers who made DES at the time in question are still in business or that they are subject to the jurisdiction of the California courts. There are, however, forceful arguments in favour of holding that plaintiff has a cause of action.

In our contemporary complex industrialized society, advances in science and technology create fungible goods which may harm consumers and which cannot be traced to any specific producer. The response of the courts can be either to adhere rigidly to prior doctrine, denying recovery to those injured by such products, or to fashion remedies to meet these changing needs. Just as Justice Traynor in his landmark concurring opinion in *Escola v Coca Cola Bottling Co* (1944) 24 Cal 2d 453 [at] 467–468, 150 P 2d 436, recognized that in an era of mass production and complex marketing methods the traditional standard of negligence was insufficient to govern the obligations of manufacturer to consumer, so should we acknowledge that some adaptation of the rules of causation and liability may be appropriate in these recurring circumstances.

. . .

[5] Where, as here, all defendants produced a drug from an identical formula and the manufacturer of the DES which caused plaintiff's injuries cannot be identified through no fault of plaintiff, a modification of the rule of *Summers* is warranted. As we have seen, an undiluted *Summers* rationale is inappropriate to shift the burden of proof of causation to defendants because if we measure the chance that any particular manufacturer supplied the injury-causing product by the number of producers of DES, there is a possibility that none of the five defendants in this case produced the offending substance and that the responsible manufacturer, not named in the action, will escape liability.

But we approach the issue of causation from a different perspective: we hold it to be reasonable in the present context to measure the likelihood that any of the defendants supplied the product which allegedly injured plaintiff by the percentage which the DES sold by each of them for the purpose of preventing miscarriage bears to the entire production of the drug sold by all for that purpose. Plaintiff asserts in her briefs that Eli Lilly and Company and 5 or 6 other companies produced 90 percent of the DES marketed. If at trial this is established to be the fact, then there is a corresponding likelihood that this comparative handful of producers manufactured the DES which caused plaintiff's injuries, and only a 10 percent likelihood that the offending producer would escape liability.

If plaintiff joins in the action the manufacturers of a substantial share of the DES which her mother might have taken, the injustice of shifting the burden of proof to defendants to demonstrate that they could not have made the substance which injured plaintiff is significantly diminished. While 75 to 80 percent of the market is suggested as the requirement by the Fordham Comment (at p 996), we hold only that a substantial percentage is required.

The presence in the action of a substantial share of the appropriate market also provides a ready means to apportion damages among the defendants. Each defendant will be held liable for the proportion of the judgment represented by its share of that market unless it demonstrates that it could not have made the product which caused plaintiff's injuries. In the present case, as we have seen, one DES manufacturer was dismissed from the action upon filing a declaration that it had not manufactured DES until after plaintiff was born. Once plaintiff has met her burden of joining the required defendants, they in turn may cross-complaint against other DES manufacturers, not joined in the action, which they can allege might have supplied the injury-causing product.

Under this approach, each manufacturer's liability would approximate its responsibility for the injuries caused by its own products. Some minor discrepancy in the correlation between market share and liability is inevitable; therefore, a defendant may be held liable for a somewhat different percentage of the damage than its share of the appropriate market would justify. It is probably impossible, with the passage of time, to determine market share with mathematical exactitude. But just as a jury cannot be expected to determine the precise relationship between fault and liability in applying the doctrine of comparative fault . . . the difficulty of apportioning damages among the defendant producers in exact relation to their market share does not seriously militate against the rule we adopt. As we said in *Summers* with regard to the liability of independent tortfeasors, where a correct division of liability cannot be made 'the trier of fact may make it the best it can.' (33 Cal 2d at p 88, 199 P 2d at 5.)

We are not unmindful of the practical problems involved in defining the market and determining market share, but these are largely matters of proof which properly cannot be determined at the pleading stage of these proceedings. Defendants urge that it would be both unfair and contrary to public policy to hold them liable for plaintiff's injuries in the absence of proof that one of them supplied the drug responsible for the damage. Most of their arguments, however, are based upon the assumption that one manufacturer would be held responsible for the products of another or for those of all other manufacturers if plaintiff ultimately prevails. But under the rule we adopt, each manufacturer's liability for an injury would be approximately equivalent to the damages caused by the DES it manufactured.

The judgments are reversed.

Bird C J, and **Newman** and **White JJ** concur.
Richardson Justice, dissenting.

I respectfully dissent. In these consolidated cases the majority adopts a wholly new theory which contains these ingredients: The plaintiffs were not alive at the time of the commission of the tortious acts. They sue a generation later. They are permitted to receive substantial damages from multiple defendants without any proof that any defendant caused or even probably caused plaintiffs' injuries.

Although the majority purports to change only the required burden of proof by shifting it from plaintiffs to defendants, the effect of its holding is to guarantee that plaintiffs will prevail on the causation issue because defendants are no more capable of disproving factual causation than plaintiffs are of proving it. 'Market share' liability thus represents a new high water mark in tort law. The ramifications seem almost limitless, a fact which prompted one recent commentator, in criticizing a substantially identical theory, to conclude that 'Elimination of the burden of proof as to identification [of the manufacturer whose drug injured plaintiff] would impose a liability which would exceed absolute liability.' (Coggins *Industry-Wide Liability* (1979) 13 Suffolk L Rev 980, 998, fn omitted; see also, pp 1000–1001.) In my view, the majority's departure from traditional tort doctrine is unwise.

. . .

I would affirm the judgments of dismissal.
Clark and **Manuel JJ**, concur.
Rehearsing denied; **Clark, Richardson** and **Manuel JJ**, dissenting.

1. The plaintiff class alleged consists of 'girls and women who are residents of California and who have been exposed to DES before birth and who may or may not know that fact or the dangers' to which they were exposed. Defendants are also sued as representatives of a class of drug manufacturers which sold DES after 1941.
2. DES was marketed under many different trade names.
3. In a recent New York case a jury found in the plaintiff's favor in spite of her inability to identify a specific manufacturer of DES. An appeal is pending. (*Bichler v Eli Lilly & Co* (Sup Ct NY 1979).) A Michigan appellate court recently held that plaintiffs had stated a cause of action against several manufacturers of DES even though identification could not be made. (*Abel v Eli Lilly & Co* (decided Dec 5, 1979) Docket No 60497.) That decision is on appeal to the Supreme Court of Michigan.
4. Eg *Gray v United States* (SD Tex 1978) 445 F Supp. 337. In their briefs, defendants refer to a number of other cases in which trial courts have dismissed actions in DES cases on the ground stated above.

NOTES

It is obvious that such cases raise issues of great complexity for the common law but the factual situation on which *Sindell* was based is by no means unique or even unusual. For example the dangers of asbestos are by now well known and it would be surprising if the passage of time did not reveal the carcinogenic properties of many other products. For comment on the case see Teff, 'Market Share Liability—A Novel Approach to Causation' (1982) 31 ICLQ 840; Kors, 'Refining Market Share Liability' 33 Stanford LR 937 (1981). For further discussion of class actions see below, Ch 8 pp 352–373.

Questions

1. How would English law deal with the following aspects of the *Sindell* case: (i) the fact that the injuries were pre-natal; (ii) the time-lapse associated with the minimum latent period of ten or twelve years before the manifestation of cancer; (iii) the inability to identify any particular manufacturer as being responsible for a given plaintiff's condition?
2. If an English court were to accept that petrol with its present permitted lead content was 'defective' because of its well-established effect on the brains of young children and others would the problems of causation be (i) essentially the same as those of the *Sindell* case or (ii) significantly

different? How should they be resolved? For an attempt to raise the issue see *Budden v BP Oil Ltd* (1980) 124 Sol Jo 376, above p 156.

The advantages of strict liability have been recognised by United Kingdom claimants some of whom have attempted to sue in the courts of the United States. However, as the following case illustrates, not all claims have succeeded in being heard on their merits.

McCracken v Eli Lilly & Co (Johnson Circuit Court State of Indiana) (5 June 1984)

Judge McKinney. More than 400 United Kingdom claimants in 17 cases charge Eli Lilly and Company and two individuals with negligence; strict liability and fraud in marketing a prescription medicine which allegedly injured the claimants. The Defendants have moved to dismiss each United Kingdom claim on the ground that this forum is a *forum non conveniens*. The Court has had the benefit of extensive evidence in support of the contentions of the parties. The difficult issues raised have been addressed with great effort and skill by counsel for both parties. After careful consideration. I have concluded to grant the Defendants Motions To Dismiss.

In support of their Motions, the Defendants point to the many connections which these claims have with the United Kingdom. The United Kingdom claimants allegedly took the drug Benoxoprofen, called Opren in the United Kingdom, as a prescription medicine for reducing inflammation symptomatic of arthritis. Benoxoprofen was discovered, patented and developed in the United Kingdom by scientists working for Lilly's UK subsidiary, Lilly Industries Limited. The British government's Department of Health and Social Security regulated the development, manufacture and distribution of Opren, including its uses, dosages and side effect warnings and reported adverse reactions. In addition, the drug was prescribed and sold in the United Kingdom for ailments suffered by persons living there. Moreover, it was there that alleged adverse reactions occurred, injuries resulted and treatment was given. The Defendants further contend that United Kingdom law would apply to these cases and that most evidence and virtually all evidence of causation and injury is in the United Kingdom, thereby making the United Kingdom the more convenient forum for trying these claims. The Defendants have agreed to submit to the jurisdiction of appropriate forums in the United Kingdom.

The Plaintiffs on the other hand oppose the Defendants' Motions To Dismiss on the grounds that Eli Lilly and Company's principal place of business was Indianapolis, Indiana, and that the allegedly tortious conduct occurred in Indianapolis and that the evidence of Defendants' 'wrongs' is available here, making this the most convenient forum. In addition, the Plaintiffs express numerous criticism of their own legal system contending that it does not provide an adequate alternative forum.

The doctrine of *forum non conveniens* is recognized in Indiana. In *Drexel Burnham Lambert Inc v Merchants Investment Counseling Inc* 451 NE 2d 348 (Ind Appl 1983) the Court stated:

> 'The doctrine of *forum non conveniens* permits an action to be litigated in another jurisdiction upon a showing that litigation in the initiating forum is so inconvenient to the parties and witnesses that substantial injustice is likely to result.'

. . .

Factors to be considered in determining issues of *forum non conveniens* are listed in Ind Trial Rule 4.4C:

> In the exercise of that discretion the court may appropriately consider such factors as:
> (1) Amenability to personal jurisdiction in this state and in any alternative forum of the parties to the action;
> (2) Convenience to the parties and witnesses of the trial in this state and in any alternative forum;
> (3) Differences in conflict of law rules applicable in this state and in the alternative forum; or,
> (4) Any other factors having substantial bearing upon the selection of a convenient, reasonable and fair place of trial.

. . .

In balancing each of these factors, I find first that the relative ease of access to sources of proof and availability of compulsory process for attendance of unwilling witnesses strongly favor trial in the United Kingdom. All of the claimants involved in the issue now before this Court were United Kingdom residents taking a drug made, marketed, regulated, sold and prescribed in the United Kingdom. The injuries allegedly suffered occurred and were treated in the United Kingdom. Thus, most evidence on issues of causation and damages is located there. Further, most witnesses, including the physicians who prescribed the drug and were treating each claimant's original condition as well as physicians treating alleged adverse reactions reside in the United Kingdom. The Defendants, in order to adequately defend themselves in these actions, must discover each claimant's pre-existing medical condition, what each treating and prescribing physician knew about the drug and about the claimant's condition, how that condition was actually treated, the nature and extent of claimed adverse reactions, the medical care given for any adverse reactions and the damages allegedly sustained. The evidence, witnesses and documents, concerning these matters is in the United Kingdom. There is no compulsory process of this Court to secure the attendance of unwilling witnesses or the production of their documents. Depositions are an inadequate substitute for live testimony and the cost of transporting to this Court live UK residents willing to testify is substantial. See *Jones,* 444 NE 2d at 161.

A second factor favouring trial in the United Kingdom is that this Court would be required to apply the law of the United Kingdom if these cases were to be tried here. Indiana follows the traditional rule of *lex loci delicti* in selecting applicable substantive law in tort cases. Under the *lex loci delicti* rule 'the tort is committed, the wrong occurs, and the cause of action arises where the injury or death occurred'. *Maroon v State Department of Mental Health* 411 NE 2d 404 at 409 (Ind App 1980); . . .

Thus, with respect to the United Kingdom claims before this Court, injury or death occurred in the United Kingdom and fraud, if any, occurred in the UK. Therefore, its laws must be applied. The identical result would follow even if a 'most significant contacts' test were applied. See *Jones* at 161 and cases cited. The court has already had ample experience with the difficulties of applying foreign law, eg, the disagreement in the solicitor and barrister affidavits already submitted in this cause and the failure of those affidavits to make clear agreed statements as to the law of the United Kingdom. The need and difficulty of applying foreign law is an important factor favoring dismissal. *See eg, Reyno* 102 S Ct at 263; *Jones,* 444 NE 2d at 161.

Although other public interest factors such as administrative difficulties flowing from a heavy trial calendar and the local costs and burdens of jury trials favour trial in the United Kingdom, I have given these considerations little relative weight. This Court is open to foreign citizens when this Court is an appropriate and not a *forum non conveniens.*

Finally, the Plaintiffs complain that the United Kingdom does not for a variety of reasons provide them with an adequate remedy. No such showing was made here. In ruling upon a similar plea, the Supreme Court of the United States in *Reyno* 102 S Ct at 265, said:

> 'Of course, if the remedy provided by the alternative forum is so clearly inadequate or unsatisfactory that it is no remedy at all, the unfavourable change in law may be given substantial weight; the district court may conclude that dismissal would not be in the interests of justice. In this case, however, the remedies that would be provided by the Scottish courts do not fall within this category. Although the relatives of the decedents may not be able to rely on a strict liability theory, and although their potential damage award may be smaller, there is no danger that they will be deprived of any remedy or treated unfairly.'

I also conclude, as have numerous other courts in similar circumstances, that the courts of the United Kingdom do provide its citizens with adequate remedies and fair treatment.

Consequently, the claims of the United Kingdom claimants are hereby ORDERED dismissed on the grounds of *forum non conveniens.* These dismissals are conditioned upon the Defendants having agreed in their Motions as follows:

  (a) to consent to suit in any action timely filed by the United Kingdom claimants in the United Kingdom;

  (b) to waive any statute of limitations defense against the present Plaintiffs under United Kingdom law that may have arisen after these claims were filed in Indiana; and,

  (c) to comply in the United Kingdom, at their own expense, with all discovery obligations in any actions instituted against them in the United Kingdom.

NOTES

In spite of the barrier imposed by the *forum non conveniens* doctrine other United Kingdom claimants are reported as having been granted the right to sue in the courts of the United States: see *The Observer* 7 October 1984 (Norinyl contraceptive pill) and see also *The Times* 30 August 1984 (Debendox). For the position within EEC countries see the Convention on Jurisdiction and the Enforcement of Judgments in Civil and Commercial Matters 1968 and the Civil Jurisdiction and Judgments Act 1982.

THE MODEL UNIFORM PRODUCT LIABILITY ACT

In the 1970's concern within the United States over escalating insurance rates and the threat of corporate bankruptcy led to the setting up by the Department of Commerce of a Task Force on Product Liability. The Task Force produced detailed legal and insurance studies and published its final report in November 1977. This led to the issuing of a model Uniform Product Liability Act for voluntary adoption by individual States. The intention was to 'introduce uniformity and stability into the law of product liability' thereby stabilising product liability insurance rates. The general intention of the Act is to retain manufacturers' strict liability for construction defects and non-compliance with express warranties but to introduce a requirement of fault where liability is based on design defects or inadequate warnings or instructions. In the case of product sellers other than manufacturers liability would be based on a failure to exercise reasonable care. Although some thirty states have now introduced product liability legislation some of which includes provisions of the Act there has been no widespread adoption of the Model Act as such. Nonetheless its principal provisions are of sufficient interest to warrant the inclusion of extracts in this text.

Department of Commerce Model Uniform Product Liability Act [44 FR 62714, 31 October, 1979]

Sec. 100. Short Title
    This Act shall be known and may be cited as the 'Uniform Product Liability Act.'

. . .

Sec. 103. Scope of This Act
    [A] This Act is in lieu of and preempts all existing law governing matters within its coverage, including the 'Uniform Commercial Code' and similar laws; however, nothing in this Act shall prevent the recovery, under the 'Uniform Commercial Code' or similar laws, of direct or consequential economic losses.
    [B] A claim may be asserted under this Act even though the claimant did not buy the product from, or enter into any contractual relationship with, the product seller.

. . .

Sec. 104. Basic Standards of Responsibility for Manufacturers
    A product manufacturer is subject to liability to a claimant who proves by a preponderance of the evidence that the claimant's harm was proximately caused because the product was defective.
    A product may be proven to be defective if, and only if:
    (1) It was unreasonably unsafe in construction (Subsection A);
    (2) It was unreasonably unsafe in design (Subsection B);

(3) It was unreasonably unsafe because adequate warnings or instructions were not provided (Subsection C); or

(4) It was unreasonably unsafe because it did not conform to the product seller's express warranty (Subsection D).

Before submitting the case to the trier of fact, the court shall determine that the claimant has introduced sufficient evidence to allow a reasonable person to find, by a preponderance of the evidence, that one or more of the above conditions existed and was a proximate cause of the claimant's harm.

(A) *The Product was Unreasonably Unsafe in Construction.*
In order to determine that the product was unreasonably unsafe in construction, the trier of fact must find that, when the product left the control of the manufacturer, the product deviated in some material way from the manufacturer's design specifications or performance standards, or from otherwise identical units of the same product line.

(B) *The Product Was Unreasonably Unsafe in Design.*
(1) In order to determine that the product was unreasonably unsafe in design, the trier of fact must find that, at the time of manufacture, the likelihood that the product would cause the claimant's harm or similar harms, and the seriousness of those harms outweighed the burden on the manufacturer to design a product that would have prevented those harms, and the adverse effect that alternative design would have on the usefulness of the product.
(2) Examples of evidence that is especially probative in making this evaluation include:
(a) Any warnings and instructions provided with the product;
(b) The technological and practical feasibility of a product designed and manufactured so as to have prevented claimant's harm while substantially serving the likely user's expected needs;
(c) The effect of any proposed alternative design on the usefulness of the product;
(d) The comparative costs of producing, distributing, selling, using, and maintaining the product as designed and as alternatively designed; and
(e) The new or additional harms that might have resulted if the product had been so alternatively designed.

(C) *The Product Was Unreasonably Unsafe Because Adequate Warnings or Instructions Were Not Provided.*
(1) In order to determine that the product was unreasonably unsafe because adequate warnings or instructions were not provided about a danger connected with the product or its proper use, the trier of fact must find that, at the time of manufacture, the likelihood that the product would cause the claimant's harm or similar harms and the seriousness of those harms rendered the manufacturer's instructions inadequate and that the manufacturer should and could have provided the instructions or warnings which claimant alleges would have been adequate.
(2) Examples of evidence that is especially probative in making this evaluation include:
(a) The manufacturer's ability, at the time of manufacture, to be aware of the product's danger and the nature of the potential harm;
(b) The manufacturer's ability to anticipate that the likely product user would be aware of the product's danger and the nature of the potential harm;
(c) The technological and practical feasibility of providing adequate warnings and instructions;
(d) The clarity and conspicuousness of the warnings or instructions that were provided; and
(e) The adequacy of the warnings or instructions that were provided.
(3) In any claim under this Subsection, the claimant must prove by a preponderance of the evidence that if adequate warnings or instructions had been provided, they would have been effective because a reasonably prudent product user would have either declined to use the product or would have used the product in a manner so as to have avoided the harm.
(4) A manufacturer shall not be liable for its failure to warn or instruct about dangers that are obvious; for 'product misuse' as defined in Subsection 112(C)(1);[1] or for alterations or modifications of the product which do not constitute 'reasonably anticipated conduct' under Subsection 102(G).[2]

---

1. This provides as follows: '*Misuse of a Product.* "Misuse" occurs when the product user does not act in a manner that would be expected of an ordinary reasonably prudent person who is likely to use the product in the same or similar circumstances.'
2. This provides as follows: '*Reasonably Anticipated Conduct.* "Reasonably anticipated conduct" means the conduct which would be expected of an ordinary reasonably prudent person who is likely to use the product in the same or similar circumstances.'

(5) A manufacturer is under an obligation to provide adequate warnings or instructions to the actual product user unless the manufacturer provided such warnings to a person who may be reasonably expected to assure that action is taken to avoid the harm, or that the risk of the harm is explained to the actual product user.

For products that may be legally used only by or under the supervision of a class of experts, warnings or instructions may be provided to the using or supervisory expert.

For products that are tangible goods sold or handled only in bulk or other workplace products, warnings or instructions may be provided to the employer of the employee-claimant if there is no practical and feasible means of transmitting them to the employee-claimant.

(6) *Post-Manufacture Duty to Warn.*
In addition to the claim provided in Subsection (C)(1), a claim may arise under this Subsection where a reasonably prudent manufacturer should have learned about a danger connected with the product after it was manufactured. In such a case, the manufacturer is under an obligation to act with regard to the danger as a reasonably prudent manufacturer in the same or similar circumstances. This obligation is satisfied if the manufacturer makes reasonable efforts to inform product users or a person who may be reasonably expected to assure that action is taken to avoid the harm, or that the risk of harm is explained to the actual product user.

(D) *The Product Was Unreasonably Unsafe Because It Did Not Conform to an Express Warranty*
In order to determine that the product was unreasonably unsafe because it did not conform to an express warranty, the trier of fact must find that the claimant, or one acting on the claimant's behalf, relied on an express warranty made by the manufacturer or its agent about a material fact or facts concerning the product and this express warranty proved to be untrue.

A 'material fact' is any specific characteristic or quality of the product. It does not include a general opinion about, or praise of, the product.

The product seller may be subject to liability under Subsection (D) although it did not engage in negligent or fraudulent conduct in making the express warranty.

. . .

Sec. 106. Unavoidably Dangerous Aspects of Products
(A) An unavoidably dangerous aspect of a product is that aspect incapable, in light of the state of scientific and technological knowledge at the time of manufacture, of being made safe without seriously impairing the product's usefulness.
(B) A product seller shall not be subject to liability for harm caused by an unavoidably dangerous aspect of a product unless;
(1) The product seller knew or had reason to know of the aspect and with that knowledge acted unreasonably in selling the product at all;
(2) The aspect was a defect in construction under Subsection 104(A);
(3) The product seller knew or had reason to know of the aspect and failed to meet a duty to instruct or warn under Subsection 104(C), or to transmit warnings or instructions under Subsection 105(A); or
(4) The product seller expressly warranted that the product was free of the unavoidably dangerous aspect under Subsection 104(D) or 105(B).

Sec. 107. Relevance of Industry Custom, Safety or Performance Standards, and Practical Technological Feasibility
(A) Evidence of changes in (1) a product's design, (2) warnings or instructions concerning the product, (3) technological feasibility, (4) 'state of the art', or (5) the custom of the product seller's industry or business, occurring after the product was manufactured, is not admissible for the purpose of proving that the product was defective in design under Subsection 104(B) or that a warning or instruction should have accompanied the product at the time of manufacture under Subsection 104(C).

If the court finds that the probative value of such evidence substantially outweighs its prejudicial effect and that there is no other proof available, this evidence may be admitted for other relevant purposes if confined to those purposes in a specific court instruction. Examples of 'other relevant purposes' include proving ownership or control, or impeachment.
(B) For the purposes of Section 107, 'custom' refers to the practices followed by an ordinary product seller in the product seller's industry or business.
(C) Evidence of custom in the product seller's industry or business or of the product seller's compliance or non-compliance with a non-governmental safety or performance standard, existing at the time of manufacture, may be considered by the trier of fact in determining

whether a product was defective in design under Subsection 104(B), or whether there was a failure to warn or instruct under Subsection 104(C) or to transmit warnings or instructions under Subsection 105(A).

(D) For the purposes of Section 107, 'practical technological feasibility' means the technological, mechanical, and scientific knowledge relating to product safety that was reasonably feasible for use, in light of economic practicality, at the time of manufacture.

(E) If the product seller proves, by a preponderance of the evidence, that it was not within practical technological feasibility for it to make the product safer with respect to design and warnings or instructions at the time of manufacture so as to have prevented claimant's harm, the product seller shall not be subject to liability for harm caused by the product unless the trier of fact determines that:

(1) The product seller knew or had reason to know of the danger and, with that knowledge, acted unreasonably in selling the product at all;

(2) The product was defective in construction under Subsection 104(A);

(3) The product seller failed to meet the post-manufacture duty to warn or instruct under Subsection 104(C)(6); or

(4) The product seller was subject to liability for express warranty under Subsection 104(D) or 105(B).

. . .

Sec. 110. Length of Time Product Sellers are Subject to Liability

(A) *Useful Safe Life.*

(1) Except as provided in Subsection (A)(2), a product seller shall not be subject to liability to a claimant for harm under this Act if the product seller proves by a preponderance of the evidence that the harm was caused after the product's 'useful safe life' had expired . . .

(2) A product seller may be subject to liability for harm caused by a product used beyond its useful safe life to the extent that the product seller has expressly warranted the product for a longer period.

(B) *Statute of Repose.*

(1) *Generally.* In claims that involve harm caused more than ten (10) years after time of delivery, a presumption arises that the harm was caused after the useful safe life had expired. This presumption may only be rebutted by clear and convincing evidence.

(2) *Limitations on Statute of Repose.*

(a) If a product seller expressly warrants that its product can be utilized safely for a period longer than ten (10) years, the period of repose, after which the presumption created in Subsection (B)(1) arises, shall be extended according to that warranty or promise.

(b) The ten- (10-) year period of repose established in Subsection (B)(1) does not apply if the product seller intentionally misrepresents facts about its product, or fraudulently conceals information about it, and that conduct was a substantial cause of the claimant's harm.

(c) Nothing contained in Subsection (B) shall affect the right of any person found liable under this Act to seek and obtain contribution or indemnity from any other person who is responsible for harm under this Act.

(d) The ten- (10-) year period of repose established in Subsection (B)(1) shall not apply if the harm was caused by prolonged exposure to a defective product, or if the injury-causing aspect of the product that existed at the time of delivery was not discoverable by an ordinary reasonably prudent person until more than ten (10) years after the time of delivery, or if the harm, caused within ten (10) years after the time of delivery, did not manifest itself until after that time.

(C) *Statute of Limitation.* No claim under this Act may be brought more than two (2) years from the time the claimant discovered, or in the exercise of due diligence should have discovered, the harm and the cause thereof.

NOTE

For a detailed critique of the model Act see Twerski and Weinstein, 'A

Critique of the Uniform Product Liability Law—a Rush to Judgment' 28 Drake Law Review 221 (1979). Recently there have been moves to introduce Federal legislation (the Kasten Bill) superseding the legislation of individual States. The Bill is similar in many respects to the proposed model Act: see Frumer and Friedman *Products Liability* Vol 2A, Ch 3E.

Questions

Is the distinction taken in the model Act between construction and design defects sufficiently clear-cut to enable a different basis of liability to be applied to the two types of defect?

Into which category should one place *Cronin v JBE Olson Corpn* 104 Cal Rptr 433 (1972), the facts of which were outlined above p 181?

What are the main reasons which might suggest that courts should be less willing to impose liability in cases of allegedly defective design?

SOME CANADIAN EXAMPLES

The statutes of some Canadian provinces also have introduced a wide measure of liability for damage or loss caused by defective products. In some cases an entitlement to recover is dependent on there being a breach of contract (for example of the implied term as to quality) although there is no requirement that there be privity of contract between the parties. In others liability is based on tort and hence is not dependent on showing a breach of contract. Some provisions are confined to 'consumer products' whereas other proposals for reform are not so limited—no doubt in recognition of the fact that other products are capable of injuring consumers who come into contact with them. The following extracts illustrate some alternative approaches.

The Consumer Products Warranties Act 1977, Saskatchewan

2. Interpretation
In this Act:

. . .

    (l) *'retail seller'* 'retail seller' means a person who sells consumer products to consumers in the ordinary course of his business but, subject to subsection (1) of section 13, does not include a trustee in bankruptcy, receiver, liquidator, sheriff, auctioneer or a person acting under an order of a court;

    (m) *'sale'* 'sale' means a transaction whereby the retail seller transfers or agrees to transfer the general property in a consumer product to a consumer for a valuable consideration and includes but is not restricted to:

        (i)   a conditional sale;

        (ii) a contract of lease or hire;

        (iii) a transaction under which a consumer product is supplied to a consumer along with services;

        and any reference in this Act to 'buy', 'buying', 'bought', 'sell', 'sold' or 'selling' shall be construed accordingly;

. . .

5. User

A person who may reasonably be expected to use, consume or be affected by a consumer product and who suffers personal injury as a result of a breach, by a retail seller or manufacturer, of a statutory warranty mentioned in paragraphs 3, 4, 5 and 6 of section 11 shall be entitled to the remedies mentioned in section 27.

. . .

27. User may recover damages

A person mentioned in section 5 shall, as against the retail seller or manufacturer, be entitled to recover damages arising from personal injuries that he has suffered and that were reasonably foreseeable as liable to result from the breach.

NOTES

1. This Act was based on the Report of the Ontario Law Reform Commission on Consumer Warranties and Guarantees in the Sale of Goods (1972). For comment see also the Commission's 'Report on Products Liability' (1979), pp 39–41.

2. The non-excludable statutory warranties of s 11(3), (4), (5) and (6) relate respectively to description, acceptable quality, fitness for a particular purpose and sales by sample. All apply only where 'a consumer product is sold by a retail seller'. For the definition of 'consumer' and 'consumer product' see s 2(d) and (e) of the Act, above p 17. By s 4(1), above p 30 subsequent consumer owners (for example by way of purchase or gift) are deemed to be given the same statutory warranties as the original consumer. By s 13(2)

> the manufacturer of consumer products shall be deemed to give to consumers of his products the same statutory warranties with respect to his products as the retail seller is deemed to have given . . .

Both provisions are subject to qualifications but the general effect is to confer on consumer buyers and those who derive title through them additional rights going beyond those conferred in the case of personal injury by ss 5 and 27.

Questions

1. Which, if any, of the following are consumer products within the meaning of s 2(e) (see above p 17): (i) a coin-operated washing machine used for example in a university launderette, (ii) an anti- nauseant medicine sold by chemists to combat morning sickness during pregnancy and (iii) a defective seat being one of a row of joined seats in a public cinema?

2. Is it defensible to provide or withhold a statutory remedy (see ss 5 and 27) according to whether a pedestrian is physically injured by a defective car or a defective bus?

3. It is said that sections 5 and 27 of the Saskatchewan Act provide a remedy based on strict liability. Is it clear that they do? Do the words 'reasonably foreseeable' in s 27 import an element of fault or do they affect only the question of remoteness of damage?

A somewhat different approach, which, however, also applies only in the case of consumer products, is to be seen in the following extracts from another Canadian statute.

Consumer Product Warranty and Liability Act 1978, New Brunswick

1(1) In this Act

. . .

'consumer loss' means
    (a) a loss that a person does not suffer in a business capacity; or
    (b) a loss that a person suffers in a business capacity to the extent that it consists of liability that he or another person incurs for a loss that is not suffered in a business capacity;
'consumer product' means any tangible personal property, new or used, of a kind that is commonly used for personal, family or household purposes;

. . .

23. Remedies where no privity of contract
Where the seller is in breach of a warranty provided by this Act, any person who is not a party to the contract but who suffers a consumer loss because of the breach may recover damages against the seller for the loss if it was reasonably foreseeable at the time of the contract as liable to result from the breach.

. . .

27. Product liability
(1) A supplier of a consumer product that is unreasonably dangerous to person or property because of a defect in design, materials or workmanship is liable to any person who suffers a consumer loss in the Province because of the defect, if the loss was reasonably foreseeable at the time of his supply as liable to result from the defect and
    (a) he has supplied the consumer product in the Province;
    (b) he has supplied the consumer product outside the Province but has done something in the Province that contributes to the consumer loss suffered in the Province; or
    (c) he has supplied the consumer product outside the Province but the defect arose in whole or in part because of his failure to comply with any mandatory federal standards in relation to health or safety, or the defect caused the consumer product to fail to comply with any such standards.
(2) For the purposes of paragraph (1)(b), where a person has done anything in the Province to further the supply of any consumer product that is similar in kind to the consumer product that caused the loss, it shall be presumed that he has done something in the Province that contributed to the consumer loss suffered in the Province, unless he proves irrefragably that what he did in the Province did not in any way contribute to that loss.
(3) A person is not liable under this section
    (a) for any loss that is caused by a defect that is not present in the consumer product at the time he supplies it; or
    (b) for any loss that is caused by a defect that he has reason to believe exists and that he discloses to the person to whom he supplies the consumer product before the loss is suffered, if the defect does not arise in whole or in part because of his failure to comply with any mandatory federal or provincial standards in relation to health or safety and the defect does not cause the consumer product to fail to comply with any such standards.
(4) The liability of a person under this section does not depend on any contract or negligence.

NOTES

1. These provisions were based on the recommendations of the New Brunswick Department of Justice, Third Report of the Consumer Protection Project (1976).

2. The warranties implied by the Act and to which reference is made in s 23 are set out in ss 8–12. Some are commonplace (for example, as to fitness for purpose: s 10(2)). Others are less usual (for example a warranty that the consumer product will be 'durable for a reasonable period of time': s 12(1)). Whereas s 23 depends on a breach of warranty s 27 does not.

The following draft Bill is appended to the 'Report on Products Liability' (1979) of the Ontario Law Reform Commission. The report contains a helpful and detailed analysis of the area and its provisions may be compared and contrasted with those of the United States Uniform Product Liability Act (above p 188) and the proposed EEC directive (below p 197). The clauses which are omitted are concerned inter alia with contribution between joint tortfeasors and jurisdictional matters. It will be noted that the Act is not confined to consumer products but is of more general application.

Ontario Law Reform Commission, 'Report on Product Liability' (1979)

**An Act to impose Liability
on Business Suppliers
of Defective Products**

HER MAJESTY, by and with the advice and consent of the Legislative Assembly of the Province of Ontario, enacts as follows:

1. *Interpretation.* (1) In this Act,
   (a) 'defective product' means a product that falls short of the standard that may reasonably be expected of it in all the circumstances;
   (b) 'false statement' includes any misstatement of fact, whether made by words, pictures, conduct or otherwise;
   (c) 'product' means any tangible goods whether or not they are attached to or incorporated into real or personal property;
   (d) 'to supply' means to make available or accessible by sale, gift, bailment or in any other way, and 'supplied', 'supplies' and 'supplier' have corresponding meanings, but a person who transports a product is not by that act alone a supplier.
   (2) *Standards established by law.* In determining whether or not a product is a defective product, any relevant standard established by law may be taken into account.

2. *Crown bound.* The Crown is bound by this Act.

3. *Strict liability for defective products.* (1) Where in the course of his business a person supplies a product of a kind that it is his business to supply and the product is a defective product which causes personal injury or damage to property, that person is liable in damages,
   (a) for the injury or damage so caused; and
   (b) for any economic loss directly consequent upon such injury or damage.
   (2) *Exception for business losses.* A supplier is not liable under clause a or b of subsection 1 for damage to property used in the course of carrying on a business.

4. *Strict liability for false statements about products.* (1) Where in the course of his business a person supplies a product of a kind that it is his business to supply and makes a false statement concerning the product, reliance upon which causes personal injury or damage to property, that person is liable in damages,
   (a) for the injury or damage so caused; and
   (b) for any economic loss directly consequent upon such injury or damage,
   whether or not the reliance is that of the person suffering the injury or damage.
   (2) *Exception for business losses.* A supplier is not liable under clause a or b of subsection 1 for damage to property used in the course of carrying on a business.

5. *New business and promotions.* A person may be liable under section 3 and 4 notwithstanding that he has not previously supplied products of the same kind as the product supplied or that he supplied the product for promotional purposes.

6. *Contributory negligence.* (1) Where injury or damage is caused or contributed to partly by a supplier of a product under section 3 or by reliance upon a false statement made by a supplier concerning a product under section 4 and partly by the fault or neglect of the person suffering the injury or damage, damages shall be apportioned in acordance with the degree of the responsibility of each for the injury or damage.
(2) *Where parties deemed equally responsible.* Where under subsection 1 it is not practicable to determine the respective degree of responsibility of the supplier and of the person suffering the injury or damage, the parties shall be deemed to be equally responsible for the injury or damage suffered, and damages shall be apportioned accordingly.

· · ·

10. *Restriction on liability void.* Any oral or written agreement, notice, statement or provision of any kind purporting to exclude or restrict liability under section 3 or 4 or to limit any remedy thereunder is void.
11. *Other rights not affected.* The rights and liabilities created by this Act are in addition to rights and liabilities otherwise provided by law.

· · ·

17. *Applications of Act.* This Act applies only to injury or damage occurring on or after the day on which this Act comes into force.
18. *Short title.* The short title of this Act is *The Products Liability Act, 198* .

United Kingdom and European proposals for reform

Since the early 1970s there has been widespread debate in the United Kingdom and the rest of Europe over the desirability of introducing a wider measure of strict liability for defective products. Within the United Kingdom the principal studies have been carried out by the Law Commissions and the Royal Commission on Civil Liability and Compensation for Personal Injury (the Pearson Commission): see respectively the Law Commissions' joint report, 'Liability for Defective Products' (Law Com No 82, Scot Law Com No 45, Cmnd 6831, 1977) and the Pearson Commission report (Cmnd 7054, 1978) Ch 22. Both reports recommend that strict liability be imposed on producers of defective products which cause death or personal injury. At European level a similar proposal is to be found in the Council of Europe (Strasbourg) Convention on Products Liability in regard to Personal Injury and Death: see Miller *Product Liability and Safety Encyclopaedia*, Div V, para [173] et seq. However the major potential source for reform has been a proposal for an EEC directive. All these proposals are confined to 'producers' of defective products, although this word is defined broadly: see, for example, Article 2 of the proposed EEC directive, below. They do not extend to others who sell or supply products in the course of a business. Contrast in this respect the provisions of the *Restatement of Torts* (2d) §402A, above p 179 and the draft bill accompanying the Ontario Law Reform Commission 'Report on Product Liability' (1979), above p 195. With the benefit of hindsight one can now see that it is regrettable that reform should have been concentrated on this particular European initiative which Sir Gordon Borrie has described as 'a well-intentioned directive but one damaging to national initiatives': see *The Development of Consumer Law and Policy—Bold Spirits and Timorous Souls* (1984), p 116. The reason for the damage is the inevitable delay associated with seeking the necessary uniformity among countries whose legal systems have no common basis of liability. For example French law has a wide measure of strict liability (see generally Mazeaud *La Responsabilité des Fabricants et Distributeurs* (Economica, 1975) and the Quebec case *General Motors Products of Canada Ltd v Kravitz* (1979) 93 DLR (3d) 481 (Supreme Court of Canada, above p 28) whereas in West Germany negligence or fault is required but the onus of proof is on the defendant manufacturer: see the decision of the 6th Civil Senate of 26 November 1968 (BGHZ 51.91) in the 'fowl-pest' or defective chicken vaccine case, extracted with helpful comments in Lawson and Markesinis *Tortious Liability for Unintentional Harm in the Common Law and Civil Law* Vol II, p 84 et seq (1982).

The latest 'official' version of the proposed directive as submitted by the Commission to the Council on 1 October 1979 is printed below with modifications to the original version printed in italics. The explanatory memorandum and preamble are omitted.

Proposal for a Council directive relating to the approximation of the laws, regulations and administrative provisions of the member states concerning liability for defective products (presented by the Commission of the European Communities to the Council, pursuant to the second paragraph of Article 149 of the EEC Treaty)

. . .

Article 1
The producer of an article shall be liable for damage caused by a defect in the article, whether or not he knew or could have known of the defect. *This provision applies also if the article has been incorporated in immovable property.*

The producer shall be liable even if the article could not have been regarded as defective in the light of the scientific and technological development at the time when he put the article into circulation.

The producer is not liable under the provisions of this Directive if the defective article is a primary agricultural product, a craft or an artistic product when it is clear that it is not industrially produced.

Article 2
'Producer' means the producer of the finished article, the producer of any material or component, and any person who, by putting his name, trademark, or other distinguishing feature on the article, represents himself as its producer.

Where the producer of the article cannot be identified, each supplier of the article shall be treated as its producer unless he informs the injured person, within a reasonable time, of the identity of the producer or of the person who supplied him with the article.

Any person who imports into the European Community an article for resale or similar purpose shall be treated as its producer.

Article 3
Where two or more persons are liable in respect of the same damage, they shall be liable jointly and severally, *each person retaining the right to compensation from the others.*

Article 4
A product is defective when, *being used for the purpose for which it is apparently intended,* it does not provide for persons or property the safety which a person is entitled to expect, *taking into account all the circumstances, including its presentation and the time at which it was put into circulation.*

Article 5
The producer shall not be liable if he proves:
   (a) that he did not put the article into circulation,
   (b) that, *having regard to all the circumstances,* it was not defective when he put it into circulation;
   (c) *that the article was neither produced for sale, hire or any other kind of distribution for the commercial purposes of the producer nor produced and distributed within the course of his business activities.*

If the victim or any person for whom he is liable has by his fault contributed to the damage the compensation payable may be reduced or no compensation may be awarded.

Article 6
For the purpose of Article 1 'damage' means:
   (a) death or personal injuries;
   (b) damage to or destruction of any item of property other than the defective article itself where the item of property:
      (i) is of a type ordinarily acquired for private use or consumption; and
      (ii) was not acquired or used by the claimant *exclusively* for the purpose of his trade, business or profession.
   (c) *damages for pain and suffering and other non-material damage.*

Article 7
The total liability of the producer provided for in this Directive for all personal injuries caused by identical articles having the same defect *may be limited to a maximum amount which is to be determined by a qualified majority of the Council acting on a proposal from the Commission. Prior to any such determination by the Council this amount shall be fixed at* 25 million European units of account (EUA).

This amount also includes the damages specified in Article 6(c) when they are related to death or personal injury.

The liability of the producer provided for by this Directive in respect of damage to property shall be limited *per capita*:
—in the case of moveable property to 15,000 EUA, and
—in the case of immoveable property to 50,000 EUA.

This amount also includes the damages specified in Article 6(c) when they are related to material damage.

The European unit of account (EUA) is as defined by *Article 10 of the Financial Regulation of 21 December 1977.*

The equivalent in national currency shall be determined by applying the conversion rate prevailing on the day preceding the date on which the amount of compensation is finally fixed.

The Council shall, *on a report from the Commission,* examine every three years *the amounts specified in this Article.* Where necessary, the Council shall, acting by a qualified majority on a proposal from the Commission, revise *or cancel the amount specified in paragraph 1 of this Article or revise the amounts specified in paragraph three,* taking into consideration economic and monetary movement in the Community.

Article 8
A limitation period of three years shall apply to proceedings for the recovery of damages as provided for in this Directive. The limitation period shall begin to run on the day the injured person became aware, or should reasonably have become aware of the damage, the defect and the identity of the producer.

The laws of Member States regulating suspension or interruption of the period shall not be affected by this Directive.

Article 9
The liability of a producer shall be extinguished if an action is not brought within ten years *from the date* on which the producer put into circulation the individual product which caused the damage.

Article 10
Liability as provided for in this Directive may not be excluded or limited.

Article 11
Claims in respect of injury or damage caused by defective articles based on grounds other than that provided for in this Directive shall not be affected.

Article 12
This Directive does not apply to injury or damage arising from nuclear accidents.

Article 13
Member States shall bring into force the provisions necessary to comply with this Directive within 18 months and shall forthwith inform the Commission thereof.

Article 14
Member States shall communicate to the Commission the text of the main provisions of internal law which they subsequently adopt in the field covered by this Directive.

Article 15
This Directive is addressed to the Member States.

NOTES

Since the publication of this revised (*italicised*) text the matter has been examined further by the Working Party on Economic Questions (Defective Products). The principal areas of controversy (apart from whether the matter is one on which the EEC is competent to act: see the 22nd Report of the House of Lords Select Committee on the European Communities, HL 1977–78 131 p 10) are (i) the desirability of a development risks or 'state of the art' qualification to liability; (ii) the extension of strict liability to certain types of property damage (see Article 6) as well as to cases of death and personal injury and (iii) whether there should be an overall limit to liability along the lines of that envisaged by Article 7. These issues are discussed in the materials printed below.

DEVELOPMENT RISKS AND THE STATE OF THE ART

The availability of a qualification to liability based on development risks and the so-called 'state of the art' is the single most important issue in the debate over whether there should be an extension of strict liability beyond its contractual confines. One of the present co-authors has discussed the position as follows.

C J Miller 'Product Liability and Safety Encyclopaedia.' Division V

DEVELOPMENT RISKS AND THE STATE OF THE ART

The desirability of introducing a qualification for development risks and compliance with the state of the art has divided the European Commission and the European Parliament. It is also the principal point of controversy dividing representatives of consumer and business interests in the United Kingdom, although the extent of the differences may have been exaggerated by lack of agreement as to what precisely is included within the two concepts. The same problem has bedevilled discussion within the United Kingdom Parliament where the issue has similarly been regarded as of central importance.
123.   The EEC proposed directive, Article 1, states that:

'The producer of an article shall be liable for damage caused by a defect in the article, whether or not he knew or could have known of the defect.'

It continues:

'The producer shall be liable even if the article could not have been regarded as defective in the light of the scientific and technological development at the time when he put the article into circulation.'

124.   In reaffirming this position in September 1979 the Commission declined to accede to the view of the European Parliament that the basic principle of liability in Article 1 should be qualified by a provision whereby: 'The producer shall not be liable if he can produce evidence that the article cannot be considered defective in the light of the state of scientific and technological development at the time when the article was put into circulation'.[1]
125.   The United Kingdom government has now committed itself to the introduction of a 'state of the art' defence in any resultant directive, thus preferring the view of the European

Parliament to that of the Commission. In reaching this conclusion it has declined to follow the recommendations of both the Pearson Commission and the Law Commissions.[2] As Minister for Consumer Affairs, Mrs. Sally Oppenheim justified this position in the following terms:[3]

'I turn now to the importance that the Government attach to the inclusion of a state of the art defence in the final directive, as do a number of other member States. The European Parliament has said that it would be wrong to impose this burden on manufacturers and has voted for a state of the art defence, but that was subsequently overturned by the Commission . . . The Government have considered this problem very carefully. We are conscious of the need to protect the consumer, particularly the innocent victim of a defective product that he or she has not purchased. At the same time, we recognise the benefits that consumers as a whole derive from innovation. We also recognise the importance of encouraging British industry to innovate, because it is on innovation that our industrial success has been based. We believe that it is important, therefore, that a state of the art defence should be included in any product liability directive . . .'

126.   This decision has been welcomed by manufacturing and commercial organisations and regretted by those representing the interests of consumers. The latter make a number of telling points,[4] noting, for example, that the present strict contractual liability for defective products is not qualified by any similar defence.[5] Equally there can be little doubt that a qualification along these lines would do much to undermine the introduction of a more general strict liability, at least in cases of alleged design defects.[6] No doubt it would become common practice for manufacturers to resist claims or promote favourable out of court settlements by claiming that the product when marketed met all relevant scientific and technological demands. It has also been suggested that with a state of the art defence the United Kingdom would become the 'guinea pig' of Europe and the testing ground for potentially dangerous products, a fear which is hardly allayed by the fact that another government Minister has conceded that 'some of the thalidomide victims might have been deprived of a remedy by a state of the art defence'.[7]

127.   Much of the debate in this area has been confused by failure to distinguish between a number of different meanings which have been attributed to the notion of the 'state of the art'. Strict liability is not the same as absolute liability but by the same token it should remain distinct from liability which is avowedly based on negligence. The lines are often blurred, especially in cases involving allegedly defective designs, through running together two issues, namely (i) the setting and applying of the appropriate standard against which the product is to be judged and (ii) the possibility of knowing of or discovering the product's characteristics, dangers and accompanying side-effects. The expression 'state of the art' is sometimes used indiscriminately to cover both these issues which, for convenience, may be termed the issue of reasonable safety and that of knowledge.

128.   When discussing the first issue it is sometimes argued that compliance with current safety standards should be conclusive proof that the product was reasonably safe. However this is not a view which commands much informed support since it is generally recognised that such standards may set only minimum requirements or indeed be seriously out-of-date. Evidence of compliance is relevant but not conclusive where liability is based on negligence and it can hardly have a higher status where proof of negligence is not required. To this extent at least it would be wrong to introduce a complete state of the art defence if such a 'defence' is regarded as extending thus far.

129.   A closely related question is the date at which the appropriate standard of reasonable safety is to be applied. There are, as the Law Commissions noted, two possible solutions: 'One is to judge the defectiveness of the product as at the time of the accident and the other as at the time that the producer put the product into circulation'[8]. The choice between these two dates becomes especially important where there has been a marked rise in safety standards in the intervening period. An example frequently cited is the introduction of refrigerator doors which can be opened from inside, thus removing much of the risk to children associated with older models. Although some American decisions have questioned the application of the standards which prevailed when the product was distributed[9] such an approach would constitute a considerable disincentive against improving safety standards over the years.[10] Accordingly it is thought that the Law Commissions were right to come out firmly in favour of judging the product in the light of the standards which prevailed when it was put into circulation . . .

130.   If advocates of a 'state of the art' qualification to product liability have in mind only that improved safety standards should not be applied retrospectively then the proposition seems unexceptional. This is especially so if the onus is on the defendant to prove that a product which was defective at the time of the accident was nonetheless reasonably safe when first put into circulation.[11]

131. A third possibility is that the product contained an unknown characteristic which was (for the sake of argument) both scientifically undiscoverable and yet such as to render it unacceptably dangerous, at least when distributed without a warning. Such dangers are associated primarily, although by no means exclusively, with drugs and the argument relates to the possibility of *discovering* the defect rather than to its actual existence. Cases of this nature are normally readily distinguishable from the refrigerator door . . . cases mentioned above . . . For example, no one would contend that thalidomide was reasonably safe; the argument relates solely to the relevance of the hypothesis that its dangers could not reasonably (or even possibly) have been appreciated when it was first put into circulation.[12] Those who argue for a 'state of the art' defence in such cases are saying in effect that liability for design or composition defects should continue to be based on negligence or fault so that it is the injured party rather than the morally blameless producer who should ultimately run the risk of undiscoverable side-effects. This is a perfectly tenable point of view but it is not one which is consistent with purporting to introduce a system of strict liability along the lines which had been envisaged by the Pearson Commission or the Law Commissions. In fact there would be remarkably little change in the law in practice if the extension of strict liability were to be confined to construction defects, that is to cases where the design is fundamentally safe but where something has gone wrong in the production process.

1. For the requests formulated in the Resolution of the European Parliament of 26 April 1979 see doc. PE 57.516/fin. The Commission stated in its Explanatory Memorandum of 26 September 1979 that it did not 'feel able to accept this proposal. If liability for damage occasioned by development risks were excluded—and such risks are in any event extremely rare—the effect would be to require the consumer to bear the risk of the unknown. The only satisfactory solution for the consumer is to make the rule of liability irrespective of fault apply to these cases as well . . .'
2. The Pearson Commission justified its recommendation that the producer should not be allowed a defence of 'development risk' by saying that: 'To exclude development risks from a regime of strict liability would be to leave a gap in the compensation cover, through which, for example, the victim of another thalidomide disaster might easily slip'; see Cmnd 7054, 1978, para 1259. The Law Commissions had reached a similar conclusion: see 'Liability for Defective Products', Law Com No 82, 1977, para 105.
3. HC Deb Vol 991, cols 1110–1111, 4 November 1980.
4. These are presented in a document dated January 1981 prepared by the 'umbrella' organisation 'Consumers in the European Community Group'.
5. See . . . the *Ashington Piggeries* case [1972] AC 441 at 498, HL, [where] Lord Diplock agreed that:
> in the then state of knowledge, scientific and commercial, no deliberate exercise of skill or judgment could have prevented the meal having its toxic effect on mink. It was sheer bad luck.
6. Speaking in the House of Lords debate of 12 November 1980 Lord Scarman put the point well when he suggested that 'this particular defence, if introduced, would really be like a torpedo hitting the ship below the water line': HL Deb Vol 414, col 1411.
7. Lord Mackay of Clashfern (the Lord Advocate): see HL Deb Vol 414, col 1455, 12 November 1980.
8. See 'Liability for Defective Products' (Law Com No 82, 1977), para 49.
9. See, eg *Bailey v Boatland of Houston* 585 SW 2d 805 (Tex Civ App 1979); *Gelsumino v E W Bliss Co* 10 Ill App 3d 604, 295 NE 2d 110 (1973) and in general Vol 2 *Frumer and Friedman* s 16A [4] [i] and cases there cited.
10. Cf the position where it is sought to lead evidence of the fact that the defendant has adopted further safety measures etc after the accident which is the subject of the present claim . . .
11. As is the case under Art 5(b) of the proposed directive which provides that: 'The producer shall not be liable if he proves . . . that, having regard to all the circumstances, it (ie the article) was not defective when he put it into circulation'.
12. This dichotomy admittedly does not exhaust the theoretical posibilities. For example there may be cases where there is a known risk which is statistically predictable in general terms but (in the then state of scientific knowledge) quite unpredictable in the individual case. Some of the American blood transfusion/serum hepatitis cases might fall into this category. In *Cunningham v MacNeal Memorial Hospital* 47 Ill 2d 443, 266 NE 2d 897 (1970) the Supreme Court of Illinois adopted an uncompromising position, saying: '[W]e believe that whether or not defendant can, even theoretically, ascertain the existence of serum hepatitis virus in whole blood employed by it for transfusion purposes is of absolutely no moment. Any other ruling would be entirely inconsistent with the concept of strict tort liability'.

NOTE

For further discussion see Cane, 'Unsafe Products and the State of the Art: UK Proposals' (1979 3 Journal of Products Liability (1979); the Ontario Law Reform Commission 'Report on Products Liability' (1979) pp 95–96. See also the United States Model Uniform Product Liability Act 1979, ss 106–107, above p 190.

THE TYPES OF DAMAGE OR LOSS COVERED

Another important issue on which opinions differ is the type of damage or loss which should be included within the proposed new system. On this the Law Commissions reached a conclusion which differed from that favoured by the EEC in Article 6 of its proposed directive.

'Liability for defective products' (Law Com No 82, Scot Law Com No 45, Cmnd 6831, June 1977)

Compensation for property damage and other losses

117.   Our recommendations, above, assume that the claim arises out of personal injury or death. It is necessary to consider whether the regime of strict liability on producers should be enlarged to cover property damage and other kinds of loss as well, such as pure economic loss. If property damage and other losses were to be included it would be necessary to reconsider such questions as the meaning to be given to the words 'defect' and 'defective', contracting out of liability, the imposition of financial limits, the burden of proof and the setting of time-limits. On all these matters different considerations apply depending on whether the liability is for personal injury and death only or whether liability for property damage and other loss is to be included.

118.   We devoted a whole section of our consultative document to property damage[1] and received many interesting comments. A large number favoured including property damage within the regime; of those, however, some said that property damage should only be included where it was linked to a claim for personal injury. A greater number of others who favoured including property damage stressed that it should not go beyond personal belongings.

119.   On the other side an impressive body of opinion favoured excluding property damage altogether. Insurers warned that the inclusion of property damage in a regime that imposed strict liability on producers would mean a significant increase in the cost to the producer of insurance. If damage to commercial property, such as to a factory or a piece of factory machinery, were included, then plainly the ultimate liability on the producer could be very heavy indeed. The cases of *Vacwell Engineering Co Ltd v B D H Chemicals Ltd*[2] and *Harbutt's Plasticine Ltd v Wayne Tank and Pump Co Ltd*[3] illustrate the very extensive losses that can be caused in the commercial area by defective products. The incidence loss is shifted, under the existing law, by the proof of a breach of contract or of fault; the impact in this area of strict liability in tort or delict might have serious economic consequences.

120.   As we indicated at the outset, general considerations of policy require that first party insurance should be encouraged where it is usual and appropriate. Damage to commercial premises and property is usually covered by the owner's taking out first party insurance and this seems appropriate. In the non-commercial sector first party insurance is much more common in regard to damage to property than it is in regard to personal injury. Most householders insure their own homes, and where the premises are rented the premises are usually insured either by the tenants or by the landlords. A large number of people insure the contents of their homes and their cars against damage or destruction, and 'all-risks' policies for damage to property outside the home are frequently taken out. The information obtained on consultation does not allow us to go too deeply into the statistics of property insurance in the United Kingdom, but we are advised that first party insurance in respect of damage to property is usual and is generally regarded as prudent and appropriate.

121. What then would happen if property damage were included in the regime of strict liability? Provided that the claimant had taken out first party insurance his new remedy against the producer, in strict liability, would be of no immediate benefit to him but only to his insurers. On the other hand the extra cost to the producer of insuring against third party claims for damage to property would be passed on to the general public in the price of the product. Overall, those members of the public who took out first party insurance would be worse off than they are under the existing law, as they would be paying the same for their own insurance but would have to pay more for the products. We believe that first party insurance in relation to property ought generally to be encouraged, and we are worried that including property damage in the regime of strict liability would add to the cost of products without a commensurate increase in benefit to the public. We accordingly recommend that strict liability for defective products should provide compensation for personal injury and death, but not for property damage or for other heads of damage, such as pure economic loss . . .

1. Paras 84–93, comprising Part V. [See Law Com Working Paper No 64, 1975].
2. [1971] 1 QB 88. £74,689 was claimed for damage to factory premises and £300,000 for loss of profits.
3. [1970] 1 QB 447. £146,581 plus interest was awarded in respect of damage to factory premises and loss of profits.

NOTES

1. The definition of a 'defect' favoured by the Law Commission was as follows (see para 125(g) of its report):

> A product should be regarded as defective if, at the time when it is put into circulation by whoever is responsible for it as its producer, it does not comply with the standard of reasonable safety that a person is entitled to expect of it; the standard of safety should be determined objectively having regard to all the circumstances in which the product has been put into circulation, including, in particular, any instructions or warnings that accompany the product when it is put into circulation, and the use or uses to which it would be reasonable for the product to be put in these circumstances.

2. The issue was discussed in some detail by the Ontario Law Reform Commission in its Report on Products Liability' (1979), Ch 7, where the majority view favoured the exclusion of pure economic loss. However damage to consumer property would be included (see draft clause 3, above p 195).

Questions

1. Are the Law Commissions' reasons for excluding property damage to consumer assets convincing? First party insurance may be 'prudent and appropriate' and sometimes sufficient, for example where index-linked house insurance runs alongside a mortgage. However is it likely that most consumers are in fact insured sufficiently (or at all) in respect of damage to their personal belongings?

MAXIMUM LIMITS TO LIABILITY

Another controversial feature of the proposed EEC directive is its maximum limit on a producer's liability for all personal injuries caused by identical articles having the same defect: see Article 7, above p 198. There are limits also on individual claims for property damage but these are less controversial. The following extract indicates the reasoning behind the suggested limitation and some of the problems it creates.

'Liability for defective products', House of Lords Select Committee on the European Communities (Session 1979–80, 50th Report, HL 236)

Limit on liability (Article 7)

. . .

44. A good deal of anxiety has been expressed about the meaning of the expression 'identical articles'. The limit on the producer's liability is expressed to be 'for all personal injuries caused by identical articles having the same defect'. When do mass produced articles cease to be identical? Does a minor change in design cause a loss of identity so as to subject the producer to a fresh maximum liability? Definition would certainly be called for.

. . .

46. The Directive . . . appears to provide for a mandatory global limit: in their Sixty-third Report (paragraphs 13–14), the Select Committee were highly critical of this provision. The only advantage to be gained from the limit would be that it would assist producers in assessing the risk involved in putting a product into circulation and there would be no need for insurance beyond the stated limit. The disadvantage would be that, until all the claims in respect of a single product were established and quantified, it would be impossible to know whether the limit had been exceeded. As a result of this, it would be inadvisable to meet an individual claim until all claims were registered—a process which could take at least as long as the maximum limitation period under the Directive (ie 10 years from the time of circulation of the product). Such a situation would be contrary to the interests of the consumer, especially since interim awards could not even be made on account; to do so, would, as the Committee pointed out, need express provision for concentrating the control of interim awards in a single national court and laying down the criteria for determining which court that shall be. The Royal Commission (paragraph 1264) were of the opinion that: 'An equitable division of the total sum would be impossible without unacceptable delay, and the outcome could be to leave those last in the queue uncompensated'.

47. The Committee reiterate and emphasise the urgent need for a full revision of Article 7. As has been pointed out in a memorandum sent to the Committee by the Law Society, the result of the revision which has so far been made is that the Article, which was previously impracticable, is now incomprehensible. If the Article is to be retained the following questions must be answered:

(1) Is the Article intended to be mandatory or optional?

(2) Is the 25 million EUA limit intended to apply throughout the Community (as seems to have been generally assumed) or in each Member State? Would it be reasonable to apply the same limit to States varying so greatly in population?

(3) How is the permitted amount to be shared out among claimants, recollecting that the claims may be spread over many years?

(4) Why is no limit provided for individual claims?

The Committee are of the opinion however that the Article is, in its present form, unworkable and should be deleted. If there is to be a limit of this kind, a fresh start should be made in drafting the relevant Article.

NOTE

At the time of writing an EUA is equivalent to about £0.62.

CHAPTER 5

Aspects of consumer credit

The problem of consumer credit

The 1960s saw a dramatic increase in consumer awareness and, parallel with this development, a widespread dissatisfaction with the complexities of the law governing consumer credit. On 24 September 1968 the Secretary of State for Trade and Industry appointed the Crowther Committee with the following terms of reference:
- (i) to enquire into the present law and practice governing the provision of credit to individuals for financing purchases of goods and services for personal consumption;
- (ii) to consider the advantages and disadvantages of existing and possible alternative arrangements for providing such credit, having regard to the interests of consumers, traders and suppliers of credit including depositors;
- (iii) to consider in particular whether any amendment of the Moneylenders Acts is desirable; and
- (iv) to make recommendations.

The reason why the law affecting credit was complex and unsatisfactory at the date of the appointment of the Crowther Committee is outlined in the following extract.

Consumers and credit (National Consumer Council, 1980) (pp 14–15)

Credit law by the 1960s
By the 1960s, law affecting credit was complex, because of the way that different types of credit had, as it were, each spawned their own pieces of legislation.

Moneylenders were particularly strictly regulated. As well as needing a licence, they were for example allowed to advertise only in a very restricted way, were not allowed to employ people to canvass for loans, had to include an interest rate in loan contracts, and risked having the terms of a loan altered by a court if they were judged 'harsh and unconscionable'—interest over 48 per cent a year was taken to be excessive unless there was some evidence to the contrary.

Hire purchase, credit sale and *conditional sale* advertising had to give a comprehensive picture of costs (if it mentioned any financial terms), and any interest rate if quoted had to approximate to a true annual rate of interest, but the formula used was different from the one in the Moneylenders Acts. Contracts for these types of credit had to include a certain amount of cost information, though not the amount of the finance charge, nor an interest rate. The layout and type size of contracts was regulated, for legibility.

Termination of the agreement by the HP finance company if the consumer stopped paying was allowed only if he had disregarded a default notice allowing him at least a week to pay up.

Repossession of the goods, if payment stopped after at least one-third of the credit price had been paid, was allowed only by court order. Instead, courts would in practice normally set a new payments schedule, allowing repossession (or perhaps some form of money sanction instead) if the new schedule was not kept up. With credit sale, the lender had no right of repossession.

With HP or conditional sale, but *not* credit sale, there were some further legal conditions. For example, an HP buyer could make much the same sort of claim against his finance company over faulty goods as the Sale of Goods Act would have allowed against a shop. And if an HP buyer returned the goods and terminated his agreement, what he had to pay was subject to regulation.

With *doorstep sales*, the buyer had a right to cancel an HP or credit sale contract, recovering any payment already made, within four days of receiving a second copy of the agreement. This did not apply to credit sale agreements for under £30.

Bank loans, and loans made by the bigger finance houses or by bodies such as insurance companies, were not in general subject to credit legislation. Nor were hire purchase, conditional or credit sale transactions involving over £2,000. Credit sale was exempt if there were less than five instalments, and was generally subject to less regulation. Most forms of shop credit were not clearly covered by the legislation.

The Crowther Committee reported in March 1971 (Cmnd 4596) and their two volume Report made far-reaching criticisms of the then law and extensive proposals for reform. Whatever views may be held about the success of the hugely complex Consumer Credit Act 1974 and the Regulations made thereunder, as an exercise in law reform, it serves as something of a model. The Report was the product of the minds of lawyers, economists, statisticans and others knowledgeable in the credit area and the translation of the policy evolved into law was itself a masterly, if perhaps over ambitious, exercise. But law reform on this scale does involve the setting aside by the Government of a very large sum of money (the cost of preparing the Report alone being £65,230). Their diagnosis of the situation was expressed in the Committee's Report (para 4.2.1) as follows:

The defects in the present law fall broadly into seven groups:
  (i) Regulation of transactions according to their form instead of according to their substance and function.
  (ii) The failure to distinguish consumer from commercial transactions.
  (iii) The artificial separation of the law relating to lending from the law relating to security for loans.
  (iv) The absence of any rational policy in relation to third party rights.
  (v) Excessive technicality.
  (vi) Lack of consistent policy in relation to sanctions for breach of statutory provisions.
  (vii) Overall, the irrelevance of credit law to present day requirements, and the resultant failure to provide just solutions to common problems.

A coherent economic policy for dealing with the problem of consumer debt, as well as the more technical matter of rationalising the law, was an essential pre-condition for proposing radical legislation. In the field of consumer credit there has been steadily increasing legislative regulation since the first Hire-Purchase Act in 1938. This has not only controlled the form and contents of credit agreements together with the rights and duties of the parties; it has extended so as to give the Secretary of State power to impose restrictions on the disposal, acquisition or possession of articles of any description under hire-purchase agreements etc, and this power has been used since 1943 to restrict excessive credit, primarily by governing the minimum amount of any deposit. Although the Crowther Committee stated that 'terms control should find no place among the weapons of economic policy' (para 8.2.24), these powers have in fact been used continuously since 1971 as a way of restraining demand and combatting inflation. Contraventions of Orders made under the Act constitute criminal offences.

As indicated above, this policy was not in accordance with the Crowther Committee's view of economic policy, which it expressed thus:

Chapter 3.9 Guidelines for Social Policy

3.9.1   Given the principles of economic policy which we have advocated, our general view is that the state should interfere as little as possible with the consumer's freedom to use his knowledge of the consumer credit market to the best of his ability and according to his judgment of what constitutes his best interests. While it is understandable and proper for the state to be concerned about the things on which people spend their money and even to use persuasion to influence the scale of values implied by their expenditure patterns, it remains a basic tenet of a free society that people themselves must be the judge of what contributes to their material welfare.

3.9.2   Our examination of the social effects of consumer credit has not uncovered any strong social reasons for departing significantly from this view. Since the vast majority of consumers use credit wisely and derive considerable benefit from it, the right policy is not to restrict their freedom of access by administrative and legal measures but to help the minority who innocently get into trouble to manage their financial affairs more successfully—without, however, also making conditions easier for the fraudulent borrower. The basic principle of social policy must, therefore, be to reduce the number of defaulting debtors. This is in every-body's interest.

The Crowther Committee proposed two separate new statutes. One was designed to regulate, in particular, security interests in any goods by recording and safeguarding them. The other was designed to confer substantial consumer protection along uniform lines for all forms of credit and to regulate credit advertising. Only one statute was passed—the Consumer Credit Act 1974—though it incorporated a few aspects of the proposed Lending and Security Act. It now seems unlikely, however desirable, that many other features of the proposed legislation to deal with security interests will be enacted in the foreseeable future.

The Report was followed by a White Paper, 'The Reform of the Law on Consumer Credit' (Cmnd 5472) which commented:

> The recommendations of the Crowther Committee were generally welcomed by all. Passage of the Bill outlined in this White Paper will mean the start of a new era in consumer credit. The industry will be freed from outdated restrictions and, for the first time, the consumer will have comprehensive protection and that truth in lending which is so necessary if he is to choose rationally. There will also be sufficient flexibility to allow for the development of new types of credit business. Thus a framework will have been established for further development of the industry which will be fair both to the provider of credit and to the consumer.

The licensing system

The Act produced a potentially powerful regulatory weapon by requiring all proprietors of consumer credit or hire businesses to be licensed by the Director General of Fair Trading, the latter having been charged with the central enforcement of the Act. The licensing provisions are to be found in Part III of the Act and the following article by Sir Gordon Borrie, presently Director General of Fair Trading, explains the background to the licensing system and how the system is operated.

'Licensing practice under the Consumer Credit Act' by Gordon Borrie, Director General of Fair Trading (1983) JBL 91 (Footnotes omitted)

The objectives of licensing

First, let us recall the objectives of licensing. The Report of the Committee on Consumer

Credit, chaired by the late Lord Crowther, considered that:

> 'the more unscrupulous type of credit grantor may well take the view that the occasional check on his malpractices . . . in an isolated transaction is not a serious deterrent, and is outweighed by the financial advantages he may derive from evading the law;'

and, later, came to the conclusion that:

> 'many of the difficulties, anomalies and confusions that now exist have arisen from past attempts to regulate part of a field where functions are constantly overlapping . . . Our basic approach is that . . . the law should treat all who grant consumer credit . . . as far as possible in the same way . . . It follows that in respect of licensing, everyone should likewise be treated in the same way . . . we do not think it would be right simply to abolish these [the then existing licensing] provisions without putting anything else in their place.' [see paras 6.3.3 and 7.2.1].

Professor Goode, a leading member of the Crowther Committee, expands on this in his Consumer Credit Legislation Manual:

> 'No consumer legislation, however sophisticated, is likely to have more than a marginal impact if not under-pinned by effective enforcement machinery.' [para 324].

I entirely agree.

. . .

Validity of applications

The terms of section 25 (1) of the Act make it clear that, provided a person satisfies me as to his fitness and that the names under which he wishes to trade are not misleading, I must, on application, grant him a licence. There is, however, a first step. An application must be made, and this must be in valid form, because section 6 of the Act provides that an improperly made application is 'of no effect.' . . .

The 'right' to a licence

Once I have a valid application, section 25 (1) of the Act gives an apparent 'right' to a licence. This right, is, however, blurred by the fact that I have to be satisfied as to the trading name or names of the applicant and as to his fitness. In considering fitness I am obliged under section 25 (2) to take into account not only 'any circumstances appearing to [me] to be relevant' but also specific matters relating to the applicant, his employees or associates. The 'right' to a licence is, therefore, more akin to a limited administrative decision—limited because I can only refuse a licence if there has been a failure to satisfy me on one of the grounds set out in section 25(2).

Further, while section 25 (1) of the Act appears to put the formal burden of proof on an applicant to show that he is a fit person to hold (or continue to hold) a licence, that onus is also blurred because that section has to be read in conjunction with section 27 (1) under which I have a statutory obligation not only to give the applicant written notice that I am 'minded to' refuse his application or to grant it in different terms and give him an opportunity to make representations to me but—more important—I am also obliged to give *reasons* why I am minded to take such action. These reasons must obviously be put in such a way that they identify the matters I am concerned about, so that appropriate representations may be made by the applicant. If in any individual case I were unable to quote adequate reasons for refusal, etc, backed up by the relevant evidence, I would be bound to grant the application.

The 'minded to refuse' notice

If I consider that I have material to warrant refusal of a licence application, I have to follow a precise procedure laid down in the Act and regulations. (The procedure for granting a licence in different terms, or for revocation, suspension or variation of a licence is much the same and my comments below can be read as generally applying equally to these other forms of action as to refusal of an application.)

The first step I have to take is to issue a *minded to refuse notice* ('an MTR') . . .

In section 25 (2) I am required, in considering fitness, to have regard to any relevant evidence about the applicants, his employees, agents or associates but in particular to whether any such person has:

 (a) committed any offence involving fraud or other dishonesty, or violence,
 (b) contravened any provision made by or under the Act, or by or under any other enactment regulating the provision of credit to individuals or other transactions with individuals,
 (c) practised discrimination on grounds of sex, colour, race or ethnic or national origins in, or in connection with, the carrying on of any business, or

(d) engaged in business practices appearing to me to be deceitful or oppressive, or otherwise unfair or improper (whether unlawful or not).

In general, therefore, an MTR will contain any material coming within section 25 (2) that raises serious and reasonably reliable doubts and reservations as to fitness. The policy of the Office of Fair Trading has been to regard the standard of fitness imposed by the Consumer Credit Act as a high one; I have a statutory duty to be satisfied that an applicant is a fit person to hold a licence and I cannot possibly be fully satisfied in this respect if doubts and reservations are raised and not answered.

In assembling an MTR the relevance of evidence to the licence category applied for is borne in mind. Any applicant for any category of licence who has been convicted of a serious criminal offence which is not spent or very old must expect to go through the full scrutiny of licensing procedure. Even here, however, there is a degree of 'weighting' for different categories of licence. A conviction for violence is always a serious matter, but vitally crucial to an application for a debt-collecting licence. Similarly, convictions for fraud and dishonesty are serious, but very serious indeed in respect of a debt-adjuster or for a person who is constantly dealing with other people's money. More generally, conviction for VAT and income tax evasion indicate an individual's lack of integrity which could easily spill over into relations with consumers should financial problems arise.

The least easily refuted evidence likely to be cited in an MTR consists of details of convictions and convictions which are not spent. They figure very highly in the material cited in MTRs. Generally speaking, we would not expect an isolated unspent conviction many years ago—other than for a very serious offence—to figure in an MTR. By contrast, however, such a conviction would take on much greater relevance if it were repeated or if it were one of a long series of similar convictions for serious offences continuing over many years.

The most difficult kind of MTR, however, is where a case has been constructed solely of complaints sent in by Trading Standards Officers or members of the public. It is in the nature of complaints, even where these take the form of formal witness statements, that they comprise only one side of the story and are in a form where the applicant or his legal representatives are often unable to test their veracity and accuracy during the course of representations. It is also in the nature of complaints that, whilst the complainant considers that he remembers very clearly the transaction he is complaining about—because to him it is a special transaction—to the trader that transaction may be just one of very many and he may not be able to recollect it at all. It follows that counterstatements designed to show that the complaint is misconceived may raise sufficient questions about the validity of the complaint that we are unable to make a finding of fact on the issues raised. In short, it is very difficult for me to arrive at a decision which is *not* favourable to the applicant in those cases which are comprised solely of complaints. Such cases are, however, very rare indeed, for we would try to obtain other supportive evidence to lend weight to the proposed case . . .

Some, if not the greater part, of the material used in an MTR is not likely to be contemporaneous. As a basic rule we would use the most up to date evidence we can. However, section 25 (2) (d) of the Act refers to a trader who '*has committed* offences,' '*has engaged* in business practices,' not '*is committing*' offences or '*is engaging*' in business practices. Therefore the material which my Office has to use in an MTR is evidence that shows the applicant has—in the past—committed offences or engaged in a business practice, which must mean that, in this latter context, the practice has been carried out over a period of time. Of course I accept that the relevant time for deciding fitness is the moment when the licensing decision is made.

A great deal of the evidence that is likely to be cited in an MTR comes within section 25 (2) (d) of the Act which requires me, *inter alia*, to take into account in considering an application whether the appplicant has engaged in business practices appearing to me to be 'deceitful or oppressive, or otherwise unfair or improper (whether unlawful or not).' The inclusion of this phrase specifically in this section, wherein I am already required to have regard to any relevant circumstances, is a clear indication that I can object to certain trading practices and use the licensing system either to compel a course of conduct which the applicant or licensee may not be legally obliged to adopt at present or to require him to refrain from activities which he is at present legally entitled to pursue . . .

Representations

In general I think it right that I should set a high standard of fitness; that I should use the licensing powers to improve trading standards; that if there is material questioning fitness it should be tested by being put to the applicant. But in doing this I am conscious that, especially as far as the smaller trader is concerned, my Office must bend over backwards to help him with what will seem a difficult procedure. Nowhere is this policy more apparent than in our procedures for representations.

When an MTR is sent out it is accompanied by an OFT leaflet explaining how to make representations and also by a form on which written representations can be made and which can also be used, if desired, to express a wish to make oral representations. Written representations vary a great deal in style and content. Some applicants submit a few words scribbled on the form whilst others write long character testimonials but do not address themselves at all to the matters that are adduced in the MTRs. In such cases we always try to help, especially the small trader, and to make it clear to him that he really ought to try to argue against the matters put in the MTR.

Those traders who ask for oral representations will find that they are very informal. There is no question of one of the adjudicating officers presiding on a dais and everyone rising to their feet when he comes in! It is more in the nature of a discussion round a table with usually, from the Office of Fair Trading, only the Adjudicating Officer, a lawyer and, perhaps, a note taker, being present . . .

The Adjudicating Officer's final decision is given in writing. In the event of a decision favourable to the applicant nothing is put on the Register and there is no public indication that the application was questioned although, where the application has generated considerable public interest, I may consider it necessary to make some public announcement. If the decision is adverse to the applicant the Adjudicating Officer will set out in his determination his reasons and the findings of the fact upon which they are based. The decision will be placed on the Public Register and may then become a matter of public comment. In sending an addressed determination to the applicant, attention is drawn to the procedure for an appeal to the Secretary of State against the decision.

Results of licensing

As at the end of September 1981, 112,608 licences have been issued. In total, since the beginning of licensing, we have issued 532 notices of being minded to refuse, grant in different terms, revoke, vary or suspend. Of those that have been determined, the decision has been in 157 cases to refuse an application or revoke or vary a licence. But in the large majority of the remainder, a letter has accompanied the favourable decision warning the applicant/licensee of the serious view I have taken of his past behaviour and giving a severe warning that his future behaviour will be carefully monitored and that future breaches are likely to endanger his continuing fitness. In many of these cases the licensee/applicant has, in the course of proceedings, given assurances to me about his future behaviour.

But I do not think that the test of the efficacy of licensing control is shown by the number of MTRs issued or the number of final refusals or revocations, etc. First, I think it significant that of the applications received so far, nearly 4,000 were subsequently withdrawn or became of 'no effect' because the applicant failed to provide subsequent information requested. Although some of these were obviously cases where the business had changed hands or where the proprietor decided not to offer credit for commercial reasons before the licence was issued, I think I am fairly safe in assuming that the vast majority of subsequently withdrawn or of 'no effect' applications concerned businesses that, once they applied, themselves come to the conclusion that they were unlikely to get a licence and thus withdrew. Secondly, added to this, must be the unknown number of businesses who decided they would have little or no chance of passing safely through a screening process and therefore gave up credit operations and did not apply for a licence. Thirdly, in about 400 to 500 cases so far we have sent letters to licensees (with their licences), warning them about their behaviour, which was not serious enough to warrant the issue of an MTR but which might be included in an MTR if subsequent adverse behaviour is reported.

Results can often be obtained without going to the extreme of refusing, revoking or suspending a licence, including the drawing up of fairer agreements and the provision of compensation to members of the public who have been overcharged and unfairly treated. Another unmeasurable benefit of licensing consists of those businesses which have declined, after consideration, to carry on or launch a particular scheme because they think it might endanger their licences; or those businesses which, in order to safeguard their licence, are now issuing firm instructions to employees on their behaviour; or those businesses which have tightened up their own procedures and redrafted their agreements and publicity material to the same end.

. . .

The following extracts from the Annual Report of the Director General of Fair Trading for 1983 (HMSO, 1983) indicate the progress of licensing applications and 'minded to revoke' and 'minded to refuse' notices to the end of 1983. An indication is also given as to the attempts used by some traders to circumvent fitness standards.

Annual Report of the Director General of Fair Trading 1983 (pp 17–21)

Licensing under the Consumer Credit Act 1974

General progress
For three successive years, as the table [see below] indicates, the number of licence applications has shown a marked increase—representing rises of 13 per cent, 15 per cent and 10 per cent respectively.

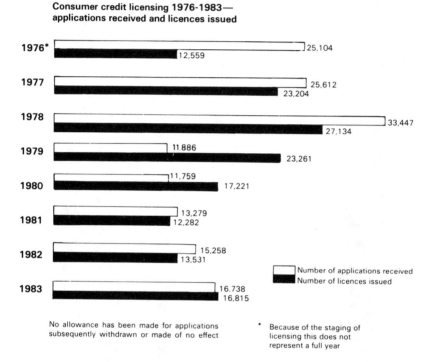

Consumer credit licensing 1976-1983—
applications received and licences issued

1976* — 25,104 / 12,559
1977 — 25,612 / 23,204
1978 — 33,447 / 27,134
1979 — 11,886 / 23,261
1980 — 11,759 / 17,221
1981 — 13,279 / 12,282
1982 — 15,258 / 13,531
1983 — 16,738 / 16,815

☐ Number of applications received
■ Number of licences issued

No allowance has been made for applications subsequently withdrawn or made of no effect

* Because of the staging of licensing this does not represent a full year

The continuing upward trend led to a considerable backlog of applications in the early part of 1983. At one time it was taking 16 weeks to consider even straightforward cases where a trader's fitness was not in question. By the end of the year, however, the period had been reduced to a maximum of six weeks with the help of some temporary staff. Overall, the year's output of 16,815 licences represented an increase of 24 per cent compared with that for 1982.

Existing licences also gave rise to a considerable amount of work. There were just over 13,000 formal communications in all: applications for variations; notifications of changes; and licence surrenders. Detailed statistics concerning applications and licences appear in Part D of Appendix One. Current group licences were listed in the Annual Report for 1980.

Considering fitness for a licence
During the year, 250 notices were served on licencees or applicants regarding their fitness to hold a licence. This is the highest in any one year since licensing began, and a milestone was reached in December with the issue of the 1,000th notice.

The pattern of businesses and trades affected by fitness notices in this and earlier years is shown in the chart [see p 212]. The number issued in 1983 included 89 indicating that the Director General was 'minded to refuse' a licence, and 154 that he was 'minded to revoke' one. There were seven similar notices that licence variations or unlicensed trading orders should be refused.

Not only were there a record number of notices, but more cases reached a final decision than in any year before. Changes in business practices, or the trader's assurances as to future trading behaviour, satisfied the Director General in 123 cases that a licence should be issued

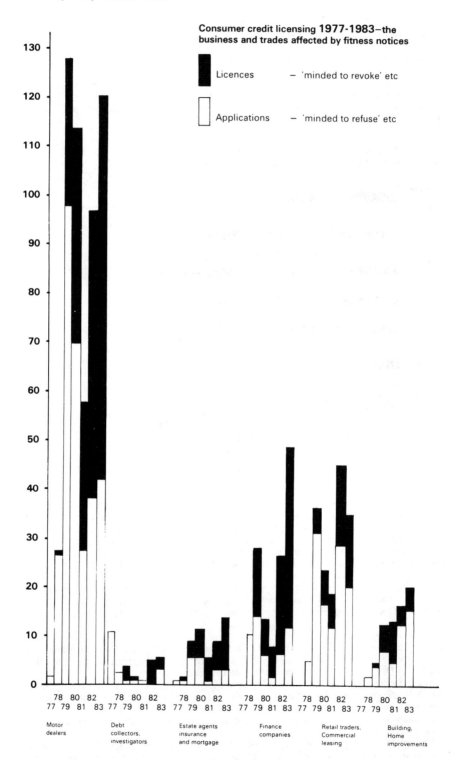

Consumer credit licensing 1977-1983–the business and trades affected by fitness notices

or that an existing one should continue. However there were 114 adverse decisions (including three concerning unlicensed trading orders) and another 34 where the trader withdrew his application or surrendered his licence. Part E of Appendix One lists the licences refused or revoked and the variations refused.

Three appeals against licensing decisions were upheld by the Secretary of State in 1983. Details of these, and the other appeals disposed of, can be found in Part E of Appendix One, and Part G provides statistics of both licensing decisions and appeals for the last three years. The procedures were described in the Annual Report for 1980.

Examples of licensing action
Action was taken in response to illegal or unfair practices in several sectors, as described below; it also took account of more general circumstances. For example, the officers of companies which had ceased trading featured increasingly as the directors of companies applying for a licence. This might be expected in times of recession but in all such cases the Office looks carefully at the effects of the earlier companies' failure in order to assess whether there is risk of detriment to consumers in the future. Another and an unwelcome development has been the provision of false or misleading information in licence applications. One prosecution by local enforcement authorities was successfully completed (see Part C of Appendix One) and another three were in progress at the end of the year.

Moneylending—there were an increasing number of cases involving unfair practices, particularly among doorstep moneylenders. Types of abuse have been described in earlier annual reports (1980 and 1981); they include getting consumers to sign uncompleted agreements and the practice of 're-loaning'. In 1983, the retention of customers' pension and allowance books led to one moneylender losing his licence; a number of others received notices regarding their fitness but their cases remain to be decided.

Retailers—mainly those selling domestic electrical appliances, attracted many adverse licensing decisions. Among the grounds for these decisions were: the supply of faulty or misdescribed goods; the use of void and/or illegal exclusion clauses; and the imposition of penalties for breach of contract when goods were repossessed. One television retailer was refused a licence because he had been convicted for theft and several complaints against him indicated breaches of contract. Another firm retained its licence only after changing its terms and conditions of hire.

The motor trade—as in past years, this sector accounted for the largest share of adverse decisions. Practices included: the falsification of mileage readings; selling unroadworthy vehicles; misleading finance companies about prices and deposits; and posing as a private seller in local newspapers' advertisements. A number of dealers were refused licences because of past convictions for theft, handling stolen goods and forgery; another had his licence revoked when it came to light that he had been convicted of supplying cars with false trade descriptions and had failed to disclose this in his licence application.

Unlicensed trading
During the year, 33 orders in all were made to enable credit or hire traders to enforce their agreements; two were refused. Further details are given in Part F of Appendix One.

The following decision illustrates an unsuccessful attempt to evade the licensing requirement imposed on persons engaged in credit brokerage within section 145 of the Act.

Hicks v Walker (1984) 28 May (Lexis transcript), (1984) 148 JP 636, Queen's Bench Divisional Court

Watkins LJ. This is an appeal by way of case stated from a decision of the deputy stipendiary magistrate for the County of West Midlands acting in and for the Petty Sessional Division of Wolverhampton in respect of her adjudication at the magistrates' court in that town.

On the 6 May, 1982, the Appellant preferred a number of informations against the Respondents who are Graham Walker, Frank Reynolds, the company Frank Reynolds Ltd. and Kenneth Purchase . . .

The informations were directed to contraventions of the Consumer Credit Act 1974, in particular section 39(1) which provides: 'A person who engages in any activities for which a licence is required when he is not a licensee under a licence covering those activities commits an offence.' In the informations it was alleged . . . that Walker on or about 1 June, 1980, unlawfully engaged in the activity of credit brokerage without a licence on behalf of a customer named John Charles Broadmeadow. Arising out of that transaction it was further alleged that Frank Reynolds, Frank Reynolds Ltd and Kenneth Purchase aided, abetted, counselled or procured the commission by Walker of the offence.

. . .

Walker is a motor car dealer. He had applied for and failed to obtain a licence under Part III of the Act, entitling him to carry on credit and hire business. He had made application under section 25 of the Act. His application failed because the Director was not satisfied that Walker was a fit person to hold such a licence. Nevertheless, he leased premises at Fallings Park Service Station, Cannock Road, Wolverhampton. He was the proprietor there of a firm called 'All Quality Cars'. He was acquainted with the Respondent Frank Reynolds who was a director of Frank Reynolds Ltd. Walker sub-let a part of the premises which he had rented to the company which had a Consumer Credit Act licence.

The Respondent Kenneth Purchase was employed upon the premises sub-let by Frank Reynolds Ltd. He was described in the course of evidence as a salesman. So far as one can tell from the evidence Frank Reynolds Ltd at no time had cars to sell at the sub-let premises. The only cars which were available for sale at the Service Station were the property of Walker. It was the practice of Purchase to act not only in the capacity of a servant of the company, but also so as to assist Walker in his dealings with persons who came to the premises to buy motor cars.

So if a person came to the premises and purchased a car and paid outright for it with cash or by cheque the transaction was exclusively between Walker and that customer, although Purchase may have played a part by acting as agent for Walker in that transaction. If a customer came to the premises who was unable to pay outright for a motor car which he wished to purchase, that person was informed either by Walker or by Purchase that credit facilities could be arranged. If the customer was agreeable to such an arrangement being made it was customary for Purchase to inform his employers that a customer of Walker's was anxious to obtain hire purchase facilities. Thereupon the company got in touch with the United Dominions Trust or some other hire purchase company and made the necessary arrangements. The car in question was sold by Walker to the company and therefore the company was able to give a good title of that motor car to the hire purchase company.

From time to time a customer came to the premises who wished to put his own car in in part exchange. In that event the company took over the car as part of the hire purchase transaction and sold it to Walker thus enabling him, if he wished, to offer that car for sale.

Evidence was provided of the understanding of the hire purchase companies as to who it was they were dealing with in the numerous transactions which went on by the combination of Walker, Purchase, the company and the hire purchase companies. The hire purchase companies thought that they were dealing exclusively with the company. They had no idea that they were dealing with Walker. Had they been so informed they would have enquired whether Walker was licensed under Part III of the Act.

The understanding of Broadmeadow, Swadkins and Hyden was that they were dealing with either Walker or Purchase or Purchase on behalf of Walker. In entering into the hire purchase agreements into which they all three entered they were assisted primarily by Purchase, but upon at least one occasion by Purchase with the assistance of Walker.

At the close of the case for the prosecution it was contended on behalf of the Respondents that there was insufficient evidence to show that Walker had at any time been responsible for effecting an introduction either to Purchase or directly to the company of a customer so that that customer could be the recipient of hire purchase arrangements in respect of a car offered for sale by Walker. He had, so it was submitted, merely been an errand boy by collecting on occasions the necessary forms for the hire purchase arrangements to be made.

Mr Parker, who appeared for the Appellants in the court below, submitted that the evidence established, firstly, that Walker had no licence; secondly, that the initiation of the transactions took place upon his premises; thirdly, that Purchase was on occasions although a servant of the company, an agent for him; and fourthly, he was well aware that the object of Purchase being upon the premises in those dual capacities was so as to facilitate the granting of hire purchase facilities to Walker's customers.

The opinion of the stipendiary magistrate was that the Appellant had failed to make out a prima facie case of unlawfully engaging in the activity of credit brokerage as defined in section 145 of the Consumer Credit Act 1974. She was of the view that Walker's title to the cars in question was insufficient for that purpose. She asks this question: 'The question for the opinion of the High Court is whether the Appellant had produced sufficient evidence to establish a prima facie case that the Respondent Walker had effected introductions to persons within the meaning of section 145(2) (a) (i) or section 145(2) (c) of the Consumer Credit Act 1974.'

The provisions, so far as they need to be read, of section 145 are these: '(1) An ancillary credit business is any business so far as it comprises or relates to—(a) credit brokerage . . . (2) Subject to section 146(5), credit brokerage is the effecting of introductions—(a) of individuals desiring to obtain credit—(i) to persons carrying on businesses to which this sub-paragraph applies' and '(c) of individuals desiring to obtain credit, or to obtain goods on hire, to other credit-brokers.' The allegation of the Appellant was that Walker introduced credit brokerage business to a credit broker, that the evidence was sufficient to create at least a prima facie case that Walker had done that and that the others had counselled or procured him to do it.

I am left in no doubt whatsoever that the deputy stipendiary magistrate was in error in coming to the conclusion that there was no prima facie case of contravention by Walker and the others of the provisions of the Act, section 145 especially. One has only to examine the activities of Purchase to see that what he did was consistent with an unlawful arrangement come to by Walker on the one hand and Reynolds and his company on the other. Purchase in his two guises moved from one role to the other as circumstances demanded. At one moment he was merely assisting Walker in the straightforward business of selling motor cars either for cash or other outright payment, and at another moment he was introducing to his employers a customer of Walker who could not pay for a motor car and therefore needed credit facilities. From that time onwards the company took over the transaction and obtained credit facilities from the hire purchase company of its selection.

It seems to me to be an inescapable inference from the way in which Purchase was said to have acted that when he was informing his employers that hire purchase facilities were needed he was acting as an agent for Walker and on his behalf effecting an introduction of credit brokerage facilities to a credit broker.

For the reasons I have outlined there was in my opinion a prima facie case and the deputy stipendiary magistrate was wrong to find to the contrary. Seeing that we are not asked to remit this case to the court below for the hearing to be resumed I would merely allow this appeal.

[**Forbes J** agreed.] *Appeal allowed; no order as to costs.*

The 'positive licensing' system developed (though not, strictly, introduced by the 1974 Act) has attracted criticism on the ground of its administrative cost both to the Office of Fair Trading and to prospective licensees. Proponents of this system argue that there are commensurate benefits to the public by the positive control which can be exercised over a wide sector of the retail market. An interesting contrast to the 1974 Act in terms of licensing policy is provided by the Estate Agents Act 1979. The overall supervision and enforcement of the 1979 Act is also the responsibility of the Director General of Fair Trading. However, no positive system of licencing or registration is imposed. Subject to ss 22 and 23 (dealing respectively with standards of competence to be provided by Regulation and prohibition of bankrupts) any person may practise as an estate agent until such time as he is shown unfit to do so. The question of an agent's fitness or unfitness is a matter for the Director who may, if the requirements of the Act are satisfied, either make a warning order under s 4 or make an order prohibiting the unfit estate agent from doing estate agency work under s 3. For a prohibition order to be made the person in question must either have been convicted of one of the offences listed in the Act (particularly one involving fraud or other dishonesty or violence), committed discrimination, failed to comply with an obligation imposed under the Act or have been engaged in a practice which, in relation to estate agency work, has been declared undesirable by an Order made by the Secretary of State.

It must also be borne in mind that many other professions are regulated by their own professional body. Solicitors, for example, are subject to the disciplinary regulations of the Law Society under statutory powers which now emanate from the Solicitors Act 1974 (See also *Pickles v Insurance Brokers Registration Council* [1984] 1 All ER 1073, [1984] 1 WLR 748 for a decision on the exercise of the IBRC of the power to refuse registration of a firm of insurance brokers under the Insurance Brokers (Registration) Act 1977).

Question

Assess the advantages and disadvantages of the positive licensing system which operates under the Consumer Credit Act 1974. Do you think that the administrative complications and expense that are involved justify the results? Can you identify sectors of the market for goods or services whose operations are likely to fall outside the ambit of the licensing control under the 1974 Act and, if so, identify what other statutory regulation may be available to control undesirable activities?

Credit tokens

The volume of credit transactions initiated through, for instance, Access or Visa (Barclaycard) credit cards is such that it is necessary to regulate both the issue of credit tokens and the agreement between the debtor and the credit card company. With regard to the issue of credit cards, when Access was first launched in Britain some 3,800,000 cards were printed and distributed. Problems inevitably arise if such cards get lost and misused, particularly where they were unsolicited in the first place.

Sections 14 and 51 of the 1974 Act are of particular interest in this connection. They state as follows:

14.   Credit-token agreements
(1) A credit-token is a card, check, voucher, coupon, stamp, form, booklet or other document or thing given to an individual by a person carrying on a consumer credit business, who undertakes—
      (a) that on the production of it (whether or not some other action is also required) he will supply cash, goods and services (or any of them) on credit, or
      (b) that where, on the production of it to a third party (whether or not any other action is also required), the third party supplies cash, goods and services (or any of them), he will pay the third party for them (whether or not deducting any discount or commission), in return for payment to him by the individual.
(2) A credit-token agreement is a regulated agreement for the provision of credit in connection with the use of a credit-token.
(3) Without prejudice to the generality of section 9 (1), the person who gives to an individual an undertaking falling within subsection (1) (b) shall be taken to provide him with credit drawn on whenever a third party supplies him with cash, goods or services.
(4) For the purposes of subsection (1), use of an object to operate a machine provided by the person giving the object or a third party shall be treated as the production of the object to him.

. . .

51.   Prohibition of unsolicited credit-tokens
(1) It is an offence to give a person a credit-token if he has not asked for it.
(2) To comply with subsection (1) a request must be contained in a document signed by the person making the request, unless the credit-token agreement is a small debtor-creditor-supplier agreement.
(3) Subsection (1) does not apply to the giving of a credit-token to a person—
      (a) for use under a credit-token agreement already made, or

(b) in renewal or replacement of a credit-token previously accepted by him under a credit-token agreement which continues in force, whether or not varied.

NOTE

The definition of 'credit-token' in s 14(1) covers such examples as credit cards issued by individual stores, such credit cards as Access and Barclaycard, cheques and vouchers, and cash cards used to obtain cash from banks' computerised cash machines (but not cheque cards guaranteeing cheques up to a stated amount). Section 9 (1), referred to in s 14 (3), states that 'In this Act "credit" includes a cash loan, and any other form of financial accommodation.'

In the following case the Director General of Fair Trading instigated what was thought to be the first prosecution under this section, which has been in force since 1 July 1977. The facts are stated concisely in the judgment of Lord Lane CJ.

Elliott v Director General of Fair Trading [1980] 1 WLR 977, [1980] ICR 629, Queen's Bench Divisional Court

Lord Lane CJ. This is an appeal by way of case stated from Surrey justices sitting at Kingston and arises under the provisions of the Consumer Credit Act 1974. The facts are scarcely in dispute and they are these. The defendant company deals in footwear and the first defendant, Mr Elliott, is a director of the company. There is no dispute that the guilt or innocence of the director depends upon the guilt or innocence of the company.

The company devised an idea to increase its sale of footwear to the public. The method adopted which has come under the scrutiny of the Director General of Fair Trading was as follows. There was sent to selected members of the public an envelope containing certain materials. The envelope itself was, so to speak, an advertising ploy because it contained, when opened out and cut away, first of all an illustrated advertisement for the Elliott Caterpillar shoe and then the only other material part was an insert in the centre of the piece of paper which represented the envelope saying:

> 'Your Elliott credit account card valid for immediate use. With your card in your hand, walk into any Elliott shop: give us your signature, show us simple identification, such as a cheque card and walk out of the shop with your purchase *and all the credit you need*. Please remember to sign your card as soon as you receive it. It is perfectly secure; it cannot be used by anyone until we have their signature in the shop.'

At the head of that page where it is cut away, it says, with two arrows, 'Cut away front of envelope to see offer inside.' Inside there were a number of other documents. First of all, there was a document stating:

> 'Elliott will pay your fare one way from any part of the British Isles to the value of half a cheap day return rail ticket against the purchase of a pair of Elliott boots, or the equivalent in shoes, bags or leather clothes. This is an unconditional offer. Valid during 1977 only.'

On the other side it repeats the information:

> '"If you have bought a cheap day return ticket, show it to your assistant when you purchase, and half the purchase price of the ticket will be deducted from your bill" and so on.'

The other item which was contained in the envelope is the central feature of the case. It is a piece of paper measuring about two inches by three or thereabouts, the size and shape of the ordinary credit card. It may not be plastic, but it is plasticised and gives the appearance at any rate of being a plastic card, again like the ordinary bank credit card. On the face of it it contains this lettering: 'The Elliott Account T Elliott & Sons Ltd London valid September 1, 1977—August 30, 1978,' and below that are a series of what I may describe as computer figures or figures which are intended to look like computer figures again as, for example, on an American Express card, but nothing, be it noted, embossed.

On the reverse side appears this: first of all, the word 'signature' and then a box again such as you get on a credit card designed obviously for the signature to be placed in it, and then these words:

> '1. This credit card is valid for immediate use. 2. The sole requirement is your signature and means of identification. 3. Credit is immediately available if you have a bank account. Sign the card as soon as you receive it; it is perfectly secure because it can only be used when a signature has been accepted at an Elliott shop. T ELLIOTT & SONS.'

In those circumstances the Director General of Fair Trading preferred four informations against the first defendant and four informations against the company, each based upon an allegation that those documents, including that card, had been sent to specified individuals in contravention of section 51 (1) of the Consumer Credit Act 1974, which reads: 'It is an offence to give a person a credit-token if he has not asked for it.'

There is no dispute that these documents were sent to the persons alleged. There is no doubt that the persons alleged had not asked for them. The only question is: was this a credit-token within the meaning of the Act. In order to discover the definition of 'credit-token,' one turns to section 14 (1) of the same statute and that reads:

His Lordship recited s 14(1) above and continued:

To narrow the problem down still further, the real contest in this case is whether the word 'undertakes' in that definition has been fulfilled by the defendants to these summonses.

The defendant's case, argued as always by Mr Beloff with great skill and persuasion and charm, is this. Mr Beloff submits that the word 'undertakes' means 'makes an offer which is capable of being accepted by the customer so as to impose upon the trader a legally binding obligation to supply to the customer goods on credit.' He goes on to submit that, since the production of the card here did not entitle the customer to the supply of goods on credit but only enabled him to apply for a credit card which would be given when he had signed a certain form of mandate to which I will come in a minute and also other documents, on that basis what the justices found to be a credit card, namely, this little bit of board which I have described before, was not in fact a credit card at all. In fact, despite the wording on this card which I have already read, the credit card was not valid for immediate use. The sole requirement was not the customer's signature and means of identification. Credit was not immediately available if the customer had a bank account. Thus, one reaches the interesting, if somewhat unattractive, proposition that, because those statements on the back of the card are not true, therefore this document, which prima facie appears to be a credit-token, is not in fact one at all. The fact of the matter was that when the customer arrived at the shop, before any credit was in fact extended to the customer, he or she would have to fill in a direct debiting mandate to the bank, and would have to sign other documents.

The submission made by Mr Beloff is that, since all those other matters had to be carried out before credit could be extended, therefore this card cannot constitute a credit-token agreement within the Act.

In my judgment, that argument fails at the outset. The word is 'undertakes,' and there is no necessity for any contractual agreement or possibility of contractual agreement to exist. One looks at the card and one asks oneself whether, on the face or on the back of that card, the defendant company is undertaking that on the production of the card cash, goods and services (or any of them) will be supplied on credit. The answer is yes. The card says 'This credit card is valid for immediate use. The sole requirement is your signature . . . Credit is immediately available if you have a bank account.' The fact that none of those statements is true does not absolve the card from being what it purports to be, namely, a credit-token card.

The argument of Mr Beloff that it is so obvious to anybody who stops to think for a moment that this card cannot do what it says without further agreements being entered into strikes me as being irrelevant. The card on the face of it and the back of it is a credit-token card, and that is all that is required. On that basis alone I would dismiss this appeal.

But there is a further basis on which I would found my judgment. Assume for the purposes of argument that the first half of Mr Beloff's argument is correct and that this cannot amount to the necessary undertaking. One then turns to inquire what about the rest of the agreements and so on which have to be signed before credit in truth can be obtained by the customer.

I repeat the words of section 14 (1):

> 'A credit-token is a card, check, voucher, coupon, stamp, form, booklet or other document or thing given to an individual by a person carrying on a consumer credit

business, who undertakes—(*a*) that on the production of it (whether or not some other action is also required) he will supply cash, goods and services . . . on credit . . .'

The other matters which had to be filled in, in my judgment, plainly fall within the words '(whether or not some other action is also required).' Even if the card cannot be looked at on its own, as I believe it can, nevertheless the further matters which have to be completed before credit is extended fall clearly within the words and parenthesis which I have read. On that basis too the justices were right in coming to the conclusion that they did. For those reasons I would dismiss this appeal.

Woolf J I agree.

Appeal dismissed with costs.

NOTE

Section 84 limits the debtor's liability arising out of accidental loss to a credit token to £50, though there is no such limit if the misuse is by a person acquiring possession with the debtor's consent. Liability for subsequent misuse ceases altogether after giving notice of loss to the creditor. Agreements for the issue of credit tokens are subject to Part V of the Act, relating to entry into, withdrawal from and formalities governing regulated agreements, and s 85 requires the creditor to give the debtor a copy of any executed agreement.

Extortionate credit bargains

Under the Moneylenders Act 1900 courts were given the power to reopen moneylending transactions and set aside agreements if satisfied that the interest was excessive and that the transaction was harsh and unconscionable. The Moneylenders Act 1927 laid down that there was a rebuttable presumption that an interest rate in excess of 48% per annum was excessive and the transaction harsh and unconscionable. The 1974 Act has greatly expanded these principles. Sections 137–140 enable the court to reopen credit agreements *whatever the amount of the credit.* The only limitation is that the debtor must be an individual as defined in the Act and by s 189 (1) this includes 'a partnership or other unincorporated body of persons not consisting entirely of bodies corporate'. It will be seen that the way these sections operate is not with reference to a stated rate of interest which must not be exceeded but rather to a number of criteria which the court is directed to consider.

Consumer Credit Act 1974

137. (1) If the court finds a credit bargain extortionate it may re-open the credit agreement so as to do justice between the parties.
(2) In this section and sections 138 to 140—
    (a) 'credit agreement' means any agreement between an individual (the "debtor") and any other person (the "creditor") by which the creditor provides the debtor with credit of any amount, and
    (b) 'credit bargain'—
        (i) where no transaction other than the credit agreement is to be taken into account in computing the total charge for credit, means the credit agreement, or
        (ii) where one or more other transactions are to be so taken into account, means the credit agreement and those other transactions, taken together.

138. (1) A credit bargain is extortionate if it—
    (a) requires the debtor or a relative of his to make payments (whether unconditionally, or on certain contingencies) which are grossly exorbitant, or
    (b) otherwise grossly contravenes ordinary principles of fair dealing.
(2) In determining whether a credit bargain is extortionate, regard shall be had to such evidence as is adduced concerning—
    (a) interest rates prevailing at the time it was made,
    (b) the factors mentioned in subsections (3) to (5), and
    (c) any other relevant considerations.
(3) Factors applicable under subsection (2) in relation to the debtor include—
    (a) his age, experience, business capacity and state of health; and
    (b) the degree to which, at the time of making the credit bargain, he was under financial pressure, and the nature of that pressure.
(4) Factors applicable under subsection (2) in relation to the creditor include—
    (a) the degree of risk accepted by him, having regard to the value of any security provided;
    (b) his relationship to the debtor; and
    (c) whether or not a colourable cash price was quoted for any goods or services included in the credit bargain.
(5) Factors applicable under subsection (2) in relation to a linked transaction include the question how far the transaction was reasonably required for the protection of debtor or creditor, or was in the interest of the debtor.
139. (1) A credit agreement may, if the court thinks just, be reopened on the ground that the credit bargain is extortionate—
    (a) on an application for the purpose made by the debtor or any surety to the High Court, county court or sheriff court; or
    (b) at the instance of the debtor or a surety in any proceedings to which the debtor and creditor are parties, being proceedings to enforce the credit agreement, any security relating to it, or any linked transaction; or
    (c) at the instance of the debtor or a surety in other proceedings in any court where the amount paid or payable under the credit agreement is relevant.
(2) In reopening the agreement, the court may, for the purpose of relieving the debtor or a surety from payment of any sum in excess of that fairly due and reasonable, by order—
    (a) direct accounts to be taken, or (in Scotland) an accounting to be made, between any persons,
    (b) set aside the whole or part of any obligation imposed on the debtor or a surety by the credit bargain or any related agreement,
    (c) require the creditor to repay the whole or part of any sum paid under the credit bargain or any related agreement by the debtor or a surety, whether paid to the creditor or any other person,
    (d) direct the return to the surety of any property provided for the purposes of the security, or
    (e) alter the terms of the credit agreement or any security instrument.
(3) An order may be made under subsection (2) notwithstanding that its effect is to place a burden on the creditor in respect of an advantage unfairly enjoyed by another person who is a party to a linked transaction.
(4) An order under subsection (2) shall not alter the effect of any judgment.
(5) In England and Wales an application under subsection (1)(a) shall be brought only in the county court in the case of—
    (a) a regulated agreement, or
    (b) an agreement (not being a regulated agreement) under which the creditor provides the debtor with fixed-sum credit not exceeding [£5,000] or running-account credit on which the credit limit does not exceed [£5,000].

. . .

140. Where the credit agreement is not a regulated agreement, expressions used in sections 137 to 139 which, apart from this section, apply only to regulated agreements, shall be construed as nearly as may be as if the credit agreement were a regulated agreement.

These provisions were considered in the following case.

Ketley v Scott [1981] ICR 241

The defendant, Mr Scott, had contracted to buy a flat at a favourable price and then paid a deposit of £2,500. Mr Scott was unable to complete (because of lack of funds) on the final day allowed for completion. He therefore applied for and obtained a loan from the plaintiffs of £20,500 secured (inter alia) by a legal charge, to enable him and his wife to complete. The interest was expressed as being 12% over 3 months, this being equal to 48% per annum. He did not declare to the plaintiffs that he had given a legal charge on the property to his bank to cover an overdraft and was liable under certain further guarantees to third parties.

The plaintiffs sued for payment due and possession and obtained judgment, but an enquiry was ordered into the question of whether the interest was 'extortionate'.

Foster J.

. . .

Conclusion

In my judgment the rate of interest charged was not extortionate within the meaning of section 138 in all the circumstances of the case. But even if I am wrong in this conclusion, the court can reopen the bargain under section 139—and I quote—'if the court thinks just.' In this case I do not think that the court should do so, for the following reasons: (a) Mr Scott failed, on the application form, to disclose his overdraft with the bank. (b) He never disclosed the guarantee up to £5,000 which he had given to some of his companies. (c) He failed to disclose that he had given a legal charge to his bank to secure his overdraft which, if registered first, would have given it priority. (d) He failed to disclose the valuation of £24,000 given to him in August 1978. It was a professional valuation. But he put in the application form a value of £30,000. In view of these four deceitful acts I would not be prepared to reopen the transaction.

In the answer to the inquiry I shall declare that the interest payable under the said legal charge should remain.

Declaration accordingly.

The Court of Appeal in *Wills v Wood* (1984) 128 Sol Jo 222, took a similar hard-headed policy decision, as is indicated in the concurring judgment of Fox LJ:

Wills v Wood (1984) (Lexis transcript), 128 Sol Jo 222, Court of Appeal

Fox LJ: The plaintiff, Mr Wills, is now about 73 years of age. He was a hotelier, but in 1967 he retired because of ill health. He sold his hotel and received a net sum of £26,000. So he had some capital to invest. The judge found that he sought and received advice from solicitors, Messrs Hubbards, as to the best way of 'investing' that capital so as to provide him with an income. On the solicitors' advice he used part of the £26,000 to buy stocks and shares. Subsequently, and again on the solicitors' advice, he lent money on security of mortgages. This latter type of 'investment', said the judge, was thereafter repeated, in each case to clients of the solicitors who in each case effected the arrangements and drew the deeds. Mr Wills never met any of the borrowers personally. Over the period 1972–6 (inclusive) loans on mortgage were made to some 13 different borrowers. Loans were at the rate of about 9%–12% It is not suggested that such rates were unreasonable. As a result, Mr Wills drew a modest income from the mortgage interest. In 1972–3 it was £1,292; in 1973–4 it was £771; in 1974–5 it was £743, and in 1975–6 it was £1,143.

In June 1973, at the instigation of his solicitors, Mr Wills lent £2,000 to Miss Wood on mortgage of her house at 12 per cent. In October 1973 and August 1974 Mr Wills advanced to Miss Wood two further sums of £500 upon the same security and at the same rate of interest.

In the present proceedings Mr Wills seeks to recover the amount of the loan which (apart from the defences raised by Miss Wood to which I will refer) is due and owing to him. The judge, however, dismissed the claim and ordered repayment to Miss Wood of some £2,392 in respect of interest which she has paid to Mr Wills in respect of the loans since they were made. Miss Wood, under this decision, thus relieves Mr Wills of some £5,300 at no cost to herself.

This result is said to be justfied by defences raised on Miss Wood's behalf and accepted by the judge.

The first is that Mr Wills was an unlicensed moneylender.

The judge held that Mr Wills was 'a person whose business is that of moneylending' within section 6 of the Moneylenders Act 1900.

In my opinion the only thing that Mr Wills had in common with persons whose business is that of moneylending is that from time to time he lent money at interest. But you do not carry on the business of moneylending simply by lending money at interest. You do not necessarily carry on any business at all by doing that. You may be simply an investor. In her narrative of the facts, the judge used the words 'invest' and 'investment' in relation to Mr Wills' disposition of his £26,000 and the lending on mortgage. She was quite right to do so. 'Investment' is exactly what Mr Wills was engaged in. But there is a fundamental difference between investment and carrying on a business. That can be seen, for example, in income tax law where a mere investor was not taxable as a trader. In the present case, in my view, the indications are strongly against any conclusion other than that this was a man engaged on quite ordinary investment. I refer, in particular, to the following circumstances. He lent only to clients of the solicitors whom they put forward; he lent only on mortgage and not on personal security; the rates of interest were in line with ordinary institutional rates and there were lengthy periods when he lent nothing at all.

In my view the argument that Mr Wills was carrying on business as a moneylender is quite without substance and must be rejected.

The second contention advanced on behalf of Miss Wood is that each of the loans was an 'extortionate credit bargain' within section 138(1) of the Consumer Credit Act 1974. The judge accepted that; she held that the bargain, in each case, 'grossly contravenes the principles of fair dealing' within section 138(1) (b).

It is not suggested that the terms of the loans were oppressive or in any way objectionable. They were, in fact, quite ordinary mortgage transactions at reasonable rates of interest. What Miss Wood is really complaining of is that she should have been lent money at all. Her financial position, it is said, was such that borrowing could only be harmful. The judge said: 'Had the Defendant received independent advice I am satisfied that she would have been strongly advised against borrowing more money.' But if Miss Wood acted to her detriment in borrowing these sums, that may be because she was not properly advised by her solicitors or because she chose to act on her own judgment. It was not, however, because of any unfairness of dealing as between herself and Mr Wills. She was of full age and capacity; she wanted loans on reasonable terms and that is what she got. Mr Wills had no contact with her and had no knowledge of her private circumstances. Nobody acting on his behalf misled her or induced her to grant the mortgages. It is quite true that his solicitors were also Miss Wood's solicitors. But in their capacity as Mr Wills' solicitors they did nothing wrong or unfair. Let me suppose that they failed to advise Miss Wood properly. That was in their capacity as her solicitors and is a matter between her and them. In relation to the establishment of a gross contravention of the ordinary principles of fair dealing, I do not see on what basis Mr Wills can in any way be responsible for such failure or its consequences or be fixed with knowledge of it.

In my opinion the case is altogether outside the provisions of section 138 (1) of the Consumer Credit Act, and there was no contravention of any principle of fair dealing.

For the above reasons . . . I would allow the appeal.

[**Sir John Donaldson, MR** delivered a concurring judgment and Stephen Brown LJ agreed.] *Appeal allowed.*

Implied terms as to quality

In consumer credit transactions the legal supplier of goods is subject to standard obligations as to correspondence with description, quality and fitness for purpose. In the case of a credit sale these obligations are to be found in the Sale of Goods Act 1979, ss 13–14, above pp 61–62. In the case of a hire-purchase agreement equivalent obligations are set out in the Supply of Goods (Implied Terms) Act 1973 ss 9 and 10, as amended, above pp 62–63. The general content of these obligations, including the remedies available on breach, are discussed in Ch 2, at p 67 et seq especially. Control over attempts to exclude or restrict liability as against one who 'deals as consumer' within s 12 of the Unfair Contract Terms Act 1977, below p 242, is discussed in Ch 6, at pp 258–260 especially.

Antecedent negotiations

Section 56 of the Consumer Credit Act 1974 deals with 'antecedent negotiations', that is negotiations with the debtor or hirer by the creditor, owner or a credit-broker, in relation to the making of any regulated agreement. Here, and for the purposes of the Act generally, a 'regulated agreement' is defined by s 189 to mean 'a consumer credit agreement, or consumer hire agreement, other than an exempt agreement'. Exempt agreements are those described in s 16 of the Act or in regulations made thereunder. Broadly speaking these comprise agreements with local authorities, building societies, insurance companies and other specified institutions, and for short-term credit, low cost credit, credit to finance foreign trade, short-term credit to finance the purchase of land, and certain land mortgages: see Diamond, *Commercial and Consumer Credit* (1982) at pp 32–33 and Ch 8.

In the case of a typical hire-purchase agreement, a dealer will negotiate with a 'customer' with a view to the formation of an agreement whereunder a finance company buys the goods from the dealer and then as creditor lets them on hire (with an option to purchase) to the debtor. Section 56(2) states that in the case of any debtor-creditor-supplier agreement, negotiations with the debtor shall be deemed to be conducted by the negotiator in the capacity of agent of the creditor as well as in his actual capacity. The Law Reform Committee had recognised the problems that might be experienced by a customer if dealers were not deemed to be the finance company's agent (see the Tenth Report, 'Innocent Misrepresentation', Cmnd 1782, 1962) and it was as a result of its recommendations that the policy now reflected in s 56 was previously to be found in s 16 of the Hire-Purchase Act 1965. See also the extract from the Crowther Committee report, below pp 225–227. The practical effect of s 56 (read with s 189(1)) is that any statements, representations, conditions, warranties or undertakings, oral or written, made by the credit-broker to the debtor confer upon the debtor the right to sue the creditor if there is a breach of any of these matters. This liability is not excludable (s 56(3)). Section 56 states as follows:

56.   Antecedent negotiations
(1) In this Act 'antecedent negotiations' means any negotiations with the debtor or hirer—
   (a) conducted by the creditor or owner in relation to the making of any regulated agreement, or
   (b) conducted by a credit-broker in relation to goods sold or proposed to be sold by the credit-broker to the creditor before forming the subject-matter of a debtor-creditor-supplier agreement within section 12(a), or
   (c) conducted by the supplier in relation to a transaction financed or proposed to be financed by a debtor-creditor-supplier agreement within section 12 (b) or (c),
and 'negotiator' means the person by whom negotiations are so conducted with the debtor or hirer.
(2) Negotiations with the debtor in a case falling within subsection (1) (b) or (c) shall be deemed to be conducted by the negotiator in the capacity of agent of the creditor as well as in his actual capacity.

(3) An agreement is void if, and to the extent that, it purports in relation to an actual or prospective regulated agreement—

    (a) to provide that a person acting as, or on behalf of, a negotiator is to be treated as the agent of the debtor or hirer, or

    (b) to relieve a person from liability for acts or omissions of any person acting as, or on behalf of, a negotiator.

(4) For the purposes of this Act, antecedent negotiations shall be taken to begin when the negotiator and the debtor or hirer first enter into communication (including communication by advertisement), and to include any representations made by the negotiator to the debtor or hirer and any other dealings between them.

Creditor's liability for the acts of the supplier

In many transactions the creditor and the legal supplier will be one and the same person. For example this is true of hire-purchase agreements where, as has been noted above p 222, the supplier's obligations as to quality are governed by the Supply of Goods (Implied Terms) Act 1973, ss 9 and 10, as amended. However the 1974 Act goes further than this and affects other types of 'debtor-creditor-supplier agreements'. Professor Diamond summarises the position as follows:

Diamond, 'Commercial and Consumer Credit: An Introduction' (1982) (pp 53–54)

Debtor-creditor-supplier agreements
The name 'debtor-creditor-supplier agreements' does not describe the parties to the agreement. Indeed, in many agreements within this class there are only two parties, for the creditor and 'supplier' may be the same person. It does, however, indicate that the credit agreement is closely related to the supply of goods or services.

    The following are examples of debtor-creditor-supplier agreements:
    a hire-purchaser agreement,
    a conditional sale agreement,
    a credit-sale agreement,
    an account or budget account at a shop,
    a credit card agreement under which goods or services are obtained,
    a trading check agreement.
In the first four examples there are only two parties, for the goods are supplied by the creditor. In the Act's terminology there is no separate 'supplier' in these cases. In the other two examples arrangements exist between the creditor and the supplier.

Section 75 contains the, at first sight, startling principle that in certain circumstances the creditor who makes possible the supply by a third party of goods (the 'connected lender') should be jointly and severally liable with the supplier in respect of a relevant misrepresentation or breach of contract. The Crowther Committee, commenting on the relationship between a lender who makes advances to borrowers pursuant to a regular business relationship between the lender and supplier, pointed out that to a considerable extent the financier and the dealer are engaged in a joint venture. This joint venture has many features. Suppliers who advertise credit card facilities, such as Access or Barclaycard, do so because they believe (normally correctly) that this increases the volume of business. A commission of various sizes is paid to the credit card company on each sale. The Crowther Committee explained these problems and added recommendations as follows:

Report of the Committee on consumer credit (Cmnd 4596, 1971)

Responsibility of Lender for Misrepresentations and Defects in Goods

6.6.20 We have mentioned earlier that for historical reasons the technique usually adopted in this country for effecting a hire-purchase transaction is for the finance house to buy the goods from the dealer and let them on hire-purchase to the hirer. The finance house thus contracts directly with the hirer and is responsible to him for observing and performing all the terms of the agreement, including those implied in favour of the hirer under the Hire-Purchase Act. If the goods are defective, the hirer's claim is usually against the finance house, not against the dealer who supplied the goods, though in certain conditions the hirer may have a right of action against the dealer either for breach of a collateral warranty or in tort for deceit or negligence. The duty laid upon the finance house by the Hire-Purchase Act is reinforced by provisions which make the dealer the agent of the finance house as regards any representations made by the dealer or his servants or agents relating to the goods during the negotiations leading to the conclusion of the hire-purchase agreement. The dealer is also made the agent of the finance house for the purpose of receiving notice from the hirer exercising a right to rescind or withdraw from the transaction.

6.6.21 Although this liability for defects in the goods has been a constant source of irritation and concern to finance houses—who argue that in reality they are merely lenders of money—it has a sound policy basis. By contracting direct with the hirer or buyer—instead of merely taking an assignment of a contract concluded between him and the dealer direct, as is the established practice in North America—the finance house makes it difficult for the hirer to pursue any effective claim against the dealer who supplied the goods. Proof of collateral contract between the hirer and the dealer is usually difficult, and it is the finance house's own procedure which has brought it into contractual relations with the hirer. It can therefore scarcely complain if it is made answerable for breaches of contract.

6.6.22 But the reason for making the finance house liable for acts and defaults of the dealer up to the time the hire-purchase agreement is made can be put on a wider footing than the purely contractual nexus between the parties. Even if one ignores the legal form of the transaction, the finance company is not in the position of a purely independent lender to whom the borrower comes for a loan. To a considerable extent the finance house and the dealer are engaged in a joint venture. The finance house controls the contract documents used by the dealer in his instalment credit business. It competes keenly with other finance houses for the privilege of obtaining the dealer's credit business. On motor vehicle business it pays the dealer a substantial commission (currently 20 per cent of the finance charge) for introducing a hire-purchase contract, thus giving the dealer a positive incentive to procure the customer's signature to a hire-purchase agreement instead of selling for cash. It provides general financial support for the dealer, the cost of which may be materially influenced by the volume of retail instalment credit business introduced to it by the dealer. When business is slack, the finance house will continually press the dealer to increase the volume of transactions put through. In every sense, therefore, the finance house relies on the dealer as a medium for promoting its own business and it cannot be equated with a wholly independent lender such as a bank approached by the borrower himself.

6.6.23 If our proposals for new legislation are adopted, it is to be anticipated that finance houses will move away still further from hire-purchase and credit sale and engage in straightforward lending, since many of the serious problems now posed by the Moneylenders Acts and the Bills of Sale Acts will disappear: and in any event, what is in form a hire-purchase agreement will, under our proposals, be treated as a loan contract in relation to its financial provisions. It is therefore necessary to consider what impact this changed situation should have on the responsibility of a finance house for defects in title to the goods or for failure of the dealer to supply goods of proper quality and fit for the required purpose. If the sale contract is made by the dealer and the finance house merely advances the price under a loan agreement, is there any longer a justification for holding it responsible for these matters?

Obligations of the Connected Lender

6.6.24 We think that once more a distinction has to be drawn between a lender who is completely independent and one whose relationship with the seller makes him a connected lender as defined by paragraph 6.2.22. We consider that there is no ground for making an independent lender answerable for defects in goods supplied with the aid of the loan, or for giving a borrower a right to set off loss or damage suffered in respect of defective goods against a claim for sums due under the loan contract. But where the lender is a connected lender, then for the reasons we have indicated different considerations apply. If, with all the pressure for business exerted by the lender and the financial inducements the lender offers, the seller seeks to boost sales by making false representations, or supplies goods which are defective, is it right that the lender should be able to disclaim all responsibility and insist on repayments of the loan being punctually maintained? We do not think so. We accept that the person who should bear ultimate responsibility is the seller who made the misrepresentation or supplied the defective goods, but we do not consider that it is sufficient to leave the borrower with his remedy against the seller, even assuming that with a changed legal structure the sale is made direct to the customer, so answering the problem referred to above of the absence of a contractual nexus.

6.6.25   There are many reasons why in practice a legal right which the buyer may have against his seller is not sufficient protection. Where the seller is reputable he will usually be prepared to deal with justified complaints and rectify the matters complained of. The majority of the cases in which the buyer is likely to suffer are those where a seller is of doubtful repute and is able to continue in business only because of the financial support he receives from the lender. The buyer supplied with defective goods may find that to secure redress from such a seller he has to incur the worry and expense of litigation, in which the burden of taking the initiative lies on him; and that in some cases the seller's financial position is so poor that it is doubtful whether he will be able to meet the judgment even if the buyer is successful. The buyer's difficulties of pursuing a claim against the seller are enhanced if, whilst wrestling with the financial problems of litigation, he has to go on paying the lender under the loan agreement. Problems of this kind are particularly prevalent in relation to agreements for the installation of central heating. There have been many cases where the supplier has either not delivered at all or has provided an ineffective heating system, and has then gone into liquidation before the consumer has been able to obtain redress, so that the consumer is left to meet a liability on a loan contract entered into with a third party. Especial hardship is caused where the buyer was induced to take the goods because they were represented as capable of producing income—eg knitting machines—which would enable the buyer to maintain payment of the instalments due under the loan agreement. If the machine is found to be inoperable, the whole basis of the buyer's financial calculation falls to the ground.

Liability of Connected Lenders

6.6.26   There are three different ways in which the borrower might be given relief against a connected lender. The first is to make the lender answerable in damages for misrepresentations made by the seller in antecedent negotiations and for breaches of any term of the agreement relating to title, fitness or quality of the goods. An alternative and intermediate measure is to provide that, while the lender shall not incur a positive liability in damages, the borrower shall, by way of defence to a claim for sums due under the loan agreement, be entitled to set off any claim that he has for such a misrepresentation or breach. The third approach is to require the borrower to pursue his remedies against the seller in the first instance, the lender becoming liable to the consumer only if the latter is unable to obtain redress from the seller because of his insolvency. This is the solution advocated by the finance houses, who accept that a seller-linked lender must accept a measure of responsibility for misrepresentations or breaches of contract by the seller, but who urge that this should be limited to the secondary liability of underwriting the seller's solvency.

6.6.27   We have reached the conclusion that the first of these approaches is that which should be adopted. If the borrower's claim does not arise, or is not made, until after he has repaid a substantial part of the loan a mere right of set-off will not give him adequate protection. Indeed, the borrower who pays his loan instalments promptly will be worse off than one who has been dilatory and thus has a substantial accrued indebtedness against which to exercise his right of set-off when the nature and extent of his own claim become clear. The third alternative would not in our view adequately protect the borrower. It imposes on him what is for the average consumer the heavy burden of initiating litigation instead of merely defending an action and exercising a right of set-off and counterclaim. Moreover, the obligation to pay the loan instalments while pursuing his claim against the seller may substantially diminish his ability to prosecute his claim.

6.6.28   We therefore recommend that where the price payable under a consumer sale agreement is advanced wholly or in part by a connected lender that lender should be liable for misrepresentations relating to the goods made by the seller in the course of antecedent negotiations, and for defects in title, fitness and quality of the goods. Further, we consider that where the sale and the loan are made by separate contracts, the borrower should nevertheless have the right to set off against any sum payable by him under the loan contract any damages he is entitled to recover from the lender for breaches of the sale agreement by the seller.

6.6.29   In reaching this conclusion we have been influenced by the additional fact that if the delinquent seller is worth powder and shot it ought to be easier for the lender to put pressure on him to deal with the complaint than it is for the borrower. The lender is not likely to be so inhibited by expense from suing the seller; and in most cases proceedings by the lender would be unnecessary because the lender is in a position to say to the seller that future financing facilities will be withdrawn unless the seller attends to the complaint and takes greater care in the conduct of his business.

. . .

6.6.31   It is of course implicit in our recommendations that a lender who incurs a liability to the borrower in the circumstances we have described should have a right of indemnity from the dealer or supplier who caused the trouble. To avoid any doubt, this right of indemnity should be expressly stated in the enactment.

Section 75 states as follows:—

75.   Liability of creditor for breaches by supplier
(1)   If the debtor under a debtor-creditor-supplier agreement falling within section 12 (b) or (c) has, in relation to a transaction financed by the agreement, any claim against the supplier in respect of a misrepresentation or breach of contract, he shall have a like claim against the creditor, who, with the supplier, shall accordingly be jointly and severally liable to the debtor.
(2)   Subject to any agreement between them, the creditor shall be entitled to be indemnified by the supplier for loss suffered by the creditor in satisfying his liability under subsection (1), including costs reasonably incurred by him in defending proceedings instituted by the debtor.
(3)   Subsection (1) does not apply to a claim—
   (a)   under a non-commercial agreement, or
   (b)   so far as the claim relates to any single item to which the supplier has attached a cash price not exceeding £100 or more than £30,000.
(4)   This section applies notwithstanding that the debtor, in entering into the transaction, exceeded the credit limit or otherwise contravened any term of the agreement.
(5)   In an action brought against the creditor under subsection (1) he shall be entitled, in accordance with rules of court, to have a supplier made a party to the proceedings.

NOTES

The essence of s 75(1) is that connected-lender liability applies to debtor-creditor-supplier agreements in which the creditor and the supplier are not one and the same person. Accordingly s 75 does not apply to hire-purchase agreements, conditional sale agreements or credit sale agreements. Thus where the debtor buys goods by using his Access card or Barclaycard the creditor is jointly and severally liable with the seller to the debtor for damages in respect of any misrepresentation or breach of contract. It should be noted that this liability does not attach to such credit card agreements as Diners Club and American Express where the entire debt must be discharged monthly, since these are exempt DCS agreements under s 16(5) of the Act.

As was noted above p 222, where the agreement is eg a hire-purchase agreement, and thus outside s 75, the debtor's rights are against the finance house which is both the creditor and supplier. These rights can be in respect of misrepresentations etc made in the course of antecedent negotiations (see above, s 56) or in respect of breaches of express or implied terms in the hire-purchase agreement. The finance house may well have a separate 'recourse' agreement against the dealer in respect of these express or implied contractual obligations, in addition to any claims against him under the Sale of Goods Act 1979.

The effect of s 75 was considered in the following case.

United Dominions Trust v Taylor [1980] SLT (Sh Ct) 28

The facts are set out in the judgment of the Sheriff Principal.

The Sheriff Principal (R. Reid QC). The pursuers made a loan to the defender for the purchase of a motor car from a supplier, who is not a party to the action. The defender avers that the car was represented to him as being in good condition, roadworthy and fit for use on public roads and that it was none of these things. He has intimated the alleged mis-representation and breach of contract to the supplier and the pursuers and has refused to pay the monthly instalments of loan repayment as they fall due. In the present action the pursuers sue for the balance of the loan and interest. The defender has pleaded the supplier's misrepresentation and breach of contract as a defence to the action and contends that he is entitled to do so under the terms of s 75 (1) of the Consumer Credit Act 1974 . . . The pursuers admit that the agreement with them is covered by the Consumer Credit Act 1974 and the parties' agents were agreed that the whole transaction was a debtor-creditor-supplier agreement in terms of s 11 (1) (*b*) and 12 (*b*) of the Act.

In opening the appeal the defender argued that he had relevantly averred that the contract had been rescinded on the ground of the supplier's misrepresentation and breach of contract and that, by virtue of s 75 (1), the rescission affected both the contract of sale with the supplier and the contract of loan with the pursuers. The question, according to the appellant, was whether the words 'any claim against the supplier' included a claim of rescission of the contract with the supplier and the answer he proposed was that, as a matter of ordinary English usage, they plainly did. The pursuers' reply to this argument was that there were two contracts and that the grounds of rescission of the contract with the supplier, namely, misrepresentation and breach of contract, could only apply to that contract. These grounds could not constitute 'a like claim against the creditor' because there was no question of the contract of loan having been induced by misrepresentation or of there being a breach of contract in relation to it. The pursuers' agent also presented the wider argument that s 75 (1) was intended to enable the debtor to exercise claims against the creditor, such as claims for restitution or damages, but not to plead a right as a defence to an action by a creditor because the claims referred to in the subsection were limited to those whose enforcement would make the creditor jointly and severally liable with the supplier to the pursuer. The pursuers' agent accepted that there would be anomalous results if these limited rights were exercised while the loan contract remained operative but he contended that these difficulties arose from the wording of the subsection.

I do not agree with the pursuers' argument. The subject-matter of the section is 'any claim against the supplier in respect of a misrepresentation or breach of contract'. The claims which leap to mind as being open in these circumstances are claims to rescind the contract, to claim restitution of any sums paid to the supplier and to claim any damage which the debtor has sustained. It would be odd, to say the least, if the right to rescind was not available against the creditor and the right to restitution, which depends on rescission, was available. The section goes on to provide that, where such claims against the supplier exist, the debtor shall have 'a like claim against the creditor'. The section does not require that the claim against the creditor shall be justifiable on like grounds to the claim against the supplier, merely that it shall be the same sort of claim. The words 'a like claim' are thus wide enough to include a claim for rescission although the creditor has given no grounds for rescission of the loan contract.

This view of the subsection has been confirmed by a consideration of other provisions of the Act, particularly as they relate to debtor-creditor-supplier agreements. The long title of the Act narrates inter alia that the Act establishes a new system of licensing and other control of traders concerned with the provision of credit and their transactions. A reading of the Act discloses that it has created a completely new system of classifications and remedies to take effect whenever consumer credit is associated with the contracts of sale and hire. These statutory remedies have been superimposed on existing contractual remedies. One of the innovations of the Act is to treat two or more contracts which are economically part of one credit transaction as transactions which are legally linked. Where these linked transactions contain two contracts the fate of each contract depends on the other, even where the parties to the contracts are different. This approach leaves no room for the idea of privity of contract which is fundamental to the common law of contract. It is for that reason that I am unable to agree with the learned sheriff's use of the principle of privity of contract to throw light on the meaning of the subsection.

The present contract between the parties is agreed to be a debtor-creditor-supplier agreement under the Act, ie a consumer credit agreement regulated by the Act of the type in which credit is given for a restricted purpose or use in a transaction between a debtor and the supplier (who is not also the creditor) and made by the creditor under pre-existing arrangements between himself and the supplier (ss 11 (1) (*b*) and 12 (*b*)). In such circumstances the contract of sale between the debtor and the supplier is a transaction linked to the credit agreement (s 19 (1) (*b*)). Withdrawal from the credit agreement operates as withdrawal from the contract of sale and cancellation of the credit agreement as a similar effect on the contract of sale (ss 57 (1), 69 (1)); and there are other circumstances in which a credit agreement and the transaction linked to it stand or fall together (see Goode on *Consumer Credit Act 1974,* para 19.9). All these are instances of cases in which events affecting the credit agreement operate also in the transaction linked to it. In precisely the same way s 75 (1) ensures that rescission of the contract of sale shall operate as rescission of a credit agreement linked to it where both form part of a debtor-creditor-supplier agreement.

[The sheriff principal then considered the defender's averments and decided to allow a proof before answer.]

[The pursuers appealed to the Court of Session but subsequently abandoned the appeal. It is understood that the decision was however set aside on the facts.]

NOTES

1. The decision in *United Dominions Trust Ltd v Taylor* has been criticised (see eg Goode, *Consumer Credit* (para 681) and F.B. Davidson, (1980) 96 LQR 343). The question is whether if a debtor has a claim to rescind the contract of sale for, for example, misrepresentation, he will by virtue of s 75 then have a 'like claim' to rescind the credit agreement. The more obvious meaning and effect of s 75(1) is that the creditor is required to accept liability as an additional or alternative defendant where the debtor has a claim against the legal supplier for breach of contract or mis-representation etc. On appropriate facts this may extend to recovery of the contract price and an indemnity against liability to pay interest etc under the credit agreement: see Diamond *Commercial and Consumer Credit* (1982), pp 268–269. However it seems that there is no right to rescind the credit agreement as such, since this agreement is distinct from the contract of supply to which it is linked. Admittedly the position may be different if a credit-broker (dealer) makes a false statement about the *credit* agreement itself. By s 56, above, such a statement would be regarded as having been made by the 'negotiator' (dealer) as an agent for the creditor, so giving rise to a possible entitlement to rescind the credit agreement.

2. Consider the possible civil liability (if any) of the parties in the following cases with particular reference to the statutory or common law sources of any such liability:

(i) Jake, the sole proprietor of Bombsite Garages, tells Richard, a would-be purchaser of a Mini that it has had 'one careful lady owner'. Richard acquires the Mini on hire-purchase from Sharkville Finance Company. Later he learns that the car had previously been owned by a hire company and moreover that it is unmerchantable.

(ii) Rupert decides to have his house double-glazed and he employs Samuel to do the work. Samuel arranges finance through Lendit Finances which advances a loan of £1,000 to Rupert. The loan is repayable over twelve months. The work is done very badly and Samuel is now insolvent. Would it affect the position if Rupert had borrowed the money from his bank?

(iii) Xavier buys an electric carving knife and a dishwasher from his local department store. The knife costs £35 and the dishwasher £280 and Xavier uses his Access card to pay for both. Two days later the dishwasher floods his kitchen causing extensive damages to the basement below, and Xavier is electrocuted when using the knife. Both the dishwasher and the knife are defective. How, if at all, might it affect the position if the shop assistant had assured him that the knife was 'absolutely safe'?

CHAPTER 6

Exemption clauses and unfair contract terms

Introduction

For many years the obligations concerning contracts for the supply of goods and services (referred to in Chs 2 and 3 respectively) could be excluded or limited by a suitably-worded exemption or limitation clause. Indeed such clauses were commonplace and prima facie binding on consumers and others even though they were neither understood nor read. This was but a reflection of the classical freedom of contract theory but the effect on individuals was described by Lord Denning MR as 'a bleak winter for our law of contract' (see *George Mitchell (Chesterhall) Ltd v Finney Lock Seeds Ltd* [1983] QB 284, [1983] 1 All ER 108, below p 234). Of course the problem was exacerbated by the growth in the use of standard form contracts or contracts of adhesion. Professor Slawson has noted the prevalence and typical nature of such contracts in an influential article.

'Standard Form Contracts and Democratic Control of Lawmaking Power' by Slawson (1971) 84 Harvard LR 529, at pp 529–31:

Standard form contracts probably account for more than ninety-nine percent of all the contracts now made . . . The contracting still imagined by courts and law teachers as typical, in which both parties participate in choosing the language of their entire agreement, is no longer of much more than historical importance . . . The predominance of standard forms is the best evidence of their necessity. They are characteristic of a mass production society and an integral part of it . . . But the overwhelming proportion of standard forms are not democratic because they are not, under any reasonable test, the agreement of the consumer or business recipient to whom they are delivered. Indeed, in the usual case, the consumer never even reads the form, or reads it only after he has become bound by its terms. Even the fastidious few who take the time to read the standard form may be helpless to vary it. The form may be part of an offer which the consumer has no reasonable alternative but to accept.

. . .

Forms standardised to achieve economies of mass production and mass merchandising will also, under the present system, almost certainly be unfair, because if they were not, their issuers would probably lose money. An unfair form will not deter sales because the seller can easily arrange his sales so that few if any buyers will read his forms, whatever their terms, and he risks nothing because the law will treat his forms as contracts anyway. The user of an unfair form does not even stand to lose any significant number of future sales because the contingencies against which his forms provide him protection are normally of a kind which only infrequently occur (although when they do, the buyer may lose a great deal). When such a contingency arises the buyer will not usually be in a position to compare the form he bought with others he might have bought instead. Most buyers probably believe (correctly) that the forms they could have bought from a competing seller would have been just as bad anyway. An unfair form thus normally constitutes a costless benefit which a seller refuses at his peril . . .'

In most Western legal systems such considerations have led to statutory control of exemption clauses and in some jurisdictions of unfair contract terms generally. Some statutes (for example the West German Act of 1976) apply to standard form contracts specifically; others are of more general application although they may also have particular provisions applicable to such contracts. The United Kingdom Unfair Contract Terms Act 1977 falls into the latter category.

Incorporation and principles of construction

Even before the advent of statutory control the full rigours of the common law were often mitigated in practice by the court's insistence that an exemption clause be incorporated in the contract and apt to cover the plaintiff's claim. Such matters are no longer important where the clause is in any event void by virtue of the Unfair Contract Terms Act 1977. However there are many consumer transactions where exemption clauses are not void but are subject rather to the 'test of reasonableness' under the 1977 Act. For example a consumer's goods may have been lost or damaged in a house removal or when being cleaned or processed or a holiday may have gone disastrously wrong. In any such case it is possible theoretically for a court to conclude that an exemption clause is both reasonable and yet ineffective, for example because it has not been incorporated into the contract. For this reason the common law rules of incorporation and construction cannot be ignored and are indeed the logical starting point for any inquiry.

The basic requirement for incorporation is that there be either a signed contractual document (as in *L'Estrange v Graucob Ltd* [1934] 2 KB 394) or that reasonable notice of the exempting provision be given before the contract is concluded. Precisely what constitutes 'reasonable notice' is often unclear (see *Woodman v Photo Trade Processing Ltd,* below p 245). The point is discussed in the standard texts on exemption clauses and on the law of contract: see for example Yates *Exclusion Clauses in Contracts* (2nd edn, 1982), Cheshire and Fifoot *The Law of Contract* (10th edn, 1981), pp 138–172 and Smith and Thomas *A Casebook on Contract* (7th edn, 1982), Ch 12. See also Lawson, *Exclusion Clauses.* For examples of cases with a consumer context see *Parker v South Eastern Rly Co* (1877) 2 CPD 416; *McCutcheon v David MacBrayne Ltd* [1964] 1 All ER 430, [1964] 1 WLR 125, HL; *Hollier v Rambler Motors (AMC) Ltd* [1972] 2 QB 71, [1972] 1 All ER 399, CA and *Thornton v Shoe Lane Parking Ltd* [1971] 2 QB 163, [1971] 1 All ER 686, CA.

The operation of the principles of construction and the general development of common law and statutory controls have been traced by Lord Denning MR in a commercial case which, as Lord Diplock was to remark ([1983] 2 All ER 737, 739), was probably also the last in which the House of Lords would have the opportunity of enjoying Lord Denning's 'eminently readable style'. Its valedictory nature provides a further reason for these extracts.

George Mitchell (Chesterhall) Ltd v Finney Lock Seeds Ltd [1983] 1 All ER 108, [1983] QB 284, Court of Appeal

Lord Denning MR

In outline

Many of you know Lewis Carroll's *Through the Looking-Glass*. In it there are these words (ch 4):

> "'The time has come,' the Walrus said,
> 'To talk of many things:
> Of shoes—and ships—and sealing wax—
> Of cabbages—and kings . . .'"

Today it is not 'of cabbages and kings', but of cabbages and whatnots. Some farmers, called George Mitchell (Chesterhall) Ltd, ordered 30 lb of cabbage seed. It was supplied. It looked just like cabbage seed. No one could say it was not. The farmers planted it over 63 acres. Six months later there appeared out of the ground of a lot of loose green leaves. They looked like cabbage leaves but they never turned in. They had no hearts. They were not 'cabbages' in our common parlance because they had no hearts. The crop was useless for human consumption. Sheep or cattle might eat it if hungry enough. It was commercially useless. The price of the seed was £192. The loss to the farmers was over £61,000. They claimed damages from the seed merchants, Finney Lock Seeds Ltd. The judge awarded them that sum with interest. The total comes to nearly £100,000.

The seed merchants appeal to this court. They say that they supplied the seed on a printed clause by which their liability was limited to the cost of the seed, that is £192. They rely much on two recent cases in the House of Lords: *Photo Production Ltd v Securicor Transport Ltd* [1980] 1 All ER 556, [1980] AC 827 and *Ailsa Craig Fishing Co Ltd v Malvern Fishing Co Ltd* [1983] 1 All ER 101 (the two *Securicor cases*) . . .

Are the conditions part of the contract?

The farmers were aware that the sale was subject to some conditions of sale. All seed merchants have conditions of sale. They were on the back of the catalogue. They were also on the back of the invoice each year. So it would seem that the farmers were bound at common law by the terms of them. The inference from the course of dealing would be that the farmers had accepted the conditions as printed, even though they had never read them and did not realise that they contained a limitation on liability.

But, in view of modern developments, it is to be noticed that the conditions were not negotiated at all between any representative bodies. They were not negotiated by the National Farmers' Union. They were introduced by the seed merchants by putting them in their catalogue and invoice, and never objected to by the farmers.

It is also to be noticed that the farmers never thought of insuring against any breach of contract by the seedsmen. It would be difficult to get any quotation. It might be possible for the seed merchants to insure themselves, something in the nature of a product liability insurance. Some seed merchants do so . . .

The natural meaning

There was much discussion before us as to the construction of that condition. I am much impressed by the words I have emphasised. Taking the clause in its natural plain meaning, I think it is effective to limit the liability of the seed merchants to a return of the money or replacement of the seeds. The explanation they give seems fair enough. They say that it is so as to keep the price low, and that if they were to undertake any greater liability the price would be much greater.

After all, the seed merchants did supply seeds. True, they were the wrong kind altogether. But they were seeds. On the natural interpretation, I think the condition is sufficient to limit the seed merchants to a refund of the price paid or replacement of the seeds.

The hostile meaning

Before the decisions of the House of Lords in the two *Securicor* cases, I would have been inclined to decide the case as the judge did. I would have been 'hostile' to the clause. I would have said that the goods supplied here were different *in kind* from those that were ordered, and that the seed merchants could not avail themselves of the limitation clause. But in the light of the House of Lords cases, I think that that approach is not available.

I am particularly impressed by the words of Lord Wilberforce in the *Ailsa Craig* case [1983] 1 All ER 101 at 102–103, where he said:

'. . . one must not strive to create ambiguities by strained construction, as I think the appellants have striven to do. The relevant words must be given, if possible, their natural, plain meaning. Clauses of limitation are not regarded by the courts with the same hostility as clauses of exclusion; this is because they must be related to other contractual terms, in particular to the risks to which the defending party may be exposed, the remuneration which he receives and possibly also the opportunity of the other party to insure.'

To my mind these two cases have revolutionised our approach to exemption clauses. In order to explain their importance, I propose to take you through the story.

The heyday of freedom of contract

None of you nowadays will remember the trouble we had, when I was called to the Bar, with exemption clauses. They were printed in small print on the back of tickets and order forms and invoices. They were contained in catalogues or timetables. They were held to be binding on any person who took them without objection. No one ever did object. He never read them or knew what was in them. No matter how unreasonable they were, he was bound. All this was done in the name of 'freedom of contract'. But the freedom was all on the side of the big concern which had the use of the printing press. No freedom for the little man who took the ticket or order form or invoice. The big concern said, 'Take it or leave it.' The little man had no option but to take it. The big concern could and did exempt itself from liability in its own interest without regard to the little man. It got away with it time after time. When the courts said to the big concern, 'You must put it in clear words,' the big concern had no hestitation in doing so. It knew well that the little man would never read the exemption clauses or understand them.

It was a bleak winter for our law of contract. It is illustrated by two cases, *Thompson v London Midland and Scottish Rly Co* [1930] 1 KB 41, [1929] All ER Rep 474 (in which there was exemption from liability, not on the ticket, but only in small print at the back of the timetable, and the company were held not liable) and *L'Estrange v F Graucob Ltd* [1934] 2 KB 394, [1934] All ER Rep 16 (in which there was complete exemption in small print at the bottom of the order form, and the company were held not liable).

The secret weapon

Faced with this abuse of power, by the strong against the weak, by the use of the small print of the conditions, the judges did what they could to put a curb on it. They still had before them the idol, 'freedom of contract'. They still knelt down and worshipped it, but they concealed under their cloaks a secret weapon. They used it to stab the idol in the back. This weapon was called 'the true construction of the contract'. They used it with great skill and ingenuity. They used it so as to depart from the natural meaning of the words of the exemption clause and to put on them a strained and unnatural construction. In case after case, they said that the words were not strong enough to give the big concern exemption from liability, or that in the circumstances the big concern was not entitled to rely on the exemption clause. If a ship deviated from the contractual voyage, the owner could not rely on the exemption clause. If a warehouseman stored the goods in the wrong warehouse, he could not pray in aid the limitation clause. If the seller supplied goods different in kind from those contracted for, he could not rely on any exemption from liability. If a shipowner delivered goods to a person without production of the bill of lading, he could not escape responsibility by reference to an exemption clause. In short, whenever the wide words, in their natural meaning, would give rise to an unreasonable result, the judges either rejected them as repugnant to the main purpose of the contract or else cut them down to size in order to produce a reasonable result. This is illustrated by these cases in the House of Lords: *Glynn v Margetson & Co* [1893] AC 351, [1891–4] All ER Rep 693, *London and North Western Rly Co v Neilson* [1922] 2 AC 263, [1922] All ER Rep 395, *Cunard SS Co Ltd v Buerger* [1927] AC 1, [1926] All ER Rep 103; and by these in the Privy Council: *Canada SS Lines Ltd v R* [1952] 1 All ER 305, [1952] AC 192, *Sze Hai Tong Bank Ltd v Rambler Cycle Co Ltd* [1959] 3 All ER 182, [1959] AC 576, and innumerable cases in the Court of Appeal, culminating in *Levison v Patent Steam Carpet Cleaning Co Ltd* [1977] 3 All ER 498, [1978] QB 69. But when the clause was itself reasonable and gave rise to a reasonable result, the judges upheld it, at any rate when the clause did not exclude liability entirely but only limited it to a reasonable amount. So, where goods were deposited in a cloakroom or sent to a laundry for cleaning, it was quite reasonable for the company to limit their liability to a 'reasonable amount, having regard to the small charge made for the service. These are illustrated by *Gibaud v Great Eastern Rly Co* [1921] 2 KB 426, [1921] All ER Rep 35, *Alderslade v Hendon Laundry Ltd* [1945] 1 All ER 244, [1945] KB 189 and *Gillespie Bros & Co Ltd v Roy Bowles Transport Ltd* [1973] 1 All ER 193, [1973] QB 400.

Fundamental breach

No doubt had ever been cast thus far by anyone. But doubts arose when in this court, in a case called *Karsales (Harrow) Ltd v Wallis* [1956] 2 All ER 866, [1956] 1 WLR 936, we ventured to suggest that if the big concern was guilty of a breach which went to the 'very root' of the contract, sometimes called a 'fundamental breach', or at other times a 'total failure' of its obligations, then it could not rely on the printed clause to exempt itself from liability. This way of putting it had been used by some of the most distinguished names in the law, such as Lord Dunedin in *W & S Pollock & Co v Macrae* 1922 SC (HL) 192 Lord Atkin and Lord Wright in *Hain SS Co Ltd v Tate & Lyle Ltd* [1936] 2 All ER 597 at 603, 601, 607–608 and Devlin J in *Smeaton Hanscomb & Co Ltd v Sassoon I Setty Son & Co* [1953] 2 All ER 1471 at 1473, [1953] 1 WLR 1468 at 1470. But we did make a mistake, in the eyes of some, in elevating it, by inference, into a 'rule of law'. That was too rude an interference with the idol of 'freedom of contract.' We ought to have used the secret weapon. We ought to have said that in each case, on the 'true construction of the contract' in that case, the exemption clause did not avail the party where he was guilty of a fundamental breach or a breach going to the root. That is the lesson to be learnt from the 'indigestible' speeches in *Suisse Atlantique Société d'Armement Maritime SA v Rotterdamsche Kolen Centrale NV* [1966] 2 All ER 61, [1967] 1 AC 361. They were all obiter dicta. The House were dealing with an agreed damages clause and not an exemption clause and the point had never been argued in the courts below at all. It is noteworthy that the House did not overrule a single decision of the Court of Appeal. Lord Wilberforce appears to have approved them (see [1966] 2 All ER 61 at 92–93, [1967] 1 AC 361 at 433). At any rate, he cast no doubt on the actual decision in any case.

The change in climate

In 1969 there was a change in climate. Out of winter into spring. It came with the first report of the Law Commission on Exemption Clauses in Contracts (Law Com no 24) which was implemented in the Supply of Goods (Implied Terms) Act 1973. In 1975 there was a further change. Out of spring into summer. It came with their second report on Exemption Clauses (Law Com no 69) which was implemented by the Unfair Contract Terms Act 1977. No longer was the big concern able to impose whatever terms and conditions it liked in a printed form, no matter how unreasonable they might be. These reports showed most convincingly that the courts could and should only enforce them if they were fair and reasonable in themselves and it was fair and reasonable to allow the big concern to rely on them. So the idol of 'freedom of contract' was shattered. In cases of personal injury or death, it was not permissible to exclude or restrict liability at all. In consumer contracts any exemption clause was subject to the test of reasonableness.

These reports and statutes have influenced much the thinking of the judges. At any rate, they influenced me as you will see if you read *Gillespie Bros & Co Ltd v Roy Bowles Transport Ltd* [1973] 1 All ER 193 at 200, [1973] QB 400 at 416 and *Photo Production Ltd v Securicor Transport Ltd* [1978] 3 All ER 146 at 153, [1978] 1 WLR 856 at 865:

> 'Thus we reach, after long years, the principle which lies behind all our striving: the court will not allow a party to rely on an exemption or limitation clause in circumstances in which it would not be fair or reasonable to allow reliance on it; and, in considering whether it is fair and reasonable, the court will consider whether it was in a standard form, whether there was equality of bargaining power, the nature of the breach, and so forth.'

The effect of the changes

What is the result of all this? To my mind it heralds a revolution in our approach to exemption clauses; not only where they exclude liability altogether and also where they limit liability; not only in the specific categories in the Unfair Contract Terms Act 1977, but in other contracts too. Just as in other fields of law we have done away with the multitude of cases on 'common employment', 'last opportunity', 'invitees' and 'licensees' and so forth, so also in this field we should do away with the multitude of cases on exemption clauses. We should no longer have to go through all kinds of gymnastic contortions to get round them. We should no longer have to harass our students with the study of them. We should set about meeting a new challenge. It is presented by the test of reasonableness . . .

Applying the test of reasonableness then imposed by the Supply of Goods (Implied Terms) Act 1973, s 4, his Lordship concluded that it would not be fair or reasonable to allow the seed merchants to rely on the clause to limit their liability. Oliver and Kerr LLJ concurred in dismissing the appeal but held that the clause did not as matter of construction limit the defendant's liability.

Appeal dismissed. [On further appeal the House of Lords dismissed the appeal on grounds which reflected the reasoning of Lord Denning (see [1983] 2 All ER 737 and below p 263)].

The introduction of statutory control

As was noted in Lord Denning's judgment in *George Mitchell (Chesterhall) Ltd v Finney Lock Seeds Ltd* [1983] QB 284, [1983] 1 All ER 108, CA, above, statutory control over exemption clauses was introduced into English law following two reports by the Law Commission. The first (Law Com No 24) was concerned with the implied terms of ss 13–15 of the Sale of Goods Act and exemption clauses in relation to such terms. The following extracts from para 65 et seq of the report indicate the background to the introduction of statutory control over exemption clauses in consumer sales.

Exemption Clauses in Contracts First Report: Amendments to the Sale of Goods Act 1893 (Law Commission) (Law Com No 24) (1969)

65. During the past few decades the habit of ousting the implied terms by express contractual provisions has become a widely practised technique of the law of sale at all levels of commerce; it has received a steadily growing impetus from the ubiquitous appearance of standard contracts on the economic scene. By the time the Molony Committee published their Final Report, they were firmly of opinion that the main criticism that could be levelled at the law of sale of goods concerned

> 'the ease and frequency with which vendors and manufacturers of goods exclude the operation of the statutory conditions and warranties by provisions in guarantee cards or other contractual documents'.

. . .

67. The Molony Committee collected a great deal of evidence on the question whether the practice of contracting out was widespread in consumer sales. The results were stated in the following terms:

> 'The answer is that it [ie the practice of contracting out] is universal in the motor vehicle trade, and general in respect of electrical and mechanical appliances. In all these cases it is associated with guarantees or 'warranties' as the motor car manufacturers term them; and is inspired, no doubt, by the fact that the goods are complex and mass produced. These classes of goods are comparatively expensive. The practice also appears in many other types of business conducted by means of catalogues or requiring an order form to be completed by the purchaser. In these no guarantee is given in return. Our conclusion is that it would be unwise to regard the contracting out practice as the prerogative of particular trades or to assume that it may not spread beyond its present limits.'[1]

68. On the strength of the evidence which they had collected, the Molony Committee declared themselves compelled to view the practice of contracting out as a general threat to consumer interest, in the sense that 'heavy and irrecoverable loss may fall upon the consumer who is unlucky enough to get a defective article.'[2] . . .

After reviewing and rejecting a certain number of objections to a prohibition of 'contracting out' (into the merits of which we need not go apart from stating our broad agreement with the Molony Committee's reasoning)[3] they found an overriding argument in favour of prohibiting 'contracting out'. The mischief was that this practice enabled well-organised commerce 'consistently to impose unfair terms on the consumer and to deny him what the law means him to have.'[4] On the whole, the consumer did not even know how he was being treated; but where he was alive to the postion, he found it difficult and sometimes impossible to avoid submitting to the terms of business universally adopted, because he had no bargaining power of sufficient weight. This being the essence of the case for intervention in support of the consuming public, the Molony Committee endorsed the soundness of the case and accepted the need to ban 'contracting out'. They took the view that in order to be effective the prohibition must extend to the efforts of any person to relieve the retailer of liability, whether made before, at or after the moment of sale. The sanction was to be a denial of legal effect to any provisions relieving the retailer of his statutory liabilities.

. . .

72. Our Working Party found themselves in agreement with the Molony Committee's main proposal that in sales to private consumers any exclusion of the statutory conditions and warranties should be void. They were led to this conclusion partly by the evidence reviewed by the Molony Committee, partly by the evidence submitted to the Working Party, and finally by such relevant information as members possessed in their individual, professional, official or representative capacities. The Working Party were persuaded that there was general dissatisfaction among private consumers with the way in which the law of sale was affected by exemption clauses, and that there was an increasing demand for better protection. In particular, there was dissatisfaction with the manufacturers' guarantees that were widely regarded as insufficient compensation for those rights which private consumers believed, rightly or wrongly, they had surrendered in exchange for guarantees. Those forms of guarantee which had come to the notice of the Working Party very often excluded consequential loss or damage; this was a serious matter in the case of 'high risk' products. Again, the frequent imposition on the customer of liability for the labour costs incurred in the repair or replacement of defective articles or components worked unfairly in many cases, particularly where the labour costs greatly exceeded the price of the replaced component itself. The Working Party were not inclined to attach undue weight to the fact that relatively few complaints by private consumers were coming to the attention of solicitors. This, the Working Party thought, did not mean that there were no real grievances and no injustice; the paucity of litigation could be reasonably explained on the ground that in most cases relatively small sums were at stake, and that many a private consumer was deterred from taking legal proceedings by the high cost of litigation, the uncertainty of the outcome or the belief that under the terms of the guarantee he had no remedy.

. . .

76. The proposal that in sales to private consumers any purported exclusion of the statutory conditions and warranties should be made ineffective by statute has received substantial support; but the support was by no means unanimous. As was to be expected, all the consumer organisations were wholeheartedly in favour of an unqualified ban; broad support came also from various representative organisations of commerce, including the retail trade; and outright opposition was confined to The Law Society, a distinguished firm of auctioneers and an individual contributor. But in between these two extreme positions there were a fair number of critical comments and alternative proposals. The suggestions included the restriction of the ban to selected fields where there was positive evidence of abuse; the provisions of facilities for the validation of exemption clauses by some such body as the Restrictive Practices Court; the mitigation of the ban by the introduction of a reasonableness test; exceptional treatment for second-hand or imperfect goods; preservation of the seller's right to exclude any reliance on his skill and judgment; and various points of detail.

. . .

79. . . . [It] is clear to us that there is widespread public misunderstanding and uncertainty about the purchaser's legal rights against the retailer where the manufacturer's 'guarantee' is offered and accepted. It is our view that legislation, in addition to providing a remedy against effective and oppressive contracting out, can perform the important function of clarifying the legal position of the private consumer. Whatever rights a buyer may have against the manufacturer, and they may be valuable rights, it may be the local retailer rather than the distant (possibly overseas) manufacturer with whom the buyer can most conveniently discuss a complaint and perhaps come to terms, or, in the last resort, litigate his claim. In our view the rights of the private consumer against his seller under the statutory conditions and warranties should be expressly and clearly maintained and safeguarded by the law.

80. Accordingly we unanimously recommend that the statutory conditions and warranties implied by sections 13–15 of the Sale of Goods Act should apply to a sale to private consumers notwithstanding any term of the contract express or implied to the contrary . . .

1. Final Report, paragraph 427.
2. Final Report, paragraph 431.
3. ibid, paragraphs 432–434.
4. ibid, paragraph 435.

This recommendation was implemented in relation to contracts for the sale of goods and also to hire-purchase agreements and agreements for the redemption of trading stamps by the Supply of Goods (Implied Terms) Act 1973. Following the Law Commission's Second Report on Exemption Clauses (Law Com No 69, 1975) much more extensive controls were introduced by the Unfair Contract Terms Act 1977.

The Unfair Contract Terms Act 1977

INTRODUCTION

This Act, the main provisions of which are printed below, gives effect, with modifications, to recommendations made by the Law Commissions in their Second Report on Exemption Clauses (Law Com No 69; Scot Law Com No 39, August 1975). Apart from s 8 which is concerned with the avoidance of liability for misrepresentations the controls introduced or restated by Part I of the Act generally apply only to 'business liability' (see s 1(3) and s 14). The scheme of the Act is to render certain exemption clauses or notices void and certain others ineffective except insofar as they satisfy the requirement of reasonableness of s 11 of the Act. The position may be summarised as follows:

Product Liability and Safety Encyclopaedia by C. J. Miller

> Subject to the above and to the exceptions made by s 29 and Sch 1, the following are void: (1) terms or notices which exclude or restrict liability for death or injury caused by negligence (s 2(1)) and certain choice of law clauses (s 27); (ii) 'guarantees' of consumer goods which, whether through a term or a notice, exclude or restrict liability for loss or damage resulting from negligence (s 5); (iii) in contracts for the sale or hire purchase of goods terms which exclude or restrict liability for breach of implied undertakings as to title (s 6(1)), or, as against one who 'deals as consumer' (s 12), breach of implied undertakings as to conformity with description or sample, quality or fitness (s 6(2)); (iv) in other consumer contracts for the supply of goods such as contracts of hire or for work and materials, terms which exclude or restrict liability for breach of implied undertakings as to conformity with description or sample, quality or fitness (s 7(2)); (v) in any such contract within s 2 of the Supply of Goods and Services Act 1982 implied undertakings as to title etc (s 7(3A)). The following contract terms or notices are valid only in so far as they satisfy the requirements of reasonableness of s 11 of the Act:
> (i) terms or notices which exclude or restrict liability for negligence resulting in loss or damage other than death or personal injury (s. 2(2)); (ii) terms which exclude or restrict liability for breach of contract as against one who 'deals as consumer' or on the other's written standard terms (s 3) or which stipulate for an indemnity from one who 'deals as consumer' (s 4); (iii) terms which exclude or restrict liability for misrepresentation (s 8); (iv) in non-consumer contracts (s 12) for the sale or hire purchase of goods terms which exclude or restrict liability for breach of implied undertakings as to conformity with description or sample, quality or fitness (s 6(3)); (v) in other non-consumer contracts for the supply of goods such as contracts of hire or for work and materials terms which exclude or restrict liability for breach of implied undertakings as to conformity with description or sample or quality or fitness (s 7(3)).

The Unfair Contract Terms Act 1977 (as amended by the Sale of Goods Act 1979, the Supply of Goods and Services Act 1982 and the Occupiers' Liability Act 1984)

PART I AMENDMENT OF LAW FOR ENGLAND AND WALES AND NORTHERN IRELAND

Introductory

1. Scope of Part I
(1) For the purposes of this Part of this Act, 'negligence' means the breach—
    (a) of any obligation, arising from the express or implied terms of a contract, to take reasonable care or exercise reasonable skill in the performance of the contract;
    (b) of any common law duty to take reasonable care or exercise reasonable skill (but not any stricter duty);
    (c) of the common duty of care imposed by the Occupiers' Liability Act 1957 or the Occupiers' Liability Act (Northern Ireland) 1957.
(2) This Part of this Act is subject to Part III; and in relation to contracts, the operation of sections 2 to 4 and 7 is subject to the exceptions made by Schedule 1.
(3) In the case of both contract and tort, sections 2 to 7 apply (except where the contrary is stated in section 6 (4)) only to business liability, that is liability for breach of obligations or duties arising—
    (a) from things done or to be done by a person in the course of a business (whether his own business or another's); or
    (b) from the occupation of premises used for business purposes of the occupier;
and references to liability are to be read accordingly but liability of an occupier of premises for breach of an obligation or duty towards a person obtaining access to the premises for recreational or educational purposes, being liability for loss or damage suffered by reason of the dangerous state of the premises, is not a business liability of the occupier unless granting that person such access for the purposes concerned falls within the business purposes of the occupier.
(4) In relation to any breach of duty or obligation, it is immaterial for any purpose of this Part of this Act whether the breach was inadvertent or intentional, or whether liability for it arises directly or vicariously.

Avoidance of liability for negligence, breach of contract, etc

2. Negligence liability
(1) A person cannot by reference to any contract term or to a notice given to persons generally or to particular persons exclude or restrict his liability for death or personal injury resulting from negligence.
(2) In the case of other loss or damage, a person cannot so exclude or restrict his liability for negligence except in so far as the term or notice satisfies the requirement of reasonableness.
(3) Where a contract term or notice purports to exclude or restrict liability for negligence a person's agreement to or awareness of it is not of itself to be taken as indicating his voluntary acceptance of any risk.

3. Liability arising in contract
(1) This section applies as between contracting parties where one of them deals as consumer or on the other's written standard terms of business.
(2) As against that party, the other cannot by reference to any contract term—
    (a) when himself in breach of contract, exclude or restrict any liability of his in respect of the breach; or
    (b) claim to be entitled—
        (i) to render a contractual performance substantially different from that which was reasonably expected of him, or
        (ii) in respect of the whole or any part of his contractual obligation, to render no performance at all,
except in so far as (in any of the cases mentioned above in this subsection) the contract term satisfies the requirement of reasonableness.

4. Unreasonable indemnity clauses
(1) A person dealing as consumer cannot by reference to any contract term be made to indemnify another person (whether a party to the contract or not) in respect of liability that

may be incurred by the other for negligence or breach of contract, except in so far as the contract term satisfies the requirement of reasonableness.

(2) This section applies whether the liability in question—
  (a) is directly that of the person to be indemnified or is incurred by him vicariously;
  (b) is to the person dealing as consumer or to someone else.

Liability arising from sale or supply of goods

5. 'Guarantee' of consumer goods

(1) In the case of goods of a type ordinarily supplied for private use or consumption, where loss or damage—
  (a) arises from the goods proving defective while in consumer use; and
  (b) results from the negligence of a person concerned in the manufacture or distribution of the goods,
liability for the loss or damage cannot be excluded or restricted by reference to any contract term or notice contained in or operating by reference to a guarantee of the goods.

(2) For these purposes—
  (a) goods are to be regarded as 'in consumer use' when a person is using them, or has them in his possession for use, otherwise than exclusively for the purposes of a business; and
  (b) anything in writing is a guarantee if it contains or purports to contain some promise or assurance (however worded or presented) that defects will be made good by complete or partial replacement, or by repair, monetary compensation or otherwise.

(3) This section does not apply as between the parties of a contract under or in pursuance of which possession or ownership of the goods passed.

6. Sale and hire-purchase

(1) Liability for breach of the obligations arising from—
  (a) [section 12 of the Sale of Goods Act 1979] (seller's implied undertakings as to title, etc.);
  (b) section 8 of the Supply of Goods (Implied Terms) Act 1973 (the corresponding thing in relation to hire-purchase).
cannot be excluded or restricted by reference to any contract term.

(2) As against a person dealing as consumer, liability for breach of the obligations arising from—
  (a) [section 13, 14 or 15 of the 1979 Act] (seller's implied undertakings as to conformity of goods with description or sample, or as to their quality or fitness for a particular purpose);
  (b) section 9, 10 or 11 of the 1973 Act (the corresponding thing in relation to hire-purchase),
cannot be excluded or restricted by reference to any contract term.

(3) As against a person dealing otherwise than as consumer, the liability specified in subsection (2) above can be excluded or restricted by reference to a contract term, but only in so far as the term satisfies the requirement of reasonableness.

(4) The liabilities referred to in this section are not only the business liabilities defined by section 1 (3), but include those arising under any contract of sale of goods or hire-purchase agreement.

7. Miscellaneous contracts under which goods pass

(1) Where the possession or ownership of goods passes under or in pursuance of a contract not governed by the law of sale of goods or hire-purchase, subsections (2) to (4) below apply as regards the effect (if any) to be given to contract terms excluding or restricting liability for breach of obligation arising by the implication of law from the nature of the contract.

(2) As against a person dealing as consumer, liability in respect of the goods' correspondence with description or sample, or their quality or fitness for any particular purpose, cannot be excluded or restricted by reference to any such term.

(3) As against a person dealing otherwise than as consumer, that liability can be excluded or restricted by reference to such a term, but only in so far as the term satisfies the requirement of reasonableness.

[(3A) Liability for breach of the obligations arising under section 2 of the Supply of Goods and Services Act 1982 (implied terms about title etc. in certain contracts for the transfer of the property in goods) cannot be excluded or restricted by reference to any such term.]

(4) Liability in respect of—
  (a) the right to transfer ownership of the goods, or give possession; or

(b) the assurance of quiet possession to a person taking goods in pursuance of the contract,

cannot [in a case to which subsection (3A) does not apply] be excluded or restricted by reference to any such term except in so far as the term satisfies the requirement of reasonableness.

(5) This section does not apply in the case of goods passing on a redemption of trading stamps within the Trading Stamps Act 1964 or the Trading Stamps Act (Northern Ireland) 1965.

Other provisions about contracts

8. Misrepresentation

(1) In the Misrepresentation Act 1967, the following is substituted for section 3—

'3. Avoidance of provision excluding liability for misrepresentation

If a contract contains a term which would exclude or restrict—

(a) any liability to which a party to a contract may be subject by reason of any misrepresentation made by him before the contract was made; or

(b) any remedy available to another party to the contract by reason of such a misrepresentation,

that term shall be of no effect except in so far as it satisfies the requirement of reasonableness as stated in section 11(1) of the Unfair Contract Terms Act 1977; and it is for those claiming that the term satisfies the requirement to show that it does.'

(2) The same section is substituted for section 3 of the Misrepresentation Act (Northern Ireland) 1967.

9. Effect of breach

(1) Where for reliance upon it a contract term has to satisfy the requirement of reasonableness, it may be found to do so and be given effect accordingly notwithstanding that the contract has been terminated either by breach or by a party electing to treat it as repudiated.

(2) Where on a breach the contract is nevertheless affirmed by a party entitled to treat it as repudiated, this does not of itself exclude the requirement of reasonableness in relation to any contract term.

10. Evasion by means of secondary contract

A person is not bound by any contract term prejudicing or taking away rights of his which arise under, or in connection with the performance of, another contract, so far as those rights extend to the enforcement of another's liability which this Part of this Act prevents that other from excluding or restricting.

Explanatory provisions

11. The 'reasonableness' test

(1) In relation to a contract term the requirement of reasonableness for the purposes of this Part of this Act, section 3 of the Misrepresentation Act 1967 and section 3 of the Misrepresentation Act (Northern Ireland) 1967 is that the term shall have been a fair and reasonable one to be included having regard to the circumstances which were, or ought reasonably to have been, known to or in the contemplation of the parties when the contract was made.

(2) In determining for the purposes of section 6 or 7 above whether a contract term satisfies the requirement of reasonableness, regard shall be had in particular to the matters specified in Schedule 2 to this Act; but this subsection does not prevent the court or arbitrator from holding, in accordance with any rule of law, that a term which purports to exclude or restrict any relevant liability is not a term of the contract.

(3) In relation to a notice (not being a notice having contractual effect), the requirement of reasonableness under this Act is that it should be fair and reasonable to allow reliance on it, having regard to all the circumstances obtaining when the liability arose or (but for the notice) would have arisen.

(4) Where by reference to a contract term or notice a person seeks to restrict liability to a specified sum of money, and the question arises (under this or any other Act) whether the term or notice satisfies the requirement of reasonableness, regard shall be had in particular (but without prejudice to subsection (2) above in the case of contract terms) to—

(a) the resources which he could expect to be available to him for the purpose of meeting the liability should it arise; and

(b) how far it was open to him to cover himself by insurance.

(5) It is for those claiming that a contract term or notice satisfies the requirement of reasonableness to show that it does.

12. 'Dealing as consumer'
(1) A party to a contract 'deals as consumer' in relation to another party if—
  (a) he neither makes the contract in the course of a business nor holds himself out as doing so; and
  (b) the other party does make the contract in the course of a business; and
  (c) in the case of a contract governed by the law of sale of goods or hire-purchase, or by section 7 of this Act, the goods passing under or in pursuance of the contract are of a type ordinarily supplied for private use or consumption.
(2) But on a sale by auction or by competitive tender the buyer is not in any circumstances to be regarded as dealing as consumer.
(3) Subject to this, it is for those claiming that a party does not deal as consumer to show that he does not.

13. Varieties of exemption clause
(1) To the extent that this Part of this Act prevents the exclusion or restriction of any liability it also prevents—
  (a) making the liability or its enforcement subject to restrictive or onerous conditions;
  (b) excluding or restricting any right to remedy in respect of the liability, or subjecting a person to any prejudice in consequence of his pursuing any such right or remedy;
  (c) excluding or restricting rules of evidence or procedure;
and (to that extent) sections 2 and 5 to 7 also prevent excluding or restricting liability by reference to terms and notices which exclude or restrict the relevant obligation or duty.
(2) But an agreement in writing to submit present or future differences to arbitration is not to be treated under this Part of this Act as excluding or restricting any liability.

14. Interpretation of Part I
In this Part of this Act—
'business' includes a profession and the activities of any government department or local or public authority;
'goods' has the same meaning as in the [Sale of Goods Act 1979];
'hire-purchase agreement' has the same meaning as in the Consumer Credit Act 1974;
'negligence' has the meaning given by section 1(1);
'notice' includes an announcement, whether or not in writing, and any other communication or pretended communication; and
'personal injury' includes any disease and any impairment of physical or mental condition.

[Part II which applies only to Scotland is omitted.]

PART III—PROVISIONS APPLYING TO WHOLE OF UNITED KINGDOM

Miscellaneous

26. International supply contracts
(1) The limits imposed by this Act on the extent to which a person may exclude or restrict liability by reference to a contract term do not apply to liability arising under such a contract as is described in subsection (3) below.
(2) The terms of such a contract are not subject to any requirement of reasonableness under section 3 or 4: and nothing in Part II of this Act shall require the incorporation of the terms of such a contract to be fair and reasonable for them to have effect.
(3) Subject to subsection (4), that description of contract is one whose characteristics are the following—
  (a) either it is a contract of sale of goods or it is one under or in pursuance of which the possession or ownership of goods passes; and
  (b) it is made by parties whose places of business (or, if they have none, habitual residences) are in the territories of different States (the Channel Islands and the Isle of Man being treated for this purpose as different States from the United Kingdom).
(4) A contract falls within subsection (3) above only if either—
  (a) the goods in question are, at the time of the conclusion of the contract, in the course of carriage, or will be carried, from the territory of one State to the territory of another; or

   (b) the acts constituting the offer and acceptance have been done in the territories of different States; or

   (c) the contract provides for the goods to be delivered to the territory of a State other than that within whose territory those acts were done.

27. Choice of law clauses

(1) Where the proper law of a contract is the law of any part of the United Kingdom only by choice of the parties (and apart from that choice would be the law of some country outside the United Kingdom) sections 2 to 7 and 16 to 21 of this Act do not operate as part of the proper law.

(2) This Act has effect notwithstanding any contract term which applies or purports to apply the law of some country outside the United Kingdom, where (either or both)—

   (a) the term appears to the court, or arbitrator or arbiter to have been imposed wholly or mainly for the purpose of enabling the party imposing it to evade the operation of this Act; or

   (b) in the making of the contract one of the parties dealt as consumer, and he was then habitually resident in the United Kingdom, and the essential steps necessary for the making of the contract were taken there, whether by him or by others on his behalf.

(3) [applies to Scotland]

28. Temporary provision for sea carriage of passengers

(1) This section applies to a contract for carriage by sea of a passenger or of a passenger and his luggage where the provisions of the Athens Convention (with or without modification) do not have, in relation to the contract, the force of law in the United Kingdom.

(2) In a case where—

   (a) the contract is not made in the United Kingdom, and

   (b) neither the place of departure nor the place of destination under it is in the United Kingdom,

a person is not precluded by this Act from excluding or restricting liability for loss or damage, being loss or damage for which the provisions of the Convention would, if they had the force of law in relation to the contract, impose liability on him.

(3) In any other case, a person is not precluded by this Act from excluding or restricting liability for that loss or damage—

   (a) in so far as the exclusion or restriction would have been effective in that case had the provisions of the Convention had the force of law in relation to the contract; or

   (b) in such circumstances and to such extent as may be prescribed, by reference to a prescribed term of the contract.

(4) For the purpose of subsection (3)(a), the values which shall be taken to be the official values in the United Kingdom of the amounts (expressed in gold francs) by reference to which liability under the provisions of the Convention is limited shall be such amounts in sterling as the Secretary of State may from time to time by order made by statutory instrument specify.

(5) In this section,—

   (a) the references to excluding or restricting liability include doing any of those things in relation to the liability which are mentioned in section 13 or section 25(3) and (5); and

   (b) 'the Athens Convention' means the Athens Convention relating to the Carriage of Passengers and their Luggage by Sea, 1974; and

   (c) 'prescribed' means prescribed by the Secretary of State by regulations made by statutory instrument;

and a statutory instrument containing the regulations shall be subject to annulment in pursuance of a resolution of either House of Parliament.

29. Saving for other relevant legislation

(1) Nothing in this Act removes or restricts the effect of, or prevents reliance upon any contractual provision which—

   (a) is authorised or required by the express terms or necessary implication of an enactment; or

   (b) being made with a view to compliance with an international agreement to which the United Kingdom is a party, does not operate more restrictively than is contemplated by the agreement.

(2) A contract term is to be taken—

   (a) for the purposes of Part I of this Act, as satisfying the requirement of reasonableness; and

   (b) [applies to Scotland]

if it is incorporated or approved by, or incorporated pursuant to a decision or ruling of, a competent authority acting in the exercise of any statutory jurisdiction or function and is not a term in a contract to which the competent authority is itself a party.

(3) In this section—

'competent authority' means any court, arbitrator or arbiter, government department or public authority;

'enactment' means any legislation (including subordinate legislation) of the United Kingdom or Northern Ireland and any instrument having effect by virtue of such legislation; and

'statutory' means conferred by an enactment.

30.   Obligations under Consumer Protection Acts

(1) In section 3 of the Consumer Protection Act 1961 (provisions against marketing goods which do not comply with safety requirements), after subsection (1) there is inserted—

'(1A) Any term of an agreement which purports to exclude or restrict, or has the effect of excluding or restricting, any obligation imposed by or by virtue of that section, or any liability for breach of such an obligation, shall be void.'

(2) The same amendment is made in section 3 of the Consumer Protection Act (Northern Ireland) 1965.

General

31.   Commencement; amendments; repeals

(1) This Act comes into force on 1 February 1978.

(2) Nothing in this Act applies to contracts made before the date on which it comes into force; but subject to this, it applies to liability for any loss or damage which is suffered on or after that date.

(3) The enactments specified in Schedule 3 to this Act are amended as there shown.

(4) The enactments specified in Schedule 4 to this Act are repealed to the extent specified in column 3 of that Schedule.

32.   Citation and extent

(1) This Act may be cited as the Unfair Contract Terms Act 1977.

(2) Part I of this Act extends to England and Wales and to Northern Ireland; but it does not extend to Scotland.

(3) [applies to Scotland].

(4) This Part of this Act extends to the whole of the United Kingdom.

SCHEDULE 1—SCOPE OF SECTIONS 2 TO 4 AND 7

Section 1(2)

1. Sections 2 to 4 of this Act do not extend to—

   (a) any contract of insurance (including a contract to pay an annuity on human life);

   . . .

2. Section 2(1) extends to—

   (a) any contract of marine salvage or towage;

   (b) any charterparty of a ship or hovercraft; and

   (c) any contract for the carriage of goods by ship or hovercraft;

but subject to this sections 2 to 4 and 7 do not extend to any such contract except in favour of a person dealing as consumer.

3. Where goods are carried by ship or hovercraft in pursuance of a contract which either—

   (a) specifies that as the means of carriage over part of the journey to be covered, or

   (b) makes no provision as to the means of carriage and does not exclude that means,

then sections 2(2), 3 and 4 do not, except in favour of a person dealing as a consumer, extend to the contract as it operates for and in relation to the carriage of the goods by that means.

   . . .

SCHEDULE 2—'GUIDELINES' FOR APPLICATION OF REASONABLENESS TEST

Sections 11(2) and 24(2)

The matters to which regard is to be had in particular for the purposes of sections 6(3), 7(3) and (4), 20 and 21 are any of the following which appear to be relevant—

   (a) the strength of the bargaining positions of the parties relative to each other, taking into account (among other things) alternative means by which the customer's requirements could have been met;

(b) whether the customer received an inducement to agree to the term, or in accepting it had an opportunity of entering into a similar contract with other persons, but without having to accept a similar term;

(c) whether the customer knew or ought reasonably to have known of the existence and extent of the term (having regard, among other things, to any custom of the trade and any previous course of dealing between the parties);

(d) where the term excludes or restricts any relevant liability if some condition is not complied with, whether it was reasonable at the time of the contract to expect that compliance with that condition would be practicable;

(e) whether the goods were manufactured, processed or adapted to the special order of the customer.

[Schedules 3 (Amendment of Enactments) and 4 (Repeals) are omitted.]

NEGLIGENCE LIABILITY

Section 2 of the 1977 Act is based on the recommendations in Part III of the Law Commission's Second Report on Exemption Clauses. The outright 'ban' in s 2(1) of the Act on terms or notices which purport to exclude or restrict liability for death or personal injury resulting from negligence goes beyond the Law Commission's recommendations. The Commission favoured a more selective and sectoral approach which would have covered for example the liability of carriers, car park occupiers and those who operate such mechanical devices as 'Big Dippers' or lifts. The categories might be extended by statutory instrument following a recommendation by the Director General of Fair Trading (see paras 95–97 of the report).

So far as other types of loss or damage are concerned the 'requirement of reasonableness' imposed by s 2(2) of the Act covers a wide range of everyday consumer transactions. Examples include the carriage, warehousing and storage of goods, laundering, dry cleaning, film processing and damage to vehicles and other property in car parks and car washes. In such cases a consumer will be protected normally by s 3 of the Act also. This covers attempts to exclude liability by reference to contract terms (although not notices). Nothing will turn on which section the case is argued under. The following case is of general interest as indicating a broadly favourable approach to a consumer plaintiff in one such everyday transaction.

Woodman v Photo Trade Processing Ltd (1981) (unreported), Judgment of 7 May, Exeter County Court

His Honour Judge Clarke. In this arbitration pursuant to Order 19 of the County Court Rules, Photo Trade Processing Ltd ('PTP') now seek to set aside the award of Mr Registrar Lewis dated 26 June 1980. They also ask for a new trial.

By that award the Learned Registrar had upheld the claim of the Plaintiff, Mr Woodman, in which he alleged that PTP had lost certain photographic films which in June 1979 he had entrusted to a shop in Exeter named Dixons for developing and printing. Dixons at all times were agents for PTP. The loss of Mr Woodman's films was undisputed, but by way of Defence PTP sought to rely upon a clause in their contract with the Plaintiff limiting their liability to the replacement of the lost films with new ones.

In the course of the arbitration the Plaintiff submitted that the alleged clause was of no effect because it did not satisfy the requirement of reasonableness laid down by the Unfair Contract Terms Act 1977 ('The Act'). In upholding that submission the Learned Registrar in his judgment specifically considered and applied the various tests of 'reasonableness' set out in Section 11 and Schedule 2 of the Act, those matters having been drawn to his attention in the course of argument. Before me, however, Mr Meeke for PTP submitted that the terms of Sections 6 & 7 of the Act make Schedule 2 inapplicable to the type of contract in issue in this case. Hence, he argued, there was an error of law on the face of the arbitration award, thereby opening the discretion to set aside the award. (*Meyer v Leanse* [1958] 3 All ER 213). Mr Tench appearing for Mr Woodman (or, to be more accurate, for his personal representatives in view of Mr Woodman's death since the arbitration) agreed with that proposition.

I accept that Schedule 2 does not apply. The only relevant provision is Section 11; Subsection (1) of which requires that the clause should be 'a fair and reasonable one to be included having regard to the circumstances which were, or ought reasonably to have been, known to or in the contemplation of the parties when the contract was made.' There is a specific consideration to which I will refer later in Section 11 (4), but otherwise the question of what is 'fair and reasonable' is at large and undefined in the Act.

In considering that wide question of what is 'fair and reasonable' the 'guidelines' set out in Schedule 2 for other types of contract would be among the matters necessarily needing consideration in this case. But Mr Meeke submitted, and Mr Tench accepted that the Learned Registrar, by treating Section 11(1) and 11(4) and Schedule 2 of the Act as if they were exhaustive of the matters to be considered, might have construed the question of reasonableness too narrowly. Accordingly I exercised my discretion to set aside the award and proceeded to a re-hearing. It is right to say, however, now that I have heard full argument, that I do not think that the Registrar did omit any relevant consideration.

For the purpose of the re-hearing both parties agreed to accept the facts as set out in the Learned Registrar's award without calling any further evidence. I will not repeat those facts except to the extent that I find it necessary to refer to them for the purpose of my decision.

The missing items are alleged to be 23 out of a reel of 36 exposures on 35mm film which Mr Woodman had, by arrangement, taken of a friend's wedding, intending to give them to those friends as a wedding present. He did not, however, reveal the subject matter of the photographs when he handed them in to Dixons, nor did he give any special instructions. All he got back were 13 of the negatives with prints therefrom. This suggests that the 23 negatives somehow became separated and lost during the processing rather than in Dixons shop, but in any event it would (unless explained) constitute a breach of the inevitable implied term that PTP would exercise reasonable care. By Section 1(1) of the Act such a breach is classified as 'negligence.' No explanation was offered as to how these films could have become lost without fault.

The clause relied upon by PTP, and held by the Learned Registrar to have become incorporated in the contract between the parties, was printed on a card measuring 4½ inches square, exhibited on the front of the Dixons shop counter. This card was not produced in evidence, but in view of the number of words which the Registrar held to have been printed upon it, I conclude that the lettering must have been fairly small. I regard myself as bound by the Registrar's finding of fact that that notice was 'adequately displayed' to Mr Woodman; but having regard to the quantity of advertising material usually displayed in photographers' shops I am not surprised that Mr Woodman says he did not see it. I would not wish this judgment to be regarded as any indication that a card of this size would constitute adequate notice except in exceptional circumstances.

The important part of the notice read as follows:—

> 'All photographic materials are accepted on the basis that their value does not exceed the cost of the material itself. Responsibility is limited to the replacement of films. No liability will be accepted, consequential or otherwise, however caused.'

I accept that such a clause, if upheld under the Unfair Contract Terms Act, would be sufficient to exclude liability for any loss including loss by negligence on the part of PTP. It is therefore a 'contract term or notice' within the meaning of Section 2 (2) of the Act which raises the requirement of reasonableness.

Evidence was given before the Registrar that similar exclusion clauses were 'standard practice throughout the trade.' In their Defence PTP plead that it is 'the custom among photographic processors.' In the course of argument Mr Meeke submitted that firms did exist who would, at a cost, carry out film processing and accept liability for their work, but there was no evidence before the Registrar of any such alternative. Specialist firms may exist, but I am bound to conclude on the evidence that Mr Woodman had no realistic alternative.

Any analysis of the clause in question in this case shows that it preserves liability for what may be called the 'tangible loss', namely the value of the film itself, but it excludes liability for the intangible value of the picture itself. That intangible value would vary enormously. A few, such as an owner's photograph of his house or garden, could be re-photographed without difficulty. Most would be in the nature of holiday photographs the loss of which would cause at least disappointment. In some cases, such as the wedding photographs in the present case where no other photographer attended, real distress would be caused by their loss. A few photographs, such as a picture of a loved-one shortly before death, would be almost priceless to grief stricken relatives. In the circumstances of the present case I conclude that virtually all the photographs handed in at Dixons would be of a personal nature rather than for any commercial or industrial use, so the consequence of loss are emotional rather than economic.

The consequences of loss to Mr Woodman consisted of his disappointment in having failed his friends expectations, rather than the disappointment of being unable to see the photographs themselves, but such consequences are all of the same nature. They are all losses of expected enjoyment. On the evidence I conclude that it was foreseeable to PTP that Mr Woodrow would suffer some loss of enjoyment if they lost his films.

. . .

I now turn to consider the 'requirement of reasonableness' in relation to the clause in question. I was asked, particularly by Mr Meeke and to some extent by Mr Tench, if I found this particular clause to be unreasonable, to go further and suggest what type of clause would be reasonable. To some extent I must consider the reasonableness of alternatives in order to throw light upon the reasonableness of the clause in question. But I must stress that it is no part of my function to lay down what type of clause PTP should use. That must be for them to decide.

PTP argue that the clause they use is reasonable, and for the benefit of the public and themselves, because it enables them to operate a cheap mass-production technique. No evidence was adduced as to the extent of their cost savings as a result of the absence of claims and the absence of checking mechanisms to prevent loss, but I suspect that it amounts to more than the 'few pence' on every film suggested by Mr Tench. In these cost-concious days I accept that a cheap mass-production service is desirable, and it is probably good enough for the vast majority of ordinary photographers who could well complain if they have to pay more in order to protect the interests of a minority whose pictures are of greater value.

The Act, however, does not require me to consider only what is reasonable for the majority of the public. I have to consider whether the term in this particular contract is fair and reasonable 'having regard to the circumstances which were, or ought reasonably to have been, known to or in the contemplation of the parties when the contract was made.' Dixons did not know what I would call the 'picture value' of Mr Woodman's photographs, but I conclude that it ought reasonably have been within their contemplation that:—

(1) His photographs might have a high 'picture value', and
(2) He might be entrusting the film to them because he had no alternative.

I was told that there are, as yet, no reported authorities on the Unfair Contract Terms Act itself; but I was referred to three cases which provide some guidance.

Firstly there is *Peek v North Staffordshire Rly Co* (1863) 10 HL Cas 493), a decision on Section 7 of Railway and Canal Traffic Act 1854 which permitted transport undertakings to impose conditions limiting their liability if adjudged by a Court to be just and reasonable. The clause under scrutiny in that case excluded all liability for loss or injury to various categories of fragile goods 'unless declared and insured according to their value.' It is a clause less onerous to the customer than that in the present case to the extent that PTP excluded liability without any option of declaring and insuring a special risk. And yet the House of Lords found the North Staffordshire Railway clause to be unreasonable.

Three main reasons emerge for the decision in *Peek*'s case:—

1 because it excluded liability for the consequences of negligence as well as mere accident,
2 because the railway was in a monopoly situation which realistically forced the customer to agree to their terms of business, and
3 because the only alternatives offered to the customer were either total exclusion of liability or insurance at a fixed rate which the Court regarded as so exorbitant as to compel customers to accept exclusion of liability.

Peek's case is complicated by the obligation laid upon common carriers to carry for reasonable remuneration; but it has strong bearing upon the present case because PTP, by adopting the same terms as the rest of the trade, also offers its customers no choice.

The present case is also similar because of the exclusion of liability for negligence as well as accident, but I do not regard this feature with the same degree of horror as did the House of Lords in *Peek*'s case. The mischief is the same in that the trader is enabled to drop his standards with impunity, but the pressure of public opinion upon traders to maintain standards are stronger than they were in 1863. Furthermore it must be less objectionable to exclude liability for negligence where the items are comparatively small in value. A common carrier may handle cargoes of immensely greater value than any photograph.

The exclusion clause in the present case is marginally more reasonable than that in *Peek*'s case because it at least preserves liability for the 'tangible value' of the films. But it is less reasonable in that it offers no insurance facility whatever. Insurance is a matter that I am specifically required to consider by Section 11 (4) of the Act. No doubt PTP could insure, but in the circumstances of this particular trade where no claims are likely to be really heavy, it would be more reasonable to satisfy claims out of their resources boosted by increased charges to their customers.

If there is to be insurance, it would have to be remembered that only the customer knows the 'intangible value' of his films. A system could be devised whereby a customer discloses the insurance value of his films when he hands them in for processing, but I do not regard insurance as a requirement of reasonableness in the film processing trade. The customer cannot buy a replacement photograph with his insurance moneys. What he really wants in some assurance that the processor will take extra care not to lose his more precious pictures.

Next I was referred to *Levison v Patent Steam Carpet Cleaning Co Ltd* [1977] 3 All ER 498, where Lord Denning, MR, anticipating the introduction of the Unfair Contract Terms Act, held that a limitation of liability clause was unreasonable because the cleaning company had not specifically drawn it to the attention of the customer and advised him to insure. Comparing that with the present case, Mr Woodman's attention was not specifically drawn to the exclusion clause, nor was he advised to procure his own insurance (not that insurance would readily be available to him in such circumstances).

Thirdly I was referred to A *Schroeder Music Publishing Co Ltd v Macaulay* [1974] 1 WLR 1308 where Lord Diplock, dealing with a contract alleged to be an unreasonable restraint of trade, posed as a test of fairness the question of 'whether the restrictions are both reasonably necessary for the protection of the legitimate interests of the promisee and commensurate with the benefits secured to the promisor under the contract.'

Applying that test to the present case, I think that PTP do have a legitimate interest in keeping their costs down in order to remain competitive in the trade. But it cannot be regarded as reasonably necessary to protect that interest by compelling everybody, including the few who have high value photographs, to take their chance with the PTP mass-production system. For the majority of customers the lower prices resulting from excluded liability may be a commensurate benefit, but even then the balance is uncertain because he does not know the extent of the risk he runs to get those lower prices.

No evidence was offered as to the frequency with which films are lost during the PTP process. However, on this particular contract with Mr Woodman the balance must be to his disadvantage because of the importance of his particular photographs.

I conclude therefore that the clause in question is unreasonable having regard to almost all the criteria mentioned in the three authorities I have referred to. I have also considered the criteria set out in Schedule 2 of the Act, but in the circumstances of this case they seem to add nothing new, except that only to the extent that account should be taken of 'alternative means by which the customers' requirements could have been met.' It is the feasibility of those alternatives which I must now consider.

Mr Tench suggested three possible alternatives, one of which was that PTP should accept all liability for negligence but exclude it for 'mishap.' This would certainly be reasonable from the customer's point of view, provided that the burden of proving 'mishap' falls upon PTP once the customer has proved the loss of films entrusted to them. But there would be few such 'mishaps' and in practice it would be virtually equivalent to the acceptance of full liability. As such I think it leans unreasonably against PTP.

A further suggestion by Mr Tench was that there should be some standardised level of compensation for the loss of 'picture-value' in every case. For example, 10 times the film cost or processing cost. I was referred to the 'Code of Practice for the Photographic Industry,' and paragraph 47 of that code states 'The Consumer may be informed of the reasonable compensation offered in the event of a film being lost or damaged by the processor or retailer.' This appears to envisage some sort of pre-arranged formula for compensation (another example of which is paragraph 76 which suggests a 'refund' as appropriate where developing and printing work is considered unsatisfactory because of an irreparable defect). However, I do not think that such a system, by itself, can be fair and reasonable in this trade because of the degree of uniformity in film costs and processing charges. In some industries servicing charges vary widely according to the delicacy or amount of work needing to be done, and in those instances compensation calculated as a multiple of servicing charges would achieve a sort of rough justice. But photographic film is reasonably uniform in price, and the developing and printing process is more or less uniform in cost. Compensation as a multiple of either figure would therefore also fall within a narrow range, and what is fair to the bulk of customers would be less than fair to a minority.

The Code of Practice appears to recognise this difficulty in that paragraph 49 adds a further recommendation for the benefit of that minority. This paragraph reads:—

'The Retailer will advise the laboratory if an order being placed for processing is of exceptional value or importance, before the order is accepted, provided he has been informed by the consumer. There may be a special service combined with a higher price.'

The authors of the Code therefore do envisage the need for additional care in some cases, and it is that element that is totally lacking in the PTP terms of business. The so-called 'Special Service' was Mr Tench's third suggestion. He called it a 'two-tier System' of a normal service with total exclusion of liability and a special service at a higher charge with full acceptance of liability.

Even if such a special service were to provide for a standardised level of compensation at an appropriately high level to suit the needs of the minority, such a system has all the benefits to the customer of giving him a choice. It presents him with an alternative where he can reasonably expect more than normal care to be taken of his photographs.

But it is not necessarily the case that PTP should have to set up such a special service for themselves. If Mr Meeke is right and specialised laboratories do exist who accept liability and who are accessible to the general public, then PTP only have to refer their customers who want it to that laboratory. Such a system would certainly require that the choice be brought to the attention of all customers. Furthermore the Special Service option would have to be identified (ie name and address) and made convenient so that the customer is not indirectly compelled to accept the normal service.

Not many customers would opt for such a special service at a higher price (although Mr Woodman might well have been among that few if he had had the option) and I conclude that it would still leave ample scope for PTP to continue its low-cost mass-production technique for ordinary holiday photography.

In the light of the Code of Practice I reach the conclusion that some such form of two-tier system is not only reasonable but practicable. Accordingly PTP (on whom the burden lies under Section 11(5) of the Act) have failed to persuade me that the clause which they applied to Mr Woodman's contract satisfies the statutory test of reasonableness.

It remains for me to consider the question of damages. It seems to me that the disappointment and distress suffered by Mr Woodman was quite exceptional and yet well within the range of what was foreseeable to PTP. I would not differ from the view of the Learned Registrar that the sum of £75 is appropriate.

In accordance with an arrangement with Counsel I will not state what order as to costs I consider appropriate in the absence of argument on the point. My proposal on the matter will only become an order if neither party has, within 21 days, given notice of an intention to argue it.

I appreciate that the Defendants succeeded in persuading me that the arbitration award should be set aside, but in the event I conclude that the error of law did not invalidate either the outcome of the litigation or the processes by which the Learned Registrar reached his decision. Costs should follow the event. The Plaintiff should have his costs on Scale 3.

It was a case involving difficult questions of law where the assistance of Solicitor and Counsel was invaluable, and I am indebted to them both. The Registrar will have his discretion on taxation.

NOTE

The facts of *Levison v Patent Steam Carpet Cleaning Co Ltd* [1978] QB 69, [1977] 3 All ER 498, CA, are set out above p 131.

Questions

1. Should the printed card have been regarded as giving adequate notice of the relevant provisions?

2. Consider the following cases:

(1) Al takes his cashmere coat for which he has recently paid £200 to the

Topclass Cleaners for cleaning. He is handed a ticket which states that 'All clothes are accepted for cleaning subject to our standard conditions'. He does not ask what these standard conditions are. When he comes to collect the coat he is informed that owing to a fault in the cleaning process it has been irreparably damaged. The 'standard conditions' limit liability to £20 in the case of any one item.

Advise Al whether the conditions form part of his contract with Topclass. Consider also the position if the standard conditions had been displayed (at some length) behind the counter but Al had not delayed the Saturday morning queue by stopping to read them.

(2) Fastprint Films advertises its film processing service as follows: 'Send Fastprint Films your pictures and you need never have the bother of buying another film again . . . That's because for each film you send us, we'll give you a free film back . . . with your developed prints'. This statement is contained on the envelopes used by customers to send their films to Fastprint. The envelopes also contain the following statement in somewhat smaller print:

> **IMPORTANT:** We seek to take every care of photographic material in our possession but if it should be lost or damaged our liability is limited to the cost of the unexposed film plus the refund of the processing charge and postage. Except as above all liability for any loss or damage, including consequential loss, however caused (even if it is our fault) is excluded. If you consider your film is of exceptional value, please arrange your own insurance.

Cannon sends six films to Fastprint for processing. The work is done satisfactorily and he receives six free films along with his developed prints. Cannon then leaves for his holiday of a lifetime, touring the USA. He uses the six films to take pictures of his wife against a background of the Grand Canyon and other unforgettable sights. On returning to England he posts the films to Fastprint for developing, using Fastprint's envelopes. Owing to Fastprints carelessness the films are damaged when being developed. Cannon has not arranged his own insurance and Fastprint is relying on its limitation clause. Cannon seeks your advice as to (i) the terms of his contract with Fastprint and (ii) whether the limitation clause is binding on him.

Advise Cannon.

Consider also the position if the cause of the unsatisfactory results lay in a fault in the films which had been supplied.

(3) The Downtown Garage displays the following notice in a prominent position in front of the car wash on its premises: 'No liability whatsoever can be accepted for any damage to cars using this facility whether such damage is caused by a malfunction of the equipment or otherwise. All aerials must be fully retracted'. Art forgets to retract his radio aerial and it is damaged beyond repair. Bert's back windscreen is broken when a malfunction in the equipment causes it to go out of control.

Advise Art and Bert.

Waldron-Kelly v British Railways Board (1981) (unreported), 17 March, Stockport County Court

The plaintiff's claim was for damages for breach of contract or negligence following the defendants' loss of a suitcase which was to have been carried by rail from Stockport to Haverford West. The cost of carriage at "owner's risk" was £6.03 and the evidence suggested that the suitcase had been put on the train to Crewe and not seen thereafter. The plaintiff claimed agreed special damages of £320.32 and a further sum for inconvenience and stress arising out of the loss of the luggage. Having stated the facts of the case His Honour Judge Brown QC continued:

The questions raised on these facts can I think be best identified by reference to part of the judgment of Denning LJ (as he then was) in *J Spurling Ltd v Bradshaw* [1956] 1 WLR 461 at 466

'Another thing to remember about these exempting clauses is that in the ordinary way the burden is on the Bailee to bring himself within the exception. A Bailor, by pleading and presenting his case properly, can always put on the Bailee the burden of proof. In the case of non-delivery, for instance, all he need plead is the contract and failure to deliver on demand. That puts on the Bailee the burden of proving either loss without his fault (which, of course, would be a complete answer at common law) or, if it was due to his fault, it was a fault from which he is excused by the exempting clause:'

This was expressly followed by Orr LJ and Sir David Cairns in *Levison v Patent Steam Carpet Cleaning Co Ltd* [1977] 3 All ER 498. The issues then are:
1. Have the Defendants proved that the loss was without their fault? The answer on the evidence must be no. Indeed the arrangements described in the evidence for the secure carriage of a suitcase, which was obviously an attraction to a thief, I regard as unsatisfactory, although no express findings of failure to take reasonable care or negligence causative of the loss can be made.
2. On the basis that the loss was the fault of the Defendants as common carriers who have not delivered the article on demand and who have not proved that it was not their fault, is that a fault from which they are excluded by an exemption clause?

This raises the only point of substance in the case. The contract is one to which the Unfair Contract Terms Act 1977 applies and however one looks at the various factors which are in point, the question comes back to this: Have the Defendants shown that the terms of their contract satisfy the requirement of reasonableness within the meaning of the Act?

The contract is contained in the Defendants' 'General Conditions for Carriage of Goods'. Clause 5B states

'Where goods are accepted by the Board for carriage at Owner's risk the Board shall not be liable for any loss or misdelivery of or damage or delay to the goods except upon proof by the Trader that the same was caused by the wilful misconduct of the Board. Provided that the Board's liability for non-delivery of a consignment or of any separate package forming part of a consignment (not being attributable to fire or to an accident to a train or vehicle) shall be determined as if the goods had been accepted for carriage at the Board's risk'.

Clause 5A(i) contains a proviso namely:

'Where loss, misdelivery or damage arises and the Board have failed to prove that they used all reasonable foresight and care in the carriage of the goods the Board shall not be relieved from liability for such loss, misdelivery or damage;'

Clause 6 sets out the calculation which by the weight of 18 kilogrammes (the weight of the suitcase) produces an agreed figure of £27.00. Liability is limited by that clause to that amount. The consignment note signed by Mrs Waldron-Kelly as Agent for her husband contains in bold type 'Goods (other than dangerous goods) carried at owner's risk'. Both the Plaintiff and his wife knew these words appeared on the documents. Mrs Waldron-Kelly knew what they meant, namely that the Board would disclaim liability for loss, knew about insuring luggage because she had insured luggage on a holiday to Newquay two years earlier but no one mentioned insurance and she forgot about it when the suitcase was sent by rail. This is not however decisive of the matter . . .

Judge Brown then quoted from sections 2(3) and (2), 3, 11(1) and (4) of the Unfair Contract Terms Act 1977 and continued:

In my judgment, the limitation of liability terms do not satisfy the requirement of reasonableness. The parties do not have similar bargaining strength, and on the evidence had other companies been employed, the Plaintiff would have faced similar but not identical exemption clauses, and no great advantage was to be had in 'shopping around'. The resources of the Defendants are obviously substantial and the Defendants could if they chose cover themselves by insurance and by appropriately weighted charges in respect of a consignment of personal luggage. Figures were given by Mr Steel of the carriage of 100,000,000 items over 30,000 miles of track in the course of a year. An exercise had been carried out some years ago to assess the increased cost of insurance. To increase the amount payable 10 fold would require a 15% increase in charges. These figures are not as helpful as they might be since Mr Steel's evidence was that the bulk of the Defendants' traffic is commercial, and proportionately the amount of passenger luggage is very small. It is the passenger luggage however which is particularly attractive to the opportunist thief and in my view calls for separate treatment in the Board's contractual arrangement. The Board's general conditions give the strong impression of being geared to commercial business eg the consignor is called 'the Trader'.

For ordinary domestic passengers the exception can work unreasonably and on the facts of this case I am not prepared to hold that the Board has discharged the burden on them of showing reasonableness.

It was argued for the Board that the result would make the Board insurers. I do not agree. The effect of the 1977 Act is to prevent the Board from escaping from the consequences of its own negligence or want of care in a consumer case.

. . .

Accordingly in my judgment the Defendants cannot rely on the exemption clause and the Plaintiffs are entitled to their special damages claim of £302.32. So far as their claim for inconvenience and distress over the loss of the luggage is concerned, I find this to be too remote as likewise the claim in respect of the holiday, and I award nothing under this head.

NOTES

1. In another case involving lost luggage Mr Assistant Recorder Alan Hitching held that regulation 6(1)(a) which created a relationship between the weight of the article consigned and the compensation to be paid was 'reasonable': see *Wight v British Railways Board* (11 October (1982) Bloomsbury and Marylebone County Court).
2. Since January 1983 British Rail's conditions have been changed to incorporate the following provision:

Section III—conditions of carriage of passengers' luggage

. . .

5. Liability
(1) Subject to the succeeding paragraphs of this condition and to the succeeding conditions of this Section the Board shall be liable for loss of or from or for damage or delay to luggage brought on to premises or taken into the trains of the Board upon proof that such loss, damage or delay was caused by the neglect or default of the Board, or their staff. Provided that when luggage is being carried in the guard's or luggage van the Board shall be liable for such loss, damage or delay unless they prove that it was not caused by the neglect or default of the Board, or their staff.
(2) In the event of the Board being liable under these conditions such liability shall in respect of any one claim:—
    (a) be limited to £500 per passenger; and
    (b) be based on the assessed value of the luggage.
(3) The Board shall not in any event be liable:—
    (a) for the loss of or from or for damage or delay to any luggage caused by—
        (i) its being improperly or insufficiently packed or labelled, or
        (ii) its comprising or containing any fragile or brittle article or any article liable to be broken and to damage any other article;
    (b) for loss of or from or for damage or delay to any luggage caused by the act, neglect or default of the passenger;

(c) for loss of or from or for damage or delay to any passenger's luggage which does not travel in the same train as the passenger unless the Board would apart from this paragraph of this condition be liable and either—
  (i) such luggage is carried on the terms that the passenger is not required to accompany it, or
  (ii) the passenger's failure to accompany it is due to the neglect or default of the Board or their staff;

(d) for loss of or from or for damage or delay to any luggage which is due to the failure of the passenger to comply with any of the Board's conditions;

(e) for loss of or from or for damage or delay to any luggage unless the same occurred on the Board's trains, road vehicles or premises and then only subject to the conditions applicable thereto;

(f) for indirect or consequential loss or damage.

LIABILITY ARISING IN CONTRACT

Section 3 of the 1977 Act is potentially of considerable importance in consumer transactions, especially in relation to the holiday trade. The section, which applies inter alia where one party 'deals as consumer' is based on recommendations in the Law Commission's Second Report on Exemption Clauses (Law Com No 69, 1975) paras 143–146 especially. Although s 3(2)(a) presupposes a breach of contract by the other contracting party, s 3(2)(b) does not. Rather it is concerned with a contracting party who so defines his obligations as to leave himself considerable latitude in the manner of performing them. Here there is a difficult distinction to be drawn between acceptable precision in defining a limited obligation and a clause which prima facie falls within the control of the subsection. The Law Commission provides the following example for the former type of case in para 143 of its report:

> If a decorator agrees to paint the outside woodwork of a house except the garage doors, no-one can seriously regard the words of exception as anything but a convenient way of defining the obligation; it would surely make no difference if the promise were to paint the outside woodwork with a clear proviso that the contractor was not obliged to paint the garage doors, or if there were a definition clause brought to the promisee's attention saying that 'outside woodwork' did not include the garage doors. Such provisions do not . . . deprive the promisee of a right of a kind which social policy requires that he should enjoy, nor do they, like the provisions excluding liability for breach of contractual obligations. . . give the promisor the advantage of appearing to promise more than he is in fact promising.

A probable example of the latter situation is to be found in a case decided well before the coming into force of the 1977 Act but which is still helpful as indicating a situation where s 3(2)(b) might now be applicable. Although the plaintiffs were travel agents they might just as easily have been disappointed holiday-makers.

For further discussion of the distinction between clauses which define obligations and those which provide defences see generally Coote *Exception Clauses* (1964) Chs 1 and 8 especially; Yates *Exclusion Clauses in Contracts* (2nd edn, 1982) Ch 4, and compare the speeches of Lord Wilberforce and Lord Diplock in *Photo Production Ltd v Securicor Transport Ltd* [1980] AC 827, [1980] 1 All ER 556, HL.

Anglo-Continental Holidays Ltd v Typaldos Lines (London) Ltd [1967] 2 Lloyd's Rep 61, Court of Appeal

This was an appeal by the defendants, Typaldos Lines (London) Ltd, from a decision of his Honour Judge Herbert at Westminster County Court ordering them to pay £447 10s damages to the plaintiffs, Anglo-Continental Holidays Ltd, for breach of contract in connection with a holiday cruise in August, 1965. The facts appear in the judgment of Lord Denning MR.

Lord Denning MR: The plaintiffs are a firm of travel agents. The defendants are shipowners who run cruises in the Mediterranean. In November, 1964, the travel agents made a booking with the shipowners. They booked 10 cabins on a ship called the *Atlantica* for a round trip starting on Aug 12, 1965. The *Atlantica* was a large ship of 22,000 tons built in 1931. She was to start from Venice and go to various places in Greece and on to Israel. In particular, she was to go to Haifa and stay there two days. On one of those days there was to be an excursion to Jerusalem and on the next day a full-day excursion to Galilee. The ship was to get back to Venice after a 14 days' cruise.

The travel agents have a considerable connection with the Jewish community. They arranged for a party of young Jewish boys and girls, with two leaders—in all 28 people—to go on this trip in the Mediterranean for their holidays in August, 1965. But there was trouble because the defendants did not issue the tickets. The plaintiffs made several inquiries and the defendants said for some time it would be all right. But then came a bombshell. About a week before the holiday was to begin, the shipowners told the travel agents there had been an error in the bookings. They were sorry but they could not take this group on the *Atlantica*. Instead they were ready to give them good cabins on another ship called the *Angelika*. The *Angelika* was to leave on the same day and was to do the same itinerary, but she was going to omit two short calls at Split and Izmir.

The travel agents were very upset. They did not know what to do. At first they wrote letters to the young people suggesting that they might accept this new proposal. But on the very next day they had second thoughts. Some of the group had begun to complain. The travel agents then decided that it would not be right to accept the new proposal at all. So they cancelled the arrangement altogether: and they claimed damages against the shipowners.

It appears that the proffered ship, the *Angelika*, was much inferior to the *Atlantica*. She was a very old ship built in 1910, and was only 9000 tons, much smaller than the *Atlantica* and she had not got the swimming pools or accommodation such as the *Atlantica* had. Most important of all, the *Angelika* did not go to Haifa for two whole days. She was only there for some eight hours. That was only time enough to go for a short trip to Tiberias. There would not be time to go to Tel-Aviv and Jerusalem.

In answer to the claim the shipowners relied on a clause in the handbook which they issued to travel agents. It said:

Steamers, Sailing Dates, Rates and Itineraries
are subject to change without prior notice.

The scope of this clause is of some importance: because we are told it is the first time it has been considered by the Courts in relation to passengers.

Let me say at once that I have some doubt whether this clause formed part of the contract. It is printed on the back of a handbook which gives an account of all the voyages which were going to take place in the coming year. It is mixed up with clauses which are plainly not contractual, such as:

'All passengers are required to possess valid passports . . .'

These clauses may be said to be only notes for the information of those about to travel: and not contractual conditions at all.

We were shown, however, specimen passenger tickets issued by the steamship line. These tickets contain (in small print, of course) equally wide conditions which purport to enable the shipowners to change the ship or the sailing dates, or to omit itinerary ports, and the like. (But not, it appears, the rates chargeable.) The travel agents must have seen these tickets, and in the circumstances I am prepared to assume that the clause did have contractual force.

In my opinion a steamship company cannot rely on a clause of this kind so as to alter the substance of the transaction. For instance, they could not say: 'We will change you from this fine modern ship to an old tramp'. Nor could they say: 'We are putting the sailing dates back a week'. Nor could they say: 'We are taking you to the Piraeus instead of to Haifa'. The law on the subject is settled by the cases starting with *Glynn v Margetson & Co* [1893] AC 351, and finishing with *Sze Hai Tong Bank Ltd v Rambler Cycle Co Ltd* [1959] AC 576, [1959] 2 Lloyd'd Rep 114 [see also [1959] 3 All ER 182]. No matter how wide the terms of the clause, the Courts will limit it and modify it to the extent necessary to enable effect to be given to the main object and intent of the contract.

Applied to this case, we have to ask ourselves: Was the proposed trip by the *Angelika* in substance a performance of the contract or was it a serious departure from it? To my mind there is only one answer. It was a radical departure. The change over from the 22,000-ton *Atlantica* (with two swimming pools and lots of accommodation) to this small old 'crate' (as one of the witnesses called the *Angelika*) was itself a substantial departure. But most important of all was the shortened time at Haifa. The climax of the trip for these Jewish boys and girls was two days at Haifa, whereas they only were to have eight hours. The defendants cannot excuse it by reliance on the clause.

I am quite satisfied that the steamship company were guilty of a breach of their contract. They had, as we now know, heavily over-booked. They had too many people for the *Atlantica* and they tried to switch their group over to the *Angelika*. They had no right to do this. The travel agents were entitled to cancel the booking and are entitled to damages.

It was suggested that, in mitigation of damages, the travel agents ought to have accepted the proffered cabins on the *Angelika,* but I do not think that it would be reasonable to expect them to do so.

The remaining question is: How much damages? The travel agents are entitled to damages for the loss of profit of £377 10s and £20 for calls and postage. They also claim damages for loss of custom or goodwill. The Judge put it as reputation. He awarded a sum of £50 on this head. The steamship company challenge this award of £50.

It is most unusual in a case of breach of contract for damages to be given for loss of goodwill. But in principle I see no reason why it should not be given if it is a loss such as might be reasonably foreseen to be a consequence of the breach. In this case I think it was reasonably foreseeable. A cancellation at the last moment would affect the goodwill and standing of the travel agents. The only difficulty is proof of loss. There was some proof of general loss of business but that was all. The Judge said this:

> 'I think that this is too vague to prove special damage. But some loss of the plaintiffs' reputation can, I think, be assumed to have flowed in the ordinary course from the defendants' breach . . .'

He awarded £50 as a reasonable sum. I do not think it is necessary in cases of this kind to prove any specific loss of business. If the breach is such as to be calculated to cause loss of goodwill, the Judge can assign a reasonable sum as damages without requiring positive proof of loss. I think the sum of £50 was justifiable in the circumstances of this case.

In my view the appeal should be dismissed.

Lord Justice Davies: I agree in every respect with my Lord's judgment and do not wish to add anything.

Lord Justice Russell: I assume (though I am not sure on the point) that the reference to the **'Steamers, Sailing Dates, Rates and Itineraries'** on the back of the brochure did form part of the contract between the parties. Nevertheless a reasonable construction must be put upon such a term, and as a matter of construction the defendants were not enabled thereby to alter the substance of the arrangement. Whether they attempted to do so must be, in a sort of package deal like this, a question of degree and perhaps to some extent of general impression. But in my view a combination of all the matters which were in fact involved in the substitution of the *Angelika* for the *Atlantica* together did constitute an alteration of the substance of the arrangement . . .

[His Lordship then considered the question of damages for loss of goodwill, agreeing with the County Court Judge, and continued]:

I would only add this. The case below went really mainly on the assumption that the so-called special condition, that the

Steamers, Sailing Dates, Rates and Itineraries

are subject to change without prior notice was an exemption clause, and the learned County Court Judge treated it as an exemption clause. Then it was sought to find out if there had been a breach of a fundamental term. With deference, I think the learned County Court Judge was wrongly led into that approach. It is not an exemption clause, as is pointed out. It is a clause under which the actual contractual liability may be defined, and not one which will excuse from the actual contractual liability. In the end of the day the approach as to the scope of the clause may not be substantially different. As I have said, I prefer to state it as being a matter of construction of a general clause, and the propounder of that clause cannot be enabled thereby to alter the substance of the arrangement.

I agree that the appeal fails.

The appeal was accordingly dismissed, with costs.

Question

Did Lord Denning MR and Russell LJ approach the 'subject to change without prior notice' clause in the same way? If not which approach is correct?

NOTES

For a not dissimilar example (again where the facts occurred before the coming into force of the 1977 Act) see *Askew v Intasun North Ltd* [1980] CLY 637 (Judge Stretton: Ashby de la Zouche County Court: clause in the defendants' brochure entitling them to change the place of holiday insufficient to provide protection as being worded inadequately).

2. The following term is included in the conditions of a shipping company here called XYZ:

9. Alteration of the contract

(1) Every reasonable effort will be made to adhere to the advertised route and timetable but any route or port may be altered or omitted or times or dates changed for any cause which XYZ and/or the Master of the Ship in their absolute discretion shall consider to be just and reasonable.

(2) XYZ has the right to charge the fare in force on the date of sailing. In the case of a return booking, the fare payable shall be that in force on the date of sailing of the return voyage. Where such fare is more than that shown on the ticket the difference must be paid before the Passenger embarks. For the purposes of these Conditions the word 'fare' shall include any surcharge imposed by XYZ up to the date of sailing.

(3) XYZ and/or the Master of the Ship may at any time, if in their absolute discretion they consider it necessary to do so, transfer the Passenger from one berth to another adjusting the fare accordingly.

(4) A Passenger shall not have the right to exclusive occupancy of a cabin with two or more berths unless he has paid the full supplement for exclusive occupation.

Questions

1. Is it likely that the above conditions would be effective to enable the company to (i) omit a port which was a major attraction or (ii) transfer a passenger from first-class to 'steerage' without being in breach of its contractual obligations?

2. What is the effect of the following: (i) a notice outside a cricket ground, 'Play Cannot be Guaranteed: No Refunds', (ii) a statement in an opera company's booking conditions, 'The Management Reserves the Right to Make Changes in the Cast Without Notice', (iii) a label sewn into a blouse stating: 'Dry Clean Only' and (iv) a notice in a china shop: 'Breakages must be Paid For'? (See also s 13 of the Unfair Contract Terms Act, above p 242).

Problem

In the light of ss 2, 3 and 4 of the 1977 Act and the extract from the Law Reform (Frustrated Contracts) Act 1943 printed below, consider the following:

The standard form booking conditions of the Moneypenny Travel Company which operates its own hotels provide in part as follows:

Although Moneypenny Travel Company (hereinafter Moneypenny) always uses its best endeavours to provide its valued customers with a peaceful and enjoyable holiday, all bookings are expressly subject to the following conditions:

(i) Moneypenny cannot accept liability for death, personal injury or inconvenience caused to or suffered by its customers, howsoever caused;

(ii) in the event of loss of or damage to customers' luggage Moneypenny's liability is limited to £20 per suitcase or similar container. All other liability for damage to customers' property is hereby expressly excluded;

(iii) in booking with Moneypenny, customers hereby undertake to indemnify the company in the event of injury or damage being caused by Moneypenny's employees or agents when dealing with customers' property;

(iv) although Moneypenny endeavours to accommodate clients in hotels which they have specified it reserves the right to use other hotels at its absolute discretion;

(v) in the event of Moneypenny being obliged to cancel the arrangements for a holiday by virtue of events wholly outside its control it is regretted that because of its commitments to airlines and foreign operators no refunds can be made and no compensation paid.

Bond and Goldfinger have booked a holiday on these conditions and they seek your advice in respect of the following matters:

Bond's first complaint is that he was not housed in the Sunny Hotel, as he had specified on the booking form, and which has splendid views over the mountains, but rather in the Hotel Poubelle which has an uninterrupted view over the local rubbish dump. It seems that the Sunny Hotel was overbooked. He adds that when dining in the Poubelle's restaurant a waiter stumbled and poured hot fat down his neck, burning him severely and ruining his expensive suit. He complains also that one of his suitcases was lost in transit and that the value of the suitcase and its contents was £500. He adds that, to compound his problems, one of Moneypenny's porters dropped his (Bond's) other suitcase on the toe of another client, the well-known ballet dancer, Dr No, causing No severe bruising. Moneypenny has paid £500 compensation to Dr No and is now claiming this sum from Bond.

Goldfinger explains that twelve hours before his departure time English air traffic controllers announced a strike of indefinite duration with the result that his flight was cancelled. Moneypenny had offered alternative travel facilities by rail and coach but it was agreed that this would allow for only four nights at the hotel rather than the six originally contracted for. Goldfinger had declined the offer and Moneypenny had declined to make any refund of the full cost of the holiday (£500) which has been paid in advance, still less to offer compensation.

Advise Bond and Goldfinger generally, and with particular reference to the *precise* source of any statutory protection which may be available to them when Moneypenny Travel Company is relying on its standard form booking conditions.

(The Law Reform Frustrated Contracts Act 1943 provides in part as follows:

1. Adjustment of rights and liabilities of parties to frustrated contracts.

(1) Where a contract governed by English law has become impossible of performance or been otherwise frustrated, and the parties thereto have for that reason been discharged from the further performance of the contract, the following provisions of this section shall, subject to the provisions of section two of this Act, have effect in relation thereto.

(2) All sums paid or payable to any party in pursuance of the contract before the time when the parties were so discharged (in this Act referred to as 'the time of discharge') shall, in the

case of sums so paid, be recoverable from him as money received by him for the use of the party by whom the sums were paid, and, in the case of sums so payable, cease to be so payable:

Provided that, if the party to whom the sums were so paid or payable incurred expenses before the time of discharge in, or for the purpose of, the performance of the contract, the court may, if it considers it just to do so having regard to all the circumstances of the case, allow him to retain or, as the case may be, recover the whole or any part of the sums so paid or payable, not being an amount in excess of the expenses so incurred.

. . .

(4) In estimating, for the purposes of the foregoing provisions of this section, the amount of any expenses incurred by any party to the contract, the court may, without prejudice to the generality of the said provisions, include such sum as appears to be reasonable in respect of overhead expenses and in respect of any work or services performed personally by the said party.)

(See generally Andrew Tettenborn (1979) NLJ 62).

GUARANTEES OF GOODS

General concern about the misleading nature of some guarantees was apparent from the extracts from the Law Commission's First Report on Exemption Clauses in Contracts (Law Com No 24) printed above pp 236–38. The problems were recognised also in the Molony Committee report of 1962 (Cmnd 1781, paras 474–78 especially) which said with particular reference to the so-called guarantees then current in the motor trade that:

> In return for discretionary, limited and unenforceable promises of attention to defects of manufacture, the consumer is induced unknowingly to forfeit the only right he might be able to maintain against the manufacturer; as well as apparently conceding his Sale of Goods Acts rights against the retailer.

Of course there are problems of a more general nature associated with 'guarantees' and reference is made to these elsewhere (see above pp 46–52).

Section 5 of the 1977 Act nullifies in the circumstances specified any effect which 'guarantees' of consumer goods might otherwise have had as exclusion clauses in the relationship between manufacturers and the consumers of their goods.

Question

It has been suggested by some commentators (see eg Yates *Exclusion Clauses in Contracts,* pp 136–37) that this may sometimes coincidentally render unenforceable any additional obligations which a manufacturer would otherwise have been regarded as undertaking vis-à-vis consumers.

Consider why s 5 might have this effect.

SALE AND RELATED TRANSACTIONS: DEALING AS CONSUMER

Many consumer transactions will fall within ss 6 and 7 of the 1977 Act, thereby giving complete protection against exemption clauses to anyone who 'deals as consumer' (see s 12 of the Act). Such transactions include contracts of sale and hire-purchase (s 6) and a wide range of other contracts whereby the property or possession in goods is transferred to consumers (s 7). This latter category includes contracts for work and materials and contracts of hire. Where the transferee does not 'deal as consumer' any such exemption clause must satisfy the 'reasonableness' test (s 11). The notion of dealing as consumer was considered in the following case.

Peter Symmons & Co v Cook (1981) 31 March (Lexis Transcript), (1981) 131 NLJ 758 Queen's Bench Divisional Court

The facts of this case are stated more fully, above p 77, in the context of implied terms in contracts of sale. Here it is sufficient to recall that the plaintiffs were a firm of surveyors comprising two partners, Mr Symmons and Mr Buckley. The firm had bought a Rolls Royce car from the defendant motor dealer for the use of Mr Symmons. Having discussed a preliminary issue the trial court judge continued:

Mr R. Rougier QC: . . . The second preliminary point concerns the nature of the sale. Were the Plaintiffs 'dealing as consumers' within the meaning of s 12 of the Unfair Contract Terms Act, 1977? For if so, then by virtue of s 6 of that Act, any implied terms arising by virtue of s 14 of the Sale of Goods Act can [sic] be excluded by an express term to that effect. For the Defendant it was boldly but nevertheless cogently submitted that since business by s 14 is specifically interpreted to include a profession, it is enough that any professional body buys a car using that body's name and money, be it a company or a firm. That, it is submitted, is sufficient to show that the professional body is buying in the course of a business. I find this proposition too startling to be acceptable. Bearing in mind that the object of the 1977 Act was to try and prevent an unfair inequality of bargaining strength and knowledge between two parties to a contract of sale, it seems to me that for a sale to fall outside the category of a consumer sale by virtue of the Plaintiffs' buying in the course of business, the buying of motor cars must form at the very least an integral part of the buyer's business or a necessary incidental thereto. Only in those circumstances could the buyer be said to be on an equal footing with the trader/seller. In this view I am fortified by considering such cases as *Havering London Borough Council v Stevenson* [1970] 3 All ER 609, [1970] 1 WLR 1375 and the case of *Rasbora Ltd v JCL Marine Ltd* [1977] 1 Lloyd's Rep 645.

The former case concerned a man whose main business was car hire. However, as part of that business he sold his fleet of cars approximately every two years. The matter fell to be decided under the Trade Descriptions Act where a similar phrase is used, and it was held that since the selling of cars was a necessary part of the business of car hire, a description as to the quality of those cars made by the Defendant to the subsequent criminal proceedings, was made in the course of the business, but it was stressed that that decision turned on the fact that the sale of the cars was an integral part of the Defendant's business.

In the *Rasbora* case to which Miss Bowman helpfully referred me, the ultimate purchaser was a Jersey company, novated to the person who had originally ordered the boat, and who incidentally controlled the company; and it was quite obvious that such an arrangement was no more than a device for the purpose of evading VAT (I should perhaps say avoiding VAT). Lawton J effectively equated the company with its owner and held that despite the avowed sole purpose of the company, that is to say, buying the boat, the purchase was not in the course of business.

Now the plaintiff firm does not deal in motor cars. They may, it is true, use their motor cars in the course of their profession as surveyors, but I have absolutely no evidence that they make a habit of doing so, nor any evidence that they intended to use this one in that fashion, either wholly or in part. Indeed, Mr Buckley's own evidence to the effect that he regarded the Rolls Royce as something to be used on high days and holidays points to the contrary. It is agreed that the burden of proving a non-consumer sale rests upon the Defendant, and on the evidence, or rather upon the lack of it, I am unable to hold that the Defendant had discharged that burden. I should add that in my view such a defence should have been advanced on the pleadings but my view of the law and the facts makes it unnecessary to decide this issue against the Defendant on such a relatively unsatisfactory basis as that.

NOTES

For a reference to the *Havering London Borough* case see below p 471, and for criticism of this aspect of the *Rasbora* case see Yates *Exclusion Clauses in Contracts* (2nd edn) p 106.

The general question was discussed in the following terms by the Law Commission in its First Report on Exemption Clauses (Law Com No 24):

> 83.   We have considered in the light of the evidence some of the types of case in which it might be appropriate to extend the proposed protection to purchasers buying otherwise than for private use or consumption. Obvious cases are motor cars, typewriters and electric heaters sold to doctors or members of other professions; here, as a matter of justice and common sense, the sale may, in all material respects, be indistinguishable from a sale to a private purchaser.
>
> . . .
>
> 84.   It is our conclusion that provision should be made to extend protection from exemption clauses to purchasers in the types of case illustrated in paragraph 83. There are two ways in which this could be achieved. One way would be to extend the definition of 'consumer sale' so as to cover cases of this kind. Alternatively, if in accordance with the proposals favoured by some of us protection from exemption clauses were to be afforded to business sales generally by a test of reasonableness applied by the courts, purchasers in the above-mentioned type of case would have the benefit of that protection.

Question

In the result the statutory reform which followed opted for the 'alternative' approach of applying a test of reasonableness to business sales. Was the 'second preliminary point' in the above case decided correctly?

For the exclusion of purchasers at auction sales from the category of those who deal as consumer see para 114 et seq of the above report.

Consider the following cases:
1. Recently Max has acquired a large deep-freeze with a view to bulk buying for himself and his family. He approaches Giles a local farmer who agrees to sell him a quantity of fifty chickens at a discount price. Later the chickens are found to be diseased. Max seeks your advice as to whether he was dealing as consumer.

Advise Max on the assumption that the chickens were supplied (i) loose and (ii) in a pack usually reserved for hotels and restaurants.
2. Jerrybuilder is a builder and plumber whose standard-form contract contains the following provisions: 'Whilst Jerrybuilder always endeavours to carry out work with the maximum speed in no case will time be of the essence of the contract. Jerrybuilder regrets that he cannot accept liability for defects in materials bought-in from third party suppliers or for any negligence on his own part howsoever arising'.

You are asked to advise consumers as to the precise source and extent of the protection afforded by the 1977 Act in the following circumstances:
(i) Jerrybuilder has replaced Gullible's central heating boiler with a new boiler manufactured by Higlow. The installation is carried out correctly but the boiler is defective and does not work. Higlow is now in liquidation.
(ii) Jerrybuilder has serviced Horace's central heating boiler incorrectly, leaving it in a dangerous condition. This causes an explosion damaging Horace's property.

MISREPRESENTATIONS

Perhaps predictably most of the reported cases concerning exemption clauses in relation to misrepresentations have been about the sale of real property (see eg *Overbrooke Estates Ltd v Glencombe Properties Ltd* [1974] 3 All ER 511, [1974] 1 WLR 1335; *Collins v Howell-Jones* (1980) 259 Estates Gazette 331, CA; *South Western General Property Co Ltd v Marton* (1982) 263 Estates Gazette 1090; *Walker v Boyle* [1982] 1 All ER 634, [1982] 1 WLR 495 and see *Howard Marine and Dredging Co Ltd v A Ogden & Sons (Excavations) Ltd* [1978] QB 574, [1978] 2 All ER 1134, CA (hire of barges).

The following case is about property but the approach of the Court of Appeal is potentially helpful in the context of consumer transactions and it makes a distinction of general importance.

Cremdean Properties Ltd v Nash (1977) 244 Estates Gazette 547, Court of Appeal

This was an appeal by the first defendant against a decision of Fox J (1977) 241 Estates Gazette 837 on a preliminary issue arising in proceedings brought by the plaintiffs in respect of the sale to them of a block of properties. The plaintiffs were seeking rescission of the contracts of sale and in the alternative damages on the ground of alleged misrepresentation in the invitation to tender as to the amount of available office space. The preliminary issue to be tried was whether certain clauses contained in a footnote to the conditions of sale were effective to exclude liability for inaccuracy of the information. Fox J had ordered that the action should proceed to trial.

Bridge LJ. Mr Newsom's able argument on behalf of the defendant can really be summarised very shortly. In effect what he says is this. The terms of the footnote are not simply, if contractual at all, a contractual exclusion either of any liability to which the defendant would otherwise be subject for any misrepresentation in the document, or of any remedy otherwise available on that ground to the plaintiff. The footnote is effective, so the argument runs, to nullify any representation in the document altogether; it is effective, so it is said, to bring about a situation in law as if no representation at all had ever been made. For my part, I am quite unable to accept that argument. I reject it primarily on the simple basis that on no reading of the language of the footnote could it have the remarkable effect contended for. One may usefully analyse the footnote by dividing it into three parts. The first part is embodied in the words: 'These particulars are prepared for the convenience of an intending purchaser or tenant and although they are believed to be correct their accuracy is not guaranteed . . .' That is something quite different from saying 'any representation in this document shall be deemed not to be a representation.' On the contrary, this part of the footnote is clearly intended to exclude contractual liability for the accuracy of any representation; so far from saying that there has been no representation, it is reinforcing the fact that there have been representations by indicating that they are believed to be correct.

The second part of the footnote is embodied in the words: '. . . any error, omission or misdescription shall not annul the sale or be grounds on which compensation may be claimed'—that, I think Mr Newsom concedes, is nothing more or less than a purported exclusion of liability which would otherwise accrue on the ground of any misrepresentation in the statements to be found elsewhere in the document.

Finally, the third part of the footnote is embodied in the words: 'Any intending purchaser or tenant must satisfy himself by inspection or otherwise as to the correctness of each of the statements contained in these particulars.' That part of the footnote may have considerable importance when this action comes to trial, as bearing upon the question of fact that will arise at the trial, as to whether the plaintiffs relied upon any misrepresentation. But for present purposes we, of course, have to assume the truth of what is pleaded, namely, that the representation as to office space was false and that the plaintiffs relied upon the alleged misrepresentation. Clearly the third part of this footnote, again on any reading of its language, does not amount even to a purported annulment of the very existence of any representation embodied in the earlier parts of this document.

In support of his argument Mr Newson relied upon a decision of Brightman J in a case called *Overbrooke Estates Ltd v Glencombe Properties Ltd* reported in [1974] 1 WLR 1335 [also (1974) 232 Estates Gazette 829]. That was a case where the plaintiff vendors were seeking to enforce a contract of sale made through auctioneers and where the defendant purchasers sought to rely upon an alleged misrepresentation by the auctioneers to avoid their liability under the contract. It was a case in which the auction particulars included a sentence in the following terms: 'The vendors do not make or give, and neither the auctioneers nor any person in the employment of the auctioneers has any authority to make or give any representation or warranty in relation to these properties.' It was alleged that, that clause notwithstanding, subsequently the auctioneers, before the defendants contracted to purchase the property, had made certain oral and inaccurate representations about some of its attributes, and it was argued on behalf of the defendants that the clause in the auction particulars purporting to limit the auctioneers' authority to make any representations on the vendors' behalf, was a clause excluding, or purporting to exclude, or limit, liability, which could only take effect subject to the provisions of section 3 of the Misrepresentation Act 1967.

Brightman J deals with that argument . . . [as follows]

> 'In my judgment section 3 of the Act will not bear the load which Mr Irvine seeks to place upon it. In my view the section only applies to a provision which would exclude or restrict liability for a misrepresentation made by a party or his duly authorised agent, including of course an agent with ostensible authority. The section does not, in my judgment, in any way qualify the right of a principal publicly to limit the otherwise ostensible authority of his agent. The defendants' second argument fails.'

I respectfully agree entirely with the whole of that reasoning. With respect to Mr Newsom's argument I am unable to see that it has any application at all to the facts of the present case, because there never was any question here but that the agents acting for the first defendant and the other defendants, when they published the document on which the plaintiffs rely as embodying the relevant misrepresentation, had the full authority of their principals to say what they did say in the document. It is one thing to say that section 3 does not inhibit a principal from publicly giving notice limiting the ostensible authority of his agents; it is quite another thing to say that a principal can circumvent the plainly intended effect of section 3 by a clause excluding his own liability for a representation which he has undoubtedly made.

I am quite content to found my judgment in this case on the proposition that the language of the footnote relied upon by Mr Newsom simply does not, on its true interpretation, have the effect contended for. But I would go further and say that if the ingenuity of a draftsman could devise language which would have that effect, I am extremely doubtful whether the court would allow it to operate so as to defeat section 3. Supposing the vendor included a clause which the purchaser was required to, and did, agree to in some such terms as 'notwithstanding any statement of fact included in these particulars the vendor shall be conclusively deemed to have made no representation within the meaning of the Misrepresentation Act 1967,' I should have thought that that was only a form of words the intended and actual effect of which was to exclude or restrict liability, and I should not have thought that the courts would have been ready to allow such ingenuity in forms of language to defeat the plain purpose at which section 3 is aimed . . .

Agreeing, **Scarman LJ** said: I agree in particular with the observations that my Lord made about the submissions put to the court by Mr Maurice, following his leader. Nevertheless, the case for the appellant does have an audacity and a simple logic which I confess I find attractive. It runs thus: a statement is not a representation unless it is also a statement that what is stated is true. If in context a statement contains no assertion, express or implied, that its content is accurate, there is no representation. *Ergo*, there can be no misrepresentation; *ergo*, the Misrepresentation Act 1967 cannot apply to it. Humpty Dumpty would have fallen for this argument. If we were to fall for it, the Misrepresentation Act would be dashed to pieces which not all the King's lawyers could put together again . . .

Buckley LJ agreed with both judgments and did not wish to add anything.

The appeal was dismissed with costs, to be taxed and paid forthwith.

Consider the following case.

Angus wishes to sell his Victorian house and he puts it in the hands of Messrs Locke and Key, estate agents. Their particulars refer to the house as having been 'recently rewired throughout'. In fact this is untrue since only the lighting has been recently rewired whilst the power circuit is old and seriously defective. Bert has bought the house having read these particulars which also contain the following statements:

> These particulars do not constitute or form part of any contract. Whilst Messrs Locke and Key take every care in the preparation of these particulars they hereby state both on behalf of themselves and the Vendor that no intending purchaser should rely on any of the statements herein as statements or representations of fact and the intending purchaser should make his own inspection and enquiries in order to satisfy himself of their authenticity and no reponsibility is accepted for any error or omission herein.

Some two months after completion Bert discovers the state of the wiring and seeks your advice as to whether he has a remedy against (i) Angus; (ii) Locke and Key. Advise Bert.

NOTE

As to an agent's personal position under s 2(1) of the Misrepresentation Act 1967 see *Resolute Maritime Inc v Nippon Kaiji Kyokai, The Skopas* [1983] 2 All ER 1, [1983] 1 WLR 857.

Question

What is the effect, if any, of the following provision taken from a manufacturer's guarantee: 'The Purchaser agrees that apart from the express terms contained herein no statement or representation has been made by the Company relating to the goods supplied, or if any such statements or representations have been made, the Purchaser warrants that he understood them to be statements of opinion only, and did not rely upon them.'?

THE TEST OF REASONABLENESS

In many consumer transactions exemption clauses will not be void but rather will be subject to the test of reasonableness of s 11 of the Act. Sch 2 to the Act lists a number of guidelines to be considered specifically in relation to ss 6 and 7. Although Sch 2 will not affect consumers directly, since a relevant clause would be void in their case, the guidelines may be thought to be no more than expressions of common sense matters to which the courts would wish to have regard more generally. The case of *Woodman v Photo Trade Processing Ltd* (above p 245) is helpful as discussing the requirement of reasonableness in the context of a consumer transaction. In the following case the House of Lords considered it in the context of a commercial transaction but made a number of points of general interest and application. (For another commercial case see *RW Green Ltd v Cade Bros Farms* [1978] 1 Lloyd's Rep 602).

George Mitchell (Chesterhall) Ltd v Finney Lock Seeds Ltd [1983] 2 All ER 737, [1983] 2 AC 803, House of Lords

The facts of this case are as stated in Lord Denning's judgment in the Court of Appeal (above p 233) from which the sellers of the cabbage seed were now appealing. (Section 55(5) of the Sale of Goods Act 1979 to which Lord Bridge refers is the equivalent of Sch 2 to the 1977 Act.)

Lord Bridge of Harwich . . . This is the first time your Lordships' House has had to consider a modern statutory provision giving the court power to override contractual terms excluding or restricting liability, which depends on the court's view of what is 'fair and reasonable'. The particular provision of the modified s 55 of the 1979 Act which applies in the instant case is of limited and diminishing importance. But the several provisions of the Unfair Contract Terms Act 1977 which depend on 'the requirement of reasonableness', defined in s 11 by reference to what is 'fair and reasonable', albeit in a different context, are likely to come before the courts with increasing frequency. It may, therefore, be appropriate to consider how an original decision what is 'fair and reasonable' made in the application of any of these provisions should be approached by an appellate court. It would not be accurate to describe such a decision as an exercise of discretion. But a decision under any of the provisions referred to will have this in common with the exercise of a discretion, that, in having regard to the various matters to which the modified s 55(5) of the 1979 Act, or s 11 of the 1977 Act direct attention, the court must entertain a whole range of considerations, put them in the scales on one side or the other and decide at the end of the day on which side the balance comes down. There will sometimes be room for a legitimate difference of judicial opinion as to what the answer should be, where it will be impossible to say that one view is demonstrably wrong and the other demonstrably right. It must follow, in my view, that, when asked to review such a decision on appeal, the appellate court should treat the original decision with the utmost respect and refrain from interference with it unless satisfied that it proceeded on some erroneous principle or was plainly and obviously wrong . . .

The only other question of construction debated in the course of the argument was the meaning to be attached to the words 'to the extent that' in sub-s (4) and, in particular, whether they permit the court to hold that it would be fair and reasonable to allow partial reliance on a limitation clause and, for example, to decide in the instant case that the respondents should recover, say, half their consequential damage. I incline to the view that, in their context, the words are equivalent to 'in so far as' or 'in circumstances in which' and do not permit the kind of judgment of Solomon illustrated by the example.

But for the purpose of deciding this appeal I find it unnecessary to express a concluded view on this question.

My Lords, at long last I turn to the application of the statutory language to the circumstances of the case. Of the particular matters to which attention is directed by paras (a) to (e) of s 55(5), only those in paras (a) to (c) are relevant. As to para (c), the respondents admittedly knew of the relevant condition (they had dealt with the appellants for many years) and, if they had read it, particularly cl 2, they would, I think, as laymen rather than lawyers, have had no difficulty in understanding what it said. This and the magnitude of the damages claimed in proportion to the price of the seeds sold are factors which weigh in the scales in the appellants' favour.

The question of relative bargaining strength under para (a) and of the opportunity to buy seeds without a limitation of the seedsman's liability under para (b) were interrelated. The evidence was that a similar limitation of liability was universally embodied in the terms of trade between seedsmen and farmers and had been so for very many years. The limitation had never been negotiated between representative bodies but, on the other hand, had not been the subject of any protest by the National Farmers' Union. These factors, if considered in isolation, might have been equivocal. The decisive factor, however, appears from the evidence of four witnesses called for the appellants, two independent seedsmen, the chairman of the appellant company, and a director of a sister company (both being wholly-owned subsidiaries of the same parent). They said that it had always been their practice, unsuccessfully attempted in the instant case, to negotiate settlements of farmers' claims for damages in excess of the price of the seeds, if they thought that the claims were 'genuine' and 'justified'. This evidence indicated a clear recognition by seedsmen in general, and the appellants in particular, that reliance on the limitation of liability imposed by the relevant condition would not be fair or reasonable.

Two further factors, if more were needed, weigh the scales in favour of the respondents. The supply of autumn, instead of winter, cabbage seed was due to the negligence of the appellants' sister company. Irrespective of its quality, the autumn variety supplied could not, according to the appellants' own evidence, be grown commercially in East Lothian. Finally, as the trial judge found, seedsmen could insure against the risk of crop failure caused by supply of the wrong variety of seeds without materially increasing the price of seeds.

My Lords, even if I felt doubts about the statutory issue, I should not, for the reasons explained earlier, think it right to interfere with the unanimous original decision of that issue by the Court of Appeal. As it is, I feel no such doubts. If I were making the original decision, I should conclude without hesitation that it would not be fair or reasonable to allow the appellants to rely on the contractual limitation of their liability.

I would dismiss the appeal.

[Lords Diplock, Scarman, Roskill and Brightman concurred in dismissing the appeal for the reasons given by Lord Bridge.]

Appeal dismissed.

Towards a general power to review unjust contracts

Apart from s 3 the Unfair Contract Terms Act 1977 is drafted tightly and in the traditional English style. Other jurisdictions have adopted much more broadly-based statutory provisions, conferring a general power of review over contracts which may be variously described as unfair, unjust or unconscionable. A selection of these is printed below. First however it must be said that English law has other more specific statutory provisions the general purpose of which is to control contracts which might otherwise be unfair. As examples one may cite the Consumer Credit Act 1974, ss 137–139 (above pp 219–222) dealing with extortionate credit bargains and ss 67–73 concerning the cancellation of agreements concluded off business premises. In addition equity and the common law have developed a recognised pattern of control in certain well-established areas, for example in cases of undue influence and relief against penalty clauses (but not excessive deposits). Although it is doubtful whether these categories have the capacity for expansion to the general benefit of consumers Lord Denning MR, attempted to bring the cases within one unifying principle.

Lloyds Bank Ltd v Bundy [1974] 3 All ER 757, [1975] QB 326, Court of Appeal

The defendant farmer, his son and the latter's failing plant-hire company all banked at the Salisbury branch of the plaintiff bank. In an attempt to keep the company going the defendant signed a guarantee of the company's account in the sum of £11,000 and gave the bank a further charge of £3,500 on his home, Yew Tree Farm. This made the total charge £11,000, the house being worth only about £10,000. This was done in the presence of the son and a new assistant bank manager who had made it clear that it was likely that the bank would otherwise withdraw its support. However the respite was short-lived and the company failed. The bank then agreed to sell the house and sought to evict the defendant. In the county court the bank was successful in obtaining an order for the possession of the property and it was against this judgment that the defendant was now appealing. Lord Denning MR, stated the facts and continued:

3.   *The general rule*
Now let me say at once that in the vast majority of cases a customer who signs a bank guarantee or a charge cannot get out of it. No bargain will be upset which is the result of the ordinary interplay of forces. There are many hard cases which are caught by this rule. Take the case of a poor man who is homeless. He agrees to pay a high rent to a landlord just to get a

roof over his head. The common law will not interfere. It is left to Parliament. Next take the case of a borrower in urgent need of money. He borrows it from the bank at high interest and it is guaranteed by a friend. The guarantor gives his bond and gets nothing in return. The common law will not interfere. Parliament has intervened to prevent moneylenders charging excessive interest. But it has never interfered with banks.

Yet there are exceptions to this general rule. There are cases in our books in which the courts will set aside a contract, or a transfer of property, when the parties have not met on equal terms, when the one is so strong in bargaining power and the other so weak that, as a matter of common fairness, it is not right that the strong should be allowed to push the weak to the wall. Hitherto those exceptional cases have been treated each as a separate category in itself. But I think the time has come when we should seek to find a principle to unite them. I put on one side contracts or transactions which are voidable for fraud or misrepresentation or mistake. All those are governed by settled principles. I go only to those where there has been inequality of bargaining power, such as to merit the intervention of the court.

4. *The categories*

The first category is that of 'duress of goods'. A typical case is when a man is in a strong bargaining position by being in possession of goods of another by virtue of a legal right, such as, by way of pawn or pledge or taken in distress. The owner is in a weak position because he is in urgent need of the goods. The stronger demands of the weaker more than is justly due, and he pays it in order to get the goods. Such a transaction is voidable. He can recover the excess: see *Astley v Reynolds*[1] and *Green v Duckett*[2] . . .

The second category is that of the 'unconscionable transaction'. A man is so placed as to be in need of special care and protection and yet his weakness is exploited by another far stronger than himself so as to get his property at a gross undervalue. The typical case is that of the 'expectant heir'. But it applies to all cases where a man comes into property, or is expected to come into it, and then being in urgent need another gives him ready cash for it, greatly below its true worth, and so gets the property transferred to him: see *Evans v Llewellin*[3]. Even though there be no evidence of fraud or misrepresentation, nevertheless the transaction will be set aside: see *Fry v Lane*[4] where Kay J said:

'The result of the decisions is that where a purchase is made from a poor and ignorant man at a considerable undervalue, the vendor having no independent advice, a Court of Equity will set aside the transaction.'

This second category is said to extend to all cases where an unfair advantage has been gained by an unconscientious use of power by a stronger party against a weaker: see the cases cited in Halsbury's Laws of England[5] and in Canada, *Morrison v Coast Finance Ltd*[6] and *Knupp v Bell*[7].

The third category is that of 'undue influence' usually so-called. These are divided into two classes as stated by Cotton LJ in *Allcard v Skinner*[8]. The first are these where the stronger has been guilty of some fraud or wrongful act—expressly so as to gain some gift or advantage from the weaker. The second are those where the stronger has not been guilty of any wrongful act, but has, through the relationship which existed between him and the weaker, gained some gift or advantage for himself. Sometimes the relationship is such as to raise a presumption of undue influence, such as parent over child, solicitor over client, doctor over patient, spiritual adviser over follower. At other times a relationship of confidence must be proved to exist. But to all of them the general principle obtains which was stated by Lord Chelmsford LC in *Tate v Williamson*[9]:

'Wherever the persons stand in such a relation that, while it continues, confidence is necessarily reposed by one, and the influence which naturally grows out of that confidence is possessed by the other, and this confidence is abused, or the influence is exerted to obtain an advantage at the expense of the confiding party, the person so availing himself of his position will not be permitted to retain the advantage, although the transaction could not have been impeached if no such confidential relation had existed.'

Such a case was *Tufton v Sperni*[10].

The fourth category is that of 'undue pressure'. The most apposite of that is *Williams v Bayley*[11] where a son forged his father's name to a promissory note, and, by means of it, raised money from the bank of which they were both customers. The bank said to the father, in effect: 'Take your choice—give us security for your son's debt. If you do take that on yourself, then it will all go smoothly; if you do not, we shall be bound to exercise pressure.' Thereupon the father charged his property to the bank with payment of the note. The House of Lords held that the charge was invalid because of undue pressure exerted by the bank. Lord Westbury said[12]:

> 'A contract to give security for the debt of another, which is a contract without consideration, is, above all things, a contract that should be based upon the free and voluntary agency of the individual who enters into it.'

Other instances of undue pressure are where one party stipulates for an unfair advantage to which the other has no option but to submit. As where an employer—the stronger party—had employed a builder—the weaker party—to do work for him. When the builder asked for payment of sums properly due (so as to pay his workmen) the employer refused to pay unless he was given some added advantage. Stuart V-C said:

> 'Where an agreement, hard and inequitable in itself, has been exacted under circumstances of pressure on the part of the person who exacts it this Court will set it aside':

see *Ormes v Beadel*[13]; *D & C Builders Ltd v Rees*[14].

The fifth category is that of salvage agreements. When a vessel is in danger of sinking and seeks help, the rescuer is in a strong bargaining position. The vessel in distress is in urgent need. The parties cannot be truly said to be on equal terms. The Court of Admiralty have always recognised that fact. The fundamental rule is:

> 'If the parties have made an agreement, the Court will enforce it, unless it be manifestly unfair and unjust; but if it be manifestly unfair and unjust, the Court will disregard it and decree what is fair and just.'

See *Akerblom v Price*[15] per Brett LJ applied in a striking case, *The Port Caledonia and The Anna*[16], when the rescuer refused to help with a rope unless he was paid £1,000.

5. The general principles

Gathering all together, I would suggest that through all these instances there runs a single thread. They rest on 'inequality of bargaining power'. By virtue of it, the English law gives relief to one who, without independent advice, enters into a contract on terms which are very unfair or transfers property for a consideration which is grossly inadequate, when his bargaining power is grievously impaired by reason of his own needs or desires, or by his own ignorance or infirmity, coupled with undue influences or pressures brought to bear on him by or for the benefit of the other. When I use the word 'undue' I do not mean to suggest that the principle depends on proof of any wrongdoing. The one who stipulates for an unfair advantage may be moved solely by his own self-interest, unconscious of the distress he is bringing to the other. I have also avoided any reference to the will of the one being 'dominated' or 'overcome' by the other. One who is in extreme need may knowingly consent to a most improvident bargain, solely to relieve the straits in which he finds himself. Again, I do not mean to suggest that every transaction is saved by independent advice. But the absence of it may be fatal. With these explanations, I hope this principle will be found to reconcile the cases.

1. (1731) 2 Stra 915.
2. (1883) 11 QBD 275.
3. (1787) 1 Cox Eq Cas 333.
4. (1888) 40 Ch D 312 at 322, [1886–90] All ER Rep 1084 at 1089.
5. 3rd Edn, vol 17, p 682.
6. (1965) 55 DLR (2d) 710.
7. (1968) 67 DLR (2d) 256.
8. (1887) 36 Ch D 145 at 171, [1886–90] All ER Rep 90 at 93.
9. (1866) 2 Ch App 55 at 61.
10. [1952] 2 TLR 516.
11. (1866) LR 1 HL 200.
12. (1866) LR 1 HL at 218, 219.
13. (1860) 2 Giff 166 at 174.
14. [1965] 3 All ER 837 at 841, [1966] 2 QB 617 at 625.
15. (1881) 7 QBD 129 at 133.
16. [1903] P 184.

His Lordship then applied this principle to the facts of the case noting the inadequacy of the consideration provided by the bank, its relationship of trust and confidence with the father, the father's affection for his son, the bank's conflict of interest and the father's lack of independent advice. He continued:

> These considerations seem to me to bring this case within the principles I have stated. But, in case that principle is wrong, I would also say that the case falls within the category of undue influence of the second class stated by Cotton LJ in *Allcard v Skinner*[1]. I have no doubt that the assistant bank manager acted in the utmost good faith and was straightforward and genuine. Indeed the father said so. But beyond doubt he was acting in the interests of the bank—to get further security for a bad debt. There was such a relationship of trust and confidence between them that the bank ought not to have swept up his sole remaining asset into their hands—for nothing—without his having independent advice. I would therefore allow this appeal.

1. (1887) 36 Ch D at 171, [1886–90] All ER Rep at 93.

Sir Eric Sachs (with whose judgment Cairns LJ concurred) held that 'on the particular and somewhat unusual facts of the case' the bank's relationship with the defendant was one of fiduciary care. The manager had 'failed to apprehend that there was a conflict of interest as between the bank and the defendant' and 'he should have insisted on the obvious need for independent advice'. He continued:

The conclusion that the defendant has established that as between himself and the bank the relevant transaction fell within the second category of undue influence cases referred to by Cotton LJ in *Allcard v Skinner* is one reached on the single issue pursued on behalf of the defendant in this court. On that issue we have had the benefit of cogent and helpful submissions on matter plainly raised in the pleadings. As regards the wider areas covered in masterly survey in the judgment of Lord Denning MR, but not raised arguendo, I do not venture to express an opinion—though having some sympathy with the views that the courts should be able to give relief to a party who has been subject to undue pressure as defined in the concluding passage of his judgment on that point.

Appeal allowed; judgment below set aside. Judgment for defendant on claim and counterclaim. Legal charge and guarantee dated 17th December 1969 set aside; documents to be delivered up for cancellation. Leave to appeal to the House of Lords refused.

NOTES

A Schroeder Music Publishing Co Ltd v Macaulay [1974] 3 All ER 616, [1974] 1 WLR 1308, HL, and *Clifford Davis Management Ltd v WEA Records Ltd* [1975] 1 All ER 237, [1975] 1 WLR 61, CA, also involved inequality of bargaining power, unconscionable bargains and (in both cases) standard-form contracts between impressarios and 'pop stars'. The analogy between pop stars and consumers is recognisable but the cases also fall within an acknowledged category of protection for contracts in restraint of trade. For an analysis of the former case see Trebilcock, (1976) 26 Univ Toronto LJ 359. For a recent case discussing unconscionable bargains see *Alec Lobb (Garages) Ltd v Total Oil GB Ltd* [1985] 1 All ER 303, CA.

Inequality of bargaining power is relevant in other areas also, for example in relation to exemption clauses and the test of reasonableness (see Sch 2 to the Unfair Contract Terms Act 1977 above p 244). In his article 'Unconscionability in Contracts' (1976) 39 MLR 369 Professor Waddams has argued persuasively for the recognition of a general principle. Having discussed the areas in which relief has traditionally been granted he continues, at pp 390–91:

I have attempted to show that, despite lip service to the notion of absolute freedom of contract, relief is every day given against agreements that are unfair, inequitable, unreasonable or oppressive. Unconscionability, as a word to describe such control, might not be the lexicographer's first choice, but I think it is the most acceptable general word. It has historical antecedents . . . it occurs consistently throughout the cases in the various branches of the law discussed; it has been accepted as a general ground of relief in modern Canadian cases . . . and it is recognised by statute both in Commonwealth and American jurisdictions.[1] . . .

Another compelling reason for adopting a general principle of unconscionability is the need to fill the gaps between the existing islands of intervention. The clause that is not quite a penalty clause[2] or not quite an exemption clause[3] or just outside the provisions of the Moneylenders' Act[4] or the Misrepresentation Act[5] will fall under the general power to relieve and anomalous distinctions like those castigated by Lord Denning in *Bridge v Campbell Discount*[6] will disappear.

1. Moneylenders' Act 1900 (now replaced in the United Kingdom by Consumer Credit Act 1974 with test of 'extortionate'), Law of Property Act 1925, s 174 (2), Uniform Commercial Code, ss 2–302.
2. Because it is a deposit in advance, or because there is no breach of contract.
3. Because the obligor has an option to perform in a variety of ways, or because the effect of the clause in question is to narrow the basic contractual obligation.
4. Because the lender is not in the business of moneylending within the statutory definition.
5. Misrepresentation Act 1967, s 3. See *Overbrooke Estates Ltd v Glencombe Properties Ltd* [1974] 1 WLR 1335.
6. [1962] AC 600 [at] 629. [The distinction was between a penalty which operates on breach and termination under an option provided for by the contract.]

See also Tiplady, 'Judicial Control of Contractual Unfairness' (1983) 46 MLR 601 and the discussion of fair trading provisions, below Ch 10.

There are many examples of broadly-based statutory provisions in other jurisdictions, some of which embody additional requirements of good faith in exercising contractual rights (contrast *White & Carter (Councils) Ltd v McGregor* [1962] AC 413, [1961] 3 All ER 1178, HL). For example the West German Civil Code (BGB) has both a duty of good faith (para 242) and the following provision (para 138) (translation from Peden *The Law of Unjust Contracts* (1982)):

> 1. A legal transaction which is contrary to public policy is void.
> 2. A legal transaction is also void whereby a person exploiting the need, carelessness or inexperience of another, causes to be promised or granted to himself or to a third party in exchange for a performance, pecuniary advantages which exceed the value of the performance to such an extent that, under the circumstances, the pecuniary advantages are in obvious disproportion to the performance.

In addition the Law of Standard Contract Terms of 1976 contains both a list of clauses which are invalid per se (§11) or unless requirements of reasonableness are satisfied (§10) and a further and more general provision (§9) (translation by Nina Galston 26 AJCL 568):

§9 General clauses
(1) Stipulations in standard contract terms are invalid if the contracting partner prejudices unreasonably the command of good faith.
(2) In case of doubt, an unreasonable prejudice is presumed if a stipulation
    (a) cannot be reconciled with the fundamental idea underlying the legal rule from which it deviates, or
    (b) so limits essential rights or duties inherent in the nature of the contract that attainment of the purpose of the contract is jeopardized.

For discussion of BGB paras 138 and 142 see Angelo and Ellinger, 'Unconscionable Contracts—A Comparative Study' (1979) 4 Otago LR

300 and Peden *The Law of Unjust Contracts* (1982) p 5 et seq. For discussion of the Standard Contract Terms Act 1976 see Von Marshall, 'The New German Law on Standard Contract Terms' (1979) Lloyd's MCLQ 278 and Sandrock, 'The Standard Terms Act 1976 of West Germany' (1978) 26 AJCL 551. See also below p 279 for further extracts from the 1976 Act.

In common law the United States of America provides the most familiar example of a broadly-based statutory provision controlling unconscionable conduct. The text of this provision and some of the issues raised by it may be seen in the following extracts:

Report on Sale of Goods 1979 (Ontario Law Reform Commission), Vol 1, p 153 et seq:

A. THE DOCTRINE OF UNCONSCIONABILITY

1. The General Issue

The right to bargain to one's best advantage is inherent in the very concept of contract, and is recognized in section 53 of the Ontario Sale of Goods Act. All civilised legal systems, however, have long recognized the need to balance freedom of contract with the need to protect the weaker party against over-reaching by the stronger party.[1] The challenge that confronted the draftsmen of Article 2 of the *Uniform Commercial Code* was whether their constituents were ready to confer a generalized power upon the courts to grant relief from unconscionable bargains, such as is now contained in the celebrated section 2-302. Predictably, their earliest efforts provoked great controversy. The provision was substantially altered in later drafts,[2] and the current version of section 2-302 emerged in the Official Text adopted by the sponsoring organizations in 1952. It reads as follows:

(1) If the court as a matter of law finds the contract or any clause of the contract to have been unconscionable at the time it was made the court may refuse to enforce the contract, or it may enforce the remainder of the contract without the unconscionable clause, or it may so limit the application of any unconscionable clause as to avoid any unconscionable result.

(2) When it is claimed or appears to the court that the contract or any clause thereof may be unconscionable the parties shall be afforded a reasonable opportunity to present evidence as to its commercial setting, purpose and effect to aid the court in making the determination.

The Code's doctrine of unconscionability and its subsequent handling by the courts have attracted an immense amount of learned comment.[3] However, the initial excitement generated by the appearance of this radical departure from accepted contract learning has subsided. Subsequent legislative and judicial developments have fully vindicated the judgment of two American authors[4] that the section embodied an idea whose time had arrived. We share this view and, subject to the more detailed comments offered below, recommend the adoption of an unconscionability provision in the revised Ontario Act . . .

2. Specific Questions

. . .

(b) Should the doctrine be restricted to cases of procedural unconscionability?

The distinction between substantive and procedural unconscionability is one that has been heavily emphasized by some American scholars. Professor Leff,[5] in particular, has argued that the court's power to interfere should be restricted to cases of procedural unconscionability. According to this line of reasoning, the mere existence of a harsh clause, or of a bargain that is improvident in its entirety, should not attract the operation of the doctrine unless the transaction is accompanied by elements of procedural unconscionability; that is, some form of exploitation of the weakness, ignorance or gullibility of the other party . . .

While not questioning the importance of procedural factors, the distinction between substantive and procedural is, in our view, too rigid. We do not, therefore, recommend its adoption. What is 'procedural' and what is 'substantive' will frequently result in a sterile debate. These are not terms of art.

. . .

(c) Should there be a list of criteria to guide the court in its determination of the issue?

A recurring complaint about the unconscionability concept as enshrined in section 2-302 of the Code, has been that it is too abstract, too elusive, and too subjective, and that it provides the court with little assistance with respect to the factors that should be taken into consideration in making a finding one way or the other. This weakness is inherent in many value concepts, and is one that can never be totally removed without destroying the utility of the concept in question. Nevertheless, we consider that a list of non-exhaustive critera would be useful, and should be incorporated in the revised Act.

. . .

(e) What types of relief?

Open textured as it is in one respect, section 2-302 is very circumscribed in the types of relief a court may allow from an agreement or a clause that it finds unconscionable.[6] It seems that the court is confined to three remedies: (a) the court may refuse to enforce the contract; (b) it may enforce the remainder of the contract without the unconscionable clause; or, (c) it may so limit the application of any unconscionable clause as to avoid any unconscionable result. In our opinion, these powers are too restrictive and may prevent the court from doing full justice. Particularly noteworthy is the court's inability to allow rescission of the agreement or, on one construction of alternative (c), to order repayment of part of the price where the court finds the price to be excessive . . .

Section 2-302 confers no power to award damages[7] and we do not recommend the addition of such a provision . . .

A power to award damages for intentional or negligent misrepresentations, which are actionable wrongs, is not necessarily appropriate in the case of an agreement which, although regarded as unfair, was not induced by misrepresentation and which, therefore, has traditionally attracted only equitable forms of relief. In view of the uncertain boundaries of the doctrine of unconscionability, especially in the non-consumer area, it would be unwise, in our view, to treat an unconscionable bargain as grounding an action in tort. Our recommendation would not, however, preclude a court from allowing damages where the impeached contract, as well as being unconscionable, was accompanied by other conduct constituting a recognized form of tort, such as fraud or duress.

. . .

3. Legislative proposal

Having canvassed the various facets of a legislative doctrine of unconscionability, it may be convenient now to reproduce our recommended version of UCC 2-302:[8]

5.2.-(1) If, with respect to a contract of sale, the court finds the contract or a part thereof to have been unconscionable at the time it was made, the court may

(a) refuse to enforce the contract or rescind it on such terms as may be just;

(b) enforce the remainder of the contract without the unconscionable part; or

(c) so limit the application of any unconscionable part or revise or alter the contract as to avoid any unconscionable result.

(2) In determining whether a contract of sale or a part thereof is unconscionable, or whether the operation of an agreement is unconscionable under section 5.7(3), the court may consider, among other factors:

(a) the degree to which one party has taken advantage of the inability of the other party reasonably to protect his interests because of his physical or mental infirmity, illiteracy, inability to understand the language of an agreement, lack of education, lack of business knowledge or experience, financial distress, or similar factors;

(b) gross disparity between the price of the goods and the price at which similar goods could be readily sold or purchased by parties in similar circumstances;

(c) knowledge by one party, when entering into the contract, that the other party will be substantially deprived of the benefit or benefits reasonably anticipated by that other party under the transaction;

(d) the degree to which the contract requires a party to waive rights to which he would otherwise be entitled;

(e) the degree to which the natural effect of the transaction, or any party's conduct prior to, or at the time of, the transaction, is to cause or aid in causing another party to misunderstand the true nature of the transaction and of his rights and duties thereunder;

(f) the bargaining strength of the seller and the buyer relative to each other, taking into account the availability of reasonable alternative sources of supply or demand;

(g) whether the party seeking relief knew or ought reasonably to have known of the existence and extent of the term or terms alleged to be unconscionable;

(h) in the case of a provision that purports to exclude or limit a liability that would otherwise attach to the party seeking to rely on it, which party is better able to safeguard himself against loss or damages; and
(i) the general commercial setting, purpose and effect of the contract.
(3) The court shall not make a finding of unconscionability based solely upon
   (a) the factor mentioned in clause d of subsection 2; or
   (b) the fact that the contract varies or excludes a provision of this Act or other legal rights.
(4) The court may raise the issue of unconscionability of its own motion.
(5) The powers conferred by this section apply notwithstanding any agreement or waiver to the contrary.

. . .

4. A cautionary note
   Section 2-302 is not a universal panacea to all the difficulties that afflict the modern marketplace; nor was it intended to undermine the binding character of freely concluded bargains. As an American court put it eloquently,[9] 'the doctrine of unconscionability is not a charter of economic anarchy . . . a promisor can be relieved of his obligation . . . only when the transaction affronts the sense of decency without which business is mere predation and the administration of justice an exercise in bookkeeping'. UCC 2-302 is designed, rather, to make explicit a power that the courts have long exercised covertly and to put it on a more rational basis. We appreciate that businessmen may not welcome this additional layer of uncertainty. We should emphasize, however, that there has been no disposition on the part of American courts to use section 2-302 as a general dispensing agent for contractual obligations,[10] and we are confident that the power would be exercised at least as responsibly by Ontario courts.

   1. For a general discussion of the doctrine of unconscionability, see Trebilcock, 'Fair Exchange of Values in Sales Transactions; the Doctrine of Unconscionability', Research Paper No III.4; and Waddams, 'Unconscionability in Contracts' (1976), 39 Mod LR 369.
   2. See, Trebilcock, supra, pp 30–32.
   3. See, among others: Note, 'The Doctrine of Unconscionability' (1967), 19 Maine L Rev 81; Harrington, 'Unconscionability under the Uniform Commercial Code' (1968), 10 South Texas LJ 203; Spanogle, 'Analyzing Unconscionability Problems' (1969), 117 U Pa L Rev 931; Younger, 'Judge's View of Unconscionability' (1973), 5 UCC LJ 348; Duesenberg, 'Practioner's View of Contract Unconscionability' (1976), 8 UCC LJ 237.
   4. White & Summers *Handbook of the Law Under the Uniform Commercial Code* (1972), p 115.
   5. 'Unconscionability and the Code—the Emperor's New Clause' (1967), 115 U Pa L Rev 485; Trebilcock, footnote 1 supra, pp 32–33. Compare, White & Summers, footnote 4 supra, pp 128–29.
   6. White & Summers, footnote 4 supra pp 131–32.
   7. Compare, *Pearson v National Budgeting Systems Inc* 297 NYS 2d 59 (N.Y. App Div 1969).
   8. See, Draft Bill, s 5.2.
   9. See, *Gimbel Bros, Inc v Swift* 307 NYS 2d 952 (NY City Civ Ct 1970) 954.
   10. Compare, White & Summers, footnote 4 supra p 114.

NOTE

The distinction between procedural and substantive unconscionability which is stressed by Professor Leff in his article 'Unconscionability and the Code: The Emperor's New Clause' (1967) 115 U Pa LR 485 is based in part on Official Comment 1 to the Code. This states that 'The principle is one of the prevention of oppression and unfair surprise and not of disturbance of allocation of risks because of superior bargaining power.' The following examples and summary are provided by Peden in his book *The Law of Unjust Contracts* (1982) at p 36:

   Any of the following elements may constitute procedural unconscionability: absence of meaningful choice, superiority of bargaining power, the contract being an adhesion contract, unfair surprise, sharp practices and deception. Examples of substantive unconscionability include overall imbalance, unfair price, and individual clauses which disclaim implied warranties, exclude or limit remedies, accelerate payments and give a right to enter premises, repossess or terminate without notice.

While elements of procedural unconscionability can be enumerated and discussed in the abstract, they may not make the contract unconscionable if the overall result is fair. Conversely, the courts have tended to baulk at relieving a party from a contract which has produced an unfair result unless there was present some element of procedural unconscionability.

Question

In the light of the above comments is the Unfair Contract Terms Act 1977 concerned with (i) procedural matters, (ii) substantive matters or (iii) both?

In respect of contracts of sale to what extent are the guidelines of the Ontario Draft Bill, clause 5.2(2) similar to (or different from) s 11 of and Sch 2 to the 1977 Act?

The Ontario Law Reform Commission proposal is confined to contracts of sale, no doubt because this was the subject of the reference. Were such a provision to be adopted in English law presumably it would be extended to other transactions, for example contracts for the supply of goods and services generally. To an English lawyer the single most striking clause in the Ontario proposal is perhaps 5.2(1)(c) which would enable a court 'to revise or alter the contract so as to avoid any unconscionable result'. A not dissimilar provision is contained in the New South Wales Contracts Review Act 1980 which enables a court to provide wide-ranging relief against oppressive, unconscionable or unjust contracts. (The term 'unjust' is defined by s 4(1) to include 'unconscionable, harsh or oppressive' and detailed guidelines are provided by s 9.)

New South Wales Contract Review Act 1980

PART II—RELIEF IN RESPECT OF UNJUST CONTRACTS

7. Principal relief.
(1) Where the Court finds a contract or a provision of a contract to have been unjust in the circumstances relating to the contract at the time it was made, the Court may, if it considers it just to do so, and for the purpose of avoiding as far as practicable an unjust consequence or result, do any one or more of the following:—
    (a) it may decide to refuse to enforce any or all of the provisions of the contract;
    (b) it may make an order declaring the contract void, in whole or in part;
    (c) it may make an order varying, in whole or in part, any provision of the contract;

    . . .

(2) Where the Court makes an order under subsection (1) (b) or (c), the declaration or variation shall have effect as from the time when the contract was made or (as to the whole or any part or parts of the contract) from some other time or times as specified in the order.

    . . .

8. Ancillary relief.
Schedule 1 has effect with respect to the ancillary relief that may be granted by the Court in relation to an application for relief under this Act.

SCHEDULE 1

Ancillary relief
1. Where the Court makes a decision or order under section 7, it may also make such orders as may be just in the circumstances for or with respect to any consequential or related matter, including orders for or with respect to—

(a) the making of any disposition of property;
(b) the payment of money (whether or not by way of compensation) to a party to the contract;
(c) the compensation of a person who is not a party to the contract and whose interests might otherwise be prejudiced by a decision or order under this Act;
(d) the supply or repair of goods;
(e) the supply of services;
(f) the sale or other realisation of property;
(g) the disposal of the proceeds of sale or other realisation of property;
(h) the creation of a charge on property in favour of any person;
(i) the enforcement of a charge so created;
(j) the appointment and regulation of the proceedings of a receiver of property; and
(k) the rescission or variation of any order of the Court under this clause,
and such orders in connection with the proceedings as may be just in the circumstances.
2. The Court may make orders under this Schedule on such terms and conditions (if any) as the Court thinks fit.

. . .

Problem

Gullible takes her old Ford car to the Downtown garage for repair saying that the engine is working badly. She asks Downtown to 'fix it'. Downtown does so at a cost of £400 which it is agreed is the going rate for the labour and materials involved. Before starting the work Downtown noticed that the car's chassis was corroded so badly that the car was fit only for scrap. However he was glad of the work and did not say anything to Gullible until she had paid her bill. Is Downtown's conduct to be regarded as 'unconscionable'? Would it be subject to control (i) in English law, (ii) under the provisions of the New South Wales Act?

Controlling the use of exemption clauses and unfair contract terms

INTRODUCTION

Although the Unfair Contract Terms Act 1977 is of great importance as a consumer protection measure its true effect will depend largely on the extent to which its provisions are observed in practice. If exemption or limitation clauses continue to be used by businesses it is probable that most consumers will not realise that they are legally ineffective. That such clauses are used is quite clear. For example a recent Report on the Holiday Industry by the Metropolitan County Councils Regional Investigation Team (1983) contains the following information at p 2:

> (e) A survey of 100 brochures covering a wide variety of holiday options was undertaken to determine the extent of usage of exclusion clauses subject to the provisions of the Unfair Contract Terms Act 1977. The findings were as follows:— (i) 10 brochures included clauses which were void under s 2(1); (ii) 99 brochures included clauses which were subject to the test of reasonableness; (iii) 24 brochures reproduced booking conditions in print which were substantially smaller than the rest of the brochure. It is suggested that, although void clauses have no effect in law, it is possible that a consumer with a genuine claim may be dissuaded from pursuing it when the clause is brought to his attention.

No doubt similar results would be obtained from surveys of other areas, for example home removals and car hire. Of course it is possible that most (or indeed all) of the clauses in the 99 holiday brochures referred to satisfy the test of reasonableness but this seems unlikely. If non-observance of the Act's intentions is widespread it may be necessary to look to methods of control going beyond making such conditions unenforceable. Certainly the Office of Fair Trading is aware of the problem. The Director General has commented as follows:

Annual Report of the Director General of Fair Trading 1983, p 14.

Void contract terms
During the year, just over 50 individual firms and several trade associations were asked to stop using a number of exclusion clauses revealed by the Office's investigations. Although their use (representing an attempt by traders to restrict or exclude certain liabilities) in itself is not a criminal offence, it might mislead consumers—contract terms of this kind were made void five years ago by the Unfair Contract Terms Act 1977. The clauses related to one or other of the following liabilities:
　　for death or personal injury resulting from negligence;
　　for the quality, fitness, etc, of goods supplied on hire or under a contract for work and materials;
　　in the case of a guarantee from a manufacturer or distributor, for loss or damage due to his negligence.
Most responses to the Office's approach were positive but a watch will be kept on the practice.

Although such responses are encouraging the fact remains that there are many other responsible bodies which continue to use such terms. For example one Council car-park issues tickets which state, 'The council accepts no responsibility for loss or damage to any vehicle or its contents or for injury to any person'.

SOME TECHNIQUES OF CONTROL

A variety of techniques is available to control the use of unfair contract terms including (i) encouraging the inclusion of fairer contract terms, for example through codes of practice, (ii) subjecting standard-form contracts to a system of prior validation, (iii) seeking assurance that particular terms will not be used, and if they are not forthcoming injunctive relief, and (iv) creating criminal offences based on the use of such terms. In this and in other areas discussed in Chs 8 and 10 it is likely that there will be a role for public agencies and perhaps consumer organisations. Francis Reynolds has discussed some of the above techniques and their possible application in English law when commenting on a paper presented by Professor Hellner at an Anglo-Swedish seminar in 1979. Both papers are perceptive and informative and now appear in *Law and the Weaker Party* Vol 1, editor Alan Neal, (Professional Books 1981). Reynolds comments at p 100 et seq in relation to the Swedish Consumer Ombudsman and Market Court:

Law and the Weaker Party, Vol 1

The second line of reflection . . . concerns the Consumer Ombudsman and the Market Court. It again arises from the limited nature of the United Kingdom Unfair Contract Terms Act; for not only is that Act confined to exemption and indemnity clauses, its effect on the use of such clauses is limited to empowering courts to ignore in whole or (perhaps) in part such a clause in particular litigation. There is no power to prevent even the particular proponent from using and relying on such a clause again and again. Again, there are more extensive powers in Sweden (and Germany).

It is perhaps the central point of Professor Hellner's paper that statutory control of unfair contract terms tends to move from the objective of 'weeding out' unfair terms into that of promoting suitable contract relations: 'The policy of counteracting unfair contract terms recedes behind a policy of providing suitable contract rules.' But this leads to legislation which is either too detailed; or refers to vague and shifting standards such as 'reasonableness'; or in the effort to provide rules for every type of a particular contract adopts a compromise which is appropriate only to some cases, and may be too strong or weak for others. The only solution, he suggests, is the adoption of a two-stage system, with a first-level official or body (in Sweden the Consumer Ombudsman) who is able to refer at a secondary level to some form of administrative, legal or quasi-legal body with coercive powers (the Market Court). It should be noted that the Swedish system does not involve prior validation of terms (an experiment tried in Israel and normally reported as not successful[1]), but rather a mechanism for prior (or subsequent) invalidation. In Sweden the first level negotiations are conducted by a Governmental official and the second level powers exercised by a body which is at least quasi-legal: this may be contrasted with the system under the German *AGB-Gesetz* where the first level is in a sense entrusted to private consumer and commercial organizations and the second to the ordinary courts. The orders made under the German Law seem however to have a more general effect than the injunctions issued by the Market Court, and this is strengthened by provisions for the official registration of judgments against particular clauses.[2]

There is of course no system of either type in the United Kingdom: but what is worth noting and is indeed striking is that most of the ingredients of the Swedish system exist here somewhere, if differently arranged. There is a Governmental official who exercises some measure of first-level control over contracts, the Director-General of Fair Trading (who also of course has functions in relation to uncompetitive trade practices); and he is reinforced in some cases at least by a special court, the Restrictive Practices Court (and it should be noted that the Swedish Market Court was originally created to deal with Restrictive Practices, its consumer functions being a later addition). These powers are not, of course, confined to exemption clauses. Although the Director-General has no power officially to approve contract terms, he is specifically required by the Fair Trading Act 1973[3] to encourage the adoption of codes of practice safeguarding the interests of consumers; and several have in fact been produced. It is true that there are limits on this. The Codes are only voluntary. Disapproval by the Director-General can only remove the privilege of stating that the Code was prepared in consultation with the Office of Fair Trading. The Director-General also has power to bring persons and bodies before the Restrictive Practices Court[4], but only in the case of persistent breaches of the criminal or civil law detrimental to consumers, as the undertakings secured, printed in his Annual Report, show. There is no power, for example, to require a trader not to use contract terms which are plainly contrary to the Unfair Contract Terms Act, or have been held unreasonable by a court. In such and related cases there are only indirect powers—perhaps reluctance to issue a licence under the Consumer Credit Act 1974 to a trader whose terms of business are unsatisfactory; where the terms used fall within the definition of a restrictive trade practice, to secure their alteration as a prerequisite to reporting to the Secretary of State that they are not of such significance as to call for investigation by the Court[5]. On the other hand there is one power which is perhaps novel: it has been termed 'acceleration of the legislative machinery'[6]. The Director-General has power to make recommendations for the prohibition of specific practices by delegated legislation. Two Acts under which such legislation may be and is now frequently made are the Consumer Protection Act 1961 (which was for many years little used) and the Consumer Safety Act 1978, which provides stronger powers and will eventually supersede the former Act. But the Fair Trading Act 1973 itself creates a special procedure for the creation of delegated legislation by way of a referral to a special body, the Consumer Protection Advisory Committee. It does however appear from the outside as if the procedure is cumbersome: and the statutory Orders which have emerged make illegal particular practices very specifically defined in the tight style of English Parliamentary draftsmen[7]. Nevertheless, once a practice has been made illegal by this method, the Director-General can take those who continue in it to the Restrictive Practices Court.

So the ingredients are there, but disordered.

1. See Hondius, (1978) 26 Am J Comp L 525, 529–532; Berg, (1979) 28 ICLQ 560.

2. See in general von Marschall, [1979] Lloyd's Maritime and Commercial Law Quarterly 278.

3. s 124(3).

4. s 35.

5. Under the Restrictive Trade Practices Act 1976, s 21(2).

6. Hondius, (1978) 26 Am J Comp L 525, 547.

7. They are the Mail Order Transactions (Information) Order 1976 (S.I. 1976 No 1812) which requires disclosure of advertisers' addresses; the Consumer Protection (Restriction on Statements) Order 1976 (SI 1976 No 1813, amended by SI 1978 No 127), which prohibits certain wrong or misleading statements by sellers as to consumer rights; and the Business Advertisement (Disclosure) Order 1977 (SI 1977 No 1918), which prohibits business advertisements so presented as to appear private advertisements.

Of course none of the techniques mentioned by Reynolds is without its difficulties.

Promoting fair contract terms

Many of the codes of practice associated with the Office of Fair Trading contain provisions which are intended to promote the use of fair contract terms. The following are examples:

Code of Practice for domestic laundry and cleaning services

Exclusion Clauses

14. Any clause which is intended to exclude, limit or restrict the launderer's/cleaner's liability at Common Law is contrary to the Code. Members of the Association will therefore not attempt to restrict either their liability for certain types of damage caused by their negligence, or the amount of fair compensation which they will pay. They may however wish to ask the customer, at the time the article is accepted, for an indication of the value which the customer places on the article; this may be done when the article is clearly of exceptional value or of unusual manufacture.

Code of Ethical Practice (Glass and Glazing Federation)

7. Installation

. . .

7.3   The delivery period for the order shall be that stated on the contract. If at the expiry of the delivery period so defined the delivery and installation has not been completed, the customer is entitled to make time of the essence of the contract and to give notice to the member in writing to this effect. The Federation would expect members to accept that in such circumstances notice of six weeks would be reasonable. If the work is then not completed in that six-week period then cancellation of the uncompleted work, without penalty to the householder, shall be accepted by the member. Notwithstanding the foregoing clause the member shall not be liable for any delay in the completion of the work which arises from causes beyond the reasonable control of the member and in the event that time has been made the essence of the contract. time shall not run during any period when delay on that account is operating.

7.4   It is a requirement of this Code that members' contracts shall include a clause setting out the cancellation rights that exist at the expiry of the delivery period in the manner defined in Clause 7.3 above. For the convenience of members a suggested draft clause is set out in Appendix A of this Code.

. . .

Appendix A

In order to meet the requirements of paragraph 7.4 of this Code, the following text is suggested to members for inclusion in their contracts:

'If the work is not completed within the delivery period stated in the contract, the customer may serve notice on the supplier in writing, requiring that the work be completed within such reasonable period as the customer may specify (in general the company would accept six weeks as being reasonable). If the work is not completed within such extended period, the customer may cancel the uncompleted work covered by the contract without penalty to himself by the service of a written notice to that effect on the supplier. Notwithstanding the foregoing the company shall not be liable for any delay in the completion of the work which arises from causes beyond the reasonable control of the company and in the event that time has been made the essence of the contract, time shall not run during any period when delay on that account is operating.'

Codes of practice are discussed below Ch 10.

Prior validation

This technique was discussed in some detail by the Law Commission in its Second Report on Exemption Clauses (Law Com No 69 paras 290–314) and rejected. The Commission felt that the advantages of such a system, including the fostering of certainty, were outweighed by the disadvantages. There are indeed practical and theoretical problems in any attempt to apply a test of reasonableness in the abstract. As the Law Commission noted (para 311) the circumstances which are relevant, for example the relative strength of the bargaining positions of the contracting parties, are much easier to apply in 'the particular circumstances of a particular contract between particular parties' than in a vacuum. This is true but it is easy to overstate the difficulties. In particular it is probable that most consumers entering standard-form contracts do so against a background of broadly similar strength (or weakness) when compared with the supplier of the goods or services in question. Nevertheless most commentators seem to agree that the most frequently cited example of a system of prior validation, the Israeli Standard Contracts Law (ISCL) 1964, has been something of a failure. Sinai Deutsch comments as follows in his book *Unfair Contracts* (1977) at pp 246–247 (footnotes omitted):

The most original innovation under the Israeli statute is, however, administrative control of standard contracts. The body designated to administer standard contracts was the board originally established by the Restrictive Trade Practices Law, 5719–1959. In order to regulate standard contracts, the board sat as a special tribunal composed of a judge and two other members, the latter presumably representing both commercial and consumer interests. A supplier who wants to ensure that the restrictive terms used in his standard contracts will not be invalidated by courts can apply to the board for prior approval of these terms. If such approval is granted, the restricted terms cannot be challenged in court during the ensuing 5-year period. Should the application for approval be refused, the 'restrictive terms' are void.

This act aroused considerable interest and was soon discussed and analysed by scholars and writers in several countries. The principal remedy which aroused the commentators' curiosity was, of course, the proposed administrative control. In view of the deficiencies of litigation as a remedy for solving unfairness in standard contracts, administrative control was welcomed as a worthwhile potential solution to this problem. Theoretically, it offered all the elements missing in the use of court litigation: certainty, impartial determination, and uniformity of result. An administrative board is clearly better suited to determine the relative interests of suppliers and consumers; its advance determination will ensure that unfair terms will not be used in standardised contracts, and that once the contract is approved, it will not be vulnerable to attack in court. This in turn avoids the considerable expenses involved for both customers and suppliers in separately litigating each case.

. . .

The act's sponsors expected the board to be overburdened with requests to approve 'restricted terms' for standard contracts. There was considerable public indifference to this act, however, and all that the mountain of labour brought forth was 'a mouse.'

(For further comments see Berg, 'The Israeli Standard Contracts Law 1964' (1979) 28 ICLQ 560.) Although there is no immediate prospect of a system of prior validation being adopted in the United Kingdom it is of interest to note that the present Director General of Fair Trading has commented in relation to the Law Commission report that, 'It is perhaps unfortunate that this idea [that is prior validation] was not pursued': see Gordon Borrie, 'Standard Form Contracts in England' [1978] JBL 317, 323.

Injunctive relief

An alternative technique is to seek assurances from, and if necessary injunctive relief against, individual traders who use unenforceable contract terms. West Germany provides a model of this approach which is notable for the involvement of consumer organisations and other bodies.

Act Concerning the Regulation of the Law of Standard Contract Terms (1976) (AGB—Gesetz)

CHAPTER THREE—PROCEDURE

§ 13 Claims for Discontinuance and Retraction
(1) One who applies or recommends the application to legal transactions of stipulations in standard contract terms which are invalid under §§ 9 through 11 of this act may have a claim for discontinuance or retraction brought against him.
(2) Claims for discontinuance and for retraction may validly be brought only
(1) by associations with legal capacity whose statutory duty it is to protect the interests of the consumer by giving information and advice, if these associations have as members other associations active in this sphere, or at least seventy-five natural persons;
(2) by associations with legal capacity to advance commercial interests, or
(3) by chambers of industry and commerce or chambers of artisans.
(3) The associations mentioned in paragraph 2 number 1 may not advance claims for discontinuance and retraction if the standard contract terms are applicable against a merchant and the contract belongs within the scope of his business or if the standard contract terms are recommended for application exclusively between merchants.
(4) Claims within paragraph 1 must be brought within two years commencing with the time when the claimant has acquired knowledge of the application or recommendation of invalid standard contract terms and, even without such knowledge, within four years commencing with the time of the appplication or recommendation.

Otto Sandrock in his article 'The Standard Terms Act 1976 of West Germany' (1978) 26 AJCL 551 (from which the above translation by Nina Galston is taken) comments (at p 567) in relation to this provision:

> [The] number of authorised plaintiffs is still very restricted: the 'common man' has no right to drag an enterprise into court on the public charge of using unlawful standard contract terms. This privilege has been reserved for a small number of organizations which are considered experts in this field.
> If the court deems the action well founded, the text of the order shall, according to § 17, set forth verbatim the standard contract terms objected to; state the kinds of legal transactions in which the standard contract terms may not be used because their use has been discontinued; order discontinuing the application of standard contract terms similar in content; and finally, in the event of an order for retraction, order publication of the judgment in the same manner in which the recommendation was publicized.
> Finally, § 20 sets up a scheme for registering claims and judgments. The court must inform the federal antitrust office (*Bundeskartellamt*) not only of all complaints introduced to prohibit the use of unlawful standard contract terms, but also of all judgments rendered thereon. Hence it will be easy to discover what proceedings have

already been instituted on the unlawfulness of certain standard terms and what stage these proceedings have reached. Nor is there any need to introduce claims on clauses the use of which has already been declared unlawful. For § 21 extends the effect of *res judicata*: once the use of a certain clause by a proponent has been declared illegal, all of his customers are able to claim the protection granted by the earlier order of court.[1]

A further example is provided by the following provision of Swedish law:

Act Prohibiting Improper Contract Terms[2]

s 1(1) If any tradesman in his commercial activities, when offering any goods, service or other commodity to a consumer for primarily personal use, applies a term which, in regard to the payment and other circumstances, is to be considered as improper on the part of the consumer, the Market Court may, if so is called for from a public point of view, issue an injunction prohibiting the tradesman from using that term or in the main the same term in similar cases in the future. The injunction shall be issued under penalty of a fine, unless for special reasons this is deemed unnecessary.

. . .

s 3 Questions concerning the issuing of an injunction shall be considered upon an application. Such an application shall be ade by the Consumer Ombudsman. If, in a certain case, the Ombudsman decides not to make an application, an application may be made by any association of tradesmen, consumers or employees.

. . .

s 4 Decisions concerning the issuing of an injunction shall constitute no obstacle to reconsideration of the matter in question, where altered circumstances or other special reasons give cause for it.

s 5 If special reasons give cause for it, an injunction may be issued also in respect of the period before a final decision is reached *(interim injunction)*.

s 6(1) Questions concerning the issuing of an injunction may, in cases which are not of great importance, be dealt with by the Consumer Ombudsman by submitting to the tradesman a cease and desist order for acceptance.

(2) If such an order has been accepted it shall have the effect of any injunction issued by the Market Court. An acceptance which takes place after the time set out in the submission of the order has expired is, however, without effect.

(3) Further provisions on the submission of cease and desist orders for acceptance shall be issued by the Government.

s 7 Proceedings for the imposition of a fine shall be instituted in an ordinary court of law by the Public Prosecutor. Such proceedings may be instituted only after notification by the Consumer Ombudsman, or, in respect of prohibition under pain of a fine, by any other person who has applied to the Market Court for the injunction.

The Swedish approach seems somewhat more restrictive than that of the West German Act (AGB-Gesetz, above) at least in relation to the apparently limited effect of a judgment against a trader. Professor Hellner describes the position as follows (at pp 89–90) of *The Law and the Weaker Party* Vol I (editor Alan Neal):

The Act to Prohibit Improper Contract Terms

The Act to Prohibit Improper Contract Terms, which dates from 1971, has been mentioned already.[1] At present it constitutes the most important weapon in Sweden for combating unfair

---

1. For further discussion of consumer redress in West Germany see below pp 381–383.
2. The translation is from *The Law and the Weaker Party*, Vol III: The Swedish Statutes (editors Alan Neal and Anders Victorin).

contract terms. Under this Act, a special Court, the Market Court (which has other tasks as well), can issue injunctions against the future use of terms which are considered improper. Such an injunction may only be issued against a merchant, and the power of the Market Court is limited to contracts where the other party is a consumer. The injunction must be directed against a particular merchant (or an employee of a merchant), and it will prohibit him from using the term found improper, or anything which constitutes essentially that same term, in the future. If the merchant does not comply with the injunction, he will be liable to pay a monetary penalty, the amount of which is set in association with the issuing of the injunction.

An injunction has effect only in relation to the merchant against whom it is directed. It does not invalidate the term found improper, even if the merchant uses it after the injunction has been issued. Any other merchant, against whom no injunction has been issued, may also use the same term, and he can do so without risk of any penalty until he himself is made the subject of an injunction. However, it is possible that in such a case a court will set the term aside, under §. 36 of the Contracts Act.

. . .

The Act does not apply only to standard terms, since individual terms, too, may be made subject to injunctions. However, in practice, the terms to which the Act is applied are standard terms; it is not worth taking up individual terms for consideration. A term can be made the subject of an injunction even if it does not yet form part of a contract; it is sufficient that it is included when the merchant presents an offer for a contract . . .

1. Lag om förbud mot oskäliga avtalsvillkor (SFS 1971:112). The following survey is based on the author's report 'Non-judicial control of standard terms' for the 8th Colloquy of European Law, Neuchatel, 6–8 June 1978, arranged by the Council of Europe. Parts of the report are reproduced verbatim.

If English law were to adopt a similar system whereby public agencies (for example the Office of Fair Trading) or consumer organisations seek injunctions restraining the use of unenforceable (or 'unfair') contract terms it would be surprising if it differed markedly from the Swedish model with its individualised approach. As Francis Reynolds noted (above p 275 et seq) the Office of Fair Trading already has powers under Part III of the Fair Trading Act 1973 (below p 424) to deal with traders who are persistently in breach of criminal or civil obligations. However this does not extend to traders who use terms which are simply unenforceable.

The criminal law

The final technique to be noted here is the creation of criminal offences based on the use of void or unenforceable terms. In principle it may be argued that any such power should be used sparingly and only in relation to terms which are unambiguously void. The demands of certainty in the criminal law must preclude any question of creating offences based on the use of terms which are unenforceable only if they fail to satisfy a test of reasonableness (for example under s 2(2) or 3 of the Unfair Contract Terms Act, above). In English law Part II of the Fair Trading Act 1973 (below p 415) confers a power to create offences where it can be established that a practice operates to the economic detriment of consumers but this has been used only infrequently. The scope and interpretation of one such offence based on the use of void terms is to be seen in the following case.

Hughes v Gillian Hall, Hughes v owen Hall [1981] RTR 430, Queen's Bench Divisional Court

Donaldson LJ. These are two appeals by case stated from the decisions of Staffordshire Justices who were confronted with charges against the two defendants alleging offences under article 3(*d*) of the Consumer Transactions (Restrictions on Statements) Order 1976, as amended, and section 23 of the Fair Trading Act 1973.

The facts which gave rise to these offences were that both defendants were involved in a second-hand car business, and they sold cars in circumstances in which the purchasers were given documents which included the magic phrase 'sold as seen and inspected'.

It was argued before the justices that the giving of such a document did not offend against the Order of 1976 and the justices came to the conclusion that that submission was well founded.

In order that the justices' conclusion and my view may be understood, it is necessary to refer first of all to the Order of 1976. The relevant paragraph is in the article 3, which provides:

'A person shall not, in the course of a business . . . (*d*) furnish to a consumer in connection with the carrying out of a consumer transaction or to a person likely, as a consumer, to enter into such a transaction, a document which includes a statement which is a term of that transaction and is void or inconsistent as aforesaid, or, if it were a term of that transaction or were to become a term of a prospective transaction, would be so void or inconsistent.'

The reference to the document being 'void . . . as aforesaid' is a reference to an earlier part of article 3 namely, paragraph (*c*) as amended consequent on section 6 of the Unfair Contract Terms Act 1977. The other thing which is to be said before leaving article 3(*d*) is that it is important to notice that it applies to a document furnished not only in connection with or as part of a transaction, but to a document including a term which *might* have been included in the contract and, if so included, would have been void under section 6 of the Act of 1977. The use of the word 'void' perhaps is not as happy as it might have been, because the effect of section 6 of the Act of 1977 is perhaps not to avoid the term but to prevent the term having the effect contemplated by the section.

Section 6(2) of the Unfair Contract Terms Act 1977 provides:

'As against a person dealing as consumer, liability for breach of the obligations arising from—(a) section 13, 14 or 15 of the '—Sale of Goods Act 1893—'. . . (b) section 9, 10 or 11 of the'— Supply of Goods (Implied Terms) Act 1973—' . . . cannot be excluded or restricted by reference to any contract term'.

The justices stated:

'We were of the opinion that the defendant would be guilty if he had furnished a statement which was void by virtue of section 6(2) of the Unfair Contract Terms Act 1977.'

That conclusion thus far is accepted by both parties. They go on to state:

'The statement "sold as seen and inspected" would be void if its effect was to exclude the consumer's legal rights.'

I think that perhaps, subject to adding 'under the Sale of Goods Act', that too would be accepted by both parties. Then the justices . . . continue:

'The consumer's legal rights would not be avoided because the term used is too vague, it does not express clearly what its intention is, and if construed strictly, against the defendant's interests, and without extrinsic evidence, it would not enable the defendant to avoid civil liability. The term would not, therefore, be void by virtue of the above Act, and accordingly we upheld the submissions of no case to answer and dismissed the two informations.'

It is that last conclusion which lies at the heart of this appeal. It is said by counsel for the defendants that the justices are not only right in saying that the term is too vague, but that it would have no effect anyway. If the car was sold by description, it would make no difference to the purchaser's right, that the implied warranty of description was negatived. He could rely upon the express terms of the contract. He says again that, if the buyer in fact examines the goods before the contract is made, then there is no warranty as to merchantability as regards defects which that examination ought to have revealed. Similarly he says in relation to section 14 (3) of the Act of 1893 that there is no implied warranty of fitness for a particular purpose, unless the buyer expressly or by implication had made known to the seller the particular purpose for which the goods are bought. If the purchaser did make the purpose known, then this clause will not affect the matter one way or another.

I do not accept these submissions. I think that, if a clause was included in the contract saying 'sold as seen and inspected', prima facie and subject always to what else might be expressly said in the contract, that would negative a sale by description. It would be a sale of a specific object as seen and inspected. That would exclude the implied warranty under section 13 of the Sale of Goods Act 1893 and whether or not or how much it left in the way of an express obligation would depend upon the rest of the contract. For example, it would still be open to the purchaser to complain that he got a different car from the one he had seen and inspected. But in my judgment he would lose some of his rights, even if he might till have other rights. This to my mind is quite sufficient to create an offence under this Act, because anything which has that effect would be voided by section 6(2) of the Unfair Contract Terms Act 1977.

For these reasons I think that the justices were incorrect.

I have not expressly referred to their suggestion that it was too vague. It must be implicit in what I have said that it is not too vague. The clause has to be considered in the context of people who buy and sell secondhand cars, and not in the context of marine insurance brokers. In the context in which it is used, I have no doubt as to what it should be understood as meaning.

I would allow the appeal.

Bingham J. I agree.

Appeal allowed with costs. Case remitted to the justices with a direction to continue the hearing.

NOTES

1. In *Cavendish-Woodhouse Ltd v Manley* (1984) 148 JP 299, 82 LGR 376, DC it was held that the words 'bought as seen' on a cash sale invoice for furniture did not contravene the above provision. In the judgment of the court the words merely confirmed that the purchaser had seen the goods that he had bought. They did not purport to exclude implied terms as to fitness or quality in respect of defects which had not been seen. At best this distinction is a very fine one.

2. In addition to the offence indicated by the above case article 3 of the Order applies also to a person who displays on business premises a notice containing a statement purporting to apply a term which would be void by virtue of s 6 of the 1977 Act. There are similar provisions for void terms in advertisements or on the goods themselves or their containers. (For article 5 of the Order which is concerned with manufacturers' guarantees see above p 47).

Consider the following cases in terms of any potential liability arising by virtue of article 3 of the 1976 Order and the Fair Trading Act:

1. Angus runs a corner shop where he has a prominent notice reading: 'Goods Cannot be Exchanged: Examine your Change: Mistakes Cannot be Rectified'.

2. Art, a car dealer, agrees to sell and Bert, a private purchaser, to buy a second-hand car standing on Art's forecourt. Its mileometer reading is 25,000 miles but Art has placed a sticker above it stating: 'Mileage Not Guaranteed'. The terms of the written contract provide that 'The Buyer shall inspect the goods and buy in Reliance on his Own Judgment. No Liability can be accepted for Defects which are Discoverable on Inspection'.

Would it affect the position if the car (a) had done 55,000 miles or (b) was badly corroded as should have been obvious on inspection?

3. Pancho runs a car-hire business. The terms of his standard-form contract provide inter alia that 'No Liability can be Accepted for any Damage Loss and Inconvenience resulting from the use of vehicles However Caused'.

4. Montague runs a safari park a main feature of which is a pride of lions. At the entrance to the park is a large notice stating: 'DANGER. Visitors Enter the Park at their Own Risk. No Liability can be accepted for Personal Injury However Caused.'

Some exempted contracts

Not all contracts are within the scope of the Unfair Contract Terms Act 1977 and indeed some of the exempted contracts are of particular importance to consumers. In this section a brief reference is made to contracts of insurance, and contracts for the carriage of passengers and their luggage by sea and air.

CONTRACTS OF INSURANCE

By para 1(a) of Sch 1 to the 1977 Acts, ss 2 to 4 of the Act do not extend to 'any contract of insurance'. Sir Gordon Borrie has recently described this exemption as 'amazing': see *The Development of Consumer Law and Policy—Bold Spirits and Timorous Souls* (1984), at p 110. It was defended by Mr John Fraser during the Committee stage of the then Avoidance of Liability (England and Wales) Bill as follows:

> Insurance is excluded because, generally speaking, exemption clauses used in insurance contracts define the risk, rather than constitute real exemption clauses. Secondly, contracts of insurance involving international trade are beneficial to this country. It might put our insurance industry at a considerable disadvantage if it had to comply with the provisions of the Bill. Therefore for practical reasons Schedule 1 leaves out insurance contracts from the scope of the Bill.

(See HC Official Report, SC C, 9 March 1977, col 44.)

As is apparent from the cases which are printed above pp 134–146 insurance law can be very harsh so far as ordinary consumer contracts are concerned. Admittedly the statements of practice which have been issued by the insurance companies and which are printed above pp 144–146 go some way towards alleviating the problems and the same is true of the establishment of the Insurance Ombudsman Bureau: see above p 146 and below pp 324–326. It is likely that legislation will be introduced in the near future.

CARRIAGE BY SEA

The United Kingdom is a party to the Athens Convention which contains the following provisions.

Athens Convention Relating to the Carriage of Passengers and their Luggage by Sea, 1974 (Cmnd 6326)

The States Parties to this Convention,
Having recognized the desirability of determining by agreement certain rules relating to the carriage of passengers and their luggage by sea;
Have decided to conclude a Convention for this purpose and have thereto agreed as follows:

Article 1

Definitions
In this Convention the following expressions have the meaning hereby assigned to them:
1. (a) 'carrier' means a person by or on behalf of whom a contract of carriage has been concluded, whether the carriage is actually performed by him or by a performing carrier;
    (b) 'performing carrier' means a person other than the carrier, being the owner, charterer or operator of a ship, who actually performs the whole or a part of the carriage;
2. 'contract of carriage' means a contract made by or on behalf of a carrier for the carriage by sea of a passenger or of a passenger and his luggage, as the case may be;
3. 'ship' means only a seagoing vessel, excluding an air-cushion vehicle;

. . .

9. 'international carriage' means any carriage in which, according to the contract of carriage, the place of departure and the place of destination are situated in two different States, or in a single State if, according to the contract of carriage or the scheduled itinerary, there is an intermediate port of call in another State;

. . .

Article 2

Application
1. This Convention shall apply to any international carriage if:
    (a) the ship is flying the flag of or is registered in a State Party to this Convention, or
    (b) the contract of carriage has been made in a State Party to this Convention, or
    (c) the place of departure or destination, according to the contract of carriage, is in a State Party to this Convention.

. . .

Article 5

Valuables
The carrier shall not be liable for the loss of or damage to monies, negotiable securities, gold, silverware, jewellery, ornaments, works of art, or other valuables, except where such valuables have been deposited with the carrier for the agreed purpose of safe-keeping in which case the carrier shall be liable up to the limit provided for in paragraph 3 of Article 8 unless a higher limit is agreed upon in accordance with paragraph 1 of Article 10.

. . .

Article 7

Limit of liability for personal injury
1. The liability of the carrier for the death of or personal injury to a passenger shall in no case exceed 700,000 francs per carriage. Where in accordance with the law of the court seized of the case damages are awarded in the form of periodical income payments, the equivalent capital value of those payments shall not exceed the said limit.
2. Notwithstanding paragraph 1 of this Article, the national law of any State Party to this Convention may fix, as far as carriers who are nationals of such State are concerned, a higher per capita limit of liability.

Article 8

Limit of liability for loss of or damage to luggage
1. The liability of the carrier for the loss of or damage to cabin luggage shall in no case exceed 12,500 francs per passenger, per carriage.
2. The liability of the carrier for the loss of or damage to vehicles including all luggage carried in or on the vehicle shall in no case exceed 50,000 francs per vehicle, per carriage.
3. The liability of the carrier for the loss of or damage to luggage other than that mentioned in paragraphs 1 and 2 of this Article shall in no case exceed 18,000 francs per passenger, per carriage.
4. The carrier and the passenger may agree that the liability of the carrier shall be subject to a

deductible not exceeding 1,750 francs in the case of damage to a vehicle and not exceeding 200 francs per passenger in the case of loss of or damage to other luggage, such sum to be deducted from the loss or damage.

. . .

Article 10

Supplementary provisions on limits of liability
1. The carrier and the passenger may agree, expressly and in writing, to higher limits of liability than those prescribed in Articles 7 and 8.
2. Interest on damages and legal costs shall not be included in the limits of liability prescribed in Article 7 and 8.

. . .

Article 11

Defences and limits for carriers' servants
    If an action is brought against a servant or agent of the carrier or of the performing carrier arising out of damage covered by this Convention, such servant or agent, if he proves that he acted within the scope of his employment, shall be entitled to avail himself of the defences and limits of liability which the carrier or the performing carrier is entitled to invoke under this Convention.

. . .

Article 13

Loss of right to limit liability
1. The carrier shall not be entitled to the benefit of the limits of liability prescribed in Articles 7 and 8 and paragraph 1 of Article 10, if it is proved that the damage resulted from an act or omission of the carrier done with the intent to cause such damage, or recklessly and with knowledge that such damage would probably result.
2. The servant or agent of the carrier or of the performing carrier shall not be entitled to the benefit of those limits if it is proved that the damage resulted from an act or omission of that servant or agent done with the intent to cause such damage, or recklessly and with knowledge that such damage would probably result.

Article 14

Basis for claims
    No action for damages for the death of or personal injury to a passenger, or for the loss of or damage to luggage, shall be brought against a carrier or performing carrier otherwise than in accordance with this Convention.

Article 15

Notice of loss or damage to luggage
1. The passenger shall give written notice to the carrier or his agent:
    (a) in the case of apparent damage to luggage:
        (i) for cabin luggage, before, or at the time of disembarkation of the passenger;
        (ii) for all other luggage, before or at the time of its re-delivery;
    (b) in the case of damage to luggage which is not apparent, or loss of luggage, within fifteen days from the date of disembarkation or re-delivery or from the time when such re-delivery should have taken place.
2. If the passenger fails to comply with this Article, he shall be presumed, unless the contrary is proved, to have received the luggage undamaged.
3. The notice in writing need not be given if the condition of the luggage has at the time of its receipt been the subject of joint survey or inspection.

. . .

As may be expected, major shipping companies avail themselves of the benefits of these limitations. The extract which follows is taken from the conditions of such a company.

Conditions (The Peninsular and Oriental Steam Navigation Company)

The contract
1.   The contract shall be between P&O and the Passenger. 'P&O' means The Peninsular and Oriental Steam Navigation Company and/or P&O Cruises Ltd. 'The Passenger' means every person whose name appears on the booking form and/or a P&O ticket.

. . .

Liability
15.   P&O shall not be liable in respect of:–
  (i)   the death, injury or sickness of any Passenger or in respect of the loss of or damage to any luggage or goods (other than valuables deposited at the Purser's Office for the agreed purpose of safekeeping) belonging to or travelling with any Passenger unless the same is due to the negligence of P&O, its Master, crew, servants or agents in which event P&O's liability shall be limited to the amounts contained in Articles 7 and 8 of the Athens Convention Relating to the Carriage of Passengers and their Luggage by Sea, 1974.
  (ii)   the loss of or damage to any valuables or other articles specified in Article 5 of the said Athens Convention howsoever caused unless the same have been deposited at the Purser's Office for the agreed purpose of safekeeping in which case P&O shall only be liable up to the limits provided in Article 8(3) of the said Athens Convention.
16.   Any damages payable by P&O up to the said Athens Convention limits shall be reduced in proportion to any contributory negligence by the Passenger and by the maximum deductible specified in Article 8(4) of the said Athens Convention.
17.   In accordance with Article 15 of the Athens Convention, luggage shall be deemed to have been delivered undamaged to the Passenger unless written notice of any loss or damage is given to P&O:—
  (i)   before or at the time of disembarkation in the case of apparent damage, or
  (ii)   within 15 days from that date of disembarkation or redelivery or from the time when such redelivery should have taken place in the case of loss or damage which is not apparent.
18.   P&O shall in no circumstances be liable in respect of consequential loss or damage, detention, delay or overcarriage howsoever caused.

. . .

22.   P&O shall in any event be entitled to the maximum protection allowed by law in respect of the liability of or any limitation on damages recoverable from Shipowners.

Actions, claims & time limits
23.   Any action covered by the Athens Convention may be brought in any Court specified in Article 17 thereof. Any other action, suit, or proceeding arising out of or connected with any contract between P&O and the Passenger shall only be brought in London. All proceedings including arbitration shall be governed by English Law both as to liability and the amount of damages whether or not they are covered by that Convention and wherever they may be brought, heard or disposed of.
24.   If despite Condition 23 hereof the Court or Tribunal applies any other law P&O shall in respect of all exclusions and limitations of liability contained herein be entitled to the maximum protection allowed by that law including any statutory protection as to the amount of damages recoverable.
25.   Any claim which is not covered by the Athens Convention must be notified in writing to P&O within 28 days of disembarkation or of the date when the claimant first had knowledge of the material facts giving rise to the claim, whichever date is the later, and any action thereon must be commenced within two years of such date. Unless these time limits are complied with P&O shall be under no liability to the Passenger whatsoever. Any action or proceeding covered by the Athens Convention shall be time barred after a period of two years in accordance with Article 16 thereof.

The Peninsular and Oriental Steam Navigation Company

Note re Liability/Limitations
P&O's liability under the Athens Convention is limited to amounts which currently approximate to £33,037 sterling in respect of death or personal injury; £590 sterling for loss of or damage to cabin luggage and £849 sterling for loss of or damage to other luggage. The deductible is about £9 sterling.

CARRIAGE BY AIR

Similar limitations apply to the carriage of passengers and their luggage by air. The following short extracts from recent cases are concerned with loss of luggage and injury to passengers respectively.

Collins v British Airways Board [1982] 1 All ER 302, [1982] QB 734, Court of Appeal

The facts are set out in the judgment of Lord Denning MR.

Lord Denning MR. When you travel by air to a foreign country and your baggage is lost or damaged, what compensation can you recover from the airlines? Usually you can only recover a limited amount under the Warsaw Convention. Many people are aware of this limitation. So they insure so as to cover the full value. It is only a small premium. But suppose you do not insure and are relegated to the Warsaw Convention, what damages you get? It depends on the terms of the ticket. Most of us know the procedure, but for those who do not, I will tell you what happens when you go on international carriage. You have your ticket beforehand. It is described as a 'Passenger ticket and baggage check'. It has tear-off strips for the stages of the journey. You go to the reception desk with your baggage. You keep your hand luggage to take with you on the aircraft. You put the heavier baggage onto the weighing machine. The young lady fastens the baggage tags onto the pieces and clips the corresponding tags onto your ticket. They go off down the conveyor belt. (You do not see your baggage again until you retrieve it, if you are lucky, at your destination.) The young lady hands you back your ticket with the tags clipped on it. Off you go to wait for the time when your flight is called. She may, or may not, have written anything onto your ticket, but you do not read it at that time. You probably do not read it at all, unless you do so on the aircraft for want of anything better to do.

Now suppose your luggage is lost and you sue the airline for damages. What amount of damages can you recover? According to the judge in this case, it depends on what the young lady has written on your ticket. There is a little tiny space in which she can insert the number of pieces and the weight of your baggage. If she has written something there (it is probably quite undecipherable), you can recover only a limited amount. The limit is that stated in the Warsaw Convention. But, if she has written nothing, you can recover the full value of your baggage, regardless of the Warsaw Convention. So says the judge in this case. This does seem a strange state of the law. We have to see whether it is right or not.

The facts

To come to the facts of this case. On 8 November 1977 British Airways issued two tickets to Mr and Mrs Collins for a round trip from Manchester to Los Angeles and back, with stops at London on the way out and New York on the way back. The tickets were marked plainly 'Passenger ticket and baggage check'. On the outward journey the young lady at the desk at Manchester filled in the little space for 'baggage check' with the figures '2/46', meaning two pieces weighing 46 kg.

On arrival at Los Angeles, Mr and Mrs Collins collected their two pieces quite safely. They did some shopping in Los Angeles and came back with three pieces. They arrived, however, late at the airport. There was no time to check in their baggage and put it on their plane. So they went aboard the aircraft with their tickets and no entry whatever in the little space for 'Baggage checked'. There was no time for it. They were told that the baggage would be forwarded on to Manchester by the next British Airways flight. That was done. But, owing to the delay, some thieves were able to ransack the three pieces. They stole the contents and forwarded the three pieces to Manchester. They arrived 24 hours later. When Mr and Mrs Collins took delivery of the three pieces, they were nearly empty. Thereupon Mr and Mrs Collins claimed the value of the contents, £2,000. British Airways said that the limit under the Warsaw Convention was £580.20, and paid that sum into court.

It is obvious that the airline had no opportunity at all of filling in the little space on the baggage check. Nevertheless because nothing was written there, Mr and Mrs Collins claim full damages. This does seem strange to me. But it all turns on the true interpretation of the Warsaw Convention which has the force of law by s 1 of the Carriage by Air Act 1961.

[His Lordship then held that the omission to fill in the baggage check at Los Angeles was merely an 'irregularity' which did not bar the airline from claiming the benefit of the limited liability under the Convention. Hence the appeal should be allowed. Eveleigh LJ agreed that the appeal should be allowed. Kerr LJ dissented.] *Appeal allowed.*

Goldman v Thai Airways International Ltd [1983] 3 All ER 693, [1983] 1 WLR 1186, Court of Appeal

The facts as stated in the headnote to the report were as follows:

The plaintiff was a passenger on a flight from London to Bangkok aboard an aircraft owned and operated by the defendant airline. During the flight the pilot failed to illuminate the seat belt sign when the aircraft entered an area for which moderate clear air turbulence had been forecast and when severe turbulence was encountered in that area the plaintiff, whose seat belt was not fastened, was thrown from his seat and sustained severe injuries. The plaintiff brought an action for damages against the defendants under the Warsaw Convention, as amended at The Hague in 1955 and as set out in Sch 1 to the Carriage by Air Act 1961. Article 22(1) of the convention limited the amount of damages recoverable to approximately £11,800, but art 25 provided that the limitation on the amount recoverable did not apply if it was shown that 'the damage resulted from an act or omission of the carrier [which was] done with intent to cause damage or recklessly and with knowledge that damage would probably result'.

The trial court judge found that the pilot's conduct fell within the provisions of Art 25 and he awarded damages of some £41,000. The defendants appealed.

O'Connor LJ. . . . A passenger injured during a flight governed by the Warsaw Convention as amended at The Hague in 1955 can recover damages up to a limited sum without proof of fault (arts 17 and 22). Article 20 allows the airline to avoid even the limited payment in certain circumstances. Article 25 allows the passenger to escape the limitation of art 22 if he proves—

> 'that the damage resulted from an act or omission of the carrier, his servants or agents, done with intent to cause damage or recklessly and with knowledge that damage would probably result . . .'

It must be remembered that art 22 imposes limits not only for personal injury, but also for loss of or damage to goods, so that 'the damage' referred to in art 25 may be personal injury or damage to goods. This makes the provisions of an act 'done with intent to cause damage' more readily intelligible. This provision shows that the limited recompense is to be the normal liability, and that only exceptional wrongdoing is to avoid the limit. It is in this context that the provision 'recklessly and with knowledge that damage would probably result' has to be construed.

In the present case the plaintiff had to prove that his injury resulted from an act or omission of Captain Swang, done recklessly with knowledge that damage would probably result.

The judge has found that Captain Swang flew the aircraft into an area where CAT was forecast without illuminating the seat belt sign in breach of the requirements of the airline's manual of instructions, and that in so doing he acted recklessly. This finding was based on the judge's acceptance of the evidence of the plaintiff's expert witnesses, in preference to those of the defendants, and on his assessment of Captain Swang as a witness. Having read the whole of the evidence, I would not have come to the same conclusion, but I am conscious that in this court we must be slow to differ from the findings of the trial judge which depend on his assessment of the witnesses. There was evidence that it was good practice to belt up before entering an area where moderate CAT was forecast. Equally there was evidence that careful pilots exercised a discretion and waited for tell-tale signs of light turbulence before pinning the passengers to their seats. There is not, and indeed there could not have been, a finding that that evidence was deliberately dishonest. It follows that even if I accept the judge's finding that Captain Swang's omission to light the seat belt sign was reckless, I do not think that there was any evidence from which the judge could conclude that Captain Swang had knowledge that damage would result from his omission.

I cannot construe art 25 by such considerations as wine glasses falling off trays. The damage must be connected with the act or omission, and there was no evidence that Captain Swang knew that injury to passengers would probably result from this omission. The judge seems to have thought that any sort of damage was enough. I think he fell into error in so doing. I do not think that the plaintiff came anywhere near proving that Captain Swang knew that damage would probably result, and accordingly the plaintiff cannot invoke the relief given by art 25 of the convention.

Eveleigh and **Purchas LLJ** agreed that the appeal should be allowed.

Appeal allowed. Judgment for plaintiff for £11,700. Leave to appeal refused.

CHAPTER 7

The enforcement of private law remedies: I Some problems of individual redress

Introduction

The notable changes in substantive laws of relatively recent years, recorded in previous chapters, have been intended (at least in part) to benefit consumers. But such changes, however desirable, are insufficient without genuine access to justice for those whom the laws are intended to serve. Here the record is patchy. The New Law Journal commented in September 1979:

> If legislation specifically enacted for the protection of ordinary consumers is not to be seen as a mere 'paper tiger', changes in procedural law are likely to be required in aid of its enforcement. Without such changes, substantive law reform may well prove a pointless exercise. It is a measure of the failure of existing procedures that recourse to the courts is not universally available to wronged individuals. In that situation, it is manifestly a fraudulent claim that equality of access to justice is one of the hallmarks of our legal system.

The barriers to effective redress take many forms and it would be unrealistic to believe that all can be removed or even diminished significantly. The individual consumer must both perceive that he has a legitimate grievance and be prepared to do something about it. This will depend in part on the general level of consumer education and on access to information and advice. Many will fall at the first hurdle. Redress may depend on there being an accessible procedure for dealing with 'small claims', whether through the courts or through conciliation or arbitration facilities. This in turn may be affected by the availability of legal aid. However even the most accessible court will be a disappointment if the debtor is insolvent or if a successful plaintiff runs up against problems in enforcing a judgment debt. These and other issues of individual redress are illustrated by the materials and cases in this chapter. In the following chapter attention is focused on some aspects of what Professor Mauro Cappelletti has termed the 'second wave of the access to justice approach', namely the problems of providing legal representation to diffuse and collective interests (see Cappelletti and Garth, 'Access to Justice: The Newest Wave in the Worldwide Movement to Make Rights Effective' (1978) 27 Buffalo LR 181, 197). Here concern is with such matters as representative and 'class' actions which some have found increasingly attractive as a means of dealing with collective grievances. This leads to discussion of a possible role for both consumer organisations and public agencies in taking on public interest litigation. Accordingly the ground covered by the two chapters is very extensive although it all falls within the one broad connecting theme.

There is a wealth of comparative information on these topics in the Florence 'Access to Justice' series (1978–79): see Vol 1 *Access to Justice: A World Survey* (eds M. Cappelletti and B. Garth); Vol 2, *Access to Justice: Promising Institutions* (eds M. Cappelletti and J. Weisner); Vol 3 *Access to Justice: Emerging Issues and Perspectives* (eds M. Cappelletti and B. Garth); Vol 4 *Access to Justice: Anthropological Perspective* (ed K. F. Koch). For other general surveys see Duggan, 'Consumer Redress and the Legal System' in A. J. Duggan and L. W. D. Darvall (eds) *Consumer Protection Law and Theory* (1980) Ch 4; R. Cranston, 'Access to Justice for Consumers: A Perspective from Common Law Countries' (1979) 3 Journal of Consumer Policy 291; I. Ramsay, 'Consumer Redress Mechanisms for Poor-Quality and Defective Products' (1981) 31 Univ Toronto LJ 117; C. J. Miller, 'Some Problems of Individual and Collective Consumer Redress in English Law' in S. D. Anderman (ed) *Law and the Weaker Party* Vol II (1982) p 121.

Problems and complaints

The annual statistics published by the Office of Fair Trading provide information about the range and quantity of complaints in any given year. The latest figures available and published in the Annual Report of the Director General of Fair Trading for 1983 are given in the table on p 1 above. Although such figures are helpful there is no doubt that they represent only the tip of the iceberg. Faced with such problems many consumers will simply do nothing. Others will take a conscious decision to transfer their custom elsewhere ('exit' as it is sometimes known) and others will voice their complaint only to their supplier. None of these will appear in the returns of advice agencies and trading standards departments from which the Office of Fair Trading figures are derived.

'Dispute processing' and complaint handling are areas in which there is an enormous amount of American literature, much of which is replete with sociological jargon. One study which is more accessible than most was conducted by Best and Andreasen and published under the heading 'Consumer Response to Unsatisfactory Purchases: A Survey of Perceiving Defects, Voicing Complaints, and Obtaining Redress' (1977) 11 Law and Society Review, 701. (For further discussion in this general area see the 'Special Issue on Dispute Processing and Civil Litigation' in (1980) 15 Law and Society Review, p 401 et seq; Cranston *Regulating Business: Law and Consumer Agencies* (1979), p 57 et seq and Diener and Greyser, 'Consumer Views of Redress Needs' [1978] Journal of Marketing, p 21).

The Best and Andreasen study was based on telephone interviews with some 2,419 respondents in thirty-four American cities and it revealed that problems (other than those involving only the price of the goods and services) were 'perceived' in some twenty per cent of cases overall. Some other conclusions have been summarised helpfully by Iain Ramsay in his article 'Consumer Redress Mechanisms for Poor-Quality and Defective Products' (1981) 31 University of Toronto Law Journal 117. Ramsay writes at pp 123–125 (footnotes omitted):

> Only 39.7% of consumers who perceived a problem took any kind of action. The most common response was to voice a complaint to the seller and ask for a refund,

replacement, or repair. The other significant response was exit—making a conscious decision to change the seller patronized or brand purchased. Only 1.2% of consumers perceiving problems voiced a complaint to a third party (for example, a Better Business Bureau, Consumer Affairs Department, media ombudsman). Important factors in affecting the rate of voicing complaints were the cost of purchase, the complexity of the problem, and the cost of repairing the defect. Manifest problems— for example, breakage or the wrong product—were voiced more frequently than judgmental problems such as durability or product design. After a complaint was voiced satisfactory solutions were reached in 56.5% of cases (manifest problems 61%, judgmental 50%). When complaints were presented to a third party, one third of all resolutions were satisfactory to the buyer.

The general conclusions of the study were that 'voiced complaints overrepresent problems that are simple, that involve high cost, and that are experienced by high socio-economic status households' and that 'third parties deal only with a small segment of the problems people perceive and the complaints people voice.' They also noted a general disinclination among consumers in general either to be identified as a victim of a consumer problem or as a person who complained . . .

A central finding of Best and Andreasen's study for those interested in consumer redress mechanisms was the almost perfect monopoly that sellers had on complaint handling. Few consumers made use of third-party mechanisms even if they were dissatisfied with the seller's response.

Whatever the methodological strengths or weaknesses of the Best and Andreasen study there is little reason to doubt the correctness of at least the broad picture which it paints. Although the United Kingdom can claim to have a better system of agencies to facilitate the seeking of independent advice (notably Citizens Advice Bureaux) (see below p 295 et seq) it is doubtful whether the position is markedly different here. Indeed the National Consumer Council's Consumer Concerns Survey (1981) said (at p 5) 'There is a further—and rather depressing—conclusion from our study. The vast majority of people with a problem or complaint about public and private sector goods and services did nothing about it.' (See also the NCC Special Paper 1 'Faulty Goods' (1981)). It is not difficult to guess at the reasons, which include apathy, a reluctance to tackle large institutions, and the time and cost involved.

The extracting of the above comments is not intended to suggest that consumers should invoke the assistance of an independent third party whenever they have a complaint. On the contrary there are obvious advantages in matters being resolved by complaining directly to the suppliers concerned. Such complaints will no doubt meet with a variety of responses. One possibility is that suggested by Alan Milner when he notes ('Settling Disputes: The Changing Face of English Law', (1974) 20 McGill, LJ 522, 523):

> One technique of dispute settlement which I shall mention but briefly is that of *settlement by inertia*. By this I mean that when a dispute arises, one party to it, although recognising the existence of the dispute, accepts a situation unfavourable to himself and does little or nothing about it. This is in all probability the most common way in which disputes are 'settled' . . . For example, I was recently told with obvious cynicism by a public relations officer in a large commercial concern that customer inertia always operated in favour of the company. More often than not, dissatisfied customers did not complain; if they did, and received no reply for some considerable time, the chances were better than 50% that they would take no further action. The company then treated the complaint as 'settled'.

A slightly more optimistic picture is suggested by another American study by Ross and Littlefield ('Complaints as a Problem-Solving Mechanism' (1978) 12 Law and Society Review 199). It is linked to the complaint-handling procedures of a major distributor of television sets with a middle-class clientèle in Denver. It notes (at p 211) that both this distributor and others within the area operated 'extremely liberal policies in the matter of repairs, exchanges and refunds, typified by slogans such as "satisfaction always or your money refunded".' Such policies often went well beyond the strict requirements of the law as in the case of the following extract from the manual of the giant Sears Roebuck company:

> The basic policy of the Company is '*Satisfaction Guaranteed or Your Money Back.*'
> The purchaser of any product or service sold by Sears, who, *within a reasonable time after purchase*, advises that he is dissatisfied with his purchase *for any reason,* will obtain prompt and courteous action in accordance with his wishes on the part of the Sears unit contacted. It is Company policy that we accept the customer's judgment of what it takes to satisfy him, including refunding his full purchase price, or the service charges paid.

Similarly, and in the United Kingdom, generous refund policies are operated by such organisations as Marks and Spencer. One assumes that they are commercially sound, especially in the case of a large organisation and where there is a likelihood of repeat purchases (see generally Ramsay, (1981) 31 University of Toronto Law Journal 117, 126 et seq). Ross and Littlefield draw the following broad conclusions (at pp 214–215 of their survey):

> The characterisation of the complaint mechanism as a cheap and effective instrument for solving consumer problems entails policy implications. From the viewpoint of consumer protection, enhancing the complaint mechanism is superior to expanding the use of formal legal institutions, even when the latter are simplified and adapted to consumer problems. Two-party negotiation is generally simpler, quicker, and less costly than any third-party institution, even when the latter is modified to handle small claims. Similarly, changing the substantive law of sales is unlikely to produce outcomes as favourable to consumers as those they can obtain through the complaint mechanisms . . .
> Although modifications of legal institutions and rules have their place, consumer activists would do well to attend to the conditions under which complaint is likely to be effective.

A similar message about the commercial value of an effective complaints system is to be found in Colin Adamson's report for the NCC entitled 'Consumers in Business' (1982). Adamson notes (at p 15) an American study commissioned by the United States Office of Consumer Affairs (Consumer Complaint Handling in America: Final Report, White House Office of Consumer Affairs, Washington DC, 1979) which shows 'a strong correlation between decisions to buy again from the same company and the satisfactory resolution of complaints'. He adds, 'The people most likely not to repurchase were those who never complained at all . . . Business is lucky to have customers who complain'. In similar vein Laura Nader has noted how complaints often serve to alert business and government agencies to potentially severe problems (See Nader *No Access to Law: Alternatives to the American Judicial System* (1980), p 9).

In general, therefore, it is important to realise that although the bulk of this chapter is concerned with ways of facilitating *legal* redress—in the sense of redress through the courts and arbitration schemes—such redress is but a small part of the total picture. It seems that most problems do not lead to a complaint and of those which do few are likely to be brought to the attention of an independent third party.

Some general considerations

There are other, more general, considerations which have been discussed in the American literature and elsewhere and which may be seen as placing the consumer litigant at an inherent disadvantage. Some, such as the question of legal aid and the specific problems of small claims, are noted later in this chapter. Others, which have been outlined by for example Professors Cappelletti and Garth (see (1978) 27 Buffalo LR 181, at p 186 et seq) include the greater financial resources of organisations, their ability to withstand the delays of litigation and their competence to recognise and pursue a claim of defence. Having discussed these points, the authors note a further advantage (at p 191; footnotes omitted):

> Professor Galanter has developed the distinction between what he calls 'one-shot' and 'repeat-player' litigants, based primarily on the frequency of encounters with the judicial system.[1] He has suggested that this distinction corresponds to a large extent to that between individuals, who typically have isolated and infrequent contacts with the judicial system, and ongoing organizations, with a long-term judicial experience. The advantages of the repeat player, according to Galanter, are numerous: (1) experience with the law enables better planning for litigation; (2) the repeat player has economies of scale because he has more cases; (3) the repeat player has opportunities to develop informal relations with members of the decision-making institution; (4) he may spread the risk of litigation over more cases; and (5) he can utilize strategies with particular cases to secure a more favorable posture for future cases. It appears that because of these advantages, organizational litigants are indeed more effective than individuals. There are clearly fewer problems in mobilizing organizations to take advantage of their rights, often against just those ordinary people who in their posture as consumers, for example, are most reluctant to seek the benefits of the legal system.
>
> This gap in access can be most effectively attacked, according to Galanter, if individuals find ways of aggregating their claims and developing long-term strategies to counteract the advantages of the organizations they must often face . . .

Similar points have been made by, for example, Professor Ison (see 'Small Claims' (1972) 35 MLR 18).

A possible way of helping to redress the imbalance and stimulate litigation is suggested by the following extract from the (American) Consumer Credit Protection Act:

§ 1640. Civil liability

Individual or class action for damages; amount of award; factors determining amount of award
(a) Except as otherwise provided in this section, any creditor who fails to comply with any requirement imposed under this part, including any requirement under section 1635 of this title, or part D or E of this subchapter with respect to any person is liable to such person in an amount equal to the sum of—
   (1) any actual damage sustained by such person as a result of the failure;
   (2)(A)(i) in the case of an individual action twice the amount of any finance charge in connection with the transaction, or (ii) in the case of an individual action relating to a consumer lease under part E of this subchapter, 25 per centum of the total amount of monthly payments under the lease, except that the liability under this subparagraph shall not be less than $100 nor greater than $1,000; . . .

Although it is most unlikely that English law would adopt a similar provision stipulating the recovery of 'minimum damages', such provisions may (at least in theory) help to benefit those who would not otherwise sue for relatively small sums of money.

---

1. See Galanter, 'Why the "Haves" Come out Ahead: Speculations on the Limits of Legal Change' (1974) 9 Law and Society Review 95; Afterword: Explaining Litigation (1975) 9 Law and Society Review 347.

Consumer advice and legal aid

The availability of advice and, where appropriate, of legal aid is of major importance to the effective enforcement of consumers' rights. For convenience the materials in this section are divided into two parts covering first, aspects of non-specialist and typically free advice (for example from Citizens Advice Bureaux) and second, professional legal advice and the operation of the civil legal aid scheme. Some of the principal sources of information in this area are to be found in the following papers and reports:

'Information and Advice Services in the United Kingdom: Report to the Minister of State for Consumer Affairs' (NCC, 1983); Gillian Borrie, 'Advice Agencies: What they do and who uses them' (NCC, 1982); The Fourth Right of Citizenship: A Review of Local Advice Services (NCC, 1977); Review of the National Association of Citizens Advice Bureaux (the Lovelock Committee) Cmnd 9139, 1984; Report of the Royal Commission on Legal Services (the Benson Commission) Cmnd 7648, 1979, Chs 7 and 8 especially.

CITIZENS ADVICE BUREAUX AND SIMILAR SOURCES OF ADVICE

Within the United Kingdom the principal source of local and non-specialist consumer information and advice is the Citizens Advice Bureau (CAB) service. Begun at the outbreak of war in 1939 and built on the work of existing voluntary organisations the service traditionally covers a wide field. Recently it has been the subject of a report by Sir Douglas Lovelock and his committee who had been appointed by the Secretary of State with the following terms of reference: 'To review the functioning of the National Association of Citizens Advice Bureaux and to make recommendations, with a view to ensuring that the Association offers the best possible service and support to local citizens advice bureaux; and that the monies available to the Association are spent in the most effective way'. (See the Review of the National Association of Citizens Advice Bureaux, Cmnd 9139, 1984). The review had been announced by Dr Gerard Vaughan, then Minister for Consumer Affairs, against a background of increased government funding to the central body of the service (NACAB). Dr Vaughan had stated earlier that he 'felt it proper to inquire if the money was being used effectively' (see Hansard 40 HC Official Report (6th series), col 676, 12 April 1983). The other aspect of concern to the Minister was 'allegations of changing attitudes within some CABs and the taking up of campaigns that some people have seen as going outside the generally accepted scope of the service' (ibid. (As to this latter point the Lovelock Committee found 'relatively few and relatively minor instances to justify this concern' (para 1.9)). The report itself contains much helpful information on the growth, work, aims and funding of the service.

After discussing the establishment of the service and a period of contraction in the years 1945–1960 the report continues as follows:

Review of the National Association of Citizens Advice Bureaux, Cmnd 9139, 1984

. . .

Resurgence: 1960–73
4.12. The CAB movement emerged from this period of financial stringency to a more favourable climate in the 1960s. There was a growing recognition of the need for advice

services. The Younghusband Committee, for instance, reporting on 'Social Workers in the Local Authority Health and Welfare Services' in 1959, said that 'good information services have become an essential feature of modern life and should be an integral part of the whole range of social services provided by local authorities'[1]. The Report of the Ingleby Committee on Children and Young Persons commented similarly on the need for a comprehensive, generalist service of information and advice[2]. There were also several initiatives to establish specialised advice services alongside the generalist advice service provided by the CAB. The Consumer Association opened its first Consumer Advice Centre in Kentish Town in 1969; following the recommendation of the Seebohm Report in 1968 two Housing Advice Centres were set up in London; and in 1970 the first Law Centre was established in Kensington, offering a free and wide range of legal services, including representation in court. All these centres were precursors of others of their type. These developments were accompanied by the setting up of independent neighbourhood advice centres and local authority advice bureaux, particularly in London.

4.13.   The CAB Service benefited from this general interest in advice work.

. . . In 1962, the Report of the Molony Committee on Consumer Protection remarked 'it is plain that the Citizens Advice Bureaux have already developed an advisory and informative service of great consumer interest, and that they are closely in touch with consumer problems in a way unequalled by any other organisation. Because of the bureaux's current work in the field and the organisation's inherent capacity to enlarge the scope of its operation, we favour the establishment of a country-wide advisory service for the consumer through their agency'[3]. In 1963-64, following the publication of this report, the Board of Trade contributed a grant of £25,000 for the promotion of new bureaux and the strengthening of existing ones. Thereafter the flow of central funding increased steadily with occasional but substantial contributions being made by the Civil Service Department and the Home Office. By 1972–73 the National Committee's funding from central Government was £109,000.

. . .

1974-83
4.15.   This was a period of expansion unparalleled since 1940. As before, the motor force was provided by increased central Government funding, which came in two phases. The first phase was initiated by the offer to the National CAB Council in December 1973 by the then Minister for Trade and Consumer Affairs, Sir Geoffrey Howe, of a Development Grant of £1.45 million over 5 years starting in 1974–75, and the second by the increase in NACAB's grant announced by the then Minister of Consumer Affairs, Mrs Oppenheim, in 1979. The aim of Sir Geoffrey Howe's Development Grant was, in the words of a discussion document produced by the Department of Trade and Industry at the time, to bring about 'a substantial improvement in consumer advice and complaint services over the next few years, both in the number of centres (whether CAB'x with local authority support or centres directly operated by local authorities) and in the quality of advice they give'. Similar support was also given in succeeding years to Consumer Advice Centres (CACs): local authorities received £4.4 million between 1974 and 1977 from the Department of Prices and Consumer Protection for the setting up of CACs, with the consequence that there were some 120 by 1979.

4.16.   The then Department of Trade and Industry's primary objective in offering the Development Grant to the CAB Service was to improve the availability and quality of advice on consumer matters. In accepting the grant, however, the National CAB Council made it clear that the CAB'x provided a generalist advice service and that there was therefore no question of earmarking the money for consumer matters: it would instead be used to improve the quality and coverage of the CAB Service as a whole. In this aim the National CAB Council was generally successful. It was now in a position to offer short-term funding to set up bureaux in partnership with local authorities or to pay for the improvement of existing bureaux by capital improvements, increased staff or special experimental projects. Inevitably the distribution of finance between the bureaux was somewhat uneven, since it was usually carried out on the basis of immediate need, and some areas of the country remained underprovided with advice services. But the number of bureaux and extensions in the United Kingdom as a whole increased by 33 per cent from 615 in 1973–74 to 818 in 1978–79. More significantly, demand for the CABx' services increased: enquiries went up from 1.9 million to 3.3 million, an increase of 74 per cent.

4.17.   The Department of Trade and Industry (and subsequently its successor Department, the Department of Prices and Consumer Protection) was one of a number of Departments providing funding to a CAB Service in the early and middle 1970s. Others which had interests in different areas of the Service's work were the Civil Service Department which provided £34,000 in 1973–74 and the Home Office which provided a total of £105,000 in 1974–75 and 1975–76. It was clearly unsatisfactory for planning purposes for the Service to be funded piecemeal in this way and a meeting was accordingly called in February 1975 of interested parties, including these three Departments and the Departments of Environment, Health and Social Security and the Lord Chancellor's Office, to appoint a single departmental sponsor. The Department of Prices and Consumer Protection (DPCP), as the largest provider of funds, emerged from this meeting with the sponsoring role. This role was subsequently taken on by the Department of Trade when the latter absorbed the DPCP in 1979 and the Department of Trade and Industry in 1983.

4.18.　In 1979 the Minister of Consumer Affairs, Mrs Oppenheim, decided to end the scheme of Government grants to Consumer Advice Centres (CACs) from 1980. In announcing the end of the scheme Mrs Oppenheim said 'I recognise that this may lead to the closure of some centres and so increase the workload of other advisory services . . . In particular, the Citizens Advice Bureaux may well have a good part to play in the future . . . I am anxious to encourage the CAB because it is a voluntary service which is both cost effective and economical'. In November 1979 she announced that the Department of Trade's grant to NACAB would be doubled from £1.85 million in 1979–80 to £4 million in 1980–81.

4.19.　NACAB took the view that the new money should be used partly to develop support services to bureaux from Area Offices and Central Office, and partly to help those bureaux most affected by closure of CACs. It was not used, as the Development Grant had been, specifically to increase the number of bureaux, though the number did increase steadily each year. (The number rose from 859 in the United Kingdom as a whole in 1979–80 to 936 in 1982–83 (9 per cent).) Because the CACs had been concentrated in inner city areas, on Merseyside, and in the Manchester, Yorkshire and Humberside, West Midlands, South Wales and Greater London Areas, the great bulk (68 per cent) of the grants in 1980–81 went to bureaux in these Areas. Bureaux elsewhere found themselves little better off.

. . .

4.22.　Better funding and the achievement of independence allowed the Association to increase its staff. The staff at Central Office increased from 26 in 1973–74 to 98 in March 1983. Though precise figures are not available, staff in Area Offices increased in parallel stabilising at 127 in March 1983. The new paid staff tended to be of a different type from the traditional CAB volunteer. A survey in 1978 of CAB workers in the North West Midlands[4] found that volunteers were predominantly female (73 per cent), predominantly drawn from social classes I and II ('professional and intermediate occupations') (73 per cent) and either middle-aged or elderly (76 per cent were over 50). They wanted to preserve the Service's voluntary nature and independence, they were suspicious of specialization and wary of, though not hostile to, NACAB. The new workers in NACAB were of a different type, generally younger and with careers in advice work or related fields. Their approach was also different. In the words of a group of them: 'They recognised the potential of the Service and the need to develop and expand its work at a fast pace'[5].

4.23.　The Service was expanding anyway in response to the pressures of demand. During the period from 1973–74 to 1982–83 demand for advice and information increased dramatically, with enquiries going up from 1.9 million to 5 million. The type of enquiry also changed in response to changing economic and social conditions. Consumer enquiries, including debt problems, for instance, increased steadily throughout, reflecting the effect of inflation on people's income and spending patterns. In the late 1970s and early 1980s, as the recession began to bite, the fastest growing category of enquiry related to social security. A feature of these categories of enquiry was that many of the cases involved were increasingly complicated and difficult to deal with. Another feature of the development of the Service's workload during this period was an increasing involvement in representing clients at tribunals.

4.24.　Under NACAB's prompting, the Service adapted to this larger and more complex workload by adopting increasingly rigorous and professional standards of performance at the bureau level and by developing a limited degree of specialization. Standards were raised by the laying down of more demanding training requirements, an increase in the minimum number of hours expected of bureau workers, the introduction of a compulsory retirement age and the encouragement of the appointment of paid Organisers in bureaux to ensure continuity and consistency of service. As far as specialization was concerned, the most notable development was the setting up of Tribunal Representation Units (TRUs) to provide technical back-up for bureau workers representing clients at tribunals. The first TRU was set up by a bureau in Newcastle in 1976 and NACAB set up another with assistance from the EEC Anti-Poverty Programme in Wolverhampton in 1976. A dozen more were set up in the next few years. The units were generally staffed by between two and five specialist workers with clerical support. Within the limitations of their catchment areas the units were successful in persuading bureaux to take on tribunal representation work (roughly half of all bureaux now do so) and, on the basis of a good track record, in encouraging claimants to bring cases to bureaux. There was also a modest degree of specialization in the field of legal services, following a NACAB Council decision in the late 1970s to encourage bureaux in the major centres to hire in-house community lawyers. There are now 12 such lawyers employed in various city bureaux.

4.25.   These developments prompted considerable debate from a variety of different standpoints within the Service. At one end of the spectrum it was argued that the increasing emphasis on professional standards and specialization not only threatened the role of the volunteer but would, if allowed to proceed, change the nature of the Service, making it more bureaucratic and less responsive to local needs. At the other end, it was maintained that they were necessary for the efficiency of the Service and to ensure a comprehensive service to clients. The debate was conducted with some vigour at Annual Conferences and in other fora in the late 1970s and early 1980s and is not yet resolved.

1. Report of the Working Party on Social Workers in the Local Authority Health and Welfare Services. London HMSO 1959, paragraphs 1018–1026.
2. Report of the Committee on Children and Young Persons' Command 1191 London HMSO 1960 paragraph 49.
3. Final Report of the Committee on Consumer Protection. HMSO London 1962 para 493.
4. 'Developing a Voluntary Service: the Volunteer's Reply' by Roger Lawrence, NACAB Occasional Paper, November 1978.
5. Combatting Poverty: CAB'x, Claimants and Tribunals by the West Midlands Tribunal Representational Unit, NACAB Occasional Paper, September 1981.

Later in the report the Lovelock Committee notes the main principles which govern the conduct of the CAB service, namely that it is impartial, confidential, free of charge, independent and generalist. It discusses its aims and what is involved in the process of giving advice as follows:

5.1.   The Aims
The CAB Service defines its aims as being:
  (a) To ensure that individuals do not suffer through ignorance of their rights and responsibilities or of the services available; or through an inability to express their needs effectively.
  (b) To exercise a responsible influence on the development of social policies and services, both locally and nationally.

5.2.   These aims, which are known respectively as the First and Second Aims, were approved by the Council of the National Association of Citizens Advice Bureaux (NACAB) in April 1977 after an extensive process of consultation lasting two years with Area Offices and other interested parties . . .

5.7.   The First Aim
There has been a wide consensus since the Second World War that the provision of an advice service is a necessary and useful function in modern society. The need for such a service has been recognised in a series of major reports over the last 40 years. Sir William Beveridge's report on Social Insurance and Allied Services in 1942[1], for instance, recommended that there should be an advice bureau in every local security office which could be able to tell every person in doubt or difficulty 'not only about the official provision for social security but about all the other organs—official, semi-official and voluntary, central or local—which may be able to help him in his difficulty'. The Rushcliffe Report on Legal Aid and Legal Advice[2] recommended in 1945 that the CAB Service continue to offer first level advice and help after the war. We have already referred to the recommendations in the same vein by the Younghusband, Ingleby and Molony Committees (paragraphs 4.12 and 4.13). Most recently the Benson Commission on Legal Services[3] concluded in 1979 that a 'competent, accessible, independent national network of generalist advice agencies is needed' and that CAB's should be the 'basic generalist advice service'. It has even been asserted by the National Consumer Council in its pamphlet *The Fourth Right of Citizenship*[4] and by NACAB in representations to us that access to information and advice is a right. We accept that a citizen has a right to information on matters such as legislation which affect his life and livelihood, though such a right would be hard to define and expensive to finance. We are not convinced that the right to information implies a right to advice. However, there is no need to go so far. The operations of both the welfare state and the market economy have become bewilderingly complex and, like our predecessors in this field, we see a clear need for a generalist advice and information service.

5.8. It is sometimes assumed that a generalist advice and information service simply provides information to enquirers in the manner of, say, a tourist office. NACAB has been at some pains to explain to us that 'advice work is more than the simple activity of looking up answers to questions and telling the client what the advice worker would do if he or she were in the client's shoes'. It has suggested that the following breakdown gives a better picture of the process of advice-giving:

   (a) *Diagnosis.* This is in some ways the most important stage. The diagnosis of the problem is often straightforward, in which case the advice worker may move directly to the next stage of the process. But in a proportion of cases the client's questions do not reveal his or her real concerns and, where this is so, these concerns must be uncovered before proceeding further;

   (b) *Information-giving.* The presentation of relevant facts in a way which can be understood by the client;

   (c) *Advice-giving.* The presentation of the options open to the client and their implications;

   (d) *Referral.* There will be some enquiries which the bureau cannot answer or which can be more appropriately answered elsewhere, in which case it should refer to a specialist agency, such as a solicitor, Law Centre, Money Advice Centre, Housing Advice Centre, etc, or to the appropriate Government Department, local authority department or statutory body;

   (e) *Action/Advocacy.* The worker may become involved in a direct attempt to resolve the client's problem. This may mean writing a letter or contacting an agency by telephone on behalf of the client; or representing a client's case, for example at a tribunal hearing. These are the activities justified by the last clause of the First Aim . . .

1. Special Insurance and Allied Services, HMSO, 1942, para 397.
2. Report of the Committee on Legal Aid and Legal Advice in England and Wales, HMSO 1945, para 185.
3. The Royal Commission on Legal Services: Final Report, HMSO 1979, para 44.5.
4. Fourth Right of Citizenship, National Consumer Council, July 1977.

It is apparent from the above extracts that the CAB service is now a major organisation operating on a nationwide basis. In 1982–83 there were some 936 bureaux in the United Kingdom—including extension bureaux—all autonomous, charitable and voluntary organisations staffed by some 13,700 workers of whom some 12,500 are volunteers. In 1983–84 government funding to the central organisation, NACAB, was some £6.041 million. The level of funding had risen sharply in 1980–81 to compensate for the withdrawal of central Government grants from the specialist consumer advice centres with full-time salaried staff (CACs) which the incoming Conservative Government did not consider to be cost-effective. (According to Mr John Fraser, MP, there were some 120 such centres in Great Britain in November 1978 with grants totalling approximately £3¾ million: see 958 HC Official Report (5th series) 958, written answers col 308, 16 November 1978). It is estimated that apart from this central funding the bureaux receive some £10 million per annum (including £1 million in kind) from local authorities and a small additional amount comes from donations. The Lovelock Committee found that the advantages of dual funding outweighed the disadvantages and recommended (see generally Ch 13 of the report) that an additional £900,000 per annum be made available to NACAB, primarily to strengthen its management.

The following table from the Lovelock Committee report indicates the range and numbers of enquiries dealt with by the CAB service. It will be noted that the highest figure is for 'Consumer, Trade and Business', although this category includes enquiries relating to fuel problems and general debt and finance problems as well as more conventional consumer queries. Similar information is to be found in the NACAB Annual Reports and Accounts.

Table 9.2.: Workload in England, Wales and Northern Ireland

Category	Enquiries 1981–82 000's	% of Total Enquiries 1981–82	Enquiries 1982–83 000's	% of Total Enquiries 1982–83	% Increase in Enquiries 1982–83 over 1981–82
Consumer, Trade and Business	790	17.3	870	17.3	10.1
Social Security	595	13.2	768	15.3	29.1
Housing, Property and Land	684	15.1	761	15.1	11.3
Family and Personal	607	13.4	626	12.4	3.1
Employment	467	10.3	536	10.6	15.3
Administration of Justice	375	8.3	419	8.3	11.7
Local Information	192	4.3	200	4.0	4.2
Health	156	3.4	165	3.3	5.8
Enquiries about CAB'x	134	3.0	153	3.0	14.2
Taxes and Duties	164	2.8	143	2.8	14.8
Travel, Transport and Holidays	123	2.7	115	2.3	– 6.5
Leisure	80	1.8	71	1.4	–11.2
Education	55	1.2	63	1.3	14.2
Immigration and Nationality	39	0.9	60	1.2	53.8
National and International	66	1.5	55	1.1	–16.7
Communication	28	0.6	29	0.6	3.6
TOTAL	4,515		5,034		11.5

Apart from CABs and solicitors in private practice additional sources of information and advice include law centres, with a staff which will include full-time lawyers, and the news media. A description of the work of law centres and recommendations for the introduction of a new service of Citizens' Law Centres is to be found in the Report of the Royal Commission on Legal Services (the Benson Commission), Cmnd 7648, 1979, Ch 8. See also Zander *Legal Services for the Community* (1978) Chs 2 and 3 and Gillian Borrie, 'Advice Agencies: What do they do and who uses them' NCC, 1982, pp 3–4.

The National Consumer Council Report on 'Information and Advice Services in the United Kingdom' (1983) contains the following general description of the scope and role of information and advice services through the 'media' (at p 32):

(e) The Media
There are numerous information—and sometimes advice—services provided by the media; for example, straightforward information items in the press; phone-ins on local radio; readers' advice columns in the national, provincial and local press; readers' advice columns in a multitude of magazines; information slots on national and regional television; information slots on national and local radio; and public service announcements. The number of people asking for information and/or advice either as a direct result of a broadcast or following media requests for people to send in their problems, shows the major role played by the media in this connection.

Examples of the types of service referred to in the NCC report include

Radio London's *Take our Advice*, BBC 1's *That's Life* (which is said to receive 15,000 letters a week during the series, at least half of which are requests for information and advice), Channel 4's *For What it's Worth* and readers' services in the national press and in magazines.

LEGAL AID AND ADVICE

However valuable the work of such agencies as Citizens Advice Bureaux, it must be desirable in principle that consumers should have access to specifically legal and professional advice. This is so even if one accepts that there is an element of truth in Stewart Macaulay's observation that lawyers rarely go beyond an essentially conciliatory and therapeutic role when dealing with consumers as clients (see Macaulay, 'Lawyers and Consumer Protection Laws' (1979) 14 Law and Society Review 115). In England and Wales the main source of legal advice is the legal aid scheme. This falls into three parts, namely (i) the legal advice and assistance or Green Form scheme, (ii) the civil legal aid scheme, and (iii) the criminal legal aid scheme. This section is concerned with only the first two parts to which there is a useful 'Legal Aid Guide' produced by the Lord Chancellor's Department and the Law Society (November, 1982). Further material of general interest and importance in this area is to be found in, for example, the following sources: the Report of the Committee on Legal Aid and Legal Advice in England and Wales (the Rushcliffe Committee), Cmnd 6641, 1945; the Report of the Royal Commission on Legal Services (the Benson Commission), Cmnd 7648, 1979, Chs 5 and 10–13 especially; the Legal Aid Annual Reports made by the Law Society and by the Lord Chancellor's Advisory Committee on Legal Aid (HMSO); and in Zander *Legal Services for the Community* (Temple Smith, 1978).

Legal advice and assistance

The 'Legal Aid Guide' explains (at para 2.1) that the purpose of the scheme is to enable 'people of small or moderate means to get help from a solicitor free or for a contribution', until his charges reach a certain sum—£50 in non-matrimonial cases as at 26 November 1984. (The figure is somewhat higher in matrimonial cases—£90 from 1 February 1985.)

In order to come within the green form scheme the applicant must qualify financially by showing that both his savings and income are within the current financial limits. As the pamphlet 'Legal Aid—financial limits' explains: 'These limits are based on what is called "disposable" capital and "disposable" income'. 'Disposable' means that appropriate deductions are made (for example for the value of the applicant's house, furniture and fittings) and appropriate allowances) for example for dependants, tax, national insurance contributions etc). The limits are updated annually (in November) and as from 26 November 1984 the limit for eligibility in the case of capital for a person without dependants is £765. In the case of income a person in receipt of supplementary benefit or family income supplement, or who has a weekly disposable income of less than £51 will be eligible for free legal advice and assistance (subject to satisfying the requirements as to capital). A person with a weekly disposable income of more than £108 will not be eligible for such assistance. Between the lower and upper limits contributions are assessed on a scale.

That the green form scheme is of considerable benefit to people of modest means is evident from the tables in the Law Society's annual reports on the operation and finance of the scheme. According to the 33rd Annual Report, a sum in excess of £33 million was paid out in 1982–83, although only a small proportion of this was accounted for by consumer problems, hire-purchase and debt. The relevant percentages for recent years were as follows:

	1978–79	1979–80	1980–81	1981–82	1982–83
Hire-Purchase and Debt	2.54	2.41	2.81	3.29	3.68
Consumer Problems	1.12	1.25	1.43	1.50	1.56

Civil legal aid

The green form scheme does not extend to court work (other than assistance by way of representation in magistrates' courts) for which provision is made by the related scheme for legal aid in civil court proceedings. The Royal Commission on Legal Services (1979) (the Benson Commission) outlined the non-monetary requirements for qualifying for civil legal aid as follows:

The tests to be applied
13.24.   An applicant for civil legal aid is required to show that he has reasonable grounds for taking, defending or being a party to proceedings. In addition, he may be refused legal aid if it appears unreasonable that he should receive it in the particular circumstances of the case. Under the first part of this test an applicant has to show that he has a good case in law and in fact. In our view, this test should be retained unchanged.
13.25.   The second part of the test is concerned with the merits of the case generally and the extent to which there would be real advantage in pursuing it. This involves wider considerations going beyond the legal merits. The time honoured method used by legal aid committees in applying this test is, as the Law Society have told us in evidence, to ask:—

> 'What advice would be given to the applicant if he were a private client with means which were not over-abundant but were adequate to meet the probable costs of the case without involving him in hardship?'

. . .

13.26.   The matter was considered in 1956 by the Select Committee on Estimates of the House of Commons which took the view that it is wrong to adopt the actions of the man of adequate but not over-abundant means as the test of whether legal aid should be granted . We agree with the Select Committee and, while we believe that it is important that legal aid committees should continue to apply strict criteria in sifting the applications for legal aid which come before them, we think that they should take into account any factors peculiar to the applicant or his case which might justify the grant of legal aid. For the reasons given by the Select Committee, the factors to be considered should include such matters as injury to an applicant's reputation, status, civil rights or personal dignity; in such cases, we think that a certificate will often be justified though the sums of money involved may be small. We agree with the change in the criteria which enables legal aid to be granted where a case is of such a nature that success by an applicant would benefit a large number of other people in similar situations. This might include claims by consumers and social security or employment cases of potentially wide application though involving relatively small claims.

The financial qualifications are again dependent on the applicant's disposable capital and income (see above p 301) being within the current financial limits. These limits differ from those which apply to the green form scheme which, as the Benson Commission noted (at para 12.34) 'assumes the provision of a smaller range of services at lower cost'. From 26 November 1984 the free limit of disposable capital was £3,000 and the eligibility limit £4,710. The corresponding figures for disposable income were £2,145 and £5,155 per annum, with the maximum contribution from income being one quarter of the amount by which disposable income exceeds £2,145.

Some points of criticism

Inevitably certain aspects of both the green form and the civil legal aid scheme have attracted criticism. One criticism is of the relatively low levels of the free limits of disposable capital. The civil legal aid capital limit is now aligned with the supplementary benefit limit. As the Law Society noted in its 33rd Legal Aid Annual Report (1982–83) para 97, this has the great advantage 'that the fact of payment of supplementary benefit to an applicant can be used as a passport to legal aid without assessment and without contribution'. Yet as the Lord Chancellor's Advisory Committee on Legal Aid has noted on several occasions there is no such correspondence between the supplementary benefit and the green form limits (see, for example, the 33rd Annual Report (1982–83) paras 47–48 especially). So a person who is entitled to supplementary benefit will not necessarily be entitled to free legal advice. Moreover it is certainly arguable that the lower limit for civil legal aid is in any event unrealistic. This was the view of the Benson Commission whose criticisms have not been met by the increases which have occurred since the Commission reported: As Benson noted:

The free limit—capital
12.41. The present free limit of disposable capital is £1,200 . . . . It is arrived at after deducting from the gross capital the value of the principal dwelling house, the tools of the trade and, save in exceptional cases, household furniture and effects. All applicants are treated on the same basis and no deductions are made for married couples, children or other dependants. The whole of the applicant's capital above the free limit is required as a contribution and it is normally paid in a single lump sum.
12.42. We have no reliable information as to the disposable capital which might now be held, or have been accumulated, by the bulk of the population and the circumstances of the applicants are in any event likely to be widely different. Sometimes capital assets are the result of a windfall, sometimes, with increasing frequency, the result of a redundancy payment. The thrifty applicant who has saved all his spare income is required to contribute the whole of his savings above a disposable figure of £1,200 up to the eligibility limit of £2,500. The applicant who has spent up to the limit of his income and made no effort to put savings aside will not be required to make any contribution from capital because he will have none available. There is unfairness in this situation. Other inequalities are likely to arise, depending on whether the applicant is married or single because the calls on resources of married couples with children are greater and they have less opportunity for saving. If, however, both spouses are in work and there are no children, the opportunity for saving is greater. The age of the applicant is also a factor which can be expected to have a bearing on the capital available because those in the higher age brackets will have had more opportunity for saving and may have inherited some assets on the death of parents or relations.
12.43. There are the same difficulties in making an assessment of the appropriate free limit of capital as there are in the case of income limits. It must be borne in mind that disposable capital includes not only cash in hand but also assets such as motor cars and insurance policies whose cash value can be realised; also that experience has shown that the overall contribution from capital is very small. Bearing these factors in mind, we think it right, as before, to give our own view of the appropriate free limit. We consider this to be £10,000.

A further criticism is that the eligibility limits for civil legal aid operate unfairly, especially in relation to people who are moderately well off. The Benson Commission commented as follows:

Eligibility limits

12.29. The present financial limits are based on the principle adopted by the Rushcliffe Committee that legal aid should be directed both to the poor and to those of moderate means. In observing this principle, imposing an upper limit of eligibility has the advantage that those of more than moderate means can with certainty be excluded. But this is not necessarily desirable. People with higher incomes pay higher taxes and should, in principle, be entitled to benefit when need arises from schemes provided out of public money. They may need less help than others. If so, an adjustment in the legal aid scheme can be made by appropriate levels of contribution. It does not follow that they should have no help at all.

12.30. An upper limit of eligibility is arbitrary and may operate unfairly. A person whose resources fall above the line is denied assistance of any kind. It is true that a person whose resources fall just below the line may be required to make a substantial contribution. Nevertheless he will still enjoy a considerable benefit as compared with someone who is ineligible for assistance, because the fixed nature of the contribution operates as a limitation on his liability regardless of the outcome of the case and its total cost. Even when the contribution is large, the benefit of the security provided by such an arrangement is considerable.

. . .

12.32. We are satisfied that, as long as eligibility limits exist, the effect will, in some cases, be to create unfairness and to expose some individuals to a choice between abandoning their legal rights and accepting the risk of suffering an undue financial burden. The eligibility limits for both capital and income should, therefore, be abolished.

However the present government was clearly not in sympathy with this view as may be seen from the following extract from 'The Government Response to the Report of the Royal Commission on Legal Services', Cmnd 9077, 1983, pp 10–11:

The Government believes that legal aid should be available to assist those of small or moderate means, by giving them the same chance to pursue or defend their legal rights as those in a position to instruct lawyers privately; provided that it has been shown that there are reasonable grounds for pursuing or defending the right in question. The Government therefore believes that the eligibility limits must be retained, and that the limits both for legal aid and for legal advice and assistance (which in general covers a different range of services at lower cost) must be kept under close review . . . The Government is satisfied that the lower limits are fixed at an appropriate level and does not consider that the contributions payable by those who are above the limits are greater than an assisted person could reasonably be expected to pay.

It should also be noted that civil legal aid will, in any event have only a modest role to play in everyday consumer transactions. As will be seen later (at p 305 et seq), in respect of small claims for a sum not exceeding £500 the general rule is that the matter is referred to arbitration and that following such a reference legal costs will not be awarded. Consequently civil legal aid is usually not granted in respect of small claims which are regarded as being an appropriate subject for do-it-yourself litigation. For sums in excess of £500 the general rule is that the losing party is expected to pay the costs of the successful opponent. (For a reference to proposals by Justice for a Contingency Legal Aid Fund (CLAF) see para 16.7 et seq of the Benson Commission report).

Obtaining compensation: small claims and other procedures

INTRODUCTION

A consumer who seeks to obtain compensation in respect of faulty or misdescribed goods or services will, depending on the circumstances, probably have three main avenues of redress. The first and most important is a civil action in the county court. County courts now have jurisdiction in cases sounding in contract and tort if the sum claimed does not exceed £5,000 (see the County Courts Jurisdiction Order 1981, SI 1981 No 1123). Obviously the vast majority of claims in consumer transactions will fall well within this limit and very few will come before the High Court. Accordingly the position with respect to proceedings in the High Court is not considered further. The second possibility is that the dispute will be resolved through the conciliation and arbritration procedures established under a trade association code of practice negotiated under the auspices of the Office of Fair Trading. Finally there will be cases in which compensation may be provided under the Powers of Criminal Courts Act 1973, as amended. For example the defendant may be convicted of an offence under the Trade Descriptions Act 1968 and a compensation order might then be made in favour of an aggrieved consumer. Some of the general issues which arise when considering the above avenues of redress are indicated in the cases and materials which follow.

COUNTY COURTS AND 'SMALL CLAIMS'

The general problems associated with 'small claims' and consumer litigants have been well documented (see eg Ison, 'Small Claims' (1972) 35 MLR 18; Foster, 'Problems with Small Claims', (1974) 2 British Jo of Law and Society, p 75; Yngvesson and Hennessey, 'Small Claims, Complex Disputes: A review of the small claims literature' (1975) 9 Law and Society Review, 219; 'Simple Justice, A Consumer view of small claims procedures in England and Wales', National Consumer Council, 1979, Ch 11 especially; George Applebey, 'Small Claims in England and Wales' in *Access to Justice* (eds Cappelletti and Weisner) Vol II, Book II (1979) p 685).

An early and influential critique was provided by the Consumer Council Study 'Justice out of Reach: A Case for Small Claims Courts (HMSO 1970). This was especially useful in drawing attention to the way in which county courts were being used in practice. The research was carried out in 1979 and based on a random two per cent sample of the summonses recorded in six county courts. Some 1,238 entries were examined and the picture which emerged is seen in pp 13 et seq of the study:

Who uses the courts?

We found out that nearly 90 per cent of the summonses in our sample were taken out by a firm or a utility board (nearly always a gas or electricity board). An individual was the plaintiff in nine per cent of summonses. The remaining 1.6 per cent were taken out by local authorities or government departments . . .

Where individuals did sue, they mainly sued each other for debt (72 summonses as opposed to 1,075 summonses by companies suing for debt); but a good proportion of the plaintiffs in these 72 cases were probably small businesses suing in the proprietor's name. Damage to person or property was the next biggest category (17 summonses); but probably most of these were car accident cases, where insurance companies would often have been standing behind the individuals . . .

Trader cases

The chief purpose for which the county courts are used is for debt collection by firms who sell on credit. Nearly three-quarters (71.5 per cent) of our total sample of summonses were 'trader cases', by our definition: that is, summonses by firms against individuals for debt for goods or services. The proportion of trader cases varied from court to court, between 66 per cent and 79 per cent. In contrast, we did not find a single case of an individual suing a firm in a consumer matter, excepting a possible one in Bolton, where the subject of the claim could not be identified precisely and the papers unfortunately were not available when our researcher was there. Consumer cases must be few and far between for us to have failed to have come upon one in our sample. Court officers and registrars confirm that this is so.

. . .

Defending a claim

Although we did not find any actions brought by consumers, we did find some defences. The defendant filed a defence or counterclaim in 50 of our sample of trader cases—which amounts to seven per cent of the summonses actually served by traders on consumers. We examined the case papers for each of these. The most striking thing that emerged was that in 32 cases (64 per cent) the action was withdrawn after the defence was filed. We could rarely tell why from the case papers. The reason may have been that the firm thought the defence sound, or that it preferred simply not to fight. But there must surely be a lesson here for solicitors consulted by consumers who are being sued for arrears of hire purchase or other forms of debt: it may well be worth defending . . .

Partly as a result of this survey changes were introduced in 1971, 1973 and again in April 1981 with the general intention of facilitating access to the courts by consumer litigants. Richard Thomas of the National Consumer Council discusses the present position within England and Wales (and some of the background to it) in his article 'Small Claims—The New Arrangements' (1981) 131 NLJ 429–431. Thomas writes as follows (the numbering of the rules has since been altered by the County Court Rules 1981, SI 1981/1687):

Small Claims—The New Arrangements

New arrangements for the resolution of small claims in the county courts are coming into operation on April 21, 1981.[1] This article examines the changes and some of the background to their introduction.

Apart from the 'private' courts in Manchester and London, both of which are now defunct, there have never been small claims courts in England and Wales. Instead, largely in response to *Justice Out of Reach,* a report of the (old) Consumer Council, special small claims procedures were introduced into county courts in 1973. Claims below the prescribed limit (last increased to £200) could be referred to arbitration on the application of one party, could be heard by the registrar and were to be subject in most cases to a 'no-costs' rule for legal costs . . .

In 1979, the National Consumer Council (NCC) published *Simple Justice,* a consumer view of the small claims procedures as they then operated. The arrangements were examined according to criteria of accessibility, simplicity, informality, cost, speed, effectiveness and fairness. It was concluded that there were a number of important ways in which the system needed to be improved. NCC called for the establishment of a Small Claims Division, clearly labelled and recognised as such, within each county court. It was proposed that there should be a code of procedure, separate from the main body of the county court rules, to regulate proceedings in these divisions. The report spelt out the various improvements which this procedure should incorporate.

The County Court Rule Committee published a consultation document in 1980. This expressly accepted NCC's diagnosis of problems relating to the appropriate financial limits, the arrangement to determine which disputes went for trial and which for arbitration, and the no-costs rule. The consultation document did not accept the case for separate small claims divisions, but did propose a number of reforms on the lines of those recommended in NCC's report. The new rules have followed after that consultation process, and include some important modifications to the original proposals.

The principal changes are as follows:—
(i) Increase of the 'small claims limit' from £200 to £500;
(ii) Automatic referral of small claims to arbitration;
(iii) Provision for a referral to arbitration to be rescinded;
(iv) New procedural rules for arbitration;
(v) A simplified 'no-costs rule' for small claims determined by arbitration.

In broad terms, the new rules will create and emphasise a sharper distinction between cases which will go to arbitration (the majority of claims below £500) and those which will go to trial (the majority of claims above £500 and a few below that). It is intended that arbitrated small claims should follow a simple, informal and flexible procedure. An almost absolute no-costs rule will discourage legal representation. On the other hand, where a case proceeds to formal trial legal costs *will* be allowed, even where the claim falls below £500. The criteria permitting rescission of an arbitration referral, which are considered in detail below, will therefore assume considerable importance.

Small Claims Limit

When the arbitration scheme for small claims was introduced in October 1973, the limit was £75. This was subsequently increased to £100 and then to £200. In 1977 about half the advice agencies who participated in a survey undertaken by NCC thought that the limit of £200 was too low. NCC argued that a small claims procedure should cover the purchase of most consumer durables with the exception of cars and suggested that the limit should be set at £500. This new limit, at least for the time being, takes into account inflation since the last increase and will cover most 'consumer' disputes.

Automatic Referral to Arbitration

. . .

The new rule (Ord 19, r 1(4)) [now r 2(3)] adopts an NCC recommendation and provides that any proceedings involving £500 or below shall stand referred for arbitration by the registrar as soon as a defence to the claim has been received. The registrar may, on the application of any party, refer the proceedings for arbitration by the judge or by an outside arbitrator instead of himself. It is hoped that greater use will be made of outside arbitrators than has been the case in the past.

Although the new rule effectively creates a presumption that all disputes involving less than £500 will proceed to arbitration with the consequences that are spelt out below, it is widely recognised that not all small claims are simple claims. There has to be a mechanism to sift out claims which are clearly not suitable for a simplified procedure. The new rule (Ord 19, r 1(5)) [now r 2(4)] allows the registrar to rescind an arbitration referral where an application is made by one of the parties. He can only do this in fairly narrow circumstances. He must first be satisfied:—

(a) that a difficult question of law or a question of fact of exceptional complexity is involved; or
(b) that a charge of fraud is in issue; or
(c) that the parties are agreed that the dispute should be tried in court; or
(d) that it would be unreasonable for the claim to proceed to arbitration having regard to its subject matter, the circumstances of the parties or the interests of any other person likely to be affected by the award.

Even if the registrar is satisfied on one of these points, he still has a discretion in the matter and is not bound to refer the case to trial. The plaintiff and the defendant will be told about the need for a written application to rescind in the request for summons, the form of defence and the notice of reference to arbitration.

. . .

The rule setting out these grounds represents the boundary line between the formal and the informal approach to adjudication in the county court. Although the onus will be upon the person seeking trial, solicitors may (for the sake of the costs rule) be tempted to argue that their client's case falls within one of these grounds. Given that it will rarely make economic sense for private individuals to be legally represented when bringing or defending claims of low financial value, it is to be hoped that registrars will not easily be satisfied that one of the grounds has been established and will exercise their discretion sparingly. If the new rule achieves its purpose, it will only be the genuinely complex or exceptional case below £500 which will proceed to trial. In such cases, it is hoped that the legal aid committee will recognise the exceptional nature and will grant legal aid to those who are eligible. Ideally, in such cases, the proceeds of a successful claim should be exempt from the statutory charge imposed by s 9(6) of the Legal Aid Act 1974. The Law Society has argued that small amounts of damages should be made available to the claimant and not to the Legal Aid Fund.

Arbitration Procedure

. . .

The new rule, Order 19, r 1(10) [now r 5(2)], now requires (except where the court other-wise directs) that proceedings which are referred to arbitration should be conducted according to a number of stated terms of reference. These terms are similar, but not identical, in substance to the schedule to the 1973 Practice Direction.

The first term requires the arbitrator to appoint a date for the preliminary consideration of the dispute and ways of resolving it. This preliminary consideration appears to parallel, but on a more informal basis, the pre-trial review (Ord 21). The pre-trial review, in that name, will now only be held for appropriate cases which are to proceed to trial. The preliminary consideration will, however, serve a similar purpose. The arbitrator will usually fix a date for the hearing of the dispute and will give directions regarding steps which it is necessary or desirable to take before and at the hearing. The new rules give the arbitrator considerable freedom at this stage and, without saying so, encourage the 'activism' on the part of the adjudicator which has been the feature of successful small claims procedures throughout the world. The directions do not have to be applied for by any party and it will largely be up to the arbitrator to decide what steps are necessary or desirable. In many cases, it is likely that the arbitrator will use the preliminary consideration as an opportunity to explore the possibilities of a settlement and generally to help unrepresented parties to get their tackle in order for the full hearing. If the parties consent, it is open to the arbitrator to decide the entire dispute on the basis of statements and documents submitted to him. In that case, of course, no hearing date will be fixed.

It should be noted that a preliminary consideration will not take place in every case. *Simple Justice* revealed considerable disagreement over the necessity of any preliminary review. The occasion can be useful in helping unrepresented litigants to prepare cases and indicating what to expect in court. But there are those who regard it, especially in straightforward cases, as an unnecessary formality, requiring the parties to appear twice at court instead of once. The new rules recognise this dilemma and provide that the arbitrator need not arrange a preliminary consideration where 'the size or nature of the claim or other circumstances make such a course undesirable or unnecessary'.

A novel feature, now effectively incorporated into statutory form, is the procedural term which enables the arbitrator to consult any expert or call for an expert report on any matter in dispute. This may be done before or after the hearing. Alternatively, the arbitrator may invite an expert to attend the hearing as an assessor. These steps can only be taken, however, where the parties give their consent. This new rule does not, however, spell out how this expertise is to be paid for. It seems most likely that the arbitrator will use his discretion to order the losing party to pay all or part of the costs of using an expert. Although party consent is required, the initiative available to the arbitrator with regard to experts is to be welcomed as a further encouragement for judicial activism and it is to be hoped that imaginative use will be made of this power.

At the hearing itself, the arbitrator again has a reasonably free hand. 'Any hearing shall be informal and the strict rules of evidence shall not apply'. The arbitrator is expressly entitled to adopt any method of procedure which he may consider to be convenient and to afford a fair and equal opportunity to each party to present his case. It is suggested that as a matter of good practice the arbitrator should, at a preliminary consideration, outline the general procedure which will be followed at the full hearing. More importantly, if these procedures are going to work well, it will be essential that arbitrators do not seek to emulate trial judges by remaining aloof from the proceedings. Where both parties are represented at formal trial, it may be sufficient to leave it to the lawyers to advance the case and to undermine the opposing case. Where one or both sides are unrepresented at the hearing, the role of the court needs to change fundamentally. It cannot be left to unrepresented parties to know what needs to be done and to do it. It is suggested that at the hearing the arbitrator should, without compromising his impartiality, go out of his way to elicit all relevant facts, himself to test the evidence and to introduce relevant points of law. It would perhaps be impossible for the letter of the new rules to spell out this sort of approach explicitly, but their spirit indicates that this is the way in which small claims and arbitrations should be conducted.

Costs

For a supposedly simple procedure, the old rules on cost in small claims cases had become something of a nightmare. There was one rule for cases below £5, another for cases between £5 and £100, another for cases between £100 and £200, another for personal injury cases and a general overriding rule in complex cases. NCC criticised these rules as exceedingly complex and called for a radical simplification with no legal costs being allowed at all in cases heard by arbitration.

In general, this is what the new rule (Ord 19, r 1(11)) [now r 6] achieves. For any small claim (£500 or below) which is heard by way of arbitration, 'no solicitor's charges shall be allowed as between party and party'. The only exceptions are the costs stated on the summons, the costs of enforcing the award and such costs as are certified by the arbitrator to have been incurred through the 'unreasonable conduct' of the opposite party. This last exception to the general position reflects the rule now in operation in industrial tribunals. What constitutes unreasonable conduct must depend on the circumstances of the particular cases, but a defendant who merely pursues a defence that fails is unlikely, because of that, to be acting unreasonably. It may, however, be unreasonable to file a defence and then, with no change of circumstances, to fail to defend it. It should be noted that costs other than solicitors charges, such as court fees, travelling expenses and the reasonable costs of preparing the case, are not subject to the no-costs rule and remain in the discretion of the arbitrator. They can be allowed in the same way as costs are awarded at a normal county court trial. The award of the arbitrator, and any order as to costs, can be enforced (at least in theory) as a county court judgment.

Conclusions

It may be convenient to summarise how a disputed small claim will be resolved under the new rules. The plaintiff will commence proceedings by completing the request for summons and filing the particulars of claim. Most county courts make available forms for particulars of claim in questionnaire format covering the most frequently encountered sets of circumstances. Once the summons has been served, the defendant who disputes the claim must file the defence (using the supplied form if desired). Solicitors may be consulted about the merits of a claim or defence and, without intending to represent, may help clients to prepare these documents. The green form scheme may be used for these purposes. It is to be hoped that solicitors will remember that, at the hearing, the client will be 'solo' and so the language of such pleadings should not be unduly legalistic.

Upon receipt of the defence, the proceedings will automatically be referred to arbitration by the registrar. Application may be made for the arbitration to be conducted, instead, by the judge or by an outside arbitrator. If a party seeks to rescind the reference to arbitration on one of the available grounds, application has to be made . . .

Lawyers will be permitted to represent clients at arbitration hearings, but this is still discouraged as they are unlikely to be awarded their costs. In any event, as was pointed out in *Simple Justice*, 'there was unanimous agreement that lawyers should not be necessary in the arbitration procedure'. Given the relatively small amounts involved, it can by definition rarely be profitable or satisfactory for lawyers to represent parties in small claims cases. The wise solicitor will be the one who points out in appropriate cases to both private and business clients, that a 'do-it-yourself' approach is both possible and desirable and who explains to his clients the various steps that will be involved.

It remains to be seen how these latest refinements to the small claims procedures will work in practice. One fear is that, unless registrars are sparing in exercising their discretion to take a case out of arbitration, consumers and other private claimants may be reluctant to commence proceedings in case legal costs are awarded against them. More generally, NCC would have preferred a more comprehensive reform. It has argued that the creation of 'self-contained' small claims divisions would have introduced a more distinctive image and would have made the system more approachable. NCC believes that separation of small claims rules would underline the departure from conventional techniques of litigation. It is unfortunate, perhaps, that the new arrangements should be tucked away in an all-purpose statutory instrument whose first concern is with proceedings taken against foreign States. Much also remains to be done on such matters as publicity, training for registrars and court staff, the simplification of court forms and, in particular, improving the procedures for the enforcement of county court awards.

The handling of small claims calls for a quite different approach from that adopted for conventional trials. This is a crucial point which has to be recognised by registrars, court staff, lawyers and by litigants. If the new arrangements do not achieve this difference of approach, the case for separate Small Claims Divisions will become irresistible.

1. County Court (Amendment No 3) Rules S1 1980/1807.

NOTES

1. A helpful guide to procedure in the county courts has been written by Michael Birks, then Registrar of the West London County Court, and issued by the Lord Chancellor's Department: see 'Small claims in the county court: How to sue and defend actions without a solicitor' (November 1981).

2. On the Manchester and London courts see, respectively, Foster, 'Problems with Small Claims' (1974) 2 British Jo of Law and Society, p 75; Egerton, 'The Birth and Death of the London Small Claims Court (1980) 13 NLJ 488.

3. For further material and discussion of arbitration within the county court framework see the Model Code of Procedure for Small Claims Divisions of County Courts (NCC, May 1980); Richard Thomas, 'A Code of Procedure for Small Claims: A response to the demand for do-it-yourself litigation' (1982) Civil Justice Quarterly 52.

Before turning to some cases which have been decided on the basis of these new rules there are certain points of a general nature which merit attention. One is the question whether legal representation should be allowed. The National Consumer Council commented as follows in 'Simple Justice' (1979), pp 95–96:

Legal representation
22.   We have argued that a system for settling small claims must be informal enough to allow individual litigants to present their own case, and cheap to use. Our evidence suggests that solicitors increase the formality of procedures, and even the chance of being opposed in court by lawyers acts as a deterrent to bringing an action. So one of the principal conditions of a small claims system is that legal representation should not be necessary.
23.   The county court arbitration procedure is designed to be simple enough for the layman to use, and legal representation is already discouraged by not allowing their costs to be awarded against the loser. However, our evidence reveals that the system is not working satisfactorily. Whatever the intention of the 'no costs' rule, solicitors are still appearing in arbitration cases. We do not know the extent of the use of solicitors, as the Lord Chancellor's Department does not keep statistics. In 1975, however, one or both parties were represented in roughly half of all arbitration cases. If anything like this use of legal representation is continuing, the arbitration procedure must be considered a failure.
24.   In all our discussions on this issue—with advice agencies, registrars, consumer organisations, the legal profession and so on—there was unanimous agreement that lawyers should not be necessary in the arbitration procedure. But there is no consensus on whether this aim should be achieved by improving the system gradually so that the need for representation diminishes, and its use disappears; or whether the issue should be tackled by an outright ban on legal representation. Many of the arguments for and against such a ban are contained in Chapter 9. Essentially these arguments are, on the one hand, that arbitration will never be a simple, informal and cheap means of redress that enables consumers to claim their rights if lawyers are present at hearings. On the other hand, there is the feeling that restricting one's right to obtain the services of a lawyer is a restriction of individual freedom and choice and may limit the chances of getting justice. It is also argued that lawyers and legal argument can be necessary in certain cases involving small amounts of money; and that some individuals are not confident enough to bring their case without some form of legal or lay representation. These opposing views are difficult to reconcile.
25.   As we saw in Chapter 9, the old Consumer Council recommended that legal representation should not be allowed in small claims arbitration, although not without searching consideration. As the Council said, 'the principle that a man should be entitled to have a lawyer speaking for him at a judicial hearing is one deserving of great respect'. However, as the Council pointed out, this was a principle and not practice, and the majority of individuals would not have lawyers even if they were permitted to do so.
26.   *On balance we conclude that arbitration as a procedure for the effective disposal of small claims cannot work satisfactorily, in the majority of cases, if representation as such is permitted. We therefore call for a ban on representation in the vast majority of cases heard by arbitration.* The only exceptions, to answer some of the arguments against such a ban would be:
  * where the registrar certifies that the claim involved a difficult question of law, or questions of fact of exceptional complexity (which cases, as we have already argued, would be referred to trial);
  * where the registrar certifies that the interests of justice require that legal or lay representation should be permitted;
  * where both parties agree to the use of representation.
27.   Even where representation at an arbitration is permitted in accordance with the last two exceptions, no legal costs would be allowed . . .

This recommendation was discussed in February 1980 by the County Court Rule Committee which concluded that 'no restriction should be placed by the Rules of Court on the litigant's right to be represented in county court arbitrations' (see the Consultative Paper referred to by Richard Thomas in his article in the New Law Journal, above p 306 et seq).

Another, and on the face of it even more radical, solution to the problems of small claims is pointed to in the following extracts from the chapter by A. J. Duggan ('Consumer Redress and the Legal System') in Duggan and Darvall *Consumer Protection Law and Theory* (1980), pp 216–217. Discussing the position in some Australian States and elsewhere Duggan writes:

(b) Court substitutes
(i) Small claims tribunals. The Victorian *Small Claims Tribunals Act* 1973 is reasonably representative of legislation in four Australian States which has established special tribunals outside the formal court system for the resolution of consumer grievances.[1]

The tribunals have jurisdiction over small claims which are defined in the Victorian Act as a claim between a consumer and a trader for the payment of money or the performance of work not exceeding $1,000 that arises out of a contract for the supply of goods or provision of services. 'Consumer' is defined, in effect, as a natural person who acquires goods or services otherwise than in a business context and 'trader', as a person in the business of supplying goods or services or who regularly so holds himself out. The parties to proceedings instituted before a small claims tribunal are referred to as the 'claimant' and the 'respondent'. 'Claimant' is defined as a consumer who has duly referred a small claim to a tribunal; 'respondent' is defined as a trader against whom a claim has been lodged with a tribunal.[2] These definitions imposed a radical limitation on the tribunals: of the two classes of person over whom they have jurisdiction (consumers and traders), only the former may sue; the latter is irrevocably consigned to the role of respondent. This limitation was imposed, perhaps at the risk of creating the appearance of a pro-consumer bias in the tribunals, because early experience with small claims tribunals in Canada and the United States had indicated that with open access they rapidly degenerated into debt collection agencies, up to 90 per cent of actions being brought by traders and creditors *against* consumers [footnote omitted].

1. See also *Small Claims Tribunals Act* 1973–1978 (Qd); *Small Claims Tribunals Act,* 1974–1978 (WA); *Consumer Claims Tribunals Act,* 1974 (NSW). Small Claims procedures have also been adopted in South Australia and the Territories, but they are annexed to the existing court system.
2. For all these definitions, see *Small Claims Tribunals Act* 1973 (Vic), s 2 (1).

For arguments in support of the view that claims for debts arising out of retail transactions should not be permitted within the small claims procedure see Ison (1972) 35 MLR 18, at p 24 et seq. See also Cranston, 'Access to Justice for Consumers' (1979) Journal of Consumer Policy 291, 296, who states: 'To prevent businessmen from colonizing small claims courts, the best approach seems to be to exclude them from being plaintiffs . . .'. Different conclusions on this point were reached in 'Justice out of Reach' and 'Simple Justice', where the National Consumer Council concluded (at p 94):

Who should be allowed to sue in arbitration?
16.   The old Consumer Council, in *Justice Out of Reach,* recommended that to be a genuine people's court all companies, partnerships, associations and assignees of debts should not be allowed to sue in the simplified arbitration procedure. Individual defendants sued by firms should, if they entered a defence or counter claim, be able to transfer the case to the arbitration procedure. After careful considerations we do not support this recommendation, largely because we consider that individuals who are being sued by companies will be more likely to submit a defence if it is clear from the start that the case will be heard by arbitration. An additional procedure for applying for a case to be transferred to arbitration might prevent individuals submitting a defence.

For further discussion of the position in Australia see Taylor 'Special Procedures Governing Small Claims in Australia' in *Access to Justice*, Vol II, Book 2 (eds Cappelletti and Weisner), 597; Turner, 'Small Claims in the County Court in England—A Contrast to the Australian approach' (1980) Anglo-Am LR 150, at p 168 et seq especially.

Other criticisms are pointed to by Jenny Levin ('Small Claims—A Small Advance': LAG Bulletin, June 1981, p 140) who writes:

Whether these new rules will encourage more individual litigants to press small claims depends partly upon how they are operated. If registrars are frequently persuaded to exercise their discretion to refuse arbitration on the ground that the case is complex or that arbitration is unreasonable (see above) then the object of the new procedure will be defeated. But even where a case is dealt with by arbitration a losing party may still be faced with an order to pay the winner's costs apart from legal costs and these could be quite substantial. Cost will still, therefore, deter many from using the procedure.

Another deterrent is the complexity and inaccessibility of the law. Nothing has been done to make the pre-arbitration procedure any more comprehensible to individual litigants. The new rules themselves are not even accessible to the non-lawyer, being contained in a statutory instrument which deals also with state immunity, charging orders, leasehold valuation tribunals and other miscellaneous matters. It is still not possible to refer litigants to comprehensive consolidated rules on small claims. No significant changes have been made in the forms used or in the rules of pleading which often defeat litigants unless they are well advised.

Questions

In the light of the above comments do you consider that within the small claims procedure it is desirable on balance to exclude or admit (i) legal representation and (ii) traders as plaintiffs?

Writing from the standpoint of consumer advocates both Richard Thomas (above, p 306 et seq) and Jenny Levin agree that it is in the interests of consumers that the automatic reference to arbitration of claims for sums not exceeding £500 should be rescinded, for example under head (d) of Order 19, rule 1(5) (now rule 2(4)), only in truly exceptional cases. Certainly this is the received wisdom and the generally held view. It is not clear to what extent doubt has been cast on these assumptions by the following case—

Pepper v Healey [1982] RTR 411, Court of Appeal

The facts are stated in the judgments of Sir Sebag Shaw and Waller LLJ.

Sir Sebag Shaw. This is an appeal from a decision of Judge Edward Jones given on 21 September 1981 at the Liverpool County Court, when he upheld the order of the registrar which had rescinded the statutory reference to an arbitration that, in the absence of a contrary direction, would have operated in relation to the claims that the plaintiff made in the present action, being claims which do not exceed £500.

The question arises under the new rule set out in Ord 19, r 1(4) of the County Court Rules 1936 (as amended). That came into operation after the plaintiff in the action had issued proceedings, but before the defence had been filed. Accordingly, it would have applied to the present action. Ord 19, r 1(4) reads:

'Any proceedings in which the sum claimed or amount involved does not exceed £500 shall stand referred for arbitration by the registrar upon the receipt by the court of a defence to the claim . . .'

There follows this qualification in paragraph (5) of the rule:

'Where any proceedings are referred for arbitration by the registrar under paragraph (4), he may, on the application of any party, rescind the reference if he is satisfied . . . (*d*) that it would be unreasonable for the claim to proceed to arbitration having regard to its subject matter, the circumstances of the parties or the interests of any other person likely to be affected by the award.'

Mr Waldron has quite rightly argued here that the policy of the rule is to ensure that small claims, that is, claims under £500, are dealt with expeditiously, with as little expenditure of the court's time as possible and as little burden of costs as might be. That is the general policy. There are some situations, however, in which a claim which does not exceed £500 may give rise to special considerations. Hence the scope of the discretion which is reposed in the registrar and also in the judge of the county court.

It is necessary to look at the facts of this case to see if any part of sub-paragraph (*d*) can relate to this matter. The claim is of the most ordinary kind in a running-down action. The plaintiff was driving her car on 14 November 1980 at Central Square, Maghull, and while she was manoeuvring her car, according to her, a car driven by another lady, the defendant, reversed into her (the plaintiff's) car and damaged it. The impact can hardly have been a very severe one because the cost of repairing the damage was assessed at £133, which is a very modest sum these days. That is the principal amount which the plaintiff seeks to recover in the action, and she adds a claim for a sum in excess of £5, in respect of the shock and the fright which she had when the collision took place.

The defence has a somewhat unusual feature in that the defendant denies that she was involved in any collision at all with the plaintiff's vehicle. In order to establish that there was no collision and that her driving had no connection with whatever mishap befell the plaintiff, it is proposed to call an expert witness on behalf of the defendant to show that, if there was damage to the plaintiff's vehicle, it could not have resulted from anything disclosed by an expert examination of the defendant's vehicle.

Now it so happens that the defendant is covered by a comprehensive policy and so her insurers have taken an interest in the conduct of the defence on her behalf. The plaintiff is a lady who, for whatever reason—perhaps because of limited means—has a policy covering her only against third-party claims, with the result that in the proceedings which ensued from the issue of the plaint in this action she would not have the advantage of being represented by a solicitor or by counsel at the expense of the insurance company.

But in order to meet the impact of the evidence of an expert on the defendant's side, it is proposed to call an expert on her side as well, and apart from the respective parties it seems that there are in contemplation two other witnesses as to this matter.

Thus the action, although in itself of the most ordinary kind as the history indicates, has one or two unusual features. The registrar took the view that this was the kind of case in which it might be said that it was unreasonable for a claim to be dealt with by arbitration having regard to the circumstances of the parties. Although the matters to be decided were not of exceptional difficulty or complication, justice might be frustrated if the plaintiff was under the disadvantage that even if she won, she could not recover the costs of representation which would be involved if solicitors had appeared for her. That of course might well have this consequence, that in a small claim of this kind if she got in all something under £200 (because she limits her claim to that figure) she might in the end be left destitute of any substantial recompense for the damage to her car.

The judge thought that the view taken by the registrar was a justifiable view. In the course of his careful judgment, to which I would wish to pay my respectful tribute, he said:

'The main ground advanced before me was the unequal contest which would ensue. The plaintiff will have to pay out of her own pocket all the not inconsiderable legal costs if her case is to be properly presented. The defendant is represented by an insurance company. The presentation of the case is really impossible for a lay person such as the plaintiff.'

I agree with this view, for the defendant is protected by her policy with the insurance company, who will arrange for legal representation, and pay any costs which may be incurred. That makes the contest unequal. The judge went on:

'It is certainly in the interest of insurance companies to have arbitration. By this means they would in all such cases, have no costs to pay to a successful plaintiff. In a claim such as this, any damages recovered will be totally absorbed by the legal costs, and this could be so even if the plaintiff handled the case herself. Indeed the costs would in all probability greatly exceed the sum recovered.'

It may be that it is just an accident of fate that the difference in strength of the parties results from the fact that one side has the protection of an insurance company and the other has not, but it is the sort of situation which might arise very frequently. It is for that reason that Mr Waldron has urged on this court that this involves an important question of principle, though, speaking for myself, I would wish to emphasise that one is dealing with the facts of *this* case and with the exercise of the judge's discretion and the application of his discretion to the facts of this case. I would not, for myself, wish to see any general principles affecting contests in which insurance companies are involved either on one side or another, emerge from this case.

But Ord 19, r1(4) clearly confers a discretion on the registrar and that discretion is also vested in the judge when he comes to hear the matter by way of appeal. It seems to me that the judge applied his mind to the legitimate consideration of all the circumstances in this case—and there was material on which he could properly exercise his discretion—in order to determine whether the qualification provided by paragraph 5 (*d*) of the rule applied.

. . .

Accordingly I would dismiss this appeal.

Fox LJ. For the reasons given by Sir Sebag Shaw, I too would dismiss this appeal.

Waller LJ. I also agree that this appeal should be dismissed. I would only say this, that the short question which we have to consider is whether or not it can be said that no reasonable tribunal considering this particular problem could have come to the conclusion to which the registrar and the judge came. In my opinion that cannot be said.

This was a running-down case with expert witnesses to be called; it was not a complicated case but it was not one which could easily be conducted without representation.

. . .

The subject matter was a running-down action in which experts were to be called; the circumstances of the parties were that on the one hand the plaintiff would have to depend on her own resources, and on the other side the defendant would be covered by insurance. If there was arbitration, under Ord 19, r 1(11) no solicitor's charges would be allowed as between party and party in the proceedings unless they were incurred through the unreasonable conduct of the other party.

The simple situation here is that, if this matter is tried in the county court and the plaintiff wins she will recover her costs; it is dealt with by arbitration and she wins, she will not recover her costs.

This is a case where she needs to be represented, and in my judgment the judge was perfectly entitled to come to the conclusion to which he did, which was that this was a case which should be tried by the county court.

Appeal dismissed with costs. Legal aid taxation of plaintiff's costs to be taxed in Liverpool. Leave to appeal to the House of Lords refused.

Questions

Is there something wrong with a small claims arbitration procedure where the 'claim is of the most ordinary kind' and yet its presentation is agreed to be 'really impossible for a lay person such as the plaintiff'? If there is would you (i) prevent insurance companies from being legally represented; (ii) make legal aid more readily available to private litigants or (iii) make further efforts to ensure that registrars give assistance to private litigants and so redress the inequality to which they are subject?

What would have been the plaintiff's position in relation to costs had she *lost* the case? Does the answer suggest that when exercising his discretion under rule 1(5) [now rule 2(4)] the registrar had formed at least a preliminary view as to the merits of the case? Is this desirable?

The 'no-costs' rule is a central feature of the small claims arbitration procedure applicable to claims for a sum not exceeding £500. The rule is intended to benefit the consumer litigant who can thus (so the theory goes) afford to litigate without the spectre of a general liability for an opponent's legal costs to act as a disincentive. Nonetheless some may feel that there is no reason in principle why such a litigant should be put in a position of *having* to forego legal costs no matter how strong his case. Do-it-yourself litigation may have its attractions for some, but others may prefer to engage a 'professional'—perhaps because they are inarticulate or simply have better or different things to do with their time. It is clear also that insurance companies have learned to use (some may say abuse) the 'no-costs' rule to their advantage. The following case suggests that the qualifications to which it is subject are less helpful to consumers than had been imagined.

Newland v Boardwell: MacDonald v Platt [1983] 3 All ER 179, [1983] 1 WLR 1453, Court of Appeal

Cumming-Bruce LJ. These two appeals involve identical questions. Both cases were originally determined by Mr Registrar Wilkinson in the Liverpool County Court and on appeal by his Honour Judge Edward Jones, who heard the two appeals together and delivered a single judgment in both of them. They raise what appear to be questions of general interest and some importance. It will be convenient to deal with them in relation to the facts in *Newland v Boardwell.*

In May 1981 a collision occurred between a motor vehicle owned and driven by the plaintiff and another driven by the defendant. The plaintiff sued the defendant for damages in the county court. Her particulars of claim were in these terms:

'1. On the 14th May 1981 in Bedford Road at its junction with Stuart Road a collision occurred between a motor vehicle owned and driven by the Plaintiff and a motor vehicle driven by the Defendant and caused by the negligence of the Defendant.

2. The Defendant has stated that liability will not be in issue.

3. By reason of the premises the Plaintiff, who is aged about 45 years, suffered injury loss and damage and was deprived of the use and enjoyment of his [sic] said vehicle and suffered inconvenience thereby.

PARTICULARS OF INJURY

Shock and general shaking up.

PARTICULARS OF SPECIAL DAMAGE

Estimated cost of repairs   £296.07

And the Plaintiff claims damages in all not exceeding £500.00.'

The effect of that limitation on the amount of damages claimed was to bring the case within the scope of CCR 1936 Ord 19, r 1(4) which, so far as relevant, provides:

'Any proceedings in which the sum claimed or amount involved does not exceed £500 shall stand referred for arbitration by the registrar upon the receipt by the court of a defence of the claim . . .'

On 12 September 1981 the registrar issued a summons addressed to the defendant enclosing a copy of the plaintiff's particulars of claim, stating that the costs already accrued were court fee £28 and solicitors' charge £21, and summoning the defendant to appear at the court office on 22 September 1981, when the registrar would consider giving directions for securing the determination of the action. On 18 September the defendant gave notice to the plaintiff and to her solicitors that he had paid into court the sum of £350 in satisfaction of the plaintiff's claim. On 22 September before the pre-trial review fixed for that day the defendant filed the following defence:

'1. The defendant admits paragraph 1 of the Particulars of Claim.

2. For the purpose of this action alone, the Defendant admits that he was negligent.

3. The injuries, loss and damage alleged are not admitted.'

As a result, the proceedings were automatically referred to arbitration under CCR 1936

Ord 19, r 1(4). Mr Registrar Wilkinson gave directions for discovery, inspection and expert witnesses and ordered the action to be set down for arbitration before a registrar.

Before the action commenced the defendant's insurers had intimated to the plaintiff or her advisers in open correspondence that liability was not in issue and that they would meet any reasonable claim; but the effect of the defence, para 3, was to put liability in issue notwithstanding the admission of negligence.

On 5 October the plaintiff's solicitors filed her list of documents, limited to special damage, comprising only an estimate for motor vehicle repairs of £257.10 plus value added tax. On 20 October the plaintiff gave notice of acceptance of the sum paid into court in full satisfaction of her claim. On 25 November the registrar, after hearing solicitors for both parties, made an order for costs (as drawn up) as follows:

> 'There be no order for costs save that the plaintiff's costs of this action be taxed on new scale 1.'

It is, however, common ground that that order was wrongly drawn up. It appears clearly from the written reasons of the registrar that he gave a certificate in favour of the plaintiff under CCR 1936 Ord 19, r 1(11)(c) and ordered that her costs of the action taxed under scale 1 should be paid by the defendant by reason of the defendant's unreasonable conduct in defending the action.

Counsel for the plaintiff contended before the registrar that the defendant had no other reason for refusing to submit to interlocutory judgment than the avoidance of the payment of the plaintiff's costs. He argued that, if the registrar did not give a certificate of unreasonableness, the plaintiff would have to bear her own solicitors' costs out of the damages which she had recovered. Counsel for the defendant contended that the defendant had every right to file a defence in order to preserve his position on the assessment of damages.

It appears from the registrar's written reasons that counsel for the defendant conceded in argument that the defendant had never sought to argue that no damage followed from his negligence: he merely wanted to be heard on quantum. The registrar said that he could think of no reason (other than costs) why the defendant did not consent to interlocutory judgment with damages to be assessed, in which case he would have been entitled to call witnesses and to cross-examine the plaintiff's witnesses as to the extent of the damage. The registrar said:

> 'The small claims jurisdiction of the county court was never intended to operate as an indemnity charter against the payment of costs for the benefit of insurance companies in running-down cases . . . It seems to me to be fundamentally wrong to leave a successful plaintiff (where liability has never been an issue) to pay his own solicitor out of his own damages. Defendants who file specious defences solely for the purpose of seeking the protection of the no-costs rule ought to be flushed out by a certificate of unreasonableness.'

The defendant applied to the judge to set aside the registrar's award on the grounds that the matter was subject to the provisions of Ord 19, r 1(11), that the registrar had been wrong in law in certifying that the defendant had acted unreasonably or alternatively that he had failed to exercise his discretion judicially. The defendant also submitted that it was not unreasonable for the defendant to file a defence admitting negligence but not admitting the alleged loss and damage.

That application was heard by the county court judge at the same time as the appeal in the other case now before this court, *MacDonald v Platt*. He delivered a reserved judgment covering both cases together. I will return to *MacDonald v Platt* later for its facts, but here it should be stated that the plaintiff in each of the two cases employed a solicitor throughout to conduct his or her case, and that in each case the effective defendant was an insurance company . . .

[His Lordship referred to the facts of *Macdonald v Platt* and continued]:

We think that there is no significant difference for present purposes between the two cases. In each the first question is whether it was unreasonable conduct on the part of the defendant for the purposes of Ord 19, r 1(11) to file a defence admitting negligence but putting damage wholly in issue, thereby putting liability in issue, notwithstanding that the defendant had in fact no defence on liability and no real intention to dispute liability except as to quantum.

The defendants contend that in any action in which the plaintiff claims unliquidated damages quantum is in issue, and that must be so; but in each of these cases the defendant did more than put quantum in issue: he put liability in issue, notwithstanding that he admitted negligence; in other words, each defendant put in issue the question whether his negligence had occasioned any or all of the damage suffered by the plaintiff. In the county court, where a plaintiff claims unliquidated damages, if the only issue is the quantum of those damages, the usual practice is for the registrar to enter interlocutory judgment for the plaintiff for an amount of damages to be assessed. On the reference for assessment each party can adduce evidence and cross-examine his opponent's witnesses. There is a full opportunity to litigate the question of quantum. There can be no prejudice to either party on the quantum being assessed in this way instead of being adjudicated in a formal trial. There can consequently be no advantage in pleading issues of fact which go only to quantum: this would only be likely to occasion extra expense. This must be otherwise, however, if the defendant puts in issue the entire question of liability by pleading that whatever damage or loss the plaintiff may have suffered was not a consequence of the alleged and admitted negligence of the defendant. Such an allegation by a defendant could not be adjudicated on by means of an assessment of damages before a registrar; it must necessitate a formal trial of the issue.

The function of pleadings in our mode of judicial proceedings is to define and clarify the issues between the parties. A party can properly make such allegations of fact as he thinks he has some hope or chance of establishing, and can admit, refuse to admit, or deny such allegations of his opponent as he thinks fit. He can in this way compel his opponent to establish affirmatively any fact in respect of which the burden of truth rests on the opponent; but, if he ventures to put in issue some fact the truth of which can be demonstrated to have been known to the party purporting to put it in issue, he will be at risk of having his pleading in respect of it struck out as being frivolous, vexatious or an abuse of the process of the court, or at the least he will be at risk as to the costs of that issue.

In *Newland v Boardwell* paras 1 and 2 of the defence consist only of admissions. The sole ground of defence pleaded in the document is contained in para 3. The position in *MacDonald v Platt* is similar. The judge found, as already mentioned (and indeed this was conceded), that on the facts the defendants 'simply cannot contend, and indeed do not contend, that it could ever have been argued that no damage flowed from their negligence'. The denial of liability implicit in each defence is clearly a device to take advantage of Ord 19, r 1(4) and counsel for the defendants makes no bones about this. Indeed, he says that it was the duty of the defendants' solicitors to employ this device in order to protect their clients from liability for costs to which they would otherwise be exposed. The device, in our judgment, involves a misuse of the pleading process. So far from clarifying the real issues between the parties, it obfuscated them. It speciously purported to raise an issue between the parties which the defendant in neither case genuinely intended to pursue. It was designed to exclude the plaintiff in each case from the benefit of the summary procedure of interlocutory judgment for damages to be assessed, while at the same time debarring the plaintiff from seeking the exercise of the court's discretion to award costs in his favour occasioned by a specious defence.

In our judgment, there were sufficient grounds in each of these cases to justify certificates under CCR 1936 Ord 19, r 1(11)(c) and to the extent that 'through' the filing of the defences the plaintiffs respectively incurred solicitors' charges which they would not otherwise have incurred. 'Through' in this context must, in our opinion, have the meaning 'in consequence of'. The words 'to have been incurred through the unreasonable conduct of the opposite party' cannot affect any costs incurred before the occurrence of the unreasonable conduct of the defendant. If either plaintiff incurred further solicitors' charges for services rendered between the date of the summons and the filing of the defence, those charges would seem to be made unrecoverable by para (11). But what about solicitors' charges incurred after the occurrence of the unreasonable conduct? Either plaintiff, as soon as he became aware that a defence had been filed in his or her action and as soon as he or she had been advised about the terms and effect of that defence could have determined his solicitor's retainer so as to avoid further solicitors' charges occurring. Neither plaintiff did so. Can it be said in these circumstances that any solicitors' charges accruing thereafter have been incurred through the unreasonable conduct of the defendant in filing the defence? We think not. The plaintiff has expressly restricted his claim to the limit of the small claims procedure. He must be taken to have known that, if a defence were filed, the case would be automatically referred for arbitration, in which event, if he continued to employ a solicitor, he would be prohibited from recovering any solicitors' charges from his opponent except under Ord 19, r 1(11)(c). If he does not protect himself by determining the solicitor's retainer, his liability to pay any solicitors' charges arising thereafter will, in our judgment, have been incurred as a consequence of his own failure to protect himself and not as a consequence of the reference to arbitration or to the filing of a defence which occasioned that reference.

We should perhaps add that at no stage has either of the plaintiffs sought to get the defence in his or her action struck out, or to have the reference of his claim to arbitration made under Ord 19, r 1(4) rescinded under r 1(5) of that order. We accordingly express no view whether any application for either of these forms of relief could have succeeded at any stage.

For these reasons, and with some regret, we allow all these appeals and set aside both awards, since it seems to us (subject to anything that counsel may say) that no useful purpose is likely to be served by remitting either arbitration to the registrar for reconsideration in the light of this judgment. The consequence of this will be that each plaintiff will only recover against the defendant in his or her action the solicitors' charges referred to in the summons.

We think there is room for doubt whether this result really accords with what the rule-making authority intended to be a proper consequence of CCR 1936 Ord 19, r 1(11)(*c*).

Appeals allowed. Order for costs before the registrar varied. Costs before the judge varied to no order for costs. No order for costs of appeal, save legal aid taxation where requisite.

Question

With respect to the solicitors' charges incurred after the occurrence of the unreasonable conduct do you agree that they were incurred as a consequence of the plaintiff's own failure to protect herself by determining her solicitor's retainer? Was the defendant's unreasonable conduct not at least a contributory cause? Was this not sufficient to justify a certificate under the then Ord 19, r 1(11)(*c*)?

NOTE

In January 1984 the County Court Rule Committee issued a consultative document inviting comments on the suggestion that the wording of the rule covering restriction on allowance of costs should be modified in the light of the above decision. By the County Court Rules 1981 SI 1981/1687, as amended by SI 1984/878, reg 13, Ord 19, r 6 (formerly Ord 19, r 1(11)(c)) now provides:

> No solicitors' charges shall be allowed as between party and party in respect of any proceedings referred to arbitration under rule 2(3), except—
> (a) the costs which were stated on the summons or which would have been stated on the summons if the claim had been for a liquidated sum;
> (b) the costs of enforcing the award, and
> [(c) such further costs as the arbitrator may direct where there has been unreasonable conduct on the part of the opposite party in relation to the proceedings or the claim therein.]

Venue

Another issue of considerable practical importance is where the proceedings are to be commenced. The relevant provision is contained in the County Court Rules 1981, Ord 4, r 2 which provides in part as follows:

General provisions as to actions
2.—(1) An action may be commenced—
(a) in the court for the district in which the defendant or one of the defendants resides or carries on business, or
(b) in the court for the district in which the cause of action wholly or in part arose.

. . .

(3) Where the plaintiff's claim—
(a) is founded on a hire-purchase agreement but is not for the delivery of the goods, or
(b) is founded on a contract for the sale or hire of goods under which the purchase price or rental is payable otherwise than in one sum,

the action shall be commenced only in the court for the district in which the defendant or one of the defendants resides or carries on business or resided or carried on business when the contract was made.

. . .

If proceedings are commenced in the wrong court then by Ord 16, r 2

'. . . the judge or registrar may, subject to rule 3—
(a) transfer the proceedings to the court in which they ought to have been commenced, or
(b) order the proceedings to continue in the court in which they have been commenced, or
(c) order the proceedings to be struck out.'

In his helpful booklet 'Small Claims in the County Court' (1981) Michael Birks writes as follows (at pp 14–15):

Selecting the right court

. . .

a An action may be commenced in the court for the district in which the defendant resides or carries on business [or]
b *An action may be commenced in the court for the district in which the cause of action (ie the events giving rise to the claim) occurred.* Thus if you lent some money to your next-door neighbour who has moved to another area without repaying you, he can be sued either in the district where he now lives or in the district where the loan was made. In the case of a road accident you have the additional choice of the district in which the accident occurred. Contracts made by post may be more difficult. Two examples will show why this is so. If in response to an advertisement offering to send goods upon receipt of a letter containing the purchase price, the contract is made (ie the cause of action arises) when you post the letter. But if you write to a firm saying that you wish to order some goods, the contract is only made when the firm accepts your order. Therefore the cause of action may arise in the district where the firm carries on business. If you have chosen the wrong court this can always be put right, for the court can transfer an action from one district to another . . .

Question

Do you agree with Birks' suggested answer to the first of his examples? Consider the following cases—
1. The Angus Mail Order Co which has its place of business in Westshire advertises as follows in the *Sunday Excess*: 'Thousands of Bargain Offers for Sale. Quickcount Minicomputers only £150, plus post and package. Send your money now.' Bert who lives 500 miles away in Eastshire sends his cheque for the full amount and a Quickcount Computer is duly despatched to him. It arrives safely but soon develops serious faults. The opinion of a local expert whom Bert has consulted is that the faults will never be remedied satisfactorily. Angus Mail Order refuses to refund the purchase price or to provide a replacement. Hotel accommodation in Westshire is expensive. Bert wishes to institute proceedings in the county court and seeks your advice as to whether he may sue in Eastshire. Advise Bert.
2. Pamela, who is on holiday in Northshire, takes her expensive leather coat to the Upmarket Cleaners for dry-cleaning. When she collects it the lining is badly shrunk. Upmarket claims that the shrinkage has been caused by a defect in the material and they refuse to offer any compensation. Pamela has now returned home to Southshire where an independent expert has reported that the fabric is not defective and that the fault lies in the cleaning. She seeks your advise as to where she should sue. Advise Pamela. [See generally the cases cited in Smith and Thomas *A Casebook on Contract* (7th edn, 1982) Chs 1 and 2].

CONCILIATION, ARBITRATION AND CODES OF PRACTICE

Conciliation and arbitration procedures intended to resolve disputes without invoking the traditional courts have been developed within several areas of English law. These include labour relations (eg the Advisory Conciliation and Arbitration Service and the Central Arbitration Committee) and race relations (the Commission for Racial Equality). The same has been true of consumer disputes where there has been something of a proliferation of codes of practice containing provisions for conciliation, arbitration and independent testing. More recently we have seen the development of the office of the Insurance Ombudsman Bureau.

These sectoral developments raise a number of problems which have been noted by consumer organisations (see eg 'Simple Justice' (NCC, 1979, Ch 10) but there is general agreement that at least within certain areas they offer sensible alternatives to litigation. As an example one may note the facilities for the independent testing of footwear for which provision is made by the Voluntary Code of Practice for Footwear prepared by the Footwear Distributors Federation. In such cases litigation can rarely be sensible (no matter how accessible a 'small claims' procedure) and the obvious solution is the one for which provision is made by the code.

The whole issue of redress procedures under codes of practice has been reviewed by the Office of Fair Trading which has published a consultative document (September 1980) followed by its conclusions (December 1981). The following summary of the Office's conclusions is helpful as indicating some of the general issues which have been raised:

Consumer Redress Procedures (1982) Trading Law 70

A number of ways of improving methods of resolving consumers' disputes with traders subscribing to codes of practice covering a wide range of goods and services—including package holidays, cars, electrical goods, shoes, mail order and furniture—are set out in an Office of Fair Trading report entitled *Redress Procedures under Codes of Practice— conclusions following a review by the Office of Fair Trading, . . .*

The report summarizes and assesses the responses to the OFT's [Office of Fair Trading] consultative document on the redress procedures provided under 20 codes of practice supported by the OFT. The document was sent to trade associations, consumer bodies and government departments in September 1980.

Gordon Borrie, Director General of Fair Trading, commenting on the report said:

'The report sets out recommended improvements to codes to practice conciliation and arbitration arrangements. I shall ask trade associations and other organizations sponsoring codes of practice, and the Chartered Institute of Arbitrators, to discuss with me how these proposals can be implemented.

'My aim is to strengthen the codes of practice arbitration system so that it will more effectively offer the essential ingredients of fairness, simplicity and speed at a minimum cost to all concerned.'

Mr Borrie also pointed out that since consumers had shown some reluctance to seek redress through the county court small claims scheme (which in any case is limited to claims of not more than £500), it was important that the option of arbitration under a code of practice should be available; that the system should be improved where appropriate; and that when new codes of practice were introduced they should include fully effective conciliation and arbitration arrangements.

Among the suggested improvements put forward by the OFT and set out in the report are:

Documents-only arbitration
The OFT thinks that arbitration under codes of practice should be on a documents-only basis

except in the very limited circumstances when the arbitrator is able to arrange a local hearing at no cost to the parties involved in the dispute.

There was a mixed reaction from consumer bodies to the suggestion in the consultative document that 'documents-only' should be the rule. Some felt that a consumer benefited psychologically by having 'a day in court' where he or she could put their case. On the other hand, the Chartered Institute of Arbitrators has said that since arbitrators are spread so thinly throughout the country, such 'in person' hearings would seldom be practical and, were they to become a regular feature of code arbitrations, costs would rise substantially.

Except in the limited circumstances mentioned above, the OFT does not favour allowing attended hearings, where customers might put themselves at risk of incurring further substantial costs. If an attended hearing is required, the county court should be the forum.

Time Targets

A common criticism was about the length of time taken to complete code redress cases. Trade associations expressed concern about the apparently slow progress made by the Institute on some arbitration cases. The Institute, in turn, was concerned about the problems which could arise when the associations prolonged the conciliation stage.

Although OFT would not wish to see rigid time limits set, it suggests that trade associations should set targets, preferably not exceeding three months, for the completion of the conciliation stage. There is no intention to halt cases which are progressing smoothly towards settlement, but if parties to a dispute are aware of time targets unwarranted delays may be reduced.

The Institute has also expressed itself 'very happy' to set time targets for the arbitration stage and the OFT will now formally ask the Institute to adopt them on the following basis:

> twenty-eight days for the claimant to submit details of his or her case; 28 days for the respondent to prepare a reply; and 28 days for the arbitrator to consider the case and deliver his decision.

The OFT will also ask trade associations and the Institute to produce and submit an annual review of performance against the time targets set.

Reasons for Decisions

The consultative document proposed that, on the grounds of natural justice and as an aid to understanding the basis of a decision, reasons should always be given for the arbitrators' decisions. One or two organizations did not support this idea. A motor trade association argued that the losing party, who might accept the arbitrator's decision without explanation, might feel aggrieved on seeing the reasons. Another association felt that giving reasons might re-open any latent ill-feelings in the dispute.

Other trade associations found giving reasons helpful in that they might point to possible weaknesses which may have contributed to the complaint and thus enable the weaknesses to be rectified or eliminated. The comments received reinforce the OFT's initial view that the giving of reasons makes an important contribution to the credibility of the arbitration process and that in future reasons should be given in all cases.

In addition, the report recommends that those trade associations whose codes include arbitration provisions, should arrange for technical advice to be provided should the arbitrator request it; on the consumer's payment for arbitration, that a standard scale of fees should be introduced; and that limited information on arbitration cases (not identifying the parties concerned) should be published. The OFT also hopes to publish a leaflet giving guidance to the consumer on the use of the Code arbitration system.

NOTES

1. The Annual Report of the Director General of Fair Trading 1983 contains the following information (at p 15):

Arbitration of disputes

Independent low-cost arbitration is a key feature of most of the 20 codes of practice with which the Office has been associated. During 1983 agreement was reached with the Chartered Institute of Arbitrators on a new model arbitration scheme incorporating improvements recommended by the Director General (see Annual Report for 1981) and the Institute was in touch with trade associations to amend their existing arrangements. The Office plans to publish an advice booklet on arbitration in the new year.

(See now 'I'm going to take it further: Arbitration under codes of practice,' Office of Fair Trading 1984.) The Office monitors the working of codes of practice with the results being published as 'Beeline' Special Edition Research Papers.

2. A good example of a scheme for resolving disputes on a documents only basis is provided by the AMDEA Code of Practice (1984), printed below, pp 388–392.

3. Further information on conciliation and arbitration is to be found in the Annual Reports of the relevant trade associations. For example the Annual Report of the Association of British Travel Agents (ABTA) for the year ending 30 June 1983 contains the following description of the working of the ABTA conciliation and arbitration services together with some useful facts and figures.

Annual Report of the Association of British Travel Agents (year ending 30 June 1983)

THE ABTA CONCILIATION SERVICE

This free service may be utilised by any customer of any ABTA member. It normally involves an appeal by the conciliation officer on behalf of the customer to an agent or tour operator for consideration or reconsideration to be given to a grievance or misunderstanding.

Problems that urgently require a settlement prior to departure are handled verbally. Such cases are increasing because of the public's tendency to book holidays at very short notice and without fully comprehending the nature of the contract or the class of accommodation on offer. Nevertheless, the bulk of complaints handled by the Conciliation Department relates to holidays that have already taken place and which people felt to be disappointing for one reason or another.

Analysis of Complaints

8,167 written complaints were received by the Conciliation Department in 1983, (besides a very large number of telephone calls which are not logged), of which 7,737 related to tour operators and 430 to retail agents. The corresponding figures for 1982 were 7,363 and 513 respectively. There was a large increase in the number of criticisms of point to point coach journeys to Europe and of continental camping sites, reflecting the rise in popularity of long distance coach and self catering holidays. The volume of follow-up letters from customers has continued to increase. As the overall quality of tour operators' passenger/staff relations is improving, it seems to follow that customers are increasingly prepared to correspond at greater length and over longer periods in their endeavours to obtain compensation.

THE ARBITRATION SCHEME FOR THE TRAVEL INDUSTRY

Any customer of an ABTA tour operator who feels that the free ABTA Conciliation Service has not resolved his dispute satisfactorily may use the independent Arbitration Scheme for the Travel Industry negotiated by ABTA with the Chartered Institute of Arbitrators.

The claimant currently pays a registration fee of £17.25 for himself plus £5.75 for each additional claimant within his immediate family of 12 or more of age. Other members of the party pay £9.20 each except for children under 12 years of age who pay no fee. The claimant's liability for costs is restricted to double the amount of the registration fee. The balance of the Institute's costs of administering the scheme is divided between ABTA and the respondent tour operator. ABTA pays £55 per case and the tour operator pays a deposit matching the claimant's registration fee and also pays £40 per case whatever the result. Generally, the wholly or partially successful applicant has his registration fee returned to him by the respondent under the terms of the Award.

All arbitrations are now dealt with on an 'on documents' basis, provision for attended hearings having been abolished from 1 April 1982. The amount of claims permissible under the scheme is limited to £1,000 per person or £5,000 per booking form, whichever is the greater. Claims arising from illness or physical injury are excluded.

Analysis of Cases

The number of cases submitted to arbitration in the last six years is as follows:

1978	101
1979	120
1980	208
1981	292
1982	240
1983	335

An analysis of those awards over the last four years made available to the Secretariat is given in Section I of the table below and Section II analyses the sums involved in awards and claims, where known.

SECTION I

	1980	1981	1982	1983
Cases settled by 31 December:				
Awards in favour of customer (tour operator normally required to reimburse customer's registration fee as well as paying amount awarded)	133	207	143	225
Cases dismissed (no amount awarded to customer: customer required to reimburse tour operator's deposit)	8	31	34	66
Nil awards (no amount awarded to customer: customer forfeits registration fee and tour operator forfeits deposit)	8	6	3	2

SECTION II

	1980	1981	1982	1983
Number of Cases in Section I where specific amount claimed	102	215	162	289
Total of claims submitted	£58,650	£103,630	£63,877	£149,379
Total amount awarded	£23,562	£51,385	£26,799	£71,690
Average sum claimed	£575	£482	£478	£517
Average sum awarded	£231	£239	£198	£248
Awards as percentage of claims	40%	49%	41.5%	48%

Of course the availability in a code of practice of an option to arbitrate does not preclude a consumer from suing in the ordinary courts. However if there is an agreement to arbitrate by the parties to the dispute it is unlikely that it will be open to either party to withdraw. Moreover the grounds for objecting to an award are very limited (see generally the Arbitration Act 1979). The following case illustrates the binding nature of contractual agreements to arbitrate:

Ford v Clarksons Holidays Ltd [1971] 3 All ER 454, [1971] 1 WLR 1412, Court of Appeal

Davies LJ. This is an appeal from an order made by his Honour Judge Willis at the

Shoreditch County Court on 10th February 1971, when he dismissed a summons taken out by the defendants, who are a well-known travel agency, to stay an action brought by the plaintiff for damages for breach of contract in respect of a 'package' holiday cruise in the Adriatic. I need not go into the details of the claim at all, save just to outline that the plaintiff claims the return of the whole of the £200 paid by him and his wife to go on this trip. They complain about the food; they complain about the cabin; they complain about practically everything. Whether those complaints are justified or not we have no idea. They are denied by the defendants.

The appeal turns really on the meaning of an arbitration clause, perhaps not very elegantly framed, in the conditions of contract. I will read it as set out in the judgment of the learned judge.

'The condition containing the arbitration clause reads as follows: "In the event of any dispute arising under this clause, any of these Booking Conditions, any guarantee, warranty, representation, condition or other matter whatsoever affecting any services sold or offered by [the defendants] the decision of a mutually acceptable independent arbitrator shall be accepted by all parties as final and, in the absence of agreement upon an arbitrator, the arbitrator shall be appointed by the President for the time being of the Law Society. Arbitration shall be in England and these conditions are subject to English Law".'

The vital words are 'shall be accepted by all parties as final'.

The major contention on behalf of the plaintiff, who resisted the defendants' application to stay under s 4 of the Arbitration Act 1950, was that that clause was an attempt by the defendants to oust the jurisdiction of the court, ie to prevent there being any application under the Arbitration Act 1950 to set aside the award or to order the arbitrator to make an award in the form of a special case. And I suppose also it must follow, as I ventured to suggest to counsel for the plaintiff in the course of the argument, if his contention for the plaintiff is right, it would prevent the court from removing an arbitrator for misconduct under s 23.

The point was dealt with with admirable brevity, if I may say so, by counsel for the defendants. He pointed out first of all that the words 'final and binding' occur in s 16 of the Arbitration Act itself, which provides:

'Unless a contrary intention is expressed therein, every arbitration agreement shall, where such a provision is applicable to the reference, be deemed to contain a provision that the award to be made by the arbitrator or umpire shall be final and binding on the parties and the persons claiming under them respectively.'

. . .

What is contended is this. It is admitted that if this agreement said 'the decision of a mutually independent arbitrator shall be final", that would be all right. But because of the intrusive word '*accepted* by all parties as final', it is contended by counsel for the plaintiff, and was so held by the learned judge, that that was ousting the jurisdiction of the court. I can myself see no validity in that contention.

. . .

I can myself see here no valid reason why this case should not go to arbitration, as the plaintiff and the defendants have contracted that it should. In those circumstances, I would allow this appeal and order that the action be stayed.

[Edmund-Davies and Stephenson, LL J delivered concurring judgments agreeing that the appeal should be allowed.] *Appeal allowed: action stayed.*

INSURANCE OMBUDSMAN BUREAU

The Bureau was opened in March 1981. The way in which it operates, together with its objects and the Ombudsman's powers and duties, are as indicated in the following extracts:

The Insurance Ombudsman Bureau Annual Report 1983

APPENDIX (I) CONSULTING THE OMBUDSMAN

(1) When a policyholder writes to the Bureau:—
    (a) if it is a general question it is answered by a letter of advice. If his dispute falls outside

the terms of reference he is advised where he may seek help, eg a broker, solicitor, the British Insurance Association or one of the life offices' associations.

   (b) if it is a dispute with a member company, the policyholder is advised to approach the Chief Executive of his company. If still dissatisfied he refers again to the Bureau.

(2) When a policyholder who has already had his problem considered by the Chief Executive of his company writes to the Bureau:—

   (a) if his dispute comes within the Ombudsman's terms of reference (see Appendix II) he is asked to complete an application form and support it with all relevant evidence, reports and letters.

   (b) on receipt of a completed application form the Bureau obtains from the company concerned all its files on the case and makes up a dossier which is passed to the Ombudsman for investigation.

(4) The Ombudsman reads first the policyholder's papers and then the company's files. When satisfied as to the point or points at issue he may:—

   (a) seek further information on the facts;

   (b) seek technical professional help and advice from a consultant;

   (c) enter into discussions with the company concerned;

   (d) conduct research into the law relevant to the point;

   (e) call a meeting between the parties at which he will take the chair;

   (f) personally interview the policyholder or carry out any combination of these courses of action.

(5) The Ombudsman will *either* reach a decision *or* negotiate a settlement satisfactory to both parties. If he fails to achieve a settlement he has power to make an award against a company but he has so far not had to use the power.

(6) According to the procedure adopted for dealing with the dispute the Ombudsman will send to both parties by the same post:—

   (a) a Decision which binds neither party until accepted in writing by the policyholder, when it binds both policyholder and company; or

   (b) a Report which records the settlement reached. No confirmation is required; or

   (c) an Award which, if under £100,000 (or £10,000 per annum in permanent health insurance cases) requires acceptance by the policyholder only to be binding on both. Above that sum it requires acceptance by the company as well.

All these documents set out the facts and, where relevant, the reasons for the Decision or Award.

(7) If the policyholder either fails to acknowledge a Decision or Award or rejects it, his legal rights remain unaffected and he is free to seek a remedy in the Courts.

(8) The Ombudsman is not empowered to reconsider his decisions or awards save on the emergence of further facts and with the leave of the Council.

APPENDIX (II) ABSTRACT OF THE BUREAU'S MEMORANDUM AND ARTICLES OF ASSOCIATION AND OF THE OMBUDSMAN'S TERMS OF REFERENCE

The Objects of the Bureau are:

To receive references in relation to complaints, disputes and claims made in connection with or arising out of policies of insurance effected with Members of the Bureau.

To facilitate the satisfaction, settlement or withdrawal of claims whether by an award or other such means.

To collaborate with government or any other authorities in matters relating to the business of insurance.

To do all such things incidental or conducive to these objects.

The Ombudsman's powers and duties are:

To attend Council Meetings and give assistance, provide reports and information as Council may direct.

To administer day-to-day conduct of Bureau within Terms of Reference.

To act as counsellor, conciliator, adjudicator or arbitrator in relation to references. Subject to Council's consent, to appoint advisers.

To make awards up to £100,000—or up to £10,000 per annum in personal health insurance cases—binding on members.

When making an award, to have regard to the terms of the contract, to act in conformity with any applicable rule of law or relevant judicial authority, general principles of good insurance practice, his Terms of Reference and the standards of insurance practice and codes of practice, but not to be bound by precedent.

To make representations or recommendations relating to complaints, disputes or claims to the Council or persons named in the reference.

To request information from members and report any non-compliance to Council.

To submit annual reports to Council, Members and Board.

The Ombudsman has no power to entertain or comment upon any reference which:
Is made other than by the person who effected the policy which is the subject of the reference or by some person who has acquired legal title to it (not for value).[1]

Relates to a policy of insurance other than one effected by or on behalf of or for the benefit of natural persons.[2]

Relates to any policy which is not a UK policy.

Relates to industrial assurance policies.

Questions areas within the competence or discretion of the appointed actuary of a member.

Rules for Reference
Complaint must have been considered by senior management of member and result not been accepted by complainant.

Complainant must not have instituted proceedings in Court of law or made reference to arbitration unless proceedings have been discontinued or arbitration reference withdrawn prior to final judgment.

Complaint must not have been considered previously (unless new evidence is now available).

Complaint must have been received by Ombudsman within six months of member company making its decision known to the complainant.

1 This exclusion forbids entertainment of third party disputes.
2 Ie, no policy taken out by a business will qualify.

NOTES

1. According to the Council Commentary on the above report, 'Of the 301 cases he dealt with the Ombudsman revised the previous company decision in 52 cases. In addition, however, 475 cases were resolved after referral to the company without requiring adjudication'.
2. For a further reference to the Bureau see above, p. 146.

COMPENSATION ORDERS

A further method of obtaining redress is through the making of a compensation order following a conviction under the Powers of Criminal Courts Act 1973, s 35(1), as partly replaced by the Magistrates' Courts Act 1980, s 40, and the Criminal Justice Act 1982, s 67. Such a power is a matter of discretion rather than entitlement and it exists in both magistrates' courts and in the Crown Court, although in the former there is a limit of £2,000 in respect of each offence of which the defendant is convicted. The provision is especially important in relation to offences under the Trade Descriptions Act 1968. Sir Gordon Borrie has noted, 'The number of compensation orders made under the Trade Descriptions Act have been 194 (1978–79), 138 (1979–80), 107 (1980–81) and 94 (1981–82). The average amount of the compensation was £147 (1978–79), £173 (1979–80), £183 (1980–81) and £308 (1981–82)': see *The Development of Consumer Law and Policy* (1984), p 69. Of course in this area use of compensation orders is very much incidental to their principal areas of use. In 1982 121,000 persons were ordered to pay compensation (other than for summary motoring offences) by magistrates' courts and about 6,000 in the Crown Court: see 'Criminal Statistics for England and Wales 1982', Cmnd 9048, September 1983, pp 169–170 and 193–196. Theft, handling and burglary featured prominently. Although there is no separate entry for consumer protection statutes one may infer that the numbers are low. Indeed the report on which the power to make compensation orders was based (see the Report of the Advisory Council on the Penal System, 'Reparation by the Offender', HMSO 1970) positively discouraged the making of orders in respect of 'regulatory offences', saying (at para 61):

> Our general approach to this matter is that compensation should be available in criminal proceedings in respect of what might be termed 'common law' offences and not regulatory offences. We recognise that it may not be possible to legislate to give effect to this intention; and if no satisfactory provision can be drafted, it will be necessary to leave the matter to the discretion of the courts and to rely on their good sense to resort to their powers to order compensation only in cases where this is justified by the character of the offence. In theory, a power to order compensation in criminal proceedings in respect of any offence might make it possible for compensation to be awarded in situations where there is no civil liability, but the risk of this happening seems somewhat remote.

The facts of the following case are far removed from the context of consumer protection legislation. However it is helpful as raising a number of issues.

Bond v Chief Constable of Kent [1983] 1 All ER 456, [1983] 1 WLR 40, Queen's Bench Divisional Court

Griffiths LJ. This is an appeal by way of case stated from an order of the magistrates sitting in the petty sessional division of Gravesham who, on 15 January 1982, after the appellant had pleaded guilty to a charge of causing damage to property contrary to s 1(1) of the Criminal Damage Act 1971, made an order that he pay the sum of £25 as compensation to the occupier of the house that he had damaged because of the distress and anxiety suffered by the occupier as a result of the appellant's behaviour.

The facts of the case are briefly these. In the early hours of 30 August 1981 the occupiers of the house were aroused by noises coming from their front garden, and became aware of the presence of a man behaving strangely and stumbling about. They telephoned the police but before the police arrived a stone was thrown through the window of the house. The occupier of the house was terrified, fearing that there would be a sustained attack and felt compelled to gather his wife and children into one room for safety. The police, on arrival, found the appellant to be in a drunken state. He was then arrested and taken to Gravesend police station.

The magistrates were asked by the prosecutor to consider awarding £25 compensation which was the cost of replacing the damaged window, but of their own motion they also considered whether or not they should not award some modest sum to compensate the occupier of the house for what must undoubtedly have been a most terrifying and frightening experience.

They considered the terms of s 35(1) of the Powers of Criminal Courts Act 1973, which provides that 'on application or otherwise' they may make 'an order . . . requiring [the appellant] to pay compensation for any personal injury, loss or damage resulting from that offence . . .' The magistrates rightly considered that there was a sufficient nexus between the behaviour and the terror caused to the occupier. Indeed, it was the only cause of the occupier's terror.

In those circumstances it appears to me that the only question for consideration by this court is whether the fright and distress suffered can be fairly covered by either the words 'personal injury' or 'damage' contained in s 35.

We have been referred to three authorities by counsel for the appellant but the first two, in my view, carry the matter that we have to decide nowhere.

. . .

The next case was *R v Vivian* [1979] 1 All ER 48, [1979] 1 WLR 291. In that case the defendant had been convicted of taking and driving away a motor car, and driving it recklessly. In the course of that he collided with and damaged another car, the estimate of repairs being £209. The judge in that case ordered him to pay compensation in the sum of £100. However, the estimate was fiercely contested by the defendant as being grossly excessive, and this court held that a compensation order should not be made unless the sum claimed by the victim as compensation for damage resulting from the offence was either agreed or had been proved. That case is clearly limited to what I will call 'quantifiable physical damage'. It has no application to small sums of money awarded for personal injury or for the results of behaviour with which we are concerned in this case.

The final case was *R v Thomson Holidays Ltd* [1974] 1 All ER 823, [1974] QB 592. In that case, Thomson Holidays Ltd had sold a package holiday and they were convicted of an offence under the Trade Descriptions Act 1968, the nature of which was that they had recklessly made a false representation in the course of their trade or business as to the amenity or accommodation provided by their hotel, contrary to s 14(1)(*b*) of that Act. The facts revealed that the hotel fell very, very far short of the legitimate expectations of anyone reading the brochure and, as a result, the customers had been very gravely disappointed in their holiday. They were awarded the modest sum of £50 by way of compensation for that disappointment.

. . .

If the disappointment and inconvenience of a ruined holiday falls within the word 'damage' in s 35 of the Powers of Criminal Courts Act 1973, I for my part have no doubt that the terror directly occasioned by this attack on the occupier's house falls either within 'personal injury' or alternatively within the word 'damage' in s 35 of the 1973 Act, and the magistrates were fully entitled to award the modest sum of £25. I would dismiss this appeal.

McCullough J. I agree. In *R v Thomson Holidays Ltd* [1974] 1 All ER 823 at 829, [1974] QB 592 at 599 Lawton LJ said:

> 'Parliament, we are sure, never intended to introduce into the criminal law the concepts of causation which apply to the assessment of damages under the law of contract and tort.'

In my judgment, the sense of that observation is this: that in assessing whether compensation should be awarded under s 35 of the Powers of Criminal Courts Act 1973 the court should approach the matter in a broad commonsense way and should not allow itself to become enmeshed in the refined questions of causation which can sometimes arise in claims for damages under the law of contract or tort. The court simply has to ask itself whether the loss or damage can fairly be said to have resulted from the offence. The court plainly did that. *Appeal dismissed.*

Questions

Is there a necessary equivalence between the disappointed customers in the *Thomson Holidays* case and the claimant in the above case? What would the position have been if the claimant had been neither (i) the occupier of the property on which the damage occurred nor (ii) the victim, it seems, of an assault?

NOTES

1. For further discussion of compensation orders generally see H. Street, 'Compensation Orders and the Trade Descriptions Act' [1974] Crim LR

345; R. Tarling and P. Softley, 'Compensation Orders in the Crown Court' [1976] Crim LR 422; P. S. Atiyah, 'Compensation Orders and Civil Liability' [1979] Crim LR 504; J. Vennard, 'Magistrates' Assessments of Compensation for Injury' [1979] Crim LR 510.

2. In *R v Chappel* [1984] Crim LR 574 the court refused to accept a contention that the existence of a potential civil liability to compensate was a precondition for the making of a valid compensation order. The case concerned an order to compensate the Customs and Excise in respect of a loss arising out of failure to make VAT returns.

3. In *R v Maynard* [1983] Crim LR 821 the court was concerned with a case in which a compensation order for £3,236 had been made following six convictions for obtaining money by deception by altering car mileages. Reducing this sum it was held that compensation orders could take account of only the actual loss suffered by the victim. They could not be used as a punitive measure to remove the profit from the crime.

4. Section 35(1) of the Powers of the Criminal Courts Act 1973 has been amended by the Criminal Justice Act 1982, s 67, which provides:

67. Compensation Orders

In section 35 of the Powers of Criminal Courts Act 1973 (which gives a court power to make a compensation order in addition to dealing with an offender in any other way)—

  (a) the following subsections shall be substituted for sub-section (1)—

    "(1) Subject to the provisions of this Part of this Act and to section 40 of the Magistrates' Courts Act 1980 (which imposes a monetary limit on the powers of a magistrates' court under this section), a court by or before which a person is convicted of an offence, instead of or in addition to dealing with him in any other way, may, on application or otherwise, make an order (in this Act referred to as 'a compensation order') requiring him to pay compensation for any personal injury, loss or damage resulting from that offence or any other offence which is taken into consideration by the court in determining sentence.

    (1A) Compensation under subsection (1) above shall be of such amount as the court considers appropriate, having regard to any evidence and to any representations that are made by or on behalf of the accused or the prosecutor."; and

  (b) the following subsection shall be inserted after subsection (4)—

    "(4A) Where the court considers—

      (a) that it would be appropriate both to impose a fine and to make a compensation order; but

      (b) that the offender has insufficient means to pay both an appropriate fine and appropriate compensation,

    the court shall give preference to compensation (though it may impose a fine as well).".

In the House of Commons second reading debate on the Criminal Justice Bill (16 HC Official Report (6th series), 20 January 1982) the following comments were made (at cols 301–2):

The Secretary of State for the Home Department (Mr William Whitelaw):

. . .

The Bill provides a timely opportunity to extend and to clarify, in the interests of the victims of crime, the general compensation power in section 35 of the Powers of Criminal Courts Act 1973. We consider it right that where an offender's means are limited and he cannot afford to pay both an appropriate fine and the appropriate compensation, the interests of the victim should prevail over the interests of the Crown and preference be given to the ordering of compensation. Moreover, if the court in a particular case sees fit to dispense with a fine completely, leaving the compensation order as the only sentence imposed, we think that it should be free to do so. That is already the situation in Scotland under the Criminal Justice (Scotland) Act 1980.

We also want to make it clear that the courts can order the compensation that they think appropriate in a particular case, without the precise value of the victim's loss necessarily having been agreed or proved. That will rectify the results of certain court cases, which have had restrictive effects on the use of the powers of the courts to make compensation orders. Clause 44 gives effect to those changes.

It remains to be seen whether in the light of this provision the courts will take a somewhat less restrictive approach to the making of compensation orders than that suggested by the *Vivian* case, above. As Sir Gordon Borrie has rightly commented, op cit p 69, 'Surely it is timely for a little more boldness to be encouraged'. Significantly Lord Hailsham LC commented in *Wings Ltd v Ellis* [1984] 3 All ER 577 at 583, [1984] 3 WLR 965 at 973, that had this provision been in force he, 'would have hoped that a compensation order would have been made in whole or in part in preference to a fine.' See further below p 521.

LITIGANTS IN PERSON

Do-it-yourself litigation may have an appeal for some (although by no means all) consumer litigants. It was in recognition of this fact that the Litigants in Person (Costs and Expenses) Act 1975 made provision for the recovery of costs and expenses by litigants in person in civil proceedings. In the case of actions in the High Court the detailed provisions are contained in RSC Ord 62, r 28A which provides in part:

'(1) On a taxation of the costs of a litigant in person there may, subject to the provisions of this rule, be allowed such costs as would have been allowed if the work and disbursements to which the costs relate had been done by or made by a solicitor on the litigant's behalf.

(2) The amount allowed in respect of any item shall be such sum as the taxing officer thinks fit not exceeding, except in the case of a disbursement, two-thirds of the sum which in the opinion of the taxing officer would have been allowed in respect of that item if the litigant had been represented by a solicitor.

(3) Where in the opinion of the taxing officer the litigant has not suffered any pecuniary loss in doing any work to which the costs relate, he shall not be allowed in respect of the time reasonably spent by him on the work more than £2 an hour . . .'

Equivalent provisions for the county courts are contained in CCR 1981, Ord 38, r 17. Of course these provisions apply only to civil proceedings, the private prosecutor being less favourably treated: (see *R v Stockport Magistrates' Court, ex p Cooper* (1984) 148 JP 261. For a detailed discussion of the implications of RSC Ord 62, r 28A see *Hart v Aga Khan Foundation (UK)* [1984] 2 All ER 439, [1984], 1 WLR 994, CA.

Questions

1. Is the cost of giving up time which would have been spent on leisure priced fairly at £2 per hour?

2 In the case of county court proceedings CCR 1981, Ord 38, r 17(1) provides in part that, 'there may be allowed to the litigant in person such costs as would have been allowed if the work and disbursements to which the costs relate had been done or made by a solicitor on his behalf . . .' How, if at all, is this provision to be applied to claims for sums not exceeding £500 (see above p 304 et seq)?

Note that by Ord 38, r 13(1), the judge or registrar may allow a sum in respect of the attendance at court of a witness, including a party to the proceedings).

The enforcement of judgment debts in the county court

INTRODUCTION

Consumers who have succeeded in obtaining a county court judgment might be forgiven for assuming that enforcement would follow as a matter of course. However this is far from the case. The onus of enforcement is placed rather on the successful litigant and the process can be expensive, time-consuming and ultimately frustrating – especially where the debtor proves to be a man of straw. Such factors have led to continual demands for the reform of enforcement procedures. In 'Simple Justice', the National Consumer Council report on Small Claims Procedures (1979), the difficulties with enforcement were said (at p 44) to 'undermine the whole system of redress for civil claims'. Drawing on the results of surveys of both consumers and advice agencies in England and Wales, the NCC concluded that:

> It is pointless trying to make it easier to bring a small consumer claim in the courts if, at the end of the day, the claimant is left with a hollow victory. We consider that this brings the law and the courts into disrepute. We therefore conclude that the improvement of enforcement procedures must become a priority for the Lord Chancellor.

The results of the NCC's own survey are indicative of the extent of the problem. The report notes (at p 41) that:

> In the end, 72 out of 127 people who won all or part of their claim received all of the money owing. Eighteen people (a quarter) received no money at all; a further four received some – but not all; eleven were still trying to recover the money; while twenty-two people did not tell us what happened. Not only did so many people not get their award, but a considerable number spent more money in enforcement fees which they did not get back.

This section is concerned with the methods available for the enforcement of judgment debts in the county court and the problems associated with them. In addition to the Simple Justice report reference may be made to the following: 'Enforcing Money Judgments in the County Court' (1980) (a booklet written by Michael Birks and issued by the Lord Chancellor's Department), the 'Report of the Review Committee on Insolvency Law and Practice' (the Cork Committee) Cmnd 8558, 1982, Ch 5, the 'Report of the Joint Working Party on the Enforcement of Judgments, Orders and Decrees of the Courts in Northern Ireland' (1965) (the Anderson Report), the 'Report of the Committee on the Enforcement of Judgment Debts' (February 1969) (Cmnd 3909) (the Payne Report), the New South Wales Law Reform Commission, 'Draft Proposal Relating to the Enforcement of Money Judgments' (1975), the New Brunswick Department of Justice, Law Reform Division, 'Third Report of the Consumer Protection Project, Vol II, Legal Remedies of the Unsecured Creditor After Judgment' (1976) and the National Consumer Council Report, 'Consumers and Debt' (1983).

METHODS OF ENFORCEMENT

Several methods of enforcement are available to a judgment creditor and a prescribed fee is payable for each. The two principal methods are a warrant of execution against goods and an attachment of earnings order. Other methods include garnishee proceedings, a charging order and the appointment of a receiver.

Michael Birks in his booklet 'Enforcing Money Judgments in the County Court' (1980) stresses that the creditor ought initially to determine whether the debtor has the ability to pay. Obviously this is sensible. To this end, and on payment of a fee (currently £6), he can apply for an order directing the debtor to attend the court, produce relevant books and documents, and answer, on oath, questions put to him as to his means and resources. Refusal to attend the court or answer questions constitutes contempt of court. Mr Birks describes the principal method of enforcement and some of the problems associated with it as follows (the text being addressed to the litigant in person):

Warrant of Execution against goods
This is the simplest method of enforcement and the one most frequently used. The court bailiff is instructed to call at the debtor's house, business premises or wherever he has reason to believe that goods belonging to the debtor may be found. He will then remove and sell sufficient goods to pay the debt and costs of sale. If the debt is substantial this may involve the removal of a great deal of furniture or other goods and the cost of transport to the auction rooms is expensive. In addition there are the auctioneers' fees for valuation and sale. Modern furniture does not always realise high prices at auction because it is easy to buy new furniture on credit.

Often the most valuable goods in a house, such as a television set or washing machine, are on hire purchase and do not become the property of the debtor until all the instalments are paid. Sometimes the furniture belongs to the debtor's landlord or to his wife or a relative. The bailiff can only sell goods owned by the debtor, and if he seizes property belonging to someone else, that person may claim it and the court will have to decide who is entitled to it . . .

Although the warrant of execution against goods is an appropriate method to use against a trade debtor with business assets this is often not the case with a private debtor. With the exception of motor vehicles (which in any event will often be the property of a finance company) secondhand consumer goods have little value, especially when sold by auction. (See in the different context of repossession by finance companies, the Report of the Crowther Committee on Consumer Credit, Cmnd 4596, 1971, para 6.646).

Some of the main problems associated with enforcing judgments through an attachment of earnings order and the limits to which the process is subject are noted in the following paragraphs from the Cork Committee report:

254. This procedure attracts substantial criticism. It was introduced for judgment debts in 1971 as a result of the Payne Committee's recommendations.[1] and has met with limited success. Debtors who frequently change jobs or who are unemployed or self-employed are able to avoid this type of enforcement. The Payne Committee also recommended the endorsement of the Employee's P45 Income Tax Form (which is issued on termination of employment) with a note or code reference indicating the existence of an Attachment of Earnings Order. The new employer would be aware of this and would be obliged to take

---

[1]See the Report of the Committee on the Enforcement of Judgment Debts (the Payne Committee), Cmnd 3909, 1969 para 580 et seq.

action to comply with the order or to notify the debtor's local County Court that he had commenced employment. This proposal has not been implemented and several of those who have given evidence to us have argued that it should be. We consider that further consideration should be given to this or some other solution to the problem of the debtor in respect of whom an Attachment of Earnings Order is in force and who frequently changes his job.

. . .

257. We recommend that the definition of 'earnings' be amended so as to bring within the scope of Orders for the Attachment of Earnings those self-employed persons who work regularly for one employer at an hourly or piece rate, or on commission. We have received representations that the procedure for obtaining Orders for Attachment of Earnings is too slow and involves unnecessary paperwork. We believe that a careful review of the procedure is likely to show that the elimination of some steps is feasible without reducing the overall effectiveness of the procedure and that this will result in a saving of the time of clerical staff and bailiffs.

THE PAYNE COMMITTEE PROPOSALS

The problems associated with the enforcement of judgment debts were the concern of the Payne Committee which reported in 1969 (see the Report of the Committee on the Enforcement of Judgment Debts, Cmnd 3909, 1969). A central recommendation of this committee was that there should be established 'an entirely new organisation enjoying exclusive jurisdiction in the enforcement of all civil judgment debts' (para 337). The organisation would build on the foundations of the county court system, using the skills and experience of its staff, but would nonetheless be a new, separate and autonomous body enjoying all the attributes of an ordinary court of law. Commenting on the powers and role of this Enforcement Office the committee said:

370. The available methods of enforcement should be capable of being employed through the Enforcement Office simultaneously, if the circumstances of the case so require, and power so to employ them should be expressly conferred upon the Enforcement Office.
371. Moreover it should be expressly provided that, after a judgment debtor has become the subject of an enforcement order, the available methods of enforcement should be capable of being employed against him until his debts are discharged or satisfied or enforcement is abandoned. Thus enforcement through the Enforcement Office will be a continuous process so long as a debtor remains the subject of an enforcement order.

. . .

377. A difficult question arises at this point. After an application for enforcement has been made, should the Enforcement Office proceed at its own discretion or should it seek the specific authority of the judgment creditor or creditors?
378. On the one hand it is argued by the Law Society in their memorandum to us that,

'Once a transfer has been ordered it would be for the Debtors' Court of its own motion to see that what was owing was paid as soon as practicable. The initiative would rest no longer with the creditor alone, it would be the duty of the Debtor's Court to see to it that the debtors who could comply with court orders should do so . . .'

. . .

Similarly, the Northern Ireland report[1] recommended that the Enforcement Office should itself consider what order or orders are appropriate for enforcing the particular judgment, but

---

[1] See the Report of the Joint Working Party on the Enforcement of Judgments, Orders and Decrees of the Courts in Northern Ireland (1969) (the Anderson Report).

should give the debtor and creditor seven days notice in writing of the proposed order or orders, leaving either party free to make such representations as he might wish to the Office within that period.

379.   On the other hand, it is held that the true function of the Enforcement Office is to provide machinery to enable creditors to obtain the fruits of their judgment.

380.   We accept this view and hold that a private debt does not cease to be private by being transformed into a judgment debt. The use of judicial institutions to convert a claim for a debt or damages into a judgment debt does not impose the duty of collecting that debt upon the State. The creditor retains the initiative as to how he should proceed to enforce judgment.

These recommendations were never implemented in England and Wales. In 1979 the National Consumer Council attempted to revive interest in the matter, stating: 'We recommend that the report of the Payne Committee, in particular the establishment of an enforcement office, should provide the basis for improving the way judgments are enforced . . .': see 'Simple Justice', p. 45. (See also the Cork Committee report (Cmnd 8558, 1982 at para 244 especially). However in Northern Ireland the position is different and an Enforcement of Judgments Office was established in 1971.

Question

Do you consider that the Payne Committee was right in its view (see para 380 of the report) that, 'The use of judicial proceedings to convert a claim for a debt or damages into a judgment debt does not impose the duty of collecting that debt upon the State'?

But first find your defendant

A successful civil action must of necessity depend on the plaintiff being able to trace an appropriate defendant. Sometimes this will be impossible, as when a receipt is lost or a product is unlabelled. There is another aspect of the problem which may prove just as intractable when it comes to issuing a summons or enforcing a judgment. This can be done only if the correct name and address of the defendant can be established, and fears have been expressed that this will be made that much more difficult by the abolition on 26 February 1982 of the Registry of Business Names. (The change does not affect limited liability companies trading under their corporate names.) The government's case was in essence that the old register was far from complete and that both creditors and consumers are protected more adequately by the disclosure requirements of the Companies Act 1981, ss 28 and 29.

The general nature of these requirements was summarised as follows by Reginald Eyre MP (Under-Secretary for Trade) in an interview with *British Business* (22 January 1982, p 152):

> But in order to enable those dealing with such businesses to know the identity of the owners, any business which is carried on under a name other than that of its owner must display particulars of its ownership – and addresses where documents can be served – at its business premises and on its business stationery. In addition, these particulars must be given on request to any person with whom business is being done or discussed. So customers and suppliers will have an important new right. I hope they

will not hesitate to point this out to any business which is not complying with the act from 26 February onwards. This requirement doesn't apply to businesses trading under the name of the owner, including companies trading under their registered names. Incidentally, the abolition of the registry of business names will mean considerable savings in staff and costs.

However not everyone was convinced and opposition had been expressed by both industry and consumer groups. Some of the main arguments for retaining the register were put by Mr Donald Anderson MP when speaking in the Second Reading debate on the Companies (No 2) Bill (see 5 HC Official Report (6th series) col 690 (1981)). He summarised the case put by the National Consumer Council as follows:

The council says, in short, that the abolition of the registry could

'produce a paradise for shady traders, who would find it much easier to conceal their true identity, from consumers, trading standards officers and investigative journalists and broadcasters trying to track them down.'

The council concludes that the Government should retain the Registry of Business Names in a new, revitalised and self-financing form. If the Government are so concerned about the hard cash of this matter, it is not difficult to increase the registration fee.

In points of detail, the council states that consumers need to be able to trace the correct name and address of the trader whom they wish to sue, which is essential if they are to pursue a court judgment to enforcement.

The council refers to the problems of investigative journalists. The Minister will know of the complaints that have been made not only by the Esther Rantzen show, *That's Life*, but also by that extremely valuable BBC *Checkpoint* series in which I have been involved in relation to some matters. I find that an ideal weapon against the fraudulent trader. Such programmes have shown considerable concern about the extent to which the work that they do, albeit as troublemakers but on behalf of the consumer, will be hampered by the Government's decision to abolish the registry.

As to particular flaws in the Bill relating to consumers seeking to enforce their rights, the Minister will know that the NCC has mentioned that the new system will be of no use to consumers where a business has ceased trading, and therefore the information that is available within the premises or on the business stationery will be of no assistance. It will be impossible to trace the owners, even though those owners of a business may have personal assets upon which creditors might be entitled to claim in seeking to enforce their judgments.

Similar problems could arise where a business does not have premises which are open to customers or may move its address frequently. The NCC has asked:

'How will the new requirements be enforceable against mobile-van traders, itinerant "hotel sale" traders or market stall holders? It won't be easy for a mail-order customer in Nottingham to find out, who owns a defaulting business in Exeter.'

Question

Section 29(1) (b) of the Companies Act 1981 requires traders to display in a prominent position on premises to which their customers 'have access' the names and addresses 'at which service of any document relating . . . to the business will be effective'. Is there a satisfactory answer to the NCC's question?

NOTE

For further discussion see A. J. Slee 'Who's Who in Trade? – A View of the Companies Act 1981' (1982) 90 ITSA Monthly Review, 240.

Prepayments and insolvency

INTRODUCTION

In recent years much attention has been focused on the problems faced by consumers who have made payments in advance for goods or services. The practice of requiring prepayments is widespread both in mail order and other transactions and the associated problems have been reviewed on several occasions, notably by the Office of Fair Trading. The following extract from an Office of Fair Trading Consultative Paper is helpful as indicating the variety of goods and services involved.

Pre-payment in non-mail order transactions – A consultative paper on a proposed reference to the Consumer Protection Advisory Committee (Office of Fair Trading, January 1979)

1. This paper reviews the problems faced by consumers who make pre-payments and seeks views upon a proposed reference by the Director General of Fair Trading (DGFT) to the Consumer Protection Advisory Committee (CPAC) recommending that traders (other than mail order traders) who accept pre-payment from consumers should be required to give standard written statements about despatch times and about the consumer's entitlement to a refund if goods and/or services are not supplied within a specified or reasonable time.

The problem
2. Consumers who have paid in advance frequently complain of delays in the delivery of goods or the peformance of services. About 24,000 such complaints are reported to the OFT by Trading Standards Officers each year, about half of which concern full or partial pre-payments made to shops or to suppliers of services. . . . Although the precise nature of the problem varies with each kind of transaction – made to measure or specially ordered goods, standards goods stocked elsewhere, services which may be subject to the availability of materials – the essential weakness is that many consumers do not have a clear idea of their rights or how to secure them. As a consequence delivery or completion dates are often not stated or are uncertain and this weakens the ability of consumers to pursue complaints effectively. The economic effects of the delay upon the consumer may consist in the impaired utility of goods needed by a particular date, vulnerability to price increases, loss of interest on the pre-payment and, where insolvency on the part of the trader intervenes, complete loss of money.

NOTES

1. The immediate result of this consultative process was that the Office of Fair Trading concluded that 'legislation was not practicable and that the improvements which are needed should instead be sought through self-regulation': see *Beeline*, No 21, December 1980, p 5. However the problem is still under review, both generally and within the mail order area: see the Annual Report of the Director General of Fair Trading 1983, pp 14–15.

2. An earlier reference to the Consumer Protection Advisory Committee had led to the Mail Order Transactions (Information) Order 1976, SI 1976/1812, requiring that mail order companies include their name and address in advertisements. See 'Prepayment for Goods, A Report on Practices Relating to Prepayment in Mail Order Transactions and in Shops', (HC 285 Session 1975/76) and the Supporting Dossier (17/2) prepared by the Director General of Fair Trading. For more general

discussion of Part II of the Fair Trading Act 1973 under which the order was made see below, p 415 et seq.

SOME APPROACHES TO THE PROBLEM

Several approaches to the problems associated with consumer prepayments have been suggested in recent years. A recent survey is to be found in an Office of Fair Trading discussion paper, 'The Protection of Consumer Prepayments' (October 1984). The building trade is an area in which it is likely that the problems will be especially serious because of both the large sums of money which may be involved and the relatively high risk of business failure. In the period January to September 1982 the construction industry accounted for some 18.4 per cent of bankruptcies analysed on an industrial basis (by far the largest single category) and between 10.6 and 11.7 per cent of company liquidations: see *British Business* 28 January 1983, p 170, Tables 2 and 3. These figures must themselves be seen against a background of rising insolvencies which can only exacerbate the problems of lost prepayments.

The Office of Fair Trading discussed the problems of prepayments within the construction industry in its 'Home Improvements' Discussion Paper (March 1982) and in a resultant Report (June 1983).

Home improvements: A discussion paper (Office of Fair Trading, 1982)

Payment in Advance

3.21   A requirement for a pre- or staged payment, ie paying for goods and services in advance or making interim payments to a contractor as the job advances, is a common feature in the home improvement sector and the building trade. This is often because a substantial proportion of the cost of the job relates to materials which the supplier has to purchase in advance, and many tradesmen are reluctant or unable to wait until all of the work is completed before obtaining some payment. Builders merchants usually give a month's credit. If a contractor asks for payment in advance it may indicate that he is not considered credit-worthy by local merchants. If householders have been asked to pay in full or to pay a substantial deposit, they may in fact have paid out a considerable sum of money before they know whether they will be satisfied with the job when it is completed. Advance payment may also affect the chances of the consumer obtaining effective redress if he has a dispute with the supplier.

3.22   Moreover, payment in advance for work to be undertaken can be followed by the disappearance of the supplier before the work is started or completed or the trader may become insolvent and go into liquidation before the work is completed. Householders should recognise the possible risks of making payments in advance, before satisfactory completion of the work, which may not be related to any actual costs incurred. They should always approach requests for payment in advance with healthy scepticism and, before agreeing to payment, should satisfy themselves, first that the trader concerned has an established business, secondly, that the advance payment is reasonably related to the costs which the trader may be expected to have incurred, and thirdly, that there is every likelihood of the contract being completed.

3.23   It has also to be said that there are major shortcomings in the protection available to consumers in the event of the insolvency of the supplier. Some progress has, however, been made on the basis of voluntary action by certain trade interests. A useful measure of protection for householders who pay deposits for double glazing work is provided by the Deposit Indemnity Fund operated by the Glass and Glazing Federation.

. . .

3.24   Valuable, however, as schemes such as that operated by the Glass and Glazing Federation may be, the experience of recent years suggests that the protection available to householders in the event of the insolvency of the supplier requires strengthening. . . .

As the above paper notes, codes of practice certainly have a part to play in protecting prepayments, whether through a bonding scheme or simply through seeking to ensure reasonable delivery dates. Codes of practice are considered in more detail in Ch 9 below. The following examples are of interest.

Code of ethical practice of the Glass and Glaziers' Federation 1981

5 Security and Deposits
5.1 It is a requirement of members of this Federation that all those who take deposits from private individuals in relation to glazing work on any private domestic premises shall be covered by the Deposit Indemnity Fund which is known as the GGF Fund Limited and shall take such action as the Rules of the GGF and the Rules of the Fund require.
5.2 If for any reason a member of the GGF is unable to carry out work for which a deposit has been taken, or shows to the Federation that it does not have the financial resouces to conclude the work or even to refund the deposit, or any part thereof, then the GGF Fund Limited will ensure that the work is carried out at a fair market price for that work less the value of the lost deposit, or at the discretion of the GGF Fund Limited it will repay the deposit.
5.3 This Fund covers contracts of the type described above up to a total value of £6000, where a deposit has been placed with a member company and it covers deposits of up to 25% on supply and fix contracts, or up to 50% on supply only contracts.
5.4 The Fund is financed entirely by members of the Glass and Glazing Federation and is operated for them by the GGF Fund Limited.

Code of practice for the selling and servicing of electrical and electronic appliances

4.1 Any retailer who accepts an advance payment or deposit for goods shall indicate the period during which delivery of the goods will be made to the customer. If delivery is not made to the customer within this period then the retailer shall offer the customer the option of a refund.

. . .

Voluntary code of practice for furniture

3.1 Retailers will ensure that their sales staff quote realistic delivery dates in line with the retailer's assessment of current information supplied by the manufacturer.
3.2 When deposits are taken, the delivery dates should be quoted in writing except when delivery should take place within one month.
3.3 Retailers should periodically check with manufacturers on the delivery position and must advise customers immediately it becomes apparent that the quoted delivery date is not likely to be met.
3.4 When an order has been accepted for delivery by a specific date, any deposit will be refunded on request, if a revised delivery date is unacceptable to the customer.

. . .

The preliminary conclusions of the Office of Fair Trading as expressed in its resultant Home Improvements report (1983) para 5.10 were that: 'the most extreme remedy of a ban on pre-payments is not an acceptable or desirable solution: more feasible would be a requirement that pre-payments should be placed in a separate trust account and used only when the trader has fulfilled the terms of the contract.' The same approach is to be seen in the Customers' Prepayments (Protection) Bill which was introduced by Mr Robin Squire MP under the Ten Minute rule. Although the Bill did not make any further progress it succeeded in attracting some publicity for the problems which it sought to tackle. Having noted that an exercise carried out by the National Federation of Consumer Groups based on mail order complaints had shown that 'of 2,641 such complaints between July 1977 and March 1982, 26 per cent involved the liquidation of a company or the cessation of trading', he continued 22 HC Official Report (6th series) Cols 847–849, 28 April 1982):

My Bill will require that every advance payment, prepayment or deposit, however described, paid by a consumer to a company will be placed in a separate account to be known as a "customers' prepayment account". At all times that sum will be held in trust on behalf of the consumer and would not be available as capital, for loan, guarantee or other business purposes for the supplying company. Title in that money should remain in the customer's hands at all times. After, not before, the performance of the contract—the delivery of goods or the supply of services—the firm, individual or company concerned may then withdraw from the customer's account the amount paid by the consumer for that purpose.

In the event of any insolvency or bankruptcy, the sums held by the company shall not only remain the property of the consumer but shall be repaid to him or her one month after the declaration of liquidation or bankruptcy. Any failure to observe that would, as in the case of failure under any other aspect of company law, lead to fine or a prison sentence or both and the disqualification of the directors for the appropriate period.

No new principle is involved here. For many years solicitors have been required to maintain separate client accounts. More recently, the same requirement has been imposed upon estate agents under the Estate Agents Act 1979. Many other trading undertakings today voluntarily follow similar procedures. The BBC holds money from the sale of its microcomputers in a separate trust account—I do not suggest, incidentally that the BBC is in any danger of insolvency or liquidation . . . On 28 March my hon Friend the Minister for Consumer Affairs addressed the national consumer congress in Guildford. He said:

> 'As far as insolvency is concerned, I want to put it on record that I strongly condemn the use of liquidation as a commercial device for the exploitation of consumers, including consumers who have paid in advance for goods or services from traders who then go out of business.'

Many business men insist on a ROMALPA clause in their contracts which has the effect of reserving title to them in goods sold and delivered unless and until payment is received, thus protecting them should the buyer become insolvent. I submit that what is legitimate business practice in selling to consumers should equally apply to consumers attempting to purchase.

The Cork Committee has reported to the Minister on many aspects of liquidation and bankruptcy. I am sure that the House awaits with great interest, and perhaps with trepidation, the publication of its findings. It is certain that they will be involved and that legislation will consequently be delayed.

The problem that I have described is with us now and can be dealt with separately and urgently outside any post-Cork legislation. No other solution could give the consumer the chance to compete effectively with preferred creditors in a liquidation. Every reputable business man should welcome a system that promises honest and fair dealing to the public. Therefore, I seek the leave of the House to bring in the Bill.

NOTE

This idea is developed in a National Federation of Consumer Groups paper, "Prepayments: Protecting Consumers' Deposits" (1984).

Question

Is it practicable to require that 'every advance payment' be placed in a separate trust fund? If not, which, if any, of the following might be subjected to such a requirement—(i) the payment of a train fare for travel the following day; (ii) an annual subscription to the Automobile

Association or a London Club; (iii) the payment of an annual premium to an insurance company, or (iv) an advance payment to a vehicle repairer undertaking work on a car?

Another approach to the problem is indicated in the following passages from the Home Improvements Discussion Paper.

Home improvements: A discussion paper (Office of Fair Trading, 1982)

5.5   The ease with which the directors of a company which has failed can set up a new company and often do so, trading in the same line of business is worrying. In extreme cases, traders can be prosecuted for fraud or theft[1] but there are many cases in which hard evidence of offences is difficult to find, but consumers suffer persistently whether as a result of fraudulence or incompetence on the part of a trader. Although the Insolvency Act 1976 (recently amended by the Companies Act 1981) provides for the disqualification of directors of failed companies in certain circumstances, this has proved in practice to be a rarely used power . . .
5.6   Against this background the Office suggested in evidence in 1979 to the Committee appointed by the Department of Trade to investigate changes necessary in insolvency law, chaired by Sir Kenneth Cork, that consumers' claims should be given preferential status or at least equal status with preferential claims. It is understood that the Cork Committee is to report shortly, and the Office hope that the Committee will, in their report, support this change in the law. Such a change would provide substantial benefit to householders with claims against traders in the home improvement sector.

The Cork Committee reported as follows:

Review Committee on insolvency law and practice, Cmnd 8558 (1982)

Payments in advance for goods and services
1048.   We have received many complaints that members of the public who pay in advance for goods or services have no remedy except as unsecured creditors in the event of the insolvency of the trader. They do no see themselves treated as ordinary providers of unsecured credit, though this is how they find themselves, except in those cases where special schemes have been established for their protection. Payments of this kind are made, for example, to mail order houses, to travel and entertainment promoters and, frequently, to building and repair contractors for house repairs and improvements.
1049.   Programmes on television and radio, and articles in the press and other media have expressed concern that the present law is thought to be unjust to members of the public paying in advance for goods and services. The Committee has heard evidence to the effect that a considerable number of companies, dealing direct with the public, which become insolvent, have accepted or required payment prior to the delivery of the goods or services. In many cases they have started business with a totally inadequate capital, often a minimal £2. We have been urged to recommend that legislation should require all such money to be paid into special accounts having trust status, from which it could not be withdrawn by the trader for use as part of his general funds.
1050.   We understand the sense of grievance felt by those who have lost money in such circumstances, but we are satisfied that the proposal is impracticable. In many cases, advance payments are an essential part of the trader's working capital. For example, a mail order company often has to purchase and pay for the goods which have been ordered by the customer, or for materials from which to manufacture them, before delivery; a tour operator often needs to use the deposits received from his clients in paying a deposit to the foreign hotel. In any case it would not be within our terms of reference to make a recommendation of this nature, unrelated to insolvency or possible insolvency.
1051.   The trader's right to mix the money with his own and use it as part of his general funds

---

[1] See *R* v *Hall* [1973] QB 126, [1972] 2 All ER 1009, CA, below, p 343.

is fatal to the existence of a trust. Some of those who have given evidence to us, recognising that it is not practical to require a separate account to be maintained, have urged that nevertheless payments in advance for goods or services should be repaid in full in the event of the trader's insolvency. In effect, this is to call for the creation of a new class of preferential claim.

1052. In our view, this attitude is misguided. The customer who pays in advance for goods or services to be supplied later extends credit just as surely as the trader who supplies in advance goods or services to be paid for later. There is no essential difference. Each gives credit; and if the credit is misplaced, each should bear the loss rateably.

1053. One of our members on the other hand is of the opinion that a purchaser of future goods should not be expected to provide the working capital and he would therefore recommend that:

(a) any company dealing direct with the public and accepting payment in advance for goods or services must have sufficient working capital; and

(b) payments made in advance should become trust money, and placed in a trust account until the goods paid for are delivered;

but the rest of us do not agree.

1054. Of course, any trader is free, by taking the appropriate steps, to create a trust which will prevail in the event of his insolvency. In *Re Kayford Ltd* [1975] 1 WLR 279, the Court had to deal with a company whose chief suppliers got into financial difficulties and could not meet the company's orders; from that stage on, the company opened a special account for the receipt of moneys from customers for goods not yet delivered to them and from which withdrawals would only be made if the goods were later delivered; this account was held to have been validly constituted as a 'trust account'.

1055. We welcome the sympathetic attitude to this problem shown by Mr Justice Megarry, as he then was, in his judgment in that case where he said: . . .

> 'No doubt the general rule is that if you send money to a company for goods which are not delivered, you are merely a creditor of the company unless a trust has been created. The sender may create a trust by using appropriate words when he sends the money (though I wonder how many do this, even if they are equity lawyers), or the company may do it by taking suitable steps on or before receiving the money. If either is done, the obligations in respect of the money are transformed from contract to property, from debt to trust. . . .
>
> In cases concerning the public, it seems to me that where money in advance is being paid to a company in return for the future supply of goods or services, it is an entirely proper and honourable thing for a company to do what this company did, upon skilled advice, namely, to start to pay the money into a trust account as soon as there begin to be doubts as to the company's ability to fulfil its obligations to deliver the goods or provide the services. I wish that, sitting in this court, I had heard of this occurring more frequently; and I can only hope that I shall hear more of it in the future.'

1056. If our proposals for wrongful trading are implemented, they will give further encouragement to the practice described in *Re Kayford*. . . .

Question

Do you agree with the Cork Committee (para 1052) that there is 'no essential difference' between the customer who makes prepayments for goods or services and the trader who supplies goods or services on credit? Ought consumers to see themselves as 'ordinary providers of unsecured credit'?

NOTES

As may be seen from the above extracts the Cork Committee did not favour either the preferential status or the compulsory trust account approach. Rather it sought to improve the position of unsecured creditors generally, for example by reducing or eliminating various types of preferential debts (see Ch 32 of the Report). The details of the proposals for subjecting directors to civil liability for 'wrongful trading' are to be found in Ch 44 of the Report. In essence there would be wrongful trading where liabilities, including the receipt of prepayments, were incurred 'with no reasonable prospect of meeting them' (para 1783) and where a director ought to have known that this was so—an objective test, unlike the subjective test for fraudulent trading of the Companies Act 1948, s 332. The proposals were backed up by recommendations (see Ch 45 of the Report) for the easier disqualification of 'delinquent directors' and for subjecting directors of small under-capitalised private companies to a period of personal liability in the event of their involvement in a second company which in turn becomes insolvent. Generally the Committee was concerned to end the mischief reflected in what it termed the 'widespread dissatisfaction at the ease with which a person trading through the medium of one or more companies with limited liability can allow such a company to become insolvent, form a new company, and then carry on trading much as before leaving behind him a trail of unpaid creditors, and often repeating the process several times' (para 1813)—a phenomenon sometimes known as the 'Phoenix Syndrome'.

The government's reponse to the Cork Committee proposals was published in a paper 'The Revised Framework for Insolvency Law', Cmnd 9175, 1984 and it was not entirely encouraging. The Office of Fair Trading commented as follows in the discussion paper, 'The Protection of Consumer Prepayments' (October 1984):

Insolvency law reform
6.32   The Cork Committee on Insolvency Law and Practice reported to the Government in 1982. The report (Cmnd 8558) recommended, amongst other things, changes in the status of types of creditor and in the way the directors of companies which went into liquidation should be treated. The Office had urged the Committee to recommend that preferential status should be granted to consumers and while the Committee's proposals were by no means as radical as this, it regarded them as helpful and, considered that they would have made a significant contribution towards the protection of prepayment consumers. In February of this year, the Government published 'A Revised Framework for Insolvency Law (Cmnd 9175) in which it indicated that it was not prepared to implement many of the Cork Committee's proposals. (Minor modifications to its plans were published in August.) The Office was very disappointed by this response.
6.33   The Cork Committee recommended that the preferential status of the State in matters such as taxes and rates should be abolished. It also recommended a change in the law on floating charges and suggested a fund for ordinary unsecured creditors, which would be calculated as a fixed proportion (10 per cent) of the net realisation of assets subject to a floating charge. The Cork Committee thus recognised the need to provide greater protection for unsecured creditors (of which consumers represent a significant proportion). The Government was not, however, prepared to accept these proposals. In consequence, consumers will continue to be at an unfair disadvantage vis-à-vis other creditors.
6.34   The Government also decided to accept only in part the Cork Committee's proposals concerning the tightening of the disqualification provisions for delinquent directors and the institution of a new concept of wrongful trading triggering a measure of personal liability. The Government's proposals in this field will to some extent provide extra protection for consumers, but the Office questions whether they go far enough. The Committee recognised the degree of public concern about the adequacy of the law to deal with malpractice by directors of companies, and put forward some radical changes. The Office welcomed their acknowledgement of the need for action and endorsed their conclusions . . . It welcomed in particular the proposed new provision relating to 'wrongful trading', and agreed generally with the Committee's proposal for tightening up the rules on the disqualification of directors.
6.35   The Office is disappointed that the Government's proposals for personal liability are

considerably more limited than those proposed by Cork. In particular, it regrets the dropping of the proposal that personal liability should be more or less automatic if anyone becomes a director of a second company within two years of the previous one being liquidated. The Cork Committee clearly saw this provision as a most important deterrent to reckless and irresponsible trading. They recognised that many directors were innocently caught up in company failure, but they did not consider it an undue burden for a director to have to convince the court of his innocence. . . .

6.36 The Office has pressed the Government to think again about the Cork proposals which it has so far rejected. In particular, it hopes it will reconsider its position on the provision relating to second insolvencies, which appear a much more effective deterrent than those parts of the Cork package which have been accepted. Without this, and especially now that a minimum petition debt of £750 is necessary, the Office is concerned that there will continue to be insufficient protection for consumers against the consequences of reckless and irresponsible trading.

The following case is of interest as illustrating the possible application of the law of theft where consumer deposits or prepayments are involved.

R v Hall [1973] QB 126, [1972] 2 All ER 1009, Court of Appeal, Criminal Division

The facts appear in the judgment of the Court.

Edmund Davies LJ read the judgment of the court. Geoffrey Hall appeals, by leave of the single judge, from his conviction at the Manchester Crown Court in September 1971 on seven counts of theft, in respect of which he received concurrent sentences totalling two years.

During 1968 the appellant and two others started trading in Manchester as travel agents under the title of 'People to People'. The other partners received no remuneration, played purely insignificant parts, and were called as Crown witnesses. Each of the seven counts related to money received by the appellant as deposits and payments for air trips to America. In some instances a lump sum was paid by schoolmasters in respect of charter flights for their pupils; in other instances individuals made payments in respect of their own projected flights. In none of the seven cases covered by the indictment did the flights materialise, in none of them was there any refund of the moneys paid, and in each case the appellant admitted that he was unable to make any repayment. In some cases he disputed all liability on the grounds that the other parties had unjustifiably cancelled the proposed trips, in others he denied dishonesty. He claimed to have paid into the firm's general trading account all the sums received by him, asserted that those moneys had become his own property and had been applied by him in the conduct of the firm's business and submitted that he could not be convicted of theft simply because the firm had not prospered and that in consequence not a penny remained in the bank.

Two points were presented and persuasively developed by the appellant's counsel: (1) that, while the appellant has testified that all moneys received had been used for business purposes, even had he been completely profligate in its expenditure he could not in any of the seven cases be convicted of 'theft' as defined by the Theft Act 1968; there being no allegation in any of the cases of his having *obtained* any payments by deception, counsel for the appellant submitted that, having received from a client, say, £500 in respect of a projected flight, as far as the criminal law is concerned he would be quite free to go off immediately and expend the entire sum at the races and forget all about his client; (2) that s 1 (1) of the Theft Act 1968 dealing with a person who '*dishonestly* appropriates', it is essential that the Crown establish that the appellant was acting dishonestly *at the time he appropriated*. . . .

[His Lordship considered point (2), concluding that the summing-up had dealt adequately with this aspect of the offence and continued:]

Point (1) turns on the application of s 5 (3) of the Theft Act 1968, which provides:

> 'Where a person receives property from or on account of another, and is under an obligation to the other to retain nd deal with that property or its proceeds in a particular way, the property or proceeds shall be regarded (as against him) as belonging to the other.'

Counsel for the appellant submitted that in the circumstances arising in these seven cases there arose no such 'obligation' on the appellant. He referred us to a passage in the Eighth Report of the Criminal Law Revision Committee[1] which reads as follows:

'*Subsection* (*3*) [of cl 5 "Belonging to Another"] provides for the special case where property is transferred to a person to retain and deal with for a particular purpose and he misapplies it or its proceeds. An example would be the treasurer of a holiday fund. The person in question is in law the owner of the property; but the subsection treats the property, as against him, as belonging to the persons to whom he owes the duty to retain and deal with the property as agreed. He will therefore be guilty of stealing from them if he misapplies the property or its proceeds.'

Counsel for the appellant submitted that . . . the position of a treasurer of a solitary fund is quite different from that of a person like the appellant, who was in general (and genuine) business as a travel agent, and to whom people pay money in order to achieve a certain object—in the present cases, to obtain charter flights to America. It is true, he concedes, that thereby the travel agent undertakes a contractual obligation in relation to arranging flights and at the proper time paying the airline and any other expenses. Indeed, the appellant throughout acknowledged that this was so, although contending that in some of the seven cases it was the other party who was in breach. But what counsel for the appellant resists is that in such circumstances the travel agent 'is under an obligation' to the client 'to retain and deal with . . . in a particular way' sums paid to him in such circumstances.

What cannot of itself be decisive of the matter is the fact that the appellant paid the money into the firm's general trading account. As Widgery J said in *R v Yule*[2], decided under s 20 (1) (iv) of the Larceny Act 1916:

'The fact that a particular sum is paid into a particular banking account . . . does not affect the right of persons interested in that sum or any duty of the solicitor either towards his client or towards third parties with regard to disposal of that sum.'

Nevertheless, when a client goes to a firm carrying on the business of travel agents and pays them money, he expects that in return he will, in due course, receive the tickets and other documents necessary for him to accomplish the trip for which he is paying, and the firm are 'under an obligation' to perform their part to fulfil his expectation and are liable to pay him damages if they do not. But, in our judgment, what was not here established was that these clients expected them 'to retain and deal with that property or its proceeds in a particular way', and that an 'obligation' to do so was undertaken by the appellant. We must make clear, however, that each case turns on its own facts. Cases could, we suppose, conceivably arise where by some special arrangement (preferably evidenced by documents), the client could impose on the travel agent an 'obligation' falling within s 5 (3). But no such special arrangement was made in any of the seven cases here being considered. . . .

It follows from this that, despite what on any view must be condemned as scandalous conduct by the appellant, in our judgment on this ground alone this appeal must be allowed and the convictions quashed. . . .

Appeal allowed. Conviction quashed.

1. Theft and Related Offences, Cmnd 2977 (1966), p 127.
2. [1963] 2 All ER 780 at 784, [1964] 1 QB 5 at 10.

NOTE

For discussion of the Theft Act 1968, s 5 (3) see J. C. Smith, The Law of Theft, (5th edn, 1984) para 68 et seq, Smith and Hogan *Criminal Law* (5th edn, 1983) p 482 et seq. On appropriate facts a trader may of course be guilty of dishonestly obtaining property (which term includes money) by deception, contrary to s 15 of the Theft Act 1968.

Questions

1. Trader enters a contract with Householder whereby he agrees to supply and fit double-glazing in Householder's London flat. He asks for and receives £1,000 in cash, saying, 'I need it to buy materials for the job'. Trader pays the money into his business account at the Dogger Bank. The following week he withdraws £1,000 in cash from this account, spending £500 in buying materials for another customer, Ivan, and the remaining £500 at the races. Trader then becomes insolvent. Discuss Trader's criminal liability under the Theft Act, s 5 (3). Would it affect the position if the money had been spent directly without it passing through his bank account?

2. In May 1982 Oenophile receives a catalogue from Bin End Vintners advertising 1981 claret at 'opening prices'. In June 1982 he orders ten cases of 'Chateau La Mission Haut Brion' at £195 per case. The wine is to be bottled in early 1983 and delivered in early 1984 when shipping, duty and VAT charges will be invoiced separately. In July 1982 Oenophile's cheque for £1,950 is cashed by Bin End and in December 1982 Oenophile is informed that Bin End is in liquidation. Advise Oenophile

3. Carpetbaggers Ltd places a notice in the window of its shop reading, 'Thousands of Rolls of Top Quality Carpet. Only £10 per square metre. Order Now'. On 1 June Partridge orders 50 square metres of carpet from the shop, paying £500 in advance. On 3 June the carpet is cut according to Partridge's measurements and placed in a corner of Carpetbaggers warehouse for delivery at the end of the month. The following day Carpetbaggers goes into liquidation.

Advise Partridge who is claiming to be entitled to the carpet as against the liquidator. [See generally the Sale of Goods Act 1979, ss 17 and 18; Atiyah *Sale of Goods* (6th edn, 1980), Ch 17.]

BONDING ARRANGEMENTS

In a number of areas there are bonding arrangements which operate to the benefit of consumers. The example of the code of practice of the Glass and Glaziers' Federation has already been noted above, p 338. A further example is provided by the Newspaper Publishers Association Mail Order Protection Scheme (MOPS).

Mail Order Protection Scheme

MOPS dates from April 1975 and covers the national newspapers and their supplements. (Similar schemes are operated by the Newspaper Society— covering the regional and local press—and by the Periodical Publishers Association). The scheme is funded by annual fees paid by mail order advertisers and advertising agencies. From time to time newspapers print a Readers' Notice drawing attention to the scheme's existence. The scope of the bonding scheme is as indicated in the following extract:

Mail Order Protection Scheme (1984 edition)

II THE SCOPE OF THE SCHEME

The Central Fund of the Scheme protects a reader if—
(i) the ADVERTISEMENT—
    (a) is inserted in a national newspaper.
    (b) describes a product, giving details of price and the address from which it may be obtained;

(c) directly asks readers to order the product by post by sending a remittance with the order.

(ii) the ADVERTISER has been recommended for acceptance. (Should an advertisement be inserted without the Committee's recommendation of acceptance then any readers' losses are the sole responsibility of the newspaper concerned).

Many advertisements are protected by the Central Fund, but the present time the following are NOT.

(a) the sale of foodstuff of any description.

(b) the sale of contraceptives and kindred products (these may be advertised under classified advertisements eg 'Personal');

(c) any product which appeals to fear or superstition, eg lucky charms, horoscopes, etc;

(d) those asking readers to send for catalogues, brochures or details of products, which are supplied free or for a price of £1 or less. Subsequent sales from catalogues, brochures etc, inserted with goods ordered in response to Mail Order advertising are also not protected by the Central Fund;

(e) those inviting readers to visit retail premises;

(f) those offering a 'service' such as membership of clubs, magazine subscriptions, theatre tickets, film processing etc. However, in the case of film processing advertisers, if a replacement film is offered which can be purchased in addition to the film processing charge then readers are protected for the replacement film cost but not the processing;

(g) those inviting readers to purchase products costing 25 pence or less;

(h) those offering goods on a self-liquidating or other premium basis, eg where readers have to send remittances for products together with coupons from products obtained through retail outlets;

(i) those that appear under the newspapers' own Classification headings or in Classified columns, such as 'PERSONAL', 'MOTORING', 'HOUSE and GARDEN', etc;

(j) those appearing under a 'GARDENING' Classification heading offering trees, shrubs, plants and other growing things, chemicals and fertilisers. The Central Fund however, protects readers if the products are 'hardware' products such as greenhouses, gardening implements etc;

(k) those offering goods on approval or for 'Cash on Delivery' or where a reader is required to send a small remittance to cover carriage costs only.

In the following advertisements there is only limited protection—

(i) claims where payment is made by Access or Visa card and where the cost of the goods is over £100. In these cases claims should be made to the credit card company concerned. Where the cost of the goods is under £100 claims should be made as shown in section VI, 'COMPLAINTS AND CLAIMS'.

(ii) those offering a series of items to be despatched in sequence at stated intervals and readers are asked initially to pay for the first item of the series and then pay on invoices sent before, or with, the despatch of the remaining items.

III LOGO/SYMBOL

THE NATIONAL NEWSPAPER

MAIL ORDER PROTECTION SCHEME

An advertiser who is an approved member of the Scheme is permitted by the Management Committee to embody the above logo/symbol in all his 'cash-off-the-page' advertisements. This logo may not be employed in Classified advertisements nor in those advertisements which do not seek 'cash-off-the-page', eg those advertisements which merely invite readers to send for brochures, catalogues and similar literature. An advertiser may not employ this logo/symbol in his advertising literature, nor on his headed notepaper. In small advertisements an alternative logo/symbol embodying the initials MOPS is permitted.

IV THE ADVERTISEMENT AND THE PRODUCT AND ITS DESCRIPTION

All mail order advertisements must comply with the British Code of Advertising Practice, especially Appendix F, and anyone interested may obtain a copy from Advertising Standards Authority, Brook House, 2/16 Torrington Street, London, WC1. (telephone 01–580 5555) Advertisements must also comply with recommendations made by the Management Committee or any national newspaper. Newspapers try to ensure that no offensive statements or visual presentations are made and that descriptions, claims and comparisons can be substantiated, and that advertisements do not abuse the reader's trust or exploit his lack of knowledge or experience.

Before advertising the advertiser must hold and wholly own in the United Kingdom adequate stocks to meet reasonable responses from readers. Forward trading, ie receiving readers' money and then purchasing goods to fulfil orders is not tolerated and if discovered means the immediate suspension of that trader's advertising.

The advertisement must fulfil all orders, either immediately upon receipt of orders or within a time clearly stated in the advertisement. All orders, with certain exceptions, MUST be fulfilled within 28 days. This 28-day period need not apply where the manufacture of goods will not begin unless sufficient orders are received and the advertisement must clearly state the advertiser's intention. Readers are therefore advised to carefully read all advertisements before ordering.

The Management Committee also tries to ensure that products are value for money and where appropriate conform to British Standards and consumer protection regulations. The Secretariat also frequently visits advertisers to ensure that the standards laid down by the Committee are being maintained.

The value of a product is of course dependent upon a person's point of view and as such can differ with each individual. However, the consumer is protected for should he be dissatisfied with it in any way he simply returns it to the advertiser AT ONCE. The advertiser is then bound to either replace the product or refund the cost, together with the return postage.

V SAFEGUARDING THE READER'S MONEY

When products are of high value or large advertising programmes are intended, advertisers may be asked to furnish indemnities. The Management Committee solely decides the type of indemnity required and advertising is not accepted until the indemnity has been provided.

The most important type of indemnity as far as the consumer is concerned is the use of a Stakeholder or Readers' Account. By this method an independent organisation is appointed as a stakeholder who, in law, becomes the agent of the readers until such time the stakeholder receives from the advertiser good evidence that the goods have been despatched. The readers' money is thus held on their behalf and if, for any reason, the advertiser fails to send the goods the readers' money remains outside the control of the advertiser. The stakeholder then has a duty to refund it to the readers in a reasonable time.

In some cases an advertisement, though showing the advertiser and his address for personal callers only, requests the reader to make his remittance payable to and send it and the order to another address. In other instances an advertisement will ask the reader to make his remittance payable to the name of the advertiser preceded by the words 'Reader's Account'. The reader must make his remittance payable to this particular account as that account is under the control of the stakeholder. Readers are advised therefore to carefully read advertisements and make their remittances payable as specifically requested. Failure to do so may mean that their money is placed in jeopardy as a result and may leave readers unprotected.

VI COMPLAINTS AND CLAIMS

Mail Order companies, in the main, offer a very reliable service, most of them are well established businesses with many years of experience in serving the readers. However, in the unhappy event of failure of a Mail Order advertiser, readers who have lost money as a result are reimbursed from the Central Fund.

In the event of a reader having cause to complain about a Mail Order advertiser, who has failed to supply goods ordered or to refund money if goods have been returned or indeed to replace goods if that be the case, then that reader is advised to write to the Advertisement Manager of the publication in which the advertisement was inserted. Readers are therefore recommended to always retain an advertisement for future reference. The names and addresses of the newspapers in the Scheme are given below.

Any complaint should give the fullest details as appropriate, such as dates of advertisement, ordering and cheque clearance, method of payment; and correspondence with the advertiser; and should be accompanied by copies of any documents supporting the claim.

In the event of an advertiser becoming the subject of liquidation or bankruptcy, or ceasing to trade, then readers' money is protected by the Scheme. (It must be stressed that this protection only applies in these three instances).

Should this unfortunate situation arise then the Central Fund will reimburse readers, through the particular newspaper in which the advertisement was seen, subject to the following conditions;—

(a) The advertiser becomes the subject of liquidation or bankruptcy proceedings, or ceases to trade and had been one accepted under the Scheme.

(b) The advertisement to which the readers responded appeared in a publication in membership of the Scheme.

(c) The reader's claim is received by the particular publication within THREE MONTHS of the appearance of the advertisement.

(d) The reader completes a claim form and assigns the debt to the newspaper concerned.

(e) The reader forwards with his claim the ORIGINAL cancelled cheque or postal order counterfoil. Photocopies of the documents are NOT acceptable. However a letter of confirmation from a reader's bankers is sufficient. In the case of payments made through Access or Visa card where the amount involved is more than £100 claims should be sent to the credit card company concerned. Where payment by this method for goods costing less than £100 occurs, claims to newspapers must be accompanied by the credit card company's statement.

(f) Any complaint should be made NOT EARLIER than 28 days from the date of the order and NOT LATER than THREE MONTHS from the date of the advertisement to the Advertisement Manager of the newspaper concerned.

NOTES

1. In recent years the total amount of claims paid out by MOPS was as follows:

To 31 March 1979	£ 75,153
To 31 March 1980	£ 7,332
To 31 March 1981	£ 81,521
To 31 March 1982	£ 91,025
To 31 March 1983	£106,613
To 31 March 1984	£105,961

2. Since the operation of the scheme is both voluntary and time-consuming it would be churlish to complain that it is limited in scope. It does not cover 'classified' as opposed to 'display' advertisements, nor orders placed through a catalogue or leaflet which the reader has been invited to 'write off for'. Still less does it cover sales made as a result of direct mailing—based, for example, on an electoral list—or inserts in magazines. Moreover the distinction between classified and display advertisements is by no means clear-cut and may depend on no more than the layout of the newspaper. Additional protection falling short of a bonding scheme is provided by the code of practice of the Mail Order Traders' Association (catalogue mail order), the code of practice of the Mail Order Publishers' Authority (books and record clubs), the code of practice of the British Direct Marketing Association (direct marketing) and the British Code of Advertising Practice (see below, p 398 et seq). The general operation of the various schemes has been reviewed in an Office of Fair Trading discussion paper, 'The Protection of Consumer Prepayments' (October 1984).

HOLIDAY TRAVEL

There is no doubt that when compared with many sectors prepayments for holiday air travel have a wide measure of protection. However the amounts of money involved are very considerable and certain problems have arisen. The general nature of the protection afforded is indicated in the following extracts from a recent Adjournment debate in the Air Travel Reserve Fund Agency (53 HC Official Report (6th series) col 1188 et seq, 10 February 1984).

Mr Dick Douglas (Dunfermline, West): I raise the subject of the future of the Air Travel Reserve Fund Agency. It will not go amiss if, in my introductory remarks, I say a little about the agency's formation. . . . The agency was founded by Act of Parliament in the wake of the collapse of the Court Line and the attendant tour operators, Clarksons and Halcyon Holidays, among others.

The fund's concept was to make payments to or for the customers of air travel organisers in respect of losses or liabilities incurred by them. In support of that concept is the licence administered by the Civil Aviation Authority, given to air travel organisers after having been assessed as being financially able to meet their commitments. Part of the licence assessment relates to the ability to meet a bond laid down by the CAA. There is also another bond for members of the Association of British Travel Agents, which costs about one third less than the average 10 per cent bond administered by the CAA.

Parliament initially voted the fund a £15 million loan. In addition, there was a 2 per cent levy on licence holders. The loan has been repaid, and currently, the fund has a balance of £16·6 million. The agency's first reserve is the bond and its second is the fund.

If we did not have Adjournment debates it is highly unlikely that the Air Travel Reserve Fund Agency's report would be discussed in the House. The fund's latest report and the chairman's remarks give rise to the debate. Sir Kenneth Selby says in that report that he is surprised at

'the risk that so many . . . holidaymakers take in paying for their holidays so far in advance . . . thereby leaving vast sums of money at the disposal of the air travel organisers without security of any form.'

That is fairly stringent stricture on the organisers.

. . .

Within recent memory we have seen the failure of organisations associated with the Laker enterprise. The failure of Laker and Arrowsmith resulted in 52,000 claims on the bonds. The number of claims on the fund amounted to more than the bonds. According to the report, if one includes administration, the calls on the fund were likely to exceed £6 million. At that time the amount of bond money available was £5·2 million.

I have had discussions with representatives of ABTA. It claimed that the reason why its bonds were less than those of the CAA was that collectively the agents can provide services that are of considerable benefit. I do not dispute that. When a company crashes, ABTA members give assistance. The argument was that, in the case of Laker the value of the rescue operation was about £75,000. The Air Travel Reserve Fund Agency felt that the bond would have been £2·5 million larger if the CAA rate had been used rather than the ABTA rate. The fund had to bear more than would have been the case if the CAA rate had prevailed rather than the ABTA rate.

Some £2·5 million was given by customers to Laker. It was used by that enterprise, through the network of its organisation, to finance operations such as Skytrain rather than for holiday purposes.

That leads me to the area of agreement between ABTA and the Air Travel Reserve Fund Agency. I hope that the Minister will tell me the Government's thinking on the matter. There should be complete segregation between the financial affairs of any licensed organiser and any other group of companies. The practice that I referred to earlier involving holiday companies such as Court Line, and the practices of the Laker holiday organisation, going back to Skytrain should be prohibited. I want an assurance that money given for holiday purposes, because of the interlocking nature of the concerns, will not go to finance engineering or other enterprises. In my opinion, that money should be devoted exclusively to holiday purposes.

. . .

If we are to assess the adequacy of the bond and the fund, it is the responsibility of the tour operators—and of the CAA for that matter—to organise the insurance cover centrally, and to make sure that the companies have insurance to cover all expectation of losses that might be incurred by their customers. We cannot leave it to the individuals who are going on holiday. This is not on all fours with the business man who is travelling, perhaps on his own account or perhaps on his company's account, to the United States or elsewhere. We are talking about people who have saved up for some time. For them it is a large expenditure, and if they give their money to companies, they expect to be almost completely sure that the companies will deliver.

I expect that the CAA and other organisations will say that if we impose additional charges, we shall force marginal companies out of the business or inhibit new companies. However, companies operate on small margins, sometimes much less than 2 per cent, so both companies and holidaymakers are at risk. Unfortunately, the holidaymaker does not always understand the risk.

The report also mentions the use of credit cards when paying for holidays, and at page 8 it states:

> 'There is some inconsistency between the Consumer Credit Act, 1974 which controls the use of credit cards and the Air Travel Reserve Fund Act, 1975 under which the Agency was established. The Agency has no power under the 1975 Act to reimburse a customer of a failed air travel organiser unless the customer has suffered a loss. If a credit card has been used to pay for a holiday and at the time of the failure the customer has not paid the credit card company, he has suffered no loss. In such cases, the Agency is precluded by statute from making any payment from the Fund.'

That is a serious matter that requires clarification by the Government. If the agency is statutorily banned from making payments, holidaymakers might believe wrongly that they could recover their losses.

I have tried to be moderate and careful in my remarks, because I do not wish to be a scaremonger, telling all holidaymakers that they face an enormous risk. However, there is a risk, and it is the Government's responsibility to respond to the views expressed by the chairman and, through him, the agency about how it approaches consumer protection. I know that many leaflets are issued by ABTA and the CAA in an attempt to educate the public about such matters, but we must know what the Government believe so that the cycle does not begin again.

I have mentioned the segregation of funds, the adequacy of the bond and the need to emphasise to companies that they must have full insurance cover. I could also have mentioned the adequate monitoring of the cost of administration, but I hope that the Minister will respond positively to what I have said.

The Under-Secretary of State for Transport (Mr David Mitchell): . . . Since 1975, when the fund was set up, holidaymakers buying packages have had the reassurance that, harrowing though the failure might be, ultimately their money will be safe. Thanks to the system of bonds required by the CAA as a condition for gaining an air travel organiser's licence, coupled with the fund, package holidaymakers have been certain of recompense no matter how big a failure.

Since its inception, the fund has paid out over £10 million to holidaymakers. I pay tribute to the chairman of the Air Travel Reserve Fund Agency, Sir Kenneth Selby, and to the agency's members past and present—including the Hon Member—for the work that they have done in bringing financial peace of mind to so many holidaymakers.

However, the agency's recent annual report has perhaps cast something of a cloud over the travel trade. I am concerned that in some quarters there may be a fear that holidaymakers are once again threatened with financial loss because of the collapse of an air tour operator. Those fears were clearly in the mind of the Hon Member in this Adjournment debate. I hope now to set those fears at rest.

As its name implies, the fund is a reserve mechanism against the financial failure of a tour operator. The very first line of defence for the holidaymaker is the Civil Aviation Authority's licensing system. Any applicant for an ATOL who is financially unsound or simply unfit to hold a licence will be refused one by the authority. Those who aspire to a licence are expected by the CAA to have sufficient financial resources to withstand one year's adverse trading conditions. Should a company's finances cease to be sufficient, its licence will be revoked.

No system can be 100 per cent watertight—at least not without also threatening to strangle to death the industry it regulates—so there is a second line of defence. These are the bonds which must be posted by holders. Only when an holder fails and the bond proves insufficient does the fund come into play as the final line of defence for the holidaymaker's money.

. . .

In its annual report, the agency suggests that—partly because of the effects of the Laker failure—the fund may no longer be large enough to withstand another major failure, particularly if one were to occur at the wrong time of the year, when customer pre-payments are at their maximum. The chairman has therefore made a number of recommendations in his report designed to protect the fund. It must be a matter of judgment whether the fund is potentially inadequate in terms of the task it faces. I respect the views of the agency's chairman in this matter, but I see no immediate cause for alarm.

The fund stood at over £16 million at the end of the last financial year. This is over twice as big as the largest sum it has ever had to pay out as a result of a failure. Indeed, since the fund was set up there has only been one major failure. The impact of all others since 1975 on the fund has been relatively slight.

. . .

It may be difficult for the authority to insist on the complete segregation of an air travel organiser's finances from the finances of others in the same group of companies, as requested by the hon Member. Segregation could have serious effects on the borrowing capacity of the company concerned, and might even threaten the existence of the sort of integrated airline and tour operator companies which are such a successful feature of the British holiday industry.

However, as I have said, Sir Kenneth's recommendations merit the very closest attention, as does his suggestion that the insurance market might take up some of the strain. As my right hon Friend indicated on Monday, insurance may have its attractions. We are, therefore, setting in hand a special review which will consider the level of the fund, its future, whether changes should be made to the present system of licences and bonds, and whether insurance has a part to play. The present arrangements form an integrated system, and it would not be sensible to review the fund without also asking how it is affected by the licensing requirements and by bonding levels. I hope that the hon Gentleman will feel that the specific points he put to me will be well catered for in this significant review.

. . .

We would also like the review to consider whether—if the fund is to continue—it should apply to scheduled air services. That is something which from time to time has been pressed upon us by hon Members, although I have to say that it is not an idea to which we instinctively warm, given that the private sector seems already capable of affording protection to such travellers. Indeed, the Department of Trade announced in December 1982 that, having looked at the matter, it had concluded that there was no justification for introducing mandatory levies or insurance schemes to protect the scheduled airline passenger. Nevertheless, there is no logical reason why those who buy air package holidays should be in a more privileged position than others who travel in other ways by air.

. . .

The Air Travel Reserve Fund was born out of the Court Line collapse because of the financial suffering it threatened to cause holidaymakers. I am sure that the hon Member and I are at one in agreeing that, whatever the future may hold for the fund, we do not want to see holidaymakers left with no means by which they can be protected.

The hon Member mentioned credit cards. That is a complex matter. Both Access and Barclaycard have said that they will reimburse people who lost through Laker. We are giving that question very careful study and I shall write to the hon Member.

NOTE

The 'special review' has now reported and concluded that the existing arrangements should be strengthened although no fundamental changes were necessary: see 'Review of Arrangements for Protecting the Clients of Air Travel Organisers' (Sir Peter Lane, 1984).

CHAPTER 8

The enforcement of private law remedies: II Collective redress

Introduction

This chapter is concerned with some issues of collective as opposed to individual redress. It falls into two main parts: first, the role of representative and class actions and second the position of consumer organisations and public agencies.

Representative and class actions

INTRODUCTION

There will be many cases in which consumers suffer what may be termed a 'common wrong'. Such cases fall into two broad categories. First there are those in which injury, damage or inconvenience is caused in a single incident, for example an aeroplane or coach crash, a mass poisoning or a disastrous package holiday. Second there are cases in which consumers have a common or broadly similar complaint, perhaps because they have been injured individually by a drug (for example, Thalidomide, Eraldin or Opren) or bought a product with a common design defect (for example, the Lancia Beta car with its tendency to rust) or relied on the self-same advertisement. For consumers generally there are advantages in a system which permits the amalgamation or joint treatment of such claims. It is likely that an individual's bargaining strength will be increased through not standing alone and society as a whole has an interest in avoiding a proliferation of actions based on substantially similar facts. Moroever, as Richard Tur has noted when discussing the attractions of a class action procedure (see 'Litigation and the Consumer Interest: the Class Action and Beyond' (1982) 2 Legal Studies 135,153):

> [It] meets one of the most obvious restraints upon litigation by pooling the interests and possibly the resources of many plaintiffs, each of whom may have suffered modest loss. If A defrauds B of £5,000,000 the law provides a remedy; if A has the wit to defraud one million individuals of £5 each, absent any class action procedure, he runs little risk of civil action on the motion of any one of them: 'By the simple device of committing numerous small wrongs, law breakers might escape the arm of justice as long as they stay clear of criminal sanctions and the reach of repressive administrative action' [citing Homburger (1971) 71 Columbia LR 609, 641].

The literature in this area is now voluminous and it includes the following: Jolowicz, 'Protection of Diffuse, Fragmented and Collective Interests in Civil Litigation: English Law' (1983) 42 CLJ 222; 'General Ideas and the Reform of Civil Procedure (1983) 3 Legal Studies 295; Arthur Miller, 'Of

Frankenstein Monsters and Shining Knights: Myth, Reality and the "Class Action Problem"' (1979) 92 Harvard LR 664; Hinds, 'To Right Mass Wrongs: A Federal Consumer Class Action Act' (1976) 13 Harv J Leg 776; 'Developments in the Law—Class Actions' 89 Harv LR 1318 (1976); 'Access to the Courts—II Class Actions' (Australian Law Reform Commission, Discussion Paper No 11, 1979); the Law Reform Committee of South Australia, Thirty-sixth Report Relating to Class Actions (1977); Debelle, 'Class Actions for Australia? Do They Already Exist' (1980) 54 ALJ 508; 'Report on Class Actions' (Ontario Law Reform Commission, 1982); Williams, 'Consumer Class Actions in Canada—Some Proposals for Reform' (1975) 13 Osgoode Hall Law Journal 1; 'Class Actions in the Scottish Courts' (Scottish Consumer Council, 1982). For a European perspective see Fisch, 'European Analogues to the Class Action: Group Actions in France and Germany' (1979) 27 AJCL 51.

JOINDER AND CONSOLIDATION

In English law there has long been provision for the joinder of parties and the consolidation of actions involving common questions of law or fact (see respectively RSC, Ord 15, r 4 and Ord 4, r 10). The essential difference between joinder and consolidation is that in the former case the parties bring their action by means of the same writ.

Joinder may be appropriate if P1, P2 and P3 have all been injured in the same accident and the only live issue is whether the defendant (D) was negligent. However if P1 sues D separately and succeeds in his action the traditional view is that it remains open to D to deny negligence (or, as the case may be, that his product is defective or unmerchantable etc) in any subsequent action brought by P2. As between D and P1 the matter is res judicata but as between D and P2 (with whom P1 is not 'privy') issue estoppel will not prevent D from disputing even central findings of fact in the earlier action (see generally *Cross on Evidence* (5th edn, 1979) p 333 et seq). Admittedly Lord Denning MR has disputed the traditional view and espoused a doctrine which is sometimes termed non-mutual collateral estoppel. Under this doctrine P2 could invoke a judgment which was adverse to D but could not have a favourable judgment invoked against him. Lord Denning put it as follows in *McIlkenny v Chief Constable of the West Midlands Police Force* [1980] 2 All ER 227 at 237–8, CA (the notorious Birmingham 'pub bombers' case):

> Likewise it seems to me that a previous decision in a civil case—*against* a man—operates on an estoppel preventing him from challenging it in subsequent proceedings unless he can show that it was obtained by fraud or collusion; or he can adduce fresh evidence (which he could not have obtained by reasonable diligence before) to show conclusively that the previous decision was wrong . . .
> To illustrate my view of the present law, I would take this example. Suppose there is a road accident in which a lorry driver runs down a group of people on the pavement waiting for a bus. One of the injured persons sues the lorry driver for negligence and succeeds. Suppose now that another of the injured persons sues the lorry driver for damages also. Has he to prove the negligence all over again? Can the lorry driver (*against* whom the previous decision went) dispute his liability to the other injured person? It seems to me that if the lorry driver (with the backing of his employer) has had a full and fair opportunity of contesting the issue of negligence in the first action, he should be estopped from disputing in the second action. He was a party to the first action and should be bound by the result of it. Not only the lorry driver, but also his

employer should be estopped from disputing the issue of negligence in a second action, on the ground that the employer was in privity with the lorry driver.

Although this approach has the advantage of reducing the possibility of different verdicts on identical facts there is little support for it in English law.

TEST CASES

It is unlikely that joinder and consolidation will be a practical proposition where a multiplicity of potential plaintiffs is involved. In any event the approach may not help where individual claims are too small to warrant litigation. As an alternative it may be agreed to single out a particular action and treat it as a test case. In practice this may prove to be perfectly adequate as a means of vindicating multiple claims, especially where public authorities are involved. This seems to have been true of *Congreve* v *Home Office* ([1976] QB 629, [1976] 1 All ER 697, CA) where some 17,000 colour television licence holders were involved, Mr Congreve being 'their leader'. Yet in other cases the procedure may be less than completely satisfactory. As the Ontario Law Reform Commission noted in its Report on Class Actions (1982), Vol 1 p 87–88:

> First the test case procedure is not adequate where the claims are individually nonrecoverable. Since, by definition, claimants will not assert these claims, they cannot benefit from the bringing of a test case. Secondly, in the case of claims that are individually recoverable, the test case procedure suffers from a number of major drawbacks. For example, it may be very difficult to obtain the consent of all those who have commenced their own action that one of the many actions should be tried as a test case. The plaintiffs would have to come to an agreement regarding the particular action that should go forward. The choice of counsel to prosecute the test case may also give rise to disagreement among the plaintiffs. A more important drawback is the fact that the defendant may not agree to be bound by the result of the test case. In such a case, if the result of the test case is unfavourable to him, the defendant nevertheless may require the plaintiffs to proceed with their action individually, perhaps at great expense. Moreover, the trial of these claims will have been substantially delayed by the resolution of the test case, during which time the other actions will have been effectively frozen.

THE ELEMENTS OF REPRESENTATIVE OR CLASS ACTIONS

It is against this background that attention has come increasingly to be focused on the representative or class action as a means of redressing 'mass wrongs'. Although the class action procedure is associated primarily with the United States of America, it has been discussed also in other jurisdictions, notably Australia, Canada and Scotland. The Australian Law Reform Commission has described the procedure as follows in its Discussion Paper No 11 (1979) p 4:

> A class action is a legal procedure which enables the claims of a number of persons against the same defendant to be determined in the one action. In a class action one or more persons ('the plaintiff') may sue on his own behalf and on behalf of a large number of other persons ('the class') who have the same interest in the subject matter of the action as the plaintiff. The class members are not usually named as individual parties but are merely described. Although they usually do not take any active part in the litigation, they may nevertheless be bound by the result. It is, thus, a device for multi-party litigation where the interests of a number of parties can be combined in

one suit. The procedure also enables one plaintiff to bring an action against a number of defendants.

In English law the procedural rule which approximates most closely to the class action is RSC Ord 15, r 12, which provides in part:

(1) Where numerous persons have the same interests in any proceedings, not being such proceedings as are mentioned in Rule 13, the proceedings may be begun, and, unless the Court otherwise orders, continued, by or against any one or more of them as representing all or as representing all except one or more of them.

. . .

(3) A judgment or order given in proceedings under this Rule shall be binding on all the persons as representing whom the plaintiffs sue or, as the case may be, the defendants are sued, but shall not be enforced against any person not a party to the proceedings except with the leave of the Court.

(4) An application for the grant of leave under paragraph (3) must be made by summons which must be served personally on the person against whom it is sought to enforce the judgment or order.

(5) Notwithstanding that a judgment or order to which any such application relates is binding on the person against whom the application is made, that person may dispute liability to have the judgment or order enforced against him on the ground that by reason of facts and matters particular to his case he is entitled to be exempted from such liability.

. . .

The principal obstacle to extensive use of the representative action is the decision of the Court of Appeal in *Markt & Co Ltd* v *Knight SS Co Ltd* [1910] 2 KB 1021. This and some other leading English cases are discussed in the following extract from the Australian Law Reform Commission Discussion Paper (No 11) on Class Actions (at pp 7–8):

9. The rules regulating representative actions in Australian courts are modelled on a similar English rule.[1] Australian courts have therefore followed decisions of English courts on the interpretation of the rule. Representative actions have most often been used to enable actions for equitable relief by way of a declaration or an injunction.

> *Covent Garden Market Stallholders*: Covent Garden Market belonged to the Duke of Bedford but an Act of Parliament fixed the rent to be paid by stallholders at the Market. One group of stallholders belonged to a class of growers of fruit and vegetables. In 1900, six of these grower/stallholders sued the Duke in a representative action of behalf of themselves and all other members of the class of growers of fruit and vegetables who held stalls in the Market claiming a declaration that the Duke had been charging more than the statutory rent. The Duke took a procedural objection that the case was not suitable for a representative action. The growers, he argued, could not be identified as they numbered many thousands all over the country. The objection was overruled in the House of Lords.[2]

Lord Macnaghten stated a test to assist courts in deciding whether or not a common interest existed sufficient to permit representative actions to proceed:

> 'In considering whether a representative action is maintained, you have to consider what is common to the class, not what differentiates the cases of individual members . . . Given a common interest and a common grievance, a representative suit was in order if the relief sought was in its nature beneficial to all whom the plaintiff proposed to represent.'[3]

The interest which was common to the class was the interpretation of the statute fixing the rent.

> *Champagne producers*: Twelve producers of wine made in the Champagne district of France wished to prevent the sale in England and Wales of wine grown in Spain and sold as 'Spanish Champagne'. In 1959 they brought a representative action against the defendant importer 'on behalf of themselves and all other persons who produce wine in the Champagne district and supply such wine to England and Wales'. There were at least 126 other wine producers. They succeeding in obtaining a declaration that the

name 'Champagne' could only be used to describe wine made in the Champagne district and an injunction restraining the defendant importer from selling 'Spanish Champagne'.[4]

10. Damages not Permitted: The rule on representative action says nothing about claims for damages. Despite the fact that there is nothing in the rule specifically to prevent recovery of damages, Australian courts, again applying English precedent, have refused to allow damages to be recovered in a representative action. The rule appears to have been established in 1910 by a decision of the Court of Appeal in England.

> *Cargo shippers:* During the Russo-Japanese war 45 traders shipped cargo from New York to Japan on board the *Knight Commander*, a ship owned by the defendant company. A Russian cruiser captured and sank the ship because its cargo contained contraband. Two traders on behalf of themselves and the other 43 traders brought a representative action claiming damages against the shipping company for loss of their goods. They relied on the *Duke of Bedford's Case* and claimed that a common interest existed among the class of traders because there was an implied condition in each contract of shipment that the *Knight Commander* would not carry contraband. Two of the three judges held that there was no interest which was common to the class as each claim stemmed from separate contracts of shipment. The action could not, therefore, proceed as a representative action for damages. One of the judges also held that damages could not be claimed in a representative action because damages have to be proved separately in the case of each plaintiff.[5]

The decision in *Markt & Co Ltd v Knight SS Co Ltd* was not unanimous. The effect of the majority decision severely restricted the use which could be made of representative actions. Although it was the opinion of only one member of the court that damages could not be recovered in a representative action,[6] that opinion has tended to become received doctrine in England and in Australia. For example, in *The Supreme Court Practice*, a leading English manual on practice in courts, it is stated:[7]

> 'No representative action will lie to establish the right to numerous persons to recover damages, each in his own several right, where the relief claimed is to recover such damages.'

Representative actions are not the only procedure provided by court rules to enable a number of parties to combine their claims in one legal proceeding but it is the only kind of multi-party litigation in which damages cannot be claimed.[8]

1. Rules of the Supreme Court, 1965, Order 15, Rule 12.
2. *Duke of Bedford v Ellis* [1901] AC 1.
3. At 8 and 9.
4. *J. Bollinger v Costa Brava Wine Co Ltd* [1960] Ch 262, [1961] 1 WLR 277.
5. *Markt & Co Ltd v Knight SS Co Ltd* [1910] 2 KB 1021.
6. At 1040.
7. (1973 ed) Part I, 198.
8. See paras 87 and 88 below.

On the question of awarding damages it has often been noted that Fletcher-Moulton LJ was the only member of the Court of Appeal in the *Markt* case to state unequivocally that, 'no representative action can lie where the sole relief sought is damages'. In so far as this came to be regarded as a blanket rule (and it appears to be so stated in the *Supreme Court Practice* (1985) para 15/12/3) the position may have eased marginally, at least where the claim is in tort rather than contract. The following case illustrates a modest development.

EMI Records Ltd v Riley [1981] 2 All ER 838, [1981] 1 WLR 923, Chancery Division

The facts are set out in the judgment.

Dillon J. This is a motion for judgment on admissions. The action is brought by EMI Records Ltd, suing on behalf of themselves and on behalf of and as representing all other members of the British Phonographic Industry Ltd ('BPI'), against a Mrs Riley, as first defendant. There were a number of other defendants originally named in the proceedings, and the proceedings remain on foot against one of them, Mr Patrick Buckley, but no claim against him is before me today. . . .

The action concerns the sale of pirate cassettes. The statement of claim sets out in para 1 certain definitions. The definition of 'pirate record' is a 'record made directly or indirectly from a sound recording without the licence of the United Kingdom copyright owner or exclusive licensee, being a member of the class', and the 'class' is 'all members of the BPI', which is a company limited by guarantee. The statement of claim then sets out in paras 2 and 3 that the 'Plaintiff is a legitimate record company and a member of the BPI and sues on behalf of and representing and for the benefit of the Class', and that 'Nearly all records in this country are produced, made or distributed by members of the Class', and in her defence Mrs Riley agrees both those paragraphs. Paragraph 4 of the statement of claim sets out that the 'members of the Class are continually and frequently producing making or distributing records embodying new sound records. The member of the Class responsible for each sound recording owns the copyright therein or is the exclusive licensee thereunder'; Mrs Riley in her defence expressly does not deny the existence of copyright.

Paragraph 8 of the statement of claim (I shall have to come back to para 7 in a moment) asserts:

'The Defendants and each of them had been concerned in a business in this country of making pirate records and/or authorising them to be made, and/or selling and/or distributing for trade purposes records which to their knowledge were pirate. Said business occurred on a massive scale and over a considerable period . . .'

and that particulars are served separately with the statement of claim.

As to that Mrs Riley denies ever making a pirate record in her life, but she says that she did order them to be made and she did authorise her daughter to sell them for her. She denies that the business occurred on a massive scale over a considerable period, but she does say that the business was conducted for some 25 weeks on 25 Saturdays in Portobello Market, 12 days in Carnaby Street, and 32 days in Oxford Street, and she says that the total number of the tapes sold was approximately 2,980, and that the probable quantity affecting members of the class was 2,900 tapes, on the assumption that her sales affected members of the class. She claims that her sales were too small to affect the large record companies, but I take this to mean that she is accepting that 2,900 out of the 2,980 tapes she admits selling were pirated versions of recordings made by members of the class.

Paragraph 7 of the statement of claim asserts that the members of the class have consented to all pecuniary remedies granted in respect of actions for, inter alia, infringement of copyright in sound recordings and selling counterfeit records and all sums paid in settlement of such actions, being actions conducted by the solicitors to the BPI, being paid to the BPI in order to defray the expenses of detecting and suppressing the pirate and counterfeit record and like trades, and it asserts further that the action is being conducted by the solicitors to the BPI. Mrs Riley in her defence says that she has no comment on that, by which I take her to mean that she does not dispute it. She has also said that she does not want this action complicated and extended by massive inquiries.

It seems to me that on the admissions of Mrs Riley's defence and in the reply to the statement of claim, which is to the same effect and on the further admissions in a sworn statement by Mrs Riley which is dated 17th November 1978, which she has put before me, the plaintiffs are entitled to an injunction against Mrs Riley. They are entitled to relief in respect of goods seized under an Anton Piller order, and they are entitled to the costs of the action, but the entitlement is not entirely in the form of the draft minutes of order, because the draft minutes of order set forth a form of injunction which would restrain Mrs Riley, for instance, from making or assisting in the making of pirate records, and she has expressly denied that she has ever made such a record or assisted in the making of such a record. I think the plaintiffs are entitled to an injunction restraining her from ordering or selling or exposing for sale or inviting offers to acquire or parting with any pirate record, that is to say, any record made directly or indirectly from a sound recording without the licence of the United Kingdom copyright owner or exclusive licensee being a member of the class.

I think the plaintiffs are also entitled to an order that their solicitors may deliver to the plaintiffs or to their order all pirate records, including the packaging thereof, which are currently in the custody of the solicitors as a result of the Anton Piller order which was executed at the inception of the proceedings, but there should be an order that the solicitors release to the defendants all genuine cassettes which are in their possession as a result of the Anton Piller order.

The minutes of order then ask for an inquiry as to what damages the members of the class have sustained by reason of the defendant's infringements of copyright and conversion of infringing copies, the costs of the inquiry to be reserved, and that the plaintiffs do recover judgment for such sums as are found due together with interest thereon without prejudice to the plaintiffs' obligations to hold or apply the sums in such manner if any as may be required of them at law or in equity.

Counsel for the plaintiffs has taken me to the judgment of Vinelott J in *Prudential Assurance Co Ltd v Newman Industries Ltd* [1979] 3 All ER 507, [1980] 2 WLR 339, where the judge expressed the view that it was not appropriate to award damages to a plaintiff in a representative capacity. A plaintiff in a representative capacity might be entitled to relief by way of declaration or injunction, but not to relief by way of damages. Counsel for the plaintiffs has submitted that that case is distinguishable on its facts from the present case, and he has referred me to orders made by Foster and Whitford JJ who on motions for judgments in default of defence directed inquiries as to damages suffered by the plaintiffs or any other member of the BPI.

I think the fundamental factor is the special position in this particular trade of the BPI. This is not a case of a small number of manufacturers getting together as a self-constituted association where there would be a serious likelihood that other pirate cassettes which Mrs Riley may have sold would have nothing to do with the members of the association, because she herself has admitted that nearly all records in this country, and 'record' includes discs or tapes or similar contrivances for reproducing sound, are produced, made or distributed by the members of the BPI. The matter of substance that underlies this is that if the plaintiffs can only recover damages in respect of tapes in which they individually own the copyright they will have considerable difficulty in establishing which pirate EMI tapes were sold by Mrs Riley among the 2,980 tapes which she admits having sold or among whatever higher number it is found she had sold, but given the admission that nearly all records including tapes are produced, made or distributed by members of the BPI, on an inquiry as to damages suffered by all members of the BPI the task will be much simpler since it will be clear and seems to be admitted that nearly all the tapes which Mrs Riley has sold were tapes the copyright in which belongs to members of the BPI.

In the circumstances of the BPI and the pleaded allegations, including para 7 of the statement of claim, and I have already referred to the defence to these, it seems to me that it is appropriate that damages should be recoverable by the plaintiffs in the representative capacity in which they are entitled to sue for an injunction, and it would be a wholly unnecessary complication of our procedure if the court were to insist that for the purposes of the inquiry as to damages all members of the BPI must be joined as co-plaintiffs, or alternatively, all members except for EMI Records Ltd must issue separate writs and apply for them to be consolidated with the claim for damages of EMI Records Ltd.

Therefore, in my judgment, it is appropriate that the inquiry as to damages should be in the form set out in the draft minutes of order, but it must be clear that there is to be no duplication of damage in as far as there are claims outstanding against other defendants. That is a matter which counsel for the plaintiffs mentioned at an early stage in his submissions, but did not in fact elaborate as the arguments proceeded.

Finally, the plaintiffs must be entitled as against Mrs Riley to their costs of the action to date, including the costs of obtaining and executing the Anton Piller order, such costs to be taxed if not agreed, but the costs of the inquiry and all future further costs after today's date are reserved.

Order that if the plaintiffs elected to proceed on the inquiry ordered they would not be entitled to seek any further inquiry as to damages as against any other defendant in the action.

The judgment of Vinelott J in *Prudential Assurance Co Ltd v Newman Industries Ltd* [1979] 3 All ER 507, [1980] 2 WLR 339 to which Dillon J referred (see above) represented a considerable advance on the view of Fletcher Moulton LJ in the *Markt* case in as much as it countenanced a split procedure. The plaintiff company was a minority shareholder in Newman Industries and it alleged misconduct on the part of Newman's directors. The relevant class comprised the shareholders of that Company other than two named directors. His Lordship allowed an amendment of the writ and statement of claim so that the plaintiffs could seek a declaration that those shareholders who had suffered damage were entitled to damages for conspiracy. Thereafter, as his Lordship noted (at 521), 'A person coming within that class will be entitled to rely on the declaration as res judicata, but will still have to establish damage in a separate action.' His Lordship expressed his general conclusions as to the scope of the representative action in the following terms (at p 520).

> In summary, in my judgment, it is clear on authority and principle that a representative action can be brought by a plaintiff, suing on behalf of himself and all other members of a class, each member of which, including the plaintiff, is alleged to have a separate cause of action in tort, provided that three conditions are satisfied. The first I have already stated. No order can properly be made in such a representative action if the effect might in any circumstances be to confer a right of action on a member of the class represented who would not otherwise have been able to assert such a right in separate proceedings, or to bar a defence which might otherwise have been available to the defendant in such a separate action. Normally, therefore, if not invariably the only relief that will be capable of being obtained by the plaintiff in his representative capacity will be declaratory relief, though, of course, he may join with it a personal claim for damages. It is not clear how far the grant of injunctive relief is consistent with this principle in that for any member of the class represented to establish a right to injunctive relief in separate proceedings he would have to show a present apprehension of injury and might be faced with a defence of laches or acquiescence. . . .
>
> The second condition is that there must be an 'interest' shared by all members of the class. In relation to a representative action in which it is claimed that every member of the class has a separate cause of action in tort, this condition requires, as I see it, that there must be a common ingredient in the cause of action of each member of the class. In the present case that requirement is clearly satisfied. . . .
>
> The third and related condition is that the court must be satisfied that it is for the benefit of the class that the plaintiff be permitted to sue in a representative capacity. The court must, therefore, be satisfied that the issues common to every member of the class will be decided after full discovery and in the light of all the evidence capable of being adduced in favour of the claim. For unless this condition is satisfied it would be wrong (as Fletcher Moulton LJ remarked in *Markt*) to permit the representative plaintiff 'to conduct litigation on behalf of another without his leave and yet so as to bind him'.

A CANADIAN EXAMPLE

A not dissimilar approach was adopted in an interesting Canadian case the facts of which fall more obviously into a consumer law context.

Naken v General Motors of Canada Ltd (1977) 92 DLR (3d) 100, Ontario Court of Appeal

The judgment of the Court was delivered by

Arnup J A:—The single issue in this appeal is whether the action is properly constituted as a class action. Osler J, held that it was. Hughes, J, granted leave to appeal under Rule 499 (3) (b), stating that it appeared to him, in the words of the Rule, that there was good reason to doubt the correctness of the decision of Osler J, and the appeal involved matters of such importance that leave should be given.

On October 13, 1977, the Divisional Court allowed the appeal of the defendant, General Motors of Canada Limited, and struck out the statement of claim as disclosing no proper cause of action. (The action is no longer being pursued against the defendant Vauxhall Motors Limited.)

The style of cause describes the four plaintiffs as suing 'on behalf of themselves and suing on behalf of all other persons who have purchased new 1971 and 1972 Firenza motor vehicles'. Paragraph 1 of the statement of claim narrows the class by adding the qualification 'and who at the date of the writ had not sold or otherwise disposed of the vehicle'. (The writ was issued on July 13, 1973.)

The statement of claim reads, in part:

'4. The Defendants were at all material times manufacturers, assemblers and marketers of motor vehicles.

5. From in or about September 1970, until the date of the Writ in this action, the Defendants manufactured, assembled and marketed 1971 and 1972 Firenza motor vehicles in Ontario.

6. Each Plaintiff and each member of the class purchased new 1971 and 1972 Firenza motor vehicles in Ontario, manufactured, assembled and marketed by the Defendants.

7. Prior to or at the time each Plaintiff and each member of the class purchased a Firenza motor vehicle the Defendants warranted to all prospective purchasers that all Firenza motor vehicles manufactured, assembled or marketed by the Defendants, were or would be of merchantable quality, reasonably fit for use as a motor vehicle and were or would be "durable", "tough" and "reliable".

8. The warranty given to each Plaintiff and to each member of the class was breached in that an unusually large number of 1971 and 1972 Firenza motor vehicles were not of merchantable quality, were not reasonably fit for use as a motor vehicle, and were not "durable", "tough" and "reliable".

9. Because of this breach of warranty, the value of each and every 1971 and 1972 Firenza motor vehicle has depreciated in the re-sale market.

10. As a consequence, the re-sale value of each Firenza motor vehicle is approximately £1,000 less than the re-sale value of a motor vehicle of comparable age, size and purchase price on the market.

The plaintiffs, therefore claim:—

(a) The sum of £1,000 for each Plaintiff and each member of the class;'

Particulars dated March 15, 1974, read, in part (the demand for particulars is not before us):

'The Plaintiffs submit the following Reply to the Defendant's General Motors of Canada Limited Demand for Particulars:

1.(a) 4,602 persons purchased new 1971 and new 1972 Firenza motor vehicles respectively in Ontario.

(b) As of this date, the exact number who had otherwise sold or disposed of their vehicle at the date of the Writ is not known, however, upon Judgment being obtained each of the members of the class will be notified and will be entitled to recovery if they can demonstrate that they had not sold or otherwise disposed of their Firenza motor vehicles at the date of the Writ.

2. The vehicles were purchased from third parties. The purchasers took delivery at different times, and in particular they took delivery of new 1971 Firenza motor vehicles from the date that they were first marketed and delivered and new 1972 Firenza vehicles from the date when they were first marketed and delivered.

3. With respect to warranties: (1) merchantable quality, implied warranty; (2) reasonably fit for use as a motor vehicle, implied warranty; (3) "durable", "tough" and "reliable"; written warranty published in newspaper ads on various dates and advertising materials distributed by the Defendant General Motors of Canada Limited.'

Paragraph 4 of these particulars then alleged 15 defects in 'the motor vehicle'.

Particulars dated March 12, 1975, read:

'The Plaintiffs submit the following reply to the Defendant's, General Motors of Canada Limited, Demand for Particulars:

The warranties referred to in paragraphs 7 and 8 of the Statement of Claim are contained in contracts made with the Defendants. The parties to the contract are General Motors of Canada Limited and each member of the class being persons who have purchased new 1971 and 1972 Firenza motor vehicles in Ontario. The date of the said contracts are the date of the purchase of the vehicles. The contracts were partly oral and partly written. The warranties referred to were expressly made in printed materials distributed by the Defendant, General Motors of Canada Limited, and contained in newspaper advertisements placed by the said Defendant in Ontario.'

I should observe that in the course of the argument before this Court, Mr Balaban (who led for the appellant plaintiffs) made a significant concession. He expressly abandoned any allegation of implied warranty, and stated that the plaintiffs would rely solely upon the warranties expressly made in printed material distributed by the defendant and in its printed advertisements. The effect of the concession was to eliminate from the case the alleged implied warranties that the cars were of merchantable quality and reasonably fit for use as motor vehicles.

The Divisional Court discussed or referred to the various English and Canadian cases which have been cited and analyzed by counsel in each of the four Courts that have considered this case. The essential elements of the decision of the Divisional Court appear to have been these:

(1) It would not have been practical for the plaintiffs to establish that each of the 4,600-odd members of the class purchased his Firenza in reliance upon the advertised representation.

(2) There is no allegation of a common fund in which each member of the class has an interest pro rata.

(3) The action was not for damages to the class, as an entity distinct from its members, but rather was in reality the accumulation or lumping together of individual claims for losses personal to each purchaser.

Before considering these grounds, there are three comments I wish to make by way of background:

(1) These proceedings began as a defendant's motion under Rule 126. It has been recognized throughout this case that a statement of claim will be struck out under that Rule only in very clear cases. If the action could possibly succeed, the statement of claim should not be struck out.

(2) For the purposes of such a motion, the allegations of fact in the pleading must be assumed to be true, or as it is sometimes put, 'must be taken as capable of being proven' (*Shawn v Robertson et al* [1964] 2 OR 696 at 697, 46 DLR (2d) 363 at 364).

(3) In these days of mass merchandising of consumer goods, accompanied as it often is by widespread or national advertising, large numbers of persons are almost inevitably going to find themselves in approximately the same situation if the article in question has a defect that turns up when the article is put to use. In many instances the pecuniary damages suffered by any one purchaser may be small, even if the article is useless. It is not practical for any one purchaser to sue a huge manufacturer for his individual damages, but the sum of the damages suffered by each individual purchaser may be very large indeed.

In such cases it would clearly be both convenient and in the public interest if some mechanism or procedure existed whereby the purchasers could sue as a class, with appropriate safeguards for defendants, who ought not to be subjected to expensive law suits by class action plaintiffs who cannot pay costs if they lose.

These views are not original with me. Much has already been written on these questions. They have engaged increasing attention in the last 20 years in the United States, particularly in California. The subject raises complicated questions of great difficulty in the areas of the delineation of the class, identity of the causes of action of the class members, discovery and production from plaintiffs, proof of the breach of contract or tort that caused loss to the class, assessment of damages and allocation of proceeds.

. . .

At the present time, the Court has no statutory guidelines nor relevant Rules (I capitalize the 'R' deliberately) except Rule 75. The question whether Rule 75, without more, can be used as the basis for consumer class actions in Ontario emerges as the central issue in this litigation. That Rule reads:

> '75. Where there are numerous persons having the same interest, one or more may sue or be sued or may be authorized by the court to defend on behalf of, or for the benefit of, all.'

The English cases, decided on a very similar rule, which have been most frequently referred to in Ontario are *Duke of Bedford v Ellis* [1901] AC 1, and *Markt & Co Ltd v Knight SS Co Ltd* [1910] 2 KB 1021. The former came up to the House of Lords through the Chancery Division. The latter was a common law action. For a long time it was held in Ontario, following the judgment of Fletcher Moulton LJ, in the *Markt* case at 1040 that an action for damages could never be brought as a class action. Jessup JA, made it plain, however, in giving the judgment of this Court in *Farnham v Fingold* [1973] 2 OR 132 at 136, 33 DLR (3d) 156 at 160, that the statement of Fletcher Moulton LJ, so frequently relied upon had not been the judgment of the English Court of Appeal . . .

The statement of claim in this case has deliberately sought to avoid some of the stumbling blocks which have caused some other actions to fail. There is not, and in common sense there could not be, an allegation of a 'common fund', out of which all members of the class will be entitled to be paid some amount if the action succeeds. What is sought to be done by the statement of claim is to remove the objection that each plaintiff in the class really ought to be suing for his own particular damages. Paragraph 7 of the statement of claim, read with the particulars, is a plea that a warranty, contained in printed material distributed by the defendant General Motors of Canada and in newspaper advertisements placed by it in Ontario, was given to *all* prospective purchasers of Firenza motor vehicles. Paragraph 8 refers to the warranty 'given to each Plaintiff and to each member of the class'.

Further, it is alleged that each and every vehicle purchased by a member of the class depreciated in the resale market by 'approximately £1,000'. In the prayer for relief, £1,000 is claimed for each member of the class. Thus, it is argued, no individual assessment of damages is required.

Since it must be assumed, for the purposes of this appeal, that all allegations in the statement of claim are true, the plaintiffs have sought to avoid the difficulty of proving, at this stage, that a warranty was extended to every single purchaser. Clearly that has been alleged, but the concession made in argument that no implied warranties are relied upon, and the theory of the plaintiffs' case as put forward by their counsel demonstrate, on analysis, that the allegation cannot be taken as true.

The plaintiffs' theory is that each purchaser had a contract with General Motors of the type made famous in *Carlill v Carbolic Smoke Ball Co* [1893] 1 QB 256. General Motors (it is said) offered to all readers of its advertisement: 'If you purchase a Firenza from one of our dealers, we warrant that it is durable, tough and reliable.' It follows that only purchasers who saw the General Motors printed material or its published advertisement could have made a contract with General Motors, of which the warranty is a part. The plaintiffs' delineation of the class does not make this distinction or qualification.

Thus, there is not the necessary 'common interest' or identity of situation among the members of the class as presently defined in the pleadings, because the defined class includes purchasers who saw the printed materials or advertisements, and purchasers who did not. It cannot be said that 'if the plaintiffs win, everybody wins'.

. . .

As I stated earlier, the plaintiffs have skilfully attempted in their statement of claim and particulars to avoid the various obstacles that have stood in the way of other plaintiffs in reported cases. In my view they have not succeeded, in the light of their own delineation of the class on whose behalf they sue. I therefore agree with Griffiths J, that this is not a true case of damage to a class, as a class. As now put to us, it is a claim for damages by such purchasers as can show that they saw a General Motors advertisement or its printed material and in reliance upon it, bought a Firenza from a dealer. Only some, and not all, of the members of the class as presently pleaded succeed if these plaintiffs succeed.

. . .

However, our task at this juncture is not to lay down procedures governing the future progress of the action. It is simply to decide whether the action can properly be brought under Rule 75. I have found that the class as presently delineated by the plaintiffs is not a proper class under that Rule and the cases decided upon it. I have also indicated what the deficiency is. If that deficiency were corrected, the plaintiffs, in my view would have pleaded a good cause of action, properly brought as a class action.

In my view the interests of justice require that the plaintiffs should be given leave to amend their description of the class on whose behalf the action is brought, so as to conform with these reasons. It is more than five years since the action was commenced, but it is even longer since the 1971 and 1972 Firenzas were sold, and to dismiss the action (in effect) might well work an injustice to Firenza buyers on whose behalf it is brought.

In this respect my views are very similar to those expressed by Stark J, in *Cobbold v Time Canada Ltd* (1976) 1 CPC 274, a class action brought on behalf of the Ontario residents with unexpired subscriptions to the Canadian edition of Time Magazine. Stark J refused to strike out the statement of claim, holding that the contracts between subscribers and the magazine publishers were identical except as to the length of term of the subscription, that the action was not improper because of the claim for damages, but that the class should be narrowed to exclude those subscribers who had accepted a refund or an alternative subscription term. He concluded (at 278):

> 'I am satisfied that, difficult as it may be to pursue to the end the roads the plaintiff has chosen, that it would be improper at this stage to foreclose his attempt. He has made out a prima facie case which requires an answer; and though changes may be needed in the style of cause and the statement of claim, I am not convinced that I should dismiss the action at this stage.'

I would, accordingly, dismiss the appeal, but reserving to the plaintiffs leave to deliver, within 30 days from the issue of our formal order, an amended statement of claim which would include such part of the particulars as remain relevant after the concession made in argument by counsel for the plaintiffs and thus would narrow the description of the class to include only those purchasers of 1971 and 1972 Firenzas who saw the printed materials or published advertisements of General Motors and, as a result, purchased a new Firenza from a dealer.

. . .

Appeal Dismissed.

Questions

The Winterreise Travel Company publishes a brochure advertising ski holidays in Austria for the winter season 1983–84. In relation to one such holiday the brochure states incorrectly that all rooms in their Klammer Hotel have an en suite bathroom and that entertainment is provided every evening. In fact only half the rooms have such a bathroom and entertainment is provided only at weekends. A, B, C and five hundred other holidaymakers from various parts of the country have seen the brochure and booked a holiday at the Klammer Hotel. All have been accommodated in rooms without an en suite bathroom. Other holidaymakers had rooms with bathrooms but have complained about the lack of entertainment.

So far as A is concerned is there any advantage (whether in terms of costs or otherwise) in seeking to frame an action as a representative action? Is it likely that such a procedure would be adopted (i) in an English court or (ii) in Ontario? If it would, how would the relevant class (or classes) be defined and how should the action proceed? Would there be any additional difficulties in cases where the common complaint is that all have been injured (although with varying degrees of severity) by the same drug?

SOME AMERICAN DEVELOPMENTS

If the procedural developments in English law have been both gradual and relatively uncontroversial the same cannot be said of the United States of America which has seen the development of a veritable class action industry. However there has perhaps been a tendency among English and Commonwealth commentators too readily to assume that the procedure provides an all-purpose remedy which can be called in aid whenever a group of consumers has some common complaint. The reality is markedly different at least where the case falls within the jurisdiction of the federal courts. The position has been summarised by the Ontario Law Reform Commission in its Report on Class Actions (at pp 250–251) as follows (footnotes omitted):

In the United States, consumer class actions do not constitute a significant portion of class action litigation in the federal courts. This is attributable to several factors. First, . . . in order to bring an action within the jurisdiction of the federal courts, a minimum monetary requirement of $10,000 must be satisfied by each claimant. Over the years, this jurisdictional requirement has been subject to several significant exceptions and, more recently, has been removed generally for actions commenced in relation to federal questions, that is, matters arising under an Act of Congress or the Constitution. Nonetheless, the minimum monetary requirement is still applicable in relation to suits in the federal courts based upon diversity of citizenship and, of particular importance in the present context, to actions commenced pursuant to the Consumer Product Safety Act, a statute enacted in 1972 to promote greater product safety and to supplement existing remedies. Moreover, . . . in the case of a class action, individual claims may not be aggregated to meet this jurisdictional minimum monetary requirement. [See *Zahn v International Paper Co* 414 US 291, 94 S Ct 505 (1973), and *Snyder v Harris* 394 US 332, 89 S Ct 1053 (1969).] Obviously, few class actions that aggregate consumer-oriented claims will consist of members, each of whom has a claim in excess of £10,000. Accordingly, access by consumers to the United States federal courts based upon the diversity jurisdiction and the Consumer Product Safety Act remains severely curtailed.

Of course there will be 'diversity of citizenship' cases (for example in disputes between citizens of various states) where the sums involved exceed the stipulated minimum of 28 USC§ 1332. Similarly cases may raise 'federal questions' which provide an alternative basis of jurisdiction. Attention will then have to be focused on the following provisions which determine whether the case may proceed as a class action and, if so, its conduct thereafter:

Federal Rules of Civil Procedure for the United States District Courts Rule 23 (1966)

Class actions

  (a) **Prerequisites to a Class Action.** One or more members of a class may sue or be sued as representative parties on behalf of all only if (1) the class is so numerous that joinder of all members is impracticable, (2) there are questions of law or fact common to the class, (3) the claims or defenses of the representative parties are typical of the claims or defenses of the class, and (4) the representative parties will fairly and adequately protect the interests of the class.

  (b) **Class Actions Maintainable.** An action may be maintained as a class action if the prerequisites of subdivision (a) are satisfied, and in addition:

  (1) The prosecution of separate actions by or against individual members of the class would create a risk of

  (A) inconsistent or varying adjudications with respect to individual members of the class which would establish incompatible standards of conduct for the party opposing the class, or

  (B) adjudications with respect to individual members of the class which would as a practical matter be dispositive of the interests of the other members not parties to the adjudications or substantially impair or impede their ability to protect their interests or;

  (2) the party opposing the class has acted or refused to act on grounds generally applicable to the class, thereby making appropriate final injunctive relief or corresponding declaratory relief with respect to the class as a whole; or

  (3) the court finds that the questions of law or fact common to the members of the class predominate over any questions affecting only individual members, and that a class action is superior to other available methods for the fair and efficient adjudication of the controversy. The matters pertinent to the findings include: (A) the interests of members of the class in individually controlling the prosecution or defense of separate actions; (B) the extent and nature of any litigation concerning the controversy already commenced by or against members of the class; (C) the desirability or undesirability of concentrating the litigation of the claims in the particular forum; (D) the difficulties likely to be encountered in the management of a class action.

  (c) **Determination by Order Whether Class Action to be Maintained; Notice; Judgment; Actions Conducted Partially as Class Actions.**

  (1) As soon as practicable after the commencement of an action brought as a class action, the court shall determine by order whether it is to be so maintained. An order under this subdivision may be conditional, and may be altered or amended before the decision on the merits.

  (2) In any class action maintained under subdivision (b) (3), the court shall direct to the members of the class the best notice practicable under the circumstances, including individual notice to all members who can be identified through reasonable effort. The notice shall advise each member that (A) the court will exclude him from the class if he so requests by a specified date; (B) the judgment, whether favourable or not, will include all members who did not request exclusion; and (C) any member who does not request exclusion may, if he desires, enter an appearance through his counsel.

(3) The judgment in an action maintained as a class action under subdivision (b) (1) or (b) (2), whether or not favourable to the class, shall include and describe those whom the court finds to be members of the class. The judgment in an action maintained as a class action under subdivision (b) (3), whether or not favorable to the class, shall include and specify or describe those to whom the notice provided in subdivision (c)(2) was directed, and who have not requested exclusion, and whom the court finds to be members of the class.

(4) When appropriate (A) an action may be brought or maintained as a class action with respect to particular issues, or (B) a class may be divided into subclasses and each subclass treated as a class, and the provisions of this rule shall then be construed and applied accordingly.

(d) **Orders in Conduct of Actions.** In the conduct of actions to which this rule applies, the court may make appropriate orders: (1) determining the course of proceedings or prescribing measures to prevent undue repetition or complication in the presentation of evidence or argument; (2) requiring, for the protection of the members of the class or otherwise for the fair conduct of the action, that notice be given in such manner as the court may direct to some or all of the members of any step in the action, or of the proposed extent of the judgment, or of the opportunity of members to signify whether they consider the representation fair and adequate, to intervene and present claims or defenses, or otherwise to come into the action; (3) imposing conditions on the representative parties or on intervenors; (4) requiring that the pleadings be amended to eliminate therefrom allegations as to representation of absent persons, and that the action proceed accordingly; (5) dealing with similar procedural matters. The orders may be combined with an order under Rule 16, and may be altered or amended as may be desirable from time to time.

(e) **Dismissal or Compromise.** A class action shall not be dismissed or compromised without the approval of the court, and notice of the proposed dismissal or compromise shall be given to all members of the class in such manner as the court directs.

Virtually every limitation and sub-clause of this detailed provision warrants the most careful scrutiny. The plaintiff must satisfy head (a) and one of the variants of head (b)—normally, in the case of a consumer class action, rule 23(b)(3). Even then, the requirements of notice of rule 23(c)(2) may be applied so stringently as effectively to preclude the class action from proceeding. The decision of the Supreme Court in *Eisen v Carlisle and Jacquelin* 417 US 156 (1974) provides a well-known example, the court holding that individual notice had to be given to over two million readily identifiable class members. The estimated cost was $225,000, as against the plaintiff investors' estimated loss of $70, and, in the words of Lumbard CJ in the court below, this 'put an end to this Frankenstein monster posing as a class action' (391 F 2d 555, 572, US Court of Appeals Second Circuit (1968)). The following case is of general interest as indicating the potential scope and complexity of a major federal class action involving claims for personal injury.

In Re Agent Orange Product Liability Litigation MDL No 381 506 F Supp 762 (EDNY 1980), United States District Court

The defendants were some nineteen or so chemical companies who had manufactured and supplied various herbicides including 'Agent Orange' for use by the military as defoliants in the Vietnam War. The herbicides which allegedly contained dioxin had, it was claimed, been manufactured to mandatory government specifications under the provisions of the Defense Production Act. This gave rise to the possibility of a government contract or 'Nuremberg' defence (see generally Frumer & Friedman *Product Liability* Vol 3A, s 46A 03 [7]). The plaintiffs were Vietnam veterans who claimed to have been exposed to 'Agent Orange' when serving in Vietnam and to have suffered (or to be 'at risk' of suffering) physical injuries as a result. Such exposure was through direct spraying, being transported through sprayed areas, ingesting contaminated water or food, and general transportation and handling. At one stage more than eight hundred plaintiffs were named and they purported to represent 2.4 million veterans who had served as combat soldiers in south-east Asia between 1962 and 1971, as well as most of the families or survivors of those veterans. Genetic injury to the children of Vietnam veterans was also alleged. Complex jurisdictional issues as to the basis of a federal claim and questions of sovereign or government immunity were raised.

Dealing with the question whether the action might proceed as a class action, George C Pratt, District Judge, held that the prerequisites of rule 23(a) ('numerosity', 'commonality' 'typicality', 'adequacy of representation' and an identifiable class of which the representatives were members) had been satisfied. Turning to rule 23(b), he concluded that the case did not fall within either rule 23(b) (1) (A), (b) (1) (B), or (b) (2). He then turned to rule 23 (b) (3) and continued:

> Rule 23(b)(3) authorizes a class action when the court finds 'that the questions of law or fact common to the members of the class predominate over any questions affecting only individual members, and that a class action is superior to all other available methods for the fair and efficient adjudication of the controversy.' The rule lists four matters pertinent to a consideration of these issues: '(A) the interest of members of the class in individually controlling the prosecution or defense of separate actions; (B) the extent and nature of any litigation concerning the controversy already commenced by or against members of the class; (C) the desirability or un-desirability of concentrating the litigation of the claims in the particular forum; (D) the difficulties likely to be encountered in the management of a class action.'
>
> Considering the circumstances of this action, and bearing in mind the manner in which the class action will proceed, the court determines that the interest of class members in individually controlling the prosecution of separate actions is minimal, especially at this early stage of the litigation when the issues under consideration concern the relationship between the defendants and the government, issues that impact equally on every plaintiff's claim. Rule 23(b)(3)(A). Later stages of this litigation, especially those concerned with individual causation and damages, may require reconsideration of this element and possibly decertification, but at this stage, individual class members have almost no interest in individually controlling the prosecution of separate actions. Indeed, the problems inherent in every one of the individual actions are so great that it is doubtful if a single plaintiff represented by a single attorney pursuing an individual action could ever succeed.
>
> With respect to the extent and nature of currently pending litigation, almost all the Agent Orange litigation currently pending is before this court under the multidistrict litigation procedures. All those cases are advancing simultaneously, and certification of a class action will serve the goals of judicial economy and reduce the possibility of multiple lawsuits. Rule 23(b)(3)(B). In addition, it will significantly expedite final resolution of this controversy.
>
> With respect to the desirability of concentrating the litigation of the claims in this forum, the actions have already been concentrated before this court through the use of MDL procedures. Allowing it to proceed as a class action will minimize the hazards of duplicate efforts and inconsistent results. Moreover, given the location of present counsel and the widely varying citizenships of the interested parties, this court is as appropriate a place to settle the controversy as any. Rule 23(b)(3)(C).
>
> With respect to the difficulties likely to be encountered in the management of a class action, the court has carefully and humbly considered the management problems presented by an action of this magnitude and complexity, and concluded that great as they are, the difficulties likely to be encountered by managing these actions as a class action are significantly outweighed by the truly overwhelming problems that would attend any other management device chosen. While the burdens on this court might be lessened by denying class certification, those imposed collectively on the transferor courts after remand of the multidistrict cases would be increased many times.
>
> Having carefully considered the above factors and all other circumstances of this action, the court is satisfied that at this time the questions of law and fact common to the members of the class predominate over questions of law or fact affecting only individual members, and that a class action is superior to any other available method for the fair and efficient adjudication of the controversy.[1]

Because over a year ago this court requested plaintiffs not to file actions pending decision on the class action motion, because the facts and issues in all of the pending and future cases are to a great degree identical, or at least parallel, and because this action presents a variety of questions in relatively untested areas of the law, this court sees the objectives of FRCP Rule 1 and Rule 23, as well as the interests of justice, best served by determining here, and for all parties, as many legal and factual issues as may properly be decided. To achieve those ends the court will certify this to be a class action under FRCP 23(b). Formal certification will be by separate order to be processed under the court's instructions.

C. NOTICE

Rule 23(c)(2) states that 'In any class action maintained under subdivision (b)(3), the court shall direct to the members of the class the best notice practicable under the circumstances, including individual notice to all members who can be identified through reasonable effort.'

Two problems with notice must be considered: how the notice shall be given and what the notice shall say. In the order to be prepared and signed which will officially certify the class, the court will direct both the manner and content of notice.

As to the manner of notice, both the rule and the court decisions display a preference for individual notice whenever possible, and ordinarily the financial burden of giving notice falls on the plaintiffs. Individual notice to all members of the broad class to be certified may be impossible. The rule requires, however, only 'the best notice practicable under the circumstances'. Counsel are invited to submit suggestions in writing as to how 'the best notice practicable' may be given to the over two million Vietnam veterans and their families who are included in the class by January 23, 1981. Certain possibilities have already been suggested, including having the Veterans Administration mail copies of the notice to all Vietnam veterans on their mailing list, and soliciting the aid of veterans' organizations around the country to circularize their memberships.

It may be that other persons or organizations are willing to assist in resolving the notice problem. The news media in particular might volunteer space or time to assure 'the best notice practicable' to veterans and their families. Still other means by which the notice requirement can be fairly and reasonably fulfilled may exist. After considering all suggestions received by January 23, 1981, the court will determine how notice shall be given.

As to the form of notice, Yannacone and Associates is directed to serve and file by January 7, 1981 a proposed form of notice which shall include at least the following information in as simple and direct a form as possible:

1. It shall state briefly the nature of plaintiffs' suit, their causes of action and their claims for relief.
2. It shall set out the definition of the plaintiff case and in general terms the issues that will have to be determined.
3. It shall notify the recipient that at his/her request the court will exclude him/her from the class so long as the request is received by a date specified in the notice that counsel and the court will set. Rule 23(c)(2)(A).
4. It shall make clear that any findings, whether favorable or not, will be binding on all class members who do not request exclusion. Rule 23(c)(2)(B).
5. It shall explain that any class member who does not request exclusion may enter an appearance through his/her counsel. Rule 23(c)(2)(C).

Counsel for defendants shall meet on or before January 16, 1981 to discuss and, if possible, agree upon suggested modifications to plaintiffs' proposed form of notice and serve and file their suggested changes, if any, with the court by January 23, 1981. To the extent that agreement among defense counsel is not possible, they may make separate submissions.

By January 16, 1981 Yannacone and Associates shall submit to the court a list of no more than 12 persons whom they propose as representative plaintiffs for the class action. Defendants may, if they choose, submit any comments, objections or suggestions with respect to the proposed representative plaintiffs by January 23, 1981. The court will then determine who will be the named plaintiffs in the class action, and plaintiffs' attorneys will be directed by further order of this court to prepare an appropriate class action order and class action complaint.

---

1. There being no need to certify subclasses of plaintiffs at this time, the court will postpone consideration of the subclass issues to a latter time when the most efficient and logical course to follow will be clearer.

NOTE

In another part of his judgment (at 796) Judge Pratt concluded that 'a government contract defense exists and has possible application to the facts at bar'. The issue was to be tried in Phase I of the case management plan established for the trial. On 24 February 1982 the Court concluded that the defence would be made out on proof that '(i) the government established the specification for "Agent Orange" (ii) the "Agent Orange" manufactured by the defendants met the government's specifications in all material respects; and (iii) the government knew as much or more than the defendant about the hazards to people that accompanied use of "Agent Orange"'. It is understood that the litigation was settled by the manufacturers, but not the United States government, for $180 million.

Questions

1. Leaving aside the desirability or otherwise of a 'government contract defence' to a product liability action is this combination of (a) a class action and (b) the initial trial of a prima facie defence, (i) an economical use of court time, (ii) likely to advance the cause of the injured parties, or (iii) an apt means of disposing once and for all of highly publicised and embarrassing litigation?
2. In view of the provision of rule 23 (above p 364) how would you have advised a 'veteran' who had received notice of the action? What would be the position of such a veteran if the defence were established and (i) notice had never reached him, or (ii) it was only later that he had discovered that he had been affected?
3. Do you favour an 'opt in' or an 'opt out' procedure under a class action system? Which procedure is adopted under rule 23 of the Federal Rules of Civil Procedure (above)? What are the practical consequences of choosing one system rather than the other?

The 'Agent Orange' litigation was unusual in that, contrary to the general belief, class actions are not normally regarded as an appropriate means of dealing with claims for personal injuries, at least within the federal courts. Certainly this was the view of the Federal Rules Advisory Committee in its note to rule 23 (see 39 FRD 69, 102 (1966)):

> A 'mass accident' resulting in injuries to numerous persons is ordinarily not appropriate for a class action because of the likelihood that significant questions, not only of damages but of liability and defenses to liability, would be present, affecting the individuals in different ways. In these circumstances an action conducted nominally as a class action would degenerate in practice into multiple lawsuits separately tried.

The same reasoning seems equally applicable to individual disasters which share common characteristics. In a recent note Rosenberg has commented as follows (97 Harv LR 849, 908–9 (1984)):

Class Actions

. . .

Courts are often reluctant to certify class actions,[1] even in cases that fall within the conventional definition of public law litigation; when they do so, they frequently regard certification as but a grudging concession to pragmatism.[2] Their concern seems to be that the class action encourages the treatment of claims in a mass production fashion that does not sufficiently recognize differences among claimants.[3]

1. See eg *In re Northern Dist of Cal 'Dalkon Shield' IUD Prods Liab Litig*, 693 F 2d 847 (9th Cir 1982), cert denied, 103 S Ct 817 (1983); *Re Federal Skywalk Cases* 680 F 2d 1175 (8th Cir),

(cert denied, 103 S Ct 342 (1982); *Ryan v Eli Lilly & Co* 84 FRD 230 (DSC 1979); *Yandle v PPG Indus* 65 FRD 566 (E D Tex 1974), *Rosenfield v A H Robbins Co* 63 AD 2d 11, 407 NYS 2d 196, appeal dismissed, 46 NY 2d 731, 385 NE 2d 1201, 413, NYS 2d 374 (1978); *Snyder v Hooker Chems & Plastics* 104 Misc 2d 735, 429 NYS 2d (Sup Ct 1980). But see *Payton v Abbott Labs* No. 76–1514–S (D Mass Dec 6, 1983) (available Feb 1, 1984, on LEXIS, Genfed library, Dist file) (order decertifying class); *Re Federal Skywalk Cases* 97 FRD 365 (WD Mo 1982); *Re 'Agent Orange' Prod Liab Litig*, 506 F Supp 762 (EDNY 1980), modified. MDL No 381 (EDNY Dec 16, 1983) (certifying class generally under Fed R Civ P 23(b)(3), and on the question of punitive damages under Fed R Civ P 23(b)(1)(B)), writ of mandamus denied. No 83–3065 (2d Cir Jan 9, 1984); *Pruitt v Allied Chem Corp* 85 FRD 100 (ED Va 1980).
2. See, eg *General Tel Co v Falcon* 457 US 147, 155 (1982); *Califano v Yamasaki*, 442 US 682, 700–01 (1979); *Hobbs v Northeast Airlines* 50 FRD 76, 79 (ED Pa 1970); 7A C. Wright & A. Miller, Federal Practice and Procedure § 1783, at 115 (1972).
3. 7A C. Wright & A. Miller, *supra* note 2, § 1783, at 115.

A device similar to the class action is multi-district litigation under 28 USC § 1407 see *Re Air Crash Disaster at Wash, DC*, 559 F Supp 333 (DDC 1983); *Re Paris Air Crash* 399 F Supp 732 (CD Cal 1975). But here also, plaintiffs may run into strong opposition to consolidation, and consequent defeat; see *Re Asbestos Litigation* 431 F Supp 906 (Multi-Dist Judic Panel 1977).

The Ontario Law Reform Commission Report on Class Actions contains helpful discussion of some developments in the United States. Having noted the limitation placed on class actions commenced pursuant to federal diversity of citizenship jurisdiction and the Consumer Product Safety Act (see above pp 363–364) it continues (Vol 1, pp 251–253) (footnotes omitted unless otherwise indicated):

Regarding other federal legislation in the consumer area, of particular note are the Magnuson-Moss Warranty—Federal Trade Commission Improvement Act and the Truth in Lending Act, both of which contain specific provisions dealing with class actions. The Magnuson-Moss Warranty—Federal Trade Commission Improvement Act expressly authorizes suits in the federal courts for breach of express and implied warranties, and it has been said that this legislation has the potential for becoming 'a significant area of class action litigation'.[1] However, since the Act became effective in 1975, very few class actions have been commenced under the Act.[2] One of the explanations for the lack of class action litigation is the fact that the Act requires a minimum of 100 named plaintiffs, each of whom has suffered at least $25 damage, as well as a minimum aggregate injury claim for all class members of $50,000. Although consumer class actions may consist of numerous potential class members, the necessity of joining 100 named class members as proper parties to the litigation is a formidable obstacle to class actions under this Act.

An exception to the scarcity of consumer-oriented class actions under federal statutes is class litigation associated with legislation regulating consumer credit. Although there are a large number of federal statutes relating to consumer credit, '[t]he most voluminous source of class actions in the consumer credit field to date is the Truth-in-Lending Act',[3] which deals primarily with non-disclosure of credit information. Until recently, the Act guaranteed individuals a minimum recovery of $100, as well as counsel fees, for proof of violation of the Act. However, no mention was made of class actions. When it became apparent that the availability of this guaranteed recovery to all class members in a class action was producing damage awards that were out of proportion to the violation, the Act was amended expressly to except class actions from the minimum recovery provision and, moreover, to stipulate a maximum monetary recovery.[4] These requirements do not, however, impose barriers to the commencement of class actions; in fact, they make it clear that the Act may be enforced in this fashion.

Due, in part, to the jurisdictional restraints placed upon the commencement of consumer-oriented class actions in the federal courts, the state courts are becoming the more frequent forum in which these types of action are brought. That the focus is shifting to the state courts to make effective remedies available in relation to consumer claims is evidenced by the fact that an increasing number of states have adopted an expanded class action procedure modelled upon Federal Rule 23, which broadens the procedural basis in these states for the redress of consumer violations. Moreover, in terms of substantive remedies for consumers, many states have enacted consumer protection statutes designed to protect consumers and to provide remedies against unfair and deceptive trade practices. In addition, several of these consumer statutes include specific provision for class actions, usually modelled upon Federal Rule 23.

Notwithstanding the enactment in recent years of legislation designed to facilitate consumer class actions, there does not appear to have been a proliferation of such actions at the state level. The notable exception in this regard is California, where the Consumers Legal Remedies Act specifically provides a class action procedure to redress violations of that Act. In that jurisdiction, the opportunity for, and the utilization of, class actions in the consumer area has been increased significantly by a number of developments. First, judicial decisions with respect to the substantive law have facilitated, for example, proof of fraudulent misrepresentation in consumer class actions.[5] Secondly, decisions regarding the class mechanism itself, with respect to matters such as notice and novel methods of calculation and distribution of damages,[6] have facilitated the bringing of class actions. In other jurisdictions, however, at least in some areas of the law, consumer class actions have met with mixed success. This is particularly the case with respect to products liability class actions, in which damages are sought for injuries resulting from the use of a defective product.

1. Note 'In Camera' (1979) 6 Class Action Reports 1.
2. For example, in *Re General Motors Corp Engine Interchange Litigation* MDL No 308 (ND III Oct 13, 1977), a national class action was certified based on allegations that General Motors Corporation deceptively installed nearly 140,000 inferior Chevrolet engines in Oldsmobiles, but a £40 million settlement negotiated by the state attorneys general was overturned by the Seventh Circuit Court, 94 F 2d 1106 (7th Cir 1979). The matter of certification has not yet been dealt with in three other cases; see *Feinstein v Firestone Tire & Rubber Co* No 78–4342 (SDNY), which alleges that Firestone Tire & Rubber Company sold nearly 40 million defective and unsafe steel-belted radial tires; *Mullins v Ford Motor Co* No 79–2091 (SD WVa), which alleges that the Ford Motor Company sold approximately 3.8 million cars with defective lubrication systems; and *Skelton v General Motors Corp* No 79–1243 (ND III), which alleges that General Motors Corporation installed 3-4 million defective transmissions. See (1979), 6 CAR 1, where these cases are discussed.
3. Newberg *Newberg on Class Actions* (1977) Vol 4 §7755a, at 572.
4. See 15 USC § 1640(a)(2)(B). In class actions, the amount that may be recovered is limited to the lesser of £500,000 or 1% of the net worth of the creditor.
5. See *Vasquez v Superior Court of San Joaquin Cty* 4 Cal 3d 800, 484 P2d 964 (SC 1971). In that case, instalment purchasers of frozen food and freezers alleged fraudulent misrepresentation on the part of the vendor. Reliance on the part of the plaintiff upon the fraudulent misrepresentation was argued by the defendant to be an element of the cause of action. The defendant asserted that, since each class member would have to prove that he or she actually relied on the misrepresentation in purchasing the goods, the matter could not proceed as a class action. However, the California Supreme Court held that, if it was found that material misrepresentations were made to class members, an inference could be drawn that the class had relied on such misrepresentations.
6. See *Daar v Yellow Cab Co* 67 Cal 2d 695, 433 P2d 732 (SC 1967).

As was noted in the above extract some of the most interesting American developments have occurred in relation to the calculation and distribution of damages. This seems to have been especially true of cases in which the individual amounts involved may be relatively small. The Australian Law Reform Commission contains a helpful summary of some of the developments in its Discussion Paper (No 11) 'Access to the Courts—II Class Actions'. Having noted the traditional methods of assessment and the 'split trial' technique (as seen, eg in the *Prudential Assurance* case above p 358), the Discussion Paper continues (at para 45 et seq):

45. **Class-wide Assessment:** The split trial technique is useful only where
  ● the size of the class is relatively manageable;
  ● assessment will not be unduly protracted;
  ● the identity of members of the class is known; or
  ● records of either the plaintiff or the defendant are available.

However, it is quite impracticable in claims for mass economic injury where often none of these factors is present.

- In the *Antibiotics Litigation*[1] commenced in 1969, more than 100 separate actions were filed, many of which were class actions brought by States on behalf of citizens, hospitals and other consumers within their boundaries. The action claimed treble damages for breach of anti-trust laws alleging price fixing by the defendants in relation to the sale of certain antibiotic drugs. Most of the actions were settled and a sum in excess of £160 million was distributed to members of the classes. Traditional methods were entirely unsuited to assessing damages. It was plainly impracticable, if not impossible, for each member of these enormous classes individually to prove a claim.

The courts in the United States have responded by developing methods of calculating damages by assessment on a class-wide basis which is then distributed to the members of the class. Modern techniques are applied. If the defendant's records are available, the use of appropriate mathematical formulae may establish the loss to the class as a whole. If records are not available, courts have used computers, surveys, sampling and polling techniques which are supported by expert evidence to compute the loss suffered by the class as a whole and the damages which should, therefore, be paid to the class as compensation for that loss. The use of these devices may seem peculiar to a traditional lawyer. But is it really so odd? In one of the cases in the *Antibiotics Litigation* it was observed:

> 'Most important management decisions in the business world in which these defendants operate are made through the intelligent application of statistical and computer techniques and these class members should be entitled to use the same techniques in proving the elements of their cause of action. The court is confident they can be successfully utilised in the courtroom and that their application will allow the consumers to protect their rights while freeing the court and the defendants of the spectre of unmanageability. In these circumstances the court cannot conclude that the defendants are constitutionally entitled to compel a parade of individual plaintiffs to establish damages. Assuming damages are later awarded on the basis of sales figures and that the total of individual claims then filed is less than the award, the court will consider what disposition to make of the residue.'[2]

Individual claims against the total fund are often processed by special masters or committees of counsel appointed by the court.

46. Use of the defendant's records may sometimes assist in identifying members of the class for the purpose of distributing damages. In the absence of such records, individual members of the class must come forward and prove their claims on the damages fund. The procedural steps involved are

- notice of the settlement;
- submission of proof of claims;
- verification of the claims; and
- the actual distribution of damages.

Procedures for notice and verification of claims vary according to circumstances. It is not unusual when large sums are recovered for many of those who are entitled to claim to fail to do so. The surplus created is applied as directed by the court.

47. **Fluid Recovery and Cy-près:** Perhaps the most novel and controversial techniques for assessing and distributing damages which have been developed in the United States courts are fluid recovery and *cy-près* schemes. The *Yellow Cab Co Case*[3] illustrates the principles of both fluid recovery and *cy-près*.

- In violation of a city ordinance the Yellow Cab Co of California raised its fares by changing its meters. As a result many thousands of passengers were overcharged. The damage to each individual passenger was small. But the gain to the company and the damage to the taxi passengers as a group was substantial. One member of the class brought a class action on behalf of all Yellow Cab passengers in the period of the overcharge. The overcharge was incapable of individual assessment. It would be impossible to determine who had been passengers in Yellow Cabs; some passengers would not have been aware of the overcharge; some passengers aware of the overcharge either did not care or would not be able to calculate the amount of the overcharge in each individual journey or could not remember how often or when they used the defendant's taxi cabs. For the same reasons distribution of damages to individuals would be entirely impracticable. The court approved the notion of fluid recovery in order to avoid denying recovery and permitting the defendant to retain the unlawful gain. The action was settled on the basis that the defendant would undercharge for a period estimated to cut out its unlawful gains.

The amount of the overcharge was calculated and the resulting fund was returned to the class by a scheme, called a '*cy-près* scheme', of reducing cab fares in future years below the authorised maximum. Damages were thereby recovered, managed and distributed on behalf of an entire class without proof of each individual claim and without the necessity for distribution.

48.   Fluid recovery techniques could be applied where
   • individual claims are too small or cannot be proved because of absence of records;
   • individual members of the class cannot be identified; or
   • individual members of the class are unlikely to claim.

Cy-près schemes could also assist where the distributing damages could absorb the damages fund, where class members cannot be identified, or where class members fail to assert their individual claims and a surplus remains after distribution. The *Yellow Cab Case* is quite exceptional. Attempts to use fluid recovery techniques to assess damages have on subsequent occasions been denied in the United States.[4]

49.   **Dealing with the Surplus:** Where a surplus remains unclaimed, the *cy-près* scheme will also permit an application of the fund to a charitable or otherwise beneficial public use, which is seen to be preferable to permitting a defendant to retain his unjust enrichment. In one of the cases in the *Antibiotics Litigation*, the States involved were required to submit plans to use funds for court-approved public health purposes so that the unclaimed portion of the settlement fund was applied 'for the benefit of consumers generally'.[5]

50.   **Are the New Techniques Desirable?:** The techniques of proof of damage on a class-wide basis, fluid recovery and *cy-près* exhibit the capacity of the class action to be more than a procedural device to recover compensation for individual loss. By these procedures, class actions tend to assume the character of a consumer protection mechanism to deter unlawful conduct, force the wrongdoer to surrender unlawful profits and distribute those profits in a way to benefit class members. These techniques are defended as being

> '. . . completely equitable, in as much as the amount of damage arrived at is likely to correspond to the total injury inflicted by the defendant or the extent of its unjust enrichment, regardless of how small or large the number of class members who came forward in the action. In addition, establishing a single comprehensive figure of a class award in one damage proceeding might best achieve a balance between affording plaintiffs relief and deterring future statutory violations in an action brought under one of the anti-trust or securities acts or some other public policy mandate'.[6]

51.   Those critical of what they see as the abuses of class actions claim that such novel methods have altered the substantive law as to damages, have denied defendants the ability to examine each claim made against them, and are punitive in character. Fluid recovery and *cy-près*, it is said, benefit some but not all members of the class. The balance in the market place may be disturbed. Because it is required (for a time) to lower prices of goods or services to comply with a class action order, the defendant may enjoy a commercial advantage over its competitors. The damages fund in effect subsidises lower prices. Some consumers may benefit who were not the initial consumers who suffered loss. The proponents of class actions reply by asserting that certain legislation (particularly trade practices legislation) is designed to encourage private citizens to take their proper part in the enforcement of the law rather than rely on governments to do so for them. The premise of their response is that the defendant should not be permitted to retain illegal profits. To allow the defendant to insist upon proof of each claim individually will enable it, so it is said, to benefit from the cumbersome nature of legal proceedings and the lack of sophistication and indolence of the consumer, and will reward his foresight in wrongfully depriving the multitude of small amounts.

52.   **The Options:** That these procedures—class-wide assessment of damages, fluid recovery and *cy-près*—result in an effective change in the substantive law relating to assessment of damages cannot be doubted. However, unless new techniques of assessing damages are adopted to supplement traditional methods the usefulness of the class action will be very limited. At the same time the interest of defendants in being able to test the claim against them must not be overlooked. Options available include
   * to adhere to traditional methods, including the split trial. This will mean that class actions will be used on limited occasions only where claims are against a clearly established or readily computed common fund, where the class is small or where the claim can be very simply calculated;
   * to permit class-wide assessment of damages only in addition to traditional methods but require the defendant to compensate only those who come forward within a certain time and prove their claim;
   * to permit class-wide assessment as in the second alternative but require the

defendant to pay the total amount of damages as assessed by the court. Damages will be paid to those who prove a claim. Any balance will be paid into a Class Actions Fund. The purpose of such a fund is noted in para 64;
* to permit fluid recovery and *cy-près* to be available in addition to class-wide assessment of damages with any surplus being paid into a Class Actions Fund. Some may argue that these techniques should be limited to class actions by governmental agencies.

Any procedure which requires a defendant to do more than pay damages to those who come forward with a claim is seen by some to have a punitive element. Because the purpose of the proceedings has moved beyond actual compensation of those who come forward to prove a personal claim, they urge that it may be more appropriate for the availability of these procedures to be restricted to government so that the primary objective of private class actions remains one of compensation and compensation alone. The issue is whether it is preferable for the enforcement of legislation to be left

- to private individuals who come forward—in the knowledge that they will usually be few, or
- to governmental agencies.

A further alternative might be to revise methods of assessing penalties in criminal prosecutions. Instead of maximum penalties being fixed by legislation, the penalty in appropriate cases could be fixed by reference to the total amount received by the defendant from the unlawful dealing. Claims by those who have suffered this loss could be made against the amount thereby recovered.[7]

1. *Re Co-ordinated Pretrial Proceedings in Antibiotics Antitrust Actions* 333 F Supp 278 (1971). For an account of this litigation and subsequent settlement procedures see Wolfram, 'The Antibiotics Class Actions', (1976) American Bar Foundation Research Journal 253; Lebedoff, 'Operation Money Back', (1975) 4 Class Action Reports 147.
2. *Re Co-ordinated Pretrial Proceedings in Antibiotics Antitrust Actions* 333 F Supp 278 at 289 (1971).
3. *Daar v Yellow Cab Co* 63 Ca R 724 (1967).
4. See cases noted in Harvard Study 'Developments in the Law—Class Actions', 89 Harv LR 1318 at 1532–34.
5. *West Virginia v Chas Pfizer Inc* 314 F Supp 710 (1970).
6. Miller, 'Problems in Administering Judicial Relief in Class Actions under Federal Rule 23 (b) (3)', 54 FRD 501, 509–510.
7. Law Reform Commission of Canada, Criminal Responsibility for Group Actions' (1976), 39.

Consumer organisations and public agencies

INTRODUCTION

The above discussion is concerned mainly with collective redress through a representative or class action in situations in which a group of individual consumers has both sufficient incentive and the means to institute litigation. Frequently however an alternative approach will be needed. For example we have noted that it is not uncommon for businesses to use, in standard form contracts, exemption clauses which are unenforceable in law by virtue of the Unfair Contract Terms Act 1977 and yet are remarkably effective in practice (see above p 274 et seq). Where this happens adequate consumer protection may require that the use of such clauses be prevented, whether through the creation of criminal offences (for example under Part II of the Fair Trading Act 1973, below p 415 et seq) or through injunctive relief. Public agencies or consumer organisations are likely to find a role here. Such control over exemption clauses would constitute a relatively modest extension of the powers to deal with persistent 'offenders' conferred on the Director General of Fair Trading by Part III of the Fair Trading Act 1973 (see p 424 et seq). Similarly, if more ambitiously, effective consumer redress may be advanced by allowing public agencies or consumer organisations to institute or take over proceedings on behalf of individual consumers or perhaps a group of consumers. There are precedents for this in some Commonwealth and American jurisdictions and on the continent of Europe.

The general nature of the developments envisaged by some commentators has been pointed to by Richard Tur in his article 'Litigation and the Consumer Interest: The Class Action and Beyond' (1982) 2 Journal of Legal Studies 135. Having referred to the position in France and Germany Tur continues (at pp 162–163):

> There are apparent virtues in combining the class action, increasingly characteristic of common law jurisdictions, and the role of groups developed in continental systems, most particularly in France. Two types of class actions would then be possible, first, the class action simpliciter or the 'internal plaintiff class action' in which one or several individuals take action on behalf of themselves and all other members of the class on the basis of a cause of action which he or they share with all other members; secondly, a type of group action which is taken on behalf of the consumer interest or the public interest by a group or association granted statutory standing to sue wherein, quite apart from injunctive or declarative relief and quite separate from damages in its own right for injury to the interest it fosters, damages on behalf of affected individuals may be sought and awarded. To distinguish this latter type of class action it may be called a 'public interest class action' or an 'external plaintiff class action'. Given the problems of management and initiative and the need to secure conformity between conduct and legal rules there would be a place for such external plaintiff class actions even where provision had been made in the legal system for the class action simpliciter. The external plaintiff class action would meet many of the difficulties of management and initiative and ensure that collective, knowledgeable, repeat playing defendants were met by collective, well-informed, experienced plaintiffs, to the betterment of the enforcement of the law. It would meet the point, as true today as when uttered 20 years ago that 'the rights which the law gives to the consumer too often go by default.[1] And it meets in part, the observation that 'what is really needed in Britain is a procedure . . . whereby consumer protection agencies can take proceedings on behalf of consumers affected by a breach of the civil law'[2] albeit by substituting private, voluntary, extra-governmental groups for the regulatory agencies or governmental bodies originally contemplated by Ross Cranston.
>
> Consequently, the first step beyond the class action suggested by a consideration of developments on the continent is the external plaintiff class action wherein consumer groups could take action on behalf of individual consumers and obtain damages on their behalf. This could meet the potential gap as regards initiative and management caused by the absence of any functional equivalent of the public interest lawyer and the contingent fee.
>
> Continental jurisdictions have, in the main, rejected class actions and sought to stimulate litigation by relaxing the rules of standing both as relates to access to administrative courts and by way of statutory authorisation for some specified groups to facilitate action in defence of the collective interests fostered by these groups.

1. Cmnd 1781, para 403 (1962).
2. Cranston *Consumers and the Law* (1st edn) p 100.

THE UNITED KINGDOM

Certainly developments along these lines would not be without precedent in the United Kingdom. Professor Jolowicz noted in his article 'Protection of Diffuse, Fragmented and Collective Interests in Civil Litigation: English Law' (1983) 42 CLJ 222, 236–237:

> The conferment on public authorities and governmental agencies of a power to take civil proceedings in the course of exercising their public functions is now commonplace. In certain circumstances, for example, the relevant Minister may petition the court for an order that a

company be wound up if he considers 'that it is expedient in the public interest' that he should do so,[1] and in this way a civil remedy, developed for the protection of the private interests of persons such as the creditors of a company, is adopted for a public purpose. Similarly, the two Commissions concerned with the administration of the legislation against discrimination on account of race or sex are empowered not only to assist the victims of unlawful discrimination to take action before the court, but may in certain circumstances do so themselves in their own name.[2] Most strikingly, perhaps, an entirely new structure of civil litigation, with its own specialised court, has been created by the restrictive practices legislation whereby the Director of Fair Trading is put into the position of a plaintiff and placed under a duty to take proceedings in respect of 'registrable' restrictive trading agreement.[3]

1. Companies Act 1967, s 35. See eg, *Re Lubin, Rosen and Associates Ltd* [1975] 1 WLR 122.
2. The Race Relations Act 1976 is administered by the Commission for Racial Equality, and the Sex Discrimination Act 1975 by the Equal Opportunities Commission. Both Acts emphasise the Commissions' duties to work towards the elimination of discrimination and to secure compliance with the law without recourse to the courts. The power of the Commissions to bring proceedings in their own name is, in general, exercisable only in cases of persistent unlawful discrimination or where the unlawful act does not cause damage to an individual who could, with the help if necessary of the Commission, bring an action himself.
3. See now the Restrictive Practices Act 1976 and the Restrictive Practices Court Act 1976. Certain categories of agreement are, by the legislation, deemed to be contrary to the public interest unless the court is satisfied, on one or more specified grounds, that they should be approved. This creates a lis between the parties to the agreement, on the one hand, and the Director of Fair Trading on the other.

Of the examples mentioned by Jolowicz the position of the Director General of Fair Trading in relation to restrictive trading agreements is not too far removed from the type of situation with which this chapter is concerned. Yet it is not without significance that the relevant powers and duties are all conferred by statute. In the absence of such provision the position of consumer organisations is at best obscure. One of the present co-authors has made the following general observations when commenting on this point in *The Law and the Weaker Party* Vol II (1982) pp 133–134:

In the United Kingdom the Consumers' Association has a notable record in promoting legislation and it occasionally sponsors test-cases. Indeed its Legal Officer, David Tench, recently appeared before the Exeter County Court qua solicitor to argue one of the first cases decided under the Unfair Contract Terms Act 1977[1]. However, neither it nor any other consumer organisation, has, so far as I am aware, sought injunctive or declaratory relief in its own name and in the interests of its members or indeed of consumers generally. Were it to do so in circumstances in which the defendant's conduct was 'unlawful' it would have to establish that it had a sufficient interest in the matter to be allowed to proceed.

The general principle is that private individuals and (where appropriate) interest groups may prosecute in respect of criminal offences[2], yet cannot (simply as members of the public) seek injunctions to restrain breaches of the criminal law. The Attorney-General's consent to relator proceedings is required[3]. In the field of administrative law, where the action is against a public authority, the rules in relation to locus standi have been relaxed in recent years. For example, a local residents' association has been held to have a sufficient interest to challenge the granting of planning permission in its locality[4], although the National Federation of Self-employed and Small Businesses did not, on inquiry into the facts of the case, have a sufficient interest to challenge the decision of the Inland Revenue Commissioners to grant an amnesty to casual workers in Fleet Street[5]. This latter decision of the House of Lords is especially important as indicating that the rules in relation to standing to sue are not to be determined in isolation from the matter to which the application relates. However, although it is unfashionable as an idea, there still remains a divide between the assertion of 'public law' rights and assertions of 'private law' concerns which happen to affect the public generally. Were it to seek an injunction or a declaration that a term in a standard-form contract was void, or that a consumer product was unmerchantable or defective in design, a body like the Consumers' Association or the National Consumer Council could hardly be categorised as a mere 'busybody'. Yet it is unlikely that it would be regarded as having a sufficient interest to entitle it to a remedy. In any event the point is sufficiently unclear for it to be desirable to have it clarified.

1. *Woodman v Photo Trade Processing Ltd* (May, 1981) [unreported], above p 245.
2. For a general discussion of this point see Research Study No 10 on Prosecution by Private Individuals and Non-Police Agencies, prepared for the Royal Commission on Criminal Procedure.
3. *Gouriet v Union of Post Office Workers* [1977] 3 All ER 70.
4. See, eg *Turner v Secretary of State for Environment* (1973) 28 P & CR 123 and, more recently, *Covent Garden Community Association Ltd v Greater London Council* [[1981] JPL 183] (Woolf J, April 1980).
5. *IRC v National Federation of Self-Employed and Small Businesses Ltd* [1981] 2 All ER 93, HL (the famous Mickey-Mouse or Fleet Street casuals' case).

Although some may consider the involvement of consumer organisations in litigation a desirable step it is plain that the funding of major litigation is not something which can be undertaken lightly. English law has no equivalent of the American contingent fee to finance litigation and it is likely that this will prove to be a much more substantial stumbling block than technical issues of locus standi. The Royal Commission on Legal Services, Cmnd 7648, 1979 (the Benson Commission) considered the question of legal services for groups though principally in relation to advice and assistance rather than to legal aid. It reached the following conclusions:

12.62   In summary, we have come to the conclusion that:—
(a) legal advice and assistance should be made available for groups but the groups which would be entitled to receive it should be carefully defined as proposed below;
(b) no change is necessary to the principle that, for the purposes of civil litigation, legal aid should be confined to individuals save in representative actions as described in paragraph 12.60.
12.63   We suggest the following provisions should be adopted to identify the groups which would be entitled to legal advice and assistance.
(a) Groups may be constituted on a formal or informal basis, but the minimum requirements are that:—
   (i)   a register should be maintained of the names and addresses of the individuals comprising the group and regularly updated;
   (ii) the members of the group should have a personal interest in the purpose of the group;
   (iii) a secretary should be appointed;
   (iv) the purpose of the group should be recorded in writing in the register;
   (v)   the register should be available for inspection by an interested party.
(b) The group would not be entitled to legal advice and assistance if:—
   (i)   it is carrying on a trade or business or operating for profit;
   (ii) it carries on party political activities;
   (iii) it has access to adequate funds.
(c) The only purpose for which legal advice or assistance should be available should be to protect the members of the group in respect of their legal rights, duties and liabilities.

. . .

These modest proposals did not meet with governmental approval as may be seen from the following statement in The Government Response to the Report of the Royal Commission on Legal Services, Cmnd 9077, 1983, p 11;

Legal aid may be available for representative actions in certain circumstances (which are explained in the Law Society's 'Notes for Guidance' set out in the Legal Aid Handbook 1983). The Government considers it is reasonable to expect groups to pool their resources and does not accept that additional help should be provided.

Occasionally the Law Society has shown itself willing to assist in the co-ordination of claims by persons having a common complaint. A good example is provided by the following statement in the Law Society's Gazette, 25 August 1982:

The Drug 'Opren'
Members of the profession will no doubt be aware that at the beginning of August, the Department of Health and Social Security suspended, for a period of three months, the promotion and supply of the drug Opren.

The Law Society has been contacted by the Opren Action Group, who are anxious to know what potential legal rights people, who claim to have suffered adverse reactions after taking Opren, may have. The Action Group have been told that The Law Society cannot take sides in this tragic situation, but that it will do whatever it can to ensure that anyone claiming to have suffered from taking Opren does obtain proper legal advice and assistance.

According to press reports the drug has been prescribed for more than half a million arthritic patients in Britain, and the Chairman of the Committee on Safety of Medicines, Professor Abraham Goldberg, is quoted as saying that his Committee has received over 3,500 reports of adverse reactions associated with the drug.

Thus it can be seen that there may be a very considerable number of potential claimants. The Society feels that it may assist solicitors who receive instructions from Opren takers, if they can be put in touch with colleagues who receive similar instructions, with a view to co-operating generally in the handling of claims.

Any solicitor who receives such instructions is, therefore, invited to write to the Secretary, Professional and Public Relations Department, The Law Society, 113 Chancery Lane, London WC2A 1PL. The Society will compile a register of all such solicitors, copies of which will be sent to them at the beginning of October. Copies will also be available to other solicitors who receive instructions after that date.

It will, of course, be for solicitors to decide how best, in the interests of their clients, to co-operate with colleagues, and The Law Society is in no way seeking to interfere in the conduct of claims by members of the profession.

A possible stimulus to the role of consumer organisations in the United Kingdom is to be found in the following recommendation of the Council of Europe.

Recommendation No R (81) 2 of the Committee of Ministers to the Member States on the Legal Protection of the Collective Interests of Consumers by Consumer Agencies (1981)

The Committee of Ministers, under the terms of Article 15.b of the Statute of the Council of Europe.

Noting that the necessity of protecting the collective interests of consumers extends over a broad field covering both the private and public sectors;

Reaffirming the usefulness of simplified procedures to reach speedy, efficient and economical settlements of consumer disputes before a judicial or other appropriate body as a means also of protecting the collective interests of consumers;

Recognising that the general interests of consumers besides being advanced by individual consumers claiming their rights, in many cases must be promoted by collective action taken on their behalf;

Considering therefore that the setting up of consumer agencies and defining and strengthening their role as well as increasing their functions are important means of furthering the collective interests of consumers;

Seeking to identify general principles which might be taken into account for this purpose;

Recognising that owing particularly to the different types of consumer agencies and legal systems in member states the implementation of these principles by states may vary;

Recommends the Governments of member states to take or reinforce as the case may be, all measures they consider appropriate with a view to the progressive implementation of the principles set out in the Appendix to this Recommendation.

APPENDIX TO THE RECOMMENDATION

Principles
Governments of member states should, in order to implement the following principles, take the necessary steps to strengthen the role of appropriate consumer agencies to enable them to

further the collective interests of consumers, or to facilitate the establishment of such agencies where they do not exist or where their numbers or qualifications are insufficient.

I   States should empower or encourage consumer agencies to carry out the functions set out in the following paragraphs:

(1) Consumer agencies should, in particular by making use of the mass media, provide:
   (a) information for consumers on their rights and duties in general or in particular fields;
   (b) warnings concerning defective or potentially dangerous products, especially where such warnings have not been given by the supplier himself;
   (c) information or warnings concerning unfair practices of suppliers, in particular misleading or unfair advertising.

(2) Consumer agencies should, in appropriate cases, encourage or, if given such powers, require suppliers:
   (a) to give consumers information of specific interest to them, in particular:
      (i) clear information as to their rights and duties;
      (ii) warnings as to the potential danger of the goods and services;
   (b) to withdraw from the market or recall from consumers any goods which are dangerous because of a defect;
   (c) to refrain from unfair practices;
   (d) to rectify any unfair or misleading advertising.

(3) Consumer agencies should, on the request of individual consumers, give them information on their rights and duties and, in case of conflict:
   (a) provide legal advice;
   (b) promote the amicable settlement of claims;
   (c) assist consumers in asserting their rights.

(4) Consumer agencies should promote the setting up or assist in the functioning of systems for voluntary conciliation or arbitration.

II   States should take the necessary measures to enable consumer agencies to participate, in matters of direct interest to consumers, in negotiations between public authorities and trade and industry and should encourage those agencies to initiate negotiations with trade and industry, in particular by concluding agreements or participating in the preparation of codes of practice.

III   States should ensure that consumer agencies are consulted when legislation—including subordinate legislation—of direct interest to consumers is being prepared and encourage these agencies to propose new legislation or amendments to existing legislation in this field.

IV   Consumer agencies should be able, by appropriate legal means, to obtain urgent relief to prevent or stop suppliers from acting in a way contrary to the law.

V   Consumer agencies qualified by national law to do so should have the power to institute proceedings or take part in pending proceedings in order to promote or defend the collective interests of consumers.

VI   Consumer agencies should be encouraged to co-operate with each other and co-ordinate their activities.

SOME EXAMPLES FROM OTHER JURISDICTIONS

In contrast to English law there are examples in Commonwealth and continental jurisdictions of a somewhat broader approach allowing the intervention of public agencies and consumer organisations. In some instances this is linked specifically to the control of unfair contract terms, a point discussed in Ch 6. Here concern is with somewhat more general considerations.

An interesting Canadian example contains the following provisions for the bringing of actions by the Director of Trade Practices:

British Columbia Trade Practices Act 1979

18. Actions and proceedings
(1) The court, in an action brought by the director, or any other person whether or not that person has a special, or any, interest under this Act or the regulations, or is affected by a consumer transaction, may grant either or both of

   (a) a declaration that an act or practice engaged in or about to be engaged in by a supplier in respect of a consumer transaction is a deceptive or unconscionable act or practice; or

   (b) an interim or permanent injunction restraining a supplier from engaging or attempting to engage in a deceptive or unconscionable act or practice in respect of a consumer transaction.

and may then make a further order requiring the supplier to advertise to the public in the media in a manner that will assure prompt and reasonable communication to consumers, and on terms or conditions the court considers reasonable and just, particulars of any judgment, declaration, order or injunction granted against the supplier under paragraph (a) or (b) or subsection (3).

(2) In an action under subsection (1), any person, including the director, may sue on his own behalf and, at his option, on behalf of consumers generally, or a designated class of consumers in the Province.

(3) In an action for a permanent injunction under subsection (1) (b), the court may restore to any person who has an interest in it any money or property that may have been acquired by reason of a deceptive or unconscionable act or practice by the supplier.

(4) In an action brought by the director under subsection (1) (a) or (b), the court may award to the director costs, or a reasonable proportion of them, of the investigation of a supplier conducted under this Act.

(5) The director may apply, ex parte, for an interim injunction under subsection (1) (b), and, if the court is satisfied that there are reasonable and probable grounds for believing there is an immediate threat to the interests of persons dealing with the supplier by reason of an alleged deceptive or unconscionable act or practice in respect of a consumer transaction, the court shall grant an interim injunction on the terms and conditions it considers just.

(6) In an action brought under this section, or in an appeal from it, the plaintiff shall not be required to furnish security for costs.

24. Substitute action of director

(1) Where the director is satisfied that a consumer has

   (a) a cause of action;

   (b) a defence to an action;

   (c) grounds for setting aside a default judgment; or

   (d) grounds for an appeal or to contest an appeal,

and that it is in the public interest, he may, on behalf of the consumer, institute or assume the conduct of proceedings, defend any proceedings brought against the consumer, with a view to enforcing or protecting the rights of the consumer respecting a contravention or suspected contravention of those rights or of any enactment or law relating to the protection or interests of consumers.

(2) The director shall not institute, assume the conduct of or defend any proceedings under subsection (1) without first obtaining

   (a) an irrevocable written consent of the consumer; and

   (b) the written consent of the minister.

(3) In respect of proceedings referred to in subsection (1),

   (a) the director, on behalf of the consumer, shall have in all respects the same rights in and control over the proceedings, including the same right to settle an action or part of an action, as the consumer would have had in the conduct of those proceedings;

   (b) the director may, without consulting or seeking the consent of the consumer, conduct the proceedings in the manner the director considers appropriate and proper; and

   (c) any money, excluding costs, recovered by the director shall belong and be paid to the consumer without deduction, and any amount, excluding costs, awarded against the consumer shall be paid by and recoverable from the consumer; but, in every case, any costs of the proceedings awarded by the court having jurisdiction shall be borne by, or paid to and retained by, the director.

(4) Where

   (a) a party to proceedings to which this section applies files a counterclaim; or

   (b) the consumer on whose behalf the proceedings are being defended is entitled to file a counterclaim,

and that counterclaim is not related to

   (c) the cause of action; and

   (d) the interests of the consumer as a consumer,

the court having jurisdiction in the proceedings shall, on the application of the director, order

   (e) that the counterclaim be heard separately; and

   (f) that the consumer be made a party to the counterclaim in his own right,

and the court may make other orders or give directions in that behalf that it considers just.

In its Report on Class Actions (1982) the Ontario Law Reform Commission refers (at p 49) to the following example of successful proceedings being brought by the Director:

> *Director of Trade Practices v Strand Holidays (Canada) Ltd* No A771507 (BCSC) . . . was an action brought by the Director of Trade Practices on behalf of consumers who had purchased certain travel services provided by the defendant, seeking inter alia damages for breach of contract and negligent misrepresentation. We have been advised by the Director of Trade Practices, Mr Michael Hanson, that this action was settled out of court, and that the defendant agreed to pay each class member $200.

For further discussion of the Act see Belobaba, 'Unfair Trade Practices Legislation: Symbolism and Substance in Consumer Protection' (1977), 15 Osgood Hall LJ 327. See also below, p 434 et seq where the British Columbia Act is discussed in relation to fair trading.

The following example is taken from an Australian Statute:

Consumer Affairs Act 1972 (Victoria)

PROCEEDINGS ON BEHALF OF CONSUMERS

9A. In this Part unless inconsistent with the context or subject-matter, 'consumer' does not include a body corporate.

9B. (1) Where—
  (a) a consumer has made a complaint under this Act; and
  (b) the Director is satisfied—
    (i) that the consumer has a cause of action or a good defence to an action relating to a matter to which the complaint refers; and
    (ii) that it is in the public interest to institute or defend proceedings on behalf of the consumer with a view to enforcing or protecting the rights of the consumer in relation to an infringement or suspected infringement by another person of those rights or of this Act or any other law relating to the interests of consumers—
the Director may, subject to this section, on behalf of and in the name of the consumer, institute proceedings against that other person or defend proceedings brought against the consumer.

(2) The director shall not under sub-section (1) institute or defend proceedings on behalf of a consumer unless—
  (a) the amount claimed or involved in the proceedings does not exceed $10,000;
  (b) the Minister has given his consent in writing subject to such conditions (if any) as he determines; and
  (c) the consumer has given his consent in writing and has not revoked that consent.

(3) A consumer may not except with the consent of the Director revoke a consent given for the purposes of sub-section (2).

9C. (1) Where, under section 9B, the Director institutes or defends proceedings on behalf of a consumer—
  (a) the Director may settle the proceedings either with or without obtaining judgment in the proceedings;
  (b) if a judgment is obtained in the proceedings in favour of the consumer, the Director may take such steps as are necessary to enforce the judgment;
  (c) an amount (other than an amount in respect of costs) recovered in the proceedings is payable to the consumer;
  (d) an amount in respect of costs recovered in the proceedings is payable to the Director;
  (e) the consumer is liable to pay an amount (not being an amount of costs) awarded against him in the proceedings; and
  (f) the Director is liable to pay the costs of or incidental to the proceedings that are payable by the consumer.

(2) Where, in proceedings instituted or defended under section 9B on behalf of a consumer—
  (a) a party to the proceedings files a counterclaim; or
  (b) the consumer is entitled to file a counterclaim—
and the counterclaim is not or would not be related to the proceedings and to the interests of the consumer as a consumer the Director may apply to the court hearing the proceedings for an order that the counterclaim be heard otherwise than in the course of those proceedings.

(3) The court may, where it makes an order under sub-section (2), make such ancillary or consequential provisions as it thinks just.

The above provisions have their counterparts in continental jurisdictions where the debates have followed very similar lines to those in the United Kingdom. This is hardly surprising since over the last two decades the protection of collective and diffuse interests—whether in relation to consumer affairs, the environment or other matters—has been a general preoccupation of Western legal systems.

The position in West Germany has been summarised by Professor Hein Kötz writing in the Civil Justice Quarterly (1982) 237, at p 247 et seq as follows:

The traditional standing rules are by no means costless. The price we pay for them is the emasculation of the policing function of private litigation and a corresponding extension of the areas in which wrongful conduct will remain unchallenged, not because there is an absence of rules defining illegal behaviour and imposing sanctions on the wrongdoer, but because there is an absence of plaintiffs prepared to invoke available judicial controls.

In principle it is of course the Government's task to implement public policy, particularly where that policy aims at protecting large segments of the public whose individual members are in a poor position to make use of existing procedures. However, setting up regulatory agencies to enforce the applicable law and thereby to safeguard the public interest is not always a satisfactory solution. Not only is the creation of such agencies an expensive and practically irreversible step. There is also evidence that governmental agencies tend to assume a bureaucratic outlook and to lose over the years the aggressiveness and flexibility necessary to cope with ingenious attempts to flout the policy of the law. Much has been written about what is called the 'capture' of regulatory agencies by the industries they are supposed to regulate. It has been contended that

'[r]egulatory bodies, like the people who comprise them, have a marked life cycle. In youth they are vigorous, aggressive, evangelistic, and even intolerant. Later they mellow, and in old age—after a matter of ten or fifteen years—they become, with some exceptions, either an arm of the industry they are regulating or senile.'[1]

. . .

Professor Kötz then discusses a provision for reducing the cost of litigation in matters which affect the public interest, and continues:

The reduction machinery relieves the plaintiff from part of the financial risk connected with litigation, but it is of no assistance if the plaintiff is denied standing to sue. An important technique frequently used in Germany to stimulate private litigation in the public interest is to grant standing to certain groups or organisations to sue for injunctive relief in the civil court when it appears that actions brought by individuals are not a sufficiently effective means of protecting the public against illegal conduct. These grants are limited to certain fields of law, and are always based on specific statutory provisions.

The most prominent statutory authorisation for such group actions (*Verbandsklagen*) is found in the Law Against Unfair Competition.[2] Before 1965, the law conferred standing to sue only on the defendant's competitors and on trade associations. Nevertheless, the courts recognised that the policy of the law was not only to keep the competitive process free from unfair business practices, but also to secure protection for consumers at large. Because competitors and trade associations sometimes appeared to be rather slow in initiating litigation, an extension of standing to consumers' associations was made in 1965, allowing them also to seek injunctions restraining unfair business practices. This experiment has been fairly successful, perhaps not so much because of a very large number of actions brought, but principally because consumers' associations, now being able to wield the 'big stick' of a possible court action, are in a much better position to obtain 'voluntary' compliance from potential defendants. There is no doubt that consumers' associations are today making a valuable contribution to the enforcement of the policy of the Law Against Unfair Competition.

Standing to sue is granted to trade or consumers' associations by a number of other German statutes. The most recent example is section 13 of the Law on Standard Contract Terms[3] by which standing is conferred on consumers' associations to seek an injunction restraining the defendant from using or recommending standard contract terms found to be illegal under the law. If injunctive relief is granted the court order is registered in an official register kept by the Federal Cartel Office from which information is available to anybody against a nominal fee. Although the law has been in force for only three years many decisions have already been published in the legal periodicals. Most major industries and trade associations using or recommending standard terms for consumer contracts have meanwhile revised them in the light of the new law, and there is no doubt that this has occurred partly in order to escape the risk of being sued by consumers' associations.

It must be kept in mind, though, that the actions for which associations are granted a *locus standi* may only be brought for injunctive relief. Since associations are not allowed to sue for damages there exists in Germany no functional counterpart of the American class action. In recent years various proposals have been made in Germany trying to adapt the American class action to the German environment and, in some way, to provide consumers' associations with standing to sue for aggregated damages. A bill worked out by the Federal Ministry of Justice[4] and now before Parliament proposes an amendment of the Law Against Unfair Competition which would provide, first, that individual consumers shall have a claim for damages if they bought goods relying on untrue statements of the seller, and, secondly, that these claims, after having been assigned individually to a consumers' association, can be enforced by it against the seller. If the action is successful the proceeds are to be distributed to the assignors who are not required to be members of the association. This bill has met with strong resistance by the industry, and it seems unlikely that it will be passed in the near future. . . .

1. Galbraith *The Great Crash* (Boston, Houghton Mifflin, 1955) p 171.
2. § 13 Absatz 1a of the . . . [Gesetz gegen den unlauteren Wettbewerb of June 7 1909, printed below]. See Grimes, 'Control of Advertising in the United States and Germany: VW Has a Better Idea,' 84 Harv LRev 1769 (1971) where it is argued that the German system of conferring standing to sue on associations should be adopted in the United States. A good description of the mode of operation of German consumers' associations in this field is given by von Falckenstein, *Die Bekämpfung unlauterer Geschäftspraktiken durch Verbraucherverbände* (Bundesanzieger Verlagsgesellschaft Köln 1977).
3. *Gesetz zur Regelung des Rechts des Allgemeinen Geschäftsbedingungen* of December 9, 1976 (BGB1. 1 3317).
4. See the draft of a Law for Amending the Law Against Unfair Competition of 29 September 1978, *Bundestags-Drucksache* 8/2145.

The Law Against Unfair Competition to which Professor Kötz refers provides in part as follows:

Gesetz gegen den unlauteren Wettbewerb (Translation by Tony Weir, Fellow, Trinity College Cambridge)

1. Any person guilty of unethical conduct by way of trade and for purposes of competition is liable to be enjoined and sued for damages.

. . .

3. Suit for an injunction lies against any person who by way of trade and for purposes of competition makes misleading statements on commercial matters, such as the nature, origin or production of goods, the pricing of any or all goods or services on offer, price-lists, the method or source of supply of goods, the possession of awards or prizes, the reason for or the purpose of the sale and the quantity of goods available.

. . .

13(1) In cases falling under ss 1, 3, 6a and 6b, the injunction may be sought by any commercial producer or distributor of similar or analogous goods or services, or by any trade association which has standing as such to sue in private law. Such persons or associations may also seek an injunction against anyone acting in contravention of ss 6, 8, 10, 11 or 12.
13(1a) In cases falling under ss 3, 6, 6a, 6b 7(1) and 11, the injunction may also be sought by an association which is empowered by its constitution to protect consumer interests by giving information and advice, if it has standing to sue in private law. Such an association may also sue in cases falling under s 1 if the claim is based on conduct which affects essential consumer interests, be it the making of misleading statements about goods or services or any other act for the purposes of competition.
13(2) Liability in damages for the harm due to their contraventions is incurred

(1) under s 3, by anyone who knew or ought to have known that the statements he made were misleading. Editors, publishers, printers and distributors of printed periodicals are liable in damages only if they were aware that the statements disseminated were misleading;

(2) under ss 6, 6a, 6b, 8, 10, 11 and 12, by those whose contraventions were intentional or negligent.

For a further reference to the Law on Standard Contract Terms see above p 279.

Unlike the position in many other jurisdictions the French legal system does in principle make provision for the award of damages to consumer organisations suing in their own name. The background is outlined as follows in Fisch, 'European Analogues to the Class Action' (1979) 27 American Journal of Comparative Law 51, at 64–65:

> A potentially more dramatic authorization was made in 1973 in the consumer field, as part of a law enacting, inter alia prohibitions against various forms of price discrimination and deceptive advertising. Art 46 of the rather vaguely titled 'Law for the Guidance of Commerce and the Crafts' (commonly known as the Loi Royer) reads in part as follows:
>
>> '. . . (D)uly registered associations whose explicit charter object is to defend the interests of consumers may, if they are approved for that purpose, bring private actions before any jurisdiction with respect to acts causing harm directly or indirectly to the collective interest of consumers.'[1]
>
> An implementing decree contemplated by the provision requires a showing of longevity, activity and representativeness, along with certification by the Attorney General of the Court of Appeal for the district in which the organization has its seat;
>
> 1. Law No 73-1193, 27 Dec. 1973, 'd'orientation du commerce et de l'artisanat,' art. 46 JCP 1974.III.41167. The courts had previously denied the action civile in cases of improper pricing and sales practices, as affecting only the public interest, see Bourat et Pinatel ¶ 1000 at pp 941–2.

As the above extract indicates consumer organisations may institute proceedings only if they satisfy a number of criteria. Writing in *The Judicial and Quasi-Judicial Means of Consumer Protection* (EEC, 1976) (the Montpellier Symposium) Professor Jean Maury of the Montpellier Faculty of Law and Economics has summarised these as follows (footnotes omitted):

> A. The Royer Law and the implementing Decree of 17 May laid down the *conditions* that have to be met by consumers' associations claiming authorization. . . .
>
> The first requirement is that the association must show that on the date on which it submits its application for approval it has been in existence for not less than one year from the date on which it was founded. The required period is therefore quite relative; it is not a question of restricting the civil action to groups which have already provided evidence over a long period that they are effective and representative. . . .
>
> [It] is merely a question here of eliminating temporary groups set up, dare one say, ab irato, to deal with a particular offence and which would disappear as soon as their objective was achieved.
>
> Secondly, the law specifies that an association must be able to show that it has a sufficient number of members. Here again, it is a matter of eliminating bodies which are not altogether serious or representative. The criterion fixed in the decree of 17 May varies enormously, however, depending on the number of people involved in the movement concerned. In the case of national associations it is very precise: only associations with not less than ten thousand individually paid up members on the date on which the application is submitted may claim approval. . . .
>
> The requirement of ten thousand members is all the more exacting since there is an entirely different criterion for groups operating at regional or local level which is as flexible as the first is strict. Without going into greater detail the decree provides that the body 'shall show that it has a sufficient number of individually paid up members, having regard to the territory

in which its activities are carried out'. Here, everything is left to the subjective assessment of the Government department responsible for examining the application for approval or the court or tribunal competent to deal with the appeal against a refusal. The apparent contradiction is even greater since in general it should be much easier, using subjective methods, to decide on the representative nature of national associations than on that of purely local bodies. It must be noted, however, that in practice it is quite easy to get round the law: national organizations unable to show a membership of ten thousand are generally represented at local level by groups which they need only ask to institute civil proceedings in criminal cases on their behalf. . . .

The final requirement relates to the *objective* of the association, which must have taken upon itself the duty of protecting consumers. This objective must be *genuine*. The approving authorities must carry out a thorough investigation into the type of activities carried on by the various applicants so as to exclude groups (generally local groups) which use consumer protection as a screen while pursuing purely commercial objectives. The Royer Law had already required that associations applying for approval should be independent of all types of business or employment.

According to *Le Monde* (30 October 1983) there were then some fifteen national and one hundred local associations of which the most influential is the Union Federale des Consommateurs (UFC). This association publishes *Que Choisir* which contains information similar to that in the Consumers' Assocation *Which?*. It seems that in the ten years since the Loi Royer was enacted some 2,500 actions have been commenced. Some have attracted widespread attention in the press, for example the cases of the Kléber-Colombes VI2 tyres (which allegedly burst at speed); talc Morhange (and the associated death of some thirty-six babies); the 'cocktails amaigrissants' (slimming claims) and the SEITA advertising campaign ('International News' cigarettes: 'emplois abusif et délictueux de l'anglais'—or passing off).

The Loi Royer does not preclude the payment of damages to a consumer organisation to vindicate the collective interest which it represents. Yet organisations cannot claim damages on behalf of individual consumers as such. In practice awards of damages were once confined to a nominal one franc. Although this is no longer so, the sums awarded to consumer organisations as a 'partie civile' may not bear any relation to the illicit profits gained by the organisation against which it is intervening. Indeed there is something all too familiar about the criticisms of French commentators when they complain about 'les amendes derisoires' and the difficulty of establishing a 'prejudice collectif'. A good example is provided by l'Affaire des vins Margnat where wine had been marketed as in one-litre bottles when in fact the contents were only 98 centilitres. Three consumer associations acting as partie civile were awarded damages of 20,000 francs each, yet the distributors' profits were almost 14 million francs. This and other French examples suggest that the solution to the problem of protecting the collective interests of consumers has proved as elusive in France as it is likely to be in the United Kingdom. There are no obvious solutions to the problem.

For further examples and discussion of the Loi Royer see *Le Monde* 30 October 1983 and *Le Bilan de l'Action Civile des Associations de Consommateurs depuis 1973* (Institut National de la Consommation, 1983).

Questions

In principle it cannot be right that the marketer of wine in the *Margnat* case (see above) should profit from his activity and at the consumer's expense.

Yet it is very difficult to determine precisely how the matter should be tackled. Is it enough to ensure that the fine imposed in criminal proceedings is sufficiently high to remove the merchant's profit or should some attempt be made to recompense consumers whether individually or as a group? If so consider the possible solutions offered by the *Yellow Cab* case (above p 371) and the minimum damages statutes (above p 294).

Is it possible to place a meaningful evaluation on the 'collective prejudice' suffered by an organisation representing a group of consumers? If consumer groups were to be accorded *locus standi* by statute what criteria should they be required to meet if they are entitled

    (i) to sue only for declarations and injunctions or

    (ii) to sue also for damages to be distributed to their members?

Do you agree with Professor Maury when he seems to assume (see above p 383) that competent organisations must have a degree of permanence and that temporary groups will be set up *ab irato*? Would it be right to exclude an aircraft or drug disaster 'action group'?

CHAPTER 9

The consumer and codes of practice

Introduction

The main advantage of a self-regulating code is that it can be 'tailor made' to suit the problems most commonly met in any given industry. Consequently it can be more detailed and specific than is usually practicable even in subsidiary legislation and is inherently more flexible since parliamentary time is not needed to update it. Frequently codes provide an arbitration or conciliation procedure with the aim of providing a quick and cheap method of settling a dispute. This aspect is considered above at pp 320–324.

The disadvantages of such codes emanate from their essentially voluntary basis—they lack formal enforcement and are only binding on the members of the trade association in question. Often the very rogue operators that consumers complain about and that industry seeks to regulate are not members of the trade association and so are free to operate outside its ambit. Even if a trader is a member there is still controversy over the effectiveness of any sanction a trade association can enforce. Expulsion is the obvious course but may be thought to be too drastic a step or alternatively not considered much of a punishment in the first place. However the adverse publicity involved in expulsion can certainly be unwelcome to the majority of traders. More general criticism attacks the modest nature of guarantees and wide variations in the codes themselves, some going little further than 'accepting' existing common law or statutory liability. If the code is negotiated with the Office of Fair Trading, however, considerable pressure is brought to bear by the Office to make its provisions useful and relevant to known problems. Even an arbitration procedure enshrined in the code can, if the consumer loses at an oral hearing, involve him in costs comparable with or even exceeding those attaching to normal county court proceedings.

The Office of Fair Trading provides free leaflets which describe the codes negotiated by it in the 'For Your Protection' series. These are widely available from libraries and Citizens Advice Bureaux etc. Participating members are required prominently to display the appropriate code for the benefit of the public and usually will provide a copy of the code for inspection.

The statutory source of the Director General of Fair Trading's obligations in relation to codes is to be found in the Fair Trading Act 1973, s 124(3), which provides as follows:

Without prejudice to the exercise of his powers under subsection (1) of this section, it shall be the duty of the Director to encourage relevant associations to prepare, and to disseminate to their members, codes of practice for guidance in safeguarding and promoting the interests of consumers in the United Kingdom.

(The cross-reference to sub-section 1 relates to the powers of the Director to arrange for the publication of information and advice to United Kingdom consumers).

Although originating as something of a parliamentary afterthought this duty has grown into one of the Director's most important functions. Some twenty codes had been negotiated by early 1984. The importance of such voluntary codes and the problems they present have been recognised and discussed by successive Directors General of Fair Trading.

In 1975, in his Second Report, the then Director wrote at pp 9–10:

I believe that proposals to change the law should be made only when absolutely necessary because I have increasingly realised that extension of the law is no automatic panacea for consumer problems. It is all too easy to suggest measures for consumer protection which are either impractical or prohibitively costly. It is no use hankering after wide criminal prohibitions which are unenforceable; and if new laws are made there is still the problem of making sure that people know about them and understand them.

. . .

Voluntary action

I have always considered that one of my most important functions is the duty to encourage voluntary codes of practice, and I have been very pleased that during 1975 more and more sectors of trade have followed the lead given last year by The Association of Manufacturers of Domestic Electrical Applicances (AMDEA) and The Association of British Travel Agents (ABTA).

Some of the draft codes which come into my Office for scrutiny are excellent, some provide a basis for further work, and others need a good deal of effort before they merit consideration. Codes, to be effective, must be carefully constructed and precise. General expressions of goodwill towards the customer, or declarations of good intent, are not nearly enough. Once a code has been negotiated and publicised it cannot stop there. It must be kept up to date in the light of changing expectations and events, and it must be monitored to see if it is working effectively. The effectiveness of the AMDEA code is currently the subject of a market research study and the results are awaited with interest.

One criticism of codes has been that they are not subscribed to by those traders who most need to raise their standards. I am aware of this difficulty, but if the majority of traders will regulate their activities by voluntary means, the problem of dealing with the rest becomes much more manageable.

In his 1982 Report the Director referred more directly to some of the disadvantages of these codes. He wrote (at p 11):

There are many other areas of trade, industry and the professions where self-regulation keeps standards high and provides for redress of complaints. The fairly recent inception within the insurance industry of schemes under which policy-holders can seek independent adjudication on disputes with their insurers is a good example of voluntary action to meet an obvious need. Self-regulation can bring its own problems when it includes restrictions on competition, such as those preventing members of a profession from publicising their services, but there is no doubt that self-regulation can provide a good or even better safeguard to the public than legal sanctions or, as with the advertising industry, is complementary to a measure of legal regulation that would need to be extended if self-regulation was absent.

Unfortunately, some measures of self-regulation may prove in practice to be less effective than was hoped. This Office has a statutory obligation to promote self-regulatory codes of practice to be promulgated by trade associations on behalf of their members for the benefit of consumers. Twenty such codes have been promoted covering a variety of industries. Generally, they have been useful—they have encouraged those large numbers of traders who are capable of trading fairly to raise their standards, to persuade them that the higher expectations of growing numbers of the public need to be met and that this can make good commercial sense. But self-regulatory codes have two principal weaknesses. First, they cannot be enforced against non-members—this may be felt to put member-firms, who are likely to be the more responsible traders, at a competitive disadvantage. Secondly, codes are difficult to enforce, even against members.

(See also Borrie, 'Laws and Codes for Consumers' [1980] JBL 315).

An example of a code

The following provides a good example of the ground covered by a code of practice.

Principles for domestic appliance servicing (Association of Manufacturers of Domestic Electrical Appliances (1984)
The principles set out in this document are recommended for adoption by all organisations offering service for domestic electrical appliances sold in the UK

THE PRINCIPAL AIMS

* To offer service wherever possible within three working days at reasonable cost to the user.
* To carry adequate stocks of spare parts to meet reasonable demands within an acceptable period and to ensure minimum delay in their delivery. Manufacturers and suppliers should ensure that functional parts are available throughout the reasonable life of the product.
* To resolve complaints by users on any aspect of appliance servicing and provide a procedure for conciliation or simple arbitration when complaints cannot be settled directly between servicing organisations and the user.

IMPLEMENTATION OF THE AIMS

1 Function
1.1   It is the responsibility of an appliance servicing organisation to ensure that a prompt and effective service is carried out at a cost which is economic to both user and service organisations.

2   Communication with the user
2.1   Effective communication between the service organisation and the user is of vital importance. Service organisations must therefore be adequately staffed to receive and handle all requests for service and information.

The telephone
2.2   With the increasing use of the telephone it is imperative that sufficient incoming telephone lines and operators are available at the switchboard and that adequate extensions and control staff are employed at the service control centre to cope with the load. Promises to ring back must be fulfilled.

Letters
2.3   Written communications, whether requests or complaints, should be replied to quickly and fully. In the case of complaints, these must be thoroughly investigated and if this precludes immediate resolution of the problem a diplomatic telephone call is often better as an interim measure than a mere acknowledgement. The user must in any event be informed of the action being taken.

Complaint handling
2.4   Personnel handling user complaints should avoid a defensive or evasive attitude which will only serve to aggravate the situation as will protracted arguments in correspondence. Once justification or otherwise has been established, decisive action should be taken. Staff should have ready access to higher authority so that effective decisions can be speedily made and acted upon in the light of all circumstances and available information. Complaints should be referred to whatever management level is appropriate in the circumstance.
2.5   Users who are dissatisfied with the treatment of their complaint should be first advised to seek the opinion of either a Trading Standards Office, Consumer Advice Centre, Citizens' Advice Bureau or other similarly recognised body. The Association of Manufacturers of Domestic Electrical Appliances will, where the complaint concerns the service organisation of one of its Member companies, provide assistance and guidance, to such bodies to ensure a rapid and satisfactory conciliation and, when cases cannot be so resolved, users will be offered the facilities of the independent Arbitration Scheme for Domestic Appliance Servicings through which speedy and inexpensive judgement can be obtained via an independent arbitrator.

User information
2.6 All appliances should be clearly marked by brand name and model number. Explanatory literature should accompany an appliance and should contain accurate information on the following points:
(i) the correct installation of the appliance;
(ii) instruction on the use of the appliance;
(iii) availability and how to obtain service and spare parts;
(iv) the terms and conditions of the product's guarantee.
This literature should be made available to the user at the time and place of purchase.

User responsibility
2.7 Users should also be informed, in the product literature and at the point of sale, of their own responsibility which, if carried out, can do much to reduce service delays and avoid unnecessary visits by service engineers:
(i) they should ensure that the appliance is installed in accordance with the manufacturer's instructions (some appliances should only be installed by an authorised or competent organisation);
(ii) the appliance should only be used for the purpose intended and in accordance with the manufacturer's instructions;
(iii) they will be required to provide proof of the date of purchase, or previous repair, if claims are to be made under guarantee;
(iv) when requesting service; they should provide full details of the appliance, including the make and model number, and describe as accurately as possible the symptoms giving rise to the request. (See para 3.7)

3 Field service

User's telephone number
3.1 When a request is received for an engineer to make a house call, the user's telephone number should always be recorded where available.

Manpower levels and stocks of spare parts
3.2 Field Service manpower and service engineers' van stocks should be calculated and maintained at adequate levels to ensure prompt, effective and economic service:
(i) where a home repair service is required, the first visit should (wherever possible) be made within three working days from receipt of the request. In remote areas this objective may be difficult to achieve, but every effort should be made to meet it. Eighty per cent of all service repair jobs should be satisfactorily completed on this first visit;
(ii) adequate stocks of spare parts should be held in store to replenish van stocks as required;
(iii) where a subsequent visit is necessary, work should normally be completed within fifteen working days of the first visit. In cases where it becomes apparent that this is not possible, the customer should be promptly informed, at the same time being given the reason for the delay.

Referring a service request to a third party
3.3 In the interests of safety and to help ensure competent workmanship, only the manufacturer or the authorised representative may carry out service on some complex appliances. Where such is the case this must be made clear to retailers and users.
3.4 Where repair or service is not to be carried out by the organisation first receiving a request for service, the most effective and expeditious method should be used to transfer the request to the authorised service organisation and the user informed.

Appointment systems
3.5 If the customer requests a visit to his home, he should be offered an appointment preferably on an am-pm basis. If a time for the visit cannot be arranged when the request is made, the person responsible for making appointments should establish which days of the week are more convenient for the customer and subsequently fix a mutually acceptable arrangement. An alternative system may be used where it can be demonstrated that it satisfied the principles set out in this document.
3.6 Where, due to circumstances beyond control, the engineer is unable to keep an appointment, the customer should be advised wherever possible. An alternative appointment, using the same procedure as detailed in para 3.5, should be offered. Similarly users

should be encouraged to inform the service organisation if they cannot honour appointments.
3.7   The person arranging the appointment should also ask the customer to provide as much of the following information as possible in order to identify the appliance, expedite the repair and minimise costs:
   (i)   make of appliance
   (ii)   model number
   (iii)   serial number
   (iv)   description of fault
   (v)   name of user
   (vi)   address where the equipment is located (indicating any special difficulties)
   (vii)   whether it is an in-guarantee fault, out of guarantee fault or maintenance call.
3.8   Service control centres should monitor work loads and adjust as necessary to ensure the best possible use of engineers' time.

Charges
3.9   Where a minimum charge is made for work on the appliance or for call-out, it should be drawn to the customer's attention when he first seeks either a workshop repair or an appointment for a home visit. At the same time a customer should be informed of any payment arrangements required.

   Where there are no fixed charges for specific repairs in the user's home, the service engineer should, wherever possible, provide the user with an approximate estimate of the cost of the repair before undertaking the work. If requested, the customer will be given a written quotation for the repair. The user should be advised that, if it is necessary to dismantle the goods to prepare such a quotation, it may not be possible to return the goods to him in the previous condition and that a charge may be made. If a charge is to be made the customer must be informed when the quotation is requested.
3.10   Detailed invoices will always be provided. These will give details of the work carried out, of labour charges (showing rate per hour and/or time taken), of the cost of material used and VAT charges.

4   Workshop repairs
4.1   When an appliance is handed in for service, the person accepting the appliance should, when requested, provide the user with an approximate estimate of the cost of the repair and a date for collection or delivery after completion. Where available, the user's telephone number should be recorded for easy contact.
4.2   On workshop repairs the total time taken to complete the work will, in many cases, depend on the location of the workshop in relation to the point where the appliance is handed in. Workshop manpower and facilities should be calculated to achieve completion of 80 per cent of all repairs within five working days (workshop time) and the balance normally within fifteen days (workshop time).
4.3   If a promised completion date cannot be honoured the customer should be advised immediately.

5   Spare parts
5.1   To enable the correct spares to be ordered and carried in both store and van, the service organisation should ensure that it holds comprehensive spare-parts lists and service manuals covering those products on which service is undertaken. Similarly, it is the responsibility of the manufacturer or importer to ensure that service literature is adequate for the function and is issued to all authorised service organisations.
5.2   To enable service organisations to achieve the aims set out in this document, it is essential that manufacturers and importers promptly dispatch orders for spare parts. Spares should be made available from the time an appliance is first offered for sale to the public.

5.3   *Functional Parts.*   These are electrical and mechanical parts which are essential to the continued operation and safety of the appliance. Functional parts should be available for a period of not less than that indicated below after the date on which production of the appliance ceases:

Small appliances	5–8 years

Cleaners	
Direct acting space heaters	
Refrigerators and freezers	8 years
Spin and tumble dryers	
Wash boilers	

Cookers	
Dishwashers	
Washing machines	10 years
Water heaters (excluding immersion)	
Thermal storage space heating	15 years

These periods are recommended as the minimum acceptable for each appliance category. Some manufacturers and importers will continue to stock and supply spare parts for much longer periods. Additionally, the useful life of an appliance should be extended whenever possible by utilising standardised components and common parts incorporated in later models.

5.4 *Non-Functional Parts.*   These are appearance parts and other parts not essential to the operation or safety of the appliance. Non-functional parts should be made available for all types of domestic electrical appliance for a period of not less than four years after the model has ceased production.

5.5   The responsibility for ensuring that parts are available for adequate periods is equally shared at each point in the distributive chain. Where special arrangements exist between manufacturers, importers and dealers, there must be a clear understanding of the division of responsibility for stocking and the supply of spare parts. Service organisations should take particular care to ensure that they have an agreement with their suppliers about the guaranteed availability of spare parts.

6   Guarantees for repair work

All repairs, and any parts fitted during such repairs, will be guaranteed for a minimum of twelve months in the case of all appliances other than small appliances, when the period will be three months. Guarantees shall not detract from the legal right of the user.

7   Staff knowledge

7.1   All service staff and those handling complaints should receive full and regular training in matters pertinent to their work, including product knowledge, customer approach and the commercial policy of the organisation.

7.2   Personnel responsible for receiving and effecting requests for service should be expert in obtaining the correct information and establishing the nature of a reported fault, thus reducing wasted and unnecessary visits.

7.3   Adequate training must be available for service engineers—from the manufacturers where appropriate.

8   Executive information

8.   All servicing organisations should maintain an analysis of genuine complaints received from users concerning product reliability, servicing efficiency, charges, etc, as the resultant information can be used to take remedial action for improved user satisfaction in the future. Management of both manufacturer/importer and service organisation should maintain a high level of interest and involvement.

8.2   The Association of Manufacturers of Domestic Electrical Appliances will analyse those complaints referred to it for conciliation or arbitration and those where expert opinion has been provided by the Association. Results of such analysis will be published annually by the Association.

AMDEA conciliation of user complaints

The vast majority of appliance service calls are performed expeditiously and satisfactorily and those few which result in complaint are usually quickly rectified by the organisation concerned. A small miniority, however, produce problems both for the industry and for the user. The cause can often be a breakdown in communication between user and service department or serious disagreement on the need for repair, its effectiveness or cost, or the time taken to complete it. It is in these cases that AMDEA is prepared to intervene when its Members are involved or to give general help and guidance to other conciliation and arbitration bodies when comparison with accepted industrial and commercial practices becomes necessary. The following points describe the role AMDEA plays in resolving user complaints about domestic electrical appliances and their after-sales service.

1.   The AMDEA Principles for Domestic Appliances Servicing set out standards to be achieved by manufacturers and service organisations in order to ensure an efficient and effective service operation to the user.

2.   These principles are recommended by AMDEA for implementation by its Members either direct between the Member and the user or by agreement through authorised retailers and service organisations.

3.   The Principles are published and made generally available so that all sectors of the domestic appliance manufacturing, distribution and servicing industries together with consumer organisations, arbitration authorities and members of the public know what standards the Association recommends to ensure a satisfactory service to the user.

4.   The Association is available to Trading Standards Offices, Consumer Advice Centres, Citizens' Advice Bureaux and other similarly recognised bodies to assist with serious complaints in the following ways:

   (i)   by directing complaints to the correct manufacturer, importer or service organisation when difficulties in product or company identification are encountered;

   (ii)   by re-routing complaints to the appropriate person in multi-company structures;

   (iii)   by restoring communications with AMDEA members via a Director of the company concerned when a defensive or evasive attitude has been adopted;

   (iv)   by investigating cases where AMDEA members are appearing to fail to meet the standards set out in the Principles for Domestic Appliance Servicing;

   (v)   by giving impartial and expert opinion to authorised bodies on any aspect of appliance servicing to enable a reasoned judgement to be made on the justification or otherwise of a specific complaint.

5.   The Association has available an Arbitration Scheme for Domestic Appliance Servicing which is offered to users who require a speedy and inexpensive machinery for resolving complaints in which a claim against an AMDEA member is involved and which cannot be settled directly between the two parties concerned. This Scheme is based on the settlement of dispute using documents only and is handled by an independent Arbitrator appointed by the President or Vice-President of the Chartered Institute of Arbitrators. It requires a small deposit from the user and a nominal arbitration fee from the manufacturer. Details may be obtained from AMDEA.

6.   The Association is prepared to offer written or oral evidence on acceptable industrial and commercial practices to other arbitration authorities and the Courts when the activities of any organisation involved in the manufacture and servicing of domestic electrical appliances is being questioned.

7.   All user complaints referred to the Association for conciliation or arbitration are analysed in terms of appliance type, type of service organisation, nature of complaint, result of conciliation or arbitration and time taken to secure settlement. Results of the analysis are published annually.

Benefits and costs

In 1976 a survey on the working of the AMDEA code was carried out for the Office of Fair Trading by Audits of Great Britain Ltd. It showed a sharp decline in the numbers of complaints received by AMDEA's conciliation service from 251 in the third quarter of 1974 to 49 in the second quarter of 1976 and that in the main the code was being observed in such matters as the making and keeping of appointments, the customers involved describing themselves as 'satisfied' or 'very satisfied'. This suggests that self-regulating codes can give rise to a markedly improved rate of consumer satisfaction. But early criticism prompted the Director in his Annual Report of 1977 to place more emphasis on the monitoring of codes. He said:

> If performance is below par, I shall say so, loudly and publicly and, if necessary, will withdraw my blessing from a code which appears to be failing because traders are not observing it.

Results of monitoring exercises have been published periodically as 'Beeline' Special Edition Research Papers.

A helpful statement of the benefits and costs of codes of practice is contained in the following extract from a paper prepared by J. F. Pickering and D. C. Cousins.

'The Benefits and Costs of Voluntary Codes of Practice' by J. F. Pickering and D. C. Cousins (1982) (No 6) European Journal of Marketing 31, 35 (footnotes omitted)

The Impact on Consumers

From the point of view of consumer policy, the objective of a code of practice is to reduce consumer detriment which arises when consumers purchase goods or services which do not live up to their expectations prior to purchase and when they cannot obtain adequate redress to overcome their dissatisfactions and thereby to increase consumer welfare and total social welfare. While it is possible to describe theoretically the nature of such changes in consumer welfare and the influences upon it, it is much more difficult to provide an empirical measure to indicate even the direction of change, let alone the magnitude of any such changes. Even if we could effectively measure the changes it may be extremely difficult to determine their causes.

Most frequently, complaints statistics are used as an indictor of consumer dissatisfaction with purchases of goods and services. These are not, however, ideal measures for a number of reasons. In order that the data can be aggregated to give national statistics, the information collected tends to be rather generalised and may be subject to significant recording error. The propensity to complain may well vary between social class groups, regional locations and products. It appears that the lower social classes may be less prone to complain, perhaps because they are less articulate. There is evidence that the provision of consumer advice centres is positively associated with the number of complaints received, so regional variation in such provision may influence the recorded statistics of complaints. Finally, since complaining behaviour is not costless, but may be quite expensive, it is likely that complaints will be concentrated upon items of higher unit value and those problems where the costs of putting the matter right will be high for each individual affected. While such data may reflect those instances where consumer detriment *per unit* is large, it may not, therefore, identify those instances where *total* consumer detriment (average loss x the number of cases) is great.

Complaints data do not, therefore, necessarily offer any indication of the overall size of consumer welfare loss. In addition, it cannot be assumed that variations through time in the number of consumer complaints indicate a change in consumer welfare. Changes in the stock of advice centres or other points at which complaints can be lodged may influence the flow of complaints. Further, other exogenous changes such as increased awareness of the opportunity to complain or improved possibility of obtaining redress (both may be the consequence of an effective code of practice) may lead to an increase in complaints without any accompanying change in the actual level of consumer detriment. It may also be that propensity to complain varies with the business cycle, with a given problem assuming greater significance to consumers in times of recession than in times of boom.

This is not to suggest that consumer complaints data do not contain any useful information, but their limitations must be clearly recognised. It may be that a more effective way of measuring consumer welfare loss would be through a longitudinal series of consumer satisfaction/dissatisfaction surveys with random samples of households. For the time being at least, assessment of the impact of codes of practice on consumer welfare has to rely on a less quantitative approach (though individual aspects such as the proportion of traders adhering to particular requirements of a code can be more readily quantified and the trends observed). Indeed it is possible that a more qualitative approach will offer greater scope to assess the causal relationship between a code of practice and an apparent change in consumer welfare.

In assessing the impact on consumers of codes of practice generally we have drawn extensively on reports produced by the Consumers' Association and the monitoring studies carried out by, and for, OFT. In addition, we have collected our own questionnaire and personal interview information from traders and their trade associations. While the significance of the impact varies from trade to trade, certain features are apparent that seem to have fairly general validity.

There are five major ways in which consumers appear to have benefited from the development of codes of practice. First, there has been some increase in awareness among consumers of their rights and of the protection that can be available to them. Such awareness is an important first step in taking action should problems and difficulties arise and is a key element in strengthening the position of customers in the interests of achieving a more effective balance between suppliers and purchasers in the market place. Secondly, codes have reiterated legal prohibitions on certain types of undesirable practice, eg exclusion clauses, the use of 'worth and value' claims, etc. While it appears that some traders still continue to adopt such practices, the incidence is now much reduced and the consumer is thereby better protected. Allied to this is a third area of improvement—namely the provision of better information to consumers. This improvement relates to both the quantity of information provided and also its quality in terms of the clarity and relevance of the information. Advertising is more accurate and informative, statements of prices are clearer and there is a wider use of informative labelling in a number of trades.

Fourthly, an improvement in the quality of products and/or services supplied has been apparent. Greater attention has been paid to overcoming the causes of product failure. Improved handling of after-sales servicing and repairs has been achieved in some trades. Some monitoring studies have indicated that when consumer complaints concerning a particular category of products or services are analysed according to whether the trader complained about was a participant in a code of practice or not, the share of such complaints accounted for by code participants often tends to be well below their share of the total trade and to be falling through time. This is encouraging evidence though it may well be that those who now participate in the code already had superior performance compared to non-participants even prior to the adoption of the code. Finally, and perhaps of greatest significance to consumers, has been evidence that, when problems have arisen, complaints handling procedures by companies have been improved, arbitration and conciliation services (often through the trade association) have been made more readily available and consequently it has become easier for the consumer to obtain redress.

Each of these developments appears to be an unambiguous benefit to consumers so long as there have not been other, undesirable, developments consequent upon these changes. The position in respect of these improvements is still by no means ideal since it is clear that many traders fail to attain the code's standards in all respects. It is also difficult to attempt to indicate the value of the improvements in consumer welfare, but they do certainly appear to be real and worth having.

The question then arises as to whether there have been any additional costs or disbenefits to consumers as a result of codes of practice. One problem is the failure of some traders to adhere fully to the code. As we have already noted, some still attempt to exclude part of their liability and others do not attain the minimum performance standards required by the code. While in one sense this indicates a failure to maximise the potential benefits of a code, it may also be a source of disbenefit to consumers where the effect of a code and its publicity has been to lead consumers to expect that all code participants will achieve the minimum standards specified in the code. Wilful failure by participants in a code to achieve the standards set is an example of 'free riding' and may impose costs upon both consumers and other traders. Associated with this is a difficulty that arises where traders are reluctant to agree to arbitration or where they do not encourage consumers to use the conciliation and arbitration procedures available. Again, this may be more a case of benefits not maximised if consumers remain unaware of the facilities for arbitration, but those who are aware of the possibilities in this respect will incur extra costs in making use of them. There is also some concern about difficulties that have been experienced in using the arbitration schemes, particularly where it was felt the arbitration was not impartial; there was a failure to give reasons for the arbitration decision; there was difficulty in obtaining adequate information about the procedures; and the time taken to deal with the matter was protracted.

Costs may be imposed upon consumers where the effects of the code are to rule out particular mixes of quality/service and price which consumers might still wish to purchase. It could be, for example, that by specifying minimum performance standards in relation to product servicing a code rules out slower but less expensive servicing arrangements. Clearly it is important that consumers should have adequate knowledge about the price/service/quality mix they are choosing in order to make an informed and effective choice. Also, it would be unfortunate if concern over particular performance standards led to the use of prescriptive standards which specify not only *what* standards should be achieved, but also *how* they are to be achieved. This would again restrict some aspects of consumer choice and possibly hinder innovation by traders. So far such restrictions on consumer choice do not appear to have been significant costs as a result of codes of practice, but it is important to try to ensure that such undesirable consequences do not occur.

A further potential cost to consumers is the possibility of higher prices. There may be two main causes for such an outcome: the effects of additional costs incurred by traders as a result of a code and the effects of a code in possibly reducing competition in a particular trade. As we shall observe in more detail in the next section, the introduction of a code of practice does cause traders to incur some extra costs. However, it appears that these costs are frequently small in total size and certainly as a proportion of turnover. While some traders reported that costs and prices had risen as a result of a code of practice, it seems unlikely that this is a general and significant consequence. Perhaps of rather greater long-term significance in this respect is the extent to which the introduction of a code of practice has increased the cohesiveness of the traders and enhanced the status and role of the relevant trade association. It was widely held that one of the consequences of the Restrictive Trade Practices legislation was that trade associations were generally weakened. It would be ironic if the competition-restricting scope of trade associations was to be increased now as a result of action encouraged and formally approved by OFT! At present the risks seem greater than the reality, but the implications ought not to be overlooked.

While not a direct cost, as such, to consumers, we should also note that it appears that the improvement in quality and service and complaint handling has not had much effect on those traders that do not participate in codes of practice. This is of some concern as, while there are important exceptions, it is often the case that non-participants have lower standards in these respects. The benefit to consumers may have been less than might otherwise have been the case. It is possible that non-participants have not been greatly affected because the markets concerned are not as competitive as some fondly believe or that non-participants in a code tend to serve distinct market segments from those operating the code. Alternatively it may be the case that the existence of a code is not a significant influence in consumer choice of traders to patronise. Certainly, traders believe that codes of practice have not affected consumer choice of outlets. It may be that consumers consider the benefits offered by a code to be insufficient to influence their conduct in this respect. Overall, however, we think it is probably because knowledge among consumers about codes of practice remains very low (and will do so until publicity is considerably increased) that non-participants have largely been unaffected by their existence. Again, this suggests that if it is held that codes of practice are beneficial to consumers the welfare gains could be further increased by appropriate action in the future.

On balance, our view of the net welfare effects of codes of practice on consumers is that there have been some worthwhile, if unmeasurable, gains. There is scope for further increases in the benefits to consumers if appropriate enforcement and publicity action is taken. There are actual and potential welfare losses that have to be set against these benefits. Effective monitoring and enforcement can help to reduce these losses and generally they do not appear to be substantial at the present time.

Thus we may conclude that consumers have, on balance, benefited and received an increase in net welfare as a result of the introduction of codes of practice. There is potential to increase these net benefits still further.

. . .

Evidential status of codes

Codes are not generally legally enforceable. But provided a code of practice is sufficiently precise there is no objection in principle to its being given statutory form. This, as yet, is unusual in English law but one example is the Packers' Code which, by virtue of the Weights and Measures Act 1979 and regulation 19 of the Weights and Measures (Packaged Goods) Regulations 1979, is given the force of law. In other cases courts may be prepared to look at a code of practice as evidence of the better trade procedures followed in a sector of industry. It is even possible that failure to adhere to a particular provision of a code of practice by a member of the relevant trade association, who advertises that he is such, constitutes an offence under section 14 of the Trade Descriptions Act 1968 (false statements as to services), though this remains to be tested in the superior courts. (For a discussion of s 14 see below, p 500 et seq). The point is discussed by A. J. Street, 'Criminal Enforcement of Voluntary Codes of Practice' (1979) ITSA Monthly Review 63.

The Report of the Inter-Departmental Working Party on the 'Review of Legislation on False and Misleading Price Information' (Department of Trade, 1984) contains interesting proposals whereby a statutory code of practice might give practical guidance on the working of a generally worded prohibition against misleading 'bargain offers' claims. Extracts are printed below, pp 548–551. The same report discusses the possible evidential status of such a code as follows:

Review of legislation on false and misleading price information: Report of the Inter-Departmental Working Party (1984)

BASIC FEATURES OF A CODE OF PRACTICE

5.21   There remains room for debate about how much of the detailed support for the general prohibition should be in a code and how much in the legislation itself but we would expect a statutory code to deal with many of the practices recommended for control in Part II of this Report. Using these as a foundation, it would give guidance on the types of activity which would breach the general provision.

5.22   The status of a code in evidence is of prime importance. A number of existing statutory codes contain similar provisions on this. The codes are not themselves legally binding: thus, failure to observe any provision of a code does not in itself render a person liable to any proceedings. However, in any proceedings the code is admissible in evidence and, if any of its provisions appear to the judicial authority to be relevant to a question arising in the proceedings, it must be taken into account in determining that question. Section 47(10) of the Race Relations Act 1976 is an example.

5.23   An interesting variation on this pattern appears in the Health and Safety at Work etc Act 1974. In addition to the above general provisions, Section 17(2) of that Act lays down special provisions as follows:

> 'Any provision of the code of practice which appears to the court to be relevant to the requirement or prohibition alleged to have been contravened shall be admissible in evidence in the proceedings; and if it is proved that there was at any material time a failure to observe any provision of the code which appears to the court to be relevant to any matter which it is necessary for the prosecution to prove in order to establish a contravention of that requirement or prohibition, that matter shall be taken as proved unless the court is satisfied that the requirement or prohibition was in respect of that matter complied with otherwise than by observance of that provision of the code.'

This provision essentially places the onus on the accused to satisfy the Court that, although he did not observe the relevant provision of the code, the steps he took to comply with the law were as effective as if he had complied with that provision of the code.

5.24   Although we do not wish to suggest there is any similarity in subject matter between the two Acts we quote and statements about prices, we believe these examples illustrate the sort of status which could be given to a code of practice on the subject we are reviewing. In our view such a status would enable a code effectively to provide the necessary detailed backing to a general prohibition of false and misleading price information.

. . .

Trade association sanctions

The effectiveness of a code of practice depends at least in part on the willingness of the relevant trade association to impose sanctions where these prove to be necessary. Accordingly it is of interest to note that at least one code which is of major importance to consumers is backed by sanctions which have been applied in practice.

Association of British Travel Agents (Annual Report for the year ended 30 June 1983), p 14

Disciplinary Proceedings

The results of formal disciplinary proceedings by the Code of Conduct Committees during 1983 are summarised in the chart below with corresponding figures for previous years.

Findings	Tour Operators			Retail Agents		
	1975–81	1982	1983	1975–81	1982	1983
Dismissed	7	2	1	7	6	4
Reprimanded	15	2	6	16	4	3
Fined £50–£199	32	5	21	14	1	5
Fined £200–£499	28	8	4	19	9	19
Fined £500–£999	10	3	0	5	—	6
Fined £1000–£1499	1	1	1	1	2	1
Fined £1500+	5	—	—	1	3	2
TOTAL	98	21	33	63	25	40

Advertising

INTRODUCTION

Advertising provides an important example of an area which is controlled through codes of practice. The following extract is helpful as indicating the structure of control.

The self-regulatory system of advertising control—report of a working party, Department of Trade, 1980.

. . .

THE PRESENT STRUCTURE

11 Control of advertising in the United Kingdom currently takes two forms—statutory control and self-regulation—the one generally complementing the other. Some 80 separate statutes, orders and regulations are concerned with advertising to a greater or lesser extent. The main function of these provisions, insofar as they are concerned with the content of advertisements, is the negative one of restraining from publication limited categories of misleading or indecent advertisements. But many advertising parties do not lend themselves easily to precise definition and the voluntarily accepted codes of practice which underlie the self-regulatory arrangements are needed to complement and extend the legal constraints.

12 Codes of practice provide a positive approach to advertising control. They can reflect the spirit rather than the letter and can be readily reviewed and updated to take account of changing social conditions and public attitudes. They command a high degree of commitment from the business community and encourage high standards of advertising to the benefit of consumer and advertiser.

13 This report is confined to the principal self-regulatory control in the UK—that

administered by the Advertising Standards Authority in the print, cinema and poster media. The ASA was established in 1962. Since 1974 it has been financed by a surcharge of 0.1 per cent on the cost to the advertiser of advertisements (other than those appearing in the classified columns of the press). The funds generated by the surcharge are collected by the Advertising Standards Board of Finance (ASBOF), a body set up by the advertising business. The ASA is a company limited by guarantee and its directors are the Chairman and Council Members. The Chairman, presently Lord Thomson of Monifieth, is appointed by ASBOF which is obliged by its Articles of Association, before making any appointment, to consult in particular 'with the Department of Prices and Consumer Protection (or other equivalent Government Department) and with the Advertising Association'. The ASA Articles of Association provide that 'the Chairman shall not be engaged in the business of advertising' and shall be appointed only 'after consultation with the Members of the Council of the Authority'. Members of the Council, a majority of whom must also be independent, are appointed at the sole discretion of the Chairman who ensures that a balance is kept on the Council between the sexes, political persuasions, religious philosophies and social attitudes.

14.   It is present policy to ensure that the proportion of independent or industry members remains at the maximum permissible level of 2:1 . . . The preponderance of independent members on the Council as a whole (9 out of 13), the mode of appointment of both ordinary Council Members and Chairman, the separation of the funding body (ASBOF) from both the Advertising Association and ASA (which therefore is not involved in soliciting contributions or chasing up reluctant contributors), together with the nature of the levy itself are, in total, designed to ensure that the supervisory element in the control arrangements is isolated from any possibility of pressure from the advertising business to support its interests against those of the general public.

15.   The present arrangements provide for the Codes of Practice on which the control administered by the ASA is based to be drawn up by a committee of advertising interests, the Code of Advertising Practice Committee (CAP), in consultation with the ASA and trade and consumer interests. (There are two such Codes—the British Code of Advertising Practice (BCAP) and the British Code of Sales Promotion Practice.) Joint approval is required for all changes in the Codes but the ASA is effectively the senior partner, having the right to override CAP decisions. Thus, as will be seen from paragraphs 13 and 14 . . . final decisions on the content of the Codes and on other applications in contested matters are ultimately in the hands of a body with a majority of independent members.

16.   The Codes of Practice are enforced through action by the media. On the recommendation of the ASA, advertising space may be denied to or trading privileges withdrawn from those who contravene the Codes. The ASA also attaches importance to the deterrent value of adverse publicity resulting from its publication of regular reports on complaints in which details are given of offenders against the Codes.

BRITISH CODE OF ADVERTISING PRACTICE (EXTRACTS)

II GENERAL RULES

All advertisements should be legal, decent, honest and truthful

Legality
1.1   Advertisements should contain nothing which is in breach of the law, nor omit anything which the law requires.

1.2   Advertisements should not encourage or condone defiance of the law.

Decency
2   Advertisements should contain nothing which is likely, in the light of generally prevailing standards of decency and propriety, to cause grave or widespread offence.

2.1   The purpose of the Code is to control the content of advertisements, not to hamper the sale of products which may be found offensive, for whatever reason, by some people. Provided, therefore, that advertisements for such products are not themselves offensive, there will normally be no ground for objection to them in terms of this section of the Code (Cf II 4.2.2 and 4.2.6).

Honesty
3 Advertisements should not be so framed as to abuse the trust of consumers or exploit their lack of experience or knowledge.

Truthful presentation
4.1 All descriptions, claims and comparisons which relate to matters of objectively ascertainable fact should be capable of substantiation. **Advertisers and advertising agencies are required to hold such substantiation ready for production immediately to the CAP Committee or the Advertising Standards Authority.** They should compile a statement outlining substantiation and have it available *before* offering an advertisement for publication.

4.2 **Advertisements should not contain statements or visual presentations which, directly or by implication, by omission, ambiguity, or exaggeration, are likely to mislead the consumer about the product advertised, the advertiser, or about any other product or advertiser.**

4.2.1 Detailed guidance in regard to truthful presentation in certain specialised categories of advertising is given in Section IV–Health Claims and in the following Appendices:—

A. Truthful presentation—Miscellaneous guidance
B. Children
C. Slimming
D. Unacceptable claims—medical and allied areas
E. Credit and Investment Advertising
F. Mail Order advertising
G. Hair products
H. Cigarettes
J. Alcohol
K. Vitamins and Minerals

4.2.2 Value judgements are, by their nature, incapable of objective substantiation. For this reason, many general assertions made by advertisers, particularly about the quality of their products or those of their competitors, fail to command universal acceptance. This does not constitute a reason, within the terms of the Code, for objecting to such claims being made *provided there is no likelihood, as a result, that the consumer will be misled about any aspect of a product which is capable of being objectively assessed in the light of generally accepted standards of judgement.*

4.2.3 Obvious untruths or exaggerations, intended to catch the eye or to amuse, are permissible provided that they are clearly to be seen as humorous or hyperbolic and are not likely to be understood as making literal claims for the advertised product.

4.2.4 Where a substantial division of informed opinion exists, or may reasonably be expected to exist, as to the acceptability of any evidence which is required to substantiate a claim in an advertisement, that advertisement should neither state nor imply that the claim is universally true or that it enjoys universal support.

4.2.5 Where advertisement claims are expressly stated to be based on, or supported by, independent research or assessment, the source and date of this should be indicated. Where this is not possible, for whatever reason, such claims to independent support should not be made. Where a claim relating to research or testing is based on the advertiser's own work or work done at his request, it should be clear from the text of the advertisement that such is the basis of the claim.

4.2.6 It is not the wish of those responsible for the Code that its provisions should be used to hamper the legitimate exercise of the freedom of speech. Therefore, where what is advertised is a book or other product, the principal object of which is to give information about, or advocate the adoption of, unorthodox ideas, practices or opinions, provided the advertisement accurately represents the contents of the product, it will not normally be regarded as contravening the Code's rules on truthful presentation.

Prices
4.3 There is no general requirement that an advertiser should quote a price in his advertisement, except in the case of some advertisements addressed to children . . . but where he chooses to do so, the price should be stated clearly and unambiguously, should be that at which the product is available to the consumer and normally should include the prices of all fixed, non-optional extras.

Note. Section 4.4 concerning price comparisons, worth and value claims has been suspended on the introduction of the Price Marking (Bargain Offers) Order 1979 [see below p 541 et seq.]

Use of the word 'Free'
4.5   Products should not be described as 'free' where there is any direct cost to the consumer, other than the actual cost of any delivery, freight or postage. Where such costs are payable by the consumer, a clear statement that this is the case should be made in the advertisement.

    4.5.1 Where a claim is made that, if one product is purchased, another product will be provided free, the advertiser should be able to show that he will not be able immediately and directly to recover the cost of the 'free' product by such methods as (i) the imposition of packing or handling charges which would not otherwise be made, (ii) the inflation of the true cost of delivery, freight or postage, (iii) an increase in the usual price or a reduction in the quality or quantity of the product with which the 'free' product is offered.

    4.5.2 A trial may be described as free, although the consumer is expected to pay the cost of returning the goods, provided that the advertisement makes clear his obligation to do so.

'Up to . . .' and 'from . . .' claims
4.6   Claims which use expressions such as 'up to X miles per gallon' or 'prices from as low as Y' are not acceptable if there is a likelihood of the consumer being misled either as to the extent of the availability or as to the applicability of the benefits offered.

Testimonials, endorsements and related matters
4.7   Consumers are inclined to place more credence in independent assessments of advertised products than in what is said about them by the advertiser himself. For this reason, advertisers should take care when referring to or quoting from what has been said in commendation of their products to avoid, where none may properly be given, any impression of independent approval.

    4.7.1 No advertiser should make reference in an advertisement to any statement in commendation of his product by a person who is, or who is likely to be understood as being, independent of the advertiser, unless he has good reason to believe that the statement in question represents the genuinely held opinion of the person making it and is based upon a sufficient acquaintance with, and understanding of, the product in the form in which it is advertised.

    4.7.2 In particular, the advertiser should bear in mind that independent approval, even if extensive, does not itself amount to substantiation for the claims he may wish to make. He should therefore ensure that nothing appears in his advertisements in the form of a reference to, or quotation from, what has been said independently about his product, which cannot be separately substantiated, or which otherwise breaches any provision of the Code.

    4.7.3 If it is desired to picture or to quote directly, in an advertisement, a person who has expressed an opinion favourable to the advertised product, then that person should either be named (which is preferable) or identified by the use of initials. It is generally desirable that some indication be also given of the place of residence of the person concerned.

    4.7.4 Where an identifiable picture of a person is used in conjunction with a quotation commending an advertised product, the person shown should be the person whose words are quoted.

    4.7.5 Advertisers and their agencies should hold ready for inspection, by the Advertising Standards Authority or the Code of Advertising Practice Committee, the originals of any statements in commendation of an advertised product to which they refer or from which they quote in any advertisement. Such original texts should be signed and dated by the persons concerned and an address should be given at which they can be contacted for confirmation. Where a photograph of a person is used in an advertisement in conjunction with a quotation from what they have said, this also should be signed and dated . . .

    4.7.6 Where any commendation of a product, which an advertiser wishes to quote in his advertisement, inadvertently contains an expression which conflicts with the Code, the advertiser may, with the permission of the person whose words are quoted, amend the statement so as to remove the source of the conflict; provided that, in so doing, he does not distort the sense of the views originally expressed, and the version which eventually appears in the advertisement has the prior approval of the person whose words are quoted.

4.7.7 Where an advertiser wishes to illustrate an advertisement with a picture of actors or models, especially where these play the part of consumers of the advertised product, he should take care to ensure that any ostensible approval of the product shown or expressed by those pictured is understood for what it is and not confused with independent approval of the kind already considered. It should be remembered that where fictitious 'characters' are used in advertisements it may well be difficult, if the advertisement contains what appears to be direct quotations from them of a testimonial kind, for them not to be seen by the consumer as real people, especially if they are given individual characteristics such as 'names' and 'addresses' or are the subject of a detailed description or 'biography.' . . .

Identification of Advertisements

4.8 An advertisement should always be so designed and presented that anyone who looks at it can see that it is an advertisement, without having to study it closely.

4.8.1 Except as specifically provided there is no requirement under this Code that the name or address of an advertiser be given in his advertisements. The provisions of the Mail Order Transactions (Information) Order 1976 should be noted in regard to mail order advertisements.

4.8.2 When the name of an advertiser, as given in his advertisement, suggests a non-commercial organisation, he should be scrupulous in making clear any commercial motivation which may underlie his advertisement.

Guarantees, warranties and related matters

4.9 'Guarantee' and 'warranty' are used by advertisers in two distinct senses; to describe a formal written undertaking, often with legal force, to reimburse a purchaser for the cost of the product itself, or the cost of having it put right in the event of defects becoming apparent; and, more generally, as an alternative to 'promise' and without any formal (particularly legal) obligation being intended to be understood. Because the possibilities of confusion are considerable, the advertiser is under an obligation to be as clear as possible as to the sense in which he uses these words.

4.9.1 Advertisements should not contain any reference to 'guarantees' or 'warranties' which take away or diminish any rights which would otherwise be enjoyed by consumers; purport so to do; or may be understood by the consumer as so doing.

4.9.2 Where an advertisement expressly offers, in whatever form, a guarantee or warranty as to the quality, life, composition, origin, duration, etc of any product, the full terms of that guarantee should be available in printed form for the consumer to inspect—and, normally, to retain—before he is committed to purchase.

4.9.3 The duration of any such formal guarantee should be stated in the advertisement and, if the availability of the guarantee is subject to a substantial limitation, an indication of its nature (eg parts only) should also be given.

4.9.4 Where a phrase such as 'money back guarantee' is used, it will be assumed that a full refund of the purchase price of the product will be given to dissatisfied consumers, either throughout the reasonably anticipated life of the product or within such period as is clearly stated in the advertisement, provided that the consumer is, where appropriate, willing to return the unsatisfactory product to the advertiser. . . .

4.9.5 There is no objection to the use of 'guarantee' etc in a colloquial sense provided there is no likelihood of a consumer supposing that the advertiser in using the word is expressing a willingness to shoulder more than his purely legal obligations.

All advertisements should be prepared with a sense of responsibility to the consumer and to society

Fear

5 Advertisements should not without justifiable reason play on fear . . .

Superstition

6 Advertisements should not exploit belief in superstitions by making any promise that the purchase of the advertised product can ensure good fortune.

Violence
7   Advertisements should neither encourage nor condone violent or anti-social behaviour.

Protection of Privacy and Exploitation of the Individual
8   Advertisements should not, except in the circumstances noted below, portray or refer to any living persons, by whatever means, unless their express prior permission has been obtained. This requirement applies to all persons, including public figures and foreign nationals. Advertisers should also take care not to offend the religious or other susceptibilities of those connected in any way with deceased persons depicted or referred to in any advertisement.
    This ruling does not apply to the following:
    8.1 The use of crowd or background shots in which individuals are recognisable, provided that neither the portrayal, nor the context in which it appears, is defamatory, offensive or humiliating. An advertiser should, however, withdraw any such advertisement if a reasonable objection is received from a person depicted.
    8.2 Advertisements for books, films, radio or television programmes, press features and the like, in which there appear portrayals of, or references to, individuals who form part of their subject matter.
    8.3 Those occasions on which the reference or portrayal in question is not inconsistent with the subject's right to a reasonable degree of privacy and does not constitute an unjustifiable commercial exploitation of his fame or reputation.

Safety
9   Advertisements should not, without justifiable reason, show or refer to dangerous practices or manifest a disregard for safety. Special care should be taken in advertisements directed towards or depicting children or young people.

Children
10   Advertisements addressed to children or young people, or likely to be seen by them, should not contain anything, whether in illustration or otherwise, which might result in their physical, mental or moral harm, or which exploits their credulity, their lack of experience, or their sense of loyalty. *For further guidance see Appendix B.*

All advertisements should conform to the principles of fair competition as generally accepted in business

Comparisons
11   Advertisements containing comparisons with other manufacturers or suppliers or with other products, including those where a competitor is named, are permissible in the interest of vigorous competition and public information, provided they comply with the terms of this section and the following section of the Code (Denigration).
    11.1 All comparative advertisements should respect the principles of fair competition and should be so designed that there is no likelihood of the consumer being misled as a result of the comparison, either about the product advertised or that with which it is compared.
    11.2 Where an advertisement makes a comparison, whether explicitly or implicitly, it should be clear with what the comparison is being made.
    11.3 The subject matter of a comparison should not be chosen in such a way as to confer an artificial advantage upon the advertiser or so as to suggest that a better bargain is offered than is truly the case. Particular care requires to be taken:
    11.3.1 in comparisons between branded and unbranded products and between natural products and substitutes for them.
    11.3.2 in price comparisons. Comparisons should be made between prices which are based upon or equated to the same unit of measurement, so that the consumer can easily compare them. . . .

Denigration
12   Advertisements should not unfairly attack or discredit other products, advertisers or advertisements directly or by implication.

Exploitation of Name or Goodwill
13   Advertisements should not make unjustifiable use of the name or initials of any firm, company or institution nor take unfair advantage of the goodwill attached to the trade name or symbol of another firm or its product or the goodwill acquired by its advertising campaign.
    13.1 Attention is drawn to the provisions governing the use of the Royal Arms and Cypher, and the Queen's Award to Industry. (Details may be obtained from the

offices of the Lord Chamberlain and the Queen's Award to Industry respectively.)
13.2 The right to the use of the Royal Warrant is not to be understood as implying personal endorsement or use of the product by HM The Queen (or such other Royal person on whose behalf the warrant is issued) and no such suggestion may be made or implied in any advertisement.

Imitation

14 Advertisements should not be so similar to other advertisements in general layout, copy, slogans, visual presentation, music or sound effects as to be likely to mislead or confuse.

(It is understood that the Code is under review although it is unlikely that the fundamental principles will be altered). Further issues of general importance and recommendations for additional controls are pointed to in the following extracts from the Department of Trade report to which reference was made above.

The self regulatory system of advertising control—report of a working party, Department of Trade, 1980

. . .

THE SCOPE OF THE WORKING PARTY'S DELIBERATIONS

17 The Working Party have concentrated on considering improvements in the machinery for dealing with misleading advertisements in the print, cinema and poster media. (They have not, however, concerned themselves with advertisements in any of these media for ethical medicines. These are subject to statutory control under the Medicines Act and to a Code of Practice which is administered by the Association of British Pharmaceutical Industry. Neither have they examined the separate controls exercised over mail order catalogues and certain other promotional techniques . . .) It follows that no attempt has been made to consider more general issues such as the role of advertising in the economy or any general effects upon culture and society which the totality of advertisements may have.

18 The Working Party recognised the existence of public interest and concern about issues of taste and morals in advertisements; and they noted that the British Code of Advertising Practice contained provisions for applying sanctions to advertisements that caused widespread or grave offence. They were informed by OFT that a very small proportion of advertisements surveyed (see paragraph 20) raised any apparent problems in this regard. They concluded unanimously that any attempt to impose further legal restraints in this area would raise difficult problems of legal policy and of definition; and that external control would inevitably raise the spectre of censorship. There was also the danger that any attempt to impose more stringent control in this area upon advertisements alone would cause resentment in the advertising business which considers that, in matters of public decency, the standards of advertisements are already substantially higher than those of much of the editorial content of newspapers and magazines (and of many of the feature films) in the context of which advertisements are seen.

THE WORKING PARTY'S OBJECTIVES

19 Legal and self-regulatory systems of control each have their particular strengths and weaknesses. In considering how the arrangements for advertising control which apply to the print, cinema and poster media could be improved in their application to misleading advertisements, the Working Party have been particularly concerned to ensure that any reinforcement of present self-regulatory controls should be approached in ways which will
  (a) permit the continuance of the flexibility inherent in codes of practice;
  (b) maintain the existing nexus of arrangements which comprise the self-regulatory control system;
  (c) foster the co-operation of the advertising industry on which the successful operation of the self-regulatory system will continue to depend.

REPORT BY THE DIRECTOR GENERAL OF FAIR TRADING

20 Relevant to the Working Party's task was the Report of the Director General of Fair Trading on the self-regulatory system which was published in November 1978. Although the

report covered the whole field of advertising subject to the ASA control arrangements, it concentrated on the problem of misleading advertising. In general, the DGFT found that the strength of the self-regulatory system lay in the flexibility of operation of its Codes of Practice; in the fact that some advertisements could be vetted in advance; and in the willingness of those covered by the codes to obey their spirit without prompting. The principal deficiencies identified by the DGFT were the difficulty of dealing, by means of self-regulatory sanctions, with those who operated entirely outside the ambit of the trade associations which sponsored and supported the Code of Advertising Practice and the absence from the self-regulatory system of a sanction which was both immediate and compelling in its effect.

21   The DGFT concluded that there was no need to create a wider framework of statutory advertising control but considered that some measure of legislative reinforcement of the self-regulatory system was necessary. He recommended that he should be given a power to apply to the High Court for an injunction in any case where he considered that an advertisement was likely to deceive, mislead or confuse with regard to any material fact. Other recommendations which he thought would make the practical operation of the ASA's system more effective included:

(i)   reinforcement of the BCAP in relation to coverage of non-media advertising—ie point of sale material and sale brochures;

(ii)   some strengthening of the ASA Council;

(iii)   a revised complaints procedure with a strictly limited time period allowed for the substantiation of claims by the advertiser;

(iv)   the placing of greater emphasis on the monitoring and pre-vetting activities of the ASA;

(v)   action to increase public awareness of the place of the CAP Committee in the system of control and the need to publicise their findings;

(vi)   consideration to be given to additional sanctions—eg fines and corrective advertising.

. . .

ASSESSMENT OF THE DEFICIENCIES OF THE SELF-REGULATORY ARRANGEMENTS AND THE CASE FOR REINFORCEMENT

22   Against the background and findings of the DGFT's Report, the Working Party first considered possible weaknesses both in the coverage of the present arrangements, and in the effectiveness of the sanctions. They noted in particular that:

(a)   the self-regulatory arrangements do not embrace all forms of non-broadcast advertising;

(b)   in principle the ASA's sanctions can be applied effectively only in those cases where either the advertiser and/or the media subscribe to self-regulation;

(c)   self-regulation does not always permit the application of effective sanctions for dealing with those who are determined either to breach the Code or to defy a decision of the ASA: neither can immediate preventive action be taken against major misleading advertising abuses.

The Working Party agreed that this indicated that there was scope for improvement, though the AA did not think that the scale of the abuse identified by the DGFT . . . called for any statutory strengthening of the self-regulatory arrangements.

THE EEC IMPLICATIONS

23   The Working Party also took into account the implications of EEC activities on the subject of misleading and unfair advertising. The Commission presented a draft Directive to the Council of Ministers in March 1978. This draft was amended in July 1979 to take account of a recommendation by the European Parliament that there should be an effective choice of enforcement procedures—either through direct application to a court of law or through administrative arrangements operated by a recognised authority. However, . . . while the draft moves towards recognising the effectiveness of self-regulatory arrangements it continues, even if the administrative route is followed, to insist upon the right to demand judicial review of the decision of the administrative authority.

24   If the present draft of the proposed Directive were to be imposed, unchanged, on the current UK self-regulatory system of advertising control, there would be two consequences. Either the ASA would have to be constituted as a statutory body which would render impossible the continued existence of self-regulation in this country (and there would be other legislative consequences); or, the UK would have to introduce new legislation to allow access to the courts for detailed matters of advertising control. The scope, weight and extent

of this legislation would not be acceptable to the UK Government. In reaching this judgement the Working Party have taken account of the views expressed by the European scrutiny committees of both Houses of Parliament. The Working Party accordingly looked for remedies which would be consistent with existing United Kingdom law and practice and, at the same time, would meet the essential objectives of the EEC proposals—judicial review of arrangements to provide protection against unfair and misleading advertising.

PRINCIPAL OPTIONS FOR STRENGTHENING THE SELF-REGULATORY ARRANGEMENTS

25 Four main options intended to meet the possible weaknesses in paragraph 22 were considered by the Working Party:
    (a) statutory recognition of Codes of Practice;
    (b) extension of the Trade Descriptions Act 1968;
    (c) the DGFT's Injunctive Proposal;
    (d) prohibition orders.

Statutory recognition of Codes of Practice
26 The possibility of giving the Codes of Practice the force of law was considered first. This would require their statutory recognition and therefore prior Ministerial approval. Such a system would thus no longer be genuinely self-regulatory. The main purpose of this approach would be to encourage compliance with the Codes by those who do not subscribe to the existing voluntary arrangements. But if infringements of the Codes became an offence, the Codes would have to be so phrased that breaches could be seen sufficiently clearly to stand up to legal scrutiny. The text of the Codes would therefore become more legal and concentrate more on the letter than the spirit of control. Nor could the text of the Codes, if they became statutory regulations, be amended so readily and the flexibility of self-regulation would thus be reduced. This would be unfortunate. The Codes administered by the ASA are the most highly developed among a growing number of codes governing trade practices. Whether or not the notion of the statutory recognition of codes is accepted or rejected for other industries, the Working Party agreed that in the context of the control of the content of advertising, statutory recognition would be inappropriate. It would risk undermining what was commonly agreed to be an excellent example of self-regulation without substituting a mechanism which would more effectively protect the public interest.
27 An alternative form of statutory recognition would involve conferring upon the ASA Codes a status analogous to that of the Highway Code (that is the status of an officially recognised manual of good practice with persuasive authority in court proceedings). But this course would still require Ministerial approval of the Codes. It might also lead to conflict between the rulings of the courts and of the ASA on particular matters and would tend to undermine the authority of the ASA and the credibility of the self-regulatory arrangements. For these reasons the Working Party concluded that it should seek alternative measures.

Extension of the Trade Descriptions Act 1968
28 The second possibility considered by the Working Party was extension of the Trade Descriptions Act 1968 so that its provisions might more closely parallel those of the Codes and give them legal backing. The Working Party concluded that there were major objections to this course, namely that:
    (a) many of the provisions of the Code of Advertising Practice are framed in general terms, such as 'all advertisements should be legal, decent, honest and truthful' or 'all advertisements should be prepared with a sense of responsibility to the consumer'. Such general provisions would not be appropriate in the criminal law;
    (b) because many of the criminal courts are overburdened, prosecutions under the Act do not always receive high priority. In practice therefore there would be no certainty that proceedings under the Act would be sufficiently speedy to provide effective support for the existing self-regulatory arrangements.

The DGFT's injunctive proposal
29 The third possibility considered by the Working Party was based upon the DGFT's proposal to institute an injunctive procedure to restrain the publication of an advertisement. The proposal would require the prior creation by statute of a general duty which would be owed by the advertising industry at large not to publish an advertisement which was likely to deceive or mislead with regard to any material fact. The Director General would then be empowered to seek from the courts an order to prevent the publication of a particular advertisement when in his view publication would constitute a breach of the general duty.

Failure to obey such an order would be a contempt of court and punishable as such, the penalty most commonly imposed being a fine.

30   The objective of the procedure would be:

   (a) to provide a practical reinforcement of the ordinary machinery of the ASA where this had been frustrated or was unlikely to be effective (for example, because the offender did not subscribe to it or was not prepared to submit to a particular ruling by it); and

   (b) to provide a speedy remedy. It is obviously important to stop a misleading advertisement with minimum delay. (The existing powers of the DGFT under Part III of the Fair Trading Act 1973 relate to repeated infringements and cannot, therefore, be used speedily.) When, therefore, the DGFT used the power he would generally be seeking an interim injunction to prevent publication.

31   The legal rules governing the granting of interim injunctions are such that the DGFT would be successful only where he could convince the court that a serious breach of the general duty was involved and that the likely detriment to the public was great compared with the inconvenience and loss to those against whom the injunction was sought. Although in some cases the DGFT might find it difficult to satisfy these tests, it would be inconsistent with the provision of a review by the courts to change the rules specifically to disadvantage the advertiser. The Working Party agreed that this did not invalidate the proposal. They were satisfied that the remedy would be one of last resort and thus only sought in clear-cut cases. The DGFT would necessarily have to consider carefully his prospect of success in persuading the court before taking proceedings. The Working Party believed, nonetheless, that the existence of the power, together with the adverse publicity which would follow action by the DGFT, would cause advertisers to think hard before risking a breach of the general duty not to mislead or deceive.

32   The creation of the general duty would also enable the DGFT to make use of his powers under Part III of the Fair Trading Act 1973 by seeking assurances from advertisers who persistently breached the duty that they would refrain from continuing with that course of conduct. (The use of Part III would not apply to advertising directed at business consumers and amendment of the Act would be needed to make it applicable to them.)

33   The AA were not convinced of the need for legislative reinforcement *per se*. The ASA on the other hand agreed that such reinforcement would assist it to operate existing procedures with greater effect, and to extend and strengthen its enforcement of the Codes. As a whole, the Working Party recognised the merit of a procedure which they believed would both sufficiently reinforce the self-regulatory arrangements of advertising control and meet the essential objectives of the EEC proposals. Accordingly they recommend to Ministers the adoption of the DGFT's proposals for an injunctive procedure.

34   The Working Party further recommended that the general duty referred to in paragraph 29 should extend to advertising by Government Departments as it would to the public and private sectors. It would not, however, apply to those categories of advertising which for reasons concerned with the freedom of expression are not covered by the existing Code, mainly those concerned with matters of political, religious or social controversy.

Prohibition orders

35   The Working Party considered a fourth possibility which has much in common with their preferred solution—the injunctive procedure described above. This would also rest on the creation of the general duty described in paragraph 29. The DGFT would be empowered to issue an order prohibiting the publication of an advertisement where there was a breach of the general duty and where the likely detriment to the public was great compared with the likely loss and inconvenience to the advertiser. The sanction for any breach of the order would be a fine—imposed by a court after application by the DGFT. The power would need to be accompanied by a right of appeal against decisions of the DGFT to make orders—either to the Secretary of State or to the courts.

36   The prohibition order procedure would allow an administrative authority (the DGFT) to take immediate action to control the content of advertisements subject to review by an appellate body, whereas the injunctive procedure rests on direct control by judicial decision on the DGFT's application. The practical effect of the issue of a prohibition order would, however, be the same as for a *successful* application for an injunction. The power in the hands of the DGFT to issue prohibition orders would undoubtedly be a speedy and effective remedy. It would be specially valuable in dealing with flagrant breaches of the general duty by small advertisers not subscribing to the ASA arrangements in localised campaigns where the overall damage to the public might not be regarded as sufficiently great to justify the seeking of an injunction. On the other hand, because an advertiser would invariably suffer damage at the time the publication of his advertisement was prevented, the procedure would be

weighted against the advertiser unless an equally speedy appeals procedure could be provided. Moreover, the need to provide for the enforcement of the prohibition order would require the creation of a new criminal offence (although there are precedents for this in the Consumer Safety Act 1978 and in the Estate Agents Act 1979).

37 The Working Party noted that prohibition orders would, like the injunctive procedure, be a remedy of last resort to be used where the ordinary machinery of the ASA had been frustrated or was unlikely to be effective, or where a speedy remedy was needed. While it would be a more certain remedy, it would be more arbitrary and would move beyond reinforcing self-regulation towards a more direct control. This would be contrary to the objectives as set out in paragraph 19.

The IBA

38 The Working Party considered whether the proposed new general duty and linked powers to obtain an injunction should embrace the control arrangements operated by the IBA—though any review of these was agreed to be outside the Working Party's terms of reference. It was recognised that adequate statutorily-based control arrangements currently existed for broadcast advertising, and that the main task of the Working Party was to consider the case for strengthening the self-regulatory system of control. But it was also recognised that the proposed injunctive procedure could have implications for broadcast advertising—and for any new developments in the electronic media, eg Viewdata. The Working Party agreed that, if their recommendation to implement the DGFT's injunctive proposal was accepted by Ministers, any implications for broadcast advertising would need further investigation.

OTHER POSSIBLE IMPROVEMENTS

39 The Working Party also considered the following possible improvements to the existing control arrangements, referred to by the DGFT in his report.

Corrective advertising

40 The Working Party considered the case for introducing corrective advertising—that is a requirement on the advertiser to publish, at his own expense, corrections of false or misleading statements in his previously published advertisements.

41 In theory, corrective advertising seems an obvious, even attractive, sanction—fitting the punishment to the crime. But the development of corrective advertising in the United States (which probably has more experience of applying this form of remedy than any other country) has shown it to be difficult to apply in practice. The Federal Trade Commission has been successfully challenged on the grounds that it has not been able to show:

(a) that the consumer believed the false claim;
(b) that the false claim affected the consumer's purchasing decision; and
(d) that the consumer persisted in believing the false claim after the particular advertisement had been stopped.

. . .

42 United States experience suggests that it is difficult to estimate the overall damage to the consumer who has been exposed to false advertisements; but unless some reasonable estimate can be made, the financial penalty imposed on the advertiser could be disproportionately large. Moreover, our legal system and institutional arrangements differ greatly from the United States'. The legal compulsions which it would be necessary to place on advertisers to publish corrections would not be consistent with and would be likely to destroy the self-regulatory arrangements in the United Kingdom. The Working Party were therefore not convinced of the case for introducing a statutory scheme of corrective advertising in the United Kingdom.

43 While the Working Party were not persuaded of the case for legally-imposed corrective advertising they agreed that substantial benefits would accrue if the self-regulatory arrangements were to extend ASA's present practices of publishing details of complaints which they have upheld in their monthly reports and of issuing *ad hoc* press releases dealing with particularly important cases. They believed that there was also scope for the ASA to develop the practice of securing corrective action including, where appropriate, corrective statements being made direct to individuals who had responded to misleading advertisements. They also considered that the ASA should intensify its efforts to persuade advertisers and advertising agencies to take advantage of the CAP Committee's willingness to advise on advertisements before publication, and that the Code should be reviewed with the intention of extending the use of disclosures and disclaimers in advertising messages in the interests of consumers. (Current examples of disclosures and disclaimers are the requirements to show in

advertisements for toys and games if the cost of batteries is additional to the stated price, and to state in advertisements for slimming aids that these can only aid slimming as part of a calorie controlled diet.)

Fines
44   The DGFT suggested that consideration should be given to fining advertisers, agencies and publishers for persistent breaches of the Code or for any failure quickly to observe CAP Committee or ASA Council decisions. Some trade associations do indeed impose fines on their members as a measure to enforce codes of practice. The ASA, however, is not a trade association and could have no recourse to this form of penalty. The AA is a federation of trade associations and could not impose fines on these associations in respect of individual offenders. The imposition of fines would therefore have to be effected by the individual trade associations and this is a matter which they may wish to consider.

Redress for individual consumers
45   The Working Party considered the problem of redress for individual consumers who suffered economic loss because of misleading advertisements. Consumers can suffer loss, for which they cannot currently insist upon compensation, either if they spend time and money following up an advertisement which proves misleading, or if they buy a product relying on misleading information contained in an advertisement and the advertiser is not the retailer. (Many of the losses which individual consumers suffer as a result of misleading advertisements may not be large enough to justify the trouble and expense of legal proceedings; and in many other cases there may be no legal basis for any claim.) The Working Party agreed that in principle it was desirable, nonetheless, for consumers who suffer loss as a result of misleading advertisements to be compensated. The Working Party believed that the best way forward would be to explore the possibilities of setting up some conciliation and arbitration scheme run by advertisers. The ASA felt that it was not the appropriate body to manage such a scheme, since its role as arbiter of the content of advertisements might be prejudiced if it had to become involved in adjudicating upon individual consumer claims for redress. The AA representatives believed that this was a matter exclusively for advertisers rather than for the advertising business as a whole and, therefore, asked that it be referred to the Incorporated Society of British Advertisers (ISBA). It was decided, therefore, that an exploration of this subject should be carried out outside the Working Party, and discussions are taking place, under the chairmanship of the Office of Fair Trading, between the Incorporated Society of British Advertisers, the Advertising Standards Authority and the National Consumer Council.

. . .

RECOMMENDATIONS

47   The Working Party recommend that:
  (i)   The injunctive procedure proposed by the DGFT should be introduced and based on a new statutory duty not to publish an advertisement likely to deceive or mislead with regard to any material fact. They consider that such a measure should adequately reinforce the self-regulatory system of control and meet the essential objectives of the EEC proposals on the control of advertising (paragraph 33).
  (ii) The statutory duty referred to in (i) above should extend to advertising by Government (paragraph 34).
  (iii) The ASA should develop their procedures for publishing details of complaints which have been upheld, and for securing corrective action including, where appropriate, corrective statements being made to affected persons (paragraph 43).
  (iv) Advertising Trade Associations may wish to consider further the imposition of fines on their members to enforce codes of practice (paragraph 44).
  (v)   the OFT should explore with the appropriate organisations the creation of a conciliation and arbitration scheme to secure redress for individual consumers (paragraph 45).

. . .

THE EEC DIMENSION

Reference is made in the Report of the Working Party extracted above to the then draft EEC Directive Concerning Misleading and Unfair Advertising. This draft has now progressed to a final adopted directive, the first to be agreed under the European Community's Consumer Programme. Its text reads as follows:

Council directive of 10 September 1984 relating to the approximation of the laws, regulations and administrative provisions of the Member States concerning misleading advertising (84/450/EEC)

THE COUNCIL OF THE EUROPEAN COMMUNITIES

Having regard to the Treaty establishing the European Economic Community, and in particular Article 100 thereof,

Having regard to the proposal from the Commission[1],

Having regard to the opinion of the European Parliament[2],

Having regard to the opinion of the Economic and Social Committee[3],

Whereas the laws against misleading advertising now in force in the Member States differ widely; whereas, since advertising reaches beyond the frontiers of individual Member States, it has a direct effect on the establishment and the functioning of the common market;

Whereas misleading advertising can lead to distortion of competition within the common market;

Whereas advertising, whether or not it induces a contract, affects the economic welfare of consumers;

Whereas misleading advertising may cause a consumer to take decisions prejudicial to him when acquiring goods or other property, or using services, and the differences between the laws of the Member States not only lead, in many cases, to inadequate levels of consumer protection, but also hinder the execution of advertising campaigns beyond national boundaries and thus affect the free circulation of goods and provision of services;

Whereas the second programme of the European Economic Community for a consumer protection and information policy[4] provides for appropriate action for the protection of consumers against misleading and unfair advertising;

Whereas it is in the interest of the public in general, as well as that of consumers and all those who, in competition with one another, carry on a trade, business, craft or profession, in the common market, to harmonize in the first instance national provisions against misleading advertising and that, at a second stage, unfair advertising and, as far as necessary, comparative advertising should be dealt with, on the basis of appropriate Commission proposals;

Whereas minimum and objective criteria for determining whether advertising is misleading should be established for this purpose;

Whereas the laws to be adopted by Member States against misleading advertising must be adequate and effective;

Whereas persons or organizations regarded under national law as having a legitimate interest in the matter must have facilities for initiating proceedings against misleading advertising, either before a court or before an administrative authority which is competent to decide upon complaints or to initiate appropriate legal proceedings;

Whereas it should be for each Member State to decide whether to enable the courts or administrative authorities to require prior recourse to other established means of dealing with the complaint;

Whereas the courts or administrative authorities must have powers enabling them to order or obtain the cessation of misleading advertising;

Whereas in certain cases it may be desirable to prohibit misleading advertising even before it is published; whereas, however, this in no way implies that Member States are under an obligation to introduce rules requiring the systematic prior vetting of advertising;

Whereas provision should be made for accelerated procedures under which measures with interim or definitive effect can be taken;

Whereas it may be desirable to order the publication of decisions made by courts or administrative authorities or of corrective statements in order to eliminate any continuing effects of misleading advertising;

Whereas administrative authorities must be impartial and the exercise of their powers must be subject to judicial review;

Whereas the voluntary control exercised by self-regulatory bodies to eliminate misleading advertising may avoid recourse to administrative or judicial action and ought therefore to be encouraged;

Whereas the advertiser should be able to prove, by appropriate means, the material accuracy of the factual claims he makes in his advertising, and may in appropriate cases be required to do so by the court or administrative authority;

Whereas this Directive must not preclude Member States from retaining or adopting provisions with a view to ensuring more extensive protection of consumers, persons carrying on a trade, business, craft or profession, and the general public.

Has adopted this directive:

Article 1
The purpose of this Directive is to protect consumers, persons carrying on a trade or business or practising a craft or profession and the interests of the public in general against misleading advertising and the unfair consequences thereof.

Article 2
For the purposes of this Directive:
(1) 'advertising' means the making of a representation in any form in connection with a trade, business, craft or profession in order to promote the supply of goods or services, including immovable property, rights and obligations;
(2) 'misleading advertising' means any advertising which in any way, including its presentation, deceives or is likely to deceive the persons to whom it is addressed or whom it reaches and which, by reason of its deceptive nature, is likely to affect their economic behaviour or which, for those reasons, injures or is likely to injure a competitor;
(3) 'person' means any natural or legal person.

Article 3
In determining whether advertising is misleading, account shall be taken of all its features, and in particular of any information it contains concerning:
(a) the characteristics of goods or services, such as their availability, nature, execution, composition, method and date of manufacture or provision, fitness for purpose, uses, quantity, specification, geographical or commercial origin or the results to be expected from their use, or the results and material features of tests or checks carried out on the goods or services;
(b) the price or the manner in which the price is calculated, and the conditions on which the goods are supplied or the services provided;
(c) the nature, attributes, and rights of the advertiser, such as his identity and assets, his qualifications and ownership of industrial, commercial or intellectual property rights or his awards and distinctions.

Article 4
(1)   Member States shall ensure that adequate and effective means exist for the control of misleading advertising in the interests of consumers as well as competitors and the general public.

Such means shall include legal provisions under which persons or organizations regarded under national law as having a legitimate interest in prohibiting misleading advertising may:
(a) take legal action against such advertising; and/or
(b) bring such advertising before an administrative authority competent either to decide on complaints or to initiate appropriate legal proceedings.
It shall be for each Member State to decide which of these facilities shall be available and whether to enable the courts or administrative authorities to require prior recourse to other established means of dealing with complaints, including those referred to in Article 5.

(2) Under the legal provisions referred to in paragraph 1, Member States shall confer upon the courts or administrative authorities powers enabling them, in cases where they deem such measures to be necessary taking into account all the interests involved and in particular the public interest:
—to order the cessation of, or to institute appropriate legal proceedings for an order for the cessation of, misleading advertising, or
—if misleading advertising has not yet been published but publication is imminent, to order the prohibition of, or to institute appropriate legal proceedings for an order for the prohibition of, such publication,
even without proof of actual loss or damage or of intention or negligence on the part of the advertiser.

Member States shall also make provision for the measures referred to in the first sub-paragraph to be taken under an accelerated procedure:
—either with interim effect, or
—with definitive effect,
on the understanding that it is for each Member State to decide which of the two options to select.

Furthermore, Member States may confer upon the courts or administrative authorities powers enabling them, with a view to eliminating the continuing effects of misleading advertising the cessation of which has been ordered by a final decision:
—to require publication of that decision in full or in part and in such form as they deem adequate,
—to require in addition the publication of a corrective statement.

(3) The administrative authorities referred to in paragraph 1 must:
(a) be composed so as not to cast doubt on their impartiality;
(b) have adequate powers, where they decide on complaints, to monitor and enforce the observance of their decisions effectively;
(c) normally give reasons for their decisions.

Where the powers referred to in paragraph 2 are exercised exclusively by an administrative authority, reasons for its decisions shall always be given. Furthermore in this case, provision must be made for procedures whereby improper or unreasonable exercise of its powers by the administrative authority or improper or unreasonable failure to exercise the said powers can be the subject of judicial review.

Article 5
This Directive does not exclude the voluntary control of misleading advertising by self-regulatory bodies and recourse to such bodies by the persons or organizations referred to in Article 4 if proceedings before such bodies are in addition to the court or administrative proceedings referred to in that Article.

Article 6
Member States shall confer upon the courts or administrative authorities powers enabling them in the civil or administrative proceedings provided for in Article 4:
(a) to require the advertiser to furnish evidence as to the accuracy of factual claims in advertising if, taking into account the legitimate interests of the advertiser and any other party to the proceedings, such a requirement appears appropriate on the basis of the circumstances of the particular case; and
(b) to consider factual claims as inaccurate if the evidence demanded in accordance with (a) is not furnished or is deemed insufficient by the court or administrative authority.

Article 7
This Directive shall not preclude Member States from retaining or adopting provisions with a view to ensuring more extensive protection for consumers, persons carrying on a trade, business, craft or profession, and the general public.

Article 8
Member States shall bring into force the measures necessary to comply with this Directive by 1 October 1986 at the latest. They shall forthwith inform the Commission thereof.

Member States shall communicate to the Commission the text of all provisions of national law which they adopt in the field covered by this Directive.

Article 9
This Directive is addressed to the Member States.

Done at Brussels, 10 September 1984.

1. OJ No C 70, 21. 3. 1978, p 4.
2. OJ No C 140, 5. 6. 1979, p 23.
3. OJ No C 171, 9. 7. 1979, p 43.
4. OJ No C 133, 3. 6. 1981, p 1.

NOTES

1. For further materials discussing private law remedies in respect of misleading advertising, see above pp 31–52.
2. For a comment on the background to the Directive see Lawson, 'Advertising and product liability: progress of sorts' (1983) Trading Law 113; 'The Advertising Directive is Adopted' (1985) Trading Law 38.
3. The Department of Trade and Industry made the following statement in a Press notice on 10 September 1984:

The Directive, which Member States are required to implement by 1 October 1986, is intended to protect consumers, traders and the public in general against misleading advertising. Member States must ensure that adequate and effective means exist for the control of such advertising; including arrangements permitting persons or organisations to take legal action against misleading advertisements, and/or to bring such advertisements before an administrative authority empowered to take appropriate action.

Legislation to implement the Directive in the United Kingdom will be put before Parliament in due course, after consultations with commercial and consumer interests concerned. The Government propose that the Director General of Fair Trading should be empowered to seek court orders prohibiting the publication of misleading advertisements, where he considers his intervention necessary in cases which cannot be adequately dealt with in other ways.

The Director General's new power will be available as a back-up or longstop to reinforce, existing arrangements for the control of misleading advertising, particularly the controls operated by the advertising industry itself through the Advertising Standards Authority. Such reinforcement was recommended in the report of the Department of Trade Working Party on the Self-Regulatory System of Advertising Control, published in 1980.

Questions

1 The view is taken in some quarters that reliance on codes of practice to regulate the conduct of traders is misguided and ineffective, even where members of the trade association in question are concerned. As has been seen, this is not generally the view taken by successive Directors General of Fair Trading. But assuming that there is some merit in the view that a code of practice tends to be a cosmetic remedy for a more deep-seated problem, consider what alternative and practicable ways exist to improve the standard of the supply of goods and services to the consumer in any selected area.

2 The 1980 Board of Trade Working Party states (in para 11 extracted above) that there are some 80 separate statutes, orders and regulations concerned with advertising to a greater or lesser extent. Identify the main such statutes and subsidiary legislation.

3 How could the existing policy of the Office of Fair Trading of implementing voluntary and self-enforcing codes within sectors of trade be affected by (a) the imposition of a new statutory duty to trade fairly, or (b) the adoption of a 'middle system of law' whereunder a number of regulatory offences now existing would be 'decriminalised' but subject to 'penalties'? (See further Chs 10, p 428 et seq and 11, p 440).

CHAPTER 10

Aspects of the duty to trade fairly

Introduction

Although it is not strictly correct to say that the imposition of a statutory duty to trade fairly dates from the passing of the Fair Trading Act 1973, this Act is of such fundamental importance that it inevitably becomes the dominating feature in surveying the 'fair trading' scene in the United Kingdom.

The background to the Act is that on 24 November 1970 the new Conservative Government announced the abolition of the Consumer Council on the ground of 'opposition to the use of public money for objectives which should be achieved by private enterprise concerns using private money' and because of the 'emergence of adequate voluntary consumer organisations'. (See respectively 807 HC Official Report (5th series) col 229 (24 November 1970) and col 891 (30 November 1970)). As a valediction, the Chairman of the Consumer Council wrote in his final Annual Report, 'I am convinced that the axing of the Consumer Council cannot mean the axing of what we have done or what we have started. Some day someone will have to invent a new, publicly financed body to promote and protect the consumer's interests'.

Since the Fair Trading Bill, introduced into the Commons in November 1972, was not preceded by any sort of published enquiry, Green or White paper—a feature which attracted critical comment in debate (see 848 HC Official Report (5th series) col 469 (13 December 1972))—it is difficult to trace the precise processes which led up to it. It seems probable that a draft Bill had been put in hand by the Civil Service, primarily within the Department of Trade and Industry, to improve the legislation on monopolies and mergers. This coincided with the appointment with Cabinet rank of a new and energetic Minister for Trade and Consumer Affairs, Sir Geoffrey Howe, within the giant Department of Trade and Industry.

Speaking to the Bill on its second reading, and explaining its objects, Sir Geoffrey Howe remarked that the Bill had two complementary purposes, firstly, the promotion of increased economic efficiency and secondly protection of the consumer against unfair trading practices. He continued,

> just as fair trading is good business, so consumer protection is in itself an integral part of the market economy. That is why competition policy needs to be considered, as it is in the Bill, as a whole. It is this integrated view of competition policy that leads to the first institutional innovation proposed in the Bill—the appointment of a Director General of Fair Trading . . . 'The Government have concluded that given the specialist and detailed nature of the work and the need for continuity in its performance, it would best be done by an independent official body.

(See 848 HC Official Report (5th series) col 454, 13 December 1972).

The Bill with a number of amendments (about 125 of approximately 4,000 proposed) became law on 25 July 1973.

In this book space forbids a treatment of more than aspects of Parts II and III of the Act. This chapter also includes consideration of whether there should be a general statutory duty to trade fairly, imposed in wider terms than under the 1973 Act.

Dealing with undesirable consumer trade practices

Part II of the Act was designed to provide machinery for carefully considered subsidiary legislation to prohibit consumer trade practices which were thought to be undesirable. (Part I makes provision for the appointment of a Director General of Fair Trading and his duties, and also for the establishment of an Advisory Committee to be called the Consumer Protection Advisory Committee). Part II then goes on to deal with the identification of undesirable consumer trade practices and, in appropriate cases, for recommendations to deal with these to be made and translated into subsidiary legislation.

THE METHOD OF CONTROL

The first and vital question is the definition of a 'consumer trade practice'. This is defined in s 13 of the Act as follows:

13. Meaning of 'consumer trade practices'
In this Act 'consumer trade practice' means any practice which is for the time being carried on in connection with the supply of goods (whether by way of sale or otherwise) to consumers or in connection with the supply of services for consumers and which relates—
(a) to the terms or conditions (whether as to price or otherwise) on or subject to which goods or services are or are sought to be supplied, or
(b) to the manner in which those terms or conditions are communicated to persons to whom goods are or are sought to be supplied or for whom services are or are sought to be supplied, or
(c) to promotion (by advertising, labelling or marking of goods, canvassing or otherwise) of the supply of goods or of the supply of services, or
(d) to methods of salesmanship employed in dealing with consumers, or
(e) to the way in which goods are packed or otherwise got up for the purpose of being supplied, or
(f) to methods of demanding or securing payment for goods or services supplied.

Section 14 deals with the method of referring such practices to the Advisory Committee and runs as follows:

14. General provisions as to references to Advisory Committee
(1) Subject to sections 15 and 16 of this Act, the Secretary of State or any other Minister or the Director may refer to the Advisory Committee the question whether a consumer trade practice specified in the reference adversely affects the economic interests of consumers in the United Kingdom.
(2) The Secretary of State or any other Minister by whom a reference is made under this section shall transmit a copy of the reference to the Director.
(3) On any reference made to the Advisory Committee under this section the Advisory Committee shall consider the question so referred to them and shall prepare a report on that question and (except as otherwise provided by section 21 (3) of this Act) submit that report to the person by whom the reference was made.

(4) Subject to the provisions of section 133 of this Act, it shall be the duty of the Director, where he is requested by the Advisory Committee to do so for the purpose of assisting the Committee in carrying out an investigation on a reference made to them under this section, to give to the Committee—
(a) any information which is in his possession and which relates to matters falling within the scope of the investigation, and
(b) any other assistance which the Committee may require, and which it is within his power to give, in relation to any such matters.
(5) The Advisory Committee shall transmit to the Secretary of State a copy of every report which is made by them under this section to a person other than the Secretary of State, and shall transmit to the Director a copy of every report which is made by them under this section to a person other than the Director.

Sections 17, 21 and 22 then indicate the procedure for (a) references made to the Advisory Committee by the Director under s 14, (b) the ensuing report of the Advisory Committee and (c) orders made by the Secretary of State in pursuance of such references. These sections run as follows:

17. Reference to Advisory Committee proposing recommendations to Secretary of State to make an order
(1) This section applies to any reference made to the Advisory Committee by the Director under section 14 of this Act which includes proposals in accordance with the following provisions of this section.
(2) Where it appears to the Director that a consumer trade practice has the effect, or is likely to have the effect,—
(a) of misleading consumers as to, or withholding from them adequate information as to, or an adequate record of, their rights and obligations under relevant consumer transactions, or
(b) of otherwise misleading or confusing consumers with respect to any matter in connection with relevant consumer transactions, or
(c) of subjecting consumers to undue pressure to enter into relevant consumer transactions, or
(d) of causing the terms or conditions, on or subject to which consumers enter into relevant consumer transactions, to be so adverse to them as to be inequitable,
any reference made by the Director under section 14 of this Act with respect to that consumer trade practice may, if the Director thinks fit, include proposals for recommending to the Secretary of State that he should exercise his powers under the following provisions of this Part of this Act with respect to that consumer trade practice.
(3) A reference to which this section applies shall state which of the effects specified in subsection (2) of this section it appears to the Director that the consumer trade practice in question has or is likely to have.
(4) Where the Director makes a reference to which this section applies, he shall arrange for it to be published in full in the London, Edinburgh and Belfast Gazettes.
(5) In this Part of this Act 'relevant consumer transaction', in relation to a consumer trade practice, means any transaction to which a person is, or may be invited to become, a party in his capacity as a consumer in relation to that practice.

. . .

21. Report of Advisory Committee on reference to which section 17 applies
(1) A report of the Advisory Committee on a reference to which section 17 of this Act applies shall state the conclusions of the Committee on the questions—
(a) whether the consumer trade practice specified in the reference adversely affects the economic interests of consumers in the United Kingdom, and
(b) if so, whether it does so by reason, or partly by reason, that it has or is likely to have such one or more of the effects specified in section 17(2) of this Act as are specified in the report.
(2) If, in their conclusions set out in such a report, the Advisory Committee find that the consumer trade practice specified in the reference does adversely affect the economic interests of consumers in the United Kingdom, and does so wholly or partly for the reason mentioned in subsection (1) (b) of this section, the report shall state whether the Committee—
(a) agree with the proposals set out in the reference, or
(b) would agree with those proposals if they were modified in a manner specified in the report, or

(c) disagree with the proposals and do not desire to suggest any such modifications.
(3) Every report of the Advisory Committee on a reference to which section 17 of this Act applies shall be made to the Secretary of State, and shall set out in full the reference on which it is made.

22. Order of Secretary of State in pursuance of report on reference to which s 17 applies
(1) The provisions of this section shall have effect where a report of the Advisory Committee on a reference to which section 17 of this Act applies has been laid before Parliament in accordance with the provisions of Part VII of this Act, and the report states that the Committee—
   (a) agree with the proposals set out in the reference, or
   (b) would agree with those proposals if they were modified in a manner specified in the report.
(2) In the circumstances mentioned in the preceding subsection, the Secretary of State may, if he thinks fit, by an order made by statutory instrument make such provision as—
   (a) in a case falling within paragraph (a) of the preceding subsection, is in his opinion appropriate for giving effect to the proposals set out in the reference, or
   (b) in a case falling within paragraph (b) of that subsection, is in his opinion appropriate for giving effect either to the proposals as set out in the reference or to those proposals as modified in the manner specified in the report, as the Secretary of State may in his discretion determine.
(3) Any such order may contain such supplementary or incidental provisions as the Secretary of State may consider appropriate in the circumstances; and (without prejudice to the generality of this subsection) any such order may restrict the prosecution of offences under the next following section in respect of contraventions of the order where those contraventions also constitute offences under another enactment.
(4) No such order, and no order varying or revoking any such order, shall be made under this section unless a draft of the order has been laid before Parliament and approved by a resolution of each House of Parliament.

The joint effect of ss 14 and 17 taken together with s 19 is that, where a reference is made by the Director under s 17, it must
(1) specify the consumer trade practice referred to and this must be one which 'adversely affects the economic interests of consumers in the United Kingdom';
(2) the report must then state which of the effects specified in s 17(2) it appears to the Director that the consumer trade practice in question has or is likely to have;
(3) it must also specify the provision to be contained in an Order, to be made by the Secretary of State, that the Director considers necessary to prevent the continuance of, or modify, the practice.

As a result of the references made by the Director since the implementation of the Fair Trading Act, there have been four reports of the Advisory Committee. These are: 'Rights of Consumers, A Report on Practices Relating to the Purported Exclusion of Inalienable Rights of Consumers and Failure to Explain their Existence' (1974 HCP 6); 'Prepayment of Goods, A Report on Practices Relating to Prepayment in Mail Order Transactions and in Shops' (1976 HCP 285); 'Disguised Business Sales, A Report on the Practice of Seeking to Sell Goods without revealing that they are being Sold in the Course of a Business' (1976 HCP 355); and 'VAT-Exclusive Prices, A Report on Practices relating to Advertising, Displaying or otherwise Quoting VAT-Exclusive Prices or Charges' (1977 HCP 416).

Orders made under s 22 to date are as follows:— The Mail Order Transactions (Information) Order 1976 (SI 1976/1812); the Consumer Transactions (Restrictions on Statements) Order 1976 (SI 1976/1813); the Consumer Transactions (Restrictions on Statements) (Amendment) Order

1978 (SI 1978/127); and the Business Advertisements (Disclosure) Order 1977 (SI 1977/1918).

Penalties for contravention of Orders so made are dealt with by s 23 as follows:

23. Penalties for contravention of order under s 22
Subject to the following provisions of this Part of this Act, any person who contravenes a prohibition imposed by an order under section 22 of this Act, or who does not comply with a requirement imposed by such an order which applies to him, shall be guilty of an offence and shall be liable—
(a) on summary conviction, to a fine not exceeding £2000;
(b) on conviction on indictment, to a fine or to imprisonment for a term not exceeding two years or both.

Offences under s 23 of the Act are subject to the defences specified in ss 24 and 25. These follow the standard pattern of trading standards offences and provide for defences of mistake, reliance on information, act or default of another person, accident or some other cause beyond the defendant's control. Reasonable precautions and all due diligence must have been exercised. These defences are considered elsewhere in this book. (See below, Ch 14 at pp 552–563).

In recent years little use has been made of the Advisory Committee and the Report on Non-Departmental Public Bodies (Cmnd 7797, January 1980) refers to its proposed abolition. This would, however, require primary legislation and 'the saving to public funds would be negligible'. Since 1983 members have not been re-appointed and where subsidiary legislation has been considered urgently necessary, as in the case of bargain offers (see below, at p 540 et seq) subsidiary legislation has been made under s 4 of the Prices Act 1974. Amongst the controversies surrounding the bargain offers legislation is the question of whether it is intra vires the enabling section of the Prices Act. However there were doubts also as to whether the necessary economic detriment to consumers (under the then obsolescent Part II of the Fair Trading Act) could be established. The preferred solution to the many problems that have arisen in the comparative pricing area is new primary legislation (see Report of the Inter-Departmental Working Party on Review of Legislation on False and Misleading Price Information (Dept of Trade and Industry, February 1984, Part VI) and below, pp 548–551.

THE BUSINESS ADVERTISEMENTS (DISCLOSURE) ORDER 1977

The above Order provides a good example of the Part II procedure. The Order was made by the Secretary of State under powers contained in s 22 of the Fair Trading Act 1973 (above). The Order followed a reference made by the Director General under s 17 (above) and the report of the Consumer Protection Advisory Committee which was laid before Parliament (HC 355 Session 1975/76).

The Director General's dossier which accompanied his reference to the CPAC contained a summary of the practice and, in a Schedule, proposals for dealing with it.

Chapter I—summary
(1) The consumer trade practice covered by this reference is that of seeking to sell goods to consumers without revealing (whether deliberately or not) that the goods are being sold in the

course of a business. We are primarily concerned with the use of classified advertisements in the local and national press although the reference also covers advertisements displayed in, for example, newsagents' or tobacconists' windows.

(2) A trader may advertise his goods clearly indicating (implicitly or explicitly) his business interest. He may, however, conceal that interest either unintentionally or deliberately: the reference deals with both forms of concealment. At the second stage of the practice, when the consumer has responded to the advertisement, the trader may immediately divulge the fact that he is selling goods in the course of business. Alternatively, he may leave the consumer with the mistaken impression that he is buying from a private individual. Such concealment at the second stage is usually deliberate and involves often quite elaborate techniques of deception.

(3) The consumer may suffer economic detriment during both the first and second stages of the practice. First, it may mislead him into making a response which he would not have made had he known the seller to be a trader. He may, as a result, suffer an economic loss—albeit small: the cost of a telephone call, or of travelling or the loss of working time. (Section 17(2) (b) of the Fair Trading Act, 1973 refers). At the second stage he may be misled into paying more for the goods than he might have done (indeed he may not even have completed the sale had he known he was dealing with a trader) (section 17(2) (b)). Having bought the goods, the consumer can suffer two other significant economic detriments if they turn out to be defective or misdescribed: either he or his adviser may be misled by the practice into believing that he enjoys only those rights which result from a contract with a private seller. These are weaker than consumers' rights against traders, eg there is no right to goods of merchantable quality and he may therefore forgo redress (this detriment is covered by section 17(2) (a)); and there may also be deception as to the availability of compensation (under the Powers of the Criminal Courts Act, 1973) resulting from a successful prosecution under the Trade Descriptions Act, 1968, because this latter Act does not apply to private sales (section 17(2) (b) of the Fair Trading Act is again relevant).

(4) We have considered, but rejected . . . relying solely on voluntary self-regulation of the practice by the media. Instead we propose that, where goods are being sold in the course of a business, advertisements should make this fact quite clear. To help advertisers to know where they stand, we propose that certain features of advertisements should be assumed to comply with this requirement. Such features are the inclusion of the words 'agent', 'dealer' or 'trader'; the inclusion of the seller's name when it is obviously a business or corporate name; or such size or format of the advertisement itself, which makes it unlikely to be taken as a private advertisement. We propose exemptions for advertisements displayed at or near the premises where the goods may be bought and those premises are clearly trade premises; for advertisements relating to a sale by auction or tender; and for advertisements classified as traders' advertisements in any publication which segregates traders' sales. We also propose a general exemption for advertisements for vegetable produce and certain other products commonly sold at the roadside.

. . .

Schedule—proposals

(1) That it should be unlawful for any person seeking to sell goods that are being sold in the course of a business to publish or cause to be published any advertisement indicating that the goods are for sale and likely to induce consumers to buy them unless the advertisement—
   (a) describes the seller by the word 'agent', 'dealer' or 'trader'; or
   (b) refers to the seller by a business name which cannot reasonably be taken to be the name of a private seller or, where the seller is a body corporate, by its corporate name; or
   (c) is by reason of its size or format unlikely to be taken as being other than a trader's advertisement; or
   (d) otherwise makes it reasonably obvious that the goods are being sold in the course of a business.

(2) That there should be exempted from the requirements described in paragraph 1 advertisements,—
   (a) displayed on or near premises where the goods may be bought provided the premises are obviously trade premises;
   (b) relating only to sales by auction or tender;
   (c) classified as traders' advertisements in publications in which the advertisements of trade and private sellers are classified separately;
   (d) relating only to vegetable produce, eggs or dead animals, fish or birds gathered, produced, or taken by the seller.

The CPAC in its Report on the Practice of Seeking to Sell Goods without revealing that they are being Sold in the Course of a Business (May 1976) accepted the Director's proposals in the following terms:

The Proposals

19.   The Director has recommended that an order should be made by the Secretary of State under section 22 of the Act to regulate the practice referred to us. The proposals are set out in the Schedule to the reference (page 2 of this report). The scope of any recommendations to be made by the Director in a reference of this kind is governed by section 19 of the Act which requires him to propose such provision as he may consider requisite for the purpose of preventing the continuance of the practice, or causing it to be modified, in so far as it may adversely affect the economic interests of consumers in the United Kingdom.

20.   The Director's proposals deal with advertisements published by traders. They are intended to ensure that all such advertisements make it clear either expressly or by implication that the goods are being sold in the course of a business and not privately. The Director has specified four alternative requirements (paragraph 1 of the Schedule). In each case the aim is to ensure that the consumer will not be misled about the nature of the transaction. The Committee considered whether they should comment in detail on the specific requirements. However the Secretary of State under section 22 of the Act may make such provision as she considers appropriate for giving effect to them and we therefore do not consider it is necessary for us to embark on what would in effect amount to a drafting exercise. The proposals in paragraph 1 of the Schedule taken as a whole are acceptable to the Committee.

21.   The Director has specified four exemptions from these requirements. Two of these (paragraph 2(a) and (c) of the Schedule) appear to be examples of advertisements which having regard to their location or context could not reasonably be said to mislead.

22.   There is a specific exemption for advertisements relating only to sales by auction or tender (paragraph 2(b) of the Schedule). The Director has proposed this exemption because such sales are not 'consumer sales' under the Supply of Goods (Implied Terms) Act 1973. This means that the seller is entitled by law to sell on terms that exclude any responsibility for defects although it does not follow that he will necessarily do so.

23.   The Committee have considered whether this exemption could be held to extend to goods offered for sale at a price 'o.n.o.' (meaning near or nearest offer). 'Or nearest offer' and related phrases are frequently to be found in classified advertisements and though we think it unlikely that goods advertised in this way could escape control by virtue of the exemption the possibility cannot be ruled out entirely. There is therefore a risk which we accept may be small that the exemption could lead to evasion from control. Since in our view no hardship would arise if sales by auction and tender were brought within the proposals we suggest that this exemption should be dropped.

24.   The fourth exemption (paragraph 2(d) of the Schedule) concerns advertisements relating only to vegetable produce, eggs or dead animals, fish or birds gathered, produced, or taken by the seller. We agree with the Director that such advertisements should be exempt, since there is no evidence of the character of the seller being important in transactions involving such goods. We understand that the term 'vegetable produce' includes flowers, fruit and vegetables.

25.   The Director has explained that his proposals cover all sales in the course of a business, not simply sales of those goods which it is the seller's particular business to supply. We have noted that the professions are included in the definition of 'business' both in the Act and in the Supply of Goods (Implied Terms) Act 1973 and that the proposals cover a professional person selling assets used in his practice. For example a doctor wishing to sell his car which is being used wholly or partly in connection with his professional duties would have to make clear in any advertisement that the car was being sold in the course of a business. The Director considered the possibility of an exemption for advertisements of goods which it was not the seller's customary business to supply. However he concluded that this would create difficulties of definition and raise the possibility of evasion of control. We agree with the Director.

26.   The representations we received strongly supported the Director's view that the practice referred was detrimental to consumers and should be controlled. Some representations we received questioned whether the Director's proposals could be effectively enforced. A few suggested alternative approaches to the control of the practice. However, we reached the conclusion that the Director's proposals would be a significant deterrent to those who might intentionally seek to mislead consumers, that they would be enforceable and that they should help to reduce the incidence of the practice.

27. The Committee therefore agree with the proposals set out at paragraph 1 of the Schedule to the reference and would agree with the proposals at paragraph 2 of the Schedule to the reference if they were modified in the manner specified in paragraph 23 of this report.

The Order was laid before Parliament in draft and was made on 21 November 1977. It states as follows:

Business Advertisements (Disclosure) Order 1977 (SI 1977/1918)

1.—(1) This Order may be cited as the Business Advertisements (Disclosure) Order 1977 and shall come into operation on 1st January 1978.
(2) The Interpretation Act 1889 shall apply for the interpretation of this Order as it applies for the interpretation of an Act of Parliament.
2.—(1) Subject to paragraphs (2) and (3) below, a person who is seeking to sell goods that are being sold in the course of a business shall not publish or cause to be published an advertisement—
  (a) which indicates that the goods are for sale, and
  (b) which is likely to induce consumers to buy the goods,
unless it is reasonably clear whether from the contents of the advertisement, its format or size, the place or manner of its publication or otherwise that the goods are to be sold in the course of a business.
(2) Paragraph (1) applies whether the person who is seeking to sell the goods is acting on his own behalf or that of another, and where he is acting as agent, whether he is acting in the course of a business carried on by him or not; but the reference in that paragraph to a business does not include any business carried on by the agent.
(3) Paragraph (1) above shall not apply in relation to advertisements—
  (a) which are concerned only with sales by auction or competitive tender; or
  (b) which are concerned only with the sale of flowers, fruit or vegetables, eggs or dead animals, fish or birds, gathered, produced or taken by the person seeking to sell the goods.

Extract from O'Keefe, 'The Law relating to Trade Descriptions'

The order is aimed only at sales of goods to consumers, so if only business people are likely to buy the goods, the order would not seem to apply.
The business identity can be revealed in a number of ways. The name of the seller, indicated in the contents of an advertisement, could be sufficient: eg X Co Ltd, X & Co, X Enterprises etc. If a large advertisement appears in a paper, half a page for example, this size and format could be sufficient to indicate a business seller. Clearly, advertisements placed in 'Trade Sales' classified columns or trade journals, or marked '(trader)' or 'T', could also satisfy the regulations. The test is whether it is 'reasonably clear'—a question of fact for the court to decide.

Blakemore v Bellamy [1983] RTR 303, Queen's Bench Divisional Court

Webster J This is a prosecutor's appeal by case stated by justices sitting at Croydon, who, on 12 November 1981, dismissed 18 informations preferred by the prosecutor against the defendant. Of those informations 16 alleged contraventions of section 23 of the Fair Trading Act 1973 and article 2 (1) of the Business Advertisements (Disclosure) Order 1977, in that the defendant being a person seeking to sell goods, namely, a motor vehicle, in the course of business as a motor car dealer caused to be published advertisements indicating that the motor vehicle was for sale and was likely to induce consumers to buy the motor vehicle without making it reasonably clear that the motor vehicle was to be sold in the course of a business. The other two informations alleged contraventions of section 1 (1) (a) of the Trade Descriptions Act 1968, one of them alleging that the defendant in the course of trade or business as a motor car dealer applied a false trade description as to the mileage of a motor vehicle, and the other alleging that in the course of trade or business as a motor car dealer he applied a false trade description as to the circumstances in which he had acquired the vehicle.
  It is to be noted, therefore, that a material averment in each of the informations was that

in publishing the relevant advertisement or in applying the relevant false trade description the defendant was acting in the course of business as a motor car dealer in 16 cases, or in the course of trade or business as a motor car dealer in the other two cases.

The justices dismissed all the informations because they were not satisfied that the defendant was acting in the course of a trade or business as a motor car dealer. They concluded that he was selling cars as a hobby.

Two questions, essentially, are asked by them in the case stated, each of which has been pursued in argument. The first is whether they misdirected themselves as to the meaning of the expressions 'business' or 'trade or business', and the second is whether, giving to those words their correct meaning, their finding was perverse; that is to say, one which no bench of justices could reasonably have reached. As that is one of the questions for us, it is perhaps more convenient to begin with the material evidence and then to advert to the justices' findings.

So far as the material evidence is concerned, it amounted to this. Between April 1980 and 31 July 1981, the defendant had inserted a total of 21 advertisements in one or other of two newspapers relating to eight different motor cars; when interviewed by the trading standards officer, employed by the prosecutor, the defendant had stated that he was not a trader and that he did not keep a record of the cars he had sold, but that he was a car enthusiast and enjoyed cleaning them up purely as a hobby. His own evidence was that he had been a postman for over 12 years, usually on duty between 8.45 pm and 6 am. He was not a trader. He had been a car enthusiast since the age of 17. During 1979 he had sold two cars. Between April 1980 and January 1981 he sold a total of seven. He liked driving cars and frequently swapping them. He did not consider himself to be a dealer in motor cars. He repaired and worked on them himself. He usually bought the cars at auctions where he could get them cheap, and quite often he got a bargain. He bought them for his own use and he had driven all but three of them himself. On some of them he made a profit, on others a loss; overall he thought that he had probably broken even on the sale of them. He denied that he was a part-time trader. He claimed that he did not sell cars in order to make a profit, even though he did make a profit, as I have said, in some cases. He admitted that he claimed to have bought the cars for his own use and that he had not driven all of them. He admitted in cross-examination that he had not insured all of the cars and in any event that he had no garage and had to keep the cars on the road. He also admitted that he often had more than one car at a time and that sometimes he did some work on the cars before re-selling them and sometimes not.

On that evidence the justices found, first of all, not surprisingly, that the defendant was in full-time employment as a postman. They found that he had a great enthusiasm for motor cars and that at any one time he would usually own either one or two cars; that in 1979 he had two cars; and that between April 1980 and January 1981 he acquired and sold seven. They found that he did, on some sales, sustain a loss, on others break even and on three make a profit, but that overall he had made no significant profit. They found that there was no suggestion that any vehicles which he had sold were excessively priced or in any unsatisfactory condition. They made this finding:

> 'The defendant's repeated changes of motor cars were a hobby and did not constitute a trade or business as a motor car dealer. He was motivated by his enthusiastic interest in motor cars and not by commercial considerations. In particular his activities were not a professional practice, nor an undertaking carried out for gain or reward, nor an undertaking within the meaning of the Fair Trading Act 1973'.

In consequence, they decided that the prosecutor had not satisfied them that the defendant was acting in the course of a trade or business as a car dealer and they believed the defendant's evidence that his activities were merely a hobby and did not constitute a trade or business as a motor dealer. They therefore dismissed the informations.

Mr Jubb, on behalf of the prosecutor, first of all submits that a part-time activity can be a business. As to that there is no doubt. There is authority for that proposition in *Stevenson v Beverley Bentinck Ltd* [1976] RTR 543, [[1976] 2 All ER 606]. Secondly he submits that the expression 'business' is wider than that of trade, and that is so.

Thirdly, Mr Jubb refers us to the definition of 'business' in section 137 (2) of the Fair Trading Act 1973 where, except in so far as the context otherwise requires in that Act:

'. . . "business" includes a professional practice and includes any other undertaking which is carried on for gain or reward or which is an undertaking in the course of which goods or services are supplied otherwise than free of charge'.

If that definition is to be incorporated into the two expressions which the justices had to apply to the facts of the case before them, then as Mr Jubb accepts, he would have to show that their finding that his activities did not constitute an undertaking was of itself a perverse finding.

As it seems to me, the effect of that definition is simply that, for the purpose of the Fair Trading Act 1973, a '. . . "business" includes a professional practice and any other undertaking . . .' It is not a definition which affects the meaning of the expressions 'business', or 'trade or business'. As it seems to me those expressions are to be given their ordinary meaning.

If that is so, the only submission left to Mr Jubb is that the justices misdirected themselves as to the ordinary meaning of those expressions. He submits that they did so, because, he suggests, their finding that the activity constituted a hobby and their conclusion that the defendant was not acting in the course of a trade or business is to be read as a direction for themselves that if he was carrying on a hobby, then for that reason there could have been no question of his carrying on a trade or business. In other words he submits that they directed themselves that a hobby on the one hand and a trade or business on the other are mutually exclusive, and he submits that that was a misdirection.

There is one authority which seems to me to bear on that submission namely, *Rolls v Miller* (1884) 27 Ch D 71. There—on altogether different facts, to which I need not refer in detail, but they concerned a covenant in a lease where the same questions arose, namely, whether the activity in question did or did not constitute a business—Lindley LJ said, at p 88:

> 'When we look into the dictionaries as to the meaning of the word "business", I do not think they throw much light upon it. The word means almost anything which is an occupation, as distinguished from a pleasure—anything which is an occupation or duty which requires attention is a business—I do not think we can get much aid from the dictionary. We must look at the words in the ordinary sense . . .'

It seems to me that it is proper and right to treat for the present purposes the word 'pleasure' used in that case by Lindley LJ, as more or less synonymous with 'a hobby'. If it be the case—and I will assume for this purpose that it was the case—that the justices decided that the defendant was carrying on a hobby and that he therefore could not have been carrying on a trade or business, it does not seem to me that they misdirected themselves as to the ordinary meaning of the words 'trade or business'. Nor does it seem to me that the application of those words to the facts led to a conclusion which is in any sense perverse. In my view there was evidence which entitled them to find on the facts that the defendant was not carrying on a trade or business, albeit it might well have been the case that a different bench might have come to a different conclusion on the same facts. I would therefore dismiss this appeal.

Donaldson LJ I agree. I only wish to add a word about one of these informations, namely, the eighteenth. In that case it was alleged that the defendant had applied a false trade description to a Vauxhall Cavalier motor vehicle by means of the following oral statement: 'The car has been left to me by my uncle who died. He had it from new'. The justices have found as a fact that the car had not been left to him by his uncle; still less had his uncle had it from new. The defendant had in fact acquired the car by purchasing it from Central Motor Auctions at Morden Road, Mitcham, on 26 November 1980; that is to say, within three weeks of the time when he was seeking to re-sell it.

He has been acquitted by the justices because, for the reasons which Webster J has been discussing in detail, they considered that he did not seek to sell it in the course of trade or business. But I should not like it to be thought that he committed no offence. A very obvious offence to which consideration might have been given with a view to prosecution was obtaining property by deception. I inquired why this had not been considered. I understood Mr Jubb for the prosecutor to say, which I can understand, that the local authority was concerned with trading standards and the possible prosecution of people for offences under the Fair Trading Act 1973 and other similar Acts and that it was not their function to consider prosecutions in general. As I have said, I can understand that; it is an administrative division, but it would, I think, be very unfortunate if they compartmentalised their activities to such an extent that, if they come across facts which appear to disclose a criminal offence of a type with which they do not deal, they were simply to shrug their shoulders and pass by on the other side. It is very important that where conduct as anti-social and potentially criminal as this comes to the notice of a trading standards authority, they should refer it to the police authority for consideration of the question whether it is appropriate to prosecute.

In saying that, I do not wish in any way to criticise the county borough of Croydon. I am merely drawing attention to the difficulties and possible dangers of an authority concerning itself solely with prosecuting over a narrow field without also taking steps to disseminate such information as it has of possible criminal activities to other authorities who may be concerned with other parts of the criminal law. But I entirely agree with everything Webster J has said.

Appeal dismissed with costs.

NOTE

For general discussion of the expression 'in the course of trade or business' see below, at pp 470–475. See also B. W. Harvey, 'Business or Pleasure', (1983) 127 Sol Jo 163, at 179. The decision in the above case may be contrasted with *Eiman v London Borough of Waltham Forest* (1982) 90 ITSA MR 204, DC, referred to below, p 474 note 2.

Controlling persistent offenders

Part III of the Fair Trading Act 1973 contains important provisions for dealing with the activities of persistent offenders. The key sections provide as follows:

PART III—ADDITIONAL FUNCTIONS OF DIRECTOR FOR PROTECTION OF CONSUMERS

34. Action by Director with respect to course of conduct detrimental to interests of consumers
(1) Where it appears to the Director that the person carrying on a business has in the course of that business persisted in a course of conduct which—
    (a) is detrimental to the interests of consumers in the United Kingdom, whether those interests are economic interests or interests in respect of health, safety or other matters, and
    (b) in accordance with the following provisions of this section is to be regarded as unfair to consumers,
the Director shall use his best endeavours, by communication with that person or otherwise, to obtain from him a satisfactory written assurance that he will refrain from continuing that course of conduct and from carrying on any similar course of conduct in the course of that business.
(2) For the purposes of subsection (1)(*b*) of this section a course of conduct shall be regarded as unfair to consumers if it consists of contraventions of one or more enactments which impose duties, prohibitions or restrictions enforceable by criminal proceedings, whether any such duty, prohibition or restriction is imposed in relation to consumers as such or not and whether the person carrying on the business has or has not been convicted of any offence in respect of any such contravention.
(3) A course of conduct on the part of the person carrying on a business shall also be regarded for those purposes as unfair to consumers if it consists of things done, or omitted to be done, in the course of that business in breach of contract or in breach of a duty (other than a contractual duty) owed to any person by virtue of any enactment or rule of law and enforceable by civil proceedings, whether (in any such case) civil proceedings in respect of the breach of contract or breach of duty have been brought or not.
(4) For the purpose of determining whether it appears to him that a person has persisted in such a course of conduct as is mentioned in subsection (1) of this section, the Director shall have regard to either or both of the following, that is to say—
    (a) complaints received by him, whether from consumers or from other persons;
    (b) any other information collected by or furnished to him, whether by virtue of this Act or otherwise.

35. Proceedings before Restrictive Practices Court
If, in the circumstances specified in subsection (1) of section 34 of this Act,—
    (a) the Director is unable to obtain from the person in question such an assurance as is mentioned in that subsection, or
    (b) that person has given such an assurance and it appears to the Director that he has failed to observe it,
the Director may bring proceedings against him before the Restrictive Practices Court.

. . .

37. Order of, or undertaking given to Court in proceedings under s 35

(1) Where in any proceedings before the Restrictive Practices Court under section 35 of this Act—

    (a) the Court finds that the person against whom the proceedings are brought (in this section referred to as 'the respondent') has in the course of a business carried on by him persisted in such a course of conduct as is mentioned in section 34(1) of this Act, and

    (b) the respondent does not give an undertaking to the Court under subsection (3) of this section which is accepted by the Court, and

    (c) it appears to the Court that, unless an order is made against the respondent under this section, he is likely to continue that course of conduct or to carry on a similar course of conduct,

the Court may make an order against the respondent under this section.

(2) An order of the Court under this section shall (with such degree of particularity as appears to the Court to be sufficient for the purposes of the order) indicate the nature of the course of conduct to which the finding of the Court under subsection (1)(a) of this section relates, and shall direct the respondent—

    (a) to refrain from continuing that course of conduct, and

    (b) to refrain from carrying on any similar course of conduct in the course of his business.

(3) Where in any proceedings under section 35 of this Act the Court makes such a finding as is mentioned in subsection (1)(a) of this section, and the respondent offers to give to the Court an undertaking either—

    (a) to refrain as mentioned in paragraphs (a) and (b) of subsection (2) of this section, or

    (b) to take particular steps which, in the opinion of the court, would suffice to prevent a continuance of the course of conduct to which the complaint relates and to prevent the carrying on by the respondent of any similar course of conduct in the course of his business,

the Court may, if it thinks fit, accept that undertaking instead of making an order under this section.

NOTE

Part III also contains provisions to deal with the activities of persons who consent to or connive at courses of conduct detrimental to the interests of consumers (see ss 38 and 39 of the 1973 Act).

The Annual Report of the Director General of Fair Trading provides details of Part III proceedings and assurances. The following extracts are illustrative.

Annual Report of the Director General of Fair Trading 1983

Assurances and legal action under Part III of the Fair Trading Act 1973

In 1983, a total of 47 assurances were obtained from traders who had persistently broken their obligations to consumers. Five orders were made against traders who either refused to provide an assurance or had broken one they had already given. Full details can be found in Parts H to K of Appendix One.

In August, for the first time, a sentence of imprisonment was imposed in connection with these procedures. The trader, a double glazing supplier had already been before the Court once for contempt of an order: on that occasion the Court accepted an undertaking from him (see Part J of Appendix One to the Annual Report for 1982). Within months, however, he had been successfully sued by a consumer for failing to carry out work as promised and failing to return the consumer's money. This was a breach of his undertaking and, following an application by the Director General, he was sent to prison for 14 days for contempt of court with the warning that any continuation of his conduct would lead to lengthy imprisonment.

Since the introduction of this sanction, 407 assurances, undertakings or orders have been obtained. (The total includes all orders concerning the breach of an assurance—these were omitted from the overall figures shown in previous years.) The following businesses or traders were involved:

Cars and motoring	96	Carpets and furniture	24
Home improvements	63	Food and catering	28
Mail order	55	One-day and doorstep sales	19
Electrical	59	Other	63

. . .

APPENDIX ONE

. . .

Part H: Fair Trading Act 1973—court order following an application by the Director General under section 35(a) when an assurance was not given voluntarily.

Between the Director General of Fair Trading and Cyril Miller in the Shoreditch County Court

IT IS ORDERED THAT Cyril Miller do refrain from continuing the course of conduct as follows:
(1) committing offences under section 1 of the Mock Auctions Act 1961;
(2) carrying on any similar course of conduct in the course of his business which is detrimental to the interests of consumers in the United Kingdom.

AND IT IS ORDERED that the Applicant's costs be taxed on Scale 1 and paid by the Respondent.

TAKE NOTICE THAT unless you obey the directions contained in this Order you will be guilty of contempt of court, and will be liable to be committed to prison.
Dated: 28 July 1983 (as amended 15 August 1983)

*Note.*The Director General had not been able to effect service of this Order by the end of 1983.

Part I: Fair Trading Act 1973—court orders following applications by the Director General under section 35(b) regarding failure to observe assurances previously given

Between the Director General of Fair Trading and Michael Alan Hughes in the Dudley County Court

IT IS ORDERED THAT Michael Alan Hughes do refrain from continuing the course of conduct as follows:
(1) committing breaches of contract with customers by supplying television sets:
    (a) which were not fit for the purpose for which they were being bought, contrary to section 14(3) of the Sale of Goods Act 1893 as amended, and to section 14(3) of the Sale of Goods Act 1979;
    (b) which were not of merchantable quality, contrary to section 14(2) of the Sale of Goods Act 1893 as amended, and to section 14(2) of the Sale of Goods Act 1979;
(2) failing to perform contracts for the repair of television sets in accordance with the express terms of the contract:
    (a) by not carrying out the work in a proper and workmanlike manner, or at all, and/or
    (b) by not carrying out the work within a reasonable period.

AND from carrying on any similar course of conduct in the course of his business which is detrimental to the interest of consumers in the United Kingdom.

AND IT IS FURTHER ORDERED that the Respondent do pay the Applicant the cost of and occasioned by this application.

TAKE NOTICE that unless you obey the directions contained in this Order you will be guilty of contempt of court and will be liable to be committed to prison.
Dated: 21 July 1983 (as amended 3 November 1983)

. . .

Part J: Fair Trading Act 1973—court order following an application by the Director General to commit the Respondent to prison for contempt of court for failure to observe the terms of an earlier undertaking given to the court

Between the Director General of Fair Trading and Ivor Martin Gilliam in the Weston-super-Mare County Court

IT IS ORDERED THAT the Defendant be committed to prison for fourteen days.

AND IT IS ORDERED THAT the Plaintiff do recover from the Defendant costs of this application assessed at £100.00.
Dated 17 August 1983

Part K: Fair Trading Act 1973—assurances given under Part III

. . .

(4) *John Eric Murphy of 41 Thorns Drive, Greasby, Wirral, Merseyside, trading under various names including Dickenson, D. Bryant, B. Flanigan, E. Hudson, Sanderson and James.*

Assurances, dated 18 March 1983, that he will refrain from the following course of conduct as required under section 34:
(1) committing offences under section 1(1) of the Trade Descriptions Act 1968 by applying false trade descriptions to goods or supplying or offering to supply any goods to which a false trade description is applied;
(2) committing breaches of contract with consumers by supplying goods which do not correspond with the description by which they are sold, as required by section 13(1) of the Sale of Goods Act 1979;
(3) committing offences under the Business Advertisements (Disclosure) Order 1977 made under section 22 of the Fair Trading Act 1973.

. . .

(7) *Christopher Robin (London) Limited, a body corporate (registered office: 3 Newburgh Street, London W1V 1LH), by its director Martin Robert Benjamin and its secretary Pear Leigh.*

Assurances, dated 18 April 1983, that it will refrain from the following course of conduct as required under section 34:
(1) committing breaches of contract with consumers:
    (a) by failing to supply goods in accordance with the terms of a contract within a reasonable time or at all; and/or
    (b) by failing to return to consumers within a reasonable time or at all, money to which they are legally entitled, in cases where the consumers:
        (i) have lawfully rejected goods for which he/she has paid, or
        (ii) have not been supplied with the goods at all;
(2) committing breaches of contract with consumers by supplying goods which are not of merchantable quality and/or not fit for the purpose for which they are bought as required by sub-sections (2) and (3) of section 14 of the Sale of Goods Act 1979;
(3) having committed a breach of contract described in paragraphs 1(a) and 2, failing promptly to pay damages or give any other compensation to the consumer.
Martin Robert Benjamin gave assurances under section 38 with regard to this course of conduct.

. . .

NOTES

1. For a helpful comparison between Part III assurances and the complaints statistics received in the Office of Fair Trading see David Hope (1981) 89 ITSA Monthly Review 180.
2. In *R v Director General of Fair Trading, ex p F H Taylor & Co Ltd* [1981] ICR 292, importers of toys and electrical equipment, who had been

convicted on some 13 occasions for contravening safety regulations, challenged the entitlement of the Director General to publicise assurances. In dismissing the application Donaldson LJ commented (at pp 293–4):

> In 1973 Parliament established the office of Director General of Fair Trading. His duties include that of acting as a watchdog for consumers. As such he has been equipped both with a bark and a bite. . . . [In] cases in which such an assurance is given, it is the Director General's duty to monitor the future of the merchant or manufacturer concerned. He cannot do this effectively by means solely of his own staff. Accordingly, he has to ensure that others who are likely to learn of conduct which would constitute a breach of the assurance must be made aware that the assurance has been given and encouraged to report breaches to his office. The Director General needs no statutory authority to speak and write about his work and about the misdeeds of others with which he is concerned in his work. Both the Director General and his office have full freedom of speech, subject to the general law of defamation and to any special statutory restrictions.

Questions

1. Are there any special difficulties in applying the notion of 'persistent' misconduct in the case of companies which operate on a national, as opposed to local, basis?

2. Do you consider that the powers of the Director General under Part III of the 1973 Act are (i) too extensive or (ii) too restricted or tightly circumscribed? (See further the text which follows.)

Should there be a general duty to trade fairly?

INTRODUCTION

Codes of practice designed to regulate sectors of industry on a voluntary and self-enforcing basis are now comparatively widespread. Section 124(3) of the Fair Trading Act 1973 specifically states that it shall be the duty of the Director to encourage relevant associations to prepare, and to disseminate to their members, codes of practice for guidance in safeguarding and promoting the interests of consumers.

However, these codes suffer from unavoidable defects. The best known and most damaging is that by no means all relevant traders are members of their trade association and amongst those that are not are likely to be found a high proportion of the rogue traders. (Codes are discussed in more detail in Ch 9.)

PROPOSALS

This problem was felt to be particularly acute in the Home Improvements sector and prompted the Director to propose a possible change of direction, which is explained and expanded in the following extracts.

Home Improvements—A Discussion Paper—March 1982 (Office of Fair Trading)

Chapter 6—A change of direction

6.1   In the home improvements sector there are likely to be millions of transactions every year ranging from the insignificant to major building jobs. It is important to be realistic, therefore, not only about the scale of the householder's problems in this area but also about what is and what is not practicable for his protection. Satisfaction, or lack of it in this market, often involves subjective judgments—the home extension which does not blend with the rest of the house as expected or the roof insulation which fails to secure the savings in fuel bills anticipated. Vigilance by the householder is of no less importance in the purchase of home improvements than in other consumer transactions, and certain elementary rules are suggested at the end of this chapter. At the same time, while exercising normal prudence, the householder is entitled to expect that the trader intends to carry out the work competently. Moreover, any recognition of the need for care by the householder in no sense diminishes the responsibility which rests on the industry to improve its own standards: abuses are widespread and there can be no justification for complacency.

6.2   . . . Although it is tempting to look for a comprehensive solution to deal with the problems which householders experience with home improvement works, it seems unlikely that it is appropriate to think in terms of far-ranging and detailed legislation. On the contrary, the diverse and rapidly changing nature of activities in the home improvement sector, the important role of the small firm, and problems of enforcement mean that there is every advantage in maintaining flexible methods of control of varied and often novel abuses.

6.3   Self-regulation has an important part to play in this. Experience shows that trade associations acting for and on behalf of their members can take positive steps to improve the image of the industry and reduce discontent among customers by adopting a voluntary code of practice designed to deal with the specific consumer problems. The recent initiative taken by the Glass and Glazing Federation in introducing a revised code, after consultation with this Office, is a welcome development, and the Office proposes to encourage other trade associations in the home improvements sector to follow the lead of the Glass and Glazing Federation.

. . .

6.5   However, voluntary codes of practice are unlikely to provide the whole answer in improving trading standards within the home improvements sector, and perhaps the answer lies in a change of direction. Codes are only binding on members of the trade associations and, even where a code of practice exists, a substantial number of traders, including most of the rogues, are unlikely to be members of the association. The Director General already has powers which enable action to be taken against individual traders who persistently breach the civil or criminal law in a way which causes detriment to the consumer or follow unfair business practices. These powers are contained in Part III of the Fair Trading Act and the licensing provisions of the Consumer Credit Act. . . . [See above pp 424–428 and pp 207–216 respectively.] These powers can only operate in the case of Part III where there is a breach of the existing law and in the case of a Consumer Credit licensee where the supplier concerned carries on a consumer credit, consumer hire or ancillary credit business. There is no other general remedy against an unfair trader. Moreover, if codes of practice are to be effective in achieving their full potential, there are strong arguments in favour of a statutory duty on all traders to trade fairly with codes providing the detailed meaning of what such duty specifically required. This duty would provide a norm by which both traders and consumers could measure their conduct and would be a positive step towards generally high standards. A duty of this nature would provide the flexible method for establishing satisfactory trading standards without the inflexibility inherent in often complex and difficult legislation for dealing with specific abuses. Although the case for such a statutory general duty to trade fairly can be put in relation to the provision to consumers of all goods and services, this paper is concerned to do so only in relation to the home improvements sector. Here the case is particularly strong because of the paucity of strong and effective trade associations willing to promote voluntary codes of practice for their members. If a general duty to trade fairly is established in the home improvements sector, it may constitute an exemplar for the provision of consumer goods and services generally.

6.6   It would not be practical in this paper to set out in detail how a general duty to trade fairly should operate, but a number of commentators have suggested that the detailed requirements of the general duty would be set out in a code or codes of practice. If such an approach were adopted the codes would be drawn up in consultation with relevant trade associations and other interested parties. (The involvement of trade associations and consumer organisations in the development of the relevant codes of practice would enable all concerned to take a positive role in setting the standards of trading that would be regarded as acceptable for all those engaged in a particular activity.) Under an umbrella of a statutory general duty to trade fairly it would be possible to incorporate particular requirements into new-style codes of practice which would represent the standards envisaged in the general duty to trade fairly. This would include such matters as cancellation rights, identification of salesmen, high-pressure selling, quotations and estimates, completion dates and guarantee protection schemes and would apply to all traders in the field irrespective of their membership or non-membership of trade associations. It would be for discussion as to whether such a general duty and/or the supporting codes should give rise to rights which individual consumers could enforce against those traders who have in a particular transaction broken the principles of fair trading.

6.7   The primary method of enforcement would probably be an obligation on the Director General to seek from a trader who persistently followed a course of conduct in breach of the general duty, an undertaking or assurance as to his future conduct. If a trader was in breach of the code the onus would be on the trader to establish that the interests of consumers were being satisfactorily protected in some other way. The procedure could be similar to that followed under Part III of the Fair Trading Act so that failure to give an assurance could be followed by proceedings for a court order. There could thereafter be proceedings for contempt against any trader who failed to comply with a court order already given.

6.8   Although progress in reducing complaints and minimising misunderstandings can be made by voluntary action on the part of traders themselves and by statutory backing for codes of practice through a general duty in this sector to trade fairly, in the last resort the best safeguards for a householder's interests are knowledge, vigilance and realism. These safeguards—which are set out as seven golden rules in the following paragraph—are essentially matters of caution and commonsense; qualities, sadly it must be said, which are liable to desert the householder at the moment when he commissions work in the home. The many industries and trades, however, which serve the householder in making home improvements have themselves a pressing interest in improving knowledge among potential customers about various aspects of home improvements. If it were generally felt to be useful, the Office could produce guidance leaflets, but there can be no real substitute for a vigorous and determined campaign by the several industries and trades themselves which make up the home improvements sector to improve communications with their customers, to deal on the basis of effective self-regulation with the minority of traders who act unfairly, and to re-establish in the public mind a reputation for reliability, quality and craftsmanship.

After considering the responses to the Discussion Paper the Director General of Fair Trading returned to the subject the following year.

Home improvements: a Report by the Director General of Fair Trading, June 1983

. . .

Legislation

12.1   In view of the inherent limitations of codes of practice as effective means of improving trading standards, the suggestion was made in the discussion paper that there should be established by statute a general duty to trade fairly in relation to the home improvements sector.

12.2   The Office did not discuss in detail how a general duty to trade fairly would operate but the approach outlined was that, under the umbrella of such a statutory duty, particular requirements would be incorporated into new-style codes of practice. These codes would be drawn up in consultation with relevant trade associations and consumer organisations and cover such matters as non-statutory cancellation rights, the identification of salesmen, high-pressure selling, quotations and estimates, completion dates and guarantee protection schemes. A key point would be that these detailed standards would apply to all traders in the field irrespective of their membership or non-membership of trade associations. The Office suggested that the primary method of enforcement would probably be an obligation on the Director General of Fair Trading to seek from a trader who persistently followed a course of conduct in breach of the general duty an assurance as to his future conduct. Refusal or breach of such an assurance would lead to proceedings for a court order as in the present procedures followed under Part III of the Fair Trading Act.

12.3   The recommendation attracted more comment than any other, which is not surprising in view of its wide reaching ramifications. Many respondents were attracted to the concept of a general duty because they considered that it would provide an adaptable method for establishing satisfactory trading standards without the inflexibility inherent in legislation for dealing with specific abuses. Some considered that while the concept has obvious attractions, the effectiveness of a general duty would depend greatly on the means of its application. A few respondents opposed the introduction of a statutory duty, regarding it as either unnecessary or counter-productive.

12.4   The Office's own preliminary consideration of the feasibility of imposing on traders a general duty to trade fairly, as well as comments in response to the discussion paper, suggest that it would be in the interests of both traders and consumers to have as clear an idea as possible of what constituted fair trading in a particular transaction and that it would be advantageous for the duty to form the basis of a code or codes of practice.

12.5   Assuming that a general duty to trade fairly would be exemplified by a code or codes of practice, ideally these should be as comprehensive as possible, since otherwise there would still be uncertainty of interpretation which could be resolved only through the courts. The more comprehensive the code or codes of practice, however, the more detailed the necessary preparatory consultation between traders and consumer organisations would have to be.

12.6   Clearly, the question of how the general duty may be enforced is a vital one. It is suggested that the duty should be enforced only when a specific requirement provided for in one or other of the codes of practice that will underpin the general duty has been broken. Where such a requirement is broken, it would seem right that an individual consumer who can show loss or damage resulting from that breach should be able to claim compensation. The primary method of enforcement, however, would, as the Office envisaged in the consultation paper, be the use of Part III of the Fair Trading Act against traders who persistently broke code obligations.

12.7   The Office will not seek to go further in this report because the concept of and the practical issues raised by a statutory duty to trade fairly require further detailed and careful consideration. The Office proposes to consult further with interested trade bodies, consumer organisations and others on the form such a duty should take, the means by which standards would be set out and the sanctions. A detailed report with specific recommendations will then be published.

Statement from the Office of Fair Trading (30 November 1983)

The discussion document on home improvements problems published in March 1982 proposed . . . a general duty [to trade fairly] for those engaged in home improvements work and the proposal attracted considerable interest and general support. Those who commented on this proposal recognised that a general duty would have a much wider application than just to home improvements work. Contributions and comments from those who have concerns other than home improvements would be helpful in the detailed consideration the Office is now giving to the general duty and to the preparation of a further discussion paper on this subject. It is intended that the paper should discuss the form and scope of a general duty to trade fairly covering the full range of goods and services provided to consumers in the United Kingdom and the legal and practical implications of its introduction. Among the questions which will need to be considered are:

(i)   the form that such a duty should take;

(ii)   whether any general duty should be supported by more detailed requirements, such as codes of practice and, if so, how the provisions of such codes could and should be developed;

(iii) what the status in law of the general duty and any detailed codes or guidelines expressing the concept should be;

(iv)   whether persistent breaches of the general duty should be subject to the procedures provided for in Part III of the Fair Trading Act;

(v)   whether a breach of the general duty should give rise to civil rights, enforceable by the consumer and/or to criminal (or other) sanctions enforceable by public officials.

SOME PRELIMINARY COMMENTS

'Should there be a general duty to trade fairly?' by B. W. Harvey (1984) Trading Law 45

. . .

Is there such a duty already?

Although no single statute lays down a 'general' duty to trade 'fairly', it must not be forgotten that there are a significant number of statutory provisions which penalize patently unfair trading. The most obvious of these statutory powers are those contained under Part III of the Fair Trading Act 1973 [above pp 424–428] . . .

Another arrow in the DGFT's quiver is the power to refuse or revoke a licence under the Consumer Credit Act 1974 [above pp 207–216].

. . .

This very wide power is used effectively against traders in sectors heavily dependent on the provision of consumer credit such as secondhand car dealers. It will be seen that the conduct which must be taken into account is wider than that relevant to Part III of the Fair Trading Act (which is confined to civil or criminal breaches).

In addition to the powers of the DGFT, there are a number of criminal statutes penalizing specific cases of 'unfair' trading. The most common offences, as evinced by the statistics issued annually by the OFT, are a false description of goods and services under the Trade Descriptions Act 1968, the giving of short measure or the use for trade of inaccurate weighing or measuring equipment under the Weights and Measures Act 1963 (as amended) and offences relating to the quality and labelling of food under the Food and Drugs Act 1955 and allied legislation. One might also include, by way of a further example, the canvassing of debtor-creditor agreements off trade premises which is an offence under s 49 of the Consumer Credit Act 1974 unless the prospective debtor has previously requested the visit in writing.

The above paragraph relates entirely to criminal offences. The civil law has also filled out considerably over the last decade. The Judges themselves have been prepared to interfere with contracts mainly on the ground of inequality of bargaining power (see eg *Lloyds Bank Ltd v Bundy* [1974] 3 All ER 757 [above p 265]). This idea has long applied to extortionate terms in mortgages and the almost equally venerable prohibition against extortionate rates of interest has now been re-enacted as a prohibition against 'extortionate credit bargains' under ss 137–139 of the Consumer Credit Act 1974. There is now also considerable control of exemption clauses in standard form contracts, many formerly valid such clauses being made void as against a consumer by the Unfair Contract Terms Act 1977. And on the basis that economic duress is more likely to occur at home than on trade premises, the consumer is entitled under the Hire Purchase Acts to a 'cooling-off' period in the case of agreements signed off trade premises. When the relevant provisions of the Consumer Credit Act 1974 come into force on May 19, 1985, this form of protection will extend to most types of regulated consumer credit agreements signed off trade premises.

Is there a need for more protection?

The above far from comprehensive catalogue of existing common law and statutory sanctions against unfair trading raises the question of whether there is very much else, not already caught, against which to legislate. Perhaps the most obvious gap arises where a trader is not a member of a trading association having a code of practice. He sells goods for cash, and is thus not subject to the sanction of refusal or withdrawal of his consumer credit licence. He does not actually commit more than the occasional civil or criminal breach and cannot thus be said to be persistently breaking the law. Hence he escapes the sanctions of the DGFT under Part III of the Fair Trading Act.

. . .

The key proposal of the DGFT is that, since a general duty to trade fairly must be properly defined if sanctions are to be attached, it should be set out in a code or codes of practice. These codes should be drawn up in consultation with relevant trade associations and other interested parties. The OFT would no doubt introduce uniform rights and duties into these codes as far as possible. It is to be assumed that they would include such matters as cancellation rights, identification of salesmen, high-pressure selling, quotations and estimates, completion dates and guarantee protection schemes. The code would then be made applicable to all traders in the field irrespective of their membership or non-membership of the relevant trade association. The sanction against unfair trading would be a similar one to that existing under Part III—a written assurance, followed if necessary by a court order and ultimately by proceedings for contempt of court.

Pros and cons of such a system

Provided a code of practice is carefully and accurately drawn up there is no objection in principle to its being given statutory form. A precedent already exists, in fact, under the provisions of the Weights and Measures Act 1979 whereby the packers' code is given statutory effect by virtue of reg 19 of the Weights and Measures (Packaged Goods) Regulations 1979. Similarly, s 15 of the Insurance Brokers (Registration) Act 1977 gives the disciplinary committee of the insurance brokers registration council power to strike off a member who has been 'guilty of unprofessional conduct'. The unprofessional conduct is measured by reference to the council's 'code of conduct' to be drawn up in accordance with the directions in s 10.

Nevertheless, wholesale conversion of what is normally a rather informally drafted code of practice into the precision instrument that a statute laying down sanctions should be is a major exercise. It is questionable whether it is good enough simply to leave the OFT to do this work. There might be a case for giving supervision of it to the now semi-defunct consumer protection advisory committee who could make recommendations to the appropriate minister under provisions similar to those which already exist (but are currently not used) in Part II of the Fair Trading Act. The proposals could be presented to CPAC by the OFT after careful negotiation by that latter body.

Since there is no doubt that the sort of trader taken by way of example above is likely to trade both unfairly and compete with his fellow traders unfairly because he is not a member of a trade association, the DGFT's suggestion along these lines is worth very serious considera-tion. But there must be proper protection built in for the trader since quasi-criminal sanctions lie behind what could easily be a rather ill-defined duty to be 'fair'. If the OFT gives fair warning before seeking written assurances and operating further sanctions there is no reason to suppose that the system should not work well enough. (There have been few complaints about the parallel working of Part III of the Fair Trading Act). The smooth working of the Part III procedures, though not directly analogous (since *persistence* is required), provides useful experience from which to develop the idea.

A rather disturbing feature of all this, however, is the interest of the injured consumer. The consumer obtains no benefit where a fine or penalty of the contempt of court lands up in Her Majesty's Exchequer. He is left to fend for himself by taking probably expensive and time-consuming civil action. What is really needed is a much more streamlined version of the compensation order system which would, to a greater or lesser extent, in the magistrates' courts. A possible solution would be to give the OFT the right to make a compensation order for breach of general duty to trade fairly in favour of a consumer, having regard to the loss that he has actually suffered. This would, however, have to be accompanied by a right of appeal. There would appear to be no great difficulties in this since the civil wrong arising is analogous to the well known tort of breach of statutory duty. Some criminal statutes conferring consumer protection do already give the injured consumer the right to sue for breach of statutory duty—see, eg, the Consumer Safety Act 1978. It would be ironic if this important element of compensation for the injured consumer is overlooked in the excitement over the creation of a possible new duty to trade fairly. But the implications of giving the DGFT such 'originating' judicial powers would need detailed examination and proper checks and balances before it would be safe to proceed along these lines.

Questions

1. Is the de facto abolition of the Consumer Protection Advisory Committee and the consequential obsolescence of the Part II procedures in the 1973 Act a desirable slimming down of unnecessary bureaucracy, or does the present position leave a genuine gap? If the latter is so, how would you fill this gap?

2. Is there genuinely a case for a general duty to trade fairly in the light of existing criminal and civil sanctions? If so, what form should it take and what objectives should it seek to attain?

3. Bumpkin buys a country cottage with no effective water supply and decides to build a well. He employs Birch, who advertises his services as a water diviner, to find out the best place to sink a well. Bumpkin signs a contract with Birch which states that a flat fee of £100 is payable whether or not water is subsequently found. Birch surveys the property for ten minutes by walking round the garden, isolates a spot which he says should be fruitful to excavate and departs with his £100. No water is found there on expensive excavation. Bumpkin has been advised (a) that there would be little prospect of suing Birch successfully for any breach of contract (although Bumpkin now believes Birch to be a charlatan) and (b) that there is no trade association or code of practice for water diviners.

Consider Bumpkin's position on the basis that (a) there is no general duty to trade fairly under English law, and (b) that a general duty has been introduced along the lines suggested by the Director General.

SOME COMPARATIVE PROVISIONS

If English law were to adopt a broadly based provision controlling unfair trading practices a number of models would be available for possible adoption. These are comprehensively discussed in an important article from which the following extract is taken.

'Unfair Trade Practices Legislation: Symbolism and Substances in Consumer Protection' by Belobaba (1977) 15 Osgoode Hall Law Journal 327, 345.

. . .

2. THE PROHIBITED PRACTICES

An important feature of any comprehensive consumer trade practices enactment will be the statutory design of the prohibition provisions. The legislative draftsman has essentially three choices. He may choose to provide simply a general prohibition against all deceptive, misleading, or unconscionable conduct in consumer transactions. This is the approach taken in the *Federal Trade Commission Act*[1] which provides, inter alia, that 'unfair or deceptive acts or practices in commerce are declared unlawful'[2] While this blanket prohibition is definitionally capable of protecting the consumer against all eventualities, its open-textured quality promotes needless uncertainty and excessive litigation.[3] A trade practices enactment that is fair to suppliers as well as consumers requires a greater degree of precision.

This concern for specificity may persuade the legislative draftsman to adopt the UK *Trade Description Act*[4] approach, which provides an exhaustive listing of the specific practices that are proscribed by the legislation. Unlike the general prohibition technique, the exhaustive specification method cannot be criticized for lack of clarity. The problem here is one of inevitable under-inclusion. The listing of prohibited practices will invariably fall short of including every conceivable and innovative trade practice abuse.

'It is impossible to frame definitions which embrace all unfair practices. There is no limit to human inventiveness in this field. Even if all known unfair practices were specifically defined and prohibited, it would be at once necessary to begin all over again. If [a legislature] were to adopt this method of definition, it would undertake an endless task.'[5]

The third approach available to the draftsman is one that combines a general prohibition against unfair practices with a specific listing. This specific itemization of prohibited acts or practices does not limit the generality of the prohibition. This third approach seems to be the most appropriate for the effective regulation of consumer trade practices. The non-exhaustive 'shopping list' coupled with a general prohibition provides an optimal combination of specificity and flexibility.

This third alternative was adopted by each of the provinces that have enacted consumer trade practice legislation. Noticeably influenced by the *Uniform Consumer Sales Practices Act*, . . . each of the four provincial enactments under consideration utilizes both the general prohibition and the 'shopping list' of unfair practices.

(a) The General Prohibition

The Ontario Act provides the clearest example of an open-textured general prohibition: '[n]o person shall engage in an unfair practice.'[6] Another provision proceeds to itemize those practices that are deemed to be unfair practices, one sub-part being devoted to 'false, misleading or deceptive consumer representations'[7] and the other to 'unconscionable consumer representations.'[8] The inter-relationship of the general proscription and the 'shopping list' of itemized prohibitions is somewhat more complex in the BC, Alberta, and Saskatchewan enactments. In the BC and Saskatchewan legislation there exists a 'double-barrelled' general prohibition, one provision providing an open-ended proscription of deceiving or misleading acts or practices,[9] and another provision providing similar generality with respect to 'unconscionable acts or practices.'[10] The only province that lacks an open-ended prohibition of unconscionable acts or practices is Alberta. The Alberta legislation does, however, prohibit any representation or conduct that has the effect 'or might reasonably have the effect' of deceiving or misleading any consumer.[11]

(b) The Deceptive Practices Shopping List

Why would a provincial legislative draftsman prefer to itemize illustrations of the acts or practices that are deemed to be deceptive or misleading under one heading and those that are suggested as unconscionable acts or practices under another? An ordinary consumer would not really care how the draftsman has characterised the unfair practice. His only concern would be effective redress. Indeed, one might be hard pressed to articulate any meaningful definitional distinction between the so-called 'deceptive or misleading acts or practices' and the 'unconscionable' ones. Lawyers have tended to explain this dichotomy by reference to the duality of law and equity and the resulting division of responsibility for deception and unconscionability. . . . While a single listing of the deemed prohibitions may be more logical, the provincial enactments have retained the traditional distinction in drafting the 'shopping lists'.

Each of the provincial trade practices enactments has a fairly comprehensive listing of the deceptive or misleading acts or practices that are deemed to be unfair practices: sixteen specifications in the BC Act, fourteen in the Ontario Act, and twenty-one in the Alberta and Saskatchewan enactments.

1. 15 USC, s 45(a) (1) (1970).
2. ibid.
3. The FTC, however, has extensive rule-making powers which enable the agency to inject some precision into the open-textured prohibitions.
4. UK 1968, c 29.
5. *Federal Trade Commission v The Sperry and Hutchinson Company* (1914), 405 US 233, per White J at 240, quoting from HR Rep No 1142. 63d Cong 2d Sess 18–19.
6. Ontario Act, s 3(1).
7. Ibid, s 2(a).
8. Ibid, s 2(b).
9. BC Act, s 2(1); Saskatchewan Act, s 3(1).
10. BC Act, s 3(3); Saskatchewan Act, s 4(1).
11. Alberta Act, s 4(1) (d).

. . .

Of the various Canadian provisions mentioned in the above article the British Columbia statute is generally recognised as being the most comprehensive. The words 'deceptive' and 'unconscionable' are defined as follows:

British Columbia Trade Practices Act 1979 (RS Chap 406)

3. Deceptive acts or practices

(1) For the purposes of this Act, a deceptive act or practice includes
  (a) an oral, written, visual, descriptive or other representation, including a failure to disclose;
  (b) any conduct
having the capability, tendency or effect of deceiving or misleading a person.

(2) A deceptive act or practice by a supplier in relation to a consumer transaction may occur before, during or after the consumer transaction.

(3) Without limiting subsection (1), one or more of the following, however expressed, constitutes a deceptive act or practice:

(a) a representation that the subject of a consumer transaction has sponsorship, approval, performance characteristics, accessories, ingredients, quantities, components, uses or benefits that it does not have;

(b) a representation that the supplier has a sponsorship, approval, status, affiliation or connection that he does not have;

(c) a representation that the subject of a consumer transaction is of a particular standard, quality, grade, style or model if it is not;

(d) a representation that the subject of a consumer transaction has been used to an extent that is different from the fact;

(e) a representation that the subject of a consumer transaction is new or unused if it is not, or if it is deteriorated, altered, reconditioned or reclaimed;

(f) a representation that the subject of a consumer transaction has a particular prior history or usage if it has not;

(g) a representation that the subject of a consumer transaction is available for a reason that is different from the fact;

(h) a representation that the subject of a consumer transaction has been made available in accordance with a previous representation if it has not;

(i) a representation that the subject of a consumer transaction is available if the supplier has no intention of supplying or otherwise disposing of the subject as represented;

(j) a representation that is such that a person could reasonably conclude that a price benefit or advantage exists, if it does not;

(k) a representation that a service, part, replacement or repair is needed if it is not;

(l) a representation that the purpose or intent of a solicitation of, or a communication with, a consumer by a supplier is for a purpose or intent different from the fact;

(m) a representation that a consumer transaction involves or does not involve rights, remedies or obligations if the representation is deceptive or misleading;

(n) a representation such that a consumer might reasonably conclude that the subject of a consumer transaction is available in greater quantities than are in fact available from the supplier, unless the limitation of availability represented by the supplier has been given such prominence as is required by the regulations;

(o) a representation as to the authority of a salesman, representative, employee or agent to negotiate the final terms of a consumer transaction if the representation is different from the fact;

(p) where an estimate of the price of a consumer transaction is materially less, as determined by the regulations, than the price of the consumer transaction as subsequently determined or demanded by the supplier and the supplier has proceeded with his performance of the consumer transaction without the express consent of the consumer;

(q) where the price of a unit of a consumer transaction is given in an advertisement, display or representation, the failure to give, in the same advertisement, display or representation, at least equal prominence to the total price of the consumer transaction;

(r) the use, in an oral or written representation, of exaggeration, innuendo or ambiguity as to a material fact, or failure to state a material fact, if the representation is deceptive or misleading; and

(s) the other acts or practices prescribed by the regulations.

4. Unconscionable act or practice

(1) An unconscionable act or practice by a supplier in relation to a consumer transaction may occur before, during or after the consumer transaction.

(2) In determining whether an act or practice is unconscionable, a court of competent jurisdiction shall consider all the surrounding circumstances which the supplier knew or ought to have known, including, without limiting the foregoing,

(a) that the consumer was subjected to undue pressure to enter into the consumer transaction;

(b) that the consumer was taken advantage of by his inability or incapacity to reasonably protect his own interest by reason of his physical or mental infirmity, ignorance, illiteracy, age or his inability to understand the character, nature or language of the consumer transaction, or any other matter related to it;

   (c) that, at the time the consumer transaction was entered, the price grossly exceeded the price at which similar subjects of similar consumer transactions were readily obtainable by like consumers;

   (d) that, at the time the consumer transaction was entered, there was no reasonable probability of full payment of the price by the consumer;

   (e) that the terms or conditions on, or subject to, which the consumer transaction was entered by the consumer are so harsh or adverse to the consumer as to be inequitable; and

   (f) the other circumstances prescribed by the regulations.

(3) Where there is an unconscionable act or practice in respect of a consumer transaction, that consumer transaction is unenforceable by the supplier.

(4) Nothing in this section limits, restricts or derogates from the court's power and jurisdiction.

NOTES

1. The powers conferred on the Director of Trade Practices by ss 18 and 24 of the Act are printed above pp 378–379. For discussion of similar issues in the context of controlling the use of unfair contract terms see above p 274 et seq.

2. The various deceptive acts or practices listed in s 3 above may be compared with the provisions of our own Trade Descriptions Act 1968 discussed in Ch 12 below at pp 464–465 and 500. It is accepted that it is not realistic to discuss the introduction of a general duty to trade fairly on the basis that such existing legislation as the 1968 Act would then be repealed: see (1985) Trading Law 2.

Similarly broad provisions are to be found in both Swedish and Australian statutes.

The Marketing Practices Act (Sweden) (SFS 1975:1418)

. . .

Improper Marketing

s2. A tradesman who, in the marketing of goods, service or other commodity, advertises or takes other action which, by conflicting with good commercial standards or otherwise, adversely affects consumers or tradesmen, may be prohibited by the Market Court from continuing therewith or undertaking any similar action. A prohibition may also be issued to an employee of a tradesman and to any other acting on behalf of a tradesman, as well as to any other person who has substantially contributed to the action.

. . .

(Translation from *Law and the Weaker Party* Vol III, eds Alan Neal and Anders Victorin).

Trade Practices Act 1974 (Australia)

PART V—CONSUMER PROTECTION

Division 1—Unfair Practices

52. (1) A corporation shall not, in trade or commerce, engage in conduct that is misleading or deceptive or is likely to mislead or deceive.

(2) Nothing in the succeeding provisions of this Division shall be taken as limiting by implication the generality of sub-section (1).

. . .

NOTE

Sections 53 to 64 make provision for more specific practices including bait advertising (s 56), referral selling (s 57), coercion at place of residence (s 60) and pyramid selling (s 61).

CHAPTER 11

Aspects of the general criminal law relating to trading standards including consumer safety

General criminal law relating to trading standards

INTRODUCTION

Control of fraudulent or dangerous practices by producers has been exercised by the criminal law of England and Wales over many centuries. It is, for instance, possible to trace the history of hallmarking legislation back to the 14th century. The motivation for this public control of trading practices was originally probably mixed. The consumer has not, until very recent times, had an effective voice as such in government. So although it would be an over-simplification to say that the consumer interest was traditionally never considered, it is probably justifiable to say that the main motivation for encouraging government to exercise control over the fraudulent trader came from competitors whose business was threatened.

So far as the consumer is concerned the justification for the umbrella of criminal protection which he currently enjoys is that it is not usually possible, simply by inspection of an article, for him to tell whether it is as described or, even if it is so, whether it is dangerous to consume or use. The classic illustrations of this point arise in the fields of hallmarking and the sale of food. In the case of hallmarking the fundamental need for protection arises because gold, silver and platinum are too soft to be of much practical use and normally need to be alloyed with other metals. This lowers the intrinsic value of the article, and it is therefore essential to establish by chemical analysis what proportion the precious metal content bears to the whole. In the case of food, the risk of toxicity arises either from deliberate adulteration by the manufacturer or seller or from the use of dangerous ingredients.

It must not be assumed that the consumer is necessarily without a civil remedy if injured, physically or financially, by purchasing an article where the sale or supply contravenes the criminal law. Civil compensation can be direct through a compensation order made by the court (see above pp 326–330) or indirect. The indirect route will involve bringing a civil action in the County Court or the High Court either for breach of contract, or for a tort such as negligence which has incidentally been committed or, where appropriate, for breach of statutory duty. With regard to the tort of breach of statutory duty some statutes, notably the Consumer Protection Act 1961 and the Consumer Safety Act 1978 (below p 456), give a specific civil right of action where a person is affected by a contravention of the Act or regulations made thereunder. In all cases, where a criminal conviction has previously been obtained, evidence of the conviction may be pleaded in a civil case to prove that the defendant committed the offence: see s 11 of the Civil Evidence Act 1968.

DE-CRIMINALISING REGULATORY OFFENCES

There has been increasing criticism over recent years of the volume of regulatory criminal offences and many of these lie in the area of trading standards. A glance at the six volume looseleaf encyclopaedia entitled *Butterworths Law of Food and Drugs*, and at the 120 or so sets of regulations made under the Food and Drugs Act 1955 [see now the Food Act 1984], the European Communities Act 1972 or allied statutes (and bearing in mind that most of these regulations impose criminal offences) emphasizes graphically the extent of the problem. The objection to 'creating crimes like confetti' is well expressed by Lord Devlin in 'Morals and Quasi-Criminal Law and the Law of Tort' (Holdsworth Club Presidential Address, 17 March 1961) (quoted Borrie *The Development of Consumer Law and Policy—Bold Spirits and Timorous Souls*, p 55). Lord Devlin considered that the ordinary man still thinks of crime as conduct that is disgraceful or morally wrong. He adds:

> 'But he cannot be expected to go on doing so for ever if the law jumbles morals and sanitary regulations together and teaches him to have no more respect for the Ten Commandments than for the woodworking regulations. Meanwhile . . . it may cause him unnecessary distress if for some petty offence which he may not even himself have committed he is classed among criminals and if in the machinery of the law he is processed as if he were one.'

Approaching the matter from a different angle Professor Atiyah has also warned that consumer protection can often be bought only at a cost which is passed on to those who purchase the goods or services in question: see 'Consumer Protection Time to Take Stock' [1979] Liverpool Law Review, p 20.

David Tench in his book *Towards a Middle System of Law* (Consumers Association, 1981) proposes that regulatory offences should be no longer subject to criminal penalties but instead should be termed infringements or contraventions. These would attract civil penalties, a change which would supposedly remove from a person found to have committed an infringement the stigma of an infraction of the criminal law. (It is to be queried whether someone duly 'convicted' of a 'penalty' and 'fined' a large sum of money will be too concerned whether the infraction is termed criminal or not). A similar idea was floated by Justice in its report entitled 'Breaking the Rules', the report estimating that there are over 7,000 offences within this category. However there is little sign of wholesale sympathy for this idea from the legislative or executive of the UK, though the Director General of Fair Trading does give cautious encouragement to it, albeit on a selective basis (see Borrie, *The Development of Consumer Law and Policy*, Ch 3). Sir Gordon Borrie states (op cit p 58):

> It is my own view that a wider *range* of powers than exist at present, to be exercised either directly by the local authority (subject to appeal to the courts) or exercised by application to the courts, eg for an order to stop illegal trading or to close down a shop, would be a useful addition to the enforcement armoury.

MENS REA

As is explained in some detail in Chapter 14 on Statutory Defences, the usual pattern of trading standards statutes is to create offences of strict liability subject only to statutory defences which will, typically, allow the defendant to plead act or default of another and due diligence. There are a few significant divergencies from this pattern. For instance, s 14 of the Trade Descriptions Act 1968 (see below p 500) relating to false or misleading statements as to services, etc requires a defendant to make a statement 'which he *knows* to be false' or '*recklessly* to make a statement which is false'. But the question may be asked—what is the position where a statute lays down an offence which involves no requirement of knowledge or recklessness, but does not either specifically directly or indirectly indicate that the offence is an absolute one? An example occurs in s 1(1) of the Hallmarking Act 1973, and the effect of this type of provision was considered in depth by the Divisional Court in the following case.

Chilvers v Rayner [1984] 1 All ER 843, [1984] 1 WLR 328, Queen's Bench Divisional Court

Robert Goff LJ. There is before the court an appeal by way of case stated from a decision of justices sitting at Guildford, under which they found the appellant guilty of an offence contrary to the Hallmarking Act 1973.

An information had been preferred against the appellant by the respondent, a trading standards officer, that he, in the course of trade as a dealer in jewellery and precious metals, supplied to Pia Theresia Hauselmann an unhallmarked article, namely an 18 carat Russian gold bangle, to which the description 'gold' was applied, contrary to s 1(1) (b) of the Hallmarking Act 1973. That charge was found to be proved and the appellant was fined £200 and ordered to pay a sum towards the prosecution costs. The case raises the question whether the offence created by s 1(1)(b) of the 1973 Act is an absolute offence.

The facts of the case, as found by the justices, are as follows. On 12 January 1982 Mrs Hauselmann purchased a Russian bangle from Orlando jewellers, 1 Sydenham Road, Guildford, of which the appellant was the proprietor. The bangle was accurately described as 18 carat gold. It was offered at £671.77; that price was reduced by 40% as being part of a 'sale', and was further reduced to £383 in consideration of payment of £300 in cash and £63 by credit card. The appellant had purchased the bangle in 1979 from Celine Collection, with whom he had traded for some time, for £160. The bangle bore some markings, but was not hallmarked. The assay office to which the appellant sent items for hallmarking had not received this bangle to hallmark. On these facts, the justices concluded that the appellant had supplied an unhallmarked article to which the description 'gold' was applied.

Before the justices, the appellant contended that the prosecution had not established the essential ingredients of mens rea, whereupon the prosecution contended that the section did not require any proof of mental state on the part of the appellant. The justices formed the opinion that it was not necessary for the prosecution to prove mens rea and so found the case proved.

The question posed by the justices for the opinion of the court is:

'Whether the offence created by s 1 (1) (b) of the Hallmarking Act 1973 is an absolute offence so that the prosecution does not have to prove mens rea.'

I turn next to the Hallmarking Act 1973. Section 1(1) provides as follows:

'Subject to the provisions of this Act, any person who, in the course of a trade or business—(a) applies to an unhallmarked article a description indicating that it is wholly or partly made of gold, silver or platinum, or (b) supplies, or offers to supply, an unhallmarked article to which such a description is applied, shall be guilty of an offence.'

By sub-s (2) it is provided that sub-s (1) shall not apply to a description which is permitted by Pt 1 of Sch 1 to the Act and, by sub-s (3) it is provided that sub-s (1) shall not apply to an article within Pt II of Sch 1. Part 1 of Sch 1 sets out a list of permissible descriptions, eg 'plated' or 'rolled' gold. Part II sets out a list of exempted articles, such as, for example, '1. An article which is intended for despatch to a destination outside the United Kingdom'.

It is striking that s 1(1) of the 1973 Act follows very closely the wording of s 1(1) of the Trade Descriptions Act 1968, to which indeed reference is made in other subsections of s 1 of the 1973 Act. Section 1(1) of the Trade Descriptions Act 1968 has been held to create an offence of absolute liability, subject to the statutory defences, in particular the defence set out in s 24 of the Act: see *Clode v Barnes* [1974] 1 All ER 1166, [1974] 1 WLR 544 and *Macnab v Alexanders of Greenock Ltd* 1971 SLT 121.

There is no equivalent of s 24 in the Hallmarking Act 1973. However, there are certain provisions of that Act creating other offences which expressly require knowledge on the part of the accused as an ingredient of the offence. Thus, s 4(4) provides that a person who knowingly makes a false statement in furnishing any information to an assay office, for the purposes of s 4(2) (ie for the purposes of showing the assay office to its satisfaction that the relevant article was made in the United Kingdom, with a view to its being hallmarked) shall be guilty of an offence.

Section 6, which is concerned with counterfeiting, creates a number of offences, each of which requires a specified intent on the part of the accused, or knowledge or belief by him, that the relevant object is counterfeit. It is of particular interest that s 6(1)(c) provides that any person who 'utters any counterfeit of a die or any article bearing a counterfeit of a mark . . . shall be guilty of an offence . . .' and that s 6(3) provides:

> 'For the purposes of subsection (1) . . . a person utters any counterfeit die or article bearing a counterfeit of a mark if, knowing or believing the die or mark, as the case may be, to be a counterfeit, he supplies, offers to supply, or delivers the die or article.'

Here, the actus reus is very similar to that prohibited by s 1(1)(b). Yet here, unlike s 1(1)(b), knowledge or belief on the part of the accused that the die or mark is counterfeit is expressly made an ingredient of that offence.

Section 7(6) is also striking. It provides as follows:

> 'It shall be an offence for any person knowingly or any dealer to supply or offer to supply any article bearing any mark of the character of a hallmark and which under subsection (1) of this section may, if the article is in the possession of an assay office, be cancelled, obliterated or defaced, unless the article has been first submitted to an assay office to enable them at their discretion so to cancel, obliterate or deface that mark.'

In this subsection a distinction is therefore drawn between a dealer and other persons and whereas, in the case of other persons, knowledge on their part is an ingredient of the offence created by the subsection, no knowledge is required where the accused is 'a dealer'.

Having regard to these provisions of the Act, it came as no surprise that counsel for the appellant did not seek to argue that mens rea in the form of knowledge of the facts rendering the act an offence under s 1(1) was an ingredient of such an offence. Founding his argument on the speech of Lord Diplock in *Sweet v Parsley* [1969] 1 All ER 347 at 361–362, [1970] AC 132 at 163, he submitted that what had to be proved was the absence of belief, held honestly and on reasonable grounds, that the article was hallmarked. In his submission, it was not enough for the accused to escape conviction that he should have believed the article was hallmarked: he must have believed it to be so on reasonable grounds. So, he submitted, if there was absence of the relevant knowledge on the part of the accused, only if that absence of knowledge was attributable to his carelessness would he be convicted.

. . .

In *Warner v Metropolitan Police Comr* [1968] 2 All ER 356 at 360, [1969] 2 AC 256 at 271–272 Lord Reid referred to the 'long line of cases in which it has been held with regard to less serious offences that absence of mens rea was no defence'. He continued:

> 'Typical examples are offences under public health, licensing and industrial legislation. If a person sets up as say a butcher, a publican, or a manufacturer and exposes unsound meat for sale, or sells drink to a drunk man or certain parts of his factory are unsafe, it is no defence that he could not by the exercise of reasonable care have known or discovered that the meat was unsound, or that the man was drunk or that his premises were unsafe. He must take the risk and when it is found that the statutory prohibition or requirement has been infringed that he must pay the penalty. This may well seem unjust, but it is a comparatively minor injustice, and there is good reason for it as affording some protection to his customers or servants or to the public at large. Although this man might be able to show that he did his best, a more skilful or diligent man in his position might have done better, and when we are dealing with minor penalties which do not involve the disgrace of criminality it may be in the public interest to have a hard and fast rule. Strictly speaking there ought perhaps to be a defence that the defect was truly latent so that no one could have discovered it. But the

law has not developed in that way, and one can see the difficulty if such a defence were allowed in a summary prosecution. These are only quasi-criminal offences and it does not really offend the ordinary man's sense of justice that moral guilt is not of the essence of the offences.'

Again, in *Sweet v Parsley* [1969] 1 All ER 347 at 362, [1970] AC 132 at 163, immediately after the very passage on which counsel for the appellant relied in support of his submission (where Lord Diplock set out the principle in *R v Tolson* (1889) 23 QBD 168, [1886–90] All ER Rep 26), Lord Diplock said:

'Where penal provisions are of general application to the conduct of ordinary citizens in the course of their everyday life the presumption is that the standard of care required of them in informing themselves of facts which would make their conduct unlawful, is that of the familiar common law duty of care. But where the subject-matter of a statute is the regulation of a particular activity involving potential danger to public health, safety or morals, in which citizens have a choice whether they participate or not, the court may feel driven to infer an intention of Parliament to impose, by penal sanctions, a higher duty of care on those who choose to participate and to place on them an obligation to take whatever measures may be necessary to prevent the prohibited act, without regard to those considerations of cost or business practicability which play a part in the determination of what would be required of them in order to fulfil the ordinary common law duty of care. But such an inference is not lightly to be drawn, nor is there any room for it unless there is something that the person on whom the obligation is imposed can do directly or indirectly, by supervision or inspection, by improvement of his business methods or by exhorting those whom he may be expected to influence or control, which will promote observance of the obligation (see *Lim Chin Aik v R* ([1963] 1 All ER 223 at 228, [1963] AC 160 at 174).'

In my judgment, the offence created by s 1(1) of the 1973 Act falls within the category of offences so described by Lord Reid and Lord Diplock. It is not a truly criminal offence, but an offence of a quasi-criminal character. True, an offence relating to hallmarking does not fall precisely within the description 'offences under public health, licensing and industrial legislation', or within the description 'involving danger to public health, safety or morals'. But I do not understand either Lord Reid or Lord Diplock to have been giving a complete list of the relevant offences, which must, in my judgment, having regard to the authorities, extend to include such matters as trade descriptions, although in such cases the absolute offence is of course subject to any statutory defences set out in the relevant Act of Parliament. Furthermore, in accordance with the passage in the advice of the Privy Council in *Lim Chin Aik v R*, referred to by Lord Diplock in *Sweet v Parsley*, it cannot be said that there is nothing which a person on whom the relevant obligations under the 1973 Act are imposed can do, in any of the manners indicated by Lord Diplock, which will promote the observance of the obligation.

For these reasons, I am satisfied that the offence under s 1(1) of the 1973 Act is, like the offence created by s 1(1) of the Trade Descriptions Act 1968, an absolute offence. I find myself in agreement with the opinion expressed by the justices in the case stated and I would answer the question posed for our decision in the affirmative and dismiss the appeal.

Forbes J. I agree.

Appeal dismissed. The court refused leave to appeal to the House of Lords but certified, under s 1(2) of the Administration of Justice Act 1960, that the following point of law of general public importance was involved in the decision: whether it was necessary for any mental state to be established in order that a person might be convicted of an offence under s 1(1)(b) of the Hallmarking Act 1973.

The Appeal Committee of the House of Lords (Lord Keith of Kinkel, Lord Roskill and Lord Brandon of Oakbrook) dismissed a petition by the appellant for leave to appeal.

Questions

Is the suggested distinction between offences categorised by the courts as 'truly criminal' and those us 'quasi-criminal' a real one? Is it, for instance, realistic to describe the conduct of a car dealer who deliberately winds back the odomoter of a car which he then resells, as 'quasi-criminal' (since the prosecution is likely to be under the Trade Descriptions Act)? If not, how could Parliament more clearly demonstrate its intention with regard to criminal legislation to the courts? (See also *Wings Ltd v Ellis* [1984] 3 All ER 577 at 589, per Lord Scarman, below, p 518).

THE EXTENT OF PROTECTION UNDER THE CRIMINAL LAW

From data produced annually by the Office of Fair Trading it is clear that offences under the Weights and Measures Acts, the Trade Descriptions Acts and the Food and Drugs Acts give rise to the largest number of reported convictions. The position for 1982/83 is given in Table 2 (on pp 446–447) and Table 3, below:

Annual Report of the Director General of Fair Trading 1983, p 73

Table 3—Convictions in reported cases under other consumer legislation

	No	Fines (£)
Consumer Credit Act 1974	49[1]	19,735
Weights and Measures Acts		
False or unjust equipment	75	13,929
Short weight or measure	212	47,059
Average weight and quantity offences	74	34,588
Other offences	94	17,617
Total	455	113,193
Food and Drugs Acts		
Not of nature, substance or quality demanded	955	72,095
Unfit food	219	23,890
Labelling regulations and others	648	145,059
Total	1,822	241,044
Estate Agents Act 1979	1	375
Regulations under the Consumer Protection and Consumer Safety Acts	273	99,426
Other legislation enforced by Trading Standards and Environmental Health Departments	997[2]	220,943

1. Includes two sentences each of three months' imprisonment.
2. Includes six sentences of imprisonment and one suspended sentence, in all ranging from 28 days to 15 months.

An idea of the ambit of the main statutes imposing criminal liabilities in Trading Standards law can be gained from the study of the following Table.

The main criminal statutes affecting consumers

Subject Matter	*Legislation*
Inaccurate Quantities	Weights and Measures Act 1963–1967

Statement of and Control of Prices	Trade Descriptions Act 1968; Mock Auctions Act 1961; Prices Acts 1974, 1975.
Food quality and hygiene	Food Act 1984.
False descriptions	Trade Descriptions Act 1968; Trading Representations (Disabled Persons) Act 1958; Food and Drugs Act 1955; Agriculture Act 1970 (section 25); Fabrics (Misdescription) Act 1913.
Unsolicited goods and services	Unsolicited Goods Acts 1971 and 1975.
Consumer Credit	Consumer Credit Act 1974 (contains some criminal provisions).
Consumer Safety; Licensing and labelling of Dangerous Products	Consumer Protection Acts 1961 and 1971; Consumer Safety Act 1978; Diseases of Animals Act 1950; Petroleum (Consolidation) Act 1928; Explosives Acts 1875 and 1923; Poisons Act 1972; Medicines Act 1968; Farm and Garden Chemicals Act 1967.
Road Safety	Road Traffic Act 1972 as amended (selling defective motor cycle crash helmets (section 33) and offences relating to the condition of vehicles).
Insurance Policy Holders' Protection	Insurance Companies Act 1974; Policyholders Protection Act 1975.
Trading Stamps	Trading Stamps Act 1964.
Hallmarking of precious metals	Hallmarking Act 1973.
Handling stolen goods/obtaining money by cheating	Theft Act 1968 (sections 22, 15).

ENFORCEMENT

The responsibility for the enforcement of trading standards offences very largely rests on the shoulders of local authorities. Local authorities generally act through their Trading Standards Officers. Although in some quarters regarded as 'minor Town Hall officials' this is in fact far from the case. Trading Standards Officers are responsible for the enforcement of a forbidding mass of primary and subsidiary legislation, some of it of great technical complexity. They are normally graduates and are required to pass statutory examinations which test not only knowledge of law in depth but also materials technology, statistics, economics and other areas of knowledge germain to the enforcement of Trading Standards. Much of their work involves advising or warning traders, but if a prosecution is to be brought a Trading Standards Officer is likely to take the necessary initiative. The following discussion of the role of prosecuting authorities is of interest.

(Royal Commission on Criminal Procedure research study no 10) Prosecutions by private individuals and non-police agencies, pp 126–128

Trading standards prosecution
Local authorities are charged with the enforcement of much of the consumer protection legislation passed by Parliament. Since the nineteenth century local authorities have been

Annual Report of the Director General of Fair Trading 1983, pp 71–72

Table 2—Convictions under the Trade Descriptions Acts and the Fair Trading Act 1973

Reported cases 1982–83
A = number
B = fines (£)

| | Trade Descriptions Acts | | | | | | Fair Trading Act 1973[8] | | | |
| | False description of goods[1] | | False price claimed | | False statements about services | | Restrictions on Statements Order | | Business Advertisements (Disclosure) Order | |
	A	B	A	B	A	B	A	B	A	B
Goods										
Food and drink	108	34,323	52	13,600	—	—	1	200	—	—
Footwear, clothing and textiles	134	32,410	7	1,755	—	—	3	350	—	—
Furniture and floor covering	15	6,825	9	8,450	—	—	2	600	1	500
Household appliances	61	19,985	4	1,035	—	—	1	40	5	490
Toilet requisites, soaps, detergents	15[2]	1,960	15	1,555	—	—	—	—	—	—
Solid and liquid fuels	15	3,855	21	5,635	—	—	—	—	—	—
Motor vehicles and accessories	503[3]	279,395	14	3,395	—	—	32[9]	8,155	137[10]	38,835
Others	327[4]	248,806	20	5,400	—	—	2	525	1	330
Services										
Home repairs and improvements	—	—	—	—	4	1,300	—	—	—	—
Repairs and servicing to motor vehicles	—	—	—	—	33[5]	6,095	—	—	—	—
Other repairs and cleaning	—	—	—	—	18[6]	4,500	—	—	—	—
Holidays, entertainment and accommodation	—	—	—	—	43	18,215	—	—	—	—
Public utilities, professional and general services	—	—	—	—	66[7]	18,915	—	—	—	—
Total	1,178	627,559	142	40,825	164	49,025	41	9,870	144	40,155

Notes to Table 2

1. Includes 26 convictions under the Trade Descriptions Act 1972 with fines totally £10,050.

2. Includes one sentence of two years' imprisonment (18 months of this was suspended for two years).

3. Includes four prison sentences ranging from seven days to six months, three ranging from three to 12 months but suspended and one of 150 hours' community service.

4. The large increase in the number of convictions for false description of goods in the category 'others', compared to 1981–82, is due to the level of prosecutions concerning counterfeit audio and video cassettes. These led to 160 reported convictions, with fines totalling £200,075 and one prison sentence of seven days.

5. Includes a suspended sentence of three months.

6. Includes a sentence of 160 hours' community service.

7. Includes a suspended sentence of nine months.

8. There were no reported convictions under the Mail Order Transactions (Information) Order during the period.

9. Includes a suspended sentence of one month.

10. Includes one sentence of two months in prison, and three suspended sentences ranging from three to nine months.

involved in consumer protection legislation, initially through weights and measures and food and drugs legislation, but in the past decade or so there has been a rapid growth in local authority consumer protection activities following an equally rapid growth in legislation designed to protect consumers and improve standards of trading. Local authorities now enforce legislation which is within the responsibility of the Department of Prices and Consumer Protection (now Department of Trade), the Ministry of Agriculture, Fisheries and Food and the Department of Health and Social Security, and also have close links with the Office of Fair Trading.

The list of Acts of Parliament enforced by trading standards and consumer protection departments is impressive and indicates the range of activities undertaken. . . .

Despite this array of statutes and regulations, most of which carry a potential for criminal prosecution, the actual figures for prosecutions by trading standards departments are low. Table 6:9 gives the number of prosecutions by all metropolitan and non-metropolitan standards departments for the fiscal year 1977/78.

Table 6:9 Prosecutions by Trading Standards Departments 1977/78 (England and Wales)

	Persons prosecuted	Offences prosecuted	Persons cautioned
Non-metropolitan counties	3,643	7,977	10,427
Metropolitan counties	1,375	4,056	1,241
Total	*5,018*	*12,033*	*11,668*

Source: Trading standards statistics compiled on behalf of the Society of County Consumer Services Officers

The above figures represent an annual average of 95 cases prosecuted in each of the 53 county councils in England and Wales, excluding London. This is a remarkably low prosecution rate and there is doubtless a number of reasons for this. The most important identified by us are:

(a) The attitude of the enforcement officers. The primary purpose of much of the legislation in this area is educative and preventive and thus a great deal of their activity raises no prospect of prosecution. Prosecution is seen as a last resort and as an admission of failure on the part of the authority.

(b) The nature of the offences involved. The majority are of strict liability; that is, they are punishable regardless of intent. There is, however, a general reluctance to punish those who did not intend to offend. Related to this is the fact that many traders do not know or understand the law. While this is in law no excuse, in practice it is often treated as such; this approach is related to the educative function of the legislation.

(c) The publicity attendant on the prosecution of a business. This can have an adverse effect on the business out of all proportion to the seriousness of the offence committed. This and the other factors mentioned may be reflected in the number of cautions issued, more than double the number of persons prosecuted.

(d) The volume and complexity of the legislation. This creates problems for enforcement officers and traders. Departments are seldom up to establishment and increased legislation without increased resources means existing resources are spread more thinly. The complexity and frequencies of new legislation means continuous training of their staff with a concomitant reduction in active enforcement. It also requires greater efforts to educate and inform traders of the legal requirements rather than to enforce them. In one county it was reported that the number of prosecutions had reached its limit given the available resources.

(e) The education of consumers by trading standards departments, the Department of Prices and Consumer Protection, the Office of Fair Trading, and the mass media. This is in a sense too successful. Consumer complaints to trading standards departments have increased annually, exceeding one million in 1977–78. Many of the complaints do not receive a full investigation because of the lack of resources and in many cases the emphasis has had to be on obtaining recompense for the consumer rather than prosecuting offenders.

(f) The majority of firms' compliance with the legislation. Most firms recognize that compliance is good for business in an age of 'consumerism' and are ready to comply with legislation once they are aware of and understand it. One exception has been the Prices

Act 1974, which requires prices to be exhibited at the time of sale in a particular manner. This has not been welcomed by traders and requires a disproportionate amount of the officer's time to explain and persuade traders to comply. In such a situation prosecution may be necessary to overcome the reluctance to comply.

These and other factors combine to produce the comparatively low prosecution rate. Attitude and resources are major factors and while attitudes are unlikely to change, the problem of resources is likely to increase in the future as public spending cuts start to bite. One may therefore forecast little, if any, increase in prosecutions in the next few years.

(For an interesting discussion of attitudes and policies of Trading Standards Departments see Cranston *Regulating Business: Law and Consumer Agencies* (1979). See also *Smedleys Ltd v Breed* [1974] 2 All ER 21, below p 567; *Wings Ltd v Ellis* [1984] 3 All ER 577, below p 516).

In some cases, for instance weights and measures, the public is not permitted to bring a prosecution. Such a prosecution must be brought by or on behalf of a weights and measures authority or by a chief officer of police (1963 Act, 551). In other cases the public theoretically has a right of private prosecution (eg food and drugs, trade descriptions), but in practice it is usually more sensible for the consumer to make a report to his local Trading Standards Office and leave the expense of the prosecution to be handled by this arm of the local authority. In certain cases, eg most offences under the Trade Descriptions Act 1968 and offences under Regulations made under Part II of the Fair Trading Act 1973, the local weights and measures authority is under a duty to give to the Director General of Fair Trading notice of intended proceedings together with the summary of the facts on which the charges are to be founded. Proceedings must then be postponed until either 28 days have elapsed since the giving of that notice, or the Director has notified the authority that he has received the notice and the summary of the facts (Fair Trading Act 1973, s 130).

An example of the terms under which a statute makes its criminal enforcement the responsibility of a local authority is provided by the Fair Trading Act 1973. The extract which follows relates to enforcement of the Orders made under Part II of that Act, for example the Consumer Transactions (Restrictions on Statements) Order 1976 as amended. Sections 27–32 are typical of the powers conferred on officers by legislation of this sort. The relevant sections run as follows:

Fair Trading Act 1973

ENFORCEMENT OF ORDERS

27. (1) It shall be the duty of every local weights and measures authority to enforce within their area the provisions of any order made under section 22 of this Act; and section 37 of the Weights and Measures Act 1963 (power of local authorities to combine) shall apply with respect to the functions of such authorities under this Part of this Act as it applies with respect to their functions under that Act.

(2) Nothing in subsection (1) shall be taken as authorising a local weights and measures authority in Scotland to institute proceedings for an offence.

28. A local weights and measures authority may make, or may authorise any of their officers to make on their behalf, such purchases of goods, and may authorise any of their officers to obtain such services, as may be expedient for the purpose of determining whether or not the provisions of any order made under section 22 of this Act are being complied with.

29. (1) A duly authorised officer of a local weights and measures authority, or a person duly authorised in writing by the Secretary of State, may at all reasonable hours, and on production, if required, of his credentials, exercise the following powers, that is to say—

(a) he may, for the purpose of ascertaining whether any offence under section 23 of this Act has been committed, inspect any goods and enter any premises other than premises used only as a dwelling;

(b) if he has reasonable cause to suspect that an offence under that section has been committed, he may, for the purpose of ascertaining whether it has been committed, require any person carrying on a business or employed in connection with a business to produce any books or documents relating to the business and may take copies of, or of any entry in, any such book or document;

(c) if he has reasonable cause to believe that such an offence has been committed, he may seize and detain any goods for the purpose of ascertaining, by testing or otherwise, whether the offence has been committed;

(d) he may seize and detain any goods or documents which he has reason to believe may be required as evidence in proceedings for such an offence;

(e) he may, for the purpose of exercising his powers under this subsection to seize goods, but only if and to the extent that it is reasonably necessary in order to secure that the provisions of an order made under section 22 of this Act are duly observed, require any person having authority to do so to break open any container or open any vending machine and, if that person does not comply with the requirement, he may do so himself.

(2) A person seizing any goods or documents in the exercise of his powers under this section shall inform the person from whom they are seized and, in the case of goods seized from a vending machine, the person whose name and address are stated on the machine as being the proprietor's or, if no name and address are so stated, the occupier of the premises on which the machine stands or to which it is affixed.

(3) If a justice of the peace, on sworn information in writing—

(a) is satisfied that there is reasonable ground to believe either—

(i) that any goods, books or documents which a person has power under this section to inspect are on any premises and that their inspection is likely to disclose evidence of the commission of an offence under section 23 of this Act, or

(ii) that any offence under section 23 has been, is being or is about to be committed on any premises, and

(b) is also satisfied either—

(i) that admission to the premises has been or is likely to be refused and that notice of intention to apply for a warrant under this subsection has been given to the occupier, or

(ii) that an application for admission, or the giving of such a notice, would defeat the object of the entry or that the premises are unoccupied or that the occupier is temporarily absent, and it might defeat the object of the entry to await his return,

the justice may by warrant under his hand, which shall continue in force for a period of one month, authorise any such officer or other person as is mentioned in subsection (1) of this section to enter the premises, if need be by force.

In the application of this subsection to Scotland, 'justice of the peace' shall be construed as including a sheriff and a magistrate.

(4) A person entering any premises by virtue of this section may take with him such other persons and such equipment as may appear to him necessary; and on leaving any premises which he has entered by virtue of a warrant under subsection (3) of this section he shall, if the premises are unoccupied or the occupier is temporarily absent, leave them as effectively secured against trespassers as he found them.

(5) Nothing in this section shall be taken to compel the production by a barrister, advocate or solicitor of a document containing a privileged communication made by or to him in that capacity or to authorise the taking of possession of any such document which is in his possession.

30. (1) Subject to subsection (6) of this section, any person who—

(a) wilfully obstructs any such officer or person as is mentioned in subsection (1) of section 20 of this Act acting in the exercise of any powers conferred on him by or under that section, or

(b) wilfully fails to comply with any requirement properly made to him by such an officer or person under that section, or

(c) without reasonable cause fails to give such an officer or person so acting any other assistance or information which he may reasonably require of him for the purpose of the performance of his functions under this Part of this Act,

shall be guilty of an offence.

(2) If any person, in giving any such information as is mentioned in subsection (1)(c) of this section, makes any statement which he knows to be false, he shall be guilty of an offence.

(3) If any person discloses to any other person—
   (a) any information with respect to any manufacturing process or trade secret obtained by him in premises which he has entered by virtue of section 29 of this Act, or
   (b) any information obtained by him under that section or by virtue of subsection (1) of this section.

he shall, unless the disclosure was made in the performance of his duty, be guilty of an offence.

(4) If any person who is neither a duly authorised officer of a weights and measures authority nor a person duly authorised in that behalf by the Secretary of State purports to act as such under section 29 of this Act or under this section, he shall be guilty of an offence.

(5) Any person guilty of an offence under subsection (1) of this section shall be liable on summary conviction to a fine not exceeding [level 3 on the standard scale], and any person guilty of an offence under subsection (2), subsection (3) or subsection (4) of this section shall be liable—
   (a) on summary conviction, to a fine not exceeding [£2,000];
   (b) on conviction on indictment, to a fine or to imprisonment for a term not exceeding two years or to both.

(6) Nothing in this section shall be construed as requiring a person to answer any question or give any information if to do so might incriminate that person or (where that person is married) the husband or wife of that person.

31. Where any goods seized or purchased by a person in pursuance of this Part of this Act are submitted to a test, then—
   (a) if the goods were seized, he shall inform any such person as is mentioned in section 29(2) of this Act of the result of the test;
   (b) if the goods were purchased and the test leads to the institution of proceedings for an offence under section 23 of this Act, he shall inform the person from whom the goods were purchased, or, in the case of goods sold through a vending machine, the person mentioned in relation to such goods in section 29(2) of this Act, of the result of the test;

and where, as a result of the test, proceedings for an offence under section 23 of this Act are instituted against any person, he shall allow that person to have the goods tested on his behalf if it is reasonably practicable to do so.

32. (1) Where in the exercise of his powers under section 29 of this Act a person seizes and detains any goods, and their owner suffers loss by reason of their being seized or by reason that the goods during the detention, are lost or damaged or deteriorate, unless the owner is convicted of an offence under section 23 of this Act committed in relation to the goods, the appropriate authority shall be liable to compensate him for the loss so suffered.

(2) Any disputed question as to the right to or the amount of any compensation payable under this section shall be determined by arbitration and, in Scotland, by a single arbiter appointed, failing agreement between the parties, by the sheriff.

(3) In this section 'the appropriate authority'—
   (a) in relation to goods seized by an officer of a local weights and measures authority, means that authority and
   (b) in any other case, means the Secretary of State.

INJUNCTIONS IN AID OF THE CRIMINAL LAW

An incidental side-effect of inflation is that the penalties imposed by the criminal law do not always keep pace with the profits which may be derived from breaking it. The question then arises as to whether it should be permissible to allow the activity to be restrained in some other, more effective, way. The following case is in point.

Stoke-on-Trent City Council v B & Q (Retail) Ltd [1984] 2 All ER 332, [1984] 2 WLR 929, House of Lords

The facts are set out in the opinion of Lord Templeman.

Lord Templeman. My Lords, the appellants, B & Q (Retail) Ltd, challenge the right of the respondents, Stoke-on-Trent City Council, to bring proceedings to restrain the appellants from trading on Sundays from the appellants' shops in Stoke-on-Trent in breach of the Shops Act 1950.

Section 47 of the 1950 Act provides that, save for certain authorised transactions, every shop in England and Wales shall 'be closed for the service of customers on Sunday.' By s 71(1):

> 'It shall be the duty of every local authority to enforce within their district the provisions of this Act . . . and for that purpose to institute and to carry on such proceedings in respect of contraventions of the said provisions . . . as may be necessary to secure observance thereof.'

Section 71(2) directs every local authority to appoint inspectors for the purposes of the Act and provides:

> '. . . An inspector may, if so authorised by the local authority, institute and carry on any proceedings under this Act on behalf of the authority.'

I agree with the observations of my noble and learned friend Lord Roskill concerning the duty of the local authority under s 71 of the Act.

The appellants' shops at Waterloo Road, Burslem and Leek Road, Hanley are within the district of the council. The appellants' shops traded in prohibited articles on Sunday, 11 April 1982, and after a warning from a council representative, again on 18 April. The appellants were warned of legal proceedings on 19 April and traded in prohibited articles on 25 April.

By s 59 of the 1950 Act the occupier of a shop which trades on Sundays in breach of the 1950 Act was made liable to a fine of £5 for a first offence and £20 in the case of a second or subsequent offence. By s 31 of the Criminal Justice Act 1972 the penalties were increased to £50 and £200 respectively and those were the maximum penalties for offences up to 11 April 1983. By ss 35 to 48 of the Criminal Justice Act 1982 from 11 April 1983 an occupier of a shop trading in breach of the 1950 Act is liable to a maximum fine of £500 for any offence and the Home Secretary can by order, subject to a negative resolution by Parliament, increase the maximum penalty to an extent justified by any change in the value of money since July 1977.

In addition to initiating but not completing criminal proceedings which could have resulted in the imposition on the appellants of a fine of £50 for the first offence and £200 for every subsequent offence, the Council on 5 May 1982 issued a writ in the Chancery Division of the High Court for an injunction to restrain the appellants from continuing to trade in breach of the 1950 Act. On 25 June 1982 Whitford J in those proceedings granted an interlocutory injunction restraining the appellants until trial of the action or further order from trading in breach of the 1950 Act. Against that order the appellants appealed unsuccessfully to the Court of Appeal (see [1983] 2 All ER 787, [1984] Ch 1) and now appeal to your Lordships' House.

By the common law of England, a plaintiff can only sue for interference with his private rights, or for interference with a public right whereby he suffers special damage, peculiar to himself. A breach of the 1950 Act does not interfere with the private rights of the council or cause the council special damage and accordingly the council could not at common law bring civil proceedings complaining of any breach of the 1950 Act. At common law the Attorney General may institute proceedings to enforce the terms of a public Act of Parliament and—

> 'It is not necessary for the Attorney-General to shew any injury at all. The Legislature is of opinion that certain acts will produce injury, and that is enough.'

(See *A-G v Cockermouth Local Board* (1874) LR 18 Eq 172 at 178 per Jessel MR.)

The Attorney General may institute proceedings himself ex-officio, and in that event is liable to incur and possibly pay costs. In the alternative the Attorney General may authorise another person, called the relator, to institute proceedings in the name of the Attorney General and, in that event, the relator is liable for costs.

. . .

The power of the Attorney General to institute proceedings to uphold public rights and duties enables the Attorney General, whether acting ex officio or in relator actions, to invoke the assistance of civil courts in aid of the criminal law. This is an exceptional but well-recognised power: see *Gouriet v Union of Post Office Workers* [1977] 3 All ER 70 at 83, [1978] AC 435 at 481. Thus at common law the Attorney General, at the relation of the council, but only if the Attorney General in his absolute discretion thought fit, had power to seek an injunction restraining the appellants from committing breaches of the 1950 Act within the area of the council. No such proceedings were however instituted.

Thus far the common law. But Parliament may confer, and undoubtedly has in some instances conferred, limited powers on local authorities to institute and maintain proceedings to ensure compliance with public duties. For certain purposes Parliament has supplemented the power of the Attorney General to act in the national public interest with a power for a local authority to act in the interests of the public within the area administered by that authority.

. . .

Section 276 of the Local Government Act 1933, . . . provided:

'Where a local authority deem it expedient for the promotion or protection of the interests of the inhabitants of their area, they may prosecute or defend any legal proceedings.'

In *Prestatyn UDC v Prestatyn Raceway Ltd* [1969] 3 All ER 1573, [1970] 1 WLR 33 Goff J applied the dictum of Kay LJ in *Tottenham UDC v Williamson & Sons Ltd* [1896] 2 QB 353 at 354–355 and decided that the terms of s 276 were not sufficiently explicit to enable a local authority to bring proceedings in their own name.

Section 276 of the Local Government Act 1933 was replaced in an altered form by s 222 of the Local Government Act 1972, which is in these terms:

'(1) When a local authority considers it expedient for the promotion or protection of the interests of the inhabitants of their area—(a) they may prosecute or defend or appear in any legal proceedings and, *in the case of civil proceedings, may institute them in their own name,* and (b) they may *in their own name* make representations in the interests of the inhabitants at any public inquiry held by or on behalf of any Minister or public body under any enactment . . .'

Thus Parliament reversed the effect of the decision of Goff J in *Prestatyn UDC v Prestatyn Raceway Ltd* by authorising a local authority to take proceedings in their own name. The terms of s 222 are sufficiently explicit to enable a local authority to bring proceedings in their own name and to contradict the view that the powers of the local authority under s 222 are limited to requesting the Attorney General to allow proceedings to be instituted in his name at the relation of the local authority. In proceedings instituted to promote or protect the interests of inhabitants generally, special damage is irrelevant and was therefore not mentioned in s 222.

. . .

Section 222 requires that a local authority shall only act if they 'consider it expedient for the promotion or protection of the interests of the inhabitants of their area.' Any exercise by the local authority of this statutory power is subject to the control of judicial review and the application of the principles enunciated in *Associated Provincial Picture Houses Ltd v Wednesbury Corpn* [1947] 2 All ER 680, [1948] 1 KB 223. In considering the exercise of their powers the local authority must take into account matters which they ought to take into account, ignore matters which they ought not to take into account and then reach a decision which is not so unreasonable that no reasonable local authority could have come to it. Where the local authority seeks an injunction, the court will consider whether the power was rightly exercised and whether in all the circumstances at the date the application for an injunction is considered by the court, the equitable and discretionary remedy of an injunction should be granted.

In the present case, when the council decided to institute proceedings and when Whitford J decided to grant an interlocutory injunction, the appellants had committed offences under the Shops Act 1950. The council invoked the assistance of the civil court in aid of the criminal law in order to ensure that the appellants did not commit further offences under the 1950 Act. The right to invoke the assistance of the civil court in aid of the criminal law is a comparatively modern development. Where Parliament imposes a penalty for an offence, Parliament must consider the penalty is adequate and Parliament can increase the penalty if it proves to be inadequate. It follows that a local authority should be reluctant to seek and the court should be reluctant to grant an injunction which if disobeyed may involve the infringer in sanctions far more onerous than the penalty imposed for the offence. In *Gouriet v Union of Post Office Workers* [1977] 3 All ER 70 at 83, [1978] AC 435 at 81 Lord Wilberforce said that the right to invoke the assistance of civil courts in aid of the criminal law is 'an exceptional power confined, in practice, to cases where an offence is frequently repeated in disregard of a, usually, inadequate penalty . . . or to cases of emergency . . .' In my view there must certainly be something more than infringement before the assistance of civil proceedings can be invoked and accorded for the protection or promotion of the interests of the inhabitants of the area. In the present case the council were concerned with what appeared to be a proliferation of illegal Sunday trading. The council was by s 71 of the 1950 Act charged with the statutory duty of ensuring compliance with the 1950 Act. The council received letters from traders complaining of infringements of the Sunday trading legislation by other shops and intimating that the complainants would themselves feel obliged to open on Sundays in order to preserve their trade unless the 1950 Act was generally observed. The council could not treat some traders differently from others. The council wrote to warn infringing traders some of whom ceased to trade on Sundays as a result of the warnings. In one case where an ignored warning was followed by the issue of a writ the proceedings resulted in an undertaking to desist. In these circumstances there was ample justification for the council to take the view that it was expedient in the general interests of the inhabitants to take such steps as were necessary to ensure compliance by the appellants with the laws of Sunday trading.

It was said that the council should not have taken civil proceedings until criminal proceedings had failed to persuade the appellants to obey the law. As a general rule a local authority should try the effect of criminal proceedings before seeking the assistance of the civil courts. But the council were entitled to take the view that the appellants would not be deterred by a maximum fine which was substantially less than the profits which could be made from illegal Sunday trading. Delay while this was proved would have encouraged widespread breaches of the law by other traders, resentful of the continued activities of the appellants. The poor trader would be deterred by the threat of a fine; the rich trader would consider breaking the law each Sunday if illegal trading produced profit in excess of the maximum fine and costs. In *Stafford Borough Council v Elkenford Ltd* [1977] 2 All ER 519 at 528, [1977] 1 WLR 324 at 330 Bridge LJ said:

> 'We have been urged to say that the court will only exercise its discretion to restrain by injunction the commission of offences in breach of statutory prohibitions if the plaintiff authority has first shown that it has exhausted the possibility of restraining those breaches by the exercise of the statutory remedies. Ordinarily no doubt that is a very salutory approach to the question whether or not the court will grant an injunction in the exercise of its discretion, but it is not in my judgment an inflexible rule. The reason why it is ordinarily proper to ask whether the authority seeking the injunction has first exhausted the statutory remedies is because in the ordinary case it is only because those remedies have been invoked and have proved inadequate that one can draw the inference, which is the essential foundation for the exercise of the court's discretion to grant an injunction, that the offender is . . . "deliberately and flagrantly flouting the law".'

In the present case any doubt about the attitude of the appellants has been resolved by their attitude to the proceedings themselves. Whitford J concluded that the appellants were proceeding—

> 'on the basis that if an interlocutory injunction be not granted now they would be free to trade . . . they hope, if they are successful in staying the grant of an interlocutory injunction, that they are going to be able to continue to trade in defiance of the provisions of s 47 of the Shops Act 1950.'

Immediately on the opening of the appeal of the appellants to your Lordships' House, my noble and learned friend Lord Diplock inquired whether if the injunction were discharged the appellants intended to resume trading in defiance of the provisions of s 47 of the 1950 Act. No answer has been vouchsafed. Whitford J and the Court of Appeal took the view that on the law and the facts an injunction should issue and I would dismiss this appeal.

[Lords Diplock, Fraser, Keith and Roskill agreed with Lord Templeman.] *Appeal dismissed.*

Question

Since the penalties for contempt on breach of an injunction under the Contempt of Court Act 1981 are markedly more severe than those for which Parliament has made provision in the Shops Act is it desirable that these latter penalties should be effectively increased by the use of injunctions in aid of the criminal law?

Consumer safety

A considerable number of statutes and regulations are concerned with consumer safety. Many are concerned with specific types of products, for example food and drugs, medicines, and poisons. Others are of more general application. The Consumer Protection Acts 1961–71 have been important over the years as enabling the Secretary of State to make regulations imposing such safety standards as were in his opinion expedient to prevent or reduce the risk of death or personal injury from specified classes of goods. Initially this power was used only sparingly, but latterly there was an increase in the number of products covered. For the text of these regulations see Miller *Product Liability and Safety Encyclopaedia* Division IV. Some of the deficiencies in the powers conferred by the 1961 Act were identified as follows:

Consumer safety: a consultative document (Cmnd 6398) (1976)

SECTION II—DEFICIENCIES IN THE SYSTEM

39. This section seeks to identify the main criticisms of the present powers and administrative arrangements. Possible remedies, and suggestions for improvements, are discussed in Section III.

Lack of information
40. The Department will always need to rely on information from many sources. The present flow of information is not inconsiderable, but there are serious gaps in it. In particular there is a need:
   (i)   to obtain regular statistics on product involvement in accidents and on causes of home accidents generally so that particular factors may be further investigated;
   (ii) for in-depth studies to ascertain the extent to which particular products, or other factors, may have contributed to the accident;
   (iii) for regular exchange of information with local enforcement authorities and other local agencies to enable quick action to be taken to deal with product hazards as they arise;
   (iv) to obtain information from industry about new hazards of which it becomes aware; and
   (v)   for exchange of information with other countries.

Production of standards
41. It is desirable that regulations under the Consumer Protection Act should be based on the safety provisions in a British Standard or some code of practice which is known to the trade and supported by it. However, many consumer products are not covered by any British or other standards, and the extension of standards to new products tends to be a slow process (see paragraph 14).
42. The main problems associated with the use of standards as a basis for product safety are:
   (i)   the lack of any standards for many types of consumer goods and the absence of adequate safety requirements in some existing standards;
   (ii) the time taken to produce new standards or to revise existing ones; and
   (iii) slow progress in formulating international standards, so that many differing standards continue to co-exist.

Regulation making
43. Even when a suitable British Standard exists, regulations cannot be made quickly. As indicated in paragraph 33, the Consumer Protection Act imposes a duty on the Secretary of State before making any regulations to consult such persons or bodies of persons as appear requisite, and this takes time.
44. Moreover, the power available under the Act to make regulations is restricted and in some instances does not permit action of limited scope to be taken. Among other things, it:
   (i)   does not enable requirements to be imposed for all appropriate labelling of goods;
   (ii) does not permit the sale of inherently dangerous products to be prohibited outright;

    (iii) does not allow regulations to specify standards which are deemed to satisfy the prescribed requirements but leave the manufacturer free to choose other methods of complying;

    (iv) does not enable imposition of requirements that the sale of specified goods should be subject to prior approval;

    (v) does not enable the imposition of a minimum age of purchase;

    (vi) does not apply to goods supplied without payment (eg in exchange for coupons or trading stamps, or as prizes in competitions and at fair-grounds, or as wrapping with a product sold);

    (vii) does not embrace the servicing of consumer goods.

Lack of power to deal with unsafe goods not covered by regulations

45.   Regulations provide a long term safety measure by ensuring that all goods of a particular class are made to minimum safety standards. But they cannot be invoked to take speedy action to deal with a newly discovered hazard, or against dangerous goods of a sort not covered by regulations. Other procedures are required to enable action to be taken in such circumstances, and there is no power at present to order the immediate withdrawal from sale of dangerous goods.

Enforcement

46.   There is no evidence to suggest that local authorities accord lower priority to enforcement of the Consumer Protection Act than of Acts whose enforcement is mandatory on them. But there seems no reason for a distinction which appears to accord lower priority to consumer safety than to other aspects of consumer protection.

Some of the above deficiencies have since been rectified, notably through the Consumer Safety Act 1978 which was the result of a private members' bill introduced by Mr Neville Trotter MP. Its principal provisions are as follows:

Consumer Safety Act 1978

1. Safety regulations in respect of goods

(1) The Secretary of State may make regulations containing such provision authorised by subsections (2) and (3) of this section as the Secretary of State considers appropriate for the purpose of securing that goods are safe or that appropriate information is provided and inappropriate information is not provided in respect of goods; and regulations in pursuance of this subsection are hereafter in this Act referred to as 'safety regulations'.

. . .

2. Offences against the safety regulations

(1) Where safety regulations prohibit a person from supplying or offering or agreeing to supply goods or from exposing or possessing goods for supply, then, subject to the following provisions of this section, the person shall be guilty of an offence if he contravenes the prohibition.

(2) Where safety regulations require a person who makes or processes goods in the course of carrying on a business—

    (a) to carry out a particular test or use a particular procedure in connection with the making or processing of the goods with a view to ascertaining whether the goods satisfy other requirements of the regulations; or

    (b) to deal or not to deal in a particular way with a quantity of the goods of which the whole or part does not satisfy the test or does not satisfy standards connected with the procedure,

then, subject to the following provisions of this section, the person shall be guilty of an offence if he does not comply with the requirement.

(3) If a person contravenes a provision of safety regulations which prohibits the provision, by means of a mark or otherwise, of information of a particular kind in connection with goods, then, subject to the following provisions of this section, he shall be guilty of an offence.

(4) A person who commits an offence in pursuance of the preceding provisions of this section (hereafter in this section referred to as 'a relevant offence') shall be liable on summary conviction to imprisonment for a term not exceeding three months and a fine of an amount not exceeding [level 5 on the standard scale].

(5) Where the commission of a relevant offence by any person is due to the act or default of some other person, the other person shall be guilty of the offence and may be charged with and convicted of it whether or not proceedings are taken against the first-mentioned person.

(6) It shall be a defence to a charge of committing a relevant offence to prove that the accused took all reasonable steps and exercised all due diligence to avoid committing the offence; but if in any case the defence provided by this subsection involves an allegation that the commission of the offence was due to the act or default of another person or due to reliance on information supplied by another person, the person charged shall not, without the leave of the court, be entitled to rely on the defence unless, within a period ending seven clear days before the hearing, he has served on the prosecutor a notice giving such information identifying or assisting in the identification of the other person as was then in his possession.

(7) Safety regulations may contain provision—

    (a) for requiring persons on whom a duty is imposed by virtue of section 5 of this Act to have regard, in performing the duty so far as it relates to a provision of safety regulations, to matters specified in a direction issued by the Secretary of State with respect to that provision;

    (b) for securing that a person shall not be guilty of an offence by virtue of subsection (1) of this section unless it is proved that the goods in question do not conform to a particular standard;

    (c) for securing that proceedings for a relevant offence are not begun in England or Wales except by or with the consent of the Secretary of State or the Director of Public Prosecutions;

    (d) except in relation to Scotland, for enabling a magistrates' court to try an information in respect of a relevant offence if the information was laid within twelve months from the time when the offence was committed and, in relation to Scotland, for enabling summary proceedings for a relevant offence to be begun at any time within twelve months from the time when the offence was committed;

and it is hereby declared that subsection (3) of the preceding section applies to safety regulations made by virtue of this subsection.

(8) Safety regulations shall not provide for a contravention of the regulations to be an offence.

3. Orders and notices to prohibit supply of goods or give warning of danger from goods

(1) The Secretary of State may—

    (a) make orders (hereafter in this Act referred to as 'prohibition orders') prohibiting persons from supplying, or from offering to supply, agreeing to supply, exposing for supply or possessing for supply—

        (i) any goods which the Secretary of State considers are not safe and which are described in the orders, and

        (ii) any goods which are designed to be used as component parts of other goods and which would if so used cause the other goods to be goods described in the orders in pursuance of sub-paragraph (i) above;

    (b) serve on any person a notice (hereafter in this Act referred to as a 'prohibition notice') prohibiting the person, except with the consent of the Secretary of State and in accordance with the conditions (if any) on which the consent is given, from supplying, or from offering to supply, agreeing to supply, exposing for supply or possessing for supply, any goods which the Secretary of State considers are not safe and which are described in the notice;

    (c) serve on any person a notice (hereafter in this Act referred to as a 'notice to warn') requiring the person to publish, in a form and manner and on occasions specified in the notice and at his own expense, a warning about any goods so specified which the Secretary of State considers are not safe and which the person supplies or has supplied.

(2) Part I of Schedule 1 to this Act shall have effect with respect to prohibition orders, Part II of that Schedule shall have effect with respect to prohibition notices and Part III of that Schedule shall have effect with respect to notices to warn; and subsection (3) of section 1 of this Act shall apply to prohibition orders as it applies to safety regulations.

(3) A person who contravenes a prohibition order, a prohibition notice or a notice to warn shall be guilty of an offence and liable on summary conviction to imprisonment for a term not exceeding three months and a fine of an amount not exceeding [level 5 on the standard scale]; but it shall be a defence to a charge of committing an offence under this subsection to prove that the accused took all reasonable steps and exercised all due diligence to avoid committing the offence.

(4) If in any case the defence provided by the preceding subsection involves an allegation that the commission of the offence was due to the act or default of another person or to reliance on information supplied by another person, the person charged shall not, without the leave of the court, be entitled to rely on the defence unless, within a period ending seven clear days before the hearing, he has served on the prosecutor a notice giving such information identifying or assisting in the identification of the other person as was then in his possession.
(5) Where the commission by any person of an offence of contravening a prohibition order is due to the act or default of some other person the other person shall be guilty of the offence and may be charged with and convicted of the offence by virtue of this subsection whether or not proceedings are taken against the first-mentioned person.

. . .

6. Civil liability
(1) Any obligation imposed on a person by safety regulations or a prohibition order or a prohibition notice is a duty owed by him to any other person who may be affected by a failure to perform the obligation, and a breach of that duty is actionable (subject to the defences and other incidents applying to actions for breach of statutory duty).
(2) An agreement shall be void so far as it would, apart from this subsection, have the effect of excluding or restricting an obligation mentioned in the preceding subsection or liabililty for a breach of such an obligation.
(3) References in the preceding provisions of this section to an obligation imposed by safety regulations do not include such an obligation as to which the regulations state that those provisions do not apply to it.
(4) A contravention of any provision of safety regulations, a prohibition order or a prohibition notice and the commission of an offence under section 2 or 3 of this Act shall not affect the validity of any contract or rights arising under any contract except so far as the contract provides otherwise.

NOTES

1. For a list of safety regulations and prohibition orders made under this Act see Miller *Product Liability and Safety Encyclopaedia* Division IV.
2. The maximum fine which corresponds to 'level 5 on the standard scale' (see ss 2(4) and 3(3) above) is in 1984 £2000, although this sum may be varied by statutory instrument to compensate for a change in the value of money.
3. By s 9(4) of the Act the word 'safe' 'means such as to prevent or adequately to reduce any risk of death and any risk of personal injury from the goods in question or from circumstances in which the goods might be used or kept, and for the purposes of section 1 of this Act the Secretary of State shall be entitled to consider that goods containing radioactive substances are safe or not safe by reference to the radiation from the goods and from other sources and to the consequences of the radiation for users of the goods and other persons;'.

Although s 3 of the 1978 Act empowers the Secretary of State to issue prohibition orders and notices, and to require the publication of warnings, it does not contain provisions for the compulsory recall of goods which have been found to be unsafe. The possibility of introducing such a power was discussed in the following passages in the 1976 Green Paper to which reference was made above.

Consumer Safety: A Consultative Document (Cmnd 6398) (1976)

Recall of unsafe goods
96.   There is also at present no power to require those responsible for supplying dangerous goods:

    (i)   to recall distributed, but unsold, stocks;
    (ii) to warn consumers of the hazard by publicity or any other means;
    (iii) where necessary, to make every effort to recall dangerous products already in the
          hands of the public.
There are two types of circumstance in which the imposition of such requirements might be
necessary:
    (a) in respect of a particular manufacturer, importer or distributor who was in breach of a
         regulation or banning order or convicted of an offence against any general safety law of
         the kind discussed in paragraphs 80 to 84;
    (b) in respect of anyone who has supplied a product which fails to comply with a particular
         regulation (or banning order) made subsequently.
In the first case, a power to apply for a court order might be appropriate; in the second the
Secretary of State might be empowered to lay down the requirements in the relevant
regulation (or order). In either case it would seem reasonable to restrict the use of such powers
to serious hazards only and possibly also to limit the period during which a trader remained
liable to recall goods after he had supplied them.
97.   Recovery of products in the hands of the public would pose problems as it is unlikely
that, for most goods, there would be any record of the names and addresses of the purchasers.
It would therefore seem necessary to designate some authority for the purpose of specifying
the form and placing of the advertisements or other publicity which the trader must issue at
his expense.
98.   The manufacturer, importer or distributor concerned would face the prospect of liability
not only for the cost of the publicity or recall operation itself but also for compensation or
damages to the person to whom the goods have been supplied. This of course impinges on the
wider question of liability discussed in paragraph 90. In the absence of any new legislation in
the field of product liability, there might be particularly acute problems in the kind of case
envisaged at (b) above, where no offence may have been committed and where there might
therefore be more room for dispute over whether there was sufficient justification for
imposing liability on someone in the supply chain and, if so, on whom.
    **The Government invites views on whether there should be powers to require anyone who has
supplied dangerous goods to take the necessary steps, at his own expense, to recall them and
issue appropriate warnings, and on the way in which any such powers might be exercised and
enforced.**

In the result the 1978 Act conferred only the power to require the issuing
of warnings. For a comparative survey see 'Recall Procedures for Unsafe
Products Sold to the Public' (OECD, 1981); see also Lawson, 'The Safety
of Goods: Some Comparative Assessments' (1982) NLJ 863.

Problem

Coffeetime has sold some ten thousand coffee pots through various retail
outlets when it becomes apparent that all the pots are potentially
dangerous because of a defect in the glue used to stick on their handles.
On 1 June 1984 some three weeks after discovering the danger, Coffeetime
has not taken any steps to alert the public and is continuing to supply
further pots to retailers. On 3 June 1984 Adam is scalded when a handle
comes away in his hand as he is pouring coffee. His friend, Bert, also owns
a coffee pot which he has received as a gift from Adam and he decides that
he cannot safely use it any further.

Discuss what powers are available to the Secretary of State and whether
any civil remedies are available to either Adam or Bert. (On the question
of civil remedies see Cane, 'Civil Liability under the Consumer Safety Act
1978', (1979) 3 Journal of Products Liability 215).

Experience of operating the 1978 Act revealed a number of practical
problems, most notably in the areas of enforcement and the prevention of

unsafe imports. Proposals for dealing with these problems are contained in a White Paper, 'The Safety of Goods' (Cmnd 9302 (1984)). The paper also develops the idea of introducing a general safety duty in relation to consumer goods:

The Safety of Goods, Department of Trade, Cmnd 9302, pp 7–9 (1984)

A GENERAL SAFETY DUTY

33.   The 1978 Act has effect only where specific requirements have been set in regulations, orders or notices. These cover only a limited number of categories and aspects of consumer goods. But dangers to safety and health can occur in almost any category of consumer product. There is no general statutory duty on suppliers to supply safe consumer goods as there is, for example, for articles and substances for use at work under Section 6 of the Health and Safety at Work etc Act 1974. The Consumers' Association has for many years advocated the introduction of such a duty.

34.   The Government accepts that there is a case for widening the scope of the Act to place a general obligation on the suppliers of consumer goods to achieve an acceptable standard of safety where it is reasonable to expect them to anticipate and reduce risks arising from those goods. This would induce a greater sense of responsibility on the part of those suppliers who currently regard themselves as unaffected by the legislation (and who may not be adequately deterred by the common law duty of care). At the same time it would provide wider scope for swift remedial action by enforcement authorities in the case of newly identified dangerous products.

35.   Local authority departments already deal informally with complaints about the safety of unregulated goods. They often seek to persuade suppliers to withdraw or modify such goods or draw cases to the attention of the Secretary of State for consideration of possible use of prohibition powers. The introduction of a general duty would enable them to take action on the basis of a legal obligation on suppliers.

36.   Any generally expressed duty carries with it the potential risk of difficulties of interpretation. The outline proposals which follow are intended to minimise such risks but the Government will be pleased to consider suggestions for alternative formulations which might reduce still further potential areas of uncertainty. It is worth noting that in nearly ten years of experience there do not appear to have been serious problems of interpretation of the level of safety required by the general duty for industrial goods in section 6 of the Health and Safety at Work Act; the Government therefore sees no reason to expect major problems in the case of a general duty for consumer goods. International, European and British Standards could often provide an appropriate reference point. Conversely a general safety duty would be likely to stimulate the formulation and wider use of safety standards for consumer goods and thus contribute to the development of a more effective standards system, an objective to which the Government is already committed[1]. The scope for use of standards is wider in the consumer goods field than in the case of industrial goods since a greater proportion of consumer goods are mass produced.

37.   It is proposed to link the duty with a broadly defined reference to standards such as 'sound modern standards of safety'. The purpose of this linkage would be to ensure that the level of safety which can legitimately be expected is interpreted by reference to identifiable and accepted points of comparison rather than simply left to more subjective assessments of safety. Such points of comparison would have to embody established and proven technology, recognised by expert opinion in the field and already available at reasonable cost. For the purposes of the general duty no account would be taken of use for purposes which are unreasonable having regard to the type of product concerned.

38.   Where a published standard could be accepted as the benchmark for safety for the product in question it would not be obligatory for suppliers to follow its specifications to the letter. Achievement of the same level of safety by compliance with equivalent standards, or by other means, would be equally acceptable. At least in the initial stages, not all published standards would necessarily provide a definitive interpretation. Some might have been overtaken by technological developments well recognised by expert opinion or identification of new hazards. Others might be only partially relevant because they include specifications not directly bearing on safety or addressing circumstances other than those falling within the scope of the general duty.

39.   The Secretary of State would have a power formally to approve published standards as

embodying 'sound modern standards of safety' where he is satisfied that the standards are suitable for this purpose. The effect would be that those who comply with the standards, or can prove that their products afford an equivalent level of safety, could be sure of having met the general duty. This would provide an incentive to suppliers to develop suitable standards where none may exist at present.

40. As a matter of marketing practice, those who produce and distribute goods already have regard to the products of their competitors. They can reasonably be expected to be aware of safety standards for the type of goods concerned. This will not always be the case for retailers. It could be excessively harsh to expose retailers to criminal liability without their attention having first been drawn by an enforcement officer to the likelihood of a breach. The Bill would provide appropriate procedures for this. In the case of other suppliers enforcement authorities would of course retain discretion to caution offenders rather than prosecute. There would be no right of private prosecution.

41. It is possible, where there is a sound case for this to exempt from the scope of safety regulations under the 1978 Act second-hand goods and goods intended for export. This was done for example in the Upholstered Furniture (Safety) Regulations 1980[2]. In the case of the general duty it would not be possible to treat each case on its merits and the Government has concluded that it would be preferable, on balance, for the general duty not to apply to these categories. Where appropriate, second-hand sales can be restricted by regulations. In the case of exports it would often be preferable to allow manufacturers flexibility to meet the safety requirements of the overseas market concerned (which may be different from those in the United Kingdom). Abuses of this flexibility could, if necessary, be dealt with by the use of existing powers.

42. There will continue to be a need to stipulate precise requirements for certain classes of goods in regulations or, in cases of emergency, by prohibition orders or notices. This will be so where the safety of consumers is likely to be best served by requiring mandatory compliance with a given standard, where it is necessary to give effect in the United Kingdom to a European Community Directive, or where particular types of goods are intrinsically too dangerous to be allowed for sale to the general public (eg tear gas capsules). The Government does not at present intend to repeal existing regulations (except, where necessary, for the purposes of updating them).

43. The Government considers that those injured as a result of a supplier's failure to comply with a general duty should be entitled to redress. This is already the position under Section 6 of the 1978 Act with regard to breaches of regulations, orders and notices. Liability in this case is strict, ie the supplier cannot escape his liability by raising a defence of due diligence. Injured parties are entitled to sue any supplier in the chain of supply. It is proposed that civil liability for breach of a general duty should be on a similar basis. The Government will, however, welcome views on whether there is a case for making provisions different to those in Section 6 of the present Act. The Government will also take into account any developments in the current discussions on product liability in the European Community.

44. *The Government invites views on a proposal to amend the Act to introduce a general duty on all suppliers to ensure that the goods they supply are safe in accordance with sound modern standards of safety. The duty would apply to all consumer goods and components for such goods, apart from those already excluded from the Consumer Safety Act (food, medicinal products licensed under the Medicines Act, controlled drugs, fertilisers and feeding stuffs) together with certain other possible exclusions for goods where safety is already adequately covered by other statutes (eg motor vehicles, aircraft), or where application of a general duty could raise particular problems (eg tobacco). The duty would not, however, apply to second-hand goods or goods for export.*

. . .

1. 'Standards, Quality and International Competitiveness', (Cmnd 8621) published in July 1982.
2. SI 725.

Question

Do you consider that it would be desirable to introduce such a broadly based provision into English law?

NOTE

Although the above provisions are undoubtedly important they should nonetheless be kept in perspective. As the White Paper, 'The Safety of Goods', notes (at para 9) 'Each year some 7,000 people in Great Britain die in home accidents (somewhat more than on the roads). It is estimated that 3 million more sustain injuries requiring medical treatment. This is a large toll in terms of human suffering and cost to the community. The proportion of these accidents caused directly by dangerous products is believed to be relatively small.' In an attempt to ascertain the causes of accidents in and around the home the Consumer Safety Unit of the Department of Trade has, since 1976, operated the Home Accident Surveillance system. The purpose of the system is to collect data at Accident and Emergency Departments relating to patients requiring in-patient or out-patient treatment as the result of home accidents. Reports are published annually. For a further report which looks at the causes of fatal accidents in the home see 'Personal Factors in Domestic Accidents: Prevention through Product and Environmental Design' (Department of Trade, Consumer Safety Unit, 1980).

CHAPTER 12

Trade descriptions: goods and services

Introduction

At least since the Merchandise Marks Act 1887 it has been recognised that a proper function of the statutory criminal law is to protect buyers of goods against false descriptions given in the course of trade. However the Molony Committee found that the 1887 and succeeding Acts were defective in draftsmanship and enforced ineffectively. The Trade Descriptions Act 1968 was a result of the Molony Committee's recommendations. For details of the committee's criticisms and proposals see the Final Report of the Committee on Consumer Protection, Cmnd 1781 (1962) Part V at para 586 et seq.

As may be inferred from the number of convictions recorded in a year covered by the Director General of Fair Trading's Annual Report (see above p 446) the 1968 Act attracts more reported cases on the interpretation of its apparently straightforward provisions than any comparable consumer statute.

The abundance of appellate decisions in this area is in part due to the relative affluence of a significant proportion of the defendants coupled with a reluctance by retailers who enjoy a national reputation for probity to have a conviction registered against them on what they regard as a technical point. However, a very large proportion of the defendants to charges concerning false trade descriptions relating to goods have been car sellers, and the incidence of fraud in this sector has more than once led the Director General to threaten either more stringent legislation or to use his powers to refuse consumer credit licences to persistent offenders.

This chapter and the one which follows concentrate on the key offences under the 1968 Act: (i) applying a false trade description to any goods or supplying or offering to supply any goods to which a false trade description is applied (s 1); (ii) making a statement concerning the provision of services etc, knowing it to be false or being reckless in that regard (s 14); and (iii) offering to supply goods and giving by whatever means a false indication as to the price (s 11).

The act imposes strict liability with regard to false trade descriptions of goods and false statements as to prices. The offence (introduced in 1968) relating to services requires knowledge or recklessness. Thus, provided the defendant knows that a trade description has been applied (see *Cottee v Douglas Seaton (Used Cars) Ltd* [1972] 3 All ER 750, [1972] 1 WLR 1408 (below, p 476)) an offence under section 1 will have been committed *unless* the defendant can bring himself within one of the specified defences. This scheme is common to a number of trading standards offences (particularly weights and measures and food and drugs) and the defences available are discussed separately in this book: see Ch 14.

Finally, before exploring the interpretation of the key offences mentioned above, the following points about the Act's operation should be borne in mind: First, the ambit of the Act extends to transactions between traders in addition to transactions between traders and the public. Second (and subject to a possible point involving s 23 of the Act, below p 566), private persons are not subjected to criminal liability under this Act. However such other statutory offences as obtaining property (including money) by false pretences contrary to section 15 of the Theft Act 1968 may have been committed in circumstances where the defendant, had he been operating in the course of a trade or business, would have contravened the Trade Descriptions Act 1968. Third, the Trade Description Act 1972 makes it an offence to supply etc goods manufactured or produced outside the United Kingdom (unless exempted by Order) with a United Kingdom name or mark unless this is accompanied by a conspicuous indication of the country of origin. This Act is not dealt with here.

False or misleading descriptions as to goods

The following are the principal provisions of the 1968 Act which are concerned with false or misleading descriptions as to goods:

Trade Descriptions Act 1968

PROHIBITION OF FALSE TRADE DESCRIPTIONS

1. Prohibition of false trade descriptions
(1) Any person who, in the course of a trade or business—
    (a) applies a false trade description to any goods; or
    (b) supplies or offers to supply any goods to which a false trade description is applied;
shall, subject to the provisions of this Act, be guilty of an offence.
(2) Sections 2 to 6 of this Act shall have effect for the purposes of this section and for the interpretation of expressions used in this section, wherever they occur in this Act.

2. Trade description
(1) A trade description is an indication, direct or indirect, and by whatever means given, of any of the following matters with respect to any goods or parts of goods, that is to say—
    (a) quantity, size or gauge;
    (b) method of manufacture, production, processing or reconditioning;
    (c) composition;
    (d) fitness for purpose, strength, performance, behaviour or accuracy;
    (e) any physical characteristics not included in the preceding paragraphs;
    (f) testing by any person and results thereof;
    (g) approval by any person or conformity with a type approved by any person;
    (h) place or date of manufacture, production, processing or reconditioning;
    (i) person by whom manufactured, produced, processed or reconditioned;
    (j) other history, including previous ownership or use.
(2) The matters specified in subsection (1) of this section shall be taken—
    (a) in relation to any animal, to include sex, breed or cross, fertility and soundness;
    (b) in relation to any semen, to include the identity and characteristics of the animal from which it was taken and measure of dilution.
(3) In this section 'quantity' includes length, width, height, area, volume, capacity, weight and number.
(4) Notwithstanding anything in the preceding provisions of this section, the following shall be deemed not to be trade descriptions, that is to say, any description or mark applied in pursuance of—

(a) [Repealed.]
(b) section 2 of the Agricultural Produce (Grading and Marking) Act 1928 (as amended by the Agricultural Produce (Grading and Marking Amendment Act 1931) or any corresponding enactment of the Parliament of Northern Ireland;
(c) the Plant Varieties and Seeds Act 1964;
(d) the Agriculture and Horticulture Act 1964 [or any community grading rules within the meaning of Part III of that Act];
(e) the Seeds Act (Northern Ireland) 1965;
(f) the Horticulture Act (Northern Ireland) 1966;
(g) [the Consumer Safety Act 1978];
[any statement made in respect of, or mark applied to, any material in pursuance of Part IV of the Agriculture Act 1970, any name or expression to which a meaning has been assigned under section 70 of that Act when applied to any material in the circumstances specified in that section], any mark prescribed by a system of classification compiled under section 5 of the Agriculture Act 1967 [and any designation, mark or description applied in pursuance of a scheme brought into force under section 6(1) or an order made under section 25(1) of the Agriculture Act 1970.]
(5) (a) Notwithstanding anything in the preceding provisions of this section, where provision is made under the [Food Act 1984], the Food and Drugs (Scotland) Act 1956 or the Food and Drugs Act (Northern Ireland) 1958 [or the Consumer Safety Act 1978] prohibiting the application of a description except to goods in the case of which the requirements specified in that provision are complied with, that description, when applied to such goods, shall be deemed not to be a trade description.
[(b) where by virtue of any provision made under Part V of the Medicines Act 1968 (or made under any provisions of the said Part V as applied by an order made under section 104 or 105 of that Act) anything which, in accordance with this Act, constitutes the application of a trade description to goods is subject to any requirements or restrictions imposed by that provision, any particular description specified in that provision, when applied to goods in circumstances to which those requirements or restrictions are applicable, shall be deemed not to be a trade description.]

3. False trade description

(1) A false trade description is a trade description which is false to a material degree.
(2) A trade description which, though not false, is misleading, that is to say, likely to be taken for such an indication of any of the matters specified in section 2 of this Act as would be false to a material degree, shall be deemed to be a false trade description.
(3) Anything which, though not a trade description, is likely to be taken for an indication of any of those matters and, as such an indication, would be false to a material degree, shall be deemed to be a false trade description.
(4) A false indication, or anything likely to be taken as an indication which would be false, that any goods comply with a standard specified or recognised by any person or implied by the approval of any person shall be deemed to be a false trade description, if there is no such person or no standard so specified, recognised or implied.

4. Applying a trade description to goods

(1) A person applies a trade description to goods if he—
  (a) affixes or annexes it to or in any manner marks it on or incorporates it with—
    (i) the goods themselves, or
    (ii) anything in, on or with which the goods are supplied; or
  (b) places the goods in, on or with anything which the trade description has been affixed or annexed to, marked on or incorporated with, or places any such thing with the goods; or
  (c) uses the trade description in any manner likely to be taken as referring to the goods.
(2) An oral statement may amount to the use of a trade description;
(3) Where goods are supplied in pursuance of a request in which a trade description is used and the circumstances are such as to make it reasonable to infer that the goods are supplied as goods corresponding to that trade description, the person supplying the goods shall be deemed to have applied that trade description to the goods.

5. Trade descriptions used in advertisements

(1) The following provisions of this section shall have effect where in an advertisement a trade description is used in relation to any class of goods.
(2) The trade description shall be taken as referring to all goods of the class, whether or not in existence at the time the advertisement is published—

(a) for the purpose of determining whether an offence has been committed under paragraph (a) of section 1(1) of this Act; and

(b) where goods of the class are supplied or offered to be supplied by a person publishing or displaying the advertisement, also for the purpose of determining whether an offence has been committed under paragraph (b) of the said section 1(1).

(3) In determining for the purposes of this section whether any goods are of a class to which a trade description used in an advertisement relates regard shall be had not only to the form and content of the advertisement but also to the time, place, manner and frequency of its publication and all other matters making it likely or unlikely that a person to whom the goods are supplied would think of the goods as belonging to the class in relation to which the trade description is used in the advertisement.

6. Offer to supply

A person exposing goods for supply or having goods in his possession for supply shall be deemed to offer to supply them.

Section I and the subsequent five sections which explain and expand it have received detailed attention from the courts. The following selected passages from a number of these decisions are designed to show how the courts have interpreted the key words and phrases in these sections.

'ANY PERSON'

'Any person' includes a corporation: see the Interpretation Act 1978, Sch I. In the common case where a trading standards offence has been committed by a company, provisions exist for making the company's director and principal officers jointly liable and they, unlike the company, may be imprisoned—an important additional sanction. Section 20 of the Trade Descriptions Act 1968 is typical:

20. Offences by corporations

(1) Where an offence under this Act which has been committed by a body corporate is proved to have been committed with the consent and connivance of, or to be attributable to any neglect on the part of, any director, manager, secretary or other similar officer of the body corporate, or any person who was purporting to act in any such capacity, he as well as the body corporate shall be guilty of that offence and shall be liable to be proceeded against and punished accordingly.

(2) In this section 'director', in relation to any body corporate established by or under any enactment for the purpose of carrying on under national ownership any industry or part of an industry or undertaking, being a body corporate whose affairs are managed by the members thereof, means a member of that body corporate.

No doubt in most cases the person applying the false trade description to goods will be the seller or supplier of them. The following case raises the question whether the scope of the offence is thus limited or whether it is similarly applicable to buyers. It also contains a helpful summary of the relevant provisions of the Act.

Fletcher v Budgen [1974] 2 All ER 1243, [1974] 1 WLR 1056, Queen's Bench Divisional Court

The facts are set out in the judgment of Lord Widgery CJ.

Lord Widgery CJ. This is an appeal by case stated by justices for the city of York in respect of their adjudication in the magistrates' court in York on 12 October 1973. Before them on that occasion were three informations preferred by the appellant prosecutor against the respondent. Each related to 9 December 1972. Each was concerned with a Fiat 500 motor car, which at that time the respondent was considering buying from its then owner. The respondent was engaged in the trade or business of a dealer in motor cars. When this Fiat was brought to him by its potential seller for him to consider its purchase, and he examined it in the course of his trade or business as a dealer in cars, he made three disparaging remarks about the car. First of all, he said there was no possibility of repairing it. Secondly, he said the repairs would not make the car safe, and, thirdly, summing up the whole situation, he said the only possible course of action with regard to the car would be for the car to be scrapped. The then owner of the car, a Mr Durkin, discouraged, and accepting that the car was good for scrap only, sold it to the respondent for £2.

To his astonishment no doubt he discovered very shortly afterwards that the car was being advertised for sale by the respondent at a price of £135. The justices found that the respondent had done repairs to the car to the value of about £56 and thus had managed to make the car sufficiently roadworthy for it to obtain its Ministry of Transport certificate. It was duly offered for sale, as I have said. The justices also found that the statements made by the respondent in regard to the car were false to his knowledge when he made the statements.

In other words, on its facts this is a very strong case. You have the non-trader who is selling the car; the motor trader who is buying it; an examination made by the potential buyer, jacking up the car and going underneath it; three extremely positive and unequivocal comments about the unsuitability of the car for any further use, and the ultimate result of the respondent having acquired the car for £2, being able apparently to sell it for a substantial profit.

Arising out of those facts there were, as I have said, three informations laid by the prosecutor against the respondent, alleging in each case that he had applied a false trade description to the car and thus committed an offence contrary to s 1 of the Trade Descriptions Act 1968.

One must look again at the first four sections, although in this court we seem to refer to them very frequently. Section 1(1) provides:

> 'Any person who, in the course of a trade or business,—(a) applies a false trade description to any goods . . . shall, subject to the provisions of this Act, be guilty of an offence.'

It is important to bear in mind throughout that the offence is created by a person who, in the course of a trade or business, applies a false trade description to the goods in question. Section 2 tells us what is meant by the expression 'trade description', and it is in the widest possible words. It is 'an indication, direct or indirect, and by whatever means given, of any of the following matters with respect to any goods or parts of goods, that is to say', and then there are listed a number of descriptions. The relevant one in the present case is (e): 'any physical characteristics not included in the preceding paragraphs.' The case for the prosecution was that when the respondent used these three derogatory observations in relation to the motor car, the observations amounted to a trade description because they were an indication of the physical characteristics of the car.

Then the Act goes on to define 'false trade description' in s 3(1), and that not surprisingly describes or defines a false description as 'a trade description which is false to a material degree'. This is somewhat further developed in sub-ss (2) and (3) in a manner which I do not find it necessary to pursue in this case because if the remarks passed on this motor car were trade descriptions, as the prosecution contended, there is no doubt whatever that they were not only false to a material degree, but, for good measure, they were known by the repondent to be false, which is not in itself an essential of the offence charged.

In s 4 one has the important provisions dealing with what amounts to an applying of a trade description, it being remembered again that the offence in sub-s (1) is created by applying a false trade description to any goods. Section 4(1) provides:

> 'A person applies a trade description to goods if he—(a) affixes or annexes it to or in any manner marks it on or incorporates it with—(i) the goods themselves . . . (c) uses the trade description in any manner likely to be taken as referring to the goods'.

Subsection (2) provides: 'An oral statement may amount to the use of a trade description', so it is not necessary for the description to be contained in writing; an oral statement will do.

Again looking at the facts of this case, it cannot be doubted that if these words amounted to a trade description they would certainly be likely to be taken as referring to the goods, namely, the car; indeed, they could not have referred to anything else.

So at first blush one looks at the four sections and observes the wide ambit which they enjoy, and if when construing the statute, one looks at the words and sees what their natural meaning is, it seems that they cover this case.

But why? Because, according to s 1(1), the respondent was carrying on a trade or business, and it was in the course of his trade or business that he made the observations. Further, the trade description was applied to the goods because it was used in a manner likely to be taken as referring to the goods. That it was a false description is really beyond doubt, as I have already sought to demonstrate.

There is, therefore, on the face of it only one reason why the prosecution might be held unsuccessful in this case, and that would be on the fundamental proposition that, although the Act does not condescend in terms to say so, yet the scheme of ss 1 to 4 is restricted to false trade descriptions made by a seller of goods and cannot apply to a buyer of goods. If on a proper consideration of the Act it can be said with confidence that Parliament must have intended that it should not have been, so be it. If one cannot, on a consideration of the sections of the Act, conclude that buyers are necessarily excluded from its terms, then it would seem to me that a buyer is as much liable to be convicted as a seller under the terms of the sections to which I have referred.

Oddly enough, this is a point which has not arisen before. Perhaps the nearest to it is *Fletcher v Sledmore*[1]. That was a case with rather unusual facts in which the owner of a motor car had agreed to sell and, being a repairer of cars, had agreed to undertake certain repairs before the car was delivered to the buyer. The buyer was contemplating reselling it to a sub-purchaser. He brought the sub-purchaser along to see the car in the state in which it was, partly dismantled for repair purposes, and the respondent, who was the original seller of the car, was present. On enquiry being made by the prospective sub-purchaser as to the quality of the car, the respondent volunteered the information that it was all right, it was a good little engine, and he had driven it himself.

That case raised a number of points not relevant in the instant case, but in the judgment of Eveleigh J there are some useful observations as to the scope of this Act, and I find them of assistance in the present problem. Having looked at the same sections to which I have already referred, he said[2]:

> 'Reading the words of the section, one sees no limitation which specifies the nature of the transaction in which the description of the goods is made. Counsel for the prosecutor has very properly drawn the court's attention to *Hall v Wickens Motors (Gloucester) Ltd*[3]. In that case the defendants, who were car dealers, sold a car, and some 40 days later received an oral complaint from the purchaser about the steering. The defendants replied "There is nothing wrong with the car". Examination of the car revealed in fact that it was defective. The defendants were charged with applying a false trade description to the car, namely, an oral statement that there was nothing wrong with it. They were convicted and appealed to quarter sessions, where the recorder accepted their submission that no offence had been committed under section 1(1)(a) of the Act of 1968.'

Then Eveleigh J goes on to deal with certain other aspects of that case, and he continued[4]:

> 'However, on the facts of this particular case it would not be right to say that the statement was unconnected with the supply or the sale of goods. There are no qualifications in section 1 as to the time when the representation is to be made. The only qualification there specifically to be seen is that it should be in the course of trade or business, in other words should be made as part of the business activities of the person charged. There is no reason to introduce any time qualification. The question then remains whether or not there is reason to introduce the qualification that the person charged should himself be a contracting party in the matters in which the representation is made. No such limitation appears in the section itself, and I see no reason why such a limitation should be implied.'

I cite that case because, as I have said, it indicates the attitude of this court towards suggestions made from time to time that the clear language of the statute should be restricted on some assumed basis that Parliament must have so intended.

A case in which a submission was made and upheld in this court is, however, *Wycombe Marsh Garages Ltd v Fowler*[5]. This was a case in which the owner of a car had taken the car to a garage to obtain a Ministry of Transport certificate. The accused in that case examined the car and came to the conclusion that the nearside tyres were defective to such a degree as to make it impossible to issue a certificate. He, therefore, refused the certificate, certifying that the tyres suffered from this particular defect. He was wrong. He was honestly wrong, but he was wrong, and eventually it was shown that the tyres suffered from no such defect.

Somewhat to the surprise of the members of the court sitting on that occasion, the authorities then proceeded to prosecute him with a criminal offence under s 1 of the 1968 Act. It was held that he had committed no such offence, and the value of the case, I think, is that it emphasises that the Act is only concerned with false trade descriptions applied to goods in association with a contract for the sale or supply of the goods. In other words, *Wycombe Marsh Garages Ltd v Fowler*[5] is valuable for the proposition that a person who merely makes an inspection of goods as a service to its owner, and who honestly certifies his findings, is not to be convicted of an offence under s 1 because, although he may be said to have applied a trade description to the goods, he has not done so in a transaction associated with sale or supply of the goods.

There one has an example of this court imposing certain limitations on the wide words of the section, but in general we must take the Act as it stands. We must look at the language used and we must give it its natural consequences.

I confess to being surprised at the conclusion to which I have ultimately come because I confess that in considering this Act in the past I have subconsciously thought that it could only apply to false trade descriptions applied by the seller. I suppose that I had never before been required to think about the circumstances in which the public need to apply these restrictions to a buyer is every bit as much as is the public need to apply them to a seller. If one visualises the present case where the potential buyer of the goods is engaged in the trade or business of buying cars, and if one reminds oneself that this Act only applies to people who apply false trade descriptions in the course of a trade or business, then I think it becomes apparent that to allow the Act to operate according to its terms in the present case is not in any sense illogical and is not likely to run counter to any intention which Parliament may have had.

It seems to me that it is perfectly reasonable when the buyer is the expert and the seller may be the amateur, where the buyer makes an examination of the goods in his capacity as an expert and then proceeds to pronounce on the qualities or otherwise, that he should be as much liable to be restrained in his language as is a seller, who in the normal course of events is the man who knows all about the goods and who is to be restricted in any temptation to make false and misleading statements about them.

I do not believe that upholding the prosecution in the present case is going to mean that every buyer of goods runs the risk of committing a criminal offence merely because he deprecates or makes some derogatory remarks about the goods which are offered to him. It would be a sad thing if such a situation arose.

But when one remembers that it is only a buyer who is conducting a trade or business, and who, therefore, in most instances will himself be the expert on this subject, who can fall foul of this Act, it seems to me that a decision in favour of the prosecution in this case will not only accord with the language of the Act and be consistent with what we have said about it in the past, but also make very good sense in view of the fact that its effect is restricted to those who carry on a trade or business.

For those reasons I am persuaded that the justices were wrong, and I would allow the appeal and send the case back with a direction to continue the hearing in the light of this court's judgment.

Park J. I agree.

Forbes J. I agree.

Appeal allowed.

1. [1973] RTR 371.
2. [1973] RTR at 375.
3. [1972] 3 All ER 759, [1972] 1 WLR 1418.
4. [1973] RTR at 376.
5. [1972] 3 All ER 248, [1972] 1 WLR 1156.

The following comment on this case is contained in the 'Review of the Trade Descriptions Act 1968: A Report by the Director General of Fair Trading' (Cmnd 6628) (1976):

Statements by experts

107. . . . The case is to be contrasted with *Wycombe Marsh Garages Ltd v Fowler* [see above p 468] in which it was held that a person who, in the course of his business, provides an expert service which involves reporting on the condition of goods commits no offence under section 1 if he makes a false statement about their condition. We first considered whether these two decisions are right in principle.

108. It seems to us that it would be entirely wrong if a trader called upon to make an independent assessment of goods committed an offence because, acting in good faith, he made an incorrect statement about them. To make a trader liable to conviction for an incorrect statement so made might well on balance tend to inhibit the communication of honest assessments rather than improve the quality of reports. We therefore endorse the principle established by the *Wycombe Marsh* Judgment.

109.   On the other hand, we also think it right that a trader should be guilty of an offence if he deliberately asserts his expertise and then proceeds to make dishonest statements about goods offered to him with a view to purchasing them more cheaply. Such practices could be widespread. It was suggested to us for example, that some antique dealers made a deliberate practice of dishonestly misdescribing goods offered to them in the hope of persuading the seller to let them go cheaply. But it is to be noted that an offence under section 1 of the 1968 Act does not depend upon the establishment of dishonest intent; and we have reservations in this connection about the Judgment in the *Budgen* case. . . .

Problem

Gruniad has been having problems with his central heating boiler. He calls in a specialist, Chimes. Chimes examines the boiler and says, 'It is on its last legs. You need a new one'. The statement was made in good faith but was incorrect since the fault could have been cured by a cheap replacement part. Gruniad buys a new boiler from Chimes, trading in the old one in part exchange.

Consider Chimes' liability under the 1968 Act.

'IN THE COURSE OF A TRADE OR BUSINESS'

Section 1 requires the false trade description to have been applied etc 'in the course of a trade or business'. This phrase or phrases similar in intent are common to a number of civil and criminal statutes and there has been little overall consistency of approach in interpreting it. It is a common experience in the investigation of trading standards offences for the potential defendant to state that the sale in question was not in the course of a business. The following case considered the matter in relation to s 1 of the 1968 Act.

Davies v Sumner [1984] 1 WLR 405, Queen's Bench Divisional Court

The facts are set out in the judgment of Robert Goff LJ.

Robert Goff LJ   There is before the court an appeal by way of case stated by the defendant, John Barry Davies, from an adjudication by the magistrates' court sitting at Flint. The case raises a question of construction of section 1(1) of the Trade Descriptions Act 1968.

It appears from the case that an information was laid charging the defendant that, in the course of trade or business, on 1 August 1981, at Bagillt in the County of Clwyd, he applied to certain goods, namely, a Ford motor car, a false trade description to the effect that the motor car had travelled 18,100 miles whereas the true mileage was in excess of 118,000 miles, contrary to section 1(1)(a) of the Trade Descriptions Act 1968.

The justices have set out in the case certain facts found by them. In substance, they are as follows. The defendant was, and still is, employed as a self-employed courier. He was engaged exclusively by the Harlech Television Co to transport films, video tapes and other items of that nature from Mold to Cardiff in South Wales, and on occasions from and to other places. For that purpose, the defendant had to provide his own car. The car which he provided was the Ford Capri car referred to in the information, registration no UDM 230V. For his services, he was paid a fee for each journey and, in addition, a subsistence allowance. He was required to pay all the expenses involved, including the running costs of the vehicle. In respect of these expenses, the defendant claimed and was allowed tax relief as business expenses. Before the defendant bought this Ford Capri motor car for use in this work, he had rented a car. He bought the Ford Capri in June 1980. Such was the extent of his activities as a courier that between June 1980 and July 1981 he travelled over 100,000 miles. He then decided that the time had come to buy a new car to continue his business as a self-employed courier.

On 31 July 1981, the defendant went to the showrooms of a company, also called Davies, who were the Ford main dealers in Bagillt. He arranged to buy a new Ford, trading in the old Ford Capri, which had travelled 118,000 miles, in part-exchange. The defendant's car was examined by a salesman and the odomoter showed only 18,100 miles. The reason for this was that the odomoter was a five digital odometer so that, although the mileage had gone right round the clock, this did not appear on the odometer. The appearance of the vehicle was consistent with the vehicle having travelled 18,100 miles only. It was found that the salesman inquired about the mileage travelled, but nothing was said about any answers which may have been given to that inquiry. The new car was purchased for £8,270 and, receiving as he did £3,800 for his Capri motor car, the balance which the defendant had to pay to the garage was £4,470. Arrangements were made for the defendant to return to the garage on 1 August 1981 to pick up the new car. This he did, and at the same time he handed over his old car and signed a sales invoice to complete the transaction. It appears that the sales invoice included a declaration to the effect that the mileage of the old car was 18,100 miles. I think it right to record that we were told by Mr Waldron, on behalf of the defendant, that that figure was not in the original sales invoice but was added later. It is admitted by the defendant that he did not disclose the true mileage of the Ford Capri, and his contention is that he was never asked to do so.

On those facts, the justices convicted the defendant of the charge as stated, and imposed a fine of £120. He was ordered to pay costs, but no order as to compensation was made. The question stated for the opinion of the court is as follows:

> 'When a person who in the course of his occupation as a self-employed courier almost exclusively uses his car for the purpose of that occupation, disposes of that vehicle for another vehicle, is that a transaction in the course of "trade or business" for the purpose of section 1 of the Trade Descriptions Act 1968?'

. . .

Here the case against the defendant was that he did apply a false trade description to goods in the course of trade or business when, on the occasion of the trading in of his car, he did so with an odometer showing only 18,100 miles when the true mileage of the car was 118,100, and by signing a sales invoice stating that the mileage of the car was only 18,100.

The justices were referred to the decision of this court in *Havering London Borough Council v Stevenson* [1970] 1 WLR 1375. It seems that that authority influenced their decision to convict the defendant. In that case, the defendant carried on a car hire business. It was found that it was his usual practice to sell the motor cars he used in his business after about two years. He sold them at the prevailing trade price and paid the proceeds of the sales back into the business for the purchase of new vehicles. On one occasion, in accordance with that practice, he sold a motor car and falsely represented to the purchaser that the recorded mileage of the vehicle was less than the mileage which the vehicle had in fact travelled. On that basis, the case came before the justices on a charge under section 1(1)(b) of the Trade Descriptions Act 1968, but the charge was dismissed by them. The prosecutor then appealed, by way of case stated, to the Divisional Court. The court allowed the appeal. The reasons for that decision are to be found in the judgment of Lord Parker CJ who said, at p 1377:

> 'The defendant carried on a car hire business. I emphasise that it was a car hire business and not the business of a motor car vendor or dealer. He had a fleet of 24 cars and made a regular practice of selling his hire cars after he had had them for about two years, when he chose to run his fleet down or when the condition of a particular vehicle warranted it. He never bought cars and sold them for a greater price. The defendant owned this Ford Corsair car and having used it in his car hire business, he put it up for sale in accordance with his usual practice. In November 1969, it was represented to Mr Carter, who bought the vehicle, that the motor car had a recorded mileage of 34,000 miles, and the speedometer recorded that mileage. In fact, as is found by the case, the mileage was over 50,000. Pausing there, for my part on those facts it seems to me that it was almost inevitable that this application of a false trade description was in the course of trade or business. It was not "for the purposes of trade or business" or even "by way of trade or business". Once it is found that a car hire business as part of its normal practice buys and disposes of cars, it seems to me almost inevitable that the sale of a car and the application of a trade description in the course of that sale was an integral part of the business carried on as a car hire firm.'

. . .

Before us, Mr Waldron for the defendant and Mr Scrivener for the prosecutor both accepted that the problem whether or not a sale, and therefore the application of a trade description in the course of that sale, arose in the course of a trade or business is to be solved by asking the question: did the sale form an integral part of the defendant's trade or business?

Mr Waldron submitted that in the present case the sale did not form an integral part of the defendant's business. He submitted that a distinction has to be drawn between cases such as *Havering London Borough Council v Stevenson* [1970] 1 WLR 1375 and the present case because, although in the present case the defendant used the car almost exclusively in the course of his business, it did not follow that, when he came to sell it, the sale formed an integral part of his business. In this connection, Mr Waldron gave a number of examples of cases where, he suggested, a sale did not form an integral part of a person's business. In particular, he gave the example of a country doctor who has two cars, using one car for his private affairs and the other car exclusively for visiting his patients in the course of his practice. I understand that the profession of a doctor does for present purposes constitute a trade or business. The time might come when he wanted to sell his second car in order to purchase a new one. Would that sale form an integral part of that doctor's trade or business? The answer, submitted Mr Waldron, is plainly not.

Mr Scrivener, on the other hand, submitted that if a person uses a car exclusively, almost exclusively or even substantially in the course of his trade or business, then any sale of that car would be a sale which formed an integral part of his business. He relied upon the fact that such a person would claim tax relief in respect of the use of his car and submitted that it would therefore be only right and proper that the sale should be considered as an integral part of his business.

I consider that Mr Scrivener's approach is not in accordance with the test laid down by Lord Parker CJ in *Stevenson's* case. On Lord Parker's test, we have to look at the nature of the business carried on by the person concerned; we have then to look at the transaction in question, and ask ourselves the question: Does that transaction form an integral part of that person's business? Where a car hire firm, which uses a number of cars in the course of its business, from time to time trades in cars in part-exchange for new ones, no doubt the transactions of disposing of old cars in part-exchange for new cars is an integral part of the car hire business. But if we turn to the example of the country doctor given by Mr Waldron, I do not think that the occasional trading in of a car used for his practice could properly be described as a sale which formed an integral part of his business. The mere fact that the doctor used his car for the purpose of his practice is not enough. Indeed, Mr Scrivener is really proposing an entirely new test. On his submission, the test would not be whether the sale formed an integral part of the person's business, but whether a particular asset used substantially during the course of his trade or business had been sold. In my opinion, that is a different test from that established by Lord Parker CJ.

I turn then to the question posed by the justices for the opinion of the court . . . [see above].

I would answer that question in the negative. It appears to me, on reading that question, that the justices applied the wrong test. They asked themselves not whether the disposal of the car was a transaction which formed an integral part of the defendant's business as a self-employed courier, but simply whether the car was almost exclusively used by the defendant for the purposes of his occupation as a self-employed courier. They therefore applied the test that has been urged upon us by Mr Scrivener and which I am not prepared to accept. I would therefore allow the appeal.

Forbes J. I agree. The justices, having had *Havering London Borough Council v Stevenson* [1970] 1 WLR 1375 drawn to their attention, have asked themselves the question, 'Was the use of the car an integral part of the business?' and not, 'Was the sale of the car an integral part of the business?' I agree with Robert Goff LJ that the question put to this court must be answered in the negative.

Appeal allowed.

The prosecution's appeal to the House of Lords was dismissed for the following reasons given by Lord Keith and with which the other members of the House of Lords agreed ([1984] 3 All ER 831 at 834):

Any disposal of a chattel held for the purposes of a business may, in a certain sense, be said to have been in the course of that business, irrespective of whether the chattel was acquired with a view to resale or for consumption or as a capital asset. But in my opinion s 1(1) of the 1968 Act is not intended to cast such a wide net as this. The expression 'in the course of a trade or business' in the context of an Act having consumer protection as its primary purpose conveys the concept of some degree of regularity, and it is to be observed that the long title to the Act refers to 'misdescriptions of goods, services, accommodation and facilities provided in the course of trade'. Lord Parker CJ in the *Havering* case clearly considered that the expression was not used in the broadest sense. The reason why the transaction there in issue was caught was that in his view it was 'an integral part of the business carried on as a car-hire firm'. That would not cover the sporadic selling off of pieces of equipment which were no longer required for the purposes of a business. The vital feature of the *Havering* case appears to have been, in Lord Parker's view, that the respondent's business *as part of its normal practice* bought and disposed of cars. The need for some degree of regularity does not, however, involve that a one-off adventure in the nature of trade, carried through with a view to profit, would not fall within s 1(1) because such a transaction would itself constitute a trade.

In the present case it was sought to be inferred that the respondent, covering as he did such a large regular mileage, was likely to have occasion to sell his car at regular intervals, so that he too would have a normal practice of buying and disposing of cars. It is sufficient to say that such a normal practice had not yet been established at the time of the alleged offence. The respondent might well revert to hiring a car, as he had previously done. Further, the respondent's car was a piece of equipment he used for providing his courier service. It was not something he exploited as stock-in-trade, which is what the defendant was in substance doing with his cars in the *Havering* case. Where a person carries on the business of hiring our some description of goods to the public and has a practice of selling off those that are no longer in good enough condition, clearly the latter goods are offered or supplied in the course of his business within the meaning of s 1(1). But the occasional sale of some worn out piece of shop equipment would not fall within the enactment.

NOTES

1. There are a number of areas of the civil law where it is necessary to distinguish a 'business' transaction from a 'private' one. The main ones are as follows.

(a) *Taxation.* It is necessary to distinguish according to whether income is derived from a trade or profession subjected to income tax under ss 108 and 109 of the Income and Corporation Taxes Act 1970 (as amended) or a non-trading capital gain or loss such as the realisation of an investment within the separate capital gains tax legislation. 'Badges of trade' have been devised by the courts which may be summarised as involving the following criteria:

   (i)   the subject matter of the realisation;
   (ii) the length of the period of ownership;
   (iii) the frequency or number of similar transactions by the same person;
   (iv) supplementary work on or in connection with the property realised;
   (v) the circumstances responsible for the realisation;
   (vi) motive.

In connection with 'motive' there is a fundamental distinction between the person buying for profitable *investment* and the person operating a systematic, or even 'one-off' *trading* transaction.

(b) *National Insurance.* A self-employed person is liable to pay Class 2 Contributions. The Social Security Act 1975, s 2, states that such a person is one who is 'gainfully employed'.

(c) *Land use.* Business as opposed to private user of land may arise as an issue under both planning law, where planning permission is required for 'development' which can include a change of use of land from private to business purposes, and under the law relating to restrictive and positive covenants. The use by way of authority of *Rolls v Miller* (1884) 27 Ch D 71 in *Blakemore v Bellamy* [1983] RTR 303, above p 421 illustrates this point.

(d) *Sale of goods.* The conditions implied by section 14 of the Sale of Goods Act 1979 apply only if the seller sells 'in the course of a business'. Problems can arise both as to the meaning of 'in the course of' and 'a business': see above, pp 72–73.

2. Other areas of Criminal law require the defendant to have acted 'in the course of a business' or to be conducting a business. For instance, firstly, under the Consumer Credit Act 1974, s 21, it is an offence to carry on a consumer credit business without a licence. Section 189(1) defines a consumer credit business as 'any business so far as it comprises or relates to the provision of credit under regulated consumer credit agreements'. (There is an exception for carrying out such transactions only occasionally: see s 189(2)). Secondly, the Consumer Transactions (Restrictions on Statements) Order 1976 (as amended), which is discussed elsewhere in this book (see above pp 47 and 281–283), applies only to persons who in the course of a business attempt to exclude consumers' inalienable rights under the Sale of Goods Act 1979. Thirdly, a similar phrase appears in the Unsolicited Goods and Services Act 1971, s 2, where it is an offence for a person without reasonable cause and in the course of any trade or business to make a demand for payment for what he knows are unsolicited goods. In *Eiman v London Borough of Waltham Forest* (1982) 90 ITSA Monthly Review 204 DC, the appellant had sent unsolicited copies of his privately published Urdu poetry to various London public libraries accompanied by a series of letters demanding payment. The appellant argued that writing poetry was his hobby but the court upheld his conviction under s 2 since the letters were 'business' letters; it did not matter how small the activity was if it had a 'direct commercial involvement' (per Ormrod LJ). This decision of the Divisional Court contrasts oddly with its decision in *Blakemore v Bellamy* (above p 421). Finally, the same expression is used in s 14 of the Trade Descriptions Act which is concerned with false statements as to services (see below p 500) and a similar limit has been implied in s 11 which covers statements as to prices (see below pp 525–526).

3. In the *Havering London Borough* case referred to by Robert Goff LJ in *Davies v Sumner* above, there was no doubt that the defendant was operating a business. The only question was whether the supply of the car was 'in the course' of it. For other cases illustrating the application of the Act to secondary lines of business see, for example, *Southwark London Borough v Charlesworth* (1983) 147 JP 470, 2 Trading Law 93 (QBD) (sale of electric fire by shoe repairer) and *Fletcher v Sledmore* [1973] RTR 371, referred to by Lord Widgery CJ in *Fletcher v Budgen*, above p 468 (sale of car by panel beater). This latter case established also that the trade or business in the course of which the false trade description is applied need not involve a contractual relationship with the customer who is prejudiced by it. But the representation must have some connection with the supply of the goods in question. An assurance that there is 'nothing wrong with the car' given some forty days after its sale is not within s 1 of the Act: see *Wickens Motors (Gloucester) Ltd v Hall* [1972] 3 All ER 759, [1972] 1 WLR 1418, above p 468. (For a contrasting case involving the supply of services, see *Breed v Cluett* [1970] 2 QB 459, [1970] 2 All ER 662, QBD, below p 501.)

4. In yet other cass the issue will be whether the defendant's activity constitutes a 'trade or business' (the terms not being defined in the 1968 Act) or simply a pastime or hobby. For a case which perhaps goes to the limit in holding that the defendant was not trading for the purposes of the Business (Advertisements) Disclosure Order 1977, see *Blakemore v Bellamy* [1983] RTR 303 above, pp 421–424 (postman selling second-hand motor vehicles). For a review of the total picture see Harvey, 'Business or Pleasure' (1983) 27 Sol Jo 163; Lawson, 'In the Course of a Trade or Business' (1984) 128 Sol Jo 24.

'APPLIES'

The offences created by s 1(1)(a) and (b) of the Act depend on the notion of 'applying' a false trade description to goods. Section 1(1)(a) covers a person who 'applies' such a description, for example by 'clocking' a car. Section 1(1)(b) covers a person who 'supplies' or 'offers to supply' (see below p 481) goods to which such a description has been 'applied', as when an honest dealer is seeking to sell a car which someone else has clocked. Section 4 (above p 465) explains what the process of 'applying' involves. The following cases illustrate some less obvious aspects of the verb.

Roberts v Severn Petroleum and Trading Co Ltd [1981] RTR 312, Queen's Bench Divisional Court

The facts are set out in the judgment of Donaldson LJ.

Donaldson LJ In this case the prosecutor appeals against the decision of Shropshire Justices sitting at Wellington, Telford, who dismissed an information preferred by him against the defendants alleging an offence under the Trade Descriptions Act 1968.

What happened was this. A garage was run by a company called E R Thomas & Son, and in front of that garage there was the usual pole with a large 'Esso' sign. There was also a smaller 'Esso' sign over the garage itself. The petrol pumps there bore no indication of the manufacturer of the petrol. They simply indicated whether it was 2-star, 3-star or 4-star petrol.

The defendants were asked by Thomases to supply them with petrol in bulk, it being known to Thomases and of course to the defendants that the petrol would not be Esso petrol. The defendants arrived at the garage. The driver in fact saw the 'Esso' sign up and took instructions from his employers and thereafter he put the petrol into these tanks. What is said on behalf of the prosecutor is that that act of putting petrol into the tanks in a garage which displays signs which will convey to the public that the petrol sold from the garage is Esso petrol is an offence under section (1)(1)(a) of the Trade Descriptions Act 1968. Section 1(1)(a) provides:

'Any person who, in the course of a trade or business,—(a) applies a false trade description to any goods . . . shall . . . be guilty of an offence'.

A 'trade description' is defined in section 2(1), so far as it is relevant, as being:

'. . . an indication, direct or indirect, and by whatever means given, of any of the following matters with respect to any goods or parts of goods, that is to say . . . (i) person by whom manufactured, produced, processed or reconditioned . . .'

It is necessary in this case also to take account of section 4(1), which provides as follows:

'A person applies a trade description to goods if he . . . (b) places the goods in, on or with anything which the trade description has been affixed or annexed to, marked on or incorporated with, or places any such thing with the goods . . .'

Mr Carlile on behalf of the prosecutor submits that the tanks of this garage were receptacles to which a trade description, namely, that the contents were the product of the Esso Petroleum Company, had been affixed.

He refers us to the decision of this court in *Stone v Burn* [1911] 1 KB 927 where a brewer placed Bass beer in bottles which were embossed with the name of another company and was held to be guilty of an offence under an earlier statute in much the same terms, notwithstanding that he put Bass labels on the bottles as well.

In the light of that decision it seems to me that the defendants were indeed committing an offence under the Trade Descriptions Act 1968 and should have been convicted. The justices in fact acquitted, and they ask in effect whether they were right to do so. I would answer the question in the negative.

Kilner Brown J I agree.

Appeal allowed. On prosecutor withdrawing application, no order for case to be remitted to justices. Order for payment of prosecutor's costs of appeal out of central funds.

NOTES

For a case in which similar issues were raised see *Donnelly v Rowlands* [1971] 1 All ER 9, [1970] 1 WLR 1600, QBD. For the associated tort of 'passing off' see *Street on Torts* (7th edn, 1983) Ch 23.

Cottee v Douglas Seaton (Used Cars) Ltd [1972] 3 All ER 750, [1972] 1 WLR 1408, Queen's Bench Divisional Court

The facts of this complex but important case are set out in some detail in the judgment of Lord Widgery CJ, below. However it is crucial to note, as did his Lordship, that the information was preferred against the respondents under s 23 of the Act. They were not charged directly under s 1. Section 23 is discussed further in Chapter 14 below, pp 563–564. Here it is sufficient to say that in adopting this course the prosecution was probably taking on an unnecessary burden. If it is alleged that D1 (the honest dealer, Warry) committed an offence and that this was 'due to the act or default' of D2 (the respondents) D2 can be convicted usually under s 23 if, and only if, D1 would have been guilty (under s 1) if charged. So on the facts of this case the respondents' liability depended on Warry's being potentially liable also.

Lord Widgery CJ This is an appeal by case stated by justices for the county of Somerset acting in and for the petty sessional division of Crewkerne in respect of their adjudication as a magistrates' court on 16 December 1971. On that date they dismissed informations preferred by the appellant against the respondents, and to take one as being representative its terms were as follows, that between the 1 and 5 September 1970 inclusive, at Merriott in the county of Somerset, one Peter Leonard Warry, unlawfully in the course of a trade or business did offer to supply to one John Louis Shillabeer certain goods, namely a Ford Corsair motor car, to which a false trade description, namely an indication that the engine compartment body-work of the motor car was in a sound condition, was applied by means of the use of plastic filler and paint to conceal rust corrosion and holes in the bodywork, contrary to s 1 (1)(b) of the Trade Descriptions Act 1968. And further that the commission of the offence was due to the act or default of the respondents whereby the respondents were guilty of the offence by virtue of s 23 of the Trade Descriptions Act 1968.

The essential facts relating to this charge are as follows. For approximately two years prior to 28 May 1970 a Ford Corsair motor car, registration no 6505 NU, was in the ownership of a Mr Meldrum. While the car was in his ownership Mr Meldrum had occasion to effect certain repairs to the bodywork of the vehicle inside the engine compartment. These repairs were called for partly as a result of an accident in which the vehicle had been involved, and partly by extensive rust damage to the bodywork. In making these repairs Mr Meldrum had used aluminium strip which he covered with plastic filler in certain areas and plastic filler alone in others. Having placed the plastic filler in position he rough filed it and painted it over with a grey zinc primer. The rest of the paintwork inside the engine compartment was off-white. Mr Meldrum made no effort to disguise the work he had done before he subsequently traded the car in to the respondents. It is important to emphasise this last-mentioned fact because any person of experience inspecting the car when Mr Meldrum sold it would have realised that some somewhat unconventional work of repair had been done by the insertion of this body filler into the structure of the car.

· Following the acquisition of the Corsair by the respondents their manager inspected the car. He, of course, saw the plastic filler on the inside of the engine compartment, and knew that this particular car was prone to rust damage. He realised that the plastic filler was not disguised in any way. Because the car was in a generally poor condition and appearance the respondents' manager decided that it was not suitable for a retail sale by his company. He therefore offered it for sale to several local motor dealers in the used car trade, but all declined to buy it. In these circumstances the respondents' manager ordered that the car be removed to the repair shop of the respondents' parent company to have the bodywork at the relevant part repaired and tidied up as cheaply as possible. When the car was examined by the appropriate officer at the parent company's repair department he realised that to make a proper repair of this defective part of the engine compartment would be extremely expensive. Labour charges alone for renewing each panel would be about £30 and the cost to a retail customer would be between £60 and £70 per panel. He thought that this was more than the respondents could afford to spend on this car and therefore arranged that the engine compartment be steam cleaned and the rough plastic filler which Mr Meldrum had inserted be smoothed down. Thereafter the whole of the engine compartment was to be painted to blend with the manufacturer's original colours, and this would protect the metal of the compartment as well as covering up the plastic filler which Mr Meldrum had inserted. The car was then sold to Mr Warry, a motor dealer. He examined it carefully, he knew that cars of this type were liable to suffer rust damage at the point where Mr Meldrum's repairs had taken place, but he also observed that the engine compartment had been recently repainted and appeared to be in good condition, and he did not notice the repair work done by Mr Meldrum, it having now been covered by the repainting carried out by the respondents. Mr Warry bought the car on an 'as seen' basis. He would not have bought the car if the engine compartment had not looked sound. Mr Warry had the car resprayed. It was submitted to the Ministry of Transport for a certificate of roadworthiness which was granted. The Ministry of Transport examiner looked at the bodywork inside the engine compartment and did not observe Mr Meldrum's handiwork or any signs of rust damage. He accordingly passed the vehicle for use on the road and in due course it was sold to Mr Shillabeer. Mr Shillabeer drove the car for some 4,000 miles between September 1970 and March 1971 without particular incident, and nothing was done during that period about repairs to the engine body compartment. In March 1971, however, the car was again involved in a minor accident, and when work was done on it in consequence of that accident the defects to which I have referred came to light.

The issues in this case in the first instance amount to one which can be put shortly: if a motor trader carries out work of repair or restoration to a motor car, and the result of the work or restoration is that some feature of the car relating to its strength or performance is obscured and thus not readily visible to a prospective purchaser, does the trader on selling that car without disclosing the nature of the work and the defect which is obscured apply to the car a false trade description under s 1 of the Trade Descriptions Act 1968? It is of some importance to note that the sale relied on by the prosecution as being the sale to which the false trade description was applied was the sale by Mr Warry. It will be remembered that Mr Warry had not carried out the repairs which involved the insertion of the filler into the structure of the car, and, furthermore, that when he sold the car he was unaware that this work had been done. There is no specific finding on the fact but it is a reasonable inference that the justices were satisfied that Mr Warry neither knew of the nature of the repairs which had been done to the car nor was he in any sense negligent in failing to discover them. If the prosecution are right in this case it means that a seller can be guilty of this offence even though he is wholly unaware of the circumstances giving rise to his offence.

His Lordship then referred to ss 1(1), 2(1), 3 and 4(1) of the Act, above, and continued:

The appellant's argument accordingly is that the concealment of the structural weakness in this car was an 'indication' of the 'strength' of the vehicle (s 2) and false to a material degree (s 3). The resultant false trade description it is argued was incorporated with the car (s 4). Alternatively, if this did not amount to a trade description it was likely to be taken for such an indication and thus to be treated as a false trade description under s 3(3).

The statutory words are very wide, and it may be that they are capable of the meaning attached to them by the appellant, but the proposition is nevertheless a startling one. If the appellant is right the consequences will be serious for all engaged in the repair and restoration of antique furniture, china, and a variety of other goods whose skill is devoted to making repairs which cannot be detected thereafter. If goods so repaired are subsequently sold expressly as undamaged an offence is, no doubt, committed, but if the seller cannot simply keep silent, and must disclose the repair by virtue of the Act, the doctrine of caveat emptor will be deprived of much of its force.

The 1968 Act replaces the Merchandise Marks Acts 1887–1953 under which the applying of a false trade description to goods had been an offence since 1887, but counsel has not been able to draw our attention to any case in which the covering up of a defect in the goods themselves has been held to amount to such an offence. I do not think that the difference of language in the two Acts, such as it is, explains or justifies such an extension of criminal responsibility. It is, of course, important that motor vehicles should not be sold in an unroadworthy state but this is made an offence under s 68 of the Road Traffic Act 1960, and does not need to be covered by the Trade Descriptions Act 1968. The primary concern of the 1968 Act is not with the condition or quality of the goods themselves, but with the possibility that a buyer may be misled by a trade description which makes them look better than they really are. I accept that an alteration of the goods which causes them to tell a lie about themselves may be a false trade description for present purposes, but Mr Warry did not apply a false trade description to these goods since he did not himself cover up the defect in the car and, indeed, was unaware of the existence of the defect.

If the respondents had been directly charged in respect of their sale to Mr Warry it might have been open to the justices, in my opinion, to find that they were guilty of the offence, but the form of the charge employed required the prosecution to prove an offence by Mr Warry.

I cannot bring myself to accept that Parliament intended to make Mr Warry guilty of a criminal offence in the circumstances of this case, and the explanation may be that a supplier of goods does not commit an offence under s 1(1)(b) if he did not himself apply the false trade description to the goods and had no knowledge or means of knowledge that this had been done by another. If Mr Warry was not guilty of an offence the respondents in this case were not guilty either. I would dismiss the appeal.

Melford Stevenson J. I agree with the judgment which has just been delivered.

Milmo J. I agree that these appeals against the decisions of the justices must be dismissed. I have reached this conclusion with regret because I am satisfied that on the findings of fact the respondents have clearly committed an offence under s 1(1)(a) of the Trade Descriptions Act 1968 with which they were not charged but have not committed either of the offences under s 23 with which they were charged. The prosecution alleged that a Mr Warry, against whom no charge was preferred, had committed two offences under s 1 (1) (b) of having in the course of a trade or business (1) offered to supply, and (2) supplied, to a customer (Mr Shillabeer) certain goods, namely, a Ford Corsair motor car, to which a false trade description was applied and that the commission of those offences was due to the act or default of the respondents. The charges against the respondents fail unless the prosecution prove that Mr Warry committed one or other or both of these offences. . . .

There was no evidence that Mr Warry had himself applied any false description of the car or that he was at any material time aware of what had been done to camouflage the serious rust damage to the engine compartment or that any plastic filler had been used in the engine compartment. The way in which the prosecution put their case that Mr Warry had committed an offence was based on s 1 (1) (b) of the Act. They said that he had in the course of his trade or business (i) offered to supply, and (ii) supplied, to Mr Shillabeer a car to which a false trade description had been applied, not by him (Mr Warry) but by another person, namely the respondents who, by using plastic filler and paint to conceal rust corrosion and holes, had given to the car what was likely to be taken as an indication that the engine compartment was in a sound condition whereas it was in no such condition. The Trade Descriptions Act 1968 is couched in very wide language and in my judgment its intention is to make considerable inroads into the legal concept of caveat emptor. Section 1 creates two different offences. The first under s 1 (1) (a) is applying a false trade description to goods. The second under s 1 (1) (b) is supplying or offering to supply goods to which a trade description is applied. Clearly under s 1 (1) (b) it matters not by whom the false description is applied and it need not be applied by the supplier himself. Equally clearly, this section does not require actual or constructive knowledge on the part of the offender of the falsity of the description whether the charge be under s 1 (1) (a) or s 1 (1) (b). I find it impossible to read into s 1 (1) (a) or s 1 (1) (b) such words as 'a trade description which he knows, or ought to know, is false'. In my judgment therefore the supplier or would be supplier of goods is liable for the falsity of any trade description which *is*—and I stress the words *is*—attached to the goods at the time when he supplies or offers to supply them.

In this case, I have no doubt that in doing what they did to conceal the use which had been made of plastic filler in the engine compartment of the car, the respondents did something which was not only likely but obviously intended to be taken as an indication that the engine compartment was in a sound condition whereas it was far from it. In these circumstances, having regard to the very wide language of s 3 (3), they applied a false trade description to the car and therefore committed an offence under s 1 (1) (*a*). Further, if Mr Warry committed an offence, it was entirely due to this act on the part of the respondents.

However, when Mr Warry sold the car he was unaware that any trade description of any sort was then applied to the car and there is no finding and no evidence that he was in any way at fault in failing to detect what had been done to it. Had he been aware that a trade description was attached to the car at the time he sold it, I am not prepared to say that lack of knowledge of its falsity would have afforded him a defence to a charge under s 1 (1) (*b*) of the Act but I think that knowledge that, at the time of supply or offer to supply, a trade description *is* applied to the goods is an essential prerequisite of an offence being committed by the supplier under s 1 (1) (*b*) of the Act.

I therefore find that the prosecution having failed to prove any offence on the part of Mr Warry, and the information having been laid under s 23 of the Act, the justices were right to dismiss the charges. I would therefore dismiss these appeals.

Appeals dismissed.

NOTES

1. A helpful analogy with Warry's position may be seen in *Warner v Metropolitan Police Comr* [1969] 2 AC 256, [1968] 2 All ER 356, HL (knowing that one possesses an object without knowing that the object is a dangerous drug).

2. As to the position of the respondents the case suggests that if they had been charged directly in respect of their sale to W it might have been open to the justices to convict. (Milmo J went further and was satisfied that they had clearly committed an offence under s 1 (1) (a)). This means that it is at least strongly arguable that deceitfully disguising defects in goods, thus causing them to 'tell a lie' about themselves, amounts to applying a false trade description. For what may be a very fine distinction between disguising defects and carrying out effective repairs compare *R v Ford Motor Co Ltd* [1974] 3 All ER 489, [1974] 1 WLR 1220, CA, below p 484. This latter case is important also in illustrating the operation of 'applying' by virtue of s 4 (3) of the Act.

3. In *R v A F Pears Ltd* (1982) 90 ITSA Monthly Review 142, the following facts arose. Pears had supplied to A. L. Steed Ltd, a self-service chemist shop, a jar of Astral moisturising cream. The jar was marked as weighing 54 grammes and its contents (58.6 millilitres) were slightly in excess of this. A test purchase by a trading standards officer revealed that the jar was capable of holding 64.2 millilitres. However the jar was double-skinned and had the inner container followed the external contours the capacity would have been 84.83 millilitres. On a charge of 'supplying goods to which a false trade description is applied' Judge Thomas, sitting in the Crown Court at Croydon, directed the jury in part as follows:

'A trade description is an indication, direct or indirect, and by whatever means given, of any of the following matters with respect to any goods or parts of goods'; that is to say, amongst other things, quantity and, quantity is expressed to include volume. Section 3 (1) defines 'false trade description' and it provides, 'A false trade description is a trade description which is false to a material degree.' Then it goes on to say that if a description, though not false, is a misleading description then it should be deemed to be a false trade description. Lastly, Section 4 (1) (a) defines, 'Applying a trade description to goods.' Amongst other things it says, 'a person applies a trade description to goods if he incorporates it with the goods themselves or anything in which the goods are supplied.' Well now, so much for the provisions of the Act which I have tried to condense for you.

His Honour then summed up the evidence and the jury found the defendants guilty as charged. (For an unsuccessful prosecution in a not dissimilar case see (1984) 3 Trading Law, p 26).

Questions

1 No doubt some may find this and other examples of such packaging misleading (whatever the commercial justification for it) even though the weight or volume is stated accurately. However, was a false trade description *applied*? (For a full definition of this word see above p 465).

2 In *Davies v Sumner* [1984] 3 All ER 831 at 832, above p 470 et seq, Lord Keith said, 'There can be no doubt that the respondent, when he traded in his car, applied a false trade description to it . . .'. Do you agree?

In considering these and some of the following questions students of the criminal law may find a helpful analogy with a distinction which arises in the law of forgery. Professor Griew puts it as follows ([1970] Crim LR 548, 549): 'The distinction, more shortly, is that between a thing which tells a lie about itself (the term "automendacious" might be coined by analogy with similar linguistic hybrids) and that which tells a lie about a matter extraneous to the document ("extramendacious").' For the present position see Smith and Hogan *Criminal Law* (5th edn, 1983), Ch 16. Consider the following cases in terms of potential liability under s 1 of the 1968 Act:

1. Dresden, a craftsman, repairs a valuable antique vase which has been sold to him with a broken handle. The repair is undetectable by the human eye but it is accepted that such a vase is significantly less valuable than one which has never been damaged. He sells it to a customer without disclosing its history.

2. The Bombsite garage has a second-hand car with a 'For Sale' sign standing on its forecourt. The car has a seriously defective engine and is unmerchantable. Would it affect the position if Bombsite had used a special substance which would hide the defect for some fifty or so miles and the purchaser had (i) asked, (ii) not asked, to hear the engine before buying the car?

3. Chisel, an unknown but highly talented sculptor, creates a work in the distinctive style of Rodin. Even the most knowledgeable private collector would assume that the work is by Rodin but Chisel does not sign or otherwise describe it as such. He then puts the work on sale in his gallery.

Sub-section 4 (2) provides that an oral statement may amount to use of a trade description. On balance the Molony Committee was against bringing such oral misdescriptions within the Act: 'To make oral misdescriptions an offence would be to put a very powerful weapon in the hands of a disappointed shopper' (para 659). *Fletcher v Budgen* ([1974] 2 All ER 1243, [1974] 1 WLR 1056, discussed above, p 466) is one of many cases in which the offending misstatement was oral. No doubt because of anticipated difficulties of proof, a shorter time limit for prosecution was originally laid down by section 19 (4) of the Act where an oral statement was involved. However in England this provision has in effect been nullified by the general provision in section 127 of the Magistrates' Courts Act 1980 which now applies the time limits of three years from the commission of the offence or one year from its discovery by the prosecutor, whichever is the earlier, to all 'hybrid' offences (that is those triable either summarily or on indictment). *Rees v Munday* [1974] 3 All ER 506, [1974] 1 WLR 1284, a leading case on time limits in relation to prosecutions is discussed in Ch 14: see pp 570–573 especially.

'SUPPLIES OR OFFERS TO SUPPLY ANY GOODS TO WHICH A FALSE TRADE DESCRIPTION IS APPLIED'

Section 1 (1) (b) catches those who passively supply goods bearing a false trade description without necessarily having applied it 'actively' (this being caught by section 1 (1) (a)). Section 24 (3) provides a special defence peculiar to this passive offence. The defendant may prove that he did not know, and could not with reasonable diligence have ascertained, that the goods did not conform to the description or that the description had been applied to the goods (see further below p 553).

Section 6 of the Act provides that 'a person exposing goods for supply or having goods in his possession for supply shall be deemed to offer to supply them'. Obviously this is intended to avoid the distinction familiar in the law of contract between invitations to treat and offers for sale—both are caught. The following case provides a striking example of the breadth of the concept of offering to supply goods.

Stainthorpe v Bailey [1980] RTR 7, Queen's Bench Divisional Court

The defendant motor dealer advertised a van for sale knowing that the odometer incorrectly recorded a mileage of 36,000 miles, the true mileage being something over 97,000. Mr Fricker, an officer of the Trading Standards Department, visited the firm's premises and was re-directed to the home of the defendant. The van was parked outside the house. The officer asked, 'Is the van for sale?'; the defendant said, 'Yes, the keys are in it if you want to have a look round' and went to answer his telephone. When the defendant returned the officer had gone. The court was requested (inter alia) to consider whether the justices had been entitled to conclude as regards the third information that no offer to supply had been made, and thus no offence committed. Having decided that the defence under s 24 did not avail the defendant (his failure to check the mileage or to disclaim the odometer reading being fatal to the 'due diligence' defence), Michael Davies J continued, as regards the third information:

The third information involved an entirely different point. I have already recounted the facts as found by the justices. Their view was as set out in paragraph 7 of their case. They referred to the newspaper advertisement and went on:

'In considering the third information we were of the opinion that the newspaper advertisement in the *Manchester Evening News* was an invitation to treat. We were mindful of the provisions of section 6 of the Trade Descriptions Act 1968 in that a person exposing goods for supply or having goods in his possession for supply, shall be deemed to offer to supply them. We considered that, since the vehicle was not at the place of business and there was nothing to indicate to members of the public that it was for sale, then no offer to supply could be made until there had been an opportunity for the defendant to complete a preliminary conversation.'

The offence of course was under section 1. That section has to be considered in the light of section 6, to which the justices referred. Section 6 provides:

'a person exposing goods for supply or having goods in his possession for supply shall be deemed to offer to supply them.'

In my view, on the facts as found by the justices, there can be no question whatsoever but that the defendant was exposing goods for supply and also indeed that he had the goods, namely, the motor van, in his possession for supply. That seems to me to be supported by the brief conversation he had with Mr Fricker and supported by the terms of the advertisement in the evening paper which quite plainly was offering for sale that very same vehicle.

I find the justices' reasons which I have just read, namely, that

> 'the vehicle was not at the place of business and that there was nothing to indicate to members of the public that it was for sale and that there ought to have been an opportunity, before it could be said that there was such an offer, for the defendant to complete a preliminary conversation'

—presumably on the telephone—quite insufficient and wholly irrelevant to the matter which the justices had to decide. I find nothing in the case which justifies their finding that section 6 did not catch the facts here and in my judgment they were in error in that regard in respect of the third information.

In those circumstances the questions which the justices ask this court to answer, namely, whether they were entitled to conclude that the defendant had made out the statutory defence in regard to the first two informations, and with regard to the third they were entitled to conclude that no offer of supply had been made, must be answered in the negative.

I would allow this appeal and return the matter to the justices with a direction to convict on all three informations.

Robert Goff J I agree.

Lord Widgery CJ I agree.

Appeal allowed. Case remitted to the justices with a direction to convict on all three informations. Order for payment out of central funds of prosecutor's costs.

NOTE

The question of effective disclaiming of false or doubtful odometer readings is dealt with under the separate head of 'disclaimers', below p 491 et seq.

A FALSE TRADE DESCRIPTION

Neither the word 'false' nor the phrase 'trade description' is fully understandable except in the context of ss 2 and 3 (above).

With regard to the meaning of 'false' an important qualification is introduced to take out of the criminal sphere over-enthusiastic, but not essentially inaccurate, descriptions of goods and other de minimis situations where otherwise the description might strictly be false. Section 3 (1) states that the description must be 'false to a material degree'. However the wording of the rest of that section clearly encompasses descriptions which, though not false, are misleading, or which, though not trade descriptions as defined, 'are likely to be taken' for an indication of any of the matters set out in s 2. If the description *is* false, it is no defence that the buyer was not deceived (though this may affect the penalty imposed): see *Chidwick v Beer* [1974] RTR 415.

Section 2 sets out a list of indications, direct or indirect, which if given with respect to goods will constitute a 'trade description'. (This is an improved version of what was formerly in s 3 of the Merchandise Marks Act 1887). Examples of the application of s 2 have already been given. For instance, in *Roberts v Severn Petroleum and Trading Co Ltd* ([1981] RTR 312, above p 475) the offending trade description applied to petrol by the Esso sign was an indication of the 'person by whom manufactured, produced, processed or reconditioned . . .'; and in the *Douglas Seaton* case ([1972] 3 All ER 750, above p 476) there was an indication of 'strength'. In some respects this list is very wide. For example the reference in s 2 (1) (d) to 'fitness for purpose' may be thought to make most breaches of s 14 (3) of the Sale of Goods Act 1979 (see above, p 61) criminal offences. Yet there are also significant omissions. In discussing the point in the 'Review of the Trade Descriptions Act 1968' (Cmnd 6628 (1976)), the Director General of Fair Trading noted that there were doubts about such matters as 'indications of the identity of a supplier or distributor and the standing, commercial importance or capabilities of a manufacturer . . . of goods' (para 127), and 'indications of the contents of books, films, recordings etc. including their authorship' (para 128). Turning to a more general problem the report continues:

Review of the Trade Descriptions Act 1968, Cmnd 6628 (1976)

Availability of goods
130. Indications in advertisements and elsewhere that goods are available from stock may cause a prospective buyer to go to some trouble to visit the trader in question; and if the indication is untrue the former person suffers the loss of time and money. At its worst an indication that goods are available when they are not is a feature of bait advertising and switch-selling. In some cases in the past prosecutions have been taken under section 14 on the basis that the availability of goods is a 'facility', but in our view this seems to stretch the meaning of the word too far. Our preliminary conclusion was, therefore, that false or misleading indications of the availability of goods should be made a specific offence under the Act.

. . .

131. The proposed new offence was welcomed by the National Consumer Council and many of those concerned with enforcement as a substantial new weapon to deter bait-advertising and switch-selling and practices which characterise some, but not all, 'one day' sales held in hired halls. However it was clear from comments from the trade that our proposals could also have serious repercussions on the activities of reputable traders and could cause cash-flow problems forcing them to acquire stock before seeking to advertise and to hold it until the advertisement is published. In the case of advertisements in some publications this 'lead time' runs into months.

. . .

132. On reconsideration, therefore, we have concluded that the abuse with which we sought to deal is too small to justify the introduction of a measure which would clearly present great difficulties for the vast majority of traders who do not seek to deceive and for those concerned with the day-to-day administration of the Act. Problems of this kind arise mainly in connection with 'one-day' sales and mail order trading, and these are areas of trading where Part II of the Fair Trading Act might be invoked to provide any control needed by statutory order. **We make no recommendation therefore on indications of availability so far as the 1968 Act is concerned.**

NOTE

For Part II of the Fair Trading Act, see above p 415 et seq. In some jurisdictions the problems noted in the above extract are dealt with more directly. For example the Australian Trade Practices Act 1974, s 56 provides in part as follows:

Bait advertising

(1) A corporation shall not, in trade or commerce, advertise for supply at a special price goods or services that the corporation does not intend to offer for supply at that

price for a period that is, and in quantities that are, reasonable having regard to the nature of the market in which the corporation carries on business and the nature of the advertisement.

. . .

Questions

Having regard to the wording of s 2 (1) (above p 464) is a trade description confined to an indication of the 'physical characteristics' of goods or their 'history'? Is a false indication that spare parts are readily available a 'trade description'?

Problem

Ada aged 80 lives alone in a large Victorian house with many fine antiques. Trader, an antique dealer, knocks on her door and is invited in. He examines a fine Queen Anne table and says, 'A fine table that. Worth a good £200. I'll give you £250 for it.' Ada who has no idea of present-day values agrees to sell the table to Trader at that price. As Trader well knows the table is worth over £2,000.

Consider Trader's liability under the 1968 Act.

There follows a selection of cases on two areas of motor vehicle sales which cause particular trouble. These are cases of cars and other vehicles which are described wrongly as being 'new' or in 'excellent' or 'beautiful' condition and of cars etc which are 'clocked'.

'NEW' AND 'BEAUTIFUL' CARS

It is trite law that *simplex commendatio non obligat*—a mere commendation is not a warranty. Nor is the exaggeration endemic in the second-hand car trade necessarily a description 'false to a material degree' under s 3 (1). But calling a vehicle 'new' when it is not, or calling a vehicle which is significantly defective in 'excellent condition throughout' (*Chidwick v Beer*)[1], in 'really exceptional condition throughout' (*Furniss v Scholes*)[2] or in 'showroom condition throughout' (*Hawkins v Smith*)[3] have all been held to involve the application of a false trade description.

The meaning of 'new' in relation to a car was thoroughly canvassed in the following case:

R v Ford Motor Co Ltd [1974] 3 All ER 489, [1974] 1 WLR 1220, Court of Appeal

The facts are set out in the judgment of Bridge J.

Bridge J delivered the following judgment of the court at the invitation of Lord Widgery CJ.

---

[1] [1974] RTR 415.
[2] [1974] RTR 133.
[3] [1978] Crim LR 578.

On 11 March 1974 the Ford Motor Co Ltd was arraigned before the Crown Court at Dorchester on an indictment containing two counts. The first count alleged that Fords, as it will be convenient to call them, on 1 November 1971 in the course of a trade or business supplied to Parkway Garages (Dorchester) Ltd, whom I will call 'Parkway', a Ford Cortina motor car to which a false trade description was applied, namely that the same was new, that offence being in contravention of s 1 of the Trade Descriptions Act 1968. The second count alleged that Parkway in the course of a trade or business supplied to one Rogers the same Ford Cortina motor car to which a false trade description was applied, namely that the car was new, that offence being in contravention of s 1 of the Trade Descriptions Act 1968, and that the commission of that offence was due to the act or default of Fords, contrary to s 23 of that Act.

The facts can be quite shortly stated. The Ford Cortina motor car referred to in both counts of the indictment was manufactured by Fords in April 1971. It was then sent, presumably by transporter, to Liverpool where it was intended to be exported in satisfaction of an order from a customer in Malta, but in due course that order was cancelled and the Cortina was then transferred to a compound at Speke. Whilst in the compound, and in the care, it is to be inferred, of Fords' forwarding agents, the Cortina was damaged by a collision with a trailer. It is unnecessary for purposes of this judgment to go at length into the detail of the damage that was caused. Sufficient indication of its extent, which was to some extent in controversy, can be given by stating that the trade cost of the repairs effected was of the order of £50. It was in fact repaired at the expense of the insurers to Fords' forwarding agents. Later the car was delivered to Parkway and sent by Parkway, who carried on business in Weymouth, to a subagent of theirs at Bridport. On 1 December 1971 the Mr Rogers referred to in the second count of the indictment came to Parkway, wanting to buy a new Ford Cortina of just the kind which had, in accordance with the history already recited, been recently sent by Parkway to their subagents at Bridport. Mr Rogers was taken to see the car and he bought it.

The documentation as between Fords and Parkway which was in evidence relating to this transaction, although quite voluminous, nowhere shows the word 'new' being in terms applied directly to describe this vehicle, although it is correct to observe that the expression 'new vehicle' occurs in a warranty which was furnished with the motor car, albeit in a context which in the judgment of this court does not show that phrase being used as an express trade description of the vehicle. The documents passing, however, between Parkway and Mr Rogers include an invoice which in terms describes the vehicle sold to Mr Rogers as one new Ford Cortina 1600 GT four door saloon as per makers' specifications.

The trial of this matter before the Crown Court occupied five days, and much of that time was taken up by submissions made on behalf of Fords at the close of the evidence for the prosecution that there was no case for Fords to answer on the basis that there was no evidence that Fords had applied the trade description 'new' to the vehicle in question, or alternatively that, if they had, there was no evidence that the vehicle was not new. The trial judge, with whom this court feels the greatest sympathy, for he was unquestionably faced with difficult problems, with evident hesitation overruled the submissions made to him on behalf of Fords and left the matter to the jury, who in due course convicted Fords on both counts. Fords now apply to this court for leave to appeal against their conviction, the submissions before us being essentially first to the effect that there was no evidence proper to be left to the jury either that the trade description 'new' had been applied to the vehicle, or that, if applied, it had been false; secondly on the broad ground that the trial judge in leaving the issues to the jury misdirected them on certain essential matters.

Before considering the argument in further detail, it will be convenient to refer to the relevant sections of this not altogether straightforward statute. . . .

His Lordship then referred to ss 1(1), 2(1) and 3(1) of the Act, above pp 464–465 and continued:

Section 4 provides: . . .

> '(3) Where goods are supplied in pursuance of a request in which a trade description is used and the circumstances are such as to make it reasonable to infer that the goods are supplied as goods corresponding to that trade description, the person supplying the goods shall be deemed to have applied that trade description to the goods.'

For completeness one should refer to s 23, the section under which the second count of the indictment was laid, which provides:

> 'Where the commission by any person of an offence under this Act is due to the act or default of some other person that other person shall be guilty of the offence, and a

person may be charged with and convicted of the offence by virtue of this section whether or not proceedings are taken against the first-mentioned person.'

The first question which we have to determine is whether on the true construction of the relevant provisions of ss 2 and 4 there was any evidence on which the jury could be invited to find that when the car subsequently sold to Mr Rogers was supplied by Fords to Parkway, the trade description 'new' was applied to it. Counsel's argument for the Crown on this part of the case has ranged widely over the evidence relating to the course of dealing between Fords and Parkway, which he submits shows it to have been well understood by the parties on this occasion that a new car was to be supplied. The argument seems to us at times necessarily to involve the proposition, although this was disclaimed by counsel, that whenever there is an implied term of a contract of sale relating to a matter falling within one of the paragraphs from (*a*) to (*j*) of s 2(1), there must be a corresponding application of a trade description to the goods supplied under that contract. This seems to us to go much too far; it would be very startling if, for instance, the effect of the 1968 Act were to make a criminal of every seller of goods by description who delivers goods in breach of the condition of merchantable quality which is implied by s 14(2) of the Sale of Goods Act 1893.

But a very much narrower and more concentrated version of the argument can be founded not on the course of dealing between the parties, or the evidence as to what they understood or expected, but on the terms of a single document which was in evidence in the case. The document in question is before us as an exhibit and it is described in the evidence as a 'mark page order', . . .

Considering in detail the terms of that pro forma order which the evidence shows to have been used by Parkway to order the Cortina in question from Fords, although we have not the original document before us, we have come to the conclusion that this document does indicate that the vehicle ordered is contemplated as being a vehicle which will come either from manufacturers' stock at the factory or off the production line. If the words appeared at the top 'please supply the following new vehicles' it would in our judgment in substance add nothing to what the language of the document by necessary implication already shows. Accordingly we have reached the conclusion that in the terms of the statute this was a request made by Parkway to Fords which gave an indirect indication that the trade description 'new' was applied to the vehicle which Parkway requested Fords to deliver, and that being so the second part of s 4(3) was in our judgment similarly satisfied by the evidence, that is to say the circumstances were such as to make it reasonable to infer that the goods supplied pursuant to that request were supplied as goods corresponding to that trade description, and it follows therefore that Fords as the person supplying the goods in accordance with s 4(3) are deemed to have applied that trade description to the goods.

It is necessary next to turn to the trial judge's summing-up to see how this issue was left to the jury. The trial judge, if he did not withdraw from the jury entirely the argument of counsel for the Crown that the course of dealing —'the new procedure', as it was described in argument—afforded a sufficient basis to say that Fords had applied to this car the trade description 'new', he at all events treated that submission so critically that it is difficult to think the jury thereafter paid much attention to it.

He went on, however, to say:

> 'Whatever you may think about that you must consider all the evidence and the documents and the whole of the surrounding circumstances, because all the documents and evidence are before you. But I suggest that this much is true and is the law. If work is done to a car to make it look new when it is not new that can be a trade description.'

Then he repeated that sentence as one to which great importance was to be attached. Later on further down the same page he said:

> 'So if combining what I have been saying together, if work were done on a car to make it look new when it was in fact not new and if that could be a trade description, and if that trade description was so used, used in a manner likely to be taken by Parkway as referring to this car, then it would be applied to the car.'

It is apparent that the principle that the trial judge had in mind in giving the jury those directions was a principle which no doubt he thought was derived from the judgments of the Divisional Court in *Cottee v Douglas Seaton (Used Cars) Ltd*[1]. That was a trade description case concerned with a car which having sustained serious damage by rust to parts of the body work which had been extensively eaten away, had been 'repaired' by the application of plastic filler and subsequently had been painted over so that the fact that the rust damage had been replaced by plastic filler could not be detected by a straightforward examination in such a way as to give the vehicle the appearance in the relevant parts of still comprising sound metal. In giving the leading judgment Lord Widgery CJ said[2]:

'I accept that an alteration of the goods which causes them to tell a lie about themselves may be a false trade description for present purposes . . .'

Counsel for Fords submits, and we think rightly, that a clear distinction is to be drawn between 'repairs' undertaken to an article which are of such a nature as to have the effect of concealing a significant defect without removing it on the one hand, and repairs simpliciter on the other which are properly and effectively carried out and which have the effect of restoring the article repaired to a sound and satisfactory condition. We accept counsel's submission that repairs which fall into the second class of those two categories should not properly be regarded as of themselves giving such an indication as to the character of the goods repaired as to amount to a false trade description.

No doubt it was just the danger of such an argument being advanced which Lord Widgery CJ had in mind in an earlier passage in the judgment from which a citation has just been made, when he observed in respect to one aspect of the appellant prosecutor's argument in *Cottee's* case[3]:

'If the appellant is right the consequences will be serious for all engaged in the repair and restoration of antique furniture, china, and a variety of other goods whose skill is devoted to making repairs which cannot be detected thereafter. If goods so repaired are subsequently sold expressly as undamaged an offence is, no doubt, committed, but if the seller cannot simply keep silent, and must disclose the repair by virtue of the Act, the doctrine of caveat emptor will be deprived of much of its force.'

We conclude that in the circumstances of this case to seek to derive, as the trial judge's direction to the jury seemed to do, a false trade description applied to this vehicle as being new exclusively from the circumstance that it had been effectively repaired after being damaged, would open just the floodgate of which Lord Widgery CJ in the passage cited was apprehensive, and which in our judgment should be kept firmly shut. Accordingly we reach the conclusion that the trial judge left the issue to the jury 'was there here a false trade description applied to this vehicle to the effect that it was new' on the wrong basis.

The question then arises whether that misdirection must be fatal to the convictions. The answer is in our judgment: not necessarily so. If the jury could and should properly have concluded from the 'mark page order' that the trade description 'new' was applied to this Cortina by Fords before it was supplied to Parkway, then provided always that appropriate directions were given to the jury as to the tests they should apply in considering the question whether the vehicle was properly described as new, it would not in our judgment matter that the trial judge had derived, and invited the jury to derive, the trade description from an incorrect source.

It is necessary, therefore, to turn to see how the question was dealt with, what does 'a new vehicle' mean, what is involved in describing a motor car as 'new'. The trial judge deals with that matter in this way. He first refers the jury to the de minimis principle very properly; aptly enough he says 'We lawyers put it in Latin but it can equally be stated in plain English that the law takes no account of trifles'. He then sets out five tests which had been suggested by counsel for the Crown in argument as tests which a motor car must satisfy if it is to conform to the description 'new': first it must not have been sold retail before; secondly it must be a current model; thirdly it must not have had extensive use—each of those criteria are elaborated in the summing-up. Then one comes to the vital passage:

'There were two other things which [counsel for the Crown] said must also be satisfied before you can say that the manufactured article is new. He said it should be in mint condition as produced at the factory and later at the end of his case he added a fifth. He said it should not have been repaired by any third party.'

The trial judge leaves those criteria to the jury virtually without comment, save only what he added when he said:

'One other thing on this question of "new" I offer for your consideration is this. A good deal of the defence case has been devoted to showing that the car was in excellent condition when it reached Mr Rogers and that the damage had been made good. If we say about something that it is as good as new, are not we really say it is not new? If, having bought something that was not new you show it to a friend and say "It is as good as new" are you not saying "It is not new but it is as good as new."'

The effect of the summing-up, particularly in the light of that last comment when added to counsel for the Crown's fifth criterion of what qualities a new car must exhibit must have been in our judgment to leave in the jury's mind that any significant damage—meaning thereby any damage in excess of minimal damage—sustained by a new car after it leaves the factory must have the result of rendering it no longer new irrespective of how well repairs may have been done.

Before coming to grips with the question whether that was a proper way of leaving the question to the jury, it is perhaps appropriate to say a word about the earlier criteria in counsel for the Crown's list; that a car cannot be new once it has been the subject of a retail sale is obvious, then it is clearly in every sense a secondhand car. Whether or not it is an essential of newness that a car be a current model it is unnecessary to decide. That the use of the car must not be excessive is again clearly right in the sense that a car no doubt ceases to be new once the mileage it has travelled under its own power at all events significantly exceeds that to be expected as reasonably incidental to delivery from the point of manufacture to the dealer. It may not matter for the purposes of the present decision, but we must not be taken as approving the suggested criterion that a car cannot be new that is not in mint condition. If that is taken to mean that a new car must be faultless, well regrettably, though it may be very desirable that new cars should be faultless, it is a matter of common knowledge that frequently they are not.

But the heart of this case really turns on the fifth criterion, the suggestion that a car ceases to be new as soon as it sustains any significant damage and irrespective of the quality of the repairs. This is a test which we do not find it possible to accept. It seems to us that in this respect the questions to be asked when a car has sustained damage which has thereafter been repaired, both events having occurred away from the manufacturer's premises, are first: what is the extent and nature of the damage? and second: what is the quality of the repairs which have been effected? If the damage which a new car after leaving the factory has sustained is, although perhaps extensive, either superficial in character or limited to certain defined parts of the vehicle which can be simply replaced by new parts, then provided that such damage is in practical terms perfectly repaired so that it can in truth be said after repairs have been effected that the vehicle is as good as new, in our judgment it would not be a false trade description to describe such a vehicle as new.

An example suggested in the course of argument was of the engine of a new car sustaining serious damage, for instance for lack of oil on its journey from the factory to the dealer's premises. If the dealer removed the defective engine and replaced it with a brand new engine from the factory, we can see no reason in common sense why the resulting vehicle should not still be described as a new car. So also if superficial damage to part of the body were sustained, but is perfectly repaired either by panel beating followed by respraying, or by replacement of individual panels with new panels; if a perfect result can be achieved, why, one may ask rhetorically, should the car no longer qualify to be described as new? Of course, the question whether the repairs which have been undertaken in any particular case have attained the necessary degree of perfection to entitle the car to be described as new must be a matter of fact and degree to be decided by the tribunal of fact before whom the question arises. On the other hand we certainly accept that a point must be reached when damage, particularly accident damage, is so serious in its nature and extent that the car is no longer capable of being repaired in such a way as to qualify for the description 'new'. It is unnecessary and perhaps undesirable to try to define the point at which that degree of damage is reached, but an example which readily springs to mind is damage which involves distortion of the vehicle frame or chassis. For these reasons we have come to the conclusion that the question whether or not this yellow Ford Cortina sold by Parkway to Mr Rogers was falsely or truly described as a new car was not left to the jury with appropriate directions. . . .

Application granted; appeal allowed; convictions quashed. Leave to appeal to the House of Lords refused.

1. [1972] 3 All ER 750, [1972] 1 WLR 1408 (see above p 476).
2. [1972] 3 All ER at 757, [1972] 1 WLR at 1416.
3. [1972] 3 All ER at 757, [1972] 1 WLR at 1415.

NOTES

1 Compare *R v Ford Motor Co Ltd* (above) with *Routledge v Ansa Motors (Chester-le-Street) Ltd* [1980] RTR 1 where a van manufactured in 1972, converted into a caravanette, and first registered on 1 August 1975 was described on a sales invoice as 'one used 1975 Ford Escort Fiesta'. The justices accepted a submission of no case to answer. On appeal the Divisional Court held that the justices should have considered whether it was likely that on reading these words an average customer would believe was likely that on reading these words an average customer would believe that 1975 was the date of manufacture. If so, they should then have considered whether the date was 'false to a material degree'.

2 For a description of a Magistrates' Court case where two employees of Rumbelows were successfully prosecuted for selling hi-fi goods marked 'Display Stock Clearance' which would (wrongly) be likely to be taken as an indication that the goods were new, see (1985) 4 Trading Law 32.

Questions

On the application of s 4 (3) consider the following case: Alice enters Shaver's Egg Shop and says, 'I would like a dozen new laid eggs please'. Shaver sells her a dozen eggs from a tray. They are not 'new laid' but are edible and of good quality. Has Shaver committed an offence contrary to s 1 of the 1968 Act? Is he liable under s 13 of the Sale of Goods Act 1979 (above pp 61 and 67–71)?

'CLOCKED' CARS

In 1978 the Director General of Fair Trading stated that in the course of making 1,614 routine checks, over 50% of vehicles were found to have been 'clocked' at an estimated cost to the consumer of £53 million a year. He has since shown himself willing to use his powers under Part III of the Fair Trading Act 1973 to deal with 'persistent offenders' (see above p 424) and his powers to withhold, suspend or revoke a dealer's consumer credit licence when dealers are convicted of the offence which this involves. (Under the 1981 version of the Motor Code of Practice members must verify odometer readings or warn customers that this has not been done). The offence lies within s 2 (i) (j) above, being a false indication of the history, previous ownership or use of the vehicle. The following case is of general interest and importance.

Holloway v Cross [1981] 1 All ER 1012, Queen's Bench Divisional Court

The facts are set out in the judgment of Donaldson LJ.

Donaldson LJ. This is another of the odometer cases. Mr Holloway, who is a motor trader, appeals by case stated against his conviction by the magistrates for Kent sitting at Chatham on 16 August 1978.

The charges were the usual charges under ss 1(1)(*a*) and (1)(*b*) of the Trade Descriptions Act 1968 of applying a false trade description to any goods in the course of trade or business and supplying or offering to supply goods to which a false trade description is applied.

The facts were these. The appellant had bought a Triumph motor car which had been first registered in 1973. The mileage was, in fact, in excess of 70,000. When he bought it the odometer reading was slightly over 700 miles. The purchaser saw the car and asked what its correct mileage was. He was told by the appellant, as was the fact, that he did not know. However, the appellant also said that he would make inquiries. Apparently it was necessary to do some minor repairs on the car and the purchaser came back, with a view to buying the car, on 1 October 1977. He and the appellant co-operated in completing a document known as a 'used car invoice'.

The appellant asked the purchaser what was the purchaser's estimation of the car's mileage but, perhaps not surprisingly, the purchaser was unable or declined to make any suggestions initially. The appellant then asked the purchaser if he thought that a figure of 45,000 sounded correct. This was accepted by the purchaser on the basis, no doubt, that it sounded correct, and the invoice was completed by the appellant to read 'Recorded mileage indicator reading is 716 estimated 45,000'.

The magistrates found that the purchaser would not have bought the car if he had known its true mileage was 73,000. They found that the figure of 45,000 miles was an average figure for a vehicle of this make, age and appearance, and that the method of calculating mileage, that is to say on the basis of make, age and appearance, is not always accurate or reliable. The magistrates went on to find that on the same occasion, when delivery was being taken and this invoice was being made up, the appellant gave the purchaser a warranty document issued by an insurance company, which applied to cars under six years of age, which of course this car was, but only if they had covered less than 60,000 miles.

They found that the appellant, in putting forward the estimate of 45,000 miles, used his knowledge of the motor trade and the general condition of the car and the information given in Glass's Guide. On that evidence, the magistrates came to the conclusion that the description 'estimated 45,000 miles' did not come within s 2 of the Trade Descriptions Act 1968 and so was not a trade description as such. Therefore, so far as s 2 was concerned, there could have been no application of a false trade description.

However, they held that it was within the extension to the concept of a false trade description, which is provided by s 3(3). Let me therefore refer briefly to those two sections. Section 2(1) provides:

> 'A trade description is an indication, direct or indirect, and by whatever means given, of any of the following matters with respect to any goods or parts of goods, that is to say . . . (j) other history including previous ownership or use.'

What was said below, and has extensively been repeated here, is that inasmuch as this statement was a mere statement of the appellant's opinion, it could not come within s 2. Section 3(3), however, reads as follows:

> 'Anything which, though not a trade description, is likely to be taken for an indication of any of those matters and, as such an indication, would be false to a material degree, shall be deemed to be a false trade description.'

The magistrates accepted that what was said and done was not an application of a trade description in the strict sense of the words but as being within the extended meaning provided by s 3(3) . . .
The question which is left for the opinion of this court is:

> 'Whether the appellant's opinion, based on the condition and general appearance of the car, concurred in by the purchaser that it had travelled some 45,000 miles, expressed in the invoice as "estimated 45,000 miles" in the absence of any evidence or suggestion by the prosecution that the said estimate was not made bona fide, amounted in law to a false trade description.'

Counsel for the appellant, who has argued this appeal with conspicuous moderation and clarity, submits that this 'estimated 45,000' was neither a trade description within s 2 nor within the extension of s 3(3). His argument is really very simple. What it amounts to is this. The purchaser was interested to find out, since the matter was in doubt, what was the information of the appellant as to the mileage of the car. Taking the facts as a whole, the purchaser knew perfectly well that the appellant did not know what the mileage was. All he wanted was an expert opinion. He got an expert opinion, and it was a bona fide expert opinion. That, he says, is the end of the matter. He adds for good measure that it is entirely irrelevant that there was an insurance company in the background or that the warranty document was given. He says that the charge relates solely to the application of the words 'estimated 45,000 miles'.

In my judgment that is an undue simplification. If it is a valid argument in relation to s 2(1) and that the words, taken in the circumstances in which they were used, do not fall within s 2(1), which, I may say, is somewhat debatable, bearing in mind that s 2(1) relates to an indication 'direct or indirect', it seems to me almost clear beyond argument that if this was not a trade description it was likely to be taken by the purchaser as an indication of the history of the vehicle and, of course, if so taken was false to a material degree. There cannot have been any point in asking the opinion of the seller as to the mileage which seems to have been done, except with a view to obtaining an indication of what the mileage was in fact. Once I have said that, I have, I think really said everything that need be said. That was the conclusion of the magistrates. In my judgment they were entitled to reach that conclusion. I would personally have been slightly surprised if they had reached any other conclusion. I would, therefore, answer the question of law by saying that the words complained of did amount, in law, to a false trade description within the meaning of s 3(3).

Hodgson J. I agree. I would only add this. Speaking personally, I am far from satisfied that the prosecution were right to concede that this expression of opinion was not an indirect indication of previous use directly within s 2. Had that been the way the prosecution had put the case, and had the magistrates come to a decision on s 2, then I would go this far with counsel for the appellant: that many of the findings of fact would have been quite irrelevant because s 1 creates an offence of strict liability which can only be got out of by a special defence set out under s 24. But, once the prosecution were going on s 3(3), it was then necessary for the magistrates to decide whether what was said was likely to be taken for an indication, and in deciding that I think they were right to take into account the matters, or at least many of the matters, on which they made findings of fact.

Appeal dismissed.

Questions

The above case is but one of many involving 'clocked' cars. Others are noted in the section on disclaimers which follows. Undoubtedly many defendants in such cases are wholly unmeritorious. However is it desirable that criminal offences should be based on bona fide estimates or expressions of opinion, especially when such an opinion has been requested by the person prejudiced?

What advice would you give to an honest car dealer who is requested to give such an estimate?

Problem

Collector enters the Provincial Art Boutique where he sees a painting of Salisbury Cathedral which is signed 'J. Constable'. He asks the owner, Poussin, 'Is this the original painting by Constable?' Poussin replies, 'Attribution of such works of art is a matter on which judgment may differ. However the overwhelming opinion, which I share, is that it is indeed the original painting'. This is an entirely accurate statement of the expert opinion of the time. Three months later it is revealed that the painting is a modern copy by Greating.

Subject to the availability of a possible defence under s 24 of the Act, below, p 553 et seq, has Poussin committed an offence under the 1968 Act? Is he civilly liable for a breach of contract or misrepresentation? (As to the latter see also above, pp 2–10 and 67–71 especially.)

NOTE

For the problems caused by misattributed or mislabelled musical instruments (a fertile source of trouble in practice) see Harvey, 'Violin Frauds, Fakes and Misdescriptions—The Law' (1982) The Strad 93.

DISCLAIMERS

The nature of the practice

Since the passing of the Act a widespread practice has grown up whereby a trader may seek to avoid the application of a trade description by disclaiming that description in such a way that the potential purchaser should not be affected by it. The practice is especially prevalent in the case of 'clocked' cars but, as the following extracts illustrate, problems may arise in other areas also:

Review of the Trade Descriptions Act 1968, a report by the Director General of Fair Trading (Cmnd 6628 (1976))

DISCLAIMING AND VARYING DESCRIPTIONS

The need for disclaimers

146.   Section 1 of the 1968 Act makes both the application of false trade descriptions to goods and the supply of goods to which a false trade description is applied, offences. In some circumstances, however, section 1 may occasion problems for a trader who wishes to comply with the law for he may come into possession of goods to which a description has already been applied by someone else and which he knows to be false or the accuracy of which he doubts. While, if the description is a printed label, it may be an easy matter to erase it, this solution is not so readily available where, for example, the goods are of metal and the description is engraved or stamped on the goods.

147.   A trader may also find himself facing difficulties where he himself applies a description to goods to be supplied at some future date, for example in a catalogue or advertisement, and he subsequently realises that the description does not match the goods he proposes to supply. Again, there may be a simple solution in that the trader can (and should) seek to supply some other goods that do conform with the description; but one can conceive of circumstances where this is not a practical proposition, for example where the article is an antique and the prospects of finding a similar article which matches the description are remote.

. . .

149.   The existing statutory defences are relevant to the problems we are considering. Section 24(1) and (2) afford a defence where it can be established that the commission of an offence is due to a mistake or reliance on information supplied to the accused or to the act or default of another person, an accident or some other cause beyond the control of the accused and that he has taken all reasonable precautions and exercised all due diligence to avoid the commission of an offence by him or anyone under his control. Section 24(3) provides a special defence where the person is charged with supplying goods to which a false trade description is applied, namely, that he did not know and could not with reasonable diligence have ascertained that the goods did not conform with the description or that the description had been applied to the goods. The case of *Sherratt v Geralds the American Jewellers Limited* indicates, however, that it was not intended that these defences should provide an easy let-out for traders who sold goods marked with false trade descriptions by, for example, manufacturers. It would appear from this case that it remains incumbent upon traders where it is reasonably practicable to do so to check descriptions and that it is not enough to rely automatically on, for example, the reputation and experience of the person who supplies them.

150.   It did not seem to us that there should be any derogation of the responsibility of the trader for the description of his goods as at present imposed, and it was in this light that we examined how far traders should be allowed to disclaim responsibility for trade descriptions by saying in effect to prospective customers 'take no notice of this description'. This is by no means a simple issue to decide for disclaimers may take a number of different forms. The Institute of Trading Standards Administration classified them into five categories, namely:

(a)   those relating to specific goods and associated with the original description in such a way as to nullify or amend it, for example, 'X brand shirts—seconds' or 'the odometer reading is *not* a true indication of the miles covered by this vehicle';

(b)   those expressed in general terms which in fact amend but are not directly associated with particular descriptions, for example, 'all sizes quoted are approximate';

(c)   those which, although directly associated with a specific description, are of a general 'non-guarantee' nature which affects the image conveyed only to the extent of introducing an element of doubt, for example, 'the colour may not exactly correspond to that illustrated above', or 'this mileage is not guaranteed';

(d)   those of a general 'non-guarantee' nature which are not directly associated with any particular description and which affect the image conveyed (to the extent that they are seen) only by introducing an element of doubt, for example 'the colour of goods may vary slightly from the illustration in this catalogue'; and

(e)   implied disclaimers, for example, where transactions take place between two traders on terms which, by custom, are known to include a disclaimer of some kind.

Moreover different situations might arise according to whether goods are new or are second-hand. We would observe that this classification indicates that there is a very fine line between disclaiming a description and applying a qualified description or disassociating goods from a description for example by using such words as 'the colour of the goods is roughly that indicated in the illustration'. We comment on certain aspects of this latter situation in paragraphs 170–177 below.

Should the use of disclaimers be regulated?

151.   A number of people told us that they thought that disclaimers should either be banned or their use closely controlled by new legislation. Anything less was regarded by these bodies as creating a loophole which would be exploited to the full by unscrupulous traders. The National Consumer Council and a number of enforcement authorities all of which particularly favoured a ban on disclaimers in respect of self-applied descriptions said that, while it would be bad enough if a trader could escape his obligations under section 24 by saying that he could not guarantee the accuracy of a trade description, it would be intolerable if it was possible for a trader to apply a false trade description and then avoid all liability by saying that it might not be correct.

152.   Trade organisations, on the other hand, argued that it would be impossible to conduct normal business if the use of disclaimers was prohibited. In their view it was also necessary to permit the continued use of disclaimers in respect of new goods. The most commonly cited reason—and one quoted by the Multiple Shops Federation, the Mail Order Traders' Association, the Association of British Travel Agents, among other trade bodies—was the fact that catalogues and other printed material had to be prepared long before they were actually needed, and that however much care was taken subsequently the goods or services actually supplied might differ in detail. Moreover, much printed material was designed for long life and it would be impracticable to withdraw or reprint catalogues etc whenever changes were made to specifications. Sometimes it was even known in advance that changes in descriptions were possible, for example, in the case of motor vehicles, computers and other sophisticated equipment where there was continuous process of development and where it was to everyone's advantage that technological improvements should be incorporated as soon as possible even though this meant that the goods supplied differed from the original description.

The case of Norman v Bennett and Another

153.   While our Review has been in progress a certain amount of judicial guidance has been given as to the circumstances in which a false trade description could be disclaimed so as to avoid the commission of an offence under the Act. In the above case, for example, while the Lord Chief Justice emphasised that the particular facts of the case were very special, he did, nevertheless lay down the important principle that 'where a false trade description is attached to goods, its effect can be neutralised by an express disclaimer or contradiction of the message contained in the trade description. To be effective any such disclaimer must be as bold, precise and compelling as the trade description itself and must be as effectively brought to the notice of any person to whom the goods may be supplied. In other words, the disclaimer must equal the trade description in the extent to which it is likely to get home to anyone interested in receiving the goods'. He added that to be effective as a defence to a charge of supplying goods to which a false description is applied, the disclaimer must be made before the goods are supplied.

. . .

159.   There is a clear risk in permitting the use of disclaimers. We have already endorsed the proposition that whenever it is reasonable to do so, traders should be expected to check descriptions already applied to goods when the goods are received. If the use of general disclaimers were lawful, traders might cease to make such checks and simply seek to repudiate all responsibilities for the accuracy of descriptions. Dishonest traders might be tempted to apply false descriptions and then protect themselves by disclaimers in the hope that the disclaimer would not entirely negative the impact of the description on prospective customers.

160.   However, if disclaimers were to be completely prohibited, the problems we have touched upon in paragraphs 146–148 above would be virtually insuperable, particularly in relation to second-hand goods where the accuracy of descriptions on, for example, antiques often cannot be checked and where the obliteration of the description by defacement might spoil the goods. There is also the special problem of odometers on used cars. Returns from local authorities indicate that tampering with these to understate the true mileage is the most prevalent offence dealt with by enforcement authorities.

161.   In considering whether disclaimers should be permitted, we have borne in mind the scope of the statutory defences described above. These suggest to us that it is only sensible that an honest trader coming into possession of goods bearing a trade description whose truth he doubts should be entitled to avoid conviction by negating the description in appropriate cases. We must conclude therefore than an absolute ban on disclaimers is not warranted.

162.   It seems to us that in saying in the *Norman* case that disclaimers must be specific and in their later Judgments, the Divisional Court has effectively precluded the use of general disclaimers, for example, a statement in a shop window relating to any description of goods in the window. At the same time the present law does not appear to require any disclaimers which apply to all the goods or services referred to in a catalogue or brochure in full on every page of that catalogue or brochure provided that the reader is made aware that there is a disclaimer at the same time as he reads the particular description, and his eye is effectively directed towards the page on which this disclaimer is set out in full. If we are right in this view, we think that the Divisional Court has provided generous guidance about the form of permissible disclaimers. Two further questions arise, however, in consequence:

    (a) whether it is necessary to limit the occasions to which disclaimers can be used; and

    (b) whether the principles as we understand them to have been established by the Court should be incorporated in the Act itself.

Disclaiming self-applied trade descriptions

163.   The decisions in the *Norman* case related to a charge of supplying goods to which a false trade description had been applied (section 1 (1) (b) of the Act). The Court did not consider whether a trader might employ a disclaimer as a defence to a charge of applying a false trade description to goods (section 1(1)(a) of the Act). It is arguable that a trader who himself applies a false trade description to goods in his possession at that time should not be allowed to escape conviction simply by simultaneously disclaiming the accuracy of that description. On the other hand a trader who has inadvertently falsely described goods must be free to correct his description, and it would be wrong to legislate in such a way that a trader cannot seek to put things right for the future by correcting the false description, either by substituting a new one or by publishing a specific disclaimer. We see no way in which it would be possible to distinguish between these two situations in legislation. We believe however that, provided the criteria laid down in the *Norman* case and the other cases clarifying the circumstances in which disclaimers can be used are applied, little is lost from the public point of view if the matter is not covered by a specific provision in the Act.

. . .

Should the Act be amended?

165.   Since it appeared that nothing had been said by the Court in the *Norman* case or the other cases mentioned above which is at variance with our views as to the way in which disclaimers should be treated, we suggested in the Consultative Document that there was no need for immediate legislation on this subject. This conclusion was not wholly accepted by a number of bodies, particularly the Law Society of Scotland and other legal commentators. These bodies considered that it would be better to incorporate the principles into the Act, and so ensure that the courts did not stray from them in the future.

166.   We appreciate these arguments. Nevertheless we continue to see an attraction in leaving the matter to be regulated by case law. To lay down a series of statutory rules might be to provoke dishonest traders to try to circumvent them, and there may be considerable difficulties in formulating legislation covering every eventuality in an appropriate manner. We adhere therefore to our preliminary view that no amendment of the Act to regulate disclaimers is necessary.

New order-making power

167.   We do see certain attractions, however, in a provision conferring a power on the Secretary of State to regulate the use of disclaimers by statutory order. Such a power might well be regarded as a useful reserve if it proved over the course of time that the present Act permitted the use of disclaimers on a scale or in circumstances which were considered objectionable. There might also be attractions in a power which allowed the regulation of particular situations so that, for example, traders were only permitted to disclaim the accuracy of odometer readings if they provided an engineer's estimate of the mileage covered by the car in question. We quote this example purely to illustrate the nature of the power we have in mind, not to suggest that such an order is feasible or desirable. This new order-making power should, we suggest, be exercisable only after consultation of the kind envisaged by section 38 of the Act.

. . .

Questions

As para 150 of the above Review notes, 'there is a very fine line between disclaiming a description and applying a qualifying description . . .'

Do such expressions as 'the colour of goods may vary slightly from the illustration in this catalogue' and 'all sizes quoted are approximate' constitute (i) disclaimers or (ii) qualified descriptions? Are they exemption clauses for the purposes of (or otherwise controlled by) the Unfair Contract Terms Act 1977, above p 239 (see pp 253–256, especially)?

Judicial guidance

The guidance supplied by Widgery LCJ in *Norman v Bennett* [1974] 3 All ER 351, [1974] 1 WLR 1229, and extracted in paragraph 153 of the Review above, is of crucial importance. The disclaimer, to be effective, 'must be as bold, precise and compelling as the trade description itself and must be as effectively brought to the notice of any person to whom the goods may be supplied'. In the following case the practice of disclaiming motor odomoeter readings by turning them back to zero before sale of a used motor (thereby rendering any future reading false) was considered by the Divisional Court. The case also provides a further example of the 'passing-over' effect of s 23 which enables an actual or potential defendant who blames a third party for the offence to bring that party before the court. For another such case, see *Cottee v Douglas Seaton (Used Cars) Ltd* [1972] 3 All ER 750, [1972] 1 WLR 1408, above p 476 and for more general discussion of s 23 see below pp 563–567.

K Lill Holdings Ltd [trading as Stratford Motor Co] v White [1979] RTR 120, Queen's Bench Divisional Court

The facts are set out in the judgment of Lord Widgery, CJ.

Lord Widgery CJ This is an appeal by case stated by Greater London Middlesex Area Justices in respect of their adjudication as a magistrates' court sitting at Tottenham on 22 October 1976.

On that occasion there were before the court the defendants, K Lill Holdings Ltd, charged with one charge to the effect that they had, in the course of a trade or business, supplied a Rover 3500 motor car to Michael Robert Manning to which a false trade description had been applied by means of the odometer, contrary to section 1 of the Trade Descriptions Act 1968. That, of course, is a common form case of a seller of cars being charged with altering the odometer.

It is important to notice straight away that the charge against the defendants was not that they themselves applied a false trade description, but that they were responsible for it under the terms of section 23. Section 23 provides:

'Where the commission by any person of an offence under this Act is due to the act or default of some other person that other person shall be guilty of the offence, and a person may be charged with and convicted of the offence by virtue of this section whether or not proceedings are taken against the first-mentioned person.'

What happened, in fact, in this case, so far as relevant, was as follows. On 8 November 1974 the defendants bought the Rover 3500 motor car from a firm called Harvey Hudson & Co Ltd. The odometer reading then was over 59,000 miles. However, it was the practice of the defendants, who are dealers in motor cars, to wind the odometer back to zero before offering a car for sale on their forecourt.

The reason for that, no doubt, is that very few cars justify a trade description that their mileage is nought, and a prospective buyer, coming to a car on the forecourt and seeing that the recorded mileage was nought, would obviously realise that something had happened and the odometer had been wound down deliberately, and he would not be misled into thinking that that was the correct mileage.

Whilst it is no business of ours to recommend or otherwise approve practices of the trade, I feel bound to say that I can see a good deal of merit in this method of winding back the odometer, because it does seem to me that, for the time being at all events, it puts the problem of a false odometer out of the reckoning because no one will be misled by such a record. However, that is what they did for better or worse.

They also placed a disclaimer inside the cab of the motor car. That, of course, is something which has been laid down in this court as being a method of escaping responsibility for this kind of trouble. To make matters as good as possible, they also had a notice up in their office disclaiming the accuracy of the mileages displayed on their cars. They seem to have done practically everything which this court has ever recommended that dealers in motor cars should do in order to avoid this kind of problem.

The defendants, having taken those precautions, in January 1975 sold the car to a Mr Stillgman. Nothing is said about that transaction to indicate that Mr Stillgman was in any way dissatisfied, and I think it right to assume that the transaction from the defendants to Mr Stillgman was one entirely without fault, because no fault is recorded in them to which I have already referred and on which Mr Henderson relies.

So far, we have got the car into Mr Stillgman's possession, but later in 1975 a firm called Peter Judge bought the car from Mr Stillgman, and within a few days it seems Mr Judge was in negotiation to sell the car to a Mr Manning. At the time when the sale to Mr Manning was being undertaken the mileage obtaining on the milometer was only 5,000, and the prospective buyer mentioned this to the seller or his showroom attendant. The seller explained that the clock had been renewed, and he thought that the correct mileage was more like 23,000 miles. Of course, it must have been in fact a great deal more than that, but it may well be that the showroom attendant was not in a position to do any better. Mr Manning having acquired the car, he bought it and paid for it in the ordinary way, and took it away with the previous record of its sale as I have endeavoured to outline.

At the trial below it was contended, and no doubt quite properly contended, that when the car was sold by Mr Judge to Mr Manning it displayed a false trade description because on the findings we have, it must have been the case that the odometer reading was somewhere in the region of 59,000 miles, and that was clearly right. There was, on the face of it, as I am prepared to accept, a case of a false trade description having been applied on the sale by Mr Judge to Mr Manning. But, of course, the whole question here is whether or not the defendants are liable to prosecution for a criminal offence on the basis of what they did when the car was theirs or under their control.

I must say that it seems to me to be clear beyond doubt in a case of this kind that the responsibility of the seller would normally terminate when he has effectively and properly sold the car on. In this case the defendants, when they made their initial sale of the property to Mr Stillgman, obviously did comply with their duty. I expect that they put up disclaimer notices. We do not know the full detail of that. But, on the face of it, there is nothing wrong with their transaction. Once they handed the car over to Mr Stillgman, they would not be in a position to control or regulate any subsequent sales. Whether or not the Act is complied with thereafter would depend on the seller and whether he was a conscientious and careful man.

Mr Henderson, however, has raised an ingenious argument to meet there. He says, true that the defendants had no control over the details of the transaction which gave rise to this charge, yet their act in winding down the odometer was an act which required some positive further act on the part of the owner of the car before he could stop the car from being a rolling lie, which was the expression he used.

That is all very well as an argument, and it is ingenious, but it seems to me to be quite wrong, because I do not think that the obligation of the defendants can be made out under section 23 because I do not think that what they did in this case justifies the contention that the commission of the offence by the subsequent seller was due to the act or default of the defendants. It seems to me that the defendants ceased to be responsible for this before the relevant sale took place, and it cannot, in my judgment, be said that they were guilty because they, by their act or default, had produced the commission of the offence by a subsequent buyer.

For these reasons I think that the conviction was misconceived, although I sympathise with the justices in these difficult questions. I would allow the appeal and quash the conviction.

Wien J I agree. I think that there is something repellent about the idea that someone can be found guilty of an offence due to circumstances which arise long after he has had any dealing with the vehicle. Everything that the defendants did in relation to this vehicle occurred in January 1975. What they did was perfectly innocent. To say that because of the act of someone else thereafter the default can be attributed to them seems to me to go far beyond what is contemplated by section 23 of the Trade Descriptions Act 1968. It is only in the case of an act or default attributable to them that liability for the offence can be brought home.

Mr Henderson, in the course of a very interesting argument, submitted that the act or default may be lawful. I cannot possibly see how that can be the position. If someone acts perfectly lawfully in January 1975, I cannot see how he can possibly be guilty of an offence later in 1975 when it is not brought home that he ought to have foreseen that anything of the kind was likely to happen.

I still adhere to the view that I expressed during the course of argument that this is a case of causation, and that the act or default contemplated in section 23 must be a wrongful act or default.

For those reasons, and for the reasons given by Lord Widgery CJ, I agree that this appeal should be allowed.

Smith J I agree also.

Appeal allowed. Conviction quashed. Order for payment of costs of defendants and prosecutor out of central funds.

Questions

Precisely why were the defendants not liable under the s 23 procedure? Was it because the subsequent seller's offence was not 'due to'—in the sense of being caused by—the zeroing of the car; or was it because such zeroing was not considered to be 'wrongful'?

Problem

Rentaford runs a car-hire business. The odometer cable of a hire car becomes disconnected during use when the car has done 30,000 miles in a year. Twelve months later Rentaford has the cable re-connected. The car is then sold by auction to a dealer, Shark. The odometer reads 30,000 but the true mileage is about 60,000. Shark puts the car up for sale on his garage forecourt with a notice on the odometer reading 'Mileage NOT Guaranteed'.

Discuss the position of Rentaford and Shark under the 1968 Act. Would it affect the position of Rentaford or Shark if the odometer had gone all the way round the clock so that the true mileage was 130,000 rather than the 30,000 indicated? (Cf *Davies v Sumner* [1984] 1 WLR 405, affd [1984] 1 WLR 1301, HL, above p 470).

Two important points arise from the decision in the *Lill Holdings* case. Firstly although the court expressed approbation of zeroing the practice renders a vehicle thereafter a 'rolling lie'. Secondly a distinction must be made between a case where the odometer of a used vehicle is zeroed and it is obvious (at least at that date) that it cannot be taken as an indication of 'other history, including previous ownership or use' within s 2(1) (j), and a case where the odometer is deliberately turned back to a lower figure and this fraudulent act is then purportedly disclaimed.

In *Corfield v Starr* [1981] RTR 380 the defendant had had the effrontery to take an odometer from one car, put it into the dashboard of another and then place a notice on the dashboard reading. 'With deep regret due to the Customer's Protection Act we can no longer verify that the mileage shown on this vehicle is correct.' The Divisional Court directed the justices to convict but did not in terms rule out the possibility of a person both 'clocking' a car and then disclaiming the mileage. Donaldson LJ added the interesting observation that;

> 'I have no doubt that some "disclaimers" can themselves amount to a false trade description. That is not alleged in this case, but in appropriate cases those whose duty it is to enforce consumer protection legislation may like to consider laying an alternative information based upon the disclaimer itself.'

Questions

Is Donaldson LJ correct in suggesting that a disclaimer might constitute a false trade description? Which part, if any, of s 2 above would it fall within?

The application of the disclaimer doctrine to a charge of 'applying' a false trade description was considered in the following case.

Newman v Hackney London Borough Council [1982] RTR 296, Queen's Bench Divisional Court

The facts are set out in the judgment of Ormrod LJ.

Ormrod LJ This is an appeal by way of case stated from a decision made at Snaresbrook Crown Court on 30 January 1981, when the Crown Court dismissed an appeal by the defendants from justices, who had convicted them of two charges. The first charge against the defendant company was that in the course of business as motor dealers, between 1 November 1978, and 1 December 1978, in the Inner London Area, they applied a false trade description to a Triumph 2000 motor car, registration number SPP 275R, by altering the odometer reading on the said car from about 46,328 miles to about 21,000 miles, contrary to section 1(1)(*a*) of the Trade Descriptions Act 1968. The second charge was against the personal defendant, then a director of the defendant company, and was that the offence under section 1(1)(*a*) committed by the company, was attributable to his neglect and he was thereby guilty of that offence by virtue of section 20(1) of the Trade Descriptions Act 1968.

The short facts of the case are these. The car in question was sold originally at auction by a well known firm of brewers. At the time of the sale by auction, the odometer reading on the car was 46,328. The defendant company bought the car at the auction. The car was taken by them to their place of business and it is common ground that one of their employees, acting on their instructions, altered the odometer from 46,328 to 21,000 miles and then stuck a disclaimer sticker over the odometer.

In due course, a Mr McCarthy came along and purchased the car. It is not necessary to say any more than that he said in his evidence he was looking for a Triumph 2000 which had done comparatively small mileage. He eventually bought the car. He did not complain himself but enquiries were made by the prosecutor which eventually led to the discovery of the offence.

In the course of a long and very careful judgment, the circuit judge, sitting at the Crown Court, held as a matter of law that the disclaimer doctrine, which had been developed by the courts in connection with the second part of section 1(1) of the Trade Descriptions Act 1968, did not apply to cases of applying a false trade description in contrast to those cases where the charge was one of supplying goods or articles to which a false trade description had been applied. This is the point with which the court is dealing at present.

Section 1(1) provides:

> 'Any person who, in the course of a trade or business,—(*a*) applies a false trade description to any goods; or (*b*) supplies or offers to supply any goods to which a false trade description is applied; shall, subject to the provisions of this Act, be guilty of an offence'.

The distinction which the Crown drew was the distinction between applying and supplying. Mr Buckhaven [For the defendants] submits that there is no valid distinction between those two offences for this present purpose and that the disclaimer doctrine should apply equally to those who apply a false trade description.

In my judgment, there is a world of difference between the two offences. It is perfectly true that the application of a false trade description must, in some way, be related to a sale or prospective sale but, looking at the Act itself, I am disposed to take the view that the offence is committed when the false trade description is applied to the vehicle or goods and that is at the time when the odometer reading is altered to read a meaningful figure like 21,000 miles. In that light, a disclaimer has no application at all.

There seems to me to be a very good reason for taking that view, as is illustrated by what happened in this case. It is quite obvious that the defendants have indulged in what can only be described as a devious piece of work for the purpose of deceiving somebody. There could be no conceivable honest motive in re-setting the odometer and then sticking a sticker on it to say that the figures on the odometer are not guaranteed, or however it was put. It is perfectly obvious that the object of altering the odometer was to suggest that this car had done only something like 21,000 miles while, at the same time, stating that that figure should not be relied upon. It is a rather naive way of evading the provisions of the section.

Our attention has been drawn to *Corfield v Starr* [1981] RTR 380 in which Bingham J gave the main judgment. The case itself was decided on a different issue. The point on which the case was decided was as to whether or not the justices were entitled to hold that the disclaimer itself was good enough to destroy the effective false description. At the end of his judgment, Bingham J said, at p 384 E-F:

'A further point was argued by Mr Hoggett on behalf of the prosecutor drawing a distinction between the effect of section 1(1)(*a*) of the Act and section 1(1)(*b*). In view of the conclusion which I have reached on the other point I think it suffices to say that I am not persuaded that there is any ground for distinguishing between the effect of those two sections for present purposes.'

I take that to mean that although the matter was referred to in argument, Bingham J was reserving his view about it.

Having considered the matter in great detail and having had the advantage of reading the circuit judge's excellent judgment, I have little difficulty in holding that there is a distinction between section 1(1)(*a*) and 1(1)(*b*) for this purpose. It was suggested that it might lead to difficulties when a motor trader, for some perfectly legitimate purpose, might have to alter the odometer, perhaps for repair or something of that kind. I prefer to leave that case to be dealt with when it arises and not to speculate about it at this stage. In the present case, there is no possible bona fide reason for acting in the way in which the defendants acted.

I accordingly agree with the judgment of the circuit judge in this matter and I would dismiss this appeal.

Woolf J I agree.

Appeal dismissed with costs.

NOTES

For a helpful discussion of this area see Bragg, 'More Mileage in Disclaimers' (1980) 2 LS 172. See also the Office of Fair Trading Report, 'Consumer Difficulties in the Used-Car Sector' (November 1983) which contains a helpful discussion of the possibility of introducing tamper-proof odometers.

False statements as to services

INTRODUCTION

The following provision is concerned with false statements as to services.

Trade Descriptions Act 1968

14. False or misleading statements as to services etc

(1) It shall be an offence for any person in the course of any trade or business—

(a) to make a statement which he knows to be false; or

(b) recklessly to make a statement which is false;

as to any of the following matters, that is to say,—

(i)   the provision in the course of any trade or business of any services, accommodation or facilities;

(ii) the nature of any services, accommodation or facilities provided in the course of any trade or business;

(iii) the time at which, manner in which or persons by whom any services, accommodation or facilities are so provided;

(iv) the examination, approval or evaluation by any person of any services, accommodation or facilities so provided; or

(v)   the location or amenities of any accommodation so provided.

(2) For the purposes of this section—

(a) anything (whether or not a statement as to any of the matters specified in the preceding subsection) likely to be taken for such a statement as to any of those matters as would be false shall be deemed to be a false statement as to that matter; and

(b) a statement made regardless of whether it is true or false shall be deemed to be made recklessly, whether or not the person making it had reasons for believing that it might be false.

(3) In relation to any services consisting of or including the application of any treatment or process or the carrying out of any repair, the matters specified in subsection (1) of this section shall be taken to include the effect of the treatment, process or repair.

(4) In this section 'false' means false to a material degree and 'services' does not include anything done under a contract of service.

'ANY PERSON'

For a reference to this expression see above, pp 466–470.

'IN THE COURSE OF ANY TRADE OR BUSINESS'

This expression has been considered in some detail in relation to false statements concerning goods, above pp 470–475. A further aspect of general importance arose in the following case.

R v Breeze [1973] 2 All ER 1141, [1973] 1 WLR 994, Court of Appeal

The appellant had listed his name under the title 'Architects' in the Yellow Pages telephone directory and had placed the letters 'ARIBA' after his name. Further he had assured one Armitage who was seeking the services of a qualified architect that he was such a person. In reality he had passed only his intermediate examination. After holding that s 14(1)(a)(i) extended to false statements as to the qualifications of a person rendering a service (see also below p 509) Lord Widgery CJ continued:

'However, it has been argued that s 14 has no application to professions, but only to businesses. It has therefore been submitted that the activity in this case should not be regarded as being in the course of a trade or business, because it is in the course, so the argument goes, of a profession, and therefore not struck at by s 14 at all.

The first answer to that submission, and the one on which we would wish to rely, is that it does not lie in the mouth of this appellant to say that he is conducting an activity of a professional character when he lacks the professional qualifications necessary for the carrying on of that profession. We are quite unable to see how, given that the appellant's activity is of a commercial and business character, he can escape from the obligation under the section by saying that his work was really professional when at the same time he lacked the professional qualification necessary. That in itself in our judgment is enough to dispose of the argument that this case is concerned with profession and not business, and we do not, therefore, find it necessary today finally to decide whether s 14 has application to genuine professional men or not. All we would say is that we do not wish anything which is said in the course of this judgment to suggest that professional men are not within the ambit of s 14.

Accordingly, it seems to us that this conviction was properly entered as a matter of law, and that the appeal against conviction must be dismissed . . .'

Appeal against conviction dismissed. Appeal against sentence allowed and fine varied.

MAKING A STATEMENT

In many cases it will be a simple matter to pinpoint precisely when a statement is 'made' and moreover to conclude that a given person either has or has not 'made' it. However this may not be true of statements which are published to the general public, as in the case of holiday brochures and advertising, and there are additional difficulties where the defendant is a body corporate. These matters are discussed in *Wings Ltd v Ellis* [1984] 3 All ER 577, [1984] 3 WLR 965, below at pp 516–22 and pp 557–58. See also *Coupe v Guyett* [1973] 2 All ER 1058, [1973] 1 WLR 669, below p 564.

A FALSE STATEMENT

Liability under s 14 depends on the prosecution establishing that the relevant statement was 'false'. This may seem to be both obvious and straightforward but in fact the area is one of great complexity. The same is true of the related requirement of mens rea, that is knowledge or recklessness as to the falsity of the statement. The cases which follow illustrate a number of points:

Breed v Cluett [1970] 2 All ER 662, [1970] 2 QB 459, Queen's Bench Divisional Court

It was alleged that on or about 23 April 1969 the respondent builder recklessly and falsely stated to the purchaser of a bungalow that it was 'covered by the National House-Builders Registration Council ten-year guarantee'. Contracts for the sale of the bungalow had been exchanged on 3 April whereupon the purchaser had an equitable interest in the bungalow.

Lord Parker CJ stated the facts and described the informations as set out in the case stated, and continued: . . .

Here the allegation is that the respondent recklessly made a statement as to the provision in the course of any trade or business of a service. The justice dismissed the information on the ground that, the contracts having been exchanged on 3rd April, there was a binding obligation. Whatever happened and whatever representations or statements were made thereafter, there was a binding contract which the vendor and purchaser had to complete, and accordingly the statement made on 23rd April could not be an inducement to enter into or to complete a contract.

In my judgment, to approach the matter in that way is to give too narrow a construction to s 14 of the Act. The statements there referred to are not, as it seems to me, confined to statements inducing the entering into of a contract. There may well be statements made after a contract is completed, a contract for repairs to my motor car, a contract for repair to my roof, stating the effect of what has been done by way of repair which may constitute an offence if made recklessly, even though the contract has been completed and the payment has been made.

. . .

Cooke J I entirely agree.

Bridge J I also agree.

Appeal allowed. Case remitted with direction to convict the respondent.

NOTE

For a contrasting case where the charge was under s 1 of the Act and the post-contractual statement concerned the condition of goods see *Wickens Motors (Gloucester) Ltd v Hall* [1972] 3 All ER 759, [1972] 1 WLR 1418 and above pp 468 and 474.

Problem

On 1 April Shark sells to Ada a car which has defective brakes. On the very same day Bert brings his car in to Shark to have the brakes serviced. The work is not done but Bert is charged for it. On 1 May both Ada and Bert return to complain and Shark says, 'Both of your brakes were in perfect condition when they left me.'
Consider Shark's liability under the 1968 Act.

As Lord Parker CJ's examples in *Breed v Cluett* illustrate the require-ment that the statement be false may be satisfied where it relates to the past, for example, 'I have treated your attic with a preservative against dry-rot'. Similarly where it relates to the present, for example, 'This spray I am using in your attic is a preservative against dry-rot'. Much more difficult (and yet of fundamental importance) is the distinction between statements of fact and unfulfilled promises which is drawn in the following case:

R v Sunair Holidays Ltd [1973] 2 All ER 1233, [1974] 1 WLR 1105, Court of Appeal

Mackenna J read the following judgment of the court at the invitation of Stephenson LJ. Sunair Holidays Ltd, the appellants in this case, are a company selling package tours abroad. In the autumn of 1969 they published a brochure, 'Sunair Summer 1970' containing particulars of hotels in Spain, Italy and other countries in which they offered accommodation for the summer season of 1970. One of these was the Hotel Cadi at Calella on the east coast of Spain. Mr Bateman got a copy of Sunair's brochure from a travel agency in Romford some time after Christmas 1969, read it, chose the Hotel Cadi, and on 7 January 1970 bought tickets from Sunair for a Whitsun holiday at that hotel for himself and his family beginning on 27 May 1970. When they got to Calella in May they were dissatisfied with the hotel, and on their return to England Mr Bateman complained to the authorities who started criminal proceedings against Sunair. The proceedings were by way of an indictment containing six counts. Each count charged Sunair with making a false statement about the Hotel Cadi in the

1970 brochure contrary to s 14 (1) (*b*) of the Trade Descriptions Act 1968. In each case the statement was said to have been made on 7 January 1970, the date when Mr Bateman bought the tickets.

We shall quote the particulars of the six allegedly false statements, using in each case the words of the indictment:

> *Count 1* '. . . that the Hotel Cadi, Calella, had a swimming pool, whereas there was no swimming pool at the said hotel.'
>
> *Count 2* '. . . that there were push chairs for hire at the Hotel Cadi, Calella, whereas no push chairs were available.'
>
> *Count 3* '. . . that the Hotel Cadi, Calella, had its own night club, whereas there was no such night club at the said Hotel.'
>
> *Count 4* '. . . that cots were available at the Hotel Cadi, Calella, whereas no cots were available.
>
> *Count 5* '. . . that there was dancing every night in the discotheque of the Hotel Cadi, Calella, whereas there was no discotheque at the said Hotel.'
>
> *Count 6* '. . . that the Hotel Cadi, Calella, provided good food with English dishes available as well as special meals for children, whereas no English dishes or special meals for children were available.'

The case was tried at the Woodford Crown Court in October 1972 before his Honour Judge Mason QC and a jury. The judge held that there was no case for Sunair to answer on count 4, that relating to the cots. He left the other five to the jury, who convicted on counts 1, 2 and 6, those relating to the swimming pool, the push chairs and the food, and acquitted on counts 3 and 5, those relating to the night club and the discotheque. Sunair appeal against their convictions and against the fines imposed on them by the judge.

His Lordship then quoted s 14(1) and (2) (b) of the Act (see above p 500) and continued:

The two questions raised by this appeal can now be stated: (1) whether s 14, as the appellants now contend, is limited to representations of facts, past or present, or whether it includes assurances about the future, and, if the appellants' contention is right; (2) whether the jury's verdict on counts 1, 2 and 6, or any one of them, can be upheld. Before we consider these two questions we shall quote those parts of the brochure which relate to the Hotel Cadi, and state a few of the facts about the hotel.

> 'Hotel Cadi, Calella. A new, very comfortable hotel in the centre of Calella and only about 20 yards from the beach. Luxurious lounge, with local decor, looks out on the sea. Well-stocked bar. *Swimming pool.* Modern restaurant: the food is good, with English dishes also available—as well as special meals for children. The friendly, informal Hotel Cadi also has its own night club.; there is dancing every night in the discotheque. Lift to all floors. All bedrooms have a private w.c. and bath, and terrace. Cots also available. Push chairs for hire. Laundry service.'

The words 'swimming pool' were underlined in red. On the same page of the brochure particulars were given of the prices, including air travel, of a holiday at this hotel during a season beginning on 7 March and ending on 6 October, lower prices at the beginning and end of the season and higher in the middle.

The hotel had been open during the summer of 1969, though apparently it had not been used that year by the appellants. It then had a room used as a discotheque and a night club, but no swimming pool. The owners of the hotel planned to improve it during the winter of 1969–1970. The upper floors at the rear of the hotel were to be rebuilt and a swimming pool was to be constructed on the roof. The room used for the discotheque and night club was to be enlarged. The hotel closed down for the winter and did not re-open until April or May 1970. In the meantime the builders went to work, but not as quickly or as efficiently as had been hoped. When the Batemans were at the hotel, the principal meals consisted of soup, chops, steaks or chicken, always served with chips, and ice-cream and mousses and the like for a pudding. The main dish is said to have been cooked in the Spanish style, presumably in oil. Children could have their meals an hour earlier than the adults, but there were no special dishes provided for them. By 27 May, the date when the Batemans arrived, the swimming pool had been built, but because of cracks or leaks it could not be filled with water. The discovery of these cracks and leaks and making them good took time, and this work was still being done while the Batemans were at the hotel. The larger room for the discotheque and the night club had not been finished, though the artistes who were to perform at the night club were at the hotel. Push chairs were not available at the hotel itself, though they could be hired from a shop in a neighbouring street.

The appellants had made their contract with the owner of the hotel in April 1969. Under this the owners were to reserve accommodation for 130 of the appellants' customers at prices payable by the appellants and fixed by the contract. The appellants knew of the owners' intention to build a swimming pool. Because of the delay in the completion of the building work the appellants did not send any of their customers to the hotel until 27 May when the Batemans and others arrived.

So much for the facts. We come now to the construction of s 14. The section deals with 'statements' of which it can be said that they were, at the time when they were made, 'false'. That may be the case with a statement of fact, whether past or present. A statement that a fact exists now, or that it existed in the past, is either true or false at the time when the statement is made. But that is not the case with a promise or a prediction about the future. A prediction may come true or it may not. A promise to do something in the future may be kept or it may be broken. But neither the prediction nor the promise can be said to have been true or false at the time when it was made. We conclude that s 14 does not deal with forecasts or promises as such. We put in the qualifying words 'as such' for this reason. A promise or forecast may contain by implication a statement of present fact. The person who makes the promise may be implying that his present intention is to keep it or that he has at present the power to perform it. The person who makes the forecast may be implying that he now believes that his prediction will come true or that he has the means of bringing it to pass. Such implied statements of present intention, means or belief, when they are made, may well be within s 14 and therefore punishable if they were false and were made knowingly or recklessly. But if they are punishable, the offence is not the breaking of a promise or the failure to make a prediction come true. It is the making of a false statement of an existing fact, somebody's present state of mind or present means.

What we have said about s 14 agrees with the law of deceit, whether civil or criminal. In a civil action of deceit the plaintiff must prove that there was a false representation of fact as distinct from the failure to fulfil a promise: see Salmond on Tort[1]. So it was with the old criminal law of false pretences: see Archbold's Criminal Pleading, Evidence and Practice[2]. So it is with the new s 15 (4) of the Theft Act. And so it is with s 14.

This section has been considered by the Divisional Court in several cases, of which we shall cite three.

1. 15th Edn (1969) pp 514–517.
2. 36th Edn (1966), p 709, para 1945.

His Lordship then referred to *Sunair Holidays Ltd v Dodd* [1970] 2 All ER 410, [1970] 1 WLR 1037 where the Divisional Court had held that a statement in a holiday brochure 'all twinbedded rooms with . . . terrace' was accurate when made in as much as the appellants had contracted with the hotel for the provision of such rooms for their clients. Hence no offence had been committed even though in the result the hotel management provided a room without a terrace. He continued:

The second case is *Bambury v Hounslow London Borough Council*[3]. Bambury was the director of a company selling motor cars. A customer saw a Ford Cortina at the company's premises on which the word 'guaranteed' appeared. He negotiated for the purchase of the car with Bambury, who told him that the word 'guaranteed' meant that if anything went wrong with the car during the next three months the company would put it right, and that this guarantee would be recorded in a book. The customer bought the car, receiving an invoice which contained a printed condition excluding the company's liability for faults. The car developed several faults, including one in the clutch. The company made good some of them, but pretended that there was nothing wrong with the clutch which eventually was repaired by another garage at a cost to the customer of £17. Bambury was charged with having recklessly made a statement which was false—

'as to the provision in the course of trade or business of a facility, namely, a guarantee to effect repairs to the car for three months from the date of purchase.'

The justices convicted, finding—

'that the defendant's statement as to provision of the guarantee was false and made recklessly by him either well knowing that it would not be or without caring whether or not it would be honoured.'

The conviction was upheld for the following reasons given by Lord Parker CJ[4].

'In my judgment the justices here came to a conclusion to which they were fully entitled to come. . . . The fact that the contractual obligations were not complied with is consistent with one or other of two matters: one, a failure to perform their contractual obligations which they had entered into; or secondly, the fact that there never was an entering into of any contractual obligations at all. The justices. . . . found that the original statement that they were entering into contractual obligations was a false one. They might have come to a different conclusion, but in my judgment there was clearly evidence . . . that the original statement was false.'

Lord Parker CJ was distinguishing between a statement by Bambury that his company were undertaking an obligation to repair the car, which would be true or false at the time when the statement was made, and the undertaking itself, if one were given. Bambury would be liable under s 14 if the first alternative was the right one, and if the statement was untrue. That would be because he had made a false statement about an existing fact, namely his company's undertaking of an obligation. But he would not be liable on the second alternative, even if the company thereafter failed to perform the undertaking.

Beckett v Cohen[5] is the third case. There a builder had promised that he would build a garage within ten days and that it would be similar to an existing garage. He did not finish the garage in time, and the one he built was in some respects different from the existing garage. In respect of his failure to complete in time, he was charged with having made a statement, 'which was false as to the time at which a service, namely the building of a garage, would be provided.' In respect of the differences between the two garages, he was charged with having made a statement which was 'false as to the manner in which such a service would be provided'. The justices upheld the builder's submission that s 14 (1)—

'only covered false statements as to services which had already been provided or were currently being provided, whereas the informations referred to a service which "would be provided" and therefore fell outside the scope of s 14 (1) of the Act'.

The prosecutor's appeal was dismissed. This is what Lord Widgery CJ said[6]:

'. . . This section matches earlier provisions in the Act dealing with the sale of goods. The purpose of the earlier sections is to prevent persons when selling goods from attaching a false description to the goods, and in the same way s 14 is concerned as I see it, when services are performed under a contract, to make it an offence if the person providing the services recklessly makes a false statement as to what he has done. The section specifically refers to the reckless making of a statement which is false. That means that if at the end of the contract a person giving the service recklessly makes a false statement as to what he has done, the matter may well fall within s 14, but if before the contract has been worked out, the person who provides the service makes a promise as to what he will do, and that promise does not relate to an existing fact, nobody can say at the date when that statement is made that it is either true or false. In my judgment Parliament never intended or contemplated for a moment that the Act should be used in this way, to make a criminal offence out of what is really a breach of warranty.'

We accept the distinction drawn in this passage between statements of fact, past or present, and promises about the future, and agree with the view that s 14 deals with the first but not the second. A statement about the quality of a service already provided is a statement of past fact and is covered by the section. A statement of existing fact may also be covered, as, for example, if a hotel advertises that its services currently provided include the provision of afternoon tea; if that service is not being provided at the time when the statement is made an offence may be committed. A statement about existing facts would not cease to be within the section because the person making it warranted that it was true and that the facts would continue to exist in the future. In that limited sense the section can apply to warranties. But it does not apply to promises about the future unless, as we said earlier, the promise can be construed as an implied statement of a present intention or the like, in which case it may be that it is caught by s 14, as it would be by s 15 of the Theft Act 1968, which includes in its definition of deception false statements of present intentions.

In answer to the first question stated above, we hold that s 14 is limited to statements of fact, past or present, and does not include assurances about the future.

It remains to consider the second question whether, on this reading of the section, the jury's verdict on counts 1, 2 and 6 or any of them can be upheld.

In the court below the prosecution contended that the words 'swimming pool' in the appellants' 1970 brochure meant that a swimming pool had already been built and was in existence on the date in January 1970, when Mr Bateman made his bookings. They seem to have contended in the alternative that the words meant that a swimming pool would be in existence on 7 March 1970 which was the earliest date given in the brochure for bookings at the Hotel Cadi. They contended that in either case the statement was false. The appellants contended that the words related only to the future and meant that a swimming pool would be in existence on 27 May 1970, when Mr Bateman's bookings took effect. Both parties seem to have agreed that the words about push chairs, English dishes and special meals for children, related to the future in the case of this hotel which was not open in January 1970, when the statements about these matters were made. Neither party contended that if any of the statements related only to the future they were not caught by s 14. *Beckett v Cohen*[5] had not yet been decided, and the point which it established about the meaning of the section had apparently not occurred to counsel on either side or to the judge himself. The appellants' case was that the words about the pool, the chairs and the food all related to the future, and that the assurances on those matters were substantially fulfilled.

Other points of construction were raised by the appellants at the trial. What was meant by 'English dishes also available'? What was the meaning of 'special meals for children'? Did this mean special dishes or only special meal times? What was meant by 'Push chairs for hire'? Did this mean that there would be chairs for hire at the hotel itself, or would it be enough that there were chairs for hire in a neighbouring shop? Somebody had to construe the brochure to answer these questions of construction and the question whether the words about the swimming pool related to the present or the future. Both parties were agreed in the court below and before us that it was for the jury to construe the document as it would be in proceedings for libel. This was the view taken in the earlier case of *R v Clarksons Holidays Ltd*[7] and tacitly approved by this court to which the case was brought on appeal. Following this precedent we shall assume that this is the right course, observing only that if it is right statements in books on evidence which treat libel proceedings as the only exception to a rule that the construction of documents is for the judge may need to be revised: see *Cross on Evidence*[8], and the article on Evidence in Halsbury's Laws of England[9].

Treating the question of construction as one for the jury, the judge directed them as follows:

> 'You must ask first: "What do these statements mean?", beginning, as I suggest you should, by asking yourself whether when [the appellants] made those statements they were representing to the people who read the brochure that the physical facilities, if I can so describe them, of the Hotel Cadi existed, as the prosecution suggest they were, on the date when Mr Bateman booked his holiday, namely, 7 January 1970; or were they representing that those facilities would exist on what was said to be the earliest possible booking date, 7 March 1970? . . . Or, third, [were the appellants] representing that those physical facilities would exist . . . when Mr Bateman arrived at the hotel, namely, 27 May? Those are the three possibilities.'

. . .

3. [1971] RTR 1.
4. [1971] RTR at 6.
5. [1973] 1 All ER 120, [1972] 1 WLR 1593.
6. [1973] 1 All ER at 121, 122, [1972] 1 WLR at 1596.
7. (1972) 57 Cr App Rep 38.
8. 3rd Edn (1969) pp 50, 51.
9. 3rd Edn, vol 15, p 276, para 503.

His Lordship then referred to the possible distinctions (notably between the swimming pool, and the food and push-chairs) on which the judge had elaborated to assist the jury in selecting the appropriate date and continued:

What further direction ought the judge to have given the jury? If our reading of s 14 is right he should have told them, in the case of the swimming pool, that if they construed the words as relating to the future, which was the appellants' contention, they should acquit them on count 1, and that in any event, they should acquit them on counts 2 and 6 which both sides agreed related to the future. He did not do so, because this point had not been taken by the appellants. Instead he went on to direct the jury that having chosen the date to which any of these statements related, they should then consider whether it was true at that date, and if it were not and they found that it had been recklessly made they could convict the appellants. This was wrong.

Counsel for the Crown in this court, asked, what did the appellants lose by the judge's failure to give the right direction on count 1? The answer is clear. They lost their chance of an acquittal on this count, which would have been their right if the jury construed the words about the swimming pool as relating to the future, as they may have done. We cannot uphold the conviction on this count, not knowing whether the jury construed the words as relating to 7 January, or whether they construed them as relating to 27 May and convicted the appellants only because they found that the swimming pool had not been completed by that date.

Counsel for the Crown appeared to argue that even if s 14 were limited to statements of existing facts, the convictions on the three counts should still be upheld on the ground that the brochure impliedly represented that satisfactory arrangements had already been made by the appellants for the provision of these facilities or services in the future, and that such arrangements had not, in fact, been made on 7 January. This was not how the charges were framed in the indictment. It is not how the case was fought in the court below. It is not how the case was summed up by the judge. It is impossible to uphold these convictions on this or any other ground, and they must be quashed.

Appeal allowed: convictions quashed.

NOTES

1. The reasoning of MacKenna, J was approved in *British Airways Board v Taylor* [1976] 1 All ER 65, [1976] 1 WLR 13, HL, a case which arose out of the appellant's policy of overbooking flights to counteract the effect of 'no-shows'. Lord Wilberforce said (at p 68):

My Lords, the distinction in law between a promise as to future action, which may be broken or kept, and a statement as to existing fact, which may be true or false, is clear enough. There may be inherent in a promise an implied statement as to a fact, and where this is really the case, the court can attach appropriate consequences to any falsity in, or recklessness in the making of, that statement. Everyone is familiar with the proposition that a statement of intention may itself be a statement of fact and so capable of being true or false. But this proposition should not be used as a general solvent to transform the one type of assurance with another: the distinction is a real one and requires to be respected particularly where the effect of treating an assurance as a statement is to attract criminal consequences, as in the present case. As Lord Widgery CJ said in *Beckett v Cohen*[1] it was never intended that the 1968 Act should be used so as to make a criminal statement out of what is really a breach of warranty.

1. [1973] 1 All ER 120 at 122, [1972] 1 WLR 1593 at 1596, 1597.

On the facts of the case the House of Lords held that the justices had been entitled to find that the statement 'I have pleasure in confirming the following reservations for you—London/Bermuda Flight BA 679—Economy Class—29 August Dep 1525 hours Arr 1750 hours' was a false statement within s 14 (1) of the Act.

2. It is evident from the above cases that there is a very fine distinction between (i) a false statement of fact which may give rise both to civil liability and liability under s 14 of the 1968 Act and (ii) a simple promise as to the future which may give rise to civil liability for breach of warranty only.

3. Presumably the potential falsity of a statement may be affected also by an appropriately worded disclaimer. Commenting on this point the 'Review of the Trade Descriptions Act' (Cmnd 6628 (1976)) said:

Disclaiming and varying descriptions

. . .

148. At present few, if any, problems of this type occur in connection with statements about services for a number of reasons. First, it is not an offence under the 1968 Act to supply a

service which does not correspond with a description applied to it. Secondly, one cannot physically mark a description upon a service. Thirdly, inadvertent mis-statements do not give rise to an offence under section 14 which is concerned only with false statements made deliberately or recklessly.

No doubt this is true generally of blatant disclaimers but there is ample scope for suitably qualified statements as to the nature etc of the services provided (cf para 150 of the above report, above p 492).

4. Lord Wilberforce noted in the *British Airways* case that s 14 (2) (a) of the Act concentrates attention on the probable reaction of the consumer addressee of the statement, this being determined as a matter of fact. See also *Cowburn v Focus Television Rentals Ltd* (1983) 2 Tr L 89, 92 where Forbes K is reported as saying: 'So long as a reasonable person might interpret a statement in a way which would make it false, then, owing to s 14 (2) (a), as a statement "likely to be taken for such a statement", it becomes false . . .'. However the reasonable person must still understand the statement as referring to one of the matters listed in s 14 (1) (b) (i)–(v), above, p 500, and it is not in terms sufficient if he concludes that the statement is *misleading* as opposed to false.

5. In a passage in the *Sunair Holidays* cases which was cited with approval by Lord Edmund-Davies in the *British Airways* case Mackenna J states that a person who makes a promise which he does not intend to keep makes a false statement of an existing fact, namely as to his 'present state of mind or present means' (see above p 504). Undoubtedly this is so but is a false statement as to one's intentions a statement as to a matter listed in s 14 (1) (i)–(v) (see above p 500 and below)?

Consider the following cases in terms of potential liability under s 14 of the 1968 Act:

(i) Alexi calls in Furnace, a central heating specialist, and tells him that she needs a new boiler and that it must be installed by Christmas. Furnace says, 'I can make no promises but I shall make every effort to ensure that my brother Rex who has his own company does it well before then'. Rex is given the work and does not complete it on time. Furnace admits that he had never intended to persuade Rex to do so since he knew that he was already heavily over-committed.

(ii) Ada wishes to have solar heating installed in her home. Loge, a salesman of such systems, tells her, 'In my estimate you will save at least 50% on your heating bill'. Loge knew that this was highly optimistic and in the result Ada's saving was only 10%.

THE PROVISION ETC OF ANY SERVICES, ACCOMMODATION OR FACILITIES

Many of the most important cases falling within s 14 of the Act involve the holiday trade and 'services, accommodation or facilities' provided in relation to it. However the section goes well beyond this so that it covers, for example, such services as home improvements, car repairs, dry-cleaning, film processing and the like. Some assistance as to the scope of the words the 'provision' and 'nature' of any 'services, accommodation or facilities' is provided by the following cases:

R v Breeze [1973] 2 All ER 1141, [1973] 1 WLR 994, Court of Appeal

The facts of this case involving a person who described himself falsely as a qualified architect are noted above p 500 where another aspect of the case is discussed. Having stated the facts Lord Widgery CJ continued:

Lord Widgery CJ . . . In this case the prosecution relied on s 14 (1) (*a*) (i), that is to say, they said that by calling himself an architect when he was not, he in the course of a trade or business made a false statement as to the provision in the course of any trade or business of any service. It seems to this court that the first question logically for consideration, and perhaps the most difficult and fundamental question, is whether if a man carrying on a trade or business in the provision of services falsely gives himself a personal qualification which he does not possess, the giving of that personal qualification can fairly be said to come within the words which I have read of s 14 (1) (*a*) (i), namely whether the giving himself of that qualification is a false statement as to the provision of any services.

It has been argued forcefully by counsel for the appellant, to whom the court is indebted for his argument, that the phrase which I have just read, that which refers to the provision of any services, is a phrase concerned with the nature of the services performed, not with the identity or qualifications of the person who performs them. In other words, he says that given that the appellant was doing the work of an architect, the fact that he falsely described himself as an architect does not amount to a false statement as to the provision of the services.

The court has given careful consideration to this matter, because it clearly is one of considerable importance, and it has come to the conclusion that there is no reason for saying that a man carrying on business whose business is the provision of services does not commit an offence under s 14 (1) (*a*) (i) if he adopts to himself a personal qualification which he does not enjoy.

For example, and one quotes it only as an example, suppose that a motor mechanic sets up in business to repair motor cars, and suppose that he announces to his prospective customers that he did a five year apprenticeship with Rolls-Royce when that is not the fact. We think that in a case of that kind it could perfectly properly be said that the man in question, in the course of a trade or business, had made a statement which he knew to be false and that it was a statement as to the provision of services which he offered, because it goes without saying that a qualified man is likely, in general, to do a better job than an unqualified man, and the fact that a man has qualifications, such as an architect or an apprentice with five years' experience with Rolls-Royce, is the sort of factor which goes to the likely quality of the service which he will perform, and is, we think, without any straining of language, properly to be taken to be within the term that the statement is made as to the provisions of services, to quote the actual statutory words.

There is no doubt in our judgment in this case that the appellant was carrying on what on the face of it was a business. He was carrying on a continuous activity with a view to gain and profit by drawing plans for people who wanted them. There is no doubt he made this false statement in the course of that activity, and for the reasons which I have already given, we think it comes within the terms of s 14 (1) (*a*) (i).

. . .

Accordingly, it seems to us that this conviction was properly entered as a matter of law, and that the appeal against conviction must be dismissed.

Appeal against conviction dismissed. Appeal against sentence allowed and fine varied.

It seems that recently prosecuting authorities have sought to extend the scope of s 14 beyond what might be thought to be its natural boundaries. However as the following case illustrates the courts have not been over-receptive to these attempts.

Newell v Hicks (1983) Lexis transcript, 128 Sol Jo 63, Times, 7 December, Queen's Bench Divisional Court

The appellants were Renault sales managers and they had placed advertisements in newspapers. One such advertisement read:

'A video cassette recorder absolutely free with every X registration Renault. All you have to do is place a firm order at Renault Wolverhampton from July 6th.'

The justices found that this statement was false in as much as the trade-in allowance made on customers' old vehicles was reduced when they wished to take advantage of the offer. They convicted the defendants who had been charged under s 14 of the Act and they now appealed to the Divisional Court.

Robert Goff LJ, having stated the facts of the case, continued:

Under each of the informations with which these two appellants were charged, it was alleged that a certain statement was false as to 'services or facilities provided in the course of the said trade of business namely as to the provision of free video cassette recorders, contrary to Sec. 14 (1) (b) of the Trade Descriptions Act.' There is no dispute, of course, that what was done was in the course of a trade or business. That, therefore, leaves for consideration the question whether what was done constituted a statement as to the provision of a service or, alternatively, a statement as to the provision of a facility.

Mr Underhill's [who appeared for the appellants] first submission was that in no case did it do so, because the statements contained in the various advertisements or circulars related to the supply of a certain item of goods, namely, a video cassette recorder, which did not constitute the provision of a service or the provision of a facility within section 14 (1) of the Act.

Mr Underhill submitted that, in this Act, a distinction is drawn in various sections between supply of goods on the one hand and the provision of services on the other. An example is to be found in section 13 of the Act, which is headed: 'False representations as to supply of goods or services.' There are indeed other sections in the Act where a distinction is drawn between the supply of goods on the one hand and the provision of services on the other. Mr Underhill further submitted that, in any event, if the words 'services and facilities' are given their ordinary natural meaning, that meaning would not embrace, apart from exceptional cases, the supply of goods.

In this connection he prayed in aid a decision of this court in *Westminster City Council v Ray Alan (Manshops) Ltd* [1982] 1 All ER 771, [1982] 1 WLR 383. That case was also concerned with a prosecution under section 14 (1) of the Trade Descriptions Act, 1968. There it was alleged that a false statement was made as to the nature of a facility provided in the course of a trade or business by displaying a sign outside a shop, bearing the words: 'Closing Down Sale', when in fact the shop was not closing down and the accused persons continued to trade. It was held by the stipendiary magistrate, and again by this court, that that did not constitute a contravention of section 14 (1) of the Act, for the reason that the statement was not as to the provision of a facility. Ormrod LJ, who delivered the principal judgment in the case had this to say about the word 'facility' in the Act (at page 773):

'Counsel for the respondents had contended that a closing down sale in relation to a shop selling goods is not properly described as a "facility" or "the provision of a facility". She contended that a "facility" must be something ancillary to the sale. But leaving that point aside, the real point is that other sections of the Act deal with the sale of goods,'

and I pause there to say that I think Ormrod LJ must have been referring there to the supply of goods,

'whereas s 14 is primarily concerned with misleading statements as to the provision of services, accommodation or facilities. I think counsel's argument can be summarised by saying that the word "facilities" in s 14 should be construed ejusdem generis with the preceding words "services" and "accommodation".

When one looks at s 14 (1) one sees that the three nouns are grouped together in all but one of the various sub-heads under that section, namely the phrase "services, accommodation or facilities" is repeated over and over again.

I have come to the conclusion that that submission is right, that the word "facilities" where it occurs in s 14 should be construed in relation to the two words preceding it, "services [and] accommodation".

Perhaps one can illustrate the difference in this way. Hotels or businesses of all kinds provide services, meaning that they do something for the customer. Others provide facilities in the sense that various things are made available to customers to use if they are so minded in a more passive sense than the activities implied in the word "services".

In those circumstances I think the magistrate arrived at the right conclusion when he said that he was not satisfied that to advertise a closing down sale was to make any representation relating to a facility and accordingly I think he was right to reach that conclusion. The word is obviously of very wide meaning, and we have to be careful of it because it has become more and more popular in commercial circles. Almost anything can be described as a "facility" and accordingly, as this is a penal statute, we have to construe it strictly. For those reasons, as to the first information, I would hold that the magistrate was right.'

I would respectfully agree with and adopt what Ormrod LJ there said, that the word 'facility' is a word which is subject to a very wide use in commercial circles and, possibly, in ordinary speech as applying to almost anything that can be made available commercially. Even the sale of goods has been described, in some instances, as a facility. I also agree with Ormrod LJ, as we are here concerned with a criminal statute, it would be wrong to stretch the meaning of the word facility in this way.

Mr Underhill submitted that, in considering the words 'services' and 'facilities' in this context, we should regard the typical meaning of the word 'services' in this Act to be doing something for somebody. I agree with that. I would not attempt, any more than Mr Underhill did in his submission, to offer a definition of 'services'. But, generally speaking, it is correct that 'services' in this context should be regarded as doing something for somebody; that is, so to speak, the core of the meaning of that word. Typical examples of services given in the course of argument were a laundry, or dry cleaning, or repairing a car.

On the other hand, a 'facility', Mr Underhill submitted in the course of argument, is providing somebody with the 'wherewithal' to do something for himself.

Again, broadly speaking, I agree. Some typical examples of facilities which were given in the course of argument were providing the facility of a car park so that a person, to use Mr Underhill's expression, is provided with the wherewithal to park his car; or the facility of a swimming pool, so that a person is given the facility to go and swim. There may also be less simple examples than these. It appears that, for example, the provision of credit may fall within either the word 'service' or the word 'facility'. However, we do not have to decide that particular point on this occasion, although I myself incline to the opinion that it falls within the expression 'service'.

Furthermore, I for my part am satisfied that, apart from exceptional circumstances, to which I shall refer in a moment, the supply of goods does not fall within the words 'services' or 'facilities'. I am fortified in my view of the natural meaning of the words 'services' and 'facilities' by the fact that in the Act itself we can see, in the earlier sections, a contradistinction drawn between supply of goods on the one hand and the provision of services on the other.

I have said that there may be exceptional circumstances, although the point does not really arise in this case. I simply draw attention to the possibility that the word 'services', for example, may, in certain circumstances, embrace and include the supply of goods. To give examples posed in the course of argument, when a car is serviced very often oil is provided, for example for an oil change; or when laundry services are rendered, sometimes stiffeners are placed in the collars of shirts. It may be that, in those circumstances, the service may embrace and include the supply of goods. The point does not have to be decided for the purposes of the present case, but I draw attention to it as a point which arose in the course of argument. In the present case, we are concerned with persons who, concerned to promote the sale of motor cars, caused statements to be published about the cars, to the effect that if a certain car was bought within a certain period a free video cassette recorder would be provided with the car. So the main contracts of this case were not contracts for services; they were plainly contracts for the supply of goods. So, we are not here concerned with the exceptional type of case to which I have just indicated.

In this case, we are concerned with the question whether the offer of a free video cassette recorder constituted a statement as to the provision of a service or the provision of a facility. Having regard to the understanding of the words 'service' and 'facility' which I have already expressed in this judgment, I am satisfied that we are here concerned with statements as to the supply of an item of goods (albeit free, and not by way of sale), and that such statements did not constitute statements as to the provision of a service, or as to the provision of a facility. I, for my part, therefore accept Mr Underhill's first submission.

I turn then to his second submission. The complaint against his clients was that they made statements that a video cassette recorder would be supplied free with certain cars. The complaint was directed towards the word 'free'. The magistrates regarded the statement as false because they considered that the video cassette recorders would not be free. In those circumstances, submitted Mr Underhill, the allegation was that the statements were false as to the price of the goods referred to, in that it was stated that no charge would be made for the relevant goods.

Mr Underhill then turned to section 14 (1) of the Act. He submitted that the price for services or accommodation or facilities is not dealt with in that subsection. He pointed out that sub-section (1) of 14 (1) is directed towards statements as to the provision of services, accommodation or facilities; that (ii) is concerned with statements as to their nature; that (iii) is directed towards statements as to the time at which, the manner in which or the persons by whom they are provided; that (iv) is concerned with the examination, approval or evaluation by any person of them; and that (v) is concerned with location or amenities of accommodation. It follows, therefore, that there are five specified matters. It also follows, submitted Mr Underhill—and with this I agree—that since there are five specified matters, it is impossible, as a matter of construction, to read the word 'provision' in section 14 (1) (i) as referring to anything other than the fact of providing, because if it were to be read widely as to embrace, for example, the terms upon which the services, accommodation or facilities were being provided, including their prices, the effect would be to render the words of (i) so wide as to render (ii), (iii), (iv) and (v) surplusage. The ordinary presumption against surplusage must militate very strongly against any submission which is founded upon such a broad meaning of the word 'provision'.

It seems to me, therefore, to be plain that, as a matter of construction, the word 'provision' can only be read as being concerned with the fact of providing services, accommodation or facilities and not as relating to the terms upon which they are provided. That being so, it appears that nowhere in section 14 is there specified, as one of the relevant matters, the price at which the services, accommodation or facilities are provided. Therefore, nowhere does the section strike, so to speak, at a statement that certain services, accommodation or facilities are being provided free, when in fact they are going to be charged for; nor at a statement that certain services, accommodation or facilities are being provided at price X, when in fact they are being provided at a higher price, Y. It may well be that there is a lacuna in this section. If so, I draw attention to the omission. But our duty is to construe the section as it stands, and I for my part am satisfied that the matter of price is not covered by section 14 (1) of the Act. It follows, therefore, that I accept Mr Underhill's second submission also.

I wish, finally, to suggest that it is possible in this case that the prosecution might have been brought under section 11 (2) of the Act, which provides:

> 'If any person offering to supply any goods gives, by whatever means, any indication likely to be taken as an indication that the goods are being offered at a price less than that at which they are in fact being offered he shall, subject to the provisions of this Act, be guilty of an offence.'

. . .

Mann J: I agree. I would wish to add this. I share my Lord's surprise that section 14 does not comprehend statements as to price in relation to services, accommodation and facilities. Plainly it does not. The omission is, in my judgment, surprising.

Appeals allowed.

NOTES

1. For a further extract from *Westminster City Council v Ray Alan (Manshops) Ltd* see below, p 530. Section 11 (2) of the Act is discussed below, p 525 et seq.

2. In *Dixons Ltd v Roberts* (1984) 148 JP 513 the Divisional Court held that the statement, 'refund the difference if you buy Dixon's Deal products cheaper locally at time of purchase and call within seven days' was not capable of giving rise to liability under s 14 of the Act. Forbes, J is reported as saying, 'it is impossible to accept that the offer of a refund on part of the price of goods could be taken as an offer to provide services'.

3. The decision in the *Ray Alan* case attracted some criticism (see, eg, Stevenson (1982) 42 MLR 710, 712). Certainly a straightforward distinction between ss 1–6 (goods) and 14 (services) does not seem tenable. For example it has been held to be an offence under s 14 to state falsely that goods are available 'on approval' or 'carriage free' (see *MFI*

Warehouses Ltd v Nattrass [1973] 1 All ER 762, [1973] 1 WLR 307, below) or for a promotional offer to state 'Hire 20 feature films absolutely free when you rent a video recorder' when postage and packing are charged (*Cowburn v Focus Television Rentals Ltd* (1983) 2 Tr L 89).

Question

Is it potentially an offence against s 14 for a brochure to state falsely that an hotel has 'First Class Shopping Facilities Incorporated' where (i) there are no such facilities, (ii) there are facilities but they are distinctly third-rate?

Problem

The following advertisements appear in a brochure published on 1 May 1984 advertising the attractions of Senta on Sea: (i) 'XY Supermarket: Late Night Shopping until 8.00 every evening from March–September'; (ii) 'Smart Marina: Berths available for yachts up to 20 metres'. In fact the XY Supermarket always closes at 6.00 pm and the marina cannot take yachts of more than 16 metres. Discuss the publisher's potential liability under s 14 of the 1968 Act.

KNOWLEDGE OR RECKLESSNESS

This section is unusual in requiring 'mens rea'. It also follows that the defences provided for in s 24 (all reasonable precautions taken and all diligence shown) will have only a limited application: see *Coupe v Guyett* [1973] 2 All ER 1058, [1973] 1 WLR 669, below p 564, but cf *Wings Ltd v Ellis* [1984] 3 All ER 577, [1984] 3 WLR 965, below pp 516–22 and 557–58. The following is the leading case most directly in point as to the meaning of the word 'reckless' for the purposes of s 14.

MFI Warehouses Ltd v Nattrass [1973] 1 All ER 762, [1973] 1 WLR 307, Queen's Bench Divisional Court

The facts are set out in the judgment of Lord Widgery CJ:

Lord Widgery CJ read the following judgment. This is an appeal by case stated by justices for the county of Chester acting in and for the petty sessional division of Chester Castle and Ellesmere Port, in respect of their adjudication as a magistrates' court sitting at Chester on 27 March 1972. On that date the justices convicted the appellants of two offences contrary to s 14 (1) of the Trade Descriptions Act 1968. . . .

The circumstances of the case were these. For some time the appellants had been selling by mail order a wooden door which is described as a louvre door because it had slats in it through which air could pass for purposes of ventilation. The terms on which these doors were advertised and sold was that they could be had on 14 days' approval without pre-payment and that 25p carriage should be charged on each door. After a while the appellants marketed a set of sliding door gear designed to be used with the louvre doors, the purpose of which was to enable these doors to be assembled in such a way as to make a sliding partition. The intention of the appellants was that these sliding door sets should be sold only with a set of louvre doors and not separately. Their intention when the door gear was sold with the doors was that no extra carriage charge should be made in respect of the inclusion of the sliding door gear, and that the same period of approval should be available for the door gear as was for the doors. The advertisement complained of referred to the doors as being 'carriage free' which was intended by the appellants to indicate that no additional carriage charge would result if the door gear was ordered with the doors. Furthermore, the advertisement in referring to 14 days' free approval did not distinguish between an order for doors and door gear respectively, it not having been in the minds of the appellants that the gear should be sold separately in any instance.

The purchaser referred to in this case read the advertisement as meaning that the sliding door gear could be bought separately. One may say at once that he was not to be blamed for reaching that conclusion because it was one which might well have been reached by an intelligent reader of the advertisement itself. Accordingly he placed an order for door gear and was surprised to find that he was expected to pay carriage on the door gear notwithstanding the reference to 'carriage free' in the advertisement, whereas in the other case the purchaser was surprised to find that he could not obtain the door gear on 14 days' free approval but was required to make payment before despatch.

The explanation of this is that the clerk who dealt with the order treated it as one which did not entitle the buyer to the facilities of free approval or free carriage because it was an order for the gear in isolation and not coupled with an order for doors. The justices found that if the clerk in question had referred the matter to the appellants' chairman the latter would then have appreciated that the advertisement was ambiguous and would have instructed the clerk to honour the terms of the advertisement. In fact the matter was not referred to the appellants' chairman and the purchaser raised complaint, which resulted in the bringing of these charges.

. . .

The justices found that the advertisement constituted a false statement made by the appellants in the course of their trade or business in regard to the provision of facilities within the meaning of s 14 (1). The only remaining question, therefore, was whether that statement had been made 'recklessly' within the meaning of the section. The only further finding which goes to the thought given by the appellants to the correctness or otherwise of their advertisement is to be found in para 2 (j) of the stated case which states:

> 'that the [appellants] by their Chairman studied the said advertisement for 5 or 10 minutes or thereabouts prior to approving it but did not think through sufficiently the implications thereof and did not appreciate that it in fact offered the said folding door gear as an item which could be separately purchased on the terms stated.'

Argument in the court below, as in this court, centred on the meaning of the word 'reckless'. For the appellants it was argued that 'reckless' here had its familiar common law meaning derived from *Derry v Peek*[1], that is to say, that 'recklessness' implies a total irresponsibility and a total lack of consideration whether the statement was false or true. It was argued that on this construction a statement could not be made recklessly unless the conduct of the maker was on the threshold of fraud or he had shown himself ready to run a risk with the truth. Such conduct, it was said, could not be found against the appellants on the facts which the justices had accepted and, in particular, having regard to the consideration given to the advertisement by the appellants' chairman.

For the respondent it was contended that the word 'reckless' in the present context had a wider meaning than that in *Derry v Peek*[1]. It was contended that if the draftsman had intended the word 'reckless' to have its normal common law meaning, he would not have thought it necessary to include a specific definition clause in the section. Furthermore, when the definition clause was examined again it was to be observed that it referred to a statement made 'regardless of whether it is true or false'. It was contended that the normal meaning of 'regardless' is 'without having regard to'. It was accordingly contended that this Act placed on sellers a duty to give active consideration to whether their advertisements were true or false, and that unless the advertisement had been examined with this end in view it was open to the prosecution to contend that the advertisement was issued without regard to whether it was true or false. Attention was also directed to the final phrase in s 14 (2) (b) namely, 'whether or not the person making it had reasons for believing that it might be false'. It is argued that this phrase shows the intention of the legislature to require sellers to examine their advertisements for falsity even though it is not shown that they had any independent reason for suspecting that the advertisement was false.

The only reference to this question in authority on this particular section is to be found in Lord Parker CJ's judgment in *Sunair Holidays Ltd v Dodd*[2]. There, after reading the section, Lord Parker CJ observed[2]:

> 'In other words this by statute is importing the common law definition of "recklessly" as laid down in *Derry v Peek*[1] and adopted ever since.'

It does not appear that this dictum was essential to the decision in the case with which Lord Parker CJ was concerned and there is no reason to suppose that there had been argument on it. For these reasons I would be disinclined to accept Lord Parker CJ's word as being the final pronouncement on this question, and think that it behoves this court to look into the matter again. I am supported in this view by a comment made by Roskill LJ in giving the judgment of the court in *R v Clarksons Holidays Ltd*[3]; it was not necessary for him to express any final view on the point but he indicated his impression that Lord Parker CJ's observation[2] would not be accepted if the matter were fully argued. That the word 'reckless' may have more than one meaning in law is apparent from a consideration of the judgment of Salmon J in *R v Mackinnon*[4], and the judgment of Donovan J in *R v Bates*[5]. I am inclined to think that it was the fact that the word 'reckless' has more than one meaning which prompted the draftsman to give a special definition of that word in the Act with which we are presently concerned, and I think, therefore, that we should approach the problem of construction by having regard to that definition rather than to preconceived notions of what the word 'reckless' should mean. I have much sympathy with the view of Salmon J[4] that where a criminal offence is being created and an element of the offence is 'recklessness', one should hesitate before accepting the view that anything less than '*Derry v Peek*[1] recklessness' will do. On the other hand, it is quite clear that this Act is designed for the protection of customers and it does not seem to me to be unreasonable to suppose that in creating such additional protection for customers Parliament was minded to place on the advertiser a positive obligation to have regard to whether his advertisement was true or false.

I have accordingly come to the conclusion that 'recklessly' in the context of the 1968 Act does not involve dishonesty. Accordingly it is not necessary to prove that the statement was made with that degree of irresponsibility which is implied in the phrase 'careless whether it be true or false'. I think it suffices for present purposes if the prosecution can show that the advertiser did not have regard to the truth or falsity of his advertisement even though it cannot be shown that he was deliberately closing his eyes to the truth, or that he had any kind of dishonest mind. If I had taken the contrary view I would have held that the facts found in this case would not support the conviction. On the opinion which I have just expressed, however, I think that the justices were entitled to convict in this case, and that the explanation of their decision is that they considered that the appellants' chairman did not have regard to the falsity or otherwise of what was written on his behalf. Accordingly, I would dismiss the appeal.

Ashworth J. I agree.

Willis J. I agree.

Appeal dismissed.

1. (1889) 14 App Cas 337, [1886–90] All ER Rep 1.
2. [1970] 2 All ER 410 at 411, [1970] 1 WLR 1037 at 1040.
3. [1972] Crim LR 653.
4. [1958] 3 All ER 657 at 658, [1959] 1 QB 150 at 152.
5. [1952] 2 All ER 842.

NOTE

In discussing the word 'recklessness' in the criminal law Professors Smith and Hogan write as follows (see *Criminal Law* (5th edn, 1983) p 52):

> Let it be assumed that D has done an act which, objectively considered, involves an unjustifiable risk of causing the harm in question. When he acted, D must have had one of three possible states of mind regarding the risk. (1) He may have known of the risk. (2) He may not have considered whether there was a risk or not. (3) He may have believed that there was no risk.

Since the decision in the above case the House of Lords has examined the meaning of the word 'reckless' in two cases of great importance, *R v Caldwell* [1982] AC 341, [1981] 1 All ER 961 (criminal damage) and *R v Lawrence* [1982] AC 510, [1981] 1 All ER 974 (reckless driving). *R v Caldwell* is authority for the proposition that statutory recklessness encompasses a situation in which a person gives no thought to an obvious risk, that is a variant of situation (2) above. Certainly the *MFI Warehouses* case is consistent with this view.

Questions

1. Suppose that the defendant trader does have regard to the truth or falsity of the statement and concludes, quite unreasonably and wrongly, that it is true. Is this to be deemed 'reckless' within s 14 (2) (b) of the 1968 Act?
2. Is the trader who gives no thought at all to the truth or falsity of the statement (i) more or (ii) less blameworthy than the trader in Question 1 above?

A relatively recent decision of the House of Lords is of considerable interest both to the scope and interpretation of s 14 of the 1968 Act and to the question of corporate criminal liability. Only the former aspect of the case is considered in this chapter, corporate liability being discussed in Ch 14 below at pp 555–560.

Wings Ltd v Ellis [1984] 3 All ER 577, [1984] 3 WLR 965, House of Lords

The Divisional Court had certified the following question as being of general public importance:

> 'Whether a Defendant may properly be convicted of an offence under Section 14(1)(*a*) of the Trade Descriptions Act 1968 where he had no knowledge of the falsity of the Statement at the time of its publication but knew of the falsity at the time when the statement was read by the complainant.'

The facts appear in the speech of Lord Templeman.

Lord Templeman. My Lords, this appeal raises a short question of construction of certain provisions of the Trade Descriptions Act 1968. Section 14, so far as material, provides:

> '(1) It shall be an offence for any person in the course of any trade or business—(*a*) to make a statement which he knows to be false . . . as to any of the following matters, that is to say . . . (ii) the nature of any . . . accommodation . . . provided in the course of any trade or business.
> (4) In this section "false" means false to a material degree . . .'

The respondent, Wings Ltd, was convicted by magistrates of an offence under s 14, that conviction was quashed by the Divisional Court and the prosecutor appeals to your Lordships' House.

In the course of its business as a tour operator, the respondent distributed to travel agents a brochure giving details of accommodation provided for the respondent's customers. Shortly after the brochure was distributed, the respondent discovered that the brochure contained a statement which was false to a material degree, namely that the accommodation provided at the Seashells Hotel in Sri Lanka was furnished with air-conditioning.

On 13 January 1982 Mr Wade, having read the brochure, booked, through a travel agent, a Wings holiday at the Seashells Hotel for three weeks beginning on 3 March 1982. The travel agent telephoned the respondent's sales agent to make a provisional booking and Mr Wade then signed the booking form which was included in the brochure acknowledging, inter alia, that he had read and agreed to certain conditions contained in the brochure. Mr Wade was not informed by the travel agent or subsequently by the respondent that air-conditioning was not provided at the Seashells Hotel and only made that disagreeable discovery for himself when he reached the hotel. The prosecutor alleged that the respondent had committed an offence under s 14 by making to Mr Wade a relevant statement which was false to a material degree and which the respondents knew to be false.

The respondent argued that on the true construction of s 14 it only made one statement, ie when it circulated the brochure; at that date it did not know the statement was false and therefore it never committed an offence. But the statement was repeated to Mr Wade by the uncorrected description of the accommodation at the Seashells Hotel contained in the brochure furnished by the respondent to Mr Wade in the course of the negotiations which were finalised by the respondent's acceptance of Mr Wade's booking. The 1968 Act was intended to ensure that the brochure was accurate and that Mr Wade was not misled. The brochure was inaccurate, the respondent knew that it was inaccurate and Mr Wade was misled. The ingredients for an offence under s 14 were compounded. To hold otherwise would be to emasculate s 14 and to place a premium on carelessness by the respondents which, as will appear, is the subject of express provisions contained in s 24 of the Act.

The respondent never intended to make a false statement to Mr Wade. The respondent had instructed its employee sales agent to inform the travel agent that, contrary to the brochure, the accommodation at the Seashells Hotel was not furnished with air-conditioning but with overhead fans. If all had gone according to plan, the respondent would not have committed an offence. The sales agent would have told the travel agent. In turn the travel agent would have told Mr Wade and the statement made by the respondent to Mr Wade would have been the statement in the brochure as orally corrected. In the events which happened, however, the respondent committed an offence under s 14 but without intending to do so. The 1968 Act makes provision for this possibility in s 24:

> '(1) In any proceedings for an offence under this Act it shall . . . be a defence for the person charged to prove—(*a*) that the commission of the offence was due to a mistake or to reliance on information supplied to him or to the act of default of another person, an accident or some other cause beyond his control: and (b) that he took all reasonable precautions and exercised all due diligence to avoid the commission of such an offence by himself or any person under his control.
> (2) If in any case the defence provided by the last foregoing subsection involves the allegation that the commission of the offence was due to the act or default of another person or to reliance on information supplied by another person, the person charged shall not, without leave of the court, be entitled to rely on that defence unless, within a period ending seven clear days before the hearing, he has served on the prosecutor a notice in writing giving such information identifying or assisting in the identification of that other person as was then in his possession . . .'

The respondent did not attempt to put forward a defence under s 24. In order to succeed in any such defence the respondent would first have been obliged to explain the introduction of a false statement into the brochure. There was a vague suggestion that this was a typographical error. The magistrates were not asked to decide and had no evidence on which to decide whether the respondents 'took all reasonable precautions and exercised all due diligence' in the employment and supervision of the blundering typist and the blundering proof reader. Moreover, it was certainly not clear that the respondent 'took all reasonable precautions and exercised all due diligence to avoid the commission' of an offence under s 14 after it discovered that the brochure contained a false statement. By relying on an oral correction being made by the sales agent and transmitted by the travel agent, the respondent accepted the risk of committing an offence under s 14. The respondent exposed Mr Wade to the serious risk that he would not be made aware of the correction and the added risk that he would not be able to prove that he had not been made aware of the correction. It may or may not have been practicable to send out correction slips to travel agents. In any event, if the respondent, on receiving the booking form signed by Mr Wade, had written to Mr Wade, if necessary through the travel agent, confirming the oral correction which ought to have been conveyed to Mr Wade and explaining that since the publication of the brochure the respondent had discovered that the Seashells Hotel was equipped with overhead fans but not with air-conditioning, then Mr Wade could have withdrawn the booking or accepted the correction and the respondent would not have committed an offence. In the course of argument before your Lordships, counsel for the respondent, on instructions, demurred to the suggestion that written confirmation of an intended oral correction was necessary to avoid the commission of an offence and advanced the explanation, illuminating and disturbing, that the brochure contained a large number of errors. But the 1968 Act is infringed and only infringed by statements which are false to a material degree and are known to be false and it is no comfort to Mr Wade to learn that other customers of the respondent might have been deceived by other false statements. It is impossible to determine whether a defence under s 24 would have succeeded because the respondent, no doubt for good commercial reasons, did not rely on any such defence. It was not open to the Divisional Court to invent a different defence, and to make its own dubious finding and to quash the conviction by asserting that when the respondent discovered that the statement in the brochure was false 'it immediately did all that could reasonably be expected in order to neutralise the error once it had been made'.

By creating a new criminal offence under s 14 Parliament indicated that the civil remedies for breach of contract and criminal sanctions for fraud are insufficient to protect the public against false statements in mass advertisements. It is necessary that the falsity should be known but by s 24 Parliament has indicated that good intentions and mistake do not by themselves constitute a defence. The accused must plead and prove the circumstances specified in s 24 before a defence of mistake can succeed. The 1968 Act, being clear, must be enforced.

My noble and learned friend Lord Scarman has courteously considered the complicated arguments advanced on behalf of the respondent and accepted in part by the Divisional Court. This case is another example of the importance of concentrating on the language and objects of an Act of Parliament; this case is another illustration of the desirability of the simple approach.

I would allow the appeal and answer the certified question in the affirmative.

Lord Scarman stated that 'the basic issue between the parties is whether on its proper construction s 14 (1) (a) of the 1968 Act creates an offence of strict, or more accurately semi-strict, liability or is one requiring the existence of full mens rea'. Having analysed the facts as stated in Lord Templeman's speech and referred to the issue of corporate liability (see below, pp 557–558) he went on to discuss the 'proper construction of s 14 (1) (b)' as follows:

My Lords, the subject matter and structure of the 1968 Act make plain that the Act belongs to that class of legislation which prohibits acts which 'are not criminal in any real sense, but are acts which in the public interest are prohibited under a penalty', as Wright J put it in *Sherras v De Rutzen* [1895] 1 QB 918 at 922, [1895–9] All ER Rep 1167 at 1169. In construing the offence-creating sections of the 1968 Act it will, therefore, be necessary to bear in mind that it may well have been the intention of the legislature 'in order to guard against the happening of the forbidden thing, to impose a liability upon a principal even though he does not know of, and is not a party to, the forbidden act done by his servant': see *Mousell Bros Ltd v London and North Western Rly Co* [1917] 2 KB 836 at 844, [1916–17] All ER Rep 1101 at 1105 per Viscount Reading CJ.

While, however, the subject matter of the 1968 Act is such that the presumption recognised by Lord Reid in *Sweet v Parsley* [1969] 1 All ER 347 at 349, [1970] AC 132 at 148 as applicable to truly criminal statutes, 'that Parliament did not intend to make criminals of persons who were in no way blameworthy in what they did', is not applicable to this Act, it does not necessarily follow that merely because an offence-creating section in the Act is silent as to mens rea its silence must be construed as excluding mens rea. As Lord Reid said, in the absence of a clear indication than an offence is intended to be an absolute offence one must examine all relevant circumstances in order to establish the intention of Parliament (see [1969] 1 All ER 347 at 350, [1970] AC 132 at 149).

What the relevant circumstances are may now be said to have been settled in a line of cases of which the greatest is *Sweet v Parsley* and the most recent is a decision of the Privy Council in a Hong Kong appeal, *Gammon (Hong Kong) Ltd v A-G of Hong Kong* [1984] 2 All ER 503, [1984] 3 WLR 437. At the end of the day the question whether an offence created by statute requires mens rea, guilty knowledge or intention, in whole, in part, or not at all, turns on the subject matter, the language and the structure of the Act studied as a whole, on the language of the particular statutory provision under consideration construed in the light of the legislative purpose embodied in the Act, and on 'whether strict liability in respect of all or any of the essential ingredients of the offence would promote the object of the provision': see *Gammon (Hong Kong) Ltd v A-G of Hong Kong* [1984] 2 All ER 503 at 507, [1984] 3 WLR 437 at 444–445 and *Sweet v Parsley* [1969] 1 All ER 347 at 362, [1970] AC 132 at 163 per Lord Diplock.

In the light of the foregoing it is now necessary to determine the proper construction to be put on the words of s 14 (1) (a). The necessary ingredients of the offence as formulated in the subsection are that (1) a person in the course of a trade or business (2) makes a statement (3) which he knows to be false (4) as to the provision in the course of trade or business of any services, accommodation or facilities. The respondent submits that the essence of the offence is knowingly making a false statement. The appellant submits that it suffices to prove that the statement was made on a person's behalf in the course of his business and that its content was false to the knowledge of the person carrying on the business.

My Lords, I accept the appellant's construction as correct. First, it advances the legislative purpose embodied in the Act, in that it strikes directly against the false statement irrespective of the reason for, or explanation of, its falsity. It involves, of course, construing the offence as one of strict liability to the extent that the offence can be committed unknowingly, ie without knowledge of the act of statement; but this is consistent with the social purpose of a statute in the class to which this Act belongs. And the strictness of the offence does no injustice: the accused, if he has acted innocently, can invoke and prove one of the statutory defences. Second, the appellant's submission has the advantage of following the literal and natural meaning of the words used. The subsection says not that it is an offence knowingly to make the statement but that it is an offence to make the statement.

The respondent's counsel, however, in support of his submission made a number of telling points. None of them is, in my judgment, strong enough to overcome the difficulties in his way. First, he relied on the general principles governing the interpretation of the provisions of a criminal statute. They are, however, for the reasons already developed, not applicable to this statute. Second, he submitted that he who makes a statement must as a matter of common sense know that he is making it. This is not so, however, when one is dealing, as in this statute, with statements made in the course of a trade or business. It would stultify the statute if this submission were to be upheld. Third, he contrasted the wording of para (*a*) with para (*b*). Paragraph (*b*) provides that it is an offence 'recklessly' to make the false statement. The inference arises, therefore, that the offence under para (*a*) requires proof of a deliberate false statement. This, with respect, I believe to be his best point, but it cannot prevail against all the indications to which I have referred in favour of the interpretation put on para (*a*) by the appellant.

But this is not the end of the respondent's case. There remains the question: did the respondent make any statement at all as to the air-conditioning of the hotel bedroom on 13 January when Mr Wade read it? The respondent's submission was that such a statement was made only once, on publication of the brochure in May 1981. The importance of the question is not only that the prosecution pinned its case to 13 January 1982 but that in May 1981 the company did not know the statement was false whereas in January 1982 it did know it was false.

This submission was not open to the respondent company before the magistrates or in the Divisional Court. The Court of Appeal had decided in *R v Thomson Holidays Ltd* [1974] 1 All ER 823, [1974] QB 592 that a new statement is made on every occasion that an interested member of the public reads it in a brochure published by a company engaged in attracting his custom. The court considered that communication is the essence of statement. My Lords, I think *R v Thomson Holidays Ltd* was correctly decided, even though I do not accept the totality of the court's reasoning. A statement can consist of a communication to another; and in the context of this Act and the circumstances of this class of business I have no hesitation in accepting the court's view that communication by an uncorrected brochure of false information to someone who is being invited to do business in reliance on the brochure is 'to make a statement' within s 14 (1) (*a*). But there can be statements which are not communicated to others. It was unnecessary for the Court of Appeal to hold that communication was of the essence, and to that extent only I think the court erred.

The respondent's case that it only made one statement, ie on publication of the brochure, is as fallacious in its way as is the view of the Court of Appeal that without communication there is no statement. I have no doubt that a statement as to the air-conditioning in the hotel was made when the brochure was published. But further statements to the same effect were made whenever persons did business with the respondent on the strength of the uncorrected brochure, which so far from being withdrawn continued to be the basis on which the respondent was inviting business. There is no injustice in this being the effect of the statute. If the respondent believed that there was no default on its part when the false description was communicated to Mr Wade, it should have admitted that the offence was committed and called evidence to establish a s 23 or s 24 defence. Instead, the respondent chose to argue that no offence had been committed at all, an argument which for the reasons I have given, I believe to be unsustainable.

Accordingly, I hold that the respondent company did make a statement as to the air-conditioning to Mr Wade on 13 January 1982. This conclusion renders it unnecessary to deal with the ingenious, if far-fetched, analogy which the respondent sought to draw between this case and your Lordships' analysis of a 'result crime' in the arson case of *R v Miller* [1983] 1 All ER 978, [1983] 2 AC 161, and which found favour with the Divisional Court. I will say only that to construe the words 'to make a statement which he knows to be false' in the context of this Act as being capable of covering a physical act of statement completed or perfected at a later date by a damaging result when it is read appears to me to be an unhelpful and over-elaborate approach to the interpretation of an Act intended to protect the public by provisions which the public can understand without a lawyer at their elbow. Making a statement consists of the act of statement. If it has consequences, so be it: the consequences are not the statement.

For these reasons I would make answer to the certified point of law as follows. A statement which was false was made by the respondent company in the course of its business when it was read by Mr Wade, an interested member of the public doing business with the respondent company on the basis of the statement. The offence was committed on that occasion because the respondent company then knew that it was false to state that the hotel accommodation was air-conditioned. The fact that the respondent was unaware of the falsity of the statement when it was published as part of the brochure in May 1981 is irrelevant. If the respondent believed it was innocent of fault, it was open to it to prove lack of fault. It did not do so.

Like my noble and learned friend Lord Brandon (whose speech in draft I have had the opportunity of reading), I cannot think, though I understand the genuine difficulties which faced the respondent, that it was improper to prosecute in this case.

I would allow the appeal.

Lord Keith of Kinkel and Lord Brandon of Oakfield delivered concurring speeches, Lord Brandon neatly pin-pointing a central issue thus:

In the present case, I regard the false statement about air-conditioning contained in the respondent's brochures as having been a continuing false statement, that is to say a false statement which continued to be made so long as such brochures remained in circulation without effective correction. I should regard a statement made in an advertisement exhibited on a street hoarding in the same way.

Being of the opinion that the certified question is ineptly expressed, I would amend it to read as follows: whether a defendant may properly be convicted of an offence under s 14 (1) (*a*) of the Trade Descriptions Act 1968 where he has made a continuing false statement, which he did not know was false when he first made it, but which, having come to know of its falsity at some later time, he has thereafter continued to make. Having amended the certified question in that way, I should answer it with a simple Yes.

I understand, however, that the rest of your Lordships are of the opinion that the certified question can be answered satisfactorily as it stands. On that footing, I agree with the answer to such question proposed by my noble and learned friend Lord Scarman.

I would only add that, in my opinion, there was nothing unreasonable, let alone improper, in the bringing of a prosecution against the respondent in this case.

Lord Hailsham, in his long and learned opinion concurred 'without qualification with the result' as expressed by Lord Scarman 'but arrived at the conclusion by a slightly different route and with feelings of somewhat greater sympathy with the respondent'. He dealt, in particular, with the making of the statement, knowledge of its falsity and the prosecution policy as follows:

The Divisional Court held (as it clearly was right to do if it were in point) that it was bound by the decision of the Court of Appeal, Criminal Division, in *R v Thomson Holidays Ltd* [1974] 1 All ER 823, [1974] QB 592. That decision is not binding on your Lordships' House, but it is relevant to consider how it was used by the Divisional Court (see [1984] 1 All ER 1046 at 1050, [1984] 1 WLR 731 at 737). *R v Thomson Holidays Ltd* itself arose from an attempt by the travel company to plead autrefois convict in respect of an indictment under s 14 (1) (*b*) (ii) of the 1968 Act. The company had already pleaded guilty to a breach of this section in respect of the same brochure in the previous year, but the new indictment was based on further complaints by two customers who had subsequently and separately booked holidays as the result of their reading of it. The Court of Appeal (in my opinion correctly) held that the two further readings by the two new complainants constituted two new 'statements' for the purposes of s 14 and therefore disclosed two new offences. But in the instant case the Divisional Court made use of the authority to establish the general proposition, taken, with respect, out of context from the judgment of Lawton LJ in *R v Thomson Holidays Ltd* [1974] 1 All ER 823 at 828, [1974] QB 592 at 597, that 'a statement is made when it is communicated to someone'. With respect, this needs further analysis. When, in the course of a trade or business, a brochure containing a false statement is issued in large numbers through a chain of distribution involving several stages, and intended to be read and used at all or some of the stages, it does not follow that it is only 'made' at its ultimate destination. It may be 'made' when it is posted in bulk, when the information is passed on by telephone or in smaller batches by post, and when it is read by the ultimate recipient, provided that at each stage what happens is in accordance with the original intention of the issuing house. The respondent made a valiant attempt to induce your Lordships to declare that *R v Thomson Holidays Ltd* was wrongly decided. In my view the attempt fails. It does not follow from this that a prosecution policy of excessive zeal involving repeated attempts to convict a firm in respect of each separate communication of an individual copy of a brochure ought to meet with anything but reprobation from the courts. That must depend on the circumstances.

. . .

It will be apparent from what I have already said that I have no difficulty at all in deciding that the statement was made at the time Mr Wade read the brochure, ie on 13 January 1982. The statement may also have been made at various other stages in the chain of distribution and was certainly made to other recipients. What renders the charge particularly objectionable to the respondent is that, at the time when Mr Wade read the statement, the respondent quite honestly believed that it would only be read by a member of the public in a corrected and therefore accurate form. The respondent had used its best endeavours to correct the statement and it genuinely thought that these had succeeded. It had succeeded down the chain as far as Sandra Leathers and, if her 's 9 statement' is correct, one stage further down the line than this. I am not sure, in view of the drafting of the case, that I am entitled to go this far, since the finding in the case does not proceed beyond the delphic sentence: 'Mr Wade was never informed of the lack of air conditioning either by the travel agent or by [the respondent], although the travel agent *might well have known*' (my emphasis). I will, however, assume in the respondent's favour, and I think it is probably the case, that no other finding than that the correction had reached the travel agent was open to the magistrates. But it did not reach Mr Wade, and there is an unambiguous finding to this effect. The statement was made both when it was issued and when it reached Mr Wade. It was in the form originally intended by the respondent. It had followed the chain of distribution intended by the respondent, and, when it reached its destination, it was false in a material particular. If this case had been a civil claim by Mr Wade in contract, there would have been no possible answer to it, and my own opinion, for what it is worth, is that a claim in the civil courts resulting in an adequate award of damages for inconvenience and a return of his money to Mr Wade might well have been a way of disposing of this matter far preferable to what has in fact occurred, since Mr Wade would have received damages adequate to recoup his estimated loss and something in addition to compensate for him for his disappointment: see *Jarvis v Swans Tours Ltd* [1973] 1 All ER 71, [1973] QB 233 and *Jackson v Horizon Holidays Ltd* [1975] 3 All ER 92, [1975] 1 WLR 1468. Without intending in any way to express a concluded view, it may well have been that if the respondent had made a prompt and generous offer of compensation when the error was first brought to its attention it would have saved itself a good deal of trouble and anxiety.

Fortunately or unfortunately the criminal law has been invoked. There would have been no possible harm in this if the charge had been simply of an absolute offence although, had the case been heard after 31 January 1983 when s 67 (1) (*b*) of the Powers of Criminal Courts Act 1983 came into effect (see the Criminal Justice Act 1982 (Commencement No 1) Order 1982, SI 1982/1857), I would have hoped that a compensation order would have been made in whole or in part in preference to a fine. Many of the offences created by the 1968 Act, for example those created by ss 1, 11, 12 and 13, to which I need not refer in detail, come clearly within the ordinary definition of an absolute offence. But offences under s 14 emphatically are not like these. Offences under s 14 require as an essential ingredient of the offence knowledge by the maker of the statement that it was false (s 14 (1) (*a*)) or recklessness in the making of it (s 14 (1) (*b*)). Any ordinary person reading the section would think that this ingredient was an almost classic statement that to be found guilty of this offence the maker of the statement must be fraudulent in the traditional sense, and anyone reading an account of the conviction after reading the section would think that the offender had been convicted of fraudulent conduct. I can fully understand the sense of outrage felt by the owners of a decent business who in my view were not, on the facts of the case, at all dishonest, and acted throughout in good faith, when they found themselves not only convicted of such an offence but fined £500, which is by no means a negligible penalty, on each of the two summonses on which they were charged.

. . .

Having said all this, I am bound to say that I am not at all happy about the position to which I have felt constrained to come, and, without criticising the authorities who mounted the present proceedings and persisted in the present successful appeal, I would say that there is room for caution by prosecuting authorities in mounting proceedings against innocent defendants. In the case of an absolute offence, the late Viscount Dilhorne had some very salutory remarks as to the considerations which prosecuting organisations ought to bear in mind before instituting proceedings in consumer cases (see *Smedleys Ltd v Breed* [1974] 2 All ER 21 at 32–33, [1974] AC 839 at 855–857) and I consider that they should be even more careful in cases which ordinary people would read as containing an implication of fraud, but where the offender was of excellent reputation and had acted honestly. Whatever else the 1968 Act was meant for it was intended to supplement and not to substitute the ordinary law of contract, and was not designed to bring on respectable traders who had acted honestly the reputation of having been guilty of fraudulent conduct of which in fact they were innocent.

But for these reasons and with these reservations I would allow the appeal. I would answer the certified question in the affirmative but with a qualification by saying, 'Yes, unless the defendant has raised a successful defence under s 24 of the 1968 Act and provided that the reading by the complainant was part of the chain of consequences intended and authorised by the defendant prior to its receipt by the complainant.'

Appeal allowed.

NOTE

For a further reference to the *Thomson Holidays* case in the context of compensation orders see above p 328. For further discussion of s 24, see below pp 552–562. For references to the discretion to prosecute see above p 445 et seq and *Smedleys Ltd v Breed* [1974] AC 839, [1974] 2 All ER 21, HL, below p 567.

Question

In the light of *Wings*, (a) to what extent is it still true to say that mens rea is a necessary ingredient of s 14, and (b) is it possible to deduce why the respondent, 'no doubt for good commercial reasons' (per Lord Templeman) chose not to rely on the defence provided by s 24?

Problems

1. Annabelle wishes to have her dress cleaned for her Graduation Ball. She takes it to Kleaneasy whose window display has long advertised, 'Try our 24 Hour Service'. What is the position under s 14 of the Act, if (i) Kleaneasy tells her, 'Sorry dear, we had to give that up weeks ago. I must take the sticker down'; (ii) Kleaneasy accepts the dress for a '24 Hour Service' knowing he is so over-committed that it is most unlikely that he will complete the work and then by a stroke of good fortune does so; (iii) Kleaneasy accepts the dress and his system which is usually very efficient breaks down so that the dress is uncleaned for the Ball?

2. The Blue Sky Travel Company publishes a holiday brochure in January 1984, advertising a 'package-holiday' based on the Hotel Carmen in Majorca. The holiday season runs from March to September and this is the first season in which the recently build hotel will be open to guests. In its brochure Blue Sky states that, (i) the hotel is 200 yards from the nearest beach; (ii) the hotel provides English style cooking; (iii) each room has a balcony with an uninterrupted view over the sea; (iv) there is a private swimming pool and (v) disco dancing every night. An artist's impression of the swimming pool with appropriately bronzed bodies features prominently in the brochure which contains the following statements in its booking conditions: 'Not all advertised facilities may be available during your holiday. Swimming pools may have to be closed for maintenance and other activities cancelled for lack of support. Majorca is a developing tourist centre and building operations may sometimes affect your enjoyment and the view from your hotel . . .'

On 1 February 1984 Maxwell reads the brochure and books a two-week holiday for himself and his family to begin on 15 April. When the Maxwells arrive at the hotel they have the following complaints: (i) although the hotel is 200 yards from the beach 'as the crow flies' there is a railway line in between and in practice a one-mile walk: the management of Blue Sky is aware of this fact; (ii) the food is cooked in a distinctly 'Spanish' style; (iii) their room has a balcony but the view over the sea is largely cut off by two enormous cranes which were erected on 15 March 1984 for use in building another hotel. The management of Blue Star was informed of this development on 20 March but did not tell its clients until their arrival at the hotel; (iv) the swimming pool, although under construction in January, has still not been completed; (v) disco dancing has been cancelled owing to lack of support.

Discuss Blue Star's liability under s 14 of the 1968 Act.

PROPOSALS FOR REFORM

The following are some proposals for reforming s 14 of the Act:

Review of the Trade Descriptions Act 1968: a report by the Director General of Fair Trading (Cmnd 6628, October 1976)

49.   Our conclusions at this stage may be summarised as follows:
   (i)   the consumer does not readily distinguish between statements made in relation to goods and statements made in relation to services; he is as easily misled by one as the other and his loss may be as great in one case as the other;
   (ii) so far as possible the sanctions against the false statements should be the same in both cases;
   (iii) a relaxation of section 1 would not be justified; harmonisation should, therefore, be effected by bringing offences in relation to services as far as possible into line with offences in relation to goods.

. . .

106.   Our further recommendations in regard to section 14 (ie additional to those already set out in paragraph 49) may be summarised as follows:
   (i)   it should be made an offence to supply any services, accommodation or facilities to which a description has been applied and which do not correspond with that description except that a person shall not be guilty of this offence if, before he provides any services etc, he takes reasonable steps to inform the intended recipient that this is so but that he will be providing services, etc which differ in certain respects;
   (ii) the provisions of sections 4 and 5 of the Act should apply *mutatis mutandis* to this offence;
   (iii) it should continue to be an offence to make false statements about the past or present supply of services etc;
   (iv) it should continue to be an offence to make false statements in respect of the future supply of any services, accommodation or facilities but only in the following circumstances;
         (a) where the falsity of the statement can be demonstrated at the time it is made, irrespective of whether the services etc are provided; or
         (b) where the statement involves holding out or undertaking that services etc will be supplied and the person making the statement can be shown to have no intention of supplying them, or no reasonable expectation that they can be supplied by him or any other person either at all or in the form that has been described;
   (v)   the offences at (i), (iii) and (iv) (a) should be absolute, subject only to the section 24 defences.

NOTE

No action has been taken to implement these proposals. For discussion of a private members' bill which lapsed see Harvey, 'False or Misleading Statements as to Services' (1983) Trading Law 99.

CHAPTER 13

False price claims and bargain offers

The principal controls over false or misleading price claims in relation to the supply of goods are to be found in the Trade Descriptions Act 1968, s 11, and the Bargain Offers Orders made under the Prices Act 1964.

Trade Descriptions Act 1968

This Act contains the following provision:

11. False or misleading indications as to price of goods
(1) If any person offering to supply goods of any description gives, by whatever means, any false indication to the effect that the price at which the goods are offered is equal to or less than—
  (a) a recommended price; or
  (b) the price at which the goods or goods of the same description were previously offered by him;
or is less than such a price by a specified amount, he shall, subject to the provisions of this Act, be guilty of an offence.
(2) If any person offering to supply any goods gives, by whatever means, any indication likely to be taken as an indication that the goods are being offered at a price less than that at which they are in fact being offered he shall, subject to the provisions of this Act, be guilty of an offence.
(3) For the purposes of this section—
  (a) an indication that goods were previously offered at a higher price or at a particular price—
    (i) shall be treated as an indication that they were so offered by the person giving the indication, unless it is expressly stated that they were so offered by others and it is not expressed or implied that they were, or might have been, so offered also by that person; and
    (ii) shall be treated, unless the contrary is expressed, as an indication that they were so offered within the preceding six months for a continuous period of not less than twenty-eight days;
  (b) an indication as to a recommended price—
    (i) shall be treated, unless the contrary is expressed, as an indication that it is a price recommended by the manufacturer or producer; and
    (ii) shall be treated, unless the contrary is expressed, as an indication that it is a price recommended generally for supply by retail in the area where the goods are offered;
  (c) anything likely to be taken as an indication as to a recommended price or as to the price at which goods were previously offered shall be treated as such an indication; and
  (d) a person advertising goods as available for supply shall be taken as offering to supply them.

TRADE OR BUSINESS?

Unlike ss 1 and 14, s 11 does not contain the limiting words 'in the course of any trade or business'. However in *John v Matthews* ([1970] 2 QB 443, [1970] 2 All ER 643) it was held by the Divisional Court that, in effect, the words must be implied. The section did not therefore catch a supply of goods by a working man's club to a member—it applied only to transactions of a commercial nature.

'OFFERING TO SUPPLY GOODS'

The offence is based on the wide concept of an offer to supply (as defined by s 6 of the Act, above p 466), rather than an actual supply. In other words the 'false indication' must be something which occurs in the process involving the offer to supply. Typically, the courts will distinguish between an indication of price in a contractual tender, which is the yardstick against which any subsequent price indication will be judged, and a purported post-contractual invoice accompanying a supply, but having no contractual or binding effect. This point was made in *Miller v FA Sadd & Son Ltd, Miller v Pickering Bull & Co Ltd* [1981] 3 All ER 265 (QBD). This decision was explained and followed in an unreported case on appeal by way of case stated from the magistrates' court. In *Simmons v Emmett*[1] transcript DC/557/81, reproduced in [1982] TL 189, Lord Lane CJ explained the facts as follows:

Simmons v Emmett [1982] TL 189, Queen's Bench Divisional Court

Lord Lane CJ. I will read the terms of the first information which is all that is necessary to give the correct idea of what the case was about. It reads as follows: 'On the 17th day of January 1980 at 35 Durham Road, Heston, she, in offering to supply goods namely double red carnation button-holes did give an indication by means of quotation, namely 60 pence each, likely to be taken as an indication that the said goods were being offered at a price less than that at which they were in fact being offered, namely 90 pence each, contrary to s 11 (2) Trade Descriptions Act 1968.'

The facts which gave rise to that information and the two similar informations which appear with it were these. The Respondent, Kathleen Emmett, carries on a flower business, particularly the supply of flowers for weddings. She learnt that the Clack family, who live at Heston, were anxious to have flowers for a wedding which was to take place in July of 1980, so she visited the Clack home on January 17, 1980 at the Clacks' request. The purpose of the visit was to enable the Clacks to discuss the flowers which they wanted to order for the July wedding.

The justices found that the Respondent presented to the Clacks a catalogue containing pictures of various flowers and flower arrangements, and after having looked at those Mr Clack placed an order for various flowers to be supplied for the wedding on July 5, that is to say in about six months' time.

We have the document which was made out by the Respondent at that time. It sets out a large number of different types of flowers which were ordered, and alongside each order is the price which was apparently being charged by the Respondent in respect of each type of flower. The three items which are the subject of informations in this case only form a small part of the document. They are to be found at the foot of the first page and read as follows: '4 double red car b'holes at 60' (that is, 60 pence) giving a total of £2.40, '4 single red car b'holes at 30' (that is 30 pence) giving a total of £1.20 and '130 single pink/white b'holes at 30' giving a total of £39. At the end of the second page, after all the items have been totalled up, the sum for payment is stated as £131.90. A £20 deposit had been paid, so there was £111.90 to pay.

So far there were no difficulties, but what happened was this. Come the day of the wedding, 5 July, 1980, the Respondent delivered to the Clack home the flowers as ordered and payment was then requested for an amount which was higher than that given in the document to which reference has just been made. The double red carnation buttonholes had increased in price from 60p to 90p each, the single red carnations had increased from 30p to 45p and the pink/white carnation buttonholes had also increased from 30p to 45p.

It was contended on those facts by the prosecutor that the offences had been made out as alleged in the three informations, but a submission was made to the justices that there was no evidence showing that the offences had been committed and, accordingly, the submission was that the Respondent should not be put in peril and was entitled to be acquitted.

---

[1] See O'Keefe, Trade Descriptions, 3 [I33.2].

To that submission the justices acceded. The case was dismissed and the suggestion now by the Appellant is that that decision was wrong and that there was evidence on which the justices could at least have called upon the Respondent for an explanation, and that they were wrong to accede to a submission of no case.

What the justices say in the case stated is this: 'We were of the opinion that (i) the Respondent did offer to supply goods even though those goods were not in existence at the time the offer was made. (ii) Upon our interpretation of s 11 (2) Trade Descriptions Act 1968 the Respondent did not come within the ambit of this section on the facts found. (iii) The offer to supply goods and the indication of the price must be made at the same time as the demand for the higher price and that the quotation given in January 1980 was only an indication of the likely cost in July 1980.'

They then posed for the opinion of this court two questions which, in the submission of Mr Underhill on behalf of the Appellant, are not referable to the case, a submission with which I myself would agree. The problem that we have to decide is simply this; whether on the facts as stated there was any evidence upon which the magistrates, directing themselves properly on the law, could come to the conclusion that the offence was made out.

The way in which Mr Underhill put the matter is this. He submits that the evidence that the charge when the flowers were delivered was higher than the quotation in the document which I read is evidence that at the time of the quotation and the apparent contract the charge set out in the document was not the real charge. In order to make this offence out there are three principal matters which have to be established by the prosecution. First of all, an offer to supply goods, secondly an indication that the goods are being offered at price x and, thirdly, there has to be proved an intention to supply the goods at that time at a price which is, in fact, higher than price x.

It seems to me the situation here was simply and solely this. There was an enforceable contract between these two people, Mr Clack on the one hand and the Respondent upon the other hand, that the flowers of the various types set out in the document would be supplied on July 5, 1980, at the various prices which are set out in that same document. The fact that at the time when the contracts came to be performed on July 5, a price higher than that set out in the document was demanded is to my way of thinking no evidence at all that at the time when this document first saw the light of day there was any intention on the part of the supplier to charge any price other than that set out. There was, it seems to me here, an offer at a price. The price at which the offer was made is that set out in the contract and there was no evidence of any other price being in existence at that time.

. . .

We were referred to . . . a decision of this court in which Mr Justice McNeill delivered the leading judgment. It is the case of *Miller v Pickering Bull & Co Ltd* [1981] 3 All ER 265. There, the respondents contracted with the local authority to supply fruit to schools at a price calculated by reference to the prices quoted in the fruit trade's official journal. In accordance with that contract the local authority asked the respondents to deliver a quantity of apples to a school which, in fact, were delivered the same day. The delivery was accompanied by an invoice which charged the local authority with a price for the apples which was higher than the contract price. The circumstances being somewhat similar to the present case the proceedings were taken under s 11 (2) of the 1968 Act.

If one turns to p 269 of the report, at letter J, one finds these words of Mr Justice McNeill: 'Thirdly, on the facts of this case the justices were entitled to find, as they did, that "the correct price was the contract price, as contained in the original tender of July 1979. From that it follows that the only false or misleading price was that which was contained in the delivery note. . . ." Accordingly, the indication in the tenders, which was continuing to the extent that the county council's requisitions concluded contracts at the prices based on the formula, was not false; the respondents did not give any indication at that time (whether likely to be taken as an indication or not) that the goods were being offered or were to be supplied at any price other than the price calculated in accordance with the formula. It was, at worst against the respondents, the invoice which was false, not the indication. The appellant was at all times obliged to pay only the contract price and was neither bound nor, if competently served by the officers of the county council, likely to be misled by the wrongly priced invoice. The correct answer was not these proceedings but a sharp reminder that the contract price was not accurately stated on the document.'

The final paragraph reads: 'Whilst the Trade Descriptions Act 1968 is a statute for the protection of consumers, it is also a penal statute; unless Parliament has made it plain that particular conduct is criminal, the courts and the enforcement officers should not seek artificial constructions of the statutory words to make it so. In this case the relevant conduct was supplying goods; the supply was in no sense coloured by misdescription. The justices were right to refuse to engraft on to this straightforward transaction rules inappropriate to it.'

The matter, if I may say so respectfully, could not be put more plainly. Those considerations apply precisely to the present case and, in my judgment, the justices were right in the conclusion which they reached, namely that there was no evidence which the respondent was called upon to answer and in dismissing the information.

Appeal dismissed

'EQUAL TO OR LESS THAN (a) A RECOMMENDED PRICE; OR (b) THE PRICE AT WHICH THE GOODS OR GOODS OF THE SAME DESCRIPTION WERE PREVIOUSLY OFFERED BY HIM'

There are two major points to note here. Firstly, s 11 (1) does not prohibit comparisons with recommended prices unless there is a *false* indication mentioned in the sub-section. However, in specified cases the Price Marking (Bargain Offers) Orders 1979 do prohibit even true comparisons with 'recommended' prices (see below, p 541). Secondly, sub-s (1) must be read with sub-s (3) which explains the constituents of the offence much more fully. In particular, and unless the contrary is expressed, a 'recommended' price is to be taken as that recommended by the manufacturer or producer for supply by retail in the area where the goods are offered, and an indication of a previously higher price is to be taken as an indication that the goods were so offered by the person giving the indication within the preceding six months for a continuous period of not less than twenty-eight days.

Some of the difficulties associated with the statutory presumptions and the onus of proof in relation to the offence created by s 11 (1) (b) are well illustrated by the following cases.

House of Holland Ltd v London Borough of Brent [1971] 2 All ER 296, [1971] 2 QB 304
Queen's Bench Divisional Court

The facts are set out in the judgment of the court.

Cooke J read the judgment of the court at the invitation of Lord Parker CJ. This is an appeal by way of case stated from a decision of the justices for Middlesex area sitting at Harrow whereby they convicted the appellants on 15 informations alleging offences against s 11 (1) (*b*) of the Trade Descriptions Act 1968. The point raised by the appeal is the same in regard to all 15 informations, and it is sufficient to refer to one of them by way of example.

That information alleged that in offering to supply a three-in-one sunchair bed at a price of 45s by means of an advertisement published in a newspaper dated 27 July 1969 the appellants gave a false indication, namely 'All prices FURTHER REDUCED' to the effect that the price was less than that at which goods of the same description were previously offered. Now s 11 of the Trade Descriptions Act 1968, so far as material, provides:

> '(1) If any person offering to supply goods of any description gives, by whatever means, any false indication to the effect that the price at which the goods are offered is equal to or less than . . . (*b*) the price at which the goods or goods of the same description were previously offered by him . . . he shall, subject to the provisions of this Act, be guilty of an offence . . .
>
> '(3) For the purposes of this section—(*a*) an indication that goods were previously offered at a higher price or at a particular price . . . (ii) shall be treated, unless the contrary is expressed, as an indication that they were so offered within the preceding six months for a continuous period of not less than twenty-eight days . . .'

The facts as found by the justices are sufficiently set out in the case.

Now in regard to the particular information which we take as an illustration, the appellants contended before the justices, and have contended in this court, that the indication as to price in the advertisement of 27 July had not been shown to be false, since there was no evidence before the justices whether the sunchair bed was offered by the appellants earlier than June 1969 and if so at what prices. The appellants contend that under the provisions of s 11 (3) regard must be had to the full period of six months immediately preceding the advertisement of 27 July, and that it was for the prosecution to establish the falsity of the indication in that advertisement by showing that the goods had not, for a continuous period of at least 28 days within that period of six months, been offered at a higher price than that indicated in the advertisement of 27 July.

The respondents say that the fallacy in the appellants' argument lies in reading s 11 (1) together with s 11 (3) in that way. The respondents say that the proper approach is to begin by applying s 11 (1) in isolation, reading para (*b*) of the subsection as referring to the offer which last preceded the offer which is said to be accompanied by the false indication. The respondents say that if on comparing those two offers in that way it appears that the indication accompanying the later of the two offers is false, the offence is established. They say that the offence is so established in this case. Subsection (3), according to the respondents' construction of the section, only becomes relevant if on comparing the two offers it does in fact appear that the earlier offer was at a higher price. In that event, say the respondents, sub-s (3) does come into play, and its effect is that the accused is nevertheless guilty of the offence unless the earlier offer was effective for a continuous period of 28 days during the six months preceding the date on which the false indication is alleged to have been given.

Now if s 11 (3) (*a*) (ii) is read in its natural and ordinary meaning, it applies to every indication that goods were previously offered at a higher price, save only where the contrary is expressed. The paragraph is saying what every such indication is to be taken to mean, unless the contrary is expressed in the indication itself. In the present case the words in the advertisement of 27 July which were relied on as giving a false indication were the words 'All prices FURTHER REDUCED'. It was not contended before the justices that the advertisement contained any express words which would exclude the application of s 11 (3) (*a*) (ii); and the argument before the justices proceeded on the basis that the words 'unless the contrary is expressed' were irrelevant to this particular case and could be ignored. We propose to begin by considering the matter on the same basis.

On that basis it seems to us, as we have already indicated, that s 11 (3) (*a*) (ii) is saying this: 'Whenever you have an indication that goods were previously offered at a higher price, that indication is to be taken to mean that they were offered at a higher price continuously for a period of at least 28 days during the period of six months preceding the indication.' Parliament is in effect attributing a statutory meaning to every indication that goods were previously offered at a higher price. One can well understand why this was thought desirable. If goods are offered at £10 apiece with an indication that they were previously offered at a higher price, it would defeat the purposes of s 11 if some stale and ephemeral offer at a higher price (eg an offer made five years previously, and open for one day only, at £11 apiece) had the effect of taking the indication out of the scope of the section.

The method which Parliament has chosen to get over this difficulty is to invest the indication with a statutory meaning. It is sufficient, in order to show the falsity of the indication, to prove that in its statutory meaning it is untrue. But it seems to us that this also involves the converse proposition, namely, that the indication is not shown to be false unless it is shown to be untrue when bearing its statutory meaning. It is the statutory meaning which has to be shown to be untrue in order to establish falsity for the purposes of s 11 (1).

It seems to us that the construction contended for by the respondents is contrary to the plain meaning of s 11 (3) (*a*) (ii), which by its terms applies to all, and not to some only, of the cases where there is an indication that goods were previously offered at a higher price. We further think that there is no sufficient warrant for the respondents' construction of s 11 (1) (*a*), which would confine the court, in cases where a false indication is alleged, to comparing the offer which was associated with that indication with the last previous offer made by the same offeror. We see nothing in the language of s 11 (1) to restrict the scope of the subsection in that way. The subsection may have to be applied in a wide variety of circumstances, including circumstances where the provisions of s 11 (3) (*a*) (ii) have no application at all. Further, we think that such a restrictive construction is inconsistent with the provisions of s 11 (3) (*a*) (ii) in cases where those provisions do in fact apply.

We are conscious of the fact that, on the construction which we have felt compelled to place on the section, the prosecution will in many cases have to discharge a fairly heavy burden in order to establish that an offence has been committed. It will be necessary for them to deal with the whole six months' period and to adduce evidence to show that during that period there was no offer at a higher price which continued for a period of 28 days. A good deal will depend on the nature of the business with which they are dealing, but bearing in mind that justices and juries are entitled to draw reasonable inferences from the primary facts proved, we are by no means convinced that the obstacles facing a prosecution will be insuperable. In the present case the difficulty arose from the fact that the evidence covered a period of two months only, and did not deal at all with the preceding four months.

So far we have dealt with this case, as the justices did, on the basis that the advertisement of 27 July did not contain any express words which would exclude the application of s 11 (3) (*a*) (ii). However, as an alternative to their main submission, the respondents have submitted in this court that the true meaning of the words 'All prices FURTHER REDUCED' in that advertisement is that it is a plain statement that all prices have been reduced since the last previous advertisement, which on the evidence available before the justices was 4 July. To put the matter another way, it is said that the advertisement of 27 July by its express language means simply this: 'We were offering these goods at a higher price on July 4'. On that basis it is said that s 11 (3) (*a*) (ii) is by its terms excluded, that the statement in the advertisement of 27 July is false, and that an offence has accordingly been committed.

We are by no means satisfied that the advertisement of 27 July can be said by its express terms to bear the meaning which the respondents thus attribute to it, and in any event we are reluctant to make a finding of fact on a matter which the justices never considered and were not invited to consider. Accordingly we think that the alternative submission of the respondents also fails. It follows that the appeal must be allowed and the convictions quashed.

Appeal allowed.

Westminster City Council v Ray Alan (Manshops) Ltd [1982] 1 All ER 771, [1982] 1 WLR 383, Queen's Bench Divisional Court

Ormrod LJ. This is an appeal by case stated by the prosecutor from a decision which was made by Mr Branson, metropolitan stipendiary magistrate sitting at Wells Street on 5 May 1981, when he found the respondents not guilty on eight informations which had been preferred against them in respect of a shop which they own at 100 Oxford Street, London W1, under the Trade Descriptions Act 1968. It raises two interesting points and, if I may say so, it has been admirably argued on both sides, and we are grateful.

The first information was laid under s 14 of the Trade Descriptions Act 1968. . . .

The other seven informations were laid under s 11, which makes it an offence if any person offering to supply goods gives any false indication as to the price at which the goods are being offered.

His Lordship dealt with the information laid under s 14 (see above p 510) and continued:

Quite a different question arises under the seven informations laid under s 11. The relevant parts of s 11 read as follows:

'(1) If any person offering to supply goods of any description gives, by whatever means, any false indication to the effect that the price at which the goods are offered is equal to or less than . . . (*b*) the price at which the goods or goods of the same description were previously offered by him; or is less than such a price by a specified amount, he shall, subject to the provisions of this Act, be guilty of an offence . . .'

The factual background relied on by the prosecution to establish those seven informations is this. It is only necessary to deal with one of them because the others are all precisely the same. What is alleged is that from 19 July 1979 until 10 January 1980 advertisements were placed in the public press advertising this time 'Thousands of Fantastic Reductions' and offering for sale various articles, one example of which was cotton casual sweaters at 75p each. The prosecutor says that cotton casual sweaters had not been offered for sale by the respondents at a higher price than that at any time *at their shop at 100 Oxford Street.*

The respondents, however, say that, while that is true, these actual cotton casual sweaters had previously been offered for sale at other shops which they run at Rotherham and Leeds at a price of £1.50 and £1.00. Therefore, they say that these articles had been offered by them at a higher price and accordingly they say they had not committed an offence within s 11 (1).

It is unquestionably right, as the magistrate held, that on the words of the section, read in their ordinary sense, they had not committed an offence. They had indicated that the price at which the goods were being offered was less than the price at which the same goods had previously been offered by them within the relevant time.

Counsel for the appellants, however, contends that that section should be read as though it contained further words to the effect that 'the identical goods or goods of the same description must have been previously offered by the shopkeeper at the same shop at a higher price'.

While one can understand the point that the appellants have in mind very clearly, I find it impossible to construe s 11 (1) as if those additional words 'at the same place' or 'at the same shop' were inserted in it.

Counsel for the appellants also submitted that, alternatively, the words 'any person' in that section should be read in a limited way, limited in the same sense by reference to the place where the goods are being offered for sale. The same comment applies, in my judgment, to that submission.

My conclusion, therefore, is that, it having been established that the respondents had previously offered these identical articles in their other shops at a higher price, then they have not committed an offence under s 11 (1), and accordingly I agree with the stipendiary magistrate in respect of this part of the case as well. Accordingly, I would dismiss the appeal.

Woolf J. I agree that the appeal should be dismissed, saying 'I have nothing to add to what Ormrod LJ has already said on the second point raised in the appeal.'

Appeals dismissed.

Questions

1 Would the position have been the same if the statement 'Thousands of Fantastic Reductions: Now £x' had appeared on the shop window at 100 Oxford Street as well as in the press?

2 Consider the following case: Hammer owns some twenty 'Do it Yourself' shops in the Warwickshire area. On 1 March 1984 all his shops display signs proclaiming 'Giant Sale, Prices Slashed'. There are further signs within the stores saying 'Goya Gloss Paint Further Reduced. Now only £3.50 per litre'. In nineteen of the Hammer shops the price of Goya paint had never been higher than £3.50 per litre. In the twentieth shop the paint was priced at £3.20 per litre from 1 February to 1 March, and at £3.70 per litre from 1 January to 1 February.

Discuss Hammer's criminal liability under the 1968 Act.

NOTES

1. The price comparisons permitted by Article 3(2) (a) (i) of the Price Marking (Bargain Offers) Order 1979 require the comparison to be with 'a particular price . . . charged in the ordinary course of business on the same or other identified premises . . .' See below p 542.
2. It seems that the disclaimers which are impliedly permitted by the words 'unless the contrary is expressed' (s 11 (3) (a) (ii)) need not state what the contrary indication is. So such general statements as, 'These goods have not necessarily been on sale at a higher price for a period of 28 days' are sufficient to displace the statutory presumption. See also below p 539.
3. For a controversial case in which a jury at Wood Green Crown Court found that Sainsbury's had committed an offence against s 11 (1) (b) through their 'Discount '81' campaign, see *R v J Sainsbury Ltd* (1983) 91 ITSA Monthly Review 45.

The company had argued that 'discount' did not mean 'less than a price previously charged', but rather that goods within the scheme were priced lower than they would otherwise have been, or lower than competitors.

Of the two suggested meanings which is the more natural?

'ANY INDICATION LIKELY TO BE TAKEN AS AN INDICATION THAT THE GOODS ARE BEING OFFERED AT A PRICE LESS THAN THAT AT WHICH THEY ARE IN FACT BEING OFFERED'

The above is the essence of the offence contained in s 11 (2). Following a long line of cases, of which *Pharmaceutical Society of Great Britain v Boots Cash Chemists (Southern) Ltd*[1] is the best known example, a display of goods at a certain price is an invitation to treat rather than an offer capable of being accepted and enforced by the customer under the law of contract (see above p 59). However the notion of 'offering to supply' is defined much more widely by s 6 of the present Act which states that, 'A person exposing goods for supply or having goods in his possession for supply shall be deemed to offer to supply them'. Consequently it is likely that an offence will have been committed if the price advertised is less than the price asked. Furthermore on conviction the disappointed customer may request a compensation order against the shopkeeper under the provisions of the Powers of Criminal Courts Act 1973, as amended (see above pp 326–330).

An example of where the price advertised was less than the price asked (because VAT was added) occurred in *Richards v Westminster Motors Ltd*[2]. This and other cases were fully reviewed in the following case:

Clive Sweeting v Northern Upholstery Ltd[3] **(1983) Trading Law Reports 5, Queen's Bench Divisional Court**

The issue was whether an advertisement of three-piece Dralon suites for £699 which in fact applied only to one colour, other colours being more expensive, gave rise to an offence under s 11(2).

Mr Justice Forbes: This is a prosecution appeal by way of case stated by the Justices for the County of Humberside acting in and for the Petty Sessional Division of Scunthorpe when sitting at the court house in Scunthorpe.

On October 6, 1981 an information was preferred by the present appellant against the respondent, charging them on February 14, 1982 at Grimsby in the county of Humberside in offering to supply certain goods, namely an 'Envoy' three piece suite, did give an indication by means of an advertisement in the Grimsby *Evening Telegraph* of February 14, 1981, which was likely to be taken as an indication that the goods were being offered at a price, namely £699, which was less than the price, namely £739, at which they were in fact being offered, contrary to s 11(2) of the Trade Descriptions Act, 1968.

The second information was preferred against the respondent in the same terms except that it referred to an advertisement in *The Star* of March 6, 1981 and charged an offer on that date.

The magistrate found the following facts:

(a) That the respondent company is a manufacturer and retailer of furniture, which has retail premises situated at Bridge Street, Brigg, South Humberside.

(b) That an advertisement placed by the respondent company in the Grimsby *Evening Telegraph* dated February 14, 1981 and *The Star* dated March 6, 1981, indicated that the Envoy three-piece suite in superb Dralon could be purchased for £699.

(c) That the Envoy suite was available for purchase at £699 in peach king (beige) only.

(d) That the Envoy suite was available at that time in a range of colours and coverings from £595 to £1,299.

(e) That Joan Susan Keightley on February 16, 1981 chose and arranged to purchase an Envoy suite in Dralon in either green, mink, brown or rust colour for the sum of £739.

(f) That the respondent company advertised the same offer on Yorkshire television showing the Envoy suite at £699, which advertisement showed the Envoy suite in a

---

[1] [1952] 2 QB 795, [1952] 2 All ER 456, and [1953] 1 QB 401, [1953] 1 All ER 482.
[2] [1976] RTR 88 (QBD).
[3] (1982) Times 23 June.

beige coloured covering, when seen on a video recorder at the hearing. The recording was in colour, apparently correctly tuned. The advertisement was accompanied by a sound recording which gave no indication that the advertisement applied to beige suites only.

As I understand the matter, no point turns on that last finding of fact, though Mr Gripton for the appellant maintains that it was wholly irrelevant and I think that must be right.

The magistrates then set out a précis of the evidence given. I think one should refer very briefly to the evidence of Mrs Keightley, the person who actually bought the suite. It appears from her evidence that having seen the advertisement in the Grimsby *Evening Telegraph*, she and her husband went to the Bridge Street showrooms of the respondent company to look at the three-piece suite on display. They decided that they preferred the Envoy suite, although she says at the time she did not connect it with the advertisement. The manager completed an invoice and quoted the price of £739.

It was only when she got home that she looked at the advertisement again and recognized the suite she had purchased as the one which was being offered apparently at £699. She then complained to the Trading Standards Department of the Humberside County Council.

After dealing with the evidence the magistrates go on: 'It was contended by the appellant that the advertisement which appeared in both the Grimsby *Evening Telegraph* and *The Star* was such that the advertisement gave an indication likely to be taken as an indication that the goods were being offered at a price less than that at which they were in fact being offered; in that the Envoy suite was only available at the stated price of £699 in peach king (beige) and thus the advertisement contravened s 11(2) of the Trade Descriptions Act, 1968.'

. . .

Paragraph 4 reads: 'It was contended by the respondent that the advertisement was not misleading and did not contravene s 11(2) of the Trade Descriptions Act, 1968 in that the Envoy suite was available at £699, as shown in the advertisement, albeit only in beige, and indeed it was also available at a price less than £699, namely £595.'

. . .

The nub of the matter is concerned with the meaning of s 11(2) of the Trades Descriptions Act 1968. The questions which the Justices posed for the opinion of the High Court . . . were as follows: '(ii) whether the facts upon which the said Justices dismissed the information were such that the said Justices could properly have arrived at their decision.

(iii) Whether an advertisement suggesting a price for an article, namely an Envoy suite, is likely to be taken as an indication that the goods were available at that price contrary to s 11(2) of the Trade Descriptions Act, 1968, when in fact only a particular colour of suite was available at that price, other colours costing £40 more than the price advertised. Nothing in the advertisement indicated that the price was limited to only one colour, but suites in this colour were available for purchase at the advertised price'.

One should perhaps go straight to s 11 of the Trade Descriptions Act, 1968. Sub-s (1) provides for a different situation and it is sub-s (2) with which we are concerned. It reads: 'If any person offering to supply any goods gives, by whatever means, any indication likely to be taken as an indication that the goods are being offered at a price less than that at which they are in fact being offered he shall, subject to the provisions of this Act, be guilty of an offence'.

I think I should also read s 6: 'A person exposing goods for supply in his possession for supply shall be deemed to offer to supply them'.

It is against that statutory background that this matter has to be decided. I point out straightaway that the important words in sub-s (2) of s 11 raise the question of whether the indication is likely to be taken as an indication that the goods are being offered at a price less than the price at which they are in fact being offered. That is the nub of the section; is the indication likely to be taken as an indication of that kind?

The matter is not free from authority. In 1972, in the case of *Doble v David Greig Limited* this court had to consider a rather interesting case in which bottles of Ribena with a label on it (sic) were displayed in a self-service store. The label said: 'The deposit on this bottle is fourpence refundable on return'. At the cash desk, which was some way away from the place where the bottles were stacked, there was a notice: 'In the interests of hygiene we do not accept the return of any empty bottles. No deposit is charged by us at the time of purchase'.

What happened was that the shopkeepers were charged with a similar offence under s 11(2) and the Justices dismissed the information. The Divisional Court allowed the appeal on the basis that the shopkeeper should in fact have been convicted of that offence.

That case was followed in subsequent cases, and we have referred to two reported cases. The first is *Richards v Westminster Motors Limited* [1976] RTR p 88. It was a case concerned with an advertisement for a secondhand motor vehicle which did not indicate that the price was net of VAT. VAT had to be paid on it and the person who had advertised the motor car at the lower price was charged with an offence under s 11(2).

In that case the Divisional Court approved the decision in *Doble v David Greig* and referred to the judgment of Mr Justice Ashworth, who gave the leading judgment in that case. I think it is sufficient if I read a short passage from the judgment of Mr Justice Ashworth in the *Doble* case, followed in the *Richards* case. He said: 'It would be perfectly simple for Parliament merely to enact that a person by whatever means represents, or indeed gives an indication, and stop there, and that would involve any court called on to consider it with the question whether what was said or done or displayed was a representation or an indication, and no doubt in many instances opinions might differ. But in order to spread its net more widely, and as I think to protect customers more carefully, Parliament chose wider language, and what was enacted was that a person who gives by whatever means any indication likely to be taken as an indication that the goods are being offered at a price and so on. The words "likely to be taken as an indication" seem to me quite plainly to involve a wider consideration than the single word "indication". One is looking, if I may say so, at the customers and the effect on the customers of whatever is said or done or displayed. If it is likely to be taken as an indication to the effect stated, then the conditions of the subsection are fulfilled.'

It is the emphasis on looking at it from the point of view of the customer which I think is important. In a very short judgment in the same case I was concerned with a point which arose on that case which was that the indication was an equivocal indication, or could be taken as equivocal. What I said in relation to that is this: 'If it is reasonably possible that some customers might interpret the label as an indication of that kind, it seems to me that an offence is committed, even though many more customers might in fact take the opposite view. In other words the Act requires a shopkeeper, and this seems to me to be important, to take pains to resolve possible ambiguities, and if they are not adequately resolved an offence is committed'.

There was another case following that called *Read Bros Cycles (Leighton) Limited v Waltham Forest London Borough Council* [1978] RTR 397. Again *Doble v David Greig* was followed on approval and both the passages to which I have just referred from the judgment of Mr Justice Ashworth and myself were followed with approval.

That was a case concerned with an advertisement for a motor-bicycle for a particular price. When the young man who wanted to buy it wished to trade in his own bicycle in part exchange he was told that the motor-bike for sale would cost him another £40 over the advertised price. Again, the Justices had dismissed the information and the Divisional Court said they were wrong to do so and allowed the appeal.

The principal question which arises, therefore, in this case is simply this: Was it likely that the advertisement would be taken as an indication that all the Envoy suites offered for supply, whatever their colour, were available at the advertised price of £699?

We have been shown the advertisements, and they are not quite the same. The advertisement in the *Evening Telegraph* shows a picture of a three-piece suite, buttoned and upholstered. In a cloud of smoke from a miniature cannon at the bottom appear these words: 'The Envoy. All that's best in upholstered furniture. Superb Dralon quilted and buttoned by hand. The finest trimmings and polished arm facings tell a story of true quality. Just look at the price—£699 and 12 months free credit'.

There is other material in the advertisement. For instance, it says: 'Choose any item from Northern Upholstery's wide range—suites from around £300 to £2,500. Northern Upholstery are No 1 in the North for upholstered furniture. We make the bulk of what we sell in our own Doncaster factory'. The advertisement in *The Star* has a box on the picture of the same suite in which it says: 'The Envoy. Superb Dralon true quality. £699 and 12 months free credit'.

The question is whether either of those advertisements is likely to be taken as an indication that all the Envoy suites offered for supply, whatever their colour, were available at £699. I put in the words 'all the Envoy suites offered for supply' because it is quite plain from the facts that the respondents had in their possession for supply in their showrooms Envoy suites in superb Dralon in four other colours. Under the provisions of s 6 they must be deemed to offer for supply that particular description of suite in five colours.

Against that background it seems to me to be very difficult to come to any other conclusion than this, that any ordinary person faced with that advertisement would say to himself 'I can buy an Envoy suite at that price in superb Dralon', and so on. It is quite plain that no reasonable person could necessarily assume that he could buy the Envoy suite upholstered in any other material because the advertisement is confined to the suite upholstered in what is called Superb Dralon.

We have seen a price list of the various suites available from the respondents. The various materials with which they are upholstered are indicated because there are a whole set of different three and four piece suites which may be purchased with different names attached to them. Each of them can be purchased in a different range of furnishing materials from standard Dralon to hide. As one might expect, all those different materials attract different prices. Price in the range, upholstered in material described as superb Dralon in the advertisement, for this particular Envoy suite was put down as £739.

The truth of the matter, as one understands it, is that the respondents had on hand an oversupply of the Envoy suites in beige or peach king as they call it. They had ordered too many, had too many upholstered in that particular colour. They were, therefore, anxious to get rid of them in order to reduce their stock of that colour. That is why they were prepared to offer them at a price of £40 less than the other colour. But not a word of that appears in the advertisement. I return to the question that I suggested should be posed: Was it likely to be taken as an indication that all Envoy suites offered for supply, whatever their colour, were available at the advertised price? I find myself only able to answer the question in the affirmative. Mr Harris, who has argued the case for the respondents with great skill, has suggested that it is sufficient if there was available in the showrooms a suite corresponding with the description in the advertisement at the advertised price. There is no doubt that there were such suites available. There were beige suites available at the advertised price. But there were other suites properly described as Envoy suites in Superb Dralon but in different colours which were offered for supply at a higher price.

That argument, that it is a sufficient defence if there are available for sale some goods which correspond with the description and the price in the advertisement, was raised in a case called *Nattrass v Marks & Spencer Limited,* unreported, a decision of this court consisting of Lord Justice Ormrod and Mr Justice McNeill, delivered on June 25, 1980. What happened in that case was that the well known store, Marks & Spencer, in their food department, had one of those freezer cabinet. On the freezer cabinet there were display cards indicating prices. On one ticket it said 'Lower price 10 cod fish fingers'. The price of 53p was struck out and the price of 49p substituted and 'until April 1' added.

Inside the cabinet the packets of fish fingers each had a little ticket on them with the price written on it. In most cases the price was 49p, but on some of them the old price of 53p was still shown; some members of the store had forgotten to put another sticker over it. The inspector, as he was fully entitled to do, carefully selected examples of the higher price and took them to the check-out. The girl looked at the price ticket and rang up 53p for each of the packets of fish fingers. On those facts Marks & Spencer were charged with a similar offence under s 11(2).

The magistrates directed themselves exactly as Mr Harris suggested is a legitimate way of directing themselves, namely: because the majority of the packets of goods was priced in accordance with the display tickets no offence was committed even though a minority of the packets was wrongly priced.

Lord Justice Ormrod said: 'The magistrates must have misdirected themselves by asking themselves the wrong question. When they came to give their reasons they stated first, that the display tickets were "not misleading" in that the majority of the packets of goods were priced in accordance with the display ticket. In my judgment that is not the question they should have asked themselves. It is not a question of misleading, they simply had to ask themselves the question set out in s 11(2) in relation to the particular packets in question'.

You can formulate, on the basis of the facts of this case, precisely the same question that I suggested the Justices should have asked themselves in the present case; namely, was the label saying 'Fish Fingers 49p' likely to be taken as an indication that all the fish fingers in the freezer compartment were offered for supply at 49p and not 53p? If they had asked themselves that question they would have come up undoubtedly with the answer 'No'. All the fish fingers were not at the price indicated and, therefore, the advertisement was likely to be taken as an indication that they all were. They all were not, and therefore, an offence was committed.

It was suggested by Mr Harris that in the present case in so far as the magistrates passed on this matter in para 6 of the case, they were indicating in some way that there was a local variation, as it were, in relation to suites of furniture; in that locally everybody would understand that a suite of furniture might have a different price according to its colour. What they said was: 'The advertisements in question were not misleading nor were the witnesses misled, because the Envoy suite could be purchased for £699, albeit in one particular colour only'. As I have indicated, that approach seems to be negated by the case of *Nattrass.*

The magistrates went on: 'Further that it is eminently reasonable that different colours and grades of covering material would affect the price'. But we are not concerned with that matter. The grade of covering material was expressed in the advertisement. It is only the question of the different colours.

I must confess I can find nothing to indicate that the Justices were directing their minds to any question of colour variation in local understanding. I do not think it is right to suggest they were. For the reasons I have given it seems to me that faced with the question which they ought to have asked themselves, any reasonable bench of magistrates would have been forced to come to the conclusion that in this case an advertisement which indicated that the suites were available at a particular price, without any indication that it only referred to suites of a particular colour, was an advertisement likely to indicate that all the suites in the showroom were available at the advertised price, irrespective of the colour in which they were upholstered.

For those reasons the Justices were wrong and I think the appeal should be allowed and the matter should go back with a direction to convict.

[Griffiths LJ agreed that the appeal should be allowed and the case remitted to the magistrates with a direction to convict.]

Appeal allowed.

NOTE

The offence created by s 11(2) of the Act depends on establishing that the 'indicated' price is lower than the price at which the goods are *in fact* being offered. However precisely what constitutes this latter (and higher) price may not always be clear beyond argument. The case of *Nattrass v Marks & Spencer Ltd* (1981) 89 ITSA Monthly Review 211, noted by Forbes J, adopted the same approach as that of Mr Recorder Gorman QC in *J Sainsbury Ltd v West Midlands County Council* (1982) 90 ITSA Monthly Review 58. A different view was taken by His Honour Judge David QC in *Manley v Marks & Spencer Ltd* (1981) 89 ITSA Monthly Review 212 (Chester Crown Court). A display board indicated that fish fingers had been reduced in price from 34p to 31p, but the price on the packet was 34p and this was the price which the trading standards officer was charged. There was a similar discrepancy in relation to sprouts. Allowing an appeal against conviction, Judge David said:

> So the conclusion we have reached is this. On the evidence we have heard it is perfectly clear that the only price at which those fish fingers and the sprouts should have been sold was the promotional price. No-one had any authority to charge any more than the promotional price. Therefore it is that the assistant—who must unfortunately have been a little inexperienced—charged the price marked on the box, presumably because she did not realise that the correct price was the promotional price. But the fact that she charged the price marked on the box does not necessarily mean that that was the price at which the goods were, in fact, being offered. The evidence clearly establishes that the price at which they were, in fact, being offered was the promotional price.

Consider the following case:

Ada goes into the Downtown Supermarket to buy a chicken, having seen the following notice stuck on the window, 'Chickens Now Only 50p per lb'. She buys a chicken labelled '4lbs 2oz: £2.70' and presents it to the cashier. Assuming the weight to be stated correctly, has an offence against s 11(2) been committed? If so, precisely when was it committed? What is the contract price?

THE DIRECTOR GENERAL OF FAIR TRADING'S PROPOSALS

The attempt to control undesirable practices relating to pricing by s 11 has, by common consent, been at best partially successful. Some of the criticisms have related to price comparisons not caught by s 11 and other suggestions for reform have been made. These are noted below. Although the following proposals have been somewhat overtaken by events they retain their interest and contain a helpful discussion of the problems associated with the section.

Review of the Trade Descriptions Act 1968, a report by the Director General of Fair Trading (Cmnd 6628) (October 1976)

PRICE OF GOODS

. . .

Comparisons with a previous price
211. Section 11(3)(a) provides that unless the contrary is expressed an indication that the goods were previously offered at a higher price or at a particular price should be treated as meaning that they were so offered for a continuous period of not less than 28 days in the preceding six months. The purpose of these provisions is clearly to ensure, so far as possible, that comparisons with previous prices are meaningful in that they relate to prices charged for a reasonable period of time in the recent past. The provisions also have the effect of preventing goods specially 'bought-in' for sales from having fictitious previous selling prices attached to them to suggest that they have been reduced when this is not the case. However, the existing provisions have three weaknesses: first, they present enforcement authorities with a formidable task in the detection and proof of an offence since it is necessary to monitor prices over a long period of time; secondly, they permit a misleading impression to be given of how prices have changed; and thirdly, an apparent price reduction may mask a real price increase.
212. We think that the first point is self-evident, but it may be helpful if we illustrate the other points by quoting as an example goods marked '£12—£11'. This price tag is within the law provided that the goods were offered at £12 for at least 28 days even though the 28 days was at the start of the preceding six month period and are currently offered at £11. Nevertheless the price may have fluctuated considerably during the intervening period and may, in the period immediately preceding the current offer, have been less than the current offer. This situation seemed to us to be unsatisfactory, and in the Consultative Document we suggested that the Act should be amended so that the 28 day period should immediately precede the reduction in price and that the six month period should be reduced to three months. This tightening-up was intended to ensure that only genuine reduced price offers could be made without some further qualification explaining the real circumstances. At the same time, we thought that the provision would become more easily enforceable by reducing the amount of checking needed to detect offences. . . .
213. Nearly everyone who responded to our invitation to comment on this suggestion considered that our solution was the wrong one. Trade bodies objected to the shortening of the period and the new requirement in regard to the 28 day period because these would inhibit claims being made in respect of seasonal goods, taken off display and then brought back at the start of the next season. Enforcement bodies said that, even with the shortening of the periods, enforcement would continue to present an insoluble problem. At the same time a strong body of opinion expressed the view that the only practicable way to ensure that a trader's comparison with his previous prices was truthful was to place the onus of proof on the trader making the claim.

. . .

215. . . . We appreciate that to impose such an obligation in this case would mean that traders must keep records of the prices at which goods have previously been offered in order to show enforcement officers that the claims being made are correct. It might be that this would discourage some traders from offering price reductions, but we do not believe there would be any significant fall in the number of genuine price reductions. However, in dealing with comparisons with previous prices we are dealing with a situation in which all the information which would establish whether the comparison is true or false is peculiarly within the knowledge of the person making the claim. If he is unable to produce the proof that his claim is justified, it can scarcely be denied that he should not have made it in the first place, and we recommend, therefore, that section 11(3)(a)(ii) should be left unchanged, but that any person accused of an offence under section 11(1)(b) should be convicted of that offence unless he can prove that he in fact charged the higher price in the relevant period.
216. One particular aspect of the previous price problem arises from multiple outlets in the

same ownership. At the present time a supplier owning two or more retail outlets may indicate in shop A that a particular article was previously sold at a higher price when, in fact, the higher price was never charged in that shop at all, but in another shop B which may not only be a considerable distance away but possibly in an area where retail margins are normally higher than in the area of shop A.

. . .

219. . . . We recommend therefore that the provisions of section 11(3)(a)(i) should be amended so that, unless there is an express statement to the contrary, an indication of a previous higher or particular price should be taken to be the price at which the goods concerned were offered in those premises. Unless some special provision is made, implementation of this proposal could give rise to special difficulties for mail order traders who may in law be taken to offer their goods in the home of the reader of the advertisement or catalogue. We think that mail order traders should continue to be free to make comparisons with their earlier catalogues or advertisements, and the amendment of the section should provide for this to be done.

220. In considering this question, our attention was drawn to the varying interpretations which are being put on such expressions as 'normal price', 'usual price', 'regular price', etc. It appears that in trade circles these expressions are sometimes used to represent the going price in other traders' shops. We think that those buying the goods are more likely to regard these expressions as an indication that the price concerned is that trader's normal, usual or regular price. If there is any doubt that a court would so interpret them, we recommend that the Act should be amended to ensure that such indications are taken to be indications of a previous price charged by the trader using them.

Some other comparisons

221. False or misleading comparisons may be made with other suppliers' prices expressed in general terms, for example 'price elsewhere £3, our price £2'. Such claims may well induce sales, and if false, should be an offence. Even if the claim is true, this kind of statement could mislead if the other supplier concerned is many hundreds of miles away and the price levels ruling there are different from those in the area where the comparison is made. Alternatively, there may be false or misleading comparisons made with a named supplier's price for example 'Smith's price £3, our price £2'. Finally there are comparisons with an alleged worth or value of the goods. The latter type of claim is increasingly being made as more and more traders seek to compete with one another by suggesting that their particular goods represent more of a bargain than their competitors'. It is certainly arguable that some form of control is needed over the multiplicity of price comparisons in regard to goods which do not fit within the present framework of section 11.

Possible extension of section 11

222. One obvious solution to some at least of these problems would be a general prohibition on false or misleading price comparisons. There has been a general prohibition of this kind in Canadian legislation for some 15 years. In its latest form this runs as follows:

> 'No person shall, for the purpose of promoting, directly or indirectly, the supply or use of a product or for the purpose of promoting, directly or indirectly, any business interest, by any means whatever, . . .
> (d) make a materially misleading representation to the public concerning the price at which a product or like products have been, are or will be ordinarily sold; and for the purposes of this paragraph a representation as to price is deemed to refer to the price at which the product has been sold by sellers generally in the relevant market unless it is clearly specified to be the price at which the product has been sold by the person by whom or on whose behalf the representation is made'[1].

According to such information as we have been able to collect, this provision in earlier and slightly different forms is considered to have exercised considerable restraint on the use of misleading comparisons with the price charged generally in the area concerned for the goods in question or those of a comparable nature.

. . .

228. Owing to our doubts about the way in which a general prohibition on the lines of the Canadian legislation would adapt to British conditions, we have a slight preference for an amendment of the Act to cover comparisons with 'any other price', and we recommend that

section 11(1) should be amended to include a new paragraph (c) to deal with this. Our study of Reports by the Director of Investigation and Research suggests that the Canadian legislation has been effective in dealing with indications that goods are supposed to sell for much higher than the actual selling price, and a version of the Canadian provision may be successful in controlling such practices here.

229. Whatever improvements may be made in the Trade Descriptions Act in regard to price comparisons, there will still be matters which could more appropriately be dealt with under Part II of the Fair Trading Act 1973.

Rental/hire purchase transactions

230. There appears to be some doubt whether an indication of the monthly or other cost of a rental transaction is covered by the pricing provision of the Act. We think that statements of this kind should come within the ambit of the Act; and provided that no legal difficulties arise, we recommend that indications of the cost of rental—and other types of transactions including hire purchase—should be treated as indications of price and suitably covered by the Act. In making this suggestion we do not, of course, intend any reduction in the protection which the Consumer Credit Act 1974 provides in this field.

. . .

PRICE OF SERVICES, ACCOMMODATION OR FACILITIES

234. Our enquiries have shown that a number of prosecutions have been brought under section 14 where the alleged offence was that the price of services, accommodation or facilities has been misrepresented. The basis on which these cases rested seems to have been that a trader who does not provide services, etc as described at the price he quotes for them is making a false statement, either about the provisions of the services, or the nature of the services he provides. However some observers take the view that section 14 is simply the counterpart of sections 1 and 2 of the Act, and as there is no specific counterpart of section 11 which deals with false indications of the price of goods, false indications of the price of services are not covered by the Act. We are in no doubt that the Act ought to cover false or misleading indications of the price of services, etc and we propose that this be done by amending section 11 so that considerations similar to those applying to the supply of goods apply to the provisions of services, accommodation and facilities, so far as they are appropriate.

DISCLAIMERS

235. Whereas there is no specific provision in the Act for the use of disclaimers in regard to descriptions of goods or services (except perhaps by the implications of sections 4 and 5 which provide that factors making it reasonable to suppose that a description has been applied to goods have to be taken into account), section 11 expressly provides for their use in regard to indications of price. For example the various assumptions which section 11(3) makes about indications of price are only to be made 'unless the contrary is expressed'. We therefore looked at the use of disclaimers anew in regard to section 11, considering how far our general conclusions in regard to disclaimers were valid in this context; whether the principles established by *Norman v Bennett and Another* and the other cases mentioned in Chapter VI had any relevance to the use of section 11 disclaimers; and whether the existing provisions in the section were satisfactory.

236. The special problem that arises in regard to section 11 disclaimers stems from the interpretation which is being placed on the words 'unless the contrary is expressed'. This is being taken as allowing a general negation in the form of notices on the following lines:

'Some reduced articles have not been on sale at the higher price for a continuous period of not less than 28 days in the preceding six months'.

Such notices are in our view most confusing since the customer has no way of knowing which, if any, of the goods on- offer at the reduced price has ever been offered—more than ephemerally—at the higher price quoted. The consumer has therefore no means of distinguishing between any regular merchandise marked down, and any merchandise specially bought-in for the sale and which has never, effectively, been offered at the higher price shown. The use of general disclaimers in the form mentioned above defeats one of the main objectives of section 11 which was to ensure that specially bought-in goods are not passed off as regular merchandise which has been genuinely reduced.

237. It could well be that many disclaimers that are made—including the one mentioned

above—are not effective in law since the usual practice is to exhibit them in windows or place them generally about the shop and they are thus not associated with particular goods. It would be possible to meet criticisms by removing altogether the possibility of disclaiming the assumptions written into the section. If this were done the only comparisons with previous prices, for example, which would be permitted would be those where the goods *had* been offered for a continuous period of at least 28 days in the preceding six months. However as this would prevent a trader claiming the credit for reductions made in other circumstances, for example where the goods had been offered at the higher price for less than 28 days, there is a risk that it would discourage traders from making reductions in these other circumstances. Since it is not our intention that the Act should inhibit genuine reductions of any kind, nor prevent traders making any truthful statements about them, we reject this solution to the problem.

238.   Another solution would be to require that, if a disclaimer is made, it must be specific rather than general, that is, it must be directly associated with the goods to which it relates and must also state the true situation. In other words, in regard to disclaimers about prices, the Act would specifically lay down the principles which the various judgments mentioned in Chapter VI appear to have established in regard to disclaimers in respect of trade descriptions.

239.   We advocated the adoption of this course in the Consultative Document, but on reflection we think that it would be better to avoid specific legislation and to leave interpretation to the courts as this would permit them to exercise the same degree of discretion in regard to disclaimers on prices as we suggest they should have in regard to disclaimers of trade descriptions (paragraph 166). Thus we put forward no proposal for the amendment of section 11(3) in regard to disclaimers as such; but, as in the case of disclaimers of trade descriptions, we think that there would be an advantage in taking powers to regulate price disclaimers in general, or in respect of the prices of specific goods, etc by statutory order to take care of any future difficulties that may arise.

1.   Section 36(1)(d) Combines Investigation Act.

NOTES

1.   This Review was itself reviewed by Gordon Borrie, the present Director General of Fair Trading: see 'A Review of the Trade Descriptions Act 1968' [1975] Crim LR 662.

2.   For a possible argument that price is a trade description within ss 1–6 of the Act, above pp 464–465, see *Cadbury Ltd v Halliday* [1975] 2 All ER 226, [1975] 1 WLR 649 (QBD) where it was held that the words 'extra value' on bars of chocolate were not trade descriptions within s 2(1) of the Act.

3.   In recent cases the courts have not looked favourably at attempts to apply s 14 of the Act to misleading price claims about goods and services (para 234 of the above report): see *Newell v Hicks* (1983) above pp 509–513.

4.   For a further broadly based provision similar to the one noted in para 222 see the Australian Trade Practices Act 1974, s 53, which provides in part that

> A corporation shall not, in trade or commerce, in connexion with the supply or possible supply of goods or services or in connexion with the promotion by any means of the supply or use of goods or services—. . . (e) make a false or misleading statement with respect to the price of goods or services . . .

Bargain offers

INTRODUCTION

A bargain offer is usually thought of as an indication either stated or implied about other prices with which the price to be paid is being compared. In para 229 of the 'Review of the Trade Descriptions Act 1968', above p 539 the Director General recognised that, 'Whatever improvements may be made in the Trade Descriptions Act in regard to price comparisons, there will be matters which could more appropriately be dealt with under Part II of the Fair Trading Act 1973'. The subsequent history of the matter is taken up in the following extract from a major review.

Review of legislation on false and misleading price information: report of the Inter-Departmental Working Party (Department of Trade and Industry, 1984)

1.8 . . . These ideas were elaborated in the DGFT's 1975 consultative document entitled 'Bargain Offer Claims', which proposed action under Part II of the Fair Trading Act to control the terms in which such offers were made.

1.9 The consultative document attracted extensive comment from interested parties. The DGFT modified his original proposal and, in 1978, made two formal recommendations to the Secretary of State. The first applied to bargain offer claims (excluding comparisons with recommended retail prices) and the second only to claimed reductions from recommended retail prices (rrps). The DGFT recognised that detailed control of bargain offers would be complex to operate. But he considered that the only bargain offers which should be permitted were those which helped the consumer to make a properly-informed choice by providing information about the price asked for a product or service, which was both clear and relevant to the consumer's assessment of the trader's offer. He hoped that such action would protect consumers from misleading and confusing claims, and channel competition away from meaningless and irrelevant claims.

The Bargain Offers Order (1978–83)

1.10 In October 1978, Ministers announced the start of consultations on a proposed Order, broadly along the lines recommended by the DGFT, but under s 4 of the Prices Act 1974 (as amended) rather than the Fair Trading Act which was considered to be too inflexible for this purpose. . .'

The above consultation led to the Price Marking (Bargain Offers) Order 1979, SI 1979/364, as amended, made under powers in s 4(3) of the Prices Act 1974. Some aspects of this Order have been widely criticised as unduly obscure, and in an answer to a Parliamentary Question on 29 February 1980 the Minister of State for Consumer Affairs said that she recognised 'the problems which traders face and am anxious to avoid placing burdens upon them. However, I am equally concerned to ensure that misleading price and value claims should be prohibited.' See 979 HC Official Report (5th series) written answers col *796*. The above review by the Inter-Departmental Working Party attempts to meet the above points and extracts from its conclusions and recommendations are printed below. First however it is necessary to look at the scope of the Order.

THE BARGAIN OFFERS ORDERS

These orders prohibit comparisons with recommended prices in specified sectors where such prices are virtually never charged and thus are misleading. The sectors which are now listed in the Schedule to the Price Marking (Bargain Offers) (Amendment No 2) Order 1979, SI 1979/1124 are beds, electrically powered and similar domestic appliances and apparatus, consumer electronic goods, carpets and furniture. Inevitably it is likely that any such list will fail to cover all areas of potential abuse and no doubt readers can point to other areas which are not included.

The other main price comparisons controlled by the 1979 orders include those mentioned in para 221 of the 1976 'Review of the Trade Descriptions Act 1968', above p 538. The structure of the principal order (which applies to bargain offers relating to services as well as to goods) is complex. The main provisions affecting goods are as follows:

The Price Marking (Bargain Offers) Order 1979, SI 1979/364

. . .

2. Regulation of bargain offers

(1) Subject to paragraph (2) below, a person who indicates that—
  (a) any goods are or may be for sale by retail; or
  (b) any services (except services which he indicates are or may be provided only for the purposes of businesses carried on by other persons) are or may be provided,
shall not, on or in relation to those goods, indicate a price for their sale or, in relation to those services, indicate a charge for their provision, in such a manner that the indication includes a statement to which this article applies.

(2) Nothing in this article applies—
  (a) to a person who gives an indication of a price or charge only as—
    (i) a compiler of a report or survey relating to prices or charges comprising that price or charge and other prices or charges, or
    (ii) as a publisher or distributor of a publication or as an exhibitor or broadcaster of a cinematograph film or radio or television broadcast comprising the indication,
    not being a manufacturer or supplier of any goods to which, or a person who provides services to which, the indication relates; or
  (b) to a statement relating to a maximum permitted price or charge which is indicated pursuant to any enactment or Community obligation (whenever passed or created).

3. Bargain offers relating to goods

(1) Subject to the following provisions of this Order, article 2 above applies, in relation to a price, to any statement (however framed and whether express or implied) that the price indicated is lower than—
  (a) a value ascribed to goods, not being the amount of such a price as is mentioned in sub-paragraph (b) below; or
  (b) the amount of another price for the sale of goods of the same description (whether that price is, or is not, specified or quantified or is, or is not, a price which has been charged, indicated or proposed by any person).

(2) Sub-paragraph (b) of paragraph (1) above does not apply—
  (a) to a particular price which the person giving the indication—
    (i) proposes to charge or has charged in the ordinary course of business on the same or on other identified premises, or
    (ii) has reasonable cause for believing has been charged in the ordinary course of business by another identified person in identified circumstances and has no reason for believing has ceased to be a price at which that person is prepared to do business in those circumstances,
    including in each case a price for the sale of goods of the same description in a specified different condition or quantity;
  (b) to a particular price applicable to the sale by the person giving the indication of goods of the same description—
    (i) upon specified different terms as to the time or manner of payment (including the provision of credit by any person either generally or to persons of a specified class or description),
    (ii) in specified different circumstances,
    (iii) in a specified different condition or quantity, or
    (iv) to any person who is not within a class or description of persons for sales to whom the indicated price is expressed to apply; or
  (c) in a case where the indicated price applies to goods when supplied with other specified goods or with specified services, to a particular price for the sale of the goods without those other goods or services or with other specified goods or services.

. . .

5. Recommended and similar prices and charges
(1) In relation to any goods or services other than goods or services of a description for the time being specified in the Schedule to this Order, article 3(1)(*b*) above does not apply to the amount of a price and article 4(1)(*b*) above does not apply to the amount of a charge which, in either case, is recommended or suggested by any person in the course of business.
(2) In relation to any goods which are exempt goods for the purposes of the Resale Prices Act 1976, article 3(1)(*b*) does not apply to the amount of the price for the sale of those goods.

6. Treatment of additional goods or services
Where, in relation to an indication of price for the sale of any goods or of a charge for the provision of any services—
    (a) an indication is also given that other goods or services will or may be supplied with the first mentioned goods or services; and
    (b) no consideration in money is ascribed to the supply of those other goods or services,
the indication shall not, in relation to those other goods or services, include any statement of a description which would be prohibited by this Order if it were made in relation to the first mentioned goods or services.

. . .

The cases which follow have been concerned to interpret these complex provisions.

West Yorkshire Metropolitan County Council v MFI Furniture Centre Ltd [1983] 3 All ER 234, [1983] 1 WLR 1175, Queen's Bench Divisional Court

The respondent furniture company inserted two advertisements in the press. One stated that it was selling a Nicole six-drawer chest at £24.95, which it described as a 'bargain price' and 'Britain's lowest price'. The other stated that it was selling a Welsh dresser at £69.95, which it described as a 'special clearance price'. The Company was charged and convicted in respect of both advertisements as contravening arts 2(1) (a) and 3(1) (b) of the Price Marking (Bargain Offers) Order 1979 by indicating that the price of goods was 'lower than . . . the amount of another price for the sale of goods of the same description.' The Crown Court allowed the appeals in respect of both advertisements and the prosecutor appealed to the Divisional Court. In the case of the first advertisement the Crown Court had placed itself in the position of an ordinary shopper and found that such a person 'would not necessarily come to the view that "bargain price" meant the price offered was lower than another price for something of the same description; he might feel that he was getting an advantageous price in the sense of good or excellent value for money'. In the judgment of the Divisional Court this was the correct approach to adopt. The Crown Court's conclusion in favour of the respondents was regarded as one of fact rather than law and it was not appropriate to interfere.

Robert Goff LJ. . . . I turn, therefore, to the second of the two cases. This raises a different question, which is one of construction of the order. There is no doubt that this question is one of law. I have already set out the matters complained of. The words used in one case were 'Special clearance offer' and in the other were 'End of range clearance price'. The approach urged on us by counsel on behalf of the appellants is a very simple one. If you use those words, you must be indicating that the price is lower than the amount of another price for the same goods of the same description. Therefore the case is caught by art 3(1) (*b*). Furthermore he submits, and this is accepted by counsel for the respondents, that the case does not fall within any of the exceptional cases in art 3(2), so this is a case where plainly the court below should have convicted.

But they did not. They set out their reasons in para 5 of the case stated. This is what they said:

    'The Appellants argued, and the Respondents conceded, that the statements "Special Clearance Offer" and "End of range clearance price" meant that the price at which the particular goods were offered for sale had been purposely reduced to clear the stock, and so amounted to statements that the price indicated was lower than the amount of another price, namely the price for the goods before the reduction.'

Pausing there, 'So far so good', said counsel for the appellants. Then the case continues:

'The Appellants contended that, accordingly, the offences had been proved. The Respondents argued that the offences were not made out because the statements complained of referred to the amount of another price *for the sale of the same goods*, not "for the sale of goods of the same description" within the terms of the Order.'
(My emphasis.)

In para 6 the court below said:

'We were not convinced that the statements complained of offended the Order. On the facts agreed, it offended our common sense to say there had been an infringement in these circumstances. Accordingly, we allowed the appeal and quashed the convictions.'

It is possible to feel considerable sympathy with the reaction of the court below. It can be argued that, as a matter of common sense, there was nothing wrong in what the respondents were doing, because they were indicating quite plainly that this was a clearance sale and there can be nothing wrong in indicating that fact to the general public. But I fear that, in a case of this kind, we are not concerned just with common sense. We have to apply the order. There may be reasons of policy which explain why the order was drafted in its present form. It would have been perfectly possible for Parliament, if it thought right, to have included in the exceptions in art 3(2) a fourth exception to deal with this very point with which we are now concerned. They have, however, not done so, which I find very striking. So counsel for the respondents was compelled to fall back on the general words and submit that as a matter of construction, the present case does not fall within the order.

May I refer again to the relevant words of the order. The offence is committed if 'the price indicated is lower than . . . the amount of another price for the sale of goods of the same description . . .' Counsel for the respondent says: 'This was not such a case, because these were the very same goods, not goods of the same description.' In my judgment, such a submission really flies in the face of reality. Let me take the case of a vendor of goods who has 30 articles of the same description, all of which are sitting in his basement because he has not been able to sell them. He puts them up for sale as a special clearance offer. Clearly he would be indicating that the price of those goods or each of them was lower than the amount of another price for the sale of goods of the same description. That would be an almost classic example of a case where the statute applies. I cannot see how the situation would be any different if there was only one article of goods in the basement to which the offending words were applied. The same principle would apply. In other words, the words 'goods of the same description' embrace in this context a particular item of goods which is marked down, so to speak, as against itself.

So I find myself differing from the court below on the construction placed by them on art 3(1)(*b*) of the order in relation to these particular advertisements. The questions posed for our consideration are as follows:

'(1) Whether, in relation to exhibit 1 and the advertisement of a "Welsh Solid Pine Dresser", it was open to the Crown Court to conclude that the statement "End of range clearance price" did not amount to a contravention of the said Order.'

I would answer that question No.
The next question is:

'(2) Whether, in relation to exhibit 2 and the advertisement of a "Welsh Dresser", it was open to the Crown Court to conclude that the statement "Special Clearance Offer" did not amount to a contravention of the said Order.'

Again I would answer that question No.
Question (3) reads:

'Whether a statement, within the meaning of Article 3(1) of the said Order, that the indicated price of goods is lower than the amount of another price for the sale of the same goods is a statement that the price indicated is lower than the amount of another price for the sale of goods of the same description within the meaning of Article 3(1)(*b*) of the said Order.'

I would answer that question Yes.

McNeill J. Agreed.

Appeal dismissed in the first case. Appeal allowed in the second case.

NOTE

Department of Trade 'Notes For Guidance' on the interpretation of the orders contain the following statement:

> 'The Order does not prohibit a trader from comparing the price of particular goods with the price at which he has previously been seeking to sell the *same* goods where it is clear that there is no implied comparison with the price at which *similar* goods have previously been sold eg a furniture dealer may compare the price of a single suite of furniture with the price at which he originally offered it for sale. He will, however, commit an offence under the Trade Descriptions Act if he has not maintained the original price for at least twenty-eight days in the previous six months . . .

Questions

1. In the situation envisaged by Robert Goff LJ, in the above case would the position be the same (i) if the item which was marked down against itself was unique, for example a second-hand car or an antique, or (ii) in the Department of Trade's example of the single suite of furniture?
2. Which, if any, of the following statements imply a lower price or a price reduction (as opposed to a good bargain) within art 3(1)(b): 'Outstanding Value £x', 'Warehouse Prices £x', 'Special Purchase Price £x', 'Only £x', 'Just £x', 'Now only £x'?
3. Are either (or both) of the following advertisements offences by virtue of art 5 of the order, (i) 'Free trip to Paris worth £100 when you buy our micro-computer price £500', (ii) 'An XY luxury fitted kitchen with a Free dishwasher worth £300. Send for our catalogue now'?

Comet Radiovision Services Ltd v Williamson [1983] 1 WLR 766, Queen's Bench Divisional Court

The facts are set out in the judgment of the Court.

Ackner LJ read the following judgment of the court. On March 18 1982, two informations were laid by the prosecutor on behalf of the Kent County Council Trading Standards Department against the defendants, Comet Radiovision Services Ltd. The first information alleged that on December 31, 1981, at Canterbury, the defendants did indicate that certain goods, namely, a Creda Cavalier electric cooker was for sale by retail and in relation to those goods indicated a price for their sale in such a manner that the indication included a statement to which article 2 of the Price Marking (Bargain Offers) Order 1979, as amended, applied, namely, the statement, 'Comet January Sale . . . Sale Price £194.90,' contained in a display card contrary to the said article 2 and paragraph 5 (1) of the Schedule to the Prices Act 1974. The second information made a like allegation in relation to an Electrolux RA120 refrigerator where the statement in the display card read, 'Comet January Sale . . . Sale Price £64.50.'

. . .

It is of course common ground that the defendants' display card contained by implication a statement that the price indicated was lower than the amount of another price for the sale of goods of the same description within the meaning of article 3 (1) (*b*) of the Order. However the defendants contended that the statements fell within the exemption allowed by article 3 (2) (*a*) (i) of that Order, so as not to be statements to which article 2 of the Order applied. They called evidence and satisfied the justices that they had advertised the goods in question for sale in their price lists displayed in their Canterbury shop over the period immediately preceding the sale—November 29, 1981, to December 24, 1981, inclusive—at a price in respect of each article higher than the sale price. The period of the sale was from December 28, 1981, until February 6, 1982. They contended that on the true construction of article 3 (2) (*a*) (i) of the Order a person should be taken to propose at any time to charge a particular price for the sale of goods of the same description if before that time he had given notice by display or advertisement of his intention to do business at that price.

The contention for the prosecutor was that article 3 (2) of the Order only allowed a statement that the price indicated was lower than the amount of another price for the sale of goods of the same description, where the other price was specified in or calculable from the price statement made by the retailer. In short, the sale ticket had to make a comparison between the sale price and the previous higher price. The prosecutor further contended that upon a true construction of articles 3 (2) (*a*) and 7 (2) (*b*) of the Order a person could only make the comparison of price allowed by article 3 (2) (*a*) (i) if he showed that at the time he made the statement he had charged the particular price for the sale of goods of the same description in the ordinary course of business in the past or proposed to do so in the future. Thus, two quite distinct points are raised and we will seek to deal with these separately.

1. *Does the higher price have to be recorded on the statement which indicates that the goods are being offered at a lower price?*

Nothing would have been simpler than to provide, in terms, in article 3 (2) (*a*) that the particular price is to be stated in the statement. Mr Stone, however, contends that this is provided for by the use of the word 'particular' qualifying the word 'price' in article 3 (2). In our judgment this is making an excessive demand upon that one simple adjective. 'Particular' in this context means no more than special as opposed to general. The trader must be able to point to a particular—that is an actual or definite—price for the price comparison. Clearly the draftsman did not intend 'particular' to mean specified or quantified, since those very words are used in article 3 (1) (*b*).

We accept that it makes good sense to oblige the retailer who is purporting to have a sale to record on his price tickets the non-sale price. This enables the potential customer to make a judgment as to the nature of the bargain which he is being offered and it immediately identifies the higher price, the genuinessess of which the retailer must establish if challenged. However, if this is what the legislature desires to impose, and impose by penal legislation, it must make its meaning clear. Mr Stone is unable to point to any other language to be found in this or in any other article in the Order to support his contention. We accordingly find that the justices who accepted his submission were in error. This however is not the end of the matter, because there is a second point.

2. *Can a person be said to propose at any time a particular price or charge merely because before that time he has given notice by display or advertisement of his intention to do business at that price?*

It is common ground that there was no actual sale of either item in question at the defendants' premises during the period referred to above when they were advertised at prices higher than the sale prices. True, the goods were in stock and if a customer had so requested he could have purchased them at the advertised prices. In order to appreciate the consequences of this situation it is necessary now to look at article 7 (2) which defines for the purposes of the Order certain of the expressions used in article 3 (2). Article 7 (2) reads:

> 'For the purposes of this Order, a person shall at any time be taken—(*a*) to propose a particular price or charge only if at or before that time he gives notice by display, advertisement or other public notice of his intention to do business at that price or charge at or after a date specified therein or after a period so specified; and (*b*) to have charged a price or made a charge only if before that time he has sold or agreed to sell goods at that price or has performed or agreed to perform services for that charge.'

It follows that, on the facts here, there can be no question of the defendants having 'charged' a particular price. Mr Kemp, however, submits that although the word 'proposes' to charge in article 3 (2) (*a*) (i) may appear to envisage a future event, the mandatory definition provided by article 7 (2) (*a*) covers the situation where his clients have in the past given notice by display or advertisement of their intention to do business at that price. We cannot accept this submission. The words of article 7 (2) (*a*), 'before that time,' relate to the giving of the notice. It cannot relate to a proposal. Clearly a notice can be given in the past for a proposal as to the future. A retailer may advertise that the price at which he is offering the goods will be increased by £X on and after a date in the future—the not unfamiliar advertisement, 'Pre-Budget prices until the end of April.' The scheme of the Order is that any price with which the marked price is to be compared must be a genuine and not a fictitious price. If the trader relies on a past price he has to show that he has actually done business at that price and not merely that he has offered the article at a price at which no one was prepared to buy. If he relies on a future price, that is a price which he proposes to charge, he has to show that he has genuinely advertised it at that price, and he can only do that if the advertisement is put out either before or at the time of his proposal to charge the future price. Accordingly, we cannot accept the defendants' contention that a person should be taken to propose at any time to charge a particular price for the sale of goods of the same description merely because before that time he has given notice by display or advertisement of his intention to do business at that price.

It follows that the defendants were rightly convicted and we accordingly dismiss this appeal.

Appeal dismissed.
Prosecution costs out of central funds.

NOTE

In relation to the 'first point' discussed by Ackner LJ compare the view expressed in the Department of Trade, 'Notes For Guidance':

> *Article 3 (2)* defines the types of bargain offer statement permitted by the Order. Points to note are:
> (i) paragraphs (a) to (c) require any comparison to be with a *particular price*, thus precluding generalised and vague comparisons such as 'save up to 40 per cent on our previous price for these items', 'you could pay up to 50 per cent more in the high street', and '50 per cent off list price'. The particular price with which comparison is made must either be stated or be calculable—thus '10 per cent reduction, only £1' is permitted but 'reduced—only £1' is not. . . .

Questions

1. In relation to the 'second point' consider the following case. Suppose that in January 1984 Comet's display card in its Canterbury branch had read, 'January Sale: Creda Cavalier Cooker . . . £194'. If in January 1983 a customer had agreed to buy a cooker at the then advertised price of £214 but had failed to take delivery, would Comet have been liable under the order? If it had been prosecuted under the Trade Descriptions Act 1968, s 11, what requirements would it have had to satisfy to avoid liability?

PROPOSALS FOR REFORM

The general complexity of the Bargain Offers orders is well illustrated by the fact that the views expressed in the Department of Trade 'Notes For Guidance' proved to be at variance with subsequent decisions of the courts on several crucial points (see above pp 543–547). The complexity of the law in this area was one of a number of factors leading to demands that it be subject to further review. Undoubtedly the other principal factor was disquiet at its apparent capacity to catch the general advertising slogans of such respectable companies as Sainsburys and Debenhams. In addition the law was difficult to enforce especially in relation to the oral claims of market traders (see Robin Young, 'Shops that are still breaking the law', *The Times* 21 January 1981) and, in such areas as furniture and carpeting, easy to avoid by the use of meaningless comparisons with 'ready assembled prices', 'special order prices' 'after sale prices' and the like.

The various proposals for reform now seem to have culminated in the 1984 Inter-Departmental report. Previously there had been a further report by the Director General of Fair Trading entitled 'Review of the

Price Marking (Bargain Offers) Order 1979' (1981) in which the Director General had recommended that the order be strengthened. The 1984 review is very comprehensive and the following extract points to some of its conclusions and recommendations:

Review of legislation on false and misleading price information: report of the Inter-Departmental Working Party—summary of conclusions and recommendations

. . .

Conclusions

(1) It would be wrong for traders who provide false or misleading information to secure thereby custom at the expense of other traders; not only does this disadvantage those other traders through unfair competition but it also distorts the normal working of the market. (Paragraphs 1.30–1.31 and 1.34).

(2) On such an important element in a purchasing decision as price consumers should be able to rely upon the information they are given by the trader as being both true and not misleading (the two legs are necessary because on this subject it is quite possible for true information to be presented in a misleading manner); if it is false or misleading he or she can be disadvantaged. (Paragraphs 1.32–1.40).

(3) The basic principle which should therefore apply is that information a consumer is given by a trader about prices should be neither false nor misleading and there is a strong case for some form of control to achieve this. (Paragraph 1.41). We take 'misleading' to cover also information which is so obscure that reasonable consumers are likely to be misled. (Paragraph 5.8).

(4) There are two main categories of information about prices to which this basic principle should be applied:—

    (a) indications about the price a consumer will be required to pay; and

    (b) indications either stated or implied about other prices with which the price to be paid is being compared—often referred to as Bargain Offers.

On the first category we concluded that:—

(5) Traders should not indicate goods or services are for supply at one price when they are in fact for supply at another higher price. (Paragraphs 2.34–2.38).

(6) Where non-optional extras such as VAT, service or carriage charges are payable in addition to the basic price, the amount of those extras should normally either be included in the quoted price or be made clear to consumers, at least on any order form, before they commit themselves to the transaction. If this is impossible or only an estimate of the extra amount can be given the trader should make the situation clear to consumers before they commit themselves. (Paragraphs 2.39–2.42).

On the second category we concluded that:—

(7) There is a wide range of practices on price comparisons (or Bargain Offers) and similar claims where detailed guidance is necessary on how to avoid breaching the basic principle concerning false or misleading price information (Paragraphs 2.3–2.32 and 2.43–2.56). We give our view on what that guidance should be in Recommendation E below.

(8) It would not be realistic to expect an entirely voluntary (or self-regulatory) system of control to achieve compliance with the basic principle at Conclusion 3, or the more specific requirements at Conclusions 5 and 6 or the guidance referred to at Conclusion 7, (Paragraphs 3.1–3.20) so that legislative control or a mixture of legislative and voluntary control is necessary.

(9) There should be a general legislative prohibition on traders providing consumers with false or misleading information about prices. (Paragraphs 5.2–5.8).

(10) Such a general legislative prohibition on its own would lead to severe practical difficulties. In the absence of detailed supplementary provisions the trade and the enforcement authorities would be unsure as to which practices the courts would hold to be misleading. Given the wide variety and ingenuity of marketing methods it would be many years and a large number of prosecutions before a satisfactory body of case law could be built up. (Paragraphs 5.9–5.10).

(11) A combination of a rather general piece of primary legislation and very detailed provisions in secondary legislation is what exists at present (in the shape of Section 11 of the Trade Descriptions Act 1968 and the Price Marking (Bargain Offers) Order 1979). This has been found wanting in many respects and the resultant criticisms are the origin of this review (Paragraphs 1.12–1.16). An examination of the reasons for this suggests to us that a different

means of providing detailed material to support a general prohibition of false or misleading price information needs to be found. (Paragraphs 5.11–5.13).

(12) We consider a statutory code of practice containing practical guidance would be the best means of providing much of the necessary detailed support for a general prohibition on false or misleading price information. During the last ten years a number of Acts have contained provisions for such a statutory code which is not legally binding—so that failure to observe any provision of the code does not itself render a person liable to any proceedings—but which is given a status which enables it to be admissible in evidence. Thus the courts can have regard to compliance or non-compliance with it in any relevant cases which come before them and it provides both traders and enforcement authorities with guidance on the day-to-day matters they need to deal with on the subject in question. We consider that these precedents, would be useful ones to follow. (Paragraphs 5.18–5.20, 5.22–5.26 and 5.28).

(13) It is a matter for further consideration how many of the detailed provisions should go in the primary or subordinate legislation and how many in such a code. (Paragraph 5.21).

(14) Such a code should be drawn up by the Secretary of State with the advice of the Director General of Fair Trading, and in consultation with representative bodies of the trade, representative bodies of the enforcement authorities and consumer organisations. (Paragraphs 5.20 and 5.28).

(15) Before judgment can be made on such a code it is clearly necessary for its likely contents to be known. We would expect our recommendations (Recommendation E) on detailed practices on price comparisons to form the main basis for such a code (Paragraph 5.21) and for it to include guidance on substantiation of previous prices (Paragraph 5.25), on the matters covered by Conclusion 24 below and on the practices of bureaux de change (Paragraphs 2.34–2.35).

(16) The primary legislation should contain provision for the Secretary of State to have power to make subordinate legislation. We consider this should be intended generally as a reserve power, leaving the code to cover most of the details. (Paragraph 5.14).

(17) Enforcement should continue to be the responsibility of trading standards authorities (Paragraph 4.37). There is a case, though not a particularly strong one, for the Director General of Fair Trading to be given enforcement powers also. If such powers are conferred on him it may be preferable for them to be exercisable only at the request of a trading standards authority. (Paragraphs 4.38–4.44).

(18) The nature of the subject merits the continuation of criminal sanctions in this area (Paragraphs 4.18–4.19).

(19) Having considered whether small scale accidental breaches of any provisions in the primary legislation should be specially allowed for in the legislation itself we concluded that the right course, in the light of all the practical issues associated with this aspect, was that criminal sanctions should be available for all actions which result in the consumer being given false or misleading price information (Paragraphs 4.20–4.25). Conclusion 23 below deals with the related aspect of defences.

(20) On this basis, criminal sanctions should be made available for breaches of the proposed general prohibition at Conclusion 9 and of any more specific provisions in the primary legislation on the requirements of Conclusions 5 and 6.

(21) The penalties at present provided for in the Trade Descriptions Act 1968 for Great Britain are appropriate in this context for the whole of the UK. (Paragraphs 4.26–4.27).

(22) The breaches mentioned in Conclusion 20 should (as with breaches in the provisions in the existing legislation) be regarded as absolute offences—ie it is the fact that the information is false or misleading, rather than the intention to be untruthful or to mislead, which determines the offence—and the legislation should include a provision on defences. (Paragraphs 4.28–4.31).

(23) On the question of defences S. 24(1) of the Trade Descriptions Act requires the defendant to prove not only that he took all reasonable precautions and exercised all due diligence to avoid the commission of the offence by himself or any person under his control but also that the offence was due to a mistake, or an act or default of some other person, an accident or some other cause beyond his control (Paragraph 4.29). The majority of us consider that, in line with modern practice, if a person can prove that he has taken all reasonable precautions and exercised all due diligence to avoid the commission of an offence then he should not be required to do more. (Paragraph 4.32). A minority of us, consider enforcement would be more difficult and less effective unless both limbs of the defences at present in S. 24(1) are included (Paragraph 4.33).

(24) It would be valuable for any code of practice to include guidance on the exchange of information between traders and enforcement authorities when doubts arise about whether traders' control systems are meeting the requirements of 'all reasonable precautions and due diligence' and for it to give guidance on where to draw the line between genuine errors and carelessness. (Paragraph 5.26).

(25) The legislation in this area should apply not only to price indications for goods but also to those for services, (including commission charges), facilities and accommodation. Hiring, hire purchase transactions, leasing, and rental should also be covered. In principle we consider that land and buildings on it should also be covered. (Paragraphs 4.13–4.16).

Recommendations

A New primary legislation should be introduced to replace Section 11 of the Trade Descriptions Act 1968 and the Price Marking (Bargain Offers) Order 1979. (Conclusion 11).

B The Bill should make it an offence for traders to give consumers false or misleading information about prices and should include specific provisions to cover such matters as those at Conclusions 5 and 6 above, provisions for a statutory code of practice containing practical guidance, power to make subordinate legislation, provision for enforcement by trading standards authorities, penalties on the lines of those in the Trade Descriptions Act 1968 and provisions for defences. (Conclusions 1–10, 12, 14, 16, 18–25). On defences a choice has to be made between our majority view (single limb defence) and our minority view (two limb defence). (Conclusion 23).

C It is for further consideration how many of our recommendations (E below) on particular price comparison practice should be included in the Bill itself and how many in the proposed statutory code. (Conclusions 13 and 15).

D It is also for further consideration whether the Director General of Fair Trading should be given an enforcement power to supplement the general enforcement duties of trading standards authorities. (Conclusion 17).

E Our detailed proposals relating to particular price comparison practices follow. (Conclusion 7). They are fairly wide ranging but we believe they will be readily understood by traders and trading standards officers. They are aimed at providing a satisfactory measure of protection against consumers being misled, while leaving traders scope for fair and reasonable competitive marketing activities. If they are included in the primary or secondary legislation they would each have statutory force and would need to be rephrased in appropriate legislative terms. If they are included in a statutory Code, and a provision is made for the Code to be admissible in evidence, then the Court in deciding whether a false or misleading price indication had been given in any particular case would be able to have regard to compliance or non-compliance with them but they would not be legally binding in themselves; we would hope much of the present wording would be found appropriate for this purpose and as guidance to traders and trading standards officers.

(i)   The comparison should always be with another price; comparisons with 'worth', 'value' or other similar figures which are not substantiable should be regarded as misleading. (Paras 2.4 and 2.19).

(ii)   Price comparisons should be between prices for the same or similar goods or services. (Para 2.4).

(iii) The comparative price should be either stated or calculable in all price comparisons whether express or implied; implied comparisons such as 'Special Offer: £10' or 'Sale Price: £5' without a comparative price should be regarded as misleading. (Para 2.4–2.5).

(iv)   Comparisons between prices for the same or similar goods or services but in different identified conditions or circumstances should be allowed provided the comparative price refers to the conditions or circumstances in which the goods or services are generally available. (Paras 2.16–2.17).

(v)   Comparisons with 'normal' or 'usual' prices should be regarded as comparisons with the trader's own previous prices. (Para 2.19) and therefore be covered by (vi) to (x) below.

(vi)   The majority of us considered that, except for a new shop just opening, in the case of traders operating from retail premises, comparisons with a trader's own previous prices should relate only to prices in the same premises or in the trader's other premises which are identified in the price comparison and are within a reasonable shopping area of those premises. (Paras 2.10–2.12).

(vii) Comparisons with a trader's own previous prices should relate only to prices which:—
       (a) were the last prices at which the goods or services were offered for supply by the trader before the introduction of the lower price *and*
       (b) were so offered for a period of at least 28 consecutive days except in the case of food and drink and other perishables. (Paras 2.47–2.53).

(viii) Where the period of at least 28 days in (vii) during which the goods were last on offer is not the period immediately prior to the introduction of the lower price (for example where some of the previous season's goods are reintroduced after a break) the trader should indicate in his price comparison when the goods were so offered. (Para 2.52).

(ix) For food and drink and other perishables the period in (vii) may be less than 28 days provided the trader draws attention in his price comparison to the actual period (for example 'last week's price £1.25, this week's price £1.15'). (Para 2.53).

(x) The proposals at (vii) to (ix) are not intended to limit a trader's scope to make further reductions from the comparative price during a sale or special offer period. (Para 2.52).

(xi) Where general advertising slogans are used in such a manner as to suggest that the prices of particular products have been reduced or are lower than prices for those products elsewhere, they should be treated as implied price comparisons as in (iii) above. (Para 2.6).

(xii) In considering general advertising slogans in relation to (xi) above the criterion should be that when a slogan using words which (in their normal everyday usage) suggest some form of reduction, is placed on individual price tickets or in-store price displays such as shelf-edge price markings it should be treated as an implied price comparison as described in (xi) above, unless prominent notices are displayed explaining in positive terms what the slogan is intended to mean in relation to the prices. (Paras 2.7–2.9).

(xiii) Comparisons with a trader's own future prices should be limited to genuine introductory or trial promotions which make clear the intended period of the lower price, even if that period is subsequently extended. (Paras 2.13–2.14).

(xiv) Comparisons with other traders' prices should be allowed provided they name the other trader and relate to the current prices being charged by that trader for the same or reasonably similar goods or services and, in the view of the majority of us, at premises which are within a reasonable shopping area of the premises of the trader making the comparison. (Para 2.15).

(xv) Comparisons with Recommended Retail Prices (rrps) above a threshold, which we suggest should initially be £10, should be limited to comparisons where the trader can demonstrate that the rrp quoted has been generally recommended or is readily verifiable from published price lists or trade guides. (Paras 2.28–2.31). (It should be noted that we have also recommended in paragraphs 2.30 and 2.31 that if experience of these proposed arrangements should indicate that in any sector rrps are being used which do not reasonably approximate to the general level of prices at which the goods are being sold, consideration should be given to the introduction, through the Order making powers proposed, of a ban on the use of rrps in the sector concerned).

(xvi) Comparisons with prices linked to other sets of initials or abbreviations should be limited to those which, in effect, mean the same as recommended retail price and for these the proposals in (xv) should apply; other initials and abbreviations should be regarded as misleading. (Para 2.20).

(xvii) Where the manufacturer's packaging states that a specified amount less than the rrp etc will be charged for the item (the practice known as 'flash' offers) either the packaging or the in-store price marking should make it clear that the price at which the goods are being offered is net of the reduction quoted. (Para 2.32).

(xviii) Comparisons which do not comply with the proposals at (i)–(xvii) should, prima facie, be regarded as misleading. (Paras 2.54–2.55).

(xix) Where a price comparison is made the trader should ensure that he is able to show that it is true. One way of demonstrating this would be to keep adequate records. (Paras 2.4, 2.10, 4.30 and 5.25).

(xx) Where a trader indicates that a Sale or similar event is being held on his premises, clear indication should be given in those premises as to which items have been specially brought in and which items are included in the sale or similar event (for which genuine comparative prices should be provided). (Paras 2.43–2.44).

(xxi) All free offers in conjunction with items offered for sale should be subject to the same requirements not to be false or misleading as other forms of price display. (Para 2.45).

CHAPTER 14

General statutory defences in consumer protection legislation

Introduction

Trading standards offences usually involve strict liability—that is liability without mens rea. (see above pp 439–444). Nevertheless the accused should have a defence where prevailing notions of natural justice suggest that it would be wholly unfair to fasten the discredit of a criminal conviction on a trader who is morally innocent. The background and current pattern of these defences is well explained in the following extract:

'The Evolution of Statutory Defences—by A. A. Painter (1982) Trading Law 181

The concept of providing statutory defences for use by persons charged with an offence of strict liability has been gradually developed during the past 100 years. From the outset Parliament has recognised that the elimination of mens rea from offences in what may be collectively termed 'trading laws' could lead to breaches of natural justice. A situation could arise where a trader without any guilty intent and having exercised the highest standards of competence and diligence in his trade could nevertheless be judged guilty of a criminal offence and punished accordingly. It was therefore necessary to ensure that such a trader could avoid conviction whilst, at the same time, preserving the necessary degree of protection for the public.

One of the earliest attempts to introduce statutory defences may be found in s 2(2) of the Merchandise Marks Act 1887 under which a trader accused of use etc, of a false trade mark or description could seek to prove that he had taken all reasonable precautions, had no reason to suspect the genuineness of the mark etc, and had otherwise acted innocently. A further development took place in s 12 of the Sale of Food (Weights and Measures) Act 1926 under which a trader could be discharged from a prosecution if he could prove that a deficiency in quantity was due to a mistake, accident or other cause beyond his control, or was due to the action of some person over whom he had no control and he had taken all reasonable precautions and had exercised all due diligence. In s 83 of the Food and Drugs Act 1938 the defence was taken a step further in that the trader could plead that the offence was due to the act or default of another person and he had exercised due diligence etc. He was, however, required to bring proceedings against the person whose act or default he was alleging was responsible for the commission of the offence.

Statutory defences under current trading law
Statutes currently in operation, namely the Food and Drugs Act 1955, the Weights and Measures Acts 1963 to 1979, the Trade Descriptions Act 1968, the Consumer Credit Act 1974 and the Consumer Safety Act 1978 provide for defences containing one, two or three limbs as follows:
(i) Section 113 of the Food and Drugs Act 1955 requires proof that:
    (a) the commission of the offence was due to the act or default of another person, *and*
    (b) all due diligence has been used to secure that the provisions of the Act have been complied with, *and*
    (c) the other person must be brought before the court by the defendant and he must have given notice of his intention to do this to the prosecutor.
There are, therefore, three limbs to this defence.
(ii) Section 24 of the Trade Descriptions Act 1968 and s 168 of the Consumer Credit Act 1974 (the defence is also applied to the Prices Act 1974) require proof that:
    (a) the commission of the offence was due to a mistake or to reliance on information supplied to the defendant or to the act or default of another person, an accident or

some other cause beyond his control, *and*

(b) all reasonable precautions had been taken and all due diligence had been exercised to avoid the commission of the offence.

There are, therefore, two limbs to this defence.

(iii) Section 26(1) of the Weights and Measures Act 1963 (as amended), s 3(7) of the Weights and Measures Act 1979, and s 2(6) of the Consumer Safety Act 1978 require proof that:

'the defendant has used all due diligence and has taken all reasonable precautions to avoid committing the offence.'

There is, therefore, only one limb to this defence.

Reversal of the burden of proof

All of these defences reverse the burden of proof. It is for the accused to prove that he has met the requirements of each defence and although the degree of proof required by the courts is . . . not as high as that required from the prosecution in respect to the substantive elements of the offence, the burden is a heavy one. It requires the establishment of a system of control within the trading unit and a proper chain of command within the company through which the operation of the system may be supervised.

It is not sufficient for a senior manager of the defendant company to give verbal evidence that diligence was exercised and precautions were taken. Proof is required by way of documentary evidence and the operation of the system must be shown by corroborating evidence. . . .

Offence due to mistake, or reliance on or act or default of another person

INTRODUCTION

This defence has given rise to much reported litigation and, as explained above, with its two limbs, is common to the Trade Descriptions Act and the Consumer Credit Act. The position under the Trade Descriptions Act will be taken as the primary example.

Section 24 of the Trade Descriptions Act provides:

24.—(1) In any proceedings for an offence under this Act it shall, subject to subsection (2) of this section, be a defence for the person charged to prove—

(a) that the commission of the offence was due to a mistake or to reliance on information supplied to him or to the act or default of another person, an accident or some other cause beyond his control; and

(b) that he took all reasonable precautions and exercised all due diligence to avoid the commission of such an offence by himself or any person under his control.

(2) If in any case the defence provided by the last foregoing subsection involves the allegation that the commission of the offence was due to the act or default of another person or to reliance on information supplied by another person, the person charged shall not, without leave of the court, be entitled to rely on that defence unless, within a period ending seven clear days before the hearing, he has served on the prosecutor a notice in writing giving such information identifying or assisting in the identification of that other person as was then in his possession.

(3) In any proceedings for an offence under this Act of supplying or offering to supply goods to which a false trade description is applied it shall be a defence for the person charged to prove that he did not know, and could not with reasonable diligence have ascertained, that the goods did not conform to the description or that the description had been applied to the goods.

In effect the section demands a proven absence of mens rea on the part of the person seeking to rely on it and thus it will have only a limited relevance where the offence charged is under s 14: see *Coupe v Guyett* [1973] 2 All ER 1058, [1973] 1 WLR 669, below, p 564 and cf *Wings Ltd v Ellis* [1984] 3 All ER 577, [1984] 3 WLR 965, above p 516.

Section 24 merely requires the accused to show that another person was responsible—there is no requirement that he be brought before the court. However it should be noted that s 24(1) requires that the accused prove he comes within *both* paragraphs.

Section 24(2) is a procedural requirement and involves the defence giving, normally, seven days' notice to the prosecution as to the identification of the other person.

Section 24(3) is in effect a defence of innocent supply of goods. It does not apply to services (s 14) nor to the offence of *applying* a false trade description (s 1(1)(a)) nor can it apply to prices. The difference between s 24(3) and s 24(1) is that s 24(3) requires only that the exercise of 'reasonable diligence' would not have shown up the offence. The point is well illustrated by the following case.

Barker v Hargreaves [1981] RTR 197, Queen's Bench Divisional Court

A second-hand car dealer advertised a car as being 'in good condition' throughout. He had successfully submitted it for an MOT test and received a certificate bearing the usual printed warnings that it should not be accepted or regarded as evidence of the car's condition. The car was badly corroded, but this was partly hidden by undersealing and a battery. The Divisional Court upheld the justices' conviction under s 1 (1) (b) of the Trade Descriptions Act 1968.

Donaldson LJ having summarised the facts of the case remarked:

> There is a very clear distinction between the two subsections. Under subsection (1) it is necessary for the defendant to prove that he took all reasonable precautions and exercised all due diligence to avoid the commission of 'such an offence', that is to say, an offence under the Act. Subsection (3), on the other hand, is directed to the particular offence and it says that it is a defence to prove that he did not know of the facts constituting the particular offence and could not with reasonable diligence have ascertained that the goods did not conform to the description, again pointing to the particular complaint. . . . The Crown Court found that the defendant had no system for ascertaining the condition of the vehicles being sold. He relied solely on MOT tests. Accordingly, I am quite clear that he cannot rely on section 24(1).
>
> When it comes to section 24(3) it is a different defence because it relates to the specific defects which were found in the vehicle and form the basis of the charge. Those are the corrosion defects. But, unlike under section 24(1), where he can rely on information received from other people, when it comes to section 24(3) it is no answer that he was misled by others. What he has to do is to show that it was a latent defect, that is to say, a defect which could not with reasonable diligence have been ascertained.

These defences have been subject to considerable judicial interpretation and the main points are best considered individually.

ACT OR DEFAULT OF ANOTHER PERSON

The words 'another person' have caused difficulty where the defendant is a company and the offence arises out of the act or default of one of its servants. The crucial point is whether the servant alleged for the purposes of s 24(1)(a) of the defence to be 'another person' is really the alter ego of the company. *Beckett v Kingston Bros (Butchers) Ltd* [1970] 1 QB 606, [1970] 1 All ER 715 is a case in point. In the leading case on corporate criminal liability the issue arose in a slightly different way when it became necessary to determine precisely who is the 'he' who must exercise all reasonable precautions etc for the purposes of s 24(1) (b).

Tesco Supermarkets Ltd v Nattrass [1971] 2 All ER 127, [1972] AC 153, House of Lords

The appellant company owned a large number of supermarket stores and set up a reasonable and efficient system of instruction and inspection for ensuring that their employees complied with the requirements of the Trade Descriptions Act. The shop had displayed a 'flash' offer on a poster relating to money off the usual price of washing powder, but they had run out of the specially marked reduced packets and consequently a customer failed to get a packet at the reduced price. The shop manager—a Mr Clement—had failed to supervise the actions of an assistant who had put out on display the only remaining packets marked at the full price. The company was charged under s 11(2) of the Trade Descriptions Act 1968, and was now appealing against conviction to the House of Lords.

Lord Reid. . . . The relevant facts as found by the justices were that on the previous evening a shop assistant, Miss Rogers, whose duty it was to put out fresh stock found that there were no more of the specially marked packs in stock. There were a number of packs marked with the ordinary price so she put them out. She ought to have told the shop manager, Mr Clement, about this but she failed to do so. Mr Clement was responsible for seeing that the proper packs were on sale, but he failed to see to this although he marked his daily return 'All special offers OK'. The justices found that if he had known about this he would either have removed the poster advertising the reduced price or given instructions that only 2s 11d was to be charged for the packs marked 3s 11d. Section 24 (2) requires notice to be given to the prosecutor if the accused is blaming another person and such notice was duly given naming Mr Clement.

In order to avoid conviction the appellants had to prove facts sufficient to satisfy both parts of s 24(1) of the 1968 Act. The justices held that they—

'had exercised all due diligence in devising a proper system for the operation of the said store and by securing so far as was reasonably practicable that it was fully implemented and thus had fulfilled the requirements of section 24 (1) (b).'

But they convicted the appellants because in their view the requirements of s 24 (1) (a) had not been fulfilled; they held that Mr Clement was not 'another person' within the meaning of that provision. The Divisional Court[1] held that the justices were wrong in holding that Mr Clement was not 'another person'. The respondent did not challenge this finding of the Divisional Court so I need say no more about it than that I think that on this matter the Divisional Court was plainly right. But that court sustained the conviction on the ground that the justices had applied the wrong test in deciding that the requirements of s 24 (1) (b) had been fulfilled. In effect that court held that the words 'he took all reasonable precautions . . .' do not mean what they say; 'he' does not mean the accused, it means the accused and all his servants who were acting in a managerial or supervisory capacity. I think that earlier authorities virtually compelled the Divisional Court to reach this strange construction. So the real question in this appeal is whether these earlier authorities were rightly decided. But before examining those earlier cases I think it necessary to make some general observations.

. . .

In my judgment the main object of these provisions [*sc* such as s 24] must have been to distinguish between those who are in some degree blameworthy and those who are not, and to enable the latter to escape from conviction if they can show that they were in no way to blame. I find it almost impossible to suppose that Parliament or any reasonable body of men would as a matter of policy think it right to make employers criminally liable for the acts of some of their servants but not for those of others and I find it incredible that a draftsman, aware of that intention, would fail to insert any words to express it. But in several cases the courts, for reasons which it is not easy to discover, have given a restricted meaning to such provisions. It has been held that such provisions afford a defence if the master proves that the servant at fault was the person who himself did the prohibited act, but that they afford no defence if the servant at fault was one who failed in his duty of supervision to see that his subordinates did not commit the prohibited act. Why Parliament should be thought to have intended this distinction or how as a matter of construction these provisions can reasonably be held to have that meaning is not apparent.

In some of these cases the employer charged with the offence was a limited company. But in others the employer was an individual and still it was held that he, though personally blameless, could not rely on these provisions if the fault which led to the commission of the offence was the fault of a servant in failing to carry out his duty to instruct or supervise his subordinates. Where a limited company is the employer difficult questions do arise in a wide variety of circumstances in deciding which of its officers or servants is to be identified with the company so that his guilt is the guilt of the company.

I must start by considering the nature of the personality which by a fiction the law attributes to a corporation. A living person has a mind which can have knowledge or intention or be negligent and he has hands to carry out his intentions. A corporation has none of these; it must act through living persons, though not always one or the same person. Then the person who acts is not speaking or acting for the company. He is acting as the company and his mind which directs his acts is the mind of the company. There is no question of the company being vicariously liable. He is not acting as a servant, representative, agent or delegate. He is an embodiment of the company or, one could say, he hears and speaks through the persona of the company, within his appropriate sphere, and his mind is the mind of the company. If it is a guilty mind then that guilt is the guilt of the company. It must be a question of law whether, once the facts have been ascertained, a person in doing particular things is to be regarded as the company or merely as the company's servant or agent. In that case any liability of the company can only be a statutory or vicarious liability.

. . .

Normally the board of directors, the managing director and perhaps other superior officers of a company carry out the functions of management and speak and act as the company. Their subordinates do not. They carry out orders from above and it can make no difference that they are given some measure of discretion. But the board of directors may delegate some part of their functions of management giving to their delegate full discretion to act independently of instructions from them. I see no difficulty in holding that they have thereby put such a delegate in their place so that within the scope of the delegation he can act as the company. It may not always be easy to draw the line but there are cases in which the line must be drawn. . . .

In some cases the phrase alter ego has been used. I think it is misleading. When dealing with a company the word alter is I think misleading. The person who speaks and acts as the company is not alter. He is identified with the company. And when dealing with an individual no other individual can be his alter ego. The other individual can be a servant, agent, delegate or representative but I know of neither principle nor authority which warrants the confusion (in the literal or original sense) of two separate individuals.

The earliest cases dealing with this matter which were cited were *R C Hammett Ltd v Crabb, R C Hammett Ltd and Beldam*[2] and *R C Hammett Ltd v London County Council*[3]. In both a servant of the accused company had infringed the provisions of s 5 (2) of the Sale of Food (Weights and Measures) Act 1926. Section 12 (5) exempted the employer from penalty if he charged another person as the actual offender and could prove:

> '. . . to the satisfaction of the court that he had used due diligence to enforce the execution of this Act, and that the said other person had committed the offence in question without his consent, connivance or wilful default . . .'

In the earlier case the offence was committed by the shop manager personally and he knew that he was committing an offence. A conviction was quashed on the ground that the magistrate had treated the question whether the employer had used due diligence as one of law, that it was really one of fact and that there was no evidence on which the magistrate could reach his decision. In the second case the offence was committed by a subordinate; the shop manager had warned him but had not exercised due diligence to see that his instructions were obeyed. Again the justices convicted on the ground that the owners were responsible for lack of due diligence in their manager. This time the conviction was upheld by the same court. It was argued for the respondents that the employer is responsible for the acts or omissions of all persons above the actual offender. It seems to me obvious that this is a matter of law depending on the proper construction of the statutory provision. But Lord Hewart CJ, did not so regard it. He said that there was evidence on which quarter sessions could arrive at their opinion and that they were entitled to come to the conclusion that the appellants were responsible for the manager's lack of due diligence.

I find these cases most unsatisfactory. There is no explanation of how it could be a question of fact whether the provisions of s 12 (5) meant that what the employer had to prove was that he personally had used due diligence, or that he also had to prove that some or all of his servants had also done so. But the court did not deal with that. Nevertheless because the only difference between the two cases appears to have been that in the first the shop manager was himself the offender whereas in the second the fault was lack of supervision, these cases have been thought to afford authority for the proposition that an employer has a defence if the only fault was in the actual offender but not if there was fault of any of his servants superior to the actual offender. I can find no warrant for that proposition in the terms of s 12 (5). Both parts of the provision—that the employer had used due diligence and that the offence had been committed without his consent, connivance or wilful default—appear to me plainly to refer to the employer personally and to no one else.

I agree with the view of the Lord Justice-General (Lord Cooper) in a case dealing with the same Act *Dumfries and Maxwelltown Co-operative Society v Williamson*[4] that:

> 'The underlying idea manifestly is that there should not be vicarious responsibility for an infringement of the Act committed without the consent or connivance of an employer . . .'

. . .

What good purpose could be served by making an employer criminally responsible for the misdeeds of some of his servants but not for those of others? It is sometimes argued—it was argued in the present case—that making an employer criminally responsible, even when he had done all that he could to prevent an offence, affords some additional protection to the public because this will induce him to do more. But if he has done all he can how can he do more? I think that what lies behind this argument is a suspicion that justices too readily accept evidence that an employer has done all he can to prevent offences. But if justices were to accept as sufficient a paper scheme and perfunctory efforts to enforce it they would not be doing their duty—that would not be 'due diligence' on the part of the employer. Then it is said that this would involve discrimination in favour of a large employer like the appellants against a small shopkeeper. But that is not so. Mr Clement was the 'opposite number' of the small shopkeeper and he was liable to prosecution in this case. The purpose of this Act must have been to penalise those at fault, not those who were in no way to blame.

The Divisional Court[5] decided this case on a theory of delegation. In that they were following some earlier authorities. But they gave far too wide a meaning to delegation. I have said that a board of directors can delegate part of their functions of management so as to make their delegate an embodiment of the company within the sphere of the delegation. But here the board never delegated any part of their functions. They set up a chain of command through regional and district supervisors, but they remained in control. The shop managers had to obey their general directions and also to take orders from their superiors. The acts or omissions of shop managers were not acts of the company itself.

In my judgment the appellants established the statutory defence. I would therefore allow this appeal.

[Lord Morris, Viscount Dilhorne, Lord Pearson and Lord Diplock agreed that the appeal should be allowed.] *Appeal allowed.*

1. [1970] 3 All ER 357, [1971] 1 QB 133.
2. (1931) 145 LT 638, [1931] All ER Rep 70.
3. (1933) 97 JP 105.
4. 1950 JC 76 at 80.
5. [1970] 3 All ER 357, [1971] 1 QB 133.

A similar issue arose, albeit in a slightly different context, in *Wings Ltd v Ellis* [1984] 1 All ER 1046, [1984] 1 WLR 731, DC; revsd [1984] 3 All ER 577, [1984] 3 WLR 965, HL, above, p 516. On a charge of recklessly making a false statement concerning the provision of services contrary to s 14 (1) (b) of the Trade Descriptions Act 1968 Mann J, delivering the judgment of the Divisional Court, said:

> The appellant is a limited company and it is established that, where the commission of an offence under the 1968 Act requires a specific intent, then a corporate defendant is not guilty unless the requisite intent was a state of mind of one or more of those natural persons who constitute the directing mind and will of the company. Lord Widgery CJ described such persons as 'the ruling officers' in *Coupe v Guyett* [1973] 2 All ER 1058 at 1063, [1973] 1 WLR 669 at 675. . . .
>
> Although the descriptions vary, the concept is clear. A company cannot be guilty of an offence unless the specified state of mind was a state of mind of a person who is or forms part of the directing mind and will of the company. As to the personal liability of such persons, see s 20 of the 1968 Act.

Was there evidence on which a reasonable bench of justices, properly instructed, could be sure that there was recklessness by such a person in the present case?

'Recklessness' means failing to have regard to the truth or falsity of the statement (see *MFI Warehouses Ltd v Nattrass* [1973] 1 All ER 762 at 768, [1973] 1 WLR 307 at 313). We can find nothing in the evidence which suggests that a person ruling the company was privy to the selection of the photograph. In particular, we reject the respondent's suggestion that Michael Stephen-Jones, who approved the photograph and who variously called himself a 'long haul development manager' and 'the contracts manager', could be inferred to be a member of the relevant class. The most that could be said for the respondent is that the members of this class, although establishing a system, failed to establish a system which would have prevented the mistake which occurred. That failure cannot, in our judgment, constitute 'recklessness'. There may be cases where the system is such that he who establishes it could not be said to be having regard to the truth or falsity of what emerged from it, but that is not this case.

For the reasons which we have given, the appeal in regard to the conviction under s 14 (1) (b) must be allowed and the conviction quashed.

Although the prosecution appealed to the House of Lords only on the charge requiring proof of knowledge under s 14 (1) (a) of the Act, the arguments in terms of the requirements for corporate liability were essentially the same. The approach of Mann J received no support in the House of Lords where Lord Scarman said:

The 1968 Act, of course, to be of any value at all in modern conditions has to cover trades and businesses conducted on a large scale by individual proprietors, by firms and by bodies corporate. The day-to-day business activities of large enterprises, whatever their legal structure, are necessarily conducted by their employees, and particularly by their sales staff. It follows that many of the acts prohibited by the Act will be the acts of employees done in the course of the trade or business and without the knowledge at the time of those who direct the business. It will become clear that the Act does cover such acts when one comes to consider the terms of the two statutory defences to which I have already referred. The Act also makes specific provision consistent with this view of its operation in respect of businesses carried on by bodies corporate. Section 20 provides that, where an offence has been committed by a body corporate and was committed with the consent or is attributable to the neglect of a director or other officer of the company, he '*as well as the bodycorporate*' is guilty of the offence.

Both Lord Scarman and Lord Hailsham LC (see ibid p 582) were clear that the 1968 Act extended to such cases. For further discussion of the position in the case of an unincorporated employer see *Coupe v Guyett* [1973] 2 All ER 1058, [1973] 1 WLR 669, below p 564.

The refusal by the court in the *Tesco* case to hold the company responsible for the acts of its employees has given rise to disquiet in some quarters. However it should be noted that it has been held that the defendant must prove not only that the offence was due to the act or default of another but that he had done all that could reasonably be expected by way of inquiry and investigation to identify the other person. The point arose in *McGuire v Sittingbourne Co-operative Society* [1976] Crim LR 268. In defence to a charge under s 11 (2) the defendants served notices on the prosecutor pursuant to s 24 (2) alleging that the offences were due to the act or default of the managers or other persons whom the defendants could not identify. In a letter amplifying the notices they named all the assistants in the shop at the relevant time. The justices held that they had established the defence. The prosecution appealed on case stated to the Queen's Bench Division. The appeal was allowed, the Court holding that the onus was on the defendants to establish, on the balance of probabilities, that they had done all that could reasonably be expected of them in the way of inquiry and investigation as to who was responsible for the default.

Lord Widgery is reported as adding:

Unless some little care is taken in regard to these matters, we may find the administration of this Act sliding down to the sort of slip-shod level at which all a defendant has to do is say in general terms that the default must have been due to something in the shop, one of the girls or some expression like that, and thereby satisfy the onus cast upon him.

The Director General of Fair Trading's Review of the Trade Descriptions Act (Cmnd 6628 (1976)) concluded that the Act had 'by and large . . . achieved what its authors and Parliament intended it to do: encourage high standards of truthfulness in describing goods and services' (para 1). However in commenting on the *Tesco* decision the report suggests (at para 54) that it may be:

responsible for the emergence of a misleading picture of the extent to which the Act is being contravened, particularly in relation to corporate retailing. It appears that some companies trading on a national scale are willing to shoulder the blame for all offences originating within their organisation, whatever the circumstances which led to their commission. Others, however, seek to avoid conviction for offences by pointing to the precautions they have taken and blaming the member of the staff responsible for the particular offence. The enquiries mentioned above have shown that, with few exceptions, local authorities are unwilling to prosecute employees, such as shop managers, in cases where the trader has argued that an offence has arisen from the employee's act or default.

Yet, swayed by Lord Reid's reasoning in the *Tesco* case, the report concluded:

63. . . .
(i) the imposition of vicarious liability for offences arising from the act or default of employees would not be justified;
(ii) consideration should be given to adding words to the existing statutory defence to ensure that a trader is not provided with a defence by reference to the act or default of a person under his control unless he can show that the method of trading he adopts, and which led to the offence, does not involve a high inherent risk that offences will be committed through the act or default of employees, having regard to their skill, training and the complexity of the system.'

The *Tesco* decision is not without its difficulties as is evident from the following extract from Sir Gordon Borrie's Hamlyn Lectures *The Development of Consumer Law and Policy* (1984), at pp 52–53:

Justifying the result of the *Tesco* decision, Lord Reid said this[1]:

'It is sometimes argued—it was argued in the present case—that making an employer criminally responsible, even when he has done all that he could to prevent an offence, affords some additional protection to the public because this will induce him to do more. But if he has done all he can how can he do more?'

Lord Reid's point seems to be logically impeccable. Yet it may be all too easy for the employer to *appear* to have done all he can, to point to systems and precautions and the training of staff. And the mere suggestion of such a defence being raised may induce Trading Standards Departments not to proceed for the simple reason that in practice the defence is difficult to counteract. Very soon after the *Tesco* decision, the Law Commmission expressed its support of the principle that companies should be criminally liable in the regulatory field, and specifically liable to prosecution under the Trade Descriptions Act[2]:

'The main objective of criminal law is the prevention of crime and it is argued that the publicity attendant upon the prosecution of companies has a strong deterrent effect. The prosecution of a company for the commission of an offence symbolises the failure of control by the company, and it is socially desirable to have the company's name before the public. We think that it is probably true that the publicity given a corporation . . . is valuable in the field of regulatory offences the purpose of which is often to ensure adherence to proper standards, for example in respect of foodstuffs, drugs and other articles of consumption. This publicity achieves its effect in the main through reports in the local press, so having a maximum impact upon consumers. . . .'

1. [1972] AC 153, 174; [1971] 2 All ER 127, 135.

2. *Criminal Liability of Corporations*, Law Commission Working Paper No 44 (1972), para 48. See also the view of Professor Glanville Williams: 'That a company should not be liable for an offence of negligence committed by its branch manager, who after all represents the company in the particular locality, is a considerable defect in the law. . . . What is evidently needed is a statutory redefinition of the officers whose acts and mental states implicate the company.' (Glanville Williams *Textbook of Criminal Law* (2nd ed, 1983) p 973.

REASONABLE PRECAUTIONS AND ALL DUE DILIGENCE

If an individual blames, for example, his supplier he must prove additionally that he satisfied the requirements under s 24 (1) (b)—that is that he took all reasonable precautions *and* exercised all due diligence, the conditions being cumulative, not alternative. The Weights and Measures Act 1963 as amended in 1979 contains in s 26 a very similar defence and the same comments apply.

Many cases have been before the Courts on this point and two underlying principles are discernible:
   (a) the person charged must at least have done something—to sit back and do nothing is not sufficient;
   (b) the question of what are reasonable precautions must be decided on the facts of each individual case.

This section was considered in *Tesco Supermarkets Ltd v Nattrass* [1972] AC 153, [1971] 2 All ER 127, above p 555. Lord Diplock's speech contains the following helpful analysis (at p 154):

What amounts to the taking of all reasonable precautions and the exercise of all due diligence by a principal in order to satisfy the requirements of s 24 (1) (b) of the Act depends on all the circumstances of the business carried on by the principal. It is a question of fact for the justices in summary proceedings or for the jury in proceedings on indictment. However large the business, the principal cannot avoid a personal responsibility for laying down the system for avoiding the commission of offences by his servants. It is he alone who is party to their contracts of employment through which this can be done. But in a large business, such as that conducted by the appellants in the instant appeal, it may be quite impracticable for the principal personally to undertake the detailed supervision of the work of inferior servants. It may be reasonable for him to allocate these supervisory duties to some superior servants or hierarchy of supervisory grades of superior servants, under their respective contracts of employment with him. If the principal has taken all reasonable precautions in the selection and training of servants to perform supervisory duties and has laid down an effective system of supervision and used due diligence to see that it is observed, he is entitled to rely on a default by a superior servant in his supervisory duties as a defence under s 24 (1). . . .

This passage was quoted with approval and followed by the Divisional Court in *Nattrass v Timpson Shops Ltd* [1973] Crim LR 197.

Sherratt v Geralds The American Jewellers Ltd (1970) 114 Sol Jo 147

In another leading case the facts were as follows.

The defendants were charged with supplying a wristwatch marked 'divers watch' and 'waterproof' to which false trade descriptions were applied contrary to s 1 (1) (b) of the Trade Descriptions Act 1968. After being immersed in water for one hour the watch stopped and filled with water. The defendants had not carried out any tests but relied on the wholesalers' reputation and their experience that the watches had previously not caused any trouble. The magistrate found that the defendants had taken all reasonable precautions and exercised all due diligence within s 24 (1) (b) of the Act. The prosecution appealed.

Lord Parker CJ is reported as having made the following observations:

> '[The] defences in s 24 (1) (a) and (b) had to be proved on the balance of probabilities; the burden being on the defendants. Clearly they had taken no precautions, relying on previous dealings with the wholesalers. To succeed, they had to show that if no precautions were taken, there were none reasonably to be taken. Whatever "all due diligence" might mean, there was clearly an obligation to take any reasonable precautions that could be taken. The watch was designed to withstand pressures of five atmospheres at the front, but no one had suggested that it was necessary to dive 170 ft as a reasonable precaution. The elementary precaution of dipping the watch in a bowl of water would have prevented the offence. While there was evidence that the defendants had discharged the burden of proof under para (a), there was no evidence on which it could be said they had brought themselves within para (b). The case should go back with a direction to convict. The magistrate might feel that there were mitigating circumstances obliging him not to impose a very severe penalty.

[Ashworth and Talbot JJ agreed.] *Appeal allowed.*'

The above principles were upheld in *Garrett v Boots Chemists Ltd* (16 July 1980, unreported). The respondents were charged with having on sale pencils which breached the Pencils and Graphic Instruments (Safety) Regulations 1974 by having a higher lead and/or chromium content than permitted. The facts were not in dispute but the defendants pleaded that they had taken all reasonable precautions—they had previously informed their supplier about the new regulations and made it a condition in their order of supply that pencils conformed to the standards. The magistrates found that the defendants had taken all reasonable precautions and to take random samples was not necessary. The prosecution appealed to the Divisional Court. In allowing the appeal and after commenting on the facts of *Sherratt v Geralds The American Jewellers Ltd*, Lord Lane LCJ stated:

> 'All reasonable precautions' are strong words. It has been suggested by Mr Scrivener, on behalf of the appellant, that one obvious and reasonable precaution which could have been taken in the present case was to take random samples of the various batches of pencils which arrived at the premises of Messrs Boots the Chemists Limited.
>
> Of course I scarcely need say that every case will vary in its facts; what might be reasonable for a large retailer might not be reasonable for the village shop. But here, dealing with a concern the size of Boots, it seems to me that one of the obvious precautions to be taken was random sample, whether statistically controlled or not. One does not know whether the random sample would have in fact produced detection of the errant pencils. It might have, it might not have. But to say that it was not a precaution which should reasonably have been taken does not seem to me to accord with good sense.
>
> Whatever the circumstances may be so far as other retailers are concerned, on the facts of this case it seems to me that no Bench of Magistrates, properly instructed in the law, could properly have come to the conclusion that Messrs Boots the Chemists had discharged the burden here which lay upon them.'

Accordingly the case was remitted to the justices with a direction to convict.

In the context of discussing reasonable precautions O'Keefe *The Law of Trade Descriptions* states (at para 119 (1)) that the expression involves 'setting up a system to ensure that things will not go wrong: "due diligence" means seeing that the system works properly'. For further cases and discussion in point see *Taylor v Lawrence Fraser (Bristol) Ltd* (1977) 121 Sol Jo 757; *Sutton London Borough v Perry Sanger & Co Ltd* (1971) 135 JP Jo 239; *Nattrass v Timpson Shops Ltd* [1973] Crim LR 197 and *Hicks v*

Sullam Ltd (1983) 91 ITSA Monthly Review 122; R G Lawson, 'Reasonable Precautions and All Due Diligence' (1983) 147 JP 486.

Mistake, accident, cause beyond accused's control

To establish this defence it is necessary to prove something which is unexpected, beyond control, and which normal diligence and precaution would not uncover. The defence has been discussed in the Divisional Court in the context of s 26 of the Weights and Measures Act 1963. The following leading case is in point.

Bibby-Cheshire v Golden Wonder Ltd [1972] 3 All ER 738, [1972] 1 WLR 1487, Queen's Bench Divisional Court

A crisp packet marked '15 drams' was found on purchase to weigh only 9 drams. The defendants pleaded as a cause beyond their control that a normally accurate and reliable machine had for no anticipated reason proved not to be so. It was further said that the machine was set to produce overweight bags—17.5 drams which most packets did weigh—and that there was no machine accurate enough, never to produce underweight bags. The justices held that the manufacturer had satisfied s 26 (1) (a) and the prosecution now appealed to the Divisional Court.

Melford Stevenson J having stated the facts of the case continued:

The defence made available to the respondents charges them with proving (a) that the commission of the offence was due to a mistake or to an accident of some other cause beyond his control; there is here no suggestion of a mistake, no suggestion of an accident, and we have to consider the words: 'some other cause beyond his control'. It is established here that there was in use a machine, whatever may be said of it, which was of a kind which would not be expected in the ordinary course of its functioning to go wrong beyond the very slight figures of error that I have indicated, and evidence also accepted that it was the best machine available at the time when this offence was committed. For myself, those considerations on the findings of fact expressed in the case seem to me to bring this case within the words 'some other cause beyond his control', but that is not enough; one has to continue:

'. . . and that he took all reasonable precautions and exercised all due diligence to avoid the commission of such an offence in respect of those goods by himself or any person under his control.'

The matters that I have already recited, I am afraid at some length out of the case, appear to me to satisfy the phrase: 'exercise all due diligence to avoid the commission of such an offence'. The justices who heard the detailed evidence on which their findings are based, plainly came to that conclusion, and in my view they were justified in reaching that conclusion. It is true they do not in express terms exclude the possibility of a cause beyond the respondents' control, but I think that does arise by clear implication from the paragraph of the case where they express their opinion, and from the question as framed by them.

I think that they were justified in finding that the burden of establishing this offence had been discharged by the respondents, and that they were right in dismissing this information.

Milmo J and Widgery LCJ agreed. Appeal dismissed.

In other cases before the courts it has been found that a retail baker has no 'control' over a wholesale baker who supplies him with loaves: see *McIntyre & Son v Laird* 1943 JC 96; *Trickers (Confectioners) Ltd v Barnes* [1955] 1 All ER 803, [1955] 1 WLR 372. Also an unusual breakdown or unlikely defect in machinery may be a bona fide accident beyond control: see *Ashton v Derby Co-operative Provident Society Ltd* (1935) (unreported); *Wolfinder v Oliver* (1932) 147 LT 80. See also *Marshall v Herbert* [1963] Crim LR 506 for a defence in which the unexpected illness of an employee was held to be a cause beyond the defendant's control (the defence, however, failing on diligence).

It should be noted that it was held in *Birkenhead and District Co-operative Society Ltd v Roberts* [1970] 3 All ER 391, [1970] 1 WLR 1497 where the alleged offence arose out of the mis-labelling by the defendant's servant of a joint of beef, that a 'mistake' by any person other than the one charged did not come within paragraph (a). To plead 'act or default of another person' seven days' notice would have had to be given in accordance with the requirements of s 24 (2).

There appear to be no reported cases on what the nature of a 'mistake' or 'accident' amounts to under this Act. It will be noted that the *Bibby-Cheshire* case (above) specifically rejected any suggestion of any mistake or accident. The decision depended on the meaning of 'some other cause beyond his control'. It is thought that the paucity of authority on the meaning of 'mistake' or 'accident' is not so much because of the unlikelihood of such things occurring; it is rather because of the great difficulty for the defendant in establishing the second line of defence—ie that the mistake or accident occurred despite taking all reasonable precautions and exercising all due diligence. The two limbs of the defence in this respect are almost inherently contradictory.

'By-passing' provisions

The provisions to be discussed here can be found in s 23 of the Trade Descriptions Act 1968, s 100 of the Food Act 1984 (replacing s 113 of the Food and Drugs Act 1955) and s 27 of the Weights and Measures Act 1963. They allow the prosecution of a person other than the person apparently committing the offence where 'the commission by any person of an offence' is alleged to be due to the act or default of that other person. Under s 23 that other person may be charged and convicted whether or not the person actually committing the offence is prosecuted. Therefore strictly speaking the sections are not defence provisions, but are provided to streamline what could otherwise be a cumbersome process.

Although the wording in the various statutes is similar there are some procedural differences involved. Section 23 of the Trade Descriptions Act permits concurrent proceedings, unlike, for example, the Food Act 1984 which does not contemplate proceedings being taken against the first person: see *Fisher v Santovin Ltd* [1953] 2 QB 266, [1953] 2 All ER 713 (decided under s 113(3) of the 1955 Act), forbidding concurrent proceedings against the first person. For the procedural difficulties arising under s 113 see Frank Nuttall, 'Food and Drugs—Third Party Procedure' (1977) 141 JP Jo 266.

Section 23 of the Trade Descriptions Act 1968 provides as follows:

23. Where the commission by any person of an offence under this Act is due to the act or default of some other person that other person shall be guilty of the offence, and a person may be charged with and convicted of the offence by virtue of this section whether or not proceedings are taken against the first-mentioned person.

For examples of the procedure in use see *Cottee v Douglas Seaton (Used Cars) Ltd* [1972] 3 All ER 750, [1972] 1 WLR 1408, above p 476 and

R v Ford Motor Co Ltd [1974] 3 All ER 489, [1974] 1 WLR 1220, above
p 484. The following is a typical example of a charge bringing in s 23.

> AB on the — day of — in the course of a business of selling musical instruments
> supplied to CD a violin to which a false trade description, namely that the violin was
> the work of Stradivarius and made in 1720, was applied, contrary to s 1 (1) of the
> Trade Descriptions Act 1968. And the commission of the offence was due to the Act of
> EF of —, whereby the said EF is guilty of an offence by virtue of s 23 of the Trade
> Descriptions Act 1968.

Two main points to consider are firstly the procedural difficulties
involved in the phrase 'commission by any person of an offence . . .' and
secondly the requirement of showing direct causal connection between
the offence by the first person and the act or default of the second.

'. . . COMMISSION BY ANY OTHER PERSON OF AN OFFENCE'

The immediate difficult question, since s 24 of the Trade Descriptions Act
prescribes a defence where an offence occurred due to the 'act or default of
another', is what scope is left for s 23? A basic prerequisite of s 23 is that
an offence must have been committed (see *Cottee v Douglas Seaton (Used
Cars) Ltd,* above p 476) which is something s 24 apparently denies. This
problem was discussed in the following case.

Coupe v Guyett [1973] 2 All ER 1058, [1973] 1 WLR 669, Queen's Bench Divisional Court

The defendant, a car repair workshop manager, was employed by the
owner, Miss Shaw, who was registered in the Business Names Register as
the sole proprietor but took no active part in the business. In an invoice of
the business the defendant recklessly made a false statement as to repairs
carried out on a car. Charges were preferred against the owner under s 14
(1) (b) of the Trade Descriptions Act and against the defendant under s 23.
The justices hearing the charges together acquitted the owner on the
grounds that she had neither made nor authorised, nor even had been
aware of the making of the false statement and in any event had a valid
defence under s 24. They acquitted the defendant on the ground that since
the owner was acquitted a s 23 conviction was not open to them. The
prosecution now appealed to the Divisional Court.

Lord Widgery CJ having stated the facts of the case continued:

At first sight there appears to be something of a conflict between ss 23 and 24, because s 23
contemplates that the person first referred to therein shall have committed an offence by reason
of the act or default of another. When one moves on to s 24, it becomes apparent that someone
who has otherwise committed an offence but has done it through the act or default of another has a
special statutory defence. Accordingly it is difficult at first sight to see how the two sections can be
fitted together. But the conflict has been resolved, and one can seek guidance on it in the speech
of Lord Diplock in *Tesco Supermarkets Ltd v Nattrass*[1]. The solution of the conflict is this, that
when a person first named in s 23 has no defence to the charge except the statutory defence under
s 24, he or she can properly still be regarded as having committed the offence for the purpose of
s 23. On the other hand, in my judgment, if the person first referred to in s 23 has a defence on the
merits, as it were, and without reference to s 24, then it is not possible to operate s 23 so as to
render guilty the person whose act or default gave rise to the matter in complaint.

With that for background, one must now attempt to see what the justices made of the
position of Miss Shaw. The prosecution were clearly saying that Miss Shaw and the
respondent were guilty, subject of course to Miss Shaw's defence under s 24 but not
otherwise. The justices took a different view. The actual words were:

'We dismissed the summons against Miss Shaw on the grounds that although she was the registered owner of Advance Autos, she personally neither made nor authorised nor was she even aware of the making of the false statement and that in any event she had a valid defence under section 24 of the Act.'

If the justices had taken the view that Miss Shaw was to be acquitted solely because of the statutory defence, then for the reasons I have already given it would have been open to them to convict the respondent. If on the other hand they were right in saying that Miss Shaw was entitled to be acquitted on other grounds, then they would not be in a position to convict the respondent under the terms of s 23. Accordingly counsel for the appellant has been faced with the somewhat uphill task of trying to satisfy us that the justices were wrong in law when they concluded that Miss Shaw should be acquitted on grounds other than the grounds of the statutory defence. If he can do that, then of course the conviction of the respondent must follow; if he cannot, then the acquittal of the respondent was in my judgment right.

In order to allege that Miss Shaw was guilty of the offence and was able only to rely on her defence under s 24, counsel for the appellant has to urge and establish that not only the statement made by the respondent, the falsity of which gave rise to the proceedings, but also the mental state of the respondent must be attributed to Miss Shaw. I think, without deciding it, that in these circumstances it may well be right to say that the statement can properly be attributed to Miss Shaw, because after all, it was her business, and the statement was made on behalf of the business. So far as that point is concerned I could be easily persuaded that the making of the statement simpliciter could be attributed to Miss Shaw, the principal.

But that is not enough unless one can also attribute to her the state of mind alleged, namely that the statement was made recklessly. As I understand it, as a general proposition of the criminal law a principal is not to be made immediately liable, in an offence involving mens rea, merely because his servant or agent had the necessary mental intent. As a question of general principle I would have thought it wrong to allow the mental state of the respondent to be attributed to Miss Shaw so as to complete the offence so far as she is concerned.

Counsel for the appellant has ranged widely over the rest of the Act and has referred us, as I have said, to Lord Diplock's speech in the *Tesco* case[2] to show that generally speaking the scheme of this Act is to make the employer liable in the first instance, subject to his possible defence under s 24, and that that should be so in cases of strict liability is not I think surprising. It is the case that most, if not all, of the other offences under this Act are offences of strict obligation; and it seems to me consistent with principle in those cases that the employer should be the person primarily responsible when an infringement occurs.

But s 14 of the Act is peculiar in many ways. It deals with services, and deals with services for the first time, because they were not dealt with in the Merchandise Marks Acts 1887 to 1953 and also contains the specific mental element of knowledge of falsity or recklessness to which I have already referred. For my part I do not think it would be consistent with principle or required by the terms of this Act, looked at as a whole, that the mental element attributed properly to the respondent should be also attributed to Miss Shaw in the circumstances of this case.

I recognise that the situation may appear at all events to be somewhat different where the employer in a case of this kind is a limited company, because again it is established in principle that the actions and the state of mind of the ruling officers of a company may be attributed to the company. Accordingly, somewhat different considerations may apply in those circumstances. Here we have no question of a company, we have two individuals, and I think the result should be as I have stated.

This may mean, of course, that the defence under s 24 will rarely, if ever, be appropriate to a charge under s 14. I say that because, if I am right, in order to establish the charge under s 14 you have to show knowing falsity or recklessness, which themselves are inconsistent with the statutory defence. But be that as it may, I think in this case the justices were entirely justified in saying that Miss Shaw was to be acquitted on the general grounds as opposed to the statutory defence, and once they reached that conclusion it was inevitable, having regard to the form of the charge, that they should acquit the respondent as well. For those reasons I would dismiss the appeal.

Ashworth J. I agree.

Bridge J. I also agree.

Appeal dismissed.

1. [1971] 2 All ER 127 at 152, 153, [1972] AC 153 at 195–197.
2. [1971] 2 All ER at 150–159, [1972] AC at 193–203.

Section 24 (1) (a) would be clearer on this point if it referred to 'the commission of the alleged offence'.

Questions

Is the decision in this case consistent with the approach of the House of Lords in *Wings Ltd v Ellis* [1984] 3 All ER 577, [1984] 3 WLR 965, above pp 557–558? Would it make any difference if someone in Miss Shaw's position had (i) been running a 'large scale' business, or (ii) set up a limited liability company?

Problem

Art is the sole proprietor of a second-hand car business but he does not play an active part in it, leaving matters to his foreman, Bert. Bert assures a prospective purchaser of a car that it is 'a grand little runner. I would stake my life on it.' Art neither authorises the statement nor even knows that it has been made. In fact the car is unroadworthy. Discuss the liability of Art and Bert under the 1968 Act.

PRIVATE INDIVIDUALS

A further problem is whether a third party due to whose act or default an offence has been committed may be prosecuted by virtue of s 23 when he is a private individual. Though yet to be tested in the High Court it is known that such prosecutions have been brought successfully, in effect causing s 23 to create a separate offence: see P. Forman 'The Trade Descriptions Act 1968. A Lawyer's Progress Report' (1970, Consumer Council) and R. G. Lawson 139 JP Jo 223. Prima facie this procedure is improper since the section, in stating that the 'other person shall be guilty of the offence' clearly refers back to the commission by any person of 'an offence *under this Act*', and such offences must be committed in the course of a business. (Of course there is always the possibility of an individual committing an offence under another statute, for example obtaining property by deception contrary to s 15 of the Theft Act 1968.) Also on appropriate facts, at common law a private individual could be charged as a secondary party aiding and abetting another's commission of an offence against the Trade Descriptions Act itself. However mens rea would then have to be proved even though the principal offender might be subject to strict liability under ss 1 or 11 of the Act: see generally Smith and Hogan *Criminal Law* (5th edn, 1983) p 129 et seq.

For a case under the Food and Drugs Act 1955 in which an individual employee of a third party was held guilty under the s 113 (1) procedure even though he was in no way involved in the sale of food: see *Meah v Roberts* [1978] 1 All ER 97, [1977] 1 WLR 1187 (QBD) (leaving of caustic soda during cleaning of lager dispenser in restaurant, the soda being sold thereafter mistakenly as lemonade).

ACT OR DEFAULT: DIRECT CAUSAL CONNECTION

Section 23 cannot be used where there are two separate offences or possible offences not causally connected. So much is implicit in the words *'due* to the act or default'. So in *Tarleton Engineering Co Ltd v Nattrass* [1973] 3 All ER 699, [1973] 1 WLR 1261 it was held that the justices had adopted the wrong approach in holding that the commission of an offence by auctioneers in selling a 'clocked' car was due to the act or default of the defendants who had entered it in the auction. This case was followed in *Taylor v Smith* [1974] RTR 190. See also *K Lill Holdings Ltd (trading as Stratford Motor Co) v White* [1979] RTR 120, above p 495.

Specific defences

There are many examples where legislation provides specific defences for certain categories of offences to mitigate the rigour of strict liability. An example is s 25 of the Trade Descriptions Act 1968, relating to 'innocent' publication of an advertisement. This provides as follows:

25. In proceedings for an offence under this Act committed by the publication of an advertisement it shall be a defence for the person charged to prove that he is a person whose business it is to publish or arrange for the publication of advertisements and that he received the advertisement for publication in the ordinary course of business and did not know and had no reason to suspect that its publication would amount to an offence under this Act.

Another important example is s 3(2) of the Food Act 1984 (formerly s 3 (3) of the Food and Drugs Act 1955) which provides that if food contains some extraneous matter is is a defence for the defendant to show that the presence of that matter was 'an unavoidable consequence of the process of collection or preparation'. The limits to this defence are discussed in the following leading case.

Smedleys Ltd v Breed [1974] 2 All ER 21, [1974] AC 839, House of Lords

The facts are set out, in the speech of Lord Hailsham.

Lord Hailsham of St Marylebone. My Lords, on 25 February 1972 Mrs Voss, a Dorset housewife, entered a supermarket belonging to Tesco Stores Ltd and bought a tin of Smedleys' peas. It goes without saying that both Tesco Stores Ltd and Smedleys Ltd are firms of the highest reputation, and no one who has read this case or heard it argued could possibly conceive that what has occurred here reflects in any way on the quality of their products, still less on their commercial reputations.

Unfortunately, and without any fault or negligence on the part of the management of either company, when Mrs Voss got home, she discovered that the tin, in addition to something more than 150 peas, contained a green caterpillar, the larva of one of the species of hawk moth. This innocent insect, thus deprived of its natural destiny, was in fact entirely harmless, since, prior to its entry into the tin, it had been subjected to a cooking process of 20 minutes duration at 250°F, and, had she cared to do so, Mrs Voss could have consumed the caterpillar without injury to herself, and even, perhaps, with benefit. She was not, however, to know this, and with commendable civic zeal, she felt it her duty to report the matter to the local authority, and in consequence, grinding slow, but exceeding small, the machinery of the law was set in inexorable motion.

Thereafter, the caterpillar achieved a sort of posthumous apotheosis. From local authority to the Dorchester magistrates, from the Dorchester magistrates to a Divisional Court presided over by the Lord Chief Justice of England[1], from the Lord Chief Justice to the House of Lords, the immolated insect has at length plodded its methodical way to the highest tribunal in the land. It now falls to me to deliver my opinion on its case.

The Food and Drugs Act 1955, s 113, [see now s 100 of the 1984 Act] provides a means whereby, if prosecuted for an offence under the Act, a defendant can seek to cast the blame on a third party and exonerate himself, and, in order to save the needless expense of an unnecessary prosecution, the local authority is empowered, when it is reasonably satisfied that a defence of this kind could be established, to short-circuit proceedings by prosecuting the third party direct. Thus it was that Smedleys Ltd, the present appellants, and not Tesco Stores Ltd, found themselves defendants to a summons which alleged that the sale by Tesco Stores Ltd was of peas which were not of the substance demanded by Mrs Voss since they included the caterpillar and that was due to the act or default of the appellants.

The relevant sections of the 1955 Act are as follows: s 2(1) provides:

> 'If a person sells to the prejudice of the purchaser any food . . . which is not . . . of the substance . . . of the food . . . demanded by the purchaser, he shall, subject to the provisions of the next following section, be guilty of an offence.'

Although the contrary had been contended below, it was conceded before your Lordships that the peas, with the caterpillar among them, were not of the substance demanded by Mrs Voss.

Despite what has been said by my noble and learned friend, Viscount Dilhorne, to the contrary, I think this concession to have been right. I believe a housewife who orders peas is entitled to complain if, instead of peas, she gets a mixture of peas and caterpillars, and that she is not bound to treat the caterpillar as a kind of uncovenanted blessing.

Section 3(3) of the Act provides:

> 'In proceedings under section two of this Act in respect of any food . . . containing some extraneous matter, it shall be a defence for the defendant to prove that the presence of that matter was an unavoidable consequence of the process of collection or preparation.'

The principal contention of the appellants before your Lordships was that, on the true construction of this subsection, and on the facts found by the magistrates, the presence of the caterpillar amongst the peas was an unavoidable consequence of the process of collection or preparation.

. . .

In theory at least, therefore, it is a defence to a charge under s 2(1) if a defendant can establish that, on the balance of probabilities, notwithstanding that facts are proved bringing the case within s 2(1) the presence of any extraneous matter was an unavoidable consequence of the process of collection or distribution. This involves at least three elements: (1) a process of collection or distribution, (2) of which the presence of the extraneous matter was a consequence, and, (3) that that consequence was unavoidable. I am by no means convinced in the present case that the appellants have made any sort of case that the failure to eliminate extraneous matter which was always there can, on the ordinary use of language, be described as a consequence of the process of collection or preparation, and I do not regard the process of dealing with the peas after vining and podding as part of any process of collection. I agree with those of my noble and learned friends who have said that it would be more natural to describe the presence of the caterpillar to have occurred despite the processes rather than because of them. But, on any view of the case, I do not think that, if consequence it were, it was an 'unavoidable' consequence.

In construing the word 'unavoidable' in this context I must have regard (1) to the ordinary and natural meaning of the word, and (2) to the contexts in which it occurs in the Act. In applying it I must remember that the case finds that:

> 'It would have been possible but impracticable for the peas to have been collected [sic] in such a way as to avoid the possibility of a caterpillar being present in the can of peas.'

I doubt myself whether the omission of any reference to the expression 'preparation' is altogether accidental in this finding. But, on the assumption, which favours the appellants, that such might be the case, I consider that this somewhat cryptic finding refers to an argument by the appellants based on the fact that in any commercial process, manual or mechanical, some failures, human or mechanical, will take place and that statistically, out of an output by the appellants of 3,500,000 tins for 1971, there had only been four complaints involving extraneous matter, including the present case. If so, I regard the contention as irrelevant. What has to be shown in order to constitute a defence under s 3(3) of the Act is not that *some* failures are unavoidable and that, owing to the excellence of the system, statistically the failures have been few. This is matter in mitigation. What has to be shown under s 3(3) is that the 'presence of *that* matter' (ie the particular piece of extraneous matter) in the particular parcel of food the subject of the charge was 'the unavoidable consequence of the process'. As I ventured to point out in argument, over a long enough run any sort of process, however excellent, will statistically result in some failures, human or otherwise, and these are statistically predictable in the light of experience. But that will not necessarily be a defence under s 3(3). What is required is the proof, on the balance of probabilities, that the particular piece of extraneous matter was present in the particular parcel of food as the unavoidable consequence of the process itself. Thus in *Warnock v Johnstone*[2] it was established that added water in buttermilk was, at least at that time, an unavoidable consequence of the process by which buttermilk is produced, and, incidentally, was always found to a greater or lesser extent in any samples of buttermilk.

. . .

There are foods (for instance field cabbage) which are subjected to a process in collection, but suffer no process of preparation before being sold to the housewife. There are also foods, which, although collected in their natural state, are subjected to processes of preparation before being sold to the housewife. An example would be tinned peas. Section 3(3) of the Act is concerned with contamination by extraneous matters. If the consequence of one of the two processes is the presence of extraneous matter it is not for the defendant to show that its presence is unavoidable. In the case of field cabbages the nature of the process of collection, whatever process is adopted, may be such that the presence in the heart of the cabbage of a certain amount of extraneous matter (eg dust or grit) is 'unavoidable'. As there is no subsequent process of preparation, there is a defence, if, in the particular case, there is a certain amount of extraneous matter which can be said to be the unavoidable consequence of the process of collection. On the other hand, in the case of tinned peas there is a process of preparation as well as a process of collection. In that case the consequences of the processes of collection are not unavoidable unless they cannot be removed in the course of preparation.

This, however, does not beg the question how one should construe 'unavoidable'. I must read the word as being contrasted with 'avoidable', and this must mean that some human act or omission could have avoided the consequence. The only question is the standard of precaution to be exacted in deciding whether a consequence is 'unavoidable'. Obviously any consequence is avoidable by the simple expedient of not engaging in the process at all. But that clearly is not what is meant unless the process itself is open to serious criticism as unnecessary or inefficient. I do not think the words 'avoidable' or 'unavoidable' are to be construed in any strained metaphysical or absolute sense. I believe they are to be construed with common sense in the way that a jury might construe them. This, in my view, means no more, and no less, than this. If any human agency in any way concerned in a proper process could have avoided the consequence by the exercise of a high standard of reasonable care, then the consequence is avoidable. On the other hand, if no human agency concerned with the process could, by the exercise of a high standard of reasonable care have avoided the contamination, the consequence, if a consequence of the process, is unavoidable within the meaning of s 3(3).

It will be seen that this construction falls short of absolute liability. But it does not save a defendant who can only show that he himself has exercised every possible diligence, where he cannot also show that the consequence could never have been avoided by any other human agency connected with the process using the requisite degree of care and diligence. In that event to escape liability he must establish a defence under s 113, and to do so he must (i) identify the third party (who may, or may not, be, his own employee) whose act or default had as its consequence the presence of the extraneous matter, (2) adopt the prescribed procedures, and (3) exonerate himself by showing that he had used all diligence. There may be many cases where he does not choose to lay the blame on another. There may be others where he cannot do so. Indeed, if the appellants here could not identify the visual inspectors whose vigilance this caterpillar escaped, this case would be one. But if he cannot or will not avail himself of s 113, a defendant must be convicted if he cannot show that the presence of the particular extraneous matter in the particular parcel of food was a consequence of the process of collection or preparation (as the case may be) which was unavoidable by any human agency provided that all concerned exercised a high standard of reasonable care in what they were supposed to do. In other words, he must suffer conviction unless the consequence was, in the ordinary sense of the word, 'unavoidable', whether or not he could have avoided it by reasonable diligence of his own.

I find myself quite unable to construe the word 'unavoidable' by inserting any reference to the care or diligence of the defendant. It would have been perfectly simple for the draftsman to insert such a reference, had he wished to do so, and in fact, apart from s 113, to the language of which MacKenna J[3] drew attention, the draftsman did insert such a reference in s 8(3) (*b*) of the Act.

. . . In my view, the appeal fails and should be dismissed.

Viscount Dilhorne, Lord Diplock, Lord Cross and Lord Kilbrandon agreed that the appeal should be dismissed.

Appeal dismissed.

1. [1973] 3 All ER 339, [1973] QB 977.
2. (1881) 8 R (Ct of Sess) 55.
3. [1973] 3 All ER at 346, [1973] QB at 978.

NOTES

1. Viscount Dilhorne in his speech questioned the desirability of bringing a prosecution when the chances against something like this happening were about 800,000 to 1. He noted also the appellants' full disclosure and commented that in such cases where it was apparent that a prosecution does not serve the general interest of consumers the justices may think fit to grant an absolute discharge. For a more general discussion of the discretion to prosecute see Painter, 'Why Prosecute' (1974) British Food Journal, 38; Cranston *Regulating Business: Law and Consumer Agencies* (1979). See also *Wings Ltd v Ellis* [1984] 3 All ER 577, above p 516, and pp 445–49.

2. *Smedleys Ltd v Breed* was followed in *Greater Manchester Council v Lockwood Foods Ltd* [1979] Crim LR 593, DC (a beetle found in a can of strawberries). It seems that the s 3(2) (formerly 3(3)) defence is virtually a dead letter, though justices might grant an absolute discharge in appropriate cases.

Time limits

The prosecution of trading standards offences is subject to provisions as to time limits. These must be observed, and if the limits are in any case exceeded it raises, upon the appearance of the defendant, a defect which is incurable and cannot be waived notwithstanding that the defendant raises no objection (*Dixon v Wells*) (1890) 25 QBD 249).

In summary proceedings, section 127 of the Magistrates' Courts Act 1980 imposes a general time limit on trying information within six months from the time when the offence was committed. However, taking the Trade Descriptions Act 1968 as an example, all except one offence under the Act are triable either way, that is either summarily or on indictment. The current position is that, pursuant to section 19, no prosecution for an offence under the 1968 Act can be commenced after the expiration of three years from the commission of the offence or one year from its discovery by the prosecutor, whichever is the earlier. (The only summary offence in the Act (obstructing an officer under s 29) is subject to a special time limit of 12 months from the commission of the offence (s 19(2)).

Originally, if the offence was committed by the making of an oral statement there was yet a third time limit—namely the 'normal' one for summary offences of six months from the commission of the offence. This point should be borne in mind when reading the case printed below. It should also be noted that although s 19 (4) which contains this six months stipulation has not been formally repealed, it has ceased to have effect; the time limit of three years now applies to such offences, since they are triable on indictment or summarily, that is 'either way'.

The significance of time limits for present purposes is that it is necessary to identify the precise moment when the offence was committed in order to assess whether the time limit has been exceeded. For instance, if a vehicle is falsely described by advertisements in a journal and is subsequently purchased by a buyer visiting the premises on which the vehicle stands, when is the false trade description 'applied' for the purposes of s 1 of the Act? This was one of the points which came before the Divisional Court in the following case.

Rees v Munday [1974] 3 All ER 506, [1974] 1 WLR 1284, Queen's Bench Divisional Court

The facts are set out in the judgment of Lord Widgery LJ.

Lord Widgery CJ. This is an appeal by case stated by the justices for the county of Somerset sitting as a magistrates' court in Dulverton as long ago as 2 May 1973. I cannot resist the temptation to observe that the case was not stated until January 1974, a period of delay which we hope to eliminate in the future under certain new provisions now under consideration for stating magistrates' cases.

On the day in question the justices convicted the present appellant of two offences under the Trade Descriptions Act 1968. Both related to a Bedford goods vehicle registration number VLM 205G. The first information alleged that the appellant in the course of a trade or business supplied that vehicle to which a false trade description was applied, namely, that it was 'in first class condition throughout'. The second information alleged that a further false trade description was applied to the vehicle, namely, that it was of '12 yd' capacity. The vehicle was not 'in first class condition throughout', as the justices found. Indeed it had a number of substantial defects, but those are not matters into which this judgment need go because in the event the concern of this court has turned on a very narrow point indeed.

The dates are important. On 29 October 1971 the appellant advertised in a motor trade journal, Commercial Motor, that he had for sale a Bedford goods vehicle, which was 'in first class condition throughout'. In the same advertisement was the reference to it being of '12 yd' capacity. A potential buyer interested in buying such a vehicle visited the appellant at his premises in Surrey on 30 October 1971. A bargain was struck there and then, that is to say in the course of the interview, a contract for sale was made, but the vehicle was kept on the appellant's premises a short while, partly because something had to be done to it, and partly because it was desired to keep it there until the purchaser's cheque had been cleared. In fact, the vehicle was delivered to the purchaser in Somerset by a servant of the appellant on 2 November 1971. The informations in this case were both laid on 1 November 1972 and the matters that concern this court are unhappily related to whether the informations were preferred in time.

Special rules apply to cases in magistrates' courts under the Trade Descriptions Act 1968 and they are to be found in s 19 of the Act itself. Section 19(2) provides:

> 'Notwithstanding anything in section 104 of the Magistrates' Courts Act 1952, [now section 127(1) of the Magistrates' Courts Act 1980], a magistrates' court may try an information for an offence under this Act if the information was laid at any time within twelve months from the commission of the offence.'

I take that provision first of all because it is from there that the appellant's first point arises. The limitation, I remind myself, is 12 months from the commission of the offence. The offence is the supply of the goods to which the false trade description is applied. One gets that from s 1(1) (*b*) of the 1968 Act, and that indeed is the provision under which these charges were laid. So in deciding whether the information was or was not laid within the appropriate 12 months' period, it is the date of supply from which the 12 months begins to run.

As will be observed, the information is laid on 1 November 1972, within the 12 month period if the date of supply is the date when the vehicle was driven down to Somerset because that was 2 November 1971; a close-run thing perhaps, but just in time if delivery is the date when supply occurs and, therefore, the date of the commission of the offence. If, as the appellant argues, the vehicle was supplied on 30 October when the contract for sale was struck, then, of course, the informations were too late by one day. On this point the sole question for us to consider is whether this vehicle was supplied within the meaning of the 1968 Act at the date when the contract for sale was made or at the date when it was physically delivered.

For my part I think that the proper construction of this Act requires supply to be treated here as the date of delivery. I can see that there are arguments which might be advanced for applying the Sale of Goods Act 1893 to this situation and saying that an article is supplied when the property passes by virtue of that Act. But I think for my own part that that would be an unnecessary and undesirable complication to attach to this already somewhat difficult Act, and I think that the proper meaning of supply in this context is the delivery of the goods as delivered by the seller, or notification that they are available for delivery if they are to be collected by the buyer. On that basis the goods were supplied on 2 November 1971, the offence was committed on that date, the information came along on 1 November 1972, just in time, and there is nothing in the appellant's first point.

The second point, still concerned with the time of the laying of the information, arises out of s 19(4), which says:

> 'Subsections (2) and (3) of this section do not apply where—. . . (*b*) the offence was one of supplying goods to which a false trade description is applied, and the trade description was applied by an oral statement . . .'

So that if one brings oneself within sub-s (4) (*b*), the period is no longer 12 months but only six months, and quite clearly on any view of the matter the informations were laid more than six months after the commission of the offence in this case. Thus this is a wholly alternative and separate point taken by the appellant and it requires consideration of how the false trade description was applied, because if it was applied by an oral statement, then under s 19(4) it would seem that the appropriate limitation period is six months.

To consider the circumstances in which a false trade description is applied one goes back to s 4(1), again reading the words that are relevant only:

> 'A person applies a trade description to goods if he . . . (*c*) uses the trade description in any manner likely to be taken as referring to the goods.'

The contest here is between counsel for the respondent, who says that the trade description was applied when the advertisement was published and therefore was a written trade description, and the contention of counsel for the appellant, who says until the buyer arrived at the seller's yard and had the vehicle pointed out to him, no trade description had been applied to that vehicle. Accordingly he says that the situation is apt to be described by the words in s 19(4) that here the trade description was applied by an oral statement.

Just go back for a moment again to the facts found because there are one or two facts which I think are of assistance on this second point: the first is not only did the appellant publish the advertisement in Commercial Motor, as I have already described, but he had only one lorry answering that description on his premises at the relevant date. When the would-be buyer, a Mr Ridler, came up from Dulverton and visited the appellant's premises on 30 October, the appellant stated that the specific lorry, the number of which is given, was the lorry referred to in the advertisement. Mr Ridler looked at other lorries before agreeing to buy the Bedford.

Counsel for the appellant argues that it would be to ignore reality to suppose that all that happened when the buyer arrived at the seller's yard was that the seller simply said: 'There it is; take it or leave it.' No doubt certain other niceties of discussion took place. But one cannot get away from the fact, I think, that when the advertisement was published there was only one lorry of that description in the seller's possession, and I think that the description was applied to that lorry when the advertisement itself was published. I think that is an example of the trade description being used in a manner likely to be taken as referring to the goods because if there was only one lorry of that description, that fact would indicate to anybody that the trade description applied to that one vehicle. If that is right, if the trade description was applied by the written advertisement, of course there is no room for arguing that it was subsequently applied by an oral statement, and counsel for the appellant's second submission goes as well.

I do not find the second point quite as easy as the first, but on the whole my conclusion on the facts of this case is that the trade description was not applied orally within the meaning of s 19(4) and that accordingly the special period of limitation of six months does not apply in this case. That means that both informations, as the justices found, were in time, the convictions were right and the appeal should be dismissed.

Melford Stevenson J. I agree.

Talbot J. I agree.

Appeal dismissed.

Question

Should the conclusion on the first point have been different if the relevant offence had been one of selling (rather than supplying) as under the Consumer Protection Act 1961 (see above p 455)?

Index

ABTA
  annual report 1983 322–323
  conciliation service 322–323
  disciplinary proceedings, and 397
Acceptance
  buyer, by—
    meaning of 91
  intimation of 109
Acceptance note
  problems caused by 109
Accident
  statutory defence, as 562–563
Accommodation
  false price claim, and 539
  meaning of 508–513
Act or default of another person
  Trade Descriptions Act 1968, and 554–560
Advertisements
  guarantee, and 48, 401
  innocent publication of 567
  trade description used in 465–466
Advertising 397 *et seq.*
  children, and 402
  codes of practice, and 397 *et seq.*
  comparisons contained in 402
  control of 397 *et seq.*
  corrective 407–408
  Council of European Communities Directive 1984 409–412
  Cyanamid 41–43
  decency 398
  denigration by 402
  Director-General of Fair Trading's injunctive proposal 405–406
  EEC dimension 408–409
  endorsements 400–401
  exploitation of individual 402
  exploitation of name or goodwill by 402–403
  fear, and 401
  fines, and 408
  'free', use of word 400
  general rules 398 *et seq.*
  honesty 399
  IBA, and 407
  identification of 401
  'ignorant, unthinking and credulous' test 40–41
  imitation, and 403
  legality 398
  meaning of 410

Advertising–*contd*
  misleading—
    EEC implications 404–405
  prices 399
  prohibition orders, and 406–407
  protection of privacy 402
  redress for individual consumers, and 408
  Report of Department of Trade Working Party 1980 403–408
  safety, and 402
  self regulatory system of control 403–408
    deficiency of 404
  statutory recognition of codes of practice, and 405
  superstition, and 401
  testimonials 400–401
  Trade Descriptions Act 1968, and 405
  truthful presentation 399
  unliquidated damages based on 35
  'up to' and 'from' claims 400
  violence, and 402
  warranty, and 401
Affirmation
  English law of 99–100
  hire-purchase, and 100–102
  meaning of 101
Agency
  priority of contract, and 24–25
Agent Orange
  class action in relation to 365–368
Another person 554–560
  limited company, whether 544–560
  meaning of 554–560
  shop manager, and 554–560
Antifreeze
  fitness of 15–16
Any person
  meaning of 466
Applies
  meaning of 475–481
Arbitration 307–308, 320–324
  codes of practice, and 321–322
  contractual agreement for—
    binding nature of 323–324
  documents-only 320–321
  procedure 307–308
  reasons for decisions 321
  small claims, and 307–308, 311–312
    reference by registrar 312–315
  time targets 321
  travel industry, and 322–323